THE PAPERS OF
Andrew Johnson

Sponsored by
The University of Tennessee
The National Historical Publications and Records Commission
The National Endowment for the Humanities
The Tennessee Historical Commission

Frontispiece: President Andrew Johnson. A portrait by George Dury (*c*1866)
Courtesy Tennessee State Museum

THE PAPERS OF
Andrew Johnson

Volume 11, August 1866-January 1867

PAUL H. BERGERON
EDITOR

PATRICIA J. ANTHONY   LeROY P. GRAF

R. B. ROSENBURG   GLENNA R. SCHROEDER-LEIN

MARION O. SMITH   LISA L. WILLIAMS

THE EDITING STAFF

1994

THE UNIVERSITY OF TENNESSEE PRESS

KNOXVILLE

Library of Congress Cataloging in Publication Data
(Revised for volume 11)

Johnson, Andrew, 1808–1875.
    The papers of Andrew Johnson.
    Vols. 8— edited by Paul H. Bergeron.
    Includes bibliographical references and indexes.
    Contents: v.1. 1822–1851.—v.2. 1852–1857—[etc.]—
v.11. August 1866–January 1867
    1. Johnson, Andrew, 1808–1875—Manuscripts.
    2. Presidents—United States—Manuscripts.
    3. United States—Politics and government—1849–
        1877—Sources.
I. Graf, Leroy P., ed.   II. Haskins, Ralph W., ed.
III. Bergeron, Paul H., 1938–   . IV. Title.
E415.6.J65   1967   973.8'1'0924 B   67-25733
ISBN 0-87049-098-2 (v.2)
ISBN 0-87049-828-2 (v.11)

TO

Ralph M. Phinney

This eminent Greeneville, Tennessee, citizen is devoted
to all things concerning Andrew Johnson
and especially to our Johnson Project.

Contents

Illustrations

Introduction

In the late summer and early fall months of 1866 the only good news for Andrew Johnson was that Congress would not be in session. Once again, as in the summer and fall of the preceding year, the President would have the opportunity to govern without interference from the legislative branch. Perhaps he could rescue his troubled administration by demonstrating, as he had done in 1865, that he could be an effective and successful leader. Unfortunately for Johnson, however, there really were very few parallels, if any, between the experiences of 1865 and 1866, beyond the obvious fact that Congress was not in town. Historian Hans Trefousse has labelled Johnson in the period from the summer of 1866 through the early months of 1867 as the "beleaguered president" and then as the "defiant president."[1] Based upon the documents published in this volume and upon monographic studies, it must be granted that these are apt terms.

The story of Johnson in 1866–67 comes close to matching the chronicles about the plagues that afflicted Biblical Egypt or the tribulations that beset Job. But, truth to tell, he brought his troubles upon himself—through his stubbornness, his inflexibility, his pro-southern bias, his erratic behavior (especially on the speaker's platform), and his unshakable convictions about a world that no longer existed. One of the chief ironies of several that marked his presidency was that as Johnson became increasingly pro-Democratic, the nation, other than the ex-Confederate states, became increasingly Republican. From that flowed a multitude of difficulties.

If there was any high-water mark of the presidency during the summer and fall months of 1866, it was the National Union convention held at Philadelphia in mid-August. But that conclave showed beyond doubt that the Republican-Democratic coalition that had earlier been so significant was nearly fragmented beyond repair. The President, however, was either unable or unwilling to admit this new reality; instead, he persisted

1. The essay is based upon documents published in this volume, as well as pertinent historical monographs: Hans L. Trefousse, *Andrew Johnson: A Biography* (New York, 1989); Eric L. McKitrick, *Andrew Johnson and Reconstruction* (Chicago, 1960); Albert Castel, *The Presidency of Andrew Johnson* (Lawrence, Kans., 1979); Michael Les Benedict, *A Compromise of Principle: Congressional Republicans and Reconstruction, 1863–1869* (New York, 1974); Michael Perman, *Reunion Without Compromise: The South and Reconstruction, 1865–1868* (Cambridge, England, 1973); and James E. Sefton, *Andrew Johnson and the Uses of Constitutional Power* (Boston, 1980).

in his belief that his tilt toward the Democrats and indeed toward the South would reap beneficial political results.[2]

Several events and developments suggest themselves as the low-water marks of the Johnson administration in this particular time span. It could be argued that of these perhaps the lowest was the ill-fated trip to the Northeast and Midwest which the President took in late August and early September. His unfortunate antics on the speaker's podium during this "swing around the circle" damaged the public's perception of his presidency so much that little hope remained.

There was no genuine boundary line separating the earlier summer weeks from the later ones, other than the departure of Congress from Washington by August. That is to say that in the August 1866-January 1867 period Johnson had to contend with a legacy left from actions taken by Congress and from events that occurred elsewhere. Particularly noticeable were the matters of the New Orleans riot and the Fourteenth Amendment. In the weeks and months that followed, the President could not escape these.

The July riot in New Orleans had a tremendous impact upon Northern opinion, for its tragedy seemed to confirm widely-held suspicions about the South. Several correspondents informed the President about various aspects of the riot, including detailed descriptions of what they thought had happened. Johnson himself swung into action, when he requested a report from Gen. Philip H. Sheridan; within two days the general sent his analysis and description to the White House. But when the President made it public, he took extreme editorial liberties with Sheridan's account by simply deleting those portions of it which he found objectionable.[3] Johnson revived the controversies surrounding the riot during his August-September tour by calling special attention to it in his St. Louis speech.[4] Correspondence concerning the riot stretched from early August through January; the topic simply would not vanish.

By mid-June 1866 both houses of Congress had approved the Fourteenth Amendment and forwarded it to the states for action. Tennessee ratified the Amendment in July, the first and eventually the only ex-Confederate state to do so. Johnson, who opposed the Amendment, reluctantly accepted Tennessee's decision. Thereafter he made no effort to encourage states, north or south, to ratify it and in fact, took direct and

2. See Orville H. Browning and Alexander W. Randall to Johnson, Aug. 14, 1866; Johnson to Browning and Randall, Aug. 14, 1866; James R. Doolittle et al. to Johnson, Aug. 16, 1866; Reply to Committee from Philadelphia National Union Convention, Aug. 18, 1866.

3. Among the pertinent August documents, see John T. Monroe et al. to Johnson, Aug. 3, 1866; Johnson to Sheridan, Aug. 4, 1866; Sheridan to Johnson, Aug. 6, 1866; Jacob Barker to Johnson, Aug. 9, 1866; James Edmondston to Johnson, Aug. 9, 1866; Juan Jennon to Johnson, Aug. 14, 1866.

4. Speech at St. Louis, Sept. 8, 1866.

indirect steps to discourage southern approval. The National Union convention at Philadelphia, for example, scrupulously and intentionally omitted any reference to the Fourteenth Amendment, a palpable ploy to court southerners. By the time of his Annual Message in December, Johnson chose, in effect, to attack the Amendment by ignoring it.[5]

Meanwhile, southern states had already started the process of rejecting the Amendment; in fact, the month of December yielded a bumper crop of disapprovals (five in all). The first ex-Rebel state to reject the Amendment was Texas, which acted in late October. When the Texas governor notified Johnson and expressed concern about the state's restoration to the Union, the President responded with reassurances that eventually everything would be all right.[6]

A legislator from South Carolina visited Johnson and some Congressional leaders in December; and, according to the lawmaker's account, the President expressed the desire that all the southern states would "steadfastly reject" the Fourteenth Amendment; and South Carolina did. In Virginia there seemed for a time to be the possibility of support for ratification. Yet apparently Johnson intervened to influence leaders there to reject the Amendment, which they eventually did in January 1867.[7]

Although Alabama initially disapproved the Amendment in December, Governor Robert M. Patton subsequently had second thoughts and attempted to bring about a reconsideration. But former provisional governor Lewis Parsons intervened to oppose ratification, perhaps at the instigation of the President. In any event, in January the Alabama legislature stood poised to hold a new vote on the Amendment. When Parsons alerted the President to this development, Johnson immediately sent a telegram to express the conviction that no good could come from reversing the previous rejection. The legislature therefore heeded his advice and did not approve the Amendment.[8] By the end of January, nine Confederate states had rejected it; and in February, Louisiana completed the circle. It should also be noted that by the end of December 1866 three Border states, Delaware, Maryland, and Kentucky, had likewise disapproved the Amendment.

Believing that his position on the Fourteenth Amendment and all other questions could best be communicated by taking his message directly to the people, the President embarked upon a Northeastern-Midwestern trip in late August. Several days prior to his departure on the 28th, two different correspondents needlessly warned Johnson about

5. Message to Congress, Dec. 3, 1866. See Interview with Benjamin Eggleston, Dec. 22, 1866, for a somewhat controversial account of Johnson's view *re* southern approval of the Fourteenth Amendment.

6. Johnson to James W. Throckmorton, Oct. 30, 1866.

7. Castel, *Presidency of Johnson*, 102; McKitrick, *Johnson and Reconstruction*, 454.

8. Johnson to Lewis Parsons, Jan. 17, 1867; Trefousse, *Johnson*, 275; McKitrick, *Johnson and Reconstruction*, 454–55.

possible physical dangers in Chicago.[9] Yet the problems that awaited him on the "swing around the circle" were *political*, not physical. His closest friends and advisers were definitely divided about the possible virtues of the proposed trip; nevertheless Seward and Welles supported it and helped make its arrangements. Unfortunately for the President, he did not heed the counsel of his friend Senator Doolittle, who warned that he must "not allow the excitement of the moment to draw from you any *extemporaneous speeches*."[10]

An air of optimism pervaded the Johnson entourage initially, for it was well received at Baltimore, Philadelphia, and New York City. But by the time the presidential party reached Cleveland on September 3, the atmosphere had become hostile and threatening. His undignified and accusatory speech at Cleveland is usually viewed as the turning point in the trip, for afterwards there seemed to be little but trouble for the President.[11] Political leaders of local and national stature avoided Johnson at subsequent stops; and the crowds, with a few exceptions, were unruly and decidedly antagonistic toward him. His visit and speech at Chicago, however, on September 6 for the dedication of the Stephen A. Douglas monument went smoothly, but two days later came the debacle at St. Louis. The tour seemingly lurched from one disaster to another for the remainder of the time on the road. Although most of these were of Johnson's own making, the collapse of the platform at Johnstown on September 14 (which resulted in death and injury to scores) obviously was not.[12] On the next day Johnson and his traveling group at long last reached Washington, where they were welcomed by an enthusiastic crowd. But the cheers there could not offset the travail and tribulation that had hovered over the presidential party.

The media, not surprisingly, played an important role in the unfolding story of Johnson's tour. But the President evidently never fully understood or appreciated the power of the press to shape the public's understanding of his trip. Hostile newspapers along the way merely exacerbated the increasingly difficult situation; there was no question that Johnson's antics made "good copy." Indeed, his reputation has never completely recovered from the devastating work of Thomas Nast, the political cartoonist, and "Petroleum V. Nasby" (David Ross Locke), the satirical writer. Adding to the litany of his woes was the decision by both the *New York Times* and the *New York Herald* to repudiate Johnson—a reversal that occurred shortly after the President's return from his "swing

9. Ward H. Lamon to Johnson, ca. Aug. 15, 1866; John M. Johnson to Johnson, Aug. 21, 1866.

10. James R. Doolittle to Johnson, Aug. 29, 1866.

11. Speech in Cleveland, Sept. 3, 1866; Trefousse, *Johnson*, 263–64; Castel, *Presidency of Johnson*, 90–91.

12. Henry A. McPike to Johnson, Sept. 15, 1866; Castel, *Presidency of Johnson*, 91–92; Trefousse, *Johnson*, 264–66.

around the circle."[13] When these two powerful papers turned against Johnson, he had little hope of competing successfully in the propaganda wars. No wonder he was the "beleaguered president."

Even while the President was still engaged in his tour of the Northeast and Midwest, early fall election returns came in from Vermont and Maine. The tremendous Republican sweep of those two states served as a harbinger of what followed in the next few weeks: victory after victory in state after state. Most disturbing for Johnson was that the Republican party emerged with an increased majority in Congress. In their letters to a distressed president, a number of correspondents attempted to explain away the results.[14] But no sensible person could assess the elections as anything but a referendum on the Johnson administration and its Reconstruction policies. Certainly at one level these elections constituted an endorsement of the Fourteenth Amendment. For a moment or two they had a sobering effect upon Johnson, who flirted with a conciliatory approach to the Northern states and to the Republican party. Yet by the time Congress arrived in Washington for the new session, he was ready to shift to a defiant mode.

As it turned out, the second session of the 39th Congress, which convened in December 1866, was much like the first session, particularly because Johnson issued a series of vetoes. Such a strategy was evidently the only way a defiant and diminished president had of dealing with the Reconstruction agenda.

Johnson ushered in the new veto season in early January 1867, when he rejected the District of Columbia franchise law passed by Congress in mid-December. He was indisputably correct when he noted the overwhelming vote against black suffrage by District citizens. From that fact flowed his conclusion that Congress should not run roughshod over the will of the people.[15] Immediately after receipt of the veto message, however, Congress rejected the President's arguments and action.

In quick order came matters concerning the future of both Colorado and Nebraska, a subject unsuccessfully dealt with during the previous session. Once again, Congress passed separate bills admitting both territories as states; and once again, Johnson vetoed them.[16] It overrode the Nebraska veto, thereby bringing in a new Republican state. But, because of doubts within Congress about the sparse population of Colorado (a point made by Johnson), it did not override this presidential veto. Nevertheless, the second session of the 39th Congress would prevail on al-

13. Castel, *Presidency of Johnson*, 93–95; McKitrick, *Johnson and Reconstruction*, 438–42; William B. Phillips to Johnson, Sept. 16, 1866.

14. From September through early November there are numerous documents published herein regarding the fall elections.

15. District of Columbia Franchise Law Veto Message, Jan. 5, 1867.

16. Colorado Statehood Bill Veto Message, Jan. 28, 1867; Nebraska Statehood Bill Veto Message, Jan. 29, 1867.

most any legislation that it might enact—the veto having become ineffectual, more symbolic than real.

If relations with Congress over legislation were challenging and difficult, much the same could be claimed about federal patronage. More curse than opportunity, the problem of distributing the loaves and fishes beset Johnson constantly. From August through January scores of correspondents had recommendations to urge upon him, usually the removal of some sworn enemy (read, Radical) and replacement with some National Union man (read, Democrat). The Treasury and Post Office departments served as the battlegrounds for much of the strivings over patronage. It must have disturbed the President to receive several resignations in this period from office holders who elected to quit, rather than work for an administration with whose policies they disagreed. The earliest and most prominent of these was Hannibal Hamlin, who resigned as collector at Boston. Doubtless it was also annoying for Johnson to receive requests for federal appointments from important persons with whom he was at odds; a notable example is Salmon P. Chase, who twice intervened in behalf of friends. It is tempting to argue that had the President handled patronage more adroitly, he might have strengthened his presidency. Yet when considering all that was troubling the administration, one would probably agree with historian Eric McKitrick that patronage offered Johnson little opportunity for altering the balance of power.[17]

The beleaguered and defiant President was made more so by rising levels of impeachment talk and by the Stanton "problem." Benjamin Butler's speeches in the fall of 1866 advocating impeachment galvanized both the defenders and detractors of the President. Meanwhile a number of Johnson's friends endorsed the removal of Stanton as secretary of war. Indeed, different individuals and groups cautioned the President about the dangers of retaining Stanton; yet, Johnson hesitated to act upon these warnings.[18] As the President would discover, neither impeachment noises nor the Stanton question would disappear.

If weary of the multitude of other stresses, Johnson could always focus directly upon the ever-troubling matter of the South. The question of amnesty and parole, for example, persisted, albeit at a decreased level. Such prominent men as George A. Trenholm, Nathan Bedford Forrest, and Christopher G. Memminger entreated the President for absolution.

17. Hannibal Hamlin to Johnson, Aug. 28, 1866; Salmon P. Chase to Johnson, Sept. 22, Dec. 13, 1866; McKitrick, *Johnson and Reconstruction*, 379, 391.

18. Examples of letters regarding Stanton's removal include: Texas Delegates to Philadelphia Convention to Johnson, Aug. 22, 1866; James R. Doolittle et al. to Johnson, Sept. 18, 1866; Washington, D.C., Irish Committee to Johnson, Sept. 18, 1866; William D. Capron to Johnson, Sept. 19, 1866. Concerning impeachment, see John W. Price to Johnson, Oct. 7, 1866; Samuel W. Dewey to Johnson, Oct. 8, 1866; Maxwell P. Gaddis to Johnson, Oct. 11, 1866; Charles G. Halpine to Johnson, Nov. 26, 1866; George Jones to Johnson, Dec. 20, 1866; Thomas Powell to Johnson, Jan. 5, 1867; William B. Phillips to Johnson, Jan. 25, 1867.

Others pleaded in behalf of Jefferson Davis, still imprisoned, to seek either an extension of his parole or a speedy trial for him.[19] Professions from certain Southerners of admiration and support for Johnson undoubtedly served as balm for his wounded spirit.

Tennessee friends kept the President well informed about conditions there. Several of them, for instance, warned Johnson about Governor William G. Brownlow's tactics and misdeeds. In the midst of these, however, the governor's son sought a military appointment from Johnson and, remarkably enough, received it. By the beginning of 1867 a strategy to find a strong candidate to compete against Brownlow in his reelection bid was discussed.[20] Radical strength and control in his home state continued to vex the President.

Yet Johnson did not have the luxury to worry much about Tennessee problems, for during the six months from August 1866 through January 1867 tribulations of seemingly monumental proportions engulfed his presidency. (Shortly thereafter in February and March, others would arise, such as the Military Reconstruction and the Tenure of Office bills enacted by Congress.) Throughout the period under review, the President calculated that Congress and particularly its Radical leaders would press their Reconstruction program so diligently that there would be a backlash against it even in the Northern states. Essentially, this did not happen; instead, Johnson himself stirred negative reactions within and beyond the capital. Almost all of the miscalculations were his, a reality he failed to recognize. Unwittingly, his actions and policies seemed to serve as the answer to the plea of Wendell Phillips, arch-antagonist, who in November 1866 implored a victory celebration crowd: "Let us pray to God that the President may continue to make mistakes. . . ."[21]

ACKNOWLEDGMENTS

Were it not for archives, libraries, federal agencies, friends and supporters, this volume would not have been possible. We continue to be the beneficiaries of assistance from such repositories as the Library of Congress, the National Archives, the Lawson McGhee Library (Knox County), and the University of Tennessee Library, particularly its Special Collections department. These institutions and others not enumerated here have provided copies of Johnson documents as well as invaluable research assistance.

19. Trenholm to Johnson, Aug. 10, 1866; Forrest to Johnson, Nov. 25, 1866; Memminger to Johnson, Dec. 15, 1866. Regarding Jefferson Davis, see, for example, Gerritt Smith to Johnson, Aug. 24, 1866; Johnson to Henry Stanbery, Oct. 6, 1866; Stanbery to Johnson, Oct. 12, 1866; Charles J. Jenkins to Johnson, Oct. 14, 1866; James Lyons to Johnson, Oct. 30, 1866; Benjamin G. Humphreys to Johnson, Nov. 5, 1866.

20. James P. Brownlow to Johnson, Nov. 10, 1866; Sam Milligan to Johnson, Jan. 13, 1867; Johnson to Milligan, Jan. 23, 1867.

21. As quoted in Castel, *Presidency of Johnson*, 98.

Financial support is, of course, absolutely essential; and in this regard we are beholden to the National Historical Publications and Records Commission, the National Endowment for the Humanities, and the Tennessee Historical Commission. It must be observed, however, that these agencies have provided more than grant allocations, for they have helped us in a wide variety of ways. Our colleagues at the NHPRC, for example, have been especially attentive to our multitude of requests for research assistance.

Fortunately, the University of Tennessee, Knoxville continues to honor its commitment of financial and moral support for the Andrew Johnson Project. We remain grateful to Dean Lorman A. Ratner and Associate Dean Charles O. Jackson of the College of Liberal Arts. The head of the History Department, Russell D. Buhite, has successfully kept the well-traveled bridge between the department and our project in good repair. As always the University of Tennessee Press has been an indispensable partner in the enterprise of producing Johnson volumes.

Monetary endorsement of our efforts has come from additional quarters. The Tennessee Presidents Trust, located at the University, has given both financial support and public encouragement to us. Ralph M. Phinney of Greeneville, to whom this volume is respectfully dedicated, has provided pecuniary donations that have been vital, a tradition begun by his cousin, the late Margaret Johnson Patterson Bartlett. Moreover, simply by the example of his life, Mr. Phinney has continued to be an inspiration to us all.

We have had the good fortune to retain the same editing staff for this volume as completed the previous volume. The significance of this continuity factor can hardly be measured. I particularly appreciate the staff's high degree of competence and professional dedication. The names of the staff members are listed on the title page as a small but sincere recognition of their contributions to this volume. Furthermore, our labors have been enhanced by the continuing assistance offered to us by Ruth P. Graf, our longtime volunteer. All of us have worked effectively together to push forward the publication of the documents that shed such meaningful light upon the Johnson presidency and thereby upon the whole Reconstruction era.

Once again, I conclude with an expression of profound gratitude to my family who, while not always understanding what I have been up to, have nonetheless consistently supported my involvement with the Johnson Project. To my wife, Mary Lee, and to our three sons, Pierre, André, and Louis, I am most indebted and also most devoted.

Paul H. Bergeron

Knoxville, Tennessee
May 1993

Editorial Method

Since this is the fourth volume to be published during the current Editor's tenure, it is perhaps appropriate to remind the readers of some of the intricacies of our editorial methodology—many of which were initially spelled out in Volume 8.

Concerning the question of selectivity, it should be stated that we have confronted thousands of documents for the six months, August 1866-January 1867. Admittedly, not all of them merit publication; yet of the many hundreds that do, we have been able to include only approximately six hundred. We continue to subscribe to the belief that from Andrew Johnson's vantage point, the world was primarily political or closely related to it. Thus, the overwhelming majority (but not all) of the published documents herein treat these considerations in one fashion or another.

Because of the paucity of documents *from* Johnson to others, we have had to search far and wide. As before, we have broadened our selection of documents to include speeches, proclamations, and messages. These kinds of documents afford insight into Johnson's views and thought that otherwise might be missing.

The matter of Johnson speeches has presented unusual problems for us in this volume, principally because he went out on the speaking circuit in August-September. Thus, there are numerous speeches from which to choose. Because of the repetitive nature of most of these, however, we knew from the outset that we would not publish all of the speeches made on Johnson's trip. The challenge of narrowing the number and deciding upon specific speeches naturally arose. Eventually we agreed to publish five of them that either have been cited by historians as the most significant, for whatever reason, or else simply seemed to be representative of some part of the tour.

A caveat about the speeches published herein needs to be raised. In virtually every instance there are multiple and sometimes conflicting newspaper versions of these speeches. Hence, the account which we have published probably varies in some particulars from some other newspaper's rendition.

To reiterate some of our methodological guidelines with regard to the documents, we note the following. Once again we have decided to omit the inside address, if any, and the complimentary closings from all letters and telegrams. If either the provenance of the document or its date have been supplied, we offer an explanation of our decisions. We indent the first line of each paragraph in a document, whether the writer did or not.

We begin each new sentence with a capital letter, regardless of the original version. Whenever there might be some dispute about the writer's capitalization of a given word, we follow modern practice. We supply periods or question marks at the ends of sentences, if none is given by the writer; and we convert dashes at the ends of sentences to the appropriate periods or question marks. In a handwritten document when a word is underscored, we italicize it; when it has a double-line underscore, we render it as small capitals; and we treat a triple-line underscore as all capitals. We have deleted extraneous periods or dots within a sentence, as well as obvious slips of the pen.

We bring down to the line all interlineations, all superscript contractions or abbreviations. Marginalia are moved to appear at the end of a document, thus resembling a postscript. We have sparingly employed square brackets to insert a word or letter, for purposes of clarification. Whenever an original document uses square brackets, we have converted them to angle brackets. We have rendered the spelling of all words as faithfully as we are able. We have not added *sic* to accompany unusual or bizarre spellings, for fear that we would needlessly clutter the text.

As before, we have worked diligently to identify every person mentioned or referred to in the documents. In a few instances, however, we have been unsuccessful in our research efforts and have so indicated in our footnotes. Any person identified in a previous volume is *not* identified again in this volume. The Index indicates whether a person has been earlier identified and gives the exact location of such. There are isolated examples of persons who, although previously identified, have been given a brief updating in this volume. The Index tells if a particular person has written to Johnson or received a letter from him.

Suffice it to say, we have endeavored to follow a middle path in our editorial method with our goal always being the faithful rendering of all documents. But it must be remembered that, in the case of letters and telegrams, we have transformed nineteenth-century handwritten documents to late twentieth-century printed documents.

SYMBOLS AND ABBREVIATIONS

REPOSITORY SYMBOLS

CSmH	Henry E. Huntington Library, San Marino, California
CtY	Yale University, New Haven, Connecticut
DLC	Library of Congress, Washington, D.C.
DNA	National Archives, Washington, D.C.

RECORD GROUPS USED*

RG15	Records of the Veterans Administration
RG26	Records of the United States Coast Guard
RG45	Naval Records Collection of the Office of Naval Records and Library

RG48   Records of the Office of the Secretary of the Interior

RG49   Records of the Bureau of Land Management

RG56   General Records of the Department of the Treasury

RG58   Records of the Internal Revenue Service

RG59   General Records of the Department of State

RG60   General Records of the Department of Justice

RG75   Records of the Bureau of Indian Affairs

RG77   Records of the Office of the Chief of Engineers

RG92   Records of the Office of the Quartermaster General

RG94   Records of the Adjutant General's Office, 1780s– 1917

RG105   Records of the Bureau of Refugees, Freedmen, and Abandoned Lands

RG107   Records of the Office of the Secretary of War

RG108   Records of the Headquarters of the Army

RG109   War Department Collection of Confederate Records

RG110   Records of the Provost Marshal General's Bureau (Civil War)

RG153   Records of the Office of the Judge Advocate General (Army)

RG156   Records of the Office of the Chief of Ordnance

RG206   Records of the Solicitor of the Treasury

RG393   Records of U.S. Army Continental Commands, 1821–1920

*We have also used a number of microfilm collections from the National Archives, all of which are parts of the various Record Groups listed here.

ICN   Newberry Library, Chicago, Illinois

LNHT   Tulane University, New Orleans, Louisiana

NcD   Duke University, Durham, North Carolina

NjP   Princeton University, Princeton, New Jersey

NRU   University of Rochester Library, Rochester, New York

OFH   Rutherford B. Hayes Library, Fremont, Ohio

RPB   Brown University, Providence, Rhode Island

ScHi   South Carolina Historical Society, Charleston, South Carolina

MANUSCRIPTS

AD   Autograph Document

ALI   Autograph Letter Initialed

ALS   Autograph Letter Signed

ALSdraft   Autograph Letter Signed, draft

Copy   Copy, not by writer
Draft   Draft
L   Letter
LBcopy   Letter Book copy
L draft   Letter, draft
LS   Letter Signed
PD   Printed Document
Pet   Petition
Tel   Telegram

ABBREVIATIONS

ACP   Appointment, Commission, and Personal Branch
Adj.   Adjutant
Appl(s).   Application(s)
Appt(s).   Appointment(s)
Arty.   Artillery
Asst.   Assistant
Atty. Gen. Attorney General
Bk(s).   Book(s)
Brig.   Brigadier
Btn.   Battalion
Bty.   Battery
Bvt.   Brevet
c/ca.   circa
Capt.   Captain
Cav.   Cavalry
Cld.   Colored
Co.   Company
Col.   Collection/Colonel
Commr.   Commissioner
Comp(s).   Compiler(s)
Cong.   Congress
Corres.   Correspondence
CSA   Confederate States of America
CSR   Compiled Service Records
Dept.   Department
Diss.   Dissertation
Dist(s).   District(s)
Div.   Division
Ed(s).   Editor(s)
Enum.   Enumeration
Ex.   Executive
fl   flourishing
Gen.   General

Gov.	Governor
Inf.	Infantry
JP	Johnson Papers
Let(s).	Letter(s)
Lgt.	Light
Lt.	Lieutenant
Maj.	Major
Mil.	Military
Misc.	Miscellaneous
No(s).	Number(s)
n.d.	no date
n.p.	no page; no publisher
p./pp.	page/pages
Pet(s).	Petition(s)
Prec.	Precinct
Pt.	Part
Recd.	Received
Recomm.	Recommendation(s)
Regs.	Regulars
Res.	Reserve
Rev.	Revised/Reverend
Rgt.	Regiment
Sec.	Secretary
Ser.	Series; Serial
Sess.	Session
Subdist.	Subdistrict
Subdiv.	Subdivision
Tel(s).	Telegrams(s)
Trans.	Transcriber(s)/Translator/Translation
Twp.	Township
USCT	United States Colored Troops
Vet.	Veteran
Vol(s).	Volume(s); Volunteer(s)

SHORT TITLES

BOOKS

American Annual Cyclopaedia   *American Annual Cyclopaedia and Register of Important Events* (42 vols. in 3 series, New York, 1862–1903).

Appleton's Cyclopaedia   James G. Wilson and John Fiske, eds., *Appleton's Cyclopaedia of American Biography* (6 vols., New York, 1887–89).

Bancroft, *Washington, Idaho, and Montana* — Hubert H. Bancroft, *History of Washington, Idaho, and Montana, 1845–1889* (San Francisco, 1890)

BDAC — *Biographical Directory of the American Congress, 1774–1961* (Washington, D.C., 1961).

BDTA — Robert M. McBride et al., comps., *Biographical Directory of the Tennessee General Assembly* (5 vols., Nashville, 1975–).

Beale, *Welles Diary* — Howard K. Beale, ed., *Diary of Gideon Welles* (3 vols., New York, 1960).

Berwanger, *West and Reconstruction* — Eugene H. Berwanger, *The West and Reconstruction* (Urbana, Ill., 1981)

Biographical History of Indiana — *A Biographical History of Eminent and Self-Made Men of the State of Indiana* (2 vols., Cincinnati, 1880)

Bradley, *Militant Republicanism* — Erwin S. Bradley, *The Triumph of Militant Republicanism: A Study of Pennsylvania and Presidential Politics, 1860–1872* (Philadelphia, 1964).

Conrad, *La. Biography* — Glenn R. Conrad, ed., *A Dictionary of Louisiana Biography* (2 vols., New Orleans, 1988).

DAB — Allen Johnson and Dumas Malone, eds., *Dictionary of American Biography* (20 vols., supps., and index, New York, 1928–).

DNB — Leslie Stephen and Sidney Lee, eds., *The Dictionary of National Biography* (22 vols. and supps., London, 1938– [1885–1901]).

Edmunds, *Pen Sketches* — A. C. Edmunds, *Pen Sketches of Nebraskans with Photographs* (Lincoln, 1871)

Everly and Pacheli, *Records of Field Officers* — Elaine Everly and Willna Pacheli, comps., *Preliminary Inventory of the Records of the Field Officers of the Bureau of Refugees, Freedmen, and Abandoned Lands* (Washington, D.C., 1973–74)

Goodspeed's *Tennessee, East Tennessee, White* [and other counties]
Goodspeed Publishing Company, *History of Tennessee, from the Earliest Time to the Present . . .* (Chicago, 1886–87).

Guide to U.S. Elections
Guide to U.S. Elections (Washington, D.C., 1975)

Heitman, *Register*
Francis B. Heitman, *Historical Register and Dictionary of the United States Army, from Its Organization, September 29, 1789 to March 2, 1903* (2 vols., Washington, D.C., 1903).

Heller, *Northampton County*
William J. Heller, *History of Northampton County ⟨Pennsylvania⟩ and the Grand Valley of the Lehigh* (3 vols., Boston, 1920)

Hill, *Indian Affairs*
Edward E. Hill, *The Office of Indian Affairs, 1824–1880: Historical Sketches* (New York, 1974)

History of Allegheny County
History of Allegheny County, Pennsylvania (Chicago, 1889)

History of Montana
History of Montana, 1739–1885 (Chicago, 1885)

History of Nebraska
History of the State of Nebraska (Chicago, 1882)

Hunt and Brown, *Brigadier Generals*
Roger D. Hunt and Jack R. Brown, *Brevet Brigadier Generals in Blue* (Gaithersburg, Md., 1990).

Jenkins, *Fenians and Anglo-American Relations*
Brian Jenkins, *Fenians and Anglo-American Relations during Reconstruction* (Ithaca, 1969)

Johnson Papers
LeRoy P. Graf, Ralph W. Haskins, and Paul H. Bergeron, eds., *The Papers of Andrew Johnson* (10 vols., Knoxville, 1967-).

Lanman, *Biographical Annals*
Charles Lanman, *Biographical Annals of the Civil Government of the United States, during Its First Century* (Detroit, 1976 [1876])

Mushkat, *Fernando Wood*
Jerome Mushkat, *Fernando Wood: A Political Biography* (Kent, Ohio, 1990)

NCAB
National Cyclopaedia of American Biography . . . (63 vols. and

index, New York, 1893–1984 [1–18, Ann Arbor, 1967]).

NUC — Library of Congress, *The National Union Catalog: Pre-1956 Imprints* (754 vols., London, 1968–).

OR — *War of the Rebellion: A Compilation of the Official Records of the Union and Confederate Armies* (70 vols. in 128, Washington, D.C., 1880–1901).

Pomeroy, *The Territories* — Earl S. Pomeroy, *The Territories and the United States, 1861–1890* (Seattle, 1969 [1947]).

Poore, *Political Register* — Ben: Perley Poore, comp., *The Political Register and Congressional Directory* (Boston, 1878)

Powell, *Army List* — William H. Powell, *List of Officers of the Army of the United States from 1779 to 1900* (Detroit, 1967 [1900]).

Randall, *Browning Diary* — James G. Randall, ed., *The Diary of Orville Hickman Browning* (2 vols., Springfield, 1925–33)

Richardson, *Messages* — James D. Richardson, comp., *A Compilation of the Messages and Papers of the Presidents, 1789–1897* (10 vols., Washington, D.C., 1896–99).

Richter, *Overreached on All Sides* — William L. Richter, *Overreached on All Sides: The Freedmen's Bureau Administrators in Texas, 1865–1868* (College Station, Tex., 1991)

Simon, *Grant Papers* — John Y. Simon, ed., *The Papers of Ulysses S. Grant* (18 vols., Carbondale, 1967–).

Sistler, *1850 Tenn. Census* — Byron and Barbara Sistler, trs., *1850 Census—Tennessee* (8 vols., Evanston, Ill., 1974–76)

Smith, *Broome County* — H. P. Smith, ed., *History of Broome County* (Syracuse, 1885)

Taylor, *La. Reconstructed* — Joe Gray Taylor, *Louisiana Reconstructed, 1863–1877* (Baton Rouge, 1974).

U.S. Off. Reg.   *Register of the Officers and Agents,
                                         Civil, Military and Naval in the
                                         Service of the United States . . .*
                                         (Washington, D.C., 1851–).

Utley, *Frontier Regulars*   Robert M. Utley, *Frontier Regulars:
                                         The United States Army and the
                                         Indian, 1866–1891* (New York,
                                         1973)

Van Deusen, *Seward*   Glyndon G. Van Deusen, *William
                                         Henry Seward* (New York, 1967).

Wakelyn, *BDC*   Jon L. Wakelyn, *Biographical
                                         Directory of the Confederacy*
                                         (Westport, 1977).

Warner, *Blue*   Ezra J. Warner, *Generals in Blue*
                                         (Baton Rouge, 1964).

Warner, *Gray*   Ezra J. Warner, *Generals in Gray*
                                         (Baton Rouge, 1959).

West Point Register   *Register of Graduates and Former
                                         Cadets of the United States Military
                                         Academy: Cullum Memorial
                                         Edition* (West Point, 1970)

Wiley and Garner, *Niagara*   Samuel T. Wiley and W. Scott
     County   Garner, eds., *Biographical and
                                         Portrait Cyclopedia of Niagara
                                         County, New York* (Philadelphia,
                                         1892)

JOURNALS

ArHQ   *Arkansas Historical Quarterly*
AzW   *Arizona and the West*
CHQ   *California Historical Quarterly*
Contributions HSMon   *Contributions to the Historical Society of
                              Montana*
CWH   *Civil War History*
GHQ   *Georgia Historical Quarterly*
Harper's   *Harper's New Monthly Magazine*
La. Hist.   *Louisiana History*
La. Studies   *Louisiana Studies*
LCT Pioneers   *Lincoln County Tennessee Pioneers*
LHQ   *Louisiana Historical Quarterly*
Messenger & Register   *The Charleston Gospel Messenger and
                              Protestant Episcopal Register*
MVHR   *Mississippi Valley Historical Review*
NebH   *Nebraska History*
NMHR   *New Mexico Historical Review*

OHQ	*Oregon Historical Quarterly*
PHR	*Pacific Historical Review*
Records CHS	*Records of the Columbia Historical Society*
SCHM	*South Carolina Historical Magazine*
SHS Papers	*Southern Historical Society Papers*
SWHQ	*Southwestern Historical Quarterly*
TxHAQ	*Texas Historical Association Quarterly*
USNI Proceedings	*United States Naval Institute Proceedings*
Va. Cavalcade	*Virginia Cavalcade*
VMHB	*Virginia Magazine of History and Biography*
UHQ	*Utah Historical Quarterly*

Chronology

1808, December 29	Born at Raleigh, North Carolina
1826, September	Arrives in Greeneville, Tennessee
1827, May 17	Marries Eliza McCardle
1829–35	Alderman, then mayor
1835–37, 1839–41	State representative
1841–43	State senator
1843–53	Congressman, first district
1853–57	Governor
1857, October 8	Elected to U.S. Senate
1862, March 3	Appointed military governor of Tennessee
1864, November 8	Elected Vice President
1865, March 4	Inaugurated as Vice President
1865, April 15	Sworn in as President
1865, May 29	Amnesty Proclamation
1865, December 4	First Annual Message to Congress
1866, February 19	Veto of Freedmen's Bureau Bill
1866, March 27	Veto of Civil Rights Bill
1866, April 2	Proclamation *re* End of Insurrection
1866, May 15	Veto of Colorado Statehood Bill
1866, July 16	Veto of Freedmen's Bureau Bill
1866, August 4	Requests report from General Sheridan *re* New Orleans riot
1866, August 14	Reception for Queen Emma at White House
1866, August 18	Replies to National Union Convention Committee
1866, August 20	Proclamation *re* End of Insurrection
1866, August 28– September 15	Trip to the Northeast and Midwest
1866, September 25	Reply to Soldiers and Sailors Convention Committee
1866, November 20	Trip to Baltimore for Masonic ceremonies
1866, December 3	Second Annual Message to Congress
1866, December 22	Interview with Congressman Benjamin Eggleston

1867, January 1	New Year's Day reception at White House
1867, January 5	Veto of District of Columbia Franchise Law
1867, January 8	Remarks at Battle of New Orleans celebration
1867, January 28	Veto of Colorado Statehood Bill
1867, January 29	Veto of Nebraska Statehood Bill
1867, March 2	Veto of Tenure of Office Bill
	Veto of (First) Military Reconstruction Bill
1867, April 9	Senate approves purchase of Alaska from Russia
1867, June 1–8	Trip to North Carolina
1867, August 12	Suspends Stanton as Secretary of War
1868, February 24	Impeachment by House
1868, May 16, 26	Acquittal by Senate
1869, March	Returns to Greeneville
1869, October 22	Defeated for U.S. Senate
1872, November 5	Defeated for congressman-at-large
1875, January 26	Elected to U.S. Senate
1875, March 5–24	Serves in extra Senate session
1875, July 31	Dies at Stover home, Carter County

THE PAPERS OF
Andrew Johnson

August 1866

From Montgomery Blair

[ca. August 1866][1]

My dear Mr President

I have been anxious to have a conversation with you in relation to Missouri since hearing from my father what passed at his last interview.[2] I am apprehensive that you do not realize the truth of your own words on the 22 of Feby[3] to the effect that the Radicals are preparing a new war to maintain themselves in power.

Nor is it surprizing that a good man should fail to realize in his heart that such a design exists, even though the proofs of it are thickening every hour & have become irresistable to his understanding.

Your language to my father has the more significance because it was substantially reported to him by Genl Sherman who had been in conference with you.[4] The Genl after saying that there was no danger of violence in Missouri & that he intended to take all the troops with him to the plains added that my brother Genl Blair[5] was always too eager for a fight. This statement my father denied & reminded Genl Sherman of the fact that Genl Blair had in all his speeches counselled a strict observance of the law or of that law which the Supreme Court of the U S had pronounced unconstitutional so as to avoid giving Gov. Fletcher[6] the least pretext for a resort to violence: that notwith standing this, Fletcher was openly arming his followers including large numbers of negroes[7] & that the Govrs of Ills Iowa & Kansas had been taken thru the State of Missouri to proclaim their intention to march troops into that State to aid Fletcher.[8] The purpose is to intimidate the voters & drive them from the polls or massacre them if they persist in offering to vote. Genl Sherman is therefore deceived by his brothers[9] partizans in Missouri & elsewhere.

Their partizans are of course absent when collision comes to Missouri. What they now report of that collision at N.O.—that the fault is yours— nor would that collision have taken place if the commanding officer had understood the Revolutionary design of the Radicals & been in Sympathy with your views.[10] I sincerely believe it would not. But Genl Sherman also fails to comprehend the Radical programme is equally plan[ned] or he would not intend removing the troops & going away from Missouri himself at this given time.[11]

M Blair

ALS draft, DLC-F. P. Blair Family Papers.
1. Internal evidence, particularly the references to the New Orleans riot and Johnson's meeting with Gen. William T. Sherman, places this document in early August.

2. The date of Johnson's interview with Francis P. Blair, Sr., is not known.

3. See Washington's Birthday Address, Feb. 22, 1866, *Johnson Papers*, 10: 145–57.

4. Johnson met with Sherman on August 1. Sherman to Johnson, Aug. 9, 1866.

5. Francis P. Blair, Jr.

6. Thomas C. Fletcher.

7. Fletcher had armed a number of voluntary militia organizations of radicals as well as blacks who, he claimed, needed arms to protect themselves and to guard the polls during an election. He had ignored the portion of the militia ordinance which subjected all males to service, and thus had armed no conservatives. Another source claimed that few blacks, perhaps a dozen, had actually been seen armed. Thomas T. Gantt to John Hogan, Aug. 10, 1866; Roger Jones to R. M. Sawyer, Aug. 15, 1866, Johnson Papers, LC. See also Michael Concannon to Johnson, Aug. 21, 1866, ibid.

8. Governors Richard J. Oglesby, William H. Stone, and Samuel J. Crawford, respectively. Oglesby appeared at meetings in May and June 1866 to kick off and close the radical campaign while Stone made a ten-day tour in early June as a part of that campaign. Rumors of military aid from these states apparently stemmed from some immoderate remarks made by the governor and lieutenant governor of Missouri as well as some radical newspapers. William E. Parrish, *Missouri Under Radical Rule, 1865–1870* (Columbia, Mo., 1965), 83–85; Roger Jones to R. M. Sawyer, Aug. 15, 1866, Johnson Papers, LC.

9. Sen. John Sherman of Ohio.

10. When the New Orleans riot took place on July 30, Gen. Philip H. Sheridan was absent in Texas, leaving Absalom Baird in command. The riot is described in Joe Gray Taylor, *La. Reconstructed*, 106–13. For an indication of the sentiment blaming the administration for the riot, see James Dixon to Johnson, Aug. 27, 1866.

11. From mid-August until mid-October 1866 Sherman toured his department and was often out of touch with telegraphic and other communications. Robert G. Athearn, *William Tecumseh Sherman and the Settlement of the West* (Norman, Okla., 1956), 56–90.

Robert B. Mitchell

Santa Fe, N.M. [ca. August 1866][1]

Mr President

I am most desirous of calling your attention to the deplorable condition in which I find this country,[2] consequent upon the want of protection from Indian raids upon the settlements.[3]

The number of troops stationed in this Territory since the commencement of the late rebellion, has been totally inadequate for the protection of the lives and property of its inhabitants.[4]

The almost daily raids made upon the settlements by hostile Indians have reduced the people to penury and in some cases to the verge of starvation, and it is universally believed here that the muster out of the New Mexican Regt's whose time of enlistment has nearly expired, will increase the danger and misery already existing.

These troops understand Indian warfare and are familiar with the country, and can endure more hardships and privations than any troops that I have seen; and in addition they naturally feel a deeper interest in the welfare of the people than could be expected from men from other sections.

It is a fact conceded by the military as well as the civil authorities of the Territory, that much more can be accomplished in this country by New Mexican troops than by any others.

I therefore respectfully urge in behalf of an unfortunate people, the re-organization of the two remaining New Mexican Regt's to serve at least until the troops now arriving here become familiarized with the country and Indian warfare.[5]

Gen. Carleton[6] (comd'g the district) does the very best that he can with the means furnished him but he has not an adequate number of troops to protect this people. Gen Pope is now here and will I am satisfied reccommend this policy,[7] as will all the officers serving in this district.

It is a fact humiliating to every American citizen that there is not to day one half the wealth in this country, that there was at the time of its annexation to the United States, and this is due entirely to the fact that the Government has failed to give the protection it then guaranteed.

I am satisfied that when the Indians are repressed and the resources of the country can be developed, that this Territory will furnish more mineral wealth, than any equal area of the National domain.

Robt B. Mitchell

ALS, DNA-RG94, Lets. Recd. (Main Ser.), File N-134-1866 (M619, Roll 499).
    1. The first endorsement on this letter is dated August 25, 1866. It would have taken several weeks, at least, for the missive to reach Washington, D.C.
    2. New Mexico Territory.
    3. Various tribes of Apaches were the primary raiders, affecting settlers in western Texas and the Arizona Territory as well as the New Mexico Territory. Utley, *Frontier Regulars*, 169.
    4. William T. Sherman, in mid-September 1866, reported after his visit to New Mexico that General Carleton had the 3rd Cav., the 5th Inf., and two black regiments, all regular army troops. Another estimate places total troop strength, including volunteers, at 1,000–1,500 until late 1867. Ibid., 170; Sherman to John A. Rawlins, Sept. 21, 1866, *House Ex. Docs.*, 39 Cong., 2 Sess., No. 23, p. 15 (Ser. 1288).
    5. The 1st Rgt. (new organization) of infantry and the 1st Rgt. of cavalry were mustered out between mid-September and early November 1866. Selected members of both regiments, however, were transferred and organized on August 31, 1866, as the 1st Btn. of N. Mex. Vols. which consisted of two companies of cavalry and two of infantry. Despite the desire of General Sherman that all volunteers be mustered out, this batallion remained in service until late 1867. Ibid.; Utley, *Frontier Regulars*, 170; *Off. Army Reg.: Vols.*, 8: 2, 6, 8.
    6. James H. Carleton.
    7. In August Gen. John Pope toured the department he commanded, including New Mexico, and approved retaining the volunteers. Richard N. Ellis, *General Pope and U.S. Indian Policy* (Albuquerque, 1970), 123; Sherman to Rawlins, Sept. 21, 1866, *House Ex. Docs.*, 39 Cong., 2 Sess., No. 23, p. 15 (Ser. 1288).

From Isaac N. Arnold[1]

Chicago, Aug 1, 1866.

Sir—

I am preparing a *"History of Abraham Lincoln, & the Overthrow of Slavery."*

There are some circumstances connected with the Emancipation Proclamation of President Lincoln, about which, before the book comes from the press, I should be glad to be advised by You.

I understood Mr Lincoln to say that Tennesse, was not included in the proclamation, because You & others; earnest, true Union men of Tennessee, in whose patriotism, loyalty, & devotion to union, he had the greatest confidence, thought at the time, it would embarass the Union cause in that State; but, before a Year had gone by, Such was the change in public Sentiment that You, & other Union men, in Tennessee, expressed regret, that Your State had not been included, in the Proclamation: but, he added, they have remedied the mistake, if mistake it was, by abolishing & prohibiting Slavery in the new constitution of Tennessee.

This was the Substance of what I understood Mr Lincoln to Say. I do not feel at liberty however to make the Statement as a part of the history of the great event, without first submitting it to You, & respectfully asking Your recollection upon the subject.

Congratulating You upon the restoration of Tennessee, as a Free State, & expressing the earnest hope, that during Your administration, national unity based upon liberty, & justice to all may be completely restored. . . .

Isaac N. Arnold

ALS, DLC-JP.

1. Arnold (1815–1884) was first elected to the U.S. House of Representatives in 1860 as a Republican from Illinois. Immediately after his congressional career, Arnold served as an auditor in the Post Office Department (1865–66). He then returned to Chicago, where he became actively engaged in a career as historian and writer as well as a leader of the Chicago Historical Society. *DAB*. For Arnold's hostile letter of resignation, see Arnold to Johnson, Sept. 29, 1866.

From William W. Holden

Raleigh, Aug. 1. 1866.

My dear Mr. President:

Enclosed please find an Editorial of the Standard in relation to a recent letter of Judge Ruffin.[1]

You may remember I told you, when in Washington,[2] that the rebellious leaders in this State held that your whole plan of restoration was a usurpation, and that consequently they denied the validity of the acts of the Convention. Judge Ruffin is the leader of these men, all of whom are high in favor with Gov. Worth.

Our people will vote to-morrow, the next day, and next, for the ratification or rejection of the new Constitution.[3] All things considered, it is an excellent instrument. But these leaders are against it, first, because they deny the authority under which it was made, and secondly, because it abolishes the black basis and institutes the white. They also hope that if they can invalidate the Convention they will be able to pay the rebel debt, much of which is coming to them. So far as slavery is concerned, they intend to try that in the Courts, at least for compensation for them, on the ground that they agreed to the amendment abolishing it, under duress.

I hear from various parts of the State that there is a concerted movement to defeat the new Constitution. Gov. Worth may vote for it, to hide appearances, but his newspaper organs are doing all they can against it, and the Counties that gave him the largest votes last Fall, will give the heaviest votes against the Constitution. I hear from the West that Graham[4] is acting with Ruffin, while the whole East is against the Constitution. If adopted at all, which is doubtful, it will be done by the loyal men of the West.

I dislike very much, Sir, to be troublesome. I have been silent and quiet for many months, in the hope that our leaders and rulers here would prove themselves loyal, and would aid in good faith in carrying out your plan. But I have lost all hope in this respect, and hence the trouble I am giving you.

If you would aid us to the extent indicated by me, when in Washington, I am satisfied we could wrest the State from the hands of these men. Indeed if the new Constitution should be rejected, you would be Justified in taking the State again into your own hands. Our loyal people would hail such a step on your part with shouts and rejoicings.

William W. Holden

ALS, DLC-JP.
1. Not found enclosed, but it was undoubtedly from the July 31, 1866, *Raleigh Tri-Weekly Standard*, which included a portion of Thomas Ruffin's arguments against the legality of the convention and consequently the proposed new state constitution, which were refuted by the *Standard*. Ruffin (1787–1870), antebellum chief justice of the North Carolina supreme court, had been a firm Unionist until 1861, after which time he actively supported the Confederacy. *DAB*.
2. Holden had an interview with Johnson on July 11. See the two Holden letters of that date, *Johnson Papers*, 10: 669–72.
3. The proposed constitution was rejected by a vote of 19,570 to 21,552. *American Annual Cyclopaedia* (1866), 551.
4. William A. Graham.

From Fernando Wood

New York   Aug 1 1866

Dear Sir

Please read the enclosed.[1] The N Y Times edited by H J Raymond is the especial organ of Mr Seward—and he is of course supposed to be in your confidence. But we cannot believe that you lend your countenance to this intended attempt to exclude from seats in the Phil Convention anybody who "accepts the situation" and is aiding your administration in sustaining its present policy.

We represent those who ask no offices or official favors. We give you our support only because you are right.

Myself & others here have been elected by the *people* delegates to this convention & we do not intend to be excluded.

Fernando Wood

ALS, DLC-JP.

1. There are no enclosures found with this document. Wood was apparently reacting to the previous day's editorial in the *New York Times*, which questioned the right of Ben and Fernando Wood and Clement L. Vallandigham to attend the National Union Convention in Philadelphia. *New York Times*, July 31, 1866.

From Joseph H. Geiger

Private

Columbus O   Augt 2, 1866

My Dr Sir

The prospects for a good Union Convention here on the 7th inst are good. We shall have an active energetic body of men whose souls are in the work. We are hurt more by the prominence given Vallandingham than by all other causes—our people shrink from contact with him. He must be kept down at the Phila. Convention or we shall be badly crippled in Ohio. The fellows doctrines *now* are not so bad, but his name is damnation. We were delighted that you refused to see him. Campbell[1] and I will leave for Washington immediately upon the adjournment of our Convention and hope then to have an interview. If we do not beat a majority of the radical members of Congress in Ohio this fall I will agree to maul rails for a livelihood. Thos. Miller[2] a war-democrat, who opposed Vallandingham will be the Candidate here and will beat Shellabarger.[3] Gov. Tod[4] does not reply to our letters. I shall endeavour to see him and ascertain his wherabouts.

Jos. H. Geiger

P.S. The Treasy Dept is nearly all against us, and with the Post Office is formidable. "How long, Oh Lord how long"!

ALS, DLC-JP.

1. Lewis D. Campbell.
2. Miller (1817–1879), Columbus bookseller, newspaper publisher, and real estate investor, served variously as sheriff, internal revenue assessor, and postmaster. *History of Franklin and Pickaway Counties, Ohio* (Philadelphia, 1880), facing 533; Columbus directory (1862).
3. Samuel Shellabarger was reelected by 2,173 votes. Poore, *Political Register*, 620.
4. David Tod, formerly governor of Ohio.

From William F. Johnston

Washington city.   2 Augt. 1866.

My dear Sir

In pursuance of my promise of last evening, I have the pleasure to submit the names &c of our friends, whom I most earnestly desire to be appointed *forth with*.

In the 23d. Congressional Dist. Penna. Major *Wm. G. McCandless*,[1] for Collector of Int. Rev. in room of D. N. White[2] present incumbent.

Maj McCandless was nominated and confirmed by Senate & then a motion to reconsider & nothing done in the case.

Andrew Robinson[3] for Post Master, Allegheny City in room of S. R. Riddle,[4] whose resignation is on file in the P.O. Depart. Mr Robinson was rejected by Senate: I believe there is no other applicant seriously pressed among or by our friends.

Col. *Alfd. G. Lloyd*[5] for Assessor, in room of Mr Marks,[6] the present incumbent. Mr. Lloyd was nominated to the Senate; but so far as I can learn no action was taken in his case.

In the 22d. Congressional dist

James Lowry[7] Esq. for Surveyor of the Port at Pittsburg; in room of Mr Batcheler,[8] the present incumbent.

Ferdinand E Volz,[9] Esq., for Collector of Int. Rev. in room of Wm Little[10] present incumbent. Mess: Lowry & Volz were recommended at an early date. They *control* a very large influence. No nominations were made of these gentlemen. I am convinced that our success in making & carrying into effect certain arrangements in relation to our tickets & to which I briefly alluded, in our conversation, depends upon the removal of these parties, and the appointment without delay of Messrs. Volz and Lowry.

Mr *Wade Hamptin*[11] for Post Master at Pittsburg, in room of Mr Von Bonhorst.[12] This appointment will secure to us a large family & *religious* influence. It should be made at an early date, as the surveillance of *our correspondence* and *newspaper circulation* is not entirely such as might be desired under the present management and *at this particular time*.

Col. *Saml. McKelvey*[13] for Marshal of the Western Dist of Penna. in room of Mr Murdock[14] the present incumbent.

Col. McKelvey was nominated to Senate, and at the instigation of Messr. Lawrence, & Morehead[15] Members of Congress from Pa. was rejected upon *false charges & gross misrepresentation*. I have *no hesitation* in saying that the *immediate* appointment of Col McKelvey would materially aid us, in the defeat of at least three radical members of the present Congress. He is energetic, non tiring and feels *personally* aggrieved by the action of Lawrence Morehead & Williams.[16] I beg to urge this appointment upon your attention; and that the Commission be made out at once.

There are many other cases of somewhat pressing importance, but if the above named are made promptly, others may be post poned for the present.

I enclose Mr. Thomas's letter.[17] The latter paragraphs are *peculiarly rich*, in impudence, considering the relation in which he stands to the appointing power.

Hoping to be excused for this intrusion upon yr valuable time.

                                                    Wm F. Johnston.

I shall take the liberty of calling upon yr. private Secretary late in the afternoon to review what action has been taken in these appts.

ALS, DLC-JP.

1. McCandless (c1838–fl1901), who served in the 5th Pa. Cav. during much of the war, was first nominated by Johnson in May 1866 after the Senate's rejection of William F. Johnston. McCandless subsequently received a recess appointment in August; when he was renominated in January 1867, he was rejected by the Senate. McCandless later became an insurance agent in Pittsburgh. CSR, William G. McCandless, RG94, NA; Ser. 6B, Vol. 3: 161; Vol. 4: 82, Johnson Papers, LC; *Senate Ex. Proceedings*, Vol. 15, pt. 1: 80, 239–40; Pittsburgh directories (1875–1902).

2. David N. White, a staunch Republican, formerly owned and edited the *Pittsburgh Gazette*. *History of Allegheny County*, pt. 1: 240, 657; White to E. A. Rollins, Apr. 18, 1866, Internal Revenue Service, Collector, Pa., 23rd Dist., David N. White, RG56, NA.

3. Robinson (d. c1890), whose April nomination for postmaster was rejected by the Senate in July 1866, was given a recess appointment in August. Eventually his permanent appointment was rejected in 1867 and Hugh McKelvy took the appointment. Ser. 6B, Vol. 3: 161; Vol. 4: 82, 87, Johnson Papers, LC; *U.S. Off. Reg.* (1867); Pittsburgh directories (1875–91).

4. Samuel L. Riddle (1814–fl1889), a Republican and a Lincoln appointee, who co-owned the *Pittsburgh Gazette* for a number of years. *History of Allegheny County*, pt. 1: 657; pt. 2: 383–84; Pittsburgh and Allegheny directories (1865–75).

5. Loyd, Sr. (d. c1869), a former quartermaster with the 139th Pa. Inf., who had been originally nominated for the Twenty-third District assessorship in April 1866, was given a temporary commission for that post on August 6. Renominated in January 1867, he was rejected by the Senate the following month. Loyd later worked as superintendent of an iron works in Sharpsburg, Pennsylvania. *History of Allegheny County*, pt. 2: 349; Ser. 6B, Vol. 3: 161; Vol. 4: 82, Johnson Papers, LC; Pittsburgh directories (1869–71).

6. Samuel Marks is not further identified.

7. Lowry (1820–1876), a former Republican mayor of Pittsburgh (1864–66) and a coal merchant, was given a temporary commission for the surveyorship on August 6, but he was not confirmed by the Senate the following February. Afterward he served as coroner for Pittsburgh and ran a foundry. Pittsburgh directories (1865–71); *History of Allegheny County*, pt. 1: 666; Ser. 6B, Vol. 3: 161, Vol. 4: 84, Johnson Papers, LC; Melvin C. Holli and Peter d'A. Jones, *Biographical Dictionary of American Mayors: 1820–1980* (Westport, 1981). See also Appts., Customs Service, Surveyor, Pittsburgh, James Lowry, Jr., RG56, NA.

8. Charles W. Batchelor (1823–c1896) had held the surveyorship since his appointment by Lincoln in 1861. He was nominated by Johnson in January 1866 but was removed several months later. Trained as a steamboat pilot, he was also involved in banking, insurance, and the natural gas business. *History of Allegheny County*, pt. 2: 276–77; Ser. 6B, Vol. 4: 82, 84, Johnson Papers, LC; Pittsburgh directories (1889–97).

9. Johnson's recess appointment of Volz (1823–1876), a former bookkeeper and Pittsburgh mayor (1854–56) who later worked as a railroad paymaster, occurred in August 1866. Volz's permanent appointment was eventually confirmed in March 1867. Holli and Jones, *American Mayors*, 77; Pittsburgh directories (1865–77); Ser. 6B, Vol. 3: 161, Vol. 4: 84, Johnson Papers, LC.

10. Little (1809–1887) served as mayor of Pittsburgh and was associated with a canal freight transport business before moving to Ohio and then Iowa. Returning to Pittsburgh, he worked with a coal company until the start of the war. After leaving the collector's office, Little was secretary and treasurer of the Saxe Deposit Company until a few months before his death. *Pittsburgh Commercial Gazette*, Aug. 27, 1887.

11. Hampton (1810–1899) was engaged in the oil business in Pittsburgh when Johnson first nominated him as postmaster of that city in April 1866. Although that nomination was rejected, Hampton received a recess appointment in August. His renomination was turned down by the Senate in 1867. John W. Jordan, ed., *Genealogical and Personal History of the Allegheny Valley, Pennsylvania* (3 vols., New York, 1913), 3: 1106–7; Ser. 6B, Vol. 3: 161; Vol. 4: 82, 86, Johnson Papers, LC; *U.S. Off. Reg.* (1867).

12. Sidney F. Von Bonnhorst (1812–1887) worked in banking, railroad, and commission businesses before being appointed postmaster by Lincoln in 1861 and reappointed by Johnson in March 1866. Removed from office by September 1866, he later returned to the banking business. *Pittsburgh Commercial Gazette*, July 25, 1887; *U.S. Off. Reg.* (1861); Ser. 6B, Vol. 4: 82, Johnson Papers, LC.

13. McKelvy (1814–1889), founder of a cast-steel business in Pittsburgh and owner of blast furnaces in Virginia, was a Democrat who served during the war as Gen. Philip Sheridan's chief commissary. Johnson nominated McKelvy in April 1866 for the western district marshalship, but the Senate rejected the nomination the following month. Given a temporary commission for the same post on August 4, he was renominated in mid-December 1866 and rejected a second time in February 1867. *History of Allegheny County*, pt. 2: 438; Ser. 6B, Vol. 3: 161; Vol. 4: 83, Johnson Papers, LC; *Senate Ex. Proceedings*, Vol. 14, pt. 2: 728, 832. See also Appt. Files for Judicial Dists., Pa., Samuel McKelvy, RG60, NA.

14. Alexander Murdoch (*fl*1872), an attorney, had been appointed by Lincoln in 1861 and reappointed by Johnson four years later, serving two years. He was appointed to the same position by Grant in 1869 and resigned in 1872. Boyd Crumrine, ed., *History of Washington County, Pennsylvania, with Biographical Sketches* (Philadelphia, 1882), 253; Ser. 6B, Vol. 4: 82, Johnson Papers, LC; *Pittsburgh Gazette*, Apr. 5, 1869.

15. Republicans George V.E. Lawrence and James K. Moorhead.

16. Thomas Williams (1806–1872) was a three-term Republican representative from the Twenty-third District of Pennsylvania (1863–69). *BDAC*.

17. No enclosures from William B. Thomas are found with this letter. For more on the Thomas situation, see William F. Johnston to Johnson, Aug. 21, 1866.

From William R. Power[1]

Philad.   Aug. 2/66

Dear Sir,

Anxious for the success of your administration, I took the liberty about three months since of writing to you[2] marking the letter *private* that it might certainly get into your own hands and saying that I could not understand how you could expect to succeed while the entire horde of Federal office-holders in the North were either opposed to your policy or too craven to openly and manfully labor to support and defend it. I am glad to see that the work of removing such men has begun, but permit me to remind your Excellency, that there is a Scylla as well as a Charybdis in the path. Permit me most respectfully to remind you, that appointing to office men who like ex-gov. Johnston of Penna. has been so thoroughly identified with the sympathisers with the rebellion in Penna. cannot help, but will certainly injure your cause and give occasion and grounds for charging your Excellency with favoring the rebel cause, and especially in view of the fact that he is to succeed a man who has fought in the army against the rebellion, and the additional fact that you have many friends in Philad. not obnoxious to the same charge. Hoping that the report of the appointment of Wm. F. Johnston in place of W. B. Thomas is erroneous, and that a more judicious selection will be made, a selection from among the War Democrats of Philad.

W. R. Power M.D
No. 919 N. 7th St.

ALS, DLC-JP.

1. Power (*c*1800–1873) practiced medicine in Philadelphia for several years. Philadelphia directories (1867–73); *Evening Bulletin* (Philadelphia), Apr. 25, 1873.

2. Not found.

From Henry D. Smith[1]

New Haven, Conn, Aug. 2d 1866.

Dear Sir:

The conservative convention here yesterday was a complete success.[2] In numbers it was all that could be expected, and the resolutions passed and speeches made were all that any patriot could desire, and were enthusiastically applauded by conservative republicans, and by democrats who were in the convention in great numbers.

Forty delegates were appointed to attend the Philadelphia Convention on the 14th—one half of whom are conservative republicans, and the balance democrats. Among the delegates are such men as James Dixon, James E. English, James F. Babcock, Loren P. Waldo, Edward Prentis, Origen S. Seymour,[3] and may others of equal standing as prominent men in the State. In fact, the delegation is composed of forty of our very best men. Men who are proverbially cautious in all they do, and who will not be likely to perpetrate a foolish act.

Though a stranger, I congratulate you upon the prospective triumph of conservative sentiments in Connecticut.

The *people*, Mr President, are with you in your re-construction policy; and what the people will, must become the settled policy of the country.

Henry D Smith

ALS, DLC-JP.

1. Probably the Henry D. Smith (1801–1874) who formerly had served as state treasurer (1849–51) and later as secretary of the New Haven Water Company and as city auditor. *State of Connecticut. Register and Manual, 1910* (Hartford, 1910), 603; New Haven directories (1861–76); *Evening Union* (New Haven), Oct. 13, 1874.

2. For an account of the meeting, see *New York Herald*, Aug. 2, 1866.

3. Both Waldo (1802–1881) and Seymour (1804–1881) were much involved in state politics before serving with Johnson as Democrats in Congress and subsequently as superior court justices. Prentis (*fl*1869) was collector of customs at New London (1863–69) and former state comptroller (1856–57). *BDAC*; *U.S. Off. Reg.* (1863–69); *Connecticut Register and Manual, 1910*, 604.

From John B. Taylor[1]

Chicago, Aug 2nd AD 1866

Hon Sir,

Enclosed please find the Grand Abolition harangue of Last night, by Senator Trumbull & Speaker Colfax,[2] the denunciation is perfect, no slang has ever been more thorough, & they Intend to keep it up untill after the fall elections. They we have good hopes will be defeated & beaten. Our forces will soon Get under way, ["]when every Inch of ground will be disputed, and the Great masses shall have light." We all hope to see you here at an early day. It would do much Good, and Inspire our people with renewed Love and Devotion for our old & venerated

Constitution and they Could see its defender face to face. Those haranguers fear results of the Phil Convention, & well they may. They are poisoning the minds of our people thus early in the field. By perusing these speeches you can form an Idea of the Ground work of the fall campaign.

J. B. Taylor.

ALS, DLC-JP.

1. Taylor (c1821–fl1881), a native of Kentucky, was a real estate agent and provision inspector during the 1870s. 1870 Census, Ill., Cook, Chicago, 5th Ward, 260; Chicago directories (1870–81).

2. Lyman Trumbull and Schuyler Colfax. For the text of their speeches, see the *Chicago Tribune*, Aug. 2, 1866.

From W. Irving Crandall[1]

Green Bay, Wis. Aug 3rd 1866.

Dr Sir

It is five years since I have seen you—quite as long a time since I have been in washington[2] and you may have forgotten me. Then you disapproved my course, although for many years you were my friend, and I had supported you on all occasions. The Times are such that I cannot now resist the temptation of writing you and saying, that whatever caused you to dislike my actions then, does not prevent me from heartily rejoicing now to see the noble stand you have taken as President of the United States, and I trust & pray that your policy, as now set forth may be successful.

The abuse and slang of the present day remind me forcibly of the excitement in Tennessee when you ran for Governor, during which the Know-nothings threatened my Printing Office and mobbed you at the Crutchfield House at Chattanooga.[3] As you did not falter then, nor in the more trying scenes you have undergone during the rebellion, so I know that you are bound to prevail now—to badly beat these Radicals in the end, and it does me good to tell them so—freely and often. I verily believe that the steps now being taken, on all sides, will lead to a grand triumph; and that your fearless independence will be acknowledged by the masses for whom you have ever devoted your life and services regardless of favor or consequences.

As you have no time to read long letters I will close—simply adding that the great reaction has commenced—the radical tide is turning and the conservative elements are combining and hope for better days, and they have full confidence that Andy Johnson is the right man to be at the helm. It renews in me the old spirit. I hope to see your Administration thoroughly harmonized upon these great and vital issues, and I know it will be proudly sustained by the people.

It must be for there can be no permanent relief without it. Excuse this liberty of writing and believe me . . .

W. Irving Crandall
who lives near Sen. T. O. Howe of Wisconsin.

ALS, DLC-JP.
1. New York native Washington Irving Crandall (1829–1899) lived in Chattanooga from 1852 to 1857 and published the *Advertiser*. After a stint in Washington, D.C., Crandall moved to Green Bay, Wisconsin, in 1863, where he was in charge of a line of steamers. In the mid-1870s he returned to Chattanooga, where he was a printer, binder, and book publisher. Marion O. Smith, "Walker County, Georgia Saltpeter Operations," *GSS Bulletin* [Georgia Speleological Survey] (1989), 9.
2. Crandall spent five years as a postal clerk in Washington, D.C. Ibid.
3. Johnson ran for governor of Tennessee in 1853 and 1855, but nothing has been discovered about his experience with a Know-Nothing mob in Chattanooga.

From Michael C. Kerr[1]

Indianapolis, Ind.   August 3. 1866.

Mr President:

In my journey home, I have reached this point, the Capitol, and I here learn facts in Connection with the applications I filed the other day for the removal of Col Spooner[2] from the Marshalship of this State and the appointment of Col Thos Shea[3] to the same, and the removal of Thos C Slaughter from the assessorship of my Dist (2nd Ind), and the appointment of Col Wm. P. Davis[4] to the same, which, before I go further, I beg leave to Communicate to you in aid of those applications.

Col Spooner is making the most bitter & radical speeches at several points in this State in favor of the policy of Congress and against your policy. He is a very severe in his criticisms on your policy, and what is usually charged by the radicals as your inconsistencies. His removal and the appointment of Col Shea is most urgently needed to Consolidate and encourage your friends in this State. There is literally *no room to doubt the earnest hostility of Col Spooner to your entire policy*.

I also find that Mr Slaughter has his appointments out over my District and I know he is making the most radical speeches. He *expects* to be removed.

Now, Mr President, I beg leave to urge the earliest practicable action in these two cases. Whatever is done should be done speedily if it is to effect the approaching elections in this State.

M. C. Kerr.

ALS, DNA-RG60, Appt. Files for Judicial Dists., Ind., Thomas Shea.
1. Kerr (1827–1876), a lawyer by profession, served in the Indiana house of representatives (1856–57) and as a Democrat in the U.S. House (1865–73, 1875–76), serving as speaker from 1875 until his death from consumption. *BDAC*.
2. Benjamin J. Spooner.
3. Shea (c1839–fl1870) served with Indiana volunteer regiments during the war, reaching the rank of colonel just before being mustered out in July 1865. In March 1867 he

received brevet promotions to captain, major, lieutenant colonel, and colonel for meritorious service during the war. He retired from the army in December 1870 with the rank
of lieutenant colonel. Johnson did not appoint him to the marshalship of Indiana. Powell,
Army List, 582; *U.S. Off. Reg.* (1867); CSR, Thomas Shea, RG94, NA.

    4. Davis (1835–*fl*1911) was engaged in the manufacture of hydraulic cement and
woolen goods before the war. When war erupted he recruited the 23rd Ind. Vols., which he
commanded for two years and saw much action. Afterwards, Johnson appointed him internal revenue assessor. He went on to become president of the board of education for New
Albany, deputy auditor of Floyd County for four years, and trustee of New Albany Township, before eventually moving to Washington, D.C., where he was a Pension Office clerk.
Biographical History of Indiana, 1: 10; *U.S. Off. Reg.* (1901); *Report of the proceedings of the
. . . annual meeting of the Society of the Army of the Tennessee* (1911), 331.

From John T. Monroe et al.

New Orleans   3d August 1866.

Sir:

    Your Excellency is in possession of the main facts as regards the con-
spiracy which, by reviving the Convention of /64, purposed to subvert
the civil Government of the State of Louisiana.[1]

    An informal meeting of twenty nine members,—one hundred and fifty
being the whole number, and seventy six a quorum,—proceeded to depose the president of the convention,[2] (who considered the convention as
extinct, and himself *functus officio*)[3] and to elect R. K. Howell, as president *pro tem*. They adjourned to meet again; and a proclamation was issued by R K Howell, president *pro tem*., convening the convention to
meet on the 30th of July last, and directing His Excellency, the Governor
of the State, to issue writs of election to fill vacancies.

    So far the whole matter was looked upon as a harmless experiment,
although mischievously intended: the people was confident that the
Governor would not condescend to notice this proclamation, and, in case
the convention would commit any illegal act of interference, that he
would have it dispersed at once.

    Unfortunately, however, after a lapse of nearly a month, the Governor
issued writs of election to fill up fifty one vacancies in that body.[4] This
document, to which the Secretary of State[5] refused to give his attestation
under the seal of State, was issued under the attestation of the private
Secretary of the Governor!

    The people of the State became alarmed when no doubt could be en-
tertained as to the fact that their Chief Magistrate had given willing aid
and assistance to subvert the Government, the preservation of which was
especially entrusted to his keeping.

    On friday, the 27th of July, a large meeting was held in the Hall of the
House of Representatives, professedly for the advocacy of Universal Suffrage, but, in reality, to organize for the meeting of the Convention on the
monday following. The object of this meeting was to arouse the passions
and prejudices of the colored population, so as to make them the victims

of a riot by urging them headlong into a conflict with the State and municipal authorities.[6]

On the other hand we were determined to prevent all riots and bloodshed, by pursuing such a course as would baffle the nefarious calculations of these agitators. Our remedy, and the only remedy, must be by pursuing the usual process of law,—and, even then,—to proceed in such a way as to fasten upon them the responsibility of any collision whatever.

The case was submitted to the Grand Jury by the Attorney General, and, in the meantime, the Lieutenant Governor and the Mayor called upon Maj. Gen. Baird[7] to ascertain whether, if a warrant, issued upon a regular indictment, were placed in the hands of the Sheriff[8] for the arrest of the members of the Convention, the military would interfere. The answer was that the Sheriff would himself be arrested and that, the Convention meeting peacebly, could not be interfered with by the officers of the law.

It is proper to state that the Mayor had previously addressed a note to Maj. Gen. Baird, inquiring whether he would be interfered with by the military in case he would proceed to disperse the Convention as an unlawful assemblage. The answer to this communication was, that the meeting of the Convention being peaceable, could not be suppressed by the Mayor; and that the military authorities would prevent the interference of the city authorities.[9]

It was suggested by the Lieut. Governor, that the civil officers, under these circumstances, would not interfere to prevent the meeting of the Convention; but he proposed that, in case a warrant of arrest were placed in the hands of the Sheriff, the latter, before attempting to execute it, would call upon the General, who, thereupon, would endorse his objections, and the matter would at once be submitted to his Excellency, the President. This arrangement was satisfactory to both parties.

On the same day, the Attorney General and the Lieut. Governor telegraphed to the President to ascertain whether the process of Court, for the arrest of the members of the Convention, could be thwarted by the military. The answer was that, instead of obstructing, the military was expected to sustain the Courts.[10]

On Sunday, 29th, the municipal and state authorities called upon the press to advize the people as to the proper conduct to be held the next day, so as to avoid all collision and riot; and the Mayor issued a proclamation to the same effect. The press of the city, with the exception of the radical organ, gave wise and salutary counsels to the public, inviting all citizens to avoid congregating about the Capitol, and to demean themselves with prudence and discretion.[11]

On the morning of the 30th, the Lieut. Governor called upon Gen. Baird to communicate to him the President's dispatch, and also inquired from the General if he would not have some troops in the vicinity of the Hall to preserve peace and good order. Gen. Baird answered that applica-

tion had been made by members of the Convention for that purpose, and
that his reason for not complying was that he did not wish to appear to
side with either party, or to uphold the convention. The suggestion was
then made that to have too large a police force on that spot might be construed as meant to over-awe the members; and that in as much as civil-
authorities did not intend interfering with the convention until instructions received from the President as above agreed on, it was not improper
to have troops to co-operate with a small police force to preserve peace
and prevent all possible attempt to bring about a collision. This suggestion met the approbation of the General, who then stated that he would
give immediate orders to have the troops in readiness.

Before the end of this interview it was again agreed upon between
Gen. Baird and the Lieut. Governor that whatever warrant of arrest
might be placed in the hands of the Sheriff, would be submitted to him
before any attempt to have it executed, and that, upon indorsement of the
General's objections, the matter would be referred to the President.

The Mayor, being informed of this arrangement, sent but a small police force to the vicinity of the Hall; and the troops that were to act in
conjunction with them, were eagerly expected.

At noon information having reached the Lieut. Governor that in the
third District there was a commencement of effervescence, and that large
numbers of negroes were coming toward Canal Street from above and
below, he immediately sent a dispatch to the General, conveying this intelligence, and urging that the troops be sent without delay. About one
hour afterwards the riot broke out, ending in the dispersion of the Convention and the capture of the rioters, including several members of said
body.

It is not our purpose to argue the question of fact as to the actual commencement of the collision, and to fix precisely the mode and manner in
which it originated. We will, however, remark that the collision was, in
every instance, brought about by the armed mob, sustaining the convention.[12] Suffice it to say that the civil authorities took all the precautions
possible to prevent the outbreak;—that they appealed during three days
previous to have the aid of the military to preserve order at the place
where was to meet the convention;—that the authorities, State and Municipal, had come to an understanding to act in concert with the military
for that purpose;—that the citizens, no more than the police, contemplated to prevent the Convention to hold their meeting peacebly, and to
adjourn and disperse unmolested;—and that the warrant for their arrest
would have been submitted to the military, as agreed upon, although the
President's dispatch to the Lieut. Governor, and the subsequent one to
the Attorney General[13] were imperative that the military must sustain
and not thwart the Courts.

The military authorities have been, for the three days previous to the
riot, in constant communication with the Attorney General, the Lieut.

Governor and the Mayor,—with the view of preventing the impending riot. These efforts were unsuccessful and could not counteract the effects of the incendiary counsels and appeals of those who, for sinister purposes had had in view this very result, in order to reap a political harvest.

That the civil authorities have done their duty in this respect is patent; that more could have been done by them, was impossible, as they were not allowed to remove the cause of the riot, by taking the proper measures to prevent the meeting of the convention. And we doubt not a moment that the military Commander himself will be the first to corroborate these facts, and to arrest all calumnious imputation against the conduct of our people under these trying circumstances.

As regards the proclamation of martial law, the least that can be said of it is that it was inopportune; for the rioting had ceased completely, the police being master of the situation!—The colored population, as a body, did not participate in these disgraceful scenes, and freedmen in the vicinity of the riot were standing as lookers-on without being molested. The colored mob, in unison with a few white rioters who were leading them in this affair were, no doubt, well organized. That they were well armed is undoubted since forty two policemen and several citizens were either killed or wounded by them, although the conflict was over in less than two hours. Twenty seven rioters were killed, and a considerable number wounded.[14] At dark, when all was over, when those of the mob were either dispersed or in prison, and tranquillity and order were restored, martial law was proclaimed,—and the prisons where the rioters were confined, were emptied by orders from Head-Quarters. These measures, undoubtedly, were not intended for reviving the hopes of the outlaws; but were they not calculated to inspire them with false hopes? The very next morning the organ of the agitators was issued, containing, as usual, most inflammatory articles; and so the succeeding issues.

Had the military authorities on monday afternoon (30th) taken a stand solely to co-operate with the Civil authorities, the most beneficial effects would have been the result.

John T. Monroe   Mayor

Albert Voorhies   Lt. Gov. La.

Andrew S. Herron   Atty Genl. of La

ALS (Monroe), DNA-RG94, Lets. Recd. (Main Ser.), File G-536-1866 (M619, Roll 476).

1. For information on the attempt to revive the Convention of 1864, see Taylor, *La. Reconstructed*, 104–13; Jacob Barker to Johnson, July 31, 1866, *Johnson Papers*, 10: 764–65.

2. Judge Edward H. Durell.

3. Having finished one's duty; out of office.

4. Governor Wells explained his proclamation in J. Madison Wells to Johnson, July 28, 1866, Johnson Papers, LC. See also Johnson to Wells, July 28, 1866, *Johnson Papers*, 10: 752.

5. James H. Hardy (1835–1879) moved to Louisiana as a small child. His Civil War service consisted of three months in Co. K of the 3rd La. Rgt. in 1861. Elected secretary of

state on the Democratic ticket in November 1865, Hardy served, with a brief exception, until removed from office in June 1868. Conrad, *La. Biography.*

6. For differing accounts of the July 27 meeting, see Donald E. Reynolds, "The New Orleans Riot of 1866, Reconsidered," *La. Hist.*, 5 (1964): 23–26; *House Reports*, 39 Cong., 2 Sess., No. 16, pp. 1, 3 (Ser. 1304).

7. Absalom Baird.

8. Harry T. Hays.

9. Monroe to Baird, July 25, 1866, and Baird to Monroe, July 26, 1866, *House Reports*, 40 Cong., 1 Sess., No. 7, pp. 1056–57 (Ser. 1314).

10. See Albert Voorhies and Andrew S. Herron to Johnson, July 28, 1866, *Johnson Papers*, 10: 750; Johnson to Voorhies, July 28, 1866, Johnson Papers, LC.

11. *Missouri Democrat* (St. Louis), July 31, 1866; *House Reports*, 40 Cong., 1 Sess., No. 7, pp. 1068–69 (Ser. 1314).

12. For a contrasting view, see Philip H. Sheridan to Johnson, Aug. 6, 1866.

13. Johnson to Voorhies, July 28, 1866, Johnson Papers, LC; Johnson to Herron, July 30, 1866, *Johnson Papers*, 10: 760.

14. Dr. Albert Hartsuff, an army assistant surgeon in charge of the Sedgwick general hospital at Greenville, Louisiana, was ordered by General Baird to compile a list of casualties. Based on personal visits, Hartsuff determined the following statistics: members of the convention, 1 killed, 8 wounded; whites attending convention, 2 killed, 9 wounded; blacks attending convention, 34 killed, 119 wounded; policemen, 0 killed, 10 wounded; whites with police, 1 killed, 0 wounded; total known, 38 killed, 146 wounded. In addition, Hartsuff believed that ten other blacks had been killed and twenty had been wounded, but he could not get positive evidence to support these latter figures. *House Reports*, 39 Cong., 2 Sess., No. 16, pp. 176–77, 181–82 (Ser. 1304).

From Thomas H. Benton, Jr.

Washington   Aug. 4th 1866

Dear Sir

Being unable to leave my room I have requested the bearer, my friend Judge Parker,[1] to lay before you two dispatches from Mayor Harris of Cincinnati,[2] in regard to the transfer of Col Thomas B. Hunt of Iowa[3] (now on duty in the Volunteer service in Quartermasters Dept.) to the Regular Army as Captain & A.Q.M. Col Hunt is a Conservative Republican & one of the most active & efficient supporters of your Administration. Mayor Harris heads the Conservative move in Ohio where Col Hunt is now on duty, & as I am largely identified with it in Iowa his home, we feel a mutual interest in his success. I can heartily endorse the language of Mayor Harris that *his services are invaluable to us*[4] in our efforts to defeat radicalism in our respective States & Sincerely hope that it may be consistent with your duties to have him appointed. There is no question as to his *qualifications* & *efficiency as an officer.*[5]

Thomas H Benton Jr.

ALS, DNA-RG94, ACP Branch, File 3866-1871, Thomas B. Hunt.

1. Lawyer George H. Parker (1830–*fl*1878) moved from Ohio to Davenport, Iowa, in 1854. Although active in Democratic politics, he was not elected to office. A firm supporter of Johnson's policy, Parker was a delegate to and member of the executive committee of the National Union Convention in Philadelphia in August 1866. Thomas H. Benton, Jr., and George H. Parker to Johnson, Aug. 1, 1866, ACP Branch, File 3866-1871, Thomas B.

Hunt, RG94, NA; *The United States Biographical Dictionary and Portrait Gallery of Eminent and Self-Made Men: Iowa Volume* (Chicago, 1878), 741–43.

2. Leonard A. Harris. Probably Harris to Benton, July 30 and Aug. 2, 1866, ACP Branch, File 3866-1871, Thomas B. Hunt, RG94, NA.

3. Hunt (*c*1830–1891), a native of Canada, was mustered in as first lieutenant and regimental quartermaster, 4th Minn. Vols., on December 23, 1861. On April 25, 1863, he was mustered out of the state troops and appointed captain and assistant quartermaster of volunteers. Powell, *Army List*, 389; CSR, Thomas B. Hunt, RG94, NA; Pension File, Thomas B. Hunt, RG15, NA.

4. Quoting from Harris to Benton, Aug. 2, 1866, ACP Branch, File 3866-1871, Thomas B. Hunt, RG94, NA.

5. Johnson recommended Hunt's transfer to the regular army and referred the matter to Stanton "for his consideration and to know if this request can be granted." Hunt was appointed captain and assistant quartermaster in the regular army on April 2, 1867. Johnson endorsement, Aug. 1, 1866, ibid.; Pension File, Thomas B. Hunt, RG15, NA.

From Charles B. Flood[1]

Cincinnati Ohio   August 4 1866

President Johnson:

In company with the late Hon. John K Miller[2] of this state I called upon you at your lodgings in Washington in 1860, at which time you was pleased to remember me from my long connection with the "Ohio Statesmen" of which paper I was for years assistant Editor.

Although a sincere supporter of your policy of Southern Pacification, I am in the position of those who have no right to ask office at your hands, for I did not cast my vote for those Electors of President and Vice President pledged to your support. Lacking confidence in Gen. McClellen I did not vote at all. The fact that I did not support your election, does not, I hope, make me less an admirer and supporter of the stand you have taken, nor the less anxious for its success.

Enos B Reed, Esq.,[3] of this City, is, or intends to be, an applicant for an office under your Administration. He is Editor-in-chief of the "Daily Union" of this city, an able and effient supporter of the Administration. His political record and his character as a man both point him out as a proper person to be appointed.

In changing the "Union" from a weeky to a Daily, and supporting you against the radical element in Southern Ohio, Mr. Reed has sunk nearly all the fortune he had acquired by a life of toil. That the "Daily Union" will be a success in time, I do not doubt. Executive patronage, in this the hour of its sorest trial, would aid it much in weathering the storm.

May I, then, under these circumstances strongly recommend Mr. Reed to your early attention and favor?

C. B. Flood

ALS, DNA-RG56, Appts., Customs Service, Cincinnati, Enos B. Reed.

1. Flood (*c*1811–*fl*1881), a captain and commissary of subsistence during the war, was a writer for the *Cincinnati National Union*. Later he was superintendent of public printing

in Columbus. *Stark County Democrat* (Ohio), May 14, 1862, July 4, 1866; 1860 Census, Ohio, Cuyahoga, Cleveland, 4th Ward, 210; Columbus directories (1870–81).

2. Miller (1819–1863), a lawyer and longtime Democrat, had served in the U.S. House (1847–51). *BDAC*.

3. Reed (c1824–fl1869) before the war had been "Local Editor" of the *Cincinnati Times*. 1860 Census, Ohio, Hamilton, Cincinnati, 8th Ward, 325; Cincinnati directories (1849–69).

From Francis A. Fuller

Washington   Augt 4th 1866

Sir.

I respectfully ask leave to call your attention to the following facts.

That in the month of June last, my name was sent to the Senate for Confirmation as Collector of the Customs, for the district of Wilmington, N.C. That at the suggestion of His Excellency Jona. Worth Governor of the State of N Carolina, you caused my name to be withdrawn,[1] and the name of Richard Savage[2] substituted in place thereof. Mr. Savage' name however was not sent to the Senate for confirmation as I understand he could not take the required oath. The name of Col James. P. Foster,[3] was then sent in and he was confirmed.

The Record of Col. Foster shows that he was cashiered and dismissed the service.

His Excellency Governor Worth refused to endorse said Foster, and as I am informed that my name was withdrawn only on account of Governor Worth having endorsed Mr Savage *previous* to his Knowledge of my character, and my ability for said position, and Govr. Worth still refusing to endorse said Foster. I Respectfully ask leave to call your Excellency's attention to the above facts, as also to the fact as: I am informed by a personal friend of Foster, that he is an extreme Radical, and that his appointment has not carried out the object to be obtained, by the withdrawal of my name, viz to place a person in the position above referred to that met the approval of yourself and Govr. Worth.

I beg also to state, that I was appointed Surveyor of Customs at Wilmington last Septr. and am in the favour of the merchants of that place who would all endorse me for Collector.

I have been highly reccommended by the Honorable Secretary of the Treasury, and can refer to him for the correctness of the above statement.

I would most respectfully submit this letter for your consideration, believing that you will do full justice to me in the premises.[4]

Francis A. Fuller.

ALS, DNA-RG56, Appts., Customs Service, Collector, Wilmington, Francis A. Fuller.

1. Fuller had been nominated for Wilmington customs collector on June 4, 1866, but his name was withdrawn two weeks later. He remained for a time as collector at New Bern. Ser. 6B, Vol. 4: 140, Johnson Papers, LC. See R. W. King to Johnson, Aug. 11, 1866, Appts., Customs Service, Collector, New Bern, Richard W. King, RG56, NA.

2. Savage (b. *c*1829), a Wilmington native currently residing in New York City, had been associated with a silver mining company in San Francisco during the war. J. G. deRoulhac Hamilton, ed., *The Correspondence of Jonathan Worth* (2 vols., Raleigh, 1909), 1: 633, 651, 654; San Francisco directories (1859–64); 1850 Census, Calif., San Joaquin, Stockton, 306.

3. Foster (1830–1904), a prewar resident of Hudson, New York, had been a captain in the 5th N.Y. Cav. and lieutenant colonel of the 128th N.Y. Inf. His November 1864 dismissal upon charges of being A.W.O.L. was revoked in March 1867, when he proved that he had been absent sick. In 1867 he returned to New York, was ordained deacon in the Episcopal church in 1870 and priest three years later. He made his home variously in Syracuse, Cortland, Pulaski, Newark, and Geneva. Pension File, Matilda B. Foster, RG15, NA; CSR, James P. Foster, RG94, NA.

4. Fuller did not receive the appointment; instead, Foster was confirmed as Wilmington customs collector July 14, 1866, and served for a year, before he resigned. Ser. 6B, Vol. 4: 140–41, Johnson Papers, LC; Pension File, Matilda B. Foster, RG15, NA.

From John A. Martin

Atchison, Kansas, Aug. 4th, 1866.

Dear Sir:—

I have received a printed circular embodying a call for a "National Convention" to be held at Philadelphia on the 14th inst. This circular concludes with a request that "if the call meets my approbation, I will signify it by a brief letter."

You have always expressed a warm personal regard for me, Mr. President, and I am sure that since first I knew you the respect, esteem and personal friendship I have entertained for you has been as constant as it was unselfish. For many months a witness of your untiring labors in behalf of the Union; appreciating the heroic zeal with which you strove to bring back your people to reason and your State to loyalty; and knowing through what constant difficulties and dangers the splendid services you gave to the country were wrought, I honored and esteemed you as I did few other living men.[1]

Knowing you thus, and believing that an honest and truthful voice ought not to be, and I hope will not be, disagreeable to you, I prefer writing to you direct instead of to those who send the circular I have before referred to. I presume that I do not misunderstand the object they have in sending it. I am Post Master at this city, and upon my approval or disapproval of this call they propose to base the tenure of my office. Whether this test is patriotic, worthy, or honorable, they must decide. Whether it is to be enforced or not, rests with you. For the functions of the high office you fill by the free choice of the people belong to you alone, and the responsibility of stewardship you cannot divide with either Cabinet Ministers or politicians.

I propose, therefore, to speak frankly and plainly to you, and I trust you will hear me patiently and believe that what I have to say is kindly meant, even though it does not meet your approval. My Regiment gave you an unanimous vote, and in adding my suffrage to theirs I did it with

more than ordinary pleasure and satisfaction. I was a Republican, and
believed that the principles of that party were the inspiration of our institutions, and that its success at the polls was no less necessary to the permanency of the Government than was the triumph of our armies in the
field. Its organization, I believed, embodied that patriotism, and its policy those ideas which alone could bring peace to a sorely-troubled country and give enduring strength to the Republic. I have seen no reason to
change my mind. I still believe that the Union-Republican party was the
agent by which alone the country could have been carried through our
recent sanguinary struggle to success; I still regard that party as embodying in its principles all that is holy and hopeful in political ethics; and I
deem its continued existence and ascendency as essential and necessary
to give enduring tranquility to the country and effect the consummation
of the results of our victory. I do not and cannot bilieve that in order to
restore the Union it is necessary to go into council with those whose
hands are yet red with the blood of loyal men, and whose hearts yet burn
with hatred towards those who opposed their mad and wicked efforts to
destroy the Government. And although the Union-Republican party
may not be all that it should be, and some of its members may be rash and
reckless, there is, I bilieve, no other organization through whose agency
we can hope for such generous and just results.

The call for the Philadelphia Convention does not, therefore, meet my
approval. I am resolutely and inflexibly opposed to any effort which tends
to divide or distract the great party which successfully fought out the war
for the preservation of the Union and upon which devolves, as it should,
the work of perfecting that Freedom and Justice which our late struggle
has given to the triumphant Republic as a sacred heritage. If, therefore,
support of the Philadelphia Convention is made a test of Executive favor,
I cannot longer hope to retain it.

And that there may be no misunderstanding, let me say further that I
regard the Constitutional Amendments proposed by Congress as embodying the most satisfactory basis of adjustment between the North and
South that can be agreed upon. They may not be entirely what I could
wish for—I regard it as impossible that, with such a wide diversity of
opinion as must necessarily exist respecting a question so complex, all
should be agreed. But I bilieve that while they demand of the Southern
people no harsh, cruel or humiliating concessions, they embody such
changes as the altered condition of the country demands, such securities
as are essential to the safety of the Government, and such wholesome
punishments as are necessary for the vindication of offended law.

I have thus frankly and fully stated my position. I desire you to fully
understand the convictions I honestly entertain. They are founded upon
no whim of the moment; they spring from no unworthy hatred of the
Southern people; they are no hasty conclusions based upon ill-regulated
zeal. They were assumed with deliberation, and will be courteously but

none the less firmly maintained. No malice, I am sure, infects one comma of the course I have chosen, and no unmanly subserviency shall induce me to silence the convictions of my conscience. I value your friendship as beyond all price; I did not grow rich out of the troubles of my country, and do not scorn the benefits of the office I hold; but I cannot consent to retain your favor if to do so I must sacrifice the holiest impulses of my heart and the most earnest convictions of my judgment. I feel for you too warm a personal friendship and honor too highly your past services to consent to a pretence, or appear as a hypocrite. There are always to be found those who will flatter a President for the sake of securing his official favor; most of those in this State who are now assuming to be the champions of your administration, and protesting for you a friendship as false as it is selfish, belong to this class of parasites and placemen. But I, who learned to love and reverence you before you had offices to give or patronage to bestow, and who esteem you for your native strength of character as I honor you for the magnificent services you gave the country in those days of darkness and danger when you were "faithful among the faithless found,"[2] will not consent either to earn reward or escape removal by stoping a sentence of just stricture upon what I bilieve to be wrong, or rounding a single period in praise of that which my conscience does not approve.

If I were either false, or selfish, or hypocritical, or mercenary, I would keep silent or pretend an approval I do not feel. But I am neither, and much as I need the office I now hold I cannot stoop to pretence, and I will not deceive you in order to retain it. You would despise me if I did no less than I would despise myself. I prefer to retain your respect by telling you frankly what I think, rather than attempt to hold an office by deceit and hypocracy. I should be glad to retain my place, but I will not purchase it by falsehood. I hold principle far, far above the benefits to be derived from holding official place, and if, as an honest and sincere Union-Republican I cannot retain position under a Union-Republican administration, I must give it up. And in regard to this you alone can decide.[3]

Assuring you that, whatever may be your action in this matter, I will ever hold in grateful remembrance the many evidences of your friendship and regard, and continue to feel for you the warmest personal esteem. . . .

Jno. A. Martin, Late Col. 8th Kansas vet. Vol. Infty.

ALS, DLC-JP.

1. Martin and Johnson probably became acquainted while Johnson was military governor of Tennessee and Martin was provost marshal of Nashville, a post he held from December 1862 to June 13, 1863. Walter T. Durham, *Nashville: The Occupied City* (Nashville, 1985), 57, 139, 227.

2. Probably a variation of John Milton, *Paradise Lost*, book 5, line 896: "So spake the seraph Abdiel, faithful found; Among the faithless, faithful only he."

3. Johnson did not remove Martin, who retained his position as postmaster for several years. *U.S. Off. Reg.* (1861–73).

From S. P. Roberts[1]

Saint Louis   August 4th 66

My Dr Sir,

Allow me to trouble you with a few lines. I have been travelling on business in portions of this state, and have noted the present political prospects, &tc.

From present appearances, Blair, Broadhead[2] & Co conservative speakers, have dug the grave of Radicalism, Fletcherism, Drakeism,[3] and all the other *isms*, with which this state has been cursed—and next November the people will burry it so deep, that the last trump will not wake them.[4]

Let me congratulate you on the adjournment of the late Congress—The majority of which, intended mischief, and ruin to the country—but were partially foiled by the wisdom, and courage of Andrew Johnson. God grant that an assemblage of man so corrupt, may never meet in Washington again.

Have you an office in your gift that I could fill, if you have, I would like to hear from you on the subject, when convenient.[5]

S. P. Roberts

N.B This Philadelphia convention is a move in the right direction. God grant that it may be successful.

S.P.R.

ALS, DLC-JP.

1. Apparently a longtime friend of Johnson's, Roberts (*fl*1868) said he resided in Franklin County, Missouri, in 1868. Roberts to Johnson, May 30, 1868, Johnson Papers, LC.

2. Francis P. (Frank) Blair, Jr., and James O. Broadhead.

3. Gov. Thomas C. Fletcher and Charles D. Drake.

4. As in other states, by fair means and sometimes foul, the Radicals won overwhelmingly in Missouri on November 6, 1866. William E. Parrish, *A History of Missouri, 1860 to 1875* (Columbia, Mo., 1973), 140–43.

5. Roberts periodically applied to Johnson for a federal post, apparently without success. Roberts to Johnson, Mar. 20, 1861, May 30, 1868, Johnson Papers, LC.

To Philip H. Sheridan

Washington, D.C.   Aug. 4th 1866.

We have been advised here that, prior to the assembling of the illegal and extinct convention, elected in 1864, that inflamatory and insurrectionary speeches were made to a mob composed of white and colored persons, urging upon them to arm and equip themselves for the purpose of protecting and sustaining the Convention in its illegal and unauthorized proceedings, intended and calculated to upturn and supersede the existing State Government of Louisiana, which had been recognized by the Government of the United States. Further, did the mob assemble, and

was it armed for the purpose of sustaining the Convention in its usurpation and revolutionary proceedings?[1] Have any arms been taken from
persons, since the 30th ultimo, who were supposed to be or known to be
connected with this mob? Have not various individuals been assaulted
and shot by persons connected with this mob without good cause and in
violation of the public peace and good order? Was not the assembling of
this Convention and the gathering of the mob for its defence and protection the main cause of the riotous and unlawful proceedings of the civil
authorities at New Orleans? Have steps been taken by the civil authorities to arrest and try any and all those who were engaged in this riot and
those who have committed offences in violation of law? Can ample justice
be meted by the civil authorities to all offenders against the law? Will
Genl Sheridan please furnish me a brief reply to the above inquiries with
such other information as he may be in possession of.

Please answer by telegraph at your earliest convenience.[2]

Andrew Johnson.   Prest. U.S.

Tel, DNA-RG107, Tels. Sent, President, Vol. 3 (1865–68).
   1. See Albert Voorhies and Andrew S. Herron to Johnson, July 28, 1866, *Johnson Papers*, 10: 750.
   2. See Sheridan to Johnson, Aug. 6, 1866.

From Delegation of the Cherokee Nation[1]

Wilmington Delaware   Aug. 5, 1866.

To the President—

We arrived in this place last night, and to day have buried the Principal
Chief of our nation.[2]

It was with pain that we observed in the telegraphic dispatches of the
Tribune, sent from Washington, of date Augst 3, an item designed to
reflect on and injure our beloved Chief.[3]

On inquiry we learned that the data had been obtained at the Indian
office. The telegraphic agent promptly corrected it,[4] having been ignorant of its purpose, and believing what he had received from the Bureau
to be reliable.

We respectfully appeal to your Excellency against the sanction of official authority being given to a libel so cruel and vindictive, at this moment. We desire some protection against the recurrence of assaults, so
covert and injurious.

LS, ICN-Ballenger Collection.
   1. Six men signed the letter.
   2. John Ross, who died in Washington, D.C., on August 1. Gary E. Moulton, *John
Ross: Cherokee Chief* (Athens, Ga., 1978), 195.
   3. "Indian Commissioner Cooley informs me that on account of John Ross's affinity to
the rebellion during the war, and his disaffection to the United States when the treaty was
being made between the Cherokees and Creeks in September, 1865, the Commission re-

fused to recognize him as a chief, but after a satisfactory acquiescence, and giving ample proof of his repentance and renewed allegiance to the Government, a few weeks before his death, a letter was written him by the Commissioner, recognizing him chief of his tribe." *New York Tribune*, Aug. 3, 1866. For the conflict between John Ross and Commissioner of Indian Affairs Dennis N. Cooley, see John Ross to Johnson, June 28, 1866, and Jane Nave and Annie B. Ross to Johnson, ca. July 14, 1866, *Johnson Papers*, 10: 633–35, 696–97.

4. "The Cherokee Delegation, now in Washington, called upon your correspondent this evening, with regard to their new treaty. They complain of the information he had received of their Chief, John Ross, and state the imputations made of disloyalty are a libel. He never was set aside, though the Commissioner refused to treat with him at Fort Smith. Mr. Ross never made any professions of repentance, as he claimed never to have been guilty of disloyalty. The President, in an autograph letter, had recognized John Ross as Chief of the Cherokee Nation, and Secretary Harlan had treated with him as such." *New York Tribune*, Aug. 4, 1866.

To Davidson M. Leatherman

Washington, D.C., August 5 1866

Consul to Hamburg is best that can be done at present. Salary $2,000. Will the place suit you? If so, you had better return to Washington, and receive your commission and instructions.[1]

Andrew Johnson.

Tel, DNA-RG107, Tels. Sent, President, Vol. 3 (1865–68).
1. Leatherman, who was staying at the St. Nicholas Hotel in New York City at the time this telegram was sent, responded the next day to Johnson's offer. Leatherman declined on the grounds that he would rather be appointed to The Hague, Switzerland, or Rome. He was named an unpaid commissioner to the Paris Exhibition in 1867. Leatherman to Johnson, Aug. 6, 1866, Johnson Papers, LC; *U.S. Off. Reg.* (1867).

From Francis P. Blair, Sr.

Silver Spring [Md.] 6, Aug '66

My Dear Sir.

I solicited from you, the appointment vacated by Admiral Davis[1] on the Light House Board, for Commodore Lee.[2] He is well fitted for the place and deserves it by having performed the duties of Hydrographer upon our coasts for years in connexion with the Coast Survey & by more recent practical observation when engaged in the Blockade of the Seaboard.[3] The duty belongs to the Treasury Department and Lee has been selected by Secy. McCulloch to execute it. Mr. Wells objects to Mr. McCullochs request for his assignment—first because Mr. Lee enquired of Mr. Davis (who held the place as a plurality with that of the observatory) whether he was willing to resign it—& secondly because Mr. Lee made prize money during the war.[4] I understand from the asst. Secy. of the Treasury,[5] that Mr. Wells says under such circumstances it would be "demoralizing" to appoint Commodore Lee & that he will overrule the application of the Treasy. Department, unless you overrule him.[6]

It seems to me, that Mr. Wells is disposed to throw obstructions in the way of my son:in:law, no matter where he would go. Why does he object to Lee's taking service under the Secy. of the Treasury,[7] when he is so obnoxious to himself, that he can never let him escape the censure of an insulting letter, when he asks even justice at his hand? When Lee's friends sought a recognition of his services in the war through the thanks of Congress[8] he was met by the opposition of the Dept in the Naval Comee. Since a most derogatory letter written by Wells to Lee[9] was put in circulation in Congress through the same channel, & now a letter to you[10] charges him with "demoralization" of the service because he consulted an officer holding two places, whether he would willingly resign one to some brother officer, who wished for employment. Davis said it would be ungenerous to refuse so reasonable a request, but on the part of Mr. Wells it is resented as an attempt at demoralization of his Dept! and on this score refuses the application of Mr. McCulloch & tells you that he will over rule the Secretary of the Treasy., unless you overrule him! With what propriety does he put this invidious office on you? I & all my sons are your friends. He expects you to consult his resentments, more than our love. When you were staked up in the last Connecticut Election he gave his Son[11] leave of absence to go there to vote against you. He staid in Washington instead of going to his state to give our cause the countenance of his vote. Do the Blairs practice in this line in backing their friends—or supporting a public cause?

Is nepotism a mode of "demoralizing" a public service? Wells has had both his sons[12] in office and a Brother in law[13] was employed in buying ships for the Navy at a percentage that made his fortune—& called down the indignation of the Press, congress, *when it was patriotic*—& of the country.

F. P. Blair

ALS, DLC-JP.
    1. Charles H. Davis (1807–1877), naval officer, was involved in the scientific work of the navy for most of his career. He was one of the founders of the National Academy of Sciences in 1863. At the outbreak of the war, he headed the Bureau of Detail and aided in the planning of naval strategy before being given fleet commands; he returned to Washington as chief of the Bureau of Navigation in late 1862. Following the war he served at the Naval Observatory (1865–67, 1873–77) and on the Brazilian station (1867–69). *DAB*.
    2. Samuel Phillips Lee.
    3. Lee served with the Coast Survey from 1842 until 1852 and on blockade duty in 1862 and 1862–64. Robert M. Thompson and Richard Wainwright, eds., *Confidential Correspondence of Gustavus Vasa Fox, Assistant Secretary of the Navy, 1861–1865* (2 vols., New York, 1918–20), 2: 205–6.
    4. Over $150,000 according to Welles. Beale, *Welles Diary*, 2: 504–5.
    5. John F. Hartley or William E. Chandler.
    6. See Welles to Johnson, Aug. 3, 1866; Welles to McCulloch, Aug. 3, 1866, Gideon Welles Papers, LC.
    7. Hugh McCulloch.
    8. Unsuccessful attempts were made to include thanks to the navy and S. P. Lee in the resolution tendering thanks to General Thomas and the army. See Dudley T. Cornish and Virginia J. Laas, *Lincoln's Lee: The Life of Samuel Phillips Lee, United States Navy, 1812–*

1897 (Lawrence, Kans., 1986), 151; *Congressional Globe*, 38 Cong., 2 Sess., pp. 340, 358, 360, 914, 1383, 1389.

9. Possibly Welles to S. P. Lee, May 22, 1866, Blair-Lee Family Papers, NjP.

10. See Welles to Johnson, Aug. 3, 1866, Gideon Welles Papers, LC.

11. Edgar T. Welles (1843–1914) was an 1864 graduate of Yale and became a success-ful businessman. After serving as chief clerk of the Navy Department (1866–69), he was involved in a wide variety of business ventures. *NCAB*, 3: 432; Miranda C. Herbert and Barbara McNeil, eds., *Biography and Genealogy Master Index* (Detroit, 1980).

12. His third son Tom (*c*1846–1892) was appointed a midshipman in 1862, resigned in 1863, and subsequently entered the Army of the Potomac, where he attained the rank of lieutenant colonel of volunteers before mustering out in May 1866. After the war he be-came an attorney in Hartford, Connecticut. Beale, *Welles Diary*, 2: 82; Hartford directories (1869–81); John Niven, *Gideon Welles: Lincoln's Secretary of the Navy* (New York, 1973), 355, 440, 461, 465–66; Heitman, *Register*, 1: 1016.

13. George D. Morgan (b. *c*1818), Welles's wife's brother-in-law, purchased ships for the navy during the war for which he received a significant commission. This was not an unusual practice and Morgan supposedly was an excellent bargainer. *DAB*, Welles entry; John D. Hayes, ed., *Samuel Francis DuPont: A Selection from His Civil War Letters* (3 vols., Ithaca, 1969), 1: 158. For more information on Morgan as purchasing agent, see Richard S. West, Jr., "The Morgan Purchases," *USNI*, 66 (1940): 73–77.

From Anna H. Dorsey[1]

"Woodreve"   Near Washington
August 6th [1866].[2]

The profound interest with which I have followed evey step of your wise administration, the enthusiastic faith which I have felt in all your sagacious plans for the perfect and safe restoration of our dear country; the intense disgust inspired by your malicious and revolutionary political oponents, have altogether inspired me with an earnest and strong desire to do something to aid you in your grand work. Being a woman I could not aspire to the Forum, there was nothing therefore left for me except to pray for you, and in my sphere of influence earnestly defend your measures.

That was all, until by the last trick of the Radicals, I was placed in a position to do in a womanly way what I so much desired, and what will at least check mate their plans in their Fenian moves. Ten days ago, I wrote to Mr Donohoe,[3] Editor of the "Boston Pilot" urging and entreating him to come out and exert with zeal all the influence in his power to expose the Radical Tricksters to his people, and otherwise defend and sustain your policy. He responded today by the *marked Article* in the last number of the Boston Pilot which accompanies this.[4] That your Excellency may understand the value of such an ally as the Boston Pilot, I will simply state that for the last forty years it has been the Talmud, of the American-Irish, their defender: their guide: and exponent in all things relating to their interests, and has a circulation of over one hundred and fifty thou-sand. But for this Paper Gen'l Pierce[5] would have lost every Catholic Irish vote in the country for his political enemies had industriously circu-lated a statement that he had supported and voted for some bill[6] in the N.

Hampshire legislature oppressive to the foreign Catholic population of the State. Mr Donohoe went himself to the Capital of the State, examined the records of that particular Session and found that Gen'l Pierce had not only used all his influence against the bill but had voted against the obnoxious and mischievous thing. He returned to Boston, published all the official facts of the case and secured for Gen'l Pierce tens of thousands of votes which he would inevitably have lost.

This Paper is also published in the very hot bed of Radicalism and is immensely circulated throughout N. England. Mr Donohoe is a rich man and would never accept official favours, therefore all that he does for the good cause he does freely, willingly and legally. The Pilot was one of the few loyal Catholic Papers during the war, and your Excellency could not find a safer organ at this crisis through which to reach the Irish heart, for whatever the Pilot teaches and defends they receive. Mr Donohoe is my dear Friend. I wrote for his Paper some fifteen years, and only withdrew from it on account of extreme ill health; but if *furnished with outlines*, I would gladly fill up, and prepare for the Pilot any article in defence of your Excellency's views that may be thought advisable. I have no object in this beyond a true patriotism and ask neither favor, price or noteriety, my only desire being to serve my country and her best interests without being myself known.

Anna H. Dorsey

ALS, DLC-JP.
    1. Dorsey (1815–1896) for over forty years was a popular author of prose fiction and poetry that highlighted the "infallible light" of the Catholic Church. *DAB*.
    2. The Library of Congress assigned the 1866 date, and the reference to the Fenians and other Irish-Americans and the *Boston Pilot* article confirm assignment of that date.
    3. Patrick Donahoe (1811–1901), editor, publisher, and philanthropist, was known as "the richest and most influential Catholic in New England." During his career he owned and edited the *Boston Pilot* (1836–1901), then the most influential Catholic weekly newspaper in the U.S. *DAB*.
    4. Probably the column entitled "The Philadelphia Convention" in the August 4, 1866, issue of the *Boston Pilot*.
    5. Franklin Pierce, President from 1853 to 1857.
    6. Such rumors were started during Pierce's presidential campaign when religious antagonism and a large Irish population made it a dangerous issue politically. The only involvement with an issue dealing with Catholics occurred when Pierce, as a private citizen and a leader of New Hampshire Democrats, advocated removing the constitutional barrier in New Hampshire against Catholics holding office. Roy F. Nichols, *Franklin Pierce: Young Hickory of the Granite Hills* (Philadelphia, 1931), 130, 181, 209–10.

From Aaron Gregg[1]

Kingston, Jamaica, August 6 1866.

Sir:

I have this day sent through the Department of State, Report of the "Jamaica Royal Commission" on the late disturbances in this Island[2]—A subject of peculiar interest to Americans at this time.

The position to which you was kind enough to appoint me has afforded an excellent opportunity to observe the effect of emancipation both upon Master and Slave, also, the result of the mistake made by the English Gov't when they placed the negro upon an equality (by law) with the white man, before the former has proved himself an equal, and before the latter is willing to receive him as such.

Having an extensive acquaintance in the States of Kentucky, Missouri, Illinois, Indiana, Arkansas, and Tennessee I wish to be enabled to canvas those States in the fall of 68, in favor of the candidates of the National Union Party.

In order to enable me to do this, I have to ask of your Excellency the position of Minister Resident to some of the Central or South American Republics. I would prefer Venezuela.[3]

I flatter myself that I am too well known to Your Excellency to make it necessary to present testimonials as to character and ability. Should however you think favorable of my application and require them, I would respectfully refer to papers deposited in Department of State July 13, 1865.

                                              Aaron Gregg   U.S. Consul

ALS, DNA-RG59, Lets. of Appl. and Recomm., 1861–69 (M650, Roll 20), Aaron Gregg.
    1. Gregg was nominated for the consulship of Jamaica in December 1865 and was confirmed in March 1866. He served as consul until around 1869. Ser. 6B, Vol. 5, Johnson Papers, LC; *U.S. Off. Reg.* (1867–69).
    2. On October 11 and 12, 1865, blacks in Morant Bay rioted, killing 18 and wounding 31. The governor, under martial law, had 439 of the rebels put to death, 600 flogged, and 1,000 dwellings burned. In Jamaica blacks had been emancipated in 1833. Geoffrey Dutton, *The Hero as Murderer: The Life of Edward John Eyre, Australian Explorer and Governor of Jamaica, 1815–1901* (London, 1967), 265–385 passim; *Encyclopaedia Britannica* (1973 ed.).
    3. Gregg was not given a consular appointment after Jamaica. *U.S. Off. Reg.* (1871).

From Herman H. Heath[1]

                      Washington City, D.C.   Aug. 6th, 1866.
Dear Sir

I have the honor to apply to be appointed Governor of the Territory of Nebraska, in place of Alvin Saunders, Esq. who has held that position for more than five years.[2]

I have given five years & over, to the military service; have been wounded in battle; Gov. Saunders was appointed from political considerations; I supported the policy of Mr Lincoln, for suppressing the rebellion; supported his reëlection with your Excellency, and support your Administration and policy. Gov. Saunders does not support, & has not, since the beginning of the present year sustained your patriotic policy, but has constantly been in unison with your opponents in the radical ranks.

He aided in electing a radical Legislature in Nebraska on the 2d of June last, the members of which, by a majority were radical, and who refused to pass a vote favorable to your administration.[3] Gov. Saunders is a radical politician, and comes within the purveiw of a resolution unanimously passed by the late Johnson Convention in Nebraska,[4] that the Federal officials of that Territory, by reason of their universal and persistent opposition to your administration, so worthy of their support, merited dismissal from office.

Trusting that my record, and my friendship for the success of true constitutional Government, have not failed to secure the approbation of your Excellency. . . .[5]

H. H. Heath   Bvt. Maj. Genl. late U.S.V.

P.S. The news slips enclosed will show the President what my position was at the commencement of the difficulty with Congress, & prior.[6]

H.H.H.

LS, DNA-RG59, Lets. of Appl. and Recomm., 1861–69 (M650, Roll 22), H. H. Heath.

1. Heath (1823–1874), a New York native, served as captain in the 1st Iowa Cav., major on the staff of Gen. Samuel Curtis, and colonel of the 7th Iowa Cav. On March 13, 1865, he was brevetted both brigadier general and major general, particularly for his activities in frontier Indian warfare. Heath edited the *Nebraska Republican* in Omaha. Hunt and Brown, *Brigadier Generals*; Berwanger, *West and Reconstruction*, 94.

2. Saunders had been nominated by Lincoln on March 26, 1861, and confirmed and commissioned the following day. He was recommissioned on April 13, 1865, and January 9, 1866. Pomeroy, *The Territories*, 123.

3. More complaints about this election can be found in James M. Woolworth to Johnson, July 30, 1866, *Johnson Papers*, 10: 762–64.

4. Strongly promoted by Heath, it apparently met August 1, 1866, at Plattsmouth to choose four delegates to the Philadelphia convention. Newspaper clipping (ca. July 24, 1866), Lets. of Appl. and Recomm., 1861–69 (M650, Roll 22), H. H. Heath, RG59, NA.

5. While Heath received a number of recommendations, many Nebraskans did not see any reason to replace the very competent Saunders, particularly with Heath. Saunders remained governor of the Nebraska Territory until statehood. Johnson did, however, reward Heath with the post of territorial secretary for New Mexico where he served until 1870. Various letters in ibid.; Berwanger, *West and Reconstruction*, 98; Pomeroy, *The Territories,* 111, 123; Hunt and Brown, *Brigadier Generals*.

6. The three articles from Heath's paper, the *Republican*, were: December 23, 1865, "The President's Message," which lauded Johnson's first annual message; February 6, 1866, "Colorado as a State," which lambasted Sumner's "fundamental condition" of black suffrage as a requirement for Colorado statehood; and February 22, 1866, "The Freedmen's Bureau Bill," which defended Johnson's right to veto the bill without anyone concluding "that a general antagonism exists between him and his party."

From Gazaway B. Lamar, Sr.

Savannah   6 Augt 1866

Sir,

When I had the honor of an interview, about the 16th July—and to ask for the release of my nephew[1] & myself from the unjust & illegal findings of the Military Commission, which were ordered to convict us of the crimes, our accusers were guilty of—and to ask for the restoration of my

Books & Papers which they took—and of my Cotton too—the President gave an unconditional & affirmative promise—& referred me to the Secretary of the Treasury as to my Cotton.

When I saw Mr McCulloch he said he could not take up the Cotton case till after the adjournment of Congress,—nor act upon it till I was released. I informed him of the President's promise & he then promised to take up the Cotton case as soon as Congress adjourned. I tried to obtain my release from the War Department—but Mr. Stanton had heard of no order, as Genl. Townsend[2] informed me—& I was unable after 8 days & nights waiting to obtain another interview—& as my passport was expiring, I had to return home.

Since my arrival, I am informed by Maj Crofton[3] commanding here, that the order was not for my release, but for a new Bond extending my limits beyond the city—but requiring also Bond, & *my agreement* to abide by the military decree—which is so entirely different from the Presidents promise, & says nothing about my Books & Papers, for lack of which, I cannot settle accounts with many persons—& as it may prevent Mr. McCulloch from restoring my private Cotton, which he admits was taken in no other case from any other person but me. I cannot see how it should prevent, doing me justice as to my property, even if the sentence of the Court were valid & just. I have therefore to appeal again to the justice, & ask for the interposition of President Johnson—*as my only hope and stay—for my liberty, & my property*—and most respectfully entreat him to grant me a written order for my absolute release & that of my nephew also—the restoration of my Books & Papers—& of all my Cotton.[4]

G. B. Lamar

ALS, DNA-RG153, Court-Martial Records, MM-3469.

1. Gazaway B. Lamar, Jr. (c1837–fl1871), the son of George W. Lamar (who was a brother of Gazaway B. Lamar, Sr.) and a Savannah merchant, during the war was a lieutenant, 1st Ga. Regs., CSA, and a member of Gen. Lafayette McLaw's staff. Savannah directories (1866–71); 1870 Census, Ga., Chatham, Savannah, 21st Subdist., 175; Donnis M. Borchers, *Thomas Lamar the Immigrant: 300 Years of Descendants* (Omaha, 1977), 127; Lillian Henderson, comp., *Roster of the Confederate Soldiers of Georgia* (6 vols., Hapeville, Ga., 1959–64), 1: 339.

2. Edward D. Townsend.

3. Robert E.A. Crofton (c1835–1898), captain, 16th U.S. Inf., and brevet major and lieutenant colonel, was a career officer who retired as a full colonel in 1897. Powell, *Army List*, 264; *New York Tribune*, June 23, 1898.

4. Johnson initially did not respond to this plea, but late in his administration he remitted Lamar's sentence. In August 1867, when Grant was secretary of war ad interim, it was agreed to return some of Lamar's papers. With these, the elderly Georgian and his descendants pressed their cotton claims, with a large degree of success, until at least 1919. *Johnson Papers*, 10: 49; Robert Neil Mathis, "The Ordeal of Confiscation: The Post-Civil War Trials of Gazaway Bugg Lamar," *GHQ*, 63 (1979): 346, 349–50, 352.

From Macon, Georgia, Citizens

Macon Geo   Aug 6. 1866.

The National Express and Transportation company, will deliver to your Excellency A bale of New Cotton.[1] The first of The Crop of 1866, and tendered you by The Citizens of Macon, as an evidence of Their appreciation of your noble Services in The cause of consitutional liberty.[2] War has desolated our fields—inervated our powers, prostrated our commerce—but we feel assured, That if your policy of restoration could be engrafted upon every department of government, and we of The South, permitted to enjoy in peace and quiet, The benefit of constitutional rights and immunities, our wasted fields would soon smile with plenty—our ruined commerce again whiten our Seas. The energies of our people, Though Crippled are not paralized. Kindness and equality would soon restore them to an active healthy condition, and our whole country, energized by a renewed commercial intercourse, would grow in prosperity, as her limits are extended and her boundaries enlarged. Renewing our professions of allegiance to our Common government, and Thanking you again for your devotion to the cause of constitutional equality.[3]

Hardeman & Sparks
J B Ross & Son
Knott & Howes   Comm[4]
Mitchell & Smith

The cotton is from the Plantation of P. W. Jones[5] of Dougherty County.

LS, DLC-JP.

1. On August 15 the National Express and Transportation Company first notified the President that the bale of cotton from Macon had arrived at its establishment. Two days later the company agent, A. C. Jones, again noted the bale of cotton, complaining that he had received no reply about whether he should deliver the bale to the White House. Jones to Johnson, Aug. 15, 17, 1866, Johnson Papers, LC.

2. The gift of the bale of cotton received attention in various newspapers. Among them were the *Nashville Union and American*, Aug. 12, 1866; *Atlanta Daily Intelligencer*, Aug. 12, 1866; and the Washington *Evening Star*, Aug. 15, 1866. The Atlanta paper took note of Johnson's policy not to receive gifts but expressed the hope that the President would make an exception in this case.

3. Almost two weeks after the famous cotton bale arrived in Washington, Johnson acknowledged the gift in a letter to the Macon citizens. He asked them to convey "assurances of my great interest in, and warmest wishes for the success of the Southern people in the growth of the great staple of the South." In early January 1867 the bale of cotton was auctioned off in New York City for $213.29. The collector's office there had arranged for the firm of John H. Draper and Company to handle the auction. Johnson to Macon Citizens, Aug. 27, 1866, in *Augusta Constitutionalist*, Sept. 8, 1866; J. B. Wilbor to William S. Mitchell, Jan. 8, 1867, Johnson Papers, LC.

4. Thomas (first Sr. and then Jr.) Hardeman and Ovid G. Sparks were large cotton warehouse owners; John B. Ross and Son (William H. Ross) were dry goods merchants; and James W. Knott and probably Orvin Howes were cotton brokers. Mitchell and Smith's line of business has not been determined. Frances T. Ingmire, trans., *Citizens of Bibb County, Georgia 1860 Census* (St. Louis, n.d.), 1, 76, 97, 108; *Memoirs of Georgia* (2 vols.,

Atlanta, 1895), 1: 346; 1860 Census, Ky., Fayette, 1st Dist., 8; (1870), Ga., Bibb, Macon, 156, 181, 244; Subdiv. No. 8, 20, 55.
    5. Not identified.

From William H. Merritt[1]

Des Moines, Aug 6th 1866

I take the liberty of addressing you upon the subject of the Marshalship of Iowa. Peter Malindy[2] the present incumbent is a Radical Abolitionist, opposed to your policy of reconstruction and in favor of Negro suffrage. Such a man in such a position can do your administration and the country infinite mischief.

Capt J M Walker[3] of this city has been named by many of your friends as his successor. Capt Walker is an intelligent, trustworthy man with conservative principles. He served with gallantry and distinction all through the rebellion and I am satisfied that his appointment as Marshal of Iowa would give general satisfaction to your friends in this state.[4]

Wm. H Merritt

ALS, DNA-RG60, Appt. Files for Judicial Dists., Iowa, Joel M. Walker.
    1. Merritt (1820–fl1891), a New Yorker, went to the Iowa Territory in 1839 to manage a store among the Sac and Fox Indians. After a return to New York he settled in Iowa again in 1847, where he edited a newspaper, served as land register, and became a banker. After about three months in the Union army, where he achieved the rank of lieutenant colonel, Merritt again edited a newspaper and in 1866 briefly served as collector of internal revenue at Des Moines until the Senate rejected his appointment. He worked as a railroad contractor and served one term as mayor and several years as postmaster of Des Moines. *U.S. Biographical Dictionary: Iowa* (Chicago, 1878), 737–38; *Portrait and Biographical Album of Polk County, Iowa* (Chicago, 1890), 206.
    2. Peter Melendy (1823–1901), a farmer, manufacturer, railroad contractor, humanitarian, and education promoter, settled in Cedar Falls, Iowa, in 1856. Appointed marshal by Lincoln in 1865, Melendy was removed by Johnson but reappointed by Grant in 1871. He was later mayor of Cedar Falls. Benjamin F. Gue and Benjamin F. Shambaugh, *Biographies and Portraits of the Progressive Men of Iowa* (2 vols., Des Moines, 1899), 1: 336–37; 2: 638.
    3. Ohio native Joel M. Walker (1835–fl1880) moved to Iowa with his parents about 1840. He briefly practiced law before the Civil War. In 1862 he helped recruit troops and became captain of Co. B, 23rd Rgt., Iowa Vols., with whom he served three years. After the war he was a farmer and stock raiser. *The History of Polk County, Iowa* (Des Moines, 1880), 1036–37; C. A. Dodge to Johnson, Aug. 17, 1866, Appt. Files for Judicial Dists., Iowa, Joel M. Walker, RG60, NA.
    4. Johnson nominated Walker on December 14, 1866, but he was rejected by the Senate on February 6, 1867. Ser. 6B, Vol. 4: 328, Johnson Papers, LC.

From Philip H. Sheridan

New Orleans La   12 M—Aug 6th 1866

I have the honor to make the following reply to your dispatch of August fourth (4th).[1]

A very large number of the colored people marched in procession on

Friday night July 27th and were addressed from the steps of the City Hall by Dr. Dostie, Ex-Gov Hahn[2] and others. The speech of Dostie was intemperate in language and sentiment. The speeches of the others, so far as I can learn were characterized by moderation. I have not given you the words of Dostie's speech, as the version published was denied, but from what I have learned of the man I believe they were intemperate.[3]

The Convention assembled at 12. M. on the 30th, the timid members absenting themselves because the tone of the general public was ominous of trouble.

I think there were but about twenty six (26) members present. In front of the Mechanics Institute where the meeting was held there was assembled some colored men, women & children, perhaps eighteen or twenty, and in the Institute a number of Colored men, probably one hundred and fifty. Among those outside and inside, there might have been a pistol in the possession of every tenth man.

About one P M a procession of, say, from sixty to one hundred and thirty colored men, marched up Burgundy Street, and across Canal street towards the Convention, carrying an American flag. These men had about one pistol to every ten men, and canes and clubs in addition. While crossing Canal Street a row occurred. There were many spectators on the street, and their manner and tone towards the procession unfriendly. A shot was fired, by whom, I am not able to state, but believe it to have been a policeman, or some colored man in the procession. This led to other shots, and a rush after the procession. On arrival at the front of the Institute, there was some throwing of brick-bats by both sides. The police who had been held well in hand, were vigorously marched to the scene of disorder. The procession entered the Institute with the flag, about six or eight remaining outside. A row occurred between a policeman and one of these Colored men, and a shot was again fired, by one of the parties, which led to an indiscriminate firing on the building, through the windows by the policemen. This had been going on for a short time, when a white flag was displayed from the windows of the Institute, whereupon the firing ceased and the police rushed into the building.

From the testimony of wounded men and others who were inside the building, the policemen opened an indiscriminate fire upon the audience until they had emptied their revolvers, when they retired, and those inside barricaded the doors: The door was broken in, and the firing again commenced, when many of the Colored and white people, either escaped through out the door, or were passed out by the policemen inside, but as they came out, the policemen who formed the circle nearest the building fired upon them, and they were again fired upon by the citizens that formed the outer circle. Many of these wounded and taken prisoners, and others who were prisoners and not wounded were fired upon by their captors and by citizens. The wounded were stabbed while lying on the ground, and their heads beaten with brickbats in the yard of the building, whither some of the colored men had escaped, and partially secreted themselves, they were fired upon, and killed or wounded by policemen. Some were killed and wounded several squares from the scene. Members of the Convention were wounded by the police while in their hands as prisoners, some of them mortally.[4] The immediate cause of this terrible affair was the assemblage of this convention. The remote cause was the bitter and antagonistic feeling which has been growing in this community since the advent of the present Mayor,[5] who in the organization of his police force selected many desperate men, and some of them known murderers. People of clear views were overawed by want of confidence in the Mayor, and fear of the thugs, many of whom he had selected for his police force.

I have frequently been spoken to by prominent citizens on this subject and have heard them express fear, and want of confidence in Mayor Monroe. Ever since the intimation of this last Convention movement I must condemn the course of several of the City papers for supporting by their articles the bitter feeling of bad men. As to the merciless manner in which the convention was broken up I feel obliged to confess strong repugnance.

It is useless to attempt to disguise the hostility that exists on the part of a great many here towards northern men, and this unfortunate affair has so precipitated matters, that there is now a test of what shall be the status of Northern men, whether they can live here without being in constant dread, or whether they can be protected in life and property, and have justice in the courts. If this matter is permitted to pass over without a thorough and determined prosecution of those engaged in it, we may look out for frequent scenes of the same kind; not only here but in other places.

No steps have as yet been taken by the civil authorities to arrest citizens who were engaged in this massacre, or policemen who perpetrated such cruelties. The members of the Convention have been indicted by the Grand jury and many of them arrested and held to bail.[6] As to whether the civil authorities can mete out ample justice to the guilty parties on both sides I must say, it is my opinion unequivocally, that they cannot. Judge Abil,[7] whose course I have closely watched for nearly a year, I now consider one of the most dangerous men that we have here to the peace and quiet of the City. The leading men of the Convention, King, Cutler,[8] Hahn and others have been political aggitators, and are bad men.

I regret to say that the course of Governor Wells has been vacilating, and that during the late troubles, he has shown very little of the man.[9]

P H Sheridan   Maj Gen Comdg

Tel, DLC-JP.
1. Johnson to Sheridan, Aug. 4, 1866.
2. Anthony P. Dostie and Michael Hahn.

3. See Albert Voorhies and Andrew S. Herron to Johnson, July 28, 1866, *Johnson Papers*, 10: 750.
4. Various accounts of the riot can be found in *House Reports*, 39 Cong., 2 Sess., No. 16 (Ser. 1304).
5. John T. Monroe.
6. See also Andrew S. Herron to Johnson, July 31, 1866, *Johnson Papers*, 10: 766.
7. Edmund Abell, judge of the federal first district criminal court until removed by General Sheridan in March 1867. He served again from 1868 to 1879. Conrad, *La. Biography*.
8. R. King Cutler (1819–*fl*1885) moved in 1838 to Louisiana, where he practiced law and served as a constable, justice of the peace, judge, and alderman. Although he raised and led a company for the Confederacy, Cutler switched his allegiance after Union forces occupied New Orleans. A member of the Convention of 1864, he was a leader in the movement to reconvene in 1866. Elected U.S. senator in 1864, Cutler was never seated. After the riot, Cutler briefly moved to the North, but soon returned to his law practice in New Orleans. Ibid.; New Orleans directories (1867–85); Taylor, *La. Reconstructed*, 54.
9. Wells reluctantly supported the convention publicly by issuing the proclamation to call an election, returned to New Orleans only on July 27, and fled the area of the riot when he learned that his life was in danger from "well-armed Democrats." Walter M. Lowrey, "The Political Career of James Madison Wells," *LHQ*, 31 (1948): 1080–83.

From George Bartlett[1]

Binghamton [New York]   Aug 7, 1866

Dr Sir

Altho I never have had the pleasure of your personal acquaintance, yet I venture to address you in regard to political matters in this Congressional District. And you will bear with me if I take the liberty of expressing my views freely.

The issue in the campaign in this State this fall, will be, whether the President shall be sustained or whether Congress shall be sustained in their respective policies. And the fight will be made on the Cong. delegation.

Hon G. W. Hotchkiss[2] is the present representative of this (22) Dist[3] and is seeking a re-nomination. This Dist is strongly radical and his re-election can not probably be prevented unless it is done in the re-nominating Convention. His re-nomination he expects to secure through the aid and assistance of Govt officials, who recd their appointments under Mr Lincoln's Administration on his own solicitation.

The friends of your Administration in this District are in a minority, but they claim and justly too, that the patronage of the Government should not be permitted to be used to secure the renomination of Mr Hotchkiss or any other Radical. If the Administration is to be sustained in this contest, it must sustain its friends. They can not stand up against the radical majority in this section of the state, especially when the patronage of the Government is brought to bear against them.

In this Cong. District Judge Wells[4] of Tompkins County holds the position of Int. Rev. Assessor for this Dist, one of the most radical men in the country, with his deputy assessors scattered all thro' the Dist. equally

radical. Then there is the Collector, S. C. Hitchcock[5] of Broome Co. altho' he claims to be a supporter of your Policy with *his radical* deputies
scattered thru' the District. Then again, there is the Post Master at Watkins and Havanna in Schuyler Co—the Post Master at Owego in Tioga
Co, the Post Master at Ithaca Tompkins Co. and the Post Master at Binghamton Broome Co,[6] one and all of them *strongly* radical, and all working for the success of the radical party and for the support of the action of
Congress. It is from these men or officials that Mr Hotchkiss expects aid
in securing his re-nomination.

I submit in all candor whether it is right and just that these officials
should be allowed to hold their respective positions and use their political
power against the Administration and its friends in this contest between
the President and Congress. You should not, in my humble judgment,
permit your oppoments to turn your own guns against you and your
friends so long as you have the power to silence them.

The country demands peace and the two sections, North and South,
must be reconciled. And I know of no way whereby it can be done so
successfully as to carry out the policy you are pursuing.

Sir, you may not know me by reputation even, but if you should desire
any corroberation as to political matters in this District, I take the liberty
of referring you to Samuel G. Courtney Esq[7] U.S. Dist. Atty of New
York City.

Hoping that the contents of this letter may receive your favorable
consideration. . . .

                                                              Geo. Bartlett

ALS, DLC-JP.
1. A former War Democrat, Bartlett (c1817–1870) served as city attorney for a number of years and briefly edited a newspaper in Binghamton prior to his election to the New
York Assembly (1862). He was also among the delegates who attended the National Union
Convention in Philadelphia. Smith, *Broome County*, 131, 224–25; Appts., Internal Revenue Service, Assessor, N.Y., 26th Dist., Matthew D. Freer, RG56, NA. See also Bartlett to
Johnson, Aug. 12, 1861, Johnson Papers, LC.
2. Giles W. Hotchkiss (1815–1878), a Binghamton lawyer who eventually served a
total of three terms in Congress as a Republican (1863–67, 1869–71), lost his bid for re-
nomination to William S. Lincoln. *BDAC*; *Guide to U.S. Elections*, 617.
3. Although Bartlett clearly wrote "(22) Dist," Hotchkiss represented the Twenty-
sixth.
4. Alfred Wells (1814–1867), a former Ithaca attorney and Tompkins County judge, as
well as a journalist and one-time Republican congressman (1859–61), served as assessor of
the Twenty-sixth District of New York from the date of his appointment in 1862 until his
death. *BDAC*.
5. Simon C. Hitchcock (c1803–1878), a paper manufacturer before the war, was not
removed by Johnson and later became a bank president and water commissioner in Binghamton. 1860 Census, N.Y., Broome, 1st Ward, Binghamton, 6; Smith, *Broome County*,
215–16; William F. Seward, ed., *Binghamton and Broome County, New York: A History* (3
vols., New York, 1924), 1: 122; *U.S. Off. Reg.* (1867).
6. Henry M. Hillerman, Charles Harris, Charles Stebbins, John H. Selkreg, and William Stuart, respectively. Hillerman (c1819–fl1879), a former employee of Wells Fargo &
Co., continued serving as postmaster of Watkins until 1871, as did Harris (fl1871) of
Havana and Stebbins (fl1871) of Owego. On the other hand, Selkreg (fl1894), a former

Democrat-turned-Republican, was removed by Johnson in late August 1866. Afterwards
he was for several years a prominent member of the state legislature. Stuart (*fl*1870) remained as postmaster of Binghamton until 1870. Smith, *Broome County*, 220; *History of
Tioga, Chemung, Tompkins, and Schuyler Counties, New York* (Philadelphia, 1879), 443–
44, 576, 578, 581, 653; Leroy W. Kingman, ed., *Our County and Its People: A Memorial
History of Tioga County, New York* (Elmira, n.d.), 298; *NUC*; 1870 Census, N.Y., Schuyler, Watkins, Dix, 43.
    7. Courtney (1826–1885), U.S. attorney for the southern district of New York, and
son-in-law of the late Daniel S. Dickinson, under whom both Courtney and Bartlett had
read law. *New York Times*, Feb. 11, 1885; Smith, *Broome County*, 131. See also Courtney to
Johnson, Apr. 19, 1866, Johnson Papers, LC.

From Robert B. Carnahan

Pittsburgh, August 7th 1866.

Dear Sir:

I enclose a printed copy of a letter addressed by me to the Chairman of
the Union Republican Executive Committee[1] in response to a circular
letter of inquiry sent to each Federal Officer in this County. I feel it to be
my duty to lay a copy of this communication before you.

I have uniformly defended you and your administration in public
speeches, newspaper publications and in conversational argument. My
views, opinions and conduct in regard to the policy of your administration on the question of reconstruction must be known to you. These
opinions were sincerely entertained and published to the world more
than three years before you became President of the United States. I was
perhaps, the very first man in this State, to defend you when assailed, as
the records of the Harrisburg State Convention will show;[2] and certainly
the first in the City of Pittsburgh, at the meeting held on the 20th of
March last.[3] I have no hesitation in saying that the course of the Radical
majority in Congress gave origin to the trouble now existing between
your administration and a majority of the Republican party.

But these views and opinions have not seperated me from the Republican and Union party—I have no confidence in any other. I would not
associate politically with very many men whom I find accredited to the
Philadelphia Convention. When the call for this Convention was made I
approved it. I thought an assembly of loyal men gathered from every
quarter of the country to confer on the political situation, could have no
other than a good result. I expected it to moderate public opinion in our
party and to produce an abatement of an unreasoning Radical spirit. But
the Convention is to be filled up with men distinguished for little else
than inveterate, malignant hostility to the war and the policy of Mr. Lincoln, and the opinions and principles which you entertained and often
expressed. The Country will not take counsel of these men, and I do not
believe you will.

I cannot support Heister Clymer for Governor of this State, nor can I
think well of any Republican who can. Nor can I give my support to any

Copperhead Congressional and County ticket which may be got up in this District and County.

I have no reason to believe and do not believe that your views and opinions on these subjects are different from mine. I have as much faith in your ability, integrity and patriotism as I ever had, and I need not tell you that it has been large. But I do know that those here who claim to be your friends denounce every body who is not for Clymer. I do know that they expect me to be removed because of my support of Geary[4] and the Republican Ticket in this County. I will not purchase retention in office on the conditions they prescribe, and I am much mistaken if they have your favor and sanction.

If you find anything in my views, principles or conduct not in accordance with your opinions, policy or wishes, I beg you to accept my resignation of the office of U.S. District Attorney for this District, which in that event I wish you to consider as respectfully tendered.[5]

R B Carnahan   U.S. Atty

N.B. I beg you to excuse the employment of another hand in writing this letter. An accidental injury prevents the use of my own, for the present, to any much greater extent than signing my name.

R B. C

LS, DLC-JP.
1. The chairman was Francis Jordan (1820–c1900), a former Whig-turned-Republican attorney and state legislator, who in 1867 was appointed secretary of the Commonwealth of Pennsylvania. No enclosures were found. *Press* (Philadelphia), Aug. 1, 1866; Bradley, *Militant Republicanism*, 276–77; *NCAB*, 7: 120; Harrisburg directories (1900–1901).
2. See Carnahan to Johnson, Mar. 16, 1866, *Johnson Papers*, 10: 261–62.
3. See Carnahan to Johnson, Mar. 19, 1866, ibid., 271–72.
4. John W. Geary.
5. Carnahan's resignation was not accepted.

From Walter N. Haldeman

Louisville Ky   Aug 7 1866

Louisville by a majority of fifteen hundred votes for Duvall[1] & Kentucky by more than thirty thousand for him have fully & unequivocally endorsed you & your policy as we made the contest emphatically on that grounds.[2]

W. N. Holdeman [sic]
Editor Louisville Courier and Member Central Dem Com

Tel, DLC-JP.
1. Alvin Duvall (1813–1891) served in the Kentucky state legislature (1850–52) and as circuit judge (1852–54) and judge of the court of appeals (1854–64). Forced to flee to Canada because of his Confederate sympathies, he returned to Georgetown in 1866 to serve as reporter and clerk of the court of appeals. *NCAB*, 6: 509.
2. Control of the Democratic party in Kentucky was taken by the former Confederates in April 1866. For the August election they selected Duvall for the clerkship of the court of

appeals, the only important office to be filled. The Republicans, split between conservatives and radicals, finally decided on Gen. E. H. Hobson. The campaign thus became a contest between a Federal general and a wartime judge who had fled to avoid arrest by Federal troops. Duvall won by 38,000 votes in an election that drew approximately 154,000 voters. E. Merton Coulter, *The Civil War and Readjustment in Kentucky* (Gloucester, 1966 [1925]), 302–9.

From William B. Phillips
Private.

New York, Augt. 7h/66

Dear Sir,

I mentioned to Mr. Bennett Sr. that you thought it might be a good movement to bring General Dix forward as a candidate for governor. He was favorably impressed, and remarked "we will see by and by." I shall direct my attention to this matter in other quarters as well.[1] I enclose an article I wrote yesterday.[2] It is rather severe on the Secretary of the Treasury. That part was inspired by Mr. Bennett himself. There is, however, a good deal of truth in what is said. I would take the liberty of suggesting that the remarks made about the President and the Philadelphia Convention exposing to the people the reckless and corrupt legislation of Congress may be worthy your consideration. The radicals are very vulnerable on that point, and nothing touches the people more sensibly than to show them how their money is being wasted.

I saw Mr. Seward, but had no definite reply.[3] What he said was not very encouraging. I wait the return of Mr. Fred. Seward. The Secretary seemed to think I was disposed to be unnecessarily troublesome. The fact is I was determined to know if a subordinate of the State Department should say whether I could see the Secretary or not when the President of the United States had asked an interview for me. My apparent importunity implied no doubt of or disrespect to Mr. Seward. After the interview I felt assured the Secretary could send me abroad if he should think proper, having the means and there being good reasons for such a service just now.

W. B. Phillips.

ALS, DLC-JP.

1. James Gordon Bennett, Sr., and John A. Dix. An editorial written by Phillips endorsing Dix for governor appeared in the *New York Herald* on September 3, 1866. See also Phillips to Johnson, Sept. 3, 1866, Johnson Papers, LC, and Phillips to Johnson, Sept. 16, 1866.

2. Entitled "Secretary McCulloch—Movement of New York Bankers and Brokers," the editorial criticized the Treasury Department's fiscal policies—particularly for failing to regulate effectively the "vicious pet bank system"—and called on McCulloch to resign. *New York Herald*, Aug. 6, 1866.

3. Phillips had been seeking a State Department post. See Phillips to Johnson, June 25, 1866, *Johnson Papers*, 10: 626–27.

From James G. Bennett, Jr.

New York   Aug 8 1866.

Have we your permission to publish General Steadmans Report?[1]
Please answer at once as it is important it should appear tomorrow.[2]

J G Bennett Jr

Tel, DLC-JP.

1. The final report of Generals James B. Steedman and Joseph S. Fullerton, who had been sent on an inspection tour of the Freedmen's Bureau. See Francis P. Blair, Sr., to Johnson, Apr. 4, 1866, and Steedman to Johnson, June 26, 1866, *Johnson Papers*, 10: 353, 627–29.

2. The President replied immediately and curtly: "Let it appear." The *New York Herald* published the report on August 10. Johnson to Bennett, Jr., Aug. 8, 1866, Tels. Sent, President, Vol. 3 (1865–68), RG107, NA.

From James R. Doolittle

Buffalo N.Y.   Aug 8, 1866

My dear Sir:

I left Washington Sunday evening after dining with you. I went directly home to Wisconsin, Attended our Union Convention made a speech in the evening.[1]

Things are moving well. A very strong delegation will come from Wisconsin. I stopped on my way here at Chicago on Sunday. You may rest assured that the appointments made at Chicago are first rate.

I arrived here at Buffalo Monday Evening, and last evening we had a grand meeting.[2]

The leading men I mean not only Democrats but Republicans are with us. While here I have learned the wishes of our friends as to appointments.

For assessor of Internal Revenue Alonzo Tanner.

For Collector of Internal Revenue Nelson K. Hopkins.[3]

For Post Master Joseph Candee.

You may rely on these men as the true active efficient men.

Mr Richmond I am informed has recommended them.

I go to Saratoga this evening.[4]

J R Doolittle

ALS, DLC-JP.

1. For an account of this meeting, which took place in Madison on August 1, see the *Chicago Tribune*, Aug. 2, 1866.

2. The meeting in Buffalo was held in order to elect delegates to a statewide convention in Saratoga Springs, New York, where in turn delegates to the National Union Convention in Philadelphia would be appointed. *New York Herald*, Aug. 8, 10, 1866.

3. All three men were given temporary commissions and nominated by Johnson for their respective posts, but each was ultimately rejected by the Senate. Tanner (c1823–fl1884), a Republican, was a Buffalo attorney and city official, and a Lincoln-Johnson supporter in 1864. Hopkins (fl1875) was also active in politics, serving on the Buffalo city

council (1862–66) and as state comptroller (1872–75). H. Perry Smith, ed., *History of the City of Buffalo and Erie County* (2 vols., Syracuse, 1884), 1: 341; 2: 487; Truman C. White, ed., *Our County and Its People: A Descriptive Work on Erie County, New York* (2 vols., Boston, 1898), 1: 477, 480–81; Appts., Internal Revenue Service, Assessor, N.Y., 30th Dist., Alonzo Tanner, RG56, NA; ibid., Collector, N.Y., 30th Dist., Nelson K. Hopkins, RG56, NA; Ser. 6B, Vol. 3: 95; Vol. 4: 51, Johnson Papers, LC; 1860 Census, N.Y., Erie, Buffalo City, 10th Ward, 51.

4. Dean Richmond. Senator Doolittle made a brief speech at the Saratoga convention the following afternoon. *New York Herald*, Aug. 10, 1866.

From Ambrose R. Wright[1]

Augusta Ga   Aug 8th 1866.

I am a paroled prisoner of war. Have been elected to the Phila Convention from this State. Can my parole be enlarged so that I may attend the convention?[2]

A. R Wright   Editor Chronicle & Sentinel

Tel, DLC-JP.

1. Wright (1826–1872), a lawyer and former Confederate general, was an active politician. In 1872 he was elected to Congress but died before taking office. Warner, *Gray*.

2. Johnson immediately "extended" Wright's parole and the Georgian did attend the National Union Convention, where he was a member of the "Committee on Resolutions and Address." Johnson to Wright, Aug. 8, 1866, Tels. Sent, President, Vol. 3 (1865–68), RG107, NA; *New York Herald*, Aug. 16, 1866.

From Jacob Barker

New Orleans   August 9th 1866

Honored Sir,

My anxiety for the President to have accurate information in relation to the late unfortunate riot in this city, is my apology for again troubling him.

Govr. Wells, in his address to the public,[1] expresses a great desire for the admission into Congress of those elected. If his publication had been intended to perpetuate our exclusion, it could not have been concocted in a manner better calculated to effect that object.

The general population of this city, white & colored, disapprove of the riot and took no part therein; they remained quietly at their accustomed occupation.

The Governor is mistaken in considering the public feeling against his political course as a feeling adverse to the Union. The population of no section of the nation is more loyal than are the citizens of Louisiana. A majority were always opposed to Secession and the minority have learned from their sufferings the folly of their hostile acts, and could not under any circumstances, be induced again to take up arms again against the Flag, the Constitution & the Union of these United States.

As to persecuting Union men for their political opinions, the Governor is mistaken. We do not allow the cry of Union to protect the assassin, the thief, or the villifier. He is also mistaken in the number of persons who suffered by the late riot; if he had said a hundred instead of three hundred, he would have been more accurate.[2] His whole document betrays the feeling and delusion which pervade the mind of the unfortunate man. This the President cannot but understand without further comment.

The Governor is also mistaken when he says: "because I had seen enough of public sentiment to convince me that none but those who had served in the Confederate Army or who had gone into the Confederate lines, would be elected to office." The triumphant vote cast for the writer should have admonished him differently.[3]

In ancient times, when one of two boxers cried hold, enough, they shook hands and became friends. Now, when they [the] cry throughout the land is hold, enough, the victors re-double their blows. If endowed with the ordinary qualifications which dignify the human character; the bravery & self-sacrificing spirit displayed by the vanquished, would command for them the highest consideration.

We are Kind to the colored race and determined to do them full justice, and do not object so much to Military authority as we do to some of those selected to rule over us.

The President will excuse me for again Suggesting the appointment of General Fullerton, if he could be induced to accept the office of Chief of the Freedmen's Bureau at this place. By his appointment to that office perfect quiet would be restored, and the rights of both races could be protected.[4]

Jacob Barker

LS, DLC-JP.
1. J. Madison Wells's speech can be found in the *Picayune* (New Orleans), Aug. 9, 1866.
2. For the best estimate of the riot casualties, see John T. Monroe et al. to Johnson, Aug. 3, 1866.
3. Since he was born in 1779, Barker, a banker who was elected to Congress from New Orleans, was much too old to have joined the Confederate forces. *Harrisburg Patriot and Union* (Pa.), Nov. 27, 1865.
4. This was Barker's third request for Joseph S. Fullerton, who, despite Barker's importunings, was not reappointed to a post in Louisiana. See Barker to Johnson, July 31, 1866, *Johnson Papers*, 10: 765; Barker to Johnson, Aug. 2, 1866, Johnson Papers, LC; Paul S. Peirce, *The Freedmen's Bureau: A Chapter in the History of Reconstruction* (New York, 1971 [1904]), 173.

From Montgomery Blair

(Confidential)

Washington   Aug 9, 66

My dear Mr. President,
I am very anxious that Col W H Purnell should be apponted District Attorney in Md.

I will engage without seeing the men that nine tenths of the Representatives to Philadelphia—democrats & Union men will recommend him.
He is the most efficient friend you have in the State, an able lawyer as all
his associates at the bar attest & the best informed man in the State as to
the *personnel* of all the politicians. I want him appointed for your own
sake especially. Rely upon it that the appointments made on Reverdy
Johnson recommendation are Seward men not Johnson men. He combined with Creswell[1] to defeat your nominees to get such appointments.
This is the opinion of our people & I concur in it. Shriver[2] lately appointed is a capable Reverdy Johnson man and so is Dr. Reese & Dr.
Carroll[3] the principal appointees made through the joint efforts of Mr.
Reverdy Johnson & Mr. Creswell.

The members of the democratic Convention held yesterday in Baltimore are fully dissatisfied with Shrivers appointment. They understand that Mr R Johnson is cooperating with Mr. Seward in building up
an antagonist party to yours in our State.

I wish you to understand these things—not expecting or desiring to
make any break between you & Mr. R Johnson. In the present state of
things that wd. be very inpolitic but I am sure of my ground & therefore I
do not hesitate to state the facts to you.

M Blair

ALS, DLC-JP.
1. John A.J. Creswell.
2. Edward Shriver (*c*1813–*fl*1898), a lawyer who practiced in Frederick, Maryland,
and served in the state legislature, was appointed secretary of state, and was clerk of the
circuit court of Frederick County, all prior to the war. During the war he aided Maryland's
governor in fulfilling the state's quota for the Union army. Afterwards he served as Baltimore's postmaster (1866–69) and registrar of the Water Department (1882–88). *Portrait
and Biographical Record of the Sixth Congressional District, Maryland* (New York, 1898),
850; 1850 Census, Md., Frederick, Fredericktown, 29.
3. William Smith Reese and Thomas King Carroll.

From Adolph Bouchard[1]

Washington City D C   August 9, 1866

Honored Sir—

You Petitioner A Bouchard a citizen of the City of New Orleans Respectfully Represents

That he is engaged in the Commission and Cotton business, Office No
15. Carondolet Street, New Orleans La. That in the month of Nov. 63
while engaged as aforesaid he with others made an agreement with Cuthbert Bullet at that time collector of the Port of New Orleans by which
he agreed to protect and pass all cotton shipped from said Port by myself
and others named in said agreement. That a large quantity of cotton was
under said agreement protected as aforesaid. That the said Bullet was
paid in my presence for said service the sum of Fourteen thousand Eight
Hundred Dollars while he was performing the duties of Collector as

aforesaid—the same being one fifth of the proceeds of the Sale of said cotton.

That we were induced to enter into said agreement for the reason that he threatened to sieze the said cotton unless we paid him one fifth of the proceeds of sale or agreed so to do. That finding we were unable to get our cotton protected or released unless we made with the said Bullet the agreement aforesaid we did so and paid into his hands the amount stated aforesaid.

Your Deponent further states that he is able to produce a written agreement signed by the said Bullet myself and others for the purposes above stated. That the said facts are known to and can be proven by the testimony of five or six winesses citizens of New Orleans whose affidavits can be furnished if desired. Mr Bullet is now in this city.

Your Petitioner respectfully claims that the said Bullet in attempting and actually Extorting from him and others the sum above stated as a bribe under threats of seizure of their property grossly violated his duties as an officer of the government of the United States. That he should be compelled to refund to said Petitioner his proportion of the amount due him paid to the said Bullet (the same being one fourth of the amount so paid—) as also to restore to the others named in said agreement the amount extorted from them—and further that Your Petitioner stands ready to establish and prove all and every of the facts above stated.

Your Petititoner therefore requests that Your Excellency will be pleased to cause the said Bullet to be brought to trial for the extortions and misdemeanor aforesaid and compel him to refund the Money paid him as aforesaid.[2]

A Bouchard

LS, DLC-JP.

1. Bouchard (c1829–fl1874), a native of Canada, had lived in Louisiana since at least the very early 1850s. In 1868 he applied to Johnson, and in 1869 to Grant, for the post of collector of internal revenue for the Third District of Louisiana, but was not appointed. By 1870 he was an oil dealer. 1870 Census, La., Orleans, New Orleans, 4th Ward, 784; George W. White to Johnson, Sept. 4, 1868; John A. Grow et al. to Johnson, ca. Sept. 1868; A. Bouchard to U.S. Grant, Mar. 9, 1869, Appts., Internal Revenue Service, Collector, La., 3rd Dist., Adolph Bouchard; *U.S. Off. Reg.* (1869); New Orleans directories (1866–74).

2. Initially, Johnson apparently ignored Bouchard's letter but eventually the charges became an important factor in the attempt, spearheaded by William H.C. King, to remove Bullitt from his current post as U.S. marshal for Louisiana. King to Johnson, Nov. 7, 1866, Johnson Papers, LC. See also John Savage to Johnson, Oct. 10, 1866, and William H.C. King to Johnson, Nov. 6, 1866.

From James Edmonston[1]

Washington City, Augst 9th 1866.

Mr. President:

If I may be permitted, with all due deference, to make a few remarks in reference to the late commotion, arising out of temporary elements of do-

mestic discord, & party strife in Louisiana,[2] I would observe, that owing
to the well known courtesy, & kindly disposition of Governor Wells, to
treat, & entertain with respectful consideration the Advocates of opposing Theories, & Doctrines, as well as those who eagerly maintain various
shades of political creed, there are many who are ever ready to take advantage of this seeming, or somewhat apparent pliability of the Governor, to carry out designing motives, or Self agrandizing purposes!—But
of this, we may be assured; that Governor Wells is essentially & emphatically a Johnson man! and will stand by, & support the policy & principles enunciated & maintained under the Constitution by Andrew
Johnson.

J. Edmonston

ALS, DLC-JP.
    1. Edmonston (fl1872), a New Orleans civil engineer and surveyor, was in Washing-
ton, D.C., as chairman of the "People's Committee on Levees of Louisiana," to present a
memorial urging federal aid for levee repair and reconstruction. The committee met with
Johnson on August 14. New Orleans directories (1861–72); *Evening Star* (Washington),
Aug. 21, 1866; J. Edmonston et al. to Johnson, several letters August, 1866, Central Office Corres., River and Harbor Division, Lets. Recd., File 1196-L-1866, RG77, NA.
    2. The New Orleans riot.

From Elijah H. Eyer[1]

Piqua, Ohio, Aug. 9th 1866.

Dear Sir:
    Excuse the intrusion of an entire stranger, but an old soldier (a private)
during the war. This is my first attempt in asking for any position of public trust, and I would not ask it now, did I not feel that I was worthy of it.
    With the exception of conducting and editing a Democratic Journal in
this city, I am poor. But I have done well for my country. I was a private
soldier, a member of the Eleventh Ohio Infantry, and served more than
three years—until being wounded and mustered out of service.
    I supported McClellan for the Presidency believing that the Salvation
of the country depended upon his election; but when you declared your
policy in your 22d of February speech, I as readily endorsed you, and
from that time to the present, the files of the Piqua *Democrat*, of which I
am editor, will show that I have been an ardent and earnest Supporter of
your administration, and shall continue to do so to the end—office or no
office. My motto always has been:—"PRINCIPLES, NOT MEN."
    I am a Practical Printer, of eighteen years, and I present my name to
you for the position of Public Printer, as a successor to mr. Defrees.[2] I
refer you to Hon. F. C. LeBlond, Hon. Geo. H. Pendleton, Hon. Geo. W.
Morgan, and Hon. J. F. McKinney.[3]
    Mr. McKinney was a member of the 38th Congress, and is our candi-
date this fall, and will be elected by a handsome majority over Hom. Wm.
Lawrence (Radical).[4] The Soldiers vote this fall.

I have written this as to a Confidential friend and any favor will be gratefully received and duly acknoledged.[5]

E. H. Eyer

ALS, DNA-RG48, Appts. Div., Misc. Lets. Recd.

1. Eyer (c1834–1898), wounded at Chickamauga, lived after the war in Ohio, Kentucky, Tennessee, Georgia, Louisiana, California, Nebraska, Pennsylvania, and New Jersey, usually plying his trade as printer. CSR, Elijah H. Eyer, RG94, NA; Pension File, Maggie J. Eyer, RG15, NA.

2. John D. Defrees.

3. Francis C. LeBlond (1821–1902) and John F. McKinney (1827–1903) were lawyers and Democratic congressmen. The former was currently in office and the latter served during 1863–65 and in the early 1870s. *BDAC*.

4. Eyer's optimism was unjustified. McKinney lost the election to Lawrence by a margin of 2,244 votes. Poore, *Political Register*, 493.

5. Eyer's solicitation came to naught. There is no record of any intercession by Johnson in his behalf.

From Oliver B. Fairbanks[1]

Paterson [N.J.]   Aug. 9th 66

Sir

It is with grate reluctance that I take the liberty of addressing you for I am well aware of the frequancy of such applications and, nothing but the most pressing necessity would induce me to solicit such a favor.

The fact is my health has been feble ever cynce my confinement as a Prisoner of War at Andersonville Ga Prison whare I was compelled to remain 20 months was Captured in the Engagement at Stephensburg Va—being formily a member of Co. E. 9th New-York Cav.[2] My Farther[3] died at the above named Prison and this combined with the expense of a Family has rendered my facilties for gaining a livelihood extreamly precarious.

I do most earnestly solicit your favorable interposition in my behalf for the appointmet as United States Assesser of the 4th Collection Dist—of New Jersey Passaic County in the Place of N Lane CIVILIAN.[4] My edication has been liberal and I can procure the best of testimonals as to character & ability entreating your favorble consideration of my letter.[5]

Sergt Oliver. B. Fairbanks
No 11. Van Houten St
Paterson   N. Jersey
Formily of Co E 9th N Y Cav

ALS, DNA-RG56, Appts., Internal Revenue Service, Assessor, N.J., 4th Dist., Oliver B. Fairbanks.

1. A tailor before the war, Fairbanks (c1844–fl1882) worked as a hat presser and photographer in Paterson during the 1870s, before he was forced to seek admission to the Ohio branch of the National Home for Disabled Volunteer Soldiers in Dayton, where he resided for four years. CSR, Oliver B. Fairbanks, RG94, NA; Pension File, Oliver B. Fairbanks, RG15, NA; Paterson directories (1866–72).

2. According to a later rendering of his own war record, Fairbanks was captured on

October 11, 1863, escaped from Andersonville Prison on April 6, 1865, and reached
Charleston, South Carolina, early the following month. Pension File, Oliver B. Fairbanks,
RG15, NA.
    3. Not identified.
    4. Nathaniel Lane (fl1874) was a stove and tinware dealer in Paterson. Paterson direc-
tories (1855–77).
    5. Fairbanks's letter was referred to the Treasury Department. Lane was soon removed,
but the assessorship was not offered to Fairbanks. Ser. 6A, Vol. C: 74; Ser. 6B, Vol. 3: 147;
Vol. 4: 75, Johnson Papers, LC.

From George D. Foster[1]

Chattanooga Tenn.   9th August 1866

My dear sir

You must excuse me for the liberty I have taken in writing you a few
lines by our stanch Freind Capt. Crutchfield,[2] to let you know that I am
still in the land of the living and have no dread about the infernal radicals.
They had me hunted to take to nashville to do an unlawful act but they
(Brownlow & Co. never had the pleasure of having me guarded to nashville to help to pass the constitutional amendments)[3] failed in every particular as Capt. Crutchfield can tell you, and Arnell[4] who is one of the
worst Rads. among the Brownlow Click has the assurance after doing all
the devilment in the Legislature for most two years is going to Washinton
to claim his seat for the last two years with the certificate of the devil,
Brownlow, to show that he is a Tennesse member to Congress to draw his
pay from tennesse & the Genl. Government at the same time. Now my
dear freind if there is any chance in the world supercede Brownlow with
a military govenr. for I think tennessee is in a situation at this time that
it will be one among the great acts to have something done in the state
by right and not so much by might which is all that Brownlow Arnell
Mullins & Co[5] is determined shall be the way tennesse is to be managed.
My daily prayr. is give us a good Military govenr. and let him regulate tennesse and then we can get along. Excuse my haste as Capt C.
starts in 2 or 3 hours and accept the best wishes of your devoted freind for
ever.

Geo. D. Foster

ALS, DNA-RG94, Lets. Recd. (Main Ser.), File F-422-1866 (M619, Roll 472).
    1. Foster (1796–1874) had first lived in Bledsoe County before moving to Hamilton
County. An active Methodist, he was also a builder and contractor who later built the Lookout Mountain Hotel. Foster was elected to the lower house of the general assembly in the
spring of 1866 to fill a vacancy. BDTA, 2: 301–2; Zella Armstrong, The History of Hamilton
County and Chattanooga Tennessee (2 vols., Chattanooga, 1931–40), 1: 412.
    2. William Crutchfield of Chattanooga.
    3. Foster was one of the several members of the house for whom arrest warrants had
been issued in July in order to obtain a quorum in the legislature, so that ratification of the
Fourteenth Amendment could be accomplished. See James W. Patton, Unionism and Reconstruction in Tennessee, 1860–1869 (Chapel Hill, 1934), 220–21.
    4. Samuel M. Arnell, already famous for his controversial election to the U.S. House in

the summer of 1865, continued serving in the state legislature long enough to help engineer the ratification of the Fourteenth Amendment. Ibid., 223.

5. James Mullins (1807–1873) of Bedford County had served in the Union army during the war. Afterwards he was elected to the state legislature in 1865 and served as speaker. In 1867 Mullins was elected to the U.S. House. *BDAC*; *BDTA*, 2: 648.

From William T. Sherman

Saint Louis Mo.   Aug 9 1866

Sir.

During the interview to which you did me the honor to invite me at the Executive Mansion on the 1st instant you handed me certain papers relating to matters in the state of Missouri.[1]

Immediately on my arrival here I put myself in communication with Governor Fletcher[2] who agreed to meet me here this morning at 9 Am. Previous to the time appointed, I saw Mr T. T. Gantt,[3] the author and maker of one of the principal papers and told him that I proposed to show it to Governor Fletcher, and at his request to avoid the effect of certain expressions therein, calculated to inflame I permitted him to modify it somewhat in expression but not in substance, and herewith return his paper as the one used in the interview.[4] I also invited him to be present, with Mr Glover[5] a lawyer here of respectability and influence, and this morning these Gentlemen met Governor Fletcher in my office.

I handed the Governor all the papers which he read carefully, and he expressed himself not only willing but anxious that I should enquire fully into all the facts specifically alledged, charging him with endeavoring to intimidate the Conservative party in the elections of November, and with his sanction I have ordered my Inspector General Colonel R. Jones[6] to proceed to Jackson County and make a critical examination of the facts alledged, and to report in such form that it may be supplementary to this.[7]

In general terms Governor Fletcher denied any intention of inviting assistance from any quarter, Iowa or Kansas, in the affairs of the State:[8] and insisted that all he had done or intended to do, was to execute the Constitution and Laws of the State, to permit a free and open election, without violence or threat.

In order that a proper understanding of the matters political in this state may be had, you must look at the Constitution now in force here, the Militia ordinance, and the Registration Law, all of which I take the liberty to enclose herewith in the best shape & form I can obtain them.[9]

These are extremely Radical and seem obligatory on the Governor, who professes to act strictly in obedience to them, which I suppose he is bound to do, so long as they stand the undoubted Law of the State.

After a full & long conversation freely indulged in between the Governor and Messrs Gantt and Glover,[10] in which individual instances of personal violence were discussed pro & con in a fair Spirit, I thought I could detect the only real cause of difference was in the Governors Construction of the Militia Ordinance to which I invite your special attention on page 34 of the pamphlet embracing the new Constitution. That ordinance makes all the able bodied men, with the presented exceptions, members of the state militia, whereas the Governor has allowed persons subject to militia duty to form Volunteer Companies, which are naturally composed of his own friend[s] (Radicals) and some of these have been armed, and used to make arrests, and in some instances have by their language and acts given some appearance to the accusation that his partizans are to be armed, but his opponents not. In this I think him wrong, and he seemed to yield the point, but in all other respects he seems to be anxious to maintain Peace and good order within the State.

Much of the ill feeling here as elsewhere is Caused by the inflamed language of the partizan Press and of stump orators, who are irrepressable, but Messrs Gantt and Glover claimed that whatevr the Governor may have done, to punish Crime, that the impression was strong with good men, that Radicals could commit crime & violence without fear of arrest or punishment, whereas the Conservatives were harrassed by indictments and forcible arrests without warrant of Law, by the State Militia or Volunteers.

The Conservatives claim that even with the sworn oaths, and the Registration act, the wisdom and legallity of which they question, they can carry Missouri by a large majority, so that all that is asked & needed is a general Confidence that when the time does come, the qualified voters shall have a fair election.

This the Governor promised, and before we parted I understood he would very soon make official publication that would make all these points as clear as possible—of course claiming the validity of the new Constitution, the Militia Ordinance and the Registration Act—that he will make the militia to conform more strictly with the ordinance, that he will use his authority to punish Criminals & violent men by the strict forms of Law, and that he will use no force or show of force at Elections or public meetings, nor tolerate any interference from Kansas or Iowa, but freely consent to the U.S. maintaining peace at the Polls if need be. In which event Messrs. Gantt & Glover promise their influence to quiet the present apprehensions of violence which they allege to exist. I do not pretend to say all this will be done, but I do say that a peaceful Election should be had, and if you order it, and instruct me as to how far I may go, I will insure it.

W. T Sherman   Lt Genl Comdg.

Letters of parties from Jackson County, and Kansas City, taken out, and given to Colonel Jones for personal inspection and Report—will be forwarded to the president in a few days with his Report thereon.[11]

W. T Sherman   Lt Gnl.

ALS, DLC-JP.

1. These probably included Thomas C. Ready to Johnson, July 24, 1866, *Johnson Papers*, 10: 727–29, and William Douglass to [Johnson?], July 26, 1866, copy not found. Roger Jones to R. M. Sawyer, Aug. 15, 1866, Johnson Papers, LC.

2. Thomas C. Fletcher.

3. Lawyer Thomas T. Gantt (1814–1889), whose education at West Point was aborted by a leg injury, moved to Missouri in 1839. A leader of the unconditional unionists in that state, he served briefly on the staff of Gen. George McClellan and as provost marshal general for Missouri during the early part of the war. After the conflict he returned to his law practice except for two years as judge of the St. Louis court of appeals (1875–77).

4. Not found.

5. Samuel T. Glover.

6. Roger Jones (*c*1831–1889), an 1851 West Point graduate and career army officer, served in the Adjutant and Inspector General Department after 1861. Powell, *Army List*, 403–4; *West Point Register*, 224.

7. His report is Roger Jones to R. M. Sawyer, Aug. 15, 1866, Johnson Papers, LC.

8. For accusations to this effect, see Thomas C. Ready to Johnson, July 24, 1866, *Johnson Papers*, 10: 727–29.

9. Not found enclosed.

10. The meeting is described in greater detail by one of the participants in Thomas T. Gantt to John Hogan, Aug. 10, 1866, Johnson Papers, LC.

11. This was written on a separate page but was mailed with the letter.

From Ephraim K. Smart[1]

Camden Maine   Augt 9th 1866.

My Dear Sir:

Hearing that [Gen]l. F. S. Nickerson,[2] has been mentioned as a candidate for Collector of Belfast, Maine, and occupying the position I do, it is natural that I should feel an interest in the appointment to be made for that place.

Having been one of the earliest supporters of the late war, and having stood by the country, during its entire struggle, I am anxious now that we should consummate the Union, we spent so much blood and treasure to maintain.

I know all the officers of the Belfast Custom House, and I am confident there is not a man connected with it, *who is for the Union for its own sake.* Their predominant political sentiment is and ever has been, *hatred of every thing southern*—a sentiment which had its foundation in the times of Jefferson and old John Adams. They were for the *Union* if they could in taking that position antagonise the people of the southern country; and now that the people of the South are returning to the Union, under your excellent and patriotic policy, they are impeled to fight the Union by their hatred of Southern men.

Your friends in Maine who are anxious to see your policy successful, are greatly crippled by such office holders, who are faring sumptuously every day upon the bread of your administration.

If you should conclude to remove such men, you can make no better appointment than that of General Nickerson.[3] I know him well and can recommend him. Both of us took ground for the war upon the start. We had always like yourself been democrats; but when the democratic *organisation* was doubtful in its position, we like yourself refused to act with it. Whenever your Excellency can find a man for office, who like General Nickerson *has no [word?] to take back*, I need not say that such a man will give strength to your administration. But there is more to be said of Genl. N.

He rose from Captain to Brigadier General in the war and was a brave and gallant officer with not a spot or blemish upon his military history. If we could have such men appointed to office immediately, it would give the friends of your Excelency decided successes in many sections of the state. In an article in Harpers Magazine of Augt 1866, I find the following allusions to General Nickersons services upon the Gulf:

> Colonel Nickerson, of the Fourteenth Maine, had his horse shot from under him by a discharge of grape. He sprang from under his dying steed, and waving his sword called upon his men for one more charge. The men sprang forward with three roaring cheers, and drove back the advancing foe.[4]

Having served in the same Congress for four sessions with yourself I have taken the liberty to write you unreservedly. Wishing you every assistance in your great work. . . .

E. K Smart

ALS, DNA-RG56, Appts., Customs Service, Collector, Belfast, F. S. Nickerson.

1. Smart (1813–1872) had served as Democratic congressman from Maine (1847–49, 1851–53) and as collector of customs at Belfast (1853–58). Subsequently, he served as editor of two different Maine newspapers. *BDAC*.

2. A former deputy collector under Smart, Franklin S. Nickerson (1826–1917) saw military service primarily in the Department of the Gulf under Generals Butler and Banks prior to June 1864, when he was transferred to Washington. After the war he practiced law in Boston. Warner, *Blue*; *U.S. Off. Reg.* (1853–55).

3. Johnson did not nominate Nickerson as collector at Belfast or, apparently, for any other office. Instead, the President chose William G. Crosby, whom the Senate eventually rejected in January 1867. Ser. 6B, Vol. 3: 1–2, Johnson Papers, LC.

4. From John S.C. Abbott's "Heroic Deeds of Heroic Men," *Harper's*, 33 (1866): 308.

From M. S. Whiting[1]

San Francisco, August 9 1866

Dear Sir

Enclosed we have the pleasure of forwarding to you the evidences of the first earnest effort to establish and concentrate into organized action and power, on this coast, the friends of the Administration,[2] and to assure you that we firmly beleive that California will at the next general election send three Representatives to Congress who will support the union policy of the present Administration.

But without a portion of the Executive patronage our struggle for supremacy must be prolonged and our ultimate success rendered uncertain, because of the aggressive and defiant stand taken against us by the

Radicals at the present the recipients of the Government patronage—our organization is composed exclusively of original "Lincoln & Johnson" men, and we propose to make the fight within the ranks of the old Union party—the better and surer way to weaken the combination now openly working against us, after which our doors will be opened widely to all of every party who will heartily sustain the Administration policy as against an aggressive Congress.

With the countenance and approval of the Administration we shall be enabled to attract to our platform (a copy of which in enclosed)[3] at least one half of the original Union party of 1864 and certainly sufficient of the opposite party to give us a respectable plurality.

Until it is known that we receive some recognition from the Administration we shall encounter scorn vituperation and ridicule from those who should be the champions of the Administration.

We know of no single U.S. official here outside of Gen. Miller[4] the Collector of the Port, (we are constrained to say) who is not in favor of the Radical Congress as against the President.

We respectfully submit to your Excellency, that while we do not desire to monopolize the Government patronage for the Administration party in California, we feel that it is injudicious and unjust to bestow it upon those who either vilify openly the course and policy of the Administration, or refuse to join in an effort to sustain those patriotic and eminent statesmen whom they have assisted to place in position and power.

Should these views meet with a response from you then this Committee suggest either a personal interview at Washington, or a correspondence for an interchange of views on the subjects embraced herein.

The names that may be reccommended to your favorable consideration by this Committee will be such only as will stand the Jeffersonian test: viz; "Is he honest?" "Is he capable?"—on this we realize that our success greatly depends in drawing to our standard worth and numbers.

Our State Central Committee are gentlemen of acknowledged worth & respectability, a majority of whom have represented San Francisco in the Senate & Assembly of our State Legislature.

Abundant testimony will be forwarded to establish the facts as to the proper qualifications and reliability of the Gentlemen having the interests of the National Union Movement in charge.

The Movement has met and is meeting with no less favor from the press than from the people—evidences of which will be transmitted.

M. S. Whiting
Chairman Nat. Union State Central Com.

LS, DLC-JP.
  1. Whiting (*fl*1881) was in San Francisco by 1856 where he was an importer and dealer in wines and spirits. From the mid-1870s he edited, managed, or published the *Wine Dealers' Gazette*. San Francisco directories (1856–81).
  2. Not found enclosed; perhaps the "evidences" included the pamphlet, "Address of the

National Union State Central Committee to the People of California," published in 1866.
NUC.
    3. Not found enclosed.
    4. John F. Miller.

From Benjamin F. Butler

[ca. Aug. 10, 1866][1]

Sir.

With grateful respect for the honor proferred me by your appointment as Post Master of Salem I feel myself compelled to decline the Office.

I venture to suppose that the gift was conferred, as a recognition of my military services. The events of the past few months however has rendered it impossible for me to take the position consistently with the true intent with which I went into the field.

Whether justly or not its acceptance will be understood to be the adoption on my part of the principles and the action of the Philadelphia Convention, as my rule of political conduct.

To that I cannot subscribe. It is impossible for me to fail to see the effect prospectively, even of that Convention. It encourages those against whom every Union soldier has fought for four years, to hope that they may seize the Government of the Country by means of political movements, which in their unholy attempt by arms they have so signally failed to do. It has strenghtened them in their hate of the free institutions and just Laws against which they rebelled.

I may be wrong in my estimate of the Convention but it would seem that I cannot be when I see every traitor North and South in favor of it, either they or the few heretofore loyal men with it are misled as to its principles and effects. I must believe the latter. While the plan of the President for restoring the Union of the States would have met my support, had it been accepted by the late rebels and their sympathisers in the spirit in which it was offered. Yet it is sad to know that there is no element of loyalty in power in the South upon which it can operate. The riots at Memphis and New Orleans the wrongs to the black men; the murders daily occurring of my late companions in arms all over the South convinces me in my judgment, that however rightly intended, the true course of Government has not been taken toward the late insurgent States, and I cannot even impliedly sanction it. I should feel that by so doing, I was giving up that for which I have seen my comrades die.

Copy, DLC-Benjamin Butler Papers.
    1. Internal evidence suggests an August 1866 date. Moreover, a rough draft of Butler's letter (also in the Butler Papers, LC) contains an August 10, 1866 date affixed to it, albeit in a different handwriting.

From John F. McKinney

Washington D.C.   Aug 10th 1866.

Sir:

Genl. John E. Cummins[1] of Sidney, Shelby County, Ohio, is an applicant for appointment to the office District Assessor of the 4th Collection District of Ohio.

I have been personally and intimately acquainted with Genl. Cummins for the last twelve or fifteen years, and take pleasure in bearing my testimony to his high standing as a citizen and a gentleman. He is a Lawyer by prefession, and stands at the head of the bar in his district, and is well qualified by experience and business habits to discharge the duties of the office he seeks.

General Cummins entered the army soon after the breaking out of the rebellion, and served faithfully until after the close of the war. For meritorious services he has been promoted to Brigadier Genl. by Brevet.

Politically he has been an "old line Whig" and Republican, and was an active and efficient supporter of "Lincoln & Johnson" in 1864. In 1865, after his muster out of the service on account of the Close of the war, he was Elected State Senator by the Union party of his District. In the Legislature he was a bold and manly supporter of the policy of the present Executive, against the attack of the "Radicals." He is now an uncompromising supporter of "President Johnson's policy," and is doing active and efficient work to accomplish the overthrow of the Radical ascendency in the 4th Congressional District of Ohio.

The present incumbent[2] in the office of District Assessor for said District, *professes* to be in favor of the policy of President Johnson, but keeps at the head of his paper, "The Piqua *Journal*," the Radical state ticket, which was nominated and placed upon a platform directly in opposition to the Conservative policy of the President. He is also pledged to the support of the present Radical member of Congress from that District, Judge Wm. Lawrence.

If Mr. Fleming is permitted to remain in office, the power that it gives him, in holding the Conservative vote to the Radical Candidates, will be very great. If he can hold office under the President and at the same time support and vote for the Radical enemies of the Administration, it is interpreted by the Conservative friends of the President that such course is approved.[3]

I have no doubt but the immediate appointment of Genl. Cummins to the Office of Assessor of Internal Revenue for the 4th Collection District of Ohio, would increase the vote in favor of the President's policy in the 4th District, by from 500 to 1000.

The appointment of Genl. Cummins to the position he desires would give universal satisfaction to the true Union men of the District, as well as a compliment merited by his long and efficient services in the Army.[4]

J. F. McKinney

ALS, DNA-RG56, Appts., Internal Revenue Service, Assessor, Ohio, 4th Dist., John E. Cummins.

1. After service as lieutenant colonel and then colonel of three different Ohio infantry regiments, Cummins (1831–1875) was brevetted brigadier general in November 1865. Ten years later he committed suicide. Hunt and Brown, *Brigadier Generals*.

2. David M. Fleming.

3. For more on the Fleming story, see David M. Fleming to Johnson, Aug. 14, Sept. 22, Oct. 14, 1866. For an earlier account of problems facing Fleming, see Fleming to Johnson, Apr. 4, 1866, *Johnson Papers*, 10: 354–55.

4. Although Fleming was ousted and Cummins nominated in his place, Johnson, "upon a representation of the facts," concluded in September that Fleming had been "improperly removed" and asked Secretary McCulloch to "carefully examine the case." On February 6, 1867, the Senate rejected Cummins, yet the President, who reportedly still favored Fleming's reinstatement, did not renominate him. Fleming finally reattained the assessorship in July 1868. Endorsement by Johnson, Sept. 20, 1866; William G. Moore to Hugh McCulloch, Mar. 12, 1867, Appts., Internal Revenue Service, Assessor, Ohio, 4th Dist., David M. Fleming, RG56, NA; Ser. 6B, Vol. 4: 256, 257, 259, 261, 262, Johnson Papers, LC.

From Leverett Saltonstall et al.[1]

[Boston][2]   August 10, 1866.

Sir,

Among the removals of Federal Officers in Massachusetts, so indispensable to carry out the re-construction policy of the President—is that of the Collector of the District of Barnstable.

Charles F. Swift,[3] the present incumbent, owes his appointment to Thomas D. Eliot[4]—Member of Congress from this District. He is a zealous supporter of Governor Bullock[5] in all his radical measures and is now laboring to secure the re-election of Mr Eliot, and says, through the columns of the "Yarmouth Register"—*"that the People of this Country demand that their Representatives in Congress shall be sustained against the President."*

His removal would meet the approval of the conservative men of the entire District and we would therefore recommend that it be done, and Major S. B. Phinney,[6] Editor of the "Barnstable Patriot" appointed in his place.

Major Phinney received the unanimous support of the conservative party for the present Congress against Mr Eliot. He has been a zealous supporter of the President from the day of his inaugaration and is a delegate to the National Convention at Philadelphia from the First District.

With this removal and the appointment of Major Phinney, there is good reason to believe that Mr Eliot may be defeated at the ensuing election, and a conservative elected in his place.[7]

Leverett Saltonstall
President of the Faneuil Hall Convention
Joseph M. Wightman   Delegate to National Convention
R. S. Spofford   Delegate National Convention
E. C. Bailey   Delegate at Large

LS, DNA-RG56, Appts., Customs Service, Collector, Barnstable, S. B. Phinney.

1. There are four signatories: Richard S. Spofford, Jr.; Joseph M. Wightman (1812–1885), a former Democratic mayor of Boston (1861–62) whom Johnson gave a temporary appointment as revenue assessor in September 1866; Edwin C. Bailey (*fl*1869), editor of the *Boston Herald* who ran for Congress in 1868 as a Democrat but lost; and Leverett Saltonstall (1825–1895), a four-time Democratic contender for Congress who presided at the Faneuil Hall Convention in Boston, where Spofford, Bailey, Wightman, and other Massachusetts delegate-designates to the National Union Convention in Philadelphia were chosen. On August 15, Moses Bates, chairman of the Massachusetts Democratic state committee, also signed this petition. *Appleton's Cyclopaedia*; *NUC*; *National Intelligencer*, Aug. 10, 1866; *New York Times*, Aug. 14, 1866; *Guide to U.S. Elections*, 763, 772, 775, 778; Holli and Jones, *American Mayors*; Boston directories (1861–70); Ser. 6B, Vol. 3: 35, Johnson Papers, LC.

2. The provenance is suggested by the fact that the signers of the document were delegates at the recently-concluded Faneuil Hall Convention, which began in Boston on August 8.

3. Swift (1825–1903), for more than forty years editor and publisher of the *Yarmouth Register*, served in the Massachusetts senate and on the governor's council, before his appointment by Lincoln in 1861 as collector at Barnstable. Simeon L. Deyo, ed., *History of Barnstable County, Massachusetts* (New York, 1890), 43, 45, 55, 260, 504–5.

4. Eliot (1808–1870), a Radical Republican, represented the First District of Massachusetts in Congress (1854–55, 1859–69). *BDAC*; Donald, *Politics of Reconstruction*, 101.

5. Republican Alexander H. Bullock (1816–1882), a former Whig journalist and state legislator, served three consecutive terms as governor of Massachusetts (1865–69). Robert Sobel and John Raimo, eds., *Biographical Directory of the Governors of the United States, 1789–1978* (4 vols., Westport, 1978), 2: 708–9.

6. In addition to editing the *Patriot*, Sylvanus B. Phinney (*fl*1890), a Democrat, also served as customs collector at Barnstable in the late 1840s and again from 1853 to 1861, when he was replaced by Swift. In his race against Thomas Eliot for Congress in 1864, Phinney had lost overwhelmingly. Deyo, *History of Barnstable County*, 52, 55, 260; *Guide to U.S. Elections*, 769.

7. Phinney was eventually given on October 24, 1866, a temporary commission for the Barnstable collectorship. But his nomination was rejected by the Senate, and Johnson renominated Charles Swift, who was confirmed on March 22, 1867. Eliot won by an even greater margin in the 1866 congressional election than he had two years earlier. Ser. 6B, Vol. 3: 35; Vol. 4: 22, 24, Johnson Papers, LC; *Guide to U.S. Elections*, 772.

From William H. Seward

Balt. Md   Aug 10 1866.

Texas will report by telegraph herself fully organized perhaps today.[1] There will need to be an order Relieving Provisional Governor[2] and transferring the state to State authorities. The chief clerk of state dept[3] can find forms for these orders in the cases of North Carolina and South

Carolina and the attorney General can issue them by telegraph as acting
Secretary of state.[4]

Wm H. Seward

Tel, DNA-RG59, Misc. Lets., 1789–1906 (M179, Roll 243).
    1. Seward had previously instructed provisional Texas state secretary James H. Bell
that governor-elect James W. Throckmorton should be inaugurated on August 9, 1866.
When this was done, Bell was to notify the federal government which would then relieve
the provisional government. Thus, Seward had reason to expect a telegram from Texas, but
such a message has not been located. Seward to Bell, ca. July 28, 1866, Tels. Sent, Sec. of
War (M473, Roll 91), RG107, NA.
    2. Andrew J. Hamilton.
    3. After more than forty years in the State Department, Virginia native Robert S. Chew
(1811–1873) became chief clerk in July 1866. *Appleton's Cyclopaedia*.
    4. On August 11, 1866, Attorney General Henry Stanbery, as acting secretary of state,
sent a telegram to Hamilton instructing him, by order of Johnson, to turn over the Texas
government to Throckmorton. Stanbery also sent a telegram to Throckmorton. The government was transferred to the newly-elected officers on August 13. Johnson issued a proclamation on August 20 declaring the rebellion in Texas ended. Stanbery to Hamilton, Aug.
11, 1866; Stanbery to Throckmorton, Aug. 11, 1866; Throckmorton to Stanbery, Aug.
14, 1866, *Louisville Courier*, Aug. 22, 1866. See also Proclamation *re* End of Insurrection,
Aug. 20, 1866.

From D. J. Shotwell[1]

New York City   Aug 10. 1866.

Hon Sir

Learning that Mr John L Deen[2] of this city is a candidate for the position of Naval officer, I make bold to express my approval of him and to
hope that his application be favorably considered.

Mr Deen is a sterling business man intimately acquainted with the
practical details of commerce, and identified with the interests of N.Y.

Although Mr Deen has never taken an active part in Politics, he can
probably swing more votes in the U.S. than any other one man living. He
is closely allied to the Tobacco interests, and it was solely through his
exertion that Congress increased the duty on Imported Cigars,[3] thereby
protecting the Domestic Manufacturer, and putting bread and butter
into the hands of an organization numbering in this city alone over
12000— voters. These men or a vast majority of them he can control.

The organization extends to and is existent in almost every state in this
Union and Mr D is the "Head Centre."

Many members of Congress were instructed by their constituents to
do Mr Ds. bidding, that he represented them &c. Several begged Mr D.
to favorably mention them to the organization within their several
districts.

I have been thus explicit hoping your Excellency may see the Wisdom
and Expediency of appointing Mr D. The Politicians of N.Y. may have

the power to regulate the "Political Machinery," but Mr D. can manage a vast number of the workmen.[4]

D. J Shotwell
219—8th Av

ALS, DNA-RG56, Appts., Customs Service, Naval Officer, New York, John L. Deen.
  1. Not identified.
  2. Deen (c1822–fl1875), a wholesale tobacco merchant in New York City since the 1840s, had been mentioned as a possible candidate for the New York naval officer post as early as April 1866. 1870 Census, N.Y., New York, New York, 21st Ward, 21st Dist., 10; New York City directories (1866–75); Appts., Customs Service, Naval Officer, New York, John L. Deen, RG56, NA.
  3. See *Congressional Globe*, 39 Cong., 1 Sess., Appendix, p. 418.
  4. See John L. Deen to Johnson, Oct. 5, 1866.

From Albert B. Sloanaker[1]

Philadelphia, August 10th 1866

My Dear Sir

Having now got my Office reorganized I deem it my first duty to return you my sincere and grateful acknowledgements for the handsome manner in which you have recoganized my services in your personal interests and that of our common cause. I will now only say, that my gratitude shall always hereafter, as heretofore, be shown by actions, not words, when to your own interests or that of our friends.

My Political course is now marked out. I trust the Philad. Convention, will act in such a manner as to bring together the true men of the whole Country So that under your guidance we can show to the Nations of the Earth that the late war was not a failure but that we are the true supporters of Constitutional Liberty and an undivided Union.

In our District Convention I succeeded in causing the selection of our friends Messrs Orr and Randall,[2] As Delegates to the Convention, having personally declined the honor through the advice of friend Randall, through prudential reasons alone.

In closing, I beg to say, that at 9. O clock A.M. on the 4th inst. I took possession of this Office, After making an agreeable and satisfactory arrangement with the retiring Collector, John H. Taggart.[3] For his present Office, purchasing all his fixtures and lease, thus preventing any interuption in the Buisness of the Office. While feeling grateful for the kindness of the past I will say, I trust I shall fully live up to the Jefferson maxim "That he is honest, competent and worthy" of the confidence bestowed by the partiallity of the Executive.[4]

A B Sloanaker Collector

LS, DLC-JP.
  1. His nomination as collector of the First District of Pennsylvania having been rejected in early July 1866, Sloanaker was given on August 2 a recess appointment to the same

post. *Senate Ex. Proceedings*, Vol. 14, pt. 2: 906; Ser. 6B, Vol. 3: 161, Johnson Papers, LC. See also Sloanaker to Johnson, Feb. 26, 1866, *Johnson Papers*, 10: 181.

2. Republican Joseph Orr and Democrat Samuel J. Randall. Orr (b. *c*1826), a well-to-do produce dealer and former candidate for the First District assessorship, is not known to have attended the Philadelphia convention. Orr to Johnson, July 6, 1866, Appts., Internal Revenue Service, Assessor, Pa., 1st Dist., Joseph Orr, RG56, NA; Orr to Johnson, July 17, 1866, Johnson Papers, LC; 1870 Census, Pa., Philadelphia, Philadelphia, 10th Dist., 3rd Ward, 101.

3. Taggart (1821–1894), a newspaper reporter and former colonel of Pennsylvania reserves, had served as collector since the fall of 1865. Following his departure from office, Taggart became a Washington correspondent for several national newspapers prior to returning to Philadelphia in 1869 and purchasing the *Sunday Morning Times*. *NCAB*, 5: 402–3; Ser. 6B, Vol. 1: 329, Johnson Papers, LC.

4. See Sloanaker to Johnson, Dec. 22, 1866.

From Henry A. Smythe

[New York City, August 10, 1866][1]

My dear Sir.

I enclose herewith two suggestive routes—for your proposed trip in Septr.[2] The one ocupying the longer time, is by *far* the best—the other is only given, in case you have but one week to spare—instead of two—after returning from Chicago.

I have taken it for granted that you would be disposed to come via Niagara, but the whole thing is respectfully submitted for your consideration & *approval*—and I would earnestly suggest, & *urge* you to adopt the one ocupying *two weeks from Niagara*—leaving me to make all the arrangments in detail—which I am sure I can do, to your satisfaction & pleasure—rendering the whole thing *an entire success*—free comparatively from the usual anoyances.

With regard to those Brooklyn appts.[3] I am rather fearfull they would be regarded as bad selections, & loose for you many friends—at least that of Mr Kinsella for Post Master.[4] He is rather a low order of politician, & *was* strongly opposed to you—now he is a Johnson man. The other Col Pratt[5] is a better man & is better known by a better class of people.

General Slocomb who is pressing these appointments, does *not* stand so high—even with his own party—as *he* imagines.

I shall be only too happy at all times, to serve you & your interests—in my opinion of men or in any other way—& I assure you, I have *no* aim or motive—but for your good.

H. A. Smythe.

ALS, DLC-JP.

1. Both date and provenance are provided on the reverse side of the letter.

2. The enclosed itinerary provided that the President should leave Washington on September 3, arrive at Chicago on the 6th, on to Niagara on September 8, followed by an extensive tour of New York and then New England. Johnson would return to Washington on September 25. The other proposal started out the same way but cut short the visit to the Northeast and had the President back in Washington on September 17. Johnson chose a

different route and timetable from either of those proposed by Smythe. See Smythe to Johnson, Aug. 18, 1866. See also Appendix III.

3. A few days earlier Johnson had notified Smythe of his decision to nominate Thomas Kinsella and Calvin E. Pratt for two federal posts in Brooklyn and asked the collector to "inform me, by telegraphic despatch, of the result of your conference upon the subject" with Gen. Henry W. Slocum. Smythe replied the following day with a suggestion of a substitute for "one of those places in Brooklyn." Johnson to Smythe, Aug. 6, 1866, in H. W. Smith, *The Presidents of America* (Boston, 1879), Guild Library, MHi; Smythe to Johnson, Aug. 7, 1866, Johnson Papers, LC.

4. Kinsella (1832–1884) worked as a printer and wartime editor of the *Brooklyn Daily Eagle* prior to receiving a recess appointment to the Brooklyn postmastership on August 25, 1866, but his nomination was eventually rejected by the Senate. He later served one term in Congress (1871–73). *DAB*; *BDAC*; Ser. 6B, Vol. 3: 95, Johnson Papers, LC.

5. A former Massachusetts attorney and veteran of the Peninsular campaign and Chancellorsville, Pratt (1828–1896) was given a recess appointment for New York's Third District collectorship but, like Kinsella, was not confirmed by the Senate. He later was elected a judge of the New York supreme court. Warner, *Blue*; Ser. 6B, Vol. 3: 95; Vol. 4: 51, Johnson Papers, LC.

From George A. Trenholm

Charleston So Ca   Augt. 10, 1866

Sir:

I venture again to appeal to your Excellency, and respectfully to solicit a favorable consideration of my petition for the exercise of the pardoning power of the Executive, in my behalf. The circumstances of my case, being already set forth in the petition, and in the memorial of my fellow citizens in its support, it would be to trespass unnecessarily upon the time devoted to the great interests of the Country, to repeat them here. My chief reliance too is upon the magnanimity and clemency of the President. To these great qualities, so frequently and generously extended to his unhappy countrymen, I appeal. Nor will it be thought inexcusable, I trust, that I should indulge the hopes that spring from a sincere conviction of the generous sentiments and policy of the Government, and from the belief that my conduct has been such since the return of peace, as to afford them that assurance of my loyalty that they justly require.

The season is again approaching when contracts for the ensuing year must be made with the freedmen. Several hundreds of them, who have confidence in the Sentiments I entertain towards them, are looking to me for employment and for the means of subsistence; and the welfare of our people essentially depends upon the early resumption and efficient prosecution, of their agricultural pursuits. I venture with great respect, to urge this as a motive for soliciting, as I earnestly do, an early and favorable consideration of my petition.[1]

G. A. Trenholm.

ALS, DNA-RG94, Amnesty Papers (M1003, Roll 47), S.C., G. A. Trenholm.

1. Recommended by Generals Daniel E. Sickles, John A. Dix, O. O. Howard, Samuel R. Curtis, John P. Hatch, and James B. Steedman, along with numerous citizens of South

Carolina and Georgia, Trenholm was pardoned on October 25, 1866. *House Ex. Docs.*, 39 Cong., 2 Sess., No. 31, pp. 4–8 (Ser. 1289).

From Parmenas T. Turnley[1]

St. Louis, Mo., Aug: 10th 1866.

Dr Sir.

I enclose a slip from Knoxville paper[2] (East Tenn.) *my* native home— for you to read for information. I have just returnd from six weeks trip in East Tenn. to look after my property on French Broad River—that I had not seen for—(most of it of) ten years.

The whole mass of farmers are hard at work—*perfectly devotd* to the U.S. laws & their Countrys best interest—*Excepting* the class calld the *Brownlow men*. These, are doing vast injury in that poor Country—and, unless Controlld will yet do more. I *must* look after my property there— and I design to do so *prepard* to defend my own interest and those whom I may chose to have employd there.

I, and all men that I take there, or give employment to, are devotd supporters of the President of the U.S. and the Constitution and laws of our whole Country.

It is not *improbable* that *strife* may ensue, by such teachings as that containd on the enclosd slip. If such should be the Case—I wish it distinctly under stood—that I in no wise shall be the aggressor—nor will any one whom I take there.

P. T. Turnley,   (*late of U.S.* Army)

ALS, DLC-JP.

1. Turnley (1821–1911) was an 1846 graduate of West Point and a veteran of the Mexican War. Afterwards he continued in the army, eventually achieving the rank of captain before resigning in 1865. After the war he was in the banking business in Chicago and subsequently mayor of Highland Park in the late 1880s and early 1890s. John J. Halsey, ed., *A History of Lake County, Illinois* (Chicago, 1912), 424–25; Powell, *Army List*, 639; *West Point Register*, 238.
2. Enclosure not found.

From Illinois Citizens[1]

Jacksonville Illinois   [August 11, 1866][2]

Your Petitioners would respectfully represent, that John Moses[3] the present incumbent of the office of Assessor of Internal Revenue for the 10th Congressional District of the state of Illinois, is a determined and out-spoken Radical, and a bitter opposer of the present Administration. His Deputies, in each of the ten Counties Composing this District, are "Radicals" exercising like opposition to the policy of your Administration.

Isaac J. Ketcham,[4] whom we now recomend as his Successor, and whose appointment we earnestly petition, is one of our most honorable and reliable Citizens, has always been a Republican, was the first leading Republican in the State, in his writing and speeches, to endorse your policy.

He is the organizer of the "Johnson Club" in Springfield Illinois, and also of the "Johnson Club" in Jacksonville Illinois.

During the War his efforts were unceasing, sparing neither time nor money to raise Companies & Regiments to defend our Country. There are men in this District who have served their Country as Soldiers, whom we might recomend, but all the facts taken into consideration, our preference is for Mr Ketcham believing him to be the best man for that position, and his appointment would give the most general satisfaction.

Pet, DNA-RG56, Appts., Internal Revenue Service, Assessor, Ill., 10th Dist., Isaac J. Ketchum.

1. The petition was signed by fifty-eight leading citizens from the various counties of the Tenth District.

2. The date is taken from a short note, following the signatures, by Anthony Thornton, U.S. representative from Illinois.

3. Moses (1825–1898), a native of Canada, was a banker, judge, and historian. He was replaced as assessor of Illinois's Tenth District in April 1867 by James Fishback. W. Stewart Wallace, comp., *A Dictionary of North American Authors Deceased Before 1950* (Detroit, 1968 [1951]), 318; 1870 Census, Ill., Scott, Winchester, 245; *Chicago Tribune*, July 6, 1898; Ser. 6B, Vol. 3: 592; Vol. 4: 300–305, Johnson Papers, LC.

4. Ketchum (*fl*1878), a lawyer and Jacksonville trustee in 1866, was appointed assessor August 21, 1866, formally nominated on January 1, 1867, and rejected February 6. *History of Morgan County, Illinois: Its Past and Present* (Chicago, 1878), 359, 497; Ser. 6B, Vol. 3: 592; Vol. 4: 300, Johnson Papers, LC.

From William P. Johnston[1]

Louisville, Ky.   Augt 11th 1866.

Sir,

I have the honor to ask a permit to visit Mr Davis at Fortress Monroe. While he acted as Prest of the Confederate States, I was for three years his aide-de-camp and a part of that time an inmate of his house. I was the son of his friend and the recipient of much kindness at his hands, & am anxious to enjoy a privilege that has been accorded to others, [with] such conditions as your Excely may impose.

W.P.J.

L draft, LNHT-Mrs. Mason Barret Collection of Albert Sidney and William Preston Johnston Papers.

1. Johnston (1831–1899), the son of Albert Sidney Johnston, practiced law in Louisville before entering the war as a major in the 2nd Rgt. Ky. Arty. Later promoted to lieutenant colonel and colonel, he served as aide-de-camp to Jefferson Davis from May 1862 until the war's end. Captured with Davis and imprisoned, he was subsequently released and traveled to Canada. By 1867 he had returned to occupy the chair of English and history at Washington and Lee University; he was named president of Louisiana State University in 1880 and then served as president of Tulane, 1883–89. There is no evidence he was permitted to visit Davis. Wakelyn, *BDC*.

From Richard Oulahan[1]

Washington D.C.   Aug 11/66

Sir:

The enclosed document[2] from a gallant Soldier of the Republic,—Capt. P. J. Condon[3] late of the Irish Brigade,—has been forwarded to me with the request that it be placed directly before your Excellency, without passing through subordinate hands.

In responding to that request, and in respectfully approaching your Excellency on behalf of my Countryman, I may be permitted to assure you that the Irish Adopted Citizens are justly indignant at the indifference and todyism manifested by our representatives at London and Dublin, (Mr. Adams & Mr. West,)[4] in regard to the Irish Americans so mercilessly flung into the English dungeons in Ireland.

Richard Oulahan late "Corcoran's Irish Legion."

ALS, DNA-RG59, Misc. Lets., 1789–1906 (M179, Roll 243).

1. Oulahan (c1825–1895), a poet, served as a lieutenant in the 164th N.Y. Inf. from 1862 to 1863. In 1864 he was employed by the Treasury Department where he was a clerk in the Third Auditor's office until 1871. D. J. O'Donoghue, *The Poets of Ireland: A Biographical and Bibliographical Dictionary of Irish Writers of English Verse* (Dublin, 1912); *Off. Army Reg.: Vols.*, 2: 671; Irish Legion Officers to Oulahan, Oct. 16, 1866, Johnson Papers, LC; Pension File, Mary Oulahan, RG15, NA.

2. Patrick J. Condon to Johnson, Aug. 7, 1866, Misc. Lets., 1789–1906 (M179, Roll 243), RG59, NA.

3. Patrick J. Condon, alias Godfrey Massey (b. c1838), veteran of the Irish Brigade, 63rd N.Y. Inf., was arrested in Dublin on February 23, 1866, and imprisoned until mid-July 1866, when he was released on condition he return to America. In the United States Condon was the chief Fenian organizer in Louisiana and Texas. However, by the fall of 1866, suspicions that he was a British spy had grown. On January 12, 1867, Condon set sail for Ireland on Fenian business; he was arrested March 4. The following month, he appeared as a witness for the prosecution in the trial of Fenian Thomas Burke for treason in connection with the raid on Chester Castle. Ibid.; William D'Arcy, "The Fenian Movement in the United States: 1858–1886" (Ph.D. diss., Catholic Univ. of America, 1947); C. F. Adams to Seward, Apr. 30, 1867, *House Ex. Docs.*, 40 Cong., 2 Sess., No. 157, pp. 37–39 (Ser. 1339); *Off. Army Reg.: Vols.*, 2: 520.

4. Charles Francis Adams and William B. West.

From Alexander W. Randall[1]

Philadelphia Pa.   Aug 12, 1866

Dr Sir:

Every thing continues looking admirable except the ripple caused by the action of Vallandigham.[2] Our friends from the South are endeavoring to persuade him to get out of the way. The only importance his being here can have is to frighten off, at the fall elections, men whose votes we want. So far as your Administration is concerned there is but one voice. The feeling is universal for you and to stand fast by you in any event. I hope V. will be magnanimous enough yet to stand aside. The Southern men are acting noble and with a good Sense which annoys the Radical Reporters here. Nothing unusual has transpired. All are hopeful. The Convention will be very full. If we can pass through without a discord it will be a most remarkable time in the history of your Administration.

Alex. W. Randall

ALS, DLC-JP.
1. On the previous day the postmaster general wrote Johnson a brief note from the site of the National Union Convention, expressing optimism and promising to keep the President "advised from time to time as events transpire." Randall to Johnson, Aug. 11, 1866, Johnson Papers, LC.
2. Clement L. Vallandigham's arrival in Philadelphia prior to the convention greatly concerned the convention's conservative organizers, who sought to disassociate themselves and their movement from the controversial Peace Democrats. In addition to Vallandigham, who had been elected as a delegate from the Third District of Ohio, two other prominent former Copperheads, Fernando Wood of New York and Henry Clay Dean of Iowa, also had been commissioned as delegates, but they soon voluntarily withdrew, leaving only Vallandigham. On the eve of the convention several delegates, including Benjamin F. Perry and James L. Orr of South Carolina, attempted to convince Vallandigham not to attend. After much maneuvering, he eventually withdrew as a delegate. Frank L. Klement, *The Limits of Dissent: Clement L. Vallandigham and the Civil War* (Lexington, 1970), 300–303; Mushkat, *Fernando Wood*, 158; Thomas Wagstaff, "The Arm-In-Arm Convention," *CWH*, 14 (1968): 109, 113–14.

From Orville H. Browning

Philadelphia   Augt 13, 1866

The Hon W. B. Reed has asked me to do him the favor to forward the enclosed.[1]

We will have an immense convention, and I sincerely trust a successful one.

Men never came together in a better temper of mind. There seems to be complete unity and harmony of views and purposes.

There is but one cloud on the horizon, Vallandingham, who appears fatally bent upon mischief, and determined to rule or ruin.[2]

If he goes into the convention he will certainly be expelled, and all who are disposed to tie themselves to the tail of his kite will have to go with him.

He is actuated by the intensest selfishness, and had rather this grand effort in behalf of the Country should fail than that it should succeed without glorifying him.

I shall continue to hope for a happy termination of our deliberations.

O. H. Browning

ALS, DLC-JP.
1. Browning enclosed a letter from William B. Reed, who was pleased to learn that the President had approved of the preliminary resolutions he had drafted for the convention. Reed to Johnson, Aug. 12, 1866, Johnson Papers, LC.
2. This was Vallandigham's "motto," according to his fellow Ohioan Lewis D. Campbell, "particularly the ruin part." Campbell to Browning, July 31, 1866, quoted in Klement, *The Limits of Dissent*, 299–300.

From R. B. Carpenter[1]
Private & Confidential

Covington Ky   Aug 13—1866

Dear Sir

I have made careful inquiries in regard to the speech of Gen Smith[2] at this place on his return from Congress. It was a *trimming*. He did not agree with Congress about some things and he differed from the President about some things. He was in favor of your policy of restoration of the Union was opposed to the civil rights bill had voted at first for the freedmen Beaurea but upon reflection had voted to sustain your veto— had favored the last amendments to the constitution gave his reasons therefor and *advocated them to the audience* Spoke kindly and respectfully of you and your administration and thanked the people for former support. The only offensive point in his speech was his defense of the latest Constitutional amendments which he in a temporate manner most undoubtedly advocated. The proof is abundant if required.

R. B. Carpenter

P S There was no personal ill will or denunciation of yourself in that or the other speeches Gen S made in Ky.

ALS, DLC-JP.
1. Carpenter (*c*1824–*fl*1869), a native of Vermont, was an attorney. Cincinnati directories (1867–69); 1850 Census, Ky., Kenton, Covington, 6th Ward, 626.
2. The text of Green Clay Smith's speech has not been found.

From George A. Custer

Washington D.C.   Aug 13/66

Yesterday I had to honor to address Your Excellency[1] in regard to the appointment of myself in the regular army, and referred you to a recommendation in my favor from Maj Genl Sheridan now on file in Genl Grants office.[2] Genl Sheridan under supposition that a much larger increase of cavalry would be authorized by Congress, and that I preferred that arm of service, recommended me for Col of Cavalry. As but a limited increase has been provided for, I respectfully request that while I still prefer Cavalry, I may be appointed Colonel of one of the new infantry regiments, provided I cannot be appointed Col of Cavalry, but in what ever branch of the service I may be assigned I most respectfully request to be attached to an organization composed of *White* troops As I have served and wish to serve with no other class.[3]

G A Custer   (late) Maj Genl U.S. Vols.
& Brevet Major Genl U.S.A.

ALS, DLC-JP.
1. Probably a reference to his letter of August 11. See Custer to Johnson, Aug. 11, 1866, Johnson Papers, LC.

2. See Sheridan to Stanton, Apr. 6, 1866, Johnson Papers, LC.

3. On a letter from Custer to Townsend dated August 13, Grant wrote that Custer had been recommended for a lieutenant colonelcy of a colored regiment but that he, Grant, would be willing to transfer him to a white regiment. Though the original appointment was in the 9th U.S. Cav., Custer was later assigned to the 7th Cav. with the rank of lieutenant colonel to date July 28, 1866. He took up his duties later in the fall of 1866 after accompanying Johnson on a portion of his "swing around the circle." Jay Monaghan, *Custer: The Life of General George Armstrong Custer* (Boston, 1959), 269–71; *Grant Papers*, 16: 276–77; Powell, *Army List*, 269.

From Hector M. Grant[1]

Helena Ark   Aug 13 1866

Rumors going rounds of papers of riot here on 7th inst are entirely unfounded. A street fight between a drunken man & some Soldiers which was immediately stopped gave rise to the rumors. Perfect quiet & harmony prevails.[2]

H. M. Grant   Mayor City of Helena

Tel, DLC-JP.

1. Grant (c1823–fl1880) was a Helena physician. 1860 Census, Ark., Phillips, St. Francis Twp., Helena, 389; (1880), 232nd Enum. Dist., 43.

2. According to the original rumor, the 56th Rgt., U.S. Colored Inf., waiting in Helena for transportation to St. Louis, "had taken possession of the town, and were firing indiscriminately upon the whites, and swore they would burn the place and kill every white." Actually, as the mayor reported, a drunken man who had antagonized the soldiers with a pistol, was disarmed by them and turned over to the police. *Chicago Tribune*, Aug. 17, 1866.

From Hezekiah L. Hosmer

Virginia City, Montana Territory.   August 13. 1866.

Mr. President:—

Some time during the month of March, I called upon you, in company with Gen. Craig[1] of Missouri, for the purpose of informing you of a movement to effect my removal as Chief Justice of this Territory, and to request as a favor, that I might be heard with reference to any charges that should be presented against me, before any action was taken by you on the subject. You were pleased to assure me that such hearing should be afforded.

On my return to Montana, I found, that, during my absence, under the Proclamation of Gen. Meagher,[2] a Legislature had been held, by which, many of the laws passed by the first Legislature of the Territory had been repealed, many new laws had been passed; new counties had been organized; new offices created, and in fact the affairs of the Territory had undergone an entire change.[3] In the meantime Judge Munson[4] had decided the acts of the Second Legislature to be illegal. The ground of this decision, in which, both Judge Williston[5] and myself felt obliged to concur, was that the First Legislature had failed, as required by the Organic

Act of the Territory, to provide for an apportionment, which is by a *proviso* made an essential pre-requisite, to any election to a Legislature, after the first. This neglect, rendered a new enabling act necessary, before another election could be held.[6]

This decision has drawn upon us the vengeance of the Legislative party, and they publicly declare that we shall be removed. I have just learned that they have prepared a memorial in my case. This party, claiming to be your supporters, is composed of a portion of Price's Missouri Army, of men who fled to the mountains during the war, to escape the draft, and of northern sympathiser's with the rebellion.[7]

I claim Mr. President, to be numbered among your friends and supporters, and do not wish to be victimized, without a fair hearing. Permit me, to refer you to my friend Gen. Steedman, your newly appointed Public Printer,[8] to Gen. Craig, and to our delegate, Col. McLain,[9] who all understand my position, and who I believe will do justice to my character.[10]

Hez L Hosmer.

ALS, OFH.

1. A former U.S. congressman from Missouri (1857–61), James Craig (1817–1888) was appointed a brigadier general in 1862 for political reasons. He served with the federal forces until May 1863 and later held a similar position in the Missouri state militia. After the war Craig was president of several trans-Mississippi railroads. Warner, *Blue*.

2. Territorial secretary Thomas Francis Meagher, in the absence of the governor, called the legislature into session. Michael P. Malone et al., *Montana: A History of Two Centuries*, rev. ed. (Seattle, 1991), 101.

3. The second territorial legislature met during March and April 1866. Ibid., 102.

4. Associate Justice Lyman E. Munson.

5. Associate Justice Lorenzo P. Williston.

6. Goaded by several influential Radical Republicans from Montana, the U.S. Congress on March 2, 1867, agreed that the second legislature was illegal and invalidated both its acts and those of the third legislature which met during the winter of 1866–67. Ibid.; Berwanger, *West and Reconstruction*, 197.

7. In 1864 roughly 21,000 Missourians, at least half of whom supported the South, migrated west, "seeking to escape the threat of retribution for their real or suspected ties to secessionist guerrillas." Many of them settled in the Montana mining camps. Alvin M. Josephy, *The Civil War in the American West* (New York, 1991), 264, 303.

8. James B. Steedman had promptly declined the appointment as public printer, a post he had held in 1857. Warner, *Blue*. See John F. Coyle to Johnson, July 31, 1866, *Johnson Papers*, 10: 765–66.

9. After briefly serving as attorney general of the provisional Territory of Jefferson (Colorado), Samuel McLean (1826–1877) moved to Montana. He held one term in Congress (1865–67) as Montana's territorial delegate; afterwards he was president of a silver mining company. He later settled on a plantation in Virginia. *BDAC*.

10. Hosmer remained in office for the rest of his four-year term. *DAB*.

From James R.W. Johnston[1]

Augusta Ga   Aug 13 1866

The office of Mayor of this City is vacant. It is the desire of many citizens to elect Gen LaFayette McLanis to that position. If elected will he be allowed to discharge the duties of the office? He is paroled but not pardoned. Please answer at once.[2]

J.R.W. Johnston

Tel, DLC-JP.

1. Johnston (b. c1831), a native of New York, was a bookkeeper in Augusta who had moved to Georgia in the late 1850s. According to the census reports, he and his wife had three young children. 1860 Census, Ga., Richmond, Augusta, 4th Ward, 156.

2. Several months earlier, Lafayette McLaws had been elected clerk of the superior and inferior court of Richmond County but subsequently had been forbidden to hold office because he had not been pardoned by the President. McLaws had applied for pardon in January 1866 but for some reason no action had been taken on it by the White House. Finally, Johnson pardoned McLaws on October 18. *Constitutionalist* (Augusta), Jan. 3, 4, Oct. 27, 1866; *Charleston Courier*, June 27, Oct. 27, 1866; F. U. Stitt to Stanbery, Oct. 15, 1866, Amnesty Papers (M1003, Roll 21), Ga., Lafayette McLaws, RG94, NA.

From Thomas Leach, Jr.[1]

Boonsboro Washington Co. Ark.

Aug. 13th 1866

The undersigned a citizen of Washington Co. Ark., haveing in March 1864 taken the oath of allegiance to the government of the U.S. and afterward in December of the same year went to Texas within the lines of the rebel army where he remained until the close of the war—finding that by so doing he falls under one of the exceptional clauses of your Excellencies Proclamations of the 29, May/65—would represent the circumstancies which impelled him to this course.

At the Presidential Election next preceeding the inception of the rebellion I cast my vote for the Union candidate—the Hon. John Bell—was opposed to the course taken by the the rebels which brought on the war and resolved not to engage in it.

Being a minister of the Gospel I was not forced into the rebel ranks but remained at home attending to my ordinary avocations until the U.S. forces took possesson of this country. After this I was part of the time at home and part at a U.S. post until I in connection with a number of other persons reported one Maj Willet[2] of the 14th Kansas volunteers to Gen. Thayer[3] comander at Ft Smith, for conduct that could not be tolerated. At this he (Maj. Willet) became incensed and threatened the lives of a number of persons myself included, orders to this effect were given by him; after this several of my neighbors were killed, one of that number a brother of mine, who was one that reported the said Willet, and whose loyalty so far as I know was not questioned.[4] I beleave that this circumstance was the cause of his death—under these circumstances—the Book of the law being disregarded—Holiness to the Lord thought of but by a few I felt *no* security at home and was fearful that I would have but little at any contiguous post: Having relatives and old friends in Texas I went to that state.

Previous to takeing the oath of allegiance I liberated my slaves except those of minor years. These I still have charge of and expect to have until they arrive at a suitable age to provide for themselves—feeling a moral obligation resting upon me in reference to them—*unless* the Freedmans Bureau takes charge of them.

I was not connected either directly or indirectly with any army or army corps during the war.

When I took the oath of allegiance I did it in good faith and have tried to mentain it, not thinking that my going to Texas would be construed as a forfeiture. Nevertheless finding such to be the case would very respectfully ask for pardon and amnesty according to the requirements of the forementioned proclamation.[5]

Thomas Leach, Jr.

ALS, DNA-RG94, Amnesty Papers (M1003, Roll 14), Ark., Thomas Leach.

1. Alabama native Leach (1820–*fl*1889) was raised in Arkansas and settled there as a farmer and minister of the Methodist Church. *History of Benton, Washington, Carroll, Madison, Crawford, Franklin, and Sebastian Counties, Arkansas* (Chicago, 1889), 973.

2. Charles Willetts (b. *c*1841) served first in the 3rd Wisc. Rgt. In August 1863 he became captain of Co. C, 14th Kans. Cav., but was appointed major in November. He took part in actions in the Indian Territory and Missouri before resigning from the service on April 29, 1865. CSR, Charles Willetts, RG94, NA; *OR*, Ser. 1, Vol. 34, Pt. 1: 108, 111–12; Vol. 41, Pt. 1: 600.

3. John M. Thayer (1820–1906) served in the Civil War as colonel of the 1st Nebr. Rgt. and fought at Fort Donelson and Shiloh. Appointed a brigadier general, he commanded the District of the Frontier with headquarters at Fort Smith, Arkansas, from February 1864 until the following February, resigning from the service five months later. After the war Thayer became one of Nebraska's first two senators, and served as governor of the Wyoming Territory, and then of Nebraska. *DAB*; Warner, *Blue*.

4. Nothing further is known about these incidents. Leach's brother is not identified.

5. Governor Murphy recommended pardon for Leach, but no pardon date has been found.

From John H. Low[1]

McDonough Ga   Aug 13th 1866

Sir

The currency is now one of the great if not the greatest question before the country (considering the union restored) how to sustain it with the least burden to the people should be the study of every Statesman. Permit me a plain cotton planter to suggest to you the propriety of the goverment monopolizing the cotton trade as a source of revenew in the place of puting a direct tax on it. I think if properly and judiciously managed it would be best for the planters generally that it would be infinitely more productive in the way of revenew as well as a spedy and a sure way to place the goverment curency on or near an equality with gold.

In the first place the planter when he gets his cotton ready for market he usually sells it at the nearest R.R. Town off his waggon to a street buyer who receives from 50 cts. to $2.00 pr bale for buying for a merchant in said town. It then goes to the wearhouse & there pays [illegible] cts. pr bale for weighing & from 25 cts. to $1.00 pr month for storeage the purchaser paying a high interest on the money that buys it. He then ships to some port pays freight Drayage & commission for seling to another individual who buys & ships to New York there to have another roteen of expences tacked on to it & have it resold to a man who will ship it to Europe there to go through the same roteen of expences & there sold a great deal of it to speculators who holds it untill the manufacturer needs it & then he must have his profit. After all these expences it is then said to be sold to the manfacturer at prices that enable them to make the most princely fortunes of any other people.

Now taking this state of the cotton trade into consideration could not the goverment take hold of it & make an imence revenew out of it. I am a cotton planter & think they could do it & benefit in the place of injuring the planter. It is true they ought to set the price on cotton before it is made & then the planter would know how to pitch his crop and what hire to pay & should it be like it was this year that many planters had to borrow part of the capitol to raise the crop in the place of their paying to brokers & banker from $2^{1}/_{2}$ to 10 pr cent per month for money the goverment could advance part of the money on the crop without loss or risk to the goverment or interest expence to the planter & in the section that I live in such an arrangement to my opinion is imperitively necessary to the making of a crop next year for the drouth of this year will have us without either provision or capitol enough to make a half crop on next year. Could it injure the goverment to advance greenbacks prudently & hold the cotton bound without interest. It has no interest to pay on its own bill, but it would be the very life of the cotton planter.

If the Goverment had the controll of the crop of the U.S. recent events shows that it would be in their power to price it to the manufacturer at what profit they in their Judgement thought best. If the manufacturer should think fit to object to the price put on it by goverment let the goverment monopolize the manufacturing of the article. I think that would yield still greater a profit or revenew. The plan to carry it out I think would be very sinple to wit appoint a buyer & inspector for each market place and an agent to sell in every market in the world where it is manufactured. Put a price on the cotton to be paid either in green backs or gold. Let the price be the same. If green backs were depreciated here they would be bought up & carried to Europe to buy the cotton & the goverment would also have all the advantage of exchange.

I am of the opinion that no goverment ever had such power to controll currency as this would then have expecially if they included tobaco. Some would object to the goverment having such great power. The capitolist of the world now have it & I for one planter do not fear to make the exchange for the Goverment would see that the planting Interest was the great interest of this goverment & it would be able to protect it from the schemes of foreigh Capitolist & well as domestic.[2]

John H. Low

ALS, DNA-RG56, Lets. Recd. from President.
1. Low (c1815–fl1870) was listed in the census as a "farmer" with a combined prewar estate of $54,000. 1860 Census, Ga., Henry, McDonough P.O., 117; (1870), 723rd Militia Dist., 21.
2. The Executive Office routinely referred Low's letter to the secretary of the treasury.

From John L. Smith[1]

Stockwell, Tippecanoe Co. [Indiana],
August 13th 1866

Honored Sir:—

Commissioned as Collector of Internal Revenue for the Eighth District of Indiana on the 17th day of August 1862 ("to serve during the pleasure of the President") by Abraham Lincoln your martyred predecessor, I have endeavored faithfully to discharge the duties of the office until the present time. I had from the time of your memorable and manly utterances, in the United States Senate, and as Military Governor of Tennessee, against treason and traitors learned to respect and esteem you. I heartily united with the loyal and liberty loving people to do what I could to place you in the second highest position within the gift of a great nation. And when the hand of the assassin contingently elevated you to your present exalted position, the American people were wont to regard you, with the new and fearful responsibilities resting upon you, with a tenderness and devotion amounting to little less than feelings of adoration. Judging of your future policy from the foreshadowings of your able annual message to the 39th Congress,[2] I regarded myself (however humble) as one of your sincere friends and earnest supporters.

I looked upon you as the visible head and standard bearer of the great Union party, which, under God, had so far saved the country from hopeless ruin.

As President of the United States, your official act which first startled your friends in Indiana, and caused them to pause, was your veto of the Civil Rights bill.[3] As I read and reread your annual message, to my mind there was clearly traceable, and ably amplified in that great document every important principle contained in the Civil Rights bill. Next, in the category of this stultifying and stunning process, was your anomalous and inexplicable course in opposition to the finally mild and conservative action of Congress, precedent to the admission of representatives from States lately in armed rebellion against the Government. Did it occur to you in the incipiency of your opposition that in that action of Congress, evry member of that body who voted to elevate you to the Vice-

Presidency in 1864, also voted for the late proposed amendments to the Federal Constitution?

Had you, as your friends in and out of Congress had a right to expect, given your sanction and official endorsement to these measures, you would have done much to quell the fears and inspire the hopes of evry patriot throughout the land. This much your friends felt you owed both to the memories of the heroic dead, and to the vital interests, present and future, of a distracted country.

But, Sir, your crowning act (I will not say of perfidy) which has resulted in severing the last link of political friendship which bound many a loyal heart to you, was your official interference with the military, whereby it was unable to *prevent*, and your nonintervention with the traitorous (pardoned) Mayor[4] and rebel horde of the city of New Orleans to *allow*, the late bloody and fearful riot,[5] disgraceful alike to the city and the nation.

Indiscriminately in that terrible tragedy Union veterans, loyal citizens, and Christian missionaries, were beaten, stabbed, shot down, and murdered outright. Among the maltreated was the learned and accomplished Rev. Henry G. Jackson,[6] a native of Indiana, a graduate of Asbury University, a model man, sent by the authorities of the Methodist Episcopal Church to preach the Gospel in the city of New Orleans. He was first knocked down, and shamefully beaten, then shot through the body, the ball passing through both lungs:—and others, doubtless as inoffensive and worthy as he, fell victims to violence on that dreadful day. By whose hands was this foul and fearful work accomplished? I answer, not by the loyal Union-loving men who elevated you to power, and who followed the old flag through the dark hours of war, but by those who for four long years were in armed rebellion against the Government, who still hate it in their hearts, and *once* hated you with equal malignity, but who *now* for *some reason*, even amid the wild carnival of death, excite forward the infuriated mob by shouting "The President is on our side!" The blood of our brothers "cries from the ground." Who shall say that condign punishment shall not be meted out speedily to the guilty that others may fear?

Since now by comparing your late acts and present status with your former repeated declarations, I have lost all hope in the future of your administration, and yet with the highest respect for your official position, and with earnest prayer that the nation's God may prevent you from wrong-doing, and uphold you in all well-doing, and believing it to be your wish, as it certainly is your privilege, to award to your *friends* the patronage at your command, I hereby respectfully tender to you my resignation.

John L. Smith

LS, DNA-RG56, Appts., Internal Revenue Service, Collector, Ind., 8th Dist., John L. Smith.

1. Smith (1811–*fl*1880), a native of Virginia, moved to Ohio as a teenager. In the late

1830s he began to preach and in 1840 moved to Indiana, where he was actively engaged as a Methodist minister. Among other posts Smith held, he was a trustee of Asbury University. He successfully raised funds for Methodist schools and churches while also being actively involved in Republican politics. In the late 1870s Smith was appointed postmaster of Thornton. *Biographical History of Indiana*, 2: 26–27.

2. See Message to Congress, Dec. 4, 1865, *Johnson Papers*, 9: 466–85.

3. See Veto of Civil Rights Bill, Mar. 27, 1866, ibid., 10: 312–20.

4. John T. Monroe.

5. For information on the July 30 riot, see *House Reports*, 39 Cong., 2 Sess. No. 16 (Ser. 1304).

6. During the war Jackson (1838–*fl*1899) was involved in educational work; afterwards he aided in the reestablishment of the Methodist church in the South. He was an original member of the Mississippi mission conference established in New Orleans in December 1865, was the first pastor of the Ames M.E. Church in New Orleans, and was an editor of the *New Orleans Advocate*. Following the riot he returned to Indiana. *NCAB*, 19: 83–84.

From John P. White[1]

Nashville   Augst 13th 1866

Dr. Sir

On my return home I called to see Mess Allen & Weaver[2] and proposed a settlement with the two Banks on the basis talked of by us and after two or three days for consideration they declined my offer and I would have written to you the result immediately but for our mutual friend Burns[3] who you are aware was a Director in the Union Bank who is of the opinion yet that they will accept my offer—in fact he is very confident that they will come to terms but I must confess I have my *doubts* for there is very little gratidude with such monied powers and past friendship is soon forgotten. I will write you again soon and let you know how things are working and I would suggest that you pay no attention to any communication from them for some time as you have done in the past for I am satisfied they are very anxious to have the matters settled but to get all they can.

I see you are going to Chicago[4] and I know you will make one of your best speeches one that will arouse and put to work your friends in the north in fact your friends here who know your power on the stump say that if it was common for men ocupying your position, to address political gatherings that all would be right but I am one of the confident that the people will sustain you in future as in the past in doing what you believe to be right.

Our family are all very well. I will write you again soon.

John P White

ALS, DLC-JP.

1. This letter is but the first in a series of exchanges by several persons with Johnson concerning his personal finances. There is a concentration of documents in October and a few in November and January.

2. Joseph W. Allen and Dempsey Weaver. Allen (1814–1902) spent many years in New Orleans in the commission business with Nashville partners. In 1862 he returned to

Nashville, where he accepted the presidency of the Planters' Bank of Tennessee. A year later he became a cashier of the Union Bank and in 1865 he organized the Third National Bank of Nashville. *Nashville Banner*, Apr. 17, 1902.

3. Michael Burns.

4. A reference to Johnson's forthcoming "swing around the circle" trip that would begin in late August and continue until mid-September. The President would make a speech in Chicago on September 6.

From Orville H. Browning and Alexander W. Randall[1]

Philadelphia Pa   Aug 14 1866

Convention assembled in wigwam[2] at 12 M. Every state and Territory fully represented. Massachusetts and South Carolina delegates entered arm in arm.[3] The vast audience rose to their feet & gave cheer after cheer. Many were moved to tears. Band played "Star Spangled Banner" and "Dixie." Cheering renewed. Gen Dix temporary chairman[4] speech appropriate & thrilling. Prayer of chaplain[5] most impressive. Committees appointed & all going well. Nothing could be better.[6]

O H Browning & Alex W Randall

Tel, DLC-JP.

1. Before the first session of the convention ended on August 14 at 1:15 p.m., the delegates agreed to Browning's suggestion that the President be informed by telegraph of the day's proceedings. Wagstaff, "Arm-in-Arm Convention," 112.

2. The massive wooden structure, which reputedly could accommodate as many as 15,000 people, had been built on Girard Avenue specifically for the convention. Ibid., 108; Bradley, *Militant Republicanism*, 237.

3. By virtue of a prearranged demonstration, the two delegations walking, literally, arm-in-arm, were led to their seats by Gen. Darius N. Couch of Massachusetts and Gov. James L. Orr of South Carolina.

4. Later in the week Johnson received an optimistic appraisal of the convention from John A. Dix. See Dix to Johnson, Aug. 16, 1866, Johnson Papers, LC.

5. The Rev. J. M. Donald, who is otherwise unidentified. *Evening Bulletin* (Philadelphia), Aug. 14, 1866.

6. At least three other messages from convention delegates were transmitted to Johnson on the 14th. See William H.C. King to Johnson, George F. Train to Johnson, and J. D. Perryman to Johnson, Aug. 14, 1866, Johnson Papers, LC.

To Orville H. Browning and Alexander W. Randall

Washington, D.C., Aug. 14 1866.

I thank you for your cheering and encouraging despatch. The finger of Providence is unerring, and will guide you safely through. The people must be trusted, and the country will be restored. My faith is unshaken as to the ultimate result.[1]

Andrew Johnson

Tel, DNA-RG107, Tels. Sent, President, Vol. 3 (1865–68).

1. Johnson's telegram was read by Browning before the convention on August 15, prompting a "noisy demonstration." Wagstaff, "Arm-in-Arm Convention," 115.

Thomas Nast's cartoon ridiculing the National Union Convention
Harper's Weekly, September 29, 1866

From David M. Fleming

Piqua [Ohio], Aug 14th 1866

My Dear Sir:

At the radical county Convention in Troy on Saturday last, Maj. Johnston,[1] father of the Deputy Collector in this city, made a speech, during which he took occasion to speak of yourself in the most offensive terms, and closed by stating that "his son the dept'y Collector,[2] felt so outraged at your 22d February Speech that he deliberately took down your likeness, which had been suspended on the wall, side by side with the lamented Lincoln, rolled it up and cast it amongst the rubbish."

I immediately notified Collector Wright[3] of the dastardly insult—the more dastardly, because it was made without any pretext whatever, and for the purpose of exciting still further the prejudice of the people against your Administration. I now have the satisfaction of knowing that the Collector has just given notice to his Deputy to hand over the books to his successor J. M. Roe, Esq.,[4] a gentleman of integrity and high standing in this city, and withal a true friend of your Governmental policy. I make this Statement because I have understood that the name of Maj Johnston has been put upon the slate in the Departments at Washington for an appointment.

And here will you permit me to say in all candor and honesty, that you have not a better friend in the District than Collector Wright, and who from his great popularity, large acquaintance, strict integrity and fine business capacity, can do more, perhaps, than any other man towards uniting the good men in the Union party in this section in favor of your measures of restoration and policy generally. He has been a great aid to me in this effort, and for this reason I hope he will be encouraged to continue.

I speak thus freely because I learn that J. W. Frizell[5] and J. E. Cummins, who are now in Washington, publicly boasted before leaving that they intended to oust both Wright and myself from our positions and appropriate them to themselves.

Believing, Mr. President, that you have the same confidence in me now that you have heretofore expressed to others, and feeling under deep and lasting gratitude to you for your kindness to me, a poor man, struggling with the world, I would not deceive you on any account, and I know I speak truly when I say that neither of these men can take with them three votes from the Union party. Be not deceived by them, for I tell you truly they are without political character and popularity at their own homes, and can carry no strength with them whatever. To show you what they are, they could only find *four men* in the District to aid them in the Convention at Columbus—and these four are all the friends they have in the Union party at home, and these they have hield by the promise of appointments.

Having stood by you from the first, and when there was scarcely a man in the District who was your friend, and now that we are building up a little party of the very best and most active men in the District to support you and your measures, I cannot deliberately set back and allow these political charlatans to destroy our hopes and throw this great element of strength back into the ranks of the radical party and against your plans and measures for a restoration of the Union under the banner of beauty and glory.

Believing that a change of the offices in the direction I have mentioned would be a detriment to the public service and to your Administration, I have, as a friend, whose sincerity I hope will not be questioned, given you my opinion, unasked it is true, but I hope it will have consideration.

I ask this not for myself, for I shall support you and your measures as long as you continue in the good work, but for the great cause in which we are engaged. The Executive cannot afford at this time to put in responsible trusts men whose only qualifications are intemperance, profanity and a disposition to bully, and knock down every man who does not descend as low in the scale of humanity as themselves.

This letter is written in the strictest privacy, as I do not wish to incur their personal animosity, but, if you have any doubts on the subject investigate what I say by trustworthy agents, in their own towns and counties.

                                                                D M Fleming.

ALS, DNA-RG56, Appts., Internal Revenue Service, Assessor, Ohio, 4th Dist., David M. Fleming.
    1. Probably Stephen Johnston (1812–*fl*1880), a Piqua lawyer, and former sheriff, legislator, and Lincoln elector (1864), who in 1861 was briefly a captain in the 11th Ohio Inf. *The History of Miami County, Ohio* (Chicago, 1880), 599.
    2. Either Stephen C. Johnston (b. *c*1840) or William C. Johnston (b. *c*1842). The former subsequently engaged in gold mining near Charlotte, North Carolina, and the latter became a Miami County lawyer and probate judge. Ibid.; 1860 Census, Ohio, Miami, Piqua, 114.
    3. Francis M. Wright (b. *c*1811), an Urbana merchant, had been appointed by Lincoln collector of Ohio's Fourth District. 1860 Census, Ohio, Champaign, Urbana, 36; *U.S. Off. Reg.* (1863–65).
    4. James M. Roe (b. *c*1822) was a Piqua grocer. 1860 Census, Ohio, Miami, Piqua, 9.
    5. Joseph W. Frizell (1821–1874), a Greenville, Ohio, lawyer and bank cashier, during the war had risen from lieutenant colonel to brevet brigadier general. In September 1866 he was given a recess appointment as collector of the Fourth District, but was rejected by the Senate during February 1867. Ohio Delegates to the National Union Convention to Johnson, Aug. 14, 1866, Appts., Internal Revenue Service, Collector, Ohio, 4th Dist., Joseph W. Frizell, RG56, NA; Ser. 6B, Vol. 3: 494; Vol. 4: 257, Johnson Papers, LC.

From Juan Jennon[1]

                                                New Orleans   14th Aug 66
Sir
    I Reside about 150 yards from the "Mechanics Institute" on Canal St. On the 30th ult I left my place of Business Exackly at 12 ocl. for my

Room, for the purpose of having a Bath. Having attented the Street meeting of the Republicans on the previous Friday Evening,[2] and having
heard "Henderson" Dostie[3] & Co. address a mob of negroes in the Street
in the most Boisterous manner, "*shouting*" *aloud*, the most Shameful Incendiary language, I thought I would drop in for a moment and see if a
Crowd had gathered—at "Dostie's bidding, in their "Strength." I passed
through Two Crowds of negroes and mulattoes in Canal, Corner of Dryades Streets, many of them having pieces of Pine Boards and Heavy
Canes. I Surveyed them well, in all about 100 in the two Crowds. I
wended my way to the Institute, and at the door and inside I found a full
House, most of them had Canes, and I got up on a form and Surveyed the
House. The negroes were all of the lower order, none of our well dressed
population were there. I seen a few white men. I Remained about ten
minuets leaving Exackly at 12.25 by my watch. Came down Crossed the
Street, Reached my Room, Calling to Servant to close the doors of
House, as I anticipated a Row. I had Just got off my Coat when I Heard
music. Running to Hall door I seen the procession moving on Walking in
a Braggard manner and in a few minuets the Firing Commenced. I Remained in Canal St. Corner of Dryades from then to 3 ocl. Every thing
was over at $2^{1}/_{2}$. I proceeded to dinner at 3.25. And Sat down 3.35
Exackly. We had been served with Soup. I had finished mine, when I
heard music, and Rising from the table I passed through the Parler, and
on to the gallery and Seen a Regiment of Infantry *trotting*—around the
Custom House. So you will see that the troops did not Reach Canal
Street, till at least 4 ocl less 20 minutes—that is the Exact time, and at 4
ocl they grounded, or Stacked arms on the Bangnetto opposite my door,
and I ordered the yard door open and furnished the men Water, and the
officers—Wine—it was Excessively Hot. My object in writing your Excellency is to give you the Exact time, and nobody knows it better than
"General Mower,"[4] who was at the Table at that moment at dinner. We
dine *Exackly* at $3^{1}/_{2}$. At $12^{1}/_{2}$ ocl. I noticed no police, at $1^{1}/_{2}$ ocl. the whole
force was on hand, and it was fortunate the Police managed to get the best
of them. (the Negroes) I am satisfied that a dozen of Soldiers would have
prevented it—Aye Six, and an officer. No gentleman Citizen Joined the
Police, an Engine, Rider, and 2 firemen Came. No Confederate Flag, was
displayed, and a more *quiet* Riot, I never Saw, people passed and Re-
passed in Canal St. as though nothing was unusual. I assure your Excellency the people to a man deplore the death of the Colored people, but as
a Foreigner, (I am not one grown in N.O.) I must Say the language used
by Dostie & Henderson to Excite the Servile Race, merited death. A
"High official" in the Parlor of our Boarding House on the following
morning made some Remarks to a gentleman Boarder, also a friend of
mine—Regarding Your Excellency, but I will not Repeat it lest my letter
may in our P.O. be opened.

However I know Your Excellency is accustomed to be So much abused, no Epithet, is ever new to your opponents.

I know personally every thing that I have stated is true and I know the N Y. Correspondents account, is from first to last the most Infamous Falsehoods—the Correspondent Himself, Receives no more notice by the good people of N.O. than a "dog." I seen Him yesterday running out and into "Head Quarters," as familiar as a poodle.

I have no interest pro nor Con in the affairs of the U.S. but I am sorry to see the people of N.O maligned. And Heaven Knows what would become of them if Your Excellency did not deal as kindly as you do. I hear blessings prayed on your Excellency by these poor but High Minded people in every place I go.

I am a Resident of Havana for many years—and temporarily on Business Here.

Hoping your Excellency will pardon the liberty I have taken in stating the EXACT time the Troops arrived, and praying your Excellency a long and useful life.

Juan Jennon
95 & 97 Gravier St

ALS, DLC-JP.
1. Not identified.
2. For other accounts of the meeting on July 27, see Albert Voorhies and Andrew S. Herron to Johnson, July 28, 1866, *Johnson Papers*, 10: 750.
3. John Henderson, Jr., and Anthony P. Dostie.
4. Probably Joseph A. Mower.

From Robert Emmet Monaghan[1]

West Chester, Pa.   August 14th. 1866.

My Dear Sir:—

Having just finished reading the history of the Administration of Genl. Andrew Jackson, and his manner of controlling the events of his time, I, as a member of the Democratic State Central Committee of Penna., address you in relation to what, in my judgment, the best interests of the Country and your administration demand. Briefly then, the country demands that the Radicals of this nation should be defeated at the coming Elections, and removed from power; and your Administration should be used, speedily, vigorously, and without fear, favor or affection, in removing from posts of honor, influence or profit, every man who is unwilling to support you by *word, act* and VOTE, in your wise policy, and patriotic efforts to restore the unity of the States, and the fraternal unity of all the people of every section of this country.

Allow no man to use the patronage of your Administration to defeat or counteract your restoration policy. Permit no Radical to hold a place of influence and power to give force to his opposition, and effect to his efforts to defeat you and the friends of the Union of all the States under the Constitution. Let him have the control of none of those positions of power or influence to enable him to dishonor his country—none, not the most insignificant Post Office by which to circulate *his documents* to further his objects and to keep back *those* which would advance your's by a proper enlightenment of the people.

Sir, I thus freely venture this as my judgment, because having met you, conversed with you, and closely observed your course, I believe you to be the proper man in the proper place.

To be frank with you, it is due to say I voted for Genl. McClellan in 1864. But from the moment you entered your present office I had hope for the future of this government. I believed you were a man of firmness and meant well for the whole country. And although I labored for the success of the Democratic ticket in the last Presidential campaign, still I freely gave you my full support when I saw that the patriot was above party, and that you had a heart to pity and forgive for your country's sake:—that you believed justice and wisdom were as powerful at least as the weapons of war.

I went to Washington in December last at the meeting of Congress—I waited to listen to your message: for that was the object of my visit,—to hear it and witness how it should be received. It was all I could ask. In company with Mr. Johnson—(member of Congress from Pa)[2] and another friend I called and had a brief interview with you. You do not remember it. I do. I still feel the impression then made in my mind. I read men from the first interview. My object being accomplished I returned to my State, and at a meeting of several members of our Democratic State Comt., in a confidential manner I narrated our interview—gave my opinion of your message and expressed my hopes in your future course. I then stated that the 276,000 Democrats of Penna. should sustain you in your policy—that your cause was our cause; and I recommended and urged an immediate call of a full Committee at the earliest day, for the purpose of sending a communication to you assuring you of our support. Our State Committee met on the 4th of January last at Harrisburg, when I offered the enclosed resolution[3] which met the unanimous approval of the members. You remember the visit of the Committee under that resolution.[4]

Our Committee, and I believe our party, and the masses of our people, will never have cause to regret our course. Our action was private and confidential, and confined to yourself and the State Committee.

Pardon me for thus trespassing. But I have been particular in order to give some force to my letter; for I am a stranger to you.

Our party now, is an unit for your policy. It will stand or fall, if need be, with it. You will more clearly see this from the gentlemen we have selected as delegates to meet in Convention in Philada. this day.[5]

Shall I say you have no strength in this state, in the Republican party as an organization. You may—you can gain some of that party to your sup-

port by the favor of your Administration. There is a *power* in your patronage. Give your offices to friendly Republicans where ever they can be
found. Let them understand that *word*, *act* and *vote*, in support of your
policy are absolutely essential, and that the *vote* is worth more than all
else. But trust no position to a political enemy—not even the smallest X
Roads Post Office. Yield us immediate aid of this kind in Penna.—teach
them that the churches—(the offices)—must be filled with orthodox
preaches—and we will give an old fashioned Jackson result in October.[6]
We are struggling to help you, and thereby helping this suffering country. Help us! May God bless You.

R. Emmet Monaghan

LS, DLC-JP.
    1. A former schoolteacher and member of the Pennsylvania legislature, Monaghan
(1822–*fl*1893), an attorney, twice served as chairman of the Democratic State Convention
(1876, 1880) and was active in Democratic circles on both the state and national levels.
Samuel T. Wiley, *Biographical and Portrait Cyclopedia of Chester County, Pennsylvania*
(Philadelphia, 1893), 194–97.
    2. Presumably Philip Johnson (1818–1867), also a former member of the state legisla-
ture, who was elected to Congress as a Republican in 1861 and served until his death.
BDAC.
    3. The resolution called for the appointment of a committee of "seven prominent Dem-
ocrats" from Pennsylvania to meet with Johnson, assuring him of their "cordial sympathy"
and "material support."
    4. An account of the committee's interview with Johnson has not been located.
    5. The Pennsylvania delegation to the National Union Convention in Philadelphia con-
sisted of nearly sixty individuals, including former Democratic governors David R. Porter
and William Bigler, Sen. Edgar Cowan, Johnson cronies Joseph R. Flanigen and William
F. Johnston, and Monaghan's law mentor, Hamilton Aldricks of Harrisburg. *New York
Times*, Aug. 14, 1866; Wiley, *Chester County*, 195.
    6. For various reports of the fall 1866 election returns in Pennsylvania, see Alfred Gil-
more to Johnson, Oct. 10, 1866; Edwin C. Wilson to Johnson, Oct. 11, 1866; William
Bigler to Johnson, Oct. 18, 1866.

From Ward H. Lamon

[ca. August 15, 1866][1]

Mr. President
    There can be no doubt of the earnest desire of your friends to have you
make your contemplated visit to Chicago on the occasion sacred to the
memory of that great man, the late Stephen A Douglas. I as an humble
individual—a personal as well as a political friend of yours—however
humble I think it may not be deemed egotism in me to say that I have had
no less extensive than sad experience in the last five years officially and
individually—and at the same time I in common with you have full faith
in wisdom and justice of the masses of this Country. I am reminded that
there are bad passions of many disaffected towards *you* and your administration. The loss of your life at this time would be the greatest calamity
that this Country has ever sustained.

We all felt & feel deeply the loss of that great and good man Abraham Lincoln—but we were fortunate enough to have his mantle fall on the Shoulders of a patriot. Yours might rest on Enemy to the best interests of our distracted Country.

Therefore in view of our recent sad experience—the bad passions prevalent in the country—high and excited party spirit and the natural and inevitable result in case of accident, I do earnestly call your attention to these facts and ask leave most respectfully to protest against your going to Chicago however beneficial as well as pleasant the result of your visit might otherwise be.[2]

[Ward H. Lamon]

Draft, CSmH-Ward Hill Lamon Col.
   1. Since the invitation to the dedication of Douglas's monument was the catalyst for Johnson's "swing around the circle," which began on August 28, the date of Lamon's letter was probably mid-August, just before the trip.
   2. Johnson did not heed the warnings but instead attended the dedication of the Douglas Monument on September 6 and spoke to the audience. There is no record of Johnson having received this letter.

From James R. Doolittle et al.

Philadelphia Pa   Aug 16 1866

At ten (10) A M the wigwam was full to its utmost capacity. The Sacred blessing was invoked & Convention proceeded to business.

Resolutions & addres adopted amid the greatest enthusiasm without a dissenting voice from the North or South, East or West. Thanks were returned to Almight God for the good order & fraternal feeling which prevailed & at one p m the Convention adjourned with nine cheers for the President. Not a jar in the Convention since it met.[1]

J R Doolittle   James Dixon
Thos A Hendrix   O H Browning
A W Randall

Tel, DLC-JP.
   1. On the following evening Doolittle, Browning, and Secretary Welles had a lengthy conversation with the President about the convention in Philadelphia. Randall, *Browning Diary*, 2: 90; Beale, *Welles Diary*, 2: 581.

From Nevada Citizens and Delegates to Philadelphia[1]

Aug. 16th 1866.

The undersigned citizens of the State of Nevada and delegates and alternate delegates from said State to the National Conservative Convention called to meet at Philadelphia, August 14th 1866, respectfully represent.

That the result of the ensuing Nov. election to be holden in said state will be of the highest importance to that state and will bear largely upon the future interests of the whole Union, as at said election all the state officers are to be elected, together with a legislature on which will devolve the duty of electing a U.S. Senator to succeed Hon. James W. Nye.[2]

That at present the federal offices of our state are filled with incumbents appointed upon the recommendation of gentlemen, than in whom, the wise humane and patriotic policy of your Excellency's Administration meets no where with more violent and virulent opponents, and these incumbents with few exceptions faithfully adhere to and reflect the sentiments of those at whose instance they were appointed, thus securing to the opponents of your Excellency's Administration, in our State, the moral and material influence incident to the said offices and positions.

One of the most important positions referred to is that of Collector of the Internal Revenue of the United States; for the State of Nevada.

The appointment of the present incumbent of this office S. T. Gage[3] was procured at the instance of parties who have and still continue to use every effort to defeat the exertions of your Excellency to secure the full supremacy of the Constitution and the restoration of the Union under it, and he is in full harmony and accord with them.

Assured that the best interests of our state demand the change we earnestly petition your Excellency to remove the said S. T. Gage and to appoint, in his stead, to the said office of Collector of the Internal Revenue of the U.S. for Nevada, the Hon. George M. Beebe.[4]

Gov. Beebe has, from the first, been an earnest active and influential supporter of your Excellency's Administration—has been for three years a resident of the state and is a delegate at large there from to the said Philadelphia Convention.

His integrity and ability cannot be questioned and his appointment will, we are confident, give universal satisfaction to the entire conservative element of our state.[5]

LS, DNA-RG56, Appts., Internal Revenue Service, Assessor, Nev., George M. Beebe.

    1. A dozen men signed the letter.

    2. Nye was reelected. *BDAC*.

    3. An Ohio native, Stephen T. Gage (1831–1916) crossed the plains to California in 1852 where he became involved in state and local politics and was the youngest member of the state legislature. In 1862 he made his home in Virginia City, Nevada, where he exercised a strong pro-Union voice in state politics. For nearly forty years Gage was involved in the leadership of the Central and Southern Pacific railroads. *NCAB*, 17: 60; Hubert H. Bancroft, *History of Nevada, Colorado, and Wyoming, 1540–1888* (San Francisco, 1890), 187–88.

    4. New Yorker Beebe (1836–1927), a lawyer and newspaperman, had practiced his professions in Illinois, Kansas (of which he was territorial secretary and acting governor), Missouri, and Nevada. He was later much involved in Democratic politics in New York, serving in the state legislature, as well as two terms in the U.S. House of Representatives (1875–79). *BDAC*.

5. Johnson appointed Beebe to the collectorship; Beebe, however, was detained in New York by the illness of his family and then became politically involved in the New York election, so he resigned his commission without ever having actually held the office. Gage remained collector at least through September 1871, resigning in order to take a railroad post in California. *NCAB*, 17: 60; Bancroft, *Nevada*, 188; *U.S. Off. Reg.* (1867–71); Beebe to Johnson, Oct. 22, 1866; Beebe to Hugh McCulloch, Oct. 22, 1866, Appts., Internal Revenue Service, Assessor, Nev., George M. Beebe, RG56, NA.

From Andrew C. Maxwell

Bay City, Mich, Augt. 17th, 1866

Dear Sir,

John F. Driggs,[1] Member of Congress from this (the 6th) District, made a speech last Wednesday at Vassar in Tuscola County. He is a Radical Republican, and very hostile to your administration. He said that he had seen Stanton your Secretary of War a day or two before leaving Washington for home, and that Stanton assured him that he fully sympathized with the radicals in Congress and was remaining in the War office for their benefit, and that he, Driggs, urged Stanton to remain in his office as Secretary of War, saying that *it is best to have some one in that office in whom Congress can depend in case of trouble with the President.*

A. C. Maxwell

LS, DLC-JP.

1. In 1856 Driggs (1813–1877) moved from New York to Michigan, where he sold real estate, manufactured salt, and was a member of the state house of representatives. A colonel of Michigan infantry during the Civil War, Driggs, a Republican, served in the U.S. House of Representatives for three terms (1863–69). *BDAC*.

Proclamation re Maximilian's Blockade

[August 17, 1866]

Whereas a war is existing in the Republic of Mexico, aggravated by foreign military intervention; and

Whereas the United States, in accordance with their settled habits and policy, are a neutral power in regard to the war which thus afflicts the Republic of Mexico; and

Whereas it has become known that one of the belligerents in the said war, namely, the Prince Maximilian, who asserts himself to be Emperor in Mexico, has issued a decree[1] in regard to the port of Matamoras and other Mexican ports which are in the occupation and possession of another of the said belligerents, namely, the United States of Mexico, which decree is in the following words:

The port of Matamoras and all those of the northern frontier which have withdrawn from their obedience to the Government are closed to foreign and coasting traffic during such time as the empire of the law shall not be therein reinstated.

ART. 2. Merchandise proceeding from the said ports, on arriving at any other where the exise of the Empire is collected, shall pay the duties on importation, introduction, and consumption, and, on satisfactory proof of contravention, shall be irremissibly confiscated. Our minister of the treasury is charged with the punctual execution of this decree.

Given at Mexico, the 9th of July, 1866.

And whereas the decree thus recited, by declaring a belligerent blockade unsupported by competent military or naval force, is in violation of the neutral rights of the United States as defined by the law of nations as well as of the treaties existing between the United States of America and the aforesaid United States of Mexico:

Now, therefore, I, Andrew Johnson, President of the United States, do hereby proclaim and declare that the aforesaid decree is held and will be held by the United States to be absolutely null and void as against the Government and citizens of the United States, and that any attempt which shall be made to enforce the same against the Government or the citizens of the United States will be disallowed.

In witness whereof I have hereunto set my hand and caused the seal of the United States to be affixed.

Done at the city of Washington the 17th day of August, A.D. 1866, and of the Independence of the United States of America the ninety-first.

ANDREW JOHNSON.

Richardson, *Messages*, 6: 433–34.

1. American editorial remarks concerning the decree and Johnson's response were favorable to the President, especially as Maximilian had no naval or land forces in the area to enforce the blockade. *New York Herald*, Aug. 19, 1866; *National Intelligencer*, Aug. 20, 1866.

To Edwin M. Stanton

Washington, D.C.   Aug 17th 1866.

Sir.

It has been represented to me by citizens and others that there is on duty near Leesburg, Va, a detachment of the 5th U.S. Cavalry, for which there is no further necessity, and the duties of which are unpleasant to the Officers of the detachment, and irritating in a high degree to the citizens of that vicinity. Will the Secretary of War please ascertain whether these statements are correct, and, if so, take such action in regard thereto as he may deem most expedient, under the existing circumstances.[1]

Andrew Johnson
President U.S.

LS, DNA-RG94, Lets. Recd. (Main Ser.), File P-479-1866 (M619, Roll 503).

1. On July 11 Bvt. Capt. Alfred B. Taylor and his detachment of the 5th U.S. Cav. were ordered to the Leesburg, Virginia, area. Beginning August 1, Stanton, Grant, and John-

son began to receive letters complaining of damages and annoyances caused by Taylor's men. Subsequent investigation exonerated Taylor and his troops but deemed their presence there no longer necessary, and on August 28 they were relieved from that duty. See the numerous letters and endorsements in Lets. Recd. (Main Ser.), File P-479-1866 (M619, Roll 503), RG94, NA.

From Charles Brodhead[1]

Bethlehem, Pa.   Aug 18th 1866.

Dear Sir

I herewith enclose an Extract from Forneys Phila Press of Aug. 16, 1866.[2]

I happen to *know* that it was written by Gen A. V. Kautz[3] of the Army, now with Gen Baird[4] at New Orleans, to a Samuel Wetherill[5] of this place.

Kautz from what I learn of him is one of the malignant Red Republicans of Germany, of the Carl Shurz order & I have no doubt but that similar letters are being sent to all parts of the Country & published in like manner in order to influence public opinion against your self & your Administration.

I assure you that you can rely upon the statement as a fact, beyond question that Kautz wrote the letter. I can substantiate the fact when ever called upon.

As to myself, I refer you to John M Brodhead[6] of the Treasury, or Senator Buckalew[7] that you may rely on my statements.

Respectfully suggesting that a great good can be done the Country by summarily ejecting such Scribblers from the public Service. . . .

Charles Brodhead.

ALS, DLC-JP.
1. Brodhead (1824–1904), a nephew of a former Democratic congressman and U.S. senator from Pennsylvania, practiced law for a few years before venturing into the real estate business in Bethlehem, where he helped establish an iron foundry and a railroad later known as the Lehigh & Lackawanna lines. Heller, *Northampton County*, 3: 514–15.
2. Brodhead enclosed a copy of an article, entitled "The Official Massacre at New Orleans," in which "an officer of the United States army" writes a former comrade-in-arms from Pennsylvania that the late riot was the responsibility of the mayor and his police force, who were disloyal to the Federal government.
3. August V. Kautz (1828–1895) was a career army soldier who performed creditably during the Civil War in both the western and eastern theaters. Given a regular army commission after the war, Kautz continued serving for the next twenty-five years until his retirement in 1891. Warner, *Blue*.
4. Absalom Baird.
5. Wetherill (1821–1890), a chemist and inventor who operated a zinc plant in Bethlehem, had served in a Pennsylvania cavalry regiment under Kautz's command. *DAB; OR*, Ser. 1, Vol. 42, Pt. 1: 836.
6. Brodhead (c1810–1880), a son of a former Democratic congressman from New Hampshire, served as second controller of the treasury from 1863 to 1876, when he resigned. *New York Times*, Feb. 24, 1880; 1870 Census, D.C., Washington, 5th Ward, 145.
7. Charles R. Buckalew.

From John Caldwell

Knoxville   Augst 18th 1866

Dear sir

For some days the public mind has been excited by a proposition to call a convention to reorganize the state goverment.[1] If you can say or do anything to avoid the evil that will result from such a move you will recieve the warmest thanks of a people praying for and desiring peace. By your courtesy I have the permission to suggest that after fifty years consideration of the slavery question and an agency in the colonization scheme dating back in 1821 I have a strong and abiding conviction that by sending the children of Ham home to their fatherland with their own consent would be promotive of the interests of both even especially if the emigration is deliberately and wisely conducted. If it meets your views of propriety and you should in your next message recommend to congress the fostering of the schieme a shout of approval will ring along down for a hundred coming generations.

During this hour of excitement the legislative department of the goverment may hesitate to favor the policy, but ere long will be heard the utterance from the millions. American philanthropy, patriotism, justice, the right views and virtuous disposition of good men will rebuke the policy that would withhold from Africa the only human instrumentality by which her degredation can be dispelled and her redemption & regeneration accomplished.

One other suggestion and I have done. Nothing in my opinion would be more promotive of the pecuniary & social interests of the desolated southern states than a careful geological survey and report of the great metaliferous range stretching diagonally from Taladega Alabama to Richmond Va. A commission with such a man as Genl L. S. Trowbridge[2] at its head would secure the confidence and respect of capitalists both at home and abroad. A partial survey made by myself on this long line and the opening of valuable mines in three of the states on the line will enable me to render material aid to the commission if created.

Jno. Caldwell

ALS, DLC-JP.
1. Ratification of the Fourteenth Amendment stirred renewed interest among some Conservatives in Tennessee for a convention that would devise a new state constitution. Thomas B. Alexander, *Political Reconstruction in Tennessee* (Nashville, 1950), 125–26. See also Francis C. Dunnington to Johnson, Aug. 24, 1866.
2. Luther S. Trowbridge (1836–1912), a lawyer and internal revenue collector, had served in the Michigan cavalry during the war and as provost marshal general of East Tennessee. Hunt and Brown, *Brigadier Generals*.

From James Johnson

Columbus Ga   August 18th 1866

Sir

The kindness which you have manifested to me in tendering the Collectorship at Savannah Geo.[1] places me under renewed obligations to you and the least return which I can make therefore is an acknowledgement on my part to you for the favor shown me. The proceedings of the late convention has already had, & will continue to have in my opinion, a happy influence on the people of Georgia. People are becoming more quiet and considerate, and are setting about now practically and earnestly to accomodate themselves to the actual condition of the Country. The action of the Convention will be *generally* approved, but there are some who will murmur, complain & reject it. They are the sectional men, who are determined not to be reconciled but fortunately they are now impotent for evil. Your labors are exhausting & your anxiety must be great, but I trust that Providence will guard your health.

J. Johnson

ALS, DLC-JP.
   1. Just a few days earlier, the President had given former governor Johnson a recess appointment as the Savannah collector. In January 1867, however, Johnson decided that he should resign on the grounds that he was "unsuited by taste & education" for the collectorship. Ironically, the President had just nominated him for a permanent appointment; the Senate approved the appointment in late February and Johnson was commissioned. Despite his intention to resign, Johnson stayed in the job apparently throughout the remainder of the presidential administration. Ser. 6B, Vol. 3: 304; Vol. 4: 162, Johnson Papers, LC; *U.S. Off. Reg.* (1867); James Johnson to Johnson, Jan. 28, 30, 1867, Johnson Papers, LC.

From Missouri Delegates to Philadelphia Convention[1]

Washington D C   August 18th 1866

Sir

The undersigned, representatives of Missouri to the Philadelphia Convention, beg most respectfully to recommend to your favorable consideration, for the position of Secretary of War Gen Frank P Blair Jr. Gen Blair was the first civilian of any prominence in the country, who drew his sword in defence of the Union, and he fought until the surrender of Lee & Johnston brought the war to a close. He was among the first to declare for those principles which constitute the basis of your wise & patriotic policy—principles which the Philadelphia Convention have stamped with the seal of nationality. Since he left the army he has devoted himself to the promulgation of those principles in Missouri with eminent success.

He has peculiar claims on the people of Missouri, for it was largely through his instrumentality that the State was Kept in the Union when the secession mania prevailed. The peculiar condition of that State now, groaning under radical tyranny & terrorism, and the consequent necessity as far as our people are concerned, of having at the head of the War Department, a man who will cordially cooperate in carrying out the views which we Know you entertain, is our reason and apology for submitting this application to you.[2]

LS, DLC-JP.

1. A sizeable group of Missourians, for whom Col. James O. Broadhead was the principal spokesman, called on Johnson on August 20, 1866. They presented papers concerning the conditions in Missouri that they believed were unsatisfactory as well as this recommendation of Blair for secretary of war, which was signed by nineteen delegates from Missouri. *Louisville Courier*, Aug. 22, 1866.

2. Attached to the Missouri delegates' signatures was a statement signed by eleven delegates from Illinois who joined in recommending Blair as secretary of war.

Reply to Committee from Philadelphia National Union Convention[1]

August 18, 1866

Mr. Chairman and Gentlemen of the Committee: Language is inadequate to express the emotions and feelings produced by this occasion. Perhaps I could express more by permitting silence to speak and you to infer what I ought to say. I confess that, notwithstanding the experience I have had in public life and the audiences I have addressed, this occasion and this assemblage are calculated to, and do, overwhelm me. As I have said, I have not language to convey adequately my present feelings and emotions.

In listening to the address which your eloquent and distinguished chairman has just delivered, the proceedings of the Convention, as they transpired, recurred to my mind. Seemingly, I partook of the inspiration that prevailed in the Convention when I received a despatch, sent by two of its distinguished members,[2] conveying in terms the scene which has just been described, of South Carolina and Massachusetts, arm in arm, marching into that vast assemblage, and thus giving evidence that the two extremes had come together again, and that for the future they were united, as they had been in the past, for the preservation of the Union. When I was thus informed that in that vast body of men, distinguished for intellect and wisdom, every eye was suffused with tears on beholding the scene, I could not finish reading the despatch to one associated with me in the office, for my own feelings overcame me. ⟨Applause.⟩ I think we may justly conclude that we are acting under a proper inspiration, and that we need not be mistaken that the finger of an overruling and unerring Providence is in this great movement.

The nation is in peril. We have just passed through a mighty, a bloody, a momentous ordeal, and yet do not find ourselves free from the difficulties and dangers that at first surrounded us. While our brave soldiers, both officers and men, (turning to General Grant, who stood at his right,) have by their heroism won laurels imperishable, there are still greater and more important duties to perform; and while we have had their coöperation in the field, now that they have returned to civil pursuits, we need their support in our efforts to restore the Government and perpetuate peace. ⟨Applause.⟩ So far as the Executive department of the Government is concerned, the effort has been made to restore the Union, to heal the breach, to pour oil into the wounds which were consequent upon the struggle, and (to speak in common phrase,) to prepare, as the learned and wise physician would a plaster, healing in character and coextensive with the wound. ⟨Applause.⟩ We thought, and we think, that we had partially succeeded; but as the work progresses, as reconciliation seemed to be taking place, and the country was becoming reunited, we found a disturbing and marring element opposing us. In alluding to that element I shall go no further than your Convention and the distinguished gentleman who has delivered to me the report of its proceedings. I shall make no reference to it that I do not believe the time and occasion justify.

We have witnessed in one department of the Government every endeavor to prevent the restoration of peace, harmony, and Union. We have seen hanging upon the verge of the Government, as it were, a body called, or which assumes to be, the Congress of the United States, while in fact it is a Congress of only a part of the States. We have seen this Congress pretend to be for the Union, when its every step and act tended to perpetuate disunion and make a disruption of the States inevitable. Instead of promoting reconciliation and harmony, its legislation has partaken of the character of penalties, retaliation, and revenge. This has been the course and the policy of one portion of your Government.

The humble individual who is now addressing you stands the representative of another department of the Government. The manner in which he was called upon to occupy that position I shall not allude to on this occasion. Suffice it to say, that he is here under the Constitution of the country, and being here by virtue of its provisions, he takes his stand upon that charter of our liberties as the great rampart of civil and religious liberty. ⟨Prolonged cheering.⟩ Having been taught in my early life to hold it sacred, and having done so during my whole public career, I shall ever continue to reverence the Constitution of my fathers, and to make it my guide. ⟨Hearty applause.⟩

I know it has been said (and I must be permitted to indulge in the remark) that the Executive Department of the Government has been despotic and tyrannical. Let me ask this audience of distinguished gentlemen to point to a vote I ever gave, to a speech I ever made, to a single act of my whole public life that has not been against tyranny and despotism.

What position have I ever occupied—what ground have I ever assumed where it can be truthfully charged that I failed to advocate the amelioration and elevation of the great masses of my countrymen? ⟨Cries of "Never," and great applause.⟩

So far as charges of this kind are concerned, they are simply intended to delude the public mind into the belief that it is not the designing men who make such accusations, but some one else in power who is usurping and trampling upon the rights and perverting the principles of the Constitution. It is done by them for the purpose of covering their own acts ⟨"That's so," and applause;⟩ and I have felt it my duty, in vindication of principle, to call the attention of my countrymen to their proceedings. When we come to examine wh[o] has been playing the part of the tyrant, by whom do we find despotism exercised? As to myself, the elements of my nature, the pursuits of my life, have not made me either in my feelings or in my practice aggressive. My nature, on the contrary, is rather defensive in its character; but having taken my stand upon the broad principles of liberty and the Constitution, there is not power enough on earth to drive me from it. ⟨Loud and prolonged applause.⟩ Having placed myself upon that broad platform, I have not been awed or dismayed or intimidated by either threats or encroachments, but have stood there in conjunction with patriotic spirits, sounding the tocsin of alarm when I deemed the citadel of liberty in danger! ⟨Great applause.⟩

I said on a previous occasion, and repeat now, that all that was necessary in this great contest against tyranny and despotism was that the struggle should be sufficiently audible for the American people to hear and properly understand the issues it involved. They did hear, and looking on and seeing who the contestants were, and what the struggle was about, determined that they would settle this question on the side of the Constitution and of principle. ⟨Cries of "That's so," and applause⟩ I proclaim here to-day, as I have on previous occasions, that my faith is in the great mass of the people. In the darkest moment of this struggle, when the clouds seemed to be most lowering, my faith, instead of giving way, loomed up through their gloom; for, beyond, I saw that all would be well in the end. My countrymen, we all know that, in the language of Thomas Jefferson, tyranny and despotism can be exercised and exerted more effectually by the many than the one. We have seen Congress gradually encroach step by step upon constitutional rights, and violate, day after day and month after month, fundamental principles of the Government. ⟨Cries of "That so," and applause.⟩ We have seen a Congress that seemed to forget that there was a limit to the sphere and scope of legislation. We have seen a Congress in a minority assume to exercise power which, if allowed to be consummated, would result in despotism or monarchy itself. ⟨Enthusiastic applause.⟩ This is truth, and because others, as well as myself, have seen proper to appeal to the patriotism and republican feeling of the country, we have been denounced in the severest terms.

Slander upon slander, vituperation upon vituperation of the most virulent character, has made its way through the press. What, gentlemen, has
been your and my sin? What has been the cause of our offending? I will
tell you: Daring to stand by the Constitution of our fathers.

Mr. Chairman, I consider the proceedings of this Convention equal to,
if not more important than those of any convention that ever assembled in
the United States. ⟨Great applause⟩ When I look upon that collection of
citizens coming together voluntarily, and sitting in council with ideas,
with principles and views commensurate with all the States, and co-
extensive with the whole people, and contrast it with a Congress whose
policy, if persisted in, will destroy the country, I regard it as more important than any Convention that sat—at least since 1787. ⟨Renewed applause.⟩ I think I may also say that the declarations that were there made
are equal to those contained in the Declaration of Independence itself,
and I here to-day pronounce them a second Declaration of Independence. ⟨Cries of "Glorious," and most enthusiastic and prolonged ap-
plause⟩ Your address and declarations are nothing more nor less than a
reaffirmation of the Constitution of the United States. ⟨Cries of "Good,"
and applause⟩

Yes, I will go farther, and say that the declarations you have made, that
the principles you have enunciated in your address, are a second proclamation of emancipation to the people of the United States. ⟨Renewed ap-
plause⟩ For in proclaiming and reproclaiming these great truths, you
have laid down a constitutional platform on which all, without reference
to party, can make common cause, engage in a common effort to break
the tyranny which the dominant party in Congress has so relentingly exercised, and stand united together for the restoration of the States and the
preservation of the Government. The question only is the salvation of the
country; for our country rises above all party consideration or influences.
⟨Cries of "Good," and applause⟩ How many are there in the United
States that now require to be free? They have the shackles upon their
limbs and are bound as rigidly by the behests of party leaders in the National Congress as though they were in fact in slavery. I repeat, then, that
your declaration is the second proclamation of emancipation to the people of the United States, and offers a common ground upon which all
patriots can stand. ⟨Applause⟩

In this connection, Mr. Chairman and gentlemen, let me ask what
have I to gain more than the advancement of the public welfare? I am as
much opposed to the indulgence of egotism as any one; but here, in a
conversational manner, while formally receiving the proceedings of this
Convention, I may be permitted again to inquire, what have I to gain,
consulting human ambition, more than I have gained, except one
thing—the consummation of the great work of restoration? My race is
nearly run. I have been placed in the high office which I occupy by the
Constitution of the country, and I may say that I have held, from lowest to

highest, almost every station to which a man may attain in our Government. I have passed through every position, from alderman of a village to the Presidency of the United States. And surely, gentlemen, this should be enough to gratify a reasonable ambition.

If I had wanted authority, or if I had wished to perpetuate my own power, how easily could I have held and wielded that which was placed in my hands by the measure called the Freedmen's Bureau bill! ⟨Laughter and applause⟩ With an army which it placed at my discretion I could have remained at the capital of the nation, and with fifty or sixty millions of appropriations at my disposal, with the machinery to be unlocked by my own hands, with my satraps and dependents in every town and village, with the civil rights bill following as an auxiliary, ⟨laughter,⟩ and with the patronage and other appliances of the Government, I could have proclaimed myself dictator. ⟨"That's true!" and applause.⟩

But, gentlemen, my pride and ambition have been to occupy that position which retains all power in the hands of the people. ⟨Great cheering⟩ It is upon them I have always relied: it is upon them I rely now. ⟨A voice: "And the people will not disappoint you."⟩ And I repeat, that neither the taunts nor jeers of Congress, nor of a subsidized, calumniating press, can drive me from my purpose. ⟨Great applause⟩ I acknowledge no superior except my God, the author of my existence, and the people of the United States. ⟨Prolonged and enthusiastic cheering.⟩ The commands of the one I try to obey as best I can, compatible with poor humanity. As to the other, in a political and representative sense, the high behests of the people have always been, and ever will be, respected and obeyed by me. ⟨Applause⟩

Mr. Chairman, I have said more than I had intended to say. For the kind allusion to myself, contained in your address, I thank you. In this crisis, and at the present period of my public life, I hold above all price, and shall ever recur with feelings of profound gratification, to the resolution containing the endorsement of a convention emanating spontaneously from the great mass of the people. With conscientious conviction as my courage, the Constitution as my guide, and my faith in the people, I trust and hope that my future action may be such that you and the Convention you represent may not regret the assurance of confidence you have so generously expressed. ⟨"We are sure of it."⟩

Before separating, my friends, one and all, please accept my heartfelt thanks for the kind manifestations of regard and respect you have exhibited on this occasion.

National Intelligencer, Aug. 20, 1866.

1. The committee, chaired by Reverdy Johnson, consisted of two delegates from each state and one from each territory. They presented Johnson with a copy of the convention proceedings. *National Intelligencer*, Aug. 20, 1866.

2. See Orville H. Browning and Alexander W. Randall to Johnson, Aug. 14, 1866.

From Henry A. Smythe

New York, 18th Augt 1866

My dear Sir.

Everyone seems to feel "*jubilant*" over the Phila Convention, & *its results*,—but *no one* is reconciled to your making so hurried a trip—en route to Chicago. I hope you will pardon me—but I feel a great interest, in both the success & the pleasure attending this journey. And I *beg* of you, *extend it into New England*—before returning to Washn—& give the city of New York at least *another day*—the latter you can do—by leaving Washn on *Monday* instead of Tuesday—and on your return you can come direct to Albany, & then go to Pittsfield—Springfield—Worcester & Boston—then Fall River—Newport New London—New Haven &c.[1]

I am somewhat embarrasssed—with numerous applications made to me—which rather *compels* me to write you—first, the Authorities here have been to me with regard to your reception.[2] General Sanford[3] wishes to know whether the Military are wanted out—how many—bands—etc—rendering it necessary for me to know something *or nothing*. My friend Mr Stevens[4]—who owns the Continental Hotel Phila—Fifth Av NY, & Revere Boston has offered *the use of all to me for you*—but says persons unknown to him, are negociating—prominent & desirable men—are ready to recieve you, & desire to know into whose hands you may fall. You will doubtless remember my *aversion* to the thing being "*Barnumized*" or that certain "played out," officious persons, should have much to do with it.

I hope you will conclude to leave Washn. *on Monday*, going to Phila. that day—(Continental Hotel—) & here on Tuesday—(Fifth Av Hotel—) & leave here on the day named Thurday—ˣ745am—& so on, as arranged.[5]

I shall be happy to do anything in my power—without making myself in the least conspicuous. Have had notoriety *enough*[6]—have enjoyed the pleasures, *and the pains*—of holding office—have succeeded somewhat to my gratification thus far—in my "*two* ambitions"—viz. to make *a good collector*, & to support & sustain my good friend *the President*—and now so far as I am able—I desire to serve him.

H. A. Smythe.

ˣ*Private Steamer.*

ALS, DLC-JP.

1. See Smythe's suggested itinerary, which was enclosed in his letter to Johnson of August 10. A clerk's notation on the back of the letter of the 18th reveals that it was not opened until August 25, after plans for the President's fall tour already had been more or less completed.

2. For the arrangements made for the reception of the President and his entourage in New York City, see *New York Herald*, Aug. 29, 1866.

3. Charles W. Sandford (1796–1878), commander for nearly thirty years of the 1st

Div., New York State National Guard, whose troops would escort Johnson through the streets of New York City. Ibid., Aug. 29, 30, 1866; *New York Times*, July 26, 1878.

4. Paran Stevens (d. 1872) also owned the Battle House in Mobile, in addition to being an art connoisseur. *New York Times*, Apr. 26, 1872.

5. The details concerning the President's hotel and other accommodations while on his trip were handled by Secretary Seward, who accepted the invitation extended by the manager of the Continental Hotel in Philadelphia. Seward to J. E. Kingsbury, ca. Aug. 24, 1866, Tels. Sent, Sec. of War (M473, Roll 91), RG107, NA. See Smythe to Johnson, Aug. 24, 1866.

6. Smythe was perceived by several prominent New York Democrats as a political liability in the forthcoming election, and they wanted Johnson to remove him. Van Deusen, *Seward*, 463.

From Calhoun M. Deringer[1]

Phila: Aug. 19th/66.

Dear Mr. President.

The Sunday papers to-day of this City, publish your address in reply to Sen. Johnson's respecting the proceedings of the great "National Union Convention." I was so pleased with it, as well as others, who read it, that I cd. not refrain from writing to you a letter, expressing my gratification and delight for such noble sentiments contained in a speech which commends itself to every Citizen of this Great Republic and will reach the heart of all who may read it. Rest assured that the people will do you honor for the noble sentiments promulgated in that great speech as well as others heretofore delivered by our worthy President.

I wrote to Gov. Randall to-day, and suggested, that it be published in pamphlet form, and sent to every Congressional District, in the Country, for the citizens to read; before Election with the Resolutions and address of the Convention[2]—and I promise good results.

C. M. Deringer.

ALS, DLC-JP.

1. Son of the renowned gunsmith whose miniature pistols bore his name, Deringer (1824–1907), a Philadelphia attorney, was soon given a recess appointment by Johnson within the Treasury Department. John E. Parsons, *Henry Deringer's Pocket Pistol* (New York, 1952), 229. For more on Deringer's appointment, see Edgar Cowan to Johnson, Oct. 25, 1866.

2. Such a pamphlet was published. See *The National Union Convention, Its History and Proceedings* (Philadelphia, 1866).

From George Bancroft

Newport, R.I.   20 August 1866.

Dear Mr. President,

After your visit to Chicago, pray come to Newport. I have here a plain, republican cottage, in which we pray you to be our guest. We will give you, pure air, the seaside, repose, & a hearty welcome. If either of your daughters is with you we shall have a room for her, & Mrs. Bancroft will be delighted to receive her.

Pray come. We will quietly discuss the affairs of the world, leaving others to their way wardness. There are two or three public questions which you might perhaps permit me to discuss with you.

Geo. Bancroft

Pray accept our invitation & let me know when we may expect you.[1]

ALS, DLC-JP.

1. Upon receipt of this note, Johnson telegraphed Bancroft, declining his "kind invitation" but adding: "I will be happy to have you accompany me to Chicago." Bancroft, however, wrote the President that he was unable to go with him. Johnson to Bancroft, Aug. 24, 1866, Tels. Sent, President, Vol. 3 (1865–68), RG107, NA; Bancroft to Johnson, Aug. 25, 1866, Johnson Papers, LC.

From Garrett Davis

Washington City   20th August 1866

Sir.

About the last day of the Session of Congress, Mr. Guthrie, Mr. Shanklin, Mr. Ritter[1] and myself talked about the appointment of the Commission[2] for the State of Ky., to assess the value of the slaves of that State enrolled into the military service of the U.S.; and of its delegation holding a conference with you on that subject.

We concluded, that as your time would probably be much occupied about the closing days of Congress, and for some weeks afterwards, we would not, until about the beginning of the next session of Congress, ask for the appointment of that commission. I have no doubt that they would prefer, as I do myself, and respectfully ask of you to defer it until then.

Garrett Davis

ALS, DLC-JP.

1. James Guthrie, George S. Shanklin, and Burwell C. Ritter. Ritter (1810–1880) served in the state house of representatives and the U.S. House (1865–67). *BDAC.*

2. In the fall of 1866, the War Department did in fact appoint a three-man commission for Kentucky to deal with the matter of compensation for slaves who had served in the military. Evidently very little was accomplished before Congress, in late March 1867, repealed the law providing for payment for slaves. Coulter, *Civil War Kentucky*, 385; Lets. Recd. (Main Ser.), File W-684-1866 (M619, Roll 528), RG94, NA; *U.S. Statutes at Large*, 15: 29.

From Andrew Johnson, Jr.

Nashville   Augt 20th 1866

Sir.

I arrived here on Saturday morning, and after Consulting Mr East[1] and other friends, have come to the Conclusion to accept the office of Tax

Commissioner in place of Mr Cone.[2] I understand it pays between two and three thousand dollars per annum. I find all well.

Please inform me as Soon as Convenient.

Andrew Johnson Jr

Address me at Goodlettsville via Nashville.

ALS, DLC-JP.
    1. Edward H. East.
    2. There is no evidence that Johnson's nephew took over Edward P. Cone's position as direct tax commissioner. See Johnson, Jr., to Johnson, Mar. 3, 1866, *Johnson Papers*, 10: 212.

Proclamation re *End of Insurrection*

August 20, 1866

Whereas by proclamations of the 15th and 19th of April, 1861,[1] the President of the United States, in virtue of the power vested in him by the Constitution and the laws, declared that the laws of the United States were opposed and the execution thereof obstructed in the States of South Carolina, Georgia, Alabama, Florida, Mississippi, Louisiana, and Texas by combinations too powerful to be suppressed by the ordinary course of judicial proceedings or by the powers vested in the marshals by law; and

Whereas by another proclamation, made on the 16th day of August,[2] in the same year, in pursuance of an act of Congress approved July 13, 1861, the inhabitants of the States of Georgia, South Carolina, Virginia, North Carolina, Tennessee, Alabama, Louisiana, Texas, Arkansas, Mississippi, and Florida (except the inhabitants of that part of the State of Virginia lying west of the Alleghany Mountains, and except also the inhabitants of such other parts of that State and the other States before named as might maintain a loyal adhesion to the Union and the Constitution or might be from time to time occupied and controlled by forces of the United States engaged in the dispersion of insurgents) were declared to be in a state of insurrection against the United States; and

Whereas by another proclamation, of the 1st day of July, 1862,[3] issued in pursuance of an act of Congress approved June 7, in the same year, the insurrection was declared to be still existing in the States aforesaid, with the exception of certain specified counties in the State of Virginia; and

Whereas by another proclamation, made on the 2d day of April, 1863,[4] in pursuance of the act of Congress of July 13, 1861, the exceptions named in the proclamation of August 16, 1861, were revoked and the inhabitants of the States of Georgia, South Carolina, North Carolina, Tennessee, Alabama, Louisiana, Texas, Arkansas, Mississippi, Florida, and Virginia (except the forty-eight counties of Virginia designated as West Virginia and the ports of New Orleans, Key West, Port Royal, and Beaufort, in North Carolina) were declared to be still in a state of insurrection against the United States; and

Whereas by another proclamation, of the 15th day of September, 1863,[5] made in pursuance of the act of Congress approved March 3, 1863, the rebellion was declared to be still existing and the privilege of the writ of *habeas corpus* was in certain specified cases suspended throughout the United States, said suspension to continue throughout the duration of the rebellion or until said proclamation should, by a subsequent one to be issued by the President of the United States, be modified or revoked; and

Whereas the House of Representatives, on the 22d day of July, 1861, adopted a resolution in the words following, namely:

Resolved by the House of Representatives of the Congress of the United States, That the present deplorable civil war has been forced upon the country by the disunionists of the Southern States now in revolt against the constitutional Government and in arms around the capital; that in this national emergency Congress, banishing all feelings of mere passion or resentment, will recollect only its duty to the whole country; that this war is not waged upon our part in any spirit of oppression, nor for any purpose of conquest or subjugation, nor purpose of overthrowing or interfering with the rights or established institutions of those States, but to defend and maintain the supremacy of the Constitution and to preserve the Union, with all the dignity, equality, and rights of the several States unimpaired; and that as soon as these objects are accomplished the war ought to cease.[6]

And whereas the Senate of the United States, on the 25th day of July, 1861, adopted a resolution in the words following, to wit:

Resolved, That the present deplorable civil war has been forced upon the country by the disunionists of the Southern States now in revolt against the constitutional Government and in arms around the capital; that in this national emergency Congress, banishing all feeling of mere passion or resentment, will recollect only its duty to the whole country; that this war is not prosecuted upon our part in any spirit of oppression, nor for any purpose of conquest or subjugation, nor purpose of overthrowing or interfering with the rights or established institutions of those States, but to defend and maintain the supremacy of the Constitution and all laws made in pursuance thereof and to preserve the Union, with all the dignity, equality, and rights of the several States unimpaired; that as soon as these objects are accomplished the war ought to cease.[7]

And whereas these resolutions, though not joint or concurrent in form, are substantially identical, and as such have hitherto been and yet are regarded as having expressed the sense of Congress upon the subject to which they relate; and

Whereas the President of the United States, by proclamation of the 13th of June, 1865,[8] declared that the insurrection in the State of Tennessee had been suppressed, and that the authority of the United States therein was undisputed, and that such United States officers as had been duly commissioned were in the undisturbed exercise of their official functions; and

Whereas the President of the United States, by further proclamation, issued on the 2d day of April, 1866,[9] did promulgate and declare that there no longer existed any armed resistance of misguided citizens or others to the authority of the United States in any or in all the States before mentioned, excepting only the State of Texas, and did further promulgate and declare that the laws could be sustained and enforced in the several States before mentioned, except Texas, by the proper civil authorities, State or Federal, and that the people of the said States, except Texas, are well and loyally disposed and have conformed or will conform in their legislation to the condition of affairs growing out of the amendment to the Constitution of the United States prohibiting slavery within the limits and jurisdiction of the United States;

And did further declare in the same proclamation that it is the manifest determination of the American people that no State, of its own will, has a right or power to go out of, or separate itself from, or be separated from, the American Union; and that, therefore, each State ought to remain and constitute an integral part of the United States;

And did further declare in the same last-mentioned proclamation that the several aforementioned States, excepting Texas, had in the manner aforesaid given satisfactory evidence that they acquiesce in this sovereign and important resolution of national unity; and

Whereas the President of the United States in the same proclamation did further declare that it is believed to be a fundamental principle of government that the people who have revolted and who have been overcome and subdued must either be dealt with so as to induce them voluntarily to become friends or else they must be held by absolute military power or devastated so as to prevent them from ever again doing harm as enemies, which last-named policy is abhorrent to humanity and to freedom; and

Whereas the President did in the same proclamation further declare that the Constitution of the United States provides for constituent communities only as States, and not as Territories, dependencies, provinces, or protectorates;

And further, that such constituent States must necessarily be, and by the Constitution and laws of the United States are, made equals and placed upon a like footing as to political rights, immunities, dignity, and power with the several States with which they are united;

And did further declare that the observance of political equality, as a principle of right and justice, is well calculated to encourage the people of the before-named States, except Texas, to be and to become more and more constant and persevering in their renewed allegiance; and

Whereas the President did further declare that standing armies, military occupation, martial law, military tribunals, and the suspension of the writ of *habeas corpus* are in time of peace dangerous to public liberty, incompatible with the individual rights of the citizen, contrary to the genius and spirit of our free institutions, and exhaustive of the national resources, and ought not, therefore, to be sanctioned or allowed except in cases of actual necessity for repelling invasion or suppressing insurrection or rebellion;

And the President did further, in the same proclamation, declare that the policy of the Government of the United States from the beginning of the insurrection to its overthrow and final suppression had been conducted in conformity with the principles in the last-named proclamation recited; and

Whereas the President, in the said proclamation of the 13th of June, 1865, upon the grounds therein stated and hereinbefore recited, did then and thereby proclaim and declare that the insurrection which heretofore existed in the several States before named, except in Texas, was at an end and was henceforth to be so regarded; and

Whereas subsequently to the said 2d day of April, 1866, the insurrection in the State of Texas has been completely and everywhere suppressed and ended and the authority of the United States has been successfully and completely established in the said State of Texas and now remains therein unresisted and undisputed, and such of the proper United States officers as have been duly commissioned within the limits of the said State are now in the undisturbed exercise of their official functions; and

Whereas the laws can now be sustained and enforced in the said State of Texas by the proper civil authority, State or Federal, and the people of the said State of Texas, like the people of the other States before named, are well and loyally disposed and have conformed or will conform in their legislation to the condition of affairs growing out of the amendment of the Constitution of the United States prohibiting slavery within the limits and jurisdiction of the United States; and

Whereas all the reasons and conclusions set forth in regard to the several States therein specially named now apply equally and in all respects to the State of Texas, as well as to the other States which had been involved in insurrection; and

Whereas adequate provision has been made by military orders to enforce the execution of the acts of Congress, aid the civil authorities, and secure obedience to the Constitution and laws of the United States within the State of Texas if a resort to military force for such purpose should at any time become necessary;

Now, therefore, I, Andrew Johnson, President of the United States, do hereby proclaim and declare that the insurrection which heretofore existed in the State of Texas is at an end and is to be henceforth so regarded in that State as in the other States before named in which the said insurrection was proclaimed to be at an end by the aforesaid proclamation of the 2d day of April, 1866.

And I do further proclaim that the said insurrection is at an end and that peace, order, tranquillity, and civil authority now exist in and throughout the whole of the United States of America.

In testimony whereof I have hereunto set my hand and caused the seal
of the United States to be affixed.

Done at the city of Washington, this 20th day of August, A. D. 1866,
and of the Independence of the United States of America the ninety-first.

ANDREW JOHNSON.

Richardson, *Messages*, 6: 434–38.
1. Richardson, *Messages*, 6: 13–15.
2. Ibid., 37–38.
3. Ibid., 92–93.
4. Ibid., 165–66.
5. Ibid., 170–71.
6. *Congressional Globe*, 37 Cong., 1 Sess., p. 222.
7. Ibid., p. 257.
8. Richardson, *Messages*, 6: 314–16.
9. See Proclamation *re* End of Insurrection, Apr. 2, 1866, *Johnson Papers*, 10: 349–52.

From James W. Throckmorton

Austin Texas   Aug 20 1866

Sir

An Editor[1] has been fined two hundred dollars (200) and imprisoned
for strictures on conduct of freedmen teachers. Has a sub-Commissioner
the power that is destroying the freedom of the Press?[2]

J W Throckmorton   Gov Texas

Tel, DLC-JP.
1. Kentucky native Dan L. McGary (c1832–1902), "an unreconstructed rebel major,"
who edited the *Banner* at Brenham, Texas, made continuous critical editorial remarks
about the Bureau and Mr. and Mrs. James G. Whann, the teachers of the Brenham blacks.
Bvt. Maj. Gen. Joseph B. Kiddoo, head of the Bureau in Texas, insisted that Capt. Samuel
A. Craig, the Bureau agent at Brenham, arrest the editor and fine him between one and five
hundred dollars for his false statements. Despite a lack of cooperation from Bvt. Maj.
George W. Smith, commanding the federal troops at Brenham, Craig finally arrested
McGary and imprisoned him in the local jail, where he received sympathetic visits from the
townspeople. After his newspaper office was burned in the Brenham fire, McGary moved
to Houston, where he published the *Age* from 1871 to 1896. Richter, *Overreached on All
Sides*, 126–31; Walter P. Webb et al., eds., *The Handbook of Texas* (3 vols., Austin, 1952,
1976).
2. Johnson apparently forwarded Throckmorton's telegram to the secretary of war,
who referred the matter to Gen. O. O. Howard. Howard telegraphed Throckmorton, "I
know of no law or regulation for such fine, except imposed by proper court. I will send
General Kiddoo to see you and to rectify any error or wrong doing in my Department at
Austin." Kiddoo reluctantly ordered Craig to release McGary on September 3, 1866,
meanwhile highly commending Craig's attention to duty. On September 17 he sent Craig
to serve as the new subassistant commissioner at Seguin. The planned conference between
Kiddoo and Throckmorton never occurred because of the Brenham fire on September 7.
Stanton to Throckmorton, ca. Aug. 23, 1866; O. O. Howard to Throckmorton, Aug. 23,
1866; Howard to Kiddoo, Aug. 23, 1866, Tels. Sent, Sec. of War (M473, Roll 91),
RG107, NA; Richter, *Overreached on All Sides*, 131. See also O. M. Roberts and David G.
Burnet to Johnson, Dec. 6, 1866.

From George M. Curtis[1]

New York   Aug 21 '66

Dear Sir:

While in Washington some days ago, I endeavoured to see you, but pressing public business prevented you from welcoming visitors. In the legislature last winter I earnestly advocated your policy of restoration. I desire now to see this State Carried against the "Radicals" in the ensuing election.[2] If Carried, it will be by the great majorities rolled up in Southern New York. Your Excellency is aware that the major element of the vote in that section is Irish! The "Radicals" are using every endeavour to mould that vote to the uses of their organization, by expressing great sympathy with the Cause of the "*Fenians*." My own position upon that question, when the invasion of Canada was attempted, is understood correctly by every intelligent mind in America: but the Abolition press and orators are misrepresenting you in Connection with that matter, with a vigor and persistence that Causes me some alarm for the safety of this Commonwealth. I would most respectfully suggest that such action be taken by the Executive or the State Department as would show to these people, that while Andrew Johnson upheld the law, his heart beat for the liberties of all peoples. The Course of the Attorney-General today is a step in the right direction.[3] Now if our Government at Washington would attempt to secure the liberation of those unfortunate men in Canada it would exercise a most salutary influence upon the vote of this State.[4] I have presumed to address you upon this matter, because you have often told us that the views of an American Citizen would receive Consideration at your hands.

Geo. M. Curtis
3rd Assembly Dis—

ALS, DNA-RG59, Misc. Lets., 1789–1906 (M179, Roll 243).

1. Curtis (c1842–1915), an attorney and former second lieutenant, 140th N.Y. Inf., served two sessions as a Democratic New York assemblyman (1864, 1866). *New York Times*, May 15, 1915; *Off. Army Reg.: Vols.*, 2: 637; *Civil List and Forms of Government of the Colony and State of New York* (Albany, 1879), 482, 484–85; James C. Mohr, *The Radical Republicans and Reform in New York during Reconstruction* (Ithaca, 1973), 98.

2. Such a victory over the Radicals never materialized. Ibid., 108–9. For reaction to the defeat of the Johnson-backed Conservatives in New York, see David L. Seymour to Johnson, Nov. 8, 1866, and Hiram Ketchum to Johnson, Nov. 9, 1866.

3. Curtis probably refers here to the decision not to prosecute American Fenians who had been indicted in federal courts. See Henry Stanbery to William A. Dart, Aug. 14, 1866, in *New York Herald* and *New York Times*, both Aug. 21, 1866.

4. The Johnson administration continued through diplomatic channels to urge clemency on behalf of imprisoned Irish-Americans in Canada and Britain. In addition the President ordered the return of Fenian munitions which had been seized by U.S. authorities; and William A. Dart, the district attorney in New York who had indicted a number of participants in the aborted invasion, was removed from office. Various historians have viewed these actions as attempts by Johnson and Seward to manipulate the Irish vote during the 1866 elections, especially in New York. The historians disagree, however, as to whether they succeeded. See W. S. Neidhardt, *Fenianism in North America* (University Park, Pa.,

1975), 98–99; Jenkins, *Fenians and Anglo-American Relations*, passim, especially chapter 6; Van Deusen, *Seward*, 502–3. See also Irish Executive Committee to Johnson, Sept. 18, 1866; Samuel J. Tilden to Johnson, Sept. 21, 1866; and Johnson to Charles A. Eldridge, Oct. 27, 1866.

From Henry C. Harman[1]

State of Tennessee
Claiborne County   Speedwell PO
Aug 21th 1866

Dear Sir

Desiring to enter the service of the united states army as an officer commissioned I do not feel disposed to remain at my residence. I can not feel content. I wannt to be a soldier. I wannt to make my return to the roll of the drum. I enlisted in the present rebellion at the age of 17 years & was Honorably discharged. I do not desire the Position I held that was a Private. I am no Radicle whatever. I feel disposed to serve my country & not negro equality. I can fech a good recommedation with a honorable one. I do not feel a desire to intrude on your person. I desire to enter the service as 2ond Liut in the regular service or any whear you feel disposed to put me.[2] I do not crave honors to an extent. My sincer desire is not to be a Private at any time. My age is 21 years. I hope you ecuse all mistaks. I hope to see the approveal this returned to this county & state. I do not hardly know that I am worthy to adress a man of your capacity or no. I hope you will not at all take this to be an insult. It is truly from me writen by my hand & signed with my signature &c.

Henery C Harman   late C E 6" Tenn Vol Inft

ALS, DNA-RG94, ACP Branch, File H-1460-CB-1866, Henry C. Harmon [*sic*].

1. Harman (1844–1918) had been accused of desertion in 1864 and arrested; in 1871, however, these charges were removed from the record. Earlier in the war he had been captured by the enemy but then paroled a few months later, in February 1863. Harman was a Claiborne County farmer and by 1880 had a wife and five children. A few years later, he moved to Kansas. CSR, Henry C. Harmon[*sic*], RG94, NA; 1880 Census, Tenn., Claiborne, 2nd Dist., 105th Enum. Dist., 3; Pension File, Henry C. Harman, RG15, NA.

2. Evidence of an appointment for Harman has not been located.

From John M. Johnson[1]

Alexandria, Va.   Augt. 21/66

Dear Sir,

I have made several unsuccessful efforts to see you since my return from Chicago where I spent the last winter, and remained until June. My main object was to say that, I believed you would be in great danger of taking the Cholera, were you to visit Chicago before the frost falls as there is always an offinsive and sickening odour arising from the Chicago River during warm weather, calculated to produce disease, and the spread of Cholera, particularly when it prevails in the country. The Chicago river is a very sluggish stream into which nearly all the sewers in the city empty. It passes nearly through the centre of the city, and the principal Hotels are not very remote from it, and I have no doubt the atmosphere in their vicinity is impregnated with the offensive odours. When I left Chicago in the latter part of last June there was then a very offensive odour arising from the River.[2]

Believing that, the preservation of your life, is important to the welfare of our country, I have taken the liberty of addressing you this letter.

Jno. M. Johnson

ALS, DNA-RG56, Appls., Asst. Treasurers and Mint Officers, Philadelphia, Charles Hall.
    1. Unidentified.
    2. Cholera arrived in Chicago in early August, having already made appearances in several other major U.S. cities. While starting slowly, it soon reached epidemic proportions, killing 673 in the month of October alone. Though evidence had existed since the 1850s that cholera was spread by contaminated water supplies, many Americans still believed that it only affected persons with particular "predisposing causes." *Chicago Tribune*, Aug. 15–18, Nov. 10, 1866; Charles E. Rosenberg, *The Cholera Years: The United States in 1832, 1849, and 1866* (Chicago, 1987 [1962]), 197–99.

From William F. Johnston

Philadelphia   August 21. 1866.

My Dear Sir

I have had an interview with Mr. Thomas,[1] the late Collector of this District. He proposes, peaceably and quietly to vacate the office & surrender it to me on the 1st of next month. This proposition is entirely agreeable to me, as it places me in charge of the business of the office at the beginning of a month, avoids contests and enables me to spend a few days in the *Western* part of the State *where* I know I can be usefully employed in the good work of organizing friends. If the arrangement meets your approval or otherwise—please direct Col Moore—to reply—direct to Pittsburg.[2]

Wm. F. Johnston

ALS, DLC-JP.
    1. William B. Thomas.
    2. Later that day William G. Moore wrote Johnston indicating that he had shown his note to the President, who believed Johnston should have insisted upon Thomas's departure from office, but the President was unwilling "to interfere in the matter." Johnston officially assumed control of the collectorship on August 31. Moore to Johnston, Aug. 21, 1866, Johnson Papers, LC; *Press* (Philadelphia), Sept. 1, 1866.

From Ulysses S. Grant

Washington, D.C.   Aug. 22d 1866.

Sir:

In regard to the requisition of the Gov. of Va.[1] refered to me by your direction, in relation to furnishing Arms for the Va. Mil. Institute, and 10,000 stand of Arms for the use of the state, I have refered the papers to Gen. Schofield,[2] Comd'y Dept. of Va. requiring him to have an interview with the Governor of the state on the subject refered to in the papers presented by W. H. Richardson,[3] Adj. Gen. of the State, and to report the necessity and expediency of making such issue.[4] I am inclined to doubt the expediency for making such issue for reasons which I have explained to Gen. Richard[son] but have invited the opinion of Gen. Schofield who has a better opportunity of judging of the matter. I would approve however the issue of Arms for the use of the Military Institute of Virginia without reference to the Department Commander.

U.S. Grant   General.

ALS, DLC-JP.
  1. Francis H. Peirpoint.
  2. John M. Schofield.
  3. William H. Richardson (1795–1876) was appointed adjutant general of Virginia in 1841, a post he held until his death, with the exception of a short time immediately after the Civil War. He also was an "agricultural apostle" to his state's farmers because of his efforts to develop and improve Virginia's agriculture. Charles W. Turner, "William H. Richardson: Friend of the Farmer," *Va. Cavalcade*, 20 (1971): 15–20.
  4. On August 25 Richardson, unable to see the President's secretary concerning the furnishing of arms to the Virginia Military Institute, wrote Grant with the hope he could expedite the matter in time for the Institute's September 10 ceremony commemorating the return of the statue of George Washington. Grant referred the matter to Schofield, who recommended the organization and arming of volunteer militia companies from the loyal white population of the state. He remained silent, however, on the return of arms to the Institute. Grant did not favor the rearming of a militia, but his original recommendation to Johnson concerning VMI stood and the arms were provided in time for the ceremony. Richardson to Grant, Aug. 25, 1866, Simon, *Grant Papers*, 16: 302–3; Schofield to George K. Leet, Aug. 27, 1866, Lets. Recd., Executive (M494, Roll 85), RG107, NA; *Dispatch* (Richmond), Sept. 3, 1866; Grant to Johnson, Nov. 9, 1866, Lets. Recd., Sec. of War (M494, Roll 85), RG107, NA.

From Oliver O. Howard

Washington, D.C.   Aug. 22d 1866

The following statements are respectfully submitted for your consideration.

The last report of Generals Steedman and Fullerton of an inspection of the Bureau[1] under my charge contains so many statements differing from those I have received from other inspecting officers and Assistant Commissioners, and furnishing deductions so widely varying from those I have formed and offered, that I deem it my duty to review the main points of this report; and more especially is this course necessary for me, that I have been assigned to duty by yourself, and have administered the Bureau in accordance with your instructions, verbal and written, keeping constantly in view a thorough and practical execution of the law by which myself and my officers have been bound.

The ostensible object of the inspection is to detect and correct abuses of administration, and furnish yourself with information of the actual state of things.

Had the Inspectors made a thorough examination and report to yourself, or to the Secretary of War, in accordance with their written instructions, so that I could have corrected the wrong doings of individual agents, or modified any policy that was faulty, I would not complain, but be grateful for the aid and encouragement thus offered. This method of inspection and report is the one that has always been pursued in the departments of the service with which I have been connected.

The Inspectors have pursued an extraordinary course. I understood they took as clerks several newspaper reporters, who gave to the press the substance of their reports, and, sometimes, the reports themselves, before you had time to give them consideration. The effect of this course has been to concentrate the attention of the public upon certain individual acts of officers and agents, or accusations against them carelessly drawn in such a way as to keep the faults committed, and not the good done, prominently in view.

Some things they have held up as criminal which are not so in reality: erroneous conclusions have been drawn from a state of affairs now existing in many places for which the Bureau is not responsible:—e.g. they charge to the account of the Bureau all the evils of the labor system they find, while they attribute to the state governments and citizens, in great part, the good accomplished. Certainly this is the impression received from reading the report.

In what I have to say I have no desire to screen any officer from Just charges; in fact, I have taken instant measures to bring to trial any officer against whom there seemed to be any well-founded accusation. It is a fact well worth considering here that of 13 Assistant Commissioners there has been but one whom the Inspectors were able to condemn, viz:—the Assistant Commissioner of North Carolina;[2] and he, though held up to the country as a liar and a dishonest speculator, has been, I believe, acquitted, by the decision of a fair and honorable court, so far as these charges are concerned.

Again, in the Departments of Virginia and North Carolina, from over two hundred agents, accusations were brought against ten only—Viz: seven officers and three civilians. The majority of them have been honorably acquitted of the charges preferred against them. The Reverend Mr. Fitz,[3] of such terrible notariety, who was having his case investigated on the arrival of the Inspectors, proves to be not a Reverend, but a young man of eighteen years, a Quartermaster's clerk during the war, and personally guiltless of the cruelties imputed to his charge. All these cases will soon be officially reported. I need not refer to them further.

I may say, however, that the charge against one officer[4] of putting men in a chain-gang had no foundation in fact: but in an other part of the same State an officer[5] especially selected by the Inspectors for unqualified commendation, had issued an order to place delinquents or vagrants in a chain-gang.

They give the number of officers in each State without commands. I would say that I have made great efforts to reduce the number of military officers. I was partially influenced by this motive when I advocated the consolidation of the office of Assistant Commissioner and Military Commander, deeming it worth a trial as the business could be easily conducted by one head, provided the right kind of man could be placed in charge. The Inspectors have endorsed this plan, and given their testimony to the benefit derived from its operation.

Their final objection is to Citizen Agents and in order to reduce expenses they recommend that all such agents be discharged, in the following language:

"A great reduction in the expenses of the Bureau, and a reform which would render it far less objectionable than it is now, would be effected by the discontinuance of all paid employe's not in the military service of the Government."

I assent to this principle, though the Inspectors do not seem to do so, as they have given unqualified praise to the administration of the Bureau in Georgia, where the greatest number of citizen agents are employed. Could I obtain details from the Army, I should certainly do so, but the smallness of the military force in most of the states has rendered it impossible.

They next speak of Georgia, saying, "that the amended laws of the State are fully as liberal as those of any northern State, and place the negro in all respects on a perfect equality with the white man as to his civil rights," conveying the impression that the Freedmen are thoroughly protected under the execution of those laws.

General Tillson,[6] who is highly commended by the Inspectors, and is known to be a man of integrity and good Judgement, in a late report to me, says: "there are many instances where, through the prejudice of the people, or the incompetency of the magistrates, the freedmen are denied the protection of the law, and where the interference of the Bureau is absolutely essential to secure Justice. Where this influence has been wisely directed, and the authority of the Bureau brought to bear firmly but kindly, the happiest consequences have followed, not only protecting the freedmen in individual cases, but changing the tone and temper of the people so as to prevent the recurrence of acts of injustice and oppression. The continuance and agency of the Bureau is still a necessity."

The case of maladministration of Capt. Louis J. Lambert[7] is the only one mentioned in this State, among 273 agents. This will be thoroughly investigated by General Tillson. I am thankful for so great purity of administration in Georgia. I may say here with reference to legal Justice, that the policy pursued constantly has been to transfer jurisdiction to civil tribunals whenever there was a prospect of its impartial exercise under Just laws; in fact, it has been the practice in most Bureau courts to use the State laws, when no distinction existed on account of color.

No fault is found with Alabama, except that a few officers are reported as engaged in planting. The Inspectors must mean that these officers have invested some of their private funds in planting. All I can say is that a great many, in fact nearly all, the officers of the government have invested their funds in planting, or something else. If they have not prostituted their official position for private gain, I can not complain, though I have lately forbidden such investments within the limits of official Jurisdiction, in order to avoid even the appearance of evils.

General Wood,[8] Assistant Commissioner of Mississippi is commended for improving upon the administration of Col. Samuel Thomas. The policy of the latter is declared not calculated to produce harmony between the races.

In this statement the Inspectors have doubtless been misinformed, for I have testimony from General Wood and from Inspectors that the policy pursued by Colonel Thomas has not been changed.

They next admit a state of affairs in Mississippi that demands some other remedy than the removal of the military force, that is, if freedmen and peaceable citizens are to be protected. The murder of one U.S. officer, and the firing upon others without cause, are admitted, and there is evidently a reign of terror in portions of the State.

The agent at Columbus, Major Smith,[9] can not be defended for telling large stories to the Inspectors.

The case of Chaplain Livermore[10] is cited, but the fact that he was relieved and placed under arrest for his crimes as long ago as last February, is creditable to the administration of the Assistant Commissioner.

The agents at Columbus, long ago discharged, are suspected by the Inspectors of robbing. If they had taken pains to send me a single receipt from any man who had paid fees or fines, I could tell them at once whether these gentlemen were robbed or not.

Louisiana.

The Inspectors complain of expenses, and recommend reduction: They allege that the main part of the money has been expended for schools. Had they inquired of General Baird,[11] he would have told them that as soon as the taxes were suspended by your order, the schools were closed or continued as private enterprises, or by employers of Freedmen under their contract stipulations.

The admirable system of education in New Orleans was established by military commanders long prior to the existence of the Bureau. No facts have been presented to me from their statements that the money under Mr. Conway,[12] the late Assistant Commissioner, was squandered as charged.

The corruption of a few officers under his administration, may possibly be true, but whether so or not, it does not affect the present administration of the Bureau in that State.

It is a little singular that the officers long ago relieved from duty should be chosen as exponents of the present management of the Freedmen's Bureau.

The report with reference to Texas rather commends than censures the administration in that state. One officer, Captain Sloan[13] is condemned for perjury and for his conduct in office. A subsequent examination of his case has furnished a more favorable report. The case will have a thorough investigation.

Arkansas, Kentucky, and Tennessee, were not visited by the Inspectors, and it is fair to suppose that the administration of the Bureau in those states is as it has been represented by the Assistant Commissioners and other officers, and by reliable citizens.

It should be noticed with regard to expenses that aside from Commissary, Quartermaster, and Medical issues, the entire expenses of the Freedmen's Bureau have been defrayed from its organization up to July last without an appropriation, and without incurring a debt. The Quartermaster, Commissary, and Medical issues were being made by the army proper, when I took charge of the Bureau, and have been reduced as much as possible consistent with the pressing necessities of the people, blacks and whites.

I now come to by far the most important part of what the Inspectors have to say; the summary of their conclusions after four months inspection of the Bureau, in which they assert that "there is an entire absence of system or uniformity in its constitution." They have never asked me for one word of information with reference to records, reports, and orders. They have made no examination of my office, and asked no reason for any action taken. The records or information they desired that could not be found in the offices of the South, may be here. What would be the result, if they should make a general inspection of the Quartermaster's, Commissary, or other Departments in the same way. Those officers who had been relieved, or were beyond their reach are supposed to have made improper disposition of all records or papers connected with their offices. There is not a Bureau in Washington with a more complete set of reports, books, and records, &c. than can be produced at this office for inspection at any time. They attempt to prove their assertion by the statement that in one state its officers exercise Judicial powers; in one, adjoining, all cases are referred to civil authorities, while in a third state, Bureau officers collect the cases and turn them over to military courts. Their own inspection reports will refute this. In the States of Kentucky, Tennessee, Mississippi, Louisiana, Alabama, Florida, Virginia, and North Carolina, Bureau agents do not exercise judicial powers of any kind, and in the other states, the powers exercised by the officers of the Bureau are modified by the feelings and conduct of the people toward the Freedmen. They admit there is great difference in this feeling of whites toward the blacks. What other principle more uniform is it possible to adopt than to regulate the power of agents of the Bureau by the disposition and conduct of the people; favoring them as they approximate equal Justice.

It will be seen by referring to the regulations from this Bureau, Circular 5, Series 65,[14] approved by yourself that a gradual transfer of Jurisdiction was implied, and Just as soon as practicable, we have made trial of the civil court in every state. I have sought the provost courts as well as the civil, to relieve me of the exercise of Judicial powers.

Bureau officers have never attempted to regulate wages, and no order ever existed, making any regulations on the subject. Demand and supply controlled the matter. Of course wages, manner of payment and all the questions entering into the labor subject differed widely throughout the South, and from the nature of things, could not be uniform.

Although importuned from all parts of the South to take Some action about wages, I steadily refused. The following has been the standing order for all the states:

"No fixed rates of wages will be prescribed for a district, but in order to regulate fair wages in individual cases agents should have in mind minimum rates for their own guidance."

Assistant Commissioners are required to furnish me with copies of all orders and circulars issued by them, and a close examination of all they have written on the subject, fails to produce any attempt upon their part to regulate wages or contracts. The Freedmen and employer have been left to manage the matter for themselves.

They say that schools in Louisiana have been supported by the Government. Their report shows however that they were supported by a military tax, and perhaps to some extent by the income from abandoned property.

They say that agents interfere in an arbitrary manner in favor of freedmen sometimes, and at others in favor of Planters. This is simply a crime according to Bureau regulations, and the Inspectors should have preferred charges against those officers, that they might have been tried and punished.

It is true that the expenses of the Bureau are not the same in all the States, as it is a plain proposition, that these expenses must be regulated by the work to be done. As the necessity for Bureau agencies differs according to the temper of the people, it is not singular that expenses should be apportioned accordingly. I am not aware that the Bureau in any state was supported by funds from the U.S. Treasury, till after the late appropriation. In fact no funds had ever been drawn directly for the purpose of supporting the Bureau organization, till that appropriation was made by Congress.

They say it was impossible to examine the accounts of Bureau Quartermasters, as they were compelled to take personal statements &c., yet admit that they examined the accounts of Gen. H. M. Whittlesey[15] of Mississippi, and found them all correct and complete. Of course his predecessor[16] was entitled to his retained papers, and one complete set is on file in my office. They can find out how much money was collected from every legitimate and proper source in Mississippi by calling on me and asking for such information.

They say this system of receiving and disbursing money is loose. The same blanks, forms, reports, and regulations used in the Quartermaster's Department have been adopted by this Bureau, as far as possible, and are as complete a check upon Bureau officers in the discharge of their duties as is imposed upon officers of the Quartermaster's Department who originate and disburse funds.

They next refer to the case of Colonel Reno's[17] report of the deficit of $7000 in Louisiana, and Lieutenant Foster[18] who is said to be a defaulter. It can not be possible that General Fullerton, who as one of the Bureau officers, assisted in bringing this matter to light, can fail to remember that this subject has been undergoing an investigation for the last six months. The whole matter originated before the Bureau was in existence, and has been brought to light and prosecuted by the Assistant Commissioner in order to fix the guilt on the proper persons and secure their punishment.

It is not Justice to the officers of this Bureau to charge them with crimes that were committed against the Freedmen in time prior to its organization, and to suppress dates, and the location of grave charges, so as to shift the responsibility upon those not guilty.

The Inspectors next admit the necessity of the Bureau last year, and acknowledge that it did much good for all classes. If this be true, it is bad logic to condemn the workings of the Bureau this year for mistakes and errors that were committed last year, and were particularly for the year before its organization. Nearly every charge made against officers in this final report, is for acts of last year, and upon which these officers have already been called to account by the Bureau or the War Department.

I can not agree with the Inspectors altogether, as to a complete revolution in the sentiment of the Southern people, which insures protection sufficient to the Freedmen, when U.S. officers and Freedmen are murdered, and the Freedmen abused and mutilated, as is reported even by the Inspectors themselves.

They say the good feelings of the whites toward the blacks are owing to their interest in securing their labor. This I regard as insufficient security, when trusted to, absolutely without some other principle, e.g. the guarantee of equal laws. For years, slave-holders have deemed compulsory measures the best security of labor.

The Inspectors declare that "the Bureau has been in the aggregate productive of more harm than good," and give as their reasons, substantially, the reliance upon it of the negroes, and their consequent distrust of the property-holders, and the provocation of espionage creating mutual suspicion and bitterness.

I deny the whole statement. It is not founded on facts, but upon theories constantly put forth by the enemies of good order. A few bad agents have been sent, and have doubtless done much harm. Yet the Bureau agency has been mediatorial and pacific as a whole. It has relieved this very suspicion and bitterness that existed when it was first organized—riots, murders, and wicked deeds have recently sprung up, but these are in no way initiated or recognised by the officers of the Government.

The Inspectors charge the Bureau with being responsible for the low wages paid Freedmen under contracts on plantations. I shall refer to contracts again, but will take up wages first. This Bureau never regulated wages, but did urge all Freedmen to labor on plantations and elsewhere, in order to relieve the Government of their support, and to demonstrate to the Country that they were not to become a shiftless, dependent race. The people North and South, as well as an evident necessity, demanded that the Freedmen should go to work at the beginning of the year. My officers entered the field and urged the Freedmen to take this course—providing for themselves. You are fully aware that at this time, planters in different parts of the South formed combinations against high wages; some counties fixing as low a rate as five dollars per month for the able-bodied. The Bureau officers urged that the standard be placed as high as possible, yet they could not compel a higher rate of compensation. What were the Freedmen to do? If they failed to contract, they would incur the odium of being a "lazy, idle, and worthless race," besides running the risk of starving. They went to work on plantations at the highest wages they could get. As soon as planters began to find that labor would be scarce, that the Freedmen were going to work, they saw that their interest was to secure laborers for their cotton-fields before it was too late, and offered higher wages. Nothing could be more natural. Yet it is not difficult to see that the Planters of the South who represented the Capital were associated against labor, and compelled low rates. Bureau officers did all in their power to get the highest wages possible for the Freedmen, but as the Georgia Railroads and Mississippi steamboats would not and could not give $1.50 per day for all the plantation laborers last January and February, when they were compelled to seek employment, the Freedmen were forced to go to work at the Planters' rates. Yet we find these Inspectors complaining about the present wages, and advising a transfer of the interests of laborers to the men who, by firmly resisting all advance, kept wages where they now are. They say: "In all the large towns of Mississippi, Planters were offering $1.00 a day in May and June, while, under the sanction of the Government, thousands of Freedmen were working for $10. per month. I do not doubt this, yet the Planters and other employers, not the officers of the Bureau, are responsible for compelling laborers to accept the ten dollar terms last January or starve.

Now that the planter's crop is near the gathering, and the cotton-fields need severe and unremitting labor, no doubt they are willing to give $1.00 per diem for a few laborers to finish up the work. They say their contracts were sanctioned by Bureau officers. This may be so. Bureau officers could not have done otherwise. If they had, they would have been accused of defeating the objects of the Bureau law, and would have introduced a principle which impairs the very nature of a contract. All the arguments of the Inspectors fall to the ground unless they can prove that the Freedmen could have obtained from property-holders without compulsion $1.50 per day last January, when necessity compelled them to go to work.

The principles that apply to wages induced the present contract system. I would have been glad to have adopted precisely the same methods of regulating labor as obtained in the Northern States, but neither the planters nor the Freedmen were yet prepared for this.

Planters complained that Freedmen under a free system of labor could not work till the crop was saved, but would remain only till they obtained money to keep them a short time, and then desert the crops at a most critical period. Nearly every Southern State has provided laws by which the Freedmen are to be contracted with, for one year. Planters refused to employ Freedmen at all, unless they would agree to remain one year. Of course, Freedmen were driven into those obligations by the same force that compelled them to work for low wages. Any one who will remember the current news of the day, as reported during the months of last January and February, will remember that all the power that capital can exercise was brought to bear upon the laborers of the South to make them contract.

I claim, and the facts will prove it, that the Bureau has labored successfully to elevate wages, and defended the interests of Freedmen in their contracts, being constantly resisted by the inertia of the peculiar opinions of Southern property holders. The evils in the contracts will disappear Just as soon as free labor shall have a permanent foot-hold under its necessary protection of equal laws properly executed.

From the course pursued by the Inspectors, I cannot help thinking that the object of the inspection, as they understood it, was to bring the Freedmen's Bureau into contempt before the country, and, to do this, they have endeavored to prove maladministration.

On the contrary, I am prepared to prove to yourself, or any other candid mind, that I have fulfilled the trust you committed to me with care, conscientiousness, and faithfulness; I have obeyed your orders and instructions, making no other objections than those I have made to yourself and the Secretary of War: that my system of operation has been a thorough one, and as complete and uniform as was possible in an institution intended to be temporary and to meet a transient necessity. Could the Freedmen's Bureau be now administered with your full and hearty sanction, and with the coöperation of the other branches of the Government, it would fulfil the objects of its creation in a short time, and be made while it existed to conduce to industry, enlightenment, and Justice for all classes of the people. The work committed to it may doubtless be done by the Army, without a Bureau, but not with much less expense; yet, if the Government would keep good faith with its new made citizens, some sort of U.S. agency must be maintained in the Southern States until Society shall have become more settled than it now is.

O. O. Howard   Maj. Gen., Commissioner.

LS, DNA-RG94, Lets. Recd. (Main Ser.), File W-324-1866 (M619, Roll 526).

1. Dated July 20, the report was printed in the *National Intelligencer* on August 10, 1866.

2. Eliphalet Whittlesey. Court-martialed, Whittlesey was found guilty of "conduct to the prejudice of good order and military discipline" because of his pecuniary interest, while on duty, in a plantation but was acquitted of the charge that he denied that fact to General Steedman. In December 1866 he was sentenced to be reprimanded by General Howard. *New York Herald*, Dec. 7, 1866.

3. Edward S. Fitz (c1842–1902) was appointed assistant superintendent of the Trent River Settlement around New Bern in April 1865 after serving in the 43rd Mass. Inf. and as pastor and teacher to the freedmen. It was alleged he had exercised arbitrary and despotic power and practiced revolting cruelties on freedmen. On April 24, 1866, a court of inquiry found him guilty of mistreating prisoners. He was dismissed a couple of days after the arrival of Steedman and Fullerton. CSR, Edward S. Fitz, RG94, NA; Pension File, Edward S. Fitz, RG15, NA; Fitz to Steedman, May 3, 1866; Steedman and Fullerton to Stanton, May 8, 1866, Lets. Recd. (Main Ser.), File W-324-1866 (M619, Roll 526), RG94, NA; George R. Bentley, *A History of the Freedmen's Bureau* (Philadelphia, 1955), 126.

4. Charles I. Wickersham.

5. Unknown.

6. Davis Tillson.

7. Lambert (d. 1867) entered the war as a captain in the volunteers and eventually attained the rank of brevet colonel in the volunteers before mustering out in June 1866. The next month he was commissioned first lieutenant in the regulars; the following year he attained the brevet ranks of captain, major, and lieutenant colonel for his services at the battles of Chickamauga, Chattanooga, and Pocotaligo River. Lambert's actions were in question because of the disappearance of money only reported stolen after Steedman and Fullerton discovered it missing and his loose style of record keeping. Powell, *Army List*, 422; *National Intelligencer*, Aug. 10, 1866.

8. Thomas J. Wood.

9. There are three possible George S. Smiths from Ohio—a merchant in Dayton (b. c1811), a railroad contractor in Cleveland (b. c1813), and a laborer in York (b. c1822). From 1863 to 1868 Smith served with the 3rd Rgt., Vet. Res. Corps. 1850 Census, Ohio, Montgomery, Dayton, 2nd Ward, 173; (1850), Cuyahoga, Cleveland, 1st Ward, 135; (1850), Tuscarawas, York Twp., 6; *Off. Army Reg.: Vols.*, 8: 34, 321.

10. Lark S. Livermore had supposedly acquired fortunes by keeping fines and fees and by selling government animals. Bentley, *Freedmen's Bureau*, 130.

11. Absalom Baird, assistant commissioner in Louisiana.

12. Thomas W. Conway. After Congress passed the Freedmen's Bureau bill over Johnson's veto on July 16, no further investigation of Conway was conducted by Fullerton and Steedman, who wished to close the cases. Bentley, *Freedmen's Bureau*, 70, 131.

13. Sam C. Sloan (b. c1811) had served as captain of the 116th Rgt., USCT; he was discharged in March 1867. He became a relatively well-off farmer in Dallas after the war and his Bureau service. *Off. Army Reg.: Vols.*, 8: 297; 1870 Census, Tex., Dallas, 2nd Prec., 353.

14. See *House Ex. Docs.*, 39 Cong., 1 Sess., No. 70, pp. 10–11 (Ser. 1256).

15. Henry M. Whittlesey (1821–1873), a native of Connecticut and a lawyer, served during the war as quartermaster to various units, attaining the rank of brevet brigadier general of volunteers in 1865. Eventually he served as city comptroller of Washington (1870–71). Hunt and Brown, *Brigadier Generals*.

16. Unidentified.

17. Marcus A. Reno (1834–1889) graduated from West Point in 1857 and served in the cavalry during the war where he attained the rank of brevet brigadier general of volunteers. After mustering out of the volunteers he was commissioned a major in the 7th Cav. of the regulars, serving until dismissed in 1880. Hunt and Brown, *Brigadier Generals*; Powell, *Army List*, 550.

18. Joseph T. Foster (b. c1839), a clerk and later farmer in Lyons, Iowa, served as a sergeant, lieutenant, and captain in the 1st Iowa Cav. before mustering out in February 1866. The following July he was appointed first lieutenant in the 8th Cav. and dismissed two years later. Powell, *Army List*, 315; 1860 Census, Iowa, Clinton, Lyons Twp., 354; (1870), 290.

From Nathan M. Knapp[1]

Winchester Illinois   Aug 22d 1866

In the month of May last I was nominated, in the month of June confirmed, and on the first inst. qualified and entered upon duty as collector of Internal Revenue for the 10th District of Illinois. I had no idea that in accepting I was in the least compromising my personal independence. Recent events have satisified me that I cannot, with propriety, retain the position. Some of my personal and political friends, who efficiently aided in your Excellency's elevation, and who were noted for capacity and fidelity in their official positions have recently been superseded, obviously for no other reason than that they entertain the same opinions they did when they voted for your Excellency in 1864. If that is cause against them it is against me. I belong to a party that has always been opposed by the Rebels of the South, and their apologists in the North. They now, with singular unanimity, approve the policy which office-holders seem expected to endorse in order to obtain, or retain their positions. I am not prepared to follow. The grave of Lincoln is too near me.

Thanking your Excellency, therefore, for any past manifestation of kindness, I respectfully tender my resignation, and request that it be accepted at once.[2]

N M Knapp

ALS, DNA-RG56, Appts., Internal Revenue Service, Collector, Ill., 10th Dist., N. M. Knapp.

1. Knapp (b. c1815), a native of Vermont, was a lawyer. 1870 Census, Ill., Scott, Winchester, 247.

2. Knapp's resignation, accepted by Secretary McCulloch, was to take effect when a successor was appointed and qualified. In November Knapp requested to withdraw his resignation, as no successor had been named and as harmonious relations once more existed

between himself and certain others. Knapp to E. A. Rollins, Nov. 13, 1866; Knapp to O. H. Browning, Nov. 21, 1866, Appts., Internal Revenue Service, Collector, Ill., 10th Dist., N. M. Knapp, RG56, NA.

From Texas Delegates to Philadelphia Convention[1]

Washington D.C.   August 22. 1866.

Sir:

We citizens of Texas, a part of the delegation to the Phila Convention, having learned of the probable speedy retirement of the Head of the War Dept, beg to assure you, that there is no event, of which we can conceive, that would so sincerely gratify our people or inspire them with greater confidence in your administration.

Such has been the arbitrary and despotic action of this functionary, that numbers of Texans are enduring wrongs from military oppression today, rather than subject themselves to the humiliation of rude insult in seeking redress at his hands.

We have heard Maj Gen Steadman[2] mentioned as the probable successor of Mr Stanton—a gentlemen now well and favorably known in Texas, and to part of the undersigned, after a personal acquaintance of many years. His appointment as Secretary of War, would meet general approval and command the fullest confidence in the people of Texas.

L D Evans   D G Burnet
Geo W Carter   Geo W White

LS, DLC-JP.
    1. Carter is the only one of the four signers who has not been previously identified. Virginia native Carter (1826–1901), a Methodist minister and college professor, moved to Texas in 1860 to head the new Soule University. An outspoken secessionist, Carter raised three regiments of Texas troops, becoming colonel of the 21st Tex. Cav. with which he served in the Trans-Mississippi West. After the war he became involved in Louisiana reconstruction politics and served as speaker of the state house (1871–72). Anne J. Bailey, *Between the Enemy and Texas: Parsons's Texas Cavalry in the Civil War* (Fort Worth, 1989), 17–19, 23, 29, 206–7, and passim; Conrad, *La. Biography*.
    2. James B. Steedman.

From Samuel J. Tilden[1]

(Private)

N.Y.   Aug 22d 1866

My Dear Sir,

After we had the pleasure of an interview with you,[2] we had a consultation, among other things, in respect to the Naval Office, and considering the political position of Col. Ludlow[3]—his military services—his experience in party organization,—we concluded that, in the present posture of things, the best advice we could give you was to select that gentleman. I understand that Mr Stanbury will now give you an offical opinion that you have authority to fill such vacancies as the present during the recess of the Senate.[4]

S. J. Tilden

ALS, DLC-JP.
1. Tilden (1814–1886), a prominent and successful New York lawyer, was influential in the pre-Civil War Democratic party in his state. He played no active part in the war and became a staunch supporter of Johnson in the immediate postwar period. Tilden was elected governor of New York in 1874 and received the Democratic party's presidential nomination two years later. In this famous disputed election, Tilden lost to the Republican contender, Rutherford B. Hayes. *DAB*.
2. Tilden possibly refers to himself and various members of the New York delegation to the Philadelphia convention, of which Tilden served as chairman. Although the date of their interview is not known, it probably took place sometime during the days immediately following the convention, when some delegates traveled from Philadelphia to Washington to pay their respects to the President. *Press* (Philadelphia), Aug. 16, 1866; *New York Times*, Aug. 17, 18, 21, 1866.
3. For more on William H. Ludlow's possible appointment, see John B. Haskin to Johnson, Sept. 28, 1866, and Ludlow to Johnson, Dec. 12, 1866.
4. For Henry Stanbery's ruling, which was that the President certainly had such powers, see Stanbery to A. W. Randall, Aug. 30, 1866, in Benjamin F. Hall et al., eds., *Official Opinions of the Attorneys General of the United States* (43 vols. to date, Washington, D.C., 1852-), 12: 32–42.

From William B. Phillips
Private.

82 East 23d. Street,
New York, Augt 23d./66

Dear Sir,

I learn from persons entitled to credit and who are well informed about the matter, that there is an undoubted understanding between the radical leaders and some of the Fenian leaders, Roberts[1] is cheifly named, to carry a part of the Irish vote for the radicals at the approaching congressional elections. Roberts, who calls himself the president of the Fenian Brotherhood, disavows, in a card published in the Herald to-day,[2] any intention of using the Fenians for political purposes, but I have reason to doubt the truth and sincereity of his disavowal. Colfax[3] and the other radical leaders have given Roberts assurances of reward.

The plan is to win over the Irish if possible by such clap trap as was used by Gov Ogelsby, Gen. Logan, and others at Chicago.[4]

Then, it is intended to get up another armed expedition to invade Canada,[5] not, of course, with any expectation of taking Canada, but to place you in a dilemma. The mass of ignorant Irishmen will know nothing about the object, but will think, as they thought before, that it must be a grand flank movement to liberate Ireland. The radicals expect you will be compelled to execute the laws and prevent the invasion, or the pretended attempt to invade Canada, and then they would denounce you and your administration. They know how silly and excessively sensitive the Irish people are about Ireland and making an Irish republic, and their calculation is that they can force you into such a position as will enable them to turn a large part of the Irish vote against you.

Another part of the programme is to keep up an excitement and large bodies of Fenians on the border to invade or under pretense of invading at the time of the elections, and thus withdraw a considerable vote from the conservative party.

There is no doubt that the radicals in their extremity are going to use the Fenians if possible, as well as all other means in their power to save themselves from the defeat that now threatens them: and we all know that they will resort to the most unscrupulous means.

There may be some little sensation and wild speculation in this programme for getting the Irish vote, but there is enough in it to give it some attention, or at least to watch it.

Hoping you are well and that God may preserve you to see your saving policy successful. . . .

W. B. Phillips.

ALS, DLC-JP.

1. William R. Roberts.

2. Roberts warned his constituents against being deceived by both Democrats and Republicans who sought to "injure our cause and organization." *New York Herald*, Aug. 23, 1866.

3. Schuyler Colfax.

4. Here Phillips refers to the "Great Fenian Pic Nic" of August 15, featuring speeches by Richard J. Oglesby, John A. Logan, and Colfax, among others, who criticized the President's handling of the Fenian crisis and encouraged Irish-Americans to vote Republican. Jenkins, *Fenians and Anglo-American Relations*, 188–89.

5. Canadian officials evidently took the report of a second invasion attempt seriously, but it ultimately proved to be a false alarm. Ibid., 188–92.

From Texas Delegates to Philadelphia Convention[1]

Washington   Aug 23 1866

Sir:

The undersigned delegates from Texas to the late Philadelphia Convention, respectfully but *earnestly request* that you will appoint Giles H. Lyon[2] collector of customs at El Paso Texas. Mr Lyon is a loyal citizen of Texas, & a *firm supporter of your administration*, & the importance of having such men in public positions on the western border of our state cannot be over estimated.

Mr Lyon's appointment was recommended by Judge Hancock[3] of Texas & we are informed that his commision was made out.[4] Afterwards, Mr Mills[5] was appointed. This appointment will prove highly objectionable to your friends in Texas, & we ask his immediate removal.

We are informed that it was shown by the Delegate in Congress from New Mixico,[6] that Mills was guilty of malfiasance in office at the same place prior to the war, and removed in consquence.[7]

He is not identified with our people, & we do not believe that his appointment was recomended by any of the *Loyal men of Texas* of influence & high standing who support the policy of your administration.[8]

L D Evans   D G Burnet

G. H. Giddings   Geo. W White

Geo W Carter

LS, DNA-RG56, Appts., Customs Service, Collector, El Paso, Giles H. Lyon.

1. Of the five signers only Giddings has not been previously identified. Pennsylvania-born George H. Giddings (1823–1903) went to Texas in 1846 and worked as a mail carrier and agent establishing the San Antonio-San Diego Mail Line. He was a lieutenant colonel in the Confederate army. In the 1880s Giddings tried unsuccessfuly to get federal compensation for damages to his stage coach line caused by Indians. Webb et al., *Handbook of Texas*; *OR*, Ser. 1, Vol. 41, Pt. 3: 931; Emmie Giddings W. Mahon and Chester V. Kielman, "George H. Giddings and the San Antonio-San Diego Mail Line," *SWHQ*, 61 (1957): 220–39.

2. Allegedly a loyal Union man during the Civil War, Lyon, formerly of San Antonio, had recently moved to El Paso to establish a business. John Hancock to Johnson, May 9, 1866, Appts., Customs Service, Collector, El Paso, Giles H. Lyon, RG56, NA.

3. John Hancock.

4. On May 10, 1866, Edmund Cooper endorsed a note to Treasury Secretary McCulloch asking him to send a nomination for Lyon to the President's office. The form withdrawing William W. Mills's nomination and nominating Lyon was duly prepared, but on May 14 William G. Moore returned it to McCulloch, "the President having decided not to withdraw the nomination of Mr. Mills." Nomination, May 10, 1866, and endorsements, May 10 and May 14, 1866, ibid.

5. William W. Mills, the collector for El Paso and New Mexico since 1862 (one post covered both places beginning in 1863), had already been reappointed in March 1866. Nomination, May 10, 1866, ibid.; W. W. Mills, *Forty Years at El Paso, 1858–1898*, ed. by Rex W. Strickland (El Paso, 1962), xvi-xvii, 83. See also New Mexico Citizens to Johnson, Feb. 5, 1866, *Johnson Papers*, 10: 35.

6. J. Francisco Chaves.

7. Chaves wrote that "Mr. Mills, while in the exercise of the functions of that office [collector of customs] in the year 1863, received a bribe from one W. H. McKee, and for a consideration, permitted McKee to transport articles contraband of War over the line into Mexico. The evidence of this fact was in Mills' own hand writing, and attested to" by two El Paso men. A certified copy of this evidence was in the possession of the U.S. Senate committee on commerce. It does not appear that Mills had been removed from office for the infraction, however. Chaves also recommended Lyon to replace Mills. J. Francisco Chaves to Johnson, May 10, 1866, Appts., Customs Service, Collector, El Paso, Giles H. Lyon, RG56, NA.

8. This August correspondence did not change Johnson's mind and Mills remained collector until 1869. Mills, *Forty Years*, xix.

From Elijah Thurman[1]

Chattanooga   August 23th 1866

Dear Sir

It has Ben a Long time Since I Saw you. I herd you make the first Speach you ever made in the County of Hamilton. I am the first and the oldest Citizen of Hamilton County. I Congratulate you on the action of the National Union Convention at Philadelphia. The Platform is Broad and Sufficent for all who Loves there County. We Long for the day when we git a Chance to turn Brownlow out of office. I am now a old Man but I have never herd of a Convention that has done So much good that has given So hearty Surpot to the President as the one had on the 16 of Augst 1866. In my umbler opinion there has been non Such Since 1776. The Peopel who you have had the honor of Serving Since 1840 Still love you and ar ansious to Elect you as President of the *U Sates*. We will Swep the Brownlow party Like a whirle wind. We ar up and Doig. We old men ar at work to help you to Guide the Ship of State in this hour of trouble. Rest assred we will help you and may a merciful God watch over you protect and help you to administer the Law as a Just and a good Presidet Should.

Johnston If there has Ben no U S Revenu Colletor apointed for the Third Congressionel Districk I would ask that you have my Son Capt M. R. Thurman[2] apinted. I will give you for Reffer Col *John H James* as to honesty Loyalty &c. I am now old and my Son is my only help he is and has Stood by you from his Boy Hood up. It was him who Nominated Goerge D. Foster and Beat the Brownlow party in our County. Twice he has Stood firmer and Squarer for you than any man. This I no the people will Say. If you wish any more Reffer it will be given. I ask this as a favor. Tis the only one I ever asked from you. I knew you when you first Started out in the world as a political man. I Refer you to Judg *J. C. Gaut* Maj D. M. Key[3] and othrs that the facts ar true. If [convenient?] please grant my Request. . . .

Elijah: Thurman

ALS, DNA-RG56, Appts., Internal Revenue Service, Tenn., 3rd Dist., M. R. Thurman.
   1. Thurman (b. *c*1805) was a Hamilton County farmer who in 1860 had six children. 1860 Census, Tenn., Hamilton, 5th Dist., Chattanooga, 207; (1870), 17th Dist., 42nd Subdiv., 6.
   2. Monroe R. Thurman (b. *c*1836), not otherwise identified. The following year he represented Hamilton County at a nominating convention of the Third Congressional District, held at McMinnville. 1860 Census, Tenn., Hamilton, 5th Dist., Chattanooga, 207; *Nashville Union and American*, June 7, 1867.
   3. John C. Gaut and David M. Key.

From William Aiken et al.[1]

Charleston S C   Aug 24 1866

Learn that Genl Scott[2] is to be mustered out first of September. In his absence we entreat you to suspend this order until the present crop is harvested and settlements made between planters and negroes.[3] Gen Scott is the best man we can have just now. More at large by mail.

Tel, DLC-JP.
   1. This wire was sent by six men, with Aiken as the first signatory.
   2. Robert K. Scott.
   3. The next day Scott's muster out was suspended and rescheduled for December 1,

1866. However, he remained on duty until July 1868, when he resigned prior to becoming governor. Johnson to Aiken, Aug. 25, 1866, Tels. Sent, President, Vol. 3 (1865–68), RG107, NA; E. D. Townsend to R. K. Scott, Aug. 25, 1866, Tels. Sent, Sec. of War (M473, Roll 91), RG107, NA; Warner, *Blue*; Powell, *Army List*, 817; Kibler, *Perry*, 470.

From George M. Ashenfelter[1]

Salem N.J.   Aug. 24, '66

Sir,

Aside from party considerations, and in a spirit of entire frankness, I wish to call your Excellency's attention to a few facts regarding Mr. James M. Scovel[2] of this State. Within the past month there has been a marked change in this gentleman's purposes, as well as in the language which is supposed to indicate his sentiments.[3] He has concluded that by following out a certain course of policy he can obtain the Republican nomination for Congress, in this District;[4] and in furtherance of this end, he is now most unreserved in his denunciation of your personal & political character—speaking of you as a "traitor, a liar and a murderer." I deem it but just that you should Know this.

Georg. M. Ashenfelter   Ed. Nat. Standard

ALS, DLC-JP.

1. Ashenfelter, though not further identified, served as a lieutenant in the 104th Pa. Rgt. during the war. William W.H. Davis, *History of the 104th Pennsylvania Regiment, From August 22nd, 1861, to September 30th, 1864.* (Philadelphia, 1866), 350, 362.

2. Scovel (*c*1829–1904) was a prominent lawyer in Camden, New Jersey, before serving in the state senate during the war. A former Democrat, he joined the Republican ranks in disagreement over Johnson's reconstruction policies. *New York Times*, Dec. 3, 1904; Hermann K. Platt, ed., *Charles Perrin Smith: New Jersey Political Reminiscences, 1828–1882* (New Brunswick, 1965), 29, 248.

3. Less than two weeks earlier, Scovel had publicly called for New Jersey's legislature to ratify the proposed Fourteenth Amendment. Later he urged Johnson to abandon the Democratic party and "stand by the amendment." Scovel to Johnson, Aug. 13, Oct. 10, 1866, Johnson Papers, LC; *Philadelphia Inquirer*, Aug. 13, 1866.

4. He was not given the nomination.

From William T. Dowdall[1]

[ca. August 24, 1866][2]

Mr President

In behalf of the people of the city and county of Peoria, I am requested and authorized by that time honored organization The Masonic Fraternity to ask that you continue your trip farther West when at Chicago and be present and participate with us in laying the corner Stone of the Soldiers Monument now erecting by Peoria County.

A Special train will be at your Service and a Six hours ride from Chicago through the most beautiful and fertile portion of our State will land you in the "central city" the Second in Size and importance and the first in beauty, location and hospitality of its inhabitants in Illinois.

Sir the duty and privilege of thus being permited to invite you to visit our city is to me gratifying for more reasons than one; our people were the first to Speak in Mass meeting endorsing the policy of your Administration as made known through your freedmans bureau veto and immediately thereafter ratified Such endorsement at the ballot box Since which time they have had no occasion to regret their act. "Time but the impression deeper makes As Streams their channels deeper wear"[3] And they feel and know that they only did their duty as you did yours.

Again the high and Sacred work of conducting the ceremonies of this truly patriotic and commendable token of respect to the memory of the honored dead has been entrusted to the care of the Masonic Fraternity and none knowing better than yourself the Sound of the Gavil or points of the compass and also that no one Surpasses you in love and respect for the Soldiery who fell in defense of our common country. Therefore for these and many other reasons it is to me a most pleasant task to invite you to our home that you may participate with us in doing honor to the memory of the Fathers, Sons and brothers of Peoria County who fell while gallantly battling under the folds of that glorious old Flag the Star Spangled banner for the Supremacy of the constitutional laws of our country and the unity of the States one and inseparable.[4]

W. T. Dowdall

LS, NRU-William Henry Seward Col.

1. Dowdall (c1842–fl1880), a very successful newspaperman, had been on the staff of the *Cairo Times* and *Delta* and published the *Alton Daily Democrat* before founding Peoria's *National Democrat* in September 1865. He and his *Democrat* were strong advocates of Democratic principles. 1870 Census, Ill., Peoria, Peoria, 5th Ward, 389; *History of Peoria County, Illinois* (Chicago, 1880), 490–91.

2. We have assigned this date because on August 25 the *New York Times* reported the President's visit with Dowdall and his state delegation at which occasion the Peoria invitation was given.

3. From "To Mary in Heaven," a poem by Robert Burns.

4. While it appears Johnson was initially favorable to this request, there is no evidence he made the trip to Peoria from Chicago. *New York Times*, Aug. 25, 1866. See also Seward to Dowdall, Aug. 26, 1866, Tels. Sent, Sec. of War (M473, Roll 91), RG107, NA; and Dowdall to Johnson, Sept. 3, 1866, Johnson Papers, LC.

From Francis C. Dunnington

Union & American Office.
Nashville   Aug. 24, 1866.

Permit me to congratulate you upon the more hopeful condition of the country. I have never believed there was any safety for republican institutions upon any other principles than those of Jefferson & Madison—the principles of the Constitution. In politics I have been like the Romanists in religion. I have never believed there was but *one* Constitutional party in the country—the party originating with those very two men in the inception of the government. I have always believed that whenever that *other* party—under whatever name—obtained permanent ascendancy, that our form of government would change. I regarded this as the real issue in the recent calamitous civil war. You thought differently—that only the question of *Union* was involved, and that that being preserved, the other could be maintained. God grant that you may have been correct & that I have been wrong in that judgment. The war is at an end but the real question of a Constitutional government is still in issue. If the American people sustain you in the noble stand you have taken it will be the brightest chapter in the history of governments. It will furnish the strongest evidence, by far, that has ever been given that the American people are capable & are disposed to perpetuate free institutions. It all depends upon the virtue of the people. I do not question their intelligence. To them alone you must adjourn the question.

Since the renewal of our paper I have been laboring, to the extent of its influence, to quiet the public mind, and bring every thing as much as possible in harmony with your administration. I have endeavored to educate the people to a spirit of toleration, conciliation, patience and confidence. If my duty as a citizen, in my humble sphere, has not been fully discharged it is only because I did not correctly comprehend what that duty was. I flatter myself that the Union & American has done much good. I trust you have had time to look occasionally to its columns, though I have not even had a line of friendly recognition from any one connected with the White House indicating that our paper was so much as read there.

If I were permitted to consult my own feelings I would seek some secluded spot—such a vally as you once described to me as existing somewhere in East Tennessee—where I would be shut out from the jaring discords of the world. But as this cannot be I must do my duty in the great battle of life, looking beyond the horizon of time for those sweet comforts which we are permited to conceive but never to realize in this existence.

I am satisfied you are fully advised as to the condition of affairs in Tennessee. They are bad indeed, and I see no means of a speedy correction. Under the ridgid partizan ruling of the present disfranchising law[1] I am sure there are some counties in which there will not be fifty men permited to vote. There is a great purpose on the part of the people in favor of a Convention to amend their organic law,[2] & according to the bill of rights I think they have the power, but from motives of policy, in a national point of view, I have discouraged such action, at least for the present. If we only knew that our Supreme Court would maintain the just & impartial dignity which should characterize such a body, I should feel satisfied that it was far better to submit to temporary evils & trust to that source for relief against the usurpations & abuses of official tyranny. But with the exception of Judge Milligan I have no confidence in its decisions.

There is no doubting the fact that Executive patronage may be used for evil. I sincerely trust it may not be permited to weigh in the balance against that policy which you deem essential to the future peace & safety of the government. And yet if you have a friend in Nashville or vicinity— except our Post Master at Columbia[3]—among the Federal officeholders, he has not been sufficiently active for me to find him out.

I have already written more than, probably, you will have patience to read. I have written, not because I had any thing to relate that would profit you, but merely to attest my friendly regard, and to awaken in your mind some faint recollection of an old friend. I can scarcely expect an answer to this letter, nevertheless, if there is or should be at any time any subject upon which you would like to have me advised I trust you will do so with the freedom of former days, remembering that I have never proven untrue to former confidence or failed to exercise that liberality of sentiment which should characterize all true & honorable friendship.

F. C. Dunnington.

ALS, DLC-JP.
  1. A reference to the 1866 franchise law which authorized the governor to appoint special voting commissioners and virtually eliminated all ex-Rebels from the right to vote. See Alexander, *Reconstruction*, 110.
  2. See John Caldwell to Johnson, Aug. 18, 1866.
  3. Undoubtedly the reference here is to John D. Moore (b. *c*1810 or *c*1817), a brick mason who served as Columbia postmaster during part of the war and for several years thereafter. *U.S. Off. Reg.* (1865–67); Nashville directories (1868–69); 1860 Census, Tenn., Maury, 9th Dist., Columbia, 39; (1870), Columbia, 2nd Ward, 38.

From Gordon Granger

Washington, August 24, 1866.

Sir—

In obedience to instructions, dated May 9, 1866, directing me, while carrying out a specific mission, "to examine carefully into the disposition of the people of the Southern States through which I might pass, towards the government of the United States," I have the honor to report:—

That in all the States I visited I found no sign or symptom of organized disloyalty to the general government. I found the people taking our currency, and glad to get it; anxious for Northern capital and Northern labor to develop the resources of their wasted country, and well disposed towards every Northern man who came among them with that object in view.

In some localities I heard rumors of secret organizations pointing to a renewal of the rebellion. On investigating these secret societies I could discover in them nothing more than charitable institutions, having for their principal object the relief of the widows and orphans of confederate soldiers who had fallen in the war.

During the whole of my travels I found it to be as safe and as convenient to mingle with the people of the South, freely discussing any and every topic that came up, as in any other section of the United States. I was often among them unknown, and the tenor of their acts and conversation was then the same as when my name and official position were thoroughly understood.

The people of the South may be divided into two classes. There is the industrious class, laboring earnestly to build up what has been broken down, striving to restore prosperity to the country, and interested mainly in the great question of providing food and clothing for themselves and families. These form the great majority of the people. Then there is another class, an utterly irresponsible class, composed mainly of young men who were the "bucks" of Southern society before the war, and chiefly spent their time in lounging round the courtrooms and bars, in chicken fighting and gambling. These have been greatly broken up by the war; many of them have been killed, but those who remain are still disturbing elements in the community, and are doing much mischief. It is this class of men, and a number of the poorer whites, who have formed gangs for horse stealing. It is they who in some instances have made attacks on officers of the Freedmen's Bureau, and have ill treated the freedmen. It is they who afford the main pretext for saying that there is among the people of the South a feeling of hostility towards the United States government. But they are not the representatives of the Southern people. They form but an insignificant minority in the community, and even they are actuated not so much by a feeling of opposition to the government as by a reluctance to earn their own livelihood by honest labor and individual exertion.

That cases of authentic outrage have occurred in the South is patent to every one familiar with the current news of the day. But these cases are few and far between, and it is both unjust and ungenerous to charge the responsibility for such acts of lawlessness upon the whole Southern people. For some malicious purpose accounts of these isolated disorders have been collected and grouped together and sown broadcast over the North so as to give to the public mind an utterly erroneous impression as to the condition of Southern society. The fact is, that wherever disaffection and turbulence have manifested themselves outside the class to whom I have above alluded, there has been some local or specific cause to account for it. Lawlessness, like an epidemic has extended over particular belts of the country, and, like an epidemic, is equally traceable to some initiatory cause. Chief among these causes must be named bad government, pillage and oppression.

For five years the Southern people have been the subjects of gross mis-

rule. During the war their government was a military despotism, dependent solely on the dictum of an individual. Since the war they have been
left more or less in a chaotic state—their government semi-civil, semi-
military, or rather a division of rule between the military, the Freedmen's
Bureau and the provisional governments. What might have been the result of a different policy it is not altogether idle to speculate. Every military man who served in the South during the war will agree that the heart
of the great mass of the people was not thoroughly in the struggle. The
number of desertions from the rebel armies abundantly establishes this
fact. Had a policy of wise and statesmanlike conciliation been followed
out immediately after the close of the war it is more than probable that the
condition and disposition of the people would now be far better than they
are. But on the subjugation of the South the national authority in the
lately rebellious States was divided and broken up into opposing factions, whose action greatly hindered the re-establishment of civil law and
good order so much needed among a people demoralized by the most
demoralizing of all agencies—civil war. The country was flooded with
Treasury agents who, with their accomplices and imitators, fleeced the
people right and left, returning into the United States Treasury for all the
enormous amount of property they seized and confiscated barely enough
to pay the cost of confiscation. Agents of the Freedmen's Bureau stepped
between the planter and the laborer, stirring up strife, perpetuating antagonism and often adding their quota of extortion and oppression. On
every hand the people saw themselves robbed and wronged by agents
and self-appointed agents professing to act under the sanction of the
United States government. Need it be wondered at that among a community thus dealt with, powerless to resist and too weak and prostrated
for successful complaint, some bitterness and ill feeling should arise?
None but a brave and well meaning people could have endured unre-
sistingly all that the South has undergone.

In prosecuting this inquiry I hardly deemed it fair to ask more than
what had been the actions of the people of the South towards the general
government. With their private opinions, their sympathies and their
prejudices I had nothing to do. Yet for a more thorough understanding of
the question I made it a part of my mission to investigate even these. I
found they had universally complied with the conditions granted and accepted at the final surrender of their armies and cause. I found that they
were carrying out with good faith and alacrity the requirements of the
constitutional amendment abolishing slavery, and that in all the States
except Mississippi and Texas, the famous Civil Rights Bill had been anticipated by the action of the State Legislatures previous to its passage by
Congress. Further than this, I found that in the repudiation of every dollar known as the Confederate debt, the same prompt action had been
taken by the State authorities, and had been universally endorsed by the

people; and I neither saw nor heard any disposition, or anything that pointed toward a disposition, to repudiate the national debt or to revive the institution of slavery.

But whilst the Southern people are thus loyal, and have fulfilled all the requirements asked of them by the federal government, it is impossible to disguise the fact, and the better class of citizens do not attempt to disguise it, that there is among them a deep feeling and a strong apprehension as to the cause of their long continued exclusion from Congress. They believe that it is part of a set plan for perpetuating the existence of the political party now in the ascendant, and that the question of suffrage, readjustment of representation and taxation are but excuses for still longer delay. Thus regardless of the great interests, not only of the suffering South, but of the whole country, burdened with debt and laboring under severe embarrassment, I found the prevailing opinion among the most intelligent citizens, as well as among those most anxious for an early restoration of the Union, to be that, if representation and an equal and just co-operation in the administration of federal affairs were much longer withheld from the Southern States, a feeling of indifference would spring up towards taking any part in filling federal offices, and more particularly towards re-filling their seats in Congress—that the people, in fact, would stay away from the polls, and allow the elections to go by default, to the great detriment of the country at large. This feeling of indifference indeed is already manifesting itself, and is rapidly increasing, so much so that were it not for a few persons in each Southern State who have found it necessary for their existence to live upon and hold office, and whose haunts and occupations have hitherto been at the federal capital, I do not believe that any clamor for representation would be heard.

What is needed to restore harmony and prosperity to the entire country, both North and South, is closer and better acquaintance with each other. I have been astonished to notice how little people, even whose social relations are all Southern, know of the true state of feeling in that section of the country. We need greater political, social, and commercial freedom, more frequent intercourse, and a kinder appreciation of each other's peculiarities. The advantages to the country in its present financial stress of a reunion of heart and sentiment would be beyond enumeration. The broad lands of the fertile South are now lying almost in waste for want of means and capital to cultivate them, when every acre of its beneficent soil might be a gold mine to its possessor were the political relations of the people better understood and acted upon.

GORDON GRANGER,
Brevet Major General,   United States army.

New York Herald, August 28, 1866.

From Russell Houston

Columbia [Tenn.]   August 24, 1866—

I am pretty well acquainted with Philip Speed,[1] the Collector of Internal Revenue at Louisville, & fully concur, with Mr A. D. Hunt[2] the writer of the foregoing letter. Mr Philip Speed is a brother of James Speed, but differs, as I have always understood, from his brother, in regard to the great questions of the times. I do not know that any efforts will be made to have a change in that office—but I think more good will be effected by retaining him in office than by his removal. His retention, *under the circumstances & with his connexions & political opinions*; I think, would be best for the cause we advocate.

I am obliged, occasionally, to write you about such matters, but you must always understand that I am the partisan of no applicant for office. I simply give you my opinions, to be weighed with the opinions of others, that the best possible thing on the matter in hand, may done. Of this character, was my letter of a recent date, in regard to the Postmaster at Nashville.[3]

Russell Houston

ALS, DLC-JP.

1. Speed (1819–1882), brother of Lincoln's attorney general, James Speed, was a prominent Louisville merchant who served as a U.S. Army paymaster during the war and as Louisville's collector of internal revenue from 1866 to 1868. *Louisville Courier-Journal*, Nov. 2, 1882; Ser. 6B, Vol. 5, Johnson Papers, LC.

2. Probably Abraham D. Hunt (1809–1885), a native of Kentucky and a successful lawyer, businessman, and eventually banker in Louisville. His enclosed letter to Houston, dated August 20, supported Speed and requested assistance in finding out whether he was to be removed from office. During August and September Johnson received several letters from Louisville endorsing Speed and requesting his retention as collector. 1860 Census, Ky., Jefferson, Louisville, 5th Ward, 143; Louisville directory (1861); T. M. Sherley to Johnson, Aug. 22, 1866; James Guthrie to Johnson, Aug. 21, 1866; John B. Smith to Johnson, Aug. 21, 1866, Appts., Internal Revenue Service, Collector, Ky., 5th Dist., Philip Speed, RG56, NA; *Louisville Courier-Journal*, May 25, 1885.

3. Adrian V.S. Lindsley.

From Edward J. Lowber[1]

Brooklyn   August 24th 1866.

Dear Sir

Being fully conscious that the perpetuity of our Government in a great measure depends upon the action of the next congress, and of the importance of returning thereto our best, and most conservative citizens, and that to this end the spirit of harmony and good will which was so marked a characteristic of the Philadelphia convention, which I am proud to say I had the honor to attend, should be early and widely disseminated, and believing that no effort should be spared to elect such men I have taken the liberty of calling your attention, directly to the political situation of our county which embraces the Second and Third Congressional districts. The second district requires no consideration on your part, nor more than the usual attention on ours, as it is largely democratic. Not so with the Third however. In that the parties are nearly equally divided, the majority being with the Republicans. It can only be carried by the most judicious management, and with the aid of the conservative republicans, and the patronage within your control, especially that of the Navy Yard which in a great measure controls the district. Many of the wards composing this district are intensely radical, and very wealthy. That the contest will be fierce and desperate there is no doubt, nevertheless we are determined to succeed, and to elect a member who will thoroughly and efficientlty support your policy of restoration. To this end it is my intention to call a meeting of the leading men of the several wards of both parties to take into consideration the selection of such candidates as will carry the district beyond a doubt, and as two from this district are to be elected, one to fill the vacancy occassioned by the death of Mr Humphrey.[2] I doubt not such division can be made as will be satisfactory to both parties and insure success. I find however—and to which I especially wish to call your attention—that the retention in office of Mr Lincoln Post Master and Mr Bowen[3] collector of the Third district we encounter a serious obstacle to the work in hand. We have had so many rumors of their removal resulting in no official announcement of the fact, that many of your earnest supporters begin to doubt whether they will be removed at all, and so objectionable are they to every conservative, that many are becoming indifferent to the coming canvass. This state of feeling should not exist, and is exceedingly injurious and adds seriously to the difficulty of harmonizing the parties. If continued in it may result in spite of all we can do, in returning a radical member. To avoid so great a calamity we request that a change may be made in the incumbents of those offices at the earliest practicable moment so that we can avail ourselves of the aid such change will give us.[4]

Trusting that the cause we all have so much at heart and upon which so momentus events are pending may be my excuse for addressing you. . . .

E. J. Lowber   Chairman of the General Democratic Committee
of Kings Co. N.Y.

ALS, NRU-Thurlow Weed Col.

1. Lowber (1818–1883) was a New York City grocer and distiller and Brooklyn water commissioner. Several months after this letter Lowber applied for appointment as naval officer of New York, and was recommended for the same post over the next two years, but he was not successful. *New York Tribune*, Sept. 8, 1883; Appts., Customs Service, Naval Officer, New York, Edward J. Lowber, RG56, NA.

2. James Humphrey (1811–1866), a lawyer, moved to New York in 1838 and later served two terms as a Republican congressman (1859–61, 1865–66). *BDAC*. For more on this election, see Henry W. Slocum to Johnson, Nov. 7, 1866.

3. George B. Lincoln and Henry C. Bowen. Bowen (1813–1896) was a prominent New York merchant, publisher, and editor. *DAB*. For related correspondence concerning their posts, see Henry A. Smythe to Johnson, Aug. 10, 1866.

4. Bowen's retention as collector had been in question, owing largely (or as he himself

believed) to his relationship with the anti-Johnson *Independent*. Secretary McCulloch, on the other hand, denied that Bowen was to be removed because of the newspaper's criticisms of the President, but rather for certain "irregularities" Bowen had permitted while in office. His replacement, Calvin E. Pratt, had been given a temporary commission for the post some two weeks prior to the date of Lowber's letter. Bowen to McCulloch, July 9, 1866, Appts., Internal Revenue Service, Collector, N.Y., 3rd Dist., Henry C. Bowen, RG56, NA; William E. Chandler to Theodore Tilton, Mar. 8, 1866, Lets. Sent *re* Customs Service Employees (QC Ser.), Vol. 2, ibid.; Ser. 6B, Vol. 3: 95, Johnson Papers, LC. See also Henry W. Beecher to William Claflin, July 14, 1866, ibid.

From Levin R. Marshall

Pelham, Westchester Co. N. Y'k　24—Augt. *1866.*

My Dear Sir,

Allow me to congratulate you upon your success in resisting the Radical crew in Congress, and to assure as far as my observation extends that your measures must be triumphant in the reconstruction of our distracted country.

I passed the greater part of the winter in the South, and recently made a visit to the west. I was not unobservant of public sentiment, and am more than ever convinced of the deep hold you have on the public mind. With few exceptions the expressions of opinion were most favorable to your course. Persevere (as I am sure you will) in the policy you have adopted, and the nation will be unanimous in gratitude for your benevolent and statesmanlike administration. GOD, grant that your Life may be spared to consummate the good work you have undertaken. I see changes already in this section, since the meeting of the Philadelphia Convention.

Mr. Tobias Gibson,[1] a large sugar Planter of Louisa., now here as a commissioner to raise funds for repairing the Levees, will apply for Pardon under your proclamation act of last year. He is a man of Conservative views, had nothing to do with the war, and beyond the age of active service. He thinks it advisable to have your pardon altho' He has committed no act of forfeiture of his property—but in the event of a sale of any portion of his real estate it might be desirable to show his pardon in making title.

His son Randal,[2] a young man, has been in the Confed: service, and also applies to be reinstated as a citizen of the Legitimate Govt. You will do me a favor, if you will comply with the wishes of Mr. Gibson and his son.[3]

I hope the excursion you have in view will benefit your health, and give renewed vigor to enable you to support the labor of body and mind consequent upon your arduous duties.

L R Marshall of Natchez, Missisi.

ALS, DNA-RG94, Amnesty Papers (M1003, Roll 27), La., Tobias Gibson.

1. Gibson (1800–1872), a native of Mississippi and the owner of a large plantation in Terrebonne Parish, Louisiana, held several local offices and served in the Louisiana state legislature (1865–67). Conrad, *La. Biography.*

2. The younger Gibson, Randall L. (1832–1892), one of ten children, was born in Kentucky. He graduated from Yale and from the law department of the University of Louisiana. During the Civil War he rose to the rank of brigadier general, for which he required a pardon. He served four terms in the U.S. House of Representatives (1875–83) and from 1883 until his death was a U.S. senator. Ibid.; *DAB*.

3. Johnson endorsed the letter: "The Atty Genl will please pardon in this Case if found to be good upon examination." Both Gibsons were pardoned on September 25, 1866. Amnesty Papers (M1003, Roll 27), La., R. L. Gibson, T. Gibson, RG94, NA.

From Annie P. Shepherd[1]

Berryville, Va.   Aug. 24.   1866

Dear Sir.

We are orphans, five of us; we are in trouble, out of which no human power, save yours, can lift us. Will not your Excellency use that power?

I approach you with the more confidence, knowing, as all who hear of you must know, how your true heart throbs in unison with every kindly, generous impulse of humanity.

My eldest brother,[2] when the war broke out, was just entering his youth and we hoped to see him prepared for some useful, honorable profession of quiet civilian life. Providence ordered it otherwise. Illinois was called upon for her "quota" and throwing aside books and the bright promises of his future, my young brother was among the first to take the field; he was mustered out of service only when peace was declared. The time that should have been spent by him in preparation for the work of manhood was passed amid the shock and smoke of battle, and he came out of the army, loving the life of a soldier, really knowing nothing else, and withal bearing written testimonials of his soldierly character and integrity from the officers of his Regiment. Those testimonials, I still hold.

You must often be wearied with such communications as mine; but please bear with me; I will be brief as possible.

After months of often impatient waiting and working he was commissioned L'ft. T. D. Shepherd; 11th Inf. and ordered to Richmond, Va. where he entered with enthusiastic ardor upon his duties. Being for some weeks somewhat unwell, he undertook his own case; his prescription was *ether*; he was discovered under its influence and reported to Gen. Terry, who made it a case of "INTOXICATION" and placed him under arrest. Fearing dishonorable dismissal, brother tendered his resignation, which, I am told, you accepted last week.[3] I have no wish to excuse my brother's error; tho' I do think there are palliating circumstances; moreover, he is a child of the Covenant, the son and brother of many prayers and withal a member of the M. E. Church and I cannot believe him to have been derelict, wilfully and habitually.

Will you not pardon—reinstate him?[4] Night and morning we pray for you as our President, give us the privilege of asking Divine blessing on our "*friend*!" I trust this may come under your own eye and hope I have not been biased in my statement by sisterly affection.

May that God whom we both acknowledge "bless and keep you; cause his face to shine upon you and grant you peace" in all the land whose good fortune it is to call you 'Ruler.' I would I could tell you how in our home-circles and in our hearts we cherish and love the name of Andrew Johnson, but even though I might, it would perhaps be mal a propos here.

Annie P. Shepherd.

ALS, DNA-RG94, ACP Branch, File S-79-CB-1869, T. D. Shepherd.

1. Unidentified.
2. Thomas D. Shepherd (1844–1917), a druggist, served during the war with the 70th Ill. Inf. and the 9th Ind. Cav. Powell, *Army List*, 583; CSR, Thomas D. Shepherd, RG94, NA.
3. In 1866 while serving as a second lieutenant in the 11th Inf., his group was detailed to keep the peace between blacks and whites in the Chimbarago Hill area. Instead he allowed his men to visit the brewery where they and he became intoxicated and were discovered by superiors. Rather than be tried, he was allowed to tender his resignation; however, it appears not to have been accepted. Powell, *Army List*, 583; Endorsements, Annie P. Shepherd to Johnson, Aug. 27, 1866, ACP Branch, File S-79-CB-1869, T. D. Shepherd, RG94, NA.
4. Shepherd continued to serve until June 18, 1866, when he resigned. In January 1869 Johnson recommended appointing Shepherd a second lieutenant. In March 1869 the request was cancelled by the secretary of war. Ibid.; Powell, *Army List*, 583.

From Gerrit Smith

Peterboro, N.Y.   August 24, 1866.

Honored Sir,

I have this day subscribed a memorial to yourself in behalf of Jefferson Davis. I have done so with great satisfaction—for I deem his very long confinement in prison without a trial an insult to the South, a very deep injustice to himself, and a no less deep dishonor to the Government and the country.

I trust that Mr. Davis may either have a speedy trial, or be admitted to bail. There are many men, who have no sympathy with his political views, and who opposed Slavery as strenuously as he upheld it, that would eagerly become his bail. I am one of them.

Gerrit Smith.

ALS, NcD-Jefferson Davis Papers.

From Henry A. Smythe

Private

New York, 24th Augt 1866

My dear Sir

A meeting has just been held in this office—of the Merchts—and others that have invited you to dine with them on Wednesday next.[1]

The Mayor[2] presided—& arrangts were made for your reception—

and for the full turn out of the military who will escort you through the city—to your hotel.

The dinner you have accepted (through the Secy of State—) is to be given at Delmonico's—and it seems to be understood that you & the party, stop there also.

Now I hope you will excuse me—& appreciate my motives—which are only to promote your cause. It strikes me I would stop at the Fifth Av hotel—(which was placed at your disposal early—) where you can return after dining at Delmonico's restaurant—(& where you would be escorted on arrival—) and where you can be serenaded—& what is more important—receive the many prominent citizens of New York—who may not be included in this perhaps rather exclusive affair.[3]

Do not think I am thin skined except for you—*for I am in it* & am in the dinner arrangment—but think you should stop at the largest & most central hotel—though you dine at another.[4]

H A Smythe

ALS, NRU-William Henry Seward Col.

1. For an account of the meeting of the "Citizens' and Merchants' Reception Committee," see *New York Herald*, Aug. 25, 1866. Among those present were Smythe, former collector Richard Schell, General Sandford, Surveyor Wakeman, businessman Alexander T. Stewart, and Mayor John T. Hoffman.

2. John T. Hoffman (1828–1888), lawyer, moved to New York City in 1849. A member of the Tammany Society, he served terms as city recorder (1861–65), mayor (1866–68) and governor (1869–73), before returning to his law practice. *DAB*.

3. As Smythe explained in a follow-up letter to Johnson, the President's appearance at the Fifth Avenue Hotel would at least "give '*the people*' a better opp[ortunit]y to see you." But Secretary Seward saw nothing wrong with the President's spending the night at Delmonico's Hotel, since "The House is certainly free from all prejudice. It was Genl [Winfield] Scotts home." Smythe to Johnson, Aug. 25, 1866, Johnson Papers, LC; Seward to [Johnson?], ca. Aug. 1866, William Henry Seward Col., NRU.

4. In the margins of this letter, Seward wrote: "It would now I think give great offence to change the plan. I would refer Smythe to Richard Schell." Three days before the President's scheduled visit to New York City, Seward warned Smythe against any changes in arrangements. In the end Johnson remained at Delmonico's, while several members of his official party spent the night at the Fifth Avenue Hotel. Seward to Smythe, Aug. 26, 1866, Tels. Sent, Sec. of War (M473, Roll 91), RG107, NA; *New York Herald*, Aug. 30, 1866.

From Thomas H. Benton, Jr.

Washington   Aug. 25th 1866

As I am about leaving the city I feel that it is due to the gentlemen who sent me the enclosed dispatch,[1] relative to the appointment of Col Small[2] as U. States Marshal for the State of Iowa, to lay it before you, having shown it to the Atty. General yesterday. He advised me that the impediment to Col Smalls appointment was that he had been rejected by the Senate when nominated for Collector of his (the 2d) District.[3] It is also due to the gentlemen whose names are appended to the dispatch to say that they are *leading* men in the District, three of them Democrats & one of them a Conservative Republican & all supporters of the Administration, & the last named the present Administration candidate for Congress[4] against Mr Price.[5] The applicants are both my friends[6] & both qualified for the office, but having recommended Col Small I cannot do otherwise than urge his claims. With this explanation I leave the matter with your Excellency & the Attorney General, and shall be satisfied with such disposition as you may deem proper to make of the case.[7]

Thomas H Benton Jr.

ALS, DNA-RG60, Appt. Files for Judicial Dists., Iowa, William E. Small.

1. Not located.
2. William E. Small (1822–1907) was in the lumber business in Iowa from 1856 until he joined the 10th Iowa Inf. in September 1861. He served as lieutenant colonel of these troops until discharged because of disability in August 1863. After the war he was justice of the peace, deputy U.S. assessor, and, for more than twenty years, in the grain business. Pension File, William E. Small, RG15, NA; CSR, William E. Small, RG94, NA.
3. Small was nominated as collector on January 31, 1866, but rejected by the Senate on March 6, 1866. Ser. 6B, Vol. 4: 328, Johnson Papers, LC.
4. New York native John P. Cook (1817–1872) went to Iowa, where he was admitted to the bar in 1842. He served a single term in Congress (1853–55) as a Whig. *BDAC*; *History of Scott County, Iowa* (Chicago, 1882), 610.
5. Hiram Price.
6. The other candidate was Joel M. Walker.
7. Small was not nominated as marshal, but he was nominated as assessor for the Second District of Iowa on February 25, 1867. The Senate, however, took no action. Ser. 6B, Vol. 4: 329, Johnson Papers, LC. See William H. Merritt to Johnson, Aug. 6, 1866.

From Robert J. Goode[1]

Fayette County Texas   August 25th 1866

Mr President

I held the Office of Assessor of Taxes under the so-called Confederate States, and considering myself one of the Excepted Classes to your Amnesty Proclamation on account *only* of having held said Office, I took the oath of Amnesty prescribed, made out my application for Pardon, obtained thereon the recommendation of Governor Hamilton, and sent it on with the Amnesty Oath, by mail, addressed to you, over a year ago.[2] Others here sent on by the same mail their applications, and have received their pardons, and of the Excepted Classes in this County, I am the only one that has not received a pardon, and as there was no opposition to my pardon, and nothing peculiar in my case, I fear that my application never reached you, and therefore I hereby renew it, and most respectfully pray your early action. I now wish to accept and qualify in a County Office here, and some question is made as to my right to do so, and hence my anxiety to be relieved as early as possible of my unpleasant position. I abide the results of the war—am loyal to the government of the United States—and support your restoration policy with all my heart. I have again taken the Amnesty Oath and herewith send it.[3]

Robt. J. Goode

ALS, DNA-RG59, Misc. Lets., 1789–1906 (M179, Roll 243).
    1. Virginia native Goode (c1829–fl1870) moved to Texas in 1860, favored secession, and briefly served as a private in the "Dixie Grays" in 1861. Appointed tax assessor for Fayette County, he held the post for at least three years. By 1870 he was clerking in a store. Amnesty Papers (M1003, Roll 53), Tex., Robert J. Goode, RG94, NA; 1870 Census, Tex., Fayette, La Grange, 26; Leonie R. Weyland and Houston Wade, *An Early History of Fayette County* (La Grange, Tex., 1936), 273–74.
    2. Goode wrote his letter and took the oath on September 1, 1865. Hamilton added his recommendation on October 20. Amnesty Papers (M1003, Roll 53), Tex., Robert J. Goode, RG94, NA.
    3. Goode had been pardoned on January 12, 1866. On September 14 Johnson ordered a certified copy of the pardon sent to him. Ibid.; Andrew K. Long endorsement, Sept. 14, 1866, Misc. Lets., 1789–1906 (M179, Roll 243), RG59, NA.

Response to National Labor League Committee[1]

[Washington, August 25, 1866][2]

I am very much obliged to you and the committee accompanying you for this visit, and for thus affording me an opportunity of making your acquaintance. I feel gratified that you thought proper to pay me so much respect and deference. In reply to the various propositions to which you have alluded, I will not attempt to make a speech or anything of the kind, but just in simple conversation refer you simply to my past acts, without making any professions or declarations now. I might rather invert the order and begin where you left off. For instance, with reference to the question of convict labor; that is a subject with which I have been familiar for a long time. Years ago—I think about the year 1843 or 1844—I introduced a resolution in Congress upon that subject,[3] not only to show its evil effects with regard to the manufacturing of articles, but even to show the deteriorating and degrading tendency it had upon labor and those employed in it. It is no new thing to me; and possibly I might claim priority with some of you upon that subject. Hence, there is no new expression I could make upon the subject, my own experience since having only confirmed me in what I then thought. I think labor ought to be elevated in the various forms in which it exists. It ought certainly to be elevated and respected. The laboring man ought to participate in the affairs of the General Government, because upon him all rests. As I said before, that is no new position to me, and my past life is an ample evidence of that. Now, in reference to the homestead policy and public lands, I was also an old laborer in that cause. As far back as 1846 I introduced the subject in Congress, and it was finally consummated in the House of Representatives in the shape of a bill. Notwithstanding that it met with taunts and jeers from a good many members, it finally passed in the House of Representatives. It then went to the Senate, and was there lost. Afterwards I was transferred from the House to the Senate, and I again took up the subject there, when it was passed, and, as you know, subsequently vetoed by Mr. Buchanan, then President of the United States.[4] My whole history every speech I made, and every vote I cast, clearly shows that I am against this wholesale monopolizing of the public lands, which should be given to individuals at low prices. I made many speeches discussing that subject, and you will see various estimates to prove that by dividing the lands among the settlers it would have the effect of not only increasing the revenue of the Government, but of bettering the condition of the people. It would give every man a domicile, a place for his wife and children, and make him a free and independent man. And touching the question of independence, we might return to other points upon which the people of the United States require emancipation. There are a great many cords and bonds upon the people that ought to be broken and thrown aside. You cannot be more sincere, more zealous, or more determined in this matter than I have been. A very short time ago I gave evidence of this,[5] and there is nothing that I could say now that could give any additional expression of what my feelings are upon the subject. It would be embracing the general idea by saying that I am in favor of, and have always been in favor of, that system that would have a tendency to advance and elevate the condition of the great masses. They ought to have a certain time for labor and a certain time for rest and intellectual culture. That is a true proposition and self evident to my mind, and I am glad the country has taken hold of it. The people ought to maintain their position. And here I cannot help acknowledging that although a democrat, there has been always one kind of aristocracy I was in favor of, and that is, the aristocracy of labor. The laboring men, when virtuous and intelligent, constitute the true aristocracy of the country. I like to see the aristocracy of the laborers, for upon them all rests and depends.

As to the precise number of hours that a person should work, that is a matter of debate which must be considered and settled as we go along. But the shortest number of hours possible, consistent with the interests of all, and that would enable the working portion of the people to better their condition, would receive my sanction. Summing up all the propositions, although I do not want to assume anything not strictly mine, I may say that if I am not in advance of some of you upon these subjects, I started at least as soon. All I can now say in this simple conversation is, that I thank you for the compliment you have paid me, and I assure you that you will ever have my sympathies and, as far as it goes, my influence, to carry out the great object of the work in which you are engaged. My acts correspond with what I now say. Once more, gentlemen, I thank you for the compliment you have paid me in coming here.

National Intelligencer, Aug. 27, 1866.

1. The National Labor League or Workingman's Convention convened in Baltimore on the 20th of August to discuss what were deemed necessary reforms, such as the eight-hour day. A committee of twenty, chaired by John Hinchcliffe, was appointed, and Johnson agreed to meet with them. *Chicago Tribune*, Aug. 11, 1866; *National Intelligencer*, Aug. 27, 1866; Hinchcliffe to Johnson, Aug. 22, 23, 1866, Johnson Papers, LC; Johnson to Hinchcliffe, Aug. 23, 1866, Tels. Sent, President, Vol. 3 (1865–68), RG107, NA.

2. Johnson's telegram on Thursday, August 23, said he would meet with them on Saturday next, i.e., the 25th of August. Ibid.

3. In Johnson's second congressional term, beginning in December 1845, he introduced a resolution against convict labor. He even considered abolishing the penitentiary system completely. Hans L. Trefousse, *Andrew Johnson: A Biography* (New York, 1989), 63.

4. On March 27, 1846, Johnson introduced "A Bill to authorize every poor man in the U.S. who is the head of a family, to enter one hundred and sixty acres of the public domain, 'without money and without price.'" Buchanan vetoed the Homestead Bill eventually sent to the President on June 22, 1860. Ibid.; Richardson, *Messages*, 5: 608–14.

5. See Johnson's Veto of the New York & Montana Iron Co. Land Purchase Bill, June 15, 1866, in ibid., 6: 416–22.

From James W. Throckmorton

Austin Texas   Augt 25th 1866.

Sir

The pressure of my official duties connected with, and arising out of the session of the Legislature, now being held, allows me but little time to give my attention to matters of general interest to the People of the State, not immediately connected with measures of legislation. But there is one subject of such serious moment to a large number of the citizens of this State, and in regard to which my sympathies are so deeply enlisted that I am impelled, not only by a sense of duty, but of humanity, to make an appeal to you in their behalf.

For a year past, the whole line of North Western Frontier of this State, has at one point and another, been the object of Indian attacks, characterized by their usual ferocity, resulting in robberies and murders and outrages even worse than murder.

I do not propose to inflict upon your Excellency a detailed recital of these out rages and atrocities, of which the people upon our frontier have all been witnesses, and many the sufferers and victims, but will satify myself with assuring you that full and indubitable testimony is before me, of the facts and of the attendant horrors.

Within the past three or four months, embolden by the impunity with which they had waged their savage warfare upon a defenseless people, the Indians have repeated their usual outrages, and depredations, at more frequent periods, at shorter intervals and with more aggravated atrocities, pushing indeed, in several instances, their forays into the very heart of the settlements driving off large herds of horses and cattle, in which consist the principal property of our frontier settlers, murdering men and carrying into captivity women & children.

The boldness and systamatic energy with which their movements are Conducted, the judgment with which they apply their force at points, and direct them into the settlements offering the richest and safest fields for plunder, suggest the opinion and encourage the belief that they are incited and led by white men, whose presence and guidance render these forays more successful, but in no degree mitigate the brutalities by which Indian warfare is usually marked. The success which has attended their recent inroads into the Settlements; the valuable spoils which they have taken and the almost intire impunity with which they have escaped, instead of satisfying, will no doubt, stimulate their Cupidity and set in motion still more numerous bodies of savages against our frontier.

Many settlers have already been driven from their homes and if this condition of things is allowed much longer to continue, will inevitably break up a broad belt of frontier, once settled by a Thriving and industrious population, and drive them back into the interior, a homeless and impoverished people.

I have addressed a communication to Maj Genl Wright,[1] Commanding the Department of Texas, on this subject, refering to him some of the representations coming from the frontier. He replied that he had no authority to establish new posts, the authority to do so residing with Maj Genl. Sheridan, Commanding the military Division, including Texas. He further stated that there was not sufficient force in Texas for the protection of her frontier, unless the policy of maintaining interior garrisons was discontinued. I replied to Genl. Wright, requesting him to refer my letter to Genl. Sheridan and through him to the Government.

In this connection I beg the privilege of saying a word to your Excellency, on the Policy of maintaining interior garrisons, in this State, and expressing my deliberate and unqualified conviction, that to enforce the laws, and preserve order, not a soldier is required at any interior point in this State. Order can be preserved and the laws promptly and justly enforced by the agency of our Civil and Judicial Officers, without the presence or aid of arms. Our people are now loyal, their interest and their Conscientiousness will keep them so, even if the bitter experience of the immediate past, had brought to them no profitable lesson.[2]

I hope it may not be amiss briefly to present my views as to the number and description of troops necessary, in my opinion, to secure adequate protection to our frontier. Exclusive of the requisite garrisons on the route to El Paso which is a measure of National interest and importance, as well as auxilliary to a general system of protection, it is believed that a line covering the settlements from a point on the Northern boundary of the State: say the confluence of the Wichita and Red River to Fort Clarke on the route to El Paso, can be garrisoned by two Regiments of mounted men. These if made efficient will yield the desired protection to that line. It will also be necessary to station a force at some proper point designated, on our Northern frontier, for the reason that large bodies of Indians assemble in the winter at, and near the Wichita Mountains in easy striking distance of these settlements.

In conclusion I beg to press this subject upon the early and favorable consideration of your Excellency.[3]

J. W. Throckmorton   Governor of the State of Texas

ALS, DNA-RG108, Lets. Recd., Book D, No. 85 (1866).

1. Horatio G. Wright.

2. "Interior garrisons" were those posted to protect freedmen from attacks and exploitation by whites. Sheridan was reluctant to send more troops to the frontier since he felt that reports of outrages there were exaggerated for the specific purpose of removing troops from the interior and interfering with Reconstruction. William L. Richter, *The Army in Texas During Reconstruction, 1865–1870* (College Station, Tex., 1987), 69, 88.

3. Throckmorton's request for troops for the frontier was not answered as quickly as he wished. Therefore, he sent a telegram to Johnson on September 26 informing the President that he was about to raise a thousand-man militia for frontier defense, a threat he attempted to carry out despite the vehement objections of Sheridan. In 1867 Sheridan sent most of his cavalry to the frontier, reactivating several pre-Civil War posts and beginning the construction of several others. Throckmorton to Johnson, Sept. 26, 1866, Tels. Recd., President, Vol. 5 (1866–67), RG107, NA; Stanton to Throckmorton, Oct. 11, 1866, Tels. Sent, Sec. of War (M473, Roll 91), RG107, NA; Stanton to Grant, Oct. 11, 1866, Johnson Papers, LC; Utley, *Frontier Regulars*, 166–68; Richter, *Army in Texas*, 66–71. For an account of frontier Indian problems under Throckmorton's predecessor, see Andrew J. Hamilton to Johnson, Mar. 1, 1866, *Johnson Papers*, 10: 202–3.

From Albert M. Lea[1]

Galveston, Texas, August 26th 1866.

Sir,

I graduated at the U.S. Mil. Academy in 1831, and remained in the Army until 1836,[2] when I resigned.

In 1861, as a Citizen of Texas,[3] I found myself obliged to choose between the conflicting authorities of my State and that of the United States. Although opposed to Secession, I deemed it my duty to support the government *de facto* under which I lived, and deeming it cowardly to shrink from duty, I entered the Army of the Confederacy, and remained therein, as a Major on Staff duty, until the surrender of the forces in Texas, in 1865,[4] when I came to Galveston, where I have since remained.

The force of Arms having decided the questions in controversy, I accepted the decision as final, and desire to live henceforth as a loyal Citizen of the United States; and to that end respectfully request that the benefit of Amnesty and pardon contained in your proclamation of the 29th May 1865, may be extended to me, being liable to none of its exceptions, but that just named, of having graduated at West Point.[5]

Albert Miller Lea

ALS, DNA-RG94, Amnesty Papers (M1003, Roll 54), Tex., Albert M. Lea.

1. Lea (1808–1891), a native of East Tennessee, studied at East Tennessee College and, in the 1840s, taught mathematics there. Neal O'Steen, "The Leas of Tennessee," *Tennessee Alumnus*, 57 (Fall 1977): 28–30; O'Steen, "The Leas of Tennessee: A Civil War Tragedy," ibid., 58 (Winter 1978): 26–28.

2. While in the service Lea participated in an expedition to present-day Iowa, Minnesota, and Wisconsin, with the result that both a Minnesota lake and town are named "Albert Lea." O'Steen, "The Leas of Tennessee," 29–30.

3. He was in Texas as the chief engineer for a prospective railroad. O'Steen, "Leas: A Civil War Tragedy," 26.

4. Lea was involved with the defenses of Cumberland Gap and Chattanooga and then sent to do engineering in Texas. The Confederate government seems rather pointedly to have ignored or underutilized Lea's skills. Ibid., 26–28.

5. Five Galveston officials endorsed Lea's request. He was pardoned on September 20, 1866, and remained in Texas for the rest of his life, engaging in civil engineering and other projects. Ibid., 28; Amnesty Papers (M1003, Roll 54), Tex., Albert Miller Lea, RG94, NA.

From Black Citizens of Tennessee[1]

Nashville, Tenn. 27th Augt. A.D. 1866

We your Petitioners, Colored Citizens of Tennessee, In view of late promises made to us by the "Executive" Ask as our first and only favor, that Brvt. Major Gen Clinton B Fisk, be retained as Commissioner of the Bureau of this State;[2] beleiving that our entire future well being depends upon the policy he has in the past so faithfully carried out toward us, and our White fellow Citizens.[3]

Thus have we enrolled & Subscribed the names of 143 of the Business Colored Citizens of Nashville & Vicinity, and had we time Could Swell the number to thousands, for throughout the State it is the wish for the continuation of the Person named in the Petition as soon as it was known to them that Gen C B Fisk's time had expired.[4]

Pet, DNA-RG107, Lets. Recd., Executive (M494, Roll 85).

1. Apparently the collection of signatures occurred at a meeting of blacks, for when Frank Parrish signed his name he added, "Pres. of the Meeting." Unfortunately, no published account of such a gathering is available.

2. In late August it was publicly known that Fisk had received orders from the War Department to relinquish his Freedmen's Bureau post and to be mustered out by September 1. See *Nashville Press and Times*, Aug. 28, 1866.

3. At this point in the document are the scores of signatures. The concluding paragraph follows the signatures.

4. On August 29 a group of black leaders invited Fisk to address them at the state capitol building on Saturday, September 1. General Fisk delivered his farewell address to a very large assemblage of black citizens in the house chamber at the capitol. In mid-September, John R. Lewis replaced Fisk. *Nashville Press and Times*, Sept. 1, 3, 19, 1866; Howard to Lewis, Sept. 14, 1866, Records of the Commr., Lets. Sent (M742, Roll 2), RG105, NA.

From James Dixon

Hartford Aug 27, 1866

Dear Sir,

Before you leave for your western tour, I desire to call your attention to a subject of great importance. I allude to the effect produced on the public mind by the late riot at New Orleans. The radical press is exciting popular opinion most deeply, and I fear we are losing ground in consequence of it. What I would suggest is that some action be taken to show that the administration is unjustly accused in regard to it. Some such step as the displacement of Mayor Monroe, by orders through Gen Sheridan, would entirely counteract the radical effort to make Capital.[1]

Depend upon it, Sir, we are in danger of losing thousands of votes in the coming elections by the falsehoods circulated on this subject. It is all important that this effect should be counteracted.

James Dixon

ALS, DLC-JP.
1. General Sheridan did remove Mayor John T. Monroe, but not until March 27, 1867. Joseph G. Dawson, III, *Army Generals and Reconstruction: Louisiana, 1862–1877* (Baton Rouge, 1982), 47.

From George R. Helmick[1]

Washington   Aug 27th 1866

Sir,

As I do not wish to occupy your time by seeking a personal interview, I take this method of makeing to you, a statement of facts regarding an application which I made for a position in the Quartermasters Dept.

When you issued your order for the appointment of honorably discharged to positions in the Depts,[2] I was in Phila. out of employment, and was advised by friends to come here and make an application for a position, which I did. The first I made by letter to you[3] (not knowing at the time the proper method of proceeding.) which was kindly refered by you to the Interior Dept. After waiting for two weeks, I called on Secretary Harlan, when he informed me that there was no vacancy, and as there was some two or three hundred applications ahead of mine, he could give me no hope. I then addressed you again,[4] asking you to transfer my application to some other Dept. In a couple of weeks, I received a communication from the Asst Sec. of the Treasury,[5] telling me that he could give me no encouragement to hope for a position.

After all this had taken place I was told by a friend the proper way to proceed. I then made an application to Gen Eaton[6] of the subsistance Dept. which was endorsed by the Hon Edgar Cowan and the Hon Samuel Randall of Pa. together with a letter from, the Hon James Dixon of Conn. (all knowing my claims for a position). This application I carried personally to Gen Eaton. He said that he would like very much to comply with the request of the gentlemen named, but it was impossible as they were then discharging clerks, from that Dept but he kindly refered the application to Gen Meigs, by endorseing it with the request that he might find a vacancy for me in his Dept.[7] I then carried the application to Gen Meigs, who informed me that the Secretary of War, made all the appointments for the Quarter Masters Dept., and that it would be necessary for me to make out another application to him (Gen Meigs) and he would refer my papers to the Sec of War,[8] "And then in a few days, if I would get one of my endorsors to give me a letter to the Secretary calling his attention to my application, that he had no doubt that the Secretary would recomend me to him for an appointment." I waited one week and then carried the Hon Secretary a letter from the Hon Mr Cowan, calling the Secretary's attention to my application, and asking that I might be appointed to a position.[9] The Secretary told me that they were making no appointments in that Dept—only to disabled Soldiers. I informed him that I was a disabled, honorably discharged Soldier. He then asked me if I had a medical certificate to that effect. I told him that I had not but I could procure one from the surgeon[10] who attended me at the time of my injurys. He requested me to do so, "*And he would recomend me to Genl. Meigs for an appointment to the first vacancy in his Dept.*" I wrote to Philadelphia for the required Certificate and in a few days, received it from the surgeon who attended me. I carried it together with one from surgeon Baxter[11] of this city to the Secretary, and after looking over them he said that he would place them on *file*. I undertook to remind him of what he had said at the former interview but he appeared to be in a bad humor and would not listen to me. This interview discouraged me a little, but I did not give the matter up, but got another letter from the Hon James Dixon[12] which I carried to Gen Eckart[13] the Asst Sec. He read the letter but could do nothing for me. I then waited a week or so and not hearing any thing from my application, I came to the conclusion to withdraw them[14] and lay the matter before you which I have done and enclosed you will find the papers of application just as I received them from the War Dept. If you can do nothing for me yourself I would like you once more to refer my papers to the Interior Dept.

I regret that I have made this statement so long but I hope that you will give it the attention which I think it merits, as well as a favorable consideration.

Geo R Helmick

372 north 9th st   Washington D C

ALS, DNA-RG107, Appls. Sec. of War (1847–87), George R. Helmick.

1. Probably Helmick (c1832–c1869), who served as a second lieutenant in the 95th Pa. Inf. from the fall of 1861 to the fall of 1862. There is confusion over whether he received an appointment in Washington because his father, of the same name, was employed as a clerk in the Agriculture Department from 1866 until his death in 1875. Washington, D.C., directories (1866–75); *Evening Star* (Washington), Oct. 27, 1875; *Off. Army Reg.: Vols.*, 3: 920; CSR, George R. Helmick, RG94, NA.

2. See Circular *re* Appointments to Office, Apr. 7, 1866, *Johnson Papers*, 10: 368.

3. Probably the letter which was received at the White House on April 13 and referred to the interior secretary three days later. Ser. 6A, Vol. B: 116, Johnson Papers, LC.

4. Probably the letter received at the President's office on May 21 and referred to the secretary of the treasury. Ibid., 120.

5. A letter from William E. Chandler or John F. Hartley has not been found. Hartley (b. c1810) was a native of Maine. 1870 Census, D.C., Washington, 3rd Ward, 576.

6. Amos B. Eaton.

7. See James Dixon to A. B. Eaton, May 28, 1866; Helmick to Eaton, June 5, 1866, Civilian Personnel Div., Personnel Papers, RG107, NA.

8. Helmick to Montgomery C. Meigs, June 9, 1866, ibid.

9. Edgar Cowan to Edwin M. Stanton, June 15, 1866, ibid.

10. Not identified.

11. Jedediah H. Baxter (1837–1890) served in the U.S. Army from 1861 until his death, at which time he had attained the rank of brigadier general surgeon general. Wallace, *North American Authors*, 32; Powell, *Army List*, 184. For his medical statement, dated June 26, 1866, see Civilian Personnel Div., Personnel Papers, RG107, NA.

12. Dixon to Stanton, July 11, 1866, ibid.

13. Thomas T. Eckert.

14. On July 20 Helmick wrote Eckert once more calling attention to his application. A month later, on August 21, he withdrew his application. See Helmick to Eckert, July 20, 1866; Helmick to Stanton, Aug. 21, 1866, ibid.

From John C. Jacobi[1]

Kalorama U.S. General Hospital[2]

Washington DC   August 27th 1866

The petition of John C. Jacobi, Hospital Chaplain, Kalorama Hospital, Washington DC. respectfully represents:

That he is a regularly ordained Clergyman of the Protestant Episcopal Church in good standing, and connected with the Diocese of New York, a Native of Poland and Citizen of the United States since 1825.

That in 1837, he volunteered from Muscogee County, Georgia, as a sergeant in a Company known as the "Muscogee Blues" in the war with the Creek Indians,

That in 1862 he was commissioned as Chaplain of the 4th New York Cavalry and was honorably discharged from said Regiment by reason of disability,

That in 1864, after recovering his health, he was appointed by President Lincoln, Hospital Chaplain and assigned to duty at Kalorama Hospital, then and now, used as a Hospital for cases of Small Pox and has during his term of service at that post, been in constant attendance as Chaplain, administering to the wants, both spiritual and temporal, of the patiens, many of whom were cases of most virulent and aggravated nature,

That, for the past year, most of the patiens, in this Hospital have been colored, so that this petitioner has had an oppertunity of becoming acquainted with the caracteristics and deposition of this class more fully than usually happens to Officers in the Army.

In view of these facts, which your petioner believes should entitle him to a careful hearing, and believing that the present Hospital at Kalorama is about being discontinued, your petioner would respectfully request an appointment as Chaplain to one of the Colored Regiments, provision for which is now made by law, or for a transfer to the Freedmen's Bureau.

John C. Jacobi   Chaplain Kalorama Hosp.

U.S.A. Washington DC.

LS, DNA-RG94, ACP Branch, File J-755-1874, John Jacobi.

1. Jacobi (d. 1874) served as chaplain for the 9th Cav., a new black regiment, from March 1867 to his retirement in July 1868. Powell, *Army List*, 396–97; Howard R. Lamar, ed., *The Reader's Encyclopedia of the American West* (New York, 1977), 819.

2. Before the war Kalorama was an estate north of Washington. Kalorama served as the hospital where contagious diseases were isolated, especially during the smallpox epidemic in Washington in 1863. Margaret Leech, *Reveille in Washington, 1860–1865* (New York, 1941), 14, 205, 283.

From Jones M. Withers et al.[1]

Mayors Office City of Mobile Ala
Aug 27th 1866

Supplies from New Orleans are indispensable. We desire that boats be permitted to run for freight without passengers. Quarantine officers to visit each boat and none of the crew when sick to be brought to the City not deemed necessary, but if required the boats can meet at quarantine & exchange freight. The above application was made to Maj Gen Woods[2] & the reply was no authority to change the time of Quarantine of fifteen days for all vessels from New Orleans.[3]

J M Withers   Mayor
Geo A Ketchem Md   President Board Health
R Milon [*sic*] MD   Secy Board Health

Tel, DLC-JP.

1. Besides Withers (1814–1890), a West Point graduate, lawyer, Mexican War colonel, and Confederate general, the signers were Mobile physicians George A. Ketchum (1825–1906) and Robinson Miller (1824–1871). Ketchum was also a prewar city council member and a teacher at the Medical College of Alabama. Warner, *Gray*; *NCAB*, 8: 211; Mobile directories (1861–72); Helen A. Thompson, comp., *Magnolia Cemetery* (New Orleans, 1974), 187.

2. Charles R. Woods.

3. A quarantine on all ships from the West Indies had been in effect since early March 1866. In late July, Mayor Withers informed General Grant that there was "no valid reason for continuing the Quarantine." He asked if the Mobile city authorities could abolish it, but a subordinate replied that it "should be strictly enforced." However, four days after Withers's wire to Johnson, Stanton authorized General Woods to modify and relax quarantine regulations "as you on conference with the local authorities may deem right & proper." Simon, *Grant Papers*, 16: 38–39, 91–92; E. M. Stanton to C. R. Woods, Aug. 31, 1866, Tels. Sent, Sec. of War (M473, Roll 91), RG107, NA.

From Beriah Frazier[1]

Knoxville   Aug. 28" 1866

Dear Sir

Is General Cooper of this county holding an office under you as collector of internal revenue?[2] If so it may be well for you to know that he is traveling round all over this Congressional district, *trying* to make speaches in which he abuses you in most unmeasured terms. I heard him make a speach on last saturday in which he called you a treator and a tyrant.[3] Judge Houk also made a speach abusing you in languge which decency and propriety forbid me to repeat.[4] This was applauded by Genl Cooper with every evidence of intense satisfaction. All men should have a right to their opinion. But surely a decent respect for those on whose bounty they feed should induce them to abstain from calumny and vituperation against their benefactors.

B Frazier

ALS, DLC-JP.
    1. Frazier (1814–1886) was a physician who had practiced for a number of years in Hamilton County before moving to Knoxville some time prior to the war. A unionist, Frazier served as a delegate to the Knoxville convention in May 1861; after the war he served one term in the state senate (1865–67). He was also a trustee of East Tennessee University and an elder in the Presbyterian church. *BDTA*, 2: 308.
    2. Joseph A. Cooper held the post of collector at this time, but he was removed by Johnson and replaced in October 1866 with James T. Abernathy. Ironically, Cooper was reappointed in 1869 by President Grant. *DAB*. See also John Williams Jr. to Johnson, Oct. 23, 1866.
    3. This is probably a reference to the rally held outside of Knoxville on August 25; it had been organized by Frazier. Both Cooper and Leonidas C. Houk spoke at the meeting. *Brownlow's Knoxville Whig*, Aug. 29, 1866.
    4. The abusive language referred to by Frazier was probably Houk's declaration that "Andrew Johnson is as vile a traitor as Jeff. Davis or Benedict Arnold." Ibid.

From Hannibal Hamlin

Custom House. Boston.
Collector's Office Aug 28 1866

To The President,

    One year ago, you tendered to me, unsolicited on my part, the position of Collector of Customs for the District of Boston and Charlestown. I entered upon the duties of the office, and have endeavored faithfully to discharge the same; and I trust in a manner satisfactory to the public interested therein.

    I do not fail to observe the movements and efforts which have been and are now being made to organise a party in the country, consisting almost exclusively of those actively engaged in the late rebellion, and their allies who sought by other means to cripple and embarrass the Government. These classes of persons, with a small fraction of others, constitute the organisation.[1] It proposes to defeat and overthrow the Union Republican party, and to restore to power without sufficient guaranties for the future and protection to men who have been loyal, those who sought to destroy the Government.

    I gave all the influence I possessed to create and uphold the Union Republican party during the war, and without the aid of which our Government would have been destroyed and the rebelion a success.

    With such a party as has been inaugurated, and for such purposes, I have no sympathy, nor can I acquiesce in its measures by my silence. I therefore tender to you my resignation of the office of Collector of Customs for the District of Boston and Charlestown, to take effect from the time when a successor shall be appointed and qualified.[2]

H. Hamlin

ALS, DNA-RG56, Appts., Customs Service, Collector, Boston, Hannibal Hamlin.

1. A few days earlier the Maine delegation to the National Union Convention at Philadelphia had requested the President to remove Hamlin on account of "his well known hostility" to Johnson's policies. Bion Bradbury to Johnson, Aug. 25, 1866, Appts., Customs Service, Collector, Boston, Hannibal Hamlin, RG56, NA.

2. Received on September 4, the resignation was referred the following day to the Treasury Department. Once out of office, Hamlin publicly took the offensive against Johnson's administration in various speeches. Ser. 6A, Vol. C: 107, Johnson Papers, LC; Hunt, *Hamlin*, 204–5.

From Henry P. Ross[1]

Doylestown Bucks Co Pa   Aug 28. 1866.

It is earnestly to be desired that an immediate removal be made of the Collector of Internal revenue for the 5th District of Pennsylvania. The District is one of the closest—if not the closest in the State. The present incumbent, A. S. Cadwallader, is a radical—he has subscribed money for the purpose of aiding the election of Radical members of the State legislature. He has announced that an office holder, who is fool enough to let the President know he is opposed to him deserves to be guillotined; and to his friends, has explained this declaration by saying, "that if Radicals retain the offices until after the election, the President and his policy will be defeated, and that he is not going to aid the Administration by permitting it to turn him out." He is supported and sustained in office by the Editors of the Radical press of the County: and boasted but two days ago in his own office, that the Radicals Knew where he was—and the Conserva thought they knew.

In one word, if retained in office until after the election, every influence he can bring to bear will be exerted actively to defeat a Conservative member of Congress, and elect radicals to the Legislature.

As I will be the nominee of the Democratic party—and will be sustained by every friend of the Administration in the District, I have a deep interest in his removal—and further, that his removal shall be immediate.[2]

I ask therefore that a Commission shall be issued at once to William B. Brown of Bucks County.[3] This gentleman is now, and has always been, a member of the Republican party; he is a warm adherent of the Administration—of an old stock in the County—and will add to its Conservative vote. If the present incumbent be retained, it will decrease the Conservative strength in the District, to an extent which may be fatal.

I have written strongly, for I feel the necessity of immediate action; and I know that the action I recommend will aid me to an extent, which will insure success.[4]

Henry P. Ross

ALS, DNA-RG56, Appts., Internal Revenue Service, Collector, Pa., 5th Dist., William B. Brown.

1. Ross (1836–1882) was elected district attorney during the war. Twice an unsuccessful candidate for Congress, he served as judge of the seventh judicial district of Pennsylvania for nearly a dozen years preceding his death. William W.H. Davis et al., *History of Bucks County, Pennsylvania*, 2nd ed. rev. (3 vols., New York, 1905), 3: 82–83.

2. Cadwallader was removed, but not until after the election, owing to Secretary McCulloch's determination "to make no changes in the Revenue service." Actually, according to McCulloch, Cadwallader's commission expired with the adjournment of the Senate in July, and therefore he continued to function as collector without official standing. Ross to Johnson, Oct. 20, 1866, Appts., Internal Revenue Service, Collector, Pa., 5th Dist., Algernon S. Cadwallader, RG56, NA; Hugh McCulloch to Johnson, Dec. 20, 1866, ibid., Nathan C. James.

3. Less than a month later, Ross withdrew his support for Brown (d. 1875), who was also recommended by Senators Cowan and Buckalew, and instead urged the appointment of Nathan C. James, a Democrat. James was nominated by Johnson in January 1867 but rejected by the Senate later that same month. Ross to Johnson, Sept. 21, 1866, ibid.; Davis et al., *History of Bucks County*, 3: 352–53; Ser. 6B, Vol. 4: 83, Johnson Papers, LC.

4. Ross narrowly lost the race in Pennsylvania's Fifth Congressional District to Republican newcomer Caleb N. Taylor. *Guide to U.S. Elections*, 617.

From William Wheeler[1]

Faribault Minnesota   August 28th 1866

Your Excellency.

As a friend of your Administration and a firm supporter of your reconstruction policy, I make bold to address you asking and praying you to appoint to some office of trust and profit John C. Morrow Esq.[2] of Faribault Minnesota.

Mr. Morrow is a firm supporter of your administration amidst a community of radicals. He is a young and rising lawyer of this place. Served in the 92d Regt. O. Vol. Inf. until the close of the war. He was Lt. Col. of his regiment, and had command of it during Sherman's great Campaign. When his regiment was mustered out of the service soon after the great review at Washington, he came to Minnesota, and made this place his home.

Your doctrine of the status of the states lately in rebellion, and your line of policy to be pursued toward them is the *line* upon which the late war was successfully fought with the rebels; and is the line upon which the war with the radicals must be fought at the polls. I regret, however, to say that in Minnesota very few of the Federal office holders are your supporters. Most of them are rampant in denunciation of you and your policy. And much of the money they receive for their services will be used in the coming campaigns to defeat your friends, and further their own radical and incendiary ends. Col. Morrow is, and has been a republican. He supported your election for Vice President, and has supported your policy from the beginning. I had the honor to serve under him as Capt. in the 92d Regt. O. V. Inf. and, besides, having had a lifelong acquaintance with him, I know him to be honest, capable, and reliable; and that he would fill with honor any office your excellency might be graciously disposed to confer upon him.

It is impossible to send a list of petitioners praying for the removal of any present incumbent and the appointment of an Administration man;—Minnesota Republicans are generally radical—*here*, all are *radical*, with a few honorable exceptions.

The office of Surveyor General of Minnesota, is now held by a rampant radical.[3] This is quite a nice little office—paying a good salary and employing quite a number of Clerks and others at good salaries. This office could be as well filled by Col. Morrow as by a radical.

The office of Assessor of Internal Revenue for the 1st District of Minn. is another desirable office that might be filled by an Administration man.

Hoping that my recommendation may meet your approval, and that my friend Morrow may receive an appointment at your hands. . . .[4]

Wm. Wheeler

ALS, DNA-RG56, Appts., Internal Revenue Service, Assessor, Minn., 1st Dist., John C. Morrow.
1. Wheeler (1832–1923), an Ohio school teacher, served in the 92nd Ohio Vol. Inf. from July 1862 to October 1864, when he was discharged because of a disability. He was nominated as deputy postmaster at Faribault on April 11, 1867, but the Senate apparently took no action on the nomination. He later lived and taught in Kansas. Pension File, William Wheeler, RG15, NA; Ser. 6B, Vol. 4: 365, Johnson Papers, LC.
2. Morrow (b. c1840) was mustered in as captain of Co. C, 92d Ohio Inf., in September 1862. Later promoted to major and lieutenant colonel, he was mustered out of the service on June 10, 1865. In 1867 he was brevetted colonel of volunteers for gallantry in the battles before Atlanta. CSR, John C. Morrow, RG94, NA.
3. Levi Nutting (1819–*fl*1890), a native of Massachusetts, moved to Minnesota in 1853. Settling at Faribault two years later, Nutting engaged in farming and all sorts of manual and construction labor. He was appointed surveyor general in 1865 and after his tenure in that post served as a special agent for the Customs Department (1869–75). *The United States Biographical Dictionary and Portrait Gallery of Eminent and Self-made Men: Minnesota Volume* (New York, 1879), 277–79; John H. Stevens, *Personal Recollections of Minnesota and Its People, and Early History of Minneapolis* (Minneapolis, 1890), 200.
4. Nutting continued as surveyor general until 1869. There is no indication that Morrow was appointed to any office. *U.S. Biographical Dictionary: Minnesota*, 278.

From Israel Porter Williams[1]

East. Boston Masstts.   Augst. 28th 1866

Dear. Sir.

Allow me to present, to you, two petitions,[2] from the Merchants of Boston, and Salem, of the highest respecability, being the richest firms in the two places, representing at least $12,000,000, and who have contributed large sums of money in support of the Government, during the late war, and I think, you will agree with me, that their wishes should be complied with. At the present time there is not a man in the Custom House, from the Collector[3] down to the lowest office; but opposes your reconstruction policy. They know I differ from them, in regard to the reconstruction of this government, which I have no doubt is the reason that the Collector will not grant the prayer of the petitioners. I tell them if Charles Sumner and Henry Wilson and others of that stamp is allowed to go on in the manner they have done during the last Congress, and do not heed your advice, in regard to the reconstruction of this Government, we shall have nothing but anarchy and confusion, in this country the next four Years; and this is the opinion of very many good and true, National Union party men here; that we must have a National Union paty to keep in check these radicals in Congress, is conceded by all parties here. And it behoves the National Union party to see that all these Custom House officers are removed, for their is a host of them, and their places should be filled by, the National Union party which supports the president; and his policy of reconstruction: and that too before they have a chance to vote.

Trusting that this very respectful petition, from the Merchants of Boston and Salem, will receive your favourable, consideration.

What I have petitioned for, is the, Store Keepers birth, in the Bonded Stores on the *National, Dock*, and, *Warehouse Companies, North Wharf family Lombards North Wharf.*

Trusting you will be able to comply with the wishes, of the importing Merchants, of Boston & Salem, in the India & European Trade.— Excuse me my dear Sir for addressing this Letter and petition to you. For I have good cause to suppose that the Collector will not appoint a National Union man to office if he can help it. This office does not require the confirmation of the senate.[4]

Israel. Porter. Williams

ALS, DNA-RG56, Appts., Customs Service, Subofficer, Boston, Israel P. Williams.

1. Williams (*fl*1867) had briefly worked as a storekeeper in the Boston customhouse before the war. Boston directories (1858–67); *U.S. Off. Reg.* (1859).

2. Not found with this letter.

3. Hannibal Hamlin.

4. Williams's letter was routinely forwarded to the secretary of the treasury. Not hearing from Johnson after nearly two months, Williams wrote again, this time informing the President that he had been unsuccessful in obtaining an appointment and asking that his petitions be returned. The Treasury Department complied with this request shortly thereafter. Williams to Johnson, Oct. 23, 1866, Appts., Customs Service, Subofficer, Boston, Israel P. Williams, RG56, NA.

From James R. Doolittle
Confidential

Rochester N Y   Aug 29t 1866.

My dear Sir:

Gov Parsons[1] and myself are here on our way to Warsaw to speak in my old District in Western N.Y.[2]

I will join you at Buffalo.[3]

I am prompted to write you and in the spirit of that true friendship which enables me to speak in all frankness to say, that I hope you will not allow the excitement of the moment to draw from you any *extemporaneous speeches*.[4]

You are followed by the reporters of a hundred presses who do nothing but misrepresent. I would say nothing which had not been most carefully prepared beyond a simple acknowledgement for their cordial receptions.

Our Enemies your Enemies, have never been able to get any advantage from any thing *you ever wrote*. But what you have said extemporaneously in answer to some question or interruption has given them a handle to use against us.

My sincere desire for your triumphant success in your great work emboldens me thus to write you as none but a sincere friend would do.

J. R. Doolittle

ALS, DLC-JP.
1. Lewis E. Parsons.
2. In the past few days, Doolittle had attended at least two "ratification meetings" in New England, where he defended and sustained the reconstruction policy of the President and the action of the National Union Convention in Philadelphia. Both he and Parsons were scheduled to participate in the meeting in Warsaw, Wyoming County, on August 30. *New York Times*, Aug. 27, 29, 31, 1866.
3. Doolittle and his wife joined the President's tour in Buffalo on September 3. *New York Herald*, Sept. 4, 1866.
4. Apparently this was not the first time that the Senator had given the President such counsel, for Doolittle recalled having advised the President on the morning of February 22, 1866, not to make "any extemporaneous speech." On the eve of the President's departure for his Chicago trip, both Browning and Hugh McCulloch warned Johnson against making speeches on his tour. Randall, *Browning Diary*, 91, 93.

Speech in New York

[August 29, 1866]

GENTLEMEN—

The toast which has just been drank, and the kind sentiments which preceded it in the remarks of your distinguished representative, the Mayor of this city, is peculiarly, under existing circumstances, gratifying to me; and in saying it is gratifying to me I wish not to indulge in any vanity. If I were to say less I should not speak the truth, and it is always best to speak the truth and to give utterance to our sincere emotions. In

New York Mayor Hoffman welcomes Andrew Johnson to City Hall, August 1866
Frank Leslie's Illustrated Newspaper, September 15, 1866

being so kindly attended to, and being received as I have been received on this occasion—here to-night, and in your city to-day by such a demonstration—I am free to confess that this overwhelms me. But the mind would be exceedingly dull and the heart almost without an impulse that could not give utterance to something responsive to what has been said and been done. (Cheers.) And believe me on this occasion, warm is the heart that feels and willing is the tongue that speaks, and I would to God it were in my power to reduce the sentences and to language the feelings and emotions that this day and this night have produced. (Cheers.) I shall not attempt, in reference to what has been said and the manifestations that have been made, to go into any speech, or to make any argument before you on this occasion, but merely to give utterance to the sincere sentiments of my heart. I would that I could utter what I do feel in response to this outpouring of the popular heart which has gone forth on this occasion, and which will as a legend spread itself and communicate with every heart throughout the confederacy. (Cheers.) All that is wanting in the great struggle in which we are engaged is simply to develop the popular heart of the nation. It is like latent fire. All that is necessary is a sufficient amount of friction to develop the popular sentiment of the popular feeling of the American people. (Cheers.) I know, as you know, that we have just passed through a bloody, perilous conflict; that we have gentlemen who are associated with us on this occasion, who have shared their part and participated in these struggles for the preservation of the Union. (Great applause.) Here is the army (pointing to the right, where sat General Grant), and here the navy (pointing to the left in the direction of Admiral Farragut[)], they have performed their part in restoring the government to its present condition of safety and security; and will it be considered improper in me, on this occasion, to say that the Secretary of State has done his part. (Cheers.) As for the humble individual who now stands before you, and to whom you have so kindly and pleasantly alluded, as to what part he has performed in this great drama, in this struggle for the restoration of the government and the suppression of rebellion? I will say that I feel, though I may be included in this summing up, that the government has done its duty. (Cheers.) But though the government has done its duty, the work is not yet complete. Though we have passed through fields of battle, and at times have almost been constrained and forced to the conclusion that we should be compelled to witness the Goddess of Liberty, as it were, go scourged through fields of carnage and of blood, and make her exit, and that our government would be a failure; yet we are brought to a period and to a time in which the government has been successful. While the enemy have been put down in the field there is still a greater and more important task for you and others to perform. (Cheers.) I must be permitted—and I shall not trespass on you a moment—must be permitted to remark in this connection, that the government commenced the suppression of this rebellion for the express purpose of preserving the union of these States. (Cheers.) That was the declaration that it made, and under that declaration we went into the war and continued in it until we suppressed the rebellion. The rebellion has been suppressed, and in the suppression of the rebellion it has declared and announced and established the great fact that these States had not the power, and it denied their right by forcible or by peaceable means to separate themselves from the Union. (Cheers—"Good"). That having been determined and settled by the government of the United States in the field and in one of the departments of government—the executive department of the government—there is an open issue; there is another department of your government which has declared by its official acts, and by the position of the government, notwithstanding the rebellion was suppressed, for the purpose of preserving the Union of the States and establishing the doctrine that the States could not secede, yet they have practically assumed and declared, and carried up to the present point, that the government was dissolved and the States were out of the Union. (Cheers.) We who contend for the opposite doctrine years ago contended that even the States had not the right to peaceably secede, and one of the means and modes of possible secession was that the States of the Union might withdraw their representatives from the Congress of the United States, and that would be practical dissolution. We denied that they had any such right. (Cheers). And now when the doctrine is established that they have no right to withdraw, and the rebellion is at an end, and the States again assume their position and renew their relations, as far as in them lies, with the federal government, we find that when they present representatives to the Congress of the United States, in violation of the sacred charter of liberty which declares that you cannot even by amendment of the Constitution of the United States, deprive any one of them of their representation, we find that in violation of the Constitution, in express terms as well as in spirit, that these States of the Union have been and still are denied their representation in the Senate and in the House of Representatives. Will we then, in the struggle which is now before us, submit—will the American people submit to this practical dissolution, a doctrine that we have repudiated, a doctrine that we have declared as having no justice or right? The issue is before you and before the country. Will these States be permitted to continue and remain as they are in practical dissolution and destruction, so far as representation is concerned? It is giving the lie direct—it is subverting every single argument and position we have made and taken since the rebellion commenced. Are we prepared now, after having passed through this rebellion; are we prepared after the immense amount of blood that has been shed, are we prepared after having accumulated a debt of over three thousand millions of dollars; are we prepared after all the injury that has been inflicted upon the people North and South of this confederacy, now to continue this disrupted condition of the country? (Cries, "No! no!" "Never!" Cheers.)

Let me ask this intelligent audience here to-night, in the spirit of Christianity and of sound philosophy, are we prepared to renew the scenes
through which we have passed? ("No! no! no!") Are we prepared again
to see one portion of this government arrayed in deadly conflict against
another portion? Are we prepared to see the North arrayed against the
South, and the South against the North? Are we prepared, in this fair
and happy government of freedom and of liberty, to see man again set
upon man, and in the name of God lift his hand against the throat of his
fellow? Are we again prepared to see these fair fields of ours, this land that
gave a brother birth, again drenched in a brother's blood? (["]Never,
Never." Cheers.) Are we not rather prepared to bring from Gilead the
balm that has relief in its character and pour it into the wound? (Loud
cheering.) Have not we seen enough to talk practically of this matter?
Has not this array of the intelligence, the integrity, the patriotism, and
the wealth a right to talk practically? Let us talk about this thing. We
have known of feuds among families of the most respectable character,
which would separate, and the contest would be angry and severe, yet
when the parties would come together and talk it all over, and the differences were understood, they let their quarrel pass to oblivion; and we
have seen them approach each other with affection and kindness, and felt
gratified that the feud had existed, because they could feel better afterwards. (Laughter and applause.) They are our brethren. (Cheers.) They
are part of ourselves. (Hear, hear.) They are bone of our bone and flesh of
our flesh. (Cheers.) They have lived with us and been part of us from the
establishment of the government to the commencement of the rebellion.
They are identified with its history, with all its prosperity, in every sense
of the word. We have had a hiatus, as it were, but that has passed by and
we have come together again, and now, after having understood what the
feud was, and the great apple of discord removed; having lived under the
Constitution of the United States in the past they ask to live under it in
the future. May I be permitted to indulge in a single thought here? I will
not detain you a moment. ("Go on;" "Go on;" "Go on." Cheers.) You
(turning to Mayor Hoffman) are responsible for having invoked it.
(Laughter.) What is now said, gentlemen, after the Philadelphia Convention has met to pronounce upon the condition of the country? What is
now said? Why, that these men who met in that Convention were insin-
cere; that their utterances were worthless; that it is all pretense, and they
are not to be believed. When you talk about it, and talk about red-handed
rebels, and all that, who has fought these traitors and rebels with more
constancy and determination than the individual now before you—who
has sacrificed and suffered more? (Cheers.) But because my sacrifices and
sufferings have been great and as an incident growing out of a great civil
war, should I become dead or insensible to truth or principle? ("No, no."
Cheers.) But these men, notwithstanding they may profess now loyalty
and devotion to the union of the States, are said to be pretenders, not to

be believed. What better evidence can you have of devotion to the government than profession and action? Who dare, at this day of religious and
political freedom, to set up an inquisition, and come into the human
bosom to inquire what are the sentiments there? (Cheers.) How many
men have lived in this government from its origin to the present time that
have been loyal, that have obeyed all its laws, that have paid its taxes, and
sustained the government in the hour of peril, yet in sentiment would
have preferred a change, or would have preferred to live under some
other form of government? But the best evidence you can have is their
practical loyalty, their professions, and their actions. ("Good," "good,"
and applause.) Then, if these gentlemen, in convention from the North
and South, come forward and profess devotion to the Union and the Constitution of these States, when their actions and professions are for loyalty
who dare assume the contrary? (Cheers.) If we have reached that point in
our country's history, all confidence is lost in man. If we have reached that
point, that we are not to trust each other, and our confidence is gone, I tell
you your government is not as strong as a rope of sand. It has no weight; it
will crumble to pieces. This government has no [life?], this government
has no binding and adhesive power beyond the confidence and trust in
the people. (Hear, hear. Loud applause.) But these men who sit in convention, who sit in a city whose professions have been, in times gone by,
that they were a peace-loving and war-hating people; they said there, and
their professions should not be doubted, that they have reached a point at
which they say peace must be made; they have come to a point at which
they want peace on earth and good-will to men. (Loud cheers.) And now,
what is the argument in excuse? We won't believe you, and therefore this
dissolution, this practical dissolution, must be continued to exist. Your
attention to a single point. Why is a Southern man not to be believed?
and I do not speak here to-night because I am a Southern man, and because my infant view first saw the light of Heaven in a Southern State.
("They are to be believed.") Thank God, though I say it myself, I feel
that I have attained opinions and notions that are coextensive with all
these States, with all the people of them. (Great applause. The whole
audience rose and waved their handkerchiefs at this sentiment. Voice—
"That's the best thing to-night.") While I am a Southern man, I am a
Northern man—that is to say, I am a citizen of the United States—
(cheers), and I am willing to concede to all other citizens what I claim for
myself. (Sound.) But I was going to bring to your attention, as I am up,
and you must not encourage me too much (good, good), for some of those
men who have been engaged in this thing, and pretty well broken down,
requires sometimes a little effort to get them warmed. (Laughter.) I was
going to call your attention to a point. The Southern States or their
leaders proposed a separation. Now, what was the reason that they offered for that separation? Your attention. The time has come to think—
the time has come to consult our brain and not the impulses and passions

of the heart. The time has come when reason should bear sway, and feeling and impulse should be subdued. (Cheers.) What was the reason, or one of the reasons at least, that the South gave for separation? It was that the Constitution was encroached upon, and that they were not secured in their rights under it. That was one of the reasons, whether it was true or false—that was the reason assumed. We will separate from this government, they said, because we cannot have the Constitution executed; and, therefore, we will separate and set up the same Constitution, and enforce it under a government of our own. But it was separation. I fought then against those who proposed this. I took my position in the Senate of the United States, and assumed then as I have since, that this Union was perpetual, that it was a great magic circle never to be broken. (Cheers). But the reason the South gave was that the Constitution could not be enforced in the present condition of the country, and hence they would separate. They attempted to separate, but they failed. But while the question was pending they established a form of government; and what form of government was it? What kind of constitution did they adopt? Was it not the same, with a few variations as the Constitution of the United States? (Cheers, and "That's so.")—the Constitution of the United States under which they had lived from the origin of the government up to the time of their attempt at separation. They made the experiment of an attempted separation under the plea that they desired to live under that Constitution in a government where it would be enforced. We said you shall not separate, you shall remain with us, and the Constitution shall be preserved and enforced. (Cheers.) The rebellion has ceased. And when their arms were put down by the army and navy of the United States, they accepted the terms of the government. We said to them, before the termination of the rebellion, "Disband your armies, return to your original position in the government, and we will receive you with open arms." The time came when their armies were disbanded under the leadership of my distinguished friend on the right (General Grant.) (Three cheers for General Grant.) The army and the navy dispersed their forces. What were the terms of capitulation? They accepted the proposition of the government and said, "We have been mistaken; we selected the arbitrament of the sword, and that arbiter has decided against us, and that being so, as honorable and manly men we accept the terms you offer us." The query comes up, will they be accepted? Do we want to humiliate them and degrade them and tread them in the dust? ("No, no," cheers) I say this, and I repeat it here to-night—I do not want them to come back into this Union a degraded and debased people. (Loud cheers). They are not fit to be a part of this great American family if they are degraded and treated with ignominy and contempt. I want them when they come back to become a part of this great country an honored portion of the American people. I want them to come back with all their manhood—then they are fit, and not without that to be a part of these United States. (Cheers—

three cheers for Andrew Johnson.) I have not, however approached the point that I intended to mention and I know I am talking too long. ("Go on," "go on," "go on."[)] Why should we distrust the Southern people and say they are not to be believed? I have just called your attention to the Constitution under which they were desirous to live, and that was the Constitution of their fathers, yet they wanted it in a separate condition. Having been defeated in bringing about that separation and having lost the institution of slavery, the great apple of discord, they now, in returning, take up that Constitution under which they always lived, and which they established for themselves even, in a separate government. Where, then, is the cause for distrust? Where, then, is the cause for the want of confidence? Is there any "No, no." I do not come here to-night to apologize for persons who have tried to destroy this government; and if every act of my life, either in speeches or in practice, does not disprove the charge that I want to apologize for them, then there is no use in a man's having a public record. (Cheers.) But I am one of those who take the Southern people with all their heresies and errors, admitting that in rebellion they did wrong. The leaders coerced thousands and thousands of honest men into the rebellion who saw the old flag flap in the breeze for the last time with unfeigned sorrow, and welcomed it again with joy and thanksgiving. The leaders betrayed and led the Southern people astray upon this great doctrine of secession. We have in the West a game called hammar and anvil and anvil and hammar, and while Davis and others were talking about separation in the South, there was another class, Phillips, Garrison, and men of that kind, who were talking about dissolution in the North; and of these extremes one was the hammer and the other was the anvil, and when the rebellion broke out one extreme was carrying it out, and now that it is suppressed the other class are still trying to give it life and effect. I fought those in the South who commenced the rebellion, and now I oppose those in the North who are trying to break up the Union. (Cheers.) I am for the Union. I am against all those who are opposed to the Union. (Great applause.) I am for the Union, the whole Union, and nothing but the Union. (Renewed cheering.) I have helped my distinguished friend on my right, General Grant, to fight the rebels South, and I must not forget a peculiar phrase that he was going to fight it out on that line. (Applause and laughter.) I was with him, and I did all that I could; and when we whipped them at one end of the line, I want to say to you that I am for whipping them at the other end of the line. (Great laughter and applause.) I thank God that if he is not in the field, militarily speaking, thank God he is civilly in the field on the other side. (Cheers for Grant.) This is a contest and struggle for the Union, for the union of these States. (Applause.) The North can't get along without the South, and the South can't get along without the North. ("That's so," and applause.) I have heard an idea advanced that if we let the Southern members of Congress in they will control the government. Do you want to be governed by rebels? (Cries of "Never," "no, no.") We want to let loyal men in—("hear, hear"), and none but loyal men. ("Good, good.") But, I ask here to-night, in the face of this intelligent audience, upon what does the face of the observation rest, that men coming in from the South will control the country to its destruction? Taking the entire delegation of the South, fifty-eight members, what is it compared with the two hundred and forty-two members of the rest of the Union? ("Good boy.") Is it complimentary to the North to say we are afraid of them? Would the free States let in fifty-eight members from the South that we doubt, that we distrust, that we have no confidence in? If we bring them into the government, these fifty-eight representatives, are they to control the two hundred and forty-two? There is no argument that the influence and talent and the principles they can bring to bear against us, placing them in the worst possible light—(A Voice—The Sumner argument)— can be a cause for alarm. We are represented as afraid of these fifty-eight men, afraid that they will repudiate our public debt; that they can go into the Congress of the United States under the most favorable conditions they could require, the most offensive conditions to us, and could overwhelm a majority of a hundred and fifty to a hundred and eighty—(a voice—"ridiculous")—that these men are going to take charge of the country. Why it is croaking; it is to excite your fears, to appeal to your prejudice. Consider the immense sums of money that have been expended, the great number of lives that have been lost, and the blood that has been shed; that our bleeding arteries have been stayed and tied up; that commerce, and mechanical industry, and agriculture, and all the pursuits of peace restored, and we are represented as cowards enough to clamor that if these fifty-eight men are admitted as the representatives of the South the government is lost. We are told that our people are afraid of the people of the South; that we are cowards. (Cries of "We are not.") Did they control you before the rebellion commenced? Have they any more power now than they had then? Let me say to this intelligent audience here, to-night, I am no prophet, but I predicted at different times, in the beginning of the late rebellion, what has been literally fulfilled. (Cries of "That's so."[)] I told the Southern people years ago, that whenever they attempted to break up this Union; whenever they attempted to do that, even if they succeeded, that the institution of slavery would be gone. (Good, good.) Yes, sir, (turning to Mr. Seward) you know that I made that argument to Jeff. Davis. You will bear witness to the position I then occupied.

Mr. Seward—I guess so. (Applause.)

Mr. Johnson—Yes, and you were among the few that gave me encouragement. (Applause.) I told them then that the institution of slavery could not survive an attempt to break up this Union. They thought differently. They put up a stake; what was it? It was four millions of slaves, in which they had invested their capital. Their investment in the institution of slavery amounted to three thousand million of dollars. This they put up at stake and said they could maintain it by separating these States. That was the experiment; what are the facts of the result? The Constitution still exists. (Great cheering.) The Union is still preserved. (Cheers.) They have not succeeded in going out, and the institution of slavery is gone. (Hear, hear.) Since it has been gone they have come up manfully and acknowledged the fact in their State conventions and organizations, and they ratify us full now and forever. (Cheers.) I have got one other idea to put right alongside of this (Applause and laughter.) You have got about $3,000,000,000. ("That's so") How are you going to preserve the credit of that? Will you tell me. (Voices—"You tell us.") How are you to preserve the credit of this $3,000,000,000? Yes, perhaps when the account is made up your ddbt will be found $3,000,000,000 or $4,000,000,000,000. Will you tell me how you are to secure it, how the ultimate payment of the principal and interest of this sum is to be secured? Is it by having this government disrupted. (Mr. Stewart[1] and others—"No, no.") Is it by the division of these States? ("No.") Is it by separating this Union into petty States? ("No.") Let me tell you here tonight, my New-York friends, I tell you that there is no way by which these bonds can be ultimately paid, by which the interest can be paid, by which the national debt can be sustained, but by the continuity and perpetuity and by the complete union of these States. (Applause.) Let me tell you who fall into this fallacy, and into this great heresy, you will reap a more bitter reward than the Southern brethren have reaped in putting their capital into slavery.

Mr. Seward—(*sotto voce*)—The *argumentum ad hominem*. Good.

Mr. Johnson—Pardon me, I do not exaggerate. I understand this question. You who play a false part, now the great issue is past, you who play into the hands of those who wish to dissolve the government, to continue the disreputable conditions to impair and destroy the public credit. Let us unite the government and you will have more credit than you need. (Applause.) Let the South come back with its great mineral resources; give them a chance to come back and bear a part, and I say they will increase the national resources and the national capacity for meeting these national obligations. I am proud to say on this occasion, not by way of flattery, to the people of New-York, but I am proud to find a liberal and comprehensive and patriotic view of this whole question on the part of the people of New-York. I am proud to find, too, that here you don't believe that your existence depends upon aggression and destruction; that while you are willing to live, you are willing to let others live. (Applause.) You don't desire to live by the destruction of others. Some have grown fat, some have grown rich by the aggression and destruction of others. It is for you to make the application, and not me. These men talk about this thing and ask what is before you? What is before you? New-York, this great State, this great commercial emporium—I was asking your Mayor to-day the amount of your taxation, and he informs me it is eighteen millions of dollars! Where did your government start from but the other day? Do you remember that when General Washington was inaugurated President, that your annual bill was $2,500,000 for the entire general government? Yet to-day I am told that my distinguished friend on my left controls the destinies of a city whose taxes amount to $18,000,000, and whose population numbers four millions—double what the entire nation had at the time when it commenced its existence.

General Sandford[2]—Our taxation by the general government is fifty millions.

Mr. Johnson—I am simply trying to get at the amount collected to sustain your municipal establishment. Thus may we advance, entertaining the principles which are co-extensive with the States of this Union, feeling like you that our system of government comprehends the whole people, not merely a part. (Applause.) New-York has a great work to perform in the restoration of this great Union. As I have told you, they who talk about destroying the great elements that bind this government together, deny the power, the inherent power of the government, which will, when its capacities are put to the test, re-establish and re-adjust its position, and the government be restored. (Applause.) I tell you that we shall be sustained in this effort to preserve the Union. It would be just about as futile to attempt the resistance of the ocean wave, or to check the wind, as to prevent the result I predict. You might as well attempt to turn the Mississippi back upon its source as to resist this great law of gravitation that is bringing these States back and be united with us as strong as ever. I have been called a demagogue, and would to God that there were more demagogues in the land to save it. (Applause.) The demonstration here to-day is the result of some of these demagogical ideas; that the great mass of the people when called to take care of the people will do right.

A Voice—Sure as you are born. (Laughter.)

Mr. Johnson—I tell you you have commenced the grand process now. I tell those present who are croaking and talking about individual aggrandizement, and perpetuation of party. I tell them that they had better stand from under—(laughter and cheers)—they had better get out of the way (cheers); the government is coming together, and they cannot resist it. Sometimes, when my confidence gives out, when my reason fails me, my faith comes to my rescue, and tells me that this government will be perpetuated, and this Union preserved. (Cheers). I tell you here to-night, and I have not turned philanthropist and fanatic, that men sometimes err, and can again do right; that sometimes the fact that men have erred is the cause of making them better men. (Applause.) I am not for destroying all men, or condemning to total destruction all men who have erred once in their lives. I believe in the memorable example of Him who came with peace and healing on his wings; and when he descended and found men condemned unto the law, instead of executing it, instead of shedding the blood of the world, he placed himself upon the cross, and died that man might be saved. If I have pardoned many, I trust in God that I have erred on the right side. If I have pardoned many, I believe it is all for the best interests of the country; and so believing and convinced that our Southern brethren were giving evidence by their practice and profession that they were repentant, in imitation of Him of old who died for the preservation of men. I exercised that mercy which I believed to be my duty. I have never made a prepared speech in my life, and only treat these topics as they occur to me. The country, gentlemen, is in your hands. The issue is before you. I stand here to-night, not in the first sense in the character of the Chief Magistrate of the nation, but as a citizen, defending the restoration of the Union and the perpetuation of the Constitution of my country. Since becoming the Chief Magistrate I have tried to fulfill my duty, to bring about reconciliation and harmony. My record is before you. You know how politicians will talk; and if you people will get right, don't trouble yourselves about the politicians, for when the people get right the politicians are very accommodating. (Cheers.) But let me ask this audience here to-night what am I to gain by taking the course I am taking if it was not patriotic and for my country? Pardon me, I talk to you in plain parlance. I have filled every office in this government. You may talk to me as you will, and slander—that foul whelp of sin—may subsidize; a mercenary press may traduce and vilify, mendacious and unprincipled writers may write and talk, but all of them cannot drive me from my purpose. (Bravo and cheers.) What have I to gain, I repeat? From the position of the lowest alderman in your city to President of the United States I have filled every office to the country. Who can do more? Ought not men of reasonable ambition to be satisfied with this? And ought not I to be willing to quit right here, so far as I am concerned? (Applause.) I tell this audience here to-night, that the cup of my ambition has been filled to overflowing, with the exception of one thing. Will you hear what that is? (Cries of "yes," and "what is it?") At this particular crisis and period of our country's history, I find the Union of these States in peril. If I can now be instrumental in keeping the possession of it in your hands, in the hands of the people; in restoring prosperity and advancement in all that makes a nation great, I will be willing to exclaim, as Simeon did of old— (Three cheers)—as Simeon did of old, of him who had been born in a manger: That I have seen the glory of thy salvation, let thy servant depart in peace. (Applause.) That being done, my ambition is complete. I would rather live in history, in the affections of my countrymen as having consummated this great end than to be President of the United States forty times. (General Sandford called for "Three cheers for Andrew Johnson, the restorer of the Union." The cheers were given.) In conclusion, gentlemen, let me tender to you my sincere thanks on this occasion. So long as reason continues to occupy her empire, so long as my heart shall beat with one kind emotion, so long as my memory shall contain or

DINNER

BY

The Citizens of New York,

To His Excellency

President Johnson

IN HONOR OF

HIS VISIT TO THE CITY

Wednesday, Aug. 29th, 1866.

Menu.

Potages.

Consommé à la Chatelaine:
Bisque aux quenelles.

Variés. Hors d'oeuvres. Variés.

Timbales de gibier à la Vénitienne.

Poissons.

Saumon à la Livonienne:
Paupiettes de King-fish à la Villeroy.

Relevés.

Selle d'agneau aux Concombres.
Filet de boeuf à la Pocahontas.

The dinner menu for Johnson and guests at Delmonico's, New York City
Courtesy Special Collections, University of Tennessee Library

be capable of recurring to one event, so long will I remember the kindnesses, so long will I feel the good that has been done on this occasion, and so long will I cherish in my heart the kindness which has been manifested toward me by the citizens of New-York. (Immense applause.)

The band played "The Star-Spangled Banner," the audience enthusiastically joining in the chorus. President Johnson, having seated himself, again arose, and said: Gentlemen, in conclusion, after having consumed more of your time than I intended, I fear unprofitably, let me propose, in sincerity, "the Union, the perpetual Union of these States." (The toast was drunk with cheers.)

World (New York), Aug. 30, 1866.
  1. Alexander T. Stewart.
  2. Charles W. Sandford.

From Henry Stanbery

                                    Attorney General's Office,   August 29, 1866.
Sir.—

I have the honor to give my opinion in the matter of John N. Tazewell,[1] on the following statement of facts:—

Mr. Tazewell is now, and was during the rebellion, and for a long time before, a citizen of Norfolk, Virginia. At the commencement of the rebellion, he held and yet holds, as owner, several bonds issued by the United States under the loan of 1842. Part of these bonds belonged to his father, Littleton W. Tazewell,[2] and were payable to his order. He died in 1860, and in the distribution of his estate, the bonds were transferred by the executors to the present holder. The other bonds are registered bonds, all payable to the order of John N. Tazewell. Mr. Tazewell has never taken any active part in the rebellion. No proceedings of confiscation have at any time been taken against his property or against these bonds. The question arises upon this state of facts whether these bonds are now valid obligations against the United States in the hands of Mr. Tazewell, and as such, may be lawfully paid to him.

The rule is well established by Public Law that private debts are not annulled by war.

The relation of creditor and debtor existing between the subjects of one belligerent and those of another, is not abrogated by war. The remedy only is suspended, and upon the return of peace, the debt and the remedies for its enforcement come again into full force.

The same rule is equally well established, and with even stronger sanction, as to public debts;—that is to say, debts due by one of the States at war to the subjects or citizens of the other State. Debts of this nature are regarded as of the highest obligation, and esteemed more sacred in time of war than private debts.

Vattel says of them: "The State does not so much as touch the sums which it owes the enemy; money lent to the public is everywhere exempt from confiscation and seizure in case of war."[3]

Whether these liberal rules which prevail in lawful war between independent States, extend in full force to a civil war, or a rebellion, need not now be considered, as the rule or policy to be applied in this case is quite clear upon the legislation of Congress.

By the Confiscation Act of 1861, only property used in aid of the rebellion is made liable to seizure and confiscation. By the Confiscation Act of 1862, it is made the duty of the President to cause the seizure of all the property real and personal of certain classes of persons acting in an official capacity under the Rebel authority, and of property situate in a loyal state belonging to a person who thereafter should give aid to the rebellion.

According to the statement of facts, Mr. Tazewell did not fall within any of these designated classes.

It will be observed that these classes do not embrace persons, (other than those holding an official character,) who have been engaged in armed rebellion or who have given aid to the rebellion; but as to such persons, their property is only made liable to seizure in the event that after sixty days' notice by proclamation of the President that they shall cease to aid and abet the rebellion, they fail to comply.

The statement of facts does not bring Mr. Tazewell within the operation of this provision.

I have, therefore, to advise that the bonds held by Mr. Tazewell are valid obligations in his hands, and lawfully payable.

Henry Stanbery   Attorney General

LS, DLC-JP.
1. Tazewell (c1804–fl1866) had personal property valued at $100,000 in 1860. 1860 Census, Va., Norfolk, Norfolk, 450.
2. Tazewell (1774–1860), a lawyer, served several terms in the state legislature, and also in the U.S. House (1800–1801) and Senate (1824–32). In 1834 he was elected governor of Virginia, serving until 1836, when he resigned. *DAB.*
3. Emmerich von Vattel. The quote is from Vattel's *The Law of Nations; or Principles of the Law of Nature, Applied to the Conduct and Affairs of Nations and Sovereigns*, trans. by Joseph Chitty, 4th American ed. (Philadelphia, 1835), 323.

From San Jose National Union Club[1]

San Jose, Cal.   Augt. 30th 1866.

The members of the San Jose National Union Club, have thought it not unbecoming in them to address your Excellency upon matters of public interest. In order that you may fully understand why we think so and appreciate the extent of the interest we take in this matter, we make the following statement:

More than a year ago, a number of intelligent union Republicans of this City and neighborhood believing that you were right in principle and that your administration policy ought to be sustained, withdrew from the radical union party, organized a National Union Party, and at a Grand mass meeting distinctly avowed our principles in a platform[2] and made nominations of candidates for various county offices. We approved so much of the platform as relates to National affairs. The State election was vigorously contested, but resulted as we expected in a Radical majority of between four & five hundred in a vote of 3000. During the Canvass we had to contend with a party occupying all the County offices, and also with the active opposition of all Federal appointees in the County. Owen, Inspector of Quick Silver[3] constantly poured out his abuse upon you. Cutler, the Post master at San Jose[4] was constant in his efforts against us, interfered to prevent musical bands from performing at our public meetings, and on election days was active at the polls against us. Savage & Slocum the assessor & Receiver of Internal revenue,[5] although less demonstrative, are and have been steadily opposed to us, throwing all their influence against us. Not discouraged by defeat, the members of this Club have maintained their organization intact and have met from time to time. Upon the call of a National Union Convention to meet at Philadelphia on the 14th August, the San Jose Union Administration Club was the only organized body in this State favorable to your administration, and its President, F. B. Murdoch immediately called the Club together at his office, the San Jose Patriot Editorial rooms, and the Club thereupon issued a call, for the meeting of a State Convention at San Francisco for the purpose of appointing delegates to represent California in the Philadelphia Convention, and to organize the party for the State by the appointment of a State Central Committee. The State Convention met on the 3d August. Your Excellency has probably seen an account of these proceedings in the public papers.[6]

These are the reasons which induce us to hope, that you will not regard any suggestions which we may make in regard to California appointments as impertinent and intrusive. The State Central Committee while informing us of its purpose to address you on this subject, also suggested, in view of our long efforts in behalf of the administration, the propriety of this Club also writing to your Excellency.

The members of this Club, are all Republicans, original republicans, not Radicals. We were decidedly Union men during the struggle for the life of the Nation, and we believe that the principles you so ably maintain are the principles of the Republican party, founded upon a true view of the Constitution. We think those principles so clearly just and true, that they must be adopted by a majority of the Union Party, so soon as reason has had time to act and prejudices which a narrow selfish and malignant party spirit has instilled are removed by the force of truth. We entertain no hope however of being able to accomplish this result in California, if persons long known as democrats are appointed to public office. For here, all loyal men of that party long since united with the Union Party, and many of them are now the most radical and bitter in the denunciation of your policy.

Those who did not join the Union Party are strongly rebel in sympathy, and although most of them sustain your measures, yet all of them are secretly hostile to you—they hope to use you for a time and then at some future time, to bring out some one upon whom they can rely with more confidence. The aristocratic southern men, of whom we have many in this state, have really no sympathy with Andrew Johnson.

The appointment of men of that kind to office would have the effect of repressing the tendency of the old republicans to join the party and would undoubtedly tend to delay the time, when we may hope to attain the ascendency in California.

ALS (Murdoch), DLC-JP.
1. Eight men signed the letter which was written by the club president, Francis B. Murdoch (1805–*fl*1881), a lawyer who had practiced in Pennsylvania, Michigan, Illinois, and Missouri before he moved to California in 1852. His first newspaper, the Whig *San Jose Weekly Telegraph*, founded in 1853, became Republican in opposition to the Kansas-Nebraska Act. Murdoch retired from this paper in 1860, but in 1863 established the *San Jose Patriot*, which he edited until 1875. *History of Santa Clara County, California* (San Francisco, 1881), 721.
2. A part of the platform in an undated, unidentified newspaper clipping was attached to the letter.
3. This is probably a tongue in cheek reference to rival editor James Jerome Owen (1827–1895) of the San Jose *Mercury*. A New York printer, Owen settled in California in 1861. He and a partner purchased the *San Jose Telegraph* about 1861 and changed its name to the *Mercury*, in which Owen supported the Republicans. He remained associated with the paper until 1885. Benjamin Bronston Beales, "The San Jose *Mercury* and the Civil War," *CHQ*, 22 (1943): 223–24.
4. Simon M. Cutler (*fl*1869) was postmaster by 1863 and served, according to available evidence, through most of 1869. *U.S. Off. Reg.* (1863–69).
5. Assessor Richard Savage had assumed his post by 1863 and retained it until at least 1867. William N. Slocum (*c*1831–*fl*1870), collector of internal revenue from approximately 1865 to 1867, was farming in 1870. Ibid., (1863–67); 1870 Census, Calif., Santa Clara, San Jose, 1st Ward, 278.
6. A brief article summarizing the resolutions of the group and listing the delegates (all persons then on the east coast, some of whom were not Californians) appeared in the *National Intelligencer*, Aug. 7, 1866.

From Mary Minor[1]

Cheraw. [S.C.]   August 31st 1866

Respected Sir.

I hope you will pardon the liberty I have taken in addressing these few lines to you, concerning those who are very dear to me. Five years ago, I was sold by a man living in this place by the name of W. L. J. Reid,[2] to a man in Atlanta Georgia. Mr Reid sold me from my children[3] the youngest being a babe not a year old: the man who bought me tried to buy my children so as they could be with me, but Mr Reid would not sell them. Since I have been a free woman I have not had the means to come back here for my children until the present time. I applied for them, and to my astonishment was refused them. Mr Reid says they were bound to him by Capt. E R. Clark[4] Pro Marshal of the 30th Mass V Vol, for 20 years. I have to day applied to Gen Giles[5] of the Freedmen's Beauro, who says he has no authority to undo, what another has done. I wish most respected and honoured Sir, that you will as the President of the U S, let me know if the laws of my country, are such, that after a poor slave badly, treated, and separated for year's from her own children, cannot be allowed the privilege of haveing her children with her. I would be more than thank ful to you most highly respected Sir, if you will order it to be settled by some one competent to give justice to the coloured woman, and at your earliest convenience, as I am away from my husband,[6] who is in Atlanta Georgia, and I am here at expense. I think very hard that they should have been bound, without my consent and without my knowledge.[7]

Mary Minor
Cheraw   So. Car.

ALS, DNA-RG56, Lets. Recd. from Executive Officers (AB Ser.), President.

1. Minor (c1832–fl1870) continued to reside in Atlanta. 1870 Census, Ga., Fulton, Atlanta, 1st Ward, 39.

2. William L.J. Reid (c1817–fl1870) was a Cheraw merchant. Apprenticeship paper of Henry [Minor], Jan. 13, 1866, Lets. Recd. from Executive Officers (AB Ser.), President, RG56, NA; 1860 Census, S.C., Chesterfield, Cheraw, 174; (1870), 10.

3. Dock (b. c1853), Scilia [or Celia] (b. c1854), Henry (c1857–fl1874), and Sallie Minor (b. c1859), the oldest born in Alabama, the others in South Carolina. Dock and Henry became Atlanta barbers. 1870 Census, Ga., Fulton, Atlanta, 1st Ward, 39; Atlanta directory (1874).

4. Edwin R. Clark (c1842–1891), a prewar student from Lowell, was a captain in the 30th Mass. Inf. (1862–66) before transferring to the regular army (1867–83) as a lieutenant. CSR, Edwin R. Clark, RG94, NA; Lowell directory (1861); Heitman, *Register*, 1: 303.

5. George W. Gile (1830–1896), an actor before the war, served as colonel, 88th Pa. Inf. and 9th Vet. Res. Corps, before being brevetted brigadier general of volunteers. After a few years in the regular army he became an insurance agent in Philadelphia. Hunt and Brown, *Brigadier Generals*.

6. Jackson Minor (c1831–fl1898) apparently remained in Atlanta the rest of his life. For a time he was a boot and shoe maker, then for decades he was a barber. 1870 Census, Ga., Fulton, Atlanta, 1st Ward, 39; Atlanta directories (1871–98).

7. Mary was supposedly sold by Reid as a punishment for an attempt to poison his wife. On January 13, 1866, her children, Celia and Henry, were apprenticed to Reid to become house servants. Johnson referred Mary's letter to Freedmen's Bureau chief Howard, who in turn passed it down the chain of command to General Gile to investigate. Gile reported on September 21 that the terms of the indenture were "not Such as would be likely to meet the approval of the Bureau. Still the contract seems to be valid . . . with the . . . official Signature of an officer of the Genl Govt." Four days later his commander, Gen. Robert K. Scott, claimed that Mary "should have her children without regard to the interest of her former owner. If she can come for them." After General Sickles, commander of the Department, authorized Scott to "promote the welfare of the children," Gile, on October 1, was again ordered personally to investigate the case "to secure the good of all concerned." George W. Gile's endorsement, Sept. 21, 1866, and Celia and Henry [Minor's] apprenticeship papers, Jan. 13, 1866, Lets. Recd. from Executive Officers (AB Ser.), President, RG56, NA; Records of the Commr., Lets. Sent (M742, Roll 2), RG105, NA; Records of the Commr., S.C., Endorsement Bk., Vol. 19, RG105, NA.

September 1866

From Jo Daviess County, Ill., Democratic Committee[1]

[ca. September 1866][2]

We understand that the principles of the Philada Convention of the 14th Augt 1866 required a united and energetic effort on the part of all true friends of the Constitution, to strengthen and support you, in your defence of the government; and that there should be no distinction made in the distribution of offices, between Democrats or Republicans.

To our surprize we learn that at a recent meeting held at Freeport[3] in the 3d Congl. District Illinois,—a number of persons met together and made a general distribution of the offices in this District without any consultation with the Democracy through its regularly organized committees; and entirely ignoring their right to be consulted. Moreover the persons who assumed to represent the friends of the President in this County have no influence outside of their own votes, while the entire mass of the Democracy who are with a few exceptions the only friends of the President in Jo Daviess County, were not consulted in the proposed appointments.

We supposed that these offices were to be distributed to promote the general good, and that could only be ascertained by a joint consultation & recommendation of the Conservative element, and the Democracy, through their respective organizations.

This being the District represented by Washburne,[4] who in bitterness & venom is not exceeded by Thaddeus Stevens—and Galena being his home, and the largest City in the District, and also thoroughly democratic—and having the most prominent powerful & influential Democratic newspaper[5] in the District located & owned here, the Democracy of this County claim that the office of Assesser for this 3rd Congl. District, and the Post Office at Galena should be allotted to them.

We fear that any action in regard to the appointment of an Assesser for the 3d Congl. District or of a Postmaster at Galena,[6] unless by the express recommendation of the Democracy of this County, will operate very injuriously to our prospects for success in the coming election in this District.

We earnestly hope that no action will be taken in regard to the appointments to office in this Congressional District until we can be heard in the matter.

LS, DNA-RG56, Appts., Internal Revenue Service, Assessor, Ill., 3rd Dist.

1. The document was signed by Frederick Stahl and five others. Stahl (1809–*fl*1878) was engaged in the mercantile business, smelting, and lead shipping in the 1830s and 1840s, and became director, and later president, of the Galena branch of the Illinois State Bank. In 1857 he became president of the Galena Marine Insurance Company, serving until 1865, when it merged with the Merchants National Bank. He was director of the latter from 1865 until at least 1878. *The History of Jo Daviess County, Illinois* (Chicago, 1878), 652.

2. Internal evidence suggests a September date. Since the Philadelphia convention of August 14 and the Freeport meeting of September 13 are mentioned, the letter probably dates to the latter half of September. Since the committee alluded to the upcoming assessor appointment and an assessor was appointed on September 25, the letter was written sometime prior to that date. *Chicago Tribune*, Sept. 19, 1866; Ser. 6B, Vol. 3: 592, Johnson Papers, LC.

3. On September 13 a meeting was held in Freeport, calling itself the National Union Convention. *Chicago Tribune*, Sept. 19, 1866.

4. Elihu B. Washburne.

5. A descendant of the *Galena Jeffersonian* and its successor, the *Courier*, the *Galena Democrat* was owned by a stock company controlled by leading Democrats. Established in December 1862 with L. S. Everett as editor, the *Democrat* fell deeply into debt and the stockholders sold out to H. H. Savage, who operated the paper until 1868 when it was sold to pay off the debts. *Jo Daviess County*, 435.

6. U. D. Meacham was appointed assessor on September 25 and Warren W. Huntington was renewed as postmaster on the next day. Meacham has not been otherwise identified. Huntington (1820–*fl*1878) was employed by several publishers before moving to Galena and entering into a partnership in the publication of the *Daily Advertiser and Galena Gazette*. From 1857 to 1862 he bought and ran the job office and bookbindery connected with the paper. President Lincoln appointed him postmaster in March 1861, a position he held until May 1873. Afterwards he was appointed special agent to the Post Office Department, continuing in that capacity until May 1877, when he again became Galena's postmaster. Ser. 6B, Vol 3: 592, Johnson Papers, LC; *Jo Daviess County*, 641.

From Albert Pike

Memphis, Tennessee   2d September, 1866.

Mr. President:

I some time since received, with gratitude for your kindness, your warrant of Pardon, for acts done by me during the late Civil War.[1]

It is proper that I should inform you of the reasons why I have not yet notified the Department of State of my acceptance of its conditions. It is the more proper, because these reasons are somewhat of a public nature, and, as I think, in some degree affect the character of the Nation and of its present Chief Magistrate, to whose sense of justice I am glad to be able to submit them.

In 1864, in the summer, libels were filed in the District Court in Little Rock, against property of mine in West Tenn, of the value of some $30,000, renting annually to the United States for perhaps $3,000. In the fall of the same year, my life-interest, so confiscated, was sold, for (I think) $2,250. The *Costs*, as allowed by the Judge,[2] for services worth perhaps $15, were some $320. The money was reported paid into Court; and the residue after deduction of costs, into the Treasury of the United States. The Marshal's return did not show to *whom* the property was sold: but one Bliss,[3] Lieutenant Governor of the State, soon turned up as purchaser; and after a time the property was conveyed to the wife of Robert E. Schenck of Ohio.[4] And in February, 1866, when ample time had been allowed for the money to be realized from the rents, it was paid into the Treasury of the United States.

Mean while, another Confiscation suit was instituted, in the District Court for the *Western* District of Arkansas, against 3,200 acres of land, of which 640 acres has long since been conveyed by me to a purchaser. That suit is still pending.

And an indictment for Treason is pending against me in Little Rock.

To the indictment and the confiscation suit still pending, I have pleaded in bar your Excellency's permission to return home; and the stipulation that, so long as I obey the laws and keep my parole of honor, I shall not be molested or interfered with by the Civil or Military authorities.

Since the filing of these pleas, I have the pardon in due form, granted by your Excellency. To avail myself of it, I must bind myself.

First: Never to claim my property which has been confiscated, or the proceeds of it, even if such proceedings should be judicially declared wholly void; and however clear my right to have them annulled.

Second: To pay the costs of the prosecution by indictment, and also these in both confiscation cases, as well as that in which my property has been sold, and I am never to claim it or the proceeds, as in that where it would be restored to me.

As I have not yet forwarded to the Department of State my acceptance of the pardon, a just respect for the President, and gratitude for his kindness, requires, I think, that I should make known to him the reasons of my delay.

In doing this, I hope the President will permit me to speak with the frankness which has always been so natural to himself.

I am not able to pay the costs in question; and it is surely sufficient that I should be required to abandon all claim to the confiscated property, without being *also* required to pay those costs.

But I should not trouble the President in regard to that. Nor, if such provisions were for the benefit of the United States, should I complain of any conditions by which the Treasury should be enriched. I bring the matter to the notice of the President because the provision is for the exclusive benefit of those, as justly odious as Roman delators under the later Caesars, who ask the aid of the President to secure them in the enjoyment of the property of others, purchased, generally, for small sums, and paid for out of the rents; and the other is for the benefit of officers of the Courts and to secure to them exorbitant and extortionate fees.

I hope the President will not deem it disrespect for me to beg him to consider whether these conditions ought to be annexed to an Act of Grace? Such an act, it seems to me, to have its due weight and excellent generosity, ought to be trammelled with no such conditions. If the *law* requires the payment of costs, when such a pardon is pleaded in bar of a pending indictment or libel for confiscation, let it be so. It is well: the pardoned can not complain of *that*, and, if the law *does* require it, it *needs* not be made a condition of the pardon: if it *does* not require it, then it *ought* not to be made such a condition.

Still less, it seems to me (and I say it with entire and respectful deference), ought it to be made a condition that one shall not exercise a legal and Constitutional right. If the proceedings for confiscation were illegal, it is not, it seems to me, consistent with the generosity or honor of a great Nation, to annex to its graces and mercies a condition that the recipient shall sanction and submit to the wrong. If the proceedings were valid, the titles of the purchasers are good, and can not be affected by the grant of a pardon.

Mr. President, has not the time come when measures of vengeance should be foregone? Those, Sir, who admire and love you most, so far as I know, are of the same opinion with myself, that not every such pending suits for confiscation ought to be dismissed; but that true wisdom and sound policy require a general and unconditional amnesty. You gain nothing and are losing much, by delaying it.

Albert Pike

ALS, DLC-JP.
    1. Pike had been granted a special presidential pardon on April 23, 1866. See Pike to Johnson, June 24, 1865, *Johnson Papers*, 8: 287; and Representatives of "Disloyal" Indians to Johnson, Jan. 13, 1866, ibid., 9: 598–99.
    2. Henry C. Caldwell.
    3. Calvin C. Bliss (1823–1891), a native of Vermont and former land agent, was elected lieutenant governor in 1864. Dallas T. Herndon, ed., *Centennial History of Arkansas* (3 vols., Little Rock, 1922), 1: 287; Mrs. William H. Counts, comp., *A Compendium of Arkansas Genealogy* (North Little Rock, 1977), 1: 40; 1860 Census, Ark., Independence, Batesville, Ruddell, 15; (1870), Pulaski, Little Rock, 4th Ward, 34.
    4. Unidentified.

Speech in Cleveland

[September 3, 1866]

FELLOW CITIZENS OF CLEVELAND:

It is not for the purpose of making a speech I came here to-night. I am aware of the great curiosity that exists on the part of strangers in reference to seeing individuals who are here amongst us. ⟨Louder.⟩ You must remember there are a good many people here to-night, and it requires a great voice to reach the utmost verge of this vast audience. I have used my voice so constantly for some days past that I do not know as I shall be able to make you all hear, but I will do my best to make myself heard.

What I am going to say is: There is a large number here who would like to see General Grant, and hear him speak, and hear what he would have to say; but the fact is, General Grant is not here. He is extremely ill. His health will not permit of his appearing before this audience to-night.[1] It would be a greater pleasure to me to see him here and have him speak than to make a speech of my own. So then it will not be expected that he will be here to-night, and you cannot see on account of his extreme indisposition.

Fellow Citizens: In being before you to-night, it is not for the purpose of making a speech, but simply to make your acquaintance, and while I am saying how do you do, appear at the same time to tell you good bye. We are here to-night, on our tour towards a sister State, for the purpose of participating in and witnessing the laying of the chief corner stone over a monument to one of our fellow citizens who is no more. It is not necessary for me to mention the name of Stephen A. Douglas to the citizens of Ohio. It is a name familiar to you all, and being on a tour to participate in the ceremonies, and passing through your State and section of country, and witnessing the demonstration and manifestation of regard and respect which has been paid me, I am free to say to you, that so far as I am concerned, and I think I am speaking for all the company, when I say we feel extremely gratified and flattered at the demonstration made by the country through which we have passed, and in being flattered, I want to state at the same time, that I don't consider that entirely personal, but as evidence of what is prevailing in the public mind, that there is a great issue before the country, and that this demonstration of feeling, is more than anything else, an indication of a deep interest among the great mass of the people in regard to all these great questions that agitate the public mind. In coming before you to-night, I come before you as an American citizen, and not simply as your Chief Magistrate. I claim to be a citizen of the Southern States, and an inhabitant of one of the States of this Union. I know that it has been said, and contended for, on the part of some, that I was an alien, for I did not reside in any one of the States of the Union; and that therefore, I could not be Chief Magistrate, though the States declared I was. But all that was necessary was simply to introduce a resolution declaring the office vacant or depose the occupant, or under some pretext, to prefer articles of impeachment, and the individual who occupies the Chief Magistracy would be deposed and deprived of power.

But, fellow citizens, a short time since you had a ticket before you for the Presidency and Vice Presidency; I was placed upon that ticket, in conjunction with a distinguished fellow citizen who is now no more. ⟨Voice, "a great misfortune too."⟩ I know there are some who will exclaim, "unfortunate." I admit the ways of Providence are mysterious and unfortunate, but uncontrollable by those who would exclaim unfortunate. I was going to say, my countrymen, but a short time since, I was selected and placed upon a ticket. There was a platform prepared and adopted by those who placed me upon it, and now, notwithstanding all kinds of misrepresentation; notwithstanding since after the sluice of misrepresentation has been poured out, notwithstanding a subsidised gang of hirelings have traduced me and maligned me ever since I have entered upon the discharge of my official duties, yet I will say had my predecessor have lived the vials of wrath would have been poured out on him. ⟨Cries of never, never, never.⟩ I come here to-night, in passing along, and being called upon, for the purpose of exchanging opinions and views as time would permit, and to ascertain if we could who was in the wrong.

I appear before you to-night and I want to say this: that I have lived and been among all American people, and have represented them in some capacity for the last twenty-five years. And where is the man living, or the woman in the community, that I have wronged; or where is the person that can place their finger upon one single hair breadth of deviation from one single pledge I have made, or one single violation of the Constitution of the country? What tongue does he speak? What religion does he profess? Let him come forward and place his finger upon one pledge I have violated. ⟨A voice. "Hang Jeff. Davis."⟩ ⟨Mr. President resumes.⟩ Hang Jeff. Davis? Hang Jeff. Davis? Why don't you? ⟨Applause.⟩ Why don't you? ⟨Applause.⟩ Have not you got the Court? Have not you got the Court? Have not you got the Attorney General? Who is your Chief Justice—and that refused to sit upon the trial? ⟨Applause.⟩ I am not the Prosecuting Attorney. I am not the Jury. But I will tell you what I did do: I called upon your Congress, that is trying to break up the Government. ⟨Immense applause.⟩ Yes, did your Congress order hanging Jeff. Davis? ⟨Prolonged applause, mingled with hisses.⟩ But, fellow-citizens, we had as well let feelings and prejudices pass; let passion subside; let reason resume her empire. In presenting myself to you in the few remarks I intended to make, my intention was to address myself to your judgment and good sense and not to your anger or the malignity of your hearts. This was my object in presenting myself on this occasion, and at the same time to tell you good-bye. I have heard the remark made in this crowd to-night, "Traitor, Traitor!" ⟨Prolonged confusion.⟩ My countrymen, will you hear me for my cause? For the Constitution of my country? I want to know when, where and under what circumstances Andrew Johnson, either as Chief Executive, or in any other capacity, ever violated the Constitution of his country. Let me ask this large and intelligent audience here to-night if your Secretary of State, who served four years under Mr. Lincoln, who was placed under the butcher's blow and exposed to the assassin's knife, when he turned traitor? If I was disposed to play orator, and deal in declamation, here to-night, I would imitate one of the ancient tragedies we have such account of—I would take William H. Seward, and open to you the scars he has received. I would exhibit his bloody garments and show the rents caused by the assassin's knife. ⟨Three cheers for Seward.⟩ Yes, I would unfold his bloody garments here to-night and ask who had committed treason? I would ask why Jeff. Davis was not hung? Why don't you hang Thad. Stevens and Wendell Phillips? I can tell you, my countrymen, I have been fighting traitors in the South (prolonged applause), and they have been whipped and say they were wrong, acknowledge their error and accept the terms of the Constitution. And now, as I pass around the circle, having fought traitors at the South, I am prepared to fight traitors at the North, God being willing, with your help ⟨"You can't have it," and prolonged confusion,⟩ they would be crushed worse than the traitors of the South, and this glorious Union of ours will be preserved. In coming here to-night, it was not coming as Chief Magistrate of twenty-five States, but I came here as the Chief Magistrate of thirty-six States. I came here to-night with the flag of my country in my hand, with a constellation of thirty-six not twenty-five stars. I came here to-night with the Constitution of my country intact, determined to defend the Constitution, let the consequences be what they may. I came here to-night for the Union, the entire circle of these States. ⟨A Voice: "How many States made you President?"⟩ How many States made me President? Were you against secession? Do you want to dissolve the Union? ⟨A Voice, No.⟩ Then I am President of the whole United States, and I will tell you one thing, I understand the discordant notes in this audience here to-night. And I will tell you furthermore, that he that is opposed to the restoration of the government and this union of the States, is as great a traitor as Jeff. Davis, and I am against both of them. I fought traitor at the South, now I fight them at the North. ⟨Immense applause.⟩ I will tell you another thing; I know all about those boys that have fought for their country. I have been with them, down there when cities were besieged. I know who was with them when some of you, that talk about traitors, had not the courage to come out of your closets, but persuaded somebody else to go.

Very courageous men! While Grant, Sherman, Farragut and a long list of the distinguished sons of the United States were in the field of battle— you were cowards at home, and now when these brave men have returned, many of them having left an arm or a leg on some battle-field, while you were at home speculating and committing frauds upon your government, you pretend now to have a great respect and sympathy for the poor fellow who left his arm on the battle-field. I understand you, who talk about the duty of the president and object to his speech of the 22d of July—(Voice, "22d of February."[)]—22d of February. I know who have fought the battles of the country, and I know who is to pay for it. Those brave men shed their blood, and you speculated, got money, and now the great mass of the people must work it out. (Applause and confusion.) I care not for your prejudices. It is time for the great mass of the American people to understand what your designs are in not admitting the Southern States when they have come to terms, and even proposed to pay their part of the national debt. I say, Let them come; and those brave men, having conquered them and having prostrated them in the dust, with the heel of power upon them, What do they say? (Voice,

"What does Gen. Butler say?") Gen. Butler! What does Gen. Grant say? And what does Gen. Grant say of Gen. Butler? What does Gen. Sherman say? He says he is for restoration of the government, and Gen. Sherman fought for it.

But fellow-citizens, let this all pass. I care not for malignity. There is a certain portion of our countrymen that will respect their fellow citizen whenever he is entitled to respect and there is another portion that have no respect for themselves, and consequently have none for anybody else. I know a gentleman, when I see him. And furthermore, I know when I look a man in the face—⟨Voice,—"Which you can't do."⟩ I wish I could see you, I will bet now, if there could be a light reflected upon your face, that cowardice and treachery could be seen in it. Show yourself. Come out here where we can see you. If ever you shoot a man, you will stand in the dark and pull your trigger. I understand traitors. I have been fighting them for five years. We fought it out on the Southern end of the line, now we are fighting in the other direction. And those men—such a one as insulted me to-night—you may say, has ceased to be a man, and in ceasing be to a man shrunk into the denomination of a reptile, and having so shrunken, as an honest man, I tread upon him. I came here to-night not to criminate or recriminate, but when provoked my nature is, not to advance, but to defend, and when encroached upon, I care not from what quarter it comes, it will find resistance, and resistance at the threshold. As your Chief Magistrate I have felt, after taking an oath to support the Constitution of my country, that I saw the encroachments of the enemy upon your sovereign rights. I saw the citadel of liberty trenched upon, and, as an honest man, being placed there as a sentinel, I have dared to sound the tocsin of alarm. Should I have ears and not hear; have a tongue and not speak when the enemy approaches?

And let me say to-night that my head has been threatened. It has been said that my blood was to be shed. Let me say to those who are willing to sacrifice my life ⟨derisive laughter and cheers,⟩ if you want a victim, and my country requires it, erect your altar, and the individual who addresses you to-night, while here a visitor, ⟨"No, no," and laughter,⟩ erect your altar if you still thirst for blood, and if you want it, take out the individual who now addresses you and lay him upon your altar, and the blood that now courses his veins and warms his existence, shall be poured out as a last libation of Freedom. I love my country, and I defy any man to put his finger upon anything to the contrary. Then what is my offence? ⟨Voices, "You aint a Radical," "New Orleans," "Veto."⟩ Somebody says "Veto." Veto of what? What is called the Freedmen's Bureau Bill, and in fine, not to go into any argument here to-night, if you do not understand what the Freedmen's Bureau Bill is, I can tell you. ⟨Voice—"Tell us."⟩ Before the rebellion there were 4,000,000 called colored persons, held as slaves, by about 340,000 people living in the South. That is 340,000 slave owners paid expenses, bought land, and worked the negroes, and at the expiration of the year, when cotton, tobacco, and rice was gathered and sold, after all paying expenses, these slave owners put the money in their pocket—(slight interruption)—your attention—they put the property in their pocket. In many instances there was no profit, and many come out in debt. Well, that is the way things stood before the rebellion. The rebellion commenced and the slaves were turned loose. Then we come to the Freedmen's Bureau Bill. And what did the bill propose? It proposed to appoint agents and sub-agents in all the cities, counties, school districts and parishes, with power to make contracts for all the slaves—power to control, and power to hire them out—dispose of them, and in addition to that, the whole military power of the Government applied to carry it into execution. Now, (clamor and confusion.) I never feared clamor. I have never been afraid of the people, for by them I have always been sustained. And when I have all the truth, argument, fact and reason on my side, clamor, nor afront, nor animosities can drive me from my purpose.

Now to the Freedman's Bureau. What was it? Four million slaves were emancipated and given an equal chance and a fair start to make their own support—to work and produce; and, having worked and produced, to have their own property and apply it to their own support. But the Freedmen's Bureau comes and says we must take charge of these 4,000,000 slaves. The Bureau comes along and proposes, at an expense of a fraction less than $12,000,000 a year, to take charge of these slaves. You had already expended three thousand millions of dollars to set them free and give them a fair opportunity to take care of themselves—then these gentlemen, who are such great friends of the people, tell us they must be taxed twelve million dollars to sustain the Freedmen's Bureau. (Great confusion.) I would rather speak to five hundred men who would give me their attention than to one hundred thousand that would not. (With all this mass of patronage he said he could have declared himself dictator.)

The Civil Rights Bill was more enormous than the other. I have exercised the veto power, they say. Let me say to you of the threats of your Stevenses, Sumners, Phillipses and all that class, I care not for them. As they once talked about forming a "league with hell and a covenant with the devil." I tell you my countrymen here to-night, though the power of hell, death and Stevens with all his powers combined, there is no power that can control me, save you the people, and the God that spoke me into existence. In bidding you farewell here to-night, I would ask you, with all the pains Congress has taken to calumniate and malign me, what has Congress done? Has it done anything to restore the Union of the States? But, on the contrary, has it not done everything to prevent it?

And because I stand now as I did when the rebellion commenced, I have been denounced as a traitor. My countrymen here to-night, who has suffered more than I? Who has run greater risk? Who has borne more than I? But Congress, factions, domineering, tyrannical—Congress has undertaken to poison the minds of the American people, and create a feeling against me in consequence of the manner in which I have distributed the public patronage.

While this gang—this common gang of cormorants and blood-suckers, have been fattening upon the country for the past four or five years—men never going into the field, who growl at being removed from their fat offices, they are great patriots! Look at them all over your district. Everybody is a traitor that is against them. I think the time has come when those who stayed at home and enjoyed offices for the last four or five years—I think it would be no more than right for them to give way and let others participate in the benefits of office. Hence you can see why it is that I am traduced and assaulted. I stood up by these men who were in the field, and I stand by them now.

I have been drawn into this long speech, while I intended simply to make acknowledgments for the cordial welcome; but if I am insulted while the civilities are going on, I will resent it in a proper manner, and in parting here to-night, I have no anger nor revengeful feelings to gratify. All I want now—peace has come and war is over—is for all patriotic men to rally round the standard of their country, and swear by their altars and their God, that all shall sink together but what this Union shall be supported. Then in parting with you to-night, I hang over you this flag—not of 25 but of 36 stars—I hand over to you the Constitution of my country—though imprisoned, though breaches have been made upon it—with confidence, hoping you will repair the breaches, I hand it over to you, in whom I have always trusted and relied, and, so far, I have never deserted; and I feel confident, while speaking here to-night, for heart responds to heart of man, that you agree to the same great doctrine.

Then farewell! The little feelings aroused here to-night, for some men have felt a little ill; let us not cherish them. Let me say, in this connection, there are many white people in this country that need emancipation. Let the work of emancipation go on. Let white men stand erect and free. ⟨A voice, "What about New Orleans?"⟩ You complain of the disfranchisement of the negroes in the Southern States, while you would not give them the right of suffrage in Ohio to-day. Let your negroes vote in Ohio before you talk of negroes voting. Take the beam out of your own eye before you see the mote in your neighbor's eye. You are very much disturbed about New Orleans—but you will not allow the negro to vote in Ohio.

This is all plain, we understand this all and in parting with you to-night let me invoke the blessing of God upon you, expressing my sincere thanks for the cordial manner in which you have received me.

Cleveland Plain Dealer, Sept. 4, 1866.
    1. It was widely believed that Grant was too inebriated at Cleveland to make a public appearance. Trefousse, *Johnson*, 263.

A satirical depiction of Johnson's Cleveland speech, September 1866
Harper's Weekly, October 27, 1866

From William B. Campbell

Lebanon Tennessee   September 4th 1866

Sir

I most earnestly recommend to you, my neighbour & friend Doct John D. Owen[1] for the place of commissioner of Internal Revenue for the State of Tennessee in the place of Mr Cone,[2] who I learn will vacate the place or be removed.

Doct Owen is a most worthy gentleman of as high standing as any man in our community, and well qualified to discharge the duties of the office, and may be relied on to be honest faithful & true to your policy & administration.

I most earnestly recommend his appointment as it would meet the approval of our whole community.[3]

W B Campbell

ALS, DNA-RG58, Direct Tax Commission for Tenn., Records Relating to Personnel Actions (1864–66).

1. Owen (1825–1889) studied medicine first under his brother, Benjamin R. Owen, and then at Philadelphia where he graduated. He moved from Smith County to Lebanon in the early 1850s. After the war he became involved in the banking business. Goodspeed's *Maury, Williamson, Rutherford, Wilson, Bedford & Marshall*, 1110; Dixon Merritt, ed., *The History of Wilson County* (Nashville, 1961), 153, 154.

2. Edward P. Cone had held the post since the late summer of 1865. But Alvan C. Gillem had repeatedly warned Johnson that Cone was a dangerous enemy. See Gillem to Johnson, Feb. 13, June 29, 1866, *Johnson Papers*, 10: 91, 636.

3. The Owen file contains several September letters written to Johnson, Secretary Mc-Culloch, and Rep. John W. Leftwich from various local leaders. Congressman Leftwich responded to Campbell's plea by also writing to Johnson in behalf of the appointment of Owen. No record of an Owen appointment has been located.

From Alfred T. Goodman[1]

Cleveland Ohio   Sept 4 1866.

⟨Private⟩

My dear Sir:

During your recent visit to this city—the hospitalities of which were unanimously voted you by our city council, you delivered a speech which recomends itself to the calm & patient judgement of every lover of his country. As you are well aware during that speech—you were constantly interrupted by men—if men they can be called—in various portions of the crowd. It now turns out, that these men—some thirty or forty in number *were hired* by notorious abolitionists in this vicinity for the purpose of disturbing you on the occasion, and were paid for their services out of the Union League fund. This gang of "bullies" of "roughs" & I might say "perjured villians" who went to the meeting with the avowed purpose of insulting you & your cabinet, have made more votes for the

cause of the Union & the Constitution than a dozen campaign meetings
could have done.

Here in the western reserve where Joshua R. Giddings & Benj. F.
Wade have preached treason for thirty years, I anticipated your illustrious
party would not escape insult. The men here have no respect for law or
authority. They snear at the Constitution—and have for thirty years
called all men "traitors" who defended it. Could Gen. Jackson, rise from
his grave—and speak in this section for his bleeding country, he would
receive nought but insult from the men whom you justly style "cormorants" & "blood-suckers."

The whole plan at the meeting here, as I am truthfully informed, was
arranged before hand, and every one with whom I have spoken pro-
nounces the course of the "bullies" & their "abettors" to have been not
only disgraceful, but palpable in the extreme.

God bless you in your efforts to restore and make permanent the Government of our fathers. God bless you for what you have already done,
and may He give you strength to carry out your patriotic purposes. May
you stand firm by the Constitution & the Union regardless of traitors in
the North. The people will sustain you, and those that now persecute and
denounce you, will a year hence, wonder that they ever were so led astray
by fanatical demagogues, as to doubt the wisdom of your measures, or
your devotion to the principles of civil & religious liberty.

A. T. Goodman

ALS, DLC-JP.
   1. Goodman (1845–1871), alternately an editor and law student, became secretary of
the Western Reserve Historical Society and wrote a book about Ohio supreme court judges.
NUC; Cleveland directories (1867–71).

From Robert W. Johnson

personal

Home   Pine Bluff [Arkansas]   Sept. 4th/66

Dear Sir

Judging others by myself as the fairest rule I know of, a true man
would prefer to be *valued for himself*, since he is always the same, rather
than for his office, or position, or fortune, which may be brief & in-
constant.

It is natural and manly I hold it, to acknowledge favor, & the more so,
when, as in my case, it is confered, under circumstances of personal pecu-
liarity I can not forget, & which marks your action with a virtue of rare
character, and *that of magnanimity*, virtue in the display of which, so few
of our greatest men of this & all other ages, have indulged.

I have recd your signature which aquits me of my unfortunate political
offences, which releaves me of the penalties of secession, & protects me

against the dishonest exageration of Radical vindictiveness, and arrests the confiscation of my property, *all* of which will be needed to pay up large debts to a few creditors who have acted a forbearing & friendly part towards me.[1]

I thank you Sir for all this, and without professions, so commonly used but to be abused, I may include the unaffected cordiality & honourable sincerity of your reception & declarations to me at Washington, & say further that these will not be likely to be forgotten.

I send my acceptance of the pardon & its conditions by this mail.

Mrs Johnson[2] says to present her very kindest regards to Mrs Patterson, who was a much loved school mate of my Sister Irene.[3]

I may now without suspicion of object or interest of a personal character, & addressing you in your personal & not official capacity, subscribe myself with the highest respect.

R. W. Johnson

ALS, DLC-JP.
    1. Johnson wrote to the President pleading for a pardon when his property was libeled for confiscation in early April. He was pardoned on April 23. R. W. Johnson to Johnson, Apr. 7, 1866, Johnson Papers, LC; R. W. Johnson to Johnson, June 27, 1865, *Johnson Papers*, 8: 301.
    2. Johnson's second wife, Laura Smith Johnson. Ibid.
    3. Irene M. Johnson (1835–1878), the youngest of eight siblings, married Dr. John A. Jordan and had five children. Josiah H. Shinn, *Pioneers and Makers of Arkansas* ([Chicago], 1908), 205.

From R. M. Pickel[1]

"*Private*"

Mount Pleasant [Iowa], Sept 4th 1866

My Dear friend

It is reported from tollerable reliable authority that my removal from the office of U S. Assessor of this District is a fixed fact. Being raised, Educated, and knowing you personally and always your political advocate and friend up to the present time and see no reasons to desert you now, I am unable to assign any reason on political grounds for my removal.[2] I have held the office for the past four years and have faithfully and impartially discharged the duties and feel well assured that my administration of the Law has been very acceptable to our people and all the complaint that can be made is that I have held the office so long or that some one very anxious for office desires my removal to secure the position for himself or friend. It is true I have no claims to the office but would if consistent with the public interest, desire to continue Therein, and in the future as in the past, I will faithfully discharge the duties of the office. It is true that the political issues of the day are Exciting, but in my opinion the only policy that will restore the relations of the States of the Union and forever perpetuate universal liberty to our people is your Endorsement of that patriotic policy *"That* the relations of the Rebellious States to the Government were never disolved and that when the people of those" States formerly in Rebellion elected loyal Senators and Representatives that could take the oath prescribed by the Constitution and Laws they should at once be admitted each house being the judge of the election and qualifications of their own members. These are my political views as a Tennesseean and as a Citizen of Iowa. I will stand by them and whether I may or may not be retained in office by you it will be the same with me. I will stand by the old flag and those principles you advocate. Hoping to be advised by you and frankly dealt with at an early day.[3]

R. M. Pickel   Dist. Assessor

ALS, DNA-RG56, Appts., Internal Revenue Service, Assessor, Iowa, 1st Dist., R. M. Pickel.

1. Pickel (*c*1821–*fl*1870), a lawyer born and raised in Knoxville, Tennessee, had been assessor of the First District of Iowa since about September 1, 1862. 1870 Census, Iowa, Henry, Center Twp., Mt. Pleasant, 6; Pickel to Johnson, Mar. 14, 1861, Johnson Papers, LC; Pickel to Johnson, Oct. 23, 1866, Appts., Internal Revenue Service, Assessor, Iowa, 1st Dist., R. M. Pickel, RG56, NA.

2. Pickel eventually discovered that the alleged reason for his removal was his inability to pay $200 for campaign funds in 1866. Pickel to Hugh McCulloch, Feb. 14, 1867, ibid.

3. Although Pickel wrote several more letters trying to retain his post, he was removed despite his claimed long-term friendship with Johnson. When his successor was rejected by the Senate, Pickel requested reappointment but was not successful. Pickel to Johnson, Oct. 23, 1866, Nov. 15, 1866; Pickel to McCulloch, Feb. 14, 1867; S. L. Pickel to McCulloch, Feb. 15, 1867, ibid; Ser. 6B, Vol. 4: 329, 330, Johnson Papers, LC.

From Charles W. Griffith[1]

Fort McPherson, N.T.[2]   September 5th, 1866.

Sir:

I have the honor to submit the following facts in relation to the trial, by Court Martial of Capt Geo. O. Sokalski[3] at Fort Kearney, N.T. in May last. Being now the only member of that Court remaining in the Service, I have sometimes thought that a brief review of what I know of the trial might be of service to Captain S. in procuring his reinstatement in the U.S. Service.

The trial commenced about May 1st 1866. Captain Sokalski being unable to procure counsel, was obliged to conduct his defence himself, a task for which he, by reason of his long service in the field and consequent inattention to books on the subject of Military Law & Courts Martial, was in my humble opinion entirely unfit. By reason of his want of knowledge of the practise of Courts Martial he failed to procure the attendance at the trial of his own principal witnesses. He made known to the Court at the commencement of the trial that he wished to have Brevet Brig Gen'l Heath, Brevet Maj Chambers, 18th U S Infantry, and Dr W. T. McClelland,[4] 1st Neb Vet. Cavalry as witnesses for the defense; but in consequence of a want of proper understanding between himself and the

Judge Advocate,[5] the affidavit, that these witnesses were material to the defense of the accused, was not made until about the time that the examination of witnesses for the prosecution closed. It required some days for either of these witnesses to arrive, the nearest one being one hundred miles distant another two hundred and the third at Washington City or on the way thither. The Court refused to adjourn long enough to permit these witnesses to arrive, and thus the accused lost the testimony of *three* material witnesses. I would remark in this connection that the guard house at Fort Kearney was then crowded with prisoners awaiting trial and that in my own opinion strict justice to the prisoner required that they should, as is always done in civil courts have postponed the consideration of his case till the arrival of his witnesses, and spent the interval in disposing of other cases, of which there were many, in considering which their time might have been profitably employed. This, however, the Court failed to do the reason therefor assigned by Judge Advocate, being that the court could not properly commence another case till they had concluded the one on which they were engaged. It may also be mentioned here that the Regimental Quartermaster of the 7th Iowa Cavalry Lieut B. T. Giger,[6] was a member of the court martial by which Captain Sokalski was tried, in opposition to what I understand to be the uniform custom of the U.S. Service; no *staff officer* being ever made a member of a Court Martial when it is possible to avoid it. ⟨Benet's Military Law, Page 19.⟩[7]

Two of the officers belonging to the Court Martial[8] had their pay stopped at the time of the trial and for sometime previous to its commencement; which stoppage of pay I am informed by Captain Sokalski, was made in consequence of disclosures by Captain Sokalski to the War Dept of illegal practices of theirs in Connection with the purchase and sale of Goverment horses—the said disclosures having been made when Captain S. Commanded the Post of Fort Kearney in the winter 1865–6. I have no doubt whatever of the correctness of Captain Sokalski's statement that the stoppage of these officers' pay was in consequence of disclosures made by himself and being admitted as true it is scarcely conceiveable that it should not bias those officers more or less against him. It should also be borne in mind that the original misunderstanding between Captain Sokalski and Brevet Brig Gen Heath had its origin in the refusal by Captain S. to approve what he conceived to be a fraudulent Sale of Government horses, when required to give it his official approval by the Said General Heath, who then Commanded the East Sub-District of Nebraska. The charge of "disobedience of orders"—on which with others Captain S. was tried[9]—was preferred against him by order of Gen Heath. Captain S. also wrote an apology to General Heath, for this disobedience of orders, the original draft of which I have seen in the Captain's possession; but General Heath appears never to have received it. The Court Sentenced Captain Sokalski "*to be dismissed the Service of the United States.*" The sentence has been returned approved by Your Excellency and he ceases to be an officer in the Service of the United from July 10th 1866.

In view of the fact above mentioned that the legal constitution of the court may at least be questionable from the fact that one of its members was a *Staff officer*; in view of the further fact Stated by Captain Sokalski and of the correctness of which I have no doubt, that two of its members were at the time of the trial under stoppages of pay, caused by disclosures made by him—a circumstance which he thinks can hardly have failed to bias those members against him; in view above all of his long and faithful services in the field, during the late rebellion, a period of five years during great part of that time serving as Assistant Adjutant General of an Army Corps, in which, and in various other military positions, he has shown himself a gallant officer and an upright and honest man, having during the war participated in nearly twenty battles; in view of all these and of the further circumstance, that he was educated a Soldier and by long service in the Army is totally disqualified for earning a livelihood in any other calling, and has moreover an amiable and accomplished young wife[10] dependent upon him, with, so far as I am advised, no means whatever aside from his pay as an officer which is now cut off; in view of all these facts, I cannot but strongly hope that his appeal to your Excellency to restore him to his commission, will not have been made in vain. His services to his Country have surely been deserving of a better fate. Trusting that your Excellency may find it not inconsistent with duty and the interests of the Service to restore him to his former rank in the Army.[11]

Charles W. Griffith   Capt. 6th Infantry U S Vols

ALS, DNA-RG94, ACP Branch, File A-22-CB-1869, G. O. Sokalski.

1. Griffith, formerly a lieutenant in the 5th USCT, had been brevetted lieutenant colonel in March 1865 and was discharged from the army October 10, 1866. *Off. Army Reg.: Vols.*, 8: 139, 174.

2. Nebraska Territory.

3. New York native Sokalski (c1839–1867) graduated from West Point in 1861 and saw service in Missouri and Arkansas, for awhile as an aide-de-camp and assistant adjutant general. Although a lieutenant colonel of volunteers, he achieved the regular rank of captain. Powell, *Army List*, 600; *West Point Register* (1970), 255.

4. Herman H. Heath, Alexander Chambers, and William McLelland. Chambers (1832–1888) served with the 5th Inf. on the frontier and in garrison. Assigned to the 18th Inf., Chambers later fought with Iowa troops, was twice wounded at Shiloh, and brevetted major in the regular army. Later he was brevetted lieutenant colonel and colonel and appointed a brigadier general. Although this appointment was soon withdrawn by the Senate, he received the rank by brevet in March 1865. Omaha resident William McLelland became assistant surgeon of the 1st Nebr. Cav. in July 1861 and was promoted to surgeon on September 7, 1862. He was mustered out of service on July 1, 1866. Warner, *Blue*; *History of Nebraska*, 256.

5. Capt. Lee P. Gillette (1832–1894) of the 1st Nebr. Cav. moved to Nebraska in 1857. He entered the military as a first lieutenant in June 1861. His service included a few months as inspector and chief of cavalry, command at Fort Kearney, and judge advocate of the General Court Martial at the fort. After the war he served in the cavalry until December 1868; then he farmed and sold farming implements for the McCormick Harvesting Machine Company. Simon, *Grant Papers*, 16: 344; *History of Nebraska*, 1066; Pension File, Julietta B. Gillette, RG15, NA.

6. Benjamin F. Giger (b. c1829), a prewar "mechanic," served as a private, member of a

regimental brass band, and as a third sergeant before his promotion to first lieutenant and regimental commissary of the 7th Iowa in July 1863. He nearly received a dishonorable muster-out in the spring of 1866 "for fraudulent practices in connection with the appraisal and sale of horses the property of the U.S." The situation was somehow resolved and Giger received an honorable discharge. CSR, Benjamin F. Giger, RG94, NA.

7. Florida-born Stephen Vincent Benet (1827–1895) graduated from West Point and after several years as an ordnance officer, returned there to teach (1859–64). He was eventually chief of ordnance for the U.S. Army (1874–91). The book referred to is his *A Treatise on Military Law and the Practice of Courts-Martial* (1862). *NCAB*, 30: 446–47; *NUC*.

8. Giger and Gillette. Simon, *Grant Papers*, 16: 344.

9. Sokalski was charged with 1) "disobedience of orders" for refusing to provide a surgeon's certificate attesting to his illness; 2) "conduct to the prejudice of good order and military discipline" for returning the above order to General Heath "with disrespectful and unofficerlike endorsement," as well as hitting 2nd Lt. S. H. Norton and calling him "a d—d dirty little pup" on the public parade ground; and 3) "conduct unbecoming an officer and a gentleman" for the Norton incident, opening a piece of mail which supposedly did not belong to him, and collecting money without authority. He was found guilty of everything except collecting the money. Gen. Court-Martial Order No. 177, July 10, 1866, RG94, NA.

10. Sokalski's wife has not been identified.

11. Although Judge Advocate General Holt urged that Sokalski remain dismissed, General Grant further investigated the court-martial records. These substantiated the truth of the injustices reported by Griffith, as well as some not mentioned by the latter. Grant therefore urged reinstatement and Johnson agreed. Sokalski's dismissal was revoked on October 26, 1866. Apparently Sokalski got into trouble again and was arrested by February 1, 1867. No court-martial was ever held on these charges, however, because Sokalski died on February 12. Gen. Court-Martial Order No. 206, Oct. 26, 1866, RG94, NA; Endorsements attached to George O. Sokalski to Johnson, Oct. 18, 1866, ACP Branch, A-22-CB-1869, G. O. Sokalski, RG94, NA; Grant to Stanton, Oct. 19, 1866, Simon, *Grant Papers*, 16: 342–44.

From George S. Houston

Athens [Ala.].   5th Septr 1866

Sir

I find considerable trouble and feeling all over this community growing out of prosecutions begun & threatened prosecutions for penalties for failing to Comply with Some provisions of the revanue law. The point at present Causing much disturbance is this.

It Seems that all persons who recd packages by either of the express companies were bound when receipting for them to put a two cent Stamp &c on the receipt. The people really did not know that such was the law— nor did the agent of the express Company[1] know or if he did he never So informed them—the result is that in Several Cases—many the Stamp was omitted—not from any design wish or purpose to avoid the payment of the tax or in any way or to any extent defraud the Govt. The penalty in Such cases as I understand is fifty dollars but the collector has power to examine those cases & if he becomes Satisfied that there was no purpose to defraud the Govt &c &c he has the power to have the papers Stamped &c & remit the penalty. He has done that in many cases. Yet Mr Smith[2] the Govt atty contends that the Collector has no right to take such action but that all such cases—where the party did not discover his own mistake & correct it, must go into court—let the Court hear the evidence & if the judge thinks fit under the law he will remit the penalty. But you will see that such course leaves the parties to pay the costs attys fees &c &c— when it is all wholly unnecessary & oppressive. The people here are impoverished by the war—used all of their means & pretty much their credit to live this year—the excessively wet Spring & dry Summer destroyed their prospects for a Crop & even if let alone the distress will be greater next year than this & now if you add to their present embarrassments a bill of costs which will benefit no one but the officers—Certainly not the Govt—you will have in many Cases to sell property & turn the people out of doors & all for no Criminal intent but for ignorance of the law.

Besides the people are being harrassed & distressed—and it does Seem to me that you have the power to arrest this course of action on the part of your officers. I know the people here and generally never intended to wrong the Govt. & if there was or is any case of intentional wrong it is a rare one—*an exception.*

Now I appeal to you on behalf of the people who are in much trouble to take such steps as will arrest this Course of the Govt atty who is now in Huntsville.[3]

Geo S Houston

ALS, DNA-RG60, Office of Atty. Gen., Lets. Recd., President.
1. Not identified.
2. James Q. Smith.
3. Houston's letter was routinely referred to Secretary of the Treasury McCulloch.

From George Francis Train[1]

Private.

No 50 Sherman House [Chicago]   Sept 6. [1866]

To the President.

I leave tonight with the Governor[2] & Directors Pacific Road[3] for Omaha. You having stopped a Radical State by putting the Senators Bill in your Pocket[4] Nebraska elects a Delegate in October. The Pacific Railway capitalists wish me returned and back me.[5] The Radicals of course will not nominate me, and the *Valandighammers* will cry old Democratic Party and may shut me out. In that case I shall run as an Independent Johnson Candidate.

You know how ardently I have espoused the National Cause—*I know I have addressed more audiences the last year and have more power with the masses than any dozen of your other friends*—all I ask of you is that you will direct Col. Moore[6]—if you cannot write a line in your own handwriting—to say that I am on the right Track and that you are my friend—or rather that you appreciate my independent action.[7]

Geo. Francis Train

ALS, DLC-JP.
    1. Train (1829–1904), a shipper and author of travel books and other articles, was becoming increasingly eccentric during the 1860s. He had located in Nebraska "to further Johnson's policy and thereby receive an appointment for himself." *DAB;* Charles E. Ames, *Pioneering the Union Pacific: A Reappraisal of the Builders of the Railroad* (New York, 1969), 27; Berwanger, *West and Reconstruction*, 94.
    2. Probably Alvin Saunders of Nebraska.
    3. The *Chicago Tribune* noted that the directors of the Pacific Railroad, Charles T. Sherman, president, Jesse L. Williams, Springer Harbaugh, Timothy J. Carter, Col. Silas Seymour, the consulting engineer, and others, "left on Thursday night for Omaha in the President's car of the Northwestern Railroad." *Chicago Tribune*, Sept. 8, 1866.
    4. Presumably Train refers to Johnson's late July 1866 pocket veto of the bill for the admission of Nebraska as a state. See James M. Woolworth to Johnson, July 30, 1866, *Johnson Papers*, 10: 762–63; Nebraska Statehood Bill Veto Message, Jan. 29, 1867.
    5. Train was a good friend of Union Pacific vice president Thomas C. Durant. Ames, *Pioneering the Union Pacific*, 27; James B. Potts, "Nebraska Statehood and Reconstruction," *Nebraska History*, 69 (1988): 78–79.
    6. Johnson's secretary, William G. Moore.
    7. Train did run for Congress as an independent candidate but never received any letter from Moore or other indication of support from Johnson. He apparently withdrew from the contest at the last moment. Train soon moved on to Kansas, where he became involved in the campaign for impartial suffrage. Train to Johnson, Oct. 3, 1866; Train to William H. Seward, Oct. 3, 1866, Johnson Papers, LC; Potts, "Nebraska Statehood," 78–79; Berwanger, *West and Reconstruction*, 99, 167.

From Joseph A. Wright

Berlin   Sept 6th 1866

My Dear President,
    Do not suppose we have lost Sight of you & your Success.
    I wrote you in July last,[1] and well knowing how fully every moment of your time is occupied, have not expected to hear directly from you. My Correspondence with friends at home encourages me to believe we shall carry at least Six of the Congressional Ticket, for the *National Union Ticket.* This will be a gain of four members. In Ohio & Illinois we shall make great gains. The next House will be decidely Anti Ultraism.
    I see that Colfax[2] is fishing for the Irish vote, by advocating Fenianism. I wish we had a War Democrat running against him, then we should have more hopes of success.
    Remember you promised I should be at home in May 1868—I desire to be in the Contest, you must therefore give me leave of absence in 1868 for a few months.[3] The resolutions and address of the Philadelphia Convention are by far the most important and worthy expositions of the *true principles* upon which our Government is based, that has emanated from any body of men, since the Constitution itself was written. *We shall triumph.* Time and patience will make all right.
    We have men in some portions of Europe who are not worthy of the office they hold. You shall be advised of some of them ere long. Give us a good man at Hamburg for Consul.[4] It is one of the most important posi-

tions in Europe for us. We are all well tho we have been in the midst of Sickness and death for some months. The Cholera has been quite severe, but we have been wonderfully preserved.

Joseph A Wright

LS, DLC-JP.
1. No Wright to Johnson letter of July 1866 has been uncovered.
2. Schuyler Colfax.
3. Wright died in Berlin on May 11, 1867. *DAB*.
4. The consulship of Hamburg was offered to Davidson M. Leatherman, who declined. Samuel Williams was nominated in December 1866 and approved the following February, replacing James H. Anderson. Johnson to Leatherman, Aug. 5, 1866; Leatherman to Johnson, Aug. 6, 1866, Johnson Papers, LC; Ser. 6B, Vol. 2: 358, Johnson Papers, LC; *U.S. Off. Reg.* (1865).

From William A. Richardson

Quincy Illinois   September 8th 1866

Sir.

Let me call your attention to the importance of early removal of *radical officials* in the Territory of Nebraska.

The Congressional Election comes off in Nebraska early in October next.[1] We can carry Territory if we have the cordial co-operation of the federal officers there and by so doing endorse your Veto of the State Admission in advance.

I am informed and I beleive that the Democrats of Nebraska will not undertake to make the fight for the Administration, against the Radicals, against State, and federal officials unless these radical office holders are removed immediately.

. The recommendations already made by J. Sterling Morton and Dr. Geo. L. Miller Editors of the two largest papers in Nebraska[2] and the only papers which ably and sincerely support the Administration should be heeded.

Gen H H Heath[3] has been recommended by some for Governor of Nebraska and Major General John M. Corse of Burlington Iowa has been advocated for the same position.[4]

E. B. Taylor Sup't of Indian Affairs;[5] Royal Buck and W H H Waters Land Officers at Nebraska City;[6] George H. Smith Postmaster at Omaha City;[7] Robt W. Furnas Agent[8] of the Omaha Indians are *active radicals* and they should be ousted immediately and those gentleman already recommended appointed.

Unless these things are accomplished at once the effect on the fall elections will be lost.[9]

I am anxious to carry the election there in October that the fact may be established that the State was carried by fraud—which is the fact.

W A Richardson

ALS, DNA-RG59, Lets. of Appl. and Recomm., 1861–69 (M650, Roll 41), W. A. Richardson.

1. October 9, 1866. *American Annual Cyclopaedia* (1866), 736.

2. Morton was the editor of the *Nebraska City News*, while Miller (1831–1920) edited the *Omaha Herald* (1864–87). A physician, Miller moved from New York to Omaha, practiced his profession and served in the territorial legislature. From 1861 to 1864 he was the sutler at Fort Kearney, but spent the rest of his life in Omaha. *DAB; NCAB*, 19: 135; James W. Savage and John T. Bell, *History of the City of Omaha, Nebraska* (New York, 1894), 565–66; *History of Nebraska*, 785.

3. See Herman H. Heath to Johnson, Aug. 6, 1866.

4. Neither man was appointed, for Alvin Saunders remained governor until statehood. Pomeroy, *The Territories*, 123.

5. Edward B. Taylor (1821–1872) was involved with newspaper publishing and railroads in Ohio before Lincoln appointed him register of the land office at Omaha in 1861. On July 1, 1865, he was appointed superintendent for the Northern Superintendency, which was comprised of a variety of Indian tribes in the upper Midwest. Edmunds, *Pen Sketches*, 393; Hill, *Indian Affairs*, 119–20; Frazer E. Wilson, *History of Darke County, Ohio: From Its Earliest Settlement to the Present Time* (2 vols., Milford, Ohio, 1914), 1: 337.

6. Former Wisconsin schoolteacher and newspaper editor, Buck (1820–fl1871) moved to Nebraska in 1860 and was appointed register of the land office at Nebraska City in June 1861, a post he held until removed by Johnson. He then was assistant assessor of internal revenue for Cass and Otoe counties. William H.H. Waters (1835–fl1885) traveled to California and Oregon before settling in Nebraska in the late 1850s, where he edited several newspapers, one of them briefly with Royal Buck. He was receiver of the land office at Nebraska City (1863–66). In 1875 Waters moved to Salem, Oregon, where he edited a newspaper, practiced law, and sold real estate. Edmunds, *Pen Sketches*, 216–17, 230–33; Herbert O. Lang, ed., *History of the Willamette Valley* (Portland, 1885), 791.

7. George R. Smith (c1839–fl1891), a city engineer and later surveyor, was postmaster from May 16, 1861 until March 31, 1867. He was again in office in 1869–70. *U.S. Off. Reg.* (1861–71); Omaha directories (1866–74); 1870 Census, Nebr., Douglas, Omaha, 6th Ward, 17; Savage and Bell, *History of Omaha*, 79, 95, 411; *History of Nebraska*, 707.

8. Furnas (1824–1905) migrated to the Nebraska Territory from Ohio in 1856 and established the *Nebraska Advertiser* in Brownville. A prewar territorial legislator, he served in the regular army during the Civil War. Appointed agent for the Omaha Agency in March 1864, Furnas was later elected governor in 1872. *DAB*; Hill, *Office of Indian Affairs*, 122.

9. Johnson removed only Buck and Waters before the election. However, on October 26, 1866, he appointed a successor for Furnas and on October 29 for Taylor. Smith remained postmaster until March 31, 1867. Most of the replacements were later rejected by the Senate. Ser. 6B, Vol. 3: 708, Johnson Papers, LC; Hill, *Office of Indian Affairs*, 120, 122; *U.S. Off. Reg.* (1867); Berwanger, *West and Reconstruction*, 98–99. See also J. Sterling Morton to Johnson, Oct. 16, 1866.

Speech at St. Louis

[September 8, 1866]

FELLOW CITIZENS OF ST. LOUIS;

In being introduced to you to-night it is not for the purpose of making a speech. It is true I am proud to meet so many of my fellow citizens here on this occasion, and under the favorable circumstances that I do. ⟨Cry, "how about our British subject?"⟩ We will attend to John Bull after awhile so far as that is concerned. ⟨Laughter and loud cheers.⟩ I have just stated that I was not here for the purpose of making a speech, but after being introduced, simply to tender my cordial thanks for the welcome you have given to me in your midst. ⟨A voice: "Ten thousand welcomes;" hurrahs and cheers.⟩ Thank you sir. I wish it was in my power to address you under favorable circumstances upon some of the questions that agitate and distract the public mind at this time. Questions that have grown out of a fiery ordeal we have just passed through, and which I think as important as those we have just passed by. The time has come when it seems to me that all ought to be prepared for peace—the rebellion being suppressed, and the shedding of blood being stopped, the sacrifice of life being suspended and stayed, it seems that the time has arrived when we should have peace; when the bleeding arteries should be tied up. ⟨A voice: "New Orleans"; "go on."⟩

Perhaps if you had a word or two on the subject of New Orleans, you might understand more about it than you do. ⟨Laughter and cheers.⟩ And if you will go back ⟨cries for Seward⟩—if you will go back and ascertain the cause of the riot at New Orleans, perhaps you would not be so prompt in calling out New Orleans. If you will take up the riot at New Orleans and trace it back to its source, or to its immediate cause, you will find out who was responsible for the blood that was shed there.

If you will take up the riot at New Orleans and trace it back to the Radical Congress ⟨great cheering and cries of "bully"⟩, you will find that the riot at New Orleans was substantially planned—if you will take up the proceedings in their caucuses you will understand that they there knew ⟨cheers⟩ that a convention was to be called which was extinct, by its powers having expired; that it was said, and the intention was that a new Government was to be organized; and in the organization of that Government the intention was to enfranchise one portion of the population called the colored population, who had just been emancipated, and at the same time disfranchise white men. ⟨Great cheering⟩ When you begin to talk about New Orleans ⟨confusion⟩ you ought to understand what you are talking about.

When you read the speeches that were made or take up the facts—on Friday and Saturday before that convention sat—you will there find that speeches were made incendiary in their character, exciting that portion of the population, the black population, to arm themselves and prepare for the shedding of blood. ⟨A voice, "that's so!" and cheers.⟩ You will also find that that convention did assemble in violation of law, and the intention of that convention was to supersede the recognized authorities in the State Government of Louisiana, which had been recognized by the Government of the United States, and every man engaged in that rebellion— in that convention, with the intention of superseding and upturning the civil government which had been recognized by the Government of the United States—I say that he was a traitor to the Constitution of the United States, ⟨cheers,⟩ and hence you find that another rebellion was commenced, having its origin in the Radical Congress. These men were to go there: a Government was to be organized, and the one in existence in Louisiana was to be superceded, set aside and overthrown. You talk to me about New Orleans! And then the question was to come up, when they had established their government—a question of political power—which of the two governments was to be recognized—a new government inaugurated under this defunct convention—set up in violation of law, and without the consent of the people. And then when they had established their government, and extended universal or impartial franchise, as they called it, to this colored population, then this Radical Congress was to determine that a government established on negro votes was to be the government of Louisiana. ⟨Voices—"never," and cheers and "hurrah for Andy."⟩

So much for the New Orleans riot—and there was the cause and the origin of the blood that was shed, and every drop of blood that was shed is upon their skirts, and they are responsible for it. ⟨Cheers.⟩ I could trace this thing a little closer, but I will not do it here to night. But when you talk about New Orleans, and talk about the causes and consequences that resulted from proceedings of that kind, perhaps, as I have been introduced here, and you have provoked questions of this kind, though it don't provoke me, I will tell you a few wholesome things that *has* been done by this Radical Congress. ⟨Cheers.⟩

In connection with New Orleans and the extension of the elective franchise, I know that I have been traduced and abused. I know it has come in advance of me here, as it has elsewhere, and that I have attempted to exercise an arbitrary power in resisting laws that *was* intended to be enforced on the Government. ⟨Cheers, and cries of "hear."⟩ Yes, that I had exercised the veto power, ⟨"Bully for you,"⟩ that I had abandoned the power that elected me, and that I was a *t-r-ai-tor* ⟨cheers⟩ because I exercised the veto power in attempting to, and did arrest for a time, a bill that was called a Freedmen's Bureau bill. ⟨Cheers.⟩ Yes, that I was a *t-r-ai-t-o-r*! And I have been traduced, I have been slandered, I have been maligned, I have been called Judas—Judas Iscariot, and all that. Now, my countrymen here to-night, it is very easy to indulge in epithets, it is very easy to call a man Judas, and cry out t-r-ai-t-o-r, but when he is called upon to give arguments and facts, he is very often found wanting.

Judaas, Judas Iscariot, Judaas! There was a Judas once, one of the twelve apostles. Oh! yes, and these twelve apostles had a Christ. ⟨A voice, "and a Moses, too." Great laughter.⟩ The twelve apostles had a Christ, and he couldn't have had a Judas unless he had had twelve apostles. If I have played the Judas, who has been my Christ that I have played the Judas with? Was it Thad. Stevens? Was it Wendell Phillips? Was it Charles Sumner? ⟨Hisses and cheers.⟩ Are these the men that set up and compare themselves with the Saviour of men, and everybody that differs with them in opinion, and try to stay and arrest their diabolical and nefarious policy, is to be denounced as a Judas? ⟨"Hurrah for Andy," and cheers.⟩

In the days when there were twelve Apostles and when there ware a Christ, while there ware Judases, there ware unbelievers, too. Y-a-s; while there ware Judases there ware unbelievers. ⟨Voices—"hear." "Three groans for Fletcher."[1]⟩ Yes, oh! yes! unbelievers in Christ: men who persecuted and slandered and brought him before Pontius Pilate and preferred charges and condemned and put him to death on the cross, to satisfy unbelievers. And this same persecuting, diabolical and nefarious clan to-day would persecute and shed the blood of innocent men to carry out their purposes. ⟨Cheers.⟩ But let me tell you—let me give you a few words here to-night—and but a short time since I heard some one say in the crowd that we had a Moses. ⟨Laughter and cheers⟩ Yes, there was a Moses. And I know sometimes it has been said that I have said that I would be the Moses of the colored man. ⟨"Never," and cheers.⟩ Why, I have labored as much in the cause of emancipation as any other mortal man living. But while I have strived to emancipate the colored man, I have felt, and now feel, that we have a great many white men that want emancipation. ⟨Laughter and cheers.⟩ There is a set amongst you that have got shackles on their limbs, and are as much under the heel and control of their masters as the colored man that was emancipated. ⟨Cheers.⟩ I call upon you here to night, as freemen—as men who favor the emancipation of the white man as well as the colored ones. I have been in favor of emancipation. I have nothing to disguise about that. I have tried to do as much, and have done as much, and when they talk about Moses and the colored man being led into the promised land, where is the land that this clan proposes to lead them? ⟨Cheers.⟩ When we talk about taking them out from among the white population and sending them to other climes, what is it they propose? Why, it is to give us a Freedmen's Bureau. And after giving us a Freedmen's Bureau, what then? Why, here in the South it is not necessary for me to talk to you, where I have lived and you have lived, and understand the whole system, and how it operates; we know how the slaves have been worked heretofore. Their original owners bought the land and raised the negroes, or purchased them, as the case might be; paid all the expenses of carrying on the farm, and in the end, after producing tobacco, cotton, hemp and flax, and all the various products of the South, bringing them into the market, without any profit to them while these owners put it all into their own pockets. This was their condition before the emancipation. This was their condition before we talked about their "Moses." ⟨Laughter.⟩ Now what is the plan? I ask your attention. Come, as we have got to talking on this subject, give me your attention for a few minutes. I am addressing myself to your brains, and not to your prejudices; to your reason and not to your passions. And when reason and argument again resume their empire, this mist, this prejudice that has been incrusted upon the public mind must give way and reason become triumphant. ⟨Cheers.⟩ Now, my countrymen, let me call your attention to a single fact, the Freedmen's Bureau. ⟨Laughter and hisses.⟩

Yes; slavery was an accursed institution till emancipation took place. It was an accursed institution while one set of men worked them and got the profits. But after emancipation took place they gave us the Freedmen's Bureau. They gave us these agents to go into every county, every township, and into every school district throughout the United States, and especially the Southern States. They gave us commissioners. They gave us $12,000,000 and placed the power in the hands of the Executive, who was to work this machinery, with the army brought to his aid, and to sustain it. Then let us run it, with $12,000,000 as a beginning, and, in the end, receive $50,000,000 or $60,000,000, as the case may be, and let us work the 4,000,000 of slaves. In fine, the Freedmen's Bureau was a simple proposition to transfer 4,000,000 of slaves in the United States from their original owners to a new set of taskmasters. ⟨Voice: "Never," and cheers.⟩ I have been laboring four years to emancipate them; and then I was opposed to seeing them transferred to a new set of taskmasters, to be worked with more rigor than they had been worked heretofore. ⟨Cheers.⟩ Yes, under this new system they would work the slaves, and call on the Government to bear all the expense, and if there was any profits left, why they would pocket them, ⟨laughter and cheers,⟩ while you, the people, must pay the expense of running the machine out of your own pockets, while they got the profits of it. So much for this question.

I simply intended to-night to tender you my sincere thanks. But as I go along, as we are talking about this Congress and these respected gentlemen, who contend that the President is wrong, because he vetoed the Fredmen's Bureau bill, and all this; because he chose to exercise the veto power, he committed a high offense, and, therefore, ought to be impeached. ⟨Voice, "never."⟩ *Y-e-s, y-e-s*; they are ready to impeach him. ⟨Voice, "let them try it."⟩ And if they were satisfied they had the next Congress by as decided a majority as this, upon some pretext or other— violating the Constitution—neglect of duty, or omitting to enforce some set of law, upon some pretext or other, they would vacate the Executive Department of the United States. ⟨A voice, "too bad they don't impeach him."⟩ *Wha-t?* As we talk about this Congress, let me call the soldiers' attention to this immaculate Congress. Let me call your attention. Oh! this Congress, that could make war upon the Executive because he stands upon the Constitution and vindicates the rights of the people, exercising the veto power in their behalf—because he dared to do this, they can clamor, and talk about impeachment. And by way of elevating themselves and increasing confidence with the soldiers, throughout the country, they talk about impeachments.

So far as the Fenians are concerned, upon this subject of Fenians, let me ask you very plainly here to-night, to go back into my history of legislation, and even when Governor of a State let me ask if there is a man here to-night, who, in the dark days of Knownothingism, stood and sacrificed more for their rights? ⟨Voice, "good," and cheers.⟩

It has been my peculiar misfortune always to have fierce opposition, because I have always struck my blows direct, and fought with right and the Constitution on my side. ⟨Cheers.⟩ Yes, I will come back to the soldiers again in a moment. Yes, here was a neutrality law. I was sworn to support the Constitution and see that that law was faithfully executed. And because it was executed, then they raised a clamor and tried to make an appeal to the foreigners; and especially the Fenians. And what did they do? They introduced a bill to tickle and play with the fancy, pretending to repeal the law, and at the same time making it worse and then left the law just where it is. ⟨Voice—"That's so."⟩ They knew that whenever a law was presented to me, proper in its provisions, ameliorating and softening the rigors of the present law, that it would meet my hearty approbation. But as they were pretty well broken down and losing public confidence, at the heels of the session they found they must do something. And hence, what did they do? They pretended to do something for the soldiers. Who has done more for the soldiers than I have? Who has periled more in this struggle than I have? ⟨Cheers.⟩ But then, to make them their peculiar friends and favorites of the soldiers, they came forward with a proposition to do what? Why, we will give the soldier $50 bounty—$50 bounty—your attention to this—if he has served two years; and $100 if he has served three years. Now, mark you, the colored man that served two years can get his $100 bounty. But, the white man must serve *three* before he can get his. ⟨Cheers.⟩ But that is not the point. While they were tickling and attempting to please the soldiers, by giving them $50 bounty for two years' service, they took it into their heads to vote somebody else a bounty, ⟨laughter⟩ and they voted themselves not $50 for two years' service; your attention—I want to make a lodgment in your minds of the facts, because I want to put the nail in, and having put it in, I want to clinch it on the other side. ⟨Cheers.⟩ The brave boys, the patriotic young men, who followed his gallant officers, slept in the tented field, and perilled his life, and shed his blood, and left his limbs behind him and came home, mangled and maimed, can get $50 bounty, if he has served two years. But the members of Congress, who never smelt gunpowder, can get $4,000 extra pay. ⟨Loud cheering.⟩

This is a faint picture, my countrymen, of what has transpired. ⟨A voice, "Stick to that question."⟩ Fellow-citizens, you are all familiar with the work of restoration. You know that since the rebellion collapsed, since the armies were suppressed in the field, that everything that could be done has been done by the Executive Department of the Government for the restoration of the Government. Everything has been done, with the exception of one thing, and that is the admission of members from the eleven States that went into the rebellion. And after having accepted the terms of the Government, having abolished slavery, having repudiated their debt, and sent loyal representatives, everything has been done, excepting the admission of Representatives which all the States are constitutionally entitled to. ⟨Cheers⟩ When you turn and examine the Constitution of the United States, you can find that you cannot even amend that Constitution so as to deprive any State of its equal suffrage in the Senate. ⟨A voice, "They have never been out."⟩ It is said before me, "they have never been out." I say so, too. That is what I have always said. They have never been out, and they cannot go out. ⟨Cheers.⟩ That being the fact, under the Constitution they are entitled to equal suffrage in the Senate of the United States, and no power has the right to deprive them of it, without violating the Constitution. ⟨Cheers.⟩ And the same argument applies to the House of Representatives. How, then does the matter stand? It used to be one of the arguments, that if the States withdrew their Representatives and Senators, that that was secession—a peaceable breaking up of the Government. Now, the Radical power in this Government turn around and assume that the States are out of the Union, that they are not entitled to representation in Congress. ⟨Cheers.⟩ That is to say, they are dissolutionists, and their position now is to perpetuate a disruption of the Government, and that, too, while they are denying the States the right of representation, they impose taxation upon them, a principle upon which, in the revolution, you resisted the power of Great Britain. We deny the right of taxation without representation. That is one of our great principles. Let the Government be restored. Let peace be restored among the people. I have labored for it. Now I deny this doctrine of secession; come from what quarter it may, whether from the North or from the South. I am opposed to it. I am for the Union of the States. ⟨Voices, "that's right," and cheers.⟩ I am for the thirty-six stars, representing thirty-six States, remaining where they are, under the Constitution, as your fathers made it, and handed it down to you. And if it is altered, or amended, let it be done in the mode and manner pointed by that instrument itself, and in no other. ⟨Cheers.⟩ I am for the restoration of peace. Let me ask this people here to-night if we have not shed enough blood. Let me ask, are you prepared to go into another civil war. Let me ask this people here to-night are they prepared to set man upon man, and, in the name of God, lift his hand against the throat of his fellow. ⟨Voice "Never."⟩ Are you prepared to see our fields laid waste again, our business and commerce suspended and all trade stopped. Are you prepared to see this land again drenched in our brothers' blood? Heaven avert it, is my prayer. ⟨Cheers.⟩ I am one of those who believe that man does sin, and having sinned, I believe he must repent. And, sometimes, having sinned and having repented makes him a better man than he was before. ⟨Cheers.⟩ I know it has been said that I have exercised the pardoning power. *Y-e-s*, I have. ⟨Cheers and "what about Drake's Constitution?"[2]⟩ *Y-e-s*, I have, and don't you think it is to prevail? I reckon I have pardoned more men, turned more men loose and set them at liberty that were imprisoned, I imagine, than any other living man on God's habitable globe. ⟨Voice, "bully for you," and cheers.⟩ Yes, I turned forty-seven thousand of our men who engaged in this struggle, with the arms we captured with them, and who were then in prison, I turned them loose. ⟨Voice, "bully for you, old fellow," and laughter.⟩ Large numbers have applied for pardon, and I have granted them pardon. Yet there are some who condemn and hold me responsible for doing wrong. Yes, there are some who stayed at home, who did not go into the field on the other side, that can talk about others being traitors and being treacherous. There are some who can talk about blood, and vengeance, and crime, and everything to "make treason odious," and all that, who never smelt gunpowder on either side. ⟨Cheers.⟩ Yes, they can condemn others and recommend hanging and torture, and all that. If I have erred, I have erred on the side of mercy. Some of these croakers have dared to assume that they are better than was the Savior of men himself—a kind of over righteousness—better than everybody else, and always wanting to do Deity's work, thinking he cannot do it as well as they can. ⟨Laughter and cheers.⟩ Yes, the Savior of man came on the earth and found the human race condemned, and sentenced under the law. But when they repented and believed, he said, "Let them live." Instead of executing and putting the whole world to death, he went upon the cross and there was painfully nailed by these unbelievers that I have spoken of here to-night, and there shed his blood that you and I might live. ⟨Cheers.⟩ Think of it! To execute and hang, and put to death eight millions of people. ⟨Voice, "never."⟩ It is an absurdity, and such a thing is impracticable even if it were right. But it is the violation of all law, human and divine. ⟨Voice, "hang Jeff. Davis."⟩ You call on Judge Chase to hang Jeff. Davis, will you? ⟨Great cheering.⟩ I am not the Court, I am not the jury, nor the judge. ⟨Voice, "nor the Moses."⟩ Before the case comes to me, and all other cases, it would have to come on application as a case for pardon. That is the only way the case can get to me. Why don't Judge Chase— Judge Chase, the Chief Justice of the United States, in whose district he is—why don't he try him? ⟨Loud cheers.⟩ But, perhaps, I could answer the question; as sometimes persons want to be facetious and indulge in repartee, I might ask you a question, why don't you hang Thad. Stevens and Wendell Phillips? ⟨Great cheering.⟩ A traitor at one end of the line is as bad as a traitor at the other.

I know that there are some who have got their little pieces and sayings to repeat on public occasions, like parrots, that have been placed in their mouths by their superiors, who have not the courage and the manhood to come forward and tell them themselves, but have their understrappers to do their work for them. ⟨Cheers⟩ I know there is some that talk about this universal elective franchise, upon which they wanted to upturn the Goverment of Louisiana and institute another; who contended that we must send men there to control, govern, and manage their slave population, because they are incompetent to do it themselves. And yet they turn round when they get there and say they are competent to go to Congress, and manage the affairs of State. ⟨Cheers.⟩ Before you commence throwing your stones, you ought to be sure you don't live in a glass house. Then, why all this clamor! Don't you see, my countrymen, it is a question of power; and being in power as they are, their object is to perpetuate their power? Hence, when you talk about turning any of them out of office, oh, they talk about "bread and butter." ⟨Laughter.⟩ Yes, these men are the most perfect and complete "bread and butter party" that has ever appeared in this government. ⟨Great cheering.⟩ When you make an effort, or struggle to take the nipple out of their mouths, how they clamor! They have staid at home here five or six years, held the offices, grown fat, and enjoyed all the emoluments of position; and now, when you talk about turning one of them out, "oh, it is proscription;" and hence they come forward and propose in Congress to do what? To pass laws to prevent the Executive from turning anybody out. ⟨Voice, "Put 'em out."⟩ Hence, don't you see what the policy was to be? I believe in the good old doctrine advocated by Washington, Jefferson and Madison, of rotation in office. These people who have been enjoying these offices seem to have lost sight of this doctrine. I believe that when one set of men have enjoyed the emoluments of office long enough, they should let another portion of the people have a chance. ⟨Cheers.⟩ How are these men to be got out— ⟨Voice, "Kick 'em out." Cheers and laughter⟩ unless your Executive can put them out, unless you can reach them through the President? Congress says he shall not turn them out, and they are trying to pass laws to prevent it being done. Well, let me say to you, if you will stand by me in this action, ⟨cheers,⟩ if you will stand by me in trying to give the people a fair chance, soldiers and citizens, to participate in those offices, God being willing, I *will* "kick them out" just as fast as I can. ⟨Great cheering.⟩ Let me say to you in concluding, what I have said, and I intended to say but little, but was provoked into this rather than otherwise, I care not for the menaces, the taunts and the jeers. I care not for the threats; I do not intend to be bullied by my enemies nor overawed by my friends ⟨cheers⟩; but, God willing, with your help, I will veto their measures whenever they•come to me. ⟨Cheers.⟩ I place myself upon the ramparts of the Constitution, and when I see the enemy approaching, so long as I have eyes to see, or ears to hear, or a tongue to sound the alarm, so help me God, I will do it and call on the people to be my judges. ⟨Cheers.[)⟩] I tell you here tonight that the Constitution of the country is being encroached upon. I tell you here to-night that the citadel of liberty is being endangered. ⟨A voice—"Go it, Andy."⟩

I say to you then, go to work; take the Constitution as your palladium of civil and religious liberty; take it as our chief ark of safety. Just let me ask you here to-night to cling to the Constitution in this great struggle for freedom, and for its preservation, as the ship wrecked mariner clings to the mast when the midnight tempest closes around him. ⟨Cheers.⟩ So far as my public life has been advanced, the people of Missouri, as well as other States, know that my efforts have been devoted in that direction which would ameliorate and elevate the interests of the great mass of the people. ⟨Voice: "That's so."⟩ Why, where's the speech, where's the vote to be got of mine, but what has always had a tendency to elevate the great working classes of this people? ⟨Cheers.⟩ When they talk about tyranny and despotism, where's one act of Andy Johnson's that ever encroached upon the rights of a freeman in this land? But because I have stood as a faithful sentinel upon the watch tower of freedom to sound the alarm, hence all this traduction and detraction that has been heaped upon me. ⟨"Bully for Andy Johnson."⟩ I now, then, in conclusion, my countrymen, hand over to you the flag of your country with thirty six stars upon it. I hand over to you your Constitution with the charge and responsibility of preserving it intact. I hand over to you to-night the Union of these States, the great magic circle which embraces them all. I hand them all over to you, the people, in whom I have always trusted in all great emergencies—questions which are of such vital interest—I hand them over to you as men who can rise above party, who can stand around the altar of a common country with their faces upturned to heaven, swearing by Him that lives forever and ever that the altar and all shall sink in the dust, but that the Constitution and the Union shall be preserved. Let us stand by the union of these States, let us fight enemies of the Government, come from what quarter they may. My stand has been taken. You understand what my position is, and in parting with you now, leave the Government in your hands, with the confidence I have always had that the people will ultimately redress all wrongs and set the Government right. Then, gentlemen, in conclusion, for the cordial welcome you have given me in this great city of the Northwest, whose destiny no one can foretell. Now, ⟨Voice: "Three cheers for Johnson,"⟩ then, in bidding you good night, I leave all in your charge, and thank you for the cordial welcome you have given me in this spontaneous outpouring of the people of your city.

Missouri Democrat (St. Louis), Sept. 10, 1866.
   1. Thomas C. Fletcher, governor of Missouri.
   2. Charles D. Drake, the principal architect of Missouri's constitution drafted in 1865.

From John West[1]

                                        Ellsworth, [Maine]   Sept 8th 1866
Sir
   I had the honor to be appointed and Commissioned in the year 1862, by your predesessor to the office of Collector of Internal Revenue in the Fifth District of the State of Maine.
   I have to the best of my ability discharged the duties of the office and I flatter myself to the satisfaction of the tax payers of the district and I hope & trust measurebly to the acceptance of the departments at Washington with which I have had to do in my official capacity.

I can but observe by your recent addreses to the people of the Country[2] you are in favor where practicable the offices of the Goverment be filled by meritorious honorably discharged offices and soldiers that have served the Goverment in its late terriable conflict with Rebels, and I perceive such policy is being caried out in this vicinity by your recent appointments.

As such policy is in accord with my own views, I feel constrained to vacate the office I now hold to make room for some one of those deserving men.

I therefore tender to you my resignation of the office of Collector of Internal Revenue which I have had the honor to hold for the last four years to take effect at the end of the present Quarter or at any time it may suit your convenience and pleasure to appoint some one of those deserving men my successor.[3]

John West

ALS, DNA-RG56, Appts., Internal Revenue Service, Collector, Maine, 5th Dist., John West.

1. On the eve of the war, West (b. c1799), who worked as a merchant in nearby Franklin, had a combined estate worth an estimated $17,000. 1860 Census, Maine, Hancock, Franklin, 501.

2. See Johnson's Circular re Appointments to Office, Apr. 7, 1866, Johnson Papers, 10: 368. A more "recent" address by Johnson on this topic has not been located.

3. West's resignation was accepted and George W. Berry, a brother of the late Gen. Hiram G. Berry, was given a recess appointment to the post in early October 1866. But the Senate rejected Berry's formal nomination a few months later. Appts., Internal Revenue Service, Collector, Maine, 5th Dist., George W. Berry, RG56, NA; Ser. 6B, Vol. 3: 13; Vol. 4: 2, Johnson Papers, LC; Warner, Blue.

From Samuel B. Franks[1]

Woodbury, Cannon Co. Tenn
September 10th, 1866

Sir,

You will please pardon me, an obscure private individual, for thus presuming, to occupy a small portion of your time, in the perusal of this letter. My subject is the grievances of our downtrodden people, and knowing you to be an ardent friend of the people I feel encouraged to inform you of the military despotism, under the regime of Brownlow that we are forced to live under. Here in the quiet village of Woodbury we have a garrison of U.S. soldiers, fifteen in number of the 16th Regulars, sent here by Gen Thomas from Nashville, at the urgent request of Brownlow, for no other purpose than to intimidate the people, and if possible to prevent the assembling of loyal men, endorsing the Convention which met in Philadelphia on the 14th of August, and "*your policy*" of restoration. These soldiers as is natural commit all manner of depredations on private property, and the people have no recourse whatever, as Genl Thomas,

and Brownlow, are radicals, and exult in the miseries of our people, supposing you to be ignorant of the continuation of martial law, after your
Peace Proclamation.[2] I appeal to you sir, as the Chief Executive of the
nation, and as the friend of liberty, in behalf of our people, to cause the
removal of these troops from our midst. Seventeen twentieth of the entire
population of your native state, Tennessee are for your policy of reconstruction, but the voice of the patriot and Statesman is silent, and none
but the wicked and malicious Brownlow, and his minions have authority
to speak or act. Withdraw the military from our midst, and radical military leaders, and Brownlow will then be disarmed, and next summer will
find Tennessee redeemed from those who are trying to build up a monarchy amongst us. Your Policy will be endorsed and we will be on the
high road to happiness and prosperity again.

S. B. Franks
In behalf of the people of Cannon County Tenn

ALS, DLC-JP.
   1. Franks (b. c1845) was a Cannon County farmer whose household in 1870 consisted
of himself, his wife, one young daughter, and a domestic servant. 1870 Census, Tenn., Cannon, 2nd Dist., Woodbury P.O., 7.
   2. A reference to Johnson's April 2 proclamation, which declared an official end to the
war everywhere, except in Texas. See Proclamation re End of Insurrection, Apr. 2, 1866,
Johnson Papers, 10: 349–52.

From John P. Hale

Legation of the United States of America,
Madrid, Sept 10, 1866

Sir

The long and uninterrupted friendship which has existed between us,
commencing with the 28th Congress in 1843 emboldens me to address
you frankly at the present time. I have seen in various newspapers, reports that I am to be shortly relieved of my present position. Indeed a
Spanish newspaper published as lately as the 8th of the present month,
says that the newspapers at Washington give it as a settled thing that I am
to be recalled, & they mention also the gentleman who is to occupy the
place.[1] I trust that I am not over sensitive in regard to newspaper notices,
but as this gives it as a settled thing that I am to be removed, I have
thought I might, without impropriety, make it the subject of a communication to you.

This situation was conferred on me by the late President Lincoln,
without any solicitation on my part, or on the part of my friends, so far as I
know or believe. Upon coming here, I found the compensation inadequate to support me in the same style that a great majority of the Foreign
ministers live. From my own private means independent of my salary, I
have been compelled to expend over two thousand dollars towards fur-

nishing a house, & if I am to remain here, shall be obliged to add to that two thousand more before winter to complete it. For a portion of this, I am still in debt, & if I were to be recalled at this time, I should consider myself more fortunate than I expect to be, if I could dispose of my furniture at a loss of only fifty per cent.

Under these circumstances, if in your judgment, the public good requires my removal or resignation, I have no word of complaint to utter, but would ask as a favor that I may not be compelled to leave here abruptly, but would respectfully ask, that in case, my resignation is deemed desirable, I may have as much notice as is practicable, with six months leave of absence, so that my coming here & bringing my family may not result in more pecuniary loss to myself than is absolutely unavoidable. By rigid economy, I hope to be able to live here on the salary & do not wish to resign, unless it is wished by the U S Government.[2]

John P Hale

ALS, DLC-JP.
1. While no evidence has been found in the Washington papers, the *New York Herald* reported in mid-August that the talk was that Secretary of War Stanton, following his resignation, would be given the mission to Spain. *New York Herald*, Aug. 19, 21, 1866.
2. Hale remained minister until July 1869, when he was replaced by Daniel E. Sickles. *Register of the Department of State* (Washington, D.C., 1872), 72.

From John J. Otis[1]

Columbia Tuolumne County   State of California
September 10th 1866

Dear Sir

Your old friends and neighbors of Tennessee who have emigrated to this distant country are I understand generally uniting in requesting you to appoint Judge James McCabe[2] of San Francisco to the office of Judge of the District Court of the United States for the Southern District of California. I, as an old Tenessean have concluded to put in my oar because I Knew Judge McCabe in Memphis about the year 1844, when Jimmy Polk cleaned out Henry Clay of Kentucky. I am from Henderson County and I Know You for the Same reason that there is not a man, woman nor child in western Tennessee who does not Know Andy Johnson. I voted for you for Governor and for Vice President and I expect to live to vote for you for President; and I have a right to talk to you pretty plain.

I came out to California in 1858 and have been mining here with pretty good luck—have saved about $25,000 and am going back to old Tennessee next year. Our mining company got Sued about a year ago; we had borrowed some money from a Frenchman in Columbia and gave a mortgage on the mine, mill &c. He undertook to foreclose on us before the mortgage was due. I Knew that McCabe was practicing law in San Francisco and having Known him in Tenessee I went after him to defend the Suit. He came up and cleaned out the French gentleman and I have tied to McCabe ever Since. He is a young Sound and rising lawyer, like you was in 1840 when your fame and Eloquence began to be talked about in the backwoods of Tennessee. I want you to appoint McCabe.[3] If Old Hickory could rise up from his grave he would say appoint him too. We call you Young Hickory out here and think you are as good a man as Jackson was. I shall meet you some time in Tennessee and remind you of some things which will make you remember your old friend and fellow Statesman.

John J. Otis

I Send this down to San Francisco by one of our boys to be mailed there in time for the outgoing Steamer.

ALS, DNA-RG60, Appt. Files for Judicial Dists., Calif., James McCabe.
    1. Not further identified.
    2. A native of New York, McCabe (fl1880) moved to Michigan, where he was admitted to the bar; afterwards, due to ill health, he moved to Tennessee. Health problems caused him to move to the Pacific Coast about 1850 and to locate in San Francisco about 1854, where he continued to practice law until at least 1880. William A. Cornwall to Johnson, Aug. 11, 1866; McCabe to Johnson, Sept. 17, 1866, Appt. Files for Judicial Dists., Calif.,James McCabe, RG60, NA; San Francisco directories (1865–80).
    3. Johnson did not appoint McCabe, at least in part because in 1866 Congress abolished the southern judicial district of California, thereby making all persons who had business with the federal courts travel to San Francisco. Hubert H. Bancroft, *History of California* (7 vols., San Francisco, 1884–90), 7: 238.

From Edward Bates

St Louis, Sept 11. 1866.

Honored Sir,

    When, but a few days ago, you honored me with a personal visit, in my own sick room,[1] I little thought that, in so short a time, I should appear before you in the troublesome attitude of an applicant for a personal favor. Believe me Sir, that I would not have done it, but that my repugnance was overcome by the manly desire, (may I not say, the reasonable wishes) of my youngest son, *Charles Woodson Bates*—a youth, in his 22d year.[2] His letter, addressed to you personally, & herewith sent, will speak for itself. It states distinctly what favor he asks at your hands;[3] and I can only vouch for the truth & honesty of his statements, and add a few particulars which he has omitted.

    By the kindness of President Lincoln, he was appointed a Cadet at West Point, & as such served for two years or more.[4] And here, I must confess that my ambition was mortified & my hopes disappointed—for I did expect him to take rank with the foremost youths of the Academy, for

I knew that he was not addicted to any degrading vice, and I confidently believed that he had good, fair talents and unusual bodily powers of strength & activity. But, by exuberant animal spirits & lack of diligence in study, he failed in some of the higher branches taught in the institution;[5] and I believe the mortification of that failure precipitated his resignation, and forced him (as he thought) to give up his profession.

His connection with the Academy, being thus ended, an application was made to the War Dept, by some of his official friends at the Point, for a commission in the army, and although that application failed, he had the satisfaction to know that his late associates, the Corps of Cadets, generously waived all opposition to his appointment, which might, in the contingent future, interfere with their own promotion.[6]

This is his case sir, and I can but add to his solicitation, my own earnest request that you will be pleased to grant the favor.

He is, in fact, an ingenuous youth, & has already suffered severely, the penalty of his past negligence; and if you now, generously, restore him to his lost profession, I make no doubt that his sense of gratitude will be a sure guarantee of his future good conduct; and that no fears need be entertained that the Public will suffer loss or you discredit by his appointment.[7]

Edw. Bates

ALS, DNA-RG94, ACP Branch, File B-1022-CB-1866, C. Woodson Bates.

1. Johnson, Seward, and Gideon Welles visited Bates on September 9. Marvin R. Cain, *Lincoln's Attorney General: Edward Bates of Missouri* (Columbia, 1965), 329.

2. Bates (c1845–fl1881) became a bookkeeper, teller, and clerk with two different St. Louis banks. St. Louis directories (1868–81).

3. C. W. Bates asked for a commission as lieutenant in the regular cavalry. Bates to Johnson, Sept. 10, 1866, ACP Branch, File B-1022-CB-1866, C. Woodson Bates, RG94, NA.

4. Young Bates entered the military academy in July 1862 and resigned in March 1866. Ibid., endorsements.

5. According to Edmund Schriver, the inspector of the military academy, by 1865, Bates stood at the bottom of his class (63rd) and had 189 demerits for the year. He was held back a year and would not have graduated until 1867. In January 1866 he apparently failed at least the philosophy examination. Ibid.; Howard K. Beale, ed., *The Diary of Edward Bates, 1859–1866* (Washington, D.C., 1933), 537.

6. C. Woodson Bates to Lorenzo Thomas, Apr. 24, 1866, ACP Branch, File B-1022-CB-1866, C. Woodson Bates, RG94, NA. This letter contained petitions from the First and Second classes at the military academy, both dated March 27, 1866.

7. On September 18, 1866, Johnson's secretary, William G. Moore, by order of the President, referred Edward Bates's letter to the secretary of war, "who will please make this appointment if it can be done consistently with the law." However, when the request was referred to the officials at the academy, Inspector Schriver noted the academy regulations which prohibited a cadet who left before completing his studies to secure a military appointment until after his class graduated. Thus, Bates could not receive an appointment until after June 1867. C. Woodson Bates to Johnson, Sept. 10, 1866, ACP Branch, File B-1022-CB-1866, C. Woodson Bates, RG94, NA.

From J. McDowell Sharpe[1]

Chambersburg Pa   Sept 11th 1866

I would most respectfully request your Excellency—to remove the present Collector (Mr. Scull[2] of Somerset) and the present Assessor (Mr. Harper[3] of Gettysburg) both of whom are Revenue officers in this Congressional District. The reasons upon which I base my request are the following—In the first place—these gentlemen are both violent and bitter opponents of the Presidents policy—and traducers of the President himself. Their subordinate officers in the District are if possible more radical and virulent than they are themselves. We have nothing to hope from the present incumbents—and they can not be removed a moment too soon—if it is desired at Washington—that the wisdom and patriotism of the Presidents plan of reconstruction shall be vindicated by the people—at the approaching elections.

In the next place—their immediate removal becomes almost an imperative necessity—in order to save this Congressional and Legislative District—the most doubtful in the state.

The last reason I urge against the retention of the present officials is—that their places can be filled by worthy and honest men—friendly to the President and earnest advocates of his measures.

If these reasons shall seem to your Excellency sufficient to justify the removal of the officers above named—I would respectfully request that Hon A. H. Coffroth[4] of Somerset shall be appointed Assessor—and Col Rufus C. Swope[5] of Adams County—Collector of this District.

The appointment without delay of these gentlemen would give universal satisfaction to the friends of the administration in the District.

The Post Master at Chambersburg (John W. Deal)[6] is obnoxious to the same objections as those which I have urged against the assessor & Collector. I would also respectfully request his immediate removal; and the appointment of Matthew P. Welsh[7] of Chambersburg—a Johnson Republican—a good citizen and an honest man.[8]

J. McD. Sharpe

ALS, DNA-RG56, Appts., Internal Revenue Service, Collector, Pa., 16th Dist., Rufus C. Swope.

1. Sharpe (1830–1883) was a prominent attorney and member of the state legislature for several terms. In his 1866 election bid for Democratic congressman, he lost to the Republican incumbent, William H. Koontz, by fewer than seven hundred votes. *History of Franklin County, Pennsylvania* (Chicago, 1887), 687–90; *Guide to U.S. Elections*, 617.

2. A former attorney and editor of the *Somerset Herald* (1852–87), Edward Scull (1818–1900) had served as collector of Pennsylvania's Sixteenth District since 1863. Scull was appointed assessor for the same district in 1869 and reappointed collector four years later, prior to his election as a Republican to Congress for three consecutive terms. *BDAC*.

3. Robert G. Harper (c1800–fl1867) held various county and municipal offices and edited *The Centinel*, a Conservative Republican newspaper, before his appointment by Lincoln as assessor. *History of Cumberland and Adams Counties, Pennsylvania* (Chicago, 1886), pt. 3: 94–95, 138, 144, 151, 191–92; *U.S. Off Reg.* (1863–65); Appts., Internal

Revenue Service, Assessor, Pa., 16th Dist., R. G. Harper, RG56, NA; 1860 Census, Pa., Adams, Gettysburg, 49.

4. Alexander H. Coffroth (1828–1906), a Democrat, served one term in Congress (1863–65) and began serving a second term until July 18, 1866, when he was unseated by William H. Koontz, who successfully contested his reelection. Sharpe urged Coffroth's appointment as assessor upon Secretary McCulloch. *BDAC*; Sharpe to Hugh McCulloch, Sept. 7, 1866, Appts., Internal Revenue Service, Collector, Pa., 16th Dist., Rufus C. Swope, RG56, NA.

5. A former draft commissioner and quartermaster of volunteers, Swope (1822–1908) worked variously as a tanner and lightning rod salesman. *Cumberland and Adams Counties*, pt. 3: 447–48; Pension File, Rufus C. Swope, RG15, NA.

6. Deal [Diehl] (b. *c*1828) had worked as a railroad conductor before his appointment as postmaster at Chambersburg in 1861. *History of Franklin County*, 224; 1860 Census, Pa., Franklin, Chambersburg, 180.

7. A former coach maker, Welsh (b. *c*1815) was postmaster at Chambersburg for three years (1866–69). Ibid., 189; *History of Franklin County*, 224.

8. Sharpe's letter was endorsed by Democrats William A. Wallace and William Bigler. Within a few days both Scull and Harper were removed from office and Swope and Coffroth given temporary commissions for their posts. Moreover, Welsh replaced Deal as Chambersburg's postmaster. But only Welsh eventually won Senate confirmation. Ser. 6B, Vol. 3: 161; Vol. 4: 84, 88, 90, Johnson Papers, LC.

From Peter Cooper[1]

Newyork   Sept. 12/66.

My dear sir,

It has been with heartfelt sorrow that I have witnessed the conflict of opinion that has unfortunately prevailed between yourself, and the Congress of the United States, in relation to matters believed to be vital to the welfare of our common country.

Such differences of opinion, when honestly entertained (and sometimes violently contended for), show the reason why charity is the greatest of all virtues, because the exercise of charity is so constantly required to enable us to bear with the weaknesses, and imperfections of each other.

There is, I believe no better way to reconcile differences of opinion, than to get a full understanding of the causes out of which such misunderstandings originate.

To do this effectually it is necessary to begin by admitting the fact that all effects, physical, moral, and political are the results of causes that are equal to their production. A little reflection on the almost Almighty power that the circumstances of birth, education, climate, and country have exerted to form, and fix erroneous opinions that often lead men, like Paul of old, to believe that they are doing God service, when they are hailing men, women, and children to prison, and to death—reflection on these facts will show how very wise it is for those who have never made a mistake to send the first stone at those who honestly entertain opinions different from their own.

It has always been to me a source of sorrow, and regret to hear of men in Congress or any other department of government, who destroy their influence for good by calling each other hard names, which never better the condition of themselves or their country.

I am sure if Mr Sumner could have been born of your parents, and subjected to all the circumstances, and conditions that have fallen to your lot through life, he would then have been the man that would have declared the many patriotic truths that have been proclaimed by yourself. And if you could have been born, and subjected to all the conditions that have made Mr Sumner what he is, you would then have been exerting, as he has done, all the powers of a mighty mind to abolish Slavery in all its forms from the face of the earth, as one of the most corrupting evils that ever brought death, and desolation as the scourge of God, to teach us to do to others as we would that others should do unto us: you would then have been like Sumner reading what Solon said two thousand six hundred years ago.—*that whatever day makes man a slave takes half his worth away.*[2]

If it were possible for us to see ourselves as others see us, it would inspire us with charity and teach us to overcome the evils of which we complain with kindness, instead of returning railing for railing, and evil for evil.

I have thought it strange, and unaccountable that you should so severely censure the large majority in Congress for adopting so mild a form of measures as a means for the guaranty of a Republican form of government in the states so lately in rebellion: measures so much more mild than those so forcibly recommended by yourself where you said:[3] "Treason against the government is the highest crime that can be committed, and those engaged in it should suffer all its penalities," and when you declared: "That treason must be made odious; that traitors must be punished and impoverished."

You say "They must not only be punished, but their social power must be destroyed." "If not they maintain an ascendency, and may again become numerous enough for treason to become *respectable.*"

You go further, and say: that "after making treason odious every Union man should be remunerated out of the pockets of those who have inflicted this great suffering on the country."

Again you say:—"I hold it a solemn obligation in every one of these states where the rebel armies have been beaten back, or expelled, I care not how small the number of Union men, if enough to man the ship of state, I hold it to be a high duty to protect, and secure to them a Republican form of government until they again gain strength. They must not be smothered by inches."[4]

In calling a convention to restore states, you ask. "Who shall restore it? Shall the man who gave his influence, and his means to destroy the government?" Is he to participate in the great work of reorganizing the government who brought this misery on the state? If this be so then you say in truth that all the precious blood of our brave soldiers, and officers will have been lost, and all our battlefields will have been made memorable in vain.

You ask "why all this carnage?" It was that treason may be put down, and traitors punished. Therefore you say: "That traitors should take a back seat in the work of restoration."

You say: "The traitor has ceased to be a citizen, and in forming the rebellion became a public enemy."

You further say: "he forfeited his right to vote with loyal men when he renounced his citizenship, and sought to destroy the government."

You say "their great plantations must be seized, and divided into small farms, and sold to honest, and industrious men."

You then add "The day for protecting the lands, and negroes of these authors of rebellion is past."

You say "I have been deeply pained by some things that come under my observation." "You say we get men in command who under the influence of flattery, fawning, and caressing grant protection to rich traitors, while the poor Union man stands out in the cold." You add ["]Traitors can get lucrative contracts while the loyal man is pushed aside." I indulge the hope that such a practice will no longer be tolerated in any branch of the government.

In relation to the reconstruction of the government you have wisely said, "We must not be in too much of a hurry." You add. ["]It is better to let them reconstruct themselves than to force them to it."[5]

In conformity with your own wise recommendation, the majority of Congress have devised, and adopted an Amendment to the Constitution that renders it conveniently practicable for all the rebel states to reconstruct themselves, and come again into the possession of those rights which they have forfeited by rebellion—a rebellion that has cost the lives, and limbs of untold thousands, and thousands of millions of debt that remains yet to be wrung from the toiling labor of our people.

The rebel states will certainly accept, and adopt the Amendment that renders reconstruction so favorable, and convenient before the assembling of another Congress, unless they are encouraged to delay in the hope that those who were half traitors during the war will come to their relief, and reinstate them in power, when they would hope to get payment for, or reenslave their negroes by legislation, which they fairly forfeited by rebellion.

After having read the many patriotic sayings, and denunciations that you have made against rebels, and their rebellion, I was lead to believe that you would be about the last man that would recommend, or accept of any terms for reconstruction that would not offer a full security for the future, even if you might be persuaded by myself and others to waive all indemnity for the past.

I was grieved, and disappointed while showing my respects to you[6] as

President of the United States to find myself listening to what appeared to me an unjust, and unmerited censure of the measures which a large majority of the peoples representatives believed to be right, and the mildest measures for reconstruction that could be adopted, with any chance of "establishing justice, or of promoting the general welfare." I with thousands of others, who labored to aid the government in putting down the rebellion would have rejoiced if Congress could have found all the reports of the continued persecution of Union men throughout the South to be groundless, and false.

The whole Republican party would have rejoiced if Congress could have found it safe to admit the members offered from southern states at once to full share in the government.

This being my wish, does not authorize me to denounce the majority in Congress and accuse them of being radicals, and traitors, hanging on the skirts of a government which they are trying to destroy.

It was said of old—the sin of ingratitude is worse than the sin of witchcraft.

To my mind our nation must live in everlasting infamy if we fail to secure a full measure of justice to an unfortunate race of men who were originally hunted down in their own country, and carried off, and sold like beasts into an abject slavery with all their posterity.

This enslaved race has the strongest possible claims for kindness, as well as for justice at the hands of the people, and government of the whole country and more especially from the people of the South. These unfortunate slaves have done a great portion of the labor that has fed, and clothed the whites, and blacks of the southern Country.

As true as the laborer is worthy of his hire, so true is it that we as a nation cannot withhold justice, and equal rights from a race of men that has fought and bled and labored to defend, and protect the Union of states in the hour of our nation's greatest extremity. The enemies of our country, and government are now trying to persuade the community to believe that a war of races would result from giving the *black* man the same measure of justice, and rights, which the white men claim for themselves. This will be found to be a groundless fear. Our national danger will always result from unequal, and partial laws.

We cannot make laws which will oppress and keep in ignorance the poor without bringing ourselves, and our country the just judgement of a righteous God who will reward us as a nation according to our works.

I indulge the hope that you will see before it is entirely too late, the terrible danger of taking counsel from northern men in sympathy with rebels who fought the government with all the energy of desperation to accomplish the destruction thereof instead of taking counsel from those friends who elected you.

Friends who have been, and are as desirous as you can possibly be to secure the adoption of every measure calculated to promote the substantial welfare of all parts of our common country.[7]

Peter Cooper

LS, DLC-JP.
1. Cooper (1791–1883) was a renowned industrialist/inventor and philanthropist. *DAB.*
2. Found in Homer's *Odyssey*, book 17, line 392.
3. Here, and in the following three paragraphs, Cooper quotes liberally and not altogether accurately from Johnson's Speech to the Indiana Delegation, Apr. 21, 1865, *Johnson Papers*, 7: 612–14.
4. Actually "not smothered by its enemies." Ibid., 614.
5. From Interview with George L. Stearns, Oct. 3, 1865, *Johnson Papers*, 9: 179.
6. Cooper had attended the banquet at Delmonico's. *New York Times*, Aug. 30, 1866.
7. Cooper's letter was also published in pamphlet form. There is no record of a reply from Johnson.

From Robert M. Patton

Montgomery   September 13 1866.

Sir:

When I had the pleasure of meeting you last week at Chicago, I hoped to have found an opportunity for a free and general conversation in reference to Alabama affairs. That, however, was not practicable; hence, I was content with submitting to our mutual friend, Gen. Steedman, some considerations upon the subject, with a request that he would confer with you in reference thereto.

I am happy to say that, under all the circumstances, we have as favorable a condition of things politically speaking, as could be reasonably expected. Our people are a unit in upholding the General Government in its Constitutional integrity. We regret our inability to do more in behalf of the great conservative cause which is now being prosecuted with such patriotic eneregy in the North. We appreciate the vast importance of the contest. Though you know that we are so peculiarly situated that we can do little else than applaud the right.

I wish I could say that our people were doing as well in matters of material prosperity, as they are politically. But unfortunately such is not the case. It is needless to speak of the desolation which the war brought upon our land. It is sufficient to say that we have had a hard struggle to relieve the suffering which resulted from the short crop of last year. We had fondly hoped, however, that the present year would yield us a crop that would place us above want; or at least above suffering. But this fond hope proved a delusion. Last year when our young and middle aged men returned home after the surrender of the Southern armies, it was too late to plant and raise a crop. This year the seasons have been most lamentably against us.[1] The General government has been bounteous in its assistance; the appeals which have gone abroad for voluntary contributions, have been liberally responded to. Still, our suffering is great.

I am sure I do not exaggerate, when I put down the number of actual sufferers in the State, at from seventy to eighty thousand; the larger portion of whom are widows and orphans. Three-fourths of this number are absolutely dependent upon governmental, or charitable contributions for subsistence. They are not only destitute, but entirely helpless. Our State Treasury is depleted; our credit is greatly embarrassed by the national political troubles. The State, therefore, can not feed them. As for the growing crop it will be wholly inadequate. In the most favorable parts of the State, the grain crop is short; in a majority of counties there will not be enough produced to support the county population; in the others the yield varies; in some half a crop; some a fourth, and some nothing worth naming.

Under these very discouraging circumstances, we have no other alternative than to continue our appeals to the generosity of the General Government. I regret to do this, but the case is so urgent that it can not be avoided. The Secretary of War, upon the recommendation of Gen. Howard, has ordered a discontinuance of rations from the first of October. It is earnestly hoped, that this order will be so modified as to allow us some relief to prevent actual starvation.

I herewith transmit a copy of a report of M. H. Cruikshank,[2] the State Commissioner to co-operate with Freedmen's Bureau in distributing supplies. This report will show, more, in detail, the extent and character of the suffering in our State.[3] It is proper to observe, in this connection, that Gen. Swayne has been freely consulted on this whole subject. He is so fully convinced of the extreme necessity of our case, that he will recommend to the proper Department that the supplies be not wholly discontinued. In his recommendation he will suggest a mode of relief somewhat different from that heretofore practiced. It is proposed, for instance, instead of undertaking to issue regular rations, that corn and bacon be furnished. Corn is the great necessity. This article, to the value of one half the aggregate value of the rations heretofore furnished, with a limited proportion of bacon, would afford far more relief than has heretofore been found.[4]

I have heretofore, officially and personally, spoken in terms of liberal commendation of Gen. Swayne. I here reiterate all that I have formerly said. I consider him a just man, and a faithful officer. Our personal relations have always been kind; and our official action harmoneous. But candor compels me to say that the Freedmen's Bureau, as a governmental agency in this State, is doing much mischief. It has a bad influence upon the freedmen; and an injurious effect upon the politics of the State.

R M Patton   Governor of Alabama

LS, DNA-RG107, Lets. Recd., Executive (M494, Roll 85).

1. Excessive spring rains were followed by a drought. By June 1866 poor crop yields were already apparent; corn and cotton were "seriously injured," oats were "ruined," and wheat was "almost a total failure." *Picayune* (New Orleans), June 24, 1866; *Republican Banner* (Nashville), Aug. 26, 1866.

2. Marcus H. Cruikshank (1826–1881), Talladega lawyer, mayor, and newspaper editor, had been a Confederate congressman late in the war. Wakelyn, *BDC*.

3. Cruikshank reported that the corn crop was a "failure" and that the entire yield would not supply half the necessities of the people of Alabama. He recommended that the secretary of war be asked to modify his recent order to cut rations and to secure from the federal government a "limited supply of corn and bacon . . . or corn alone" to be "furnished regularly each month." M. H. Cruikshank's report, [Sept. 1866], Lets. Recd., Executive (M494, Roll 85), RG107, NA.

4. General Swayne did recommend that supplies continue to be furnished to the destitute of Alabama. At first Bureau chief Howard proposed that $200,000 be allowed for purchases of corn and bacon for a full year following October 1, 1866. But this was modified and approved by Secretary Stanton not to exceed $40,000 per month for three months. O. O. Howard to Stanton, Sept. 27, 28, 1866, Records of the Commr., Lets. Sent (M742, Roll 2), RG105, NA.

From James Speed

Louisville, Sept. 13th 1866.

Sir;

On reaching my home I find that the Associated Press had telegraphed me as having said "the Tyrant" of the White House. Such was not my language. I said "Tenant of the White House."

It may be needless for me to make this statement and correction as you may not have seen the report of the speech. But I feel that it is due to our relations that I should do so.

The papers of Phila reported me correctly.[1]

James Speed

ALS, DLC-JP.

1. The first week of September, the Southern Unionist Convention convened in Philadelphia and chose Speed as its president. The *Chicago Tribune*, in its verbatim account of his address, quoted him as saying "tyrant of the White House." The *Press* of Philadelphia, in a similar verbatim account, recorded him as saying "occupant of the White House." *Chicago Tribune*, Sept. 5, 1866; *Press* (Philadelphia), Sept. 5, 1866.

From Thomas N. Stilwell[1]

Anderson Indiana   Sep 13, 1866

Dear Sir

Your kind suggestion at Indianapolis[2] to give me some position in connection with my trip to New Orleans and the South would be very acceptable and highly appreciated.

Anything I can do for yourself or any of your Department's shall have prompt attention.

If there has been no investigation of the riot at New Orleans in justice to you against the lying reports, would not a report of that by a Committee be important?[3]

Please let me hear from you by Telegraph, if you can find any place where I can serve you, as I wish to start in a few days.[4]

There is a tremendious reaction over the outrageous proceedings of the radical mob at Indianapolis.[5]

Thos. N Stilwell

LS, DLC-JP.
1. Stilwell (1830–1874), a native of Ohio, studied law, was admitted to the bar in 1852, and practiced in Indiana. He served one term in the state house of representatives and fought in the Union army. A single-term Republican congressman from Indiana (1865–67), he held the post of minister to Venezuela (1867–68), and then presided over a bank. *BDAC*.
2. Johnson arrived in Indianapolis on September 10, 1866. *New York Herald*, Sept. 11, 1866.
3. When Congress met in December 1866, the House of Representatives appointed a committee of three who interviewed 197 persons in both Washington, D.C., and New Orleans between December 11, 1866, and February 2, 1867, producing a substantial report. *House Reports*, 39 Cong., 2 Sess., No. 16 (Ser. 1304).
4. Apparently Johnson gave Stilwell no assignment despite two more offers to assist, one on October 1, the day Stilwell was leaving for New Orleans. Stilwell to Johnson, Sept. 18, 1866, Tels. Recd., President, Vol. 5 (1866–67), RG107, NA; Stilwell to Johnson, Oct. 1, 1866, Johnson Papers, LC.
5. When Johnson attempted to address the crowd from a hotel balcony on September 10, the people made so much noise shouting, interrupting, and telling Johnson to "Shut up!" that he was unable to speak. *New York Herald*, Sept. 11, 1866; Eric L. McKitrick, *Andrew Johnson and Reconstruction* (Chicago, 1960), 431.

From John F. Miller

San Francisco   14 Sept 1866

To cultivate friendly relations with the Sandwich Islands & for the interests of commerce our leading citizens believe it would be good policy for the Government to convey Queen Emma[1] home to Honolulu in the Vanderbilt.[2] The British Govt having conveyed her in a War Vessel from the Islands to Panama.[3] In this opinion I concur. The Vanderbilt is ready if ordered by the Navy Dept.[4]

John F. Miller

Tel, DLC-JP.
1. Widow of the Hawaiian king Kamehameha IV, Queen Emma (1836–1885) left the islands on May 6, 1865, for a journey to England and France to recover from the sorrow of losing both her only son and her husband in little more than a year. On her way home she arrived in New York on August 9, 1866, met with President Johnson in Washington on August 14, and visited Niagara Falls. Her final stop was San Francisco. *New York Herald*, Aug. 9, 1866, and various articles and notes, Aug. 8–28, 1866; *New York Times*, Aug. 15, 1866; *Chicago Tribune*, Oct. 7, 8, 1866; Ralph S. Kuykendall, *The Hawaiian Kingdom* (3 vols., Honolulu, 1938–67), 2: 78, 83–84, 95, 124, 201–2, 205; 3: 3–16, 191, 280.
2. The *Vanderbilt*, a steamer, was the flagship of U.S. Navy Rear Admiral H. K. Thatcher. Ibid., 2: 205.
3. The British vessel was the *Clio*. Ibid., 202.
4. The *Vanderbilt* did take Queen Emma home, leaving San Francisco on October 14, 1866, and arriving in Honolulu on October 22. Ibid., 205; *Chicago Tribune*, Oct. 15, 1866.

From Albert Smith

Boston   14 Sept. 1866

My dear Sir

I crave your attention for a single moment.

Having graduated from the Military Academy at Norwich Vt. before he was twenty years of age, Col. Edmund Rice,[1] late of the 19 Regt Mass. Volunteers, was appointed to a captaincy of that Regt. in August 1861. He served through the war & was in all the battles, under McLellan, Burnside, Hooker, & Meade, in which that Regt. was so distinguished. He was in command of it at the first Fredericksburgh fight in which he was severely wounded, until peace was proclaimed. Was twice wounded at Gettysburgh[2] & once at Antietam, & was soon after made a full Colonel. Modest & generous & brave to a fault, he made no effort, other than his services in the field to be retained in the service. But, now, since Congress has provided for the appointment in the regular Army, of meritorious officers in the volunteers, he & his numerous friends desire that he may be included in that number.[3]

Educated from boyhood for a Military life, he is peculiarly qualified for it. It has become to him a sort of second nature.

Did you know him as I do, *I know* you would not hesitate to confer upon him an appointment in the army, commensurate with his services & his personal merit.[4]

Albert Smith

N.B. It may not be amiss to say that Col R. is among your warm friends.

A. S.

ALS, DNA-RG94, ACP Branch, File R-775-CB-1866, Edmund Rice.

1. Receiving a commission in the regular army, Rice (1842–1906) later saw service in the West against the Ute and Sioux, as well as overseas, prior to his retirement as brigadier general in 1903. *Who Was Who in America* (5 vols., Chicago, 1943–73), 1: 1026; *New York Times*, July 21, 1906.

2. For his actions during this battle Rice received the congressional Medal of Honor in October 1891. Powell, *Army List*, 552; *Medal of Honor Recipients, 1863–1973* (Washington, D.C., 1973), 206.

3. A number of letters were written recommending Rice's appointment. ACP Branch, File R-775-CB-1866, Edmund Rice, RG94, NA.

4. Johnson's nomination of Rice as first lieutenant, 40th Inf., was confirmed by the Senate in March 1867. Ser. 6B, Vol. 2: 279, Johnson Papers, LC.

From William L. Hartley[1]

Osgood Ripley Co Indiana
Sept 15 /66

Dear Sir

Being borned and raised in Hawkins County E. Tennessee Your old Congressional District and always being both your personal & political friend I take the privilege of addressing you these few lines. You always

Received my Vote and influence from the time I was a voter which was in 1838 till the year I moved to Indiana which was 1850 when you was a candidate. I have since then always advocated your claims for the presidency. In 1853 I had a son Born which I called Andrew Johnson and told my neighbors then I called him after a man that would some day be President of these U.S.A. Though unfortunately he Died when he was about 1 year old. I believe I told you the circumstance when I saw you at Mr. Cobbs[2] on the hill at Aurora Indiana in the fall of 1861. Doubtless you recollect Judge Gray[3] and my self comeing to see you when thare. I also Introduced to you my Son[4] while thare who was Lieut in the 37 Reg Ind Vol who sickened and Died at Bolinggreen Ky while on his way to Nashville under General Buell[5] (in Aprl 1862). About the time he started out he urged me to purchase apiece of land lying near me for him which I did and went in Debt for it. His Death caused me to have it to pay for. On the top of that Morgan[6] made his raid through Ind, and took all my horses and the goverment never has paid for them. So it has embarrassed me to Some extent. And as John Ferris[7] who is Revinew collector of this District the 4th has turned his back on you and advocating the policy of the Radicals or Rump congress the supposition here is among your friends that he will be removed. The object of this letter if such is the fact and you are not pledged to some one else is to solicit of you that appointment. It is supposed by some that Col James Gavin[8] of Decator County will get it. Col Gavin is my personal friend and much of a gentleman and a strong advocate of your Reconstruction policy. There is an other Gentleman Col Ben Spooner of Lawrenceburgh Ind who is Marshal of the State who is canvassing the 4 Congressional District Denouncing you as a Dam Traitor &c which I think ought to be removed. If such should be the case and I cannot get the other position I would like very much to have that. As to my honesty fidelity and integrity to the policy enumerated by you from the commencement of your Admr, I can refer you to Thomas A Hendricks our United States Senator and our exmember of congress from my District which is the 4th viz Hon Wm. S. Hoalman. I have twice Represented my County in the Legislatur and once in the Senate.

So I must close hoping and trusting in God that nothing may cause you to swerve from the policy you have laid down.

William L. Hartley

ALS, DNA-RG56, Appts., Internal Revenue Service, Collector, Ind., 4th Dist., William L. Hartley.

1. Hartley (b. c1818) was a moderately well-off farmer. 1860 Census, Ind., Ripley, Center, 57.

2. Oliver P. Cobb (1817–fl1885) was a successful river trader, pork packer, and shipper from the Midwestern states to New Orleans. During the Civil War he served as a quartermaster's agent for the federal government, charged with providing forage for the Union armies. In addition to these activities, after the war he served the Aurora Iron & Nail Company in a variety of capacities, including president. *History of Dearborn and Ohio Counties, Ohio* (Chicago, 1885), 666; *Biographical History of Indiana*, 1: 83–92.

3. Henry L. Gray (b. c1806), a native of Tennessee, was a farmer in Ripley County, Indiana, at the outbreak of the war. 1860 Census, Ind., Ripley, Center, 57.

4. James J. Hartley (c1840–1862) served as a second lieutenant in the 37th Ind. Inf. He died of disease at Osgood, Indiana, on April 26, 1862. Ibid.; *Off. Army Reg.: Vols.*, 6: 91.

5. Don Carlos Buell.

6. John Hunt Morgan.

7. Ferris (b. c1819), a very successful druggist in Lawrenceburgh, Dearborn County, was commissioned collector in May 1866 and served until November, when James Earvin was appointed. 1860 Census, Ind., Dearborn, Lawrenceburgh, 58; Ser. 6B, Vol. 2: 90; Vol. 3: 553, Johnson Papers, LC.

8. Gavin (1830–1873) began as a schoolteacher before studying law. When the war began, he helped organize the 7th Ind. Vol. Inf., in which he served as lieutenant, adjutant, and lieutenant colonel. After resigning in 1863 because of wounds received, he unsuccessfully ran against W. S. Holman for Congress and, instead, was elected clerk of Decatur County. In 1864 he took command of the 134th Ind. Vols.; following their return he was reelected clerk, serving until 1867. *Biographical History of Indiana*, 1: 26–27.

From Francis W. Kellogg

Mobile, Sept 15th 1866

Sir

Hon J M Withers[1] Mayor of the City of Mobile is Chairman of a Com—app'ted by the Chamber of Commerce to visit Washington & confer with the Sec'y of the Treasury in order to obtain some modification of the "*Regulations*" for the collection of the tax on Cotton.

The People here regard you as the especial guardian of their interest & I most respectfully request your attention so far as possible to the grievances which this Committee complain of in behalf of the Cotton Planters of the South and for which they ask relief.[2]

F W Kellogg   Col of Int Rev

ALS, DLC-JP.

1. Jones M. Withers.

2. Within a few days Withers and a delegation of southern business leaders, primarily cotton factors and planters, did journey to Washington. There they presented a memorial from the chambers of commerce of New Orleans and Mobile, which contended that the "payment of the three per cent. tax before the cotton leaves the plantation . . . works great injury to the planter." Withers's delegation had an interview with Secretary McCulloch, who seemed willing to modify the regulations "so far as the existing law gives him any discretion" but doubted if any change in the law was warranted. The delegation then met with Johnson and successfully asked that the question of McCulloch's authority under the law be referred to the attorney general. *Picayune* (New Orleans), Sept. 26, 1866; *National Intelligencer*, Sept. 22, 1866; *Evening Star* (Washington), Sept. 24, 1866.

From Henry A. McPike[1]

Johnstown [Pa.], Sept. 15th '66

Dear Sir—

As you must be painfully interested in the details of the sad catastrophe which occurred here yesterday,[2] I trust you will not consider it too pre-

sumptive on part of an humble citizen to address you. The deaths immediate and since resulting, up to time of writing, from the best information
I can obtain, amount to five. The number injured are believed to be
somewhere in the neighborhood of three hundred, but with the exception of about twenty-five or thirty, their wounds are not of a serious character. Of the latter, three or four are dangerously injured, and death is
looked for—a number of others will doubtless be crippled, perhaps for
life, but the greater part will eventually recover. It is the greatest calamity
that ever befell this community, rendering nearly every other house a
hospital. It is nevertheless wonderful that so many escaped from serious,
not to say fatal, injury, and the Providence of God, which overruleth all
things, can alone be recognized in the preservation of so comparatively
many from serious injury. For my own part, I have great reason to be
thankful to the Almighty. In company with wife and child[3] I visited the
station to look upon yourself and the other distinguished visitors, but
while waiting for your arrival my wife fortunately became tired and faint,
and retired to the ticket office, where she was at the time of the accident.
With the child in my arms, however, I followed the crowd and went down
amid the struggling mass of appalled humanity. Strange to say, the child
escaped without a scratch, and I myself suffered but little more.

What must have been your own feelings upon witnessing the sad catastrophe you are of course the best judge, but your noble conduct in remitting the handsome sum you did in aid of the sufferers[4] is evidence sufficient that you amply sympathized with a distressed community. Yet there
are those amongst us who would willingly blame you for the sad occurrence, and within my own hearing a leading Radical of to-day (but a leading any thing else to-morrow, if it paid better,) made the remark that you
manifested any thing but a humane feeling in moving off at the very
height of the people's distress. It was not inhuman in General Grant (all
honor to his glorious name) or the other members of your party, but in
you it was an act worthy of condemnation. And the radical organ here to-
day[5] in a portion of its edition informed the public, that by order of Gen
Grant one of the surgeons of your party remained here to render assistance to the wounded. I said in a portion of the edition, for, either because
said surgeon did not stop off, or because it was by your orders and not
General Grant's, this information was not given in the *last* of its edition.
But not a word had it to say of your magnaminous generosity to the injured, although the fact was patent upon ever tongue. But such is the
vindictiveness of party hate, and had it not been for the lamentable occurrence there is no doubt but that demonical spirit would have manifested
itself in your presence. Like their ancient prototypes, the Radicals are not
willing to admit that any "good can come out of Nazareth." But in the
words of a dying Redeemer, may "God forgive them, they know not what
they do."[6]

In conclusion, permit me to hope that God may sustain you in the noble work you are laboring to accomplish, and spare your life until long after you again see this great country reunited, happy and free.

H. A. McPike

ALS, DLC-JP.

1. McPike (c1832–fl1909), a journalist, owned, published, and edited at least two Democratic newspapers in Pennsylvania before removing to Washington, D.C. Henry W. Storey, *History of Cambria County, Pennsylvania* (3 vols., New York, 1907), 1: 381–82, 384, 387; 1870 Census, Pa., Cambria, Ebensburg Borough, Ebensburg, 2; *U.S. Off. Reg.* (1903–11).

2. Not long after the President's train had stopped at Johnstown on September 14, a wooden platform near the depot collapsed, causing the multitude which had gathered upon the structure to plunge some twenty feet. Although sources differ, as many as six people died as a result of the accident and nearly four hundred were injured. A suit later filed against the Pennsylvania Railroad Company for damages and negligence in building an unsafe platform was dismissed, and the state supreme court ultimately upheld the dismissal. Storey, *Cambria County*, 1: 448–56; *Press* (Philadelphia), Sept. 16, 18, 1866; *Evening Bulletin* (Philadelphia), Sept. 15, 1866. See also Daniel McLaughlin to Johnson, Jan. 12, 1867, Johnson Papers, LC, a letter from one of the attorneys involved in the suit.

3. Ann (b. c1841) and Frank P. (b. c1864) McPike. 1870 Census, Pa., Cambria, Ebensburg Borough, Ebensburg, 2.

4. After arriving in Altoona later in the day, Johnson sent five hundred dollars for the "relief of the most needy of the bereaved and wounded." Storey, *Cambria County*, 1: 449; Daniel J. Morrell to William G. Moore, Sept. 17, 1866, Johnson Papers, LC.

5. The *Johnstown Tribune*.

6. From John 1: 46 and Luke 23: 34, respectively.

From Thompson B. Oldham[1]

Mtsterling, Ky.   Aug [Sept.] 15th 1866[2]

Dear Sir

After my thanks to you for favors I have receved first the appointment as collector for the 9th Collection Dis for Ky, which I declined for reasons of my own then again by A. E. Rolins[3] that of Inspector for the same district which I now hold, I wish to say that while I have never for one moment doubted your patriotism or Loyalty, yet I did differ a little with you on some miner matters, but more with the Congress of the U.S. I hoped for a long time that the split between you & them was not perminent, but I find they would not allow you to a gree with Them without Seff stultification. It dose seem to me that it would have been better to have admited the Ten' delligates to seats at the opening of the Sission & then Arkansas & so on as fare as they could have taken the oath. This would have tended to consiliating them, & the temper of the Southern people was much better then than now. I spent two months south last winter & my opinion was then & is now that they were more Loyal & in a better condition to be reprresented in Congress than we are here in Ky. They then seemed to me to be so completely conquered that we ought to do all that we could to consiliate & help them. I have wached your excursion trip & speaches[4] & was please with the reception give you with the exception of the rowdies & blackgards wo tryed to insult you at Cleavland

& one or two other points on the rout. I take it that none but a low dirty scoundral & blackgard will interrupt a public speaker. My opinion is that the late rebelious states were never out of the union & that when ever they laid down their arms & showed a disposition to resume their former relations & submit to existing state of affairs that they ought to be permitted to do so. I was well pleased with the proseeding & resolutions of the Philadelpia convention, While the one that met on the 3rd Sept tember[5] in their riotous prosedings in trying to force Negroe suffereg was disgusting to me & I think will have a good effect in arousing te masses of the People to see where we are drifting. In the darkest hours of the ware, I was strengthened by a remark you made in a private conversaation with myself & Gen Willians[6] in Paris Ky in the summer of 1861. It was this "That you had an abiding faith that any caus the foundation of which was so mostrously wrong as was that of the Rebels was could not suckseed unless all of our Religious teaching were rong, That right must & would in the end triumph over wrong that if it did not that shipreck of the faith of thousands of pious persons would be the consequence, that right would ultimately prevail over wrong." So I think at this time, Though I own that things at this time looks dark & ugly but right will in the end triumph.

T. B. Oldham

P S. I did not vote in the last Election having lost my right to vote by leaving the State but should have voted for Hobson[7] he being a true man & soldier & a Johnson union while his opponent Duvall[8] was a Rebel & no friend of your course.

T. B. Oldham

ALS, DLC-JP.
1. Possibly the Thompson Oldham (b. c1819) of Montgomery County, who had been a farmer and would become a gauger employed by the U.S. government, and also a grocer. 1860 Census, Ky., Montgomery, Mt. Sterling, 90; (1870), 1st Prec., Mt. Sterling, 18; (1880), 4th and 1st Wards, 77th Enum. Dist., 11.
2. Although Oldham wrote the date as August, it should be September because of the references to the Southern Unionist Convention and to Johnson's speech at Cleveland.
3. Edward A. Rollins.
4. Johnson's "swing around the circle" in late August and early September 1866.
5. The Southern Unionist Convention convened in Philadelphia on September 1. Northern Unionists withdrew because the Southern Unionist majority favored black suffrage. Later, border states (the majority) and deep South states (the minority) split and adopted their own resolutions. *American Annual Cyclopaedia* (1866), 758.
6. Possibly Thomas J. Williams (1838–1866), who served during the war as captain, 23rd Ky. Inf., and lieutenant colonel, 55th Ky. Inf., before being brevetted brigadier general in 1865 for his war service. In civilian life he was a bookkeeper. Hunt and Brown, *Brigadier Generals*.
7. Edward H. Hobson (1825–1901), businessman, served in the Mexican War and was director and president of the Greensburg Branch Bank of Kentucky prior to the Civil War. During the war he served with the 2nd and 13th Ky. Inf. and attained the rank of brigadier general of volunteers in November 1862. Following the war President Grant appointed him internal revenue collector for Kentucky's Fourth District; he continued his business interests in railroads, lumber, real estate, and merchandise. *DAB*.
8. Alvin Duvall.

From John Savage

Fordham N.Y[1]   Sept. 15/66

I beg your Excellency will suspend action in the matter of the Collectorship of the 10th district of this state, until I see you. Understanding that a change would be made I made application for the same on the 1st inst.[2] Last evening a New York paper gave the name of a violent copperhead as the successor;[3] but I learn by telegraph from Washington that the change has *not* been made.

I will go on immediately after our demonstration on Monday.[4] It will be the greatest affair ever gotten up here; and we look for a word in response to the letter I had the honor of writing to you at Cincinnatti.[5]

John Savage

ALS, DNA-RG56, Appts., Internal Revenue Service, Collector, N.Y., 10th Dist., John Savage.

1. After leaving New Orleans, Savage, apparently in the spring of 1866, removed to New York, which he represented at the National Union Convention in Philadelphia. *DAB*; John B. Haskin to Hugh McCulloch, Sept. 1, 1866, Appts., Internal Revenue Service, Collector, N.Y., 10th Dist., John Savage, RG56, NA.

2. See Savage's letter to McCulloch which, though undated, was received at the Treasury Department on September 3. The President notified McCulloch: "I am anxious to Serve Mr Savage. He is my friend." Savage to McCulloch, n.d.; Johnson to McCulloch, n.d., ibid.

3. We are not sure to whom Savage refers. An article naming a successor has not been found in the New York papers.

4. A reference to a "ratification" meeting at Union Square in New York City, which featured speeches by such notables as General Dix, ex-Governor Parsons, Henry J. Raymond, and Samuel J. Tilden. *New York Times*, Sept. 18, 1866.

5. Savage's letter to Johnson has not been found. Exactly what happened next is difficult to reconstruct. Evidently, Savage did meet with the President sometime before September 21, when his temporary commission as collector was forwarded to the White House for Johnson's signature. Yet for some reason the appointment was soon suspended. Meanwhile, Thurlow Weed had recommended Savage's appointment. Apparently the incumbent, John M. Mason, remained in the collectorship for several more years, despite all the stirrings. Haskin to McCulloch, Nov. 8, 1866; Thurlow Weed to [Johnson?], Sept. 21, 1866, Appts., Internal Revenue Service, Collector, N.Y., 10th Dist., John Savage, RG56, NA; John A. Stewart to McCulloch, Oct. 6, 1866; Ser. 6B, Vol. 3: 95; Vol. 4: 53–54, Johnson Papers, LC; *Senate Ex. Proceedings*, Vol. 15, pt. 1: 301, 326; pt. 2: 554, 573; *U.S. Off. Reg.* (1867–73).

From Edwin M. Stanton

Washington   Sept 15 1866

Your Telegram received.[1] All necessary arrangements have been made at Mr Sewards house for his comfort[2]—the People here have made arrangments for your reception.[3]

Edwin M Stanton

Tel, DLC-JP.

1. Not found.

2. After leaving Louisville on September 11, Seward became seriously ill. By the eve-

ning of the 14th it was questionable whether Seward would survive the illness, and his family had been sent for. His daughter, Fanny, arrived at Harrisburg the following morning and accompanied him to Washington and home that evening. Van Deusen, *Seward*, 462; Beale, *Welles Diary*, 2: 594–95.

3. Shortly after 7 p.m. on the 15th Johnson arrived in Washington and proceeded to City Hall where the mayor made a welcoming speech and Johnson spoke in reply. A festive procession accompanied the President back to the White House, where Johnson again addressed the crowd. *New York Times*, Sept. 17, 1866.

From Richard H. Stanton

Maysville, Ky, Sep 15, 1866.

Sir,

Upon the recommendation of Mr. Davis, Mr. Guthrie,[1] the Ky members of the Philadelphia Convention, myself and others, Mr. Throckmorten Forman,[2] who was a soldier in the Union Army, was appointed Assessor in this District, in the place of Samuel L. Blaine.[3]

I am informed by the Secretary of the Treasury,[4] that because Mr. Blaine has telegraphed to him, that he is your friend and approves your "general policy," the Secy feels it his duty to withhold Mr. Forman's commission, and will submit the matter again to you. I have learned too, that Martin P. Marshall,[5] and other equally open radicals, have certified to Mr. Blaine's friendship for you and your measures.

This is an impudent attempt to deceive you, for I know personally that until the apprehension of his removal, Mr. Blaine was as openly opposed to you and your policy, and in favor of the radical measures of Congress as any man in the community. To keep his place and prevent the offices for going into the hands of your friends he now chooses to claim to be your friend.

Every deputy of Mr. Blaine in the District is a radical, and are using their influence and power to prevent the success of your measures. Mitchell,[6] of Lewis Co, Patton[7] of Greenup and Warder[8] of Fleming are especially bitter and hostile. If we wish to carry this District against McKee[9] these men must be removed.

Mr. Blaine voted for McKee, whose violent hostility to you in Congress and out of it, is notorious, and in the late canvass in this State, Mr. Blaine and his friends brought McKee to this place to make a speech, gave him an ovation, and applauded his violent and disgraceful denunciation of you. Mr. Blaine attended that meeting and was prominent in his approval of the speaker's coarse and offensive attacks upon you and your administration. Mr. Blaine also voted for Col L B. Goggin[10] for the State Senate, when it was well known that he was an open and notorious advocate of every radical measure; and when the Legislature vacated his seat Blaine voted again for him against one of your best friends, William C. Halbert,[11] the present State Senator, an earnest Union man, and at a time when the lines were distinctly drawn between your policy and that of the radical Congress. Goggin has within a few weeks published a card approving of the late Philadelphia radical convention, to which he was appointed a delegate by the radical party.

All these facts have been certified to the Secretary of the Treasury, and overwhelmingly show that Mr. Blaine has not been your friend, nor the friend of your measures, no matter what he may now pretend, and that the withholding of Mr. Forman's commission for that reason, is injustice to thousands of your sincere and ardent friends here, who desire the success of your present noble efforts to save the country from disunion and ruin above every other consideration. Hundreds of the good people in this District, who were startled and surprised at the attempt to deceive the department by representing Mr. Blaine as your friend, have sent to the Secy of the Treasury their protest against his retention in office,[12] and I believe if appealed to, ten thousand more would do the same thing.

I earnestly hope Mr. Forman will be commissioned. He is a good and accomplished business man, served gallantly in the Union Army, and has been supporteg your measures with zeal and enthusiasm all the time.

R. H. Stanton

ALS, DNA-RG56, Appts., Internal Revenue Service, Assessor, Ky., 9th Dist., Throckmorton Forman.

1. Garrett Davis and James Guthrie.

2. Forman (c1842–1932) served with the 10th Ky. Cav. in 1862 and 1863, when he mustered out. CSR, Throckmorton Forman, RG94, NA; Pension File, Throckmorton Forman, RG15, NA.

3. Blaine (c1810–fl1873), a native of Pennsylvania and involved primarily in mercantile interests, was assessor from 1864 to 1873. *The Biographical Encyclopaedia of Kentucky of the Dead and Living Men of the Nineteenth Century* (Cincinnati, 1878), 519; 1870 Census, Ky., Mason, Maysville, 3rd Ward, 431.

4. Hugh McCulloch.

5. Possibly Marshall (b. c1816), a farmer. 1860 Census, Ky., Owen, 1st Dist., Monterey, 67.

6. Probably either John Mitchell (b. c1809), a clerk in a clerk's office in Vanceburg, or Thomas W. Mitchell (b. c1831), a circuit court clerk also in Vanceburg. 1870 Census, Ky., Lewis, Vanceburg, 528–29.

7. William M. Patton (1803–1872), iron manufacturer, was a teacher, engineer, and mercantilist, before managing and owning furnaces in Ohio and Kentucky. In 1865 he was appointed assistant assessor and collector for Johnson, Lawrence, and Floyd counties, and assessor of Carter County in 1868. He remained in office until 1871, at which time he retired from business. *Biographical Encyclopaedia of Kentucky*, 371.

8. Luther F. Warder (1840–1901), businessman, fought for the Union (1861–63) before resigning for health reasons. Following the war he served as assistant assessor for the Ninth District under Johnson until the district was consolidated. Thereafter he engaged in the hotel business until appointed internal revenue storekeeper in 1868. In 1870 he unsuccessfully ran for local office and then moved to Jeffersonville, Indiana, where he was involved with the railroads and served on the city council. In 1873 he was admitted to the bar, and in 1875 was elected mayor, a position he held for about fifteen years. *History of the Ohio Falls Cities and Their Counties* (2 vols., Cleveland, 1882), 2: 478–82; Pension File, Elizabeth A. Warder, RG15, NA.

9. Samuel McKee.

10. Lucien B. Goggin (c1811–fl1877) served in the Kentucky house (1853–55) and senate (1865–69), however, his senate seat was declared vacant in December 1865. In 1870 Goggin was a farmer with extensive land holdings in Mason County. Lewis and

Richard H. Collins, *History of Kentucky* (Louisville, 1877), 547–48; 1870 Census, Ky., Mason, Washington, 528.

11. William C. Halbert (1817–1877), lawyer, was admitted to the bar in 1856 after having served three years as a deputy sheriff in Arkansas and six as acting sheriff of Lewis County, Kentucky. He was a successful lawyer with a wide reputation and large practice in Lewis County and the county leader of the Whigs and later Democrats. In 1862 and 1870 he was elected county attorney and in 1865 was elected to the state senate to fill Lucien Goggin's seat and retained that post until 1869. E. Polk Johnson, *A History of Kentucky and Kentuckians* (3 vols., Chicago, 1912), 815–16.

12. For the numerous letters and petitions protesting against Blaine, see Appl. and Recomm., Internal Revenue Service, Assessor, Ky., 9th Dist., Samuel L. Blaine, RG56, NA.

From Jonathan Worth

Personal

Executive Dept. of N C
Raleigh, Sept. 15 1866

Sir

Nobody, not demented by party rage, doubts your devotion to the Union. You have been, as I have been, the constant opponent of Secessionism and all other issues which fostered Sectionalism & Disunion. When the terrible task devolved on you as the head of the nation to compose the jarring passions & restore a harmonious Union, your object doubtless was to select as your agents men who like yourself had constantly opposed Sectionalism & Disunion. In this State your selection was unfortunate. No man in this State had done so much to teach secession & create sectional alienation as W. W. Holden. Others had equal zeal, but not equal adroitness & opportunity to effect the end. Just before the breaking out of the war he took sides with the Union men,—an immense majority of this State; but sought a seat in the Convention of 1861, and voted to dissolve the Union, and fervently labored to make Disunion perpetual. In the Progress of the war he became alienated from the leaders of the Rebellion, and made *Peace & Independence his motto—but scouted Reunion*. As a consequence his former Secession friends hated him, & the true Union men despised him. Your friends then & now excuse you for his appointment on the ground that you were not posted as to your antecedents. When you offered a free election to the people of this State the most constant Union men induced me to become a Candidate & sustained me on account of my better Union record: but many of the best Union men of the State, who preferred me, voted for him, on the idea that you preferred him. Most of the Secessionists voted for me, because they hated him as a renegade from their ranks, who after deserting, reviled them: and as all regarded the Union restored and then intended, in good faith to sustain it, they preferred a more constant & consistent Union man. Every man in the State knows well that I never had any affinity, or gave the slightest countenance to Sectionism, North or South, and that I adhere now, most firmly, to these convictions—, and hence I support your views because they look to National Conciliation & Concord. In Novr. last you sent to Govr. Holden a telegram which he published, declaring that the recent *elections* in this State, "had greatly damaged the prospects of the State, in the restoration if its governmental relations." *Elections* had just been held for members of Congress and the Genl Assembly as well as for Govr. Govr. Holden has kept this telegram as a standing article in his paper, and construes it as a having special reference to *my* election. He insists that I have been a stumbling block in the way of your restoration policy. From his supposed intimacy with you many believe his interpretation is all right. For aught I know, it may be that you have confidence in him & not in me:—but I *know* that the great body of the intelligent Union men of this State have confidence in me, and have not confidence in him.

He now advocates the ratification by this State, of the Howard amendment:—and publishes without dissent, the electioneering documents of the Radicals, and is endeavoring to get up radical opposition to me, which he puts on the ground that my election would be unacceptable to you.

If there be any thing in my political record or private life, before, or since, or during the war, which warrants your alleged partiality for him, and aversion to me, I cannot imagine what it is. If the fact be so, it must rest on some misinformation. The unceasing reiteration of this thing by a man claiming, with much plausibility to be in your confidence, impairs the efficacy of my exertions to aid you in your noble efforts to restore a fraternal Union.

Jonathan Worth

I inclose the last issue of the Standard.[1]

ALS, DLC-JP.
  1. Not found.

From William B. Phillips
Confidential.

72 East 23d. Street,
New York, Sept. 16, 1866.

Dear Sir,

You have noticed, probably, that the Herald has commenced a new course, and one less cordial to your administration and the conservative party than heretofore.[1] I need hardly say that I regret this very much and that I was unable to prevent it. As far as I am concerned I shall employ my pen on other topics—on financial, foreign, and other questions, and not on those relating to political issues against my own convictions.

The Herald cares nothing for party and likes to "pitch in," (to use its own peculiar expression,) to all parties in turn. Nor does it care about individual public men, though for some there exists always a personal regard and for others a persistent dislike. It aims to be independent, and like the London Times in this respect, but its course is directed more by capricious moods or personal feeling than by large and liberal views or fixed principles. Yet at the bottom Mr. Bennett is not without patriotism or generous sentiments; nor are these apparent fitful moods without a motive. While he is naturally disposed to change with the changing tide, or when he beleives the tide is going to change, he makes this subservient to his business interests. His business is in the midst of a mercurial and an excitable people and he attracts attention to his paper by doing startling or exciting things. Young Mr. Bennett, who has begun to interest himself in the paper, and in whose ability the old gentleman has an overweening confidence, is more changeable than his father, while his judgement is more defective and his information limited. I mention these things to show you upon what principle, or want of fixed principles, the paper is conducted.

The disposition to take a course unfavorable to your administration some time ago, and which was then more strongly shown in young Mr. Bennett than in his father, was kept in check, and finally took a decided turn in favor and in support of the conservative Philadelphia Convention movement. The election in Vermont and Maine,[2] and particularly the election in Maine, has impressed Mr. Bennett with the beleif that the whole of the States will go the same way this fall, that, in fact, the voice of the majority of the Northern people is in favor of the republicans and the republican organization. I can not here give his arguments. These may be seen in the Herald. I only state what his convictions are. He does not beleive, however, that the country will go with the ultra republicans or radicals, and he will continue to assail the radicals as feircely as ever. He thinks your trip to Chicago was unfortunate, and has done you no good. Another motive for the course he is now taking is his opposition, on personal grounds in part, to Mr. Hoffman,[3] the nominee of the State conservative convention for governor. Had General Dix been nominated he would have supported him.

Mr. Bennett thinks now that in view of public sentiment at the North being in favor of the republican majority in Congress that the only safe course for the country and to bring about an early restoration of the South is for the States, and particularly the southern States, to adopt the Constitutional Amendment.

With regard to your own position, he says you have done all you could to restore the South, and that now you should leave it to Congress and no longer make an issue with that body on the subject. On the other hand he thinks you should strike out a fresh course on other questions; that a strong national policy in our foreign relations and affairs and an able financial policy would give *eclât* to your administration. This, he argues, would divert the public mind from the distracting and embittered partisan issues of the day and help to settle them.

I hope the coming elections may result differently to what Mr. Bennett expects, and that I may see him take another conservative turn agreeable to the expressed conservative sentiment of the country. Although I differ with him in some things it must be confessed he is very sagacious and a man of great experience. The views I have communicated here are the substance of a conversation between Mr Bennett and myself the night before last when I went out to Washington Heights with him.

W. B. Phillips

ALS, DLC-JP.
1. See, for example, the editorial entitled, "President Johnson and the True Policy for His Administration," which, after taking note of the unfavorable election results in Maine, pronounced Johnson's reconstruction policy a failure and called on the President to get rid of Seward and others in the cabinet. *New York Herald*, Sept. 14, 1866.
2. In each of these elections which took place in early September 1866, Republicans prevailed in the gubernatorial races, maintained a sizable majority in the legislatures, and captured all eight of the congressional seats. *American Annual Cyclopaedia* (1865), 524, 813; (1866), 468, 763; *Guide to U.S. Elections*, 616–17.
3. John T. Hoffman.

From John Commerford

New York   Sept 17th/66

Honored Sir

Permit me to congratulate your Excellency upon your safe return to Washington. From the extreme hatred which I have seen manifested towards you by the radicals I was very fearful that some one or more of their associates less cautious of life than their leaders might be instigated to assasinate both you and Mr Seward.

Perhaps you may think it strange that I should thus presume to address you and more especialy after such silence on my part, for as near as I can remember I have not written to you since before the first election of Mr Lincoln.[1] I did not seek to trouble you for the sufficient reason that I conceived that you had more important matter to attend to.

After the election of your predecessor, the whole of the members of the Executive Committee of the land reform association with the addition of some of our responsible and wealthy citizens signed a Petition asking the President to appoint me to the office of Marshall for this District. Many of my friends urged me to go to Washington, offering at the same time the money to pay my expenses ⟨for I had none of my own as I had been financialy injured by aiding those who abused my confidence⟩. This I refused, telling them that as I had not been a follower of Mr Seward I could not expect him to take up my cause to the exclusion of those who sustained him through his political career.

After the election of Mr Lincoln Greely sent to me to apply to be one of the Assistant Collectors of this Port. I did not follow his advice. Mr Greely did this although he knew that I consented to run for Congress in a hopeless District with the Homestead Bill as my only avowed issue. In this unequal contest I took the stump and ran Five Hundred ahead of the regular ticket.[2] I hope Your Excellency will excuse me for thus alluding to myself and I only revert to these incidents for the reason that you may have not heard any thing appertaining to my conduct during the last 5 or 6 years. Unlike Mr Greely and many of his retainers and associates I opposed Secession from first to last. Week after week I have met at the Peoples meeting in the Bowery with the most rabbid of these disunionists and discussed this and all other questions in which the welfare of our country is at stake. One of my speeches against Secession was published in a Sunday Paper—a Paper which by the by is now opposed to your present honest generous and patriotic course. Some little while after your accession to your present position the Executive Committee of land reformers sent a Petition[3] directed to your Excellency in my behalf, asking for some governmental situation, and it appears that your private Secretary Col. Browning did not present it. Informing me of this action on their part and ascertaining that they intended to draw up another and transmit it for your consideration I requested them to desist from the undertaking as I did not like to have men asking favors for me, that were individually opposed to your policy and to my own conviction of its aptness and Justice.

Your Excellency may recollect that while you were struggling for the success of the Homestead Bill, by invitation you visited this city to address a meeting[4] to forward the cause. Whilst with us that you advised us to refrain from intermingling Abolition with land reform. That advice I endeavoured to carry out and have always regarded as wise and most Judicious, that is I mean as to the period to which it was properly confined.

During that part of the War when the Emperor of France was about entering Mexico I wrote him a somewhat lengthy letter[5] on the expediency and policy of distributing the lands of that country among the indigent portion of its population; and I wished him to extend this benefit to such French emigrants as his majesty might see fit to transport to that unsettled region of this Continent. I done this whilst doubtful of its adoption, but at the same time hoping that some necessity of state would cause him to get rid of a portion of what is deemed the disturbing element of all overcrowded nations. Beside with a great many others I did not know how the great revolt might terminate. Any how if that Napoleon would give the lands of Mexico to the necessitous there was not a doubt that any other than the real essence of a permanent Republic must be established.

Having attempted to give you a brief history of my doings let me leave such narrative and approach something which is more worthy of your attention. Your excellency is aware of the existence of an organisation of the various Mechanical trades in this and other cities. I say that you are acquainted with this fact because I read the proceedings and action of the Committee that waited upon you.[6] From the tenor of your remarks it was evident that you could teach the delegation in respect to the nature, history and substance of the Homestead Bill. I felt very happy in your escape from the exaction of the eight hour system. Being one of the delegates that waited on Mr Van Buren to solicit the establishment of the Ten Hour system[7] I say that Mr Van Buren risked nothing in granting it, simply for the reason that all of the trades in which the days work was the rule of laboring had for years been regulated by the ten hour system. Now I do not know of a solitary trade in our City that does not work ten hours, for a days work. In the trade which has the great honor of claiming you as one of its most distinguished members the great body in fact I may sall[say] all save with the exception of a few Cutters work by the piece. So it is with the trade in which I have and am now working journey work, we all work by the piece. I think that three fourths of all the trades work in this manner. Your excellency wil not I trust regard me as being opposed to the movement for I am in favor of it—so much so is this the case that I have endeavoured to get my trade to organise that they might assist to shorten the hours of their more exposed and laborious brethern. The motive which guides me in this matter is that which springs from a wish to see you beyond the danger of placing yourself in a position where the concentrated hatred of bad men may be supplied with the material for your destruction. I am one of those who feel proud of your elevation and notwithstanding that the captious and learned asses whom Burns said went into College dunces and came out asses[8] will not agree that your style of language is classical. Yet I cannot discover from whence they draw this unwanton deduction. Pretension is the principal stock of these College mongers, and nothing grieves them so much as to know that no College has ever produced a Shakespeare or Franklin.

I have as far as able endeavoured to instill a sort of pride in my felow workingmen by pointing to you as an example. If I were placed with regard to means as I was a few years ago I would have had a Workingman's meeting for the purpose of showing them the necessity of supporting one of themselves.

I hope that Mr Seward will recover from his illness.[9] The loss of such a man at this time would be a serious calamity. The noble and patriotic stand which he has taken entitles him to the affection of every friend of our Country. I trust that you and him will both live to see the establishment of the true policy of our free government.

I see that one of your pretended friends General John Cochrane has bolted and joins Field Marshall Greely.[10] I was rather astonished at this as he told me a few months ago that you would be sustained and that in all probability he would be the Collector of this district.[11]

John Commerford

ALS, DLC-JP.
1. See Commerford to Johnson, Feb. 9, 1858, Dec. 17, 1859, *Johnson Papers*, 3: 10–11, 356–58, and Brotherhood of the Union to Johnson, July 22, 1861, ibid., 4: 593.
2. Running as a Republican, he had finished a distant third in this election, behind the Democratic and "Fusion" candidates. See Charles C. Commerford to Johnson, Mar. 9, 1865, ibid., 7: 512, 514.
3. Not found. The list of incoming letters at the White House indicates receipt of a January 1866 recommendation of Commerford by the National Land Reform Association of New York City. Evidently the petition was returned to the association the following day. Ser. 6A, Vol. B: 40, Johnson Papers, LC.
4. Probably when Johnson spoke to the New York Land Reformers on May 27, 1852. See *Johnson Papers*, 1: 57–60.
5. Commerford's son enclosed a copy of this letter when writing President Lincoln. See Charles C. Commerford to Johnson, Mar. 9, 1865, ibid., 7: 512–13.
6. See Response to National Labor League Committee, Aug. 25, 1866.
7. Van Buren's executive order of March 31, 1840, granted a ten-hour work day to federal public works employees. Richard B. Morris, ed., *Encyclopedia of American History* (New York, 1976), 763.
8. A variation of stanza 12, line 69, in the *Epistle to J. L*****k, an old Scotch Bard, April 1, 1785,* by Robert Burns.
9. See Edwin M. Stanton to Johnson, Sept. 15, 1866.
10. Commerford probably had read where Cochrane and Greeley had spoken during a "Radical Ratification Meeting" of New York veterans a few nights earlier. *New York Times*, Sept. 15, 1866.
11. Cochrane had indeed asked Johnson for the appointment. See Cochrane to Johnson, Nov. 16, 1865, *Johnson Papers*, 9: 391–93.

From James Dixon

Confidential

Hartford   Sept. 17, '66

Dear Sir,

I heartily congratulate you on your safe return to Washington.

I desire now to call your attention to a matter of Great importance to the interests of our cause in New England. I refer to the appointment of Collector of Customs for the Port of Boston. This office ought to be so placed as to build us up, instead of conducing to our injury.

In Massachusetts our cause is hopeless. Connecticut is the only New England State where we have any hopes of success. Here we greatly need a Newspaper, as we have now no Conservative organ. If I had the control of this important office, I could by its aid, start a daily paper of vast influence in this section. You will at once see the immense value of such an organ. Public opinion is now benighted. Your views and policy are misrepresented and misunderstood, and we have no means of reply, except the Democratic papers which reach few Republicans. Give me the appointment of this office, and I will change all this, and diffuse light where thick darkness now reigns. Is it asking much—standing as I do *alone* in New England?[1]

James Dixon

ALS, DLC-JP.
1. There is no extant reply from Johnson.

From John Fisk[1]

Suspension Bridge N.Y.   Sept. 17th. 1866

There is but one other step the radicals can take. They have succeeded in passing the Civil Rights Bill, so called, over the veto. The next step is to impeach the President, and expel him from the Seat in which the People, by the Grace of God, have placed him.

The masses are with you. Can you rely upon the Military now about the Capitol? If not call upon those in whom you can trust. The moment Stevens, Sumner, and their fellow conspirators make their first move in their treasonable designs, arrest them the moment they are clear of the Capital, and have them quietly lodged in the old Capitol[2] or some other safe place until they can be brought to trial for the crimes they are committing against the American people and the President of these States— and believe me the people will sustain you and sheild you with lives. That you may have about you those in whom you can confide at the the trying moment, is the prayer of him who pens these lines.

John. Fisk   Late Colonel 2nd Mtd. Rifles N.Y.V.

P.S. This is a copy of a letter written you 12th. last, but not sent. If it was then applicable to the state of things, sincerely do I beleive it to be now.[3]

ALS, DLC-JP.

1. Fisk (c1813–1891), a veteran of the Appomattox campaign, was discharged from the army on May 18, 1865. CSR, John Fisk, RG94, NA; *Off. Army Reg.: Vols.*, 2: 317; Pension File, Maria H. Fisk, RG15, NA.

2. Old Capitol Prison.

3. A week later Fisk, as chairman of a meeting of veterans, called for the removal of Franklin Spalding as collector for the port of Niagara and James Low, Jr., as postmaster at Suspension Bridge, and the appointment in their places of "sound and reliable Conservative Andrew Johnson men." But neither one was removed. See Fisk et al. to Johnson, Sept. 24, 1866, Appts., Customs Service, Collector, Suspension Bridge, Franklin Spalding, RG56, NA. See also Niagara County, N.Y., Citizens to Johnson, ca. Nov. 13, 1866.

From John W. H. Underwood

Rome Ga.   Sept. 17. 1866

Dear Sir

Last July was one year ago. I made out & sent to you my application for Pardon, and one month or so afterwards I sent you one more formal that was properly approved by James Johnson Provisional Governor of Georgia. I have never heard from it directly. I asked Gen Geo. S. Houston Senater elect from Alabama, to See you on the Subject, also Gen. W. T. Wofford Member of Congress elect from this district. I also requested the Hon. R. F. Lyon[1] to See you on his return from the Philiadelphia Convention. I have not heard from the latter but I am informed by Gen Houston & Gen Wofford that they have had an interview with you on the

Subject, and were only informed that the pardon could not now be granted.

I have performed Since the summer all the duties of a good Citizen and cannot conceive of any reason why the clemency of the Department Should not be extended to me, and I am induced to believe that Some enemy of mine has falsely represented me to you. I am too poor to pay any agent to look after this matter for me. I have a wife & five children[2] dependent on my personal exertions for a support and I appeal directly to you in the matter if there is any explanation you may want inform me at once and it will be given. I can procur the favourable recommendation of any man in Georgia you will name.

My condition is weighing like a millstone around my neck, I ask in the name of Common humanity and for my innocent children to ask your clemency in the matter. Please let me hear from you.[3]

John W H Underwood

ALS, DNA-RG94, Amnesty Papers (M1003, Roll 24), Ga., John W.H. Underwood.
    1. Richard F. Lyon (1817–1892) was a Macon lawyer who served on the state supreme court during the war years (1859–66). Allen D. Candler and Clement A. Evans, eds., *Georgia: Comprising Sketches of Counties, Towns, Events, Institutions, and Persons, Arranged in Cyclopedic Form* (3 vols., Spartanburg, 1972 [1906]), 2: 508–9; Amnesty Papers (M1003, Roll 21), Ga., Richard F. Lyon, RG94, NA.
    2. Mary A. Wyly Underwood (1824–1892) and her husband had nine children, of which six, four girls and two boys, ranging in age from about two to fifteen, apparently comprised their 1866 household. Shirley Kinney, Madge Tate, and Sandra Junkins, eds., *Floyd County, Georgia Cemeteries* (2 vols., Rome, Ga., 1985–89), 1: 520; William J. Northen, ed., *Men of Mark in Georgia* (7 vols., Spartanburg, 1974 [1907–12]), 3: 104; 1870 Census, Ga., Floyd, Rome, 1st Ward, 4.
    3. Underwood was pardoned on September 29, 1866. Amnesty Papers (M1003, Roll 24), Ga., John W.H. Underwood, RG94, NA.

From Orville H. Browning

Washington D.C.   Sep 18 1866

Sir

I have the honor to enclose herewith, for your consideration a communication from the Commissioner of Indian Affairs of the 29th ult;[1] with other papers, relative to a proposed reservation for certain Indians,[2] upon Shoalwater Bay, in Washington Territory.

By the accompanying report of the Commissioner of the General Land Office of the 15th inst;[3] it will be seen that the land indicated upon the enclosed diagram is vacant,[4] and I therefore respectfully recommend that you direct the land in question be set apart for the purposes mentioned.[5]

O. H Browning   Secretary

LS, DNA-RG48, Patents and Misc. Div., Lets. Recd.
    1. Dennis N. Cooley to James Harlan, Aug. 29, 1866, Office of Indian Affairs, Report Books (M348, Roll 15), RG75, NA.

2. The Shoalwater Bay reservation was one of two provided for some bands of the Upper and Lower Chehalis and Chinook tribes. Cesare Marino, "History of Western Washington Since 1846," in Wayne Suttles, ed., *Northwest Coast* (Washington, D.C., 1990) [vol. 7 of William C. Sturtevant, gen. ed., *Handbook of North American Indians*], 171.

3. Joseph S. Wilson's report has not been found.

4. The enclosed plats show over 300 acres allotted for the reservation.

5. On September 22, 1866, Johnson endorsed Browning's letter, "Let the tract of land as indicated on the with in diagram be reserved from sale and set apart for Indian purposes as recommended by the Secretary of the Interior in his letter of the 18th inst. said tract embracing portions of sections 2 & 3, in Township 14. N.R. 11. West, Washington Territory."

From James R. Doolittle et al.[1]

Cleaveland, O.   Sept 18th 1866

In discharge of a duty which we owe to you, to the country and to ourselves, we beg leave to say that Hon. E. M. Stanton, Secty. of War, does not possess the confidence, politically or otherwise, of any considerable number of your friends, or the supporters of your policy; and that his continuation in that position greatly tends to weaken your administration.

J. R. Doolittle

LS, DLC-JP.

1. Among the other eleven signatories were John E. Wool, Gordon Granger, Lovell H. Rousseau, George P. Este, and Lewis D. Campbell.

From Edward H. East

At Home [near Nashville]   Sept 18/66

Your Despatch in regard to the Post Office at Nashville,[1] was recieved by me in the country wither I have come, to escape the Cholera. I can not imagine how the fact, that I had any desire for the office, could have been circulated. I certainly have none in the world, and am exceedingly grateful to you, for this manifestation of your continued kindness and appreciation.

While writing to you, I desire to say a word or two, in regard to Tennessee, and suggest what I think will be the efforts of the future. The Legislature will assemble in November next. There will be an effort to arm about 30,000 soldiers (whites & negroes[)]. I think the balance of the *Bank* of Tennessee will go for that purpise, *School fund* and all. The hatred and bitterness indicated by Stokes[2] (William Brownlow & others,[)] some of whom one year since, were apparently your sworn friends, is a feeling common to all of that party (radicals) in Tennessee, and they will go any length, to carry their point.

If you have any policy, or basis in your mind, in regard to what should be done in Tennessee, I would be glad to know it. I think many of our political friends in the state, have too much *personal* ambition, and there is too much spirut of rivalry, among those recognized as leaders to attain a thorough success. All are, or pretend to be, your friends, and may be. I believe are, but they are jealous of each other, and are not ready co-workers. I think I could so use any views, or policy you may chose to give out or indicate, in such manner, as to aid us with all these men.

Edward H East

ALS, DLC-JP.
    1. See Robert Johnson to East, Sept. 17, 1866, Tels. Sent, President, Vol. 3 (1865–68), RG107, NA.
    2. William B. Stokes.

From William McEwen[1]

Columbus Ind.   Sep 18th 1866
Dear Sir

Permit me to remind you of what transpired between you & I on the cars (between Indianapolis & Columbus) on the morning you left Indianapolis for Louisville.[2] I informed you that Mr Stansifer[3] the collector of Revenue for the Third Collection district (which is the district in which I live) was sustaining the Radical party; giving all the aid of his personal & pecuniary influence in support of that party. I also suggested the name of Smith Jones[4] as one who would fill the position of Collector in a manner that would be satisfactory to the Treasury Department, and at the same time, give an earnest support to the conservative ticket in the pending election.

I merely call your attention to the subject assuring you that the change indicated would meet the approbation of your active and devoted friends here and promote the success of the Conservative party. Secretay McCulloch has on file letters and papers, from some of your most prominent friends in the state urging this change—including such names as Senator Hendricks, Gen. Manson, D. W. Vorhees & Capt. Powell[5] of Madison (the latter a business partner of mine) well known to Sec. McCulloch, who also knows me and knows that I am not a politician and have no interest except in the general good of the whole country. I have no doubt that Mr. Stansifer professes to be a supporter of yours and in favor of your reconstuction policy but I know that he is in league with the Radicals—furnishing Counsel and pecuniary aid in their war on the President. I think it all important that this and all similar cases have immediate attention. I want nothing left undone that will tend to advance the interests of the Country and secure the support of the state of Indiana to your policy of reconstruction as against the Radical Congress. Trusting that these suggestions may meet your approval & have prompt attention. . . .

Wm McEwen

ALS, DNA-RG56, Appts., Internal Revenue Service, Collector, Ind., 3rd Dist., Smith Jones.

1. McEwen (1816–1876), a businessman, ran a pork packing business in Madison, Indiana, before moving to Columbus, at which time he became a founder and principal stockholder in the Kentucky Stock Bank. From 1857 to 1870 he was president of the bank, while also engaging in real estate and serving as a director of the Indianapolis & Madison Railroad. *Biographical Record of Bartholomew County, Indiana* (Indianapolis, 1904), 514–15.

2. September 11.

3. Simeon Stansifer (1826–1902) began practicing law in 1848 at Covington, Kentucky; he moved to Columbus, Indiana, in 1851. In 1863 he was appointed provost marshal and later was commandant of Camp Rendezvous until 1865, at which time he was appointed collector of Indiana's Third District. In 1866 he resumed his legal career at Columbus, practicing there until his death. Ibid., 368–69.

4. Smith Jones (b. *c*1815), a farmer, was commissioned collector of Indiana's Third District on March 2, 1867, following the rejection of the previous nominee. Ser. 6B, Vol. 4: 286, Johnson Papers, LC; 1860 Census, Ind., Bartholomew, Wayne, 34.

5. Thomas A. Hendricks, Gen. Mahlon D. Manson, Daniel W. Vorhees, and Capt. Nathan Powell. Powell (1814–*fl*1880) was a successful river trader, moving grain, produce, pork, and flour to New Orleans and other cities. He also helped organize the Madison Life, Fire, and Marine Insurance Company in 1848 and served as its president from 1851 until at least 1880. During the war he supplied provisions to federal armies. Afterwards, he became president in 1865 of the newly-organized National Branch Bank. *Biographical History of Indiana*, 50; 1860 Census, Ind., Jefferson, Madison, 6th Ward, 40.

From Richard Vaux

Phila.   18 Sep 66.

Mr President

Your safe return to Washington is cause for joy among all your friends. That mischief, if not worse, was intended by the New England traitors to be consumated, for their plans of revolution, I have no doubt.

The issue is now made, your policy is to save the country, theirs is ruin, impeachment, civil war, and a war of races.

In this state of affairs, to countenance these people in public positions, is unbelief in their purposes, or weakness in the exercise of duty joined with will.

I thank you for what has been done in Philadelphia. Chambers McKibbin is the best appointment that could have been made.[1]

There are others that should be removed, and I trust you will act in these cases. The district attorney of the U.S here Mr Gilpin[2] should be removed. In the State, where I have been addressing meetings, it is sad to find federal officers doing all they can to defeat the purposes of your administration, not openly only, but by the most miserable tricks.

I beg you will consider the most pressing need of an amnesty, or proclamation of Pardon, for the so called *desserters*.[3] It is most important: I cannot impress this too forcibly. It is vital. I do not trouble you with visits or letters, but I am none the less most anxious for your success in restoring the Union and preserving the constitution.

Your position is so like that of President Jackson, that I trust and be-

lieve, like him, Standing on the ramparts of the constitution and appealing to the People you each will share in history the same homage of all
patriots.

Richard Vaux

ALS, DNA-RG60, Appt. Files for Judicial Dists., Pa., Charles Gilpin.

1. McKibbin, Sr. (d. 1891), a former military storekeeper and hotel proprietor, had
been given a temporary commission on September 17 as assistant treasurer of the Philadelphia mint. McKibbin's nomination, supported by several leading Pennsylvania Democrats, was confirmed by the Senate in January 1867. Philadelphia directories (1865–75);
Powell, *Army List*, 471; Lets. Recd. *re* Asst. Treasurers and Mint Officers, Pa., Chambers
McKibbin, RG56, NA; Ser. 6B, Vol. 4: 84, Johnson Papers, LC; Heitman, *Register*, 672.
See also J. Glancy Jones to Johnson, Sept. 20, 22, 1866, Johnson Papers, LC.

2. Charles Gilpin (1809–1891), a former Philadelphia lawyer and mayor (1850–53)
whom the Senate had confirmed in 1864, was not removed by Johnson. However, at the
expiration of his four-year term in 1868, Gilpin was replaced. Holli and Jones, *American
Mayors*; Ser. 6B, Vol. 4: 91, Johnson Papers, LC; Appt. Files for Judicial Dists., Pa., John
P. O'Neill, RG60, NA.

3. In July 1866 the War Department offered pardon to deserters of the regular army
who turned themselves in before August 15 of that year. But Johnson is not known to have
extended a similar pardon. Simon, *Grant Papers*, 16: 241.

From Washington, D.C., Irish Committee[1]

[September 18, 1866][2]

Mr. President

The Executive Committee of Irish Citizens in the District of Columbia, in approaching Your Excellency, beg leave, in the first instance to
tender their heartfelt congratulations at your safe return to the National
Metropolis: and hope that that Providence which has so happily watched
over you thus far, will, for the sake of the nation, continue to preserve you.

This Committee formed of Irish Citizens in this District, would have
but slight claims on your excellency's consideration, & little right to obtrude on you their views on the present political Crisis, did they express
merely the sentiments of their individual members; but placed as they
have been in communication with their countrymen in the large Cities of
the Union, and finding their own views adopted and approved wherever
known, they are confident that they thus far represent their brethren, and
thus supported, they are anxious to place before the President their views
upon the present attitude and leanings of the adopted Citizens of Irish
birth and extraction.

And in the views to be put forward and the language in which they are
expressed, should aught appear in the slightest degree dictatorial or un-
courteous, the Committee desire to disclaim all such intention, guided as
they have been in seeking this interview solely by a desire that the line of
policy which has been marked out by the President may be sustained by
our Countrymen, and that they may support him in his efforts to carry
them into practice.

Having thus far made the object of our interview clear the Committee beg leave to represent, that,

However apparently antagonistic to the administration, the attitude of a large body of Irishmen may be, yet the Current of democracy flows through their whole political life and influences all their acts; and hence it is that when in this Campaign, our Countrymen have been called upon to declare their favor for & sympathy with the Administration as Contrasted with the radical party they naturally turn their eyes to Washington and see in the Cabinet and in all high places of authority the same *personel* which filled those seats during the period of active Civil War. The War has ceased many months since, and the active machinery of War should be put out of sight. The policy of the president should be self-Evident in the stamp of his Cabinet: the high officials who served under a radical administration are still the apparently favored advisers of the president: and thus viewing those who manage the destinies of this Country, few Irishmen can draw any conclusion other than this, that so long as those officials remain, so long will the same policy which placed and retained Mr. Lincoln in power be the policy to be meted out from these stations. The War department, and the bureau of Military justice have been engines of great despotism, and cruelty during the last few years, and Irish Citizens as well as others have been sufferers from them: and while therefore the present head of the War department remains in office, so long will Irishmen feel, that that Consitution which has been fought for so hardly by them in the battles of the South, has received severe shocks at his hands in the North; and that if the President be placed at one side, there is not a single liberal element in the Cabinet recognisable by them.

The Committee therefore ask that Mr. Stanton be removed as speedily as possible, because they believe that an additional liberal element in the Cabinet, while it would give more force to the Carrying out of the policy of restoration, would also show an approach toward democratic views, so acceptable to the Irish American Citizen.

You are aware Sir, that by far the larger number of our Irish adopted citizens while professing allegiance to this Country, and truly loving her free political institutions, have, by an ardent longing for the restoration of their native land to her former independence, been placed in apparent antagonism to the Administration, and our enemies the radicals have spared no pains, and labor still with extraordinary Zeal to fan the flame of dissatisfaction, which Fenian Irish Citizens of this Country, have felt, and with what result the Maine Election has shown.[3]

As the Fenians are the Active Irish Element, have a Common purpose in their political life, and act in a body it may be worth the attention of the head of the Executive to place himself rightly before them, therefore the Committee Suggest, that,

Inasmuch as the Conduct of the Consuls of this republic, in Ireland especially those at the Eastern ports,[4] has been such as to merit reprehension, owing to a want of Exhibition of due Zeal and interest in standing between the power of England and those American Citizens suddenly seized and Confined, the removal of these Officials and the appointment of Citizens who would perform their duty aright, would be an acceptable proof of Unity, and harmony of feeling, between the administration and the Irish-American Citizens.

Your Committee Suggest that the Citizen travelling through European nations should be allowed to go his way unmolested—that the liberty of transit thro' a foreign nation should be secured to the American adopted Citizen—they think that the flag should every where cover the Citizen: Your Committee point to the arrest in Ireland and forcible deportation therefrom of many adopted Citizens by British Officials—adopted Citizens against whom no crime was at any time charged.—and recommend this Subject to the attention of the Secretary in the hope that the Interest and Safety of American Citizens travelling thro' that portion of the British Empire may meet with more consideration than it has heretofore.

The Irish people have never acknowledged, and never will acknowledge, that in their efforts to obtain justice and liberty for Ireland, by legislative independence or otherwise, they have Committed Treason. In the State Trials which succeeded the struggle of 1848 the English government were unable to prove treason, and to meet the emergencies of supporting English rule, the British parliament at that time in session and subsequent to the alledged offences, passed a retrospective act calling it "Treason-felony"—a new Parliamentary Crime, and with that hasty legislation proceeded against and convicted the leaders of the Young Ireland party of that day.[5] In view of this The Irish American-Citizens think that the American Minister Mr. Adams,[6] overstepped his duty to his own Country by his Expressions designating as treasonable the late efforts of our brethren in Ireland. The Committee look upon such language in the mouth of an American Minister as singularly unhappy, indicating a forgetfulness of the struggles of his own nation, and evidencing a Want of Sympathy, with one of the most oppressive of modern people, and they respectfully submit, that the Appointment of a gentleman with more liberal views in the place of the present Minister to St. James' would be considered with special favor by Irish American Citizens.

It would gratify this last named element of our population, if it could be shown, that the Government of our Country, while bold, quick & powerful to preserve its international law unbroken—even at the Expense of the good will of many of the Supporters of that government— was equally bold, and willing to be equally powerful to insist upon the performance of international obligations incurred by another nation— and to exact from it that same measure of rectitude of international conduct, for which this government has received so much Credit on the other side of the Atlantic: and the Committee Suggest to the Secretary of State that the Alabama claim is yet unsettled, and a fit subject for adjustment. Action of this kind just now might Convince our Countrymen that English influence is not supreme in the State department, and it would bring the Administration closer to the Irish born Voter. The Committee beleive that much of the late Irish Majority in the State of Maine might have been Withdrawn from the radicals by a judicious diplomatic Action on the Fishery question.

While the Secretary of State reminds England on the foregoing matter it might be well for him to further contrast the principles of action in both Countries: and to call the Attention of the English Home government to the magnanimity of this people and their rulers—who at the moment when a deadly internal war had been closed—at once and freely granted pardon—not only to those in arms, but to those in Opposition—and to ask of England to imitate such act, by opening the prison doors on several hundred of her own subjects, immured in narrow cells, with no prospect of immediate release, and against some of whom there are no charges of criminality; such an action on the part of this administration would place it favorably before the Irish American Citizen.

The Citizens of Irish birth Constitute a Nation in the heart of the United States: with their lineage they Exceed five Millions; and the number of Irish here now exceed the Irish population in their island home: The Irish Citizen Soldiers furnished by them in the late war are recorded by the hundred thousand, and their military graves by the thousand: next to the native Element in number ranks the Irish: and by direct nativitity or by consanguinity more than three quarters of a Million of Votes may be cast: Yet the official lists of federal Appointments may be carefully searched and the names of few of our countrymen will appear—less than these of other Nationalities of far inferior numbers. A judicious distribution of the federal offices in the several states—so as to secure to Irish-born Citizens a share of official patronage in the ratio of their numberical Strength—is needed: The post office, internal revenue and similar federal appointments might be distributed in this way: and so of all Federal Appointments in States and Territories: such distribution is recommended to be made prior to the date of the Coming elections in the middle and western states.

Nor should the Federal patronage be distributed merely as regards state offices—the diplomatic list might be made accessible and the Consular appointments be similarly selected to a fair share. The intelligence and capability for these offices of honor can surely be found as readily in the Celtic, as well as in the Teutonic Constitution; and the appointment of such patronage to the Irish people would rally round the Administration a hearty support.

The Committee have now Sir placed their views before you; and have called attention only to those points which demand immediate Action:

and which when Conceded will form the base on which the local speakers can appeal with force to our people. This Committee is at all times ready when called on to offer assistance: and hope in Concluding that thier Suggestions will receive your patient consideration.

AD, DLC-JP.
1. Thomas Antisell, president, and James R. O'Beirne and P. A. Flynn, secretaries. Antisell (1817–1893) taught in Dublin until, as a member of the "Young Ireland" party which incited the rebellion in 1848, he was exiled and went to New York. After lecturing and practicing medicine in a variety of places, he settled in Washington where he taught at Georgetown University. During the Civil War he served as a brigade surgeon, medical director of the 12th Army Corps, and as surgeon-in-charge of Harewood Hospital. Following the war he continued at Georgetown and was also employed as chief chemist in the Department of Agriculture (1866–71). O'Beirne (1838–1917), journalist, lawyer, and government clerk, was born in Ireland but educated in New York. During the Civil War he received the congressional Medal of Honor for his conduct at Fair Oaks, Virginia. There are two possibilities for Flynn, both natives of Ireland—Patrick (b. c1812), a laborer, and John A. (b. c1804), a clerk in the Treasury Department. The committee presented these statements in person to Johnson on the 18th; he sympathized and promised that the administration would do its best to promote the interests of the Irish. *NCAB*, 19: 433; Hunt and Brown, *Brigadier Generals*; *New York Times*, Sept. 19, 1866, Feb. 18, 1917; 1870 Census, D.C., Washington, 5th Ward, 123; (1870), Georgetown, 593; *Mobile Sunday Times*, Sept. 23, 1866, clipping found in Lets. of Appl. and Recomm., 1861–69 (M650, Roll 6), Thomas Antisell.
2. Date taken from the cover letter.
3. The Maine elections of September 10 resulted in an overwhelming victory for the Republicans for the governorship, state legislature, and House of Representatives. *American Annual Cyclopaedia* (1866), 468.
4. William B. West, consul at Galway and Dublin; Gwynn H. Heap, consul at Belfast; Edwin G. Eastman, consul at Cork. Heap (1817–1887), diplomat, served as vice and acting consul in Tunis, a government clerk in Washington, and for the War Department in Turkey before the Civil War. At the outbreak of war he was a Navy Department clerk. He then entered the secret service, after which he commanded Admiral Porter's Mississippi squadron pilots (1863–64). In 1866 he was appointed consul to Belfast; from 1867 to 1878 he served as consul to Tunis. Eastman has not been identified. Ser. 6B, Vol. 2: 126, Johnson Papers, LC; *U.S. Off. Reg.* (1865–67); *Appleton's Cyclopaedia*.
5. The Irish rebellion of 1848 was part of a larger liberal movement against established authority that resulted in revolutions throughout Europe. However, the Irish movement lacked the support of businessmen, landowners, and professionals found to be necessary in the successful rebellions on the continent. The Treason Felony Act, passed by Parliament in April 1848, enabled authorities to take action against the rebellion's leaders without being forced to try them for sedition, a comparatively minor offense, or treason, which required a death sentence. R. V. Comerford, *The Fenians in Context: Irish Politics and Society, 1848–82* (Dublin, 1985), 13, 15–16.
6. Charles Francis Adams.

From William D. Capron[1]

Winchendon Mass   Sept 19th/66
Sir;
Nothing but the *Present Distracted* state of the Country would have tempted me to trouble you with my views. You are well aware that the Radicals by their course in congress during the last session, put back the cause of Reconstruction for the sole purpose of carrying the next Presidential Election. They care nothing for the Poor Negro, and are intent

wholly upon retaing power. If the elections to come off this fall, go the same as Maine it is no Secret, that when congress comes together measure will be taken, for your Impeachment and trial. I do not know myself precisely on what grounds, but I beleive on that of assumption of power. You can rest assured that is to be the programme for the coming winter. Such being the case it becomes you to have your house in order, forewarned is to be forearmed. It is not good policy for the Offices of a Government to be held by its enemies. Pardon me for making the statement, but you *should at once proceed to remove every officeholder* who denouces the coure of the admistration. The cause of the country demands no *half way* work, but the line should be drawn, friend or foe, for or against. In the person of Edwin M. Stanton Secy; of War, you have a Marplot who will prove a traitor to yourself and the Country. He is the first man to be *removed* to bring harmony into the counils of the Nation. All of the Demicrats, and Nine out of Ten Republicans, look upon him with abhorrence, and disgust. The present aspect of the Country, is such as to cause a great deal of anxiety to its true friends—and the future looks gloomy enough if the Radical policy succeeds. In my opinion the removal of Edwin M. Stanton, would do more toward restoring the union, then any other one measure, which is practicable to carry out. The question then arises, who to appoint in his place. You well recollect that Genl Jackson appointed a young man from your own state by the name of Eaton, who filled the Office acceptably.[2] (Full many a rose is born to blush unseen and waste its fragrace on the desert air.)[3] There are any quaity of young men who possess executive ability in abundance and who could fill any position in the country if the were called to it. To make a long story short, I am a Soldeir in the army of the Republic, perfectly able and competent to fill any office in your gift, except Secretary of Stat, or Attorny General, and possess as much Executive ability as any man in the Country, *not exceptng* Benj Butler. I have not got up a petition and spent time and money to procur names, but if you have any position in your gift which you think I would fill I make bold to say I would like it. I should make you a good privat Secty, or officer in the Regular Army, or Collector of Internal Revenue in the 9th Dist of Mass.[4]

I am a person who always am right to the point. I prefer to write to you rather than to spend a few weeks time, in getting the names of Politicians to a petition.

Wm. D. Capron.

ALS, DNA-RG56, Appts., Customs Service, Subofficer, Boston, Wm. D. Capron.

1. By 1870 Capron (b. *c*1838) was working in a machine shop. 1870 Census, Mass., Worcester, Winchendon, Gardner, 60.

2. John Henry Eaton (1790–1856) served a controversial stint as secretary of war, 1829–31. *DAB.*

3. A variation of Thomas Gray's *Elegy Written in a Country Churchyard*, stanza 17.

4. It was this last post that Capron evidently was most interested in filling. In fact, he

wrote McCulloch on the same date, asking that the incumbent, Daniel W. Alvord, be removed; Alvord remained in the post, however. Capron to McCulloch, Sept. 19, 1866, Appts., Customs Service, Subofficer, Boston, Wm. D. Capron, RG56, NA; *U.S. Off. Reg.* (1865–67).

From Addison H. Douglass[1]
Private

                                                                Memphis   Sept 19th 1866
Dr Sir

I take the liberty after enclosing the Communication of the Committee[2] to drop a line rather sub Rosa. On our return to the city from St Louis where we met you we found the greatest interest among the people in regard to your visit.

Great apprehension is felt among many good men here about the results of the Coming election.[3] The fear is that you will not be able to bring the whole Conservative strength into the field, and that you *may* fail not only to reverse the Radical Majority, but what is of equal concern break up the 2/3d majority. Doubts of this My dear Sir are working injuriously to all & every interest throughout the South.

This doubt is crippling, & fettering all enterprise, commercial and manufacturing, and whatever you can do towards this end either by direct or indirect means will be appreciated. Alexander (it is said) when the Gordian Knot was handed him to unravel, struck terror to the heart of his enemies and made himself respected, by boldly drawing his sword and solving the mysterious problem by Cutting the chord, instead of wasting time by pursuing the legitimate process of solution. As much as you may deprecate the necessity the fates I fear have decreed that you shall follow his example or witness the melancholy fate of a great people struck down by the hand of discord & faction.

I do not counsel violence to the Constitution & laws—far from it, but you must fight the devil with fire, he, more than all others dreads his own element. From your high stand point you are fully capable of surveying the entire field—but one like myself in the lower strata may observe what may escape your attention.

Mark this if they go into the next Congress with the same, or an increased majority they will impeach you in ten days after organization. Suppose they do? What then? Anarchy *universal disruption* and ruin. Let me beg of you to take an early step, surround yourself with your known friends at the Capitol & elsewhere, see that your Army & Navy are under the Control of officers who will obey *The President*. Where there is a doubt, *strike*, for the perpetuity of the Nation hangs upon it.

Let us hope for the best and act on the injunction of one of our Revolutionary Sires "pray to God *and Keep your powder dry*."

We have to make a fight in your own state and unless we have the countenance of the Government I say God help us. Let us entreat you Mr
President to reflect on the matter and advise us, when you come to our
city.

It will afford me great pleasure to hear from you.

A. H. Douglass

ALS, DLC-JP.

1. Douglass (1820–1894), a lawyer, was a native of Tennessee who had lived in Mississippi during the 1840s before moving to Memphis. In 1855 he was elected mayor of Memphis and almost thirty years later was elected judge of the criminal court of Shelby County.
O. F. Vedder, *History of the City of Memphis and Shelby County, Tennessee* (2 vols., Syracuse, 1888), 2: 28; *Memphis Commercial Appeal*, Sept. 4, 1894.

2. The enclosed document, signed by Douglass and others, referred to a visit at St.
Louis by a Memphis delegation which had invited Johnson to make a trip to Memphis. In
the document the committee asked the President to specify the exact time for his arrival in
Memphis. The President had arrived in St. Louis on September 8 and remained there until
his departure on the morning of September 10. His visit in St. Louis was a part of his
"swing around the circle." Johnson did not go to Memphis, despite the invitation. See
Committee to Johnson, Sept. 19, 1866, Johnson Papers, LC.

3. An obvious reference to the pending congressional elections throughout the nation.

From Caleb P. Johnson[1]

Gazette Office
Wilmington, Del.   Sept. 19, 1866

Dear Sir:

Since your accession to the Presidency I have defended you and your
administration in my paper with all sincerity and honesty, solely for the
good of my country. The Radical journals here[2] made you and Mr. Seward the special objects of abuse. During all this time whatever countenance there was in the shape of advertisements, were bestowed upon the
Radical presses, mine being the only paper in the city that gave you support. When I found the Radicals were determined to refuse to bestow the
common courtesy upon the President of the United States on his late tour
I secured the co-operation of some friends and inaugurated our delightful
little excursion to the Susquehanna, where we met you.[3] I had no
thought of office; but when I found the Federal officers here refused to
come near you and Gen. Grant and others, and even kept the National
Flag from its accustomed staff on the Custom House, Post office and
other public buildings,[4] I determined that they had disgraced themselves
and our country, and that I would run the risk of a refusal of an appointment rather than allow them to remain in position and still abuse a man
whom I believe possesses as patriotic a heart as pulsates in this union.
Although many of my Democratic subscribers were opposed to my
course, at the first, some of whom were high in social and political position, I am proud to-day, to say, that I do not know a Democrat in Dela-

ware who is not now heart and soul with me and the "*Gazette*" in favour of the policy of Andrew Johnson.

C. P. Johnson

P.S. My letters of recommendation were forwarded to you on Monday.[5]

C.P.J.

ALS, DNA-RG60, Appt. Files for Judicial Dists., Del., Caleb P. Johnson.

1. Johnson (1820–*fl*1882) was in the newspaper business in Maryland, Pennsylvania, New York, and Washington, D.C., before removing to Wilmington in 1842, when he purchased a half interest in the *Delaware Gazette*, a Democratic organ of which he served as publisher and editor for nearly forty years. J. Thomas Scharf, *History of Delaware, 1609–1888* (2 vols., Philadelphia, 1888), 1: 453.

2. Presumably Johnson refers here to the *Delaware State Journal* and perhaps the *Delaware Republican*, both advocates of the Republican party in Wilmington. Ibid., 1: 455, 458–59.

3. Johnson was among the group of Delaware citizens who met the President on August 28 at the Maryland-Delaware line and accompanied him across Delaware to the Pennsylvania state line. *Philadelphia Inquirer*, Aug. 29, 1866; *New York Herald*, Aug. 29, 1866.

4. The Wilmington city council had refused to offer an official welcome to the President. Ibid.; Phifer, "Johnson Takes a Trip," 9.

5. He had been recommended for U.S. marshal of the district of Delaware. On October 1, 1866, the President gave him a temporary commission to that post and in mid-December his nomination went to the Senate, but before Johnson was confirmed he resigned. Scharf, *History of Delaware*, 1: 453; Appt. Files for Judicial Dists., Del., Caleb P. Johnson, RG60, NA; Ser. 6B, Vol. 3: 207; Vol. 4: 102, Johnson Papers, LC.

From Hugh McCulloch

Treasury Department.

September 19th 186[6]

Sir:

I hope you will not commit yourself in favor of General Couch for Collector at Boston.[1] Should he be appointed, we should have Couch for Collector, Swift[2] for Naval Officer, and Underwood[3] for Surveyor, all meritorious and able gentlemen, doubtless, but not one of them having the necessary business qualifications for his position. While it is proper to reward soldiers in the field, the interests of the Government must not be overlooked.[4]

H McCulloch   Sec

LS, DLC-JP.

1. Darius N. Couch (1822–1897) had been recommended by a number of Massachusetts delegates to the Philadelphia convention, among others. On one of the petitions in support of Couch, Johnson noted: "The Secrety will give this application his personal and immediate attention." During the Civil War, Couch held the rank of major general and served with distinction in a number of engagements. Warner, *Blue*; Appts., Customs Service, Collector, Boston, D. N. Couch, RG56, NA.

2. A former captain in the 3rd Mass. Cav., John L. Swift (1828–1895) later penned a biography of General Grant. In support of Swift's appointment, a Boston citizen assured the President: "He [Swift] is a '*live man*'—& we want such here. Milk & water politicians are not adapted to the present state of affairs." Albert Smith to Johnson, Aug. 20, 1866, ibid., Naval Officer, John L. Swift, RG56, NA; *Off. Army Reg : Vols.*, 1: 125; *NUC*.

3. Commissioned as surveyor of the port of Boston in February 1866, Adin B. Underwood (1828–1888) had seen action in the Shenandoah Valley and at Chancellorsville and Gettysburg, before a leg wound at Chattanooga forced him from active field duty. His stint as surveyor lasted for nearly twenty years. Warner, *Blue*; Ser. 6B, Vol. 4: 22, Johnson Papers, LC.

4. Although both Couch and Swift obtained temporary commissions for their respective posts, neither man's full nomination was confirmed by the Senate in early February 1867. Ibid., Vol. 3: 35; Vol. 4: 24; Couch to Johnson, Feb. 7, 1867; Simon P. Hanscom to Johnson, Feb. 8, 1867, Johnson Papers, LC; *National Intelligencer*, Feb. 7, 1867.

To John Williams, Jr.

Washington, D.C.   Sept. 19" 1866.

Your letter of the 16" just read.[1] I regret that it will be out of my power to be with the people of my adopted home in Knoxville this day.[2] Though I cannot be with them in person, I will be with them in spirit, in feeling, and in sentiment. It is hoped that after they have struggled so long and suffered so much for the preservation of the Union, they will not now be misled by designing, bad men, whose policy, if carried out, will result in a dissolution of the Union and a change of our free institutions.

Andrew Johnson

Tel, DNA-RG107, Tels. Sent, President, Vol. 3 (1865–68).

1. Williams's letter of the 16th reiterated an earlier invitation to Johnson to attend the planned Knoxville meeting. Along with this letter Williams enclosed a September 5 letter from Frederick S. Heiskell and others; it had been inadvertently misdirected and had not reached Johnson. It entreated the President to participate in the forthcoming Knoxville mass meeting. See Williams to Johnson, Sept. 16, 1866; Heiskell et al. to Johnson, Sept. 5, 1866, Johnson Papers, LC.

2. In a telegram of September 17 Johnson had already notified Williams that he would not be able to visit Knoxville. Given the promptness of that reply, the President must have been responding either to the September 5 letter from Heiskell et al. or to some (now missing) direct invitation from Williams that antedated his letter of September 16. In other words, Johnson on the 17th could not have been responding to the Williams letter of the 16th. Heiskell et al. to Johnson, Sept. 5, 1866, Johnson Papers, LC; Johnson to Williams, Sept. 17, 1866, Tels. Sent, President, Vol. 3 (1865–68), RG107, NA.

From Francis P. Blair, Sr.

20 Sep 66   Silver Spring [Md.]

My Dear Mr. President:

I am on my way to take a [hunt?] in the mountains of Penna. Mongomery is there stumping the state & Doolittle writes me from Indiana that he also will go there. His letter is marked private and although he is the most sensitive man on earth about revealing any feeling of dissent from a friend whom he would rather suffer any personal sacrifice than say any thing that looked like fault finding, I have brought myself to believe that I ought to let you see what his observation on the Canvass prompts him to say to me. I concur entirely in his views, but I would not urge anything on my own Judgment. I am too much prejudiced to trust it.

Doolittle tells me

"For six long months I have been urging the president to call on Grant temporarily to do the duties War Department so that he could be called to council & be fully identified & committed with all his moral support to our cause.

But Stanton remains & all over my state, through the Milwauki Sentinel, the letter of a correspondent from Washington says that Stanton is not removed because it is rumored & believed at Washn. that Stanton has testimony to show that Mr. Johnson was privy to Lincoln's assassination; and in the midst of the excitement raised by the representation and misrepresentation of the Presidents speeches it gains currency & produces such a state of phrenzy & insane madness that no man can read the future.

I am as calm as most men. I study the philosophy of history & Christianity & endeavor to school myself to a Christian resignation to what I cannot control. But I cannot close my eyes to what we lose by this long delay in making the Cabinet a Unit on this great question. I begin to have my fears it is too late.

A united Cabinet last December would have controlled the last congress simply by its moral power standing upon Lincoln's policy, upon which Mr. Johnson's was an improvement so far as he changed it.

And if Mr Johnson had stood upon his written messages, he would at this moment be invinable."[1]

I have ventured here to give what one of your trusted friends writes to another in strictest confidence. It is marked "private." I am sure it cannot hurt him in your opinion, because he writes with a heart full of concern for you. And if I have passed propriety in revealing his feelings & my own on this crisis, you will pardon it for the love we bear you & our devotion to that cause you represent.

F. P. Blair

ALS, DLC-JP.
1. Not found.

To Salathiel C. Coffinberry[1]

Washington, D.C.   Sept. 20, 1866.

Dear Sir & M. W.[2] Brother.

Your acceptable letter of the 17th of June[3] was duly received, and but for the pressure of official business would have been answered at an earlier day.

The simple and touching memento, enclosed in your letter,[4] certainly does awaken in my memory a renewed appreciation of the great moral integrity and eminent ability of Lewis Cass;[5] and it will be preserved by me as an interesting memorial of that distinguished and patriotic man. Nothing could give me more unalloyed satisfaction than your assurance that he approved my political action, and that he trusted in me "as the guardian of our institutions of Government and the preserver of the sacred covenant between the fathers of our country and mankind."[6] The approval of such great and good men encourages me in my efforts for the restoration of the constitutional relations of the States, in order that a spirit of mutual conciliation may prevail, our national Union be strengthened, the rights of all our people be maintained, and their liberties sacredly preserved.

Gen'l. Cass honored every association with which he was connected, and we may well be proud that, as an eminent and consistent freemason, we could claim him as a brother.[7] The Grand Lodge of Michigan highly appreciating him while living, has fraternally exhibited its love and respect for his memory, now that his spirit has departed to the Lodge above, where the Supreme Master of the Universe presides.

Thanking you for the memento which, in such eloquent terms, you have transmitted for my acceptance. . . .

[Andrew Johnson]

L, DLC-JP.

1. Coffinberry (1809–1889) went to Michigan in 1843. The author of an article on the Potawatomi Indians and the Black Hawk War, he was, in 1866, the Grand Master of the Masons in Michigan. Sue I. Silliman, *St. Joseph in Homespun* (Three Rivers, Mich., 1931), 39, 200; Coffinberry to Johnson, June 19 [*sic*], 5866 [1866], Johnson Papers, LC.

2. Probably Most Worshipful Brother, a term of recognition and respect used in Masonic lodges, especially for prominent leaders such as Coffinberry.

3. The date on Coffinberry's letter could be read as either June 17 or June 19, but the letter could not have been written before June 20, the date of Lewis Cass's funeral. Ibid.; Frank B. Woodford, *Lewis Cass: The Last Jeffersonian* (New Brunswick, 1950), 343.

4. Coffinberry sent Johnson a piece of crepe, "a portion of the mourning drapery" which he wore for the Masonic burial ceremonies of Gen. Lewis Cass, which occurred after the funeral on June 20. Ibid.; Coffinberry to Johnson, June 19 [*sic*], 5866 [1866], Johnson Papers, LC.

5. Cass, whose final political office had been secretary of state under James Buchanan, lived in retirement, due to his advancing age and failing health, during most of the Civil War. He died on June 17, at the age of 83. Woodford, *Lewis Cass*, 334–39, 342.

6. Johnson is quoting from Coffinberry's letter. Coffinberry to Johnson, June 19 [*sic*], 5866 [1866], Johnson Papers, LC.

7. Cass was a previous Grand Master of the Michigan Masons. Ibid.

From Robert Morrow

Knoxville   Sept 20, 1866

Notwithstanding peculiar disadvantages the ratification mass meeting here yesterday was large, most harmonious and enthusiastic.[1] The preamble adopted contains a severe and critical comparision between the 14th August and the 3rd Sept Conventions in Phila[2] and the resolutions ratify without qualification the platform of the National Union Convention with an additional resolution of greeting from the fellow citizens & neighbors of Andrew Johnson to him in his present position.[3] Elaquent pointed & telling addresses were made by the Chairman Hon T.A R

Nelson by Rev W. B. Carter & John Netherland. Your dispatch[4] was read amid deafening applause and afterwards three cheers were given for you with unbounded enthusiasm.

R. Morrow   Bt Col & AAG

Tel, DLC-JP.
1. See accounts of the Knoxville meeting in the *Nashville Press and Times*, Sept. 22, 1866; *Nashville Dispatch*, Sept. 22, 1866; *Brownlow's Knoxville Whig*, Sept. 26, 1866.
2. The reference to conventions is to the National Union Convention in Philadelphia in mid-August and to the Southern Loyalists Convention, also in Philadelphia, which followed a few weeks afterwards.
3. The preamble and resolutions praised the National Union Convention and castigated the Southern Loyalists meeting. The Knoxville gathering went on record as endorsing the Declarations of Principles adopted at the National Union Convention. Moreover, the Knoxville mass meeting expressed its support of Johnson's administration. See *Nashville Dispatch*, Sept. 22, 1866.
4. A reference to Johnson's telegram to John Williams, Sept. 19, 1866.

From William J. Allen[1]

Cairo Ills   Sept 21, 1866

I am the nominee of the Democrats and conservative men, supporters of your policy, in this the 13th Congressional District of this State. I am opposed by Gen'l Raum,[2] who is a fierce and uncompromising Radical, and undergoing a heated and somewhat acrimonious contest in the District before the people. My friends think that it is important that certain things be done to secure my election, and, per consequence, secure you a friend in the next Congress. I find, in canvassing the District that many of the important offices, (post offices &c) are in the hands of the enemy. Our friends have been insisting upon proper and judicious changes being made, and I address you in behalf of what I consider our mutual interests, as well as what I esteem to be the best interests of the Country.

Will your Excellency please indicate whether myself and other friends of your policy in this section may be consulted in reference to appointments in this District and that changes may be made at the suggestion of your friends here.[3]

Wm. J Allen

ALS, DLC-JP.
1. Allen (1829–1901), a native of Tennessee, moved to Illinois, where he was admitted to the bar in 1849. In Illinois he served as prosecuting attorney for the twenty-sixth judicial circuit, state senator, and circuit court judge for the twenty-sixth. Thereafter he held two terms as U.S. representative (1861–65). A member of many state and national conventions in the ensuing years, he was appointed U.S. district judge for the southern district of Illinois in April 1887 and served until his death. *BDAC*.
2. Green B. Raum (1829–1909) practiced law in Illinois and Kansas before serving in the Union army where he rose from major to brigadier general. Following the war, he was elected to the U.S. House of Representatives (1867–69) and served as commissioner of internal revenue (1876–83) and pensions (1889–93) before retiring to his law practice. *BDAC*.

3. On the 28th, Johnson replied that he would "be glad to receive from you such information and suggestions in regard to the appointments in your section as you may deem best." Johnson to Allen, Sept. 28, 1866, Johnson Papers, LC.

From Joseph R. Flanigen

Philadelphia, Sept 21 1866

My dr Mr President

With a very full appreciation of the constant presure on your time, I venture to invite yr reading of the enclosed article from the Daily News of yesterday.[1]

The results to be obtained from a resumption of specie payments by the Goverment, are in my judgment much greater and of far more importance than most people suppose. I beleive with you, that the Radicals are trying to break up the Goverment, and hence we should seek evry means in our power to break down the Radicals.

Nearly all the immense sums of money made from the war is in their hands, and assisted by the plethoric condition of the mony market, which is produced by an excessive volume of currency they are able to spend millions of dollars for the purpose of defeating the measures of your administration. The Radical power is the monied power of the country, and the National Banks constitute the most important element of that power. The dividends which they earn and declare are without precedant, and those who controll them are lavish of their contributions to partisan purposes. The cheapness of the currency begets the impression that the country is in a most prosperous condition, and notwithstandg the fact that the people are obliged to pay most exorbitant prices for evrythig they need, they are content in the beleif that we are prosperous. The action of Congress is directed to a contination of this condition of things, because in it consists their safety, and hence Congress has a greater power with the people than is found in the administration. So long as this condition of affairs continues, we cannot break down the Radical power. We may, and will, carry some additional Congressmen, and occasionaly a state, but without a *revulsion* we have no hope in the Presidential contest. I propose that we shall produce that revulsion on the principle indicated in this article which I enclose. Let the Secretay of the Treasy deliberately and quietly determine on his policy to resume specie payments on the Goverment issues, and the work of contraction will begin at once. He needs no legislation. He does not need to interfere with the Banks. If they are effected—as they will be—it is not his fault, but their misfortune. He but does his duty to the people as a public officer, and in doing that he will save his country from Radical rule and in all probability he will save the Goverment from disruption.

Do me the favour my dear sir to consider this subject carefully.

I think we should at once adopt and urge the proposition—to resume

specie payments as a part of our political faith. I care not wether the proposition is popular to day, or tomorrow or not. If we adopt it, and cary it
out in practice the results which I have indicated will follow as sure as you
live.

The importance which I attach to this subject is the only excuse I offer
for troubling you with it at this time.

J R Flanigen

ALS, DLC-JP.
  1. Not found.

From Andrew H. McClain[1]

Carthage Tennessee   21st Sept 1866.

Sir.

On the 19th June last I addressed a communication to your Excellency[2] in reference to Military interference with the Circuit Court of
Dekalb County and informed your Excellency that in consequence
thereof the June term of the Court was not held.

I have not had any intimation as to what action your Excellency has
taken or intends taking in regard to the matter.

The time for the next regular term of the Court is now near again at
hand. The 3d monday in october being the time fixed by law.

Permit me now to say that without some action on the part of your Excellency, sustaining Civil authority in that County matters are destined to
assume an attitude and develop a result which I feel satisfied you do not
desire or intend.[3]

My communication of 19th June sets out the facts of this matter with
some particularity. I shall therefore not repeat them now.

I will only say that I am satisfied from what I have heard out of Court
(These causes having never been tried) that the assumption said to be
made that the horses in controversy were sold at Quarter masters sale is a
mere pretense wholly unfounded in the truth of the case.

The defendants in these suits were informed distinctly that the Circuit
Court of DeKalb would extend to them the full benefit of all the acts of
Congress in favor of the discharged Federal Soldier and others to which
they could show they were entitled, and that if these suits fall within the
class of cases referred to in certain acts of Congress they could have their
causes transferred to the Federal Court if they desired it to be done. After
these announcements were made in open Court they chose a resort to
military force.

To be frank I will say that matters have now assumed an attitude that
forces upon me the necessity to suspend the Court in that County unles I
can have the assurance from your Excellency that the Court will be
sustained.

My communication of the 19th June presents a state of facts showing that the process of the Court was annulled and set aside by military forces sent from Nashville and not only so a squad of Soldiers were present in smithville on the day for the meeting of the Court with orders to report to a private citizen taking an active part and probably the instigator of the whole affair. I have no assurance that these things will not be repeated, and even if I did have such assurances I do not deem it proper to attempt to hold Court in that County without at least twenty five or thirty soldiers to stand by the sheriff and protect the Court.

Andrew H McClain

ALS, DNA-RG94, Lets. Recd. (Main Ser.), File T-673-1866 (M619, Roll 521).

1. A member of the Carthage bar, McClain (1826–1913) became a circuit court judge in 1864 and held that post for four years, after which he was appointed to a brief term on the state supreme court. Years later McClain served as U.S. district attorney for the middle district of Tennessee. John W. Green, *Lives of the Judges of the Supreme Court of Tennessee, 1796–1947* (Knoxville, 1947), 178, 180.

2. Not found.

3. On October 10 McClain again pleaded with Johnson for some response. A week later on behalf of the President, Edward D. Townsend reported McClain's complaints concerning the civil courts to Gen. George Thomas. Townsend also informed Thomas that Johnson wanted a report from him about the matter. The President immediately followed with assurances to McClain that "Instructions have been given preventing all interference by the Military with the Civil Courts in Tennessee." Finally, in December, Secretary Stanton forwarded to Johnson the report from Thomas in which the general denied any military interference with the courts and insisted instead that the military had assisted the civil courts. McClain to Johnson, Oct. 10, 1866; Townsend to Thomas, Oct. 17, 1866; Stanton to Johnson, Dec. 8, 1866, Lets. Recd. (Main Ser.), File T-673-1866 (M619, Roll 521), RG94, NA; Johnson to McClain, Oct. 19, 1866, Tels. Sent, President, Vol. 3 (1865–68), RG107, NA.

From MacGregor J. Mitcheson[1]

Private.

Philadelphia   Sept. 21st, 1866.

My Dear Sir

Will you permit a personal stranger to your Excellency—(but one who has entered the campaign to speak in support of your policy)—after returning from a somewhat extended tour in Canada to express to you the assurance of the very great respect in which you are held in that Province by reason of your most honorable and neighbourly course on the occasion of the attempted *Fenian* invasion;[2] and the great confidence entertained by leading Citizens and Officers of Government that your Excellency, aided by the willing co-operation of our noble Generals and their commands, will promptly suppress any further outbreak that may be undertaken—and perhaps feel justified in prohibiting public meetings being held in furtherance of their nefarious designs.

I beg to assure your Excellency that it afforded me great pleasure at a dinner party—at which some of the most distinguished gentlemen of

Canada were present—to hear a toast proposed from the head of the table to the *good health of Your Excellency*—accompanied by some very kind and cordial expressions of respect and earnest wishes for your hearty support by our people.

I have no personal favours to ask from your Excellency as a *supplement* to this note, but could not refrain from avowing my personal admiration—as a War Democrat—of the wise measures you have so bravely indicated and advocated on behalf of the interests of the *Whole* Union, and of the active measures adopted on behalf of the people of Canada—some of whose Capitalists, at my instance, when our National Loan (first issued for war purposes) was rather dull of sale, cheerfully Subscribed to aid the cause:—and to express the hope that you may be able more fully to enforce Your policy in the future.

MacGregor J. Mitcheson.

ALS, DLC-JP.
1. Mitcheson (*fl*1886) was a Philadelphia attorney. Philadelphia directories (1865–87).
2. On June 6, Johnson issued a proclamation declaring that the Fenian invasion of Canada, begun June 1, had violated America's neutrality laws and warning citizens of the consequences of taking part in such Fenian activities. Johnson also called for the arrest of the "invaders" and empowered General Meade to use all the necessary force to carry out the law. Richardson, *Messages*, 6: 433; Neidhart, *Fenianism*, 59–72.

From E. Reed Myer

Custom House, Philadelphia,
Surveyor's Office, Sept 21st. 1866

Sir:
The time has arrived when I consider it my duty to tender you my resignation of the position of Surveyor of this Port. I am prompted to this act for the reason that I do not approve of the policy of your Administration,[1] and look upon that adopted by Congress for the Settlement of our present difficulties as the wisest Safest and best for the Country.[2]

E. Reed Myer

ALS, DNA-RG56, Appts., Customs Service, Surveyor, Philadelphia, E. Reed Myer.
1. In his letter of the same date to McCulloch, Myer complained about a recent departmental directive which stipulated that Myer's deputy would be appointed by the secretary of the treasury. See Thaddeus Stevens to Johnson, June 22, 1865, *Johnson Papers*, 8: 272–73.
2. Myer's resignation (which was accepted on September 29) naturally created a void which a host of individuals wanted to fill. See Appts., Customs Service, Surveyor, Philadelphia, Joseph Severns, Henry W. Tracy, William Harbeson, RG56, NA; Ser. 6B, Vol. 3: 161; Vol. 4: 84, 87–90, Johnson Papers, LC. See also Pennsylvania Citizens to Johnson, Oct. 16, 1866, and William H. Wallace to Johnson, Nov. 7, 1866.

From Samuel J. Tilden

(Confidential)

New York   Sep 21 1866

My Dear Sir,

Mr Humphry,[1] who bears this, desires to represent to you the propriety of the release, on proper terms, of the arms & material taken by the goverment from the Fenians, in as much as the goverment has deemed the matter so entirely at an end as to dismiss the pending prosecutions. There is no policy in holding this property as a mere pecuniary fine; and the opponents of the administration are using such demagogical art to take from it the votes of the Irish, that no pretext should be given them which clear duty does not compel.

Mr Humphry will discuss the whole matter with you; and I trust you will deem it proper to comply, in some form, with his recommendations. He is well acquainted with this aspect; and a man of excellent practical judgment.

It is important that immediate action in the matter should be had.[2]

S. J. Tilden

ALS, DLC-JP.
1. James M. Humphrey (1819–1899), was a New York Democratic congressman (1865–69) who represented the Buffalo district, where much of the captured Fenian arms and ammunition were stored. *BDAC*; Randall, *Browning Diary*, 95.
2. Presumably Humphrey met with the President, Secretary Stanton, and Attorney General Stanbery to discuss this matter on September 22. At a cabinet meeting three days later, Johnson ordered the release. But news of his order was not made public until several weeks afterwards, closer to the New York election. Ibid.; Jenkins, *Fenians and Anglo-American Relations*, 200–201; Stanton to Johnson, Sept. 24, 1866, Johnson Papers, LC. See also Humphrey to Johnson, Oct. 26, 1866, Office of Atty. Gen., Lets. Recd., President, RG60, NA.

From Samuel P. Chase

Washington, Sep 22, 1866.

My dear Sir,

When at Savannah last year[1] Mrs Marthell, wife of Capt Marthell[2] was very kind to my daughter,[3] and the Captain seemed to me a deserving man.

He has now a place in the New York Custom House with a salary of $1000, quite insufficient for their wants.

She writes me that "Collector Smythe says that if we get a letter from the President recommendig Mr. Marthell that he will give him a much better place."

Is it too much to ask you to have a note sent to Mr. Smythe to this effect? I shall be much gratified by any good done to them.[4]

If Mr. Marthell has any politics I don't know it; but I think him capable of doing good work.

S. P. Chase

P.S. I should have called; but to leave a card is an idle ceremony & having nothing to ask & no reason to think any thing I could say would be of use did not care to take time which so many are eager for. But if I can ever be useful, I shall promptly obey any summons, you may send.

ALS, DLC-JP.
   1. While on his southern tour in the spring of 1865, Chase wrote Johnson several letters. See Brooks D. Simpson, LeRoy P. Graf, and John Muldowny, eds., *Advice After Appomattox: Letters to Andrew Johnson, 1865–1866* (Knoxville, 1987), 17–38.
   2. Probably Emil G.A. Marthell (1832–1890), who served as a staff officer under Gen. John P. Hatch, headquartered in Charleston, South Carolina, and was mustered out of the army on July 31, 1865. Marthell's wife, apparently the first of two, has not been identified. Pension File, Johanna Marthell, RG15, NA; Powell, *Army List*, 804; *O.R.*, Ser. 1, Vol. 47, Pt. 2: 605; *U.S. Off. Reg.* (1867–69); Marthell to James B. Fry, Mar. 2, 1863, ACP Branch, File CB-1863-M43, Emil Marthell, RG94, NA.
   3. Janet "Nettie" Ralston Chase (1847–1925), who accompanied her father on various trips, later married William S. Hoyt. Frederick J. Blue, *Salmon P. Chase: A Life in Politics* (Kent, Ohio, 1987), 74, 251, 310, 312–13, 393; *New York Times*, Nov. 20, 1925.
   4. It is not known whether the President intervened on Marthell's behalf; he was last listed as holding a clerk's job in the New York collector's office at a salary of $1,500 per year. *U.S. Off. Reg.* (1869).

From David M. Fleming

Willard's Hotel,
Washington   Sept 22d/66

Sir:
   Permit me to thank you for the courtesy you have shown me on the subject of my removal and the interest you have manifested in my behalf, and to assure you of my continued personal regards and devotion to your cause, notwithstanding the decree of the Hon Secretary of the Treasury to submit my case to the parties who caused my removal.
   If this decison affected myself only I should not give it so much concern. The destruction of my printing business by the action of the radicals has left me without the means to support my wife and children,[1] unless I can again revive my paper as an Administration organ for I will publish no other. My opinions cannot be purchased nor will I sanction or sustain a policy I know to be wrong in principle or that will operate unjustly on any section of our common country, and could I be assured of support I would commence its publication immediately, but unfortunately I have no means to operate with.
   The Secretary has, however, at my request suspended the order for me to deliver up the office until further orders which I hope will be long deferred.
   I leave Washington for home this evening and as I may not see you

again and express in person my feelings towards you I hope this note will be kindly received.

Hoping that you may be spared many years to serve your country in this the hour of her trial, and that your Administration of public Affairs may prove eminently successful and result in a complete restoration of the Union, and that peace and harmony may prevail in all sections of the thirty six States under our glorious banner.

D M Fleming
Assr 4th Dist   Piqua, Ohio.

ALS, DLC-JP.

1. Fleming and his wife Matilda (b. c1831), a Pennsylvania native, had at least two girls and two boys, whose ages ranged from six to twelve. 1860 Census, Ohio, Miami, Piqua, 19.

From John W. Leftwich

Washington City D. C.   Sept 22d 1866

Sir

When I secured from you the appointment of R Hough Esqr[1] as Int. Rev. Collector at Memphis Tenn it was under as you will remember a promise to inform you if I became convinced—as most of your friends then were—that he was identified with the radical party.

I received numerous letters from reliable sources saying he was; and an equal number from himself saying he was not; and knowing that he controlled the political actions of F S Richards Esqr[2] of the Tenn Legislature I determined to test the matter by asking him to influence Richards to oppose the Constitutional Amendment.[3]

Instead of doing this he allowed the Radical Correspondent of the "Missouri Democrat" to make such a perverted use of my letter on that subject as to place you and myself in a false light before our friends as well as enemies.

This was to my mind *conclusive* proof but in addition, I saw that he was using his influence in favor of the "Memphis Post" one of your most foul mouthed columniators; that his deputies were open and avowed Radicals; that a Senate confirmed his nomination that rejected your known friends; and that he failed to cooperate with your friends in Memphis on *all* occasions and *especially* in the movement for the Phila. Convention which you were *known* to favor.

With these unmistakeable evidences I would have been false to you as well as to myself not to yield the point; and in doing so nominated in his stead my personal friend Mr Leake;[4] but at the Phila. Convention I was shown that Mr Saunders had strong recommendations from every county in my Dist. and the endorsement of every senator and member of Congress from Tenn except Mr Maynard and myself and almost the entire Tenn delegation to the Phila. Convention.[5]

Thus I was induced to sink my personal preferences for Mr Leake and to consent to the appointment of Mr Saunders, because it would be gratifying to a larger number of your friends and supporters.[6]

Having taken such pains to give you a reliable opinion I regret to notice an indisposition to make the change even after your friends in West Tenn have been intoxicated with joy because the Washington papers announced that the change had already been made.

I present this with a respectfull request that if the change is not made that this be returned to me with evidence that it has been read that I may show my constituents that I have done my duty.

Jno W Leftwich

ALS, DNA-RG56, Appts., Internal Revenue Service, Collector, Tenn., 8th Dist., Rolfe S. Saunders.

1. Reuel Hough had been nominated by Johnson for this post in late May 1866; the Senate approved and Hough was commissioned in June. Ser. 6B, Vol. 4: 227, Johnson Papers, LC.

2. Richards (c1825–fl1873), a civil engineer and railroad auditor, served two terms (1865–69) in the legislature, representing Shelby, Fayette, and Tipton counties. Governor Brownlow appointed him in 1868 superintendent of the Nashville and Northwestern Railroad; that same year he was also appointed U.S. consul to Leeds, England. *BDTA*, 2: 766; *U.S. Off. Reg.* (1869–73); 1860 Census, Tenn., Shelby, 6th Ward, 164; Memphis directories (1858–60); *Brownlow's Knoxville Whig and Rebel Ventilator*, Apr. 26, 1865.

3. The reference is to the ratification of the Fourteenth Amendment by the Tennessee legislature in July 1866.

4. G. P. Leake, not further identified, worked for Leftwich as an employee in the Leftwich, Cash, and Company firm. See Leftwich's support of Leake as revealed in Leftwich to Johnson, Aug. 17, 1866, Appts., Internal Revenue Service, Collector, Tenn., 8th Dist., Rolfe S. Saunders, RG56, NA; Memphis directories (1865–66).

5. Undoubtedly some of the letters and documents that Leftwich saw are the ones still located today in the files for Appts., Internal Revenue Service, Collector, Tenn., 8th Dist., Rolfe S. Saunders, RG56, NA. Pertinent documents include the letter from the Tennessee delegates to Johnson, Aug. 16, 1866; the one from the Tennessee congressional delegation to Johnson, no date; Saunders to Johnson, Aug. 18, 1866; and Saunders to David T. Patterson, Aug. 18, 1866.

6. The file cover sheet indicates that on September 29 Johnson ordered the secretary of the treasury to make the appointment of Saunders and that it was done the following day. Another source gives October 1 as the date of Saunders's recess (or temporary) appointment. President Johnson submitted the permanent nomination to the Senate in January 1867; the Senate confirmed the nomination in early March and Saunders was commissioned as collector that same day. Appts., Internal Revenue Service, Collector, Tenn., 8th Dist., Rolfe S. Saunders, RG56, NA; Ser. 6B, Vol. 3: 424; Vol. 4: 227, Johnson Papers, LC.

From James Potts[1]

Johnstown, Cambria, Co. Pa.
Sept. 22. 1866

I am sorry for the appointment, of A C Mullin[2] as Collector of the 17. District of Pennsylvania.

This is an unpardonable outrage and *must* result in the *defeat* of the democratic candidate for Congress in this district—R. L. Johnston Esq.[3]

The democracy of this district would have been successful this fall, were it not for this indignity.

Mullin is a radical of the Stevens school, and is now *cheif clerk* in the state department of Curtin's Cabnit.

If Mr. Cowan is not restrained in making *such* appointments, we will loose the state and almost every Democrat Congressman.

The democracy have no incouragement to sustain you, when you allow Cowan to perpetrate such indignaties. The peoples, nor your intrests are *not* consulted in his appointments.

I have cast my thirty sixth *annual* vote for the nominees of the democratic party because I ever beleevd, its principles were those of the patriot. And I beleev now it is the duty of every patriot, who wishis in the future as in the past, to enjoy constitutional liberty to sustain you, in preserving the Union of States. This can only be done by sustaining the democratic party against the *dis*-unionists. Now I submit what encouragemt have we, when the very means at your control for that purpose are taking out of our hands & give to the enemy? How are we to sustain you in changing the sentiment of Congress, when Cowan wont sustain us? You dont know me, nor is it important who I am. I have a deep intrest in the preservation of the Union, am no applicant for office. I wrote to assure you that if we are defeated in Pennsylvania, your appointments will be the cause of it.[4]

James Potts

ALS, DNA-RG56, Appts., Internal Revenue Service, Collector, Pa., 17th Dist., A. C. Mullen.

1. Potts (1809–1891) was a longtime Johnstown attorney, editor of the *Democratic Courier* (1846–47), and district judge (1871–74). James W. Swank, *Cambria County Pioneers* (Philadelphia, 1910), 90–98.

2. A former Whig-turned-Republican, Alexander C. Mullin (1830–1878) edited a newspaper in Ebensburg, before serving in the Pennsylvania legislature (1860–61), and securing a wartime appointment as private secretary to Gov. Andrew G. Curtin and subsequently as chief clerk in the state department at Harrisburg. Given a temporary commission on September 17 as revenue collector in place of Samuel J. Royer at Sen. Edgar Cowan's urging, Mullin later worked as a banker in Schuykill County. Ibid., 114–23; Cowan to McCulloch, Sept. 10, 1866, Appts., Internal Revenue Service, Collector, Pa., 17th Dist., A. C. Mullen [*sic*], RG56, NA; Ser. 6B, Vol. 3: 161, Johnson Papers, LC.

3. Robert L. Johnston (1815–1890), a former county treasurer and prothonotary, indeed lost the congressional race to Republican Daniel J. Morrell. *Biographical and Portrait Cyclopedia of Cambria County, Pennsylvania* (Philadelphia, 1896), 344; *Guide to U.S. Elections*, 617.

4. Despite this protest and at least one other from the ousted incumbent's brother-in-law, Mullin's nomination was sent to the Senate in January 1867 but rejected in early March. Meanwhile, Morrell, now the congressman-elect for the district, endorsed and forwarded a petition to Johnson asking that Royer be reinstated. The President apparently approved this request following Mullin's rejection and after being told by Secretary McCulloch that Royer's removal "was a blunder." But Royer's nomination was later withheld. Cyrus L. Pershing to Johnson, Oct. 12, 1866; Daniel J. Morrell to Johnson, Dec. 8, 1866; Hugh McCulloch to Johnson, Mar. 6, 1867, Appts., Internal Revenue Service, Collector, Pa., 17th Dist., Samuel J. Royer, RG56, NA; Ser. 6B, Vol. 4: 84, 87–90, Johnson Papers, LC; Swank, *Cambria County Pioneers*, 56.

From Montgomery Blair

Irvine Warren Co Pena.   Sept. 23. 1866

My dear Mr. President

I write to recommend the appointment of E. O. Perrin[1] Esq. of New York to the place of assessor of the 1st Dist of that State. I am very well acquainted with Mr. Perrin having met him frequently in such canvasses as we are now engaged in in this State. He is a very effective Speaker & is a generous warm hearted fellow, who responds promptly to the wishes of his friends & goes earnestly & without thought of himself, & in utter disregard of private business to do the party work, wherever required. "Those who serve at the altar, should be fed from the altar," is what we hear in the church, & it is not better doctrine for the church, than it is for the Govt. Our people love to see such men as Perrin provided for; & the Administration which passes over such services as he renders, to promote the cold blooded indifferent people, who are too selfish to give their time to political subjects, & then decry the active political workers will have little sympathy even from the non-political classes.

I feel a personal interest in Mr. Perrin, because he responded promptly to a call I made upon him to speak for us in Maryland this spring.

I do not think it adviseable either to *postpone* his appointment. It will do him no harm as a stumper to have it. It will on the contrary I think enable him to do much more good than he can do without it in his District. I hope therefore you will make the appt at once.[2]

M Blair

ALS, DNA-RG56, Appts., Internal Revenue Service, Assessor, N.Y., 1st Dist., E. O. Perrin.

1. Edwin O. Perrin (1820–1888) practiced law and was a civil navy agent in Memphis in the 1850s before removing first to Kansas and then to the New York City area, where he was later clerk of the state court of appeals (1868–88). He served as secretary of the Democratic national conventions (1856–72) and of the National Union Convention in Philadelphia (1866). *New York Tribune*, Dec. 20, 1888; *U.S. Off. Reg.* (1851); Frederick Cook, *Manual for the Use of the Legislature of the State of New York. 1888* (Albany, 1888), 420; Richard Schell to Johnson, Sept. 15, 1866, Appts., Internal Revenue Service, Assessor, N.Y., 1st Dist., E. O. Perrin, RG56, NA.

2. Blair's letter was referred to the Treasury Department, where recommendations from Robert J. Walker, Governor Curtin of Pennsylvania, Gen. Henry W. Slocum, among others, already had been forwarded. In reply to Perrin's own letter to Johnson, the President had written: "Special attention is Called to this application. A. J." But McCulloch delayed Perrin's recess appointment until November 26, after the fall elections, and his nomination was not confirmed by the Senate. Meanwhile, Perrin secured a temporary special agency within the Treasury Department, before Johnson nominated him in June 1868 as chief justice of the supreme court in the Utah Territory. But this nomination was likewise not confirmed. Ser. 6B, Vol. 3: 97; Vol. 4: 51, 383, Johnson Papers, LC; Perrin to Johnson, Sept. 10, 1866, Appts., Internal Revenue Service, N.Y., 1st Dist., E. O. Perrin, RG56, NA.

From James S. Brisbin
Private and Personal

Austin Texas   Sept 23d 1866

Sir

The 34th Article of war grants to officers the right to complain to their superiors when "they shall think themselves wronged." I desire however to address you as one of your constituents. I am informed that you have striken my name from the list of promotions under the new Army Bill because I made a political speech to my old comrads in arms, at Pittsburg some two months ago, and because I have at different times and places opposed your policy. Sir this is a mistake. I never made a political speech at Pittsburg nor have I at any time or place spoken against your mode of reconstruction. The only political speech I have made since entering the Army was at the City of Philad. in 1864 against Genl McClellan and in favor of your election. Before entering the Army being an Editor and politician I was in the habit of canvassing my State on the occasion of important elections but since becoming a soldier I have declined to speak on political subjects though often solicited to do so. All the appointments made for me while lately in the North I declined to fill believing that soldiers should not engage in Politics. Do not however think that I have no opinon or that I believe in your policy. I am an honest man and I tell you frankly it is wrong. True the opinion support or opposition of a poor little Captain of Cavalry without influence, can be of small importance to a great man like you but what I see every day with my eyes and hear with my ears I know to be so and I tell you there is not, there can be no mistake when I say that the mass of these southern people are unrepentent rebels, hating the union, proscribing men for their opinions, aye and they would hunt them down as they did you in Tennessee were it not for the presence of our loyal bayonets. They take your pardon for it brings immunity from crime and they smile in your face and then come home—here to hate and abuse you. If you were not President they would not let you live in peace among them. I am here on the bloody and disputed ground, in and among them and I know them. Mine is the voice of one crying in the wilderness of treason. But while I am a radical in sentiment Mr President you made a mistake in supposing I openly in speeches opposed you politically and you did me a great wrong when you struck my name from the lists of promotion. My opinions are my own but I think Presidents and Army officers ought not to make political speeches. I entered the Army as a private soldier and rose step by step to be a Brevet Major General of Vols and Captain in the Regular Army. I was present in twenty seven engagements and received three wounds in the service of my country. My Commanding Genls Pleasenten Burbridge Hooker Mead Banks[1] and others have filed in the Dept of War many recommendations in my behalf. Some were sent to your Private Secretary. I write simply to disabuse your mind of the groundless—charges some bad person has made against me and I ask no further consideration at your hands than to examine my recommendations and read my letter.[2]

James S Brisbin

ALS, DLC-Edwin M. Stanton Papers.
    1. Alfred Pleasonton (1824–1897), born in Washington, D.C., and educated at West Point, served in the Mexican War as well as in Florida and on the Indian frontier. During the Civil War he commanded cavalry in the eastern theatre, especially at the battle of Brandy Station, and, after 1864, in the Trans-Mississippi. After the war he occupied some minor federal posts. The other generals mentioned are: Stephen G. Burbridge, Joseph Hooker, George G. Meade, and Nathaniel P. Banks. Warner, *Blue*.
    2. In a note on the back of the letter, dated October 16, 1866, Johnson requested the secretary of war to "please inform me if any instructions of mine have interfered with the promotion of the writer of this communication." An unsigned reply indicated that "there has been no interference by the President or any one else." It is not clear exactly what promotion Brisbin expected. While he remained a captain, he was transferred in early September to the 9th Cav., one of the new black regiments authorized by act of Congress on July 28, 1866. He was officially nominated to and confirmed in this post on March 2, 1867, with his commission dated five days later. Brisbin was not promoted in rank until January 1, 1869, when he became major of the 2nd Cav. Powell, *Army List*, 211; Ser. 6B, Vol. 2: 73, Johnson Papers, LC; William H. Leckie, *The Buffalo Soldiers: A Narrative of the Negro Cavalry in the West* (Norman, Okla., 1967), 6–7.

From Robert M. Moore[1]

Private

Cincinnati   Sept. 24th 1866.

I feel glad to be able to say, that your visit to this City was a complete success, notwithstanding the unpatriotic course of the City Council,[2] but you must not be shocked, when informed that a few weeks ago the *same gentlemen* eulogized and made much to do over the *Hon* Mr *Trenholm Secretary* of the *Confederate Treasury*, an *unpardoned Rebel*, but mind you, his business at Cincinnati, was to build a Rail Road from *here South*.[3] I consider it one of the most unfortunate acts the City Council has ever been guilty of. Long before the War, Cincinnati, was looked upon as an Abolition City, and she has suffered greatly thereby. Now, in your advent here, she had a favorable opportunity to make amends for the past, and place herself in an advanced position before the south-western States, and to control their entire business, for I know that the southern feeling was growing strong in favor of trading largely with Cincinnati, in preference to going west. Her merchants feel this act very *keenly*. A few days ago a southern merchant called on one of our Pearl St. houses where he had been dealing for many years, paid a small balance and went on to New York with $20,000. in his pocket to lay in his goods. As I said to you in the Spencer House, (where I took the liberty of presenting to you a Rose called the "Giant of Battles,") when you are in front of the enemy, take every advantage of that enemy, but when you have subdued and have got that enemy in you power, *treat him kindly*, and you will be sure to turn his enmity to friendship. I practiced that course to a great extent while I was in the army, and it worked well. I will take the liberty, shortly, to give you the particulars of how I subdued the rebellious feelings of almost the whole people of Gilmer Co. West Virginia, when at the out-break of the war, there was but 40 men in that County who voted against secession. Genl Rosecrans, often said, that the course I pursued, and with but 80 men under my command, accomplished more than three Regiments had been able to do stationed at Glenville the Co seat. The other remarkable case was in Huntsville Aa. Acting on the same principle of kindness and human nature, "do unto others as you would have others do unto you," particularly when they are of our own Country, and the same flesh & blood, you will think it remarkable indeed, when told that at Huntsville, I marched fifty one Rebel prisoners to attend the funeral of their Commander through that Rebel City, out to the cemetery, accompanied by over three hundred citizens, (all Rebels,) and back, *Without a Guard*, and even I, had neither sword nor pistol about me, but they came back under my charge and *answered every man to his name*. I belong to that old union party. I voted for Lincoln & Hamlin, and then for Lincoln & Johnson. In less than ten days after Mr Lincolns first call for 75,000 men, I had a company of 95 men mustered in, was Co D, in the 10th Ohio Regiment, Col Lytle.[4] You must have heard of the *Bloody 10th* about Nashville. I was all through western Virginia, Kentucky Tennessee and Alabama. Was in that 21 days march from Huntsville to Louisville after Bragg, where my military career was ended at the battle of Perry-ville, in being severely wounded. It was while in Tennessee and Alabama, that you became so well known to the men of the army. Although Mr Lincoln, was President yet, the boys of the army considered you more identified with, and as one of themselves, because they had heard of your persecution by the people of your own State, as well as the noble Part you took to preserve the Union of the States. I know their feelings, as it was often expressed, for I was with them.

I think it would have been well, just at the end of the war to have banished a few of the leading spirits of secession, and then proclaimed to the people of the States lately in Rebellion, that the war is now over, and that we must all try and forgive and forget the past, reorganize the state Governments, send the best men to Congress, and all become friends once more. I think if that kind of a course had been pursued, every state would now be fully organized and represented in Congress and the whole country at pease, with a consolidated Union of states & feeling, looking forward to an endless prosperity in the future, and the admiration of the world, and a terror to all man kind.

We hear of a great many *soldiers & sailors* conventions called by both political parties, each trying to make the most out of the soldier's popularity. Now I think it wrong, because it will imbitter the soldier against each other. But the kind of a Soldiers & Sailors Convention that I would like to see, would be a Soldiers & Sailors Convention of the Union Army, with an equal number of Soldiers & Sailors of the Rebel Army and none above the grade of Orderly Sergeant, to meet at some Border City, and I will risk, the settlement of the whole question of Reconstruction in their hands. They have met before as enemies, & I think would be proud to meet as friends & peacemakers. If you think well of the suggestion, I think such a convention can be hand, & what ever they resolve upon, would be very apt to put it through.

R. M. Moore.

ALS, DLC-JP.
1. Moore (1816–1880), an Irish native who went to Cincinnati during the 1830s, was a businessman, who served as a captain during the Mexican War as well as lieutenant colonel of the 10th Ohio Inf. during the Civil War. Afterwards, he was a claim agent, real estate dealer, and during the late 1870s mayor. Charles T. Greve, *Centennial History of Cincinnati and Representative Citizens* (2 vols., Chicago, 1904), 2: 10–12; Cincinnati directories (1867–79).
2. On September 10, 1866, just before Johnson's "swing around the circle" visit, the Cincinnati city council, by an eighteen to six vote, refused "to extend the hospitalities of the city to the President and his entourage." *Cincinnati Commercial*, Sept. 11, 1866.
3. During the latter half of June 1866 a large contingent of men from South Carolina and Tennessee, of which Trenholm was the most noted, visited Cincinnati to encourage construction of a railroad to Charleston via Knoxville. They were received "with great courtesy and kindness," and on the 19th participated in a public meeting at the Merchants' Exchange, where Trenholm and others spoke. *Charleston Courier*, June 25, 1866; *Cincinnati Enquirer*, June 19, 1866.
4. William H. Lytle (1826–1863), a Mexican War lieutenant, during the 1850s was a lawyer, legislator, militia major general, and poet. During the Civil War he became colonel of the 10th Ohio Inf. and eventually was promoted brigadier general of volunteers. Although he survived a wound at Perryville in 1862, he was slain the next year at Chickamauga. Warner, *Blue*.

To Henry A. Smythe

Washington, D.C. Sept. 24th 1866.

Mr. Weed is here. His conversation in reference to yourself has been of the most friendly character, and no objections have been urged, as anticipated by you. I state this, in order that you may know what has been said here. Have you heard any thing respecting the Subject of our conversation yesterday?[1]

Andrew Johnson

Tel, DNA-RG107, Tels. Sent, President, Vol. 3 (1865–68).
1. The conversations with Thurlow Weed and Smythe apparently concerned the appointment of Gen. John A. Dix as naval officer of the port of New York City. After receiving Johnson's dispatch, Smythe responded that he hoped "for a favorable answer from the General" shortly. Soon Smythe sent a follow-up telegram, indicating that the general "will do what you think best for the interest of your administration. I hope that you will appoint him today." Dix was given a temporary commission as naval officer on the following day, September 25, and two days later personally notified Johnson that he was heading to Washington for an interview with the President. Smythe to Johnson (2), Sept. 24, 1866; Dix to Johnson, Sept. 27, 1866, Johnson Papers, LC; Ser. 6B, Vol. 3: 95, Johnson Papers, LC. See also John B. Haskin to Johnson, Sept. 28, 1866.

From Democratic Citizens of Berks County, Pennsylvania[1]

Reading   Sept. 25. 1866.

Dear Sir,

The undersigned Democratic citizens of Berks County Pennsylvania would most respectfully represent that the appointment of Sergt. Franklin B. Laucks[2] for assessor of the Eighth District of Penna. meets with our cordial approval and of our people generally.[3] He is honest, capable and trustworthy and in every respect the appointment is a proper one. We would further beg leave to say that it would be injudicious to make any more changes prior to the election. The interests of Mr. Clymer are best served in that way. It seems to us very obvious that if those gentlemen now in Washington were at home working for the ticket instead of *boring for office* success would more likely attend the efforts of those who are laboring for Mr. Clymer's election and through that to sustain the policy of the President. Disorganization is creeping into our ranks in consequence of this scramble for office.[4]

Pet, DNA-RG56, Appts., Internal Revenue Service, Assessor, Pa., 8th Dist., Franklin B. Laucks.

1. There were thirty signatories, headed by Jeremiah Hagenman (1820–*fl*1886), a prominent former district attorney and Democrat who resided in Reading. Morton L. Montgomery, *History of Berks County in Pennsylvania* (Philadelphia, 1886), 543–44.

2. Laucks (c1838–*fl*1871), a disabled veteran of the 7th Pa. Vols. and a Democratic attorney in Reading, had been appointed revenue assessor on September 18, largely on the recommendation of the outgoing Democratic congressman for the Eighth District, Sydney Ancona. Ibid., 576; 1870 Census, Pa., Berks, Reading, 3rd Ward, 77; S. E. Ancona to [Johnson], Sept. 17, 1866, Internal Revenue Service, Assessor, Pa., 8th Dist., Franklin B. Laucks, RG56, NA; Ser. 6B, Vol. 3: 161, Johnson Papers, LC; J. Glancy Jones to Johnson, Sept. 22, 1866, ibid; Reading directories (1866–72).

3. Yet Laucks had his critics, including J. Glancy Jones, who advised the President that the appointment was "*fatal*, unless revoked," and forty-five other citizens of Berks County, several of whom were Conservative Democrats, who signed a petition calling for the removal of Laucks and the appointment of Capt. Richard H. Jones. J. Glancy Jones to Johnson, Sept. 22, 1866, Johnson Papers, LC; David Kutz et al. to Johnson, ca. Sept. 25, 1866, Appts., Internal Revenue Service, Assessor, Pa., 8th Dist., Franklin B. Laucks, RG56, NA. See also Pennsylvania Citizens to Johnson, ca. Sept. 1866, Johnson Papers, LC.

4. Laucks's appointment was soon revoked. News of this fact "came upon our population like a thunderstroke" (according to one disgruntled voter in Reading), thereby costing the Democrats a thousand votes. The assessorship eventually went to Col. George W. Alexander, who had been recommended for the post as early as December 1865. Jacob Haenchen to Johnson, Oct. 15, 1866, Appts., Internal Revenue Service, Assessor, Pa., 8th Dist., Franklin B. Laucks, RG56, NA. See also J. Glancy Jones to Johnson, Dec. 22, 1865, *Johnson Papers*, 9: 528, and Berks County, Pa., Committee to Johnson, Feb. 1, 1866, ibid., 10: 8–10.

From Henry W. Harrington[1]

Madison Inda   Sept 25 1866

Sir

Our Governor[2] or some one Else has been distributing guns to the "Army of the Republic"[3] a secrete political organization. Cannot they be taken in before the Election? Floyd[4] is said to have stolen the U S Arms & President Buchanan, was Justly censured for not preventing it.[5] The Rads are trying to do the same thing.

My Competitor[6] yesterday threatened vengeance on the President at a Joint Speaking we had, and he was surrounded by 100 men & boys of a secrete organization call "boys in blue."[7] They were all brought by his brother[8] from the 4th Dist.

H W Harington   3 Dist

ALS, DLC-JP.
  1. Harrington (1825–1882), a lawyer born near Cooperstown, New York, practiced in New York, Indiana, and Missouri during his career. Following a term in the U.S. Congress (1863–65), he was collector of internal revenue for the Third District of Indiana from October 1866 to March 1867. *BDAC*.
  2. Oliver P. Morton.
  3. Probably the Grand Army of the Republic.
  4. John B. Floyd.
  5. Floyd had been accused of aiding southern secessionists by moving arms to southern arsenals, supposedly for storage. An investigation found the charges unfounded and a Senate resolution to censure Buchanan for failing to stop Floyd failed, though it was widely publicized. *DAB*; Elbert B. Smith, *The Presidency of James Buchanan* (Lawrence, Kans., 1975), 194.
  6. Morton C. Hunter (1825–1896), lawyer, served in the state house in 1858 and the U.S. House following the war (1867–69, 1873–79). During the war he commanded a brigade in the 14th Army Corps, was with Sherman on his march to the sea, and was brevetted brigadier general of volunteers. *BDAC*.
  7. The Boys in Blue societies were campaign organizations, affiliated with the Grand Army of the Republic, that promoted the Republican party and its candidates. Mary R. Dearing, *Veterans in Politics: The Story of the G.A.R.* (Baton Rouge, 1952), 100–03, 116–17, 162–64 passim.
  8. John S. Smith Hunter.

From Kentucky Democratic State Central Committee[1]

Washington D C   Sept 25. 1866.

In following up the points of a conversation held with you yesterday, the undersigned Democratic State Central Committee of Kentucky now formally protest in writing against the following appointments reported to have been made or about to be made in Kentucky

Gen. S. G. Burbridge

to a Lieut Colonelcy in the Regular army. We beg leave to represent that in our best judgment, no man is more odious (and justly so) personally and politically to the people of Kentucky than he. We are satisfied that no honest supporter of your administration in the state would for a moment favor his appointment to any position whatever. We do most earnestly request that your Excellency will give your personal attention towards saving a state which has nobly stood by the Constitution and by you in your efforts to maintain it from so great an indignity as this appointment would be deemed.

Secondly. We protest against the appointment of two persons held by

most people in Kentucky to have been instruments of Burbridges robbery & tyranny viz:

D. S. Goodloe

Supervisor of the assessor of internal Revenue or some office of that kind.
Goodloe is justly odious as one of the infamous "Board of Trads" under
Burbridge by which the people of the State were plundered and robbed
in a most shameful manner. He has been a radical of a most intense
character—fighting the friends of your policy at all times—and according to our well grounded convention really occupies the same position
now—further he has been an opposer of free elections and an active abet-
tor of attemps to suppress the conservative & Democratic vote by the use
of bayonets—and that so late as the Congressional elections of 1865.
Also

J Crockett Sayres.[2]

Assessor of Internal Revenue in the Covington district. He has been & is
a radical as we are informed. He too is odious as an instrument of Burbridge in carrying out the infamous "Hog Order"[3] by which he & others
robbed the farmers of Kentucky out of vast amounts under the false &
fraudulent pretext of Government authority. Such appointments we are
satisfied would greatly injure any administration in the estimations of the
people of Kentucky.

Lastly, but for very different reasons—We respectfully protest against
any appointment *at the present time*, to be given to

Gen. E. H. Hobson

a gallant soldier & true gentleman who according to his own representations now holds conservative sentiments—but who has just been repudiated by the people of his own state and by your friends in it, by the unprecedented majority of near 40,000. Gen H lent himself to a bad cause.
His appointment at present, has been threatened by his friends & would
be construed with considerable semblance of propriety into a smart re-
buff or affront to the great dominant party which we have the honor to
represent in this matter.

LS, DLC-JP.
    1. The seven-member committee was chaired by Robert W. Scott.
    2. Sayers (c1832–fl1870), a prosperous Kenton County farmer, was known for his pro-
pensity for office-seeking and had served as secretary of a Republican convention for the
Sixth Congressional District before traveling to Washington in August 1866 to obtain a
presidential appointment as assessor for the Sixth District. *Cincinnati Enquirer*, July 25,
Aug. 23, 1866; *National Intelligencer*, Jan. 24, 1867; 1870 Census, Ky., Kenton, Stephenson Prec., 9.
    3. In the fall of 1864, Burbridge issued a proclamation that the government wanted to
buy all surplus hogs for the military. Agents were appointed who, while promising a fair
market price, offered prices one to two cents below market values. Permits were now required to drive hogs to market; and ferries across the Ohio were patrolled which literally
forced sales to be made to the government agents. This collusion between the military and
certain Louisville packers drove prices down and made it impossible for other Kentucky
packers to transact business. While the "Great Hog Swindle" lasted only a month before
President Lincoln put a stop to it, Kentucky farmers lost an estimated $300,000. Coulter,
Civil War and Readjustment, 222–23.

Reply to Soldiers' and Sailors' Convention Committee[1]

[September 25, 1866]

MR. CHAIRMAN AND GENTLEMEN OF THE COMMITTEE:

I have no formal reply to make. But the presentation of the record of the proceedings of the Cleveland Convention is peculiarly acceptable in the present posture of our public affairs. To receive the encouragement and expression of confidence in me of gentlemen so intelligent and patriotic inspires me with renewed and increased zeal to progress in the discharge of my duties, strictly adhering to and maintaining the Constitution of the country.

You have performed your part in the field; that has become a portion of the history of the country. But, after having done that, there is, as you have just evinced, an important part to perform as citizens, equal, if not superior, to the service which you have rendered as soldiers and sailors of the Union.

While the war was a physical contest, (connected, of course, with intellect and intelligence, as far as the science of war is concerned,) the struggle now is purely of a civil character, and for the establishment of the basis on which our institutions shall hereafter rest; and the query comes up—a very serious one, I think it is—whether the genius, nature, and character of our Government shall be perverted, or mayhap subverted, or whether it shall settle down and be maintained on the basis and principles of the Constitution.

It is known to all of you the part I have borne since the civil war commenced, both in the campaign and out of it, and I must refer you to that as evidence and proof of what my course and conduct will be in the future.

I have been coöperating with you in every capacity in which you have been engaged since the struggle commenced. I think we are now at a most important crisis in the country's history; when we are to establish and fix a substantial and enduring basis on which our institutions are to rest. We must return to constitutional limits, establish the great fact that ours is a Government of limited powers, with a written Constitution, with boundaries, both national and State, and that these limitations and boundaries must be observed and strictly respected if free government is to exist; and, coming out of a rebellion, we ought to demonstrate to mankind that a free government cannot live on hate and distrust and with ill will towards one another, and that the time has come for reconciliation and restoration of confidence, and the return of the Southern States in all of their relations to the Federal Government, which I look upon as equally, if not more, important than all other work which could now engage our attention.

I have, gentlemen, said more than I intended to say; but I repeat, this encouragement, countenance, and confidence given to me, coming from the sources they do, is peculiarly acceptable to me; and, God willing, and with your help, I shall continue to pursue the course I have been pursuing in trying to restore and save the Government.

Some one has said that the founders of governments are entitled to the most conspicuous places in history; but my conviction is, that those who preserve governments are entitled to a higher honor. But few who were living when this Government was founded now remain. Let us all perform our part according to the theory and genius of our Government, and the result will be the preservation of our institutions; and we will take our places in history wherever the pen of the historian may assign them to us.[2]

National Intelligencer, Sept. 26, 1866.

1. The convention, called for on August 19 by the committee headed by Gen. George A. Custer, was to meet in Cleveland on September 17 and show support for Johnson's policy and the principles of the Philadelphia convention. National Intelligencer, Aug. 22, 1866.

2. At the conclusion of the President's remarks, Gen. Kilby Smith introduced the officers to Johnson. They then departed, "delighted with their reception and the urbanity of the President." Ibid., Sept. 26, 1866.

From John B. Weller[1]

Private

Great Salt Lake City U.T.   25th Sep 1866

My dear sir

I have now been in this City one month[2] and have had an opportunity of becoming somewhat acquainted with the Condition of affairs in this territory. I assume that the time has now arrived when it becomes absolutely necessary that the administration should put forth its whole power to sav the govement from destruction. In my mind it is clear that if the radicals retain power in Congress and attempt to carry out their mad schemes nothing short of another bloody Civil war Can sav the liberties of the people. I also assume that the administration is not disposed to retain men in office who are aiding and abetting the radicals in their efforts to undermine the Constitution and destroy the fundamental principles upon which it is established.

Various charges are made against some of the federal officers in this territory which I do not choose to investigate. It is enough for me to know that they are hostile to the administration and that all their feelings and sympathies are with the radicals who are arrayed against it. Gov Durkee[3] is well known as an extreme radical. Franklin H. Head Supt. Indian Affairs[4] (against whom the gravest charges are made) is an open and avowed radical. Judge Drake[5] it is said is another. Judges Titus & McCurdy[6] it is universally conceded are good and true men. The Secretary of the territory Judge Reed[7] (who in the absence of Durkee for the past 3 months has discharged the duties of Governor) is eminently Conservative and sustains the administration with all his energies.

It is proper to remark that I know of no one in this territory who desires either of the places to which I have alluded but I have no doubt you can readily find plenty of friends upon the other side of the mountains who would gladly accept them.

I beg you to believe that in writing this letter I am actuated by no other motive than a sincere desire to aid you in your efforts to maintain the Constitution and preserve the liberties of the people.[8]

Jno B Weller

ALS, DLC-JP.

1. Weller had been chairman of the commission to run the boundary line between the U.S. and Mexico, served as a U.S. senator from California and as governor of that state, and was minister to Mexico. After the Civil War he practiced law in New Orleans. *DAB*.

2. Weller was on a tour through Oregon, Idaho, and Utah prospecting for minerals. Ibid.

3. Charles Durkee.

4. Head (1832–1914) practiced law in Wisconsin before going west in 1866. Appointed superintendent of Indian affairs for the Utah Territory on March 21, 1866, he served until 1869, and also engaged in stockraising and mining. *NCAB*, 41: 268–69; Hill, *Indian Affairs*, 191.

5. Thomas J. Drake (c1799–fl1869) had practiced law in Pontiac, Michigan, for some years before his appointment as associate justice for Utah in 1862. Although at times not on good terms with the Mormons, Drake remained in his position until 1869. 1860 Census, Mich., Oakland, Pontiac, 620; Orson F. Whitney, *History of Utah* (4 vols., Salt Lake City, 1893), 2: 70, 95–96, 310; Gustive O. Larson, "Utah and the Civil War," *UHQ*, 33 (1965): 72; Hubert H. Bancroft, *History of Utah, 1540–1886* (San Francisco, 1889), 609, 611, 621.

6. John Titus (1812–1876) was initially nominated as U.S. attorney for the Arizona Territory in 1863, but he resigned the post before going west and instead became chief justice of the Utah Territory. When his term expired in 1868, he returned to his law practice in Philadelphia. The following year, however, he became an associate justice and in 1870 chief justice of the Arizona Territory. A native of Kentucky, lawyer Solomon P. McCurdy (c1818–fl1880) was appointed from Missouri as an associate justice for the Utah Territory in 1864. After his failure to obtain the post of chief justice to succeed Titus in 1868, McCurdy practiced law in Salt Lake City. 1880 Census, Utah, Salt Lake, Salt Lake, 9th Ward, 26; Bancroft, *History of Utah*, 621; Whitney, *History of Utah*, 2: 310, 578; John S. Goff, "John Titus: Chief Justice of Arizona, 1870–1874," *AzW*, 14 (1972): 26–28, 31, 41, 43.

7. Amos Reed, a New Yorker, served as clerk for James D. Doty when the latter was superintendent of Indian affairs for the Utah Territory. When Doty became governor in 1863, Reed soon became territorial secretary and held the office until December 1867. E. B. Long, *The Saints and the Union: Utah Territory During the Civil War* (Urbana, Ill., 1981), 129, 184; Whitney, *History of Utah*, 2: 309.

8. Johnson did not replace any of these officeholders before September 1867. *U.S. Off. Reg.* (1867).

From Joseph R. Cobb

Sub Rosa

Treasury Dept.   Sept. 26th 1866

Dear Sir

Enclosed please find "*Card*."[1] This is significant taken in Connection with the Subtle Conduct of Assistant Secretary *Chandler*. Within my own immediate observation he has prostituted his Official Power in awarding a disproportionate Number of appointments (4/5) to the little State of *New Hampshire*, and upon the late Election indirectly urging the Clerks home to vote, to consumate—an expression of opinion against your administration policy. This petty Time Server, (All things to every Man and not *one* thing to any), and his Subservient *tools* Came home Vauntingly boasting their Success, and your discomfiture, with the Unrefined Nassal twang So familiar to N.H. Yanks. I assume this vague cirography upon the enclosed Card Contains an unsolved Cipher.[2] A familiar Problem to the arch Conspirators. Though filling an humble position it may be presumptive my tilting So doughty a *Night Errant*.

Yet in view of this Radl. Champion's want of magnaminity in lending one ear to the Conspirators against myself and wife he Stooped so low as to Stop my pitiful months pay less than $160- per months to gratify that "Baker," alias *Jonathan Wild*[3] and his Political friends, who so dull for a moment to believe we were the intended game. It was a cowardly Stab at your Protection. Shakespear Says "Vaulting Ambition o'er tops itself!"[4]

Joseph. R. Cobb.

ALS, DLC-JP.
    1. The enclosed card was from William E. Chandler in which he observed: "If nothing will be done today in New Hampshire matters I won't bother you now. Will any immediate action be taken?"
    2. The reverse side of the card contains this obscure message: "Final separation on again[?]. If subsequent events show that they cannot live together &c."
    3. Lafayette C. Baker.
    4. Taken from *Macbeth*, act 1, scene 7, line 27. "Vaulting ambition, which o'erleaps itself/ And falls on the other."

From William V. Morrison[1]

Albion Michigan   Sept 26, 1866

Your Excellency will, I trust, permit me to congratulate you on your safe arrival in Washington, and to express the hope that the popular manifestations of approval received during your recent tour, will encourage you to persevere in your noble efforts to re-establish the Union of the States in conformity with the constitution.

Having a deep anxiety that every thing possible and honorable should be done to influence such action on the part of a majority of the people as to indicate by the coming elections the establishment of your national policy, I feel heartily to approve your action in the removal of your traducers and enemies from the federal offices. And as your object—in one sense—is the same as above referred to I hope you will pardon any suggestions I may make in that behalf. I am informed that there are several applicants for the office of Collector of Internal Revenue in this Congressional district (the third) two of whom reside in this (Calhoun) County. viz: Messrs Schuyler[2] and Church.[3] The former I understand has the recommendation of the Conservative Central Committee of this State,

From which recommendation I am constrained to dissent, for the following reasons.

There are two national Banks in Marshall—where both applicants reside—one of which is principally owned by, and under the direct control of C T Gorham[4] one of the most violent and vituperative radicals in this County. Mr Gs. Bank is the depository of the present Radical Collector (Mr S S Lacey)[5] and I am informed, and have no doubt as to the correctness of the information, that Mr Schuyler has been put forward at the instance of Mr Gorham through his personal or business friends in order to retain the government deposits in his Bank as heretofore.

The other Bank is principally owned by, and under the direct management of Horace J Perrin,[6] who although formerly a Republican was the first republican of prominence in that place, that identified himself with your policy and opposed the Radicalism of the majority of Congress. Mr Ennis Church was also a republican but soon became a co-laborer with Mr Perrin in the vindication of your policy; and should Mr Church be appointed he will, if approved by the department, make Mr Perrins Bank the depository of the Govnt. money collected by him thereby in a double sense promote the conservative cause, by favoring those who have abandoned radicalism.[7] Whether the facts I have named were taken into consideration by the Committee or not, I am not informed, but presume they were not. To me they appear important and deserving of due consideration. And in case the appointment is not already made in accordance with the recommendation of the Com I feel assured that your Excellency will give the subject that attention its merits deserve.

In conclusion I would say that I have no personal or direct interest in the appointment, and that I have made the above explanations without the solicitation or knowledge of Mr Church or his personal friends, my sole object being to favor that which will best subserve the great object in view.[8]

Wm. V. Morrison

ALS, DNA-RG56, Appts., Internal Revenue Service, Collector, Mich., 3rd Dist., Ennis Church.

1. Morrison (1817–*fl*1878), a native of New York, worked as a clerk and bookkeeper before ill health caused him to move to Michigan in 1837. After several years of teaching, he was involved in a prosperous business until he met financial reverses in 1871. He served as a justice of the peace for many years. *American Biographical History of Eminent and Self-Made Men: Michigan Volume* (Cincinnati, 1878), 72–73.

2. Peter S. Schuyler (*c*1827–*c*1889) joined the 2nd Mich. Cav. in September 1861 and was advanced to captain the following spring. He served as provost marshal and resigned from the service with an honorable discharge in October 1864. For the rest of his life Schuyler suffered from inflammatory rheumatism contracted in the service. John Robertson, comp., *Michigan in the War* (Lansing, 1882), 924; CSR, Peter S. Schuyler, RG94, NA; Pension File, Peter S. Schuyler, RG15, NA.

3. Ennis Church became surgeon of the 9th Mich. Inf. in November 1861. Although he attempted to transfer to the 26th Inf. in the fall of 1862, he was not permitted to do so, because he had been absent without leave from the 9th Inf. since August. Robertson, *Michigan in the War*, 796; CSR, Ennis Church, RG94, NA.

4. Connecticut native Charles T. Gorham (1812–1901) moved to Marshall, Michigan, in 1836, where he was a merchant until he opened a private bank in 1840, continuing it with great success until 1865, when it became the First National Bank and he became its president. Gorham was U.S. minister to The Hague (1870–75) and served as assistant secretary of the interior (1876–77). *Portrait and Biographical Album of Calhoun County, Michigan* (Chicago, 1891), 191–92; *Michigan Biographies* (2 vols., Lansing, 1924), 1: 339–40.

5. After a four-year residence in Arkansas, where he was judge of Hot Springs County, Samuel S. Lacey (1815–*fl*1887) moved to Michigan, where he farmed and served as county clerk and commissioner of the state land office. Collector of internal revenue from 1865 until removed in 1866, Lacey became postmaster of Marshall in 1867 and held the office until at least 1887. Ibid., 2: 6; *American Biographical History: Michigan*, 62.

6. Originally from New York, where he had learned all aspects of merchandising, Perrin (1819–1880) moved to Marshall, Michigan. There he was a merchant, made extensive real estate investments, owned several milling establishments, and was president of the National Bank of Michigan, which was organized in 1865. *Portrait and Biographical Album of Calhoun County*, 273–74; Washington Gardner, *History of Calhoun County, Michigan* (2 vols., Chicago, 1913), 1: 247.

7. According to one source, both Lacey and Church were directors of Perrin's bank. Ibid.

8. Actually the committee recommended Church, who was appointed collector on September 11, 1866, with his notice of appointment and blank bond sent care of Alfred Russell, the U.S. attorney at Detroit and the chairman of the Michigan National Union Committee. Church probably never saw his appointment, however, because on September 16 Russell returned the papers asking that the appointment be revoked "for reasons which need not be set forth in detail, but which are *perfectly conclusive*." Therefore, on September 21 Johnson appointed Andrew DeForest, who was rejected by the Senate in February 1867. Eventually the President settled on Chauncey H. Miller, whom the Senate approved in April. Alfred Russell to Hugh McCulloch, Aug. 24, 1866; George Parnell to Ennis Church, Sept. 12, 1866; Alfred Russell to McCulloch, Sept. 16, 1866, Appts., Internal Revenue Service, Collector, Mich., 3rd Dist., Ennis Church, RG56, NA; Ser. 6B, Vol. 3: 539; Vol. 4: 275, 277, Johnson Papers, LC.

From Robert W. Johnson

private

Little Rock   Sept 27/66

Mr. President

You know Judge Geo C Watkins,[1] the Head of our Bar, & ablest judge who ever sat on our Supreme Bench; a gentleman of great diffidence & sensitive modesty, & I do not therefore write any letter of introduction.

I beg of you to hear him personally, in his own behalf, & *trust & believe him*.

I also inform you that I am broke up & ruined. So, as it is honest, I have arranged to give up *every thing* to the use & benefit of my creditors—(it will or ought to pay them all) act decisively, & become a poor man at once, without tears or sighs. I have arranged to become an editor of a paper which I hope to make, *in time*, the organ of the State. I send you a number with this. Its title is indicative.[2] It will occupy no half way position, but support you unqualifiedly. I trust in God you will *never submit* to a corrupt & revolutionary process of impeachment.

I wish you would talk some, & freely with Judge Watkins of our affairs here. In his composition he has nothing & knows nothing of a partizan spirit. Our Legislature meets soon, & He and Judge David Walker[3] are in truth the proper men for Senators from our State, & I shall present their names & support them: but the lists are already full of a frightful host of adventurous gentlemen, & as usual I presume the best men will refuse to take on them the conflict with the crowd, & thus half disarm their friends from the beginning.[4]

Gather from him the condition of affairs here, & you are not likely to be misguided: in many respects we need your assistance, as matter of good government & sound policy. And in our postal facilities, offices Routes & contracts, our condition is terrible.

I think Mr. President I know you now—more thoroughly—tried as you have been, & in the freedom of a private letter like this, permit me to subscribe myself. . . .

R. W. Johnson.

ALS, DLC-JP.
    1. Watkins (1815–1872) grew up in Arkansas. After studying law in Connecticut, he returned to Little Rock to practice in 1837. He served as state attorney general and then was chief justice of the state supreme court for two years (1852–54). An ardent Confederate, he was a member of a military court during the war. *DAB*.
    2. Not found. No biographical source mentions what was apparently a very brief attempt at editing. Johnson soon became a law partner of Albert Pike, practicing in Washington, D.C. George H. Thompson, *Arkansas and Reconstruction: The Influence of Geography, Economics, and Personality* (Port Washington, N.Y., 1976), 47.
    3. Kentucky native Walker (1806–1879) moved to Little Rock in 1830 to practice law. A member of the state constitutional convention of 1836 and an associate justice of the state supreme court, Walker was president of the Arkansas secession convention. Chief justice of the state supreme court in 1866–67, Walker was also associate justice again (1874–78). *DAB*.
    4. Neither Watkins nor Walker ever became a senator.

From Charles L. Smith & Co.[1]

Bureau Co. Patriot office,
Princeton, Ill., Sept. 27. 1866.

Enclosed please find a letter signed by a number of leading friends and supporters of the administration, of this city requesting His Excellency not to accept the resignation of John H. Bryant, Collector of the 5th District of Internal Revenue.[2] (The names attached to the request were mostly Republicans in 1864.) In this Congressional District, now represented by "Rinderpest" Ingersoll,[3] the Republican party in 1864 had a majority of 6000, and it would seem to an outsider a rather hopeless district. But still there is hope, the changes are great and many in the District. We are proud to say that the 5th District will do well, many who were earnest supporters of Congress three months ago are to day with the administration and the Union of States. The soldiers in the District are making arrangements to announce in a few days General J. H. Howe,[4] of

Henry County as a candidate for Congress against "Rinderpest" Ingersoll, with a fair prospect of election. The General was formerly (as myself) an earnest Republican, and popular with the party. He is a good de-
bater, and will in our opinion have a fair chance of election, and if defeated
should have the office of Collector. Another reason why the appointment
should not be made now, is, it as an undisposed bait, will bring to our aid
a number of influential men from the Republican ranks, who we might
not get if this Collector office were disposed off. You will doubless at a
glance see the utility of the matter. Mr. Bryant will do very well for the
present, as we are confident, that if he does not vote our whole ticket, he
will at least vote, a part of it, and I think the whole. He is very hostile to
Ingersoll. The great "out side pressure," and the moment of excitement
from insult from the radical side, he forwarded his resignation. We pray
therefore that the resignation may not be accepted for the present.[5]

C. L. Smith & Co.

LS, DNA-RG56, Appts., Internal Revenue Service, Collector, Ill., 5th Dist., John H.
Bryant.
    1. Smith (1843–*fl*1885) moved to Bureau County, Illinois, in 1863 from Hennepin,
Illinois, and worked in his father's newspaper business, the *Bureau County Patriot*. He later
bought and edited the *Bureau County Tribune* (1872–81) and afterwards the *Bureau
County News*. H. C. Bradsby, ed., *History of Bureau County, Illinois* (Chicago, 1885), 653–
54.
    2. See Bureau County, Illinois, Citizens to Johnson, Sept. 24, 1866, Appts., Internal
Revenue Service, Collector, Ill., 5th Dist., John H. Bryant, RG56, NA. Bryant was resigning because he publicly disagreed with the President's policy. For Bryant's resignation, see
Bryant to Johnson, Sept. 14, 1866, ibid.
    3. Ebon C. Ingersoll. "Rinderpest" refers to an acute infectious disease of the intestinal
membranes of cattle otherwise known as cattle plague. *Webster's New Twentieth Century
Dictionary*, 2nd ed. (New York, 1983).
    4. John H. Howe (1822–1873) served during the war as a lieutenant colonel and
brevet brigadier general with the Illinois volunteers. A lawyer by profession, he was chief
justice of the supreme court of the Wyoming Territory from 1869 to 1871. Hunt and
Brown, *Brigadier Generals*.
    5. In February 1867 Bryant tried, unsuccessfully, to withdraw his resignation. See
Bryant to McCulloch, Feb. 2, 1867, Appts., Internal Revenue Service, Collector, Ill., 5th
Dist., John H. Bryant, RG56, NA.

From Richard, George W., and John P. White

Nashville Tenn   Sept. 27th 1866

Dear Sir—

Honl. W. S. Oldham late Senator in the Confederate Congress from
Texas, returned to New York a few days since, having seen the erroneous
statement in the newspapers, that he had been pardoned.[1] He is now in
Toronto. In a letter to us he expresses his wish to return to Texas, & provide for the support of his family, & who we know much need his
assistance.

He says he is ready to meet any charge that may be preferred against

him in the courts of the country, & has gone to Canada to avoid annoy-
ance by the military.

We earnestly hope & request that you will send us a parole for Judge
Oldham, or give us an assurance that he will be paroled on returning to
the United States or on his reporting to you in Washington.[2]

Richard White   Geo. W. White   John P White

ALS (George W. White), DLC-JP.
1. The W. S. Oldham, who had been pardoned, was apparently a relative of Sen. Williamson S. Oldham. Alma Dexter King, "The Political Career of Williamson Simpson Oldham," *SWHQ*, 33 (1929): 132.
2. Johnson allowed Oldham, who had initially fled to Mexico before he went to Canada,
to return to the United States in November 1866. But when the latter arrived in Washington, he refused to accept a pardon because he still believed in states' rights and he did not
believe that he had committed any crime. He did, however, take the oath of allegiance and
was permitted to return to Texas in December, where, unreconstructed, he practiced law
until his death from typhoid fever in May 1868. Ibid., 132–33; Johnson to [?], Nov. 19,
1866; Oldham to Johnson, Dec. 5, 1866, Johnson Papers, LC.

From Edwin R.V. Wright[1]

Hudson City [N.J.]   Sept 27th 1866

Sir

If you had purposely resolved to destroy my chances of reelection you
could not have done it more effectually than by the appointment of a Colonel Thorn[2] as Collector of Internal revenue for my district nor do I
know how it could have been done without consultation with the Representative from the district. Your appointee has only resided a few months
in the State of New Jersey and possesses the high merit (if such it be) of
being the Grand Commander of the Loyal League of Hudson County.
He presided as such within the past week. He was a delegate to the convention that nominated George A. Halsey[3] whom you have just removed
to give place to your real friend Col Zulick.[4] The enclosed article from
the *Radical* Jersey City Daily Times[5] will perhaps be the best means of
exhibiting the *status* of this so called Col Thorn. If you think me worthy
of a consultation I might perhaps present a name that would be entirely
acceptable to my constituents and add great strength to the efforts of
those who are endeavoring to sustain you.[6]

E.R.V. Wright

LS, DNA-RG56, Appts., Internal Revenue Service, Collector, N.J., 5th Dist., George W.
Thorn.
1. After serving but one term as a Democrat in Congress (1865–67), Wright (1812–
1871), a former attorney and mayor of Hudson City, was later elected governor of New
Jersey. *BDAC*.
2. A former Whig representative in both the New York and New Jersey legislatures,
George W. Thorn, who had been wounded at Fredericksburg and thereafter retired from
the volunteer army, was recommended for governor of the Montana Territory, as well as an
unspecified foreign consulate, prior to being given a recess appointment on September 21
as revenue collector for New Jersey's Fifth District. Johnson's nomination of Thorn in Jan-

uary 1867 was rejected by the Senate in March. *Cincinnati Enquirer*, Oct. 17, 1866; Lets. of Appl. and Recomm., 1861–69 (M650, Roll 48), George W. Thorn, RG59, NA; Ser. 6B, Vol. 3: 147; Vol. 4: 74, Johnson Papers, LC.

   3. Halsey (1827–1894) was a Newark businessman, state legislator (1861–62), and assessor for the Fifth District for several years until his removal in August 1866. After winning the election later that fall, Halsey served two terms in Congress as a Republican (1867–69, 1871–73). *BDAC*.

   4. An alternate delegate to the Philadelphia convention, Conrad M. Zulick (1839–1926), former lieutenant colonel, 2nd D.C. Inf., was appointed assessor on August 27, 1866. Officially nominated in January 1867, he was subsequently rejected by the Senate. He later served as governor of the Arizona Territory (1885–89). Ser. 6B, Vol. 3: 147; Vol. 4: 75, Johnson Papers, LC; *Off. Army Reg.: Vols.*, 3: 1091; Appts., Internal Revenue Service, Assessor, N.J., 5th Dist., C. Meyer Zulick, RG56, NA; Thomas A. McMullin and David Walker, *Biographical Directory of American Territorial Governors* (Westport, 1984), 38–40.

   5. The enclosed excerpt stated the editors' disbelief that Thorn would accept his commission as collector, since he was in their opinion a Radical Republican who had allegedly withdrawn his application for a consulship in disgust over the President's policies. But such charges were unfounded, at least according to various members of the state Democratic executive committee which had described Thorn as being a Republican who "heartily, honestly and zealously" supported the Johnson administration. Joseph T. Crowell et al. to Johnson, Sept. 18, 1866, Appts., Internal Revenue Service, Collector, N.J., 5th Dist., George W. Thorn, RG56, NA.

   6. Two days later Wright recommended that Johnson appoint Noah D. Taylor as collector of the Fifth District; Taylor was given a recess appointment on October 6. Wright to Johnson, Sept. 29, 1866, ibid., Noah D. Taylor; Ser. 6B, Vol. 3: 147, Johnson Papers, LC.

From Eunice Pomeroy Davis[1]

Private

New York. Sept 28th [1866][2]

Mr. President

   Knowing, as I do, that every loyal woman in this broad land may confidantly ask your generous hearing, I venture to ask your consideration in the case of my nephew Bvt. Col. Theodore A Dodge[3] of the Vet. Reserves, now soliciting a Major's commission in the Regular Army.

   Coming of an ancestry whose only boast was to have served God and their country—at the first call from his native land, he left a foreign University, with all its well earned honors, so dear to a youth of 18 and hastened to give his early manhood to the cause. He bravely fought its battles till he left his leg on the terrible field of Gettisburgh—and as soon as sufficiently restored, he presented himself upon his crutches, for further duty. He was rec'd at the War Dept. and how faithfully he has done his duty there—his Superior officers know.

   Will you, Mr. President with your accustomed justice & generosity give his case a hearing, and thus confer a great faver upon a large family, who, without an exception are your cordial supporters?[4]

Eunice P. Davis.

144 E. 17th St.   Stuyvesant Square

ALS, DNA-RG94, ACP Branch, File D-832-CB-1866 (filed with D-619-CB-1866),
Theodore A. Dodge.
    1. Davis (b. 1808), the daughter of Lemuel Pomeroy, was the second wife of George
T.M. Davis. *History of Berkshire County Massachusetts* (2 vols., New York, 1885), 2: 472;
New York Tribune, Dec. 21, 1888.
    2. The year is indicated by both internal evidence and supporting documentation.
    3. The son of Mrs. Davis's younger sister, Dodge (1842–1909) received academic
training at European universities before returning to the states and fighting in two New
York infantry regiments until he was disabled at Gettysburg. He served the remainder of
the war in the provost marshal-general's office in Washington. Following his retirement
from the army in 1870, Dodge moved to Massachusetts. *DAB*.
    4. Johnson referred Davis's letter to the secretary of war for action. The President's
nomination of Dodge as captain, 44th U.S. Inf., was confirmed by the Senate in March
1867. Johnson also approved Dodge's brevet promotions of major and lieutenant colonel.
Ser. 6B, Vol. 2: 62, Johnson Papers, LC; Powell, *Army List*, 285; Samuel C. Pomeroy
to Johnson, Mar. 16, 1867, ACP Branch, File D-344-CB-1867 (filed with D-619-
CB-1866), Theodore A. Dodge, RG94, NA.

From John B. Haskin

New York, Sept. 28, 1866.

My dear Mr President.

Gen. Dix has been honored with three of the most important appointments in your gift within the space of a month[1] and I respectfully suggest
that a soldier of more distinction and greater influence in the State has
been entirely overlooked. Maj. Gen. Henry W. Slocum was the most successful and brilliant officer New York produced during the war and at its
close with a generosity which amounted almost to self sacrifice he resigned his position and became the standard bearer of the Democracy to
vindicate your policy.

That he was not elected Secretary of State last fall was in great measure
owing to the efforts of Thurlow Weed and others of the old Whig regime,
who are now I am told opposing his appointment as Naval officer at this
port. When he accepted the nomination he was the most popular man in
the State and he was defeated because of the unpopularity of the Democratic party at the time and because the republican party pretended to be
the only sincere supporters of your policy. I believe that Weed & company
favored Gen. Dix's appointment and that they are now urging Col. Wm.
H. Ludlow for Naval officer.[2] Remembering as I do that Gen. Dix broke
down the Democratic party in 1848 and contributed as much if not more
than any other man in New York to make the republican party what it has
been and is and remembering also that Col. Ludlow who was on Gen.
Dix's personal staff, was also a member of the Van Buren and Adams
party in 1848 I ask you whether there are not other good and true men at
least equally deserving. Col. Ludlow could not control his election as a
delegate to the last State convention. I hope you will not be deceived by
the representation of Weed and Company as to their strength in the com-

ing campaign. I feel that they will not control six thousand votes and I believe that we made a great mistake in not nominating Gen. Slocum for Governor as his popularity would have counterbalanced the defection of Raymond.

I believe that Gen. Slocum's appointment as Naval officer is deserved by his devotion to you and if made will meet the approval of the people of the whole union.[3]

John B. Haskin

ALS, DLC-JP.

1. These appointments were naval officer of the port of New York, minister to France, and minister to The Hague, though the latter post had been tendered to Dix several months earlier. Ser. 6B, Vol. 2: 57–58, Johnson Papers, LC; Beale, *Welles Diary*, 2: 602.

2. Before he was appointed, Dix had recommended that Ludlow be chosen for the position. See Dix to Johnson, June 19, 1866, *Johnson Papers*, 10: 597. See also Dix to Johnson, Aug. 16, 186[6], as well as recommendations by others in Appts., Customs Service, Naval Officer, New York, William H. Ludlow, RG56, NA. For Weed's involvement, see Weed to Johnson, Oct. 2, 1866, and Ludlow to Johnson, Dec. 12, 1866.

3. Several others also urged the appointment of Slocum, who had requested and received an interview with the President to discuss the matter. But Dix continued to serve as naval officer until late November 1866, when he resigned and left for Paris. William S. Hillyer to Johnson, Sept. 17, 1866, Appts., Customs Service, Naval Officer, New York, William S. Hillyer, RG56, NA; Heister Clymer to Johnson, Aug. 14, 1866; Slocum to Johnson, Sept. 17, 1866, Johnson Papers, LC; Dix to Johnson, Nov. 21, 1866, Appts., Customs Service, Naval Officer, New York, John A. Dix, RG56, NA; *Evening Star* (Washington), Sept. 29, 1866. For further developments see Charles G. Halpine to Johnson, Nov. 23, 1866, and Slocum to Johnson, Dec. 8, 1866.

From Hugh McCulloch

Treasury Department.   Sept. 28, 1866.

Dear Sir,

Enclosed I hand you a letter from General T. W. Egan,[1] recently appointed Collector of Internal Revenue in the Ninth District of New York.

If Col. Sweeney's only offense was that he joined the Fenian Brotherhood,[2] it would be, in my judgment, an act of justice towards him and a politic movement on your part to have him reinstated.[3]

H McCulloch

LS, DLC-JP.

1. Of Irish lineage, Thomas W. Egan (1834–1887) had risen in rank from lieutenant colonel to brevet major general in the Army of the Potomac. Initially recommended by Generals Grant, Meade, and Hancock, among others, for naval officer of New York, Egan had received a recess appointment as collector of the Ninth District on August 27, 1866. Nominated for permanent appointment by Johnson in December 1866, Egan was rejected by the Senate, renominated, and rejected a second time. His letter has not been found, though a clerk's notation indicates it recommended that Thomas W. Sweeny be restored "to his former rank & position in the army." Warner, *Blue*; Appts., Internal Revenue Service, Collector, N.Y., 9th Dist., Thomas W. Egan, RG56, NA; Ser. 6B, Vol. 3: 94; Vol. 4: 51, 53, Johnson Papers, LC.

2. A native of Ireland and a career soldier, Thomas W. Sweeny (1820–1892) had fought conspicuously as a brigade and division commander in the western theater prior to

being mustered out of volunteer service in August 1865. Holding a commission as a major (with a lieutenant colonel's brevet) in the regular army, he had been dismissed in late December 1865 owing to his Fenian activities, though the official explanation from the War Department was that he had been absent without leave. In fact, Sweeny had helped plan and direct the foiled June 1866 invasion of Canada. Warner, *Blue*; Jenkins, *Fenians and Anglo-American Relations*, 33, 110–11, 121, 149, 197.

3. Although Secretary Stanton soon revoked the order dismissing Sweeny from the army, Sweeny's reinstatement, which required the advice and consent of the Senate, was twice rejected before it was finally confirmed on April 18, 1867. He retired from the army three years later with the rank of brigadier general. *Senate Ex. Proceedings*, Vol. 15, pt. 1: 281; pt. 2: 680, 758; Powell, *Army List*, 618; *DAB*.

From J. Bankhead Magruder

Mexico   Sepr. 28th 1866

Sir

I have the honor to apply for a Special amnesty & permission to return to the United States.[1]

I am satisfied that is my duty to assist to the extent of my humble abilities, in carrying into successful execution, the policy of your Excellency, in reference to the Southern States & I beg leave to inform your Excellency, that whist I carried into our unfortunate cause, all the energy, zeal & devotion of which I was master I undeviatingly, acted in strict accordance with the rules of civilized warfare.

J. Bankhead. Magruder.

ALS, DLC-Garrett Family Papers.

1. Magruder, one of many Confederate veterans to offer their services to Emperor Maximilian, who declined, was associated with Confederate Commodore Matthew F. Maury's immigration organization in Mexico as director of land distribution. With recommendations from Reverdy Johnson, Thomas G. Pratt, and Henry Stanbery, Magruder was pardoned on December 9, 1867. Alfred J. and Kathryn A. Hanna, *Napoleon III and Mexico: American Triumph over Monarchy* (Chapel Hill, 1971), 225–26; Reverdy Johnson and Pratt to Johnson, Oct. 10, 1866, Garrett Family Papers, LC; Reverdy Johnson to Johnson, Nov. 21, 1867; Magruder to Johnson, Nov. 14, 1867, Amnesty Papers (M1003, Roll 65), Va., J. B. Magruder, RG94, NA.

From Benjamin Rush

45 Half Moon St.   Piccadilly,
London   28' Sept. 1866.

Dear Sir,

Americans, in a foreign land, naturally watch with great interest what is passing in their own Country. I trust you will allow me, as one of your constituents, to express the great interest with which I have followed, through our papers, your late important Tour to the West, and the admiration with which I have regarded your firm, give me leave to say your *courageous*, adherence throughout, to the patriotic principles you publicly and repeatedly and fearlessly announced on first succeeding to the Chief Magistracy.

This feeling of admiration, Sir, permit me to say, is frequently expressed to me here by English people in town and country, sometimes in strong, and sometimes in calm, and therefore more deliberate, and well weighed, terms of commendation, for the English like to see *pluck*, as much as we do.

It was only last week that a well informed *Clergyman*, whose acquaintance I made that day in Buckinghamshire, about 40 miles from London, said to me very calmly, the conversation happening to turn on affairs in the United States, and particularly your course as President, "*I think he is right.*"

In the London Times of to-day there is a leading article devoted to you, which contains *some* views that are so just (and in such remarkable contrast to the course of that paper formerly) that I take the liberty to put it under cover to you[1] by this Steamer.

In the soundness of some of its *concluding views*, I do *not* concur, for I am of those who *believe*, as I ardently *hope*, that the American People will triumphantly vindicate and sustain you.

Having come abroad, with my Family, mainly for the benefit of my health, already very much improved since I left home, and expecting to pass perhaps some time in England, where I have many friendships contracted during my official residence here formerly, I will venture, from time to time, if agreeable to you, to impart to you whatever I may hear, which I think would be of interest to you.

You will receive this at about the time of the important Election in my own State of Pennsylvania. That the result may be such as your friends every where ardently hope for, is also my own most earnest hope.

Benjamin Rush.

ALS, DLC-JP.
1. The article is not found with the letter. While supportive of Johnson and his career, the article recognized the growing power of Congress and the certainty that the coming elections would result in a defeat of presidential policy. It suggested that further opposition from Johnson was useless, for Republican victory was certain, and that the President should be content with what he had achieved. For the complete text, see *The Times* (London), Sept. 28, 1866.

From Owen Thorn[1]

Young Men's National Union Club
Washington   Sept 28 1866.

Sir:

A member of the Executive Committee of this organization has just returned from Philadelphia, *and* after a conference there, one of the main difficulties ascertained in regard to the coming contests in the Congressional Districts, is that the Internal Revenue Bureau, here *and* there, except those lately appointed in all its ramifications, are using every effort to defeat any and every man who has been or will be nominated in support of the policy of the President of the United States.

The general impression was that the change should be commenced at the head of the Bureau referred to (Mr Rollins) so that orders or instructions may not be issued to the subordinates, against us.

Owen Thorn   Chairman Ex Committee

ALS, DLC-JP.
1. Thorn (c1836–fl1869), a Washington, D.C., native, was a clerk during the war, after which he became a ship broker and then a proprietor of the conservative *Evening Express* in 1868. 1860 Census, Washington, D.C., 4th Ward, 143; Washington, D.C., directories (1860–69); James H. Whyte, *The Uncivil War: Washington During the Reconstruction* (New York, 1958), 67.

From George Archdeacon[1]

29th Sept 1866

The Memorial of George Archdeacon of 1607 Helmouth Street Philadelphia Most respectfully Sheweth

That your Excellency's Memt. is a citizen of the great Republic of which you are chief Magistrate, having duly obtained his last papers of naturalization on the 1st day of december 1854

That in the year 1862 Memt. proceeded to Liverpool to obtain a sum of money due to his wife[2] but not being successful he sought for and procured a few Agencies for American and Irish Books and newspapers to enble him to support himself whilst delayed in the Country.

That on the 23d of September 1865 he was arrested in his place of business upon a warrant for high Treason signed by the Lord Lieutenant of Ireland[3] and conveyed hand cuffed by detective officers to the City of Dublin.

That altho the common Informer Nagle[4] was unable to identify him and neither arms amunition nor Treasonable papers were found upon his person nor in his house yet Memt. was fully committed for Trial on the 5th day of Octr. 1865.

That Memt. immediately after his arrest feeling conscious that there was no real charge against him and that his arrest was on mere suspicion applied to Mr. West[5] the American Consul for protection and had a lengthened correspondence with that Gentleman[6] a correspondence now in the possession of Memt and in the course of which Mr. West repeatedly and to his great surprise declared his belief that once an Irish adopted citizen touched British or Irish soil again he to all intents and purposes became a British subject—a doctrine which after his solemn oath of allegiance to the United States and abjuration of allegiance to Queen Victoria Memt. could not and would not accept.

That upon many occasions as the correspondence refered to in last paragraph will shew the consul Mr. West sought to induce Memt. to plead guilty and upon one occasion when Mr. West visited him he heard that Gentleman tell the Governor[7] that he was sent to Archdeacon to say that the British Attorney General[8] would make Memts. punishment light if he plead guilty but if he went to Trial he would give him Ten years penal servitude.

That on the 9th of Feby 1866 Memt. upon the application of his Solicitor[9] after the Attorney General admitted in Court that he had not sufficient evidence to put him on Trial was admitted to bail and made to sign a bond for two hundred pounds himself and two sureties for the sum of one hundred pounds each—the conditions of the bond being that Memt. should abide Trial at the next commission to be held in Dublin.

That Memt. at a very heavy expense returned to Dublin from Liverpool to fulfil the condition of his recognizance and remained there until his last dollar was expended without obtaining any information as to whether he would be tried or not, and finally from Liverpool and thru Mr. West the consul he made an application to have his Bail discharged and his seized property returned to him—To which application and thru Mr. West he received an answer saying that if he gave new Bail to return at once to America and not to visit England, Ireland, or Scotland for three years his former recognizance would be discharged and his books and papers not Treasonable restored to him.

That Memt. under these unpleasant circumstances—prostrated in health after 5 months close and solitary confinement—prostrated in business by the action of the British Government on mere suspicion deprived of papers Books—Family documents and other property valuable to him and subjected to a most unnecessary and irksome police espionage and totally unable to procure the high bail required resolved at once to return to the land of his adoption and lay his case before you confident that in your justice you will see reason to protect him humble a citizen as he is of the great Republic over which you preside—and not allow a foreign Country to ignore his just rights but call upon the Law officers of Britain to return Memts. property and grant him redress for the loss he has sustained.

Finally Memt. feeling a deep interest in common with hundreds of thousands of true Irish American citizens in the question of our rights as openly sworn citizens of the United States when business or pleasure induced one or more to visit Britain or Ireland respectfully prays of you in addition to his other request of personal restitution to set this grave matter at rest so that adopted citizens generally may know their real standing in foreign Countries and the value from home of that Citizenship of which they are so proud here.[10]

Memt. trusts the nature of his claim and the interests involved will induce your Excellency to pardon the length of his appeal and grant him a favourable answer.

George Archdeacon

ALS, DNA-RG59, Misc. Lets., 1789–1906 (M179, Roll 244).

1. Unidentified.
2. Not identified.
3. John Wodehouse (1826–1902), Earl of Kimberley, served as lord lieutenant of Ireland (1864–66). He continued to serve the British Empire in a variety of offices. Desmond Ryan, *The Fenian Chief: A Biography of James Stephens* (Coral Gables, Fla., 1967), 368.
4. Pierce Nagle first offered his services to the British as an informer in 1864 while in America. Prior to going to the U.S., Nagle, a teacher, absconded with school funds and ran out on debts. Returning from America, he obtained a job in the office of *The Irish People* and continued to keep the police informed of Fenian activities taking place there. Following the mass arrests of September 1865, Nagle was an important witness for the prosecution. John Rutherford, *The Secret History of the Fenian Conspiracy* (2 vols., London, 1877), 1: 138–40; D'Arcy, "The Fenian Movement," 65–67; Leon Ó Broin, *Fenian Fever: An Anglo-American Dilemma* (New York, 1971), 4, 13, 15.
5. William West.
6. See *House Ex. Docs.*, 40 Cong., 2 Sess., No. 157, pp. 9–19 (Ser. 1339).
7. Not identified.
8. Before his appointment as attorney general in 1865, James A. Lawson (1817–1887) was the crown's legal advisor in Ireland (1858–59) and solicitor general for Ireland (1861–65). In July 1865 he was elected to the seat for Portarlington, representing that place until 1868. Thereafter, he served the Queen in a variety of offices. *DNB*, 11: 733.
9. Not identified.
10. Johnson made no such foreign affairs policy statement.

From Isaac N. Arnold

Washington, Sept. 29 1866.

Sir:

I hereby resign the office of Auditor of the Treasury for the Post Office Department.

Three days before his assassination, the position was tendered to me by President Lincoln, to facilitate the preparation of a record of his Administration, and the overthrow of slavery in the Republic, which I then hoped he would live to completely consummate. When I accepted the commission from you, which death prevented him from issuing, I did it in the full faith, based upon your patriotic record during the rebellion, and your repeated declarations over the dead body of the martyred President, that your policy would make treason "odious," and that you would be faithful to the loyal men, North and South, who had saved the Republic; that you would endeavor to carry out the principles which will make Lincoln's Administration illustratious to all time.

I will do you the justice to say that I believe, if, while you were addressing the Illinois delegation who waited on you and tendered you the same support they had given their own great statesman—if at that moment when your heart seemed full of loyalty and fidelity, and you told us that "the people must understand that *treason* is the *blackest of all crimes*, and will surely be punished," and that "when the question of exercising mercy comes before me, it will be considered calmly, judicially, for we must not forget that what may be mercy to the individual, is cruelty to the State," if at that time your future course could have been held up before you, and your apostacy could have been foretold, you would have indignantly exclaimed "Is thy servant a dog that he should do this great thing?"

You have betrayed the great Union party which elected Abraham Lincoln, and which, as an incident of the election placed you in the office of Vice President. You have deserted its principles, and are today, in open cordial communion with those who sought the over-throw of the Republic; of those who for four long years made war upon our flag, and who crowned their long catalogue of crimes by the murder which placed you in the Executive Chair.

You are to-day persecuting and denouncing as traitors, the life long friends of Abraham Lincoln; those upon whom his great arm leaned for support in the hour of supreme peril for the Union; you are denouncing and persecuting these friends of Mr. Lincoln for no offense but fidelity to the principles and party which you have deserted.

You have chosen as your friends and counsellors from the lately rebellious States, not the persecuted, abused, faithful, heroic Union men, but those whose hands are yet stained with the blood of loyal men. In the loyal states, your supporters and counsellors are, to a great extent, those whose sympathies were ever with rebels and traitors.

In your present position, and with such associates, it is natural you should hate those whose fidelity must be a constant reproach to you. You are proscribing in Illinois, and elsewhere, the old personal friends of Lincoln, at the instance of his life long enemies.

Mr. President, the American people in their hour of bitterest anguish, when almost stupified with grief over the murder of the noblest grandest character which has adorned our history, heard your voice uttering bold, indignant, loyal patriotic words. They took you to their hearts and gave you their confidence. Where are you today? Who are your associates and advisers? What promise made over the dead body of Lincoln have you kept? What pledge there uttered have you not broken?

Sir, you are wielding immense power and patronage, but I tell you, not in anger but in deepest sorrow, that there are few names other than that of the rebel chief, as yet in Fortress Monroe, so odious among loyal men and so popular among traitors, as that of Andrew Johnson. With fidelity, you would to-day, have been the first of American Statesmen. With fidelity on your part there would to-day have been harmony in all departments of the Government, and peace and security throughout the Republic. With fidelity, it was yours to have saved the country. God and the people will prevent your treachey from destroying it.

I will not now contrast your policy with that of your illustrious predecessor; but I shall ask your attention to one point only. To the loyal black
man, and the loyal white man of the South, Mr. Lincoln promised protection and security. *He* kept his promise. When rebel emissaries such as
you pardon and take to your confidence, proposed to him to return to
slavery the black soldiers of the Union Army and thus win the masters
they had fought, Mr. Lincoln indignantly replied "Should I do so, I
should deserve to be damned in time and eternity!" How can you, Mr.
President occupy the Executive Mansion as the successor of Lincoln,
how could you visit his grave with the bloody outrages of Memphis and
New Orleans unpunished? Do you remember that Mr. Lincoln said "Negroes like other people act upon motives. If they stake their lives for us,
they must be prompted by the strongest motive—even the promise of
freedom, *and the promise being made must be Kept*?"

The nation promised the negro liberty and protection, for helping to
put down the rebellion. You have turned him over to his exasperated master whom he helped to subdue. When did you punish a rebel for the murder of a loyal negro? The rebels are to-day, your counsellors. They and
the copperheads constitute a large majority of those who call themselves
your friends. They control your patronage.

Believing you are today exerting your vast power in the interests of
traitors, and that your policy should be over thrown at the ballot box, that
the Republic based on liberty and justice may live, I retire from office that
I may more freely and effectively aid in that overthrow.

I N Arnold

LS, DLC-JP.

From James Johnson

Sabine Pass, Texas, Sept 29th 1866

Dear Uncle

I arrived here and entered upon the duties of the office which you were
kind enough to bestow upon me, Viz, Assessor U.S. Int Rev on the 20th
Inst relieving my Uncle Mr B. F McDonough, who you know was requested to resign in consequence of his inability to take the *Test Oath*,
which he could not do on account of his holding the office of Collector of
the Port of Sabine under the so called Confederate Government.[1] Since
the close of the war he served the U.S. Gov't faithfully for over 12 Months
as Assessor of Internal Revenue in this district, without receiving any
compensation for his Services, which is a serious loss to him as he has a
large family. Money is very scarce and the necessaries of life very high at
present in this state.

Uncle the office of United States Marshall for the Eastern District of
Texas is now filled by a Mr Breckenridge,[2] who I understand was a dele-

gate to the late Radical Convention which assembled at Philadelphia. He is an extreme radical in politics, and a known enemy to Your reconstruction policy. I respectfully ask, if you should find it necessary to remove Mr Breckenridge to give the appointment to Mr B. F McDonough who is a man of Strict integrity and excellent business qualifications and who if Necessary can be endorsed by almost every leading Man in Texas. In fact he would do honor to any position that Your excellency might see proper to bestow upon him.[3]

This leaves us all quite well with highest regards and good wishes for your health and prosperity and that of your estimable family.

                        J Johnson   Assessor 1st Dist of Texas

P.S. My uncle here met with a sad bereavement almost too sad to dwell upon. His eldest son, an excellent Young man about 21 Years of age[4] on the 23rd Inst. committed Suicide by Shooting himself in the head with a pistol. Cause unknown.

                                                             J. J.

ALS, DLC-JP.
    1. See Benjamin F. McDonough to Johnson, May 27, 1865, *Johnson Papers*, 8: 118–19.
    2. George W. Brackenridge (1832–1920), a native of Indiana, moved to Texas in 1853 and served as the surveyor of Jackson County (1857–61). A Unionist, despite having three brothers in the Confederate army, Brackenridge became a U.S. treasury agent in 1863 and worked in New Orleans. After the war he amassed a fortune as a San Antonio merchant and banker, served as a trustee of the University of Texas, and financially supported educational and other philanthropic causes. Ser. 6B, Vol. 5, Johnson Papers, LC; Webb et al., *Handbook of Texas*, 1: 202.
    3. Brackenridge, commissioned in April 1866, served for less than a year, as his successor, James J. Byrne, was commissioned in February 1867. Ser. 6B, Vol. 5; Vol. 4: 211; Johnson Papers, LC.
    4. This may have been Alonzo McDonough (b. *c*1843), the oldest son of B. F. McDonough listed in 1860, or possibly C. A. McDonough (b. *c*1846), who was more nearly the correct age. Neither is listed among the four children in the household in the 1870 census. 1860 Census, Tex., Rusk, Beat No. 1, Henderson, 5; (1870), Jefferson, Sabine Pass, 9.

From George Bancroft

                                          Newport R.I.   30 Sept. 66

My dear Mr. President,

I have just finished the volume[1] on which I have employed myself uninterruptedly this summer; as soon as it comes from the binder's hand, I shall take leave to send you a copy. And I hope you will like it. It is my tribute to *union*,— & my plea for it on historical grounds which cannot be shaken. While writing it, I have received many proofs of good will from eminent men at the South who have asked only impartiality.

I trust Mrs. Johnson & your charming daughters are well. I hope but hardly dare expect that Congress will on the first day of its meeting, admit the members from South Carolina, & for all the passion of the hour, I trust you will see before long all the states in the Union in their places. I go to New York this week.

Geo. Bancroft.

Be sure I for one very much approve the appointment of Mr. Dix to the Naval Office in New York. But pray, beware of extreme Copperheads; they are dreadfully unpopular; & as you & I know, the old nullification secession party never had one quarter of the votes of the people, from the days of White of Tennessee to those of Jefferson Davis.[2]

ALS, DLC-JP.
1. Volume nine in Bancroft's ten-volume *History of the United States*, published by both a Boston and a London firm, with preface dated New York, September 24, 1866. *NUC*.
2. The President replied several days later, congratulating Bancroft "upon the completion of another volume of your great work," expressing gratification that he approved of Gen. John A. Dix's appointment and confidence that "before long *all* the states of the Union will be permitted to resume their proper constitutional relations with the Government." Johnson to Bancroft, Oct. 5, 1866, RPB.

From Alvan C. Gillem

Nashville Tenn   Sept. 30, 1866.

Dear Sir:

Since my return from Washington I have endeavored to ascertain the political views entertained by the people of this state. Of West Tenn I can only speak from hearsay. The people of Middle Tenn with the exception of a small faction Say one *fifth* of the voters under the "Franchise law"[1] are firm supporters of your administration, and will stand by you through good & evil report come what may. The faction opposed to you in Middle Tenn. is limited in numbers and extremely bitter. It is made up of three classes—Northern men who came in *rear* of the army to make money or have settled here because of their failures elsewhere. This class includes Derby—cotton speculator, Cone, Judge Lovering,[2] Capt Brown police Commissioner of Nashville—Col Stone of Ohio—Do. Dr. Sparling of Ireland Do. & Genl Milroy (very bitter[)] & a few others.[3] The second class is composed of men who have been thrown to the service of political affairs by the waves of the revolution and who know their only hope of remaining in power is to prevent a peaceable settlement of our political difficulties—hence their cry that they are in danger of their lives, that the rebels are preparing for war & their hypocritical cries for aid from the North. To this class belongs Wines of Clarksville, Waters of Wilson Arnell of Maury—Mullins of Bedford & Bill Stokes.[4] Many of these men were early sympathizers with the rebellion. The third class small in number contains a few men of some ability who forget to be patriots to remember they were Whigs.

Such as Harrison & Trimble.[5] I think one fifth is a liberal allowance for the Radical party in Middle Tenn. That was about the proportion polled yesterday for Mayor of Nashville & I am certain their great strength lies in the city. Brown received 1645 Scovell 397.[6] Judge John S. Brien beat Dickey[7] for the Legislature—in the county by a larger ratio.

In East Tenn. The Radicals are stronger and are making great exertions to increase their strength. Maynard[8] has at last become convinced that his interests lie on that side. Judge Hall, Judge Swan Judge Houk! and General Cooper are the only radicals of note that I am acquainted with in East Tenn. if I except Fletcher.[9] The bitterest of all these men are Houk & Dan. Trewhitt.[10] The Radicals are very active in East Tenn & should be met by equal activity, which so far has not been the case. Taylor Nelson, Netherland The Kyles[11] & others should stump that section of the state. The only difficulty lies in getting the true issues before the people. The action of the Rad. Convention at Philadelphia on the subject of suffrage has somewhat opened their eyes.

It is the opinion of many of your friends that the Legislature which meets in November will pass an act giving the right of suffrage to the negro or rather striking out the word White, wherever it occurs in the laws of the state.[12]

The unconstitutionality of the proceeding will not I believe deter them from such action. If this does not provoke an outbreak, which they much desire, the assumed fear of one will be seized as a pretext to arm the malitia, which in Middle & West Tenn will be mostly *colored*. The continued political agitation has had a very bad influence on the temper of the negros. They are evidently expecting some commotion. Since my return I have received my appointment as Colonel of the 24 Regular Infantry for which I tender my heartfelt gratitude. From some conversation I had with the Secretary of war I had thought I would be assigned to command in Tennessee, but as yet I have received no orders of any kind. Genl. Fisk has been mustered out of service and Genl Lewis[13] an officer I believe of the Freedmans Bureau is at present in Command. I think by a gradual process the Bureau in Tenn might be dispensed with.

I had intended meeting you in Louisville[14] but was taken sick with fever the night before leaving here, & have not entirely recovered yet. The Cholorea rages unabated in Nashville the deaths average from fifty to one hundred daily, several thousand of the inhabitants have left the city. The appointment of second Lieutenant ordered by you for William H. French Jr.[15] at my request when in Washington has not I fear been made. He has not received it. As Capt. Peter Engels[16] 10 Tenn Inf (Govr Guard) has lost his position which paid him twelve hundred dollars pr year by accepting the position of delegate to the Cleveland Convention and supporting the administration, I would suggest that he be made a Second Lieutenant.

Hoping to be excused for intruding on your time already overburdened.

Alvan C. Gillem

ALS, DLC-JP.

1. A reference to the 1866 Tennessee franchise law which limited voting rights to thorough-going Unionists and excluded all former Rebels.

2. N. Derby, Edward P. Cone, and Amos Lovering.

3. W. Matt Brown, Henry Stone, Frederick W. Sparling, and Robert H. Milroy. Brown (c1815–1885) was mayor of Nashville (1865–66); earlier he had served as city marshal. Subsequently, he was in business as an insurance agent in Nashville. Stone (1830–1896) had held a variety of military posts during the war, including a stint as commander of the 100th USCT. Stone was brevetted colonel in March 1865. After the war he served in Nashville as U.S. claim agent and then as police commissioner. After working for the Census Bureau for several years, he moved to New York, then to Boston, where he served as a member of the State Board of Lunacy and Charity and then as state superintendent of the Department of Out-door Poor. Sparling (b. c1825) was not only a physician but also an insurance agent in Nashville. In 1869 he became assessor of internal revenue for the Fifth District. *Nashville American*, Sept. 13, 1885; *Nashville Banner*, Sept. 12, 1866; "Obituary Record of the Graduates of Bowdoin College" [1895–96], found in Pension File, Cora B. Stone, RG15, NA; Nashville directories (1867–74); 1870 Census, Tenn., Davidson, 10th Dist., 31; *U.S. Off. Reg.* (1869).

4. William G. Wines, Wilson L. Waters, Samuel M. Arnell, James Mullins, and William B. Stokes.

5. Horace H. Harrison and John Trimble.

6. W. Matt Brown defeated Hezekiah G. Scovel by a substantial margin. See *Nashville Press and Times*, Sept. 30, 1866.

7. According to one newspaper account, Brien defeated Daniel D. Dickey by a 1500-vote majority. Dickey (b. c1823) was a Nashville businessman who sold flour and feed. *Charleston Courier*, Oct. 8, 1866; 1860 Census, Tenn., Davidson, 4th Ward, Nashville, 164; Nashville directories (1865–74).

8. Horace Maynard.

9. Elijah T. Hall, James P. Swan, Leonidas C. Houk, Joseph A. Cooper, and Andrew J. Fletcher.

10. Daniel C. Trewhitt.

11. Nathaniel G. Taylor, Thomas A.R. Nelson, John Netherland, Absalom A. Kyle, and William C. Kyle.

12. The Tennessee legislature passed a black suffrage law in February 1867. See Richard O. Curry, ed., *Radicalism, Racism, and Party Realignment: The Border States during Reconstruction* (Baltimore, 1969), 63.

13. Clinton B. Fisk and John R. Lewis. Lewis (1834–1900) had been brevetted brigadier general in March 1865; prior to that he held the rank of colonel. Lewis retired from the army in 1870. Hunt and Brown, *Brigadier Generals*. See Black Citizens of Tennessee to Johnson, Aug. 27, 1866.

14. Johnson had stopped in Louisville on September 11 as a part of his overall Northeastern-Midwestern trip ("swing around the circle").

15. French (1844–1923) had entered military duty in March 1862 with the 57th N.Y. Vols. He held the rank of second lieutenant with the 19th U.S. Inf., beginning in July 1866, and the rank of first lieutenant as of May 1868. After French left the military in 1870, he was a clerk in various War Department offices. His death in 1923 was a result of his being "struck by automobile." Powell, *Army Register*, 319; *U.S. Off. Reg.* (1903–19); Pension File, Emilie O. French, RG15, NA; Washington, D.C., directories (1882–1901).

16. Engels (c1828–*fl*1870), a carpenter, began his military career during the Mexican War. During the Civil War he was an officer with the 10th Tenn. Vols.; in July 1866 he became a second lieutenant with the 24th U.S. Inf. and was promoted to first lieutenant in September 1867. Two years later he resigned from military duty. Powell, *Army List*, 301; 1860 Census, Mo., St. Louis, St. Louis, 1st Ward, 326; (1870), Miss., Adams, Natchez, 194.

From Daniel F. Miller[1]

Keokuk, Iowa, Sept 30th 1866.

Mr President,

I obtained some information two days ago, which I deem of sufficient importance to inform you about. In a private conversation between Mr. Benjamin[2] Radical M. C. of Mo, and some of his political friends, among whom was a general of the State militia of Mo, he, Mr B. among other expressions, said as follows; "*As soon as Congress meets, we will have the President arrested.*" The conversation and interview occurred about 12 days [ago] at the house of a private citizen in a Radical County of Mo. My informant is *truthful* and RELIABLE.[3]

D. F. Miller

ALS, DLC-JP.

1. Miller (1814–1895), a lawyer in Iowa since 1839, served a brief term in the U.S. House of Representatives (December 1850-March 1851). *BDAC*.

2. John F. Benjamin.

3. Miller enclosed this letter to Johnson in a missive to Charles Mason, National Union Resident Executive Committee corresponding secretary in Washington, D.C., who, in turn, forwarded it to Johnson. Miller explained to Mason that he did not give the name of his informant because the latter was a substantial property holder and businessman whose prosperity would suffer "if by any means he should be exposed as the medium of communication to me." Miller to Mason, Sept. 29, 1866; Mason to Johnson, Oct. 4, 1866, Johnson Papers, LC.

October 1866

From James Gordon Bennett, Jr.

New York   Oct 1st [1866]

Did not receive your telegram until today.[1] I regret that owing to business engagement I will be prevented from leaving the city for the present.

J G Bennett Jr

Tel, DNA-RG107, Tels. Recd., President, Vol. 5 (1866–67).

1. The President's dispatch of the previous evening read: "I will be pleased to see you in Washington. Answer." Presumably Johnson had summoned Bennett to the White House to discuss the *Herald*'s much-publicized desertion of the administration. Beginning in mid-September 1866 (after the disastrous Maine elections), the newspaper concluded that the battle between the President and Congress was "virtually decided" and urged Johnson to "shape his course accordingly" by accepting the proposed Fourteenth Amendment. In the days which followed, the paper distanced itself from Johnson even further. Johnson to Bennett, Jr., Sept. 30, 1866, Tels. Sent, President, Vol. 3 (1865–68), RG107, NA; *New York Herald*, Sept. 14, 19, 26–27, 1866; James L. Crouthamel, *Bennett's New York Herald and the Rise of the Popular Press* (Syracuse, 1989), 153; Patrick W. Riddleberger, *1866: The Critical Year Revisited* (Carbondale, 1979), 224–27.

From William Bigler

Clearfield Pa, Oct 1st 1866.

My dear Sir.

I arrived here to-day after having traversed a large portion of the state and take great pleasure in saying to you that my hopes of carrying the state have been very much elevated. We find numerous accessions to the conservative cause in all parts of the state, and whilest our defeat for Govnor is still probable, it is not possible for the Radicals to beat us largely or to save themselves from a loss of representation in Congress. We shall certainly gain from two to five members.[1] I need not trouble you with the reasons for the faith that is in me for that would occupy too much of your time, but I give you the result of a very dispassionate judgement. The ensuing reaction in N.Y. was unfortunate for us. The "Herald" & "Times" have done us much harm,[2] and when in N.Y. last week, I found every body saying that we were hopelessly gone & this did harm also. Mark what I say, Pa is sounder by far than N.Y.[3] If we are defeated, the conservatives of N.Y. will share the same fate by a much larger vote.

Wm. Bigler

ALS, DLC-JP.

1. Actually, the Democrats suffered a net loss of two seats, with narrow Republican victories by Henry L. Cake and John Covode, both of whom were Radicals, in the Tenth and

Twenty-first districts, respectively. *Guide to U.S. Elections*, 617; Bradley, *Militant Republicanism*, 249; *American Annual Cyclopaedia* (1866), 615.

2. Bigler's criticism of the *Times* evidently stemmed from the apparent reversal of its editor, Henry J. Raymond, who, as the main speaker at the Philadelphia convention, had tolerated the prevailing hostility toward the Fourteenth Amendment, but had since called on the President and the southern states to adopt it. Shortly thereafter Raymond withdrew from public life and abandoned Johnson altogether. Riddleberger, *Critical Year*, 224; *New York Times*, Sept. 27, 1866.

3. See Bigler to Johnson, Oct. 18, 1866.

From Rebecca B. Coleman[1]

Richmond   Oct 1st *1866*

Honored Sir,

Many are the petitions and cries that go up daily to the throne of God, from the widows, and orphans, of this our "desolated South." Many like the "Prodigal Son" return with groanings & sighs to the very doors of the fold they were wont to desert, and with aching heart, and bowed heads, ask alms from their more fortunate neighbours the north, who in many instances have responded nobly to the call. But Sir: none have dared like myself to approach the "Executive Chair," to plead charity, knowing how deeply ingrossed you are in the affairs of State; most noble sir; I crave your pardon for this intrusion upon your time and position.

But I feel and even know, that you do sympathize with these our afflicted people in the great calamity that now oppresses them. That we have erred I confess; but God forgives the transgressor, why should not our fellow man; Ruin and desolation stares us on every side, is not that enough to satisfy the most eager enthusiast for revenge. Yea: methinks I hear you say more than enough. You too are southern born, the warm blood of our sister state flows in swelling tide throughout your veins, and proud are we to see that in spite of all that foes threaten and enemies conspire to hate, you stand boldly in their midst, and dare their dislike by proclaiming and defending the rights of the southern people, under the laws of the "Old Constitution." Many are the prayers offered for your safety, that ascend from hearts filled with gratitude to him who has given us so firm a friend so noble a defender, in the person of our President.

It was not my intention when commencing this letter, to praise, but to plead, in my own personal behalf, but "from the fullness of the heart, the mouth speaketh." Therefore deem it not idle flattery used to obtain the end for which I labor no, no, think me no such craven creature, were I to perjure myself by using such deceit. You are a gentleman of too much reality of character to tolerate such a course in the most depraved of mankind much more so in woman; Every word that I write is as true as "holy writ."

Now to my story and its sequel. But five short years ago, I basked in the quiet of a southern home, (Memphis Tenn.) where comfort & luxury

reigned supreme. Servants to do my bidding, a kind & indulgent husband[2] in flourishing business, and two lovely children[3] which made
earth an Eden. To day, I am *widowed, childless* and *penniless*. Standing
alone in the world as I do, clasped by no shining bands of affection, life to
me is a dreary waste reminding one of a desert wild, with not an "Oasis"
to refresh or strengthen the weary pilgrim. From the first hour the deso-
lating cry of war sounded through this our once happy land, fate began to
cast her dark shadows over my pathway. My husband who was never
strong, was ordered into the field, (he like the rest of our poor deluded
people believed he was in the right,) in twelve months he returned, not to
our happy home, but to Va. his native place, to linger out his few remaining days in hopeless consumption. On the fourth of July last, I laid him in
the Cemetery beside our little children, all of whom are now in heaven.

Being stunned by the heavy strokes of misfortune that in such quick
succession fell upon me, I could not realize my situation; until aroused by
that stern monitor want. After looking into the ruined affairs of my husband, I found from the entire loss of property there was barely enough to
defray funeral expenses. God help me, or I faint, I die. What am I to do,
enfeebled in health, having been delicately reared, I am not fitted to perform the drudgery of a menials life; I know not what course to pursue. I
am but too willing to work if my strength will admit of it. With the assistance of one or two friends, I have succeeded in obtaining a few children
to teach, at the pitiful sum of three dollars per month, with that small
pittance I will not be able to procure the meagre sustenance of life much
less the necessary clothing & fuel that the coming winter with its stern
realities demand.

It is to this I have come to this end I now write to you Sir, the great &
chief head, of our country, to ask you to assist me, from your maney
stores. Perhaps you may treat this with derisive contempt, and with a
frown of impatience, cast it from you; But Oh! could you, but know the
humility it cost a refined, and sensitive woman to plead her cause before
so high a tribunal, you would not hesitate to judge her seeming *boldness*
with the greater *leniency*; and stoop from your high position to look into
the abode of suffering humanity. Will not your wife & daughters assist
you in this one, deed of mercy. I know their pathway is strewn with light
& love; but surely they have hearts that can feel for the afflicted. I too have
known joy and happiness in her brightest garb but oer all sorrow has cast
an impenetrable pall. "Alone, Alone" is the cry that goes up hourly, to
him who alone can heal the broken heart. It is the first time in life that I
ever had to ask an alm of mortal, my very pen seems to refuse to perform
its office, it is with trembling hand, and aching heart that I have traced
these lines, and may God forgive me if I commit an offence in thus addressing you. Whatever you think of the proceeding yourself, lay it not
open to public censure I implore you. I have laid bare my case before you
and should you feel disposed "to cast your bread upon the waters" mine

shall be the tongue to pray that it shall be gathered unto you before many days. Any contributions (Clothing or money) you or family may think proper to send me, will be most thankfully an[d] safely received by Adams & Co Express. Address Mrs. Rebecca B Coleman at Mrs A.D. Quarles,[4] 109 Main St Richmond Va or if by letter direct Mrs R B Coleman Care of Daniel Denoon.[5] Rich. Va: The Rev. Mr Shaver[6] Pastor of the Second Baptist Church can testify to the high Respectability of all parties. I shall direct this letter to *your lady* least it should fall into the hand of your Secretary and he might cast it aside as *one* of the many nuisances that infect the *Official Bureau*. Again I ask you to pardon my intrusion and my [may] God speed this poor attempt to beg, on its mission of mercy.[7]

Rebecca B Coleman.

ALS, DLC-JP.
1. Not identified.
2. Not identified.
3. Not identified.
4. Mrs. Augustus D. [Lisetts/Isaetta?] Quarles (*c*1836–*fl*1881), a widow. 1870 Census, Va., Henrico, Richmond, Monroe Ward, 275; Richmond directories (1869–81).
5. Denoon (*c*1829–*fl*1881), a clerk, soon became partner in a hardware business. 1870 Census, Va., Henrico, Richmond, Monroe Ward, 192; Richmond directories (1866–81).
6. David Shaver (1820–1902) of Virginia was ordained a Baptist minister in 1844; he received an honorary doctorate from Furman University in 1866. He served in pastorates in Virginia before the war and in Georgia after the war and was editor of several journals beginning in 1857. Garnett Ryland, *The Baptists in Virginia, 1699–1926* (Richmond, 1955), 294, 316; George W. Lasher, ed., *The Ministerial Directory of the Baptist Churches* (Oxford, Ohio, 1899), 655.
7. Johnson sent her ten dollars. See Coleman to Johnson, Oct. 19, 1866, Johnson Papers, LC.

From Edgar Cowan

Phila   1 Oct 1866.
Dr Sir.

I am contesting Penna as well as I can, but we must have *some money* as it is impossible to contend with the Radicals who have thrown $13,000 into my Congressional District to elect Covode over me, and my influence.[1]

I am poor myself and have no money to put into the issue of any acct. but I have found Maj. Hall[2] who wants to be a pay master and Wharton White[3] who wants to be a Leiut (2d.) in the Army and they each agree to give for the purposes of election $2000—each. This will enable me to pay the expenses of Speakers who have been Speaking day & night and to pay canvassers & wagons to bring out the votes of 2 or 3 close districts in this State. Can you give Gen Zulich[4] such assurances that Maj. Hall & Mr White will be appointed as are reliable and aid us in this?[5]

Edgar Cowan

ALS, DLC-JP.
1. John Covode was elected in this district, which comprised the counties of Fayette, Indiana, and Westmoreland, Cowan's home county. Bradley, *Militant Republicanism*, 247– 48; *Press* (Philadelphia), Oct. 1, 1866.
2. Peter P.G. Hall (c1830–1905) was an attorney in Philadelphia before joining the volunteer army during the war. Appointed as a paymaster in the regular army in January 1867, he remained in the service until his retirement in 1891. Powell, *Army List*, 349; Philadelphia directory (1861); Ser. 6B, Vol. 2: 134, Johnson Papers, LC; Pension File, Amelia M. Hall, RG15, NA.
3. Son of a navy paymaster, White (c1839–*fl*1893) was not a veteran but (according to an enclosure accompanying Cowan's letter) did work during the last few months of the war as a clerk in the Quartermaster's Department at Philadelphia. Appointed as a second lieutenant in the 20th U.S. Inf. in April 1867, White served only a few years before obtaining an honorable discharge at his own request. Afterward, he was in the real estate business in Philadelphia. Ser. 6B, Vol. 2, Johnson Papers, LC; Powell, *Army List*, 670; Philadelphia directories (1861–93); White to Johnson, ca. Mar. 1866; White to E. D. Townsend, June 20, Aug. 7, 1867, White to William M. Belknap, Dec. 19, 1870, ACP Branch, File 19-ACP-1871, Wharton White, RG94, NA.
4. Possibly Samuel M. Zulick (1824–1876), former colonel and brevet brigadier general, a veteran of the Atlanta campaign and Sherman's march, whom Johnson had nominated in April 1866 as collector of the Third Revenue District. However, Zulick's role during the 1866 Pennsylvania campaign has not been determined. Hunt and Brown, *Brigadier Generals*; John W. Geary to Johnson, Dec. 11, 1865, Appts., Internal Revenue Service, Collector, Pa., 11th Dist., Samuel M. Zulick, RG56, NA; Ser. 6B, Vol. 4: 82, Johnson Papers, LC.
5. A Treasury Department envelope, which is found with Cowan's letter, has the following endorsement written in Johnson's hand: "Application for the appointment of Pay Master & 2d Leiutentat For which they propose to pay $4,000." Johnson later approved both appointments, after each man personally applied or was recommended by other individuals. Subsequently he endorsed a March 1867 Wharton White letter: "Let the appointment be made if there is a vacancy." Johnson endorsement of Mar. 28, 1867, on Wharton White to Johnson, ca. Mar. 1867, ACP Branch, File 19-ACP-1871, Wharton White, RG94, NA; Ser. 6A, Vol. D: 104, Johnson Papers, LC.

From George B. Wallis[1]

Private

Herald Office   New York, Oct 1, 1866

Mr President:—

Some four weeks ago, I received from the Commissioner of Indian Affairs,[2] a notification of my appointment as a special Inspector of Indian Agencies, and asking my presence at Washington for instructions, if ready for the expedition. I answered that from the condition of my health & my engagements in this office, I could hardly be prepared for the undertaking till October. I have now to say, that with the heartiest thanks for your generous consideration of my case, as laid before you by Mrs. W.[3] I am prepared to visit Washington to receive my instructions, if not too late. But you must take me with a liberal margin of neutrality in regard to the Constitutional amendment. In other respects, I think, that on this trip, I may do some good service to the Administration and the Country, in the way of a reconnoissance, touching the future disposition of the Indian tribes, and the advantages offered here & there, to miners,

farmers, mechanics &c. from Kansas & Nebraska to the Rocky Mountains, or to the Pacific, if you say so. My friend Ross Browne[4] has gone
upon such a mission, I believe, but, I presume, there is "scope and verge
enough" for another of the same sort, though not an artist & not so experienced a traveller. If I go to Washington, it is at my own expense, and
every dollar with me now weighs a pound; yet I should like to have a talk
with you. I have a sure position in this office which I cannot put at hazard
upon an uncertainty, nor for an adventure which will not pay; but ever
since Capt Fremont's first western explorations,[5] I have had a desire
which still lives, for a run at least to the Rocky Mountains, and as a servant of Uncle Sam. Mrs. W. begs to be kindly remembered to your wife,
son & daughters, and with hers, please assure them of my best regards.
Wishing you a good deliverance from the Philistines, and long life & a
great name under a Union restored. . . .

                                                        Geo B Wallis
P.S. I hope to hear from you as soon as your many labors and engagements from hour to hour will offer you a few minutes for an answer.[6]

ALS, DLC-JP.
    1. Wallis (fl1866), not further identified, was in New York City by 1852, working
briefly as a reporter before becoming an editor. New York City directories (1852–67).
    2. Dennis N. Cooley.
    3. Not otherwise identified.
    4. J. Ross Browne.
    5. John C. Frémont first explored the Rockies in the early 1840s. DAB.
    6. There is no indication that Wallis actually went west.

From Benjamin R. Curtis

                                    Maplehurst   Near Pittsfield   Masstts.
                                                        Octr. 2, 1866
Mr President.
    I beg leave to address you concerning the case of Mr Fitz John Porter,[1]
lately a Major General in the Military Service of the United States, &
Cashiered by Sentence of a court Martial.
    I presume you are aware that many persons who felt no particular in-
terest in Gen. Porter, & who formed their opinion only from a perusal of
the proceedings which took place in his trial, beleive that the result of
that trial did entire injustice to a brave officer who had done important
service to his Country. I was one of those persons. I had never seen Gen.
Porter & had no relations with him in any way; but the result of that court
martial I felt to be an injury to the Military Justice of the Country.[2]
    This opinion has been, in my own judgement, made as near a certainty
as any such subject admits of, by the reports of Longstreet Hood &
Jones[3] exhibited in the "History of The Army of the Potomac" by Mr.
Swinton.[4]
    I beleive you will agree with me when I say, that there are few things

more important in government, than the preservation of public confidence in *the justice* of judicial sentences, whether civil or military. And that when, in a conspicuous instance, not only grave doubts existed at the time whether the sentence was correct, but desisive evidence of its injustice has since been discovered, the government owes it, not only to the accused, but to the sense of justice which itself entertains, & to the preservation of that confidence in its love of justice among the people, which is essential to their willing respect & obedience, to interpose & do whatever can fitly be done in such a case.

With entire confidence in your own appreciation of the merits of this subject, & in your superior knowledge of the best way of providing for the public interest therein. . . .[5]

B. R. Curtis.

ALS, DLC-JP.
   1. Porter (1822–1901) was a career military officer, who, as a corps commander under George McClellan, earned a reputation for skillful defensive fighting during the Peninsula campaign. Nevertheless, following the Second Manassas campaign, he was removed from command by John Pope, ordered to stand trial by court-martial, and eventually dismissed from the army in January 1863. Porter devoted the next two decades of his life attempting to have the findings of the military commission annulled, which was finally done in 1879. *DAB*; Warner, *Blue*.
   2. By this date, ex-Presidents Fillmore and Pierce agreed with Curtis, and several letters and petitions on behalf of Porter were sent to Johnson. See Millard Fillmore to Porter, Sept. 19, 24, 1866; Franklin Pierce to Porter, Sept. 18, 1866; Horace Binney Sargent to Johnson, Oct. 17, 1866; Darius N. Couch to Johnson, Oct. 19, 1866; and Henry Wilson et al. to Johnson, Nov. 26, 1866, all in Johnson Papers, LC. See also R. H. Eddy to Johnson, Oct. 10, 1866, Lets. Recd. (Main Ser.), File R-574-1867 (M619, Roll 580), RG94, NA.
   3. James Longstreet, John B. Hood, and David Rumph Jones. Like Porter, Jones (1825–1863) graduated from West Point and had fought in Mexico, but he had joined the Confederates, commanding a division during the Peninsula campaign, at Second Manassas, and later at Sharpsburg before developing heart trouble and dying in Richmond. Warner, *Gray*.
   4. In his *Campaigns of the Army of the Potomac* (New York, 1866), William Swinton (1833–1892), a former war correspondent for the *New York Times* who later taught English at the University of California and wrote school textbooks, asserted that Pope, rather than Porter, was to blame for the failure at Second Manassas. *DAB*; Henry Gabler, "The Fitz John Porter Case: Politics and Military Justice" (Ph.D. diss., City University of New York, 1979), 335–36, 346.
   5. Despite this and similar pleas, Johnson took no action regarding Porter's case until late the following year. Ibid., 339–44. See also Otto Eisenschiml, *The Celebrated Case of Fitz John Porter: An American Dreyfus Affair* (Indianapolis, 1950), 196–200.

From Solomon Meredith

Cambridge City Ind.   Oct 2nd 1866

Sir,

When at Washington some ten days ago I had an interview with you relative to the dismissal of my son, Capt. D. M. Meredith,[1] from the Service. I have heard nothing from the case since and fear in the multiplicity of business pressing upon you, that you have forgotten it. Both myself and family feel a deep interest as you must know in having him restored.

Capt Meredith writes me that an occurrence of that kind shall never again happen.

I am informed that a large number of the Officers in the 15th Infantry are Radicals—that since my son preferred charged against Major Curtis,[2] they have become very bitter on that account, as they are implicated to some extent. I also learn that General Wood[3] who is in Command at Mobile is a Radical, and a warm friend of Major Curtis so that it will not do to have him tried at Mobile. There are some things connected with Gen Woods administration at that place that should be examined into—will give you information about the matter when I see you. I think he should be relieved and some other officer sent there.

On account of the number of Radical Officers in the 15th Infantry and the bad feeling necessarily engendered since the unfortunate difficulty my son had I would like very much to have him transferred to some of the new Regts.

It would be agreeable to him, if not asking too much of you, to be placed in the Regiment commanded by General Reynolds[4] of this State, as I have been informed that he is to be appointed Col. of one of the new Regts. Almost all of the recent appointments in the 15th Infantry are Radicals and I fear too many of the recent appointments will turn out that way. Hope it will be otherwise.

If it is not convenient to have Capt. Meredith transferred, should he be restored to his Command, the Recruiting Service would relieve him from the unpleasant surroundings now embarassing him. He is a very successful Recruiting Officer, having been on that duty for some time. Will you please have your Sect'y write me a few lines informing me what can be done for my Son.

                                                          S Meredith

ALS, DLC-JP.
    1. David M. Meredith (c1840–1867) was a clerk before the war broke out, at which time he was appointed first lieutenant, 15th U.S. Inf. Promoted to captain in 1862 and brevetted major in 1863, he was transferred to the 33rd U.S. Inf. in September 1866 but resigned six months later. Although Meredith was found guilty in July 1866 of "Drunkenness on duty" by a court-martial and Judge Advocate General Holt concurred with the findings, Johnson did not agree to the dismissal and instead had Meredith transferred. Powell, *Army List*, 478; 1860 Census, Ind., Wayne, Centre, 69; Solomon Meredith to Johnson, Sept. 13, 1866; Joseph Holt to Johnson, Sept. 25, 1866, Court-Martial Orders No. 193, Aug. 28, 1866; Court-Martial Orders No. 201, Oct. 13, 1866, ACP Branch, File M-150-CB-1867, S. Meredith, RG94, NA.
    2. James Curtis, Jr. (c1831–1878), an 1851 graduate of West Point, had previously served in the army (1851–57) before reenlisting in 1861 with the 15th U.S. Inf. Wounded at Shiloh and Atlanta, he was brevetted major in September 1864. Curtis was brought before a court-martial in February 1867 at Mobile on general charges of disobedience of orders and neglect of duty. Found guilty, he was given only a reprimand and was restored to duty. Following the war he served in the 3rd and 10th U.S. Cav., and retired with the rank of major in 1876. Powell, *Army List*, 268; *West Point Register*, 244; ACP Branch, File CB-1873-3440, James Curtis, Jr., RG94, NA.
    3. Charles R. Woods.
    4. Joseph J. Reynolds.

To William T. Sherman

Washington, D.C.   Oct. 2d. 1866.

The publication of your letter to me of February eleventh[1] is deemed by your best friends of the utmost importance. Have you any objection to its publication?[2]

Andrew Johnson

Tel, DNA-RG107, Tels. Sent, President, Vol. 3 (1865–68).
    1. See Sherman to Johnson, Feb. 11, 1866, *Johnson Papers*, 10: 82.
    2. The telegram included instructions to the officer in charge at St. Louis to forward the message to Sherman if the general was out of town. Sherman was indeed absent on a military inspection of the west and could not be reached until he arrived at Fort Riley, Kansas, on October 16. On that date Sherman replied, "I am willing that anything I ever wrote you should be published if it will do good & if Henry Stansbery Attorney General advises it. I am very anxious if possible to keep out of all Controversies as I have had too many." Sherman's letter apparently was not published. W. A. Nichols to Johnson, Oct. 2, 1866; Sherman to Johnson, Oct. 16, 1866, Johnson Papers, LC; Sherman to Mrs. Sherman, Oct. 26, 1866, Simon, *Grant Papers*, 16: 340.

From Thurlow Weed

New-York, Oct. 2. [1866][1]

Dear Sir,

Gen Slocum has already cost our State Ticket several thousand Votes by bad influence in Appointments.[2] He seems to have purposes inconsistent with the success of our cause. I sincerely hope that no Appointments will be made for this State unless upon information wholly reliable.[3]

Thurlow Weed

ALS, DLC-JP.
    1. The year is suggested by both internal evidence and supporting documentation.
    2. Here Weed undoubtedly refers to the troublesome Brooklyn appointments mentioned in Henry A. Smythe to Johnson, August 10, 1866. For verification see Henry W. Slocum to Johnson, Nov. 7, 1866.
    3. Weed reportedly was in Washington two days later, though it is not known whether he had an interview with the President at that time. See enclosure in William B. Hancock to Johnson, Oct. 5, 1866, Johnson Papers, LC.

From James B. Bingham

Private

Memphis, Tenn., October 3 1866.

My Dear Sir—

I have this day written a letter to Hon. D. T. Patterson, particularly in reference to the policy of the Administration in reference to the Constitutional Amendment.[1] I have bitterly opposed it in the *Bulletin*, but if it's to be abandoned, after the election, I will desist, notwithstanding its unjust discriminations. If Congress may make a Constitutional Amendment a precedent condition to representation, it can impose any thing it may please. They get no authority in the Constitution, and all outside is despotism—the despotism of a majority of a moiety. I do not presume to advise you, in reference to *expediency*, but I believe we shall ultimately succeed. Still I want the Bulletin to support your Administration fully, and hence through Senator Patterson have asked for light on the future.

I have also spoken freely in my letter to him in reference to the Federal appointments in this portion of the State.[2] I hope you will act as you deem best, but *act*, and I shall be satisfied. I am now, as I have been ever since I knew you, *a friend*, and equally so whether you give me office or not.

I have given my views in reference to the Federal officholders in this section in full, in my letter to Senator Patterson, and I have asked him to communicate its contents to you. There is nothing additional that I would say now.

You have made a number of speeches to the *People* since I saw you. I have made only *one*. That was at a mass meeting in Hardeman. It has been reported and published throughout the Western District. I send you a copy,[3] and ask that you will at least read the remarks I have uttered about *you*. They are not well reported, but enough is given to give you some idea of their scope. I believe honestly all I uttered. And while Brownlow, Stokes & co. are giving their *impressions* of you, it might not do any harm to have what I have said about you published in the *Intelligencer*, as the views of another Tennesseean, who is their equal in every respect except an *infamous notoriety*.

I have been solicited to run for the legislature, to fill the vacancy occasioned by the expulsion of our members, but I have refused, hoping that in the new deal of Federal offices in this section I would not be forgotten. But at all events, give the offices to your friends, and let your enemies look out for themselves.

Still hoping almost against hope for success in the Northern elections, I remain. . . .

James B. Bingham

ALS, DLC-JP.
    1. The letter regarding the Fourteenth Amendment has not been found.
    2. For another letter that deals with Memphis area federal appointments, see John W. Leftwich to Johnson, Sept. 22, 1866.
    3. Not found.

From Albert Voorhies

New Orleans   3d October 1866.
Sir;
    Since the New Orleans riot of the 30th July last three communications from Gov. J. M. Wells have appeared in the Press,—the first his "Proc-

lamation to the Loyal people of Louisiana,"[1]—the second, his answer to the communication of the Soldiers' & Sailors' Association at
Washington,[2]—and the third, his letter to Thos. H. Jones Esq.,—a copy
of which is herewith enclosed.[3]

These documents, burdened with the Convention of 1864 and its
offspring—the riots in question,—were intended for no other purpose
than propagandism for a policy, by which the radical element in Congress aims to paralyse the Executive Department by absorbing all the
functions of government.

It is a sad spectacle to behold the Executive of a State, but yesterday
elected by an unparalleled majority of the people, and to-day charging
that very people with perjury and treason. The aspersion thus cast—
gratuitously and unsparingly, shoots in bold relief when the eye is
brought to bear on the infinitesimal constituency, which he himself de-
fines as "*the small band of Union men in our State.*" You understand the
sollicitude and uneasiness of our people on account of any thing emanating from their Governor on the subject of the Convention of 1864, more
especially since he openly assumes the leadership to subvert the government entrusted to his guardianship, and which his position enables him
effectually to assail.

The governor expresses the opinion that it is necessary to have the military force in the State increased for the maintenance of order; but for
what kind of order? The order of things consequent upon a complete
subversion of the present State and Municipal governments, through the
agency of the Convention of 1864! However well and peacefully the present State government may get along,—the Courts open to all and every
one, without distinction of color, and the judges themselves holding their
Commissions from Governors Hahn[4] and Wells, and few of them appointed since the end of the War,—that will not answer radical expectations at home!

Whilst upon the subject of the military let me add that, when it was
evident throughout the month of July last that the Governor's course
would, as it did, lead to riot and blood-shed, application was made, in
good time, by the Attorney General[5] and myself to the Military here and
to yourself in Washington,[6] for the purpose of averting the impending
catastrophe; and had Genl. Baird,[7] to whom your dispatches were
handed,[8] obeyed your orders instead of theorizing upon American politics, not a drop of blood would have been shed in the Streets of New
Orleans.

At that time Genl. Sheridan was absent: two days afterwards he arrived. His official report[9] was swift in finding its way to the War Department; but, up to this day, I have yet to learn that he called upon the civil
authorities for whatever information they might possess as to the origin,
progress and responsibility of the riot. The privilege of being heard on
such an occasion might well have been extended as an act of common

justice. There seems to be a difference between that order of talents and capacity, which will carry through a cavalry general and the judgment and statesmanship to be expected in the Commander of the Gulf Department.

These statements are made openly and frankly: their object is to attract your attention to the peculiarly unfortunate posture of our state affairs, with the abiding hope that whatever can be done within the pale of the Constitution, will be done by you for the relief of our people.

Albert Voorhies

ALS, DLC-JP.
    1. *Picayune* (New Orleans), Aug. 8, 1866 (afternoon ed.).
    2. Dated August 27, 1866, and addressed to William Short, corresponding secretary of the Soldiers' and Sailors' Union, Washington, D.C., Wells's letter had been published in the *New York Tribune*. See the *Picayune* (New Orleans), Sept. 13, 1866 (afternoon ed.).
    3. The letter to Jones (*c*1813–*fl*1870), a farmer and Unionist resident of Arcadia in Bienville Parish, was dated September 18, 1866. Ibid., Oct. 2, 1866 (afternoon ed.); 1870 Census, La., Bienville, 1st Ward, Arcadia, 20.
    4. Michael Hahn.
    5. Andrew S. Herron.
    6. See Albert Voorhies and Andrew S. Herron to Johnson, July 28, 1866, *Johnson Papers*, 10: 750–52.
    7. Absalom Baird.
    8. Johnson to Andrew S. Herron, July 30, 1866, *Johnson Papers*, 10: 760–61.
    9. Philip H. Sheridan to Johnson, Aug. 6, 1866.

From Benjamin W. Bedford[1]

Near Germantown Shelby County Tennessee
October— 4th 1866

Dr Sir

I have Seen it asserted, that you have no precedent in appointing individuals to office, who have been rejected by the Senate. During President Jacksons administration Doctr Boyd,[2] receiver of public money at the land office at Mount Salas Mississippi was a defaulter & turned out of office—Genl. Jackson appointed Col. Stokely D Hays[3] of Davidson cty Tenn a nephew of Mrs Jackson, who died on his way. He then appointed Samuel Gwin of Sumner County Tenn. a Son of his Chaplain in the Army, The Reved. Mr Gwin & brother of Dr. Wm. M. Gwin[4]—when the nomination Came to the Senate, Senator Poindexter of Missi[5] opposed the nomination, as an indignity to the State of Missi; that an honest man could not be found in Missi to fill the office—that Genl Jackson must Send to Tennessee for one—the nomination was rejected by the Senate. No further nomination was made during that Session of Congress; but after Congress adjourned, President Jackson again appointed Samul Gwin & when Congress met his nomination was Sent to the Senate and again rejected. No further nomination was made during that Session of Congress, but after congress adjourned, President Jackson appointed Samul Gwin the third time & when congress met his nomination was Sent to the Senate and Senator Poindexter Said the Senate was not likely to get rid of General Jackson nomination of Samul Gwin & he was then willing to vote for his confirmation & Samul Gwin appointment was confirmed.[6] Thus you have in the *above case* the *precedent* of Genl Jackson a man of iron will and determined effort. Senator Poindexter had previously been the warm friend of Genl Jackson—was his volunteer aid at the battle of New Orleans. But the Gwin question produced an unkind feeling between Genl Jackson & Senator Poindexter. The fact that Genl Jackson was my friend & Senator Poindexter my relative, was the case of my paying more attention to this matter at the time; which I much regretted.

If I have been mistaken in any particular, the journals of the Senate will put it right—I think it was in the time of President Jacksons first term.

Although I lived in Nashville Tenn. from 1811 to 1834 engaged in the mercantile business—I have not the pleasure of yr acquaintance—Since which time I have been planting Cotton in Missi & am Still planting there—though for the past 8 months a permanent Citizen of this county. I am your Political friend and admire your devotion to the constitution of the U.S. and determined effort to preserve it in its purity. I was taught from my cradle by my Revolutionary Sire,[7] for whom Bedford county Tenn was named to reverence that old flag and if my friends will follow my injunction—the Stars & Stripes will be my winding Sheet & the constitution of the U S (as handed to us by our fathers) my pillow in the Silent grave. I will take the liberty to remark, that I desire no office in the gift of the people or our Goverment & that I am 72 1/2 years old, with a constitution & vigour of most men of 45.

Benjamin W. Bedford.

N B. I conscientiously believe that Genl Jackson removed every man from the high to the low from office; who was opposed to his administration in doing which; he discharged his duty to himself, his country & his God.

ALS, DLC-JP.
   1. Bedford (1794–1883), a native of Tennessee, had long been a resident of Mississippi. Irene S. and Norman E. Gillis, comps., *Abstract of Goodspeed's Mississippi* (Baton Rouge, 1962), 37.
   2. Gordon D. Boyd (1801–1850), a native of Kentucky, had studied both medicine and law and evidently practiced both. He moved to Wilkinson County, Mississippi, in 1820. In the 1830s and 1840s he served in both houses of the Mississippi legislature. In late 1836 he was appointed receiver of public monies at the land office in Columbus, Mississippi. He evidently never held the post at Mt. Salus (Clinton), Mississippi. *Southron* (Jackson, Miss.), Apr. 26, 1850; *The Official and Statistical Register of the State of Mississippi, 1908* (Nashville, 1908), 47, 68.
   3. Stockley Donelson Hays (1788–1831) had been quartermaster of Tennessee volunteers in the War of 1812. Sometime thereafter he moved to Madison County, where he practiced law before moving to Mississippi. Emma Inman Williams, *Historic Madison* (Jackson, Tenn., 1946), 6, 37; Sam B. Smith et al., eds., *The Papers of Andrew Jackson* (3 vols. to date, Knoxville, 1980-), 2: 142; 3: 28.
   4. Samuel Gwin (d. 1838) had served as secretary to Gen. John Coffee in the New Orleans campaign (1814–15) and later as a postal clerk in Washington. Gwin was appoin-

ted in October 1831 as register of the land office at Clinton, Mississippi, after the death of Hays. The father was the Rev. James Gwin (c1769–1841), a Methodist preacher who was a native of Wales but had moved to the Nashville area by the late 1780s. He served as a chaplain to Jackson's army during the New Orleans campaign; he also had gained renown as an Indian fighter. Jackson compounded his difficulties over Mississippi appointments when he decided in 1833 to name Dr. Gwin as U.S. marshal for the southern district of Mississippi. Jay G. Cisco, *Historic Sumner County, Tennessee* (Nashville, 1909), 251–53; Walter T. Durham, *Old Sumner: A History of Sumner County, Tennessee from 1805 to 1861* (Nashville, 1972), 211–12, 217; Edwin A. Miles, *Jacksonian Democracy in Mississippi* (Chapel Hill, 1960), 48–49, 51; Anita Shafer Goodstein, *Nashville, 1780–1860: From Frontier to City* (Gainesville, Fla., 1989), 239; *DAB*; *Nashville Banner*, June 6, 1914.

5. George Poindexter (1779–1855) moved to Mississippi as a young man to practice law. He held numerous public offices, including governor of the state and member of the U.S. House of Representatives, before being elected U.S. senator, where he served for five years (1830–35). *BDAC*.

6. For an account of the difficulties between Jackson and Poindexter over Mississippi appointments, see Miles, *Jacksonian Democracy*, 48–54; Durham, *Old Sumner*, 211–12.

7. Thomas Bedford (1751–1804) served in the 4th Va. Rgt. during the Revolution. He later moved from Virginia to settle in Rutherford County, Tennessee. *VMHB*, 20 (1912): 197; Jill K. Garrett and Iris H. McClain, comps., *Some Rutherford County, Tennessee Cemetery Records* (Columbia, Tenn., 1971), 127.

From William C.P. Cleghorn[1]

Americus Sumter Co Ga.   October 4th, 1866

Sir

Many of the Counties in the Southern states have held public meetings to express their approbation of your "Policy"; as no meeting has been held in this County, I trust, that you will not think the liberty I am now taking *obtrusive*; We citizens of this county being "a Unit" in your favour, have thought it unnecessary to hold any such meeting, as the mere fact of doing so might leave the inference that there were parties in the South opposed to your administration, which is not the fact. Every man from the Potomac to the Rio Grande is a "Johnson man." *You alone* can save us, the prayers of every christian are offered daily, that God may strengthen you for your work, and oh! Sir, think of our weakness; the negroes here are armed, and drilling every day, while we are unarmed and helpless. Can you help us? Will you help us? I have no property to be confiscated by the Radicals, but I have a wife and children[2] who have an interst in these United States, as much so, as if I were the owner of Millions. I own nothing, have nothing, but an education received in Scotland, my native country and I have taken *this great liberty*, because I love my adopted country, and see in you the only barrier between us and ruin, and to assure you that the People here are with you, *all with you*, although no public demonstrations indorsing Your "Policy" have been given; In hopes that I have not transcended the privileges of a citizen, in thus addressing the Chief Magistrate of the United States of America and with sentiments of the highest consideration.[3]

Wm. C. P. Cleghorn

ALS, DLC-JP.
   1. Cleghorn (c1804–fl1870), a school teacher, before the war lived a number of years in Alabama. 1870 Census, Ga., Schley, Ellaville, 2.
   2. Drady J. Cleghorn (c1817)–fl1870), a South Carolina native, was the mother of at least two sons and three daughters, ranging in age from about five to eighteen. Ibid.
   3. This letter was sent to Mrs. Johnson with a cover letter asking her to hand it to her husband. On the envelope Johnson pencilled, "Answer this letter, Acknowledge the reciept and thanks for this encouragement. AJ." Under this is a notation that it was answered on October 20.

From John P. Holtsinger

Greenville, October 4 1866

Sir.

I take the privilege of writing to you, as an old friend and acquaintance,[1] as well as President of the United States. The Radicals are doing every thing in their power to carry East Tennessee; And we are suffering a great deal, for the want of some man, who has a good war character to address our people upon the political issues of the day. I am trying to beat back the *tide*, as well as I can; But have not opportunity to do a great deal. T.A.R. Nelson, and Col. Neatherland[2] are making Some telling Speeches.

I just want to Say this to you, in refference to my office, that we are wanting a Collector very badly.[3] And if it is consistant with your duties, at this time, to give one we would be pleased for you to do So. Just So it is done before the meeting of Congress it will all be right. But if not untill then they may delay it until the close of the Session, and it would almost ruin Some of us.

I know you will do all in your power to accommodate us. And we intend to do all we can to Sustain you. My best wishes, and payers are for you, and your Success in maintaining *Constitutional Liberty*.

John P. Holtsinger

ALS, DLC-JP.
   1. Holtsinger, sometime minister of the Cumberland Presbyterian church in Greeneville, had been nominated by Johnson in May 1866 to the post of assessor of internal revenue for the First District. The Senate had confirmed the appointment in early June 1866. Ser. 6B, Vol. 2: 127, Johnson Papers, LC.
   2. John Netherland.
   3. Interestingly enough, on the very same day that the President submitted Holtsinger's nomination as assessor he also submitted Elijah Simmerly's nomination as collector of the First District. But the Senate took no action on Simmerly's nomination and therefore Johnson later gave him a recess appointment. The President resubmitted Simmerly's nomination in January 1867; the Senate approved in February and he was immediately commissioned. Ser. 6B, Vol. 2: 297; Vol. 3: 424; Vol. 4: 227, Johnson Papers, LC; *U.S. Off. Reg.* (1867).

From Andrew Neat[1]

New Albany Ind   Octo 4th 1866

My dear Sir:

As the necessary work of removing *Radicals* from Office, and appointing persons in their place, upon whom you can rely, your *true* friends, has at length commenced in good earnest, induces me to make application to you for the Office of "Collector of United States Internal Revenue" for the Second (2nd) District of the State of Indiana.

This is the first time in my life that I ever asked for an Office. I was Surgeon in the Federal Army nearly two years—and while serving in that capacity, lost my health to such an extent as to unfit me for regular or constant practice.

Col. B. F. Scribner, the present incumbent, served his Country well, but no better than I labored to do. He is a high toned gentleman and discharges the duties of the office as well as any man; but he is an ultra Radical, and a bitter enemy of you and your Restoration Policy, a warm personal and political friend of Gov. O. P. Morton, a bitter enemy to the Great Democratic party.

I was first Surgeon of the 2nd Regt. East Tennessee Vols. Col. J.P.T. Carter. I first met you at Camp Dick Robinson's. Was introduced to you by Genl. Geo. W. Thomas. You may remember me as the Surgeon who asked you to have your Photograph taken for me. Was hurried off to Wild cat before getting it. I saw you frequently at London, Laurel Co. Ky. but did not have the pleasure to be in your company. While you were staying at Mark Harden's[2] or James Slaughter's you selected a Colt pistol for me from a Mr Bowyer[3] or a yung man named Shaw[4] from Lexington Ky.

While at Flat Lick, I assisted Your Son, Robt Johnson, to raise his Regt. and by his request, acted as Surgeon for him and his Regt, till it was completed, mustered into service and a Surg. furnished.

He was a warm personal friend, and spent considerable time with me, while at Flat lick.

I was an old line whig till Know-nothing-ism came into existance— then identified myself with the Democratic party. In 1856, voted for Buchanan and Breckenridge. In 1860 for S. A. Douglas and in 1864 for Abram Lincoln and Andrew Johnson.

I will not send you a list of names of personal and political friends, recomending me as a suitable person to fill the office I ask, but will simply say that such men as M. C. Kerr, McDonald,[5] Gen. Cravan[6] and hundreds of such men would do so most willingly and cheerfully—and will do so if necessary.

I was present at the reception given you in Luville[7]—had the pleasure of listening to the words of truth, wisdom and patriotism, that came from your brave and patriotic heart, and thanked God we had at the helm of the Old Ship so noble and reliable a pilot.

Now my dear Sir and more than friend, I hope you will give this your favorable consideration. I have written you the whole truth, and my appointment to the office I ask, will give universal satisfaction to your *true* friends in this District. May God bless you and preserve your life, and stand by and give you strength to carry out these great measures that will save our common Country for irredeemable ruin is my sincere prayer.

Andrew Neat, M.d.

ALS, DNA-RG56, Appts., Internal Revenue Service, Collector, Ind., 2nd Dist., Andrew Neat.

1. Neat (*c*1820–1891) was a native of Kentucky and served as surgeon for the 2nd Tenn. Inf., USA, from October 1861 to October 1862, when he resigned. He did not receive the appointment and Scribner remained until 1871. *Off. Army Reg.: Vols.*, 4: 1198; 1850 Census, Ky., Frankfort, 2nd Dist., 145; (1860), 27; CSR, Andrew Neat, RG94, NA; Pension File, Hettie R. Neat, RG15, NA; *U.S. Off. Reg.* (1867–69); *Johnson Papers*, 10: 136.

2. Hardin (*c*1820–*fl*1890), businessman and lawyer, ran a tanyard and grocery and restaurant business in London, Kentucky, during his career. 1860 Census, Ky., Laurel, London, 135; Russell Dyche, *Laurel County, Kentucky* (London, Ky., 1954), 72, 99.

3. George A. Bowyer.

4. Not identified.

5. Joseph E. McDonald (1819–1891), U.S. representative (1849–51) and senator (1875–81) from Indiana, practiced law in Crawfordsville from 1847 to 1859. He ran unsuccessfully as a Democrat for the governorship in 1864. *BDAC*.

6. James A. Cravens (1818–1893), U.S. representative from Indiana, served in the Mexican War and then as a member of the state legislature before serving in the U.S. House (1861–65). Afterwards he pursued his agricultural interests and was a delegate to the 1866 National Union Convention in Philadelphia and the 1868 Democratic National Convention in New York. *BDAC*.

7. Perhaps a reference to Johnson's stop at Louisville on September 11 during the President's tour of the Northeast and Midwest.

From Benjamin C. Truman

Hartford, Oct 4, 1866.

Sir:

I have been pretty well over this state and Rhode Island, since Chicago trip. I think that, with judicious management, an Administration member from the Western district of R.I. can be secured.[1] Late elections in this state show democratic gains in democratic strongholds and Rep. gains in Rep. districts. I am sure this state will go for your policy next spring, if Hoffman[2] is elected, and Congressional gains are made in Pa. N.J. and Ind. Let me assure you that the long haired men and cadaverous females of New England think you are horrid. I had a conversation with an antique female last night, in the course of which she declared that she hoped you would be impeached. Said I "Why should he be impeached— what has he done that he should be impeached?" "Well," replied she, "he hasn't done anything yet, but I hope to God he will."

Ben. C. Truman

ALS, DLC-JP.
1. Truman misjudged, for Republican Nathan F. Dixon, an ultra Radical, was reelected in April 1867 to his third consecutive term. *BDAC*; *Guide to U.S. Elections*, 618; David Donald, *The Politics of Reconstruction, 1863–1867* (Baton Rouge, 1965), 100.
2. John T. Hoffman, mayor of New York City, was seeking election as governor of New York.

From J. Logan Chipman[1]

Detroit   Oc. 5—66.

Sir.

I see by the papers that young Custer has evinced his devotion to you, by attacking me.[2] He admits in his leter that he does not know what he is talking about[3]—a condition of mind, which seems natural to him.

I enclose the letter. It is a gratuitous attack upon you, on a vital point.[4] I beg you to give it due consideration.

If I am to be slaughtered in the house of my friends, the fight better be abandoned.

J. Logan Chipman

ALS, DLC-JP.
1. Detroit-born Chipman (1830–1893), a lawyer and member of the Michigan house of representatives, was an unsuccessful Democratic candidate for Congress in 1866. He later served as attorney for the Detroit police board (1867–79), judge of the Detroit superior court (1879–87), and a member of the U.S. House (1887–93). *BDAC*.
2. Chipman refers to a letter from Gen. George A. Custer to Gen. Russell A. Alger, written October 3 and published in the *Detroit Advertiser* on October 4. Alger's letter to Custer of October 1, also printed, asked Custer to clarify his political views, which appeared to have been misrepresented, especially whether Custer would urge his old soldiers to support Chipman for Congress. Custer hedged somewhat but finally stated that he would never urge someone to vote for a person for whom he would not vote. Moreover, Custer would not vote for Chipman because "popular opinion" held that the candidate was "included in that class of men, who, during the war, failed to render to the Government that support which is due from every truly loyal and patriotic citizen." *Chicago Tribune*, Oct. 7, 1866.
3. Custer said that he did not know Chipman personally, but he based his opinion on hearsay from a wide variety of sources, both Republican and Democratic, none of which contradicted the impression that Chipman was a Copperhead. Ibid.
4. Not found with this document, Custer's letter never mentioned Johnson specifically, but his opposition to Chipman and his declaration that the press had misrepresented his position were considered to be attacks on Johnson, since Custer had traveled with him on the "swing around the circle." Ibid.; also Oct. 6, 1866. See also Henry Barns to Johnson, Oct. 6, 1866.

From John L. Deen

78 Water St.   N.Y.   Oct 5. 1866

Dear Sir

Permit me to thank you for your kindness to us while we were in Wash'g.[1]

I regret that I did not have another interview with you before I left, but business of importance demanded my immediate presence in New York.

We are all more or less selfish in this world and I feel some disappoint-
ment in not securing what I sought. Yet I am just enough to acknowlege
and be pleased that you selected so worthy a man as Genl. Dix. I do not
doubt but that he will give very general satisfaction.

Genl. Dix was my choice for the gubernatorial chair, and had I attended the convention at Albany N.Y. I should not have yielded him for
any less popular man: although the nominee[2] of the convention bears a
very good name—and is much of a gentleman. But he is not So widely
known as the Genl.

It is currently reported and generally beleived in New York that Genl.
Dix will soon vacate his position as Naval officer, in which event Mr President you will please consider me as an applicant.[3]

Hoping your Excellency enjoys good health, and that you may be
spared to us.

John L Deen

ALS, DLC-JP.
1. The date of the President's interview with Deen and his wife is unknown.
2. At Albany, on September 11, the Democrats nominated Mayor John T. Hoffman of
New York City for governor. Hoffman was not successful in the gubernatorial race but was
reelected as mayor in 1867 and eventually as governor. *American Annual Cyclopaedia*
(1866), 545; *DAB*.
3. Deen's wife also wrote to the President, thanking him "for the many kindnesses"
shown to them while they were in Washington and asking that Johnson appoint her husband as naval officer, once Dix had resigned the post. Over the course of the next two years,
Mrs. Deen continued urging Johnson to appoint her husband. Finally, in January 1869,
after several others had been rejected by the Senate, Deen got the nomination he had long
desired; but he was not confirmed. A. M. [Mrs. John L.] Deen to Johnson, Oct. 5, Nov. 7,
1866, Jan. 6, Feb. 2, Mar. 7, 1867, July 3, 1868, Feb. 17, 1869, Johnson Papers, LC; Ser.
6B, Vol. 4: 58, ibid. See also Mrs. John L. Deen to Johnson, Jan. 6, Dec. 18, 1868, Appts.,
Customs Service, Naval Officer, New York, John L. Deen, RG56, NA.

From R. Mathews[1]

Cincinnati   Oct 5th 1866.

Dr. Sir.

As one who never supported you before, but am now ready to stand by
you and your policy of reconstruction, I am impelled to say a word to you
more with a view to the future than the present. The democratic & national union party will no doubt be successful in this county, if not in the
entire state, and I should not be surprised if we even carried the State of
Ohio. If we had two weeks more to work in we would kill radicalism so
dead that it would never again raise its head in this region. Already the
skies are brightening. Dawn will soon appear; ere long the rays of the
coming glory will lighten our faces. It will be to us as the sun of Austerlitz.[2] Yet the clouds will follow, and it is well to look a little ahead and
provide for the future.

You will have to change some of the government offices here, Sam Carey is out in a letter this morning in favour of Congress and Thad Stevens & Co. His head should come off as well as others, but let me conjure you to be careful what you do. Your appointments should give a moral & political force. There is scarcely one of the men that I hear of now applying for place that is fit for it. But there are men that can be had. And allow me to intimate in view of the troubles that will no doubt beset you hereafter to have men of undoubted pluck and ability for their places, and dont forget that we have just such men in the democratic ranks men who are now standing by you when they think you are right, not such democrats as got frightened when the war came, left their own party and covertly acted with the other not knowing to which side they belonged. They are not reliable. They are not the men you want. Take some good old line democrats who are with you now, and they will stay with you. You will find them reliable, and if a fight comes, they will be efficient for they are not afraid, and you will triumph. Consult with Steedman Mclean Bartley Thurman Vattier Frees Farran[3] and such men as these and you will find out who are the men to back you up out here, that is of the democratic faith.

Trusting that providence may guide you safely through the coming troubles. . . .

R Mathews

ALS, DLC-JP.

1. Possibly Robert Matthews[*sic*] (*fl*1867), a bookkeeper. Cincinnati directories (1861–67).

2. For a discussion of the importance of weather conditions at the famous battle of Austerlitz, see Claude Manceron, *Austerlitz: The Story of a Battle*, trans. by George Unwin (New York, 1966), 222–28.

3. James B. Steedman, possibly Washington McLean, Thomas W. Bartley, Allen G. Thurman, John L. Vattier, possibly George Fries, and James J. Faran. Vattier (1808–1881), a physician, had been a state senator and Cincinnati postmaster. Fries (1799–1866), also a doctor, had been a Democratic congressman (1845–49) and Hamilton County's treasurer (1860–62). Faran (1808–1892), a lawyer, legislator, and congressman (1845–49), was a longtime proprietor of the *Cincinnati Enquirer*. *The Biographical Encyclopaedia of Ohio of the Nineteenth Century* (Cincinnati, 1876), 453; *New York Times*, Jan. 14, 1881; *BDAC*.

From George D. Prentice

Louisville   Oct 5 '66

Dear Sir,

I earnestly ask your good offices in behalf of the Louisville Journal so far as you can render them consistently with your views of duty. The Journal has been an expence to the proprietors during the last year. Because of our steady and resolute Unionism and especially our advocacy of the first Constitutional amendment (ours was the only paper of any consequence in this State that did advocate it) we have been to a great extent ignored by the people of the South, while the merchants here, seeking Southern trade, think it their interest to advertise in and encourage papers that have ever been Southern in spirit.

All of the papers in Kentucky, with one or two exceptions, prefer your general policy to that of the Radicals, but the Louisville Journal is the only one in Louisville and about the only one in that State, that has endorsed the leading, the paramount policy of your administration, the grand policy of restoration—the policy upon which I believe that your fame will rest more than upon any other.

The Government has a large amount of printing and advertising done. We receive what is to be published for this locality only. In the East, the papers publishing for the Government are not thus restricted. May I not beg therefore that you will do what you can to give us help.[1] We need it.

Be assured that I am *very* reluctant to obtrude my affairs upon your attention amidst the vast difficulties that surround you.

Geo. D. Prentice.

ALS, DLC-JP.
1. On October 10, William G. Moore and Robert Johnson, by order of the President, referred the letter to the various departments for their special consideration. Subsequently the State and War departments chose the *Journal* as one of the Kentucky papers to receive printing contracts. Endorsement, Prentice to Johnson, Oct. 5, 1866; *U.S. Off. Reg.* (1867).

From William Thorpe
Private.

Harrisburg, Oct. 5, 1866.

Dear Sir:—

I have been spending some days in Pennsylvania, and have used my best efforts to ascertain the real views of the citizens, with a view of forming some idea of the result of the election.

In that region lying along the Penn. Central Railroad, the Union Party seems very strong—in fact no town where I stopped but I saw the best evidences of encouragement. The Union men are active and enthusiastic in spirit, and sufficiently powerful to take care of themselves. Gentlemen from various sections of the country with whom I have conversed tell me that a similar spirit prevails wherever they have been, and it is universally conceded that the election will be a very close one.

I am greatly encouraged at what I have seen and heard, since I came here. In the West the radicals have been predicting that they would carry Penna. by a hundred thousand majority, and Gen. Geary boasted to a friend of mine recently, that he would not only get the entire republican vote but a majority of the Democratic.[1] This opinion prevails in Michigan, Illinois, Indiana, and to some extent in Missouri. In those states our friends are looking anxiously towards Pennsylvania for encouragement but are almost hopeless. They seem to fear that everything is giving way, and that you will be obliged to yield to the overpowering rush of radical fanaticism.

The feeling in this state is intense. Both parties are concentrating upon the Congressmen.

Thaddeus Stevens is not popular in his own state by any means. His private reputation is bad.

Gen. Geary arrived at Altoona to-day. Very little notice was taken of him, and no enthusiasm was manifested.

The radicals have got the best of us so far as the soldiers here are concerned.

Wm. Thorpe

ALS, DLC-JP.
1. For a report on John W. Geary's victory in Pennsylvania, see William Bigler to Johnson, Oct. 18, 1866.

From John A. Waugh[1]

Greenville Mercer County Penna.
Oct 5th 1866

Dr. Sir

I have taken the liberty of trespassing upon your good feelings, in consequence of difficulty existing in this the 20 assessment district in this State, And being a Warm advocate of your policy & hoping that every thing under your administration may be carried out in strict comformity with your plans & wishes, is the best apology I can offer for thus intruding upon you. The matter to which I want to Call your attention is this viz on the 6th of Augt last Mr Jno B Hays[2] of Meadville Crawford Co Pa was appointed assessor for the district (20th). On the first day of September last he took possession of the office. Since when Mr J H Lenhart[3] who formerly held the position, has been reappointed with instructions to resume & take possession of the office on the 20th this month. This unexpted reappointment of Mr Lenhart has created a great deal of surprise & dissatisfaction in the district not only to your warm adherants but throughout the district.[4]

The reappointment of Mr Lenhart has (I have no doubt) been prcured through misrepresentations on the part of som ones who are not your friends.[5]

Whilst Mr Hayes is a warm advocate of your policy and a man commanding great influence in the district, the other man J H Lenhart is a bitter opposer of your policy.

The desire therefore of your friends & the majority of the district is that you will adopt such measures in the premises as will continue Mr Hays & Countermand the reappointment of Lenhart.

And that is the sincere desire of your friend. . . .[6]

Jno A Waugh

ALS, DNA-RG56, Appts., Internal Revenue Service, Assessor, Pa., 20th Dist., John B. Hays.

1. Waugh (b. *c*1817) was a merchant and stock dealer. *History of Mercer County, Pennsylvania: Its Past and Present* (Chicago, 1888), 834; 1870 Census, Pa., Mercer, Greenville Borough, New Hamburg, 30.

2. Son of the founder and former editor of the *Crawford Journal*, a Republican paper, and onetime postmaster of Meadville, Hays (*c*1829–1898), a four-year veteran of the 19th U.S. Inf., before he resigned from the army in September 1865 with the rank of brevet major, was a delegate to both the National Union Convention in Philadelphia and the Soldiers' Convention in Cleveland. Given a recess appointment for the Twentieth District assessorship in early August 1866, Hays later owned and edited a newspaper in Beaver County, Pennsylvania, before relocating in New York City, where he appears to have taught school for several years and worked as a journalist. *History of Crawford County, Pennsylvania* (Chicago, 1885), 430–31, 744; Joseph H. Bausman, *History of Beaver County, Pennsylvania and Its Centennial Celebration* (2 vols., New York, 1904), 1:468; William F. Johnston to Johnson, July 20, 1866; Hays to Hugh McCulloch, Sept. 24, 1866, Appts., Internal Revenue Service, Assessor, Pa., 20th Dist., John B. Hays, RG56, NA; Hays to Johnson, Jan. 26, 1875, Johnson Papers, LC; Ser. 6B, Vol. 3: 160, ibid; New York City directories (1875–80); Powell, *Army List*, 365; Pension File, Fanny M. Hays, RG15, NA.

3. Joseph H. Lenhart (1821–1889), a merchant and banker in Meadville, had served as assessor since 1862. Samuel P. Bates, *Our County and Its People: A Historical and Memorial Record of Crawford County, Pennsylvania* (n.p., 1899), 725–26.

4. Following Hays's removal and Lenhart's reinstatement on September 18, hundreds of conservative voters in the district petitioned Johnson to reappoint Hays in order that the Democratic candidate for Congress for that district, Gen. A. M. McCalmont, would be ensured of success. Hays's reappointment came too late to aid McCalmont, who lost the election by less than two thousand votes. Appts., Internal Revenue Service, Assessor, Pa., 20th Dist., John B. Hays, RG56, NA; *Guide to U.S. Elections*, 617.

5. Here Waugh undoubtedly refers to S. Newton Pettis of Meadville who, according to Edgar Cowan and others, had agreed to use his influence against the election of McCalmont's Radical opponent, Darwin A. Finney, in exchange for Hays's removal and the reinstatement of Lenhart. "The thing to be done now," Cowan explained to Hugh McCulloch a few days after the election, "is to remove Pettis creature Lenhart and restore Maj. Hays to the Assessorship at once." Cowan to McCulloch, Oct. 12, 1866, Appts., Internal Revenue Service, Assessor, Pa., 20th Dist., John B. Hays, RG56, NA. See also Hays to McCulloch, Aug. 15, Sept. 24, ibid.

6. Across the bottom of Cowan's note of October 18 to Johnson, in which he urged that Hays's reappointment be "now made absolute," the President wrote "Approved" and signed his name. Hays was soon reappointed and when his nomination was sent to the Senate in January 1867 he was likewise confirmed. He continued as assessor until the end of Johnson's term. Cowan to Johnson, Oct. 18, 1866, ibid.; Ser. 6B, Vol. 3: 161; Vol. 4: 84, Johnson Papers, LC; *U.S. Off. Reg.* (1867–69).

From Henry Barns[1]

Detroit   Oct. 6th 1866

Sir,

I can but feel mortified and grieved at the evidence I send you herewith of the defection of another Michigan military man, who has so highly favored by you.[2] When Gen. Willcox[3] turned his back upon your friends here, on receiving the appointment to a Colonelcy, I thought the extent of ingratitude had been exhibited. Now, however, to see Gen. Custer, who had been *more* highly favored by you, turns his back upon you and your friends, as he does in the letter referred, you, and those who are exerting their utmost to stem Radical encroachments upon true Liberty and the Constitution, may well exclaim "deliver me from my friends," or "protect me from my friends, I can take care of my enemies." But, Sir, while there will be, as there is, now and then such an exhibition of baseness and ingratitude, permit me to say, Be not discouraged; you have true friends, sufficient, I sincerely believe, who will more than compensate your efforts for the losses of the Judases that may, by their treachery, sting the breast of him who has nourished them into consequence. The attempt of Gen. Custer to defeat our nominee for Congress, may injure, or seriously prejudice, the success of Mr. Chipman, as Gen. Willcox's defection did, but we shall do the best we can.[4] If Gen. Williams,[5] our candidate for Governor can be relieved from his post at St. Louis, as I hope he may be, I am strongly of the opinion that he can do very much to counteract the Judaslike conduct of Custer and Willcox. I, very respectfully, recommend that Gen. Williams be so relieved until after the election.[6] We need him here, very much. Our friends in the interior give us great encouragement that we shall materially reduce the radical majority in the State. In the fifth and sixth district, our friends are quite sanguine of success.[7]

H. Barns

ALS, DNA-RG94, Lets. Recd. (Main Ser.), File 805-W-1866 (M619, Roll 529).

1. Barns (c1815–c1871), a native of England, was in Detroit as early as 1850, spending most of his career as a newspaper editor and printer. He served as Detroit postmaster from October to the end of December 1866, and then as a pension agent. Detroit directories (1850–72); *U.S. Off. Reg.* (1867); 1860 Census, Mich., Wayne, Detroit, 6th Ward, 617.

2. Not found, but undoubtedly he was sending a clipping of the letter from Gen. George A. Custer to Gen. Russell A. Alger, dated October 3, 1866, and appearing in the *Detroit Advertiser* of October 4. See J. Logan Chipman to Johnson, Oct. 5, 1866.

3. Orlando B. Willcox.

4. Chipman lost by over 4,000 votes, but the problem was not his alone since Republicans were elected by large margins in all six Michigan congressional districts. *Chicago Tribune*, Nov. 7, 8, 1866.

5. Alpheus S. Williams (1810–1878), a Yale graduate, opened his law practice in Detroit in 1836. His prewar positions included probate judge, newspaper owner, lieutenant colonel in the Mexican War, and Detroit postmaster. During the Civil War he fought as a brigadier general in both the eastern and western theaters. He served as minister resident to the Republic of Salvador (1866–69) and U.S. congressman (1875–78). Warner, *Blue*.

6. Johnson endorsed Barns's recommendation that Williams be granted a leave of absence, referring it to the secretary of war with the comment, "Let this request be granted, unless it should be detrimental to the interests of the service."

7. The Democrats lost in the Fifth and Sixth districts, as elsewhere, and incumbent Gov. Henry H. Crapo soundly defeated Williams by 96,746 to 67,708. Willis F. Dunbar, *Michigan: A History of the Wolverine State* (Grand Rapids, 1970 [1965]), 466; *American Annual Cyclopaedia* (1866), 508.

To William H.C. King

Washington, D.C., Oct. 6th 1866

You are authorized to publish such report of the proceedings of Military Commission convened by Genl Baird as may be furnished you by Gen'l. Sheridan.[1]

Andrew Johnson.

Tel, DNA-RG107, Tels. Sent, President, Vol. 3 (1865–68).
1. King, editor of the *New Orleans Times*, had telegraphed Johnson's secretary, Robert Morrow, twice. First he asked if the report of the military commission convened by Gen. Absalom Baird to investigate the New Orleans riot had been made public. The next day he observed, "Genl Sheridan will give me copy of Bairds commission if it is officially made public by President." Newspaper summaries revealed that Generals Mower, Quincy, Gregg, and Baldey signed the report in which "The Commission gives opinion that it was a preconcerted plan among the rebel associations for the purpose of attacking the Convention if there was any plausible pretext." King to Robert Morrow, Oct. 5, 6, 1866, Tels. Recd., President, Vol. 5 (1866–67), RG107, NA; *Chicago Tribune*, Oct. 3, 1866.

From Richard Oulahan

663 Penna Ave. Capitol Hill
Washington D.C.   Oct 6th/66

Sir:

In the absence of my friend Col. O'Beirne[1] I take a liberty which I should not otherwise presume to take; and I leave a sick bed to communicate certain important facts to your Excellency:

Col. Kelly,[2] the Deputy of James Stephens C.O.I.R.[3]—and who planned the escape of the latter from Richmond Prison,—is here and has called on me, as one of the Irish Executive Committee, & also representing the Fenian Brotherhood of the District.

He wants us to join in opposition to your Excellency in the coming campaign, on account of the way certain Irish American Officers have been treated in Ireland, by our Minister & Consuls, and who have lately returned to New York.

Unless your Excellency make it known, distinctly, *that American Citizens shall be protected abroad*, these returned Officers are determined to "Stump" the State of New York against your Excellency *on that issue alone*, and I—belonging, as I do, to that State—know that they can ruin our cause before the elections; so far as the large Irish element is concerned.[4]

If Col. Kelly obtain an interview, this may be of service.[5]

Should your Excellency require any further information on this matter, I may be found in the anti-room.

Richard Oulahan

ALS, DLC-JP.
1. James R. O'Beirne.
2. Thomas J. Kelly (1833–1908), a native of Ireland, became involved in Fenian activ-

ities in America in the 1850s. When the Civil War erupted, he abandoned his newspaper and enlisted in an Irish regiment from Ohio. For a time he served as General Thomas's chief signal officer in the Army of the Cumberland before being discharged in June 1864. Following the war he went to Ireland and served as second-in-command to James Stephens and became the Fenian leader for a time when Stephens was in exile. Following his own arrest in 1867, he escaped to America where he was employed in the New York customhouse for the next thirty-plus years. Paul Rose, *The Manchester Martyrs: The Story of a Fenian Tragedy* (London, 1970), 17–18; Ryan, *Fenian Chief*, 349; *New York Times*, Feb. 7, 1908; Pension File, Anna Frances Kelly, RG15, NA.

 3. Central Organizer, Irish Republic.

 4. See D'Arcy, "The Fenian Movement," 188–89; Jenkins, *Fenians and Anglo-American Relations*, 218.

 5. Kelly wrote to Johnson the same day requesting an interview. See Kelly to Johnson, Oct. 6, 1866, Johnson Papers, LC.

To Henry Stanbery

Washington, D.C.   October 6th 1866.

Sir:

 A special term of the Circuit Court of the United States was appointed for the first Tuesday of October, 1866, at Richmond, Virginia, for the trial of Jefferson Davis on the charge of treason. It now appears that there will be no session of that Court at Richmond during the present month, and doubts are expressed whether the regular term—(which by law should commence on the fourth Monday of November next)—will be held.

 In view of this obstruction and the consequent delay in proceeding with the trial of Jefferson Davis under the prosecution for treason now pending in that Court; and there being, so far as the President is informed, no good reason why the Civil Courts of the United States are not competent to exercise adequate jurisdiction within the District or Circuit in which the state of Virginia is included, I deem it proper to request your opinion as to what further steps, if any, should be taken by the Executive, with a view to a speedy, public, and impartial trial of the accused, according to the Constitution and Laws of the United States.[1]

Andrew Johnson

LS, DLC-JP.
 1. See Stanbery to Johnson, Oct. 12, 1866.

From William B. Phillips

Private.

72 East 23d Street,
New York, Octr. 7th 1866.

Dear Sir,

 Last night we received at the office a telegram from our Washington correspondent, which is published this morning,[1] and to which we give some prominence, stating, that, in the event of the approaching elections going for the radicals or the republicans who affiliate with the radicals, you would recommend the southern states to adopt the constitutional amendment as necessary to appease the demands of the North and to place themselves in a better position to obtain restoration. Mr. Cooke,[2] who was our correspondent a few days ago, came to the office yesterday just from Washington. Upon asking him about your health and views and so forth he told me he had seen you recently, and that you were firm in your resolution to stand upon the ground you had taken on the restoration question however the elections might go. The two statements are entirely different.[3]

This is a very prominent subject in our editorial meetings, and, as you may have noticed by the paper, is a constant theme,[4] though I have written nothing about it. I would rather have continued the fight on the radicals while there was any chance of beating them. Without knowing your views particularly, and only judging from what I know of your character and views in general, I have ventured to say in our conferences that you would yeild to the popular voice if it should be clearly expressed in favor of the congressional plan of restoration. I have really thought you would consider it your duty to take such a course both out of regard to public sentiment and for the sake of healing up our troubles before they become chronic. Whether I was right or wrong in my conjecture I think the expression of such an opinion has had the effect of softening somewhat the attacks which some were disposed to make on you.

With regard to the constitutional amendment I think my views are much the same as your own. I think all the states ought to participate freely and without coercion in making any change in the Constitution, and that whatever change should be made ought to be made deliberately after restoration. I think the course that Congress is pursuing is unwise, unstatesmanlike, and contrary to good policy, that, in fact, the interests of the country are being sacrificed to the interests of party. The object should be to allay the passions evoked by the war and to bring a better state of feeling at the earliest moment possible between the two sections of the country, but Congress, and the dominant party which it represents, do not seem to care about this. I fear, too, the people of the North lack that feeling of magnanimity to the conquered which a great people should have. Even in Europe they promptly proclaim amnesties to the subjugated as soon as peace is restored, yet republican America is disposed to be proscriptive and revengeful. All this is to be deplored; but the question for the southern people and the friends of restoration to consider is not that of complaint at what is unfortunately adverse but what is best, to be done under these circumstances. If the elections go for Congress resistance to the Congressional plan of restoration would be useless and might be very injurious. It is no use talking of rights when war has placed the conquered absolutely in the power of the conquerer. The real ques-

Extract Const. Amend.

"Now, ANDY, take it right down.   More you Look at it, worse you'll Like it."

A cartoonist's rendering of attempts to coax Johnson to endorse the 14th Amendment
Harper's Weekly, October 27, 1866

tion is under these circumstances what is best to be done to get out of this difficulty as quickly as possible. Perhaps the constitutional amendment is the only way left open. We may regret this and wish there was some other and a more liberal way, but will it not be wise to take the best we gan get rather than risk greater loss and a prolonged exclusion from the government?

The feature in the constitutional amendment with regard to counting representation by actual voters, may reduce the number of southern members in the House, but not in the Senate, and after all there is a principle in this proposed amendment. The worst feature in the other portion of the amendment is the proscription of so many southerners who for the most part are the best class of the population. But better accept this than have the South kept out altogether and perhaps with confiscation and worse proscription. As to the clause about the federal and rebel debts I suppose there can be little objection to that.

I know your only wish is to do what is best for the whole country, and, therefore, I have taken the liberty to submit with all respect these views to you. The highest order of statesmanship is shown in adapting measures to the circumstances of the time.

W. B. Phillips.

ALS, DLC-JP.
1. According to the newspaper, Johnson would soon issue the following decree to southern states: "I have submitted my plan to the people, and so far as the people have had an opportunity to act upon it their verdict has been in favor of the proposed constitutional amendment. Under the circumstances, the best advice I can give is that you adopt the amendment, in order that you may be restored to the Union, so that all the people may consult upon the future of our great country." *New York Herald*, Oct. 7, 1866.
2. Probably Thomas M. Cook (*fl*1868), a former war correspondent for the *Herald*, for whom Johnson later obtained a special agency in the Treasury Department. J. Cutler Andrews, *The North Reports the Civil War* (Pittsburgh, 1955), 70, 363, 553, 572; Crouthamel, *New York Herald*, 121, 136; Cook to Johnson, Nov. 23, 1868, Johnson Papers, LC.
3. According to another story which appeared in the *Herald* some two weeks earlier, Johnson had reportedly told a member of his cabinet that if the New York elections "would follow the course of Maine," then he would advise the southern legislatures to accept the amendment. *New York Herald*, Sept. 24, 1866.
4. See, for example, the editorials in ibid., Sept. 24, 27, 29, 1866.

From John W. Price[1]

Cincinnati Ohio   Oct 7th 1866.

My dear Sir.

I hasten to send you a copy of a speech delivered last night at "Mozart Hall" in this city, by that bad, bold man, Genl Ben Butler, of Massachusetts, wherein he specifically and circumstantially sets forth the causes of impeachment against you as President.[2] I blush for the honor of the American name, to think, that any one calling himself an American citizen, and having enjoyed high military office in the gift of his country, should so far forget the honor and respect due to the President of the United States as thus to publicly and falsely seek to degrade him, and the high office he holds in the Estimation of the American People.

Comment on this most extraordinary speech is unnecessary—it is simply infamous. Were it but the utterings of this one bad man, silent contempt would be its best notice; but it may be, that this man, more bold than the others, is put forth as their spokesman; and this speech, "like coming events," may foreshadow the action of the next Congress.

At all events, I deemed it my duty to let you know what had been said on this occasion, as "to be forewarned, is to be forearmed."

Thanking you for the acknowledgment of my last letter, through Col Morrow. . . .

John. W. Price
Box 793,   Cincinnati

ALS, DLC-JP.
1. Though there were other possibilities, this Price (c1838–fl1888) was probably the one who was a Cincinnati belt manufacturer. 1880 Census, Ohio, Hamilton, 161st Enum. Dist., 4; Cincinnati directories (1870–81); Price to Grover Cleveland, June 8, 1888, Cleveland Papers, LC.
2. Although not found enclosed, one account of Butler's October 6 speech may be found in the *Cincinnati Enquirer*, Oct. 8, 1866.

From David Zigler et al.[1]

Port Byron Ills   October 7" 1866
Dear sir

We have the honor by direction of the state central committy to make to you the following report by way of a petition praying that your honor will without delay act in this matter. We have here one captan Benjamin Harding[2] who has been a soldier for some three years & whose Labours can be had with the Democratic party for either of the following positions a commition as major in the regular army with orders to report to General Rodman[3] or at Rockisland for the comeing winter a position which he is said to [be] capable of filling with much credit to himself & then insureing his servises on the side of the administration subscribeing to your policy. The above would be prefered by him but will take the apointment of Governor of Utah teritory or montana both of which are filled by ultry opposers[4] of your honor Pollicy of reconstruction & in the event that neither of the three named can be given him we believe that his servises can be retained by giveing him the apointment of surveyor genl of either of the above named teritories but it is not safe to trust him to long for the abolition party are bidding high for him & he has said this much to us that he will work in this campeign for whoever will pay him best & we have his promis not to take anny offer from them untill he hears from you which must be to him direct as he willnot allow anny to know what his bid is from us. We have promised him anny thing he may ask within your jurisdiction. Sugested the first & we would most earnistly recomend and prey that this recomendation be approved by your excelency for by secureing him we secure at least five hundred votes in this county & if he hears from you in time he will canvas this congressional district & we believe will carry votes enough to insure the election of Mr Thompson[5] the Democratic candidate for congress. The capten is one of our strongest and most influential men amongst the soldiers and it is said by the suporters of the oposition that as he goes the district goes. We should have made this report sooner but all ware afraid to aproach him in the matter as it was almost impossible to draw him out on the subject and then only to say that those who paid best would get his servises in this campaign and since he so defined his position there has been a number of propositions mad him none of which he has accepted yet and has gave us a promis not to untill he has time to hear from you. We therefore most earnestly urge and prey that your honor will act imediately and forward to the said captan a commition as majar which will insure him and his servis with our party. He has high bids one of which is if prefered to be the next anominee from the district to congress. That you will see the necessity of imediate action or we must suffer by the loss of our candidate we feel that we cannot urge the matter to strongly as the time is short & we are doomed if we lose his servises. This done at Port byron Illinois this day and year above. You will answer this by directing to the capten direct who will make known to us the facts of your answer. We have the honor to sir vary Respectfully your obedient servents all of which are suporters of Andrew Johnsons Polliy to a letter. Signed by our secratary, H B. Young[6] for the undirsyned names.

L, DNA-RG94, ACP Branch, File H-988-CB-1866, Benjamin Harding.
1. Zigler (1814–*fl*1885), tailor and merchant, moved from Pennsylvania to Illinois in 1855 and was appointed postmaster of Port Byron in 1858 and again in 1866. His and five other names were signed to this petition. *Portrait and Biographical Album of Rock Island County, Illinois* (Chicago, 1885), 306–7.
2. Harding (c1824–1903) served as a lieutenant in the 65th Ill. Inf. and then as a company captain with the 17th Ill. Cav. Unable to hold a job for any significant time, he wandered between Missouri and Iowa during the last twenty years of his life. Pension File, Benjamin Harding, RG15, NA.
3. Thomas J. Rodman (1816–1871) graduated from West Point and served in the Mexican War and Civil War, attaining the rank of brevet brigadier general in March 1865. He remained in the army until his death. Hunt and Brown, *Brigadier Generals.*
4. Charles Durkee and Green Clay Smith. *U.S. Off. Reg.* (1867).
5. John S. Thompson (b. c1806) was judge of the tenth circuit court from September 1864 to February 1867, when he resigned. He was unsuccessful in his congressional race against A. C. Harding in 1866. 1850 Census, Ill., Whiteside, 37th Dist., 433; John Moses, *Illinois: Historical and Statistical* (2 vols., Chicago, 1892), 2: 1149; D. W. Lusk, *Eighty Years of Illinois Politics and Politicians, Anecdotes and Incidents. A Succinct History of the State*, 3rd ed. rev. (Springfield, 1889), 199.
6. Unidentified.

From Charles H. Brainard

Medford Mass.   October 8, 1866.

Dear Sir,

You will doubtless remember that a few years ago I employed an artist to draw your portrait on Stone.[1]

As a likeness, as well as a work of art the drawing was universally approved, but it was not quite Satisfactory to yourself and you objected to purchasing the One hundred copies agreed upon; but to re-imburse me for my expenditure of time and money you generously offered to pay me One hundred dollars on a certain day. When I called to receive it it was not convenient for you to pay me more than Fifty dollars, which I received with your assurance that the balance should be paid at some future time. For reasons which it is unnecessary to explain I have never reminded you of the balance due, and should not now venture to trespass on your valuable time by renewing the subject, but for the simple fact that for nearly a year I have been an invalid, unable to attend to business and am in straitened circumstances. Should you therefore remember the conversation we had together at your lodgings in St Charles Hotel, and feel disposed to remit the balance, I shall be very grateful for your kindness.[2]

C. H. Brainard.

ALS, DLC-JP.
1. See Johnson to Brainard, Apr. 23, 1859, and Brainard to Johnson, Apr. 27, 1859, *Johnson Papers*, 3: 271–73.
2. A month later Brainard wrote again continuing to seek reimbursement, but there is no record of a reply from Johnson. Brainard to Johnson, Nov. 8, 1866, Johnson Papers, LC.

From Samuel W. Dewey[1]

Washington   8th Octr 1866.

Mr. President.

The accompanying basket of "glad tidings" from Lancaster County Pennsylvania,[2] the home of that arch Traitor Thad. Stevens, is respectfully presented, & at the same time you will please be informed that unless you Proclaim the Right of Habeas Corpus to be suspended in this District, the Radicals will on the assembling of Congress at once proceed to impeach you.

With the Habeas Corpus Suspended, they will be much intimidated & perhaps prevented from impeaching you & disgracing our whole Mighty Nation, but at all events, if they do attempt an impeachment, you can easily have the Conspirators convicted of High Treason & suspend them between Heaven & Earth upon the Haman-like gallows they contemplate erecting for you.

Asking no favor of you, nor having any object in view but the saving of our Country from the everlasting disgrace of an attempt to impeach the Head of our Great & Glorious Republic. . . .

Saml. W. Dewey

ALS, DLC-JP.
1. Dewey (1807–1899) was a ship broker in New York from 1836 to 1845. The next year he removed permanently to Philadelphia. During his lifetime he invested in mineral lands and discovered the largest American diamond and ruby ever found, in Virginia and New Jersey, respectively. Rossiter Johnson and John H. Brown, eds., *The Twentieth Century Biographical Dictionary of Notable Americans* (Boston, 1904).
2. According to the enclosed description, the basket contained special varieties of pears presented on behalf of Henry Conn, a master mechanic of Lancaster County, Pennsylvania.

From Adam J. Glossbrenner

York Pa   Oct. 8, 1866

I just learn that soldiers at Carlisle Barracks are ordered not to vote. Twenty (20) are entitled to vote. Please have order rescinded by telegraph. Answer by telegraph.[1]

A. J. Glossbrenner

Tel, DNA-RG94, Lets. Recd. (Main Ser.), File G-553-1866 (M619, Roll 478).
1. Johnson immediately referred the telegram to Secretary Stanton, who in turn authorized Assistant Adjutant General Townsend to "ascertain whether any such order has been made & if so when and by whose authority and order it to be revoked." Later that evening Townsend received a dispatch from Bvt. Brig. Gen. William N. Grier, commander of the Carlisle Barracks, who explained that his order forbidding soldiers at the garrison from going to town on election day without a pass was not intended to keep them from voting, but rather to avoid "trouble" with an "excited populace." After directing Grier to "Give passes to soldiers entitled to vote tomorrow," Townsend notified Congressman Glossbrenner of his actions. Johnson and Stanton endorsements; Grier to E. D. Townsend, Oct. 8, 1866, Lets. Recd. (Main Ser.), File G-553–1866 (M619, Roll 478), RG94, NA; Townsend to Grier (2), Oct. 8, 1866; Townsend to Glossbrenner, Oct. 8, 1866, Tels. Sent, Sec. of War (M473, Roll 91), RG107, NA.

From James N. Harding[1]

Port Gibson, Miss, Oct 8th 1866

Sir

I respectfully request in behalf of my son James M. Harding[2] the appointment to a cadetship in the United States Military Academy at West Point. He was born, and still resides in the town of Port Gibson, 5th Congressional District, State of Mississippi: He was seventeen (17) years of age on the 20th of last month—September 1866—no brother or other relation of his has heretofore been educated or admited in said Institution; He is five feet and ten inches in height, well built and free from any deformity, disease or infirmity whatever.

He is, at present, a student in the Mississippi University at Oxford: has studied a pretty thorough course in the Latin, and made some progress in the Greek languages. He has also studied English Grammar, Gerography, History of the United States, Arithmetic, Algebra and Geometry.

He rendered no military, naval or other service to the (so called) Confederate States, and for the political inclinations and conduct of his family relations I respectfully refer to Senator Sharkey[3] and to E. G. Peyton[4] Representativ of the 5th Congressional District.

James N. Harding

ALS, DNA-RG94, USMA, Corres. re Military Academy, 1866, S-26.

1. Harding (b. c1814) was a lawyer. 1850 Census, Miss., Claiborne, Port Gibson, 211.

2. Harding (b. 1849) did not receive an appointment to the Military Academy. *West Point Register*.

3. As early as spring 1866, William L. Sharkey had recommended young Harding for an appointment to the Military Academy; in his August and October missives to Johnson, he reiterated this endorsement. Sharkey to Johnson, Aug. 21, Oct. 18, 1866, USMA, Corres. re Military Academy, 1866, S-26, RG94, NA.

4. Ephraim G. Peyton (1802–1876), a lawyer, legislator, and local district attorney, had been a strong opponent of secession. After the war he was elected to Congress but was not seated. During the 1870s he was chief justice of the Mississippi supreme court. *NCAB*, 7: 294–95.

From John S. Hollingshead

Washington D C   Oct 8, 1866.

Sir:

A Committee from the different Temperance Associations of the City of Washington and District of Columbia was appointed to confer together and make arrangements for a Grand Temperance Demonstration to be made on the 15th of this month to assemble at LaFayette Square at 2 oclock P.M. and march from thence to the Capitol Grounds where temperance addresses will be delivered. By resolution of the Committee I was directed to request that you would issue a General Order to the effect that all employees of the General Government in the District of Columbia who are members of Temperance Societies shall be granted leave of absence at 12 oclock M on the 15th of this month.

Many working men as well as clerks are connected with our societies and we believe this endorsement of our efforts in the cause of Temperance would have a very happy effect, which we trust you will make if it can be done consistently and not to the prejudice of the public service.

It will be a great encouragement to us and to all who have an interest in the Temperance Cause.[1]

John S. Hollingshead

ALS, DNA-RG56, Lets. Recd. from President.

1. According to the endorsement, on October 10 Johnson approved the request and referred the matter to the various department heads for the needed orders. On the day of the demonstration, the parade passed through the White House carriageway, where Johnson acknowledged it. *National Intelligencer*, Oct. 12, 16, 1866.

From Edmund Cooper

Shelbyville Ten.   Octbr. 9th 1866.

Dear Mr President.

During the prevalence of the Cholera, which raged fearfuly in my village—there were a few young men, who bravely ministered to the wants of the sick—and buried the dead.

Without their courage and aid, many would have suffered. One of the most heroic was Lt Thomas Martin[1] late of the Federal Army—a native of the village—and who served during the late war on the side of the Government.

What I ask is, that you would appoint Lt Martin to a Lieutenancy in one of the new Regiments—as he desires to follow a soldiers life—and certainly has the moral and physical courage—and influenced by a genuine patriotism, to make a good soldier. I remained at home during the epidemic—and did my duty.

We have an election for Representative from Bedford county on Saturday.[2] I greatly fear the result on account of the friends of the administration having neglected to Register their names—and the "Commissioner"[3] who is an intense Radical—refusing now to open the Registration. However, we have started a strong man—and will try and win.[4]

Edmund Cooper

ALS, DNA-RG94, ACP Branch, File M-1094-CB-1866, Thomas Martin.

1. Not identified.
2. George W. Thompson, considered to be a Radical, was the victorious candidate for the Bedford legislative post in the mid-October election. *BDTA*, 2: 899; *Observer* (Fayetteville), Oct. 25, 1866.
3. Not identified.
4. The unsuccessful candidate was William L. Little (1806–1875), a Bedford county farmer and formerly, in the 1850s, a member of the state legislature. *Republican* (Shelbyville), Oct. 19, 1866; *BDTA*, 1: 450–51.

To Albert B. Sloanaker

Washington, D.C., Octo 9t 1866

I thank you for the good news from Philadelphia.[1] God bless the people. In them is my reliance for the preservation of peace and the ultimate Salvation of the Country.

Andrew Johnson

Tel, DNA-RG107, Tels. Sent, President, Vol. 3 (1865–68).

1. Correspondence from Sloanaker to Johnson regarding the early election returns in Philadelphia has not been located. If there was a reason to be optimistic, one could have pointed to the reelection by a substantial majority of Samuel J. Randall, a Johnson man, or the gain by Democrats of four legislative seats. But within a few days it became clear that the Johnson administration had not fared very well. Bradley, *Militant Republicanism*, 249–50; *New York Tribune*, Oct. 10, 1866. See also Beale, *Welles Diary*, 2: 614–15.

From Anonymous

Interior Department   Oct 10th 1866—
My dear Sir—

I wish you could know what I have seen in this office to-day among the gentlemen whom you support but who dont support you by a d—n sight. They have been to-day *laughing* at "my policy" as they call it. You cannot succeed unless surrounded by friends—and in the name of all that's good, get clear of them—and put gentlemen in their places—and especially send old Otto[1] off. He is an injury to any one—and particularly to you. Send them off and put in your friends, for they are getting tired of this delay. Mr. Ringwalt,[2] Mr. Forney's man of all work enjoys his $1600 pr year. Your friends are in the Street with nothing—many of them are.

L, DLC-JP.
    1. William T. Otto.
    2. G. B. Porter Ringwalt.

From William W. Armstrong et al.[1]

Office of the Plain Dealer,
Cleveland, O,   Oct. 10/66.
Sir:

On the 23d of August last, it was annouced from Washington that Major D. Kenny, Jr.[2] had been appointed by you Collector of the 19th (Ohio) District.

Major Kenny's appointment was at the time generally noticed by the press of Ohio as one most eminently fit to be made. For some reason, however, the Commission of Major Kenny for said position is being withheld by the Department; and it is now claimed by Gen. Garfield,[3] M.C. from the 19th District, that there will be no change made. Under all the circumstances this is exceedingly embarrassing to Major Kenny.

We are personally acquainted with Major Kenny. His record as a soldier will be found with the paper on file in his case, and will be found honorable to him. He is a warm supporter of your Administration and is a genuine Union man, having proved his devotion to the flag by four years of service in the field. In addition we know Mr. Kenny to have the requisite business qualifications for this position. In fact he has all the Jeffersonian qualifications, and we hope your Excellency will not over-look his claims for the position he has been named for.[4]

W W Armstrong   W. D. Morgan
H B Payne   R. P. Ranney

LS, DNA-RG56, Appts., Internal Revenue Service, Collector, Ohio, 19th Dist., Dennis Kinney[*sic*].
    1. The signatories were Armstrong, William D. Morgan, Henry B. Payne, and Rufus

P. Ranney. Armstrong (1833–1905), Ohio's secretary of state during the latter half of the war, edited the *Plain Dealer* (1865–84) before serving as Cleveland's postmaster and city treasurer. Morgan (d. 1887), elder brother of Gen. George W., editor of newspapers at New Lisbon and Newark, and former Ohio state auditor, briefly held a half interest in the *Plain Dealer* (1866–67) before he returned to Newark. Ranney (1813–1891) was a lawyer and former state supreme court judge. *NCAB*, 24: 352; Archer H. Shaw, *The Plain Dealer: One Hundred Years in Cleveland* (New York, 1942), 187–89; *Memorial Record of the County of Cuyahoga and City of Cleveland, Ohio* (Chicago, 1894), 908–9.

2. Dennis Kenney, Jr. (b. *c*1833), a Geneva, Ohio, merchant, had served as captain, Bty. C, 1st Ohio Lgt. Arty. (1861–62) and captain, commissary of subsistence (1862–65). 1860 Census, Ohio, Ashtabula, Geneva, 7; *Off. Army Reg.: Vols.*, 5: 29; Powell, *Army List*, 800.

3. James A. Garfield.

4. Johnson did not recommend Kenney for the collectorship.

From George Carver[1]

Huntsville Yadkin Co N C
October 10th 1866

Dear Sir

I have thought for sometime past that I would write you a letter, but am fearful you have forgotten me and will think I am writing for some favor, but such is not the case. I went from this state to Greenville Ten and lived with Dixon & Williams[2] and was there about a week before you arrived. I made your acquaintance and was in the caucus that brot you out for the legislature against John McGaughty.[3] I lived in Greenville five years. You was my tailor and made me several suits of clothing. I am glad of the progress you have made and feel proud of the position you have gained. We look on you as our only friend who can save us from the radicals and hope you will stand by us in these uncertain times. We are all loyal and anxious to regain our former place in the union. I myself was like many in the South for the union all the while, but powerless to do good. I am now the Post Master at this place, the only man who would be troubled with the office & that could take the required oaths. I will feel proud to know you have not forgotten me and with many wishes for your health and prosperity. . . .

George Carver

ALS, DLC-JP.

1. Carver (*c*1803–*fl*1870) was a miller. 1860 Census, N.C., Yadkin, 11; (1870), Fanbush Twp., 14.

2. Probably William Dickson and his son-in-law, Dr. Alexander Williams. Richard H. Doughty, *Greeneville: One Hundred Year Portrait (1775–1875)* (Greeneville, Tenn., 1975), 277.

3. John McGaughey was a Greene County, Tennessee, state representative (1827–33). Although it is possible that during one of his reelection bids Johnson may have been an opponent, no biographer mentions it. *BDTA*, 1: 477.

From Alfred Gilmore[1]

Continental Hotel   Phila   Oct 10, 1866

Penna nobly sustains the President. Geary about three thousand (3000) majority in Phila. We are gaining largely over the state. Berks indicates over eight thousand 8000 majority, Lancaster falls off. Clymer elected by a large majority.[2]

Alfred Gilmer[*sic*]

Tel, DNA-RG107, Tels. Recd., President, Vol. 5 (1866–67).

1. Gilmore (1812–1890) served in Congress as a Democrat with Johnson (1849–53) prior to practicing law in Philadelphia and later in Lenox, Massachusetts. *BDAC*.

2. Although Hiester Clymer carried Berks County by more than six thousand votes, his victory there was offset by John Geary's similar majority in Lancaster County. *Press* (Philadelphia), Oct. 11, 1866.

From Blackston McDannel

PRIVATE

Greenville [*sic*] Tennessee   Oct. 10, 1866.

Dear Sir

The time has been when I could sit down and write you an old fashioned familiar letter, and all was right. In doing so now, I hope no exceptions will be taken. I would not now trouble you, but for the fact that on the 7th inst. I received a letter from a friend at Knoxville, stating that a movement was on foot at that place to turn me out of my position as Marshal and to put in a military gentleman; probably the same individual who made a slight demonstration some twelve months ago to get the *ins*.

This is not altogather unexpected to me as I have long since been satisfied that I did not suit the scrub aristocracy of this region, and besides that I have been threatened recently with being turned out. I was born to poor. I am a plebian and Mechanic. This is a great offense to the Codfish.

I have no doubt but a strong petition will be sent up to you asking for my removal, and that it will be numerously signed by your old enemies—men who would now, as well as in the past, sacrafice you for their private or political interests—who have always denounced you and your supporters, and some of whom, no doubt, approved of the plot to assassinate you in 1861. Probably, the worst of these men, will have sagacity enough to withhold their names, while they prompt others to sign the paper. Some three or four weeks since, I had a quarrel with one E. C. Trigg, one of my Deputies, made so at the request of the Judge.[1] The quarrel was on account of his inattention to business and bad habits. I infer that this fresh movement to displace me is the result of that quarrel, because I know I greatly offended his dignity, and he then threatened to have me turned out. He now pretends to be a great friend to you, but while you was military Governor, he cursed and denounced you to my face. I would have dismissed him on the spot, but the circumstances that surrounded me prevented me from so doing. Although he is too trifling to couple with this communication, yet I do so from the fact, that I believe he has managed to get up this movement against me; and in order that you may be posted I mention the facts.

I suppose the petitioners will charge me with a little of every thing. I hope they will, just to make the matter interesting. Of course I cannot answer unknown charges. All I ask is fair play, and in the event the petition should be sent up to you, and before you act in the matter, I would respectfully ask that you give me a chance, and cause a copy of the charges to be sent to me, so that I may have an oportunity to defend myself, which I have no doubt, I can do successfully, as I am conscious of having done no wrong, intentionally either in my individual or official capacity. Probably, to give force and effect to their petition, they will charge that I am a Radical. If they do, it is false and they are liars. They may charge that I am incompetent. If they do that may be nearer the truth than the other. Judge Trigg, however, has complimented me on several occasions, by saying that he had a better set of Marshals in East Tennessee than any where else. The Clerk of the Court and District Attorney[2] as well as hundreds of others, can and will testify in my favor, if necessary. And the Records of the Court will bear witness of my efficiency as an Officer of the Court. The Third Auditor of the Treasury,[3] if consulted, might throw some light upon the subject.

I am free to say that I have performed my duty as well as any man could under the circumstances, for I have devoted my whole time, or nearly so, to my official duties. I was appointed through you first, and by you last, and on this account, I have endeavored to fill the bill, so that no reflections could be cast upon you on account of my inefficiency. I have not turned aside to meddle with or study politics, because I had no time to do so, and on this account I believe I have been suspected by both sides. The last political speech I heard, was delivered by you in 1864, a part of which only, I heard. I have not therfore kept myself posted in all the different phases of political matters. I thought it was enough for me to be an old fashioned union man and attend to my own business, and leave the rest to the wise men of the country.

My present political status is about as follows, to wit, I am and always have been opposed to the Freedmans Bureau and Negro equality, both political and social, and now in favor of Colonization as soon as possible. I have all the time said, that when a loyal representative presented himself for admission into the Congress of the U. States, he ought at once be admitted, no matter what state he might hail from.

I confess I do not understand the "Constitutional Amendments" as I have given them but little attention. I have heard some talk and speculation about them, and find that different interpretations are given. I have my own notions about them and that is this. If Congress seeks to have the power and control over the Negro franchise to the exclusion of the states, or in any other manner, not warranted by the Constitution, I stand opposed to all such assumptions of power. While the war was on hands war measures were necessary, and there was some excuse then for running over Law and Gospel in order to crush out the rebellion; but in peace, the Constitution and common sense ought to govern. There may be questions in controversy between the President and Congress of which I know nothing, but I am for right whenever I find it out.

And lastly, as to the Rebels, I have had great prejudices against them, especially toward the leaders, but the masses are not accountable for the rebellion. They were led or driven into it. Recently I have been among those who were in armed rebellion as well as citizen sympathisers, and have had frequent conversations with them and I find they are for peace and they say they will act in good faith toward supporting the Government, and I find on my recent trip, especially in Sullivan county, that [they] are quiet and seem to be well disposed. This has had the effect to lessen my prejudices against them.

These are my views, and I hope you will not consider them of such a radical character as to justify you in throwing me overboard. I would dislike very much to be turned out, by such a combination as I think exists against me at Knoxville. I am now in the midst of getting up the business for the Nov. term of the Court, and if I am to be thrown out at all, I hope the matter will be defered until after the Court adjourns.[4]

B. McDannel

ALS, DLC-JP.
1. Edward C. Trigg and Connally F. Trigg, respectively.
2. Major Leroy Hall and Crawford W. Hall, respectively. The former (1814–1899) had served for a number of years as clerk of the circuit court of Knox County prior to the Civil War. In 1864 he was appointed as clerk of the U.S. district court for the eastern district of Tennessee, a post he held until his resignation in 1870. Subsequently, Major Hall was elected judge of the criminal court of Knox County. John W. Green, *Bench and Bar of Knox County, Tennessee* (Knoxville, 1947), 47–48.
3. John Wilson (c1808–1876) was a native of Ireland who held several bureaucratic posts in the national government before becoming third auditor in 1864. After his tenure in the Treasury Department, Wilson became a claims agent and attorney. Lanman, *Biographical Annals*, 471; *Evening Star* (Washington), Jan. 11, 1876.
4. McDannel was not removed as marshal of the eastern district, despite his apprehensions. According to one source, Johnson was pleased with McDannel's position and views. See Absalom A. Kyle to Johnson, Dec. 5, 1866, Johnson Papers, LC; *U.S. Off. Reg.* (1867).

From Jeremiah Murphy[1]

Prairie du Chien Crawford Co Wisconsin
October 10th 1866

Dear President

On the 6th day of September I had the hapiness of Seeing and hearing your Excellencey in Chicago and for the awful offence of going to See the President, I have being deprived of My situation as clerk in the Rail Road office at prairie du Chien. I am now Set down as one of the Copper John- son dead ducks and all Such insulting and offensiv names for no other offence only because I Support the President of the U.S of America. Now Dear President Johnson I do most Respectfully ask you for an apoint- ment as American Consul to the City of Dublin or Cork or Wexford Ire- land. Being an Irish America Citizen and Knowing very well that Some of the American Consuls there are not doing thir duty to thir fellow Countrymen. Now Dear President if you Should not See proper to grant this apointment please grant me an apointment as Post Master in some P. O. office whare Some of the Rads now disgrace.

Haveing the honour to be Dear President your Dear Friend & strong supporter in your Present Policey.

Jeremiah Murphy

ALS, DNA-RG59, Lets. of Appl. and Recomm., 1861–69 (M650, Roll 35), Jeremiah Murphy.
1. Murphy (b. c1837), a native of Ireland, did not receive any of the requested positions, and by 1870 was once again a clerk in the railroad office at Prairie Du Chien. 1870 Census, Wisc., Crawford, Prairie Du Chien, 508.

From George W. Raff [1]

Canton, Stark Co. Ohio. Oct. 10, 1866.

President Johnson.

At the risk of appearing officious in addressing you again, I have con- cluded to present a few matters for your consideration.

We have been overwhelmingly defeated at the election held in this County, yesterday, and it is no more than what we who knew the current of public sentiment expected. Our candidate[2] for Congress was a man peculiarly odious to the people of the District by his extremely offensive course during the war; and irrespective of that, was a man of no influence, politically or otherwise. He was *worse* than a dead weight, as we who labored for the success of the party in the County learned to our sorrow. The mere fact that the Democracy of the District *could nominate such a man* was damaging in the extreme to the cause; and I have, myself, heard men say—democrats of life-long standing—that the nomination was a disgrace, and they could not support the man. Under such circum- stances, is it to be wondered at that he should be left in the rear of his ticket, and that we should be badly defeated?

But it may be asked why such a nomination was made? The simple reply is that there was not very much prospect, with a heavy majority in the District against us, of an election, and such men as McCook, Lahm,[3] and others who would have given respectability to the ticket did not de- sire the nomination, and so the nomination went by default. And we have this morning the mortifying reflection to be constantly present to our minds that had this nomination not been made we could at least have, in all probability, elected our County ticket.

I speak of these things in part for the purpose of putting you upon your guard with regard to the man. He induced the appointment of John R. Miller[4] for Collector of this District, a man who yesterday openly supported the Radical ticket; he has been laboring for the appointment of Peter Kaufman[5] as Postmaster at this place—a man who cannot carry a single vote but his own, and in whom community has no confidence—in preference to Gotshall,[6] a man who served his country in the late war, and who, as the publisher of a conservative Democratic newspaper, *has* influence.

I understand that Mr. Schaefer, and a few others who are equally obnoxious to the masses of the people, are now endeavoring to obtain the appointment of another person to the office of Collector. I can only say that I trust that if such is the case you will receive their efforts with suspicion, and make due inquiry before accepting and acting upon their suggestions.

The conservative Democracy of this County are endeavoring to induce Gen. S. Lahm to become a candidate for the Collectorship, and he will probably consent. Should he do so, it will be the very best appointment that could possibly be made. Mr. Lahm came out boldly as long ago as February last, and held a public meeting in the Court House, to sustain your administration, at a time when by so doing he brought down upon himself the abuse of Schaefer, the Editor of the Stark County Democrat, and others of the same ultra School. Even after the calling of the Philadelphia Convention these men denounced Lahm, myself and others, because we gave it our hearty support; and they only came into the measure when they found that they were left in a hopeless minority.

General Lahm not only is and has been your ardent friend during the present crisis; but possesses great influence in this County and District. He has been a prominent politician for many years; and I doubt whether any man within the District can exert as much influence favorable to your administration as he. He sat with you one term in Congress; and if any man deserves notice for warm and unflinching friendship for another, it is Gen. Lahm of you.

I may say further of Gen. Lahm that he was, during the war, a Conservative or War Democrat, making speeches in favor of suppressing the rebellion, and sacrificed two of his sons[7] for the country.

In closing, permit me to thank you for the noble and patriotic stand you have taken in support of the rights of the people, and the best interests of our common country. Time and history will do you justice, if the malignant passions of the men opposed to you will not. The very best Presidents we have ever had, the men who stand the very highest in the list, were the worst abused in their life-time. This consolation is left you amid the abuse and opprobrium that are heaped upon you. And in the hearts of the American people to-day you occupy a position which your maligners might well covet.

Geo. W. Raff.

ALS, DNA-RG56, Appts., Internal Revenue Service, Collector, Ohio, 17th Dist., Samuel Lahm.

1. Raff (1825–1888), a lawyer and former judge of the Stark County probate court, was the author of pension and other manuals. John Danner, ed., *Old Landmarks of Canton and Stark County, Ohio* (Logansport, Ind., 1904), 322–24.

2. Louis Schaefer (1815–1889), a native of France and a Canton resident since 1832, was a lawyer, avid Democrat, and frequent member of the city council, who strongly supported local economic development. During the war he was a member of a commission which went to Washington to demand the release of Clement L. Vallandigham, and in the congressional election of 1866 he was soundly defeated by a margin of over 4600 votes. Ibid., 1208–10; Poore, *Political Register*, 379.

3. George W. McCook and Samuel Lahm. McCook (1822–1877), a Steubenville resident and member of the famous "Fighting McCooks" family, was Edwin M. Stanton's law partner during the 1840s and 1850s, and a captain and colonel during the Mexican and Civil wars. He also served as state supreme court reporter and attorney general. Lahm (1812–1876), a Canton lawyer, had been an antebellum state senator, militia general, and congressman. Joseph B. Doyle, *20th Century History of Steubenville and Jefferson County, Ohio and Representative Citizens* (Chicago, 1910), 1096–97; *BDAC*.

4. Miller (1829–*fl*1881), a Canton businessman, was a grocer before switching to the dry goods trade. Schaefer had indeed helped him attain the appointment as collector of Ohio's Seventeenth District, but due to "bitter feeling" of the Republicans, Miller decided not to accept the position. William H. Perrin, ed., *History of Stark County, With an Outline Sketch of Ohio* (Chicago, 1881), 623; John R. Miller to Johnson, ca. October 1866, Appts., Internal Revenue Service, Collector, Ohio, 17th Dist., RG56, NA.

5. Kaufman (*c*1800–1869) edited German language newspapers and published a local almanac. He did not receive the postmastership. Danner, *Old Landmarks*, 1462–63; *U.S. Off. Reg.* (1865–67).

6. Martin Gotshall (*c*1838–1881), a private in the 43rd Ohio Inf., was editor of the *National Democrat* after the war. He did not become postmaster. 1860 Census, Ohio, Stark, Canton, 3rd Ward, 64; Pension File, Elizabeth P. Gotshall, RG15, NA; *Stark County Democrat*, Nov. 14, 1866; *U.S. Off. Reg.* (1867).

7. Probably Marshall (b.*c*1839) and Edward D. Lahm (*c*1841–1862), who served as privates in the 4th and 115th Ohio Inf., respectively. CSR, Marshall Lahm, Edward D. Lahm, RG94, NA.

From John Savage

private.

Fordham N.Y.   Oct. 10th 1866.

To The President.

I enclose your Excellency a letter to me from my friend King[1] of the New Orleans *Times*, which though private I deem it my duty to lay before you, and in connection with it, some facts which I would prefer to convey in person, but the complicated state of affairs in this Congressional district will not warrant my absence until after the Convention of the 18th inst.[2]

I naturally take a great interest in the Success of the N. O. *Times*, with which, as the opening of Mr. K's letter will suggest, I still hold connection.[3] In addition, Mr. K's energy, force of character, devotion to you personally and politically, of which I have already spoken to you, claim the most earnest consideration from your Excellency and those who stand by you on broad National grounds. It is such men as King who give that vitality to party which brings conviction home to the people. The persons opposing him in N. O. have no principle—save indeed Col. Nixon[4] who fought for his views in the Confederate ranks. They are completely selfish, and not to be depended upon in an emergency. When tools were scarce down there Mr. Chase used them, and they have since distinguished themselves more by the ability to desire, and the audacity to demand office; than the Capacity to deserve, or the useful virtues which might command it. Utterly without popular influence they have managed to keep up an outside show of organization by corrupt local coalitions which if allowed to continue will thoroughly demoralize the Nationality, manly spirit of justice, and faith which it is your desire should Characterize the Restoration. They are hollow and heartless, and their Antagonism to King is found in the wonderful energy and direct devotion to principle which have made him a power. Successful Industry always makes idle mediocrity jealous and malicious. They have now made a coalition by which the patronage and funds of the Marshal's and Treasurer's offices and the First National Bank can be used to Swamp King, whose business tact and clearness of political vision in identifying his journal with your faith has built up a great establishment.

The last thing I did before I went to New Orleans was to write a life of your Excellency for the Campaign.[5] Arrived in N. O. King and I became associates in the conduct of the *Times* on the same day. The paper earnestly advocated you there. I left in six months through the machinations of Mr. May,[6] their Asst. Treasurer, to get a Chase-man in my place. My Successor, soon found to be unequal to the task, is now the Asst. Treasurer.[7] May also thought to oust King for the same purpose but failed, and having been forced to sell out,[8] now strives by combination with U.S. Officials to crush the journal which has been & is the bulwark of your views in the South and South-West.

No one knows better than Mr. C. Bullitt the U.S. Marshal the character of the *Times* and its out-spoken devotion to you from before you were elected to the present. Yet he gives the printing patronage of his office to the *Picayune* which under Union *regime* had to be stopped for Anti-Union views. Then again the printing of the U.S. Laws is sedulously withheld from a conservative National Union Democrat who defended and upheld them through days of trial, and is given to one who during those same days labored for National Annihilation.

On the other hand the charges against Bullitt of corruption, levying enormous fees, using his official position for extortion &c &c fill the mouths of the New Orleans Merchants who pass through New York. They are clamorous for his removal—declare that the government is aware of the facts, and suggest the name of E. E. Norton or any other upright man for the Marshalship. In this connection, I learn on good authority that a Mr. Bouchard[9]—who says Bullitt extorted fourteen thousand dollars from him that he holds the proof and presented an affidavit of the fact to your Excellency on the 10th August last[10]—failing to draw attention to his case went to Massachusetts and was put in communication with Banks and Butler; that they eagerly entered into his affairs: advised him to keep quiet until the meeting of Congress when they would agitate it, demand a congressional investigation, and connect the President with Bullitt and his acts by tolerating both after being advised on oath of the stated facts. I never saw Bouchard and know him not, but deemed it my duty to note this programme; and waited in Washington three days after I heard it, but failed to see you through the pressure of visitors at the Executive Mansion.

The facts recounted rationally suggest two points—1st. That King should be sustained in an order directing the printing of the Marshal's office to his paper. 2nd That at this tremendous crisis important offices should not be in the hands of persons likely to create and add mean complications to the great but vexed questions in which the Administration is involved.

These are self-evident and must be admitted by your best and truest friends; among whom; as your Excellency must be aware there is not one who more fully appreciates your position, or who would do more to overcome its assailers, or expand its glory, than. . . .[11]

John Savage

ALS, DLC-JP.
1. The letter from William H.C. King has not been found.
2. The Democratic convention for New York's Tenth District met on October 18 and nominated William Radford for a third consecutive term. Savage was one of the secretaries for the convention. *New York Tribune*, Oct. 19, 1866.
3. In an earlier letter King had indicated that Savage was writing articles for the paper. King to Johnson, July 8, 1866, *Johnson Papers*, 10: 656.
4. James O. Nixon.
5. *Life and Public Services of Andrew Johnson* (1866). See King to Johnson, June 9, 1865, *Johnson Papers*, 8: 207.
6. Thomas P. May.
7. In the fall of 1866 attorney William R. Whitaker (*fl*1886) was strongly recommended for the position of assistant U.S. treasurer in New Orleans. He held that post perhaps continuously from then through the first half of 1867. Apparently he earlier had served briefly in 1865 as revenue collector. In August 1866 Whitaker attended the Philadelphia convention. He later was judge of the superior criminal court for four years (1877–80). Ser. 6B, Vol. 4: 202, 203, Johnson Papers, LC; New Orleans directories (1866–86); Appls., Asst. Treasurers and Mint Officers, New Orleans, William Whitaker, RG56, NA.
8. May was one of the co-owners of the *New Orleans Times* who sold his share of the paper to King. See King to Johnson, July 22, 1865, *Johnson Papers*, 8: 454; King to Johnson, Sept. 29, 1866, Johnson Papers, LC.
9. Adolph Bouchard.
10. According to Bouchard's account, he and the others involved in the agreement paid Cuthbert Bullitt $14,800, equal to one fifth of the amount of the cotton sale. Bouchard paid one quarter of the total, or about $3,575. See Adolph Bouchard to Johnson, Aug. 9, 1866.
11. For Bullitt's removal see King to Johnson, Nov. 6, 1866.

From Robert H. Whitfield[1]

(*Private*)

Smithfield Isle of Wight Co. Va.
Oto: 10 1866.

Sir.

I will indulge the hope, that you will bestow on this note a moments Consideration. Some time in July, or August 1865, I addressed an *appli-*

cation to you for a *pardon*.[2] It Contained (briefly) these facts. In 1860–
1861, during the agitation of the *fatal* question of secession, I spoke
against it in this and the adjacent Counties. I was elected to the Virginia
Convention (1861) as a *Union man*; and in that body spoke and voted
against secession. When the election, or nomination of Candidates for the
last Confederate Congress, was brought before the people, I was earnestly
solicited by men of all parties to allow my name to be used. I at first positively refused—alleging that I was no politician, and had no desire for
that kind of life, that my preference was for a quiet & retired life, with my
family &c. But representing that I, knew the wants of the people, having
suffered with them, by reason of the proceedings of some of our military
officers: I thought it my duty to yield, especially as the people must have
under any government, (de facto, or de jure), certain interests which
should be attended to. I furthermore stated to many of my friends, that I
must go untrammelled: and if I saw an opportunity of reconciling our
unhappy difficulties, I should use the influence of my position to secure a
result *so desirable*. I was elected in Consequence of my previous, Conservative Views—, took my seat, attended to the local interests of my Constituents, and finding there was no hope of reconciliation, after a few
weeks service resigned my seat, and came home to afford some protection
to my family liable to wrong and outrage as we all were, and to deplore
the wretched condition of our unhappy people. I started to see your Excellency in person in August 1865, but was assured that it was unnecessary, besides my health was quite feeble. I started again Nov. last, but
Gov. Pierpont[3] thought you would be so much Occupied, that an audience would probably not be granted to me. I waited until January last,
and got as far as Richmond, but was then told by some friends from
Washington, that *no pardons* would be granted for some time to members
of the Conferate Congress. I had again determined to call on you the past
month so soon as you returned from your Northern tour, but to be frank,
I had not the means of *travelling*, such is the wretched condition of our
once, happy & luxurious people. If it be agreeable to your Excellency, to
send my *Pardon*, the thanks of myself & family will in our hearts be rendered to you.[4] Probably it may be improper to touch upon political subjects; but permit me to say, that *you* have not only the sympathies, the
hearty support, feeble as it is, but the earnest prayers of us all, for your
health and your success in saving us from a doom worse than death; if the
Jacobins in Congress shall have full sway in their plans & schemes.

Ro: H. Whitfield
Smithfield Isle of Wight County Virginia.

ALS, DNA-RG94, Amnesty Papers (M1003, Roll 70), Va., Robert H. Whitfield.
    1. Whitfield (1814–1868) received his law degree in 1839 from the University of Vir-
ginia and began practicing in Smithfield. A Unionist member of the 1861 Virginia secession convention, Whitfield was elected to the Second Confederate House of Representatives from Virginia's Second District. Financially ruined by the war and in ill health, he
died in Smithfield in October 1868. Wakelyn, *BDC*; William H. Gaines, Jr., *Biographical*

Register of Members: Virginia State Convention of 1861, First Session (Richmond, 1969), 78–79.

2. See Whitfield to Johnson, July 1, 1865, Amnesty Papers (M1003, Roll 70), Va., Robert H. Whitfield, RG94, NA.

3. Francis H. Peirpoint.

4. Whitfield was pardoned November 14, 1866. See Amnesty Papers (M1003, Roll 70), Va., Robert H. Whitfield, RG94, NA.

From Charles O. Faxon

Louisville, Ky., Oct 11th 1866.

Dr Sir:

I have just been informed that Mr Hughes,[1] one of the editors and proprieters of the Louisville Democrat, is now an applicant for the Post Office in this City. But that the information reached me upon authority I could not question, I should have been slow to believe it; for after all that has occurred and with such a record as Hughes has made in the last year in connection with you and your administration; it is almost incredible that he should have the audacity to ask for an appointment from you. As I informed you on the Boat on our way up from this City to Cincinnati,[2] during the greater part of the year past the Louisville Democrat has been one of the most bitter and unreasonable opponents of your policy. It has given us of the Courier, who were defending that policy, more trouble than all other papers in Kentucky which were against it. It denounced that policy as unconstitutional and your acts as usurpations. It maintained until a few months since, that the Sherman Johnson treaty[3] was the only Constitutional mode of settleing the question. It entered the Coalition with the radicals of the State in the late Canvass and made unceasing war upon the democracy which was supporting you and which gave you and your policy near forty thousand majority.

Under these circumstances you will perceive that the appointment of Mr Hughes would be an undeserved censure of the only party in this state now sustaining you and upon which you must rely if you desire to be among your friends. We of the Courier feel that his appintment would be an undeserved rebuke to us who have stood by you and your policy from the first issue of our paper until the present time, and who intend to fight it out on that line.

If the Democrat is now your friend it is because we have pounded the true faith into it, and because it is not safe to be any where else. I make no suggestions as to who you should appoint, but I do hope that you will not afflict us with this man Hughes.

I wrote you several days since in regard to the Post Office at Clarksville and trust that you received the letter.[4]

The result of the elections has depressed us somewhat[5] but we still hope for the dawning of a more auspicious day. Our faith in you is strong and full and we say God speed you in your glorious work.

C. O. Faxon

ALS, DLC-JP.
    1. William E. Hughes (b. c1822), originally from Pennsylvania, was an editor of the
Louisville Democrat from the 1840s until 1868, when the paper closed. Hughes did not
become the Louisville postmaster; in fact, there is little evidence that he was a serious applicant for the job. 1860 Census, Ky., Jefferson, 2nd Dist., 160; J. Stoddard Johnston, ed.,
Memorial History of Louisville: From Its First Settlement to the Year 1896 (2 vols., Chicago,
1896), 2: 66; *U.S. Off. Reg.* (1865–69).
    2. Undoubtedly a reference to Johnson's journey from Louisville (September 11) up to
Cincinnati on September 12, all as part of the President's "swing around the circle."
    3. This is probably a reference to the agreement reached in April 1865 between Gen-
erals William T. Sherman and Joseph E. Johnston. The President opposed their agreement and sent General Grant to nullify it. See Jonathan T. Dorris, *Pardon and Amnesty
under Lincoln and Johnson* (Chapel Hill, 1953), 98–99.
    4. Records indicate that in early October Faxon wrote to the White House concerning
the Clarksville postmastership. See Ser. 6A, Vol. C: 78, Johnson Papers, LC.
    5. The Confederate-controlled Democratic party won strongly in the elections. See
Walter M. Haldeman to Johnson, Aug. 7, 1866.

From Maxwell P. Gaddis

Cincinnati, October 11 1866

Dear Sir

The battle in this County has been fought, and we are defeated.[1] Your friends here made a manly honorable fight, but failed to carry the day.

For one I cheerfully accept the situation, in view of the fact that their former majorities are much reduced. Thus far the majority of people is against your plan of reconstruction. This arises more however from the prejudices and passions of your opponents, (stirred up through certain members of Congress) than from any convictions that the plans of Congress are preferable to your own. They are much elated over their victory.

I understand that Mr. Eggleston[2] said last evening that he was willing to assist in your impeachment. Impeach you for what? Let them answer the question before they dare talk of impeachment. I trust they will not attempt this—if they do, your friends here will stand by you, we therefore have to acquiesce in the will of the people as expressed at the ballot box, provided said expression does not mean the impeachment of the President.

If it does, then we do not submit.

During all the struggle to re-construct and restore the Union—I have hoped and prayed for harmony between your Excellency and Congress—and that—'ere your term of Office expired, the two great potential powers would be seen standing side by side rejoicing together over a re-constructed—a restored Union.

I am now satisfied that Congress—owing to its late victories will be more vindictive than ever. On reassembling they will seek to overcome you, and drive you from your position, failing to accomplish that, they may try their hand at impeachment.

They cannot succeed in doing either without increasing our present troubles. If however as some of their friends have predicted, they evince a disposition to close up our troubles in a less vindictive or malignant manner then I trust you may see your way clear, to co-operate with them, and thus close up the struggle. Do not understand me Mr. President, as yielding up my position as expressed during the late campaign, far from it. The proposed amendment will not settle the difficulty, and until Congress presents a plan whereby all the States in the Union shall be represented in the Union according to the Constitution, and the existing laws of the land, I will adhere to my present position.

May the God of all wisdom and grace lead you by his counsel, and nerve you for these hours of trial.

M. P. Gaddis

ALS, DLC-JP.
1. The October 9, 1866, election in Hamilton County resulted in Democratic defeats in every contest, whether state or local. The county margins against the Democratic congressional candidates in the First and Second districts were 980 and 2612, respectively. *Cincinnati Commercial*, Oct. 10, 1866.
2. Benjamin Eggleston, who had just been reelected to Congress.

From Daniel Watrous[1]

Lyons, Wayne Co.   New York   Oct 11th 1866

Your excellency!

Pardon me for asking if it can be even possible that Congress has the power to dissolve the Union! It has succeeded, for eight months, in keeping the south out, and can keep the states unrepresented for eight years, if there be any doubts concerning its right to do so.

If the position of the radical majority is the true one, then the Constitution is a failure, and you are not bound to obey its behests, and all the blood and agonies of the battle fields of the Union, have been given in vain. If *not* true, then the course of Congress is *revolution* and *rebellion*, and you are as much bound to put it down as was Abraham Lincoln bound to wage the war to suppress the late rebellion.

I see but one resort left under the Constitution, to preserve the Union from the evils of dissolution. You are sworn to *preserve, protect,* and *defend the Constitution*, as well as to *transmit it to your successor even as you received it from Your predecessor*, and from this fact it becomes patent that if *Congress interferes to prevent your preservation of the Constitution*, it becomes an enemy to the *peace and well being of the government, and the people living under it*, and your duty impels you to put down all attempts to "alienate one portion of the Common Country from the rest."

You are Commander-in-chief of the army and navy. This power was given to the President to enable him to "repel invasion and suppress domestic revolution." It matters not where it occurs, whether in the states or in co-ordinate branches of the government, by majorities or minor-ities. Its intent was to secure every individual, as well as every state, their rights under the great Charter of Rights, including the right of representation in Congress, which, under the Constitution it is strictly prohibited from denying. This Constitution describes the qualifications of members. Congress has the right to judge no farther than to see that members claiming seats are duly elected, and are of the age of twenty five years, and have been citizens of the United States for the period of seven years. There ends the powers of Congress. They cannot go to the extreme, by refusing an examination of credentials, because if they do, they themselves become traitors and enemies to the rights of the states and the peoples thereof. Such a course, on the part of the sitting members surely is *revolution* if not *treason*. Truly it is against the dignity of the Commonwealth, and that is treason.

I know that the great tribulation of the hour is, to see whether republican institutions shall stand or fall. The trial, on the part of the president, is much more severe than to wage a bloody war for years, but I am satisfied the president is as fully equal to the task as his great prototype and predecessor, Andrew Jackson, (for whom I cast my first presidential vote.)

Mr. President! This cry for the Union by men who are filled to the uttermost with the rankest of disunion sentiments, and its sole object has been to hold on to power. It is all mere pretence. With the class of men now following the radical leaders, is simply party power in preference to Country. If not for power then it is bigotry, of which it has been aptly said: "Bigotry has no head, she cannot think. No heart, she cannot feel."[2]

I know the president understands it all.

Please pardon this intrusion.

Daniel Watrous

ALS, DLC-JP.
1. Watrous (b. *c*1802) was a merchant and a native of Connecticut. 1860 Census, N.Y., Wayne, Lyons, 345.
2. Of undetermined origin.

From Dempsey Weaver

Nashville, Oct 11th 1866

Dear Sir

The Philadelphia Stockholders of the Planters Bank, through Evans Rogers[1] Esq of that City, are urging me to Sue on all claims due the Bank, so as to close up the affairs of the Bank as speedily as possible. In your case I am unwilling to proceed without giving you due notice, and making you what I believe to be a liberal proposition for the settlement of the claim and one that I hope you will accept at once.

If you will pay me the face of the Bill, say Twenty Thousand Dollars, in the Notes of this Bank I will recieve it in full payment. These Notes can now be purchased at about 83 on the Dollar or I will recive from you Twenty Tennessee Six per Cent Bonds of $1000 each in paymt of the claim. The Bonds can now be purchased in New York at 72 to 75 on the Dollar.

Please let me heare from you on the subject on recipe of this.[2]

With my best wishes for your health happiness and success. . . .

D Weaver

ALS, DLC-JP.

1. Rogers (*fl*1872) was listed as a "gentleman." Philadelphia directories (1867–72).

2. There may have been an earlier response from Johnson, but the only extant one is a telegram from Johnson to Weaver, October 24, 1866, in Tels. Sent, President, Vol. 3 (1865–68), RG107, NA. In it the President expressed the hope that the financial matters could soon be "adjusted." Several communications were exchanged between Johnson and his Nashville financial connections during the next few weeks. See, for example, Johnson to Joseph W. Allen, Oct. 24, 1866; Johnson to Michael Burns, Oct. 24, 1866; and Dempsey Weaver to Johnson, Oct. 31, 1866.

From Edwin C. Wilson[1]

Erie, Penna. Oct 11, 1866

Honored Sir—

We have just got through our campaign in Pennsylvania, and we are only defeated by a few majority in the State. Our radical opponents may say with the Roman General "another such a victory and we are ruined."[2] The result of this election is a substantial victory for *you*—and had the *only* issue been with us, Congress or the President, *you* would have Swept the State. Thousands who were your friends could not be induced to vote for Clymer and other Anti-War Democrats.

In the contest they will now force upon you the *people* of this State will stand by you, and will not permit the Constitution to be overturned, and yourself impeached. Gen. Butler's programme to that purpose has aroused universal condemnation.

I have held several high positions in this State, and I know the people well, and as your personal and political friend, I ask you to stand firm in the right, and you will be triumphantly maintained, and history will record your name as the great "Defender of the Constitution."

Ever ready, myself, to defend you from all enemies. . . .

Edwin C. Wilson

ALS, DLC-JP.

1. Wilson (b. 1820) had read law under Edwin M. Stanton in Steubenville, Ohio, where he practiced his profession before relocating to Pennsylvania and serving as state adjutant general and quartermaster general on the eve of the war. Jordan, *Allegheny Valley*, 2: 673.

2. Actually "Another such victory over the Romans, and we are undone," as attributed to Pyrrhus, King of Epirus, in Plutarch's *Lives: Pyrrhus*.

From Francis A. Abbot[1]

Phila. Oct 12th 1866

As the Correspondent of the Ledger of this city for the past 21 years, I beg leave to address you a few words in reference to the telegram which appeared in that paper Thursday morning 11th instant with reference to certain "purported questions" that had been put by you to the Attorney Gen'l.[2]

My central office from whence I have telegraphed ramifications to all parts of the country is at New York. There I receive Washington and all other news of interest in the papers which I represent.

The particular dispatch to which I now allude, is that having reference to the President and the 39th Congress. Those alleged "questions" were forwarded to me by Mr Henry M Flint[3] of Washington, and received by me in good faith on the morning of Wednesday.

The precision and care with which they were written, and the positive manner in which they were stated, there being no preface of "it is rumored"—"it is reported" &c convinced me at once that they were perfectly genuine, and on this belief and the known character of Mr Flint to the writer for carefullness and correctness in his statements, I forwarded the dispatch along with others to The Ledger.

That the Proprietor of The Ledger, Mr Geo W. Childs was therefore wholly innocent in the use of the despatch and entirely free from the blame of any known fabrication is perfectly apparent. And the same remark will apply to the writer of these lines who forwarded it to The Ledger after its receipt from Mr Flint, his correspondent at Washington.[4]

I have other correspondents also at Washington besides Mr Flint. Geo. W. Adams is a regular one, and J N. Ashley[5] an occasional one. I have also received dispatches from Mr Bartlett.[6]

Occasionally the information I receive from Washington is sent by mail (when it will *keep*) and when not by telegraph. In the case under consideration (the "questions") they were forwarded by mail as I find this an additional security against the "depredations" of some not over honest Telegraphers.

(Signed) J[*sic*] A. Abbott[*sic*]

P.S. In response to Telegrams I forwarded to Washington[7] with reference to the *Canard* on the day it appeared I received ten (?) despatches confirming or pretending to, the false statements that had been made, and I also saw in the hands of a leading Banking House on Wall Street, a despatch from their own House in Washington asserting that the reported questions were probably correct.[8]

Copy, DLC-JP.
    1. Abbott (*fl*1867) is listed in city directories as an editor. His letter was among a larger group of documents which were delivered to the White House on Saturday, October 13, 1866, by the *Ledger*'s editor-in-chief, William V. McKean. New York City directories (1866–67); *National Intelligencer*, Oct. 15, 1866; George W. Childs to Robert Johnson,

Oct. 13, 1866; McKean to Robert Johnson, Oct. 13, 1866, Abbot to Johnson, Apr. 11, 1868, Johnson Papers, LC.

2. According to the Associated Press report, the President had asked the attorney general to issue written opinions on five interrogatories, namely: 1) Whether the 39th Congress, without southern representatives, was a legally constituted body; 2) Would the President be justified in withholding his next annual message from such an assemblage; 3) What constitutional right does Congress have to exclude the southern representatives; 4) Is the President empowered by the Constitution to see to it that the southern representatives are admitted to Congress; and 5) What specific action is the President authorized to take to ensure that Congress *is* legally constituted. Owing to the nature of the report, it appeared in numerous newspapers across the country. A manuscript copy is available in Johnson Papers, LC. See also Frederic Hudson, *Journalism in the United States, From 1690 to 1872* (Grosse Point, Mich., 1968 [1873]), 513–14.

3. Flint (1829–1868), a Washington correspondent for the *New York News*, *Chicago Times*, and New Orleans *Picayune*, also wrote a biography of Stephen A. Douglas and histories of Mexico and U.S. railroads. *NCAB*, 4: 278; *House Reports*, 40 Cong., 1 Sess., No. 7, "Impeachment Investigation," pt. 2, p. 45 (Ser. 1314).

4. In his sworn testimony before Congress during the impeachment investigation several months later, Flint claimed that he did not know that Abbot represented the *Ledger* or that the newspaper would publish his "news" item. Ibid., p. 46.

5. Adams (1838–1886) was a Washington correspondent for various papers, including the *Cincinnati Enquirer*, the Philadelphia *Bulletin*, the New Orleans *Picayune*, and the New York *World*. He later acquired an interest in the Washington *Evening Star* and gave up all other work to concentrate on that paper. James N. Ashley (*fl*1867), who had formerly worked for the *New York Herald*, appears to have left the District not long after this incident. *NCAB*, 15: 371–72; Washington, D.C., directories (1864–67).

6. Philip Bartlett, otherwise unidentified.

7. See the Abbot-Flint exchanges of October 11, 12, 1866, Johnson Papers, LC.

8. Still seeking confirmation after the report had been published, George Childs sent an urgent dispatch to the White House. Robert Johnson assured him that the report was false, whereupon Childs ordered a thorough investigation. Soon, the *Ledger* published a retraction of its report and declared that it had been deceived by Flint, who had obviously manufactured the story. When Congress conducted its own investigation several months later during the impeachment hearings, Flint admitted his fabrication. Attorney General Stanbery later claimed that the President had never forwarded any such questions to him. Hudson, *Journalism*, 514; *New York Herald*, Oct. 12, 1866; *Evening Star* (Washington), Oct. 13, 1866; *National Intelligencer*, Oct. 15, 16, 1866; *House Reports*, 40 Cong., 1 Sess., No. 7, "Impeachment Investigation," pt. 2, pp. 46–51, 419–20 (Ser. 1314); Robert Johnson to George W. Childs, Oct. 11, 13, 1866, Tels. Sent, President, Vol. 3 (1865–68), RG107, NA. See also the many statements and letters by Abbot, Flint, and McKean, as well as telegrams from and to Childs, all in Johnson Papers, LC.

From Pierre G.T. Beauregard

Washington   Willard's Hotel   October 12th 1866

Sir—

I have the honor to report my return to the United States from Europe.[1] I would be happy to present my respects in person to your Excellency, if you could find it convenient to receive me.[2] I will probably remain in Washington (on my way to New Orleans) until the 14th inst.

G. T. Beauregard

ALS, DLC-JP.

1. Beauregard arrived in Washington at noon on October 12. *Evening Star* (Washington), Oct. 12, 1866. See Johnson to J. Madison Wells, May 5, 1866, *Johnson Papers*, 10: 479–80.

2. Beauregard met with both Johnson and Grant in an effort to secure his pardon as well as the return of twelve trunks and boxes of personal belongings and papers that had been captured by Wilson's cavalry after Beauregard had surrendered at Greensboro, North Carolina. In November 1866 he received one trunk and one box of "private baggage" and miscellaneous books, and was "sadly disappointed in not receiving my letter books and papers." Beauregard was not pardoned until the amnesty proclamation in July 1868. T. Harry Williams, *P.G.T. Beauregard: Napoleon in Gray* (Baton Rouge, 1955), 260–61; Beauregard to Grant, Oct. 15, 1866; Beauregard to C. L. Sayre, Nov. 16, 1866, Beauregard Papers, LC.

From J. H. Black[1]

Private

                                        Pine Bluff, Arkansas, October 12th 1866.
Sir,

I have no office or favor to ask at your hands, but admiring your patriotic policy, and feeling an abiding faith in its ultimate triumph, I venture to make a suggestion for what it may be worth. When in New Orleans last winter, I met several of Gen John A Logan's intimate friends—also some of Gen Shridan's. These officers were then represented to be warmly in favor of the speedy reconstruction of the rebel states, because they hoped to be able *to lead their veteran legions into Mexico.*

The idea has often occurred since then that a foreign war was the only escape from a domestic broil, and that the thwarted ambition of these chieftains in this direction accounts for their subsequent opposition to your policy. Would it not be better to yield to this *war feeling* and retain the affection of the army? It would be a Godsend to Mexico to extend the protectorate of the United States over that factious country, and a bold and aggressive foreign policy might unite all parties in support of the administration.

With the remark that boldness is often the highest prudence, I submit the practicability of the above suggestion to your superior judgment and experience.

                                                                J H Black

ALS, DLC-JP.
1. Possibly James H. Black (b. *c*1846) of Tennessee who later ran a livery stable in Gray, Arkansas. 1870 Census, Ark., White, Gray, 325.

From Ulysses S. Grant

                                        Washington, D.C.   Oct. 12th 1866.
Sir:

Enclosed please find report of Bvt. Brig. Gen. C. B. Comstock[1] of the result of his inspection to ascertain whether any Military Organizations were forming, or being designed, in the state of Tennessee threatening the peace or security of the inhabitants of the State.[2] I am pleased to see that no cause for apprehension exists, at least for the present.

U.S. Grant   General

ALS, DLC-JP.
1. Cyrus B. Comstock (1831–1910) held several different ranks and duties during the Civil War, including being an aide to General Grant. He was brevetted brigadier general in the regular army in March 1865 and remained in the army until his retirement in 1895. The report indicated Comstock's findings after a visit to Nashville (authorized in September by Grant), where military authorities professed no knowledge of any quasi-military organizations being formed. Moreover, reported Comstock, blacks were "entirely quiet and not in the least threatening." He conversed with a number of prominent persons who assured him that they anticipated no troubles prior to the gubernatorial election in the summer of 1867; they expressed concerns about a proposed convention to be held with the intention of establishing a government that would supersede the Brownlow administration. Comstock found that the only indication of any arming of citizens was contained in Brownlow's speeches. Hunt and Brown, *Brigadier Generals*; Comstock to Grant, Oct. 12, 1866, Johnson Papers, LC; Grant to Comstock, Sept. 24, 1866, Simon, *Grant Papers*, 16: 314–15.
2. Several days prior to his formal report, Comstock had telegraphed Grant to the effect that authorities were not expecting trouble and therefore had not increased the regular force. Governor Brownlow was opposed to any proposal for federal troops to be sent into the state. Comstock to Grant, Oct. 7, 1866, ibid., 314.

From Henry Stanbery

Attorney General's Office,
October 12, 1866.

Sir,

I have the honor to state my opinion upon the question propounded in your letter of the 6th,[1] as to what further may be proper or expedient to be done by the Executive in reference to the custody of Mr. Davis, and the prosecution for treason now pending against him in the Circuit Court of the United States for Virginia.

I am clearly of opinion that there is nothing in the present condition of Virginia to prevent the full exercise of the jurisdiction of the civil courts. The actual state of things, and your several proclamations of peace and of the restoration of civil order guaranty to the civil authorities, Federal and State, immunity against military control or interference. It seems to me that in this particular there is no necessity for further action on the part of the Executive in the way of proclamation—especially as Congress at the late session required the Circuit Court of the United States to be held at Richmond on the first Monday of May and the fourth Monday of November in each year, and authorized special or adjourned terms of that Court to be ordered by the Chief Justice of the Supreme Court, at such time and on such notice as he might prescribe, with the same power and jurisdiction as at regular terms.[2]

This is an explicit recognition by Congress that the state of things in Virginia admits the holding of the United States Courts in that State.

The obstruction you refer to, it seems to me, cannot be removed by any Executive order. So far as I am advised it arises as follows:

Congress on the 22nd of May 1866, passed an act providing that the Circuit Court of the United States for Virginia should be held at Richmond on the first Monday of May, and on the fourth Monday of November in each year; and further providing that all suits and other proceedings which stand continued to any other time and place should be deemed continued to the place and time prescribed by the act. The special or adjourned session which was ordered by the court to be holden at Richmond in the present month of October was considered as abrogated by force of this act.

This left the regular term to be holden on the fourth Monday of November; and if there had been no further legislation by Congress, no doubt could exist as to the competency of the Chief Justice[3] and the District Judge[4] of that Court then to try Mr. Davis. But on the 23d of July 1866, Congress passed an act to fix the number of Judges of the Supreme Court of the United States and to change certain judicial circuits.[5] Among other changes in the circuits made by this act, is a change of the fourth circuit to which the Chief Justice had been allotted. As this circuit stood prior to this Act, when allotted to the Chief Justice, it embraced Delaware, Maryland, Virginia, North Carolina and West Virginia. It was changed by this act by excluding Delaware and adding South Carolina.

It is understood that doubts exist whether this change in the States composing the circuit will not require a new allotment. Whether this doubt is well founded or not, it is certain that the Executive cannot interfere; for although under peculiar circumstances, the Executive has power to make an allotment of the Judges of the Supreme Court, yet these circumstances do not exist in this case. A new allotment, if necessary, can only be made by the Judges of the Supreme Court, or by Congress— perhaps only by Congress.

Mr. Davis remains in custody at Fortress Monroe precisely as he was held in January last, when in answer to a resolution of Congress, you reported communications from the Secretary of War and the Attorney General,[6] showing that he was held to await trial in the civil courts. No action was then taken by Congress in reference to the place of custody. No demand has since been made for his transfer into civil custody. The District Attorney of the United States for the District of Virginia,[7] where Mr. Davis stands indicted for treason, has been notified that the prisoner would be surrendered to the United States Marshal[8] upon a capias under the indictment, but the District Attorney declines to have the capias issued because there is no other place within the District where the prisoner could be so safely kept, or where his personal comfort and health could be so well provided for. No application has been made within my knowledge by the Counsel for Mr. Davis for a transfer of the prisoner to civil custody. Recently an application was made by his counsel for his transfer from Fortress Monroe to Fort Lafayette on the ground chiefly, of sanitary considerations. A reference was promptly made to a board of surgeons, whose report was decidedly adverse to the change on the score of health and personal comfort.

I am unable to see what further action can be taken on the part of the Executive to bring the prisoner to trial. Mr. Davis must for the present remain where he is, until the Court which has jurisdiction to try him shall be ready to act, or until his custody is demanded under lawful process of the Federal Courts.

I would suggest that, to avoid any misunderstanding on the subject, an order issue to the commandant of Fortress Monroe[9] to surrender the prisoner to civil custody whenever demanded by the United States Marshal upon process from the Federal Courts.

I send herewith copy of a letter from the United States District Attorney for Virginia,[10] to which I beg to call your attention.

Henry Stanbery   Attorney General.

LS, DLC-JP.
    1. Johnson to Stanbery, Oct. 6, 1866.
    2. See *U.S. Statutes at Large*, 14: 51–52.
    3. Salmon P. Chase.
    4. John C. Underwood.
    5. See *U.S. Statutes at Large*, 14: 209.
    6. See *Senate Ex. Docs.*, 39 Cong., 1 Sess., No. 7, pp. 1–4 (Ser. 1237), for Johnson's transmittal on January 5 of Stanton's and Speed's reports.
    7. Lucius H. Chandler.
    8. John Underwood, nephew of John C. Underwood, though not further identified, was an abolitionist and did not approve of the President's policy. *OR*, Ser. 1, Vol. 21, p. 696; Underwood to Charles Knap, Sept. 27, 1866, Appt. Files for Judicial Dists., Va., Thomas C. Pratt, RG60, NA.
    9. Henry S. Burton (1818–1869) became commander of the fort after Nelson A. Miles was relieved of duty on September 1. Strode, *Jefferson Davis*, 291–92; Hunt and Brown, *Brigadier Generals*.
    10. The enclosure was an October 8 letter Chandler wrote Stanbery in order to answer his question, "Why no demand had been made upon the military authorities for the surrender of Jefferson Davis, in order that he might be tried upon the Indictment found against him in the United States Circuit Court, at the Term held at Norfolk, in May last." Chandler asserted that at a state jail Davis's safe custody could not be secured without great expense and that his health would suffer.

From Hiram Ketchum, Jr.[1]

Washington D.C.   Oct. 13. 1866

I am about to leave the City and enclose to you the accompanying suggestions with an earnest desire that you may *read* them.[2] I mingle with the people to a great extent and know their feeling. The radicals are appealing to the passions of the people with success. Why not use a *counter-irritant*? Do not allow yourself to be persuaded that there is no danger. There *is* danger. A bold action on the part of the Executive which will turn the excitement in a new direction will rob the radicals of their arms. If you can in a justifiable manner create it, why not do so? Be an *Andrew Jackson*. Resolve to win by the use of every point within your Constitutional power. I for one will stand by you; the people will stand by you.

I have not in these suggestions attempted to study grammatical construction. I send you the original draft through the hands of my friend Col: Frank.[3] I am fearfully in earnest, am addressing the people every night and I know that if we can have a sensational topic in our favor in the North, we can yet succeed. But the action must be immediate.

Excuse the assumption of this letter. The good of the cause, in which I have a deep interest, is my apology. It is not for the files but for your personal inspection.[4]

Hiram Ketchum Jr.

ALS, DLC-JP.

1. Ketchum (*fl*1881), an attorney, had seen Johnson on October 8 in reference to his bid to become general appraiser of merchandise for New York. Unsuccessful in that attempt, he later applied for a deputy collector's post in the New York customhouse; eventually Ketchum was nominated by Johnson (but was not confirmed by the Senate) as collector of customs for the district of Alaska. New York City directories (1869–81); Ketchum to Hugh McCulloch, Oct. 9, 1866; Ketchum to Johnson, Mar. 26, 1867, Appts., Customs Service, Naval Officer, New York, Hiram Ketchum, Jr., RG56, NA; Ser. 6B, Vol. 4: 399, Johnson Papers, LC.

2. Ketchum's "suggestions" warned of Johnson's all-but-certain impeachment, unless the President were to recommend the adoption of the Fourteenth Amendment or to declare war against Great Britain.

3. Paul Frank (1828–1875) was a former colonel of the 52nd N.Y. Inf. and brevet brigadier general to whom Johnson gave a consular post in Japan. Unable to deliver Ketchum's letter and enclosure in person, Frank forwarded both from Washington with his pledge of support in the forthcoming contest in New York. Hunt and Brown, *Brigadier Generals*; Frank to Johnson, Oct. 13, 1866, Johnson Papers, LC; Ser. 6B, Vol. 2: 90, ibid.

4. Some two weeks later Ketchum gave a speech in the Masonic Hall in New York City, in which he defended the President and his restoration policy and predicted that John T. Hoffman would win the gubernatorial election by a sizeable majority. *New York Times*, Oct. 26, 1866.

From James R. Doolittle

Private

Green Bay [Wis.]   Oct 14" 1866.

Sir:

I take a deep and special interest in the Case of Young Lieutenat L. Martin,[1] of Green Bay in Wisconsin. I join in urgently requesting that he may be allowed to be restored to the Army. He is a splendid young man, was a most excellent Officer, and has been educated at West Point.[2]

His father[3] once represented Wisconsin in Congress and is now in nomination by the National Union & Democratic Convention for Congress, and we hope we shall Carry this District.[4] I am now here at Green Bay in the Canvass and not altogether discouraged although we have not

Carried the October Elections. We hope we shall carry 3 out of six Districts, and have a fair chance to carry the Legislature.[5] Had Penn, Indiana & Ohio gone for us, we should certainly have Carried Wisconsin.

As it is we shall have a harder fight and the result is not certain. The course of the Times & Herald and some other Causes have operated against us.

But the triumph in the end of the great principle for which we contend is certain.

J. R. Doolittle

ALS, DLC-JP.

1. Leonard Martin (c1839–1890) graduated from West Point in May 1861 and promptly became an artillery lieutenant. He served in that post until April 1865, when he became colonel of the 51st Wis. Vols., a position he held only until mustered out in August 1865. Martin resigned from the regular army in April 1866. *West Point Register*, 255; Powell, *Army List*, 455.

2. Martin was not reappointed to the regular army. Ibid.

3. Lawyer Morgan L. Martin (1805–1887), a New Yorker who moved to Green Bay, Wisconsin, in 1827, and was a member of the Michigan and Wisconsin territorial legislatures and the Wisconsin state legislature. He served a single term in the U.S. House of Representatives (1845–47). During the Civil War he was a Union paymaster, and later an Indian agent (1866–69) and county judge (1875–87). *BDAC*.

4. Martin was not elected. Ibid.

5. The Democrats elected only one congressman. In the state senate they carried eleven out of thirty-three seats and in the state house, twenty-six of one hundred seats. *American Annual Cyclopaedia* (1866), 772.

From David M. Fleming

[Washington, D.C.]   Oct. 14, [186]6

Sir:

This day (14th Oct.) three years ago the writer of this note formed the following ticket and sent it to the World through the columns of his Journal months in advance of all papers, and had the satisfaction of seeing his suggestions carried out in the Baltimore Convention in June 1864, seven months afterwards. The ticket was as follows:

OUR TICKET FOR 1864
For President.
ABRAHAM LINCOLN
of Illinois.
For Vice President
ANDREW JOHNSON
The Patriot of Tennessee.

Three years later (Oct 14th 1866) the writer of this note left Washington for his home to give up a position he held under the Administration, given to him especially for his former act and for his continued friendship for Andrew Johnson, by *order* of the *President*.

I have no complaints to make, but were I in Andrew Johnson's place

and he in mine, every officer in the Government should go before he
should be deprived of his position.

For the truth of what I state above I refer to Col. Granville Moody and
every citizen of Piqua and Western Ohio. In conclusion, Mr. President,
permit me to express to you my earnest wish for your continued good
health and that your Administration may prove a blessing to the country,
and that you may retire with the plaudits of your countrymen.

For what you have done for me, although but little, I shall never cease
my friendship. Fleming *never forgets a friend under any circumstances.*
Good bye.

                                                                    D M Fleming

P.S. It would afford me some pleasure while laboring under the depres-
sion of a removal from my position, by one that I regarded my particular
friend to receive a kind note from him if for nothing more than to show
that his former acts are *appreciated.*

ALS, DLC-JP.

From Charles J. Jenkins

                                        Milledgeville, Ga., 14th Oct, 1866

Honored Sir

I address you with some hesitation upon a subject about which, I fear
you may think, I ought not to concern myself. Nevertheless, it has
pressed long and heavily on my mind and I have given much thought to it
in its political bearings and to the propriety or impropriety of intermed-
dling with it. I allude to the long continued imprisonment of Mr Davis.
Whilst there remained a hope that so soon as the Federal judicatories in
the State of Virginia could be reorganized a speedy and fair trial would be
given him, fully impressed with the delicate and responsible duties of
your position I felt that silence became Southern men and Southern officials. But now that reorganization has been effected—that the preliminary step of placing on the files of the proper Court a bill of indictment
against him has been taken, his trial is postponed from time to time, and
there is a seeming indisposition on the part of the Judiciary to take con-
gnizance of his case, (he being all the while anxious for a trial)—and understanding that there will certainly be no hearing until an advanced period of the next year, I venture upon approaching you in frankness but
with all possible respect.

The question to which I ask your attention is, ought Mr Davis to be
longer kept in close confinement?

I think you will concede, Mr President, that although, at the last, aiding in and advising the attempted measure of Secession, Mr Davis came
to it slowly and reluctantly—that he, in earnest words, the utterance of

deep feeling, urged the Senate to take what he deemed appropriate action, to avert the catastrophe. His last appeal to that Body must have satisfied all who heard or read it that his affections still clung about the Union.

Now as to the part he subsequently acted. It is an accepted fact at the South that he did not seek the prominent position he occupied, but was sought for it, by the general voice. From that time to the closing scene, he was, in that terribly tragic drama, but a Representative man. There were many, very many far more active and influential than he in goading the masses on to secession, who are now at large in the enjoyment of personal freedom and security. I allude to these as considerations proper to be weighed, by those who condemn him most, in mitigation of any imputed criminality, not as reasons for his exoneration without trial. If it be deemed by Federal Authorities that his position of itself, in legal or political contemplation made him the head and front of the offending, and requires that in his person the majesty of the law shall be vindicated, so let it be. I do not understnd that *he* desires to evade a trial. It is against the rigor of longer imprisonment, in his old age and injured health that I, assuming to speak for a vast majority of the People of Georgia, now appeal to your Excellency.

The U.S. Judiciary, fully aware that nothing more than a formal application is needed, to transfer him from your custody to theirs, elect to leave him in your hands, therby virtually fastening upon you whatever of unpleasnat reflection, or unfriendly criticism, may in the future grow out of death in prison, without legally established guilt. I know, Sir, full well that you retire before no rightfully imposed responsibility and it is that knowledge, pervading all classes, that causes the unhappy South, now to lean upon and to confide in you. I know that the case, like almost every great movement since the cessation of hostilities, is anomilous. And it is in that view, that I respectfully inquire, whether, seeing that the Prisoner is de facto in your custody, and that the Judiciary will not place themselves in such relation to him, as will justify an application to them for enlargment according to law, you will not put him upon his parole or on Bail to appear and answer the charge against him.

I doubt not he could give reliable bail to any amount that would be asked. I most respectfully make this plea in his behalf. Mr. President, sincerely trusting that if the communication itself or any word in it, be offensive to you, you will excuse it, as the prompting of thorough conviction, and profound feeling, possibly erroneous, but certainly free from all taint of disrespect for yourself, or indifference to your official responsibilities.

Charles J. Jenkins

ALS, DLC-JP.

From John N. Cochran[1]
Private

Washington City, D.C.   [ca. 15] Oct 1866[2]
Mr. President:

Will you allow a Stranger but a Supporter of yours, to write you a few words.

I wish to state that I am a conservative not a democrat. As all know, the course of the Democratic party during the whole of the War was most odious to all Union men, and the name of democrat, generally, was understood to be but another name for Secession and I did hope that the action of the Phila. Convention would result in burying the name so deep that it would never be resurrected by its present adherents, but most unfortunately the Convention took no measure to get rid of this rallying word so hateful to loyal men, took no measures what ever to fuse the two parties under a common and a different title but left the whole at loose ends to work as it might, and the consequence has been that, generally, and almost everywhere "*Democracy*," is the rallying cry in opposition to "*Radicalism*" instead of "National Union" or something equivalent, and every one felt that if the Radicals were defeated it would be heralded as a great Democratic victory, and these facts would necessarily keep thousands from voting with the Conservative side. Can you doubt it? I was always a democrat before this war, but, in common with yourself and thousands others acted with them no more during our struggle, and, I assure you, that *I* feel just as I have stated, and never want to hear this detested name again. And it does seem that the democrats are not only possessed of no modesty in view of their antecedents, but are absolutely crazed to expect that they can ever succeed to rule under that name again. See the action of the N.Y. Convention calling itself *democratic*, and similar action may be found in smaller bodies most generally.

In the Pa. Election just held, too, look at the kind of man selected to run for Gov.[3] A *democrat*, and an *opposer of the war*, or, simply, a *secessionist*, and how could conservative men work with any heart for such a man. The whole matter has been most bunglingly handled and until democrats are driven to learn that they at least, under no circumstances will be swallowed by this people nothing can be gained by their help.

Such things as these have carried the elections lately held to go against your position and not your principles.

Those principles are sure to be endorsed in the future, as sure as day will dawn again. The policy of removals, too, has been more hesitating than it should have been. Thousands of office holders have been operating against you whose actions would have been prevented if they had feared the loss of office the Action of the Administration being energetic in that respect. Here, in this city, are thousands in Office who are opposed to your administration and rejoicing over every defeat you may sustain either before Congress or the people and forming an immense Corps of Radical letter writers for the papers and when every one supposed that as the Cabinet was reorganized they would be noticed and made to give place to the friends of the Administration, and their rampant abuse of yourself and measures meet with the proper desert we are told, so it is said, by the Secretaries that no one is to be removed for all this, if he does his duty in the office.

So they remain on the rampage a singular way, folks think, to support a party. Energetic action all know begets the same—makes energetic friends. You certainly, see, now, very plainly, that there is nothing to expect from such a mild policy. Every effort must be used to insure success.

There is no ammunition to throw away. Every party must reward its friends. In this City out of the Departments, also, there are offices which should be filled by others, especially the Postmaster,[4] the most obnoxious man to the citizens who could be found, from his course in regard to negro suffrage, coupled with his abuse of them in a letter[5] published in the Chronicle some time ago—yet he still remains, then, Congress will shortly convene, when it is understood that he cannot be removed. It is stated very freely on the street, that the reason he is not removed, as given from himself, too, is that he appointed an employee at the request of P.M.G. Randall, and that he, also, helped to get him confirmed by the Senate when he hung fire there and that he therefore will not consent to his removal.

He, also, thinks, however, in addition that Mr. Seward is acting as a friend of his. But shall the unanimous wish of the citizens be disregarded in his case for such reasons?

Action, evidently, should be taken in the cases of this office holder and the others, also, in this City as soon as practicable, before it is rendered impossible, in his case, most especially.

I hope, in conclusion, Mr. President that you will pardon any thing I may have said if it looks like dictation, as my object was, simply, suggestion of the views of an American Citizen to the Chief Magistrate of the United States.

John N. Cochran M.D.

ALS, DLC-JP.
    1. Not identified.
    2. We suggest the circa October 15 date because of internal evidence in the document, particularly the reference to the "just held" Pennsylvania election. It occurred on October 9.
    3. Hiester Clymer.
    4. Sayles J. Bowen.
    5. Not found.

To David M. Fleming

Washington, D.C.   October 15th 1866.

Dear Sir:

I have received your letter of yesterday's date, and thank you for your kind wishes for my health and success. Fully appreciating your friendly acts, I regret sincerely the circumstances which caused your removal. In determining upon the many applications for changes in office that daily come before me, it is almost impossible to give each individual case particular attention, and it thus occasionally happens that removals are made which otherwise would not be directed. This was unfortunately so with your own removal, and I need hardly assure you that had I, at the time, fully understood all the facts in your case, the change would not have been made. When opportunity occurs, I hope to be able to give you evidence of my appreciation of your friendliness.[1]

Andrew Johnson

This note is, of course, not intended for publication.

A. J.

LS, DNA-RG56, Appts., Internal Revenue Service, Assessor, Ohio, 4th Dist., David M. Fleming.

1. Fleming responded a week later with an indication that the President's letter had not mollified his feelings. In fact, he requested that Johnson delay the transfer of his assessorship until after November 4. The stalling tactic would enable Fleming "to save a little home I purchased last fall for my family." Fleming to Johnson, Oct. 22, 1866, Appts., Internal Revenue Service, Assessor, Ohio, 4th Dist., David M. Fleming, RG56, NA.

From Thaddeus S. Seybold[1]

Private,

And is [it] is hoped that the President will have the patience to read this short note *clear through.*

Washington, D.C., Oct. 15, 1866.

Dear Sir;

I submit that my humble Article laid before you a short time ago,[2] contains the true solution of the current political difficulties. I confess my own appreciation of a "White Man's Government," if the Continent was to be settled anew; but the colored element, through slavery, has now got to be so large, on our soil, And so *diffused* (it being hard to strike the dividing line between the white and colored races), I feel that universal colored suffrage is now as inevitable, in time, as Emancipation itself, And that the south must prepare to submit as gracefully to the former as they have to the latter, having by their own secession acts, as a natural consequence, brought both upon themselves. It only requires one of the excluded states, together with the (probably) unanimous North, to carry the "Constitutional Amendment," And this the descendants of the witch burners of New England in their zeal, by hook or crook, will no doubt have, in time, right or wrong, And I think, as I have said, that the south might as well prepare themselves for the event, as an inevitable consequence of their own acts. It seems to me that they run no risk in immediately adopting the Con. Amendment, and colored suffrage with it, as they would no doubt (as I think the President himself long ago suggested) control the colored vote as effectually as the capitalists of the North do the factory vote, &c.

The greatest objection I have to the Constitutional Amendment, is to the *disfranchisement* clause, to which, as a liberal reconstructionist, I am emphatically opposed; but its impolicy, as a permanency, is anticipated even in the clause itself, and with the increased representation of the south, under universal suffrage, added to the liberal representation from the North, I think this difficulty would be almost immediately remedied. Still, it must be confessed, it is a miserable *contingency* to put in the permanent Constitution of a Country, and will require another Amendment to get it out, when it shall have served its temporary purpose.

☞   I make these humble suggestions in my zeal for the triumph of the President's liberal policy, for I consider it *not in conflict with any of these*. The President is right in urging a constant Observance of the Constitution as it stands, until it is constitutionally amended, especially when the representation of ten great States of the Constitutional compact, a representation fully guarantied by the Constitution, is the object of its Observance.

☞   I repeat that I make these suggestions in my solicitude that the Presidents Policy may prevail, or, at least, that the *President* may prevail, despite his liberal policy, *to carry out a more liberal one*, and I hope that my late article (which I flatter myself is a complete solution of the whole subject), may be corrected and returned for general publication if thought best, *or, at least*, (if it has not already been done), *that its main points may be made use of in that way, or otherwise, to the end in view*.

T. S. Seybold, Washington, D.C.[3]

ALS, DLC-JP.
 1. Seybold (*fl*1880) was a photographer. Washington, D.C., directories (1870, 1880–81).
 2. Not found.
 3. His signature was on a separate sheet of paper.

From Henry A. Smythe

New York, 15th Octr. 1866

My dear Sir.

I regretted to day on the receipt of your telegram—that I did not go to Washington *as I at first* proposed *Saturday night*—but I imagined from your reply to my suggestion that I would see you on Sunday—that you would as soon I come some other time.[1] I need not tell you my dear & much respected Sir—that it is not only my *first duty*—but it would be my greatest pleasure at all times—to pay my respects in person to you—whenever wanted.

I had some plans & matters with regard to the Election in this state that I wished to consult with you about—as well as to consult with you on other subjects—but it is as well perhaps—as I have since seen some of the leading men of the state—& things to say the least, are looking better—& from those who ought to know—I get much encouragement that Hoffman will be elected—in which case, as a matter of course—the radicals will loose members of Congress.

I shall be most happy to go on to Whn. at an hours notice—whenever you may wish to see me.[2]

H. A. Smythe

ALS, DLC-JP.

1. On Saturday, October 13, Smythe had indicated that he wanted to meet with the President for "an hour" on Sunday, the 14th. Robert Johnson promptly replied that his father would be happy to see Smythe, but later that afternoon the collector telegraphed that he would have to put off his visit to Washington for about a week, a turn of events which the President regretted. Smythe to Johnson, Oct. 13, 1866; Smythe to Robert Johnson, Oct. 13, 1866, Johnson Papers, LC; Robert Johnson to Smythe, Oct. 13, 1866; Johnson to Smythe, Oct. 14, 1866, Tels. Sent, President, Vol. 3 (1865–68), RG107, NA.

2. See Johnson to Smythe, Oct. 17, 1866.

From Frederick Koones[1]

Washington   Oct 16th 1866.

Sir

I am informed that Mr. Z. C. Robbins[2] Register of Wills of this City is making great efforts to prove his friendship for you and your views as to Reconstruction &c. That you may know somewhat of the sincerity of his friendship, as well as the honesty of his extremely sudden conversion, I will give you a slight sketch of his history. In the early days of the Rebellion this gentleman was a member of Trinity Episcopal Church of this city, to which Mess: Ingle, Torbert and Judge Chipman[3] also belonged; these gentlemen were elected Vestrymen by the congregation, some of whom it is true were not ultra radical in their ideas, and for this reason Mr. Robbins, with others, was instrumental in having them removed from Office, notwithstanding they were loyal men and were well known as such. Subsequent to this occurrence a new minister was called to the Church,[4] a good Union citizen and christian gentleman, but not endorsing all of Mr. Robbins views or radical notions. Mr. R. forsakes the Religion of his forefathers and now finds himself a communicant in the Church of the Rev. Byron Sunderland's[5] one of the most ultra woolly heads, who figured extensively not long since by giving up his pulpit to

Fred Douglass much to the disgust and disapprobation of the congregation. Next we hear of Mr. R, with others of his politics, trying to get out
an injunction to prevent this Corporation from paying the expenses of an
election held for the purpose of ascertaining the sense of the Citizens
upon the subject of Negro suffrage.

The morning after you made the speech on Feb 7.,[6] last, in which some
of the Acts of Congress as well as persons of some notoriety were shown
up in their true light, this same gentleman denounced you as being as
great a Traitor as Jeff Davis, and said that the rope ought to be put
around your neck, instead of his. These remarks were made in the presence of Judge Purcell,[7] of the Orphan's Court and his bailiff Mr. Jones.[8]
For my character and veracity I respectfully refer you to my friend the
Hon: Henry Stanbery Atty. Genl.

Fredk. Koones

ALS, DNA-RG48, Appts. Div., Misc. Lets. Recd.
    1. Koones(c1821–fl1883) was chief clerk and navy agent in 1866; the next year he be-
came a notary public and later was in real estate. Washington, D.C., directories (1866–83);
1870 Census, D.C., Washington, 4th Ward, 659.
    2. Zenas C. Robbins (1810–fl1902) lived in Boston and St. Louis before settling in
Washington in 1844. During Lincoln's administration he was register of wills for the District; however, his regular occupation was that of patent attorney. Washington, D.C., directories (1866–70); Douglass Zevely, "Old Houses on C Street and Those Who Lived
There," *Records CHS*, 5 (1902): 157.
    3. There are three possible Ingles he could be referring to—John H. (b. c1834), a
Washington native; Henry (b. c1812), a clerk from Virginia; Christopher (b. c1828), a law-
yer and native of the District. James M. Torbert (1802–1880), a bookkeeper, was from
Delaware and had lived in Washington since 1831 where he was employed as a clerk in the
Treasury Department for forty years until his death. Norton P. Chipman (1836–1924)
practiced law in Iowa prior to entering the Union army. Commissioned a major, 2nd Iowa
Inf., he was promoted to colonel and eventually brevetted brigadier general of volunteers in
March 1865 for his services in the Bureau of Military Justice. After the war he settled in
Washington and was appointed secretary and then delegate when the territorial govern-
ment for the District was established in 1871. *BDAC*; Zevely, "Old Residences and Family
History," 113; Washington, D.C., directories (1866–70); 1870 Census, D.C., Washing-
ton, 1st Ward, 48; (1870), 4th Ward, 650, 856.
    4. The Reverend Robert J. Keeling (c1828–1909) graduated from the Theological
Seminary of Virginia in 1858. He served as rector of the Trinity parish in Washington and
subsequently of St. Stephen's in Harrisburg, Pennsylvania. He died in New York City.
Washington, D.C., directories (1862–66); *New York Times*, Dec. 10, 1909.
    5. Sunderland (1819–1901), one of the foremost preachers in the Presbyterian church,
pastored two different churches in the state of New York prior to his move to Washington,
D.C., to serve as pastor of First Presbyterian church. He was chaplain of the U.S. Senate
during the war and again in the 1870s. *NCAB*, 10: 71; *NUC*.
    6. See Interview with Delegation of Blacks, Feb. 7, 1866, *Johnson Papers*, 10: 41–48.
    7. William F. Purcell (c1812–1871) was chosen a justice of the peace at Washington in
1846 and appointed a judge of the Orphans' Court in December 1848, a position he held for
at least twenty-two years. 1870 Census, D.C., Washington, 4th Ward, 722; William Henry
Dennis, "Orphans' Court and Register of Wills, District of Columbia," *Records CHS*, 3
(1900): 212; Charles S. Bundy, "A History of the Office of Justice of the Peace in the District of Columbia," *Records CHS*, 5 (1902): 279; *Evening Star* (Washington), Dec. 23,
1871.
    8. Francis Jones (c1810–fl1870), a native of Virginia. 1870 Census, D.C., George-
town, 593; Washington, D.C., directory (1866).

From J. Sterling Morton

Nebraska City   October 16th 1866

Mr President,

We have been beaten in Nebraska by a small majority.[1] In this County,[2] where the only removals in the territory had been made—two radical U.S. Land Officers here having been ousted[3] and two Conservative appointed[4]—we increased the Conservative majority to more than 450!!

We now ask a new Judge for this Dist in place of E. S. Dundy[5] a corrupt man and a raving radical. We have petitioned for the appointment of Milton Browning,[6] of Berlington, Iowa, who is I beleive a brother of the Hon, the Sec of the Interior.

Court meets on the 31 inst, and it is very important that a new Judge should arrive prior to that time. Let me hope that Your Excellency will give us Mr Browning for Judge *immediately*![7]

J. Sterling Morton

ALS, CtY-Pequot MSS Col., Beinecke Rare Book and Manuscript Library.

1. On October 9, 1866, Turner M. Marquette, the Republican candidate, beat Morton by something over 700 votes out of roughly 9,000 cast for delegate to Congress, in case Nebraska remained a territory. The election for congressman, should the territory become a state, saw Republican John Taffe defeat Conservative A. S. Paddock. *American Annual Cyclopaedia* (1866), 736; James C. Olson, *J. Sterling Morton* (Lincoln, 1942), 146–47.

2. Otoe County.

3. Register of the land office Royal Buck and receiver William H.H. Waters. See William A. Richardson to Johnson, Sept. 8, 1866.

4. Albert Tuxbury, who has not been further identified, was appointed receiver and Edward S. Reed, also not identified, register at Nebraska City, both on September 24, 1866. Neither retained office for long. Ser. 6B, Vol. 3: 708, Johnson Papers, LC; *U.S. Off. Reg.* (1867).

5. Elmer S. Dundy (1830–1896) moved from Pennsylvania to Nebraska in 1857 and practiced law until Lincoln appointed him territorial associate justice in June 1863. Edmunds, *Pen Sketches*, 399–402; *New York Times*, Oct. 29, 1896.

6. Browning (c1810–1881), who was the brother of O. H. Browning and an able lawyer and orator, moved from Illinois to Burlington, Iowa, in 1837. He served in the territorial house and four terms in the state senate. Edward H. Stiles, *Recollections and Sketches of Notable Lawyers and Public Men of Early Iowa* (Des Moines, 1916), 295–96.

7. Dundy remained territorial justice until the office was abolished by statehood. In April 1868 Johnson nominated Dundy U.S. district judge, a post he held until his death in 1896. Johnson appointed Browning U.S. district attorney for Iowa instead. He held that office from 1867 to 1869. Ibid.; *U.S. Off. Reg.* (1869–95); Edmunds, *Pen Sketches*, 399–402; *New York Times*, Oct. 29, 1896.

From Pennsylvania Citizens[1]

Philada.   Oct. 16th 1866

Among the Philadelphia appointments, by your request agreed upon, was that of *John Welsh Esq.*,[2] of Philadelphia, for the Office of *Surveyor of the Port*, vice *E. Reed Meyer*.

As Mr. Welsh had been selected by the Independent, Conservative and Democratic elements of the 4th. Cong. District of Penna. as the most fit person to oppose Wm. D. Kelley and the Radical element, it was thought best to retain the present Surveyor, until the result of the election was determined. Mr. Welsh made a noble and determined fight against Kelly—the Union League's money and an overwhelming majority. The result, although adverse, was highly honorable to Mr Welsh, Mr. Kelly's former majority being reduced over fifteen hundred.[3] As the champion of your policy in the 4th Cong. of Penna. and as the choice of the Conservative element in Eastern Pennsylvania, we now most respectfully ask his appointment as Surveyor of the Port of Philadelphia.[4]

LS, DNA-RG56, Appts., Customs Service, Surveyor, Philadelphia, John Welsh.
1. There are nine signatories, including William F. Johnston, Philadelphia collector, Joseph R. Flanigen, naval officer, Chambers McKibbin, Sr., treasurer of the Philadelphia mint, and Gen. Samuel M. Zulick, revenue collector of the Third District.
2. John Welsh, otherwise unidentified, had served as a sutler at Fort Delaware during the war. *Evening Bulletin* (Philadelphia), Sept. 12, 1866.
3. Kelley outpolled Welsh 14,551 to 12,126. *Guide to U.S. Elections*, 617.
4. Welsh's name was not among the ten nominations Johnson eventually made to fill the post of Philadelphia surveyor. Ser. 6B, Vol. 4: 84, 87–90, Johnson Papers, LC. See E. Reed Myer to Johnson, Sept. 21, 1866.

From James O. Broadhead

St. Louis   Oct: 17th 1866—

Mr. President

The condition of affairs in Missouri impels us to make a request of you, which we hope you will not hestitate to grant.

In some of the counties of the State there are regularly armed organizations of men who assume to interfere with the Registration of voters— they are armed with United States muskets—they are organized into squads & companies—they undertake to deter men from registering as voters—and obstruct the process of the law if it is attempted to be enforced against registering officers who have violated the law to the prejudice of the rights of loyal citizens—they threaten that men who have been registered and who happen to be opposed in political sentiments to themselves shall not be permitted to vote at the election—and doubtless this system of intimidation will be used by them at the election to prevent men from voting who are opposed to them—and these organizations are gotten up and maintained for that purpose.[1]

We do not ask you to interfere with the execution of the law as bad as it is—but where the civil arm is powerless—or the rights of peaceable citizens are in jeopardy from armed mobs—and the freedom of elections is invaded whether by connivance of the State Executive or not—we hold that you have the right to preserve the peace and protect the political rights of the citizen when thus invaded.

We ask therefore that you will issue an order to Maj. Genl. Hancock in command of this Department[2]—authorising him to send any part of the

United States forces under his command—to any portion of the State when in his opinion it becomes necessary to do so, for the purpose of preserving the peace of the country or of dispersing and disarming any illegal military organizations in the State.[3]

Jas. O. Broadhead   Chm. of State Advisory Committee

ALS, DLC-JP.

1. Previous complaints about the actions of the state militia include Thomas C. Ready to Johnson, July 24, 1866, *Johnson Papers*, 10: 727–29; William T. Sherman to Johnson, Aug. 9, 1866.

2. Johnson had placed Gen. Winfield Scott Hancock as commander of the Department of Missouri in August 1866. Parrish, *Radical Rule*, 93.

3. Congressman John Hogan commended Broadhead's letter to the President in a note appended to the letter. Hancock had only three companies of troops to assign throughout the state and by mid-October they were spread very thin. William T. Sherman, Hancock's superior, did not want to commit troops to Missouri which were needed elsewhere for frontier defense, but he did permit two additional companies to be stationed in Missouri during the final week before the election. Ibid., 95–96.

From William M. Daily

New Orleans, Louisiana, Oct. 17th, 1866

Personal and Private

PLEASE READ

Mr. President:

I beg leave, most respectfully to call your attention to our last *conversation together*, in the latter part of August last, soon after the meeting of the "*National Union Convention*"—in your own room.

Just before bidding you "*good bye*," as I had been some what *importunate*, previously, in pleading for some *lucrative position*, at your hand, as one of *your life long friends*—you said to me—"Now dont you become *impatient*—just go on down there to *New Orleans*—wait awhile *patiently*"— and then added, "*Now dont get impatient*"—As much as to say—"*I will not forget you—and you shall be provided for before long.*" I took my leave of you and have waited in *patience* and *hope*—toiling on in my present *beggardly*, and yet *laborious position*[1]—and now, I must renew my plea, with more importunity, if possible, than ever before. I have told you of my *poverty*, my long and continued public service—my *personal* and *political* devotion to *your Excellency*—until you must know my arguments by heart.

What more can I say? I now call upon you with all the *earnestness of my nature*, and the *urgency of pinching poverty*, to give me an *appointment*, of any kind, and in any place, or part of the country, that will *pay better*, than the one I have, without this terrible, constant toil and labor.

I am ready to go any place—any State any territory—any place where you can send me, in a capacity, or position that will pay—and relieve me from pressing want, in my advancing years. I am a kind of *a citizen of the nation at large—the whole nation,* any how—and am so recognized: So, you cannot say there is no place for me, *that has money in it*—when the whole nation is before you to select a place in. And if you would serve *a friend of unceasing devotion,* whose qualifications, I am vain enough to say, no man can doubt, who knows me—*you will grant my request,* and give me a *lucrative appointment, at once, and be done with it*—and let the nation see *your* devotion *to your true friends.* Having "waited *patiently,*" I now ask the long looked for place. *I will expect an appointment, "by return mail,"* and *no mistake.*[2]

                                                                Wm M. Daily

ALS, DNA-RG56, Appls., Asst. Treasurers and Mint Officers, New Orleans, William M. Daily.

   1. Daily was a special agent for the post office in Louisiana and Texas. Daily to Johnson, Sept. 11, 1865, *Johnson Papers,* 9: 62.

   2. Johnson did not grant Daily's request, but Daily continued his importunings. Daily to Johnson, ca. Oct. 29; Nov. 1, 5, 1866; May 15, 1867, Appls., Asst. Treasurers and Mint Officers, New Orleans, William Daily, RG56, NA.

To Henry A. Smythe

                                    Washington, D.C., October 17 1866

Your letter received: I intended to say in my dispatch, that I would see you on the day you were to come, or any other day.

I hope your information in regard to the election in New York is right. If New York can be saved, all is well.[1]

                                                                Andrew Johnson

Tel, DNA-RG107, Tels. Sent, President, Vol. 3 (1865–68).

   1. After receiving a copy of this dispatch, Samuel J. Tilden, chairman of the National Union state committee, assured Johnson that prospects for a victory in New York appeared "encouraging," with "Organization throughout the State well advanced, Our people acting every where Courageously and effectually." Tilden to Johnson, Oct. 17, 1866, Johnson Papers, LC; Jerome Mushkat, *The Reconstruction of the New York Democracy, 1861–1874* (East Brunswick, 1981), 106–8. See Johnson to Smythe, Oct. 29, 1866.

From William Bigler

                                    Clearfield Pa   Oct 18th 1866

My dear Sir.

The returns show that Pa has gone radical by a fraction over two per cent. One and half per cent of a change would have saved the State. The total vote has exceeded 600,000 and the majority over us will be about 15000.[1]

There is, therefore, nothing very disheartening for you or your policy in this result. The Constitution will yet be vindicated, and the revolutionary doctrines and actions of Congressed be rebuked.

All sorts of explanations of this result will doubtless come to your ears. Our candidate for governor, it is true was not an available man, and I did all I could to induce him to refuse the nomination, but the true source of the radical strength is found in the prejudices & passions still cherished in the hearts of the people against the States & people lately in insurrection. The radicals knew this and their whole effort was to inflame those feelings. They ignored or denied the issue of negro sufferage. On that issue alone we should have carried the state by an immense majority.

As it is, you have an organized party of 290,000 which will stand by you in maintaining the constitutional rights of the States, & perfecting the Union, and if needs be, in resisting revolution, come whence it may.

Wm. Bigler

ALS, DLC-JP.

1. By most calculations the total vote was about 597,000, with John W. Geary defeating Hiester Clymer by a majority of approximately 17,000. *American Annual Cyclopaedia* (1866), 615; Bradley, *Militant Republicanism*, 274.

From John S. Brien
PRIVATE & CONfiDENTIAL

Nashville Tenn.   October 18th 1866.

My Dear Sir.

I feel that nothing but Roman firmness upon the part of the Conservative men of the Nation Can Save the Country Since the indications of the late Elections. To this end it occurs to me, that we had best begin at once to husband our resources that we may do this in harmony and to profit. I repeat my Suggestions to you on another occasion.

Our people desire very much Some changes in places here. First, they want a man to command the United States forces in this State, who is a just man one competant to command and one friendly to, and a Supporter of your Administration, as they fear that if Brownlow Sucedes in arming the negroes and organizing them as Malitia, they may need troops to preserve the peace. The man for the command of the District of Tennessee is Brevet Major General William P. Carlin,[1] who is a major in the regular Army, Is a first rate gentleman, fought all through the Rebelion, is a first rate Commander, a Gallant and brave Solder is loved by his Soldiers, esteemed highly by the Citizens, and is withall an ardent supporter of your Administration. This latter point makes Genl Thomas his enemy—who is trying to overslaugh him. He will not recommend him for promotion or give him any prominent command. In fact he is as I understand trying to Suppress the District of Tennessee, or merge it with the Kentucky So that, he may still controle this state. There is no chance then for us to have justice done to us and to Genl Carlin, but by direct appeal to you. I Sincerely hope it will suit your views to have this appoinmt for this district of Tennessee at once made.[2]

Since writing the above, I understand that a man by the name of Coats,[3] belongin to the United States army from Ohio, is now, by recent appointment a Col, or Left Col, Sent to this place with the view of being put in comand of this district. Coats was in Ben. Butlers Cavalry in Virginia, and is supposed to be a Butler man, and is a thougher Radical. For Gods [sake] save us from such men, and especially when it can be done by putting into office such men as Genl Carlin who together with his relatives and friends in Illinois are Conservatives.

Next. The Post Office. Judge Gaut thinks he cannot take the oath, as he occupies, precisely the same position Judge Patterson[4] did. But for this he would take the appointment if offered to him. His Son John M. Gaut[5] is a first rate young man of fine business quallifications, and in every way well quallified and reliable, who can take the oath. If he should be appointed, it would be the same thing as if the Judge had been appointed, for the Judge Says he would give the office his personal Superintendence, and be responsible to the proper management of the same. The appointment would be a good one, and hailed with delight.

Cone[6] ought to be removed, and the others I mentioned to you. It is outragous that such men should hold office under and by your permission, and doing all they can to destroy your Administration. If the names I have Suggested do not Suit, Send such as you may prefer. But change at all events.

I fear we are to have trouble with Brownlow at the meeting of the Legislature. He Seems bent on the ruin of this State at least. How much further wrong he intends by hanging yourself, myself and a few others, I do not know at this writing. I may give him Some trouble before he gets intirely through his plans.

I See Chase and Underwood have again postponed the trial of Jeff Davis.[7] Is this, because they want to get clear of trying him? Or is it for the purpus of continuging, the charges against you of preventing the trial? You know Jeff Davis was indicted in the Federal Court at Knoxville, for High Treason, for one year or more before he was indicted in Va. If we had him in this State, Trigg[8] would try him, and if the proof was Sufficent convict him; and thus end the charges of Cruelty to Davis by keeping him in prison.

Now Suppose Trigg Should, as he has the right to do, Send a certified Copy of the Indictment to Underwood, and direct Underwood to issue a Capeas, have Davis arrested and sent under guard to Knoxville to be tried would it be done? Or would your Attorney General[9] direct it to be done? Please let me hear from on this point. I am anxious to see whether they will refuse to let him be tried as they will not try him themselves. If they refuse it will take all the wind out of that sail.

The cholera has prevented our ratification meeting so far. It will take place on the 27 Inst.[10] I intend to prepare and deliver a speech on that occasion, which I shall have printed,—will send you a copy. It will con-

OCTOBER 1866

tain in brief my views, as to the object and views of the Radical party. The infamous proposed Constitutional amendment and the ultimate condition of the country in the event of a continuance of radical power, &c.

The effect of the Northern Ellections, has attached your friends more closely to you. May they unde providence help you to save our dear Country.

You must excuse this baddly written letter. I have the Tetter so bad in my hands I can Scarsly write at all.

John S. Brien

ALS, DLC-JP.
1. Carlin (1829–1903) was a West Point graduate and a career officer prior to the Civil War. During the war he served extensively throughout Tennessee; he was brevetted brigadier general in 1862 and later as major general. After the war, he was a major in the regular army and held the post of assistant commissioner of the Freedmen's Bureau for Kentucky and Tennessee (1867–68). He continued his military career thereafter, eventually retiring with the rank of general in 1893. Warner, *Blue*; Everly and Pacheli, *Records of Field Officers*, pt. 3: 425.
2. In November Secretary Stanton inquired about the commander at Nashville and informed Gen. George H. Thomas that the President had suggested Carlin as a suitable officer. Stanton to Thomas, Nov. 13, 1866, Tels. Sent, Sec. of War (M473, Roll 91), RG107, NA.
3. August V. Kautz. Edward D. Townsend telegraphed Kautz on October 20 that he should join his regiment at Nashville and await his commission there. See Townsend to Kautz, Oct. 20, 1866, ibid.
4. John C. Gaut and David T. Patterson.
5. Gaut (1841–1918) graduated from Rutgers University in 1866 and thereafter began the practice of law in Nashville. In later years he occupied several important assignments with the Cumberland Presbyterian church as a lay person, including a lengthy tenure on its board of publications. Adrian V.S. Lindsley was postmaster at Nashville at this time and continued in the job until the spring of 1867. *DAB*; *U.S. Off. Reg.* (1865–67).
6. Edward P. Cone, direct tax commissioner.
7. Salmon P. Chase and John C. Underwood. There had been and would continue to be repeated delays in the trial of Davis, largely because of Chase's apprehensions about such a trial. See Frederick J. Blue, *Salmon P. Chase: A Life in Politics* (Kent, Ohio, 1987), 264.
8. Connally F. Trigg.
9. Henry Stanbery.
10. An announcement from the executive committee, chaired by Brien, appeared in the Nashville papers indicating that the convention would be postponed until October 27. At the meeting of the so-called National Union Convention in Nashville resolutions condemning the Fourteenth Amendment were adopted; Brien's lengthy speech followed. *Nashville Dispatch*, Oct. 18, 1866; *Republican Banner* (Nashville), Oct. 29, 1866.

From Orville H. Browning

Washington D.C.   Oct 18th 1866.

Sir,

I have the honor to inclose herewith a letter addressed to this Department on the 22d ultimo by the Secretary of War,[1] inclosing certain papers and requesting that the lands therein specified be reserved for military purposes under the name of Fort Bidwell.

The lands are described as in latitude 41°51′14½″, longitude

120°8′4″, situate in the north-east of California, in the upper part of Surprise valley, having for their northern boundary a true east and west line,
marked by a series of large stakes, and extending from the creek which
enters the upper lake from the north, called Big-Creek, to the crest of the
ridge bounding the valley on the west, a distance of about three miles. Its
southern boundary is a line parallel to the northern one and one mile distant from it, similarly marked by stakes and extending from the creek to
the crest of the ridge to the west, which separates Surprise valley from
Goose Lake valley. The eastern boundary is the creek and the western
one the crest of the ridge.

The Commissioner of the General Land Office[2] states that the tract
which is described above is on unsurveyed public land, and I, therefore,
recommend that the reservation be ordered as requested by the Secretary
of War.[3]

O H Browning Secretary

LS, DNA-RG49, Executive Orders, 1806–1913.
   1. Not found.
   2. Joseph S. Wilson.
   3. On October 19, 1866, Johnson endorsed Browning's letter: "Let the lands within
described be reserved for '*Fort Bidwell*,' as recommended by the Secretary of the Interior."

From the Democratic County Committee
of California[1]

San Francisco   Oct, 18, 1866

The Democracy of California deem it to be due to themselves to inform
the President of the United States, of the stand which they as a political
party have taken upon the absorbing questions of the rehabilitation and
harmonizing of all the States, and at the same time to inform the President of the attitude of our political opponents upon these questions; in
order that by a candid and critical comparison the President may determine upon which side the great weight of his official patronage ought to
be thrown; not for the purpose of aggrandizing individuals, but to foster
correct political sentiments, and to secure National unity.

In California there are but two political parties.

Ours Known as the National Democratic Party.

Our opponents Known as the Union Party.

Our party sustained the cause of the Union through the war, our
banner-cry was "*the Union and the Constitution*." We sustained the war
heart and soul for this purpose. The few Secessionist, who reside in this
State neither fraternized nor voted with us. As an evidence of our sentiments we transmit herewith, the Resolutions adopted by us both in the
State Conventions and in the largest gatherings of our Party.[2]

And we affirm to the President as gentlemen, that there never has been a sentiment expressed or entertained by our Party contrary to the scope and tenor of these Resolutions; that individuals may have cherished different views during the war is undoubtedly true. Today the Democratic Party of California is a unit in sustaining the President's policy of reconstruction. We stand as one man on this question, and we could control the State politically, were it not for the weight of Federal patronage and Federal Official influence thrown against us. We deem it unjust to ourselves, as individuals, and detrimental to the cause for which we labor in common with the President, that this should be continued. As it would have been intolerable during the war, that Secessionist should have controlled and enjoyed the patronage of the Federal Government so now it is not to be endured, that pratical disunionists, should do so. *The evidence upon which we found this charge against the officials in this State is overwhelming. And, we pledge ourselves to furnish it at any time it may be demanded.* Outside of our own organs there is not a press in this State, that sustains the policy of the President, or cordially endorsed the principles enunciated in the Philadelphia Convention.

There never has been a public meeting called to do so, except those called by us.

There never has been a public speech made to this effect except those made by us. We have invited the heads of the Custom House, Revenue Department, Mint and other Officials[3] to unite with us to ratify endorse and sustian the President and his policy, and they have, in every instance scornfully refused to do so.

We have offered directly and personally *to give way for them to call and officer the meetings, while we would defray all the expense and help to swell the audience and this they refused with contempt*, and we now charge distinctly—That the Federal officials, as a body, in California, are not only opposed to the policy of the President, but are opposed to the restoration of the Union and the harmony of these States;—or in other words they sustain Congress in its most radical measures.

These facts we deem the President ought to Know.

We do not think we have any right to suggest men to fill these positions, but we do claim the right to insist that they shall be filled by loyal Union loving men. The only endorsement of the President in this State outside of our Party is found in a printed address put forth by some obscure persons styling themselves a "National Union State Central Committee."[4]

This Committee is without a Party and from the secrecy observed about their address here, we infer that it was intended rather for circulation in Washington than in California. *The members of this Committee were personally solicited by us, to call a public meeting to ratify and endorse the Presidents Policy as enunciated in the Philadelphia Convention, and* they positively refused to do so. We again affirm that there are but two political parties in California. One sustains the President. The other opposes him, and *that the Federal officials in San Francisco to our personal Knowledge belong to, work for, and vote with the latter Party.* If there are any exceptions, they are so insignificant as to have escaped our observation.

Geo. H. Rogers chairman Democratic County Committee
W. C. Reed Secretary Co. Committee
S. B. Axtell Member of Com.

LS, DLC-JP.

1. Three members of the committee signed the letter: George H. Rogers, chairman; William C. Reed, secretary; and Samuel B. Axtell, committee member. Rogers (*c*1829–*fl*1881), an engineer and contractor, was in San Francisco by 1860. He later served in the state assembly and senate. Reed (*fl*1881), a miner, who at other times worked as a gauger, clerk, and broker, may have been in San Francisco as early as 1852 but was certainly there by 1861. Lawyer Axtell (1819–1891) moved to California in 1851 where, after engaging in mining, he resumed the practice of his profession. As a Democrat he served two terms in the U.S. House of Representatives (1867–71). He later served as territorial governor of Utah and New Mexico and chief justice of the New Mexico supreme court. 1870 Census, Calif., San Francisco, San Francisco, 12th Ward, 1st Prec., 754; San Francisco directories (1852–81); Bancroft, *California*, 7: 363, 368; *BDAC*.

2. Five clippings from unidentified newspapers dated September 1865 (two clippings), February 1866, August 1866, and September 1866, accompanied the document. Each one contained a marked resolution supporting Johnson and his administration.

3. John F. Miller, collector of customs; Frank Soulé, collector of internal revenue; Lewis C. Gunn, assessor of internal revenue; Davis W. Cheesman, assistant treasurer of the U.S. and treasurer of the U.S. Branch Mint in San Francisco; and Robert B. Swain, superintendent of the mint. Newspaper editor, historian, and poet Soulé (*c*1810–*fl*1881) arrived in California in 1849. He held his office as collector until June 1868. Gunn (1813–1892), also a "Forty-Niner," was a physician, newspaper editor, store owner, temperance lecturer, and customs surveyor. Cheesman (*c*1825–*fl*1868), a lawyer and unsuccessful Republican candidate for lieutenant governor of the state in 1857, was a California delegate to the Republican national convention in 1860, which apparently earned him his treasury appointment in 1861. He held the office until July 1868. Swain (1822–1872), a commission merchant and insurance agent, moved to San Francisco in 1855 and superintended the mint, 1863–69. 1860 Census, Calif., Butte, Ophir Twp., 763; (1870), San Francisco, San Francisco, 2nd Ward, 278; San Francisco directories (1856–81); Ser. 6B, Vol. 4: 348–49, Johnson Papers, LC; *NCAB*, 12: 237–38; Dorothy H. Huggins, comp., "Continuation of the Annals of San Francisco," *CHQ*, 16 (1937): 336; Milton H. Shutes, "Republican Nominating Convention of 1860: A California Report," ibid., 27 (1948): 97, 103; Peyton Hurt, "The Rise and Fall of the 'Know Nothings' in California, Chapter 6: The Campaign of 1856," ibid., 9 (1930): 116; Anna Lee Martson, ed., *Records of a California Family: Journals and Letters of Lewis C. Gunn and Elizabeth LeBreton Gunn* (San Diego, 1928), passim.

4. "Address of the National Union State Central Committee to the People of California" (1866), *NUC*. For more on the views of this committee, see the letter of its chairman, M. S. Whiting to Johnson, Aug. 9, 1866.

From Charles G. Halpine

32 BEEKMAN STREET, N.Y.
Oct. 18th 1866

Dear Sir:

This note will be presented to you in company with the papers & opinion of Maj. Gen. Gordon Granger in regard to the care of Lieut. Col. James Kelly, late 69th N.Y. Vols, and Captn. 16th U.S. Infy.[1]

I shall not discuss again the points referred to by Gen. Granger, but will content myself with saying:—That in a long & varied experience as Chief of Staff of various Departments, I have never seen nor heard of so gross a case of *injustice* to a brave and deserving officer. Col. Kelly is a friend of mine & is a gentleman wielding an influence second to that of no Irishman in the City or State of New York.

I ask, with Gen. Granger, the revocation of the order dismissing him as an act of Justice; and I also ask it as a favor for which many Irishmen will be personally grateful,—amongst whom will be found . . . [2]

Charles G Halpine

ALS, DNA-RG94, ACP Branch, File R-168-CB-1868, James Kelly.

1. Kelly (c1831–1871) had been commissioned in October 1861 as a captain of the 16th U.S. Inf. Later he was permitted by the War Department to help organize what became the 69th N.Y. Vols. and to serve as the regiment's lieutenant colonel. The "Fighting" 69th was subsequently consolidated into a battalion and its officers, including Kelly, were mustered out of the service; but evidently no word of this action had reached Kelly. Later he learned that he no longer was a lieutenant colonel but still held a captaincy with the 16th U.S. Inf. Kelly was with that regiment until July 1864, when he received an order dismissing him from the service on the grounds that he had intentionally defrauded the army by continuing to draw pay as a lieutenant colonel when he no longer held that rank. After having completed a "full review" of the case, Granger had written Johnson from New York asking that Kelly be restored to his "proper position" in the army. Powell, *Army List*, 408; CSR, James Kelly, RG94, NA; Thurlow Weed et al. to Johnson, ca. Nov. 27, 1865, ACP Branch, File R-168-CB-1868, James Kelly, RG94, NA; Granger to Johnson, Oct. 16, 1866, ACP Branch, File R-168-CB-1868, James Kelly, RG94, NA. For a copy of the order effecting Kelly's dismissal, see Lets. Recd. (Main Ser.), File K-117-1867 (M619, Roll 557), RG94, NA.

2. On two previous occasions Kelly had sought reinstatement but to no avail. Eventually the War Department recommended to the President that Kelly should be reinstated, since he was not actually guilty of defrauding the government. So, on October 31, 1866, by order of the President, the 1864 order dismissing Kelly from the service was revoked and he was restored to his former rank. But it was some eleven months later before he was finally appointed as captain in the 34th U.S. Inf. Joseph Holt to Johnson, Oct. 20, 1866, ACP Branch, File R-168-CB-1868, James Kelly, RG94, NA; Ser. 6B, Vol. 2, Johnson Papers, LC; Powell, *Army List*, 408.

From Thomas F. Meagher

Virginia City, October 18th 1866.

Sir,

I have the honour respectfully to tender you my resignation as Secretary of Montana Territory, the same to take effect on the 15th (fifteenth) day of December, 1866.

The arrangement would be personally agreeable to me, whilst it would enable you to appoint my successor in full time for him to enter upon the duties of the office on that date. This would obviate the occurrence of an interval or vacancy in the office, and any consequent embarrassment to the public interests of the Territory. Under present circumstances, it is most important that the gentleman, succeeding me, should enter upon his duties the time specified, as that will be the period for the adjournment of the Legislature, when funds should be on hand to pay the Members.

You will not, I trust, regard it as an informality, involving any impropriety, if I venture to suggest the appointment of Major John P. Bruce,[1] late of St Joseph, Missouri, who has been for two years a resident of this Territory, and for the last twelve months has, as Editor and Proprietor of the "Montana Democrat," signally served the great and sacred cause of National Unity, asserted so nobly by you.

An application has been forwarded to your Excellency by several of the best of our people in Montana, in favour of Major Bruce—which application was based upon the avowals made by me a short time since, of my intention to resign.

I beg you will give this earnest communication, to which I now refer the frindliest consideration as I feel satisfied that the public interests will be most influentially served by your doing so, whilst I myself shall have ample reason to feel highly gratified.

In closing this letter of resignation, I should do painful injustice to my own feelings did I not avail myself of the opportunity to assure your Excellency that my official disconnection from the government of the United States will in no way affect my relations with it as a private citizen. These shall remain sincere, eager, and devoted. Indeed, I am led to the conclusion, that, in the event I speak of, a new sphere will present itself to me, in which my services, in this position of the National fortunes, may prove more advantageous, and at the same time more generous, to the Executive of the Nation, than they have been, or can possible be, rendered by me as Secretary of Montana.[2]

                                                            Thomas Francis Meagher

ALS, DNA-RG59, Appts., Lets. of Resignation and Declination.

1. Earlier Bruce (c1813–fl1878) had been an editor in Missouri. He founded the *Montana Democrat*, a weekly at Virginia City in November 1865. When he did not become territorial secretary or delegate, he left Montana soon after the 1866 election, locating first in San Francisco and then in Washington, D.C., before returning to Montana for more newspaper work in the 1870s. He died in Kentucky. 1860 Census, Mo., Buchanan, St. Joseph, 1st Ward, 371; Henry N. Blake, "The First Newspapers of Montana," *Contributions HSMon*, 5 (1904): 254–55, 279–80.

2. It is not known why Meagher wanted to resign, although his quarrels with the territorial judiciary and other partisan squabbles certainly were not pleasant. Why he rescinded his resignation is also unclear, but he did so in a telegram to Johnson on the same day that territorial governor Green Clay Smith telegraphed Johnson, "Do not accept resignation of Gen Meagher." Malone et al., *Montana*, 100–103; Meagher to Johnson, Nov. 6, 1866; Smith to Johnson, Nov. 6, 1866, Territorial Papers, Mont. (M354, Roll 1), RG59, NA.

From Oregon Legislators[1]

Dated Salem, Oregon, October 19, 1866.

We, the undersigned, members of the Legislature of the State of Oregon, respectfully tender to you our cordial approval of the policy indicated and the measures recommended by you for the maintainance of the Union under the Constitution inviolate and the recognition of the States and the people lately in revolt as integral parts of the United States; and, in behalf of a majority of the people of Oregon—whose sentiments on that subject we have no doubt we fairly reflect—we pledge ourselves to support you in that policy in all practical ways and in all circumstances which would justify a free people in defending their liberties and Constitutional rights.

In proof that we have not mistaken the popular sentiment of our State in this respect, we beg leave to call your attention to the following facts:

1st In the recent political canvass in this State the Democratic candidates were specifically pledged to sustain your policy. Their opponents evaded the questions at issue between the Executive and the Legislative departments of the Government by adopting a resolution declaring that "loyal men may honestly differ" upon those questions. Under this pretext of supporting the Administration, the entire influence of the Federal office-holders of this State was cast against the Democratic ticket, in consequence of which an official result was declared in favor of the so-called Union candidate for Governor[2] by a majority of 277, on an aggregate vote of over twenty thousand.[3] This apparent majority was made up chiefly of returns afterwards judicially decided to be fraudulent. A fair and legal count of the votes, an honest expression of the voters upon the issues involved in the contest, or the withdrawal of the influence of the Federal office-holders from the canvass, would have shown, beyond any reasonable doubt, a large majority of the voters in favor of the conservative policy of your Administration.

2d. The Constitutional Amendments proposed by Congress have not been endorsed by the people of the State, nor received the legal sanction of the Legislature. Art. IV. Sec. 25, of the State Constitution says—"A majority of all the members elected to each House shall be necessary to pass every bill or joint resolution; and all bills or joint resolutions so passed shall be signed by the presiding officers of the respective houses." The House of Representatives is composed of forty-seven members. The joint resolution approving the Constitutional Amendments ostensibly passed the House by a vote of 25 to 22. Two of the members[4] who voted in the affirmative on that question held their seats in the House by virtue of fraudulent certificates made by one of said members, and but two days subsequent to this vote were compelled, by more than a two-thirds vote of the House, to surrender their seats to the legally elected members,[5] who immediately placed upon the journal their protest against the passage of said resolution approving the Constitutional Amendments. Had the legally elected members been permitted to vote the resolution would have been defeated by 24 to 23.

3d. On the election of a Senator[6] to succeed the Hon. J. W. Nesmith, it was again made apparent that the supporters of the radical policy of Congress had not a majority in the Legislature. An avowed Radical received the caucus nomination of his party,[7] but failed, after many trials, to receive the votes of a majority of the members, and his supporters were forced to unite upon a more conservative candidate who could command the votes of avowed supporters of your Administration which were necessary to an election.

In view of these facts, and in the light of our own observation, we feel fully justified in repeating to you the assurance that the policy of your Administration relating to the restoration of the Union meets the hearty approval of a majority of the people of Oregon. We would further assure you that the support which we accord to your Administration is actuated by no consideration of personal favor or party aggrandizement. We set up no claim to the patronage or the honors and emoluments of office of which you have the control; but we most respectfully and earnestly protest against the use of such patronage and power to thwart and defeat the policy of your Administration, in the success of which we have a common interest with you. We fully recognize the right and the duty of the President—the Tribune of the people—the sole custodian of the people's sovereign prerogatives—to maintain discipline in his political household. "A house divided against itself cannot stand."[8] From the beginning of the revolutionary attempt of the present Congress to change the policy of the Government towards the revolted States to the present time, the whole influence of Federal patronage in this State—without a notable exception—has been used unscrupulously and with sufficient effect to turn the scale against an unbiassed popular verdict, to strengthen the hand, and promote the cause of the Radical Congress against the conservative policy of the Executive. We pray not for political rewards and punishments, but for such relief as justice and sound policy dictate.

With personal assurances of our high appreciation of your services in behalf of our beloved Union, we subscribe our names hereunto.

Pet, DLC-JP.
    1. Thirty-one members of the state house and senate signed the petition.
    2. George L. Woods (1832–1890) moved with his family from Missouri to Oregon in 1847. After miscellaneous jobs, including gold mining, Woods became a lawyer and Republican activist. He was appointed to the Idaho territorial supreme court in 1865. After his term as governor of Oregon (1866–70), he was appointed territorial governor for Utah (1871–75) and later practiced law in Nevada and California. Sobel and Raimo, *Governors*, 3: 1263.
    3. Woods had 10,316 votes to 10,039 for his opponent James K. Kelley, giving a total of 20,355 votes cast. Ibid.; *Oregonian* (Portland), Sept. 15, 1866.
    4. These two delegates were from Grant County, M. M. McKean, not further identified, allegedly had served with the Union Army of the Potomac in a secret service capacity during the war and was wounded. Thomas H. Brents (1840–1916) held several local offices before his election to the state legislature. After his ouster he became a lawyer and settled in the Washington Territory, serving three terms as territorial delegate (1879–85). Ibid., Sept. 24, 1866; Hubert H. Bancroft, *History of Oregon* (2 vols., San Francisco, 1888), 2: 666; *BDAC*.
    5. The Grant County contests were the most controversial of several disputed seats in this session. Democratic members of the house pushed the ouster of the two Republicans

without giving them time to gather supporting evidence from Grant County, which was some distance away from the capital at Salem. Meanwhile they dragged their feet in the similar case of Polk County, since the men to be unseated there were Democrats. McKean and Brents were replaced by J. M. McCoy (c1830–fl1870), a miner, and S. W. Kinesley (may be G. W. Kniseley). *Oregonian* (Portland), Sept. 20, 24, 1866; 1870 Census, Oreg., Grant, Rock Creek Prec., 370.

6. The new senator, Henry W. Corbett (1827–1903), a merchant, had come from New York to Portland in 1851 to open a store. He held several local offices but served only one term in the senate (1867–73). *BDAC*.

7. Addison C. Gibbs (1825–1886), a New York lawyer, moved to Oregon in 1850 and engaged in promoting settlement in southern Oregon. He served as governor of Oregon (1862–66) and supported the Lincoln administration, after which he held the post of district attorney for Oregon and practiced law. Sobel and Raimo, *Governors*, 3: 1262; Stanley S. Spaid, "The Later Life and Activities of General Joe Palmer," *OHQ*, 55 (1854): 324.

8. Matthew 12: 25 and Mark 3: 25.

From Delphine P. Baker[1]

New York   Oct 20, 1866

Please act upon my request soon as possible that the work of "destruction" at Point Lookout may cease.[2] I postpone public notice of meeting here to wait your reply. Public sympathy & aid will attend my unceasing efforts in behalf of "the nations defenders" Sufficient reward for the struggle.[3]

Delphine P Baker
National Hotel

Tel, DLC-JP.

1. Baker (1828–fl1881) devoted her energy to caring for wounded Union veterans in Chicago and St. Louis. In March 1865 she succeeded in lobbying Congress to establish a national home for disabled Union soldiers and sailors, and several regional branches. Judith G. Cetina, "A History of Veterans' Homes in the United States, 1811–1930" (Ph.D. diss., Case Western Reserve University, 1977), 74–78, 116, 151; *House Misc. Docs.*, 40 Cong., 1 Sess., No. 45, pp. 1–2, 16–17 (Ser. 1312).

2. Since the summer of 1865, Baker had been trying to convince various board members of the military asylum to convert Point Lookout, Maryland, the former site of a Confederate prisoner-of-war camp, into a soldiers' home. But after obtaining the endorsements of General Grant, Horace Greeley, and others, she met resistance from the secretary of war, who directed that the government buildings on the site be sold at public auction. President Johnson ordered the War Department to postpone the sale indefinitely. Nevertheless, at its May meeting, the newly-constituted board of managers officially rejected the Point Lookout location. Cetina, "Veterans' Homes," 113–16; *House Misc. Docs.*, 40 Cong., 1 Sess., No. 45, pp. 2, 6 (Ser. 1312); Simon, *Grant Papers*, 15: 263.

3. A reply from Johnson has not been found.

From Frank Barrett[1]

Clearfield Penna.   October 20th 1866

Sir—

Enclosed you will find an article clipped from the Buffalo Commercial[2] recommending the appointment of Maj. Genl. Jas B. Steedman to the War Portfolio, which meets with the hearty approbation of the Democratic & conservative parties, as well as a majority of the Radicals of the 19th Congressional District. There has been various rumors afloat,[3] some of which point to Genl Sherman & Senator Cowan as Mr Stantons successor, which does not satisfy the people.[4] They think it ought to be filled by a soldier and that soldier should be Genl. Steedman who is eminently qualified and who has earned the position. Steedman is the peoples choice.[5]

Frank Barrett

ALS, DLC-JP.

1. The correspondent is, presumably, the same Frank Barrett (b. *c*1845), who was a son of a local judge. 1860 Census, Pa., Clearfield, Clearfield, 22.

2. Not found.

3. The rumor was that Stanton had resigned and that he would be tendered a foreign mission of some kind. But there was no truth in it. *Press* (Philadelphia), Oct. 18–19, 27, 1866; *New York Tribune*, Oct. 19, 1866; Beale, *Welles Diary*, 2: 399, 403. See also Horace Greeley to Johnson, Jan. 28, 1866, *Johnson Papers*, 9: 647; John P. Hale to Johnson, Sept. 10, 1866.

4. On the other hand, Johnson was encouraged a few days later to "releive the people of their suspence" by ordering William T. Sherman to replace Stanton "as speedily as possible." Samuel J. Randall to Johnson, Oct. 24, 1866, Johnson Papers, LC.

5. See Max Langenschwartz to Johnson, Oct. 23, 1866.

From Ward B. Burnett[1]

Avenue House, 7th Street,
Washington City, D.C., October 20th, 1866.

Enclosed be pleased to find a copy of a letter, sent to you by my brother-in-law, the Hon. Samuel J. Randall of Philadelphia;[2] and also a political letter of my own,[3] published extensively in the States of Pennsylvania, New-Jersey and New-York, in the canvass of 1864.

I am desirous to obtain the appointment of "Superintendent of Public Buildings," occupied and enjoyed so long, by the present incumbent.[4] My professional career as a Constructing Engineer, vouched for by Mr. Randall, will, I hope, commend me to your favour as strongly; as my military services and *constant support* of *yourself* politically.[5]

Ward B. Burnett

ALS, DNA-RG48, Appts. Div., Misc. Lets. Recd.

1. A graduate of the U.S. Military Academy (1832), Burnett (*c*1810–1884) served in the Black Hawk and Mexican wars before working as a civil engineer in various localities, including New York City. *NCAB*, 27: 52; *West Point Register*, 222.

2. The enclosed copy of Randall's September 20 letter to Johnson has the following postscript written by Burnett and dated October 20, 1866: "The original of the above letter was sent to Hon. Hugh McCullough by the President."

3. The "letter" was a clipping from a Plattsburg, New York, newspaper, dated ca. September 1864, in which Burnett reminisced about his early days as a young lieutenant stationed in South Carolina during the nullification crisis.

4. Benjamin B. French, who was not removed by Johnson but by Congress in March 1867 when the office was abolished. Donald B. Cole and John J. McDonough, eds., *Benjamin Brown French, Witness to the Young Republic: A Yankee's Journal, 1828–1870* (Hanover, N.H., 1989), 533–34.

5. Burnett's letter was referred by Johnson to the secretary of the interior, "with the hope that Something may be done for Gen'l Burnett." In January 1867, when Burnett applied for appointment as commissioner of the Pacific Railroad, that letter too was referred to the Interior Department. But it is not known whether Burnett succeeded in finding employment in the Johnson administration. Ser. 6A, Vol. D: 17, 25, Johnson Papers, LC.

From E. B. T.[1]

Savannah Ga   20 Oct 1866

Mr President

An Ex Officer in the Union Army, I hope will be excused for troubling you a few minutes. Having followed Genl Sherman on "The grand march" & liking this portion of our Country when peace followed quickly on the heel of our brilliant achievements, I determined to settle in this section & have done so & am now interested in the Culture of Cotton. I have been South long enough & seen enough of the people to have arrived at a pretty correct judgement and I do cheerfully testify that the people of the South are loyal to the Government. 'Tis true they take very little interest in politics, because they have found out by experience that it is necessary to human happiness to let politics alone & mind their own business. The people every where are intent on money making and a more industrious & orderly people cannot be found in no Country. I find that between the Former master & slave the most kindly feeling exist. The best friend the negro has, from what I have seen is his old master. The lives of Northern men being in danger South is all stuff. I actually have never lived in a community where people have been kinder to me than here. I find every body kind & courteous & ready to grant a favor or give a stranger information. The kind suggestions of my *neighbors* have been of great value to me in my planting interest.

To you this people are very much attached.

There is but one thing in this section that I dont like and that is some thing that is now going on which I believe bears the imprint of considerable political significance viz: the removal of all arms from the Arsinals of this State to Springfield Massachusetts & other points north. If our Crazy Congress intend ruining the Country and bringing on the horrors of war or God knows what, would it not Mr. President be as well to have arms distributed among your friends & decidedly to the interest of the Country & Common sense not to have them ALL in Massachusetts & other Crazy lattitudes. Every Steamer & Sailing Vessel it seems to me are taking arms off. I have never been on the wharves of this city for the last two months but what I see hundreds of boxes being shipped. Thinking you know nothing about this I concluded to let you know.

E B.T.   20th Army Corps.   *Hookers*

ALI, DLC-JP.
1. Not identified.

From Ulysses S. Grant

Washington, D.C.   Oct. 21st 1866.

Sir:

On further, and full, reflection upon the subject of my accepting the mission proposed by you in our interview of Wednesday, and again yesterday,[1] I have most respectfully to beg to be excused from the duty proposed. It is a diplomatic service for which I am not fitted either by education or taste. It has necessarily to be conducted under the State Department with which my duties do not connect me. Again then I most urgently but respectfully repeat my request to be excused from the performance of a duty entirely out of my sphere, and one too which can be so much better performed by others.[2]

U. S. Grant   General.

ALS, DLC-JP.

1. According to William Moore's version, the President met with Grant on the 17th and informed him of his plan to send Grant to Mexico to accompany Lewis Campbell; the general seemed to respond favorably. The two men met again the next day at which time the secretary of state was summoned. Seward arrived with and read the instructions for Grant's proposed commission to Mexico. When asked whether he had any suggestions to make, Grant said that he had none. Moore Diaries, Johnson Papers, LC.

2. For further correspondence concerning this matter with Grant, see Johnson to Stanton, Oct. 26, 1866, and Campbell to Johnson, Nov. 2, 1866.

From David S. Walker

Tallahassee Fla   Oct 21st 66

Some persons in Fernandina in this state wishing to get up a riot & retain possession of property which the U S tax Commissioners have allowed the original owners to redeem gave the sheriff notice that they will resist him if he attempts to execute writs of Execution issued out of the Civil Courts of the State. The Sheriff[1] applies to the officer Commanding the U S Troops at Fernandina[2] for assisstance to suppress the threatened resistance & riot. The Officer replies that the Sheriff may execute his writs. If no one resists the Sheriff he the officer will order the sheriff to suspend the Execution[3] of his writs & that if the Sheriff refuses to obey that order the officer will arrest him and put him in confinement. I applied to Maj Gen J D Foster[4] Comdg this District to order the Officer at Fernandina to withdraw his threats of arresting the Sheriff & to assist the Sheriff in quelling any disturbance. The General declined to Comply with my request. I hold that the Military has no right to arrest the Sheriff in the discharge of his municipal duties. The General holds that the officer must determine in each case whether he will prevent a writ executed. Who will arrest the Sheriff. Or assist him in the execution of his writs.[5] I respectfully request that you will give such definite instructions as will

insure the Enforcement of the Civil law without bloodshed & riot which
I daily fear.[6]

D S Walker   Gov Fla

Tel, DNA-RG107, Tels. Recd., President, Vol. 5 (1866–67).

1. James M. Bennett (c1834–fl1870), a "Tramer" before the war, became a hardware merchant after his term as Nassau County's sheriff. 1860 Census, Fla., Nassau, Fernandina, 14; (1870), 29; Walker to John T. Sprague, Jan. 12, 1867, Lets. Recd., Executive (M494, Roll 96), NA.

2. William T. Dodge (1844–1914), formerly a private and lieutenant in various Maine regiments, and now a first lieutenant, 7th U.S. Inf., temporarily commanded at Fernandina until his captain could arrive. After leaving the army in 1870 he homesteaded in Nebraska. *History of Nebraska*, 1292; Constance W. Altshuler, *Cavalry Yellow & Infantry Blue: Army Officers in Arizona Between 1851 and 1886* (Tucson, 1991), 105; W. T. Dodge to J. M. Bennett, no date, Lets. Recd. (Main Ser.), File F-408-1866 (M619, Roll 472), RG94, NA.

3. A letter from Walker dated October 20, which, according to the file sheet, was a copy of the telegram, was somewhat different in wording. The "writs of execution" were instead "writs of ejectment." The reply of the officer to the sheriff was that "the sheriff may execute his writs if no one resists him but that if anyone resists him he the officer will order the sheriff to suspend the execution." Walker to Johnson, Oct. 20, 1866, Lets. Recd. (Main Ser.), File F-408-1866 (M619, Roll 472), RG94, NA.

4. John G. Foster (1823–1874), a West Point graduate assigned to the Engineer Corps, during the recent war rose to major general of volunteers and commanded the Department of the South and subsequently the Department and District of Florida. Warner, *Blue*; Everly and Pacheli, *Records of Field Officers*, pt. 1: 88.

5. The letter again differs here with "ministerial duties" instead of "municipal duties," and the sentence following reads, "The General holds that the officer must determine in each case whether he will permit a writ to be executed, whether he will arrest the sheriff or assist him in the execution of his writs." Walker to Johnson, Oct. 20, 1866, Lets. Recd. (Main Ser.), File F-408-1866 (M619, Roll 472), RG94, NA.

6. The next day Secretary Stanton wired Walker that the President "requests that you will cause the sheriff to suspend the execution of the writs . . . and send . . . a detailed statement of the facts by telegraph that will enable him to understand the questions in dispute, and to give such direction in respect to the jurisdiction of military and civil authority as will avoid conflict." Stanton to Walker, Oct. 22, 1866, Tels. Sent, Sec. of War (M473, Roll 91), RG107, NA. For further details in the Fernandina conflict, see David S. Walker to Johnson, Jan. 12, 1867.

From Joseph S. Fullerton

St Louis Mo.   Octo. 23d. 1866.

Sir:

Col. Jno. D. Stevenson,[1] lately appointed to the regular army, appeared before the Chicago board of military examiners and passed a satisfactory examination. He was afterwards ordered to proceed to his regiment,[2] but since then the Secretary of War directed him to remain on duty as a member of the board appointed to audit the Missouri military claims vs the U.S., until the work of said board shall be completed. This will detain him here until the latter part of November, and will prevent the vacancy in the board which you mentioned to me.

Genl. Sherman will leave here today for Washington. If he is to temporarily assume the duties of Secretary of War,—according to the report—, I would like very much to work under him as Assistant—in the place vacated by Col Eckart.[3] I could not well have taken such a place under Mr Stanton even if such appointment would have been agreeable to him. I think I would be acceptable to Gen Sherman, and in said position could be of great service to you.[4]

As the case at present stands our prospect for success in the approaching elections in this State are not very encouraging. Our friends are doing all that can be done, but it is hard to accomplish much against a state government that is so completely in the hands of the radicals from the Governor to Constables. A large proportion of the voting population has been disfranchised, and in each district many who, even under the new Constitution are entitled to vote, have been rejected by the radical registers.[5] The union men are dispondent; the radicals rampant. The former have had the whip held over them so long that they are completely cowed. I think there will be no riots during the election—at least, none of sufficient importance to give alarm. Whatever the result may be, we will drive in the wedge that will shatter the radical party in this state.

J. S. Fullerton

ALS, DLC-JP.
  1. Stevenson (1821–1897), a Missouri lawyer, served in the Mexican War and had several terms in the state legislature. On June 7, 1861, he became colonel of the 7th Mo. Inf. and served in the western theater until August 1864 when he was assigned to West Virginia. In March 1863 he was promoted to brigadier general and later brevetted major general of volunteers. Appointed to the regular army in 1866, he was discharged in 1870 and resumed his St. Louis law practice. Warner, *Blue*.
  2. He was colonel of the 30th Inf. Ibid.
  3. Thomas T. Eckert.
  4. Sherman did not become secretary of war.
  5. For more information on voting restrictions, see Parrish, *Missouri, 1860 to 1875*, 121. See also James O. Broadhead to Johnson, Oct. 17, 1866.

From Max Langenschwartz[1]

New York, October 23d '66.

Honorable Sir,

I am directed to transmit to Your Excellency the following Resolutions passed by the General Committee of the League[2] on the 21st inst.—to wit:

Resolved,—after mature Re-consideration,—that we are unshakenly in favor of Sections *first, second* and *fourth* of the Howard Amendment.[3]

Resolved: That we have full faith in the Patriotism and Republican Uprightness of Andrew Johnson.

Resolved: That we heartily desire to see the War Department freed from the Person and Presence of Mr. E. D. Stanton.

Resolved: That this last name recalls to us the name of General McClellan, and that,—despising those who stood by this General only as long as he was in power, but left him when he was cast into the shade,— we herewith renew and confirm our indignation about the slanders and wrongs heaped upon him, declaring our firm belief that with regard to his Personal acts and Sentiments, George B. McClellan stands before the world as pure and irreproachable as any of our purest Patriots. Therefore

Resolved: That we expect to see General McClellan recalled to a Position worthy of his Genius and Patriotism, and of his eminent qualities, abilities and integrity.

Resolved: That we are convinced Andrew Johnsons heart will estimate the right weight of these our feelings, his own mean assailants having lately proven how easy it is to heap the most infamous falshoods upon any noble and prominent character.

Resolved: That a copy of these Resolutions be sent to His Excellency the President.

Acquitting myself of the charge by the General Committee, I have only to join the remark that Our League is not, as often published, a "*German*" one, but composed of members of all Nationalities (Germans being by far the lesser part) throughout the Union.

Col. Max Langenschwartz   H. C. Peoples League
233 East Houston Street N.Y.[4]

Besides the Resolutions sent here, there was another of *high importance*, passed in secret session, and which I could only personally submit to your Excellency.

Please to inform the League through me whether their Resolutions have been received by you.

Max Langenschwartz
233 East Houston str. N.Y. City

P.S. My History of the last events (to be published in french, english and german) progressing rapidly, I would be most happy anyhow to pay you my respects in person, and to converse about some points very interesting to you personally.

ALS, DLC-JP.
1. Langenschwartz (1801–*fl*1868) was the author of several German-language publications, including a study of Austrian politics under Prince Metternich. *NUC*.; Langenschwartz to Johnson, Oct. 12, 1868, Lets. of Appl. and Recomm., 1861–69 (M650, Roll 28), Max Langenschwartz, RG59, NA.
2. The Peoples League, which had been founded in 1853, in which Langenschwartz held the post of "Presid. Head-Central-Committee."
3. The Fourteenth Amendment, presented by Sen. Jacob M. Howard of Michigan.
4. This brief letter and postscript accompanied the longer letter which contained the resolutions of the Peoples League; it was written on a separate page.

From George W. McCracken[1]

Paris, Hotel Meurice—   October 23. 1866

Mr. President.

I have travelled a good deal in Europe during the last year, and had occasion to see something of our Ministers and Consuls in various Countries. A large majority of those, whom I met with, were bitterly hostile to you and your Administration, and expressed that hostility in so open and offensive a manner as to astonish American travellers, and to leave a very bad impression on Europeans who were present. This was particularly true of those from the New England States, of whom a large majority of our foreign representation seems to be composed, and a very indifferent set they are, individually and collectively.

Mr. Motley,[2] Minister at Vienna, does not pretend to conceal his "disgust," as he styles it elegantly, at your whole conduct. Having been appointed *exclusively* by Charles Sumner, he applauds him and his revolutionary doctrines, despises American Democracy, and proclaims loudly, that an English nobleman, is the model of human perfection. There is not in all Europe, a more thorough flunkey, or a more un-American functionary. He tells every traveller, that Sumner is entirely justified and that you have deserted your pledges and principles, in common with Mr Seward, who he says, is "*hopelessly degraded.*"

At Franckfort, the Consul Murphy,[3] who is said to have cleared more than $100,000 through his office, declared repeatedly, that the threat of his friend "Zach Chandler" would be made good and ought to be, by your impeachment. This is notorious and a public scandal. The fellow himself is vulgar, ignorant and unworthy, and is one of Chandler's tools.

Hale at Madrid[4] condemned your course in a malignant manner to various Americans, and so did Morris at Constantinople.[5]

Some of my friends who went to Morroco heard McMath at Tangier[6] rail violently and shamefully against you, saying he was ready to retire from "such a concern." Perry at Tunis,[7] was equally offensive in his language.

There are many others in the same boat and it is time, that better men were appointed—men who will at least respect the President and the dignity of his office.

Radicalism of the worst sort, makes war on you and your friends under every pretext, and yet the instruments of that faction, are blatant, all over Europe, in condemnation of both. It is a shame and a stigma to permit this longer.

Massachusetts seems to monopolise a lion's share of the Consulates, and Boston has no less than *three* of the first Missions. Mr. Adams, Burlingame[8] and Motley. Is no other part of our Country to be considered or worthy of notice? Must Sumner, Butler, Phillips, Chandler, and the like, engross all the honors for their satellites?

I want nothing at your hands of any sort, but fit and decent men should be sent abroad, who will not slander the Chief Executive and the Government. The Consul at Geneva[9] is a common drunkard and a disgrace to the Country. When sober, he abuses the President in the hearing of everybody.

Respectable Americans are very much mortified by the presence of such unworthy persons, in places of trust and responsibility, and few like the task of letting their experience be known, as I have done. There are hundreds who know much more, but prefer to remain silent.

Geo W McCracken of N.Y.

A friend will deliver this note personally.

ALS, DNA-RG59, Lets. of Appl. and Recomm., 1861–69 (M650, Roll 31), George W. McCracken.

1. McCracken was a wealthy New York Democrat, former proprietor of Fort Washington, who traveled in Europe in 1866. Van Deusen, *Seward*, 466; *Welles Diary*, 3: 36–37.

2. John L. Motley (1814–1877), historian and diplomat, served as minister to Austria (1861–67) and to Great Britain (1869–70). In November 1866 Seward confronted Motley and the others mentioned about the charges McCracken had made. Motley immediately replied with a long discourse on his views on Reconstruction and, while they differed from the President's, he insisted he had not publicly broken with the President. Resenting being questioned, he enclosed his resignation, which several months later was accepted. *DAB*; Seward to Motley, Nov. 21, 1866, and Motley to Seward, Dec. 11, 1866, *Senate Ex. Docs.*, 39 Cong., 2 Sess., No. 8, pp. 1–3 (Ser. 1277).

3. William W. Murphy (1816–1886) practiced law in Michigan (1837–61). In July 1861 President Lincoln appointed him consul general for Frankfurt-am-Main, Germany. He served until 1869 when he settled in Heidelberg and worked as an agent for several U.S. railroad companies. *DAB*.

4. John P. Hale served as minister to Spain from 1865 to 1869.

5. Edward J. Morris (1815–1881), legislator, diplomat, and author, served in the U.S. House (1843–45, 1857–61). His diplomatic posts included charge d'affaires to the Two Sicilies stationed at Naples (1850–53) and minister to Turkey (1861–70). *DAB*.

6. Jesse H. McMath (c1832–fl1880) of Ohio was consul to the Barbary States at Tangier. He later was a judge in Cleveland's common pleas court and an attorney. *U.S. Off. Reg.* (1865); Cleveland directories (1870–81); 1880 Census, Ohio, Cuyahoga, Cleveland, 6th Ward, 17th Enum. Dist., 16.

7. Amos Perry (1812–1899) was appointed consul to the Barbary States at Tunis in 1862 and served until he resigned and was replaced in March 1867. *NCAB*, 2: 297; Ser. 6B, Vol. 2: 136, Johnson Papers, LC.

8. Charles Francis Adams and Anson Burlingame. Burlingame (1820–1870), congressman and diplomat, was elected in 1855 to the U.S. Congress where he served three terms. For his services to the Republicans in the 1860 campaign, he was named minister to Peking, China. He served until 1867, when he accepted from the Chinese the post as the head of an official Chinese delegation to visit the western powers. *DAB*.

9. Charles H. Upton (1812–1877), a Virginia public official, was elected as a Republican to the U.S. House of Representatives in 1861. He served until February 1862, when the House unseated him. In 1863 Lincoln appointed him as consul at Geneva, Switzerland, where he served until his death. *BDAC*.

From James A. Rogers

Brownsville Tenn.   23rd. Oct. 1866.

D. Sir,

In as much as coming events cast their Shadows before them, I now, in time, make personal application to you for a pardon[1] for any thing I may have done during the great Rebellion whilst a citizen of Tenn. I was always a union man,[2] but even the union men, many times, were coerced by the authority over them to do things that might be construed by those in power, to be aiding the Confederates. I do not write to any agent, but from your long acquaintance with me, I take the liberty to make direct application to yourself, for this favor.

It does seem to me, that it is about as difficult a matter to get the rebellious states harnessed back into the union, as it was to suppress the rebellion. There is a fault somewhere. Before the rebellion the Negro as a slave was the eternal hobby, now the whole South admit, he is free, treat him in all respects as a freeman yet this does not answer. In the South we try to do just as we are ordered by those in authority over us, yet this does not give satisfactions. The Constitution of our fathers, once esteemed so sacred, is all wrong and must be materially amended. The wise sages, who were actuated in the framing the good old Constitution by the most patriotic feelings, were all wrong and their illustrious descendents must fix it up all at once. God only knows where we are drifting.

I believe to-day that it would be the best thing on earth that could be done for the South, if the last vestige of the negro were removed from us. Colonize them somewhere. Then, we could get white labor to come and help us develope our once happy country. Now when emigrants land at N. York, they are met at the wharves and told that the South is not a safe place for them to go, that we are a set of semi-savage, barbarians and they would not live one year in this country. This at once, causes them to change their course to the north west, with the germ of prejudice planted in their breasts against the Southern people.

You at once see, the insurmountable difficulties thrown in our way. There is but little reliance to be placed in the Negro. He is disposed to be migratory does not want to live long at the same place, has a constant desire to get into the cities & villages, to work one day & play 3. We cannot possibly keep up our farms with such labor, our fences are all going to wreck and the hand of dilapidation is manifest every where. Yet we struggle, we toil and exercise as much patience as characterized the ancient Job, hoping that a better time may dawn upon our downtrodden country.

James A. Rogers.

ALS, DNA-RG94, Amnesty Papers (M1003, Roll 51), Tenn., James A. Rogers.

1. No record of a presidential pardon for Rogers has been located.

2. Rogers's claims about being a Union man are debatable. See Rogers to Johnson, Mar. 25, 1861, *Johnson Papers*, 4: 429–30; Rogers to Johnson, Feb. 22, 1866, ibid., 10: 142.

From John Williams, Jr.

Knoxville, Tenn, Octo. 23, 1866

My dear Sir:—

You will recollect that while in Washington last August on my way to the Philadelphia Convention, I had a conversation with you in reference to the removal of Genl. Cooper[1] from the office of collector of this Congressional District, & the appointment of Col J. T. Abernathy.[2] When

Col. Robert Morrow was here I requested him on his return to Washington, to remind you of this matter. Not hearing from him, & the removal not taking place I supposed in his multiplicity of engagements, he has neglected to mention the subject to you, & therefore, I write to you direct.

Your friends here are desirous for his removal. Genl Cooper is one of your most violent enemies. He is second to no man in Tennessee except Brownlow & Houk,[3] in his denunciations of your Administration. He is making speeches against you wherever & whenever he can get a crowd to listen. He should be turned out at once—without any further delay, and Col. Abernathy appointed in his stead.

Col. Abernathy is a gentleman in the strongest sense of the term. He has been a soldier, and honorably discharged from the Army. He is a man of fine business qualifications. He is an ardent supporter of your Administration; firm & unflinching in his devotion to the cause of Constitutional Government, which you are so heroically fighting to preserve. He is acceptable to your numerous friends in this section of Country.

I hope you will not consider me importunate when I again repeat, make the change, & do it at once.

John Williams.

P.S. In a few days I will have something to say in relation to some other Federal officers in part of the Country. The patronage of the Govern[ment] in the hads of your enemies, will keep you . . .

ALS, DNA-RG56, Appts., Internal Revenue Service, Collector, Tenn., 2nd Dist., John Williams.

1. For other letters that called for the removal of Joseph A. Cooper, see Beriah Frazier to Johnson, Aug. 28, 1866; John Netherland to Johnson, Oct. 15, 1866, Appts., Internal Revenue Service, Collector, Tenn., 2nd Dist., William Rodgers, RG56, NA.

2. James T. Abernathy (b. c1832) had joined the Union army, 10th Tenn. Cav., in August 1863 in Nashville. He became lieutenant colonel in 1865 and was mustered out in August of that year. Abernathy received the appointment as collector in 1866, a post he held until his removal in 1868. CSR, James T. Abernathy, RG94, NA; *Off. Army Reg.: Vols.*, 4: 1187; *U.S. Off. Reg.* (1867); Ser. 6B, Vol. 3: 424, Johnson Papers, LC; Robert Johnson to Abernathy, Nov. 30, 1866, Tels. Sent, President, Vol. 3 (1865–68), RG107, NA; McCulloch to Johnson, July 30, 1868; Edmund Cooper to McCulloch, July 30, 1868, Appts., Internal Revenue Service, Collector, Tenn., 2nd Dist., John Williams, RG56, NA.

3. Leonidas C. Houk.

To Joseph W. Allen

Washington, D.C., Octo 24 1866

Your letter has been received.[1] I was in hopes to have seen you or some one connected with the transaction before now, to whom an explanation might be made, but have not been able to do so. I hope all will be arranged satisfactorily in a short time.[2]

Andrew Johnson

Tel, DNA-RG107, Tels. Sent, President, Vol. 3 (1865–68).
  1. It is not clear what letter Johnson refers to here. Allen sent a letter to the President in March, notifying him of an unpaid draft drawn by Johnson as military governor in 1862 in the amount of $20,000 (interest added to that sum was $3,900). Two months later Allen again wrote to Johnson about the unpaid debt of $20,000; at that time the accrued interest had reached $4,100. Allen noted that the total bill should be paid by June 1. Allen to Johnson, Mar. 6, May 19, 1866, Johnson Papers, LC.
  2. See Johnson to Michael Burns, Nov. 13, 1866, and Allen to Johnson, Jan. 5, 1867.

To Michael Burns

Washington, D.C., Octo 24 1866

Call on Dempsey Weaver, and Joseph W. Allen, and if they will take the cost of twenty (20) State Bonds, which can now be had at Seventy two (72) and Seventy three (73)—You will draw on me for the Amount payable at the First National Bank, Washington. Let me hear from you as soon as convenient.[1]

Andrew Johnson

Tel, DNA-RG107, Tels. Sent, President, Vol. 3 (1865–68).
  1. After receiving the President's telegram, Burns immediately assured Johnson that he would attend to the matter. But four days later Burns informed Johnson that Allen declined to close the transaction while Weaver agreed to close. Burns asked the President if he should deal with Weaver. Johnson's reply of several days later instructed Burns to close with Weaver. Burns to Johnson, Oct. 25, 29, 1866; Johnson to Burns, Oct. 30, 1866, Johnson Papers, LC. See also Johnson to Burns, Nov. 13, 1866.

From George W. Morgan

Mount Vernon O   Oct. 24" 1866

Mr. President,

The democracy of Ohio, polled nine thousand more votes than at any previous election; and our friends are full of hope courage and determination, and are ready for any issue which the Radicals may make. There may be difficulties and dangers ahead, but the majority of the white people of the United States, cannot, and will not be permanently governed by a minority.

George W. Morgan.

ALS, DLC-JP.

From William Patton
Strictly confidential

Towanda Pa   24 Oct. 1866

My dear Sir:

I am so committed, in my public speeches and writings, that I cannot consistently *ask you* for any office; but if you should, on the ground of your own personal knowledge of me; and our early and mutual friendship, and my known loyalty—having been a war democrat throughout—appoint me *on your own responsibility* collector of the Revenue for this District, I would accept it, thankfully. The fact is I am in debt, about $6,000, and that situation would, with my income, enable me to pay it in a year or two, or, at farthest, during your administration.

My friend, Senator Cowan, was committed in favor of Col. McKean,[1] before I had any idea of it, as I supposed your appts. wd. be of Republicans, only; and, I know, he wd. be quite as well, if not better, pleased with my appointment, as with that of Col. McKean's; and by your assuming the responsibility of appointing me, it would relieve him. Col. Smith,[2] our new Postmaster, here, and Col. McKean, belong to the same wing of the Republican party; and, I being a war democrat, I think my appt. wd. give you more strength than to confine your appointments to that wing of the Republican party; which, in fact, is but little more than nominal in this county, and the appt. of P. master, already made to Col. Smith, will hold the very few votes that are in it.

We have lost the election in this State owing to bad nominations. There was a prejudice against Clymer, although a very worthy man, that it was impossible to overcome; and two dem. candidates were renominated for congress who had been defeated before;[3] and, in this district, although we had the most popular dem. in the district for our candidate,[4] he was defeated. I advised the nomn. of a Republican, but our friends relied too much on the popularity of your measures; but, popular as they are, they were overloaded by political hacks. I spent two weeks in Phila., next preceding our election, writing and stumping; and, if we had done as well in the rural districts as we did there we wd. have carried the state by a large majority. But the truth is the election was carried by the radicals with money.

I presume you intend doing what I am going to remind you of and that is to recommend that the compensation to public officers should be all reduced to an amount so low as to make it a matter of patriotic duty to serve in them instead of a profit. I will amplify on this point hereafter.

I would suggest that if I shd. be appointed that my appt. be withheld until after the New York election. I am now helping the Empire state, which, I am in great hopes, will be the Breakwater against the tide of treasonable fanaticism.[5]

W. Patton

ALS, DNA-RG56, Appts., Internal Revenue Service, Collector, Pa., 13th Dist., William Patton.

1. Allen McKean (c1809–1886), a former prothonotary and army paymaster, was a member of the National Union Central Committee for Pennsylvania. Heitman, *Register*, 671; Joseph R. Flanigen et al. to Johnson, Oct. 1, 1866, Customs Service, Surveyor, Philadelphia, Henry W. Tracy, RG56, NA; 1860 Census, Pa., Bradford, Towanda Borough, Towanda, 22.

2. Elhanan Smith (b. c1818), an attorney, had been given a recess appointment as post-

master on August 19, 1866. He was not confirmed by the Senate, however. Ser. 6B, Vol. 3: 161; Vol. 4: 86, Johnson Papers, LC; 1860 Census, Pa., Bradford, Towanda Borough, Towanda, 14.

3. Actually, there were four such candidates: Charles Buckwalter, Henry P. Ross, Robert L. Johnston, and Theodore F. Wright, of the Third, Fifth, Seventeenth, and Eighteenth districts, respectively. All four men had run as Democrats in 1864 and lost. Buckwalter (*c*1839–*fl*1868) was a Philadelphia attorney. Wright has not been further identified. *Guide to U.S. Elections*, 614, 617; Philadelphia directories (1861–68); 1860 Census, Pa., Philadelphia, Philadelphia, 13th Ward, 146.

4. William Elwell (b. *c*1808) was an attorney. 1860 Census, Pa., Bradford, Towanda Borough, Towanda, 1.

5. Received on November 2, the letter was forwarded the following day to the Treasury Department without the President's recommendation. Patton was not nominated by Johnson to fill the collectorship of the Thirteenth District nor, apparently, for any other post. Ser. 6A, Vol. D: 206, Johnson Papers, LC.

From Edgar Cowan

Washington   25 Oct 1866

Dr. Sir.

I write this to remind you of my protest against the removal of Col Thomas Sweeny[1] and the appointment of C M. Derringer in his place.[2]

I know Sweeny was with us heartily—and I doubt if the other was—besides the latter is obnoxious to all our friends.[3] Mr. McCulloch refuses to remove your enemies—why does he remove your friends?[4]

Stop this at all events.

Edgar Cowan

ALS, DNA-RG56, Appts., Internal Revenue Service, Assessor, Pa., 2nd Dist., Thomas W. Sweeny [*sic*].

1. Thomas W. Sweney (*c*1812–1872), former commander of the 99th Pa. Inf., had served as assessor of the Second District since 1863. Later he went into the real estate business. *Off. Army Reg.: Vols.*, 3: 927; *U.S. Off. Reg.* (1863–65); *Evening Bulletin* (Philadelphia), Apr. 9, 1872.

2. Deringer had been appointed in place of Sweney on September 6, but two days later was ordered by Secretary McCulloch to delay assuming his duties until further notice. Ser. 6B, Vol. 3: 161, Johnson Papers, LC; Deringer to [McCulloch], Sept. 8, 1866, Appts., Internal Revenue Service, Assessor, Pa., 2nd Dist., Calhoun M. Deringer, RG56, NA.

3. Deringer had the endorsement of a number of Johnson Clubs in Philadelphia, which decried Sweney's radicalism and called for his removal. In fact, as one supporter put it, Deringer's appointment was the desire of Cowan's friends. See John E. Faunce to McCulloch, Sept. 14, 1866, as well as nearly two dozen other letters and petitions in favor of Deringer, in ibid.

4. The President referred Cowan's note to McCulloch "for his special attention." Nevertheless, thanks in part to Deringer's repeated visits to Washington and the lobbying by a delegation from the Second District which had an interview with Johnson in early November, Deringer was soon thereafter permitted to take office. But when his name was placed in nomination before the Senate in late January 1867, he was ultimately rejected amid allegations that he had taken a bribe. Deringer to Johnson, Oct. 17, Nov. 3, 1866, ibid.; Richard Vaux to Johnson, Nov. 3, 1866, Johnson Papers, LC; Ser. 6B, Vol. 4: 84, ibid.; *National Intelligencer*, Jan. 1, 1867. See also Joseph R. Flanigen to Johnson, Nov. 15, 1866.

To Edwin M. Stanton

Washington D.C., Oct. 25 1866.

Sir:

From recent developments, serious troubles are apprehended from a conflict of authority[1] between the Executive of the State of Maryland and the Police Commissioners of the City of Baltimore.[2] Armed organizations, it is alledged, have been formed in the State, and threats have been made that should a collision occur, armed bodies from other States would enter Maryland, with the view of controlling its people in the settlement of questions exclusively local in character. The Governor of Maryland has therefore deemed it expedient and proper to issue a proclamation, bearing date the 22d inst., warning all persons against such unlawful and revolutionary combinations.[3]

In the event of serious insurrectionary disorders, the Government of the United States might be called upon to aid in their suppression; and I therefore request that you will inform me of the number of Federal troops at present stationed in the city of Baltimore, or vicinity, that would be available for prompt use should their services be required to protect the State from invasion and domestic violence, and to sustain the properly constituted authorities of Maryland.[4]

(sgd) Andrew Johnson.

Copy, DNA-RG108, Lets. Recd. re Military Discipline.

1. Since the end of the war Maryland's voter registration law had engendered significant hostility, for it was the nation's most restrictive and more stringent than procedures used in the South during military reconstruction. As the November 1866 elections approached, the contest between Unionists and Democrats heated up, causing Gov. Thomas Swann to seek the counsel of Johnson and the War Department frequently in the weeks preceding the election. In Baltimore, Governor Swann ousted the Unionist police commissioners and replaced them with Democrats. Unionist Judge Hugh Bond arrested Swann's new commissioners. At issue was the police commissioners' power to appoint election judges sympathetic to Unionists who might prevent some Democrats from voting. Jean H. Baker, *The Politics of Continuity: Maryland Political Parties from 1858 to 1870* (Baltimore, 1973), 143–64; Beale, *Welles Diary*, 2: 620–21.

2. Samuel Hindes and Nicholas L. Wood. Possibly Wood (c1795–fl1880) who was a Baltimore store clerk in 1870. J. Thomas Scharf, *History of Baltimore City and County* (Philadelphia, 1881), 163; 1870 Census, Md., Baltimore, 14th Ward, 452; Baltimore directories (1873–80).

3. For the text of the proclamation, see *National Intelligencer*, Oct. 23, 1866.

4. There were 2,224 soldiers stationed in the vicinity of Baltimore, of whom 1,550 were on active duty. On November 1 and 2, Johnson, believing the military force present not sufficient, requested that Stanton and Grant take whatever measures they deemed necessary to contain and discourage the impending insurgency. However, the election went off calmly and without violence, and the new commissioners took office without disruption. In his July 1867 testimony before Congress, Grant declared his objection to the use of federal troops by Johnson to deal with the Baltimore troubles. For a contemporary account of the situation in Baltimore, the *New York Herald* extensively covered the action throughout October and November 1866. Grant endorsement, Oct. 27, 1866; Johnson to Stanton, Nov. 1, 2, 1866, Johnson Papers, LC; Scharf, *Baltimore City and County*, 164; Simon, *Grant Papers*, 17: 230–32.

From Henry Wikoff

New York   61 [Clinton?] Place   October 25/66
Your Excellency
Allow me to hope that the tone of the "N.Y. Herald" is more acceptable since my return here. I made known to Mr. Bennett the conversation I had the honor to hold with you;[1] & the views & expressions of Your Excellency seemed to afford him no small satisfaction. I made fully known that you attached importance to his friendship & support—that you would not be unmindful of the services already rendered.

As to the "Amendment"; I stated, you left it to the South to accept, or reject, it as they deemed fit.

I am sorry that the friends of Mr. Browning have mixed up your name with the very prolix letter just published, with reference to the "Amendment."[2] Your Message will afford an opportunity to express your opinions on this point,—and if conveyed with only half the force & elegance of thought & diction that have distinguished all your great State Papers the North will be far better satisfied than with the verbose pleading of the Secretary of the Interior. Mr. Bennett is anxious to continue his support of the Administration, but he is committed to the "Amendment." It is his honest conviction that the wisest course for Your Excellency is *not to identify* yourself with any opposition to the "Amendment." This would only enable your antagonists to inflame the public mind against you.

Forney has compromised himself with his own Party. I hope he will be indicted.[3]

If Your Excellency can give any aid to the "Hargous Grant"[4] for a Railroad across the Isthmus of Tehuantepec I shall be very thankful, as I am interested in it. Marshal O. Roberts is the owner of the grant, & he hopes you consider him a staunch Johnson-man in spite of his acquaintance with Forney.

I have urged Mr. Bennett to restore Cook[5] to his late position, & he will do so before the meeting of Congress.

Henry Wikoff

ALS, DLC-JP.
1. Exactly when Wikoff spoke with Johnson is not known.
2. On the night of October 20, Secretary Browning had gone to the Executive Mansion and read the letter to Johnson, Attorney General Stanbery, Sen. Edgar Cowan, and others, who were pleased with it and approved its publication. As Browning noted, "The President was especially solicitous it should be done." Randall, *Browning Diary*, 101. For the letter itself (which the *Herald* judged too long to be printed in its columns but criticized nonetheless), see the *New York Times* or the *National Intelligencer*, Oct. 24, 1866. For the *Herald*'s objections, see its editorial of October 25.
3. There were unsubstantiated rumors that John W. Forney would be indicted for inciting a riot, as expounded in his letter of October 17 in which he blamed the President for the Baltimore police commissioner crisis and called on Union veterans in Pennsylvania and elsewhere to march to Maryland and help resist the use of Federal force. *Press* (Philadelphia), Oct. 18, 1866; *New York Herald*, Oct. 25, Nov. 2, 1866.

4. The Hargous grant across the isthmus of Tehuantepec dates from the late 1840s and was one of many proposed routes across Central America for the purpose of faster transportation and communication between the Atlantic and Pacific oceans. The discussion of a railway and/or canal continued until the turn of the century when the U.S. chose to support the Panama route and began canal construction in 1904. *Senate Misc. Docs.*, 30 Cong., 2 Sess., No. 50, pp. 1–4 (Ser. 533); *House Ex. Docs.*, 47 Cong., 2 Sess., No. 107, pp. 76–79, 87–88, 105, 165–213 (Ser. 2112). See also *House Ex. Docs.*, 33 Cong., 1 Sess., No. 109, p. 5 (Ser. 726); *Senate Ex. Docs.*, 39 Cong., 1 Sess., No. 62, pp. 2–28 (Ser. 1238); 2 Sess., No. 25, pp. 1–30 (Ser. 1277); James M. Callahan, *American Foreign Policy in Mexican Relations* (New York, 1932), 189–213.

5. Thomas M. Cook.

To Edwin M. Stanton

Washington, D.C.   Oct. 26th 1866.

Sir:

Recent advices indicate an early evacuation of Mexico by the French expeditionary forces,[1] and that the time has arrived when our Minister to Mexico[2] should place himself in communication with that Republic.

In furtherance of the object of his mission, and as evidence of the earnest desire felt by the United States for the proper adjustment of the questions involved, I deem it of great importance that General Grant should, by his presence and advice, co-operate with our Minister.

I have therefore to ask that you will request General Grant to proceed to some point on our Mexican frontier most suitable and convenient for communication with our Minister; or (if General Grant deems it best) to accompany him to his destination in Mexico, and to give him the aid of his advice in carrying out the instruction of the Secretary of State, a copy of which is herewith sent for the General's information.[3]

General Grant will make report to the Secretary of War of such matters as in his discretion ought to be communicated to the Department.

Andrew Johnson.

Copy, DLC-JP.

1. See, for example, John Bigelow to William H. Seward, May 25, 1866, and Seward to Bigelow, June 6, 1866, *Senate Ex. Docs.*, 39 Cong., 1 Sess., No. 54, pp. 20–21 (Ser. 1238).

2. Lewis D. Campbell.

3. See Stanton to Grant, Oct. 27, 1866, William T. Sherman Papers, LC; Seward to Campbell, Oct. 20, 1866, *House Ex. Docs.*, 39 Cong., 2 Sess., pp. 569–71 (Ser. 1294). The same day, the 27th, Grant sent to Stanton his continued refusal of the mission. Grant to Stanton, Oct. 27, 1866, Johnson Papers, LC.

To Charles A. Eldredge

Washington, D.C., October 27 1866

Your dispatch received:[1]—Steps have already been taken in reference to the release of B Lynch,[2] which is hoped will result Satisfactory.[3]

Andrew Johnson.

Tel, DLC-JP.

1. Eldredge had telegraphed Johnson earlier on October 27 from Fond du Lac, Wisconsin: "Robert B. Lynch sentenced to death as a Fenian at Toronto Canada is a Citizen *US* resident of Milwaukee—I hope and beg you will interpose to the utmost of power to save him." John T. Hoffman, mayor of New York, also sent Johnson a resolution passed by the city council with a similar request. Eldredge to Johnson, Oct. 27, 1866; John T. Hoffman to Johnson, Oct. 16, 1866, Johnson Papers, LC.

2. Robert B. Lynch (*fl*1879), a native of Ireland, was in Milwaukee, Wisconsin, by 1856, where he worked as a clerk for the city council for several years. Lynch was the first of the Fenians tried for the raid on Fort Erie in Canada in June 1866. His defense claimed that he had been present as a reporter, not as a fighter, but he was nonetheless sentenced to be hanged on December 13, 1866, along with six other conspirators who were tried after him. On October 27, Secretary of State Seward wrote a letter to Sir Frederick Bruce, the British minister in Washington, requesting British government intervention for the Fenians. Milwaukee directories (1856–66); Chicago directories (1874–79); Neidhart, *Fenianism*, 101, 103, 105.

3. Not wanting to make martyrs of the Fenian prisoners, the Canadian government, with urgings from their superiors in Britain, commuted the death penalties of all twenty-five Fenians eventually convicted and sentenced them to twenty years hard labor in the Provincial Penitentiary at Kingston. All the prisoners were released long before they had served twenty years. Lynch, the fourth to be freed, was released on April 6, 1871. He eventually resided in Chicago and sometimes worked as a clerk. Ibid., 104–8; Chicago directories (1874–79).

From David H. Houston[1]

Milford Del.   Oct. 27. 1866.

Sir

I crave your indulgence for the liberty which I take in writing to you, but believing that a letter will interfere less with your engagements than a personal interview, I adobt this mode of respectfully appealing to your kindness and justice.

At an early period of your administration I made application[2] thro' the honorable Secretary of the Treasury for the Collectorship of Internal Revenue for Delaware, and filed with him recommendations which he assured us were sufficient to justify my appointment. Subsequently my brother, Judge John W. Houston,[3] who is well known to you, obtained an interview with you, and on making known to you his desire for my appointment, you very kindly told him that it would give you pleasure to gratify by giving me the appointment, and desired him to go to the Secretary, with whom he was acquainted, and tell him that it was *your* request that he should make the appointment immediately, which he did, but for reason well known and I presume satisfactory, the Secretary declined to comply with the verbal order. Subsequently being convinced that there was no further cause to doubt the Conservatism of Mr Day,[4] the incumbent, we, at the request of and by the advice of the Delegates to the 14th of August Convention, and other friends, Conservative and Democratic, made application for the Assessorship of Internal Revenue,[5] presuming of course, as all did, that as the only obstruction to my obtaining the other position was that Mr Day having become a friend of the Presidents policy it was inexpedient to remove him, there could be no question of my success in this application, for Mr McLear,[6] the incumbent was openly opposing your policy.

Such being the universal opinion, you can imagine with what sorrow, mortification and consternation we learned that Your Excellency had refused to *sanction* my appointment when asked to do so by the honorable Secretary of the Treasury a few days since[7]—but decided in favor of Mr George B. Dixon,[8] an enemy of yours always, because he having been recommended by Messr. Saulsbury, Riddle and Nicholson,[9] our congressional delegation, you could not go against them.

It is to be regretted that these gentlemen should so falsify their often repeated declarations (publicly and privately), that the offices belonged to those of your friends who voted for you for Vice President and now supported your policy and that they could not ask you to appoint a Democrat knowing that none could be confirmed, and *privately* use the influence of *their position* to induce you to repudiate your only true friends, those who voted for you, believed in your policy and desired to sustain you now and hereafter—and *upon whose votes at the November Election these very men depend* for *success* of *their* ticket. The result of their influence is that your Conservative supporters are entirely *ignored* for of all the appointments made for this state, *but one* (a village post office) has been given to them.[10] And now we learn that their *leader*,[11] a man whose record for loyalty, respectability and influence will bear the scrutiny of even the Senate of the U.S. is denied the last appointment of any consequences in the State: "the last feather broke the camels back"—these acts are the most convincing proof that Radical assertions are true and if the present feeling is not corrected before the 6th of November—the result can be foreseen.[12]

Again apologizing for this liberty and hoping that my appeal will be favorably considered.[13]

David H. Houston

ALS, DNA-RG56, Appts., Internal Revenue Service, Del., 1st Dist., David H. Houston.

1. A graduate of Jefferson Medical College in Philadelphia, Houston (1819–*fl*1878) had served during the war in the volunteer ranks, rising to the post of chief surgeon, 1st Div., 2nd Corps, Army of the Potomac, before his retirement in July 1864. Described as a Lincoln/Johnson man in 1864, he later ran twice as a Republican for the state legislature but lost both contests. *Biographical and Genealogical History of the State of Delaware* (2 vols., Chambersburg, Pa., 1899), 2: 1313–14; William O. Redden to Hugh McCulloch, Sept. 29, 1866, Appts., Internal Revenue Service, Assessor, Del., 1st Dist., David H. Houston, RG56, NA.

2. Not found, but several recommendations of Houston were received at the White House and routinely referred to the Treasury Department from early July through late September 1866. Ser. 6A, Vol. C: 98–99, 107, 109, Johnson Papers, LC. See also Reverdy Johnson to Johnson, Aug. 24, 1866, Appts., Internal Revenue Service, Assessor, Del., 1st Dist., David H. Houston, RG56, NA.

3. Houston (1814–1896) had served as a Whig in Congress (1845–51) prior to becoming associate judge of the Delaware superior court in 1855, a position he held until he

retired from the bench in 1893. He was also a member of the 1861 peace conference in Washington, D.C. *BDAC*.

4. Charles H.B. Day (1828-*fl*1899) was an attorney whom Lincoln first appointed as collector of the district of Delaware in August 1862, a position he held until May 1869. He was later elected clerk of the House of Representatives for the 1877 session. *Biographical History of Delaware*, 2: 1236.

5. See the petition written by Houston, signed by Day and other delegates, and addressed to McCulloch on Sept. 24, 1866, in Appts., Internal Revenue Service, Assessor, Del., 1st Dist., David H. Houston, RG56, NA.

6. John P. McLear (*fl*1881), a real estate agent and stock broker whom Lincoln appointed as assessor in 1862, had served as chairman of the state Republican convention which met in Dover several months earlier. He later worked in the insurance business and as treasurer of a textile firm. Redden to McCulloch, Sept. 29, 1866, ibid.; John A. Nicholson to Johnson, Aug. 15, 1866, ibid., George B. Dickson; Wilmington directories (1862–82).

7. Evidence that McCulloch made such a request has not been located.

8. Dickson (b. *c*1821), a former recorder of deeds, was a Democrat and had the endorsement of several other prominent Democrats, including Gove Saulsbury, the Democratic candidate for governor. See Saulsbury to Johnson, Aug. 15, 1866, as well as other recommendations in Appts., Internal Revenue Service, Assessor, Del., 1st Dist., George B. Dickson, RG56, NA. Actually, Dickson's appointment was not made official until mid-November 1866. Ser. 6B, Vol. 3: 206, Johnson Papers, LC; 1860 Census, Del., Kent, Dover Hundred, Dover, 4. See also James L. Houston to Johnson, Nov. 10, 1866, Appts., Internal Revenue Service, Assessor, Del., 1st Dist., James L. Houston, RG56, NA.

9. Senators Willard Saulsbury and George Read Riddle, and Rep. John A. Nicholson, all Democrats. Riddle (1817–1867) worked as a civil engineer and practiced law before entering politics and serving with Johnson in Congress (1851–55). He was elected to the Senate in 1864. Nicholson (1827–1906) was a school superintendent and an attorney prior to his two terms in Congress (1865–69). *BDAC*. For their recommendations of Dickson, see Nicholson to Johnson, and Willard Saulsbury to Johnson, both Aug. 15, 1866, Appts., Internal Revenue Service, Assessor, Del., 1st Dist., George B. Dickson, RG56, NA.

10. Among the more important offices, Joseph M. Barr had been appointed as postmaster of Wilmington and Caleb P. Johnson was given the marshalship. Both men were Democrats. See James L. Houston to Johnson, Sept. 25, 1866, ibid., James L. Houston; Ser. 6B, Vol. 3: 206, Johnson Papers, LC. See also Caleb P. Johnson to Johnson, Sept. 19, 1866.

11. Here Houston, as a Conservative Republican, probably refers to himself.

12. In the state-wide canvass Gove Saulsbury was elected governor and the Democrats maintained their sizable majority in the legislature. Moreover, Nicholson won his second term by a relatively comfortable margin. *American Annual Cyclopaedia* (1866), 264.

13. Received one day after the election, Houston's letter was referred to the Treasury Department without the President's recommendation. Less than a week later, Dickson was given a recess appointment for the assessorship. Confirmed by the Senate in March 1867, he apparently continued serving through the end of Johnson's term. Ser. 6A, Vol. D: 101; Ser. 6B, Vol. 3: 206; Vol. 4: 102, Johnson Papers, LC; *U.S. Off. Reg.* (1867–69).

From Mary Livermore[1]

Paris. France. Oct. 27th 1866.

Dear Sir.

Having addressed a letter to you in regard to the Paris Consulate,[2] whilst you were making a tour through the States, I am under the impression that you never rec'd it; and write again to inform myself, and you, whether a letter to the President of the United States can be suppressed in consequence of its political tendencies.

I can bring the name of Judge Smith,[3] an old Tennessee friend of yours to attesst my veracity and standing as a lady in St. Louis, Mo. who, with his wife, and "Tiff,"[4] boarded in the same house with me awhile, when Tennessee was too hot too hold you all.

In the letter alluded to, I informed you of what is well, and generally, known, in Paris, in regard to Mr. Nicolay's[5] politics. He has expected to be removed all summer. He is about as bitter a radical as can be found on either Continent. This I *know*, I travelled with some of his personal friends to Paris.

My husband[6] is a true blue Union, Conservative, man; and was ruined in fortune by the tyranny of a Federal Official[7] while we were under Military rule in St. Louis. As the Government ruined him, I thought it no more than right that it should help him to live.

I am dying with consumption and should think it the greatest earthly blessing if I could have my husband with me; but we are separated by our misfortunes. My husband can give you the names of the best *Johnston* men of his state, who have been deterred from applying to you in consequence of your unaccountable generosity to a political enemy. Though of Northern extraction, Mr. Livermore, has lived in some portion of the South since boyhood. Familiarity with each Section has prevented his being a fanatic.

One line from your hand will give an unhappy invalid, great satisfaction, and be prised for the autograph alone.

Mary Livermore.

12 Rue Jacob. Paris France.

Mr. Emery Livermore, 10. Commercial St, St. Louis Mo.

ALS, DLC-JP.

1. Livermore, not further identified, had moved to Paris on the orders of her physician as she suffered from consumption. Mary Livermore to Johnson, Aug. 23, 1866, Lets. of Appl. and Recomm., 1861–69 (M650, Roll 35), John G. Nicolay, RG59, NA.

2. Ibid.

3. William M. Smith.

4. Smith was married twice—first to Julia Taylor in 1853 and later to Mattie Rives. He had five sons and one daughter. *BDTA*, 1: 686.

5. John G. Nicolay.

6. Emery Livermore (*c*1809–*fl*1879) was a commission merchant during the war and a bookkeeper afterwards. 1870 Census, Mo., St. Louis, 8th Ward, 15th Subdiv., 49; St. Louis directories (1863–79).

7. The official is unidentified; for details, see Mary Livermore to Johnson, Aug. 23, 1866, Lets. of Appl. and Recomm., 1861–69 (M650, Roll 35), John G. Nicolay, RG59, NA.

From James A. Stewart

Confidential

Rome Ga   Oct 27th 1866

Dear Sir:

You will perceive from the enclosed slip from the Atlanta Intel-ligencer,[1] that the canvass for Congress in this district to fill the vacancy created by the resignation of Genl William T. Wofford, is developing the old leven of Secession. We have now, six candidates in the field,[2] all soliciting the suffrages of the people on the ground of having taken up arms in support of, or otherwise aiding the cause of secession and rebellion.

I have just returned home from Atlanta. Was there ten days. Had fre-quent opportunities to mix with the people—to hear the expression of their views, and to judge of the cincerity of their professions. You may rest assured that our aspirants for Congressional honors, have no love for you, except through your aid, to ride into power and position. There is not the shadow of a chance to elect a true and consistent Johnson man to any office. A man South, who never wavered in his attachment to a Con-stitutional Union cant be elected to congress. A man South, who like your self never gave countenance to, or sanctioned secession, cant be elec-ted to Congress.

Secessionists court the favor and support of true Johnson men; but so soon as one becomes a candidate for office, he is turned upon as fiercely as conscripts were set upon by Blood hounds.

We have a few men south claiming to be Union men who, through per-secution, or other causes, have been induced to seek protection from re-bel persecution, in the Radical party North. They are radicals to all in-tents and purposes,—Supporting, perhaps honestly, the most extreme radical measures, and as such we could not reasonably encourage their election to positions of importance.

Besides these, we have conservative Union men in point of numbers and talents enough to fill all important positions, and hence there is no excuse for the south in sending up men to congress who cant take the required oath. You may rest assured if this infernal rebellious spirit now being again fanned into life by Southern journals and unscrupulous po-litical aspirants, is not severely and promptly rebuked, that no firmness of purpose on your part—that no depth of wisdom or Statesmenship how-ever profound can prevent the "*higher law*" men north aided by madmen south from subverting and casting aside every vestage of the Old Gov-ernment.

Our Secessionists South tried to overthrow the Government. They failed, and now, some of them are willing to see it brought to ruin through the instrumentality of Northern fanatticism. I feel for you in your position, and hope you may be able to prevent the enemies of our

Government, both north and south, from again involving us in war, which may end only in the utter ruin of our country.

J. A. Stewart

ALS, DLC-JP.
1. Not found, but possibly the statement by congressional candidate James P. Hambleton, which included the following: "Let us maintain boldly, fearlessly and defiantly, if we choose, that the South in her effort to establish a Southern Confederacy, was guilty of no crime, and although failing, was simply in the exercise of an inalienable right." *Atlanta Intelligencer*, Oct. 26, 1866.
2. The candidates for Georgia's Seventh Congressional District November 28, 1866, election were: James P. Hambleton (c1832–1897), surgeon, 35th Ga. Inf., CSA, and editor of the Atlanta *Southern Confederacy*, who later practiced medicine in Washington, D.C.; James M. Calhoun (1811–1875), lawyer and ex-mayor of Atlanta; Daniel S. Printup (1823–1887), Rome lawyer and former major, 55th Ga. Inf., CSA; Nathaniel J. Hammond (1833–1899), lawyer and Confederate solicitor general of the Atlanta circuit who was later a Democratic congressman (1879–87); Jesse A. Glenn (1833–1904), a Whitfield County lawyer and colonel, 36th Ga. Inf., CSA, who became a Republican and was postmaster of Dalton under Grant; and Francis H. Little (b. c1839), a Walker County resident and colonel, 11th Ga. Inf., CSA. Incomplete election returns seem to indicate that Little was the winner. *Rome Courier*, Oct. 16, Nov. 30, Dec. 7, 21, 1866; *Atlanta Intelligencer*, July 26, Oct. 19, 21, 28, 1866; Franklin M. Garrett, *Atlanta and Environs* (3 vols., Athens, 1954–87), 1: 923; 2: 350; 1860 Census, Ga., Fulton, Atlanta, 1st Ward, 697; Floyd, Rome, 1st Ward, 3; Walker, West Armuchee Dist., 765; Henderson, *Confederate Soldiers of Georgia*, 2: 73; 3: 844; Washington, D.C., directories (1894–97); Kinney et al., *Floyd County Cemeteries*, 1: 411; *List of Field Officers, Regiments and Battalions in the Confederate States Army, 1861–1865* (Mattituck, N.Y., 1983), 98; *BDAC*; Clark Howell, *History of Georgia* (4 vols., Chicago, 1926), 2: 135–36; *Walker County Heritage, 1833–1983* (Dallas, 1984), 255.

From Saul S. Henkle[1]

Washington City   Oct 28, 1866

Sir:

I am as you probably know a conservative Republican and have been a uniform and active supporter of your administration from the beginning. I was a Delegate from the 7th Congressional Dist of Ohio to the Philadelphia Convention and was selected by the Republican wing as their member of the Committee on Resolutions in that body. During the late campaign in Ohio I spent my time and money in travelling and making speeches in favor of Conservatism. I am here at the urgent request of the leading Johnson men and some of the leading Democrats to counteract if possible the efforts of Mr Miller[2] late Democratic candidate for Congress in my Dist to induce your Excellency to make a set of appointments which if made will be considered an abandonment of your conservative friends and would leave your Administration without a supporter in our Dist outside of the Democratic party.

1st I charge Mr Miller with treachery to the Johnson men who in good faith supported him.

Upon my return from Philadelphia he called upon me and almost abjectedly solicited my support—and pledged his honor that he would not interfere in appointments saying that the Johnson men (Republicans) should have them—that he would neither recommend, nor encourage any Democrat in making application for appointments and all he asked was that appointments be withheld until after the election.

He made this pledge to me distinctly and he made to many others. If he denies I am prepared to prove it.

Some Democrats who knew him better than we did urged us to take his pledge in writing, which writing was prepared by them or at their instance and submitted to Mr Miller. He professed to be indignant because it implied a want of confidence in his word.

We supported Mr Miller in good faith and that [he] was not elected must be attribed to other causes than a want of support from us. The result probably could not have been changed by any man certainly not by a Democratic candidate but I am entirely satisfied that if we had had a suitable candidate we could have made a vastly more creditable fight than we did.

I charge that nearly all the leading Democrats in the Dist were opposed to the nomination of Mr Miller and that he procured his nomination by management and the use of money without talent and utterly without education foisted himself upon the convention as a candidate—when there was possibility of success except by taking the best man who could be induced to run. His nomination recognized as it was by nearly every one as unfit to be made, demoralized and the contest from the beginning was a hopeless one.

Besides after he got the Johnson men to work for him, he began to coquette with different persons with regard to appointments for the same place and in some instances this double dealing was observed and lukewarmness and disgust the result. Now the election is over in violation of his most solemn promises and pledges not to interfere in appointments and not to encourage any Democrat in applying for office, he comes here seeking two appointments as I am informed. One that of Post Master. The other of assessor of Internal Revenue, and it was understood at home that his programme extended also to the collector.

He recommends for Post Master at Columbus O. P. Hines.[3] Mr H is a very good man I believe, but is and has always been a Democrat and has but been heard of in Columbus as a Candidate. He is or has been the partner in business of Wm Miller[4] the brother of Thomas, who is the applicant for assessor.

Now as to Wm Miller what I say of him is upon my personal responsibility and I would rather say it in his presence than behind his back.

I charge that his reputation at home is that of a mercenary, mean and unprincipled man and that he is not only simply unpopular but is almost universally dispised in the community in which he lives. I have heard it repeatedly charged and never heard it denied that he was heretofore interested in a very disreputable business, but as I know nothing except from information—I do not charge it as true.

Now Mr Miller seeks the removal of Judge Dewey[5] recently appointed assessor and the substitution of his brother as I am informed by the Secy of Treasury upon the ground that he violated pledges to him—Did not support him &c. Mr Miller should be the last to speak of broken pledges but I say the charge against Judge Dewey is *false*, and if proof is required it can be produced in abundance. The Community in which he lives is most fiercely Radical and Mr Miller was intensely objectionable to the people of that County as a candidate. That was not Deweys fault.

The real objection to Dewey is that he appointed Conservative Republicans or Johnson men as his assistants upon the Recommendation of myself and other Johnson men and did not the men that Wm Miller recommended. This is the only reason given in the Community where the facts are known.

Since Mr Millers defeat every body concedes that he should not have been a candidate and I am satisfied that his influence is less now than before he ran.

It would now be a nice thing to turn out of office the influential friends of the Prest and give them to Mr Miller's family.

And now in conclusion Mr Prest allow me to say that we (the Johnson men) have stood by you faithfully and some of us have lost friends and business on account of the part we have taken in behalf of your Policy, and if the suggestions of Mr Miller are yielded to we shall feel that we have been abandoned by the Prest and the result you can calculate.

If my statements are not credited all I ask is time to prove them to your satisfaction.

S. S. Henkle

ALS, DLC-JP.

1. Henkle (c1828–c1899), a Columbus lawyer and wartime member of the Ohio board of enrollment, about the time of this letter became a permanent resident of Washington, D.C. 1870 Census, D.C., Washington, 2nd Ward, 230; Washington, D.C., directories (1869–99); Columbus directories (1866–67); *OR*, Ser. 3, Vol. 5, 901; *National Intelligencer*, Jan. 22, 1867.

2. Thomas Miller.

3. Oliver P. Hines (*fl*1881) operated a papermill in conjunction with William Miller before becoming a cigar maker and later banker. Columbus directories (1862–81); *George W. Hawes' Ohio State Gazetteer* (1859–60).

4. William Miller (*fl*1881), along with Oliver P. Hines, ran a papermill before going out on his own. Ibid., Columbus directories (1862–81).

5. Charles W. Dewey (*fl*1881) was a probate judge in the early 1860s. R. S. Dills, *History of Greene County . . . and the State of Ohio* (Dayton, 1881), 935.

From David B. Pickens[1]

Oregon   october the 28th 1866
Scholls Fery Twalitan River   Washington county

My friend

Mr Andrew Jonson i beg you will indulge me with your forgiveness for the liberty which i take in thus troubling you with a letter but as my name is probably familiar to you from my having been a resident from my youth up to the year of 1855 of East tennessee Sulivan county. I was 38 years old the fall i left East tennessee. I emegrated to Missoury in adair county with a wife & 9 children.[2] My wife and 3 of my children deceast in missoury. I lived thar till the Spring of 62 which i crost the plains. I have maried and has a wife and 6 children with me now.[3] I have a Son[4] in the States. He has bin in the union armey over 4 years. He was under grant till grant got to be the chief commander and then he was placed under Sherman till he was discharged. You are well a quanted with all of my relations in east tennessee. I will mension Some of them to you. Old David Bragg[5] was my grandfather and all of the Pickens & hails & hayzes & baughtmans & Mourlocks & titsworth & finks are my relations.

Well Mr Jonson i have all wais ever Sence i have bin old a nough to vote bin a warm friend of yours. I all wais Supported you in every instance in your a lections. I have often wisht for the time to come that you would be president of the united States. I at last have reacht my desire in that. Well Mr andrew Jonson i now will give you the histry of the way i have voted Sence i left East tennessee that is for the prominent men. I voted for buck hannon for president and that ticket thrue when i lived in missoury. Then i voted for douglas for president next. This was the way i voted while i lived in missoury. I voted for missoury to Stay in the union. I voted for lincorn & you this last a lection. If it had not a bin that i had all confidence in you i could not have voted for lincorn. I all wais was a democrat till this ware broke out then i tuck the name of the union party. I have watcht your corse and your percedence ever Sence you have bin in president and i can Say to you to day that i inedorse your policy and a nother a State a lection hear will prove to you that oregon indorses Andrew Jonsons policy. The people are changing ther opinion hear faste. Sence this laste a lection for governor ther was wone curnel hawkins[6] of east tennessee. He Said he lived in Knoxville. Perhaps you now him. He Stunped this State in favor of congress and the union party and Said brown low ism was constitutional. In east tennessee he trid to leave the impression on the peopels minds that you had changed Sence you had got to be president. I rite this to you that you may now wone of your Enemys. Well Mr Johnson i never was enney polatishner but if i had a bin able i would a traveled over this State with him. I could a talked Some and a told the people of oregon that i was as well a quanted with you as mister hawkins and i new you to be a Sound man & to be a pore mans friend & a Soaldiers friend.

This I tell to to all i converse with a bout you. I now you well tho you may have no recolection of me. I new your Son and Sunan law David patison. I was wone that voted for him for Sircuit Judg before i left tennessee. He was a good judge. I tuck the greenville Spy 3 years before i left Eastten-nessee. Now Mr jonsson if you think my Note and acquaintance of you is worthy of your notice i wish you to Send me Some interesting Books or docaments. I Recolect Well a hearing you Say once in Blunts ville that if you had enney thing to give you would give it to your friends. Now you have got the hiist office that is in the gift of the people and you have the power to do Something for your old long tride friends & be non the worst for doing it. Remember me i am a umble Sadler by trad & 49 years old and my means is very limited and i now you have a Simpathy for a mac-anic and the old and your long friend and wone of your own State. Those lines is not rite to flatter you. Thay are Sincear from my harte. Ther is Some radical hear in office that i think aut to be turned out and Some of your friends have them. I must bring my lines to a close by wishing you a long life and a happy won. If you think my leter worthy of your notice and feels like doing enney thing for me that is to rite to me or Send me enney book or docaments i will give you my Poste office address. Direct them to Porteland Po Multinoma co Scholls Fery Box oregon.

David B. Pickens

ALS, DLC-JP.
    1. Pickens (c1817–fl1866) was a farmer in Tennessee before moving to Missouri, where he worked as a saddler. 1850 Census, Tenn., Sullivan, 1st Dist., 190; (1860), Mo., Adair, Morrow, Twp., 76.
    2. Pickens was married to Rebecca (b. c1813), who died during the late 1850s. His nine children, of whom only seven can be accounted for, included Elizabeth (b. c1841), John (b. c1843), Thomas (b. c1845), Joseph (b. c1846), Sarah (b. c1849), Charles (b. c1853), and Nancy (b. c1855). Ibid.
    3. Unidentified.
    4. Probably John Pickens.
    5. Bragg (c1750s–fl1830) of Sullivan County, Tennessee. 1830 Census, Tenn., Sullivan, 298.
    6. Isaac R. Hawkins.

From Narcissa P. Saunders[1]

Private.

"Melrose" Near Nashville, Tenn.   October 28th 1866.
Mr President.
    For a long time past, I have been wishing to address you a letter to re-assure you of our unchanging regard, and of "your peoples'" un-diminished love. We of this state never cease to watch your every move-ment with the greatest interest—and notwithstanding the slanders and malice of union factions and parties, know full well that the *truest* friend of the *Union*—stands at the helm of "the good old ship of state." You have our *prayers*, Mr President—for a long life of usefulness—prosperity and

success—and surely that just God—who has so faithfully promised "never to forsake those who put their trust in Him"—will in the end crown your heroic and righteous efforts with His Blessing and a lasting Peace to our country. Doubtless you must meet with many vexations and trials, but then *who* of us have not those? Truly "every heart knoweth its own bitterness." Since we parted with you our little household has been in *deep troubles* and *affliction*—for my beautiful sister[2] has "passed away"—like a tender flower before the storm! Oh! Mr President, *what* a *fate* was *hers*! I fairly shudder with misery and horror, when I think of the story of her sad life, and saddest of *all deaths*! You must have heard of Ma's[3] opposition to the marriage—although, after it was consumated, on my *sisters account* we never would say any thing about her husband. But now that old ties are broken—I am free to say to you—that, in my opinion, he (Col. *W*)[4] is the *worst* man I have ever known or *heard* of. He married my sister for her *money*—and it was as much of a speculation, with him as though he had been *buying* and *selling cotton*. In *four weeks* after the wretched wedding he made her make a will in which she left him and, in event of his death, (every thing she owned or *might own*) to his "representatives." When Ma reached Philadelphia, he for half a day refused to allow her the privilege of seeing her *dying daughter*—and during the last hours of his lovely wifes life he was *cursing* and *abusing* in the most *profane* and *vilest* language, her Mother, Brother[5] & sister. In my sister's last illness, he was boasting of "*his* wealth" and in less than an *hour* after she *died*—he *escorted* home a young lady, and remained at her Fathers' until late the day following. He refused to give Ma a lock of her daughter's abundant hair, but the servant woman, Sally (*Uncle Bens'* daughter) who helped him in all his schemes—and whom he *paid* for so doing, is now in Nashville, wearing a set of *jewelry* made of *Sis'* hair which the "Col gave her." He has sworn dozens of times "to kill" Ma, Brother, and myself; in fact, has frequently sent *me* word that he "meant to *defame* my *character* until I was the most disgraced woman in the U. States." However, when he was in town some weeks ago, to have *his* will (for it was *not* my *sisters*) probated, Brother feeling so incensed at his vile language and conduct, hunted him up and denounced, him as a "coward—villian, and swindler", all of which he most amiably bore without once resenting it. So he proved himself to be what his *brother officers* have *always* pronounced him—as much of a *coward* as knave. Pardon me, Mr President—for expressing myself so plainly—but you *cannot imagine* how deeply this man has outraged our feelings and insulted us *every possible* way. He made my poor sister believe that her Mother, sister, and brother were the worst enemies she had in the world—that we *hated* her—had disinherited her—that we *refused* to come and see, while she lay weeping with mental and physical agony upon her *dying bed*. All of this and *much* more she had to hear—& so under the weight of these accumulated *woes*, she, poor child! *had to die*! And this man committed these many crimes simply for money and nothing more. As I have before remarked, I have never met with such a character, not even in the over-wrought fictions of Sue, or Victor Hugo.[6] Under ordinary circum-stances, Mr President, I should apologize for speaking of our *domestic troubles*, but as you knew my lovely sister and seemed attached to her (as she *certainly was* to *you*) and Mr Smith[7] recently told me that you had inquired into the matter, Ma, as well as myself, felt that it was *due us* that you should hear the truth concerning the treatment that our whole family met with from Col. W.[8] But enough on this unhappy subject. The citizens of Nashville were *greatly disappointed* that you did not come to see them during your late tour, but we hope ere long that you may honor us with a visit. You would receive a *heartfelt welcome*, I assure you. The changes in military affairs recently ordered in this Department, is very gratifying to the people generally—*including* the officers of the U.S. Army who are stationed here. I mean those *outside* of Gen Thomas' staff. I *know* this to be *so*—as our house is visited by almost all the Federal offi-cers in Nashville. Will you pardon me, Mr president, if I refer to a little matter that is a good deal discussed in military circles here? It is in rela-tion to the promotion of officers who are *not* considered friends of the administration, and the *non*-promotion of others warmly devoted to your course and cause. For instance—Brevet Maj Gen Carlin, who ranks as Maj. (*only*) of the 16th Regulars—(stationed *here*) was a few days since notified by Gen Kautz[9] that *he* had come to take command of the regi-ment, having very recently been appointed by Mr *Stanton* Lieut. Col. of the regiment *now* commanded by Gen Carlin. Thus, you see a soldier who distinguished himself through the war, and a man *thoroughly conser-vative* in his views, and a *friend* to *you*—kept in the same position he held during & before the war (except his *Brevet* rank) while Gen *K.* known more particularly as a *friend* of Gen Butler[10]—is *promoted over* this *more worthy* officer. I have written you of this circumstance because, as a *true friend* to *you*, Mr President, I felt it my *duty* to do so. Gen C. has no idea of my intention of writing to you on the subject; but I think he would have been particularly gratified to have been placed in command as Lieut Col of the Regiment he has been with (*here*) since the war was over. Now, you needn't accuse me of asking favors for a *beau*, as he (Gen. C.) has been *married two years*. What I have written you is *perfectly confidential* and I hope you will excuse me for having expressed myself so freely; but I *wanted* to *tell* you just what I have written; and that is my *only* apology. Ma unites with me in kindest regards to Mrs J. and your daughters & self; while I am, Mr President, your *attached friend*.

Narcissa P. Saunders.

Will you not drop me a line to say you *pardon* this *long* letter?

ALS, DLC-JP.

1. Saunders (*c*1835–1913) was one of the three children of John W. Saunders and Cynthia Pillow. Except for time spent in Washington in the late 1850s as part of the social

scene there, Saunders evidently lived her entire life in Nashville. Saunders excessive use of commas, semi-colons, and dashes in this letter made for extremely difficult reading and, therefore, some were deleted. Sistler, *1850 Tenn. Census*, 1: 204; Jill K. Garrett, comp., *Obituaries from Tennessee Newspapers* (Easley, S.C., 1980), 424–25.

2. Cynthia Saunders (c1844–1866) had married Thomas C. Williams in May 1865 and moved with him from Nashville to Philadelphia, where she died in July 1866. Ibid.; *Evening Bulletin* (Philadelphia), July 10, 1866.

3. The mother was Cynthia Pillow Saunders Brown (c1815–fl1878), who had married Aaron V. Brown in 1845. She was the sister of Gideon J. Pillow. *BDTA*, 1: 82; Sistler, *1850 Tenn. Census*, 1: 204; Garrett, *Obituaries*, 424–25. See also Cynthia Pillow Saunders Brown to Johnson, Nov. 9, 1866.

4. Thomas C. Williams (d. 1869) entered military service in August 1861 as a captain in the 19th U.S. Inf. He was brevetted a lieutenant colonel in August 1865; at one point in his career he served as an aide to Gen. Lovell Rousseau. ACP Branch, File S-302-CB-1869, RG94, NA.

5. John Edward Saunders (b. c1838), Narcissa's younger brother, was later one of the defendants in the lawsuit brought by Williams. Sistler, *1850 Tenn. Census*, 1: 204; *Tennessee Supreme Court Reports*, 5 Coldwell (1868).

6. Eugène Sue (1804–1857) and Victor Hugo (1802–1885) were both French novelists. *Webster's New Collegiate Dictionary*.

7. Not identified.

8. In October 1866 Williams requested that General Grant assign him to a post at or near Nashville, so that he, Williams, could help prepare for the lawsuit that would be going to court in early 1867. Grant bounced the request to Gen. O. O Howard, who evidently did in fact assign Williams to either Nashville or Memphis. In any event, the expected lawsuit, Thomas C. Williams v. Narcissa Saunders et al., emerged in 1867 over the question of the probate of Cynthia S. Williams's will. The case was eventually heard by the state supreme court in 1868 at which time the court found in favor of Thomas Williams. ACP Branch, File S-302-CB-1869, RG94, NA; Garrett, *Obituaries*, 424. See *Tennessee Supreme Court Reports*, 5 Coldwell (1868).

9. William P. Carlin and August V. Kautz. See John S. Brien to Johnson, Oct. 18, 1866.

10. Benjamin F. Butler.

From M. Elizabeth Young

Nashville   October 28th [1866]

President Johnson

Once more I appeal to you to aid my Aunt.[1] Her pecuniary situation is most deplorable. All that she posessed was in the Union Bank and it has gone into a state of liquidation and has failed to pay her which leaves her peneyless. The little I have will be expended in a few months. We then will both be without a home—and without the means of [obtaig?] one. Can you listen to this recital unmoved—and from persons for whom you have expressed so much regard. Why is it that you will not give her that paltry office that I asked for her. Would it inconvenience you? And it would save her from actual want. Is it so much that I ask for? Possibly you do not understand what I wish. It is the Timber Agent to care for the timber on the wild lands on the coast of Florida and else where. It is a sinecure that her nephew Robert Sommerville[2] could attend to for her without giving up his business. Why is it that I have to appeal to you so often for such a trifle? Are you going to wait until Congress meets and the Radicals put it out of your power to aid us?[3] I cannot come to Washington—else I would have been there long since to have asked you in person but the *Gossips* have put that out of my power.

Do not let me have to ask again. Do for a moment consider our situation and aid us. Is our consistent Friendship nothing? Have we made no sacrifices for you so that you should [illegible] to aid us in such a trifle— or perhaps you think that I am exaggerating our situation. I do not prevaricate and have not said all, but you alone can aid us in your *official* capacity. Will you do it or not?[4]

M E Young

ALS, DLC-JP.

1. Martha Somerville of Nashville.

2. Robert N. Somerville (b. *c*1832) was a successful cotton broker in Montgomery, Alabama, by the time of the 1870 census. 1870 Census, Ala., Montgomery, Montgomery, 50.

3. Certainly a number of friends attempted to secure Robert Somerville's appointment. There was a flurry of letters in the summer of 1867. See, for example, Edward H. East to Johnson, June 13, 1867; John Trimble to Johnson, June 17, 1867; Martha A. Somerville to Johnson, June 17, 1867; Sarah C. Polk to Johnson, June 17, 1867, Appts., Customs Service, Subofficer, Fla., Robert N. Somerville, RG56, NA.

4. Despite another plea from M. Elizabeth Young to Johnson in behalf of her aunt and Robert Somerville, Gideon Welles notified the President that there had been no timber agents appointed since the beginning of the Civil War. In fact, in his annual report Secretary Welles had recommended that no such agents should ever again be appointed. Young to Johnson, June 15, 1867, ibid.; Welles to Johnson, July 3, 1867, Lets. Sent to President and Exec. Agencies, Vol. 22 (M472, Roll 11), RG45, NA.

From Charles Glanz[1]

Easton, Penna.   Oct. 29. 1866.

Dear Sir

I find myself compelled, most reluctently, to decline the appointment of Assessor of this (11th) district, recently so graciously tendered me.[2]

I have been for many years past engaged in the business of brewing beer at this place, and for the last two years I have been anxious to dispose of that business, whenever I could do so without too severe loss.

At the time I made application for the appointment,[3] I had under consideration, offers, that were made by my partner[4] to buy out my interest and by independent parties in New York, to take the whole establishment.

I therefore very naturally supposed, that I could readily so dispose of my interest, either to my partner or to other parties as to enable me to qualify myself under the act by: at least leasing my interest in the whole establishment, which would of course cover my interest as a manufacturer for a term of years for a fixed consideration in money, the amount of which would not in any way depend upon the success of the business transacted.

In this I find myself mistaken. These parties knowing my anxiety to enter upon the discharge of the duties of my appointment and knowing too, before I can do so, I must divest myself of all interest in the manufactury of beer, now taking advantage of my situation, retract their former offers and demand of me sacrifices too exhorbitant for me to make.

Although the office is but an humble one I felt that I should be honored in the acceptance of it, because of the source from which it emanated and had hoped that one who could so divest himself of that business, as to enable him to serve two terms in the field, would have little difficulty in so disposing of it, as to enable him to discharge the duties of assessor in times of peace under the law. In this however, I am disappointed, and being anxious that the public business shall not suffer—I beg leave to recommend for appointment in my stead Daniel H. Neiman[5] of this place, who is in every way well qualified to enter immediatly upon the discharge of the duties of the office and whose appointment I know will give entire satisfaction to that class of persons who regard the office in a business point of view and also to the seven thousand majority of Conservative men who registered themselves the other day, not only as the supporters of your administration, but as the enemies of your opposers, come from whence and in whatever form they may.

Please have this declination referred to the Honorable Secretary of the Treasury with my kindest regards and accept for yourself the most profound respect and esteem. . . .[6]

Charles Glanz

ALS, DNA-RG56, Appts., Internal Revenue Service, Assessor, Pa., 11th Dist., Charles Glanz.

1. Glanz (1826–1880) served as colonel of the 153rd Pa. Vols., which was mustered out in late July 1863. A Democrat, he was elected a delegate to the state and national soldiers and sailors conventions of 1866. Heller, *Northampton County*, 3: 357; Frederick H. Dyer, comp., *Compendium of the War of the Rebellion* (Des Moines, 1908), 1619; Philip Johnson to Johnson, Sept. 18, 22, 1866, Internal Revenue Service, Assessor, Pa., 11th Dist., Charles Glanz, RG56, NA.

2. Glanz was given a temporary commission for the post on September 24. Ser. 6B, Vol. 3: 161, Johnson Papers, LC.

3. Not found, but Glanz was first recommended for the assessorship by his congressman as early as mid-September in place of Gen. James L. Selfridge. Philip Johnson to Johnson, Sept. 18, 1866, Internal Revenue Service, Assessor, Pa., 11th Dist., Charles Glanz, RG56, NA.

4. Probably Willibald Kuebler (c1826–1898), a native of Germany, who settled in Pennsylvania and established, with Glanz, Kuebler's Brewery in Easton in the mid-1850s. Heller, *Northampton County*, 1: 307; 3: 418.

5. Neiman (c1826–fl1883), owner and editor of the *Easton Sentinel*, a Democratic paper, for more than thirty years, was also recommended by Philip Johnson, Josiah P. Hetrick, revenue collector for the Eleventh District, and Daniel M. Van Auken, Democratic congressman-elect for the same district. Heller, *Northampton County*, 1: 292; 1860 Census, Pa., Northampton, Bushkill Ward, Easton, 22; Philip Johnson to Johnson, Oct. 29, Nov. 6, 1866; Hetrick to Johnson, Nov. 7, 1866; Van Auken to Hugh McCulloch, Nov. 1, 1866, Internal Revenue Service, Assessor, Pa., 11th Dist., Daniel H. Neiman, RG56, NA.

6. Glanz's declination was accepted and Neiman was given the post on November 5, 1866, only to be rejected by the Senate several months later. Ser. 6B, Vol. 3: 161; Vol. 4: 84, Johnson Papers, LC.

From Barnas Sears[1]

Providence, R.I.   Oct. 29, 1866

Under an Act of Congress to increase and fix the Military Peace Establishment of the United States, approved July 28th, 1866 the President of Brown University, in behalf of the Corporation; applies for the Appointment of an Officer in the Army to act as Professor in said University.

Brown University was Established in 1764, and has capacity to Educate two hundred male students: there being now in attendance one hundred and ninety.

The fact that the State of Rhode Island has connected with Brown University the State Agricultural College authorized by an Act of Congress reguiring Instruction in Military Tactics may be mentioned as giving emphasis to this application.[2]

B. Sears, Pres.   Brown University

ALS, DNA-RG94, Lets. Recd. (Main Ser.), File S-1103-1866 (M619, Roll 516).

1. Sears (1802–1880), an ordained Baptist minister, taught at theological institutions in Massachusetts and New York for several years before assuming the presidency of Brown University in 1855. In September 1867 he moved to Staunton, Virginia, where he served for most of the remainder of his life as a general agent for the Peabody Education Fund. *DAB.*

2. Endorsed by Sen. H. B. Anthony of Rhode Island, Sears's letter was referred to the War Department. There Secretary Stanton informed Sears that his department wished to appoint a retired disabled officer and therefore requested that President Sears designate such a man from the list provided him. Stanton to Sears, Nov. 2, 1866; Edward D. Townsend to Stanton, Nov. 8, 1866, Lets. Recd. (Main Ser.), File S-1103-1866 (M619, Roll 516), RG94, NA.

To Henry A. Smythe

Washington, D.C., Oct. 29 1866.

New York must be saved. What are the prospects? I will be pleased to see you at any time.[1]

Andrew Johnson

Tel, DNA-RG107, Tels. Sent, President, Vol. 3 (1865–68).

1. Smythe's reply indicated "prospects fair & improving." He also referred to a forthcoming meeting with Johnson, but no record of such a meeting has been located. Smythe to Johnson, Oct. 30, 1866, Johnson Papers, LC.

From E. A. Haley[1]

Salt Lake city Utah   Oct 30th/66

Mr. Johnson sir

Allow me to congratulate you upon your success in reorganizeing the southern states—and upon the faithful support of a large majority of the people to your cause. I have been a special admirer of your acts ever since the winter before the Rebllion broke out—and I was proud to know that you were there ready to take the place of the distinguished Lincon when he fell—and I am still proud of the fact—and believe I ever shall be.

Pardon me now for intruding myself upon your notice for a few moments.

I am thirty six years of age a Kaintuckian by birth and education. I have lived on the Pacific Coast the most of the time for the last twelve years. I served as a volunteer in the Indian war in Oregon and Washington Territories in 1855–6 and lost all that had in the world by depredations committed by the Indians—for which I have never received a cent—and again this season in crossing the Plains to Montana Territory I lost all I had. Now pardon me for asking you to appoint me to some office that will in part at least remunerate me for the losses that I have sustained—through the negligence perhaps of government officials. I have never asked such a favor before of anyone and would not now if I was not forced by my circumstances to do so—and under the circumstances I think I have a right and perhaps a claim to do so. I would like an office somewhere in Arizona—New Mexico—or lower Calafornia as I expect to go down that way about christmas—untill then you can address me at Salt Lake city Utah.

If the office of collector of customs at Los Angelos Calafornia is not filled at present by a man that suits you I would like such an office as that—if it is—Marshall of Arizona or New Mexico Territories or some thing of that kind—or Receiver at some land office—or a Post office. You will doutless discover that I am not posted in regard to making an application for an office. I have stated my own case in my own way—without a string of Politicians to recommend me—and I flatter myself my chances for an appointment will be none the worse for it. I claim to be an honest upright American citizen—and reasonably well quaified to fill any of the officies I have named or any other similar to them.[2]

With my best wishes for your happiness and success in all after life— allow me to subscribe myself your sincere friend and supporter— whether you see fit to give me an office or not.

E A Haley

ALS, DNA-RG56, Appts., Customs Service, Subofficer, Los Angeles, E. A. Haley.
1. Not further identified.
2. Haley is not listed as holding any customs position in California; moreover, there was no collector of customs in Los Angeles at this time. He did not become marshal of the New Mexico Territory or the Arizona Territory, nor was he appointed to any federal post in either of these territories or in California. *U.S. Off. Reg.* (1867).

From James Johnson

Galveston, Texas, October 30th 1866

Sir

Since my appointment as Assessor of this district[1] I find great difficulty existing here concerning the Operation of the New Internal Revenue Law in connection with the present arrangements of collection Districts. Nearly all of the cotton country tributary to this City is now in another collection District and the Merchants and Planters are alike unable to get their cotton to Market owing to the Complication which under the present division of Counties cannot be avoided. Thirteen Counties have petitioned to be included in the first Collection Dist. At all the Rail Road Stations in the 2d District Cotton is accumulating very rapidly Greatly to the embarassment of the Planter and Merchant alike.[2]

The difficulty would be in a manner obviated if there was a Collector in the 2nd District[3] to make the Necessary appointments of Subordinates but that would be only a partial remedy.

I Consider that under the acts of Congress passed in 1864 & 1866 the authority rests with the President to alter the arrangment of Assessment Districts whenever it shall be made apparent that such a change is needed.

Gen L. Kent Collr. of Customs[4] (who has from me a letter of introduction to You) Goes to Washington at the instance of the Merchants & Planters and the City Council to urge this and other Matters—he will explain his business to You—and I beg for him and his object Your favorable action and Consideration.

J Johnson   Assessor 1st District

ALS, DNA-RG56, Appts., Internal Revenue Service, Assessor, Tex., 1st Dist., James Johnson.

1. Johnson was nominated assessor of the First District on July 19, 1866, then confirmed by the Senate and commissioned on July 27. He was on duty by late September. Ser. 6B, Vol. 4: 211, Johnson Papers, LC. See also James Johnson to Johnson, Sept. 29, 1866.

2. The problems which Johnson reported probably stemmed from a law passed by Congress in early 1866 which taxed all cotton at three cents per pound. *American Annual Cyclopaedia* (1866), 260.

3. Actually Robert H. Lane had been nominated on July 20, 1866, receiving confirmation and his commission on July 26. He remained in office at least through September 1867. Perhaps he had not yet reported to his post. Ser. 6B, Vol. 4: 211, Johnson Papers, LC; *U.S. Off. Reg.* (1867).

4. Loren Kent (1839–1867), a telegraph operator and merchant, had served with Illinois troops during the war and been brevetted brigadier general of volunteers on March 22, 1865. He was nominated collector on March 6, 1866, confirmed a few days later, and commissioned on March 15. Kent served in Galveston until his death. Ser. 6B, Vol. 4: 211, Johnson Papers, LC; Hunt and Brown, *Brigadier Generals*.

From James Lyons

Richmond   Octo 30 1866

My dear Mr. President

I beg your indulgence while I make a little appeal to you for mercy and humanity. In a conversation with Col Simmons,[1] the medical Director of this District a few days since, he said to me that he beleived a continuance of the present rigorous confinement of Mr. Davis would probably terminate the life of Mr. Davis before the close of the coming winter, while he beleived that if he could be paroled so as to take horseback and exercise in the neighbourhood of the Fort, and the early locking up at night with the constant presence of the guard was dispensed with his life would be preserved.

Now my dear Sir, while I know you intend to do your whole duty to the Country in respect to Mr. Davis, I am satisfied that it is your purpose to blend mercy with justice, and by no indirect means to permit the worst penalty of conviction to be inflicted upon an untried man.

Most respectfully therefore I venture to ask that you will extend the parole of Mr. Davis and otherwise mitigate his confinement as suggested in the remarks of Col Simmons.

I would pledge my life that Mr. Davis will faithfully keep his parole and not exceed the prescribed limits by an inch.[2]

James Lyons

ALS, DNA-RG94, Amnesty Papers, Jefferson Davis, Pets. to A. Johnson.

1. James Simons.

2. Johnson also received word from Stanbery that others had made similar requests concerning Davis's confinement. The President referred the matter to Stanton, asking that such requests be accommodated. On October 31, Edward D. Townsend issued an order to relay Davis's regulations to Gen. H. S. Burton, commander of Fortress Monroe. In reaction to the order, Davis's family was permitted to join him in his prison rooms and the guard was removed. Stanbery to Johnson, Oct. 30, 1866; Townsend to Burton, Oct. 31, 1866; Burton to Townsend, Nov. 3, 1866, Lets. Recd. (Main Ser.), File P-606-1866 (M619, Roll 504), RG94, NA.

From John H. Phillips[1]

Edmonton Metcalfe Co. Ky.   Octr. 30th 1866

President A Johnson

It has been my misfortune to have some fifteen thousand dollars destroyed by the rebel army during the war because I adhered to the Union Cause and had a son[2] in the Federal army. I have been laboring hard since the restoration of peace to make up some of my losses, and pay off some debts, Contracted before the war. But as I have no means to opperate on, and have rather a helpless family to support, I have been unable to regain any of my losses.

As I am assured that you sympathise with those who were destroyed because they were for the Union I make an appeal to you to be placed in a position that I Can to some extent be remunerated. Can you not make me one of the Commissioners of this State to pass on the Claims of the Loyal Citizens who had slaves to enlist in the servise of the United States.

I can refer you to Governor Bramblette of this State and many others for honesty and Capability.

John H Phillips

OCTOBER 1866

ALS, DNA-RG94, USCT Div., Lets. Recd., File P-286-1866.
1. Phillips (c1811–fl1882) was a farmer. Augusta P. Johnson, *A Century of Wayne County, Kentucky, 1800–1900* (Evansville, 1972 [1939]), 216–18; 1860 Census, Ky., Wayne, Newberry, 420.
2. Harrison B. Phillips (c1845–1864), a private in the 3rd Ky. Inf., was wounded at Kennesaw Mountain and died about two months later. Johnson, *Century of Wayne County*, 218; *Report of the Adjutant General of the State of Kentucky* (2 vols., Utica, Ky., 1984–88 [1866–67]), 1: 618.

To James W. Throckmorton

Washington, D.C., October 30 1866

Your telegram of 29th inst. received.[1] I have nothing to suggest, further than urging upon the Legislature to make all Laws, involving Civil rights, as Complete as possible, so as to extend equal and exact justice to all persons without regard to color, if it has not been done.[2]

We should not despair of the Republic. My faith is strong—my confidence undiminished in the wisdom, prudence, virtue, intelligence, and magnanimity of the great mass of the people, and that their ultimate decision, will be, uninfluenced by passion and prejudice engendered by the recent civil war, for the complete restoration of the Union, by the admission of Loyal Senators and Representatives from all the States, to the respective Houses of the Congress of the United States.

Andrew Johnson

Tel, DLC-JP.
1. The telegram read: "The Legislature has rejected the proposed [Fourteenth] amendment to the Constitution. The Legislature will adjourn soon. Is there anything I can recommend to facilitate restoration that should be acted upon before its adjournment." Throckmorton to Johnson, Oct. 29, 1866, Johnson Papers, LC.
2. Actually the legislature passed a number of bills which limited the freedmen's rights: restricting their testimony to cases involving other blacks, segregating public transportation, putting blacks at a disadvantage in labor contracts, and prohibiting black political participation. Carl H. Moneyhon, *Republicanism in Reconstruction Texas* (Austin, 1980), 51.

From William E. Chandler

Treasury Department.   October 31st 1866

Sir:

I have the honor to acknowledge the receipt through Col. R. Morrow, Bvt. Col & A-A G. of your check for one thousand dollars ($1,000.) payable to the order of A. G. Mackey,[1] Esq. Collector of Customs, Charleston South Carolina, to be transmitted to him in part payment of the amount due from the Board of Missions on account of the purchase by them of the Marine Hospital at Charleston. The check will be transmitted to Collector Mackey with a request to forward his receipt for the same, accompanied by an acknowledgment of the Board of Missions of the payment of your subscription, upon the reception of which the same will be transmitted to you.[2]

Wm. E. Chandler   Assistant Secretary

ALS, Johnson-Bartlett Col., Greeneville.

1. Albert G. Mackey (1807–1881), a prominent South Carolina unionist, was a physician and noted Masonic author and editor. *DAB.*

2. Johnson had contributed the money to help pay for the purchase of the hospital, which was to be used as a school for freedmen. The receipt was sent the next month. A. Toomer Porter to Johnson, July 28, 1866, *Johnson Papers*, 10: 745; Chandler to Johnson, Nov. 10, 1866, Johnson-Bartlett Col., Greeneville.

From Dempsey Weaver

Nashville, Oct 31st 1866

Dr Sir

Mr M Burns has this day handed me his Check on the First National Bank Washington D C For Fourteen thousand Six hundred Dollars, which when paid will be payment in full of draft of Andrew Johnson M G[1] at Ninety days after date from Sept 29th 1862 with interest from date and endorsed by you individually which draft you have herewith enclosed.[2]

May God bless and protect you is the Sincere prayer of your true friend. . . .

D Weaver

ALS, DLC-JP.

1. Military governor.

2. As per the instructions from Johnson, Burns had dealt with Weaver. On the day following Weaver's letter to the President, Burns informed Johnson that he had closed with Weaver. Johnson to Burns, Oct. 30, 1866; Burns to Johnson, Nov. 1, 1866, Johnson Papers, LC.

November 1866

From Thomas Smith and N. R. Wilkinson[1]

Portsmouth Va.   Nov. 66

Sir.

Believing it to be the policy of your administration to place in positions of influence those who are known to extend to you a hearty cooperation in carrying out the great and we may say sacred right of conservatism we the Johnson Constitutional Club of Portsmouth Va. through our President and Secretary would most respectfully call your attention to the dilatory action of the Hon Gideon Wells Secretary U.S. Navy in removing from Office the most bitter radicals the evidences of whose opposition to the present administration are now and have been for some Time in his possession. The evidence is of the most conclusive kind containing certificates from responsible gentlemen that the wish for your impeachment and execution is openly expressed; of the contribution of money by master mechanics to defray the expenses of the candidates to the radical convention (Messers Clements and Brownley[2] who were discharged by the Secty on that account). We are constrained to believe that Your Excellency is unaware of this state of affairs and yet that it so is unquestionable. We have sent delegations to Washington in vain and our delegate in his last interview with Secty Wells was informed that no man should be removed on account of his voting. Surely the Secretary would not have thought so two years ago. Feeling our utter inadequacy to combat successfully the radical element whilst fortified by the positions they now retain by sanction of the Secty of Navy we appeal to Your Excellency on behalf of the friends of Conservatism to examine the papers forwarded by our Club to the Navy Dept and if deemed satisfactory grant our requests.

Thomas Smith   President
N. R Wilkinson   Secretary

ALS (Wilkinson), DLC-JP.

1. Not identified.

2. James H. Clements (c1831–fl1899), a native of Washington, D.C., was an engineer and had left Portsmouth when war erupted to join the Union forces. In 1867–68 he served as a moderate Republican delegate to the state constitutional convention and was later postmaster of Portsmouth (1869–75) and a Washington, D.C., pension clerk (1877–99). 1870 Census, Va., Norfolk, Portsmouth, Jackson Ward, 10; Washington, D.C., directories (1862–65); Norfolk and Portsmouth directories (1874–79); McKitrick, *Johnson and Reconstruction*, 37; Richard Lowe, *Republicans and Reconstruction in Virginia, 1856–70* (Charlottesville, 1991), 138; *U.S. Off. Reg.* (1869–99). Brownley has not been identified.

From Anonymous

Turn it not aside nor laugh it of[f]

                              Washington D C   Nov 1st 8666 [*sic*]

Sir,

You need not take this as an idle threat or a bombastic boast to scare or frighten you.

But if in one month from this date you are still on the side of *rebels and copperheads*, as sure as the *Devil is in hell* I will take your life. You have the privilege in the meantime of resigning or of comng back to the *radical party—openly*. I have been a prisoner at *Andersonville* and a *soldier* & by *God I will* not have traitors brought up to my equal.

Do you what you will if you do one or the other. I will take your life—do what you will to prevent it. *So help me* God. All sinners shall shurely die.

Agan you need not treat this as a Joke—or you need not laugh it off—for so shure as the sun rises and sets, if you dont mend in one month, that sure will I kill you.

One who hates you as he does the king of hell, & one who will carry out his threat if he dies for it, do what you may to prevent it.

So help me god,

                              Herewith I set my hand & seal
                              this first day of October—1866[1]

["]The way of the transgressor is hard"—Bible.

L, DLC-JP.
1. We are at a loss to explain why the anonymous writer first indicated that the date was November 1 and then at the end put October 1 as the letter's date. We have somewhat arbitrarily chosen to recognize the date at the top of the letter.

From Richard H. Jackson[1]

                              Washington, D.C.   Nov. 1st 1866.

Sir:

Permit me to respectfully tender my resignation as U.S.D. Atty. of New Mexico,[2] and to submit therefore the following reasons.

1st. The insecurity of travel and danger of personal safety from maurauding Indians between Kansas City and Santa Fe.[3]

2dly. Because (as informed by Major Cutler[4] a resident of the territory), of the practice of the U.S.D. courts requiring where there are five Natives upon a Jury that then they should be addressed by counsel in both *Spanish* and English! Perhaps this was adopted from the old territorial practice of California. It is unquestionably however, an inovation upon the established practice of our courts generally, and is practically a revival of the spirit of the exploded doctrine *"De mediatate linguae."*[5] There are in N.M. five natives to one American proper—invariably five or more are impaneled upon every Jury—and thus, in every trial is enforced this rule. I am informed that the Chief Justice of the Territory[6] has frequently to appeal in the course of a Trial to his more fortunate associate Justices,[7] who happen to be better acquainted with the native lingo, what this or that advocate may be saying when addressing a jury! A distinguished scholar once observed that, ["]it were easy to learn to speak several languages, but the work of a life-time to become eloquent or forcible in any one." Without hoping to master the language, yet being a good Latinist, was the language of the natives of N.M. Spanish, I would undertake to learn it,—beleiving I could soon do it; but it is a miserable corruption of French, Spanish, Mexican or "Greeser," English and Negro—is not to be learned in the books, and can only be acquired by intimate associations and intercourse with the people. This rule of practice being repugnant to the reason and spirit of American law and institutions, might readily be set aside unless founded and guaranteed in some Treaty regulation of 1847; for I cannot beleive that a Territorial Legislature or U.S.D. Court can legally establish any such system.

Nowithstanding the aforgoing reasons, however, I would undertake the expedition but for the following more important consideration.

I hear from a source *"ab hoste doceri*, &,"[8] that Congress intends to reject all appointments requiring their confirmations and not meeting with their *political* endorsement, made by you Mr. President, since the adjournment; and further, intends providing by positive enactment against their re-appointment by withholding from such all pay & emoluments of Office. Moreover, that it intends to impeach you if possible, unless you accede to their revolutionary demands—at least, *will attempt it anyhow*, regardless of all law, authority, justice or propriety. That Bingham of Ohio, is the controling spirit of the Conspiracy, and is even now preparing a Bill of Impeachment—aided and abetted by Butler, Banks, Wade, Forney *"et sui generis."* Wilson[9] of Mass. has declared positively to a woman with whom he is peculiarly intimate, who figures conspicuously in the political circles of Washington, and exercises a controling influence over his political intrigues,[10] that I "should not be confirmed under any circumstances." The President will readily perceive how I would be placed at the mercy of these political cutthroats whom I have offended by my speeches and writings in his support. Besides in this connexion I would not that my appointment should prejudice in any degree or in any possible manner the relations of the President with Congress. My appointment at least, however it may be with others, shall not furnish Congress with even the shadow of a pretext for complaint against him.

I have informed the Atty. Genl.[11] of my resignation, and regret that I have not had an opportunity to lay this matter before you personally.

Confident that the President will readily appreciate my motives in resigning; regretting deeply that any circumstance should have arisen to
require it; profoundly grateful for the favor; with undiminished confidence in the patriotism, integrity, and wisdom of his re-adjustment policy, and still firm and vigilant in its support; and hoping that in resigning
I may not be prejudiced in his kind consideration and respect, I have the
honor to remain . . . [12]

Richard H. Jackson

ALS, DLC-JP.
    1. Jackson had been a lawyer and journalist in Illinois and Maryland, earnestly espous-
ing the Union cause in the latter state during the Civil War. George P. Este to Johnson,
Jan. 18, 1866; John A. Rawlins to Johnson, Jan. 19, 1866; Petition from Maryland Legislators, Jan. 16, 1862[?], Appt. Files for Judicial Dists., N. Mex., R. H. Jackson, RG60,
NA.
    2. Recommended by Montgomery Blair, among others, Jackson claimed ambivalence
about whether he became attorney general for New Mexico or Montana, since he planned
to settle in the West permanently and not to become involved with politics. Attorney General Stanbery recommended his appointment, which was made on August 10, 1866. M.
Blair to Stanbery, Aug. 6, 1866; Richard H. Jackson to Stanbery, Aug. 6, 1866; Stanbery
endorsement, ibid.; Ser. 6B, Vol. 3: 720, Johnson Papers, LC.
    3. The southern plains, through which Jackson would have to pass to get from Kansas
City to Santa Fe, were relatively quiet during the summer of 1866 with only a few minor
Indian incidents. Perhaps Jackson had a limited knowledge of western geography and con-
fused his potential path with some of the northern trails where the Indians were very active.
Utley, *Frontier Regulars*, 97–98.
    4. Benjamin C. Cutler (c1834–1868), a native of New York, became first lieutenant
and adjutant of the 1st Calif. Inf. in August 1861. Resigning to take the rank of captain in
the volunteers in 1862, Cutler served on Gen. James H. Carleton's staff. Mustered out in
January 1866, Cutler settled in New Mexico and became surveyor general of the territory
just before his death. Altshuler, *Cavalry Yellow & Infantry Blue*, 91.
    5. Concerning the moderation of the tongue or of language.
    6. John P. Slough.
    7. Associate justice Joab Houghton (1811–1877), a native of New York, was a civil
engineer who emigrated to New Mexico in 1844, where he became a merchant and was
influential in politics. In the government set up by Gen. Stephen Kearny, Houghton served
as chief justice of the territory (1846–52) even though he had no legal background. During
the Civil War he was a staunch Unionist involved in prosecuting confiscation cases against
Confederate sympathizers. Appointed associate justice again in 1865, Houghton remained
in the position, despite some controversy, until removed by Grant in 1869. He then prac-
ticed law in Santa Fe. Connecticut-born Sidney A. Hubbell served as associate justice in
New Mexico (1861–63, 1864–67), resigning in 1867. Ralph E. Twitchell, *The Leading
Facts of New Mexican History* (3 vols., Cedar Rapids, Iowa, 1912), 2: 272–73; Pomeroy,
The Territories, 112; Lanman, *Biographical Annals*, 216; Ser. 6B, Vol. 4: 370, Johnson
Papers, LC.
    8. Taught by the enemy.
    9. John A. Bingham, Benjamin F. Butler, Nathaniel P. Banks, Benjamin F. Wade,
John W. Forney, and Henry Wilson.
    10. Not identified.
    11. Henry Stanbery.
    12. Stephen B. Elkins, who was already a New Mexico resident, was nominated in
Jackson's place on January 7, 1867, then confirmed by the Senate and commissioned on
February 21, 1867. Ser. 6B, Vol. 4: 370, Johnson Papers, LC.

From Isaac Ver Planck Van Antwerp[1]

Washington, Novr 1. 1866.

Sir,

I desire much to have a brief personal interview with you, which I find it difficult to obtain, in consequence of the numbers always present, when I call for that purpose.[2]

Like yourself, Sir, I am a Democrat of the old school—the school of Jefferson and Jackson, of Benton and of Silas Wright.[3] That I possessed the warm friendship, and the fullest confidence, of the two latter "Great American Senators," *as long as they lived*, I have the most ample evidence, in numerous letters, over their respective signatures.

My first vote was given for Andrew Jackson for President, and for Martin Van Buren for Governor of New York, in 1828. Ten years later, in *1838*, I went to Iowa; and, with Dodge and Mason[4] & others, organized the Democratic party there—acting with it, and never allying myself to any other.

When, however, the rebellion broke out, in 1861, *unlike* most of my Democratic associates, but, *like yourself*, I took up arms to help crush it, went forward to the field for that purpose, and *remained there* until I was *compelled* to quit it, on account of being *disabled while in the service*.

Could the war possibly have been averted, by any honorable means— any *just* and *reasonable compromise*—and had the power rested with me to avert it, I would have done so but, when the collision of arms came, and the question was reduced to one of *Union or Disunion*, I thought, and felt, with you, Sir, that it was the clear duty of the great Democratic party to do as it had done, in 1833, with Jackson, and Benton, and Wright— stand by the Union!

I accordingly went *in person*, and tendered my services to the *then* Governor of Iowa (Kirkwood—now a *Senator*),[5] asking him for a Regiment; to which my *education at the U.S. Academy at West Point*,[6] and my connection, for a long time, with military organizations, both in New York and Iowa—I had been *Adjutant General* of the latter—would seem properly to have entitled me. But, Mr. Kirkwood, while giving to more than one of his *partizan friends*, Regiments which they subsequently proved themselves *utterly* unfit to command, refused one to *me—because I was a Democrat*!

I thereupon—though ten years beyond the age requiring of me *any* military service—determined to seek some *Staff* duty, which my personal friend Hon O. H. Browning (now Secretary of the Interior) helped me to procure—see his letter, herewith enclosed, of Novr 1. *1861*.[7] I was commissioned by the President, as an Additional Aide-de-Camp, with the rank of Major.[8] I also enclose, herewith, a letter from my friend Hon A. C. Dodge *of about the same period*—and one from Colonel Wm. H. Merritt,[9] who left here a few days since, to return to Iowa.

How I performed my duty *in the field*, until, as before stated, forced to quit it, on account of being disabled—rendered a cripple—for life—I have testimonials of the highest character to show, and *which I desire to present to you in a personal interview.*

Having, as I feel in my heart, suffered *gross* injustice, at the hands of men of the class of Govr Kirkwood,—because of my former political opinions,—and that justice has never been done me yet, for my serices in the field, I now confidently ask it at the hands of one born and bred in the same political school with myself.[10]

V. P. Van Antwerp.   Late Bt Brigr Genl. U.S.V.

ALS, DNA-RG156, Lets. Recd., File 547-WD-1866.

1. Van Antwerp (1807–1875) was a lawyer, politician, and U.S. land office receiver before the war. Hunt and Brown, *Brigadier Generals.*

2. Sometime in November, Van Antwerp did have an interview with Johnson. Van Antwerp to Johnson, Nov. 1866, Lets. Recd., File 547-WD-1866, RG156, NA.

3. Missouri senator Thomas Hart Benton and Silas Wright (1795–1847), New York lawyer, Democratic politician, governor, and member of the U.S. House of Representatives and Senate. *DAB.*

4. Augustus C. Dodge and Charles Mason.

5. A native of Maryland who moved to Iowa after a sojourn in Ohio, lawyer Samuel J. Kirkwood (1813–1894) was instrumental in organizing the Republican party in Iowa. He served as governor of the state during the Civil War and then briefly held a U.S. Senate seat. *DAB.*

6. Van Antwerp was admitted as a cadet in 1823 but did not graduate. *West Point Register*, 218.

7. O. H. Browning to Abraham Lincoln, Nov. 1, 1861, Lets. Recd., File 547-WD-1866, RG156, NA.

8. Van Antwerp was appointed in January 1862 and served on the staffs of Major Generals James G. Blunt and Winfield S. Hancock. Hunt and Brown, *Brigadier Generals*; Powell, *Army List*, 642.

9. A. C. Dodge to Abraham Lincoln, Nov. 12, 1861; William H. Merritt to Johnson, Oct. 30, 1866, Lets. Recd., File 547-WD-1866, RG156, NA.

10. Van Antwerp wished to become an ordnance or military storekeeper. Robert Johnson referred the matter to the secretary of war on November 19, 1866, "whose special attention is called to this application." A. B. Dyer of the Ordnance Office returned the material to the secretary of war on November 22, noting "that there are now commissioned, *Two* (2) Military Store Keepers of Ordnance *more* than the number allowed by the Law of 28 July 1866." Despite this surplus, Van Antwerp was apparently appointed a captain and military storekeeper to date from July 28, 1866. Endorsements; Van Antwerp to Johnson, Nov. 1866, ibid.; Hunt and Brown, *Brigadier Generals*; Powell, *Army List*, 642.

From Lewis D. Campbell

Hamilton O.   Novr 2. 1866.

Dear Sir—

When I left home to make my recent trip to Washington[1] I parted with my family in a good deal of distress growing out of the fact that Mrs. Campbell's mother[2] who resides with me was dangerously sick—her life almost despaired of. This of course rendered my absence exceedingly unpleasant to me and to them. Besides, this, whilst in Washington I was myself quite unwell the result of a severe cold I took on the cars as I went on.

After the conduct of Gen. Grant in *upsetting* Mr. Seward's instructions about Mexican matters,[3] Mr. Seward's daughter became dangerously ill.[4] On Sunday I received intelligence from home rendering my immediate presence here necessary, and presuming that some time must necessarily elapse before the Secretary would have his new programme arranged I left Washington unexpectedly, and since my arrival I have been confined to my room by a severe attack—the result of over-exertions during the late political campaign and exposure in travelling. As I am convalescent to day I write this by way of explanation.

Yesterday I received from Gen Sherman a telegram[5] informing me that he had been substituted for Gen. Grant in the matter of the Mexican business,—that he was on his way to St Louis, and would meet me at Cincinnati on a day next week to be agreed on to proceed thence on the mission &c &c. I will confer with Gen. S. immediately and I presume we shall start about the 8th which is probably about as soon as he can go to St Louis and return, as he informs me he will desire two or three days there.

I think I am safe in saying, therefore, that we shall be in Washington or New York by the 10th. Of course it will be necessary for *me* to go by Washington, and it may not be desirable to the Government that I should tarry there long. As no Secretary of Legation has yet been appointed, I desire to say that *Ralph L. Plumb*[6] Esqr of New York is the gentleman that I would respectfully recommend. Mr. Hunter[7] of the State Department informed me that he knew of no man better qualified. He speaks and writes the French and Spanish languages well (accomplishments that I have not acquired.) He is a ready writer and a good translator. From my personal knowledge of him I believe him to be a gentleman. I have met no man who seems to understand Mexican matters better than he. He has been highly recommended to me. Unless there be some positive objection to him, unknown to me, I should be glad to have him appointed. I write this now, so that there should be no unnecessary delay on this subject on my arrival. I have written to Mr. Seward on the same point.

Lewis D Campbell

ALS, DNA-RG59, Lets. of Appl. and Recomm., 1861–69 (M650, Roll 39), Edward Lee Plumb.

1. Campbell arrived in Washington about October 21 to receive his instructions regarding Mexico. *National Intelligencer*, Oct. 22, 1866; Seward to Campbell, ca. Nov. 6, 1866, Tels. Sent, Sec. of War (M473, Roll 91), RG107, NA.

2. Nancy Hunter Reily (d. 1881), the widow of John Reily, was the mother of four others besides Campbell's wife, two of whom lost their lives as colonels during the war, one for the North and one for the South. *A History and Biographical Cyclopaedia of Butler County, Ohio* (Cincinnati, 1882), 84.

3. See Grant to Stanton, Oct. 21, 1866; Johnson to Stanton, Oct. 26, 1866.

4. Frances Adeline (Fanny) Seward (1844–1866) was the last child born to William

Henry and Frances Seward. She died on the morning of October 29, 1866. Van Deusen, *Seward*, 92, 416–17; Edwin M. Stanton to Thurlow Weed, Oct. 29, 1866, Tels. Sent, Sec. of War (M473, Roll 91), RG107, NA.

    5. W. T. Sherman to Campbell, Oct. 31, 1866, ibid.

    6. Edward Lee Plumb (1827–1912), diplomat, railroad promoter, and vice president of the Mexican International Railroad Company, was appointed by Johnson secretary of the legation to Mexico on November 5, 1866, and immediately accompanied Campbell and Sherman to Mexico. He did not receive Senate approval until February 1867 and was recalled in mid-1867. *NUC*; *Evening Star* (Washington), Nov. 9, 1866; Johnson to Campbell, Nov. 5, 1866, Tels. Sent, President, Vol. 3 (1865–68), RG107, NA; Ser. 6B, Vol. 2: 256, Johnson Papers, LC.

    7. William Hunter.

To Isaac Murphy

Washington, D.C., Novem. 3d. 1866

    Your telegram of the 2d received.[1] The special pardons granted to Watkins and Play[2] restore them to *all their property*, except to such property or the proceeds thereof as may have been *sold* by the order, judgment, or decree of a court under the confiscation laws of the United States. Therefore, all of their property remaining *unsold* under an order, judgment or decree of a court, as set forth in the 4th condition of the warrant, should be restored to them; with the exception of course of property in slaves.[3]

Andrew Johnson   Prest U.S.

Tel, DNA-RG107, Tels. Sent, President, Vol. 3 (1865–68).

    1. Governor Murphy of Arkansas telegraphed from Little Rock, "I respectfully ask of you to remit any forfeiture under decrees of Confiscation of property in cases against Geo C. Watkins & Gordon W Play of this state and to direct that so much of the property as remains unsold under the decrees be restored to them." Murphy to Johnson, Nov. 2, 1866, Johnson Papers, LC.

    2. Watkins had been pardoned July 12, 1865. Amnesty Papers (M1003, Roll 14), Ark., George C. Watkins, RG94, NA. No information about Play or his pardon has been found.

    3. Attorney General Henry Stanbery expressed this opinion to Johnson. However, apparently nothing was returned to Watkins, for on November 22 he wrote to Johnson in some despair about the state of his property, his debts, and his pardon. In fact, he was so distressed that he sent his pardon back to Johnson. On December 24 Johnson returned the pardon to Watkins with copies of Stanbery's opinion and Johnson's November 3 telegram. Stanbery to Johnson, Nov. 2, 1866, Johnson Papers, LC; Watkins to Johnson, Nov. 22, 1866, Amnesty Papers (M1003, Roll 14), Ark., George C. Watkins, RG94, NA.

To Green Clay Smith

Washington DC   Nov 3d 66

    The telegraph will soon flash intelligence around the entire circle of the globe.[1] I hope the day is not distant when Montana will be added to the constellation of States, with Senators and Representatives in both Houses of Congress.[2]

Andrew Johnson

Tel, DNA-RG107, Tels. Sent, President, Vol. 3 (1865–68).

1. Johnson was responding to a telegram from Smith, the new territorial governor, dated the previous day, which read: "Montana sends greeting. We are this day brought in hourly Communication with the United States & the world." Smith to Johnson, Nov. 2, 1866, Johnson Papers, LC.

2. Although Johnson was normally opposed to adding new western states, he would have favored Montana because it had a Democratic majority. However, Montana's population was too small in 1866 to merit serious consideration for statehood by the Republican-dominated Congress. Malone et al., *Montana*, 79–80.

From Andrew B. Johnston[1]

Baltimore   Nov 4 1866

Sir

In the troubles which Seem inevitable in this Country, It may appear to you desirable to have some men under Your Control, who would know no law but your will.

I am a Virginian by birth, was a Captain of Artillery in the CSA & fought to the last for the cause I thought right.

If you have need of a regiment of good fighters, I Can raise the men & should be pleased to hear from you.[2]

A B Johnston

ALS, DLC-JP.

1. Johnston (*fl*1871), a clerk, served as a lieutenant in the Army of Northern Virginia's Crenshaw Bty., Pegram's Btn., 3rd A. C. Arty. *OR*, Ser. 1, Vol. 29, Pt. 1: 403; Peter S. Carmichael, *The Purcell, Crenshaw and Letcher Artillery* (Lynchburg, 1990), 115; Baltimore directories (1866–71); Richmond directories (1866–72).

2. No evidence of a reply has been found. For other examples of offers of a regiment for Johnson's support, see Leonard G. Faxon to Johnson, Oct. 12, 1866; Charles H. James et al. to Johnson, Jan. 24, 1867; Ethan A. Allen to Johnson, Jan. 26, 1867, Johnson Papers, LC.

From Reuben Davis[1]

Aberdeen Missi   5 Nov 66

Dear Sir

You will remember that I called on you about the 22d July last[2] and asked you to do me the kindness to grant me a pardon for past political offences and refered you to my petition. You expressed a wish to favor me but thought the time unpropitious.

You invited me to call the second day after which I did but your engagement prevented your seeing me. Hon Mr Cooper[3] told me you would send pardon soon. If their is no political reason now operating will you have the kindness to pardon me.

I wish to make a *union* which I cannot do until I am pardoned.[4] This allusion you will understand.

Reuben Davis

ALS, DNA-RG94, Amnesty Papers (M1003, Roll 32), Miss., Reuben Davis.

1. Davis (1813–1890) was a prominent lawyer, Mexican War colonel, militia major general, and U.S. and Confederate congressman. A "fire eater" and strong advocate of secession, he later opposed the Jefferson Davis administration. Wakelyn, *BDC*.

2. Evidence of a July meeting between Davis and the President has not been uncovered.

3. Edmund Cooper.

4. The "union" to which Davis alluded was his upcoming second marriage. He apparently did not receive an individual pardon. *A History of Monroe County, Mississippi* (Dallas, 1988), 434, 435.

From Benjamin G. Humphreys

Jackson, Miss.   November 5, 1866.

Sir,

By a resolution of the Legislature of Mississippi, it was made my duty to appoint two commissioners to visit you, and apply for the enlargement, on bail or parole, of Jefferson Davis, at present confined in Fortress Monroe.

In performance of that duty, I have appointed and commissioned the Hon. Robt. Lowry, and the Hon. Giles M. Hillyer,[1] the former a Senator and the latter a Representative in the Legislature; who will hand you this communication.

I have chosen, in this formal manner, to address Your Excellency, in aid of the object sought to be accomplished by the resolution of the Legislature. I hope to be pardoned in adding a few reflections which occur to me as not inappropriate.

Prominent amongst the causes which induced the adoption of the resolution is the fact, that seems now to be conceded, that the accused will not be admitted to a trial before the ensuing Spring, owing to the reorganization of the Judicial Districts, under an act of Congress, and the non assignment of the Judges to the Districts thus reorganized; and the danger apprehended from a winter's imprisonment in his present feeble and precarious State of health.

From such information as they were able to obtain from those who have recently visited Mr. Davis, the Legislature were induced to believe that it would be attended with imminent risk to his life to be detained at Fortress Monroe another Winter. They were moreover fully persuaded —and I think I can speak with confidence when I say, there is not a citizen in the State, and I seriously doubt whether there is one in the United States, who is not equally well persuaded, that his imprisonment is not at all necessary to secure his presence at any time and place which may be appointed for his trial. Of this the Government must be the judge. I would not be understood as desiring to dictate and, far less, as presuming for a moment to indulge in reflections upon the justice of the course hitherto pursued in his imprisonment. Without controverting the wisdom, justice and policy of that course in the past, I confine myself to the present, and the future, and then, only, in reference to the effect likely to result to his life and health by longer confinement.

In all that I have said, and may say, my sole purpose is to put your Excellency in possession of what I believe to have been the motives and influences which actuated the Legislature in the adoption of the resolution under consideration.

Another fact, doubtless, had weight, and I cannot forbear mentioning it. I do it in a spirit of perfect candor, believing that Your Excellency has the magnanimity to appreciate it. The fact is historical and incontrovertible that the people of Mississippi by a majority unprecedented in their annals, inaugurated, at the ballot box, and by ordinance of a Convention which they believed represented the Sovereignty of the State, the policy which resulted in placing Mr. Davis where he is. It was by their mandate, he vacated his seat in the United States Senate, and by the same authority, and that of her sister states of the South, in vain essaying to establish a separate Government, that he was placed at the head of the Government they attempted to organize. I state the fact without discussing or vindicating it, that the Legislature responding to the popular sentiment in that regard, consider him neither more or less guilty than those who placed him in that position.

In connection with that fact, I desire to say, that the people of Mississippi with equal, nay greater unanimity; indeed, I might say with almost absolute unanimity, have, in perfect good faith, accepted the arbitrament of the forum, to which they referred the controversy; have returned to their allegiance to the Government of the United States, with a firm purpose to maintain its integrity, and promote its prosperity, by all the means in their power. The proof of this, if it was not found in the very necessity to which they are shut up, would be in the zeal and unanimity with which they support your administration in its struggle to preserve and perpetuate the admirable form of Government established by the framers of the Constitution. With one mind and heart they are united in that support, believing, as they do, that, upon your success in that struggle is involved the last hope of constitutional freedom, not upon this continent alone, but throughout the world.

I know of no event which would go further to heal the wounds inflicted by the late sanguinary and fratricidal war than the gratification, by your Excellency, of the wish implied in the resolution of the Legislature. It would send a thrill of joy through the hearts of the whole people of the South, irrespective of all past political differences upon the origin and causes of the war. It is believed that it would excite similar emotions in every just and generous bosom even amongst those so lately arrayed in deadly conflict with us.

As I have before remarked, we do not ask for an unconditional pardon, nor that pending prosecutions shall be dismissed. We do not seek to screen him from trial. Believing that the ends of Justice will be reached, that his imprisonment is not necessary to secure his presence when desired for trial, and can only be attended with fatal results to his health, I add my earnest entreaty, to that of the Legislature, that it may please Your Excellency to admit him to bail or enlarge him upon parole.[2]

Benj. G. Humphreys   Governor of Mississippi

LS, DNA-RG94, Amnesty Papers, Jefferson Davis, Pets. to A. Johnson.

1. Lowry (1830–1910), a Brandon, Mississippi, lawyer and Confederate brigadier general, during the 1880s served two terms as governor. Hillyer (b. c1819), a native of Connecticut and editor of the *Natchez Courier*, had been a major and chief of subsistence on the staff of Gen. Braxton Bragg. *DAB*; 1860 Census, Miss., Adams, Natchez, 89; William C. Harris, *Presidential Reconstruction in Mississippi* (Baton Rouge, 1967), 130; *OR*, Ser. 1, Vol. 30, Pt. 4: 549.

2. By November 10th commissioners Hillyer and Lowry were in Washington. On the 13th they sent to Johnson the Mississippi legislature's resolutions *re* Davis. The next day when they were "courteously" received by the President, they presented to him Governor Humphreys's letter. But Johnson would not pardon or release Davis. Subsequently the commissioners visited Davis at Fortress Monroe as well as his principal attorneys in Philadelphia and New York before returning home in January 1867. *Evening Star* (Washington), Nov. 10, 1866; *New York Herald*, Nov. 15, 1866; Dunbar Rowland, *History of Mississippi: The Heart of the South* (2 vols., Chicago, 1925), 2: 134, 137.

From James M. Spellissy[1]

Private

Universe office (Irish-American organ)
Philadelphia   Nov. 5. 66

Mr. President,

With very great respect, I return you sincere thanks for having made a direct request "for an appropriate place" in my favor, to the Custom House authorities in this City. Honb. S. J. Randall has made me acquainted with this act of kindness. I asure Your Excellency that it will not be forgotten in this office. At the same time it is proper to state, that the request has not produced the natural consequence. An appropriate position is not likely to be conferred. There is some vague intelligence of a $4 a day place—such as does not at all correspond with the full letter written to Your Excellency, some weeks ago by Mr. Randall[2]—with the natural desire of the Irish-American community to see their class recognized—with the Journalistic field I occupy—or, and strongest of all, with the direct request of the Chief Magistrate.

Certainly, it is impossible to satisfy every one, it is the part of a man of sense to take what is offered to him, and I am far, far from claiming anything as an absolute right: but "*est modus in rebus*"—there is a happy medium in things: and I take the liberty of saying to Your Excellency that I do not think you would be satisfied at seeing your request for an appropriate place for the Editor of the strongest and most varied Administration "weekly" in the country, responded to by a $4 a day position. There is no certainty even of this place. But I lay its character before you.

But, Mr. President, I would not mind the plans if your most obliging circular[3] in regard to advertising in these columns to the War Department, were observed. The War Department Quartermasters have advertisements every week: but we never hear from them. This is a very black radical city, and the decided Administration attitude of the Universe, has most materially injured its advertising patronage. The War Department is the only Department that has any thing like good advertising. May I ask authority to insert its announcements from the Washington Journals?

I return Your Excellency the most sincere thanks. You have treated me kindly in person[4]—as well as in other respects, and in admiration of your policy as well as in gratitute for your favors, this paper will continue— what it has been from the commencement of your authority—the strongest and most varied Administration *weekly* in the land. If I can make the paper a *daily* I will and its character will remain unchanged.[5]

J. M. Spellissy   Ed. Universe

ALS, DLC-JP.

1. For the past several months, Spellissy (*fl*1869), as editor and proprietor of the Philadelphia *Universe* (*Catholic Herald*), had been an applicant for a number of federal posts in Philadelphia, including U.S. emigration agent, collector or assessor for the First Revenue District, and surveyor of the port. Philadelphia directories (1865–70); Spellissy to Johnson, May 10, 1866, Lets. of Appl. and Recomm., 1861–69 (M650, Roll 46), J. M. Spellissy, RG59, NA; Spellissy to Hugh McCulloch, Aug. 26, 27, Sept. 29, 1866; Spellissy to Johnson, Oct. 4, 1866, Appts., Customs Service, Surveyor, Philadelphia, J. M. Spellissy, RG56, NA.

2. See Randall to Johnson, Sept. 22, 1866; Spellissy to McCulloch, Sept. 22, 1866, ibid.

3. See the executive order of October 1, 1866, which had authorized the *Universe* to receive government advertising. Robert Johnson to McCulloch, Oct. 1, 1866, Lets. Recd. from President, RG56, NA. A copy is also available in Johnson Papers, LC.

4. Spellissy had had several interviews with Johnson. See Spellissy to McCulloch, Aug. 26, 1866; Spellissy to Johnson, Sept. 29, 1866, Appts., Customs Service, Surveyor, Philadelphia, J. M. Spellissy, RG56, NA; Spellissy to Johnson, Sept. 22, 1866, Johnson Papers, LC.

5. Despite this and subsequent applications for office (for example, Spellissy to Johnson, Jan. 2, Feb. 23, 1867, Appts., Internal Revenue Service, Assessor, Pa., 2nd Dist., J. M. Spellissy, RG56, NA), Spellissy was not appointed by Johnson.

From William H.C. King

New Orleans La   Nov 6 1866

If I knew what needed Explanation it should be furnished. As for his having strongest Recommendations[1] If you know how they had been obtained they would be of little account. At Philadelphia Bullett acknowledged that he had studiously ignored the Times regarded as your best exponent here & that if I would let his bogus delegation in & make him vice President he would give me his printing.[2] Thereafter I was fool enough to believe him. When he knew I was out of hearing he talking behind my back & soon I heard beyond the shadow of a doubt he allied

himself to your enemies & mine who all swore they would break me
down. They have boasted here they would upset all I have done & get me
under. The very men who fought me for months to support Chase &
forced me into my present precuniary position.[3] Dr Hough Kennedy the
man who received Wells,[4] Bullitts Brother-in-law Boasted that they
would pull the wool over your eyes as he termed. In this Bullitt affair
Bullitt May & Nixon[5] are in Combination against me. The people are
with me & I could get fifty thousand (50,000) signatures against Bullitt.
If you dont stick to me I will have a hard Road to travel. You will be Rewarding false friends while my past ought to speak my sincerity. Completely in the dark as to Bullitts statements I know not what else to say. I
was candid to place the matter on personal grounds for my advantage. I
have never deceived you knowingly & never will. I have worked Hard.
Bullitt & his friends have held office, Reaped emolument & did nothing
but deceive you. If necessary I will go to Washington but Spare me this if
you Can. Please telegraph me again. I thank you for your kindness.[6]

Wm. H.C. King

Tel, DLC-JP.

1. King was responding to a telegram from Johnson which read: "The removal of C.
Bullitt needs explanation. He is here with the strongest recommendations, and has made a
statement which, without explanation, is very satisfactory." Bullitt had been removed from
his position as U.S. marshal for Louisiana a week or two previously. Johnson to King, Nov.
6, 1866, Tels. Sent, President, Vol. 3 (1865–68), RG107, NA; *New York Times*, Nov. 14,
1866.

2. Factional disputes caused Cuthbert Bullitt and his "Andrew Johnson Club of Louisiana" to send a separate slate of delegates to the National Union Convention at Philadelphia
in August 1866. See William H.C. King to Johnson, July 10, 1866, *Johnson Papers*, 10:
664–65. On the matter of the marshal's public printing, see also John Savage to Johnson,
Oct. 10, 1866.

3. King had paid "immense sums" to purchase "Entire Control" of the *Times* in order to
support Johnson. King to Johnson, Sept. 29, 1866, Johnson Papers, LC.

4. Hugh Kennedy and Gov. J. Madison Wells.

5. Thomas P. May and James O. Nixon.

6. King telegraphed Johnson several more times in the next two days with information
on the charges against Bullitt, but finally he left for Washington on November 9. Apparently his arrival in the capital city helped to keep Bullitt from reinstatement. The new marshal, J. H. McKee, was soon replaced by Francis J. Herron. King to Johnson, Nov. 7, Nov.
8 (3 telegrams), 1866, Johnson Papers, LC; *New York Times*, Nov. 14, 15, 1866; *U.S. Off.
Reg.* (1867).

To Thomas Swann

Washington, D.C.   Nov 6th 1866

I thank you for your despatch.[1] Thank God that so glorious a result
has been obtained without riot and bloodshed. When passion and prejudice have subsided and the people are permitted to reflect their true sentiments the nation will stand redeemed, and the Union restored. The news
is equally cheering from the City of New York and it is hoped it will be as
encouraging throughout the State.

A. J.

Tel, DLC-JP.
    1. Swann reported favorable election returns and the absence of violence. See Swann to
Johnson, Nov. 6, 1866, Tels. Recd., President, Vol. 5 (1866–67), RG107, NA. For more
on the story of the Maryland election problems, see Johnson to Stanton, Oct. 25, 1866.

From Henry H. Fish[1]

Utica [N.Y.], Nov 7th 1866

President Johnson

On the 20h of Sept. last I was notified of my appointment as Collector
of this district.[2] I appreciated the responsiblity of the position, and am
gratefull for the confidence implied in the appointment. But it may not be
improper to state that I accepted it soley in defference to the wishes of
friends with whom I was cooperating in support of the measures designed to restore the lately revolted States to their proper constitutional
relations. I desired no political preferment or appointment whatever.
Feeling anxious only, to see the states restored to their legal relations to
the National government, and the people of evry section reconciled with
each other, I regarded it of little moment who held the offices. It was
urged that my declination at that time might be taken for a want of con-
fiden in, or sympathy with important movements just then inaugurated,
from which we had reason to expect good results. So I accepted the position and entered upon the discharge of its duties. Heartily approving the
measures of your administration, which in the short space of seven
months, had successfully reestablished all the machinery of regular civil
government in all the lately revolted States, I could not doubt their approval by the people, Especially after they had garnered the substancial
fruit of a *legal sanction* to the Amendment of the Constitution abolishing
slavery from evry foot of our soil. I certainly had no doubt of the approval,
of a majority of the people to these wise and beneficent measures of your
administration. In this however, I have been disappointed and must patiently wait the subsidence of passion and resentments, which have so
largely marked the canvass and so disasterously determined the result.
The great masses of all parties are undoubtedly honest and patriotic, but
unfortunately for the country, their fears have become excited and their
passions aroused, to an an extent altogether in consistent with a reasonable judgment, and the verdict just pronounced is nominally against us.
My only hope now is, that these passions unduly, but purposely aroused
to further the interests of local candidates, will now become calmed, and
reason and conscience be permitted to influence the deliberations and actions of Congress, and that thus the great work of reconcilliation may yet
be accomplished. I cannot believe this doctrine of indefinite exclusion of
States from participation, in the persons of loyal representatives, in the
national legislation, can be permanently sanctioned by the American
people. I cannot think any considerable portion of the people will acquiesce in so radical a revolution in our elective structure of govmt. But for

the time being I find myself opposed by a very decided majority of the electors of this District[3] who would, I think it quite probable prefer to see the position I occupy, filled by one of political views more nearly in accord with their own. I have no means of knowing how far you may deem it expedient or desirable to make your appointments conform to the sentiments of the locality. My own views are not now likely to be changed, and I feel it is not right to embarass any action that may be desired in this regard. I therefore respectfully tender my resignation of the office of Collector of the 21st District of New York.[4]

H H. Fish

ALS, DNA-RG56, Appts., Internal Revenue Service, Collector, N.Y., 21st Dist., Henry H. Fish.

1. Fish (1813–1887) was a Utica businessman, city official, and Republican. M. M. Bagg, ed., *Memorial History of Utica, N.Y.* (Syracuse, 1892), pt. 2: 17–19.

2. Given a recess appointment on September 17, he had been recommended by, among others, Thurlow Weed, who believed that Fish's appointment would help defeat Rep. Roscoe Conkling's reelection bid. See Appts., Internal Revenue Service, Collector, N.Y., 21st Dist., Henry H. Fish, RG56, NA. See also Ser. 6B, Vol. 3: 94, Johnson Papers, LC.

3. In the election held on the previous day, Conkling received fourteen hundred votes more than his Democratic rival, Palmer V. Kellogg. *Guide to U.S. Elections*, 617.

4. Fish's letter was referred to Secretary McCulloch, who evidently asked Fish to withdraw his resignation, which he did, only to be denied confirmation by the Senate in January 1867. Ser. 6A, Vol. D: 73; Ser. 6B, Vol. 4: 51, Johnson Papers, LC; Fish to McCulloch, Nov. 19, 1866, Appts., Internal Revenue Service, Collector, N.Y., 21st Dist., Henry H. Fish, RG56, NA.

From James P.D. Rosebrough[1]

Fayetteville Tenns   Nov 7, 1866

Sir

It is with some degree of timmidity that I address you on this all important subject of oppression in our State. I have lived in this County (Lincoln) forty four years & ten in missippi. I loocked on & watched all my life & I never saw the people more Submissive and more Law abideing in all my life than they are at this time. They are all quiett & every boddy is trying to make a liveing in there own natturel way. Some by farming Some Mecanick at their trade Some Merchendising Some lawyers Some Docters. All is busy at their Daly avocation Trying to make a liveing. I never Saw the time when the people was So mutch oppressed. The hiest authorties has extended Pardon to the mass of the People tha was engaged in the Rebellion. They have become reconciled & gone to work to try to live. Now has the governer of the State or the Legislator the rite to say who Shal Vote in our Elections? Have they the rite to determing who is a qualified member to Serve in the Legislator. When the Constitution of the State Shows the qualification that a man must have before he can serve the people in that capssity after the people Elects a man that is sutch as the Constitution requires then have they the rite to Drive him out of the Legislator because he differs with them in politicks. Have they the rite to Tax they people at their will & pleasure & Compell the people to pay all taxes laid on them And not a low the people to have no Coarts attall & men ly in jale & give them no chanse to have a tryel but just ly there, then what must the People do. They beare it al verry patiently tho it hurts. I would ask you Mr President under sutch sircumstances as these [I] have Stated has not the people a rite to ask the Chief Justis of the nation for relief. Have they not the rite to ask him for advise what to doo, then I would ask yo what they (the People) must doo? Will Please tell us what we must doo. If you think that I have misrepresented the Case I would refer you To George W. Jones & Colonel Robert Farqueson[2] Men with whome you are intimately acquainted. I must say to you Mr President that I have not told half the Story. I am near Fifty four years of age and in all the histry of my life I never saw nor read of a more complete Despotic goverment than we have at this time most unconstitutional Goverment in all my life time. I ask for advise. Will you be So kind as to give it? Answer my letter if you please. I lived under your administration whe Goverer of the State of Tennessee So did my Father[3] & I heare no Complaint.

When you write Direct your leter to Fayetteville Tennessee. It is now late in the night & I have drove my Plain harde all day. Write soon.

                                                      J.P.D. Rosebrough

ALS, DLC-JP.
    1. Rosebrough (b. c1813) was a Lincoln County millwright who years earlier had married Mary Cooper Warren. 1870 Census, Tenn., Lincoln, 22nd Dist., Lynchburg P.O., 10; *LCT Pioneers*, 7 (1977): 18.
    2. The reference here is probably to Robert Farquharson of Lincoln County.
    3. James Rosebrough (d. 1849). *LCT Pioneers*, 7 (1977): 18.

From Henry W. Slocum

                                        Brooklyn N.Y.   Nov 7th 1866
Dear Sir—

At the commencement of the recent political campaign in this State, I recommended the appointment of Gen Pratt as Collector for the 3d Congressional Dist and Mr Kinsella as Post Master for this City.[1] You manifested a generous confidence in my judgement for which I assure you I felt deeply grateful.

Soon after the appointments were made I learned that rumors were being circulated in Washington that the selections were injudicious. I traced these rumors to Mr Weed and knew at once his object. Soon after a letter signed by Mr Weed appeared in the N.Y. Times,[2] a paper opposed to the success of our ticket, stating openly that you had made bad appointments here—and that the error would lose us *five thousand votes* in Kings County. I felt that it would be useless for me to attempt to combat this assertion and that a controversy at that time on the subject might injure our cause. I therefore remained silent—preferring to suffer temporarily in your estimation than to reply to these *false charges*.

The election is now over and *the result* is the best reply I can make. The 3d Congressional Dist is redeemed and sends two Representatives[3] who are not only your frinds—but who will under any circumstances be true to the best interests of the County. Kings County has given for the conservative ticket about 10,000 maj—nearly double that ever before given to any ticket—and this has been accomplished not withstanding the efforts of Mr Weed's personal and political friends have been directed to make his prediction as to the result prove true. To no men in this county are we more indebted for this brilliant success than to those you have recently appointed to office.

I earnestly desire to convince you that I have not abused your confidence, and therefore take great pleasure in submitting this reply to the charges made by Mr Weed.

H. W. Slocum

ALS, DLC-JP.

1. Calvin E. Pratt and Thomas Kinsella. See Henry A. Smythe to Johnson, Aug. 10, 1866.

2. For Thurlow Weed's lengthy letter, see the October 9 issue of the *Times*. See also Weed to Johnson, Oct. 2, 1866.

3. Democrats John W. Hunter and William E. Robinson. Hunter (1807–1900), who was chosen in a special election to fill the unexpired term of James Humphrey, later held the office of mayor of Brooklyn (1875–76). Robinson (1814–1892), a former newspaper correspondent, New York attorney, and assessor of the Third District (1862–67), was successful in the regular election. He subsequently served two additional terms in Congress (1881–85). *BDAC*; *Guide to U.S. Elections*, 617; Robinson to Johnson, Feb. 25, 1867, Appts., Internal Revenue Service, Assessor, N.Y., 3rd Dist., W. E. Robinson, RG56, NA. See also Edward J. Lowber to Johnson, Aug. 24, 1866.

From William H. Wallace[1]

Philad   Nov 7' 1866.

My Dear Sir:

I seldom afflict upon you any corrispondence, but there are times when it is the duty of all to be heard. I have been and am a true and devoted friend of your Policy and much pleased with your administration, in evry particular. When you were here on your journey west, I did all I could to have a good reception and couteract the disgrace cast upon our city by the action of the Mayor.[2] Many scenes occurred and expressions used on that occasion—if done to Lincoln when he was President would confine the culprit to a dungin in one of our Forts. Still, that has passed but allow me to assur you that let the elections go as they may the great popular heart of this Country is in favour of your wise and patriotic policy.

Never faulter or desert a principal, or a right guaranteed you under the Constitution though the *Heavens* may fall.

It is true you have made some mistakes in your appointments in this City—that will occur at all times, as you must be governed in these matters by the recommendation of your friends. One mistake most of your friends here think was in not appointing Mr Walten[3] Treasurer of the Mint. He is a man not only of great respectability, but has administrative ability, seldom equaled by one of his age—a good man in every respect, hails from that portion of our State called the 10th Legion that gave you 7500 majority. He has represented his District in the State Senate, a able Lawyer and good talker.

I learn to day he is likely to be appointed Surveyor of the Port here.[4] If so, I am sure you will be proud of him. It is said a printer[5] in Tho B Florence[6] office has been spoken of. Dont be deceived. He Could not satisfy your friends here.

John Welsh is also spoken of.[7] This would not do. He has suddenly got ritch off the misfortune of the Government, has not strength. No man could be so acceptable as Mr Walton, or add more to the success of your Administration.[8] I fear I have drawn to much on your time to read this, but comes from a Devoted Friend.

Wm. H. Wallace
1318 Chestnut St Philad

ALS, DNA-RG56, Appts., Customs Service, Surveyor, Philadelphia, James H. Walton.

1. Wallace (*fl*1872) is listed as being a clerk in Philadelphia. Philadelphia directories (1867–72).

2. Morton McMichael was on a "brief holiday" away from the city when Johnson visited Philadelphia. *Evening Bulletin* (Philadelphia), Aug. 29, 1866.

3. James H. Walton (*fl*1867), a stock and exchange broker, had served as treasurer of the Philadelphia mint during Buchanan's administration. Philadelphia directories (1861–68); Walton to Johnson, Apr. 21, 1866, Johnson Papers, LC. Chambers McKibbin, Sr., had been given the treasurer's post instead of Walton. See Richard Vaux to Johnson, Sept. 18, 1866.

4. Walton's appointment as surveyor had the support of Senators Cowan, Doolittle, and Buckalew, among others, but Walton was not chosen by the President to fill this slot. Walton to Johnson, Nov. 17, 1866, Jan. 25, 1867, Appls., Asst. Treasurers and Mint Officers, Philadelphia, James H. Walton, RG56, NA; Ser. 6A, Vol. D: 281, Johnson Papers, LC. See also E. Reed Myer to Johnson, Sept. 21, 1866.

5. Not identified.

6. Florence (1812–1875), a former Democratic congressman from Pennsylvania (1851–61), was associated with a number of newspapers in Philadelphia and Washington, D.C., throughout his career. He was also a delegate to the National Union Convention in Philadelphia. *DAB*.

7. See Pennsylvania Citizens to Johnson, Oct. 16, 1866.

8. Later, Walton applied for appointment as naval officer at Philadelphia, but he did not receive that post. In February he also sought appointment as director of the Philadelphia mint. Walton to Johnson, Jan. 25, 1867, Appls., Asst. Treasurers and Mint Officers, Philadelphia, James H. Walton, RG56, NA; Ser. 6A, Vol. D: 284, 287, 289–90, 292, Johnson Papers, LC.

From John A. Dix

Confidential

New York   8 Nov. 1866.

My dear sir:

I have not written to you since I returned from Chicago because I had no pleasant political intelligence to give. I foresaw the inevitable result in this state from the moment that the democratic party was put prominently forward in the Albany Convention[1] as the leading interest to be promoted. The understanding at Philadelphia was that in the movement we were inaugurating we were to follow the lead of the Conservative republicans. Our failure in this state is due to the utter selfishness and folly of the democratic managers. But for the liquor interest in this City, which was arrayed against Fenton,[2] the defeat would have been overwhelming.

I need not say how deeply I deplore the result—how much aggrieved you have a right to feel by the selfish policy of making the success of your measures to tranquillize the country and place the government on its constitutional footing, secondary to personal and local interests.

Hoping to have the pleasure of seeing you soon.

John A. Dix

ALS, DLC-JP.
1. The Democratic state convention was held at Albany, New York, in early September. *American Annual Cyclopaedia* (1866), 545.
2. Reuben E. Fenton.

From James Guthrie

Louisville, Nov. 8th 1866.

Sir:

On the 11th of Octo. a train on the Louisville and Nashville R.R. was thrown off the track by a band of robbers—formerly Guerrillas,—and robbed of $10,000 in money.[1]

Last night a Passenger and Mail train was thrown off the track, 3 cars burned, among which was the Mail Car, and all the Passengers robbed of their money, and valuable packages.[2]

There are regular organizations of robber bands in the states of Kentucky and Tennessee, imperilling constantly the life and property of private Citizens, as well as the lives and property of travellers over the public Highway, and Mail Route. The civil authorities are totally inefficient to afford protection under the peculiar circumstance arising from the last War, and we have to look to military authorities to clear the country of the remains of the old guerrilla bands. No effective steps can be taken to accomplish this, without authority in the military officers to arrest suspected parties, and force the attendance of witnesses. Should the parties be innocent they can be turned loose, should they be guilty they can be handed over to the civil authorities. Gen. Thomas to whom I have applied for protection, does not wish to take the responsibility of acting in the manner indicated except with your approval.

I address you for the purpose of asking you to authorize Gen. Thomas, to adopt such measures, as he in his own judgment may deem necessary to meet the exigencies of the case.[3] Some prompt and energetic action is absolutely necessary. The people in the State of Ky. & Tenn. would support any measures you would adopt to make them secure in their homes. They are now at the mercy of these robber bands.

Hoping that you will give this communication a favorable consideration.

James Guthrie   President L. & N. R.R.

Copy, DNA-RG393, Dept. of Tennessee, Lets. Recd.
    1. See the *Louisville Journal*, Oct. 12, 1866.
    2. Ibid., Nov. 9, 1866; *Nashville Press and Times*, Nov. 9, 1866.
    3. The following week General Thomas was authorized to station troops where they would be most effective against the guerrillas and to take any steps necessary while guarding against excessive use of military power. Stanton to Thomas, Nov. 15, 1866, Dept. of Tennessee, Lets. Recd., RG393, NA.

From Hugh McCulloch

Treasury Department   November 8. 1866.
Sir:

In compliance with the terms of a resolution of enquiry adopted by the House of Representatives on the 28th of May last,[1] concerning captured and abandoned cotton, a copy of which is hereto annexed and in compliance also, with the request of the Congressional Joint Select Committee on retrenchment upon the same subject, I have caused a careful examination to be made of all records, reports and other papers in this Department relating thereto, and have the honor to submit herewith various tabular statements which it is believed furnish in detail all the information desired.

It seems proper to submit in connection with these statements, a brief history of the legislation under which this Department has acted together with some of the embarrassments and difficulties encountered in carrying out the laws referred to, in order that the whole subject may be properly understood and the results accomplished may be duly appreciated.

The first legislation requiring action by this Department in relation to the recovery, care and disposition of captured and abandoned property, was the Act of Congress, approved March 12th 1863,[2] by which the Secretary of the Treasury,[3] was required to appoint Special Agents to receive and collect all captured and abandoned property in any State in insurrection. On the 31st., of same month, orders were issued by the Secretary of War and the Secretary of the Navy⁴ requiring the officers of their respective Departments to turn over all captured and abandoned property in their possession to Agents appointed by this Department. Agents previously appointed to carry out Acts of Congress concerning Commercial Intercourse between loyal and insurrectionary States were then authorized and directed by the Secretary of the Treasury to execute the provisions of the Act of March 12 1863, in addition to the duties previously performed by them and they took such measures as they could to carry its provisions into effect.

The country in which this property was found, had been or was occupied by contending armies; the inhabitants had generally deserted it or were hostile to its removal: teams and means of transportation were removed from the country so that when the property was found or received by the Agents they could do very little with it except by the aid of the military and naval arms of the public service, and could accomplish but little in the direction indicated except through their assistance and cooperation. The orders from the heads of Departments were ample. That of the War Department required Quartermasters so far as they could without injury to the service to aid Agents in collecting such property and transporting it to places of shipment. But this aid could rarely be obtained, the teams and wagons were generally otherwise employed or it was represented the exigencies and nature of the service forbade their use for the purpose indicated. In fact it was represented by some of the Agents that instead of aiding in the execution of these duties, they frequently encountered embarrassment on the part of local and subordinate military officers. The property in question while in the hands of military authorities, had been a fruitful source from which they could readily supply local needs for money, which they could not so readily obtain in any other way. It was often required and used as was alleged for secret service, for lighting and cleaning towns occupied as military posts, for sanitary purposes; for feeding and clothing the destitute and for the legitimate uses of the Commisary and Quartermasters Departments. Thus as above stated Agents found themselves almost helpless in undertaking to execute the work assigned to them.

As our armies advanced during the Summer of 1863, large quantities of this property were left in their rear. It was generally where it could not be reached without means of land transportation. These could seldom be obtained from the Quartermasters. The inhabitants of the neighborhood where it was situated would not furnish teams or other aid except upon the most exorbitant terms. They were adverse to any taking of the property by Agents of the Government. They were hostile to all persons engaged in the business and ready to do anything in their power to prevent them from finding or removing it. Marks and other evidences of its character were destroyed and the cotton itself often removed and concealed. Personal injury to Agents and others engaged in collecting it was often threatened and not infrequently executed. Most of the cotton was found on plantations which had been abandoned by the owners. Some of it was secreted in woods and swamps. When found it was generally damaged and in bad condition. The rope and bagging was mostly rotted. Nearly all of it required assorting and rebaling.

It was therefore found necessary to provide more adequate means for securing the cotton as directed by law. Accordingly regulations were made by the Secretary of the Treasury in relation to the whole subject, which were approved by the President and promulgated on the 11th of September, 1863.[5] One of these regulations authorized Agents to contract on behalf of the United States for the collection and delivery to them of such property in their respective Agencies, on the best possible terms not exceeding twenty-five per cent of the proceeds of the property, which percentage should be in full compensation for all expenses of whatever character incurred in collecting, preparing and delivering such property at points to be designated, from which it could be sent forward to market. And under this regulation considering all the circumstances above stated it was thought that the contracts authorized by it were not only the most practicable and economical, but absolutely the only way of collecting the cotton preparing it for transportation and delivering it at points from which the Agents could forward it to market. This therefore became the system generally adopted on these collections.

Another regulation provided that Agents might receive property from persons who should offer voluntarily to abandon it, giving receipts therefor to the owners, stating that the same would be forwarded and disposed of in accordance with the Act of Congress. The increasing magnitude of the business required the immediate appointment of Agents. They were appointed upon satisfactory testimonials as to character and capacity. The duties to be performed by them were entirely new, no precidents existed for thier guidance; the instructions given them were necessarily general; and the country in which their transactions were carried on was in an unsettled condition rendering frequent communication with the Department difficult and often impossible. Agents frequently misunderstood their duties. Irregularities were the necessary result of this condition of things.

During the Summer of 1863, considerable cotton was brought forward by the owners and voluntarily abandoned to the Agents upon their assurance that the Secretary would promptly hear their cases and if satisfied of their loyalty and ownership, he would at once release it. This mistake was promptly corrected, but the then Secretary felt that it would be unjust to parties who had voluntarily delivered their property to Agents of the United States, upon such assurances to retain it and send them to the Court of Claims for relief. He therefore directed releases to be made in all such cases upon payment of the expenses incurred, the internal revenue taxes and other government dues.

Under the system of contracting with parties for collecting, putting in order for shipment and delivering at designated points, many irregularities also occurred. Contractors anxious for gain, were sometimes guilty of bad faith and peculation and frequently took possession of cotton and delivered it under contracts as captured or abandoned, when in fact it was not such and they had no right to touch it under their contracts, or under the Act of Congress. Residents and others in the districts where these peculations were going on took advantage of the unsettled condition of the country and representing themselves as Agents of this Department went about robbing under such pretended authority and thus added to the difficulties of the situation by causing unjust approbrium and suspicion to rest upon officers engaged in the faithful discharge of their duties. Agents also, sometimes imposed upon and sometimes misunderstanding their duties, frequently received or collected property and sent it forward which the law did not authorize them to take. Persons thus wrongfully deprived of their property followed it, and appealed to the Secretary for its restoration. These appeals were considered by the Secretary and if he was satisfied that the property was not such as the Act authorized the Agents to receive or collect he ordered that it, or its proceeds should be returned to the owner. But this again led to other complications. The success of the bona fide applications by owners opened to bad men an opportunity for gain by imposing on the Department in representing that cotton which had come to its possession had been wrongfully taken from them by the Agents and petitioning for its release. They submitted with their petitions, proofs which although seeming conclusive, were often false. Thus the applications made in good faith and in which the parties were fairly entitled to relief, and those made, in bad faith upon fair seeming though false proofs to defraud the Government, forced upon the Department great care and labor. It was often very difficult, if not impossible to discriminate between fraudulent and bona fide cases, and no duty devolving upon the present Secretary has caused him more perplexity and care and anxiety than that connected with this subject.

The next legislation of Congress affecting the matters enquired about, was the Act of Congress approved July 2. 1864,[6] by which the purchase of cotton, naval stores, and other southern products was authorized.

Regulations under which such purchases should be made were prepared by the Secretary and approved, by the President, September 24th 1864,[7] Agents were promptly appointed and sent to prominent points in the South, to make purchases as authorized by the Act of Congress and in pursuance of the Regulations. Their transactions were profitable to the

Government and generally satisfactory and were continued until the promulgation of the Executive order of June 13th 1865,[8] which removed all restrictions upon Commercial Intercourse between the citizens of States East of the Mississippi River. This order rendered purchases no longer proper or practicable and the Agents were recalled.

After the surrender of the armies of the rebellion the Secretary desired to recall all Agents engaged in executing the Acts of Congress relating to captured and abandoned property and to receive and dispose of only such as should be delivered by military forces to Customs officers at shipping ports and circular directions were given accordingly on the 27th of June 1865.[9]

But it was urged that the Cotton, and other property which belonged to the so-called Confederate Government was scattered all through the lately insurrectionary States, and that the rapid withdrawal of the military forces would render it impossible for them to take possession of this property and deliver it to shipping points. It was also urged that all property belonging to the so-called Confederate Government at the time of the surrender should be considered and treated as captured property and the plain duty of the Secretary of the Treasury, under the Acts of Congress above referred to required him to collect and dispose of it.

The Secretary therefore felt required to continue to collect this property through the Agents in the same manner as above stated and renewed his efforts to execute the laws concerning it. But the difficulties and embarrassments previously existing as above stated were greatly increased after the surrender.

The military forces were withdrawn from the Districts where the property was located. No means of enforcing law or of punishing the violation of it were established. Lawless men singly and in organized bands, engaged in general plunder. Every species of intrigue and peculation and theft were resorted to, Agents of the Department though generally faithful and efficient were probably in some cases involved in these illicit transactions. What had been difficult before the disbanding of the hostile armies, became almost impossible during the disorganized state of affairs in the South immediately after. Still the efforts were continued until the requirements of the law seemed to be fulfilled and the results are submitted herewith.

It is proper to state that judicial proceedings have been commenced and in several cases are still pending, prosecuted for the recovery of property which had been taken and disposed of as captured property. These are vigorously defended and special counsel is generally engaged to assist the United States District Attorneys, in protecting the interests of the Government therein.

All sales of property collected have been made in large markets, at public auction upon proper notice for cash. A list is appended hereto showing the names of all Agents appointed by the Department who have been in any way connected with the business, with the rate of compensation paid to each.

The papers and proofs upon which releases have been made are on file in this Department and in any case where examination thereof may be desired they will be furnished.

I annex hereto tabular statements which have been prepared to show in detail all transactions of Agents so far as they have been reported to or are known by the Department.

The results of the whole action of the Department under the Acts of Congress above referred to as shown by the annexed statement are recapitulated as stated as follows.

Abandoned Cotton.

Number of bales of Cotton received as abandoned.	{	11,180
Number of bales improperly taken as abandoned and released by the Department.	{	1,907
Number of bales of cotton sold as abandoned.	{	9,273
Gross proceeds of sale of 9273 bales sold as abandoned.	{ $	2,682,271.69
Amount paid to claimants for cotton improperly taken and sold as abandoned.	{ $	668,028.68
Amount paid to contractors for collecting, transporting and delivering abandoned cotton to agents at designated points.	{ $	93,646.06
All other expenses including freight and charges paid to Quartermasters on account of abandoned cotton.	{ $	180,946.67
Net amount realized by the United States on account of *abandoned* cotton.	{ $	1,739,650.28

Captured Cotton.

Number of bales of cotton received as captured.	{	156,387
Number of bales improperly taken or detained as captured and released.	{	18,485

(It is proper to say in explanation of this item, that after the surrender the Secretary was reliably informed that large quantities of cotton which had been claimed by the so-called Confederate Government were being stolen and otherwise wrongfully taken by individuals, and that he thereupon directed Agents to take possession of, and detain for investigation all cotton which they had good reason to believe should be treated as captured, and to promptly examine into the facts, and if satisfied that it was captured, to forward it as such, or if not so satisfied, to deliver it back to the persons from whom it was taken. But the Agents were required to report their action in all such cases and hence a large quantity of such cotton seems to have been treated as captured, when the fact is that it was merely detained for examination and was released to owners upon failure by Agents to show a right to treat it as captured property.)

Number of bales paid to contractors for collecting	{	9,164
Number of bales lost by fire, or in transit, or taken out of the hands of the Agents by judicial process, or by military orders, &c.	{	13,223
Number of bales of cotton sold as captured.	{	115,051
Number of bales on hand	{	464
Gross proceeds of sales of 115,051 bales of cotton sold as captured.	{	19,239,320.24
Amount paid to claimants for cotton improperly taken and sold as captured.	{ $	654,918.18
Expenses, including amount paid to contractors for collecting, transporting and delivering to Agents at designated points, and freights and charges paid to Quartermasters on account of captured cotton.	{ $	2,783,229.96
Net amount realized by the United States on account of *captured* cotton.	{ $	15,801,172.10

Miscellaneous Property collected as Captured or Abandoned.

Gross proceeds of sales and collections	{ $	1,374,573.94
Amount of proceeds released to claimants by the Department.	{ $	9,856.85
Expenses of collection transportation and sale of miscellaneous property.	{ $	74,918.66
Net amount realized by the United States from miscellaneous captured and abandoned property.	{ $	1,289,798.43

Purchased Cotton.

Number of bales of cotton purchased by Agents under the Act of July 2, 1864.	{	53,838
Number of bales of cotton sold by Agents under the above Act.	{	53,837
Lost in repacking	{	1
Gross proceeds of sale of 53,837 bales of cotton.	{ $	7,537,847.77
Purchase money paid for same	{ $	3,490,695.21
Expenses incurred by Agents connected with this class of transactions	{ $	147,272.82
Net profit realized by the United States from the *purchase* of cotton.	{ $	3,935,879.74

Miscellaneous Property Purchased.
Total amount paid for same.   { $ 17,943.06
Total amount received for sale of same.   { $ 31,124.69
(The expenses incurred by Agents connected with
this class of transactions are included in the
expenses charged to cotton purchases.[)]
Net Profit realized by the United States from the
purchase of *miscellaneous* products.   { $ 13,181.63
Miscellaneous Receipts.
Other receipts connected with the execution of the
several Acts, such as rents of abandoned property,
fees for registering same &c., amounts collected
for misappropriation of this class of property and
receipts from Agents without account of details.   { $ 3,151,671.21
Expenses, such as salaries to Agents, pay to clerks,
and other employees connected with the various
Agencies and all other matters not charged in
other accounts above stated.   { $ 1,189,330.84
Net amount from this source   { $ 1,962,342.37
Total Amount received by the United States from
various sources as above stated.   { $34,052,809.54
Total amount released to claimants   { $ 1,332,803.71
Total amount of purchase money paid for
property.   { $ 3,508,638.27
Total amount of expenses paid including expenses
of collecting, transportation, Agents salaries,
compensation and all other expenses of every
description connected with the execution of the
various Acts, so far as adjusted or ascertained.   { $ 4,469,345.01
Leaving *as a total net amount* realized by the
United States from the various sources named
after payment of every expense in any way
connected therewith.   { $24,742,022.55
                           H. McCulloch   Secretary of the Treasury.

LS, DNA-RG56, Lets. Sent *re* Restricted Commercial Intercourse (BE Ser.), Vol. 15.
    1. *House Ex. Docs.*, 39 Cong., 2 Sess., No. 97, p. 7 (Ser. 1293).
    2. *U.S. Statutes at Large*, 12: 820–21.
    3. Salmon P. Chase was secretary of the treasury in 1863.
    4. *House Ex. Docs.*, 38 Cong., 1 Sess., No. 3, pp. 436–39 (Ser. 1186). Stanton was
secretary of war and Gideon Welles secretary of the navy in 1863.
    5. Ibid., pp. 408–27.
    6. *U.S. Statutes at Large*, 13: 375–78.
    7. *House Ex. Docs.*, 38 Cong., 2 Sess., No. 3, pp. 294–324, 345–50 (Ser. 1222).
    8. *New York Tribune*, June 14, 1865.
    9. Ibid., June 30, 1865.

From William B. Phillips
Private.

Editorial Rooms   Herald Office.
N. York, Nov. 8th 1866

Dear Sir,

Will you permit me to say a few words on the political situation of the time as determined by the late elections and as regarded from this point of view?

Looking over the whole feild and at the popular vote generally it seems to me that the policy of Congress for the restoration of the South has been endorsed by the people of the North. It is true the vote in the two great central states, New York and Pennsylvania, was pretty close, but that of the North West, which is rapidly becoming the seat of political power, has been more decisive in favor of the Congressional plan of restoration. Whatever we may think of this or however much deplore the want of enlightenment on the subject and want of magnanimity toward the South it is the voice of the people. Not of the whole people—not of the south, it is true—but of the great majority of those who only have a voice in the matter just now. I wish it had been otherwise and think it unfortunate that it is not, but we can not always have what we want or what is best. Under these circumstances I think you will agree with me that it will be wiser not to stem an overwhelming current but rather to use it, and control it, as far as possible, for the welfare of the whole country. To do so will be acting in accordance with the highest statesmanship and as the greatest statesmen of all countries act. Proscriptive and objectionable as the constitutional amendment is I do not think any more favorable terms can be obtained for the South, while by the delay caused in attempting to modify these conditions the political disabilities of the South may become chronic, sectional bad feeling may become intensified, and the difficulty of restoration may become greater. I regard it as of the utmost importance that the South should be restored before her excluded condition becomes chronic. The question is, then, whether it will not be better to take what she can get—to swallow even the constitutional amendment, as a man would a nauseous dose of medicine to releive himself from a painful disease, and leave the rest to the future. If the South had again a voice in Congress she could defend herself, she would then be heard by the whole country, and these very disabilities imposed by the constitutional amendment might then be modified. Some of them would wear away in time. The good of the country is paramount to every thing else, to all personal or party feeling, and the southern people ought to look at the matter in this light.

I do not presume to give you advice as to how far you should act or abstain from acting any more in the matter of restoration. You understand that far better than I do. I merely take the liberty in a friendly way

13. *Our noble President hears from Vermont, but thinks it isn't more than might be expected from Vermont.*

14. *He hears from Main.*

15. *He hears from Pennsylvania, and Indiana and Ohio.*

16. *He hears from New York.*

Nasby's version of Johnson's response to the fall 1866 election returns
From *Nasby's Life of Andy Jonsun.*
Courtesy Special Collections, University of Tennessee Library

of submitting a few remarks on the general principle which underlies the question.

I am delighted to see the able manner in which you are taking up questions pertaining to our foreign relations. This will give glory to your administration. We shall continue to give you full credit for all that in the Herald. I refer more particularly just now to the settlement of the Mexican difficulty. Mr. Bennett invited me to meet Wykoff at dinner when Wycoff returned from Washington for the purpose of hearing the good news which he brought.[1] My article on your next Message had taken the right ground and we were all much pleased.[2]

The subject of our national finances, the currency, and banks is a highly important one and a very difficult one to understand and handle. Yet it is a subject that must be handled. I hope your administration may have the great honor of establishing a sound system. I have an article in type on this[3] and will send it to you when published.

W. B. Phillips.

ALS, DLC-JP.
1. It is not known what "news" Henry Wikoff brought. See Wikoff to Johnson, Oct. 25, 1866.
2. See "The Next Message of the President to Congress," *New York Herald*, Oct. 26, 1866. Phillips thought it best for the President to avoid further confrontations with Congress over the readmission issue and the Fourteenth Amendment, and concentrate instead on developing a "broader and more decisive" foreign policy and dealing with the nation's financial woes, especially the "monstrous moneyed monopoly of the national banks."
3. See "Our National Finances—The Forthcoming Report of the Secretary of the Treasury," ibid., Nov. 9, 1866.

From David L. Seymour[1]

Troy NY   Nov 8. 1866

My Dear Sir

We are greatly disappointed at the result of the recent election in this state. There are many topics connected with it which I should like to discuss with you but I can not do it in a letter.

One thing however I think is now quite clear. It is this; every office holder who has in this election voted against your policy of reconstruction should be immediately removed & his place filled by true & loyal friends of your administration. I am quite sure that if the most of the political offices held under the U.S. Govt had during the past summer been filled by the friends in stead of the enimies of your administration we should not have suffered the sad defeat which we have & our country would be in a fair way soon to be restored to a condition of peace & prosperity.

I hope you will adopt at once the policy of creating a power in the country which will sustain your sound democratic & conservative views on the subject of reconstruction. The movement in this direction should not in my opinion be delayed.

My personal & political friend Mr N. B. Milliman[2] who was our candidate for Congress in this the 15 Cong Dist of NY will soon be in Washington to confer with you on this subject[3] & until then so far as this District is concerned I hope no changes will be made. I hope I shall be able to come & see you soon. I wish to confer with you as to the policy I have above recommended for I feel quite sure that if you have any doubt on the subject I can convince you of the correctness of my views.[4]

David L. Seymour

P.S. You may rely upon it that the sound business men of our state are with you. But when the thousands of Postmasters & others holding office under the U.S. use their influence & means against us we can hardly expect in so close a vote to succeed.

D.L.S.

ALS, DLC-JP.
1. Seymour (1803–1867), who served with Johnson as a Democrat in Congress, had written to his former colleague from time to time, advising him on various topics and endorsing his position against the Radicals. *BDAC*; Seymour to Johnson, Sept. 8, Nov. 25, 1865, Feb. 22, 1866, Johnson Papers, LC.
2. Nathaniel B. Milliman (1820–*fl*1878), a Democrat, served two terms as county clerk before running for Congress in 1866. He was also involved in the manufacturing of doors and window sashes both during and after the war. *History of Washington Co., New York* (Philadelphia, 1878), 113, 320, 498.
3. See Nathaniel B. Milliman and Thomas B. Carroll to Johnson, Nov. 16, 1866.
4. Several weeks later Seymour wrote again from New York, this time asking Johnson to consider issuing a blanket amnesty to all southerners "without any condition as to suffrage." Seymour to Johnson, Nov. 27, 1866, Office of Atty. Gen., Lets. Recd., President, RG60, NA.

From Edwin M. Stanton

Washington City   Novr. 8th 1866

Mr. President—

I beg to call your attention to the 2d Section of the Act making appropriations for the support of the Army, &c, approved June 15, 1864 (Chapter CXXIV, U.S. Statutes at large).[1] That section provides, among other things, that persons of color who shall thereafter be mustered into the service of the United States shall receive such sums in Bounty as the President shall order in the different states and in the United States, not exceeding $100. In the State of Maryland several regiments formed of a number of persons who were slaves at the time of enlistment, were mustered into the United States service in regiments and are about to be mustered out of service. Under existing laws these persons cannot receive bounty unless it be authorized by order of the President under the Section of the Act referred to. Having faithfully performed their duty there seems to be no just reason that they should not receive the benefit of that provision. I would respectfully recommend, therefore that under the authority of that Act you order bounty to be paid them, not exceeding $100. It is desirable, if this recommendation meets your approval that the order should be made before the regiments are mustered out, so that its benefit may be secured to the soldiers without the intervention of claim-agents or other persons and that they may receive it when paid off.[2]

Edwin M. Stanton   Secretary of War

LS, DNA-RG94, Lets. Recd. (Main Ser.), File A-971-1866 (M619, Roll 459).
1. *U.S. Statutes at Large*, 13: 130.
2. No evidence has been found that Johnson took action; however, Congress continued to pass legislation for the payment of bounties to "colored soldiers & sailors" at least through 1870, and the attorney general determined and directed the paymaster general that those who were slaves at enlistment were entitled to their regular bounties and the extra bounty at the time they mustered out. Ibid., 15: 302; *National Intelligencer*, Nov. 21, 1866.

From Thomas W. Bartley

Cincinnati O   Nov. 9" '66

Mr. President

I had a conversation a few days since with Genl. Sherman,[1] as he was passing through this City, & I truly regret, that, I found, that he had no adequate appreciation of the dangers & difficulties which the radicals in Congress will bring upon the country at the approaching session, if they wield the same controlling influence over Congress which they held last winter; & I was grieved to observe, that he does not express himself with his usual clearness & decission of character upon the matter of the vital political issues before the country. It is true, that he recognizes your position as to the restoration of the Union as the true one, & does not hesitate to condemn that of congress, but he is averse to taking any part in the settlement of those questions, which are essential to making the war a success. I insist, that he owes it to himself as well as the country to exert all the influence in his power to sustain your position, which makes the war a success in preserving the government, while the position of Congress makes the war *result in the distruction* of the government. The issue between your position & that of Congress must determine, whether the war has been the means of *preserving* the government or of *distroying* it. The federal government made by our forefathers was *founded on the Union of the States*, & if it be determined, that *the Union* shall *not be restored* under the present constitution, *the foundation* for the government is gone, & the government, to preserve which the war was waged, is distroyed, or revolutionized, which is the same thing. But more than this. Not only is the government established by our forefathers distroyed, but *the essential principles of civil liberty*, for the maintainance of which the government was instituted, *are absolutely repudiated* by the position of Congress. To say, that the government shall *be changed, & a different government created*, for the people of ten States, without their participation in framing such change, or new government, is to repudiate the inalienable right of self government declared in the declaration of American Independence. And to say, that seven millions of people, constituting ten distinct States, *shall be governed, & taxed, without representation*, is to make the people of those states *political slaves*, & to repudiate the most essential principles of free government. And further yet, to say, that Congress has the power to repudiate & abolish the fundamental & most essential principles of the constitution, to prevent the restoration of the Union, to defeat the great end & object of the war, & to remodel the government, by superceding the civil authority in the establishment of a military government under the name & disguise of a freedmen's bureau, is to say, that the results of the war have not only revolutionised our government, but also abolished the essential elements of free government: Your position must finally prevail, if the people of the country shall manifest their capacity for maintaining free government. Immoveable firmness on your part in defending & maintaining the Constitution gives the only ground to hope for the preservation of the government. If Congress resorts to rash & violent measures to carry out the distructive purposes of the radicals their own party will break to pieces. Excuse my troubling you with my crude views upon Subjects upon which your opinions are doubtless much more mature.

One of the most manifest causes of the total failure of the democratic party this fall is to be found in the inefficiency and short-sightedness of the democratic press.

An effort is about being made to establish a first class news paper in this city. If successful it will deserve the patronage of your Administration.

T. W. Bartley

ALS, DLC-JP.
1. Upon Johnson's request, Sherman traveled from St. Louis to Washington, D.C., between October 23 and 25, 1866, amid rumors he was to be made the temporary head of the War Department. Instead, he agreed to be Lewis D. Campbell's escort to Mexico, in place of General Grant, who had refused to go. Simon, *Grant Papers*, 16: 337–41; William T. Sherman, *Memoirs of General William T. Sherman* (2 vols., New York, 1990 [1886]), 2: 904–5.

From Cynthia Pillow Saunders Brown

"Melrose" Near Nashville, Nov. 9th, 1866
Mr President,
By the last mail, I received, a letter from a Federal officer, of high position (now in Washington) stating that Col Williams[1] was at that time, in

the Capital—making "strenous efforts," to be in command, of the Freedmens Bureau, in Tenn—with Head Quarters at Nashville. Or in event, of
his failure, to secure, the position alluded to—he desires to obtain *some
subordinate place*, in the same Department. He does not hesitate, to avow
that he wishes, to be stationed, *here*, in order, to facilitate his intention, of
still further, *traducing*, and *harassing my family*; whose peace of mind, he
has, already *destroyed*. I therefore, beg of you, as a *personal favor*, Mr
President *not* to assign him, to *any position*, in *this* state where, he thinks,
his *military position* will *protect him* in any further outrange, he may commit. Besides any personal consideration I very naturally feel, I think it
but right, that I should tell you, that he is the most bitter, and *abusive*, of
the Radicals, and denounces you, and your policy on all occasions. It is
my honest opinion, that if he is placed *here*—, he would if possible—,
delight, in getting up, a *riot*, similar to those that have been enacted, in
Memphis, and New-Orleans. With sentiments of regard, and high respect . . .

Mrs Aaron V. Brown

Do not trouble yourself, Mr President, to write—as I am aware, that
your time, is fully occupied; with important, official business.

Mrs A.V.B.

ALS, DLC-JP.
   1. Thomas C. Williams. See Narcissa P. Saunders to Johnson, Oct. 28, 1866.

From Hiram Ketchum, Sr.[1]

New York   November 9. 1866

Sir.
   The election in this State is over, and you know the result. During the
Canvass, in which I have taken a warm and active interest, the proposition which I have urged with whatever ability I possess, both in the public press, and before the people—with pen and voice, is this—that the
president was bound by his oath office, acting under the Constitution, to
do what he could to favor the admission to Congress of the representatives of the ten excluded States because *they were States in the Union*.
This duty is so plain under the express provisions of the Constitution,
that there is no room for any question of Construction. No popular expressions could obliterate or impair this duty. It is personal, explicit, and
imperative. You have performed that duty in good faith, but it would
seem, for the present at least, that the popular voice has not Sustained
you, although I have a confident belief that it will come up to your Support before the expiration of your official term.
   Now allow me to express the opinion, with great deference, that you
are released from proceeding any farther on that line of duty, while I

would take no Step backward. Fidelity to the Constitution would not allow you to do less than you have done, but, under the Circumstances, you are not required to do any thing more.

As to Constitutional amendments, the Constitution has left them to the decision of two thirds of the members of Congress; they are not required to Submit their action to the president, nor can I see that the president is bound, or perhaps even authorised to give any advice to Congress. Congress has acted on this Subject, and, in my judgment, not wisely. Please excuse these Suggestions. They proceed from a friendly Source.

Hiram Ketchum

ALS, DLC-JP.

1. Ketchum (c1792–1870) was a prominent New York City attorney who had voted for McClellan in 1864 and claimed a friendship with Charles Sumner. Although highly recommended for naval officer of New York City, he was not appointed by Johnson. Charles M. Wiltse et al., eds., *The Papers of Daniel Webster: Correspondence Series* (7 vols., Hanover, N.H., 1974–86), 5: 70; Appts., Customs Service, Naval Officer, New York, Hiram Ketchum, RG56, NA. See also John A. Dix to Johnson, Sept. 20, 1866, Johnson Papers, LC.

From John S. Brien

Private

Nashville   November 10th 1866

My Dear Sir,

I wrote you some time since.[1] I have not heard from you. At the risque of being troublesome, I write you again. You will have seen Brownlows Message,[2] before this reaches you, so that I need make no comment upon it.

There has been no quoram up to this time. It is supposed there will be one on Monday. I do not thing I will be admitted. I am sure I will not if they can find any pretex to exclude me.[3] The Radicals, as I learn are determined to stand by Brownlow in his message. If so and they pass his proposed bills there will in my opinion be trouble in this state. The people are getting sore under Brownlows oppressions and threats, and unless they can see that there is a chance to be relieved, I do not believe they will much longer tamely submit to the outrages put upon them by this radical Click.

It was to avoid such conflict, that induced me to make some suggestions to you as to the appointment of certain officers. It is very trying to our people, to be trod upon by those who would distroy the Government, and at the same time receiving pay from that Government, and wielding the offices, and well as the prestige it gives them to serve their unholy purpose. I do not know that this letter will ever reach, you I intend to send it under cover to Senator Patterson.

Now Mr President, I suggest that you fill all the offices in this state with the friends of your administration, so that we may at least communicate with our friends.

The most important thing to be done at present, under the Brownlow program, is the appointment of a proper man to Command the Millitary, and freedmans Bureau in this state, tho Genl. Carlin I suggested, is in my opinion the best man that could be selected, a Maj in the Regular Army, Brvt. Majr. Genl in the Vol. Services, fought with great gallantry through war, is a first rate man and an ardent friend to your administration. If you place him in command of the forces here, as also of the Freedmans Bureau all things will be done right, and will make our friends feel secure. Turn out these radicals, and if they fight you let them fight upon their own resources.

I have only time to hint you. I wish I could see you to explain all. I shall have to bear the burden of our cause here. I am upon the ground and understand our situation. Help me.

John S. Brien.

P.S. I can scarcely write, my hand has become so unsteady. This is my apology for this badly written letter, but you know me, and will understand what I am. Chase out these fellows before Congress meets.

J.S.B.

ALS, DLC-JP.

1. Doubtless a reference to his earlier letter of October 18. On November 13, Johnson sent a dispatch to Brien in which he assured him that he had received and read both of Brien's letters, had profited from them, and would write soon in reply to them. See Brien to Johnson, Oct. 18, 1866; Johnson to Brien, Nov. 13, 1866, Johnson Papers, LC.

2. Brien refers here to the governor's message to the general assembly. The message itself is dated as November 6; it apparently was read informally to the house on November 7 and was published in the Nashville newspapers on the following day. White mistakenly dates the message as being November 15. *Nashville Press and Times*, Nov. 8, 1866; Robert H. White et al., *Messages of the Governors of Tennessee* (10 vols., Nashville, 1952-), 5: 530–45.

3. After qualifying on November 19, Brien took his seat in the lower house and served during the November 1866-March 1867 session. Ibid., 689; *BDTA*, 1: 78.

From James P. Brownlow

Washington D.C.   Novem 10" 1866

I have the honor, to most respectfully, apply for a position in the "Regular Army" as Major or Captain,[1] or any position you may see poper to confer upon . . . [2]

James P. Brownlow

ALS, DNA-RG94, ACP Branch, File B-61-CB-1868, Jas. R. [*sic*] Brownlow.

1. In a cover sheet endorsement, Johnson on November 14 instructed the secretary of war to appoint Brownlow as captain in the cavalry if a vacancy existed. If none existed, the President told Stanton to appoint Brownlow to the infantry. Powell's reference work indicates that Brownlow was appointed a captain in the 8th U.S. Cav. in late July 1866. Regardless of the confusion surrounding the date, Brownlow was definitely appointed captain at Johnson's behest. Powell, *Army List*, 217.

2. In December a Knoxville newspaper noted that Brownlow had been appointed as captain and had been assigned to go to California in April 1867. In response to a Nashville newspaper's claim that Governor Brownlow should feel grateful to the President, the Knoxville paper indicated that the governor, had he been consulted in advance, would have advised his son against taking any appointment. Moreover, the governor believed that his son should have received a higher appointment. April found James P. Brownlow in Franklin, Tennessee, instead of in California; he pleaded with the President and subsequently with Sen. David T. Patterson that either he be granted an extension of time before he had to report to California (Johnson ordered this) or else be honorably discharged because of physical handicaps. Brownlow resigned from the army in March 1868. *Knoxville Whig*, Dec. 5, 1866; Brownlow to Johnson, Apr. 9, 1867; Brownlow to Patterson, May 23, 1867, ACP Branch, File B-61-CB-1868, Jas. R. [*sic*] Brownlow, RG94, NA; Powell, *Army List*, 217.

From Washington McKean, Jr.[1]

Toms River [N.J.]   Nov 10th 1866

Sir,

As you are disposing of the office holders that are against your policy, there is one more in this place that ought to be disposed of, and that is Edward W Ivins[2] Superintendent of the station houses along our coast, as on last Tuesday at the polls he done all in his power to elect Wm. A Newell, to Congress a man who is in opposition to you and the Laws and Constitution of the United States. I served three years to help put down the Rebellion and now to think such men as Newell being upheld when they are trying to bring on a harder rebellion than the Southern Rebellion was, by men holding office under you is going against all laws of a nation such as ours should be not as the *Radicals* wish to make it. If I have fought against the people in the South I would rather take them by the hand of friendship than a great many of the Northern fanatics. Therefore I hope that you will remove Edward W Ivins and put a good man in his place that will stand by the Constitution, but Newell is defeated and we have elected *Gen Hight*[3] a man that will stand by the Nation in its worse struggles, and all I wish is that the fortieth Congress could have been all composed of such men as Hight.[4]

Washington McKean Jr
formerly of the 14th N J vols

ALS, DNA-RG26, Life-Saving Service Executive Correspondence.

1. A carpenter before and after the war, McKean (1835–1912) was mustered out of the army in June 1865. Pension File, Washington McKean, RG15, NA; 1860 Census, N.J., Ocean, Dover Twp., Toms River, 49.

2. Probably Ivins (b. *c*1821), a prewar coal merchant. Ibid., 41.

3. Democrat Charles Haight (1838–1891), a brigadier general of militia during the war, defeated Newell by less than four hundred votes. He served in Congress for two terms (1867–71). *BDAC*; *Guide to U.S. Elections*, 616.

4. The letter was referred to the secretary of the treasury. Ser. 6A, Vol. D: 112, Johnson Papers, LC.

From Benjamin F. Perry

Greenville S.C.   Nov 10" 1866

My dear Sir

I take the liberty of enclosing to you, a printed copy of a letter, written by me, on the Constitutional Amendment.[1]

There is but one feeling in South Carolina on this subject. The Amendment will be unanimously rejected by the Legislature. Worse terms may be imposed by Congress, but they will be *imposed* & not *voluntarily accepted.*

The elections in the Northern States have greatly disappointed me, & I feel dispirited.

B. F. Perry

ALS, DLC-JP.

1. Not found, but it was Perry's October 26, 1866, letter to Charles W. Woodward of Philadelphia, published in the newspapers. See *Charleston Courier*, Nov. 5, 1866.

From Samuel T. Smith[1]

Homer N.Y.   Nov. 10 1866

The Election of the state of New York is over, and the radical flood still rolls on. In our Saratoga Convention,[2] the Conservative men of the two parties seemed to be united in a determination to bring about a change in the Counsels of the nation. At Philadelphia the same spirit, although not universal, still prevailed, and our action was harmonious, and promised the best of results. At Albany the Demon of selfishness seemed to have taken possession of our Democratic brethren. The occasion demanded the nomination of a Conservative Candidate, to give assurance of good faith to the Conservative Republicans in our state who naturally distrusted the Democrats who had the power in their hands and could use it as they saw fit—but disregarding the earnest solicitation of those of us who saw the need of this guarantee on their part, to give the people confidence in their sincerity—they nominated, after a strictly democratic speech of Judge Pierpont[3] a Democratic Candidate, as the mass of Conservative Republicans believed, to grasp the Appointments for Democratic purposes; and thus, in the contest, cast a suspicion on their sincerity—destroyed the confidence they ought to have fostered. Had they nominated Dix,[4] we could have given an increased vote in every county in the state, and in my judgment, carried the state, and had a firm corner-stone to work from hereafter. But the state is gone and who can tell the result?

By our utmost efforts we reduced the Majority in our small county about 100.—The same reduction every where would have carried the state.

What now? Are those proposed amendments to be adopted, changing the whole nature of our government.

I trust not. I think a year or two of Radicalism more, will satisfy the country that the principles contained in that old instrument are too dear to us to be frittered away, and that the balances of our government are too useful and necessary to be destroyed in favor of Congress.

I believe that with you standing firmly on the ground you have assumed and each state Organizing her Conservative men on the Philadelphia platform, two years more will have seen the end of the Radical race, and we shall have a united Country, prepared to look back on the propositions of the present Congress, as a dangerous experiment of a body of men who are insane by partisan excitement.

While I have the pleasure of knowing that one is at the head of the government who will not be induced to depart from the plain line of his duty by any consideration, I can well disregard the curses of my former political associates—and the fears of my timid political friends.

With expressions of sincere regard, allow me to declare myself the firm friend of my country—and of its distinguished president and the firm believer in the final success and vindication of Both.

Saml. T. Smith

ALS, DLC-JP.
　1. Not identified.
　2. A bipartisan, pro-Johnson meeting was held at Saratoga on August 9, 1866, to elect delegates to the National Union Convention in Philadelphia. Among the six hundred or so in attendance was Smith, who represented Cortland County. *New York Tribune*, Aug. 9, 10, 1866. See also James R. Doolittle to Johnson, Aug. 8, 1866.
　3. Edwards Pierrepont.
　4. John A. Dix.

From Edmund Cooper

Shelbyville Ten:　Novr. 12 1866.
Dear Sir:

The friends and supporters of your administration in Cincinatti, request me to write you a letter in favor of Honl Thomas Spooner[1]—who they desire to have appointed "Commissioner of Internal Revenue"—in place of the Honl E. A. Rollins—the present commissioner.

I have no information as to your intentions or that of the Department in regard to the present commissioner, but in the event, of his removal—I know of no one, who comes more highly recommended than the Gentleman mentioned above.

Gov Len Harris of Cincinatti urges the claims of Mr Spooner, upon the grounds of merit and qualification—as well as the location of the applicant, coming as he does from the great west.

If upon consultation you should conclude to make the change, would it not be advisable to make it before the meeting of congress?

Of course, I do not wish to interfere in a positional matter beyond my "bailiwick"—but feel most inclined to say a good word for Mr Spooner, who has worked earnestly during the last campaign, in promoting the interest of the administration in the State of Ohio.[2]

Edmd. Cooper

ALS, DNA-RG56, Appls., Heads of Treasury Offices, Thomas Spooner.

1. Spooner (1817–1890), a Cincinnati hardware merchant, had been clerk of the Hamilton County court of common pleas (1854–57) and collector of internal revenue (1862–66). In 1879 he moved to Glendale, Ohio, where he later served as mayor. *History of Cincinnati and Hamilton County, Ohio* (Cincinnati, 1894), 1010–11.

2. Although he had considerable support, Spooner did not replace Rollins as commissioner of internal revenue.

From Lemuel Davies[1]

Cairo [Ill.]   Nov 12/66

Dr Sir

Our election has passed over quietly; we have met the enemy, and they are ours (in this Alexander County). We formed a *Johnson Club*, early in the canvass, and it done a great deal of good, in the distribution of *Campaign Documents*. The only severe drawback we met, was that all the U.S. patronage was against us, for when we called on (which was only for form sake) them for their share of the expense, they gave us to understand, that they would not contribute a cent for the support of *My Policy*, but would contribute freely to put down that old *Traitor*. Our prospect, in the future is not as flattering as I would like, but it will not do to go backward. Prosperity demands at our hands an unimpaired Goverement, and we must obey; looking over the feild after the smook has cleared off, there is not much for the Rads to rejoice over, in every fair contest they have worsted themselves; true they have gained their old members of Congress but have not gained any accession to their number; but amongst the rank and file lost badly.

In 1868, with *A. Johnson*, as our standard bearer, we will march on to victory; even in the North, and doubly sure with the aid of the South; for by that time we will be throughly orginized. Since the contest there has been two new and essential appointments in this *destrict*, of two warm supporters of you Administration; we have two more we wish you would make. One is a Conservative *Postmaster* the other is a Conservative *Surveyor of Port* for *Cairo*, both the present encumbents are *Rads*.[2] I have applied for the *Surveyor of this Port*. If there is any other one that wants the office give it to him, so that he is one of us, as the only reason I applied for it was there was no other application, and my friends, said I must try and get it so that we can controll all the Patronage for the strugle of 1868; if you think there is any prospect of our winning the race give us a helping hand and if the Democracy can achive a victory the country is saved. If not God save us.

Lemuel Davies

ALS, DNA-RG56, Appts., Customs Service, Surveyor, Cairo, Lemuel Davies.
  1. Unidentified.
  2. Postmaster John M. Graham, not further identified, had been appointed July 23, 1866, and took office September 1. He served until 1870. The surveyor of the port was Dr. Daniel Arter (1798–1879), who served as such from 1861 until 1869. *U.S. Off. Reg.* (1865–67); John M. Lansden, *A History of the City of Cairo, Illinois* (Chicago, 1910), 233, 270; William H. Perrin, ed., *History of Alexander, Union and Pulaski Counties, Illinois* (Chicago, 1883), pt. 5: 5.

From Samuel W. Dewey

Private!

Washington   12th Novr. 1866.

Hon. Sir.

Having for many years known you to be a fearless, impartial, willing & ever prompt defender of the rights of the honest hard working men of our Country, after the manner you nobly vindicated those rights nearly twenty years since in Congress, at my individual suggestion, & prevented the almost irresistibly wealthy & powerful "*New-York State Prison Monopoly,*" from obtaining, what to them would have been a very profitable contract—the building of the Smithsonian Institute, out of their miserable New-York dingy White Marble, which was to have been quarried & dressed by Convicts in the New-York Sing-Sing State Prison, for whose labor, that Great "Monopoly", paid the Empire State, the paltry sum of (30) thirty cents per day only, for each Convict.[1] Your praiseworthy course on that occasion, should have done so, if it did not entitle you to the everlasting gratitude of not only the Mechanics of this District of Columbia, but throughout the entire United States, for, if the New-York Monopoly in question, had succeeded in getting the Smithsonian Contract, it was their intention to have secured all the contracts for our Government-Buildings, that might be in future offered "*to the lowest bidder.*" Please pardon me for this reminiscence, for in my humble estimation, it takes rank with your "Homestead Act," which caused you so many long years of toil & legislative exertion, worthy in every sense of the term of being called both herculean & masterly statesmanship!

I need not here allude to your numerous public achievements for the great mass of honest laborers throughout our mighty Empire Republic, for they are all well known to yourself, although by the late election Returns, it would seem as if the "Dead Duck" Forney, had so far succeeded in hoodwinking the Masses, as to make them forgetful of their duty towards their best Friend & the best Friend of our whole Country! A shameful fact that only goes to confirm the olden adage respecting the "Ingratitude of Republics." I am free to admit that, the late vote given for the Radical Members of Congress, is far more than sufficient to cause you to become disgusted with the forgetfulness of the Masses, even to the souring of your mind against ever again doing any more disinterested acts in their behalf, & were I not firm in believing you have too much magnanimity to be turned aside from you duty, even by the combined ingratitude of the whole world, I would not ask permission of you to give a little niche in your forth coming Message, to the Poor & Needy Nurses, who at our Country's call, left their comfortable homes, came here & accepted the slavish positions of nursing the wounded & disabled Soldirs that were crippled & diseased by exposure & otherwise during the late war!

In my humble opinion all those who rendered meritorious services as Nurses or otherwise, & thereby either seriously injured their health or their pecuniary condition by abandoning their respective avocations, should be honorably provided for by our Government. Those who from infirmity or lack of ability to serve as copying or other Clerks, should be duly & liberally pensioned, while all Nurses who have rendered meritorious services in our Hospitals or otherwise, should rank next to the needy Wives of disabled Soldiers & Soldiers Widows, so far as regards their being provided for, by Government offices, in the Female Clerk Departments, or by life Pensions. If you will but do this act of justice, millions will bless you & offer up prayers in your behalf that cannot fail to find favor with the Great Dispenser of all Great & good Gifts.

It would give me pleasure to obtain access to you for only a moment, if you could spare me the time; meanwhile I beg you to be assured I have an eye upon the movements of Forney's Minions, as set forth in the enclosed call for "The Grand Mass Welcome to Congress," a miserable attempt to intimidate & deter you from performing your duty as Chief Magistrate or Captain of our Mighty Ship of State.

Saml. W. Dewey

P.S. During a recent visit to Columbia, I called upon Mr. Robert Hamilton, one of the most staunch supporters you have in that section, & on exhibiting to himself & his Lady,[2] your kind acknowledgement of Fruit, dated 10th ult. after expressing themselves highly honored & delighted by your acceptation of their heartfelt present, Mrs. Hamilton being engaged in making Quince-Apple-Butter, remarked that, if I would see it safely delivered, she would forward by Express, two Jars of the Butter she was then preparing with her own hands. I agreed to do so & in due time, the package arrived, but unfortunately the contents of one Jar were spoiled by reason of its being broken. I can vouch for the Excellence of this little Souvenir from your Columbia Friends, & am confident you will in giving it a trial, find it to be delicious.

Saml. W. Dewey
Having Rooms at 439—West Ninth St. between F. & G. Sts.

ALS, DLC-JP.

1. Johnson, a strong enemy of the Smithsonian, does not appear to have taken any action concerning its construction, save to present a memorial from District citizens requesting that materials used be from the District area and that prison labor not be used. Trefousse, *Johnson*, 63; *House Journal*, 29 Cong., 2 Sess., p. 236 (Ser. 496).

2. The Hamiltons have not been identified.

From John McClelland

Nashville, Tenn., Nov 12 1866

Dear Sir & friend

Some 5 days since, a letter was sent to you,[1] asking for myself, the office of PostMaster in this City, provided you removed Mr Lindsley.[2]

If by giving me the Post Office you would weaken your strength, or subject yourself, or the cause you represent to danger, do not make the change for me. I will always be your friend, in my humble way, for I believe that you are earnestly, and honestly determined that the Majesty of the Constitution shall be maintained, in spite of faction or sectionalism.

Do therefore as you think best. If you do not make a change—or if you do make a change, and give the office to some other than myself, with me and my friends it will be all right.

What you have done for me, I am sincerely grateful for. But I hope that I am not selfish enough to desire that My Friend should jeopardize the cause which he represents, or bring upon himself the maledictions of a venomous party for my own advancement.

If you do make the change in my favor, I would respectfully suggest that Andrew Johnson Jr, be appointed U S Internal Revenue Assessor, for the fifth Collection district of Tennessee, in my Place.[3]

Jno. McClelland

ALS, DLC-JP.

1. Perhaps the reference is to the letter from McClelland that was received at the White House on November 14 which concerned a recommendation of him for postmaster. The letter was referred to the postmaster general. Ser. 6A, Vol. D: 168, Johnson Papers, LC.

2. Contrary to rumors, Adrian V.S. Lindsley was retained in the postmastership at Nashville for the time being; he was replaced in the spring of 1867.

3. McClelland continued on in his post as assessor at least through 1867 and perhaps beyond that time. The President's nephew did not receive the appointment. *U.S. Off. Reg.* (1865–67).

From Camillus P. Anderson[1]

Louisville   Nov 13th 1866

Sir

You will no doubt be surprised at receiving a letter from me an obscure individual of whom you have never heard of or thought of perhaps but you no doubt remember the time you in the capacity of Military Governor of Tennessee went from Wichester Tenn to Shelbyville Tenn with a small guard. I was sergeant of that guard and you made the remark that you would be pleased to do anything in the way of a favor for me if I should ever call on you. So now I am asking you for an appointment in the regular army or any civil appointment which I can fill. I am a steamboatman by proffessin was in the army three years and some months and have a good comon education. If you remember me as you said you would I shall feel grateful. . . .[2]

Camillus P. Anderson   a member of the 10th. O.V.I.

Lock Box No. 25   Newport, K.Y.

ALS, DNA-RG94, ACP Branch, File A-399-CB-1866, Camillus P. Anderson.

    1. Anderson (b. c1833), a native of Wooster, Ohio, and a moulder by trade, enlisted in 1861 and had risen to sergeant when he mustered out in 1864. CSR, Camillus P. Anderson, RG94, NA.

    2. The endorsement shows that Johnson ordered Anderson's appointment. In late November he received an appointment as second lieutenant in the 38th Inf. Rgt. Stanton to Anderson, Nov. 22, 1866, Johnson Papers, LC.

To Michael Burns

Washington, D.C., Nov 13th 1866

Are you likely to make any arrangement with the "Union Bank?" Perhaps it would be better for me to authorize Mr Allen to draw on me for the amount proposed in his letter to me Sometime since, which was fifteen thousand Dollars.[1]

Andrew Johnson

Tel, DNA-RG107, Tels. Sent, President, Vol. 3 (1865–68).

    1. On the following day, Burns telegraphed Johnson with the news that he had conferred with Joseph W. Allen who now wanted $19,960 from the President. But Burns confidently assured Johnson: "Leave this matter to me. I will I think bring him to terms." Then on the 16th Burns notified the President that he was en route to Washington within a few days and cautioned Johnson: "Dont do anything with Allen until then." Burns to Johnson, Nov. 14, 16, 1866, Johnson Papers, LC. See also Allen to Johnson, Jan. 5, 1867.

From Amos Layman[1]

⟨For the President Only.⟩

Statesman Office,

Columbus, Ohio, Nov'r 13, 1866.

As a life-long admirer and eulogist of yours; as a member of the Committee of our City Council to invite you to visit Columbus last September; as a member of the Reception Committee, appointed by our City authorities to go to Cincinnati and escort you to the Capital of Ohio; and as Editor of the Daily Central organ in this State of your Administration —I ventured to ask you, as you were leaving Columbus, on the morning of the 13th of September last, to do me the favor to promise that you would yourself read any private letters I might write you, relating to Ohio men, Ohio appointments, and Ohio politics. You were kind enough to promise me that you would. I desire now to claim the fulfilment of that promise, and to ask your attention to what follows:

When I was a mere school-boy, I became your fast friend and admirer: while at College, my friendship and admiration for you strengthened and matured. Your first speech in Congress, in favor of restoring the fine imposed upon General Jackson for placing New Orleans under martial law, completely fascinated and captivated me. Your succeeding efforts in Congress and in other public positions I watched, admired, and approved; and during your first year as Governor of Tennessee, I wrote an appreciative Biographical Sketch of Hon. Andrew Johnson, for Buell's Western Democratic Review—April, 1854—which closed with the following sentences:

"With the illustrious patriots of this country; with 'those who loved their fellow men'; Andrew Johnson will find a nobler monument than Westminster or the Memnon, in the hearts of a grateful people. His name will go down to future times, not as that of a warrior chief thirsting for the blood of the innocent and the pure, nor as a cognomen for the meteoric splendor of some useless philosophy; but it will be blazoned and heralded as a talismanic appellation for a character that gave a home to the homeless, clothed the naked, fed the hungry, and dried the orphan's and the widow's tear."

Thus I wrote early in 1854; and I have been writing and laboring ever since to insure the completest fulfilment of my predictions then made. I now write articles every day, and print them too, sustaining your administration; and I expect to continue to do so, until your successor shall be sworn in.

In view of all this, you may readily imagine that it is anything but pleasant and agreeable to learn that some members of your Cabinet will for a moment lend an ear to the silly and mischievous falsehoods and slanders that are being tailed about the Departments by S. S. Henkle, who has set himself up for a time as an office-Broker in Washington—a man who is utterly characterless here at home; an exile from all respectable Society; and without any influence whatever where he is known. He thrust himself upon our Committee in the late contest in this District, and succeeded in getting himself announced to speak on several occasions; but failed to meet appointments that he had announced, because of continued inebriation, &c. While professing to be in favor of your policy, he openly and publicly undertook to ridicule you, Mr. President, and the speeches you delivered. Such a man, aided by Jos. H. Geiger, whose political treachery is just about as black, and whose influence where he is best known amounts to just about as little, is trying to traduce and undermine the influence of Hon. Thomas Miller, the Administration candidate for Congress in this District, at the late Election.

Where Mr. Miller is known he needs no vindication or defense. One of the purest and most upright men in Ohio, he has for years been a power in the politics of the State. He can make and unmake public men here. Having held positions of trust and responsibility, he has never failed to discharge aright every duty devolved on him. Nominated by our last Congressional Convention without any solicitation on his part, he made a gallant and glorious fight in the District, legitimately spending on his own means what some would esteem a small fortune, and running ahead of his ticket in every election precinct of every county of the District—notwithstanding the secret opposition of a class of Democrats who called themselves "Sons of Liberty" during the late war, who could not forgive Mr. Miller because he favored the prosecution of the War for the Union; nor do they forgive the Ohio Statesman for the same reason. Some of them are now aiding Henkle, Geiger & Co., in their efforts to undermine Mr. Miller's just influence with certain members of your Cabinet. I do not believe that they can affect his standing with you, Mr. President; and it is only that you may set Secretary McCulloch and Post Master General Randall right, that I write you this letter, which is already too long—but I may not conclude it without adding a few sentences more.

Hon. Thomas Miller, whose irreproachable life has been devoted to the cause of his country, has given more of his hard-earned means than any other man in Ohio, to sustain The Ohio Statesman, in order that there may be a Daily Central Organ of your Administration in this State; and he is still willing to give more. But in view of all this, and in view of the further fact that he made the race for Congress here with Shellabarger, against great odds and at heavy expense to himself, and came out of it with a larger vote than anybody else now in the District could have got, he has a right, I think, to expect that you and your Administration will stand by him, and not allow mere political adventurers, without character or influence at home, to traduce him at Washington in order to undermine his influence and power. As to his character, standing, and influence, I need only refer you to Hon. S. S. Cox, now of New York, to Hon. Henry Stanbery, of your Cabinet, to Hon. Thomas Ewing, of Ohio, and to Gen. Ewing,[2] and others, in addition to what I have said in this letter. Hence, I trust that Mr. Miller will at once receive his Commission as Assessor of Internal Revenue for this District;[3] and that he may be favorably heard as to the other appointments in this (7th Ohio) District.

Amos Layman,   *Edr. Ohio Statesman.*

ALS, DLC-JP.
  1. Layman (*c*1830–*fl*1881), a lawyer and editor of Columbus's *Ohio Statesman* (1864–67), was later clerk of the state house of representatives and executive clerk to the governor.

1880 Census, Ohio, Franklin, Columbus, 33rd Enum. Dist., 42; Columbus directories (1862–81).

2. Thomas Ewing, Jr. (1829–1896), Ohio native, Kansas lawyer, and state chief justice, during the war rose to brevet major general. Resigning in early 1865, he practiced his profession successively in Washington, D.C., his hometown of Lancaster, Ohio, and New York City. While in Ohio he associated with the Greenback faction of the Democratic party and served two terms in Congress (1877–81). Warner, *Blue*.

3. Miller had been appointed assessor of Ohio's Seventh District on October 31, 1866. However, on January 26, 1867, the Senate failed to confirm him. Ser. 6B, Vol. 3: 495; Vol. 4: 257, Johnson Papers, LC.

From Niagara County, N.Y., Citizens[1]

[ca. November 13, 1866][2]

Sir.

We the undersigned supporters of Your Excellency's policy for the restoration of the Union, residing in Niagara County, State of New York, most respectfully beg to bring under Your Excellency's *immidiate* notice and consideration the following well *know facts*.

1st. That the recent defeat of Your Excellency's friends and supporters in New York state, has been brought about *solely* by the *powerful influence* of a very great many persons holding office under the General Government; using with their influence the *very means* which they receive from the same Government, in sustaining your *bitterest political enimies* in *power*.

2nd That in our own county Niagara, Frank Spalding[3] Collector of Customs at Suspension Bridge, *openly* and *warmly* sustained and Voted for the whole Republican Ticket including the Hon Burt. Van Horn[4] as member of Congress. That the Post Master James Low Jr.[5] of Suspension Bridge *also Voted* and *sustained the whole* Republican Ticket & Party. That James P Murphy the *assesor* of the 29th Congressional District *who is the Chairman of the Radical Republican County Committee*, not only voted for the *whole Radical Republican Ticket*, but has been heard *Over and Over again to denounce Your Excellency's administration in the strongest terms*.

We Cannot but express our feelings as *deeply wounded* by the *Known fact* that our defeat in *this County* has been through the influence and means of *Frank Spalding Collector James Low Jr Post Master* at Suspension Bridge and *James P Murphy Assesor 29 Cong. District*, and we do hope and trust that Your Excellency will Cause the removal from office, of the said *Frank Spalding James Low Jr* and *James P Murphy*; and restore in a *measure* our feelings of *regret at the Known cause of our defeat*.

And we recommend S. Park Baker[6] of Youngstown N.Y to fill the place of Frank Spalding Collector—Ebenezer W Williams[7] of Lockport as the *sucessor* of James P Murphy as assesor 29th Con Dist and Leander Colt[8] of Suspension Bridge as Post Master in the place of James Low Jr. *All* the above named Gentlemen are and have been *strong supporters of your Excellencys Administration*, having given *good proof* of their support at the Election just passed—and will give *General satisfaction* to the *citizens of this County*.[9]

Pet, DNA-RG56, Appts., Internal Revenue Service, Assessor, N.Y., 29th Dist., James P. Murphy.

1. There are nearly fifty signatories, including Alexander Campbell (*fl*1869), a farmer, who withdrew his name from consideration for assessor in favor of Ebenezer W. Williams. Hamilton Child, comp., *Gazetteer and Business Directory of Niagara County, N.Y., for 1869* (Syracuse, 1869), 108.

2. The document bears a receipt stamp with this date. Also, internal evidence indicates that it was drafted not long after the New York election, which occurred on November 6.

3. Franklin Spalding (1815–*fl*1892) had served as customs collector under Presidents Taylor and Lincoln. In addition, he was Niagara County sheriff for a number of years and postmaster of Niagara Falls during Chester Arthur's administration. Wiley and Garner, *Niagara County*, 140, 143.

4. Van Horn (1823–1896) was elected to his fourth and final term in 1866 by defeating his Democratic challenger by more than three thousand votes. Leaving Washington in 1869, he returned to New York, where he farmed and also served as internal revenue collector at Rochester (1877–82). Van Horn strongly opposed Spalding's removal, arguing that the administration "would gain nothing" from it but a "public disaster." *BDAC*; *Guide to U.S. Elections*, 617; Van Horn to Johnson, Nov. 13, 1866, Appts., Customs Service, Collector, Suspension Bridge, Franklin Spalding, NA.

5. Low (1836–*fl*1892) formerly served as Spalding's deputy before joining the army in 1862. Rising to the rank of major in the 129th N.Y. Vol. Inf., Low had been appointed postmaster by Johnson on July 16, 1865. He continued in that office until 1873, then he served three terms in the New York legislature. Wiley and Garner, *Niagara County*, 337–38; Ser. 6B, Vol. 5, Johnson Papers, LC.

6. Baker (1832–*fl*1892), an attorney and peach grower, was also recommended by Henry W. Slocum, A. R. Lanning, and Sanford E. Church, all prominent New York Democrats. Slocum to Johnson, Sept. 17, 1866; Lanning to Johnson, Oct. 23, 1866, Appts., Customs Service, Collector, Suspension Bridge, S. Park Baker, RG56, NA; Ser. 6A, Vol. D: 22, Johnson Papers, LC; Wiley and Garner, *Niagara County*, 391–92.

7. Williams (*c*1818–*fl*1869), who was in the livery stable business, had been mentioned earlier that summer as a possible replacement for Murphy. Alexander Campbell's name originally appeared at this point in the document. Campbell struck out his own name and inserted Williams's instead. Child, *Gazetteer of Niagara County*, 223; R. Davison et al. to Johnson, Aug. 1866, Appts., Internal Revenue Service, Assessor, N.Y., 29th Dist., Ebenezer W. Williams, RG56, NA; 1860 Census, N.Y., Niagara, Lockport, 2.

8. Colt (1824–*fl*1892) spent four years in search of California gold before returning in the mid-1850s to his native Niagara County, where he ran a shoe store in Suspension Bridge. A veteran of an Illinois cavalry unit, he was later appointed by Grant as postmaster. Wiley and Garner, *Niagara County*, 497.

9. The President referred the letter to Secretary McCulloch: "This seems to be a pretty strong case." But neither Baker, whose appointment apparently had been earlier agreed upon but since held up, nor Williams or Colt were issued commissions for their respective posts. Slocum to Johnson, Sept. 17, 1866, Appts., Customs Service, Suspension Bridge, S. Park Baker, RG56, NA; Van Horn to Johnson, Nov. 13, 1866, ibid., Franklin Spalding.

From Leslie Combs

Lexington Ky.   Nov 14/.66

My dear Sir,

I feel very much disturbed by what I See of *physical* preparations at Washington & elsewhere, to overawe you & destroy, our free government —by violence. Standing on the rock of the Constitution *as you are*; I think, it the duty of every true lover of liberty to Stand by you & uphold your measures.

You know me as a life-long, Whig, of the *Clay & Webster* School & an unwavering Union man, in our late terrible war. But we have put down all armed opposition to the Government & must have law & order again. Nothing prevents this now, but the factious avarice & love of power of the Abolition Leaders, in, & out of, Congress.

How can I Serve you, in this emergency. I am out of office, Since Sept, & think I might do good at Washington, this winter, among the *Old Whigs* in & out of Congress.

Mr. Clay relied on me always in his troubles & never was disappointed.

                                                                Leslie Combs

ALS, DLC-JP.

From Joseph R. Flanigen

                                              Philadelphia, Nov 15 1866

My dr Mr President

I understand that the struggle in regard to the assesorship of the Second district has finaly culminated in the appointment of C M Deringer. I need not say to you that I consider this as most unfortunate both politicaly & moraly. But I refer to the matter for the purpose of remarking on what I understand to be the programme of the parties who have been successfull in accomplishing the appointment of Deringer in oposition to the moral sense of this entire community.

The next movement as I am assured is to displace Mr Jno H Deihl[1] Collector of the Second district in which case the same clique would have absolute control of the district. Mr Deihl is one of the best if not *the best* collector in the State and to yeild him up to the demands of the bold bad men who will seek his removal would be to offend the people of the entire district and do us incalculable damage throughout the city. I do not know what your veiws now are, as to the Democratic party, or the propriety of placing the patronage of the government in the hands of those who belong to it but as your freind I may not conceal from you the fact that we are being seriously damaged by recent developments. The programme as I understand it is to continue to force upon you if possible democrats for all future appointments, and to assist in defeating the confirmation of your National Union freinds who are now in position and to press the arrangement untill they get controll of the entire patronage of the Government. To allow such a scheeme to succeed would be to allow your administration to be "Tylerized" and perpetuate the Radical power.

Permit me to say my dr sir that you cannot defeat the Radical party with the Democratic Organization. A *National Union party must be*

formed and wether it is necessary to abandon the Democratic organization or not is a question that need not now be considered. The radical
party can only be demoralised by drawg from its ranks men who are disposed to be conservative, and this can be done in no other way except by a
national organization which cannot be charged with Copperhead sympathies. I write you hastily and *breifly as posible* because I know the pressure
on your time, *but I beg of you if* there *is yet time revoke the Deringer Appointment.* If it is realy neccesary to remove Sweney let us find the man for
his place who will not be offensive to the public and in whom there can be
some security for an honest administration of the office.[2]

                                                                J R Flanigen

ALS, DLC-JP.
    1. Diehl (*fl*1870), a Philadelphia merchant who had been appointed as revenue collec-
tor by Lincoln, was not removed by Johnson. *U.S. Off. Reg.* (1863–69); Philadelphia directories (1861–71).
    2. Several weeks earlier Flanigen had written the President another letter protesting
Thomas W. Sweney's removal, but to no avail. Deringer's appointment went forward as
planned. Flanigen to Johnson, Oct. 25, 1866, Appts., Internal Revenue Service, Assessor,
Pa., 2nd Dist., Thomas W. Sweney, RG56, NA. See also Edgar Cowan to Johnson, Oct.
25, 1866.

From Duff Green

                                                      New York   15th Nov. 1866
    Mr. Clingman[1] of North Carolina told me, last night, that he and
others had organised or were now engaged in organising a revolutionary
movement predicated on the fact that, before the Secession of the Southern States, you were known to favor an alteration of the Constitution giving the choice of President directly to the people. The plan he said is that
you shall, in your annual message, recommend that the Constitution
shall be so amended as that the President shall be chosen by a majority of
all the qualified voters of all the States, and that, in case Congress refuses
to recommend such Amendment, the people shall nevertheless hold an
Election, and organise an army of five hundred thousand men who shall
go to Washington and inaugurate the President thus chosen. To my suggestion that this would be revolutionary and end in a military despotism,
resulting in an hereditary monarchy, he declared his preference for such a
government, and that he and others would exert thier influence in favor of
such a change!
    I deem it to be my duty to let you know that in a mixed company, where
there was no obligation of secrecy, the purpose of organising such a
movement, connected with a contemplated recommendation in your annual message, was declared to exist, for from the manner in which he
urged the measure to me, I have no doubt that he has spoken in the same
manner to others, and will continue to urge it upon others again & again
hereafter, and that therefore should you in your annual message, or even

in private conversation, indicate your wish for such a mode of electing the President, your enemies will charge that he is acting under your advice & in collusion with you, & that your purpose is revolutionary.

I am satisfied that the late Elections were carried by the Fenians & the laboring men, acting under false impressions as to their own interests and as to the bearing of the political issues involved in the revolutionary assumptions of Congress. I hope to see you in a few days, when I have some facts to submit which I think will encourage you to persevere in your effort to save the Constitution and with it the liberties of the people.

Duff Green

ALS, DLC-JP.
1. Thomas L. Clingman.

From Charles G. Halpine
PRIVATE

32 BEEKMAN STREET, N.Y.   Nov. 15th 1866

Dear Sir:

The best return I can make for the appreciative kindness with which you lent me your consideration last Tuesday evening, is to seize the earliest moment of laying before you what I find to be the public sentiment of this city and State, so far as I can judge—and few men have better opportunities—in regard to the political situation.

To prophesy smooth things would be easy, but not honest; & even at the risk of appearing to obtrude suggestions beyond my proper reach, my desire for the success of the principles which you represent, and my gratitude for the kindness with which you have invariably received me, impel me to make this statement.

I find a double influence working against Mr. Seward to the overwhelming detriment of your administration. The Radicals point to the fact that Mr. Seward has not elected *one Assembly man* in the State, and that the majority against your administration in Auburn (Mr. Seward's home) is heavier in proportion than anywhere else in New York. Their quarrel seems to be more against him than against Your Excellency, and against him, it appears to me, they are resolved to push their power to the very uttermost.

The Democratic Union party[1] also stand arrayed against Mr. Seward, and point to the fact that in the recent County Contest, Mr. Seward's friends in this City made their distinct *alliance with Fernando Wood*, by running John McCool's[2] tickets out of their [boxes?], in return for which the Mozart[3] [boxes?] ran Joseph L. Taylor[4] (Conservative Repr.) for Supervisor; but it is elsewhere, that the most serious hostility to Mr. Seward must be looked for.

I find the democratic Irish sentiment (not merely the Fenians proper, but the whole Irish element) arrayed against Mr. Seward's foreign policy with a bitterness which makes it no longer safe for any man of prominence on the Irish side to attempt to stem. They blame him for encouraging (tacitly) the Canadian raid, and then letting loose the power of the United States against men who had just purchased arms out of the U.S. Arsenals; but yet more is he blamed for tolerating, without protest, the incarceration of American officers (some of Irish birth, others born in the States) in the jails of Ireland without charges preferred or trial of any kind, & their subsequent discharge from said jails, still untried & without any effective reclammations from this government.

Not a Fenian myself, in any manner of adhering to their organization, yet my sympathies as an American citizen are with this movement; and I would be disentitled to the generous confidence which large masses of my Irish fellow-citizens repose in me, and false to the friendship which I profess and feel for your administration, if this candid statement of grievances were withheld.

Let me add that my pen only speaks what all the prominent leaders of Irish opinion in this City & State—and, so far as I can judge throughout the United States—have resolved upon with regard to Mr. Seward;—and I cannot help fearing that his continuance in power, will force *a general & permanent coalition* between the Radical party & Irish vote, such as was—fortuitously only & sporadically, I might say—shown in my case last Tuesday week.[5]

The minor patronage of the Post is of no consequence unless this stumbling block can be got rid of: that done, all else will follow. I find the Radical leaders, so far as I can judge, enlisted not against you but against Mr. Seward; and I think—and there are reasons behind my thought—that many serious difficulties might be removed, & the moral if not political weight of the State of New York be cast in your favor, if this one thing were once thought compassable.

I know that a letter such as this is a thankless office; but believe that you know me sufficiently to believe that I write sincerely; and let me add that in the views of this letter, so far as we have consulted (on the Democratic & Irish side of the question), my friend Gen. Gordon Granger shares. If there were any hope of this door being opened, I could continue the subject MORE IN DETAIL.

Thanking you for your manifold kindnesses, & trusting that in the future you shall have no cause to regret them.

Chas. G. Halpine

P.S. I send you two articles from my paper,[6] both bearing on this subject.

ALS, DLC-JP.

1. By this, Halpine meant a faction of New York State Democrats—including Daniel S. Dickinson and James T. Brady—who had been conciliatory toward Republicans both during and after the war. Mushkat, *Fernando Wood*, 117.

2. McCool (*c*1830–*fl*1866), a native of Scotland and former mason/builder and the in-

cumbent register, was the candidate of both Tammany Hall and the Mozart Democrats. *New York Times*, Oct. 29, 1866; 1860 Census, N.Y., New York, New York, 8th Ward, 3rd Div., 215; New York City directories (1861–67).

3. Another faction among New York State Democrats, organized and led by Fernando Wood for a decade (1858–68). Mushkat, *Fernando Wood*, 85, 168–69.

4. Republican Joseph B. Taylor (*c*1828–*fl*1867), a brewer, was defeated by Gerseon M. Herman, whom the *New York Times* described as the Tammany and Mozart Democratic candidate. *New York Tribune*, Nov. 5, 1866; *New York Times*, Oct. 24, Nov. 7, 1866; 1860 Census, N.Y., New York, New York, 5th Ward, 1st Dist., 370; New York City directories (1861–67).

5. Here Halpine refers to his election as register over McCool on November 6. Mushkat, *Fernando Wood*, 161.

6. Not found with this letter.

From Nathaniel B. Milliman and Thomas B. Carroll[1]

Metropolitan Hotel Washington   Nov 16 1866

Dear Sir

The undersigned being compelled to forego the pleasure of a personal interview take this method of calling your attention to the enclosed letter of Mr. Tilden[2] & to some of the reasons which led us to wish for an interview at this time.

The position we have been obliged to occupy in the recent canvass in our State has forced upon us the personal knowledge that all who represented your policy in that canvass as candidates have been violently opposed & many have been defeated by the open personal & official efforts & influence of persons holding office under Federal appointment. This opposition has been so defiantly & notoriously Exhibited by all classes of Federal officials in the 15 Congressional District as to create a very general expectation & desire among all classes of your supporters & friends that such infidelity in the perversion of official influence & patronage should be rebuked by removals from office.

The undersigned are not applicants for official favour but have been willing to give their time & means for the advancement of the policy of your administration in the hope that the peace & prosperity of the Country might be thus in some degree subserved & in the firm belief that such policy will ultimately be sustained & triumphantly vindicated.

They only ask that the administration will defend itself through its true & faithful friends & through them sustain the only political organization & the presses & persons who yield a support to its position & policy.

As circumstances compel us to leave for home tomorrow evening Your Excellency will pardon this method of communicating our views.

N B Milliman   Thos. B. Carroll
Also in behalf of Hon Gideon Reynolds[3]

ALS (Milliman), DLC-JP.

1. Carroll (c1816–fl1879), a former Democrat turned Barnburner Republican, served one term in the New York senate (1850–51) and worked as state canal appraiser, before occupying the office of mayor of Troy (1871–73). 1860 Census, N.Y., Rensselaer, 6th Ward, Troy, 50; Nathaniel B. Sylvester, *History of Rensselaer Co., New York* (Philadelphia, 1880), 65, 68, 204; Troy directories (1866–79); Samuel J. Tilden to Johnson, Nov. 16, 1866, Johnson Papers, LC.

2. After introducing Carroll, Reynolds, and Milliman, Tilden in his letter urged the President to confer with these men about adopting specific measures which would bolster the pro-Johnson forces in the Fifteenth District of New York. Ibid.

3. Reynolds (1813–1896), a member of the Republican state central committee since its organization, had served in Congress (1847–51) and as revenue collector for New York's Fifteenth District (1862–65). Both he and Carroll were also delegates to the National Union Convention in Philadelphia (1866). Ibid.; *BDAC*.

From Joseph F. Montgomery[1]

Sacramento, Cal., Nov. 16, 1866.

Dear Sir:

I have been so much pleased with the wise, just, patriotic & courageous course you have pursued in your official conduct since your accession to the Presidency, that I feel irresistibly constrained, as one who Knew you years ago, to offer to you, as every good citizen or true friend of the country should do, my earnest & cordial endorsement of that course; & the observance, founded upon firm conviction, that, in my opinion, you will eventually be triumphantly sustained by the people.

I first met you in March 1849, in the town of Lovingston, Nelson County, Virginia, (my native county & State,) & had the pleasure of travelling with you by stage, from that place to Blountville, Tennessee. The Hon: Paulus Powell,[2] then but recently nominated for the first time in that District for Congress, travelled with us from Lovingston to Amherst C.H., & I remember introducing you to him, with the expression of the hope that you might both be successful in the then approaching elections, that you might meet as members in the House of Representatives at Washington. That hope was realized, & I met you both in Washington about July 1, 1850, when on my way to this distant region. I remember calling on you, at that time, at your lodgings & renewing the acquaintance so agreeably formed during the previous year. I arrived in California in August 1850 & settled in this city the following month. I have remained here ever since, in the practice of my profession, that of medicine.

I desire no office whatever, & you will not suppose, therefore, that I am prompted by any selfish or unworthy motive in writing this letter. I have been from my earliest manhood a member of the same party to which you belonged up to 1861, & as to secession, I was as earnestly & as determinedly opposed to it as you could possibly have been. I regarded it, always, as the greatest political blunder a people ever attempted, & the result of the fruitless effort to sever the Union proves the correctness of that opinion.

But I will frankly admit that I voted for McClellan in 1864, for the reason that his success, I thought would insure a more speedy & satisfactory restoration of the Union than would be likely to follow that of his opponent. The course pursued by the Radicals since the death of Lincoln proves, I think, that I was not far wrong in that calculation, for the very sane wise policy you have urged so ably is the one which, in the main, McClellan & his party would have adopted.

I regret profoundly that the Democratic organization had not been surrendered, for the good of the country, when the Philadelphia convention was called, that all conservatives, irrespective of previous political antecedents, may have united cordially in that movement, which, under such circumstances, could not well have failed of success. And now, I see no hope for the country but the union, prior to the next Presidential election, of all true patriots, to arrest the mad & despotic rule of the party now having control of the legislative department of the Government. I pray you, Sir, to stand firmly by the proud position you now occupy, regardless of all threats & menaces, & your triumph will finally be complete, & your name be honored by succeeding generations.

It would afford me very great pleasure to hear from you, if you can ever find time or acquire the disposition to respond to one so little Known to you as I am.

I will mention, before concluding, that I am a first cousin to Hon: John Netherland of Tennessee, & I am pretty well acquainted with those who have been in public life here since the organization of the State government. My residence here at the seat of government, & the general interest I have always taken in public affairs have naturally led me into such acquaintances.

Jos. F. Montgomery.

ALS, DLC-JP.
    1. Montgomery (1812–1883) graduated with medical degrees from both the University of Virginia and the University of Pennsylvania. After practicing in Virginia and Mississippi, he moved to Sacramento, California, in 1850. He was a member of the state board of health and the city school board. William B. Atkinson, ed., *The Physicians and Surgeons of the United States* (Philadelphia, 1878), 258–59; *NUC*.
    2. Powell (1809–1874) held local offices, served in the Virginia house of delegates, and was a Democrat in the U.S. House of Representatives for five terms (1849–58). *BDAC*.

From John S. Berry[1]

Private

Baltimore   Nov. 17/66

Dear Sir:

As chairman of the Committee of the Arrangements, I am considerably exercised about your presence with us on Tuesday next, to participate with us in laying the Cornerstone of our New Masonic Temple.[2] I saw Gov. Swann to day and because of your pressing engagements he could not see you. He however left word with your Son (Robert) that you MUST BOTH come, and be his guests. I beg of you Mr President that you will both come, and we ask as *Masons* that you will remain Tuesday night and be with us at our Banquet. This, for the success of our undertaking is requisite, and I beg that you will gratify your Bretheren. . . .

Jno. S. Berry

The Governor insists that you go directly to his house* and breakfast, and join the procession at his door, by which, according to our Route it will pass.[3]

Be kind enough to telegraph me on Monday.[4]

Genl John S. Berry

Eutaw House *Baltimore*

*His private carriage will be in waiting for 7 A.M train.

ALS, DLC-JP.

1. Berry (1822–*fl*1900), adjutant general of Maryland, began his career in dry goods and brick manufacturing before entering state politics. Twice elected to the state house and to its speakership, he was then appointed adjutant general (1862–*c*70). He was three times elected Grand Master of the Masonic Order of Maryland. *The Biographical Cyclopedia of Representative Men of Maryland and the District of Columbia* (Baltimore, 1879), 55–56; Baltimore directories (1884–1900).

2. Johnson had been approached as early as the 9th with an invitation to the ceremony and on the 16th with a request from the District Grand Master that the Masons employed by the government be permitted to attend the occasion. The President made such a request of his department heads. George C. Whiting to Johnson, Nov. 16, 1866; Robert Johnson (for the President) to Stanton, Nov. 16, 1866, Lets. Recd., Executive (M494, Roll 85), RG107, NA; Edwin H. Webster to Johnson, Nov. 9, 1866, Johnson Papers, LC; W. E. Chandler to Edward Jordan, Nov. 17, 1866, Lets. Recd. from Sec. of Treasury, RG206, NA.

3. Johnson, himself a Past Grand Master of the Grand Lodge of Tennessee, arrived in Baltimore at 9 o'clock on the 20th and was taken by Governor Swann to his home. Subsequently, they joined the procession to the site of the new Masonic temple. Johnson's reception by the crowd was a positive one. *Baltimore Sun*, Nov. 21, 1866.

4. Several telegrams conveyed the President's departure and arrival times. See, for example, Johnson to Swann, Nov. 18, 1866; Robert Johnson to Berry, Nov. 19, 1866, Tels. Sent, President, Vol. 3 (1865–68), RG107, NA.

From William Cassidy[1]

Albany, Nov. 17, 1866

Dear Sir:

I was absent in Europe in the earlier part of the Controversy, which has terminated in the recent election, & did not return till October.

I may be mistaken; but it seems to me that in the presentation of your policy before the people, the press, the Speakers & the Conventions failed to give prominence to your suggestions of a Constitutional amendment basing representation (in the House) on the number of Voters & direct taxes upon property.

The recent election may be taken as a verdict in favor of some modification of our representative system, growing out of emancipation. I believe your plan would have met the popular approval if strongly urged.

In presenting your views on reconstruction in the coming Message, if you would give prominence & emphasis to the proposed amendment as part of it, I think you would make a strong impression upon the public mind—sufficient to produce a decided reaction in favor of your policy. The Message reaches everywhere & is read by every one; & now that the excitement of the election is over, its views would have a candid hearing.

Pardon me for thus intruding this suggestion. My excuse is that I do it in the sincerity of friendship.[2]

William Cassidy

ALS, DLC-JP.
1. Cassidy (1815–1873) edited and owned the *Albany Argus*, an influential organ affiliated with the Democratic party in New York. George R. Howell and Jonathan Tenney, eds., *History of the County of Albany, N.Y., From 1609 to 1886* (New York, 1886), 358.
2. On the obverse side of Cassidy's letter is found the following annotation, written by William G. Moore, one of Johnson's secretaries: "I read this note to the President."

From Simeon M. Johnson[1]

84 Franklin Street   Balto.   18 Nov. 1866

Sir—

I am always anxious for the success of your administration because I consider your measures eminently just, and for a better reason, because the country never before so much needed honest government. Judged by the constitution, the states lately in rebellion are greatly wronged in being deprived of representation in the general Congress.

I have thought, never the less, that it might happen, in the struggle, that the South would take untenable ground in some way, & thereby lose any advantage accruing to her by virtue of present position. *For instance I have thought seeing the strong feeling throughout the Slave-States against any kind of equality of the* two races, the people of those States might reject *the principle of equality*, even though the blacks should be deemed qualified, otherwise, to vote. I am satisfied this will never be answered by good ends, should the South so determine.

The tendency of all the great populations of the Earth, just now, is in the direction of general enfranchisement. We are moving with the current; and are no more radical in this respect than are the Reformers of England & scarcely more so than are the reformers of Italy under the lead of his Majesty Victor Emanuel[2] himself.

Maintaining an Elective government we must prepare for negro suffrage, and if a system (organic) can be adopted admitting the votes of the Blacks under specific qualifications of property or knowledge of the trust, I am clear that the South should accept it.

We must take many steps forward, in this movement, before we can hope, if we find it necessary, to take one backwards.

I shall be greatly surprised if the radical interest of the U. States, do not, at an early day, give some tokens of conservatism; and if we may judge them by the laws that have ever governed humanity, their complete triumph, at the late elections, is precisely what will be most likely to evoke this element amongst them. Should it appear I sincerely hope you will meet it in the spirit genuine fellowship and strive to guide it to a good end.

The prize is the grandest ever contended for; for if we close up the gulf between the North and the South, so as to effect a moral & political union, we shall in evitably become the governors of the world.

All that is required is to allay deep seated passions & prejudices, and to effect this noble achievement I dont know what sacrifices I would not make, being in your place.

S. M. Johnson

ALS, DLC-JP.

1. Johnson (c1817–fl1872) had served as U.S. consul to Matanzas, Cuba, during the Polk administration, before becoming editor of the *Detroit Free Press* and later on the editorial staff of the *Washington Union*. A former New York Democrat, Johnson appears to have spent the war years writing political treatises and practicing law in both Washington, D.C., and Baltimore. He was eventually offered appointments in the Treasury and State departments but was not confirmed for either post. Robert W. Johannsen, ed., *The Letters of Stephen A. Douglas* (Urbana, 1961), 261; S. M. Johnson to Lincoln, Dec. 14, 1861, Lincoln Papers, LC; S. M. Johnson to Johnson, June 25, 1865, June 15, 1868, Johnson Papers, LC; Ser. 6B, Vol. 2:153, ibid.; Washington, D.C., directories (1861–76); Baltimore directories (1865–68); 1860 Census, D.C., Washington, 2nd Ward, 458.

2. Victor Emmanuel II (1820–1878) was the first king of a unified Italy (1861–78). During the wars resulting in unification, Victor Emmanuel deposed his relatives ruling Tuscany, Naples, and Sicily, and conquered much of central Italy from the Pope. Robert Katz, *The Fall of the House of Savoy* (New York, 1971), Appendix 1; Denis Mack Smith, *Italy and Its Monarchy* (New Haven, 1989), 3.

From Sarah C. Polk

'Polk place'   Nashville Tenn.   Nov. 19, 1866.

Dear Sir.

Allow me to enclose you a letter from my neice Mrs. I. N. Barnett[1] of Columbia Tenn. on the subject of a pardon to Genl. George D. Johnson[2] of Marion Alabama.

Mrs. Barnett is the daughter of the late Mr. James Walker of Columbia Tenn. and the neice of my Husband. And she is extremely anxious in regard to a pardon for Genl. Johnson, who is her son in law.

I beg most respectfully your kind interest to this pardon. Genl. Johnson's application was made to you some time since[3] & presented to you by the Govenor of Alabama[4] & endorsed by others. He then had the assurance that you would grant it, and now thinks, in the press of public duties, his petition has been overlooked.

Genl. Johnson was a Brig. Genl. in the Confederate service, was a civilian before the war, a Democrat & now in private life.

To grant this pardon Mr. President will be received & acknowledged by Mrs. Barnett & their family as a great kindness & I will regard it as a personal favor.[5]

With my compliments to Mrs. Johnson & family.

Mrs. Polk

ALS, DNA-RG94, Amnesty Papers (M1003, Roll 6), Ala., George D. Johnston.
1. Jane C. Walker (1820–1899) married Isaac N. Barnett in 1842 and had five children. In the enclosed letter Mrs. Barnett noted that her son-in-law had forwarded a pardon application in the summer of 1865 but no pardon had been sent to him. Mrs. Frank M. Angellotti, *The Polks of North Carolina and Tennessee* (Columbia, Tenn., 1984), 23; Barnett to Johnson, Nov. 15, 1866, Amnesty Papers (M1003, Roll 6), Ala., George D. Johnston, RG94, NA.
2. Johnston (1832–1910) had served as mayor of Marion and also in the state legislature of Alabama prior to the Civil War. He saw considerable action during the war, especially with the Army of Tennessee, and rose through the officer's ranks from major to colonel to brigadier general. After the war Johnston was commandant of cadets at the University of Alabama, superintendent of the South Carolina Military Academy, and civil service commissioner during President Cleveland's second term. Warner, *Gray.*
3. According to the extant documents in Johnston's files, he took the oath of allegiance in September 1865 and at approximately the same time wrote to the President asking for an individual pardon. Amnesty Papers (M1003, Roll 6), Ala., George D. Johnston, RG94, NA.
4. Lewis E. Parsons recommended Johnston for pardon on September 26, 1865. See ibid.
5. Confusion and mystery surround the actual pardon date for Johnston. His files, for example, indicate that his application was filed on October 18, 1865, and that he was pardoned on November 11 (no year specified). Likewise a listing of Alabama pardons shows November 11, 1865, as Johnston's date of pardon, and that letters from Mrs. Barnett and Mrs. Polk had recommended Johnston's pardon. There is no question that the letters from the two women were written in November 1866 and that they did not believe that Johnston had yet been pardoned. Barring additional evidence, it is not possible to ascertain whether Johnston was pardoned in 1866 or in 1865; but there is no question that he was indeed granted a pardon by the President. Ibid.; *House Ex. Docs.*, 40 Cong., 2 Sess., No. 16, p. 19 (Ser. 1330).

From Thomas E. Rose[1]

Washington, D.C., Nov 20 1866

Dear Sir

I have the honor to announce to you that the note[2] sent by me to the secretary of war was returned from the Adjutant Generals office with the statement that I could not be appointed in the Cavalry being inelligible not having served two years in the Volunteer Cavalry. The note further stated that all the vacancies in the infantry were filled. I claimed that I was elligible from the fact that I was a regular Brigade commander and commanded Cavalry as well as infantry besides when ordered by the President the Board of examiners must decide whether I am eligible or not for the position—23 par Army Regulations.

I feel the most profound regret for having to trouble you so much, but I find that I will [be] thrown out altogether without your assistance.

Earnestly hoping that you will see the order obeyed . . . [3]

Thomas E Rose

ALS, DNA-RG94, ACP Branch, File R-747-CB-1866, Thomas E. Rose.

1. Rose (1830–1907) served as captain and colonel of the 77th Pa. Inf., before being captured and confined at Libby Prison (October 1863-April 1864). Exchanged in May 1864, he rejoined his regiment and served until war's end. In July 1865 he was brevetted brigadier general of volunteers for his war service; in March 1867 he was brevetted major and lieutenant colonel in the regular army. He retired in 1894 with the rank of major. *Appleton's Cyclopaedia*; Hunt and Brown, *Brigadier Generals*; Powell, *Army List*, 563.

2. Not found.

3. Twice Johnson endorsed Rose's letters that he be granted the requested cavalry appointment, if a vacancy existed, or in the infantry otherwise. Finally on December 1, 1866, Rose was appointed to a captaincy in the 11th Inf. See Endorsements, Oct. 25, 1866; Rose to N. P. Sawyer, Nov. 28, 1866, ACP Branch, File R-747-CB-1866, RG94, NA.

From Allen Pierse[1]

St. Louis Mo.   Nov 21st 1866.

Sir.

This comes from one who has warmly approved your reconstruction policy, but who, now that the elections are over & the battle lost, believes it wise to abandon a position that cannot be maintained, & fall back upon a new line. A just cause can prevail only, when a just & intelligent public opinion rules the country. *Such* a public opinion does not now rule; but a malicious, bigoted & corrupt majority now control the country, & will continue to control it, as long as resisted by the present opposition & upon present issues. The resistance they receive only keeps the majority together—let it cease, & they will dissolve into fragments. The folly of continuing the present struggle, is only equalled by that of the gamester, who after loosing heavily at the gaming table, continues to play to win back his loosings.

The statesman who continues to urge a just policy after it is obvious he cannot succeed, & that his persistency can only cement opposition & work injury to his country, may be commended for his honesty, but not for his prudence or usefulness. It is his duty to do the *best he can*, & not fail to do any thing, by trying to do more than he can do.

What then can be done under existing circumstances? This: Let the conservatives *regulate* to the extent of their ability the course of a power they cannot successfully *resist*. They may avert many of the evils that threaten the country. Let them adopt the constitutional amendment with all its villainy. It will be no very great wrong to disfranchise those who *got up* the rebellion. Many others, it is true, will suffer from the disfranchisement clause, but as true men they should not suffer their personal wrongs to stand in the way of the restoration of the Union—*Their day will come*.

And as to negroes; let them vote; those who can read & write; & let the same rule apply to whites, for the time being. This rule will make no distinction on account of color. The negroes generally will vote the way their old masters do. It is a mistake to suppose they will vote to *Northernise* the South, which is the main object of the radicals; but the longer the present struggle is continued, the more apt they will be to succeed in that object.

Let every Southern State adopt the constitutional amendment, & come into the Union, & ere long the South & the Northern democracy, will have control of the government, & then they can correct the errors of the present evil times, even to the extent of amending the constitution if necessary; & so far from radicalism ever getting a foothold in the South, it will die out in the North. You will remember that generally for the last thirty years the elections in the middle of a Presidential term have been reversed at the Presidential election.

But to the object of this letter. In coming to it I must speak of myself. I am a North Carolinian: served in the legislature of that State as long as I lived there after attaining the age of majority: was a lawyer in good standing in Louisiana thirteen years, & presided on the Bench of one of the District Courts there for a short time; & believe I have friends in both those States. But having drifted out West several years ago, & got among a population of abolitionists in Kansas, I am now utterly broke up, & without friends or means. The people would not believe me true to the Union, though I served in the Union Army, volunteering as a private at the age of 54 & serving till honorably discharged.[2] I now want to go South; to either N.C. or Louisiana. Cant you give me some position in either of those States, by which I can get there & pay expenses for a while?[3] No matter *what it is*: If it involves difficulty or danger so much the better.

My real object is to advise my old friends, if I find any of them left, to adopt the constitutional amendment, & hold themselves in reserve for better times, & to exhaust none of their strength in vain efforts. I conscientiously believe that if I can get a chance to go South & make enough to pay expenses I can do much towards hastening the downfall of that unprincipled & despotic party that is now in the ascendent. Give me a chance, if you can, & let me prove my gratitude to you & my affection for my country.

I have asked no one to recommend me, & shall not. If I get any thing from you, I do not wish to be under obligations to any one else for it.[4]

Allen Pierse

Why do you not follow your profession in St Louis, is a natural question. Ans: I have not had money enough at any one time since I have been here, to open an office—viz—furnish it, & pay a few months rent.[5]

If President Johnson has not time to read this letter: or will not have it read & listen to its contents from the reader, the writer desires it may be destroyed. It has not been written with a view of having its claim to consideration submitted to subordinates.

ALS, DLC-JP.
1. Pierse (b. *c*1809), a native of Northampton, North Carolina, was a lawyer living in Leavenworth, Kansas, with his wife and three small children in 1860. By 1863 he was a clerk. 1860 Census, Kans., Leavenworth, Leavenworth City, 4th Ward, 158; CSR, Allen Pierse, RG94, NA.
2. Pierse enlisted as a private in Co. A, 14th Kans. Cav., on August 11, 1863, in Leavenworth, Kansas. He appears to have spent most of his service in the hospital suffering from chronic rheumatism, and was discharged due to "enfeebled constitution from age" and toothlessness in August 1864. Ibid.
3. There is no indication that Johnson gave Pierse a job in North Carolina, Louisiana, or anywhere else.
4. His letter was, however, endorsed by J. F. Torry & Co., Booksellers, and D. M. Grissom, editor of the *St. Louis Dispatch*.
5. The endorsement to Pierse's letter explained that he had "for the last 18 months made a bare living in this city by carrying newspapers & pedling maps, charts, books &c. & doing odd jobs of any thing he could get to do," because of the high unemployment rate in St. Louis and Pierse's lack of contacts there.

From J. Montgomery Peters[1]

Baltimore, Novr. 22d. 1866.

Dear Sir.

Fortune has placed you in a position in which you are powerful to control events of more magnitude than ever before affected the human race. This is a continent of vast extent, and committed by the genius of the principles under which government began here, or may say, to the progressive development of the whole human race. Certainly it is not saying too much to say that America has excelled all other countries in her gigantic strides in the elevation of the whole human race. But we have now reached a point in our history in which the violence of unreasoning passions threatens to engulf all that has been done, and to convert America from the home of just and wise laws and examples, into a demoniac bedlam, in which every beast is to have his share in making discord more discordant still. It is for you, Sir, to stay the progress of this wild stream. What can be gained by making of the negro, educated or uneducated, a politician? What can be gained to this glorious government of free white men, who are amply able to manage their own affairs, by appointing negroes to assist them in their civil business? Nothing can be gained by the white race, but a great deal, a vastly great deal, may be lost. What would be the first effect of such a change in our political system? It would be to remove power from the great body of the white people of the South, and to locate it there in the hands of the negroes, and a few of the aristocrats, who would always control the negroes. The negroes have no respect for "the poor white trash" of the country, as they call the poorer classes of white people. They love power, and the symbols of power, and they will always cling to them. It isn't sufficient to say that it is only "qualified negro suffrage" that is asked for by the abolitionists of the North. The people of the South dread the voting of the negro atall, simply upon the principle that, in his nature, he is below the white man, and therefore should not be allowed to vote, or to take any share in the government of the country. Break this principle down by allowing even *one* negro to vote there, and the talismanic charm is gone at once, and the principle having been broken through they would then just as soon *all* should vote, as for one to vote, and perhaps a little rather, for they would then gain numbers by it in the Federal Congress. Rest assured, Sir, it is this principle for which they stand out. The principle that no negro shall have anything to do in a government made by white men "for themselves and their posterity." This is the principle, incorporated in the constitution of the United States, and to be found in it's opening sentence, for which the people of the South stand out. Destroy this principle there once, by letting even *one* negro vote, and they will then let them *all* vote, because the principle will then be gone. You, Sir, are sworn to protect and defend the Constitution of the United States, and yet there are those who have the boundless impudence to ask you to violate your oath of office by tendering universal amnesty to the people of the South on condition that they will so amend their state constitutions as to allow "*qualified negro suffrage.*" Of course they would then expect it to be exercised in electing members of Congress, a President of the United States &c. Now let me inquire, even if they were so to amend their constitutions as to allow "qualified negro suffrage" how could it be exercised for Federal offices in the face of that opening clause of the Constitution of the United States, by which the framers declare that one of the chief objects of ordaining and establishing the Constitution is "to secure the blessings of liberty *to ourselves and our posterity.*" Surely negroes cannot be taken as a part of "themselves or of their posterity." The *Constitution of the United States* would, then, have to be amended first, Sir, and this clause would have to be striken out, before you would be authorized to offer amnesty on any such grounds. It would simply, Sir, be a violation of your oath of office if you were to hold out this tempting fact to the people of the South to violate the Constitution of the United States. Hoping, Sir, that you will consider well this point. . . .

J. Montgomery Peters,
ex-District Judge of California

P.S. Even if the people of the Southern States were ever so anxious to let the negroes vote, the people of the other States would not be just to themselves to allow it, *unless* there had first been some solemn settlement of the right by a change of the Constitution of the United States. Suppose a negro were to appear on the floor of Congress from the State of Massachusetts, do you suppose that he could take his Seat there amongst the white representatives of other States? Certainly not. The equality principle of the several states would at once assert itself, and they would at once demand of Massachusetts to remember with whom they could associate.

They would have equally as plain a right also to object to white men *elected by negro votes*. They would say, "come to us, as our Fathers intended you should, by the votes of white men, and we will then let you in, but not before." This is a white man's government.

ALS, DLC-JP.
1. Other than the fact that Peters (*fl*1868) was a frequent correspondent with Johnson and even had at least one personal interview with him in 1868, little else has been uncovered about him. See Peters to Johnson, Apr. 25, May 8, 18, Dec. 11, 1868, Johnson Papers, LC.

From Jacob Ziegler

Harrisburg   Nov 22d 1866.

Dear Sir.

If you can find time to read this letter do so, if not burn it.

The papers state on the authority of some member of the cabinet, that you will not refuse to carry out any law which Congress may pass by a two thirds vote, and that you will reserve to yourself the Constitutional privilege of vetoeing whatever you consider unconstitutional and wrong, and also adhering to the doctrine that to the states respectively belongs the right of regulating suffrage.

You cannot refuse to carry out the law whatever it may be. The rebellion, which, happily for the country has been suppressed, was an obstruction to the due execution of the laws. The President of the United States, being charged under the constitution with the duty of seeing the laws faithfully executed, was required to see this obstruction removed. If the civil power failed to accomplish it, there was no alternative left, but the exercise of the military. Hence I have always said that it became the duty of every good citizen, to see that, that power was made effective to the end for which it was invoked. The obstruction was removed, and the laws are now being faithfully executed. If the President should assume the position of refusing to carry out a law passed by the constitutional two thirds, does he not place himself in antagonism to the law and become a rebel? He cannot plead in justification that all the states are not represented in Congress, or that Congress has deprived certain states of their just representation, because the iniquity of such deprivation attaches to Congress and not to the President—they possessing the right to judge of the qualifications of their own members. It is true, I do not believe that Congress has the authority to go outside of the requirements of the Constitution in judging of the qualifications of members, but if they do so, the responsibility of it attaches alone to themselves. Although the people in the late elections seemingly endorsed this action of Congress, yet I am far from believing they would have done so, had the single isolated question of admission been presented to them, disconnected from other and extrinsic questions.

The President then must see *all laws faithfully executed* in order to be consistent with the position assumed against the rebellion, and he can but exercise the veto power when obnoxious laws are presented to him for his approval. To the states belong the exclusive right of granting or withholding suffrage. To take this right from them and give it to Congress is virtually stealing power from the many to the few and organizing in this country a despotism. The suppression of the rebellion was not the destruction of states rights as the Charleston Mercury argues. It was simply, that a state had no right when once a member of this Union to leave it of its own volition. Nay it settled the doctrine that a state cannot without its own consent be deprived of its right as a state, or as a member of the Union. It will not be long before your traducers will have to acknowledge this plain doctrine. There are a thousand questions looming up in the future which will establish the rights of the states under the reserved powers on a more enduring basis than existed heretofore.

I was pleased to see it announced that you intended to assume the position attributed to you. Remain firm and steadfast, and a few short months more will produce circumstances which shall vindicate your policy most triumphantly.

I am but an humble citizen in these United States. But you are the head of the people and I for one wish to encourage you in your course.

J. Ziegler

ALS, DLC-JP.

From Lewis D. Campbell

U.S. Steam Ship Susquehanna　Havana　Nov. 23, 1866

Dear Sir—

You are already apprized that I am "on my way rejoicing" in the direction of the Halls of the Montezumas or "elsewhere" in pursuance to your wishes. I have delayed here a short time to meet the Consuls at Vera Cruz and the city of Mexico,[1] who left here yesterday, and arrange with them a system by which they may transmit to me when I reach the coast of Mexico any information of value touching the condition of affairs in the interior. Having accomplished this we shall depart for Vera Cruz or Tampico in a day or two[2] unless something intervenes to render it expedient to wait longer. I have information which I have officially communicated to Mr. Seward which justifies the belief that Maximilian has either left Mexico already or will do so within a very few days.[3]

We have been treated with distinguished consideration since our arrival by the Captain General[4] and other officials and have been tendered some public demonstrations by Cubans which we have felt it to be our duty to peremptorily decline. In mixing somewhat with the people here,

I find a very strong spirit of discontent with the condition of things on the Island. The spirit of revolution exists and I should not be surprized if before long it breaks out. What has surprized me most is that many of the most wealthy and influential Cubans are in favor of the abolition of slavery and of annexation to the United States or reciprocal free trade with them. These sentiments they avow frequently. Upon the subject I have of course carefully avoided expressing any opinion believing that it is a good rule for every man to attend to his own business, and that if I can attend to that well which your partiality has devolved upon me, I shall acquire as much honor as I am entitled to.

When in New York I gave to Gen Ewing[5] the recommendations of Col. Minor[6] (Kates husband) who it seems would like to be Post Master or Internal revenue Collector at Memphis. The Gen. will hand them to you if he has not already done so. My *cheek* has been hard enough to permit me to bore you about offices for those in no manner related to me, but I could not consistently with my nature insist on your conferring an appointment on my son-in-law. I can say however that the Col. served gallantly and faithfully through the war—that his integrity is beyond question—that he is temperate—of excellent moral character and good business qualifications.

Lewis D Campbell

ALS, DLC-JP.
1. Marquis D.L. Lane and Marcus Otterbourg. Lane (1825–1872), a Dartmouth graduate, practiced law in Lowell, Massachusetts, and Portland, Maine, where he served as judge of the municipal court (1857–62), before becoming consul to Vera Cruz (1862–67). After resigning the consulship he was elected a state senator, serving from 1868 to 1870. The following year he was appointed judge of the superior court and served until his death from a malarial fever in September 1872. Otterbourg (*fl*1876) worked for a Milwaukee newspaper before the war. In 1867 he was appointed minister plenipotentiary to Mexico, a position he held only briefly. *U.S. Off. Reg.* (1865); *History of Cumberland Co., Maine* (Philadelphia, 1880), unnumbered pages between 102 and 103; Milwaukee directories (1859–60); Lanman, *Biographical Annals*, 318.
2. Campbell departed from Havana on the 25th and arrived in Vera Cruz on the 29th. Campbell to Seward, Dec. 1, 1866, *House Ex. Docs.*, 30 Cong., 2 Sess., No. 76, p. 577 (Ser. 1294).
3. See Campbell to Seward, Nov. 21, 23, 1866, ibid., pp. 573–76.
4. Gen. Joaquin Manzano (1805–1867) of Spain was a much decorated career army officer who served as commanding general and captain general in Spain and her possessions. He served as captain general of Cuba from November 3, 1866, until August 1867, when he resigned and soon died. *Enciclopedia Universal Ilustrada*; *New York Herald*, Nov. 9, 1866, Aug. 25, 1867.
5. Thomas Ewing, Jr.
6. Married to Campbell's oldest daughter, Oscar Minor (*c*1831–1868) served as captain and acting adjutant general of the 75th Ohio Vol. Inf. and 1st Div., 11th Army Corps, during the Civil War before being forced to resign because of illness in late 1864. He applied for various offices until he received a commission in August 1867 for the office of assessor at Cincinnati. However, from November 1867 until his death in April 1868, he was collector of customs at Galveston, Texas. *Off. Army Reg.: Vols.*, 5: 169; Powell, *Army List*, 807; Campbell to Johnson, Feb. 22, 1867, Appts., Customs Service, Assessor, Galveston, Oscar Minor, RG56, NA; CSR, Oscar Minor, RG94, NA; Pension File, Kate C. Minor, RG15, NA; ACP Branch, File M-1864-CB-1179, Oscar Minor, RG94, NA.

From Charles G. Halpine

New York, Nov. 23rd. 1866.

My Dear Sir:—

Having consulted my democratic friends, your independent supporters, in this city, and encouraged by your expressed resolve to apply
the principle of rotation to the office-holders of this city who have lost
their hold upon the confidence of the people,—I very respectfully suggest the name of Maj. Gen. Henry E. Davies, to succeed General Dix, as
Naval Officer,[1] and John Y. Savage,[2] to be Post-master, in case you are
resolved that the present incumbent[3] shall hold that place no longer. I am
aware that my dear and honored friend, Gen. Gordon Granger, has been
named as a candidate for the Naval Office;[4] but would suggest, that, as
the Surveyorship is certainly filled by a gentleman[5] of no political influence whatever (save a power to hurt by the fact of his retention,) there
should be no difficulty between Gens. Davies and Granger on this
score,—as the latter might receive the Surveyorship and the former the
Naval Office. These three appointments, I think, could beyond question
command the approval of the Senate. Granger and Davies could not be
rejected without offending the military element of the country; and besides Judge Henry E. Davies is strong with all classes; while Mr. J. Y.
Savage, Chairman of the Democratic Union General Committee, and a
prominent "hardshell" member of the Tammany Society, would be sustained from *personal friendship* by every influence within Mr. Greeley's
control. By the way, let me say, that Greeley is greatly obliged for your
kind expressions in his favor; and will *tomorrow* publish a very striking
article on "Amnesty & Suffrage"[6] showing that he is willing to go more
than half way (I think,) toward an accommodation of differences. As to
recommenders for these gentlemen—Granger, Davies and Savage, the
two first-named have their papers already on file; while for Mr. Savage,
you have only to let me know there is a chance, and I can deluge you with
petitions, leading off with Sam. J. Tilden Sam. L.M. Barlow, Horace
Greeley, Peter Cooper, &c., thus showing that ALL CLASSES are willing to
unite in the endorsement of this sterling and honored democrat. Mr. Savage, let me add, was born in North Carolina, but has been in this City for
thirty years, and has been chairman of the Demo. Genl. Comt. on many
previous occasions. Believing that Gen. Granger will be appointed on
influences *outside of N.Y. City*, and for his services in the army and to the
party of the Constitution, I desire and am instructed to confine this special recommendation to Gen. Henry E. Davies and J. Y. Savage, for the
places of Naval officer and Postmaster. It should not be lost sight of that
there were 64,000 votes cast by my friends for me last election, of which
over 34,000 were independent democrats; and I think and believe that
the Charter Election now pending will wipe out the last vestiges of power

in the hands of the old politicians of the "regular Tammany" and "Conservative Republican" parties. Both Savage and myself are members of the Tammany Society; but this, you are aware, is NOT the "Tammany general Committee," which claims to be the exclusive organ of the "regular democracy." I think these two appointments of Davies & Savage would go far toward rebuilding an active and earnest administration party here & in the state, giving you the MORAL support of this City in your contest for the Constitution; and I can only add that if you think well of the proposition, & will so notify me, but feel that you need further assurance before taking a step so important, I will forthwith go to work to have the necessary documents and delegations sent forward in favor of Gen. Davies & Mr. Savage.[7]

Chas. G. Halpine

ALS, DLC-JP.
1. Several months earlier Halpine had recommended Gen. Daniel E. Sickles for this same post. See Halpine to Johnson, July 24, 1866, *Johnson Papers*, 10: 721–22.
2. Savage (*fl*1882), a watch dealer and jeweler, later served as Halpine's deputy register in the New York City Hall of Records office. New York City directories (1866–84).
3. James Kelly.
4. Granger, himself, had applied for this position during the previous summer. In mid-December 1866 he withdrew his application. Granger to Johnson, July 25, 1866, Appts., Customs Service, Naval Officer, New York, Gordon Granger, RG56, NA; James Dixon to Johnson, Oct. 15, 1866; Granger to Johnson, Dec. 15, 1866, Johnson Papers, LC.
5. Abram Wakeman.
6. Entitled "Southern Papers," a *Tribune* editorial concluded that the North was prepared to pardon all southerners and readmit southern states to Congress if they only consented to black civil rights and suffrage. *New York Tribune*, Nov. 24, 1866. See also ibid., Nov. 27, 1866.
7. Granger, Davies, and Savage were not appointed by Johnson. For more on Savage's post, see Halpine to Johnson, Nov. 26, 1866.

From Francis X. DeRolette[1]

Pittsburgh 24th November 1866

When your Excellency came to Pittsburgh[2] I handed to Gen. McCollam[3] a letter to your address, but in the confusion of the moment, my letter was lost. However I had previously written another[4] to Your Excellency few months under the Care of Honorable Dawson[5] the Representative of Penselvania. I hope that it did not meet with the same fate as my last. The political atmosphere is not better than it was then. The radical party in Congress mean to impeach your Excellency. Already Butler and Thadeas Stephens are at work. I compare your position to the one of Louis Napoleon when President of the Republic of France in 1852—few months before his second nomination to the Presidency. He was also threatened of Impeachment and perhaps to be incarcerated under the order of the Red Republicans of the Assembly. But his great coup d'etat Saved him and also restore peace in France.[6] Since the Elections have given to the Radicals the majority in Congress, I am of the opinion that

Fanaticism will carry them to the Extreme measures. In that alternative what is to be done? I am afraid that the only means to be adopted to Save Your Excellency and the Institutions of this Republic is to get rigorously as did Napoleon in his great Coup d'etat; I am confident that Your Excellency will have the Support of all Conservatives of the Union, and the whole Democracy who from the beginning of Your Administration has side by you. I must add that you can confidently rely on the Support of the South—the majority of the Radicals in their late Election is insignificant in Pensilvania, in N-York or else where. Corruption, Fraud by Money or other means do not represent the will of the People. Like Napoleon did, Discard all the Traitors of Congress as well as those in different States; this is the time to use your power as Chief of the States— as General in Chief of all the Armies of U.S. All the means employed by the Radicals are treasonables, they are preparing armies, militia and others means to oppose your administration at the opening of Congress. As did Napoleon, Dismiss the minister of war or any other Minister of your Cabinet who are your Ennemy's. Appoint a General in Chief in whom you have full confidence and who will *blindly* obey your Orders without consulting his personal interest.

I will not fatigue you with all the details of the *coup d'etat* of Napoleon. I hope my precedent letters were read by Your Excellency. They contain the principals means adopted by the President of France. I will only remind you that the Most Influential generals were arrested, *Cavaignac*, Changarnier, Lamorioure[7] and many others with over 60 members of the Assembly. I will also say that Napoleon did not permit any of his Ministers to remain at their Minsterial Offices any time—so as to discover their treasonable means if there was any. No pretext to settle the Affairs of the War department were allowed to be given, as the Present Minister of war is allowed to give.

I will not take your time with more details. If your Excellency is oblidged to resort to Such means to protect his life and the Institutions of this republic I have only to offer My Services and my Energy to carry your Excellency's measures to an happy result. I have by me all plans and programm ready to be submitted to your Excellency, If asked.

                                        F. X. DeRolette   Physician &c

ALS, DLC-JP.
1. DeRolette (c1800–fl1871) was a native of France. 1870 Census, Pa., Pittsburgh, 2nd Ward, 427; Pittsburgh directories (1866–71).
2. September 12, 1866.
3. Daniel C. McCallum.
4. Not found.
5. John L. Dawson.
6. First elected president in 1848, Louis Napoleon Bonaparte, supported by the army, seized control of Paris in December 1851. A republican uprising was brutally suppressed and Napoleon assumed dictatorial powers. Exactly one year later he established the Second Empire and became Napoleon III. R. Ernest and Trevor N. Dupuy, *The Encyclopedia of Military History* (New York, 1986), 770, 838.

7. Louis Eugène Cavaignac (1802–1857), Nicholas Anne Theodule Changarnier (1793–1877), and Louis Christophe Léon Juchault de Lamoricière (1806–1865), all career French army officers. They served the government in a variety of capacities but opposed Napoleon's administration and were either imprisoned or banished. *Encyclopaedia Britannica* (1973 ed.).

From George O'Reilly[1]

Montgomery, Ala, Novr. 24", 1866.

Sir:

Permit me humbly to bring before your notice a case which I think merits your gracious consideration.

When the late Rebellion broke out in the Southern States, I was in Hindostan, employed in a lucrative Situation under the British Government, I believed then that the crisis had arrived which was to determine whether civilization and liberty were to continue their progress throughout the world, or the great masses of mankind once more be enchained under the rule of a feudal aristocracy. Although not a native of America, I determined to lend my aid to the cause of freedom. I consequently resigned my Situation in India and came to New York, where I enlisted in the 78" New York Vols. My Military career in that Regt., although obscure, has not been dishonorable, for I was for almost three years first sergeant of my company, and I shared, during that period, in the perils and the glories of the 16" Army Cops. After the collapse of the Confederacy and the expiration of my term of service, having no connexions in America, I applied for and obtained a Situation, as clerk, in the Quartermaster's Office of the "Bureau of Refugees, Freedmen and Abandoned Lands," at Montgomery Ala. I remained here for Seven months, performing my duties to the perfect satisfaction of my immediate employer, the Quarter-master,[2] as may be seen by the accompanying testimonial. Toward the close of last September, General Wager Swayne, Asst Commr. of the Bureau for the State of Alabama, sent for the Quartermaster and ordered him to dismiss me from his employ; the Quarter-master asked him to assign a reason for my dismissal, stating 'that I was his chief clerk, that he had every confidence in my abilities and integrity, and that his Official business would suffer in consequence of my discharge.' General Swayne refused to assign any reason for his conduct, stating 'that he entertained no doubt of my business abilities, or my excellent character as a private individual,' but repeated 'that he required me to be discharged at once.' On my being apprized of the fact I waited on the General, he refused to admit me to an interview. I then wrote to him, requesting him to let me know the cause of my discharge. I have the honor to enclose his reply, dated Sept. 30", 1866.[3] In pursuance of the instructions contained in that letter, I waited on the Quarter-master, who informed me 'that the General wished me to leave Montgomery and "proceed to Clarke Co, Ala. make a personal Inspection and Report of the destitution Said to exist in that County, and remain there until I received further instructions." I went to Clarke Co. I made my Inspection and report and forwarded it to Head Quarters at Montgomery; I remained in Clarke Co. five weeks, and during that time received no reply to either private or official Communications which I addressed to Head Quarters. Unable to understand the reason of this continued silence, I returned to Montgomery. General Swayne was absent, but his Superintendent, O. D. Kinsman,[4] informed me that my report had been received and no immediate action was about to be taken in the matter. Mr. Kinsman futher informed 'that he very much regretted the fact, that owing to General Swayne's Express Order' it would be impossible to continue me in the employ of the Bureau at Montgomery, and I was consequently finally dismissed on the 15" Inst.

Your Excellency this my discharge was not occasioned by any contemplated reduction in the number of employees, as none such took place. Another man was immediately appointed to fill my position. Nor was it caused by my being suspected of any immoral conduct, or my being implicated in any dishonorable or dishonest transaction. Neither was it owing to any neglect of or inefficiency in my official duties. What then was the cause? Your Excellency I will tell you; It was because I, who as a Soldier, had helped to sustain the Union with my musket in battle, when Peace was restored to the exhausted Country, had dared as a free citizen to raise my voice in favor of the restoration of that Union for which I had fought. It was because I deprecated the unhappy fanaticism of radical politicians, who would goad to desperation, or condemn to slavery, their brave and high spirited Southern Countrymen, who had already atoned sufficiently for their errors, in the death of their friends, the loss of their property, and the extinction of their bright but fallacious hopes. It was because I, an employe of the Freedman's Bureau, had dared to extol President Andrew Johnson as the true friend and Saviour of his Country. It was because I praised Your Excellency as the friend of true liberty, the enemy alike of anarchy and despotism. This is the cause of my dismissal. These are my crimes. They may not indeed Seem crimes to the eye of a patriot, but they are hideous and unpardonable ones to the jaundiced vision of a Bureau General. Hence General Swayne, refusing to assign any reason for my discharge, wraps himself in his military majesty, and says "I order your discharge."

But your Excellency I know your motto is "Fiat Justitia." I refuse to accept General Swayne's decision in this matter. "I appeal unto Caesar."

Sir, pardon my egotism in troubling you with such a trivial matter, as the discharge of a clerk of the Freedmen's Bureau, but your Excellency may perceive from my case, how the unrelenting hatred of your political opponents pursues and crushes your devoted friends, no matter how humble or obscure their positions in Society. I well know the Atlantean burden you sustain, but I know also that you combine the genius of a Caesar, with the patriotism of a Cincinnattus, and I humbly trust that you will not permit a soldier, who had fought for the Country, a citizen, who desires the restoration of our glorious Constitution, and a humble admirer of the unswerving patriotism of its illustrious Chief, to be trampled beneath the feet of a military dictator of the Freedmans Bureau.

George O'Reilly.

ALS, DLC-JP.
    1. O'Reilly (b. *c*1836), an Irish native and clerk, served in the Union army from June 1863 until March 1866. CSR, George O'Reilly, RG94, NA.
    2. Salem, Massachusetts, resident George F. Browning (*c*1838–1871), a first lieutenant in the 1st Rgt., Vet. Res. Corps, formerly had the same rank in the 2nd Mass. Inf. Pension File, Adel Virginia Browning, RG15, NA.
    3. The letter stated that in the termination of O'Reilly's duties no "aspersion of your character or qualifications" was intended, and instructed him to see the quartermaster who "may place at your disposal employment in a different line." Swayne to O'Reilly, Sept. 30, 1866, Johnson Papers, LC.
    4. Oliver D. Kinsman (1835–1927), a civil engineer, served as second lieutenant, 11th Iowa Inf., and captain, assistant adjutant general of volunteers. After his muster out in October 1866 he resided variously at Montgomery, Alabama, Clinton, Iowa, Brooklyn, New York, and Washington, D.C., and vicinity. CSR, Oliver D. Kinsman, RG94, NA; Pension File, Oliver D. Kinsman, RG15, NA.

From Edwin M. Stanton

Washington City, November 24th 1866.

Sir:
    I have the honor to recall to your attention the claim for compensation for damages to the "Old Methodist Church," at Knoxville, Tennessee.
    On the 3rd ultimo I had the honor to inform you of the Quarter Master General's report[1] that, Knoxville having been a captured town, and the property having been destroyed by the unauthorized acts of troops, he could not recommend the allowance of any sum upon the claim, but of the fact that I had directed an estimate of the damages with a view to payment if the amount should not be found too large. A second report has recently been received from the Quarter Master General, in which it is stated that the estimated value of the Church is $1755, and of the fencing $141.75, and that the parties interested desire favorable consideration not so much of the former as of the latter part of the claim, as it is their wish to have the cemetery protected and ornamented. I have therefore directed that the grounds be fenced, and the palings around the family burial-places be, as far as possible, restored.

Edwin M Stanton   Secretary of War.

LS, DNA-RG107, Lets. Recd., Executive (M494, Roll 85).
    1. Stanton had acknowledged receipt of the request for compensation, which had been received by the War Department in February 1866 and referred to Quartermaster General Montgomery C. Meigs. Stanton to Johnson, Oct. 3, 1866, Lets. Sent, Mil. Bks., Executive, 58-C, RG107, NA.

From Nathan Bedford Forrest

Memphis Tennessee, Novr. 25, 1866.

It has been nearly eighteen months, since laying down my Arms, I gave my parole, to cease war, against, and to submit to the constituted authority of the United States, with the determination to do so, in all loyalty, and with full recognition of the complete restoration of the Constitutional supremacy, of the federal Union over all the States.[1] That engagement and purpose I have kept, in both spirit and letter, using my influence, as well as my example, in all possible ways to restore, amongst the people of this section, a friendly disposition towards the government, and to counteract all that tended to keep alive or inflame a hostile sentiment. I have lost no proper occasion to counsel patience, and a spirit of forbearance under a state of affairs, which your Excellency has so earnestly sought to terminate, and I have constantly sought to repress those recriminations, so natural on our side, against the wrongful and irritating imputations, to which we have been subjected.

I have earnestly labored also to incline all around me to give their chief attention to industrial reconstruction, and the development of our vast material resources, rather than to the discussion of vexations and unprofitable political affairs. So too have I endeavored to allay every phase of sectional antipathy or antagonism.

In all this, I have been animated by a sense of what was due your Excellency, in your patriotic endeavors to restore the Union, upon the constitutional foundations, laid by our fore-fathers, as well as by views of my duty to the survivors of those brave men, whom I had led in Campaign and battle, and by a feeling likewise, of obligation, under the engagement, gravely taken by me on the 9th day of May 1865.[2]

I am conscious that the loyalty of my course has not been unnoticed, nor unappreciated, in many high quarters including the most distinguished of the soldiers whom I opposed in War. Yet I am also aware, that I am at this moment regarded in large communities, at the North, with abhorrence, as a detestable monster, ruthless and swift to take life, and guilty of unpardonable crimes in connection with the capture of Fort Pillow on the 12th of April 1864. Perhaps at a time of political excitement so fierce and high as at present, this mis-judgement of my conduct and character should not surprise me. Nevertheless it pains, and mortifies me greatly; Yet if any good can be brought from it, I am still willing to rest for a time longer under this heavy wounding weight of undeserved obloqy, without any attempt at that perfect justification before the World, of my course as a soldier and commander in the storming of Fort Pillow, which I am satisfied I can make to the conviction of all fair minded people, and in complete refutation, of the *exparte* proceedings of the Congressional Committee, with their manifestly leading questions, and willing witnesses, whose prompted evidence should, thenceforward, mislead no one.

I have, however, to appeal to the judgement of your Excellency, in this regard, and to invoke your advice as to my present course, and especially, whether the time is propitious or inauspicious, for an attempt on my part to throw off the load of these widely believed, and injurious calumnies; and I have presumed to make this appeal from a sincere desire to do nothing, that shall in the least contribute to those sectional animosities, which now rend the country almost as effectually, as when great Armies were meeting in battle, and which your Excellency has been striving with such intrepidity to stifle.

Struggling as you are, with an appalling array of forces hostile to Constitutional, regulated liberty, I have been unwilling to ask you, for that Amnesty, which I felt your own sense of right had disposed you to grant me, much as it was desirable, for the proper conduct of my greatly involved private fortunes. I have preferred to endure those private embarrassments, rather than to give your vindictive enemies, an opportunity to misrepresent your motives, were you to grant my Amnesty.

In conclusion, I take occasion to say that I shall continue to do all that I can to assuage ill feeling, and promote a spirit of moderation, and accommodation. Moreover, I will say further, that should your excellency deem it as likely to subserve the purposes of pacification, I would even waive all immunity from investigation into my conduct at Fort Pillow, that might attach to my parole.[3]

N. B. Forrest

ALS, NcD.
1. Forrest took the oath of allegiance on July 1, 1865, and had his request for a special presidential pardon forwarded to Washington. See Forrest to Johnson, July 1, 1865, *Johnson Papers*, 8: 331.
2. Probably a reference to Forrest's May 9, 1865, farewell circular to his just-surrendered troops wherein he admonished them to submit and "to aid in restoring peace and establishing law and order throughout the land." John A. Wyeth, *That Devil Forrest* (New York, 1959 [1899]), 542–43.
3. In response to his letter, Forrest was granted an extension of his parole in December 1866 so that he could visit any place in the United States. But Forrest did not receive an individual pardon until July 17, 1868. Robert Johnson to Forrest, Dec. 29, 1866, Johnson Papers, LC; Wright Rives to Orville H. Browning, July 16, 1868, Amnesty Papers (M1003, Roll 49), Tenn., N. B. Forrest, RG94, NA.

From Frederick A. Aiken[1]

Brooklyn N.Y.   Novr 26/66

Sir.

There are one or two thoughts concerning the present political situation which ever since the election in this State I have been wishing to communicate but, not till the present time have I been well enough to write.[2]

Sincerely believing the policy of the President to be truly national & patriotic and in accordance with the only safe historical precedents I have labored for months as a public speaker to assist in securing the endorsement of that policy by the people.[3] The superficial and unthinking and the revilers and defamers of the President declare that the policy of Congress is endorsed by the people, but how mistaken they are is easily shown.

In the Northern States the radical party was sustained in the late elections by about Eleven millions of population and the President, or Democratic party by about nine millions. In the Southern States, exclusive of negroes the President is represented (taking late elections there as a basis) by fully Seven millions while the Radicals are not backed by more than a million, giving the Democracy a majority of Six millions. Then we see that North and South the President has among the whole people sustaining him an army of Sixteen millions & congress twelve millions giving him a majority of four millions. Now looking at the voters we find similar results.

The northern states have cast a radical vote of about two millions & a democratic vote of, in round numbers, of one million six hundred thous'd giving the radicals a majority of four hundred thousand. In the Southern States we have a voting population of Eleven hundred thousand & the Radicals two hundred thousand perhaps. North & South we have two million seven hundred thousand voters and the Radicals two millions two hundred thousand giving us a majority of five hundred thousand. This makes the sectionalism of the Radical party conspicuous. Its strength is almost entirely in the North. The radicals think they can make a party at the South out of the negroes. It is their *only* hope of continued political ascendancy and for this reason they will never consent to allow those States to resume their rightful places in the Union until the right of Suffrage is conferred on the negroes.

The policy of the President must meet with a triumph. It seems to me he has every encouragement to hold out against every form of intimidation from his enemies. A review of the electoral college is not altogether gloomy. The twenty six states represented give 246 Electoral votes of which 124 would elect. Now the Democrats are sure of Del. Md. Tenn. & Kentucky which leaves 91 to gain. New York, Penn, Inda. Conn. New Jersey, Nevada & Oregon supply the 91 votes we need. These last seven States combined in the late elections gave less than 50,000 majority (Radical). A change of 25,000 or about one in 80 would give those States to us.

A removal of the weak and uncertain props under the President in those States would soon make the change.

                                            Fredk. A. Aiken

LS, DLC-JP.
1. Aiken (d. 1876), an attorney, was affiliated with several newspapers in Washington, D.C., including the *Constitutional Union*, which he edited, and the *Washington Post*. He also briefly held a clerkship in the Treasury Department. *Appleton's Cyclopaedia*; Aiken to Johnson, Sept. 10, 1867, Johnson Papers, LC; Washington, D.C., directories (1869–71); *U.S. Off. Reg.* (1867).
2. In an earlier letter, after examining the long-range electoral scene in various northern states, Aiken had urged Johnson to concentrate on winning the election in Pennsylvania by appealing to the Masonic vote. Aiken to Johnson, Mar. 16, 1866, Johnson Papers, LC.
3. Aiken had been campaigning in Pennsylvania and New York. Aiken to Johnson, Oct. 24, 1866, Appts. Div., Misc. Lets. Recd., RG48, NA.

From Charles G. Halpine

Private

32 Beekman Street, N. Y.   Nov. 26th 1866

My dear Sir:

Mr. Greeley will tomorrow take strong ground against Gen. Butler and *the whole impeachment policy*;[1] and his efforts will be directed toward reconciling all differences for the future between both sections of the Country. Mr. Greeley authorizes me to say that he would most heartily support and endorse the nomination of Mr. J. Y. Savage for Postmaster, and would have no trouble in getting it endorsed by the U.S. Senate. Indeed Mr. Greeley is enthusiastic on the subject. I think it certain that Chanler, and Morrissey, and probable that Brooks & Fox[2] (Congressmen) would endorse Savage's name. But it is not on such influences that we urge his claim. Hoping an early communication in regard to the Postmastership.[3]

Chas. G. Halpine.

ALS, DLC-JP.
1. Although the *Tribune* printed in full Benjamin Butler's speech on impeachment, which he delivered at the Brooklyn Academy of Music on November 24, a critique by Greeley has not been located in his newspaper. *New York Tribune*, Nov. 26, 1866.
2. John W. Chanler, John Morrissey, James Brooks, and John Fox, respectively. Both Morrissey (1831–1878) and Fox (1835–1914) were newly-elected members of Congress, and each served two consecutive terms as New York Democrats. Before their election in 1866, Morrissey was the owner of gambling houses and a race course, and was a champion heavyweight boxer, while Fox held public office in New York City. Both men were elected to the state senate in the 1870s. *BDAC*.
3. Savage was not appointed.

From Edward D. Holbrook[1]

Washington D.C.   November 26th 1866.

Esteemed Sir:

I placed on file with the Secretary of State, an application of John M. Murphy,[2] for the appointment of Governor of Idaho Territory.

In addition to what is therein stated, I can assure Your Excllency, that on a long and intimate acquaintance with the applicant, there is no man on the Pacific Coast, who has labored more diligently or effectively in having your policy sustained.

He accompanied me, and materially assisted in my late canvass of the State of Nevada, where he spoke at all of the principal Cities; and as the State Centre of the Fenian Organization of Idaho Territory, he was entirely successful in bringing the organization of that State to the Support of the Conservative ticket. Although our efforts in that State did not meet with entire success, I have the satisfaction and consolation of knowing that the Radicals sustained a greater loss in that State than any other in the Union, in proportion to the vote cast. And believe that to the applicant belongs a great portion of the credit, if successful; in defeating the arch-demogogue—J. W. Nye—for the United States Senate.[3] He is an old resident of the Territory, a large property holder, and thoroughly identified with the people of the Territory, her interests and advancement.

The present incumbent, D. W. Ballard, never saw the Territory until after his appointment as Governor, has no interests in, or knowledge of the people or the Territory, always having resided in the State of Oregon, and is not considered a resident of the Territory except through his appointment. Mr Ballard was appointed upon the recommendation of Gentlemen, not one of whom resided a single day in the Territory.[4] The development of our Young and infant Territory has been greatly retarded by the appointment to office of non-residents, men who had no interests, or were not identified with the people, or with the advancement and prosperity of the Territory.

By the appointment of non-residents, large sums of money have already been lost to the Government. The former Governor Caleb Lyons of Lyonsdale, took as I am informed, about one hundred thousand dollars there two years ago, to discharge indebtedness contracted and make treaties with the Indians, (who are almost daily killing some of our people). Our people had no confidence in his integrity, and he has since proved himself unworthy of the position, by virtually retaining or appropriating nearly the entire sum to himself.[5]

One of the Secretaries, and I believe an honorable one, C. Dewit Smith,[6] died very suddenly, after receiving twenty thousand dollars to pay the members of the Territorial Legislature, his trunks and papers were immediately ransacked in private by the balance of the Territorial Officials, and the money, as I am thoroughly convinced was stolen by one of the United State Judges, (to wit) Kelly[7]—assisted by Horace C. Gilson,[8] the successor of Smith, and one Reynolds[9] the Editor of a Radical paper of that Territory.[10]

After Gilson's appointment as Secretary, (to wit) on the 27th day of December A D 1865 there was thirty thousand dollars forwarded to Horace C Gilson the Secretary of the T'y to pay the expenses of the Territorial Legislature, this sum he took and left the Territory for whence or where, remains a mystery. This was another appointment without one of our people recommending him.[11]

Both parties in the late political canvass in our Territory, passed resolutions favoring the appointment of none but actual *bona fide* residents of the Territory. I will copy the last resolution in the Platform adopted at the late Radical Territorial Convention held at Boise City, June 21st A. D. 1866.

"*Resolved*—That in the appointment of Federal Officers for the Territories, preference ought to be given to the Citizens thereof over those of Other States, who have little or no Knowledge of their local affairs, and are not identified with the interests of the Territories."

I can assure Your Excellency, that that resolution expresses the unanimous sentiment of our people, and as we never have had a single Officer appointed to any Office of importance in the Territory, who was a resident thereof;[12] is it asking too much to solicit this one at your hands? I ask it for that Territory, which was the first of all the Northern States or Territories, through its representatives, to pass a series of Resolutions warmly and sincerely approving and endorsing your policy, and sustaining the same in the recent election; and which, I in common with the applicant trust may be the last to forsake it.

My efforts to have it done last winter, whilst here, was well known to my constituency. They have returned me here by an increased majority, and insist on my once more renewing my efforts in their behalf.[13]

I have conversed with Senator Nesmith of Oregon,[14] who endorsed Mr Ballards recommendation, and have his assurance that he will not, and does not wish in anywise to interfere or object to the appointment of Mr Murphy.

If the petition of persons resident or non-resident be required, I can get and will procure as large and respectable a one, as has been at any time considered sufficient in such matters in his behalf, but at present deem it unnecessary, and shall continue so to feel until assured to the contrary.

Trusting that my request may meet with a kind and favorable consideration at your hand.[15]

E D Holbrook—Delagate   Idaho Terr'y

LS, DNA-RG59, Lets. of Appl. and Recomm., 1861–69 (M650, Roll 35), John M. Murphy.

1. Holbrook (1836–1870), a native of Ohio, was admitted to the bar in 1859 and moved that year to California to begin practicing law. In 1863 he went to Idaho, where he again practiced law and was elected territorial delegate to Congress for two terms (1865–69). In June 1870 he was shot and killed in front of his law office in Idaho City. *BDAC*; Bancroft, *Washington, Idaho, and Montana*, 470.

2. Murphy (*fl*1867) had previously resided in Oregon, where he held a local office and was allegedly indicted for embezzlement, causing him to flee to Idaho where he settled before the territory was organized and held the post of recorder for Boise County. E. D. Holbrook to Johnson, [Nov. 1866], Lets. of Appl. and Recomm., 1861–69 (M650, Roll 35), John M. Murphy, RG59, NA; *Idaho Statesman*, Sept. 27, 1866.

3. James W. Nye was, in fact, reelected to the Senate and served until March 3, 1873. *BDAC*.

4. Holbrook led the attempts in Washington to get rid of David W. Ballard. Eventually he was charged with maladministration of Indian affairs and the ouster attempt nearly succeeded. Bancroft, *Washington, Idaho, and Montana*, 470–71; W. Turrentine Jackson, "Indian Affairs and Politics in Idaho Territory, 1863- 1870," *PHR*, 14 (1945): 322–23.

5. Governor Lyon actually absconded with somewhat over $46,000. For this and other Idaho financial problems see also David W. Ballard to Johnson, July 25, 1866, *Johnson Papers*, 10: 731–32.

6. A native of New York, Clinton DeWitt Smith (d. 1865) had a legal education and spent several years as a clerk in the attorney general's office in Washington, D.C., before being appointed Idaho territorial secretary. About six months after his arrival, on August 19, 1865, Smith died suddenly "from the effects of a dismal and melancholy disease," although some alleged "from the effects of dissipation." Bancroft, *Washington, Idaho, and Montana*, 463; Merle W. Wells, "Clinton DeWitt Smith, Secretary, Idaho Territory, 1864– 1865," *OHQ*, 52 (1951): 50.

7. Milton Kelly (1818–1892), a native of New York, moved to Wisconsin, where he was admitted to the bar and practiced law. He later moved to Idaho in 1862, where he was elected to the first territorial legislature and served as a justice of the territorial supreme court (1866–70). He edited the *Idaho Statesman* in Boise (1872–89). *History of Idaho Territory* (San Francisco, 1884), 192, 254; Mark Wyman, "Frontier Journalism," *Idaho Yesterdays*, 17 (1973): 32; Ronald H. Limbaugh, "Fighter on the Bench: Milton Kelly's Idaho Legal Career, 1862–1870," *Idaho Yesterdays*, 25 (1981): 5–6.

8. Gilson (*fl*1866), originally from Ohio, was working as a "small gambling bar tender" in San Francisco when he met C. DeWitt Smith, who was en route to Idaho. Accompanying Smith as his private secretary, Gilson became the administrator of Smith's estate and succeeded him as Idaho territorial secretary. Ronald H. Limbaugh, "The Idaho Spoilsmen: Federal Administrators and Idaho Territorial Politics, 1863–1890" (Ph.D. diss., University of Idaho, 1966), 32–33; Wells, "Clinton DeWitt Smith," 51.

9. New York native James S. Reynolds (1831–*fl*1881) and some relatives published the first issue of the *Idaho Statesman*, a Republican paper, in Boise on July 26, 1864. Although Reynolds sold the paper in January 1869, he soon repurchased it and continued tri-weekly and weekly issues until he sold it to Milton Kelly in 1872. He then settled in California, where he practiced law. *Idaho Territory*, 192; Bancroft, *Washington, Idaho, and Montana*, 438; ibid., *California*, 7: 403; San Francisco directories (1877–81); 1870 Census, Idaho, Ada, Boise City, 23.

10. The probate court had appointed Kelly and Reynolds as appraisers for Smith's estate and Reynolds stated that their examination of Smith's effects took place before five witnesses. *Idaho Statesman*, July 31, 1866.

11. Gilson absconded with $8,062 which he claimed was "missing" from Smith's accounts, as well as at least $33,000 in other territorial funds, when he left for San Francisco in February 1866 to superintend the territorial printing. By April Gilson had vanished, apparently going to Hong Kong with his ill-gotten gains. In contrast to Holbrook's statement, apparently a good many "Boise dignitaries," despite a short acquaintance with Gilson, had hastened to send recommendations. Limbaugh, "The Idaho Spoilsmen," 32– 33; Wells, "Clinton DeWitt Smith," 51; *Idaho Statesman*, Jan. 31, 1867.

12. Certainly Holbrook was in error, since Judge Kelly had resided in Idaho for several years before he was appointed.

13. Holbrook was reelected on August 13, 1866, by a majority of 718 votes out of a total of 6,564 cast. *American Annual Cyclopædia* (1866), 734.

14. James W. Nesmith.

15. Johnson heeded Holbrook's request and nominated Murphy for governor on January 14, 1867, but the Senate rejected him on March 2. Although Johnson nominated two other men, they were also rejected, leaving Ballard in office to serve the longest term of Idaho's territorial governors (June 14, 1866-July 12, 1870). Merle W. Wells, "David W. Ballard, Governor of Idaho, 1866–1870," *OHQ*, 54 (1953): 6, 11, 16–17; Ser. 6B, Vol. 4: 394, 398, Johnson Papers, LC.

To Davidson M. Leatherman

Washington, D.C., Nov 26" 1866

You were appointed one of the Commissioners to attend the World's fair to be held in Paris.[1] It was supposed you would remain there until it met.[2]

The persons referred to in your dispatch must take their Chances, if they return to the United States.[3]

Andrew Johnson

Tel, DNA-RG107, Tels. Sent, President, Vol. 3 (1865–68).

1. Ten days earlier the President had appointed Leatherman as one of the unpaid commissioners to represent the United States at the 1867 Paris exhibition. Johnson to Seward, Nov. 16, 1866, Acceptances and Orders for Commissions, 1861–68, D. Leatherman, RG59, NA; *U.S. Off. Reg.* (1867).

2. On the day preceding Johnson's telegram, Leatherman had sent a dispatch from New York City indicating that personal interests had caused him to leave France and return to Memphis for a month. Leatherman assured Johnson that he would return to Europe in April. Leatherman to Johnson, Nov. 25, 27, 1866, Johnson Papers, LC. See also Leatherman to Johnson, Oct. 4, 1866, ibid.

3. In his telegram of November 25, Leatherman had mentioned John C. Breckinridge and Robert A. Toombs, both of whom sought assurances from Johnson about their return to the United States. Leatherman to Johnson, Nov. 25, 1866, ibid.

From Rufus W. Peckham[1]

Alby.   Novr. 26./66

Sir—

Pardon me for assuming to advise. I wish most earnestly to ask you to issue a general amnesty to the whole South, now—now while your authority cannot be questioned. I ask it for every reason that can influence a true man. For the sake of justice—no civilized people ever suffered more than the South in such a rebellion—added to all, they were deprived of property (their slaves) to more than $2,000,000. They have been thoroughly punished for fighting for what they erroneously believed to be their rights. For the sake of a generous humanity—For the welfare & material prosperity of the whole country, North & South—and Sir for your own sake—Perform an act of lofty statesmanship—of pure patriotism—an act that will place your name high in the records of history.

Exceptions can be made if deemed wise—But true wisdom, true manhood & true statesmanship demands none. All know that another rebellion of the South is a literal impossibility. "Guaranties" are a sham. Give peace to the South & peace to the country. Give to the South what little property the desolation of war has left to them. Give them their lives & a feeling of personal security against the ferocious partisan & personal hate that would annihilate them. All this you may do now. In one week it will be too late. The act of Congress is then repealed & your authority—yr. power is then questioned. Sir—allow me to say if you fail to do this, you will regret it when it is too late—Regret it to the latest hour of yr. life & regret it in vain.

The whole civilized world would hail such an act with joy & admiration —always excepting your Butlers & Brownlows & their followers, if that be an exception.

Though a stranger to you I am no partizan of the South. I opposed & voted in Congress against the repeal of the Missouri Compromise, fearing the excitement that followed it.

I pray you in conclusion, do not fail in decision now.

R W Peckham

ALS, DNA-RG60, Office of Atty. Gen., Lets. Recd., President.
1. After serving just one term in Congress as a Democrat (1853–55), Peckham (1809–1873) returned to New York, where he practiced law and served as state supreme court justice and later as an appellate judge. *BDAC*.

From J. H. Brown[1]

New York.   Nov 28. 1866

Sir.

Though personally unknown to you, I deem it my duty to inform you, now that the elections are over, that during the canvas you were most shamefully betrayed by many who, for purely selfish reasons, professed to be your devoted friends, the most conspicuous of whom is

Mr. Alexander T. Stewart.

After his most liberal subscriptions to Mr. Dunbar[2] and others, to sustain the noble policy which you had proposed, I have to inform you, that he also subscribed *far more* in aid of the radical republicans, and in a secret way, did all he could to defeat both Mayr. Hoffman[3] for Governor, and Mr. James Brooks for Congress. This assertion I base upon the following facts, namely:

1st. One week before the elections he invited the members of the radical republican State Committee to a private dinner party at his own residence.

2d. He subscribed the sum of $1,000. to the radical republican State Committee to aid in reelecting Gov. Fenton, for the proof of which I respectfully refer to Senator Morgan,[4] Mr. Geo. Opdyke,[5] and Mr. Waldo Hutchins.

3d. He gave $250. in one sum, to a radical republican committee to aid Col. Le Grand B. Cannon[6] in carrying on his Canvas against Hon. James Brooks, with a full knowledge of the fact that you yourself were particularly desirous that Mr. Brooks should be elected.

Honl. Wm. E. Dodge,[7] M.C. can testify to this fact, and also Col. Cannon himself.

4th. Mr. Stewart also contributed generously for the gratuitous distribution of the *Campaign Tribune*, in which your policy was constantly denounced in the most unmeasured terms.

For the truth of this, I refer to Mr. Samuel Sinclair,[8] Mr. Wm. A. Hall,[9] and to Mr. Horace Greeley himself.

It is rumored that far larger sums have been given by Mr. Stewart to *aid in defeating your policy* but of that I have no positive proof. Nevertheless credulous officials are assured that Mr. Stewart is still friendly and on intimate terms with the President, and accordingly *do his bidding*.

Is this right and just? Is such a man longer entitled either to your confidence or respect?

J H Brown

ALS, DLC-JP.
1. Not identified.
2. Not identified.
3. John T. Hoffman.
4. Reuben E. Fenton and Edwin D. Morgan.
5. Opdyke (1805–1880), a Republican who amassed a fortune before and during the war as a clothing retailer, formerly served as mayor of New York City (1862–63) and was active in state politics for a number of years. *DAB*.
6. Cannon (*c*1815–1906), a staff officer under Gen. John E. Wool, was soundly defeated for the Fourth District congressional seat by the Democrat Brooks in early November 1866. Cannon was for many years in the canal business and active in local politics. *New York Times*, Nov. 4, 1906; *Guide to U.S. Elections*, 617.
7. Dodge (1805–1883), founder and head of the New York business firm, Phelps, Dodge & Co., was the Republican incumbent for the Fourth District of New York. *BDAC*.
8. Sinclair (*c*1822–*fl*1891) was the business manager, publisher, and chief stockholder of the *New York Tribune*. From the 1870s to 1891 he was a storekeeper for the Customs Service, though he requested appointment as naval officer of New York from President Garfield in 1881. 1860 Census, N.Y., New York, New York, 20th Ward, 2nd Dist., 78; Hudson, *Journalism in the United States*, 537, 572; *U.S. Off. Reg.* (1877–91); Sinclair to Garfield, Mar. 1, 1881, Garfield Papers, LC.
9. Hall (*c*1820–*fl*1880), a native of Massachusetts, was a successful shoe merchant with a net worth of $100,000 in 1860. 1860 Census, N.Y., Westchester, Greenburgh, 451; New York City directories (1859–61, 1880).

From Mary Hindman[1]

Helena. [Ark.]   Nov 28th [1866][2]

I take the liberty of writing you a few lines to ask in *mercy* the pardon of my husband, Gen T. C. Hindman now in Mexico. I have just returned home with four little helpless children[3] without home or money, and feel assured that your heart will not *fail* to give me symphaty and a speedy pardon for my husband. We failed in Mexico even to make a support and are anxious to live in the United States with your permission. My husband promises most *faithfully* to be a quiet citizen, and devote his life to domestic duties.[4]

With bright hopes of hearing from you soon I hope you will forgive the liberty I have taken.

Mary Hindman

ALS, DNA-RG94, Amnesty Papers (M1003, Roll 13), Ark., Thomas C. Hindman.

   1. The former Mary Watkins Biscoe (c1841–1876), of Helena, Arkansas, married
Thomas C. Hindman on November 11, 1856. Her letter was enclosed in one to Johnson
from James H. O'Connor, late lieutenant colonel of U.S. volunteers, with whom the Hindman family was staying. 1870 Census, Ark., Phillips, St. Francis Twp., 143; W. J. Lemke,
"The Hindman Family Portraits," *ArHQ*, 14 (1955): 105–6; O'Connor to Johnson, Nov.
28, 1866, Amnesty Papers (M1003, Roll 13), Ark., Thomas C. Hindman, RG94, NA.
   2. O'Connor's letter is dated 1866. Ibid.
   3. The children were Susan (b. c1858), Biscoe (1861–1932), Thomas C., III (c1864–
c1934), and Blanche Carlotta (c1866–1952). 1870 Census, Ark., Phillips, St. Francis
Twp., 143; Lemke, "Hindman Family Portraits," 105–7.
   4. No pardon date is given for Hindman and Johnson made no evident response to this
letter. Hindman returned to Arkansas in 1867, where he practiced law in Helena and was
assassinated on September 27, 1868. Ibid., 105; Andrew F. Rolle, *The Lost Cause: The
Confederate Exodus to Mexico* (Norman, Okla., 1965), 196.

From John A. McClernand

PRIVATE!

Springfield Ill.   Nov. 28" 1866

Friends have put upon me the disagreeable task of bringing to your notice certain matters of complaint.

The brother-in-law[1] of Ward H. Lamon Esq has been, (as stated,) lately appointed to the P.O. at Danville, Ill. through the influence of Mr L. Without, in any way, questioning the character either of the appointee or his patron, I venture with entire respect to all concerned, and for your information, to add, that this appointment is unsatisfactory to those of your friends, in that locality, whose part in the late political contest, in Illinois, entitle them to particular consideration.

This dissatisfaction is enhanced by information received, of *quasi* official character, that Mr Lamon's cousin-in-law, W. T. Cunningham,[2] is to be retained as Collector of Internal Revenue for the same District, notwithstanding the previous signing of a commission to Mr Fithian[3] and the forwarding of his bond for approval.

Mr Fithian's case is a strong one in many respects. He is an old and honored citizen of Illinois, a man of much influence, voted for you and Mr Lincoln, sustained your administration, and the candidacy of Genl Cha's Black,[4] his step-son, who was the conservative candidate for Congress in the same District, and who made the most energetic, heroic and brilliant canvass made by any candidate in the state, during the late political campaign.

Having stated these facts from my own knowledge, or upon information, I leave them with you.

John A. McClernand.

ALS, DNA-RG56, Appts., Internal Revenue Service, Collector, Ill., 7th Dist., William
Fithian.
   1. William Morgan (*fl*1879), later an insurance agent and justice of the peace, received
a recess appointment in late September 1866 and was confirmed the following March. He

served for two and a half years. Several years prior to this he had served as a deputy collector under W. T. Cunningham. Ser. 6B, Vol. 3: 593; Vol. 4: 301, Johnson Papers, LC; *U.S. Off. Reg.* (1867); H. W. Beckwith, *History of Vermilion County* (Chicago, 1879), 416.

2. Cunningham (1834–*fl*1879) served as a clerk in various departments in Danville and Washington before being appointed collector of the Seventh District by Lincoln. In October 1866 he heard that he was to be removed and replaced by Dr. William Fithian. However, it appears that Cunningham held the collectorship at least through September 1867. Beckwith, *Vermilion County*, 380–81; *U.S. Off. Reg.* (1865–67); Cunningham to Hugh McCulloch, Oct. 18, 1866, Appts., Internal Revenue Service, Collector, Ill., 7th Dist., W. T. Cunningham, RG56, NA. See Ward H. Lamon to Johnson, ca. Oct. 18, 1866, ibid.

3. William Fithian (1799–1890), a physician, served in the Civil War as provost marshal of the then Seventh District. A leading prewar Whig in Indiana and Illinois, he served a short time as both state senator and representative. *The Past and Present of Vermilion County, Illinois* (Chicago, 1903), 825–27.

4. John Charles Black (1839–1915) served in the Union army for the entire length of the war, rising from private to brevet brigadier general. Following the war, he studied law and was admitted to the bar in 1867. He was unsuccessful in his run against Henry P.H. Bromwell for Congress. *BDAC*; Poore, *Political Register*, 301.

From John Morrissey

New York   29th Novr. 1866

Sir

Encouraged by your Excellency's Kind permission to mention one or more of the friends of your Administration in my district whose zeal and ability were most conspicuous in the late triumphant election in this City, I beg to submit the application of my valued friend Mr. James Hayes,[1] for the Collectorship of Internal Revenue in its Fifth District.

In thus rewarding Mr. Hayes for his invaluable services to the great National Cause, your Excellency will enable me to acknowledge by the patronage held under this appointment, the aid rendered to it by scores of humbler, but no less zealous aherents to the policy of your Excellency.

I might have had this application backed by any number of the Eighty Thousand "Johnson men" who stood up for the Union and the Constitution in this City on the 6th Inst, but I cannot doubt that the few and sterling names appended to Mr. Hayes' petition,[2] will more than satisfy the Conditions of such recommendations.

Messrs. *Hoffman* and *Tilden* are representative men in politics, Mr. *Dodge* (of the house of Jay Cooke & Co.) and Mr. *Crawford*[3] (of the house of Clark, Dodge & Co.) in finance; Mr. *Francis Skiddy*,[4] in Commerce, and Mr. *Barlow*, in law; while Mr. *Travers*,[5] the son-in-law of the Hon. Reverdy Johnson, stands deservedly at the head of the New York Stock Exchange.

To these estimable guarantees for the fitness of my friend Mr. Hayes, I beg to add the most earnest solicitations of your Excellency's sincere friend.[6]

John Morrissey

LS, DNA-RG56, Appts., Internal Revenue Service, Collector, N.Y., 5th Dist., James Hayes.
1. Hayes (*fl*1880) was a New York City supervisor. New York City directories (1866–81).
2. See Hayes to Johnson, Nov. 22, 1866, Appts., Internal Revenue Service, Collector, New York, 5th Dist., James Hayes, RG56, NA.
3. Both Edward Dodge (*fl*1874) and David Crawford, Jr. (*fl*1876) were Wall Street bankers, whose companies were major banking and investment firms with offices around the country. New York City directories (1866–78); Ellis P. Oberholtzer, *Jay Cooke: Financier of the Civil War* (2 vols., New York, 1968 [1907]).
4. Skiddy (c1810–1879) was a prominent sugar broker. *New York Times*, May 2, 1879.
5. William R. Travers (1819–1887), a native of Maryland, married Reverdy Johnson's fourth daughter, Maria Louisa, before removing to New York City, where he attained success on Wall Street. *NCAB*, 8: 87.
6. Johnson referred Morrissey's letter to Secretary McCulloch, but Hayes was not appointed collector.

From Antonio Lopez de Santa Anna

New Brighton St. I. [Staten Island]   Nov 30/66

Your Excellency will pardon the intrusion I make upon your time in requesting your attention to the perusal of these lines, which are of vital interest to a nations voe and wellfare.

Your Ex. has already been made avare of my coming to this country some months ago[1]—which was the result of a special invitation from a distingueshed member of Your Exs. Cabinet[2] when visiting me at St Tomas, and inducing me to leave the abode which I had selected for the remainder of my days.

When here, the courtesey due even to a private Gentleman was denied me, for, my Communications addressed to this same Gentleman of your Exs. Cabinet remained unanswered.

While here, I offered my services to the Representative of the Republican Governement of my country[3] and they were refused, and my political ennemies even published through the medium of the press—that I was a spy of Maxmilian and the french.

Both of these causes nerved me in the resolution—to go to the aid of my country and free it once more from foreign yoke as I have already done before in my life. To do this, I was encouraged by the voice of my countryman who called me to action—and I would already long ago have been on the soil of my native land were it not that I respected the *neutral position observed by Your Exs. Governement* whose laws, while enjoying the hospitality of the country I felt obliged to guard.

The arrest of General Ortega by order of a General of the Army of the U.S.[4] comfirmed me in my resolution, and I decided to return to my home in St Tomas—and await there, although not with tranquility the solution of my country's fate.

While nearly prepared to start, I received Comissioners from various parties of my country, inviting me most vehemently to go to their aid—and abandon the plan which I had adopted of retirement.

This invitations came, first, from the Clergy and conservative party of my country—second from the Chief Military leaders that serve now under the Archducke Maxmilian and with the french, and 3dly they come even from the Archducke himself—inviting me to come, not to rule, but only as a mediation—to avoid anarchy, bloodshed and revenge—that must plunge the country in an abysme after the evacuation of the french, and Maxmilians leaving the country.

The wealthier part of my Countrymen place even the sum of 5 Millions of Dollars to my disposal, in behalf of the object proposed, while the french residents of the principal cities of Mexico petition me to receive favorable the Commissiners.

These Commissiners have also manifested to me, that in case I do not comply with their wishes a new party will be formed with Ex President Miramon and General Marquez[5] at the head. These men, I am convinced, aspire to power only for their own aggrandizment, and would never combine with the present Governement of Don. Benito Juarez, while I would agree to hand over to him the situation, for the sake of the pacification of the country. Yet, firm in my resolution, to do nothing that would be against the will and politic of your Exs. Governement—and in proofe of this my assertion, I direct the present to Your Excellency—not officialy—but privatly, pledging my word of honor as a Gentleman and Soldier—to abide your Exs. decision—viz: Should it be contrary to your Exs. Governement politic that I shall answer to the call made on me, then I will retire as formerly resolved, to my abode in St Tomas. 2d Should your Ex. resolve differently than I pledge myself to your Excellency that I neither aspire for power nor anything else—but only as mediator, and will after a pacific settlement give over the position to the man, who so be called by the majority of the nation, to rule its further destiny.

Your Excellency will preceive by my frank language, the sincerity of my intentions, pledging again my word of honor as a Gentleman and Soldier that I will abide by your Ex's kindly advise.

Should it meet with your Exs. approbation and desires, to Confer verbally upon this subject, I would send a person fully authorised to represent me, under strict pledge of secrecy, to inform You more particulary; informations which I wish not trust to writing.

Hoping that my sincerity and frankness will merit a speedy answer from your Exy and that my request as well as your Exs. decision will be regarded as a matter of privacy.[6]

A. L. de Sta Anna.

LS, DLC-JP.
    1. Santa Anna arrived in New York on May 12. *New York Herald*, May 13, 1866.
    2. William Seward had visited Santa Anna in January 1866 while cruising the West Indies. Van Deusen, *Seward*, 493.

3. Santa Anna wrote Mathías Romero on May 21 offering "his services in behalf of the Republic" and tendering Juárez "his aid and support." *Picayune* (New Orleans), Aug. 17, 1866.

4. Prior to the November 22, 1866, Cabinet meeting when neither Johnson nor Stanton would accept responsibility for approving or disapproving General Sheridan's request, Sheridan arrested Gen. Jesús González Ortega, to prevent his return to Mexico for purposes of promoting the mutiny against the government. Grant telegraphed Sheridan that his conduct merited complete approval. Thomas Schoonover, ed., *Mexican Lobby* (Lexington, 1986), 146–47; James A. Magner, *Men of Mexico* (Milwaukee, 1942), 386.

5. Miguel Miramón and Leonardo Márquez. Márquez (1820–1913), a career Mexican army officer, supported the Conservative forces and fought for Maximilian against Juárez during the 1860s. He mysteriously disappeared June 19, 1867, the day Maximilian was executed, turning up in Havana where he remained the rest of his life except for a short return to Mexico. *Enciclopedia de Mexico*.

6. Following his attempts to garner support in person in the U.S. in 1866, Santa Anna was tried and condemned (in his absence) by Mexican authorities and his property confiscated. On June 3, 1867, he again returned to Mexico and sought a hearing; but American officials refused to allow him to disembark from the American vessel in Vera Cruz. Taken to another port, Santa Anna was forcibly removed from the ship and imprisoned by Mexican officials. Magner, *Men of Mexico*, 347–48.

From Jonathan Worth

Raleigh   November 30th 1866

Sir.

Col Bomford, Military Commandant of this State has transmitted to me, the enclosed General Orders from Genl Sickles No. 15, dated Oct. 1st 1866. Col Bomford Calls my special attention to paragraphs 5 and 6.[1]

These Orders seem to rest on the assumption that the Military Commandant of the Department, has a right to suspend or annul such laws of the States within his Command as he may deem inhumane or unwise. By the laws of North Carolina the penalty for Larceny, Bigamy, and sundry other infamous Crimes, is Corporal punishment—to wit, whipping. If these orders are carried out, under our existing laws, some of these Crimes must go unpunished. The 5th and 6th paragraphs of these orders, are in Conflict, as I Conceive with your Excellency's proclamation of the 20th Aug last, declaring that ["]Civil authority now exists throughout the whole of the United States."[2]

I do not apprehend any Conflict under other paragraphs of these orders, resting, as I suppose, on the Military Orders of Genl Grant of the 12th January and 1st July last, but having seen it stated through the newspapers, that Genl Grant deems these orders as essentially modified by your proclamation aforesaid.

I would be glad to know officially to what Extent he deems them modified.[3]

Jonathan Worth   Governor of N.Carolina.

LS, DNA-RG107, Lets. Recd., Executive (M494, Roll 85).

1. These sections stated that corporal punishment could only be inflicted on a minor,

"by the parent, guardian, teacher, or one to whom said minor is lawfully bound by indenture of apprenticeship," and the state laws "defining and punishing vagrancy, applicable to
white persons, may be enforced against all persons." General Orders, No. 15, Department
of the South, Oct. 1, 1866, Johnson Papers, LC.

    2. See Proclamation *re* End of Insurrection, Aug. 20, 1866.

    3. General Grant's opinion is unknown. The North Carolina legislature authorized the
governor to send a commission to Washington to obtain the revocation of the order forbid-
ding corporal punishment. Before the commission departed, Worth himself journeyed to
Washington, accompanied by David L. Swain and Thomas Ruffin. They twice met with
Johnson, on December 17 and 19, 1866, and at the latter meeting secured their object, a
directive to General Sickles to "issue orders suspending . . . paragraphs V and VI of . . .
General Orders No 15." Richard L. Zuber, *Jonathan Worth: A Biography of a Southern
Unionist* (Chapel Hill, 1965), 243–47; Edward D. Townsend to Daniel E. Sickles, Dec.
19, 1866, Johnson Papers, LC.

December 1866

From John Bigler

Sacramento   Dec 1 1866,

Dr Sir

I enclose herewith an editorial clipped from the Daily "Sacramento Union,"[1] the organ of California Radicalism, as a specimen of the malignant stuff which daily disgraces the paper named, and also to [assure?] you that the editors of the "Union"—Gov Low[2] and his Attorney General *McCullough*,[3] are the *advisers* of the removed Assesser—J. M. Avery. These men sustain Avery because *he* is your bitter opponent, and they oppose and denounce me because regarded as your friend. I opposed too because these believe that I know the people of California as well—if not better than any other man, and they greatly fear the influence I may exert with assisstants in sixteen of the largest counties including the important cities of Sacramento—Nevada—Maysville—Grass Valley and Placerville. But there are other reasons influencing Avery and his advisers in the efforts making to keep the Books and Papers.[4] I have carefully examined the returns in full in the Collector office and satisfied myself that Averys *favoriteism* within the past three years has in the aggregate reduced the Revenues of the 4th District not less than *twenty-five* thousand—perhaps as much as thirty-five thousand Dollars. *I Know* that the men who are now most active in the support of Avery, have not for the past three years paid over one-third the amounts they should have paid the Government and these men fear that I will take the authorized steps to compel them be just to their country and their fellow citizens. As I am now discharging the duties of the office kindly bestowed by you I will as soon as possible conclusively prove the correctness of the foregoing statements.

John Bigler

ALS, DNA-RG56, Appts., Internal Revenue Service, Assessor, Calif., 4th Dist., John Bigler.
1. Entitled "A Fearful Charge," the article, which discussed the possibility of Johnson's involvement in the plot to assassinate Lincoln, appeared on November 20, 1866.
2. Frederick F. Low (1828–1894) emigrated to California with the early wave of Gold Rush settlers in 1849. Subsequently he became involved in business ventures in San Francisco and Marysville. Briefly a U.S. congressman (1862–63) and collector of the port of San Francisco, Low served as governor (1863–67), and afterwards spent four years as U.S. minister to China. *DAB*.
3. Lawyer John G. McCullough (1835–1915) moved to California for his health in the late 1850s. After terms in the state house and senate, McCullough served as state attorney general (1863–67). In the 1870s he moved to Vermont, where he headed several railroads and was later elected governor. *DAB*.

4. Bigler was supposed to succeed Avery as assessor, but Avery refused to acknowledge Johnson's right to remove and replace him and, therefore, would not give up his official papers to Bigler. Bigler to Johnson, Oct. 22, 1866, Appts., Internal Revenue Service, Assessor, Calif., 4th Dist., John Bigler, RG56, NA. See also Bigler to Johnson, Mar. 14, 1866, *Johnson Papers*, 10: 253.

From Francis P. Blair, Jr.

Washington City   Dec 3rd 1866

In conversation the other day about the appointment of John D. Stevenson of Mo, as a colonel in the Regular Army[1] you said you wished me to put in writing what I had said on the subject and you also requested me to see Genl. Grant about it. I have called on the General and said to him substantially what I had previously said to you. Genl. Grant remarked that he thought Stevenson would make a better Colonel than General and that at any rate he had been appointed & accepted and placed on duty. I said "suppose the President declines to send his name to the Senate." Genl. Grant said "I would not advise the President to withhold his name, if he should do so, the senate might take exception to some whose names are sent in to them." I give you as near as I remember Genl. Grants precise words. I thought them significant and they suggested to me that Stevensons appointment was perhaps due to Senatorial influence. This only confirms me in the opinion that it was an appointment unfit to be made, and inasmuch as Stevenson is from my state—the only Colonel appointed from that State which furnished so many fine officers to the volunteer service—I desire to protest against it as derogatory to the state and to all the soldiers of the state. When Genl. Lyon was pressed by overwhelming numbers in the south western part of Missouri, Genl. Frémont ordered Stevenson, whose Regiment was at Rolla, to march to his assistance. Stevenson failed to do as he was ordered and was severely reprimanded, after the death and defeat of that brave officer at Wilson's Creek near Springfield.[2] Subsequently he was in command of the garrison at Decatur, Ala, when Sherman was marching on Atlanta. Genl Sherman told me he was compelled to relieve him from the command because of his excessive nervousness & timidity.[3] I have known Stevenson a great while and I do not think he possesses a high qualification for such an appointment.

If you should decide to withhold his nomination I would suggest the name of Genl. P. J. Osterhaus Genl. Giles A. Smith, Colonel Jo Fullerton[4] as suitable persons to receive the appointment. I am sure that Genl. Grant who knows all of these officers would not hesitate to give either of them the preference over Stevenson.[5]

Frank P. Blair

ALS, DLC-JP.
1. See Joseph S. Fullerton to Johnson, Oct. 23, 1866.

2. The battle was fought August 10, 1861.

3. Stevenson resigned from the Decatur, Alabama, post on April 22, 1864, but was reappointed brigadier general in August 1864 and stationed in West Virginia. Warner, *Blue*.

4. Originally an Ohio and Illinois businessman, Smith (1829–1876) joined the 8th Mo. Inf. as captain in June 1861. He participated in many battles in the western theater, became brigadier general of volunteers to rank from August 4, 1863, was seriously wounded at Missionary Ridge, and led a division in Sherman's "March to the Sea." Mustered out in 1866, he served as second assistant postmaster general during a part of Grant's administration (1869–72). Joseph Fullerton had begun his Civil War service as first lieutenant of the 2nd Mo. Inf. Hunt and Brown, *Brigadier Generals*; Warner, *Blue*.

5. Stevenson retained his position as colonel. After his discharge from the army on December 31, 1870, he resumed his law practice in St. Louis. Warner, *Blue*.

Message to Congress

WASHINGTON, *December 3, 1866.*

Fellow-citizens of the Senate and House of Representatives:

After a brief interval the Congress of the United States resumes its annual legislative labors. An all-wise and merciful Providence has abated the pestilence which visited our shores, leaving its calamitous traces upon some portions of our country. Peace, order, tranquillity, and civil authority have been formally declared to exist throughout the whole of the United States. In all of the States civil authority has superseded the coercion of arms, and the people, by their voluntary action, are maintaining their governments in full activity and complete operation. The enforcement of the laws is no longer "obstructed in any State by combinations too powerful to be suppressed by the ordinary course of judicial proceedings;"[1] and the animosities engendered by the war are rapidly yielding to the beneficent influences of our free institutions, and to the kindly effects of unrestricted social and commercial intercourse. An entire restoration of fraternal feeling must be the earnest wish of every patriotic heart; and we will have accomplished our grandest national achievement when, forgetting the sad events of the past, and remembering only their instructive lessons, we resume our onward career as a free, prosperous, and united people.

In my message of the 4th of December, 1865,[2] Congress was informed of the measures which had been instituted by the Executive with a view to the gradual restoration of the States in which the insurrection occurred to their relations with the General Government. Provisional Governors had been appointed, Conventions called, Governors elected, Legislatures assembled, and Senators and Representatives chosen to the Congress of the United States. Courts had been opened for the enforcement of laws long in abeyance. The blockade had been removed, customhouses re-established, and the internal revenue laws put in force, in order that the people might contribute to the national income. Postal operations had been renewed, and efforts were being made to restore them to their former condition of efficiency. The States themselves had been asked to take part in the high function of amending the Constitution, and of thus sanctioning the extinction of African slavery as one of the legitimate results of our internecine struggle.

Having progressed thus far, the Executive Department found that it had accomplished nearly all that was within the scope of its constitutional authority. One thing, however, yet remained to be done before the work of restoration could be completed, and that was the admission to Congress of loyal Senators and Representatives from the States whose people had rebelled against the lawful authority of the General Government. This question devolved upon the respective Houses, which, by the Constitution, are made the judges of the elections, returns, and qualifications of their own members; and its consideration at once engaged the attention of Congress.

In the meantime, the Executive Department—no other plan having been proposed by Congress—continued its efforts to perfect, as far as was practicable, the restoration of the proper relations between the citizens of the respective States, the States, and the Federal Government, extending, from time to time, as the public interests seemed to require, the judicial, revenue, and postal systems of the country. With the advice and consent of the Senate, the necessary officers were appointed, and appropriations made by Congress for the payment of their salaries. The proposition to amend the Federal Constitution, so as to prevent the existence of slavery within the United States or any place subject to their jurisdiction, was ratified by the requisite number of States; and on the 18th day of December, 1865, it was officially declared to have become valid as a part of the Constitution of the United States. All of the States in which the insurrection had existed promptly amended their Constitutions, so as to make them conform to the great change thus effected in the organic law of the land; declared null and void all ordinances and laws of secession; repudiated all pretended debts and obligations created for the revolutionary purposes of the insurrection; and proceeded, in good faith, to the enactment of measures for the protection and amelioration of the condition of the colored race. Congress, however, yet hesitated to admit any of these States to representation; and it was not until towards the close of the eighth month of the session that an exception was made in favor of Tennessee, by the admission of her Senators and Representatives.

I deem it a subject of profound regret that Congress has thus far failed to admit to seats loyal Senators and Representatives from the other States, whose inhabitants, with those of Tennessee, had engaged in the rebellion. Ten States—more than one-fourth of the whole number—remain without representation; the seats of fifty members in the House of Representatives and of twenty members in the Senate are yet vacant—not by their own consent, not by a failure of election, but by the refusal of Congress to accept their credentials. Their admission, it is believed, would have accomplished much towards the renewal and strengthening of our relations as one people, and removed serious cause for discontent on the part of the inhabitants of those States. It would have accorded with the great principle enunciated in the Declaration of American Independence, that no people ought to bear the burden of taxation, and yet be denied the right of representation. It would have been in consonance with the express provisions of the Constitution, that "each State shall have at least one Representative," and "that no State, without its consent, shall be deprived of its equal suffrage in the Senate." These provisions were intended to secure to every State, and to the people of every State, the right of representation in each House of Congress; and so important was it deemed by the framers of the Constitution that the equality of the States in the Senate should be preserved, that not even by an amendment of the Constitution can any State, without its consent, be denied a voice in that branch of the National Legislature.

It is true, it has been assumed that the existence of the States was terminated by the rebellious acts of their inhabitants, and that the insurrection having been suppressed, they were thenceforward to be considered merely as conquered territories. The Legislative, Executive, and Judicial Departments of the Government have, however, with great distinctness and uniform consistency, refused to sanction an assumption so incompatible with the nature of our republican system, and with the professed objects of the war. Throughout the recent legislation of Congress, the undeniable fact makes itself apparent, that these ten political communities are nothing less than States of this Union. At the very commencement of the rebellion, each House declared, with a unanimity as remarkable as it was significant, that the war was not "waged, upon our part, in any spirit of oppression, nor for any purpose of conquest or subjugation, nor purpose of overthrowing or interfering with the rights or established institutions of those States, but to defend and maintain the supremacy of the Constitution and all laws made in pursuance thereof, and to preserve the Union with all the dignity, equality, and rights of the Several States unimpaired; and that as soon as these objects" were "accomplished the war ought to cease."[3] In some instances, Senators were permitted to continue their legislative functions, while in other instances Representatives were elected and admitted to seats after their States had formally declared their right to withdraw from the Union, and were endeavoring to maintain that right by force of arms. All of the States whose people were in insurrection, as States, were included in the apportionment of the direct tax of twenty millions of dollars annually laid upon the United States by the act approved 5th August, 1861. Congress, by the act of March 4, 1862, and by the apportionment of representation thereunder, also recognized their presence as States in the Union; and they have, for judicial purposes, been divided into districts, as States alone can be divided. The same recognition appears in the recent legislation in reference to Tennessee, which evidently rests upon the fact that the functions of the State were not destroyed by the rebellion, but merely suspended; and that principle is of course applicable to those States which, like Tennessee, attempted to renounce their places in the Union.

The action of the Executive Department of the Government upon this subject has been equally definite and uniform, and the purpose of the war was specifically stated in the Proclamation issued by my predecessor on the 22d day of September, 1862. It was then solemnly proclaimed and declared that "hereafter, as heretofore, the war will be prosecuted for the object of practically restoring the constitutional relation between the United States and each of the States and the people thereof, in which States that relation is or may be suspended or disturbed."[4]

The recognition of the States by the Judicial Department of the Government has also been clear and conclusive in all proceedings affecting them as States, had in the Supreme, Circuit, and District Courts.

In the admission of Senators and Representatives from any and all of the States, there can be no just ground of apprehension that persons who are disloyal will be clothed with the powers of legislation; for this could not happen when the Constitution and the laws are enforced by a vigilant and faithful Congress. Each House is made the "judge of the elections, returns, and qualifications of its own members," and may, "with the concurrence of two-thirds, expel a member." When a Senator or Representative presents his certificate of election, he may at once be admitted or rejected; or, should there be any question as to his eligibility, his credentials may be referred for investigation to the appropriate committee. If admitted to a seat, it must be upon evidence satisfactory to the House of which he thus becomes a member, that he possesses the requisite constitutional and legal qualifications. If refused admission as a member for want of due allegiance to the Government, and returned to his constituents, they are admonished that none but persons loyal to the United States will be allowed a voice in the Legislative Councils of the Nation, and the political power and moral influence of Congress are thus effectively exerted in the interest of loyalty to the Government and fidelity to the Union. Upon this question, so vitally affecting the restoration of the Union and the permanency of our present form of government, my convictions, heretofore expressed, have undergone no change; but, on the contrary, their correctness has been confirmed by reflection and time. If the admission of loyal members to seats in the respective Houses of Congress was wise and expedient a year ago, it is no less wise and expedient now. If this anomalous condition is right now—if, in the exact condition of these States at the present time, it is lawful to exclude them from representation, I do not see that the question will be changed by the efflux of time. Ten years hence, if these States remain as they are, the right of representation will be no stronger—the right of exclusion will be no weaker.

The Constitution of the United States makes it the duty of the President to recommend to the consideration of Congress "such measures as he shall judge necessary or expedient." I know of no measure more imperatively demanded by every consideration of national interest, sound policy, and equal justice, than the admission of loyal members from the now unrepresented States. This would consummate the work of restoration, and exert a most salutary influence in the re-establishment of peace, harmony, and fraternal feeling. It would tend greatly to renew the confidence of the American people in the vigor and stability of their institutions. It would bind us more closely together as a nation, and enable us to show to the world the inherent and recuperative power of a Government founded upon the will of the people, and established upon the principles of liberty, justice, and intelligence. Our increased strength and enhanced prosperity would irrefragably demonstrate the fallacy of the arguments against free institutions drawn from our recent national disorders by the enemies of republican government. The admission of loyal members from the States now excluded from Congress, by allaying doubt and apprehension, would turn capital, now awaiting an opportunity for investment, into the channels of trade and industry. It would alleviate the present troubled condition of those States, and, by inducing emigration, aid in the settlement of fertile regions now uncultivated, and lead to an increased production of those staples which have added so greatly to the wealth of the nation and the commerce of the world. New fields of enterprise would be opened to our progressive people, and soon the devastations of war would be repaired, and all traces of our domestic differences effaced from the minds of our countrymen.

In our efforts to preserve "the unity of Government which constitutes us one people," by restoring the States to the condition which they held prior to the rebellion, we should be cautious, lest, having rescued our nation from perils of threatened disintegration, we resort to consolidation, and in the end absolute despotism, as a remedy for the recurrence of similar troubles. The war having terminated, and with it all occasion for the exercise of powers of doubtful constitutionality, we should hasten to bring legislation within the boundaries prescribed by the Constitution, and to return to the ancient landmarks established by our fathers for the guidance of succeeding generations. "The Constitution which at any time exists, until changed by an explicit and authentic act of the whole people, is sacredly obligatory upon all." "If, in the opinion of the people, the distribution or modification of the constitutional powers be, in any particular, wrong, let it be corrected by an amendment in the way in which the Constitution designates. But let there be no change by usurpation; for" "it is the customary weapon by which free Governments are destroyed."[5] WASHINGTON spoke these words to his countrymen, when, followed by their love and gratitude, he voluntarily retired from the cares of public life. "To keep in all things within the pale of our constitutional powers, and cherish the Federal Union as the only rock of safety," were prescribed by JEFFERSON as rules of action to endear to his "countrymen the true principles of their Constitution, and promote a union of sentiment and action equally auspicious to their happiness and safety."[6] JACKSON held that the action of the General Government should always be strictly confined to the sphere of its appropriate duties, and justly and forcibly urged that our Government is not to be maintained nor our Union preserved "by invasions of the rights and powers of the several States. In thus attempting to make our General Government strong, we make it weak. Its true strength consists in leaving individuals and States as much as possible to themselves; in making itself felt, not in its power, but in its beneficence; not in its control, but in its protection; not in binding the States more closely to the centre, but leaving each to move unobstructed in its proper constitutional orbit."[7] These are the teachings of men whose deeds and services have made them illustrious, and who, long since withdrawn from the scenes of life, have left to their country the rich legacy of their example, their wisdom, and their patriotism. Drawing fresh inspiration from their lessons, let us emulate them in love of country and respect for the Constitution and the laws.

The report of the Secretary of the Treasury affords much information respecting the revenue and commerce of the country. His views upon the currency, and with reference to a proper adjustment of our revenue system, internal as well as impost, are commended to the careful consideration of Congress. In my last annual message I expressed my general views upon these subjects. I need now only call attention to the necessity of carrying into every department of the Government a system of rigid accountability, thorough retrenchment, and wise economy. With no exceptional nor unusual expenditures, the oppressive burdens of taxation can be lessened by such a modification of our revenue laws as will be consistent with the public faith, and the legitimate and necessary wants of the Government.

The report presents a much more satisfactory condition of our finances than one year ago the most sanguine could have anticipated. During the fiscal year ending the 30th June, 1865, the last year of the war, the public debt was increased $941,902,537, and on the 31st of October, 1865, it amounted to $2,740,854,750. On the 31st day of October, 1866, it had been reduced to $2,551,310,006, the diminution, during a period of fourteen months, commencing September 1, 1865, and ending October 31, 1866, having been $206,379,565. In the last annual report of the state of the finances, it was estimated that during the three quarters of the fiscal year ending the 30th of June last, the debt would be increased $112,194,947. During that period, however, it was reduced $31,196,387, the receipts of the year having been $89,905,905 more, and the expenditures $200,529,235 less than the estimates. Nothing could more clearly indicate than these statements the extent and availability of the national resources, and the rapidity and safety with which, under our form of government, great military and naval establishments can be disbanded, and expenses reduced from a war to a peace footing.

During the fiscal year ending the 30th of June, 1866, the receipts were $558,032,620, and the expenditures $520,750,940, leaving an available surplus of $37,281,680. It is estimated that the receipts for the fiscal year ending the 30th June, 1867, will be $475,061,386, and that the expenditures will reach the sum of $316,428,078, leaving in the Treasury a surplus of $158,633,308. For the fiscal year ending June 30, 1868, it is estimated that the receipts will amount to $436,000,000, and that the expenditures will be $350,247,641—showing an excess of $85,752,359 in favor of the Government. These estimated receipts may be diminished by a reduction of excise and import duties; but after all necessary reductions shall have been made, the revenue of the present and of following years will doubtless be sufficient to cover all legitimate charges upon the Treasury, and leave a large annual surplus to be applied to the payment of the principal of the debt. There seems now to be no good reason why taxes may not be reduced as the country advances in population and wealth, and yet the debt be extinguished within the next quarter of a century.

The report of the Secretary of War furnishes valuable and important information in reference to the operations of his Department during the past year. Few volunteers now remain in the service, and they are being discharged as rapidly as they can be replaced by regular troops. The army has been promptly paid, carefully provided with medical treatment, well sheltered and subsisted, and is to be furnished with breech-loading small arms. The military strength of the nation has been unimpaired by the discharge of volunteers, the disposition of unserviceable or perishable stores, and the retrenchment of expenditure. Sufficient war material to meet any emergency has been retained, and, from the disbanded volunteers standing ready to respond to the national call, large armies can be rapidly organized, equipped, and concentrated. Fortifications on the coast and frontier have received, or are being prepared for more powerful armaments; lake surveys and harbor and river improvements are in course of energetic prosecution. Preparations have been made for the payment of the additional bounties authorized during the recent session of Congress, under such regulations as will protect the Government from fraud, and secure to the honorably-discharged soldier the well-earned reward of his faithfulness and gallantry. More than six thousand maimed soldiers have received artificial limbs or other surgical apparatus; and forty-one national cemeteries, containing the remains of 104,526 Union soldiers, have already been established. The total estimate of military appropriations is $25,205,669.

It is stated in the report of the Secretary of the Navy that the naval force at this time consists of two hundred and seventy-eight vessels, armed with two thousand three hundred and fifty-one guns. Of these, one hundred and fifteen vessels, carrying one thousand and twenty-nine guns, are in commission, distributed chiefly among seven squadrons. The number of men in the service is thirteen thousand six hundred. Great activity and vigilance have been displayed by all the squadrons, and their movements have been judiciously and efficiently arranged in such manner as would best promote American commerce, and protect the rights and interests of our countrymen abroad. The vessels unemployed are undergoing repairs, or are laid up until their services may be required. Most of the iron-clad fleet is at League Island, in the vicinity of Philadelphia, a place which, until decisive action should be taken by Congress, was selected by the Secretary of the Navy as the most eligible location for that class of vessels. It is important that a suitable public station should be provided for the iron-clad fleet. It is intended that these vessels shall be in proper condition for any emergency, and it is desirable that the bill accepting League Island for naval purposes, which passed the House of Representatives at its last session, should receive final action at an early period, in order that there may be a suitable public station for this class of vessels, as well as a navy-yard of area sufficient for the wants of the service, on the Delaware river.[8] The Naval Pension fund amounts to $11,750,000, having been increased $2,750,000 during the year. The expenditures of the Department for the fiscal year ending 30th June last were $43,324,526, and the estimates for the coming year amount to $23,568,436. Attention is invited to the condition of our seamen, and the importance of legislative measures for their relief and improvement. The suggestions in behalf of this deserving class of our fellow-citizens are earnestly recommended to the favorable attention of Congress.

The report of the Postmaster General presents a most satisfactory condition of the postal service, and submits recommendations which deserve the consideration of Congress. The revenues of the Department for the year ending June 30, 1866, were $14,386,986, and the expenditures $15,352,079, showing an excess of the latter of $965,093. In anticipation of this deficiency, however, a special appropriation was made by Congress in the act approved July 28, 1866. Including the standing appropriation of $700,000 for free mail matter, as a legitimate portion of the revenues yet remaining unexpended, the actual deficiency for the pay year is only $265,093—a sum within $51,141 of the amount estimated in the annual report of 1864. The decrease of revenue compared with the previous year was one and one-fifth per cent., and the increase of expenditures, owing principally to the enlargement of the mail service in the South, was twelve per cent. On the 30th of June last there were in operation six thousand nine hundred and thirty mail routes, with an aggregate length of one hundred and eighty thousand nine hundred and twenty-one miles, an aggregate annual transportation of seventy-one million eight hundred and thirty-seven thousand nine hundred and fourteen miles, and an aggregate annual cost, including all expenditures, of $8,410,184. The length of railroad routes is thirty-two thousand and ninety-two miles, and the annual transportation thirty million six hundred and nine thousand four hundred and sixty-seven miles. The length of steamboat routes is fourteen thousand three hundred and forty-six miles, and the annual transportation three million four hundred and eleven thousand nine hundred and sixty-two miles. The mail service is rapidly increasing throughout the whole country, and its steady extension in the Southern States indicates their constantly improving condition. The growing importance of the foreign service also merits attention. The Post Office Department of Great Britain and our own have agreed upon a preliminary basis for a new Postal Convention, which it is believed will prove eminently beneficial to the commercial interests of the United States, inasmuch as it contemplates a reduction of the international letter postage to one-half the existing rates; a reduction of postage with all other countries to and from which correspondence is transmitted in the British mail, or in closed mails through the United Kingdom; the establishment of uniform and reasonable charges for the sea and territorial transit of correspondence in closed mails; and an allowance to each Post Office Department of the right to use all mail communications established under the authority of the other for the dispatch of correspondence, either in open or closed mails, on the same terms as those applicable to the inhabitants of the country providing the means of transmission.

The report of the Secretary of the Interior exhibits the condition of those branches of the public service which are committed to his supervision. During the last fiscal year, four million six hundred and twenty-nine thousand three hundred and twelve acres of public land were disposed of, one million eight hundred and ninety-two thousand five hundred and sixteen acres of which were entered under the homestead act. The policy originally adopted relative to the public lands has undergone essential modifications. Immediate revenue, and not their rapid settlement, was the cardinal feature of our land system. Long experience and earnest discussion have resulted in the conviction that the early development of our agricultural resources, and the diffusion of an energetic population over our vast territory, are objects of far greater importance to the national growth and prosperity than the proceeds of the sale of the land to the highest bidder in open market. The pre-emption laws confer upon the pioneer who complies with the terms they impose the privilege of purchasing a limited portion of "unoffered lands" at the minimum price. The homestead enactments relieve the settler from the payment of purchase money, and secure him a permanent home, upon the condition of residence for a term of years. This liberal policy invites emigration from the old, and from the more crowded portions of the new world. Its propitious results are undoubted, and will be more signally manifested when time shall have given to it a wider development.

Congress has made liberal grants of public land to corporations, in aid of the construction of railroads and other internal improvements. Should this policy hereafter prevail, more stringent provisions will be required to secure a faithful application of the fund. The title to the lands should not pass, by patent or otherwise, but remain in the Government and subject to its control until some portion of the road has been actually built. Portions of them might then, from time to time, be conveyed to the corporation, but never in a greater ratio to the whole quantity embraced by the grant than the completed parts bear to the entire length of the projected improvement. This restriction would not operate to the prejudice of any undertaking conceived in good faith and executed with reasonable energy, as it is the settled practice to withdraw from market the lands falling within the operation of such grants, and thus to exclude the inception of a subsequent adverse right. A breach of the conditions which Congress may deem proper to impose should work a forfeiture of claim to the lands so withdrawn but unconveyed, and of title to the lands conveyed which remain unsold.

Operations on the several lines of the Pacific Railroad have been prosecuted with unexampled vigor and success. Should no unforeseen causes of delay occur, it is confidently anticipated that this great thoroughfare will be. completed before the expiration of the period designated by Congress.

During the last fiscal year the amount paid to pensioners, including the expenses of disbursement, was thirteen million four hundred and fifty-nine thousand nine hundred and ninety-six dollars; and fifty thousand one hundred and seventy-seven names were added to the pension rolls. The entire number of pensioners, June 30, 1866, was one hundred and twenty-six thousand seven hundred and twenty-two. This fact furnishes melancholy and striking proof of the sacrifices made to vindicate the constitutional authority of the Federal Government, and to maintain inviolate the integrity of the Union. They impose upon us corresponding obligations. It is estimated that thirty-three million dollars will be required to meet the exigencies of this branch of the service during the next fiscal year.

Treaties have been concluded with the Indians who, enticed into armed opposition to our Government at the outbreak of the rebellion, have unconditionally submitted to our authority, and manifested an earnest desire for a renewal of friendly relations.

During the year ending September 30, 1866, eight thousand seven hundred and sixteen patents for useful inventions and designs were issued, and at that date the balance in the Treasury to the credit of the Patent fund was two hundred and twenty-eight thousand two hundred and ninety-seven dollars.

As a subject upon which depends an immense amount of the production and commerce of the country, I recommend to Congress such legislation as may be necessary for the preservation of the levees of the Mississippi river. It is a matter of national importance that early steps should be taken not only to add to the efficiency of these barriers against destructive inundations, but for the removal of all obstructions to the free and safe navigation of that great channel of trade and commerce.

The District of Columbia, under existing laws, is not entitled to that representation in the National Councils which, from our earliest history, has been uniformly accorded to each Territory established from time to time within our limits. It maintains peculiar relations to Congress, to whom the Constitution has granted the power of exercising exclusive legislation over the seat of government. Our fellow-citizens residing in the District, whose interests are thus confided to the special guardianship of Congress, exceed in number the population of several of our Territories, and no just reason is perceived why a delegate of their choice should not be admitted to a seat in the House of Representatives. No mode seems so appropriate and effectual of enabling them to make known their peculiar condition and wants, and of securing the local legislation adapted to them. I therefore recommend the passage of a law authorizing the electors of the District of Columbia to choose a delegate, to be allowed the same rights and privileges as a delegate representing a Territory.[9] The increasing enterprise and rapid progress of improvement in the District are highly gratifying, and I trust that the efforts of the municipal authorities to promote the prosperity of the national metropolis will receive the efficient and generous co-operation of Congress.

The report of the Commissioner of Agriculture[10] reviews the operations of his Department during the past year, and asks the aid of Congress in its efforts to encourage those States which, scourged by war, are now earnestly engaged in the reorganization of domestic industry.

It is a subject of congratulation that no foreign combinations against our domestic peace and safety, or our legitimate influence among the nations, have been formed or attempted. While sentiments of reconciliation, loyalty, and patriotism have increased at home, a more just consideration of our national character and rights has been manifested by foreign nations.

The entire success of the Atlantic Telegraph between the coast of Ireland and the Province of Newfoundland, is an achievement which has been justly celebrated in both hemispheres as the opening of an era in the progress of civilization. There is reason to expect that equal success will attend, and even great results follow, the enterprise for connecting the two Continents through the Pacific Ocean by the projected line of telegraph between Kamschatka and the Russian possessions in America.

The resolution of Congress protesting against pardons by foreign Government of persons convicted of infamous offences, on condition of emigration to our country,[11] has been communicated to the States with which we maintain intercourse, and the practice, so justly the subject of complaint on our part, has not been renewed.

The congratulations of Congress to the Emperor of Russia, upon his escape from attempted assassination, have been presented to that humane and enlightened ruler, and received by him with expressions of grateful appreciation.[12]

The Executive, warned of an attempt by Spanish-American adventurers to induce the emigration of freedmen of the United States to a foreign country, protested against the project as one which, if consummated, would reduce them to a bondage even more oppressive than that from which they have just been relieved. Assurance has been received from the Government of the State in which the plan was matured, that the proceeding will meet neither its encouragement nor approval. It is a question worthy of your consideration, whether our laws upon this subject are adequate to the prevention or punishment of the crime thus meditated.

In the month of April last, as Congress is aware, a friendly arrangement was made between the Emperor of France and the President of the United States for the withdrawal from Mexico of the French expeditionary military forces. This withdrawal was to be effected in three detachments, the first of which, it was understood, would leave Mexico in November, now past, the second in March next, and the third and last in November, 1867. Immediately upon the completion of the evacuation, the French Government was to assume the same attitude of nonintervention, in regard to Mexico, as is held by the Government of the United States. Repeated assurances have been given by the Emperor, since that agreement, that he would complete the promised evacuation within the period mentioned, or sooner.

It was reasonably expected that the proceedings thus contemplated would produce a crisis of great political interest in the Republic of Mexico. The newly-appointed Minister of the United States, Mr. Campbell, was therefore sent forward, on the 9th day of November last, to assume his proper functions as Minister Plenipotentiary of the United States to that Republic. It was also thought expedient that he should be attended in the vicinity of Mexico by the Lieutenant General of the Army of the United States,[13] with the view of obtaining such information as might be important to determine the course to be pursued by the United States in re-establishing and maintaining necessary and proper intercourse with the Republic of Mexico. Deeply interested in the cause of liberty and humanity, it seemed an obvious duty on our part to exercise whatever influence we possessed for the restoration and permanent establishment in that country of a domestic and republican form of government.

Such was the condition of affairs in regard to Mexico, when, on the 22d of November last, official information was received from Paris that the Emperor of France had some time before decided not to withdraw a detachment of his forces in the month of November past, according to engagement, but that this decision was made with the purpose of withdrawing the whole of those forces in the ensuing spring. Of this determination, however, the United States had not received any notice or intimation; and, so soon as the information was received by the Government, care was taken to make known its dissent to the Emperor of France.

I cannot forego the hope that France will reconsider the subject, and adopt some resolution in regard to the evacuation of Mexico which will conform as nearly as practicable with the existing engagement, and thus meet the just expectations of the United States. The papers relating to the subject will be laid before you. It is believed that, with the evacuation of Mexico by the expeditionary forces, no subject for serious differences between France and the United States would remain. The expressions of the Emperor and people of France warrant a hope that the traditionary friendship between the two countries might in that case be renewed and permanently restored.

A claim of a citizen of the United States for indemnity for spoliations committed on the high seas by the French authorities, in the exercise of a belligerent power against Mexico, has been met by the Government of France with a proposition to defer settlement until a mutual convention for the adjustment of all claims of citizens and subjects of both countries, arising out of the recent wars on this Continent, shall be agreed upon by the two countries. The suggestion is not deemed unreasonable, but it belongs to Congress to direct the manner in which claims for indemnity by foreigners, as well as by citizens of the United States, arising out of the late civil war, shall be adjudicated and determined. I have no doubt that the subject of all such claims will engage your attention at a convenient and proper time.

It is a matter of regret that no considerable advance has been made towards an adjustment of the differences between the United States and Great Britain, arising out of the depredations upon our national commerce and other trespasses committed during our civil war by British subjects, in violation of international law and treaty obligations. The delay, however, may be believed to have resulted in no small degree from the domestic situation of Great Britain. An entire change of ministry occurred in that country during the last session of Parliament. The attention of the new ministry was called to the subject at an early day, and there is some reason to expect that it will now be considered in a becoming and friendly spirit. The importance of an early disposition of the question cannot be exaggerated. Whatever might be the wishes of the two Governments, it is manifest that good-will and friendship between the two countries cannot be established until a reciprocity, in the practice of good-faith and neutrality, shall be restored between the respective nations.

On the 6th of June last, in violation of our neutrality laws, a military expedition and enterprise against the British North American Colonies was projected and attempted to be carried on within the territory and jurisdiction of the United States. In obedience to the obligation imposed upon the Executive by the Constitution, to see that the laws are faithfully executed, all citizens were warned, by proclamation,[14] against taking part in or aiding such unlawful proceedings, and the proper civil, military, and naval officers were directed to take all necessary measures for the enforcement of the laws. The expedition failed, but it has not been without its painful consequences. Some of our citizens who, it was alleged, were engaged in the expedition, were captured, and have been brought to trial, as for a capital offence, in the Province of Canada. Judgment and sentence of death have been pronounced against some, while others have been acquitted. Fully believing in the maxim of government, that severity of civil punishment for misguided persons who have engaged in revolutionary attempts which have disastrously failed, is unsound and unwise, such representations have been made to the British Government, in behalf of the convicted persons, as, being sustained by an enlightened and humane judgment, will, it is hoped, induce in their cases an exercise of clemency, and a judicious amnesty to all who were engage in the movement. Counsel has been employed by the Government to defend citizens of the United States on trial for capital offences in Canada; and a discontinuance of the prosecutions which were instituted in the courts of the United States against those who took part in the expedition, has been directed.

I have regarded the expedition as not only political in its nature, but as also in a great measure foreign from the United States in its causes, character, and objects. The attempt was understood to be made in sympathy with an insurgent party in Ireland, and, by striking at a British Province on this Continent, was designed to aid in obtaining redress for political grievances which, it was assumed, the people of Ireland had suffered at the hands of the British Government during a period of several centuries. The persons engaged in it were chiefly natives of that country, some of whom had, while others had not, become citizens of the United States under our general laws of naturalization. Complaints of misgovernment in Ireland continually engage the attention of the British nation, and so great an agitation is now prevailing in Ireland that the British Government have deemed it necessary to suspend the writ of *habeas corpus* in that country. These circumstances must necessarily modify the opinion which we might otherwise have entertained in regard to an expedition expressly prohibited by our neutrality laws. So long as those laws remain upon our statute-books, they should be faithfully executed, and if they operate harshly, unjustly, or oppressively, Congress alone can apply the remedy, by their modification or repeal.

Political and commercial interests of the United States are not unlikely to be affected in some degree by events which are transpiring in the eastern regions of Europe, and the time seems to have come when our Government ought to have a proper diplomatic representation in Greece.

This Government has claimed for all persons not convicted, or accused, or suspected of crime, an absolute political right of self-expatriation, and a choice of new national allegiance. Most of the European States have dissented from this principle, and have claimed a right to hold such of their subjects as have immigrated to and been naturalized in the United States, and afterwards returned on transient visits to their native countries, to the performance of military service in like manner as resident subjects. Complaints arising from the claim in this respect made by foreign States, have heretofore been matters of controversy between the United States and some of the European Powers, and the irritation consequent upon the failure to settle this question increased during the war in which Prussia, Italy, and Austria were recently engaged. While Great Britain has never acknowledged the right of expatriation, she has not for some years past practically insisted upon the opposite doctrine. France has been equally forbearing; and Prussia has proposed a compromise, which, although evincing increased liberality, has not been accepted by the United States. Peace is now prevailing everywhere in Europe, and the present seems to be a favorable time for an assertion by Congress of the principle, so long maintained by the Executive Department, that naturalization by one State fully exempts the native-born subject of any other State from the performance of military service under any foreign Government, so long as he does not voluntarily renounce its rights and benefits.

In the performance of a duty imposed upon me by the Constitution, I have thus submitted to the Representatives of the States and of the People such information of our domestic and foreign affairs as the public interests seem to require. Our Government is now undergoing its most trying ordeal, and my earnest prayer is, that the peril may be successfully and finally passed, without impairing its original strength and symmetry. The interests of the nation are best to be promoted by the revival of fraternal relations, the complete obliteration of our past differences, and the reinauguration of all the pursuits of peace. Directing our efforts to the early accomplishment of these great ends, let us endeavor to preserve harmony between the co-ordinate Departments of the Government, that each in its proper sphere may cordially co-operate with the other in securing the maintenance of the Constitution, the preservation of the Union, and the perpetuity of our free institutions.[15]

ANDREW JOHNSON.

PD, Johnson-Bartlett Col., Greeneville.

1. From Lincoln's proclamation of April 15, 1861, calling out the militia. Richardson, *Messages*, 6: 13–14.
2. See Message to Congress, Dec. 4, 1865, *Johnson Papers*, 9: 466–85.

3. For the Senate and House resolutions, see the *Congressional Globe*, 37 Cong., 1 Sess., pp. 222, 257.

4. Richardson, *Messages*, 6: 96–98.

5. From George Washington's Farewell Address, September 17, 1796. Ibid., 1: 209, 212.

6. From Thomas Jefferson's Second Annual Message, December 15, 1802. Ibid., 1: 346.

7. From Andrew Jackson's Veto Message concerning the Bank of the United States, July 10, 1832. Ibid., 2: 1153.

8. On February 8, 1867, Congress passed the bill approving the acquisition of League Island. *Congressional Globe*, 39 Cong., 1 Sess., pp. 3026, 3277; 39 Cong., 2 Sess., pp. 27–1360 passim; *U.S. Statutes at Large*, 14: 396.

9. Section 34 of "An Act to provide a Government for the District of Columbia," passed in 1871, provided the District a delegate to the U.S. House with the same privileges as those of territories. Ibid., 16: 426.

10. Isaac Newton.

11. Johnson signed the resolution on April 17, 1866. For discussion of congressional action, see *Congressional Globe*, 39 Cong., 1 Sess., pp. 1407, 1492–94, 1928, 2052.

12. Alexander II (1818–1881) was the Russian emperor from 1855 until his assassination. For the resolution and reply, see ibid., 39 Cong., 2 Sess., pp. 2384, 2443–44, 2546, 2562; *Senate Ex. Docs.*, 39 Cong., 2 Sess., No. 1, pp. 1–2 (Ser. 1276).

13. William T. Sherman.

14. See his June 6, 1866, proclamation in Richardson, *Messages*, 6: 433.

15. Evidently Secretary Seward assisted Johnson with the preparation of this second annual message. Van Deusen, *Seward*, 469.

From Michael J. Heffernan[1]

11 Cumberland Street,
Brooklyn, N.Y., Decr. 4th, 1866.

Sir,

It pains me, an humble soldier of the Union, to trouble you with a trivial matter at a time when weighty affairs demand your almost exclusive attention; but the fact that no other course is open to me, and the hope that this note may possibly overtake you in a leisure moment, embolden me thus to tresspass on your precious time.

Being out of employment last June, I applied to the Collector, Port of New York,[2] for a situation in his department. My only recommendation for the position was an honorable discharge from the army. Three months afterwards I was appointed an Inspector of Customs.

In the meantime, I had secured employment as Associate Editor of the New York "*Irish People*." Believing, however, that the position offered me by the Collector—considering the nonpartisan grounds on which it was sought—was likely to be more permanent, as it was assuredly less laborious, I resigned my situation on the newspaper and entered upon my duties as a Customs officer.

From this latter position I was removed on the 27th ult.—having occupied it exactly two months—and am now, through strange conduct on the part of somebody, without the means of support. Having never identified myself with any political party, nor sought the interference in my behalf of those who did, I looked upon my appointment by Collector

Smythe simply as a reward for my having served honorably in the war for the Union.

I endeavoured to ascertain the cause of my removal; but no explanation was given me. I have reason, however, to attribute it to the fact of my having, to the best of my ability, defended your Administration against the attacks of certain Irish politicians. The journal I was connected with was "strictly neutral" in American politics. I, nevertheless, took several opportunities of rebutting the charge, persistently made, that the Executive of this nation was hostile to any movement for Irish regeneration. I take the liberty of enclosing some of my articles on this subject clipped from the "*Irish People*" newspaper.[3] They are insignificant in themselves; but I have reason to know that they saved at least twenty thousand Fenian votes from being carried over, by specious slanders, to your political opponents. I have not made this voluntary defence of your course the ground of any claim on the consideration of your supporters. It is clear to me, however, that it either caused my appointment to, or my removal from the little office which I held. If the former, it injured me by inducing me to abandon my employment on the "Irish People": if the latter, the injury it has done me is sufficiently evident.

I do not now advance my services as a claim to preferment: I merely entreat that you will not permit my humble, though well-meant, efforts to defend you from unjust attack, to be even the remote cause of leaving my family unprovided for.[4]

                                                        M. J. Heffernan.

ALS, DNA-RG56, Appts., Customs Service, Subofficer, New York, M. J. Heffernan.
    1. Irish-born Heffernan (*c*1840–1885), a poet and former National School teacher, worked as a journalist for several New York newspapers. O'Donoghue, *Poets of Ireland*; New York City directories (1867–85); 1870 Census, N.Y., Kings, Brooklyn, 20th Ward, 44.
    2. Henry A. Smythe.
    3. As many as seven editorials are enclosed.
    4. Heffernan's letter was routinely forwarded to the Treasury Department.

From Chambers McKibbin, Sr.

United States Treasury
Philadelphia   Decr. 4th 1866

Sir:

My attention is drawn by your private Secretary to a letter written you by Joseph Wood,[1] whom I removed from office.

Allow me to respectfully state, that a number of gentlemen of respectability & commanding influence, supporters of your policy for the peace & unity of the Country, urged the change. Representations were made to me, which I could not but regard, "That Mr Wood was covertly opposed to the President & voted the radical ticket." I have known Mr Wood for years, & always as a member of the Opposition, & am certain my predecessor Mr Brown[2] would not have retained him in office, had he not known him to be a radical, as he is one of the prominent Loyal Leaguers.

Mr Wood never intimated to me that he was or had been an advocate of your policy, until after his removal, neither did I hear a whisper from any person to that effect.

His successor in office[3] has all the qualifications required, in a eminent degree. For his character & qualifications I refer you to the Hon Saml. J. Randell.

I have made but two removals since I came into office, one for Drunkenness, & the other Mr Wood. In the case of Mr Wood there is nothing in my judgement peculiar or trying, requiring the traversing of my conduct, respecting him. In his letter he stigmatizes those who contributed to his removal, with the odious Epithet of Copperhead, which assure me he is not in sympathy with the restoration spirit of the President & his policy.

Under the circumstances I believe to notice the complaint of Wood further, might lead to insubordination in case it came to the ears of the Clerks.

Permit me to say that, whilst I continue in office, the President may rest assured I shall reccommend no changes incompatible with the best interests of the Government, your policy, & my own self respect.

I again refer you to the Hon Saml. J. Randell who knows Mr Wood & Mr Kirkpatrick his successor.[4]

                                    Chambers McKibbin   Asst. Treasurer U.S.

ALS, DLC-JP.
    1. Wood, not further identified, had worked as building superintendent and detective. The letter has not been found, but a reference indicates it was received on November 30 and referred the following day to McKibbin by Robert Johnson. Ser. 6A, Vol. D: 284, Johnson Papers, LC.
    2. Nathaniel B. Browne (1819–1875), who had served as postmaster of Philadelphia (1859–61), had been appointed as director of the Philadelphia mint in 1865. He was also a commercial attorney, legislator, temperance advocate, and insurance executive. *The Biographical Encyclopaedia of Pennsylvania of the Nineteenth Century* (Philadelphia, 1874), 355–56; *Evening Bulletin* (Philadelphia), Mar. 13, 1875.
    3. Robert Kirkpatrick (c1815–fl1872), a bookkeeper, was a native of Ireland. *U.S. Off. Reg.* (1867); Philadelphia directories (1867–72); 1870 Census, Pa., Philadelphia, Philadelphia, 13th Dist., 4th Ward, 1.
    4. Wood was not reinstated.

From Patrick V. Moyce[1]

                                    Northampton [Mass.]   4th December 1866
Dear Sir

I wrote to you some eleven months ago[2] on the subject of suppressing the Fenian organization then existing at New York under the leadership of O'Mahony & Roberts.[3]

I regret to say, that your failure to act upon my suggestions at that time, has been in great part the cause of the many calamities entailed upon some of the most deserving of my countrymen who stand convicted of Fenianism in Canada.

I write you now again requesting you to use your influence in behalf of the unfortunate men condemned to death for no proven crime other than the fact, that they are Irishmen, they are citizens of the United States, they are Catholics & one of them is a Catholic priest.

I know well Sir, that if you fail to interpose in their favor so far as to procure their release, it will only be because you sympathize with the orange bigotry that condemned them to the gallows without a fair conviction.

I have always been an earnest opponent of Fenianism since the first moment of its inception—It never did nor never could take root in any part of the mission from which I wrote to you last January—but seeing now, that the issuing of your untimely proclamation,[4] I say untimely because it was too late, has delivered so many into the clutches of the Orange hangman of Toronto. I can not refrain from demanding in their name, as well as in the name of humanity & justice, that you take immediate steps to procure their release.

But should you determine to suffer the foul murderous sentence to be carried out in their case, & that my people determine in their might to resent it, I shall be far from advising them to take any notice of a preventive proclamation at your hands, when they shall have gone forth to stamp out the last vestige of Orange bigotry in upper Canada.

P. V. Moyce

P.S. I have no objection that this letter be published over the name of an Irish Catholic Priest.

ALS, DNA-RG59, Misc. Lets., 1789–1906 (M179, Roll 247).
1. Moyce (c1823–fl1870) was a Catholic priest in Hampshire County, Massachusetts. *Wentworth's Hampden and Hampshire County Business Directory and Register* (1871); 1870 Census, Mass., Hampshire, Northampton, 287.
2. Not found.
3. John O'Mahony and William R. Roberts. O'Mahony (1816–1877), a native of Ireland, was the Fenian leader in the United States. Forced to flee Ireland, he lived in France until 1853 when he went to New York. One of the organizers of the Emmet Monument Association, the foundation of what later became the Fenian movement, O'Mahony and others encouraged James Stephens to start the same type of revolutionary society in Ireland. During the 1860s and 1870s his leadership was seriously opposed not only by his American colleagues but also by Stephens and his organization in Ireland. *DAB*.
4. See Johnson's proclamation of June 6, 1866, warning U.S. citizens against taking aggressive action towards Canada. Richardson, *Messages*, 6: 433.

From Robert M. Patton

Montgomery   Decr 4th 1866

My Dear Sir

In the Month of October last an order, was made by the Agent of the Freedmens Beaureau at Washington with the Concurrence of Secretary Stanton to Continue Supplies to the Destitute and poor of Alabama for

Three Months from that time, And the Sum of Forty thousand Dollars per Month was appropriated for that purpose. We hoped at that time the financial Condition of the State would be So improved by the Month of January as that we Could take Care of the large population of this Class of person without the further Aid of the National Government but in this I have been Mistaken. I Must therefore in addition to what has very Generously been done for the poor and destitute of this State earnestly appeal to the Government, that a Continuance of rations be allowed to the destitute of this State for the Months of January and February which will Not require An appropriation exceeding that heretofore Made per Month. I feel Assured after the first of March the State will be able to Mentain her own poor, and Not longer to appeal to the National Government, for Assistance. Without that further Assistance there Must be Much Suffering among the poor widows and orphans of Alabama without Some Concurrence, or that of the Secretary of War. I very Much fear the Freedmans Beaureau will discontinue Supplies, and leave the poor to Suffer.

It is Generally Supposed the Crop of Corn Made the present Year will Not be entirely inadequate to bread the State until another Crop Can be made. Hoping to hear from You in Reply.

R M Patton   Govr. of Alabama

ALS, DNA-RG105, Asst. Commr., Ala., Unregistered Lets. Recd.

From William H. Carroll
Private & Confidential

Washington, D.C., Dec 5th 1866

Mr. President.

I came here for a certain purpose[1] and also to collect and place before you certain *facts* bearing upon the corruption and frauds of the Treasury Dept.[2] as well as placing before you information in regard to the Radical commissions send to Canada to endeavor to find witnesses to implicate you in the assassination of Mr. Lincoln.[3]

The facts I can obtain and place before you will astound you. The immense frauds practiced in the Treasury without the knowledge or *consent* of the Secretary when exposed will give the Radicals enough to do, for the next month, if you will take hold of the matter and prosecute the affair "*Criminally*" not by congressional committees that do nothing but whitewash &c.

I have just been informed that Judge Patterson had said that if I remained here he would telegraph to Brownlow and have me arrested.[4] I have deemed it prudent to leave befor I had the opportunity of seeing you and placing the *matters* refered to before you.

I am going at 10½ oclock and beg leave to request an answer stating whether such information as I have suggsted would be of use to you or meet your approval and action. If so I will send you an abstract from New York by one of your friends stating particulars and the names of the parties who will testify to the same which you can examine before you act.

All I ask in the Premises is that the Parties I introduce to you as witnesses or otherwise shall be protected and that my name shall in no manner be known in the affair.

Mr. President I am your friend and I can give you a weapon to destroy your enemies. Mr. McCalloch, is not implicated in the frauds and I believe he will Cooperate with you. You shall have all if you desire to act by next Monday and also a suggestion as to the best course to pursue.

In my opinion there is no time to sit idely looking on. The Schemes of the Radicals are Revolutionary, and the developments of these frauds will be like a Bomb shell burst in their Camp.

If you cannot answer this by 10½ o clock, am Please address me under Cover care of Columbus Powell[5] Esq No 38 Broad Street New York.[6]

Wm. H Carroll

ALS, DLC-JP.

1. Carroll's "certain purpose" probably included his desire to receive a pardon. John W. Leftwich to Johnson, Oct. 13, 1866, and H. M. Watterson to Johnson, Nov. 14, 1866, Johnson Papers, LC.

2. There is no evidence indicating what specific treasury corruption and frauds concerned Carroll.

3. Carroll probably refers to the notorious procurer of witnesses, Charles A. Dunham (alias Sanford Conover). One motivation for Carroll's concern about the attempt to implicate Johnson in the Lincoln assassination plot was that he too had apparently been accused of complicity in the conspiracy. Carroll to Johnson, Oct. 25, 1866, Johnson Papers, LC.

4. David T. Patterson and William G. Brownlow. Carroll was still apparently without favor, at least in East Tennessee where he had commanded Confederate forces during the early part of the war and had earned Unionist wrath by trying and executing three accused bridge burners. Although Brownlow believed that Carroll had treated him badly personally, by October 1866 he was amenable to Carroll's returning to his home in Memphis. Carroll to Johnson, Sept. 20, 1865, and W. G. Brownlow to M. F. Pleasants, June 6, 1865, Amnesty Papers (M1003, Roll 48), Tenn., William H. Carroll, RG94, NA; W. G. Brownlow, Oct. 20, 1866, endorsement on F. S. Richards to Brownlow, Oct. 16, 1866, Johnson Papers, LC; Warner, Gray.

5. Powell (fl1869) was briefly a banker and commission merchant in New York City. New York City directories (1867–69); Carroll to Robert Johnson, Dec. 13, 1866, Johnson Papers, LC.

6. A week later Robert Johnson, on behalf of the President, notified Carroll that after his information had been received at the White House, he would be advised about the necessity of a trip to Washington. Carroll answered that the information was "in the hands of a gentleman in Washington." Therefore he would send Col. John Williams to said person with instructions that Williams be given an abstract of the charges. The unnamed "gentleman" could "quietly bring one or two witnesses to see the President if desirable." It is not known whether Johnson took further action on this clandestine matter. Robert Johnson to Carroll, Dec. 12, 1866, and Carroll to Robert Johnson, Dec. 13, 1866, Johnson Papers, LC.

From Jerome B. Chaffee

Washington D.C.   Dec 5th 1866

Sir

We desire to submit some evidences of the resources & increasing wealth & population of Colorado, gathered from Official sources & otherwise, as additional reasons of the propriety of admitting that State into the Union.

First. The table of votes in different elections during the years 1861, 2, 3, 4, & 5, spread before Congress and your Excellency last session to show a decreasing population, is false & obtained by fraud & deception. The true vote on the Constitution at first election under the enabling act was

For Constitution	4,219
Against "	5,006
Majority against its adoption	787 instead of

3,152 as falsely represented.[1]

2nd As evidence of the increasing prosperity of Colorado & her accessions in population during the last year, the following figures, certified to by the Officers having charge of the respective statistics will show.

Tax valuation of 1865	$ 8,836,500.00
Do. " 1866	10,610,800.00
Increas last year.	$ 1,774,300.00

Amount of Land claimed at Land office from

Jany 1st 1865. to Nov 1st 1865.	140,000. acres
Do. 1866 " " 1866.	251,000. "
Increase last ten months	111,000. acres

Amount of exchange drawn by 1st Nat Bk Denver from

May 10th 1865. to Nov 1st 1866.	$11,822,000.00
assessment of Revenue Tax 1866.	$ 141,368.80
No. of buildings erected in Denver last year	250
Cost of same	$ 476,000.00

No. of Furnaces completed for Smelting ore since Nov 1st 1865,

is, 8, & cost of same	$ 180,000.

No. of miles of Mountain Roads built since Nov 1st 1865 is, 58

cost of building	$ 60,000.

No. of miles of large Irrigating Ditches, during the year is,

136, & cost of same	$ 136,000.

The production of Gold has more than doubled during the year.

It is proper to add that there are two other national Banks & 6 or 7 Banking Offices, that do a large business each.

These facts & the fact that a census ordered by the last Territorial Legislature, by which the different Township assessors were instructed to take a Census as they assessed the property in their several districts, & which has only been done in 12 out of 18 counties, & in these generally only such were counted as owned taxable property, said census only hastly taken & imperfectly done showing a population of something over 22000 in the 12 counties—the enumeration being made in February & Mch last will show conclusively that Colorado has a population of not less than 50000 & probably over 60000 souls.[2] The rapidly approaching Rail Roads to her borders—one built more than half way from Omaha to Denver this last summer, insures to Colorado a very large increase in population in the coming year. In view of these facts & the almost vital importance it is to Colorado to be placed in a position to better assimulate & guard her interests, while the great system of Rail Roads is being fixed about her, which will forever bear upon her growth & prosperity, & the benefits arising from state government over the anomalous condition of a Territorial government we respectfully request a modification of your views regarding our admission, if not still considered incompatible with the public interests of the nation.

J. B. Chaffee

ALS, DLC-JP.
1. Colorado population statistics were a source of tremendous wrangling and confusion. For the statistics accepted by Johnson in the spring of 1866, see Colorado Statehood Veto, May 15, 1866, *Johnson Papers*, 10: 506–9. For views opposed to Chaffee's, see Alexander Cummings to Colorado Legislature (Governor's Message), Dec. 13, 1866, Johnson Papers, LC.
2. See Alexander Cummings to O. H. Browning, Jan. 4, 1867, Johnson Papers, LC; D. A. Cheever to Benjamin F. Wade, Nov. 10, 1866; Frank Hall to John Evans, Nov. 10, 1866, *Congressional Globe*, 39 Cong., 2 Sess., p. 363.

From Julia Gardiner Tyler[1]

Castleton Hill
Staten Island N.Y.   Dec 5. 1866

Sir,
I had the honor to address you some weeks since, enclosing an affadavit[2] in regard to my property in the vicinity of Old Pt. Comfort consisting of a house & lot which before & since the conclusion of the War has been held in some use by the Govt. & is at this time occupied by teachers of negro children.
Will you permit me again to draw your attention to the subject.[3]

Julia Gardiner Tyler

ALS, DNA-RG107, Lets. Recd., Executive (M494, Roll 85).
1. Tyler (1820–1889), the second wife of the tenth president, John Tyler, was an energetic advocate of the Confederacy (a partisanship which permanently estranged her from many of the Gardiners) and of federal pensions for presidential widows, a measure which Congress approved in 1882. Edward T. James et al., eds., *Notable American Women, 1607–1950: A Biographical Dictionary* (3 vols., Cambridge, 1971), 3: 494–96.
2. Wilson Barstow forwarded Tyler's affidavit, dated October 5, to Maj. Dewitt Clinton. Barstow to Clinton, Oct. 10, 1866, Lets. Recd., Executive (M494, Roll 85), RG107, NA.

3. The property in question was known as Villa Margaret (Hampton, Virginia) which the Tylers had purchased for a summer home in 1858. Its seizure in 1861 by Union forces made the Tylers one of the first southern families to lose property by an act of war. In late 1862 Julia Tyler transferred ownership of Villa Margaret to her mother who lived in New York and who began correspondence to secure compensation from the federal government. After the war's end, the situation was further complicated in early 1866 by the occupation of the property by school teachers operating a school for blacks under the auspices of the Freedmen's Bureau. However, the property was not directly controlled by the Bureau, but instead by the American Missionary Society in New York and authorized directly by the secretary of war. In October 1868 the War Department authorized payment of monthly rent; by the time Julia Tyler regained possession of Villa Margaret in 1869 it was in significant disrepair. Despite her attempts to force the government to buy the property, she was compelled to sell it in 1874 for under a third of its 1860 value. Robert Seager II, *And Tyler too: A Biography of John and Julia Gardiner Tyler* (New York, 1963), 372, 467, 477, 515–16. See also Stanton to Johnson, Feb. 2, 1867, Lets. Sent, Mil. Bks., Executive, 58-C, RG107, NA; numerous letters in Lets. Recd., Executive (M494, Roll 85), RG107, NA.

From James Brooks

(Private)

New York   Dec 6/66

Dear Sir

Mr Secretary Seward has in his possession an important Letter to you from Hon John Carter[1] of California upon the Japan and China unofficial mission,[2] I spoke to you of,—a Letter I wish you would ask for, to read.

Mr Seward entertained me with a long and somewhat insulting dissertation upon the impudence of travellers, who wanted to be Bearers of dispatches, &c &, and as I did not wish to again subject myself to such lectures upon Etiquette, Proprieties &c, I abandoned the project in disgust, and hereafter, shall do what I am ambitious to do for the administration, for myself.

I have thought this explanation due to you, because of your very kind note to Mr Welles,[3] and because of your uniform Kindness to me.

James Brooks

ALS, DLC-JP.
1. Unidentified.
2. Unknown.
3. Johnson requested that Welles have a conference with Brooks. Johnson to Welles, Dec. 4, 1866, Misc. Lets., 1789–1906 (M179, Roll 246), RG59, NA.

From Lydia Fisher[1]

Woodstock [Va.]   Dec 6th 1866

Honored & respected Sir:

I hear that you are a friend to the South and wish to make an appeal to you for assistance in my great misfortune & trouble.

During the war in a heavy skirmish below Woodstock[2]—(in the Valley)—between Gen Fremont & Ashby[3] I was so unfortunate as to be in a house situated between the contending forces. A Cannon ball passed through the house and tore & mangled one leg so badly it had to be amputated above the knee.

My parents are old—and in indigent circumstances. I am their sole support & comfort in their old age. Besides have an invalid sister[4] who is an additional charge upon me. I have no means to procure a cork leg & no opportunity (my cares at home being so great and being now rendered so helpless in the loss of my leg) to make the money to buy one.

I humbly appeal to your generosity for assistance. Will you not aid me to procure this great help & comfort to me?[5] It will be gratefully recieved and my heart will forever thank you for such a benefaction—besides the blessing that Heaven sends upon the charitable & the merciful.

Lydia Fisher

Please direct to Lydia Fisher Care of Dr. J. L. Campbell[6] Woodstock Shenandoah Co. Va.

ALS, DNA-RG107, Lets. Recd., Executive (M494, Roll 85).
1. Fisher (c1831–fl1880) was a native of Virginia. 1870 Census, Va., Shenandoah, Stonewall Twp., 33; (1880), Stonewall Dist., 84th Enum. Dist., 59.
2. On June 2, 1862, Union forces under Generals Frémont, George D. Bayard, and Julius Stahel skirmished heavily with Confederate forces under Generals George H. Steuart and Ashby in the vicinity of Woodstock, Virginia. *OR*, Ser. 1, Vol. 12, Pt. 1: 651, 731.
3. John C. Frémont and Turner Ashby. Ashby (1828–1862) was engaged in business and farming prior to the war. Rising to colonel in just a few months, he eventually was in charge of Stonewall Jackson's cavalry in the Shenandoah campaign and was promoted to brigadier general in May 1862. He was killed June 6 fighting a rear-guard action just south of Harrisonburg as Jackson withdrew up the Valley. Warner, *Gray*.
4. Jacob (c1791–fl1870), a farmer and tailor, and Isabella (c1795–fl1870) Fisher and their daughter Mary A. (c1821–fl1880). 1860 Census, Va., Shenandoah, Strasburg Dist., 238; (1870), Stonewall Twp., 33; (1880), Stonewall Dist., 84th Enum. Dist., 59.
5. Endorsements indicate the letter was referred to the secretary of war, who in turn sent it to the surgeon general. The surgeon general's office requested that authority be given to provide Fisher with an artificial leg.
6. Josiah L. Campbell (1834–1912), physician, was an organizer, officer, and regimental surgeon for the first company established from the Shenandoah Valley for civil war service, the "Muhlenburg Guards." He later served as surgeon for the 33rd, 7th, and 10th Va. Inf. From 1869 to 1871 he served in the Virginia house of delegates. John W. Wayland, *A History of Shenandoah County, Virginia* (Strasburg, Va., 1927), 764; T. K. Cartmell, *Shenandoah Valley Pioneers and Their Descendants: A History of Frederick County, Virginia* (Winchester, Va., 1909), 427; Lowell Reidenbaugh, *33rd Virginia Infantry* (Lynchburg, 1987), 115; "VERY COMPLETE ROLL of Company F, Tenth Virginia Regiment, or the Muhlenburg Rifles," *SHS Papers*, 28 (1900): 116.

From Sam Milligan
Private

Greeneville Tenn.   Dem. 6. 1866

Dear Sir:

I have just finished reading your message, and I thought that our former intimate and pleasant relations would justify me, in telling you candidly what I think of it. In advance, I must say, knowing your combattive nature, I had feared, you would under the storm of wanton abuse and misrepresentation to which you have been exposed, be betrayed into some intemperance in the message. But when I read it all over, and saw the calm, dignified, and dispashioned spirit, that marked evey line and sentence of it, I was profoundly impressed with the propriety of the tone of the whole document. Contrasted with the foul vituperatian and vulgar slander of those who oppose your policy, I could not but feel, that the one was the offspring of a mind conscious of its own rectitude; while the other, was the ebulition of passion, staid upon no other foundation, than the unnatural sectional hatred of the hour. The one will live and flourish, when the other is forgotten and condemned by the very men that now uphold it.

The sentiment of the message with reference to the reconstruction policy, is so plain, and so effectually removes all objections that have been urged against it, that the opposition, can not, without an absolute distruction of the Constitution itself, avoid yielding to it sooner or later. The Constitution authorizes no other mode, and hence, they have not, nor can they, present any substitute. They seem to have a Sectional majority, but they are nevertheless, bound hand & foot. They can carry their radical policy no further. If they attempt it, the violation of the Constitution will be so open, that they certainly will loose their power over their own people. And if they admit the seceded States, they have a clear national majority against them. Even now, they can not ratify the proposed amendment to the constitution.[1] What then can they do? Sooner or later, they must come to your policy. They only desire to postpone it now, until after the next Presidential election; and if they can accomplish that, then their will be a race between them; who shall do the most to win the favor of the South.

Your record, thank God, is made on this great subject in your message, and no time, or circumstance, can change it. It rests on the truths of the Constitution, as understood an interpreted by the father's of the Republic, as you have happily interwoven in the message. Stand by, and act firmly on it, and time and history will do you justice.

I have no space to say any thing of the other matters which it contains, more than your conciseness is certainly a great virtue. No message in the same space ever contained more real matter. It strikes me forceable, as a great paper, and one of which you may well be proud, and which will certainly satisfy all your friends.

Enclosed you will see a paper which some time since was sent me from Nashville in relation to the removal of the post master at that place.[2] I do not personally know the gentleman proposed in his place;[3] but he is said to be a gentleman of good qualifycations. Lindsly I do not think is a bad man, and I think no removals ought to be made unless you can fill the place with as good or a better man than the one removed. I send the paper that you may do as you think best.

Excuse me this long letter. My wife[4] sends her regard. Be cautious [of] Maynard.[5] He is a relentless selfish man.

Sam Milligan.

ALS, DLC-JP.
1. The Fourteenth Amendment would not finally be ratified until 1868.
2. The enclosure has not been found. Rumors were persistent in the fall of 1866 that Adrian V.S. Lindsley would be removed as Nashville postmaster; he was not.
3. It is not clear to whom Milligan refers here.
4. Elizabeth R. Milligan.
5. Horace Maynard had parted company with Johnson, although he had earlier been a supporter of the President.

From Oran M. Roberts[1] and David G. Burnet

Washington City D.C.   Decr. 6th 1866

Respected Sir

The undersigned senators elect from the State of Texas, at the request of Governor Throckmorton,[2] most respectfully submit to the decision of your Excellency whether or not the Military Officers, now stationed in Texas, shall longer assert their supremacy over the civil authority of the state, in all cases civil and criminal wherein persons belonging to the army are concerned. We respectfully submit the folloing cases which show the necessity for a prompt decision of this question.

1st Lieut Moor[3]—indicted and convicted and fined $10 for "Playing cards in a public place" under the penal laws of the state in the District Court of Gaudaloupe County (a court of general jurisdiction corresponding to the Circuit Court in other states). He was after conviction forcibly taken out of the custody of the sheriff[4] by Capt S A Craig,[5] Sup Ass Comr. B R &c. Professing to act under authority from Brevet Maj Genl comdg at San Antonio[6] informing him that "*Military law is still supreme.*" See Statement of District Attorney & Sheriff in paper marked No 1.[7]

2nd W Longworth[8]—Capt Craig forcible imprisoned the clerk of the District Court of Gaudaloupe County[9] and forcibly took from his office the papers in a civil and also in a criminal case pending in said court,—professing to do so under orders from Genl. Heintzelman.[10] See Statement of District Clk Wilcox & his Dept Arbuckle and sheriff Brown in No. 1.[11]

3rd Venia a freed-woman indicted for Assault with intent to murder in Matagorda County Texas.[12] Rescued from the sheriff by Charles F. Rand[13] Ass Comr. of R & F & A L. See No 2 statement of District Judge & Sheriff.[14]

4th A. M. Bryant[15]—county Judge of Grayson County. Indicted for false imprisonment in District Court of Grayson County.[16] He was rescued from custody of Dept Sheriff[17] by Brvt. Lt Col Wm. S Abert,[18] Capt 6th Cav'ry. Comdg. See No. 3 copy of records & returns.[19]

5th Brevet Maj G. W. Smith.[20]—Burning of Brenham in Texas.[21] See
the report of evidence taken by a Joint Committee of both Houses of the
Legislature appointed to investigate this matter;—also the Governor's
Special Message on the subject.[22] This case has excited a great deal of
attention, and it will be seen that the committee took every precaution to
have a fair investigation of it. The Governor states that this Maj Smith
has not only been retained in command at Brenham but has been promoted since the burning of the Town.[23] See No. 4 & 5.[24]

6th Indictments against Genl. Heintzelman & Capt Craig.[25]

See No. 6 Govnr. Throckmorton's letter to us;[26] the whole tone and
tenor of which will, as it is hoped, most urgently commend it to your
most serious consideration.[27]

O. M. Roberts
D. G. Burnet

ALS (Roberts), DNA-RG107, Lets. Recd., Executive (M494, Roll 85).
1. Roberts (1815–1898) practiced law in Alabama and served in the state legislature
before moving to Texas in 1841. President of the Texas secession convention, Roberts resigned his post as state supreme court justice, raised the 11th Tex. Inf. Rgt., and became its
colonel. He was elected chief justice of the state in 1864 and served until the end of the
Confederacy. Although elected to the U.S. Senate in August 1866, Roberts was never permitted to take his seat. He was elected governor in 1878 and served two terms. *DAB*.
2. J. W. Throckmorton to D. G. Burnet and O. M. Roberts, Nov. 16, 1866, Lets.
Recd., Executive (M494, Roll 85), RG107, NA.
3. First Lieutenant James B. Moore (b. *c*1841), who had served in various Massachusetts regiments from July 1861 to June 1865, was mustered into the 9th USCT as a
second lieutenant appointed from civil life at Brownsville, Texas, on October 16, 1865. He
became Freedmen's Bureau agent at Seguin, Texas, on July 26, 1866. A Bureau inspector
soon found that Moore "was drunk much of the time, solicited prostitution from any freed-
woman on the street," and embezzled bureau funds, in addition to the illegal gambling for
which he was indicted. On November 26, 1866, he was mustered out of the service in New
Orleans. Richter, *Overreached on All Sides*, 124–25; CSR, James B. Moore, RG94, NA;
USCT Div., Lets. Recd., File M-570-1865, RG94, NA.
4. B. A. Brown, the sheriff, might have been the thirty-eight-year-old farmer (b. *c*1822)
originally from North Carolina, who, shortly before 1860, had moved to Texas from Tennessee, settling in Carter, Denton County. Or he could have been the fifty-one-year-old
farmer (b. *c*1809) residing at Marlin, Falls County, a native of Tennessee. Statements of B.
A. Brown, Lets. Recd., Executive (M494, Roll 85), RG107, NA; 1860 Census, Tex.,
Denton, Carter, 451; (1860), Falls, Marlin, 159.
5. Capt. Samuel A. Craig (1839–1920), a printer, had served briefly in the 8th Pa. Vol.
Inf., and then in the 105th Pa. Inf. He was wounded at Fair Oaks, Virginia, on May 31,
1862, and at Second Manassas (Bull Run) in August. Partially disabled by his wounds, he
became a captain in the 17th Rgt., Vet. Res. Corps, in September 1863. In this capacity he
had served as a Freedmen's Bureau agent in Madison, Indiana, before being transferred to
Texas. By May 1866 Craig was stationed in Brenham, where his altercation with news-
paper editor D. L. McGary contributed to the atmosphere of hostility which caused the
Brenham fire. Craig was transferred to Seguin in September 1866 to succeed Lieutenant
Moore. Mustered out of the service in December 1866, Craig returned to Brookville,
Pennsylvania, where he became a lawyer. Richter, *Overreached on All Sides*, 126, 129–31;
William L. Richter, "The Brenham Fire of 1866: A Texas Reconstruction Atrocity," *La.
Studies*, 14 (1975): 297, 312; Pension File, Nancy R. Craig, RG15, NA. See also James W.
Throckmorton to Johnson, Aug. 20, 1866.
6. Samuel P. Heintzelman (1805–1880), a graduate of West Point and a career officer,
was appointed a brigadier general in May 1861 and a major general ranking from May

1862. He served various posts during the Civil War without notable success. His command in Texas was brief. Warner, *Blue.*

7. Lawyer John B. Rector (1837–1896) fought with Terry's Texas Rangers during the Civil War. He was district attorney for the second judicial district from 1866 until his removal in 1867. Later he served as a district judge (1871–76) and U.S. district judge (1892–96). The sheriff was B. A. Brown. Rector's statement addressed to Throckmorton dated October 20, 1866, and Brown's statement are found in Lets. Recd., Executive (M494, Roll 85), RG107, NA.

8. William Longworth (*c*1825–*fl*1870), who claimed to be a unionist, had been appointed judge of the Wilson County court by September 1865. Desiring to aid the freedmen, he secured appointment as Bureau subassistant commissioner, without pay, on December 27, 1865. His district included Wilson, Karnes, and Guadelupe counties, as well as a portion of Gonzales County, with headquarters eventually at Seguin. He was replaced in July 1866 by Lt. James B. Moore. In 1870 Longworth was serving as a district clerk. 1870 Census, Tex., Wilson, 4th Prec., Lodi, 473; Richter, *Overreached on All Sides*, 116–24.

9. The district clerk, James M. Wilcox (*c*1828–*fl*1880), who had been in Texas since at least the early 1850s, was accused of being a blatant racist and of using the local newspaper to oppose Longworth's efforts. In 1870 he was serving as justice of the peace. Ibid., 121–22; 1870 Census, Tex., Collin, 5th Prec., Plano, 459; (1880), 25th Enum. Dist., 214.

10. One of the cases involved James L. Dial of Guadelupe County whom Longworth had charged with kidnapping and false imprisonment and fined ninety dollars. After a great deal of wrangling, Dial sued Longworth for $20,000 for damages and false arrest. Captain Craig took papers for this case, as well as documents for a case brought by Dr. James M. Cox, and Longworth's bonds, when he arrested Wilcox on October 7, 1866. Under orders from General Heintzelman, Craig destroyed the papers. Richter, *Overreached on All Sides*, 119–20, 132–34; Statements of James Wilcox and C. L. Arbuckle, Lets. Recd., Executive (M494, Roll 85), RG107, NA.

11. Charles Lockhart Arbuckle (*c*1840–*fl*1880) was a farmer in 1860, still the deputy clerk in 1870, but by 1880 had become the district court clerk. 1860 Census, Tex., Guadelupe, Seguin, 324; (1870), 360; (1880), 334; Statements of James Wilcox, C. L. Arbuckle, and B. A. Brown, Lets. Recd., Executive (M494, Roll 85), RG107, NA.

12. Venia, about whom nothing else is known, was indicted for attempting to kill a white man. She was tried in the fall of 1866 but the jury, apparently for political reasons, could come to no decision, so her case was continued to the next term of court. Statement of E. J. Inglehart, Oct. 30, 1866; B. Shropshire to Throckmorton, Nov. 5, 1866, ibid.

13. While Venia was in the custody of Sheriff Edward J. Inglehart, who was supposed to transport her to the jail in Brazoria County to await the next term of court, she was rescued on October 22, 1866, by Rand. Inglehart (*c*1835–*fl*1912) had enlisted in the Confederate ranks in October 1861 and fought in the Army of Tennessee, suffering both wounds and capture. By 1870 he was a farmer. Rand (*c*1839–1908), a first lieutenant and brevet captain whose severe shoulder wound at the battle of Gaines Mill in June 1862 cost him the use of his right arm, served in the 101st N.Y. Inf. and the 2nd Btn., Vet. Res. Corps. After the war he was Bureau agent at Wharton, Marshall, Gilmer, and Clarkesville, Texas, remaining on duty until January 1, 1869. He then earned a medical degree from Georgetown University and practiced in Batavia, New York, and Washington, D.C. Statement of E. J. Inglehart, Oct. 30, 1866, ibid.; 1870 Census, Tex., Washington, Brenham, 3rd Prec., 51; Mamie Yeary, comp., *Reminiscences of the Boys in Gray, 1861–1865* (Dallas, 1912), 372; *Off. Army Reg.: Vols.*, 3: 591; 8: 79; Richter, *Overreached on All Sides*, 108; Pension File, Louise C. Rand, RG15, NA.

14. Statement of E. J. Inglehart, Oct. 30, 1866; B. Shropshire to Throckmorton, Nov. 5, 1866, Lets. Recd., Executive (M494, Roll 85), RG107, NA. Benjamin Shropshire (b. *c*1826), a lawyer, moved to Texas in the early 1850s. A captain in the Confederate forces, he was elected judge of the first district of Texas in 1866 and removed from office on September 11, 1867. 1860 Census, Tex., Fayette, La Grange, 305; Randolph B. Campbell, "The District Judges of Texas in 1866–1867: An Episode in the Failure of Presidential Reconstruction," *SWHQ*, 93 (1990): 361–62, 367–68, 375.

15. Judge Anthony M. Bryant (*c*1819–*fl*1880), a farmer, was an outspoken unionist with a concern for the freedmen. From late March to November 1, 1867, he served as

Freedmen's Bureau agent for the forty-first subdistrict, until elected to a seat in the state convention. 1860 Census, Tex., Grayson, Sherman, 153; (1870), Kentucky Town, 4th Prec., 132; (1880), 9th Enum. Dist., 226; Richter, *Overreached on All Sides*, 194–95.

16. On February 5, 1866, Bryant had J. P. Hopson (or Hobson) and William F. Stewart summoned "to appear before me and show cause if any why they hold and refuse to give up to the Agent of the United States Government a Revolver belonging to the Government." Apparently this summons resulted in the arrest of the two parties and their imprisonment for ten hours, for which imprisonment Bryant was indicted by the grand jury at the 1866 spring term of the Grayson County district court. A. M. Bryant to Grayson County Sheriff, Feb. 5, 1866; Copy of Indictment, Spring 1866, Lets. Recd., Executive (M494, Roll 85), RG107, NA.

17. Deputy sheriff James W. Vaden (c1842–fl1881) had enlisted as a private in the Confederate 11th Tex. Cav., fighting against Indians, as well as against Sherman in the Georgia campaign. After his stint in the sheriff's office he raised cattle. 1860 Census, Tex., Grayson, Sherman, 136; (1870), 78; (1880), 4th Ward, 96; William S. Speer and John H. Brown, eds., *The Encyclopedia of the New West* (Easley, S.C., 1978 [1881]), 64.

18. Abert (1836–1867), a native of Washington, D.C., and son of Col. John J. Abert, chief of the topographic engineers, was a career army man. He served on the staffs of Generals George B. McClellan and Nathaniel P. Banks, and as an artillery colonel. Brevetted brigadier general for meritorious services during the war, Abert had attained the rank of major by the time he died in Galveston, Texas, in August 1867. He freed Anthony M. Bryant on October 19, 1866, the same day Bryant was arrested. Powell, *Army List*, 154; Hunt and Brown, *Brigadier Generals*; William S. Abert to Judge Weaver, Oct. 19, 1866; Copy of Deputy Sheriff's Return, Oct. 19, 1866, Lets. Recd., Executive (M494, Roll 85), RG107, NA.

19. Enclosure No. 3 contains A. M. Bryant to Grayson County Sheriff, Feb. 5, 1866; Copy of Indictment, Spring 1866; William S. Abert to Judge Weaver, Oct. 19, 1866; Copy of Deputy Sheriff's Return, Oct. 19, 1866; and Thomas W. Randolph, clerk of county district courts, certification of copies, Oct. 22, 1866, ibid.

20. George W. Smith (c1840–1896) enlisted at Lebanon, New Hampshire, in May 1862 and served with the 17th Inf. throughout the Civil War, rising from private to brevet major and fighting with distinction in several battles, being wounded at Gettysburg and Spotsylvania. He went to Texas with his regiment in 1866 and was stationed with a detachment of troops at Brenham at the time of the fire. Afterwards he was transferred to the 35th Inf. and replaced Capt. Samuel Craig as Bureau agent at Seguin, Texas, where he was accused of embezzling Freedmen's Bureau funds and was court-martialed. Although found innocent on a technicality, Smith resigned from the army on December 31, 1869. He became a furniture manufacturer in Philadelphia. Powell, *Army List*, 594; Richter, "The Brenham Fire of 1866," 297–98, 312; Pension File, Nellie D. Smith, RG15, NA.

21. Apparently on the night of September 7, two soldiers were shot and wounded by local citizens and in revenge a number of soldiers came to Brenham, Texas, broke into the businesses of several suspects in the shooting, and set them on fire. The resulting blaze destroyed much of the business district of the town, causing over $130,000 in damages. Various investigations attempted to determine what actually happened but no participant was ever brought to justice. Richter, "The Brenham Fire of 1866," passim. See also James W. Throckmorton to Johnson, Aug. 20, 1866.

22. Probably *Report of the Joint Select Committee to Investigate Facts in Regard to the Burning of Brenham* (Austin, 1866). Throckmorton issued his message on September 13, 1866. Richter, "The Brenham Fire of 1866," 287; Lets. Recd., Executive (M494, Roll 85), RG107, NA.

23. Smith never received any promotion for his actions at Brenham. Richter, "The Brenham Fire of 1866," 312.

24. Four and five are the report of the legislative committee and Throckmorton's message. The National Archives omitted them from its microfilm collection.

25. When the contingent of protective troops in Seguin was recalled to San Antonio in December 1866, Judge John Ireland had Craig incarcerated for destroying the records of the court cases previously mentioned. The troops returned, however, to release Craig from jail. Craig promptly left Texas as he had desired to do, having made a good deal of money speculating in oil stocks in Pennsylvania. Ireland had Heintzelman indicted for ordering

Craig to destroy the legal papers and allowing Craig to escape arrest. Ibid., 312; Richter, *Overreached on All Sides*, 134–35. See also Edwin M. Stanton to Johnson, Jan. 29, 1867.

26. Throckmorton enclosed a variety of documents pertaining to "the most flagrant outrages perpetrated by the military authorities." He had previously sent much documentation to Attorney General Stanbery. Throckmorton to D. G. Burnet and O. M. Roberts, Nov. 16, 1866, Lets. Recd., Executive (M494, Roll 85), RG107, NA.

27. On Thursday, December 6, 1866, Roberts and Burnet visited Johnson to give him the papers sent by Throckmorton. Johnson directed them to submit the letters to Stanton as well. After the meeting Roberts prepared the letter printed here to be submitted with the documentation; on the following day he sent it and other papers to Johnson. O. H. Browning recalled in his diary that Stanton presented the Texas request to the cabinet. "We still thought some military force necessary in Texas at present, and, therefore, concluded to temporize and become fully informed of all the facts before we took any decided action." O. M. Roberts, "The Experiences of an Unrecognized Senator," *TxHAQ*, 12 (1908): 97; Randall, *Browning Diary*, 2: 115–16.

From Lewis D. Campbell

Point Isabel, Texas   Friday Decr. 7, 1866

Dear Sir

I am somewhat in the situation of Japhet in search of his father:[1] have searched industriously for President Juarez, but have not yet found him. I wrote you from Havana.[2] From that port we went to Vera Cruz where we lay at anchor outside the harbor for three days. I sent to the Secretary of State dispatches giving full information as to the condition of things there.[3] On the eveng of the 2nd we left Vera Cruz and arrived at Tampico on the 4th. That port being in the possession of the liberal authorities we entered and remained one day. We were well and hospitably received; but finding no probabilities of communicating with President Juarez from that point we concluded to come to the Rio Grande. To-morrow moring we go to Brownsville and Metamoras, to see Gen. Escabado[4] with a view to ascertain something as to the "local habitation" of President Juarez.

Gen. Sheridan who has just come down from Brownsville had an interview with Escabado yesterday, and was in formed that Juarez is still at Chihuahua, and contemplates being at San Louis Potosi about the 15th of January. If this shall prove to be the condition of affairs, I shall not be able to communicate with him from this *base*, and shall therefore have to return to Tampico and there await the events of the future. I confess that I am quite disappointed in not finding the Juarez Government more *progressive*. It will be by no means pleasant to house up for more than a month at Tampico on the *uncertainties* that seem to surround affairs here, and it will be still more unpleasant to be drifting about in the gulf encountering the terrible "Northers" which prevail at this season of the year. Still as you have sent me here I shall stay until you send for me to return, and will do all in my power to advance what I understand to be the policy of your Administration in regard to Mexican affairs. Should I find, however, that after a month or two of industrious effort, I shall be unable to accomplish any practical good for the Republic of Mexico, for your Administration or for myself, I may ask that you will in kindness to my family allow me to return home. After I have visited Metamoras and Brownsville, I will make a formal communication to Mr. Seward.

We are far away from the Capitol and know nothig of what is goig on. Have not recd. your message and dont know how much good or evil our virtuous Congress is likely to accomplish. I have full faith, however, that your share of the national work will be done well.

Lewis D Campbell

P.S. You must not suspect that I am home sick. What I mean is that I came here on *business*. If I cant have that to employ me I fear I shall *demoralize*.

LDC

ALS, DLC-JP.
1. This reference has not been found.
2. See Campbell to Johnson, Nov. 23, 1866.
3. See Campbell to Seward, Dec. 1, 1866 (2 letters), *House Ex. Docs.*, 39 Cong., 2 Sess., No. 76, pp. 577–78 (Ser. 1294).
4. Mariano Escobedo (1827–1902) served as chief of staff for Benito Juárez's republican army during the war involving France in Mexico. Afterwards he was president of the Supreme Court of Military Justice and deputy minister of war and navy. *Enciclopedia de México.*

From New Mexico Council of Legislative Assembly[1]

[December 8, 1866][2]

Your memorialists the Council of the Legislative assembly of the Territory of New Mexico, would most respectfully represent that the condition of our country in consequence of the constant murders and depredations by the Indians, demand prompt action on the part of the General Government, so as to dispose of the savages who are committing depredations, (coming nearly to our capital to rob and murder)[3] and to protect our citizens from their marauding expeditions. We would urge that they be immediately placed upon Reservations outside of the settlements[4] and your memorialists as in duty bound will ever pray.

Signed   "Miguel E. Pino"[5]
"President of the Council"
"Francisco Salazar"[6]
"Chief Clerk"

Copy, DNA-RG75, Gen. Records, Lets. Recd. (M234, Roll 553).
1. This memorial from the upper house of the territorial legislature was also addressed to Orville H. Browning, secretary of the interior, and Lewis V. Bogy, commissioner of Indian affairs. It included resolutions sending Col. A. Baldwin Norton, superintendent of Indian affairs for New Mexico, to Washington, D.C., to cooperate with territorial delegate J. Francisco Chaves in explaining "the present condition of our citizens, and of the Indians."
2. December 8 was the date on which William F.M. Arny, territorial secretary and acting governor, endorsed this a true copy of the original document, written in Spanish and filed in his office.

3. On November 13, 1866, alleged Navajo raiders had attacked the herd of a Mrs. Ortiz near Galisteo, only twenty-two miles southeast of Sante Fe. Gerald Thompson, *The Army and the Navajo* (Tucson, 1976), 126.

4. This memorial was part of the continuous New Mexican complaints about depredations by Navajos who had avoided deportation to the Bosque Redondo reservation, Navajos who had escaped from the reservation, and Apaches and Comanches as well. It was also part of the complaints against the Indian policy of Brig. Gen. James H. Carleton who had set up the Bosque Redondo. Ibid., 126–27.

5. Pino (*c*1821–1867), who served two terms as president of the territorial council and representative from Santa Fe (1865–67), also served three terms in the territorial house and two years as territorial auditor between 1854 and 1865. During the Civil War he fought at the battle of Valverde as colonel of the 2nd Rgt., N. Mex. Inf., a post he held, August 1861-May 1862. Hubert H. Bancroft, *History of Arizona and New Mexico, 1530–1888* (San Francisco, 1889), 635–36, 704, 706; *Off. Army Reg.: Vols.*, 8: 10; Charles and Jacqueline Meketa, "Heroes or Cowards? A New Look at the Role of Native New Mexicans at the Battle of Valverde," *NMHR*, 62 (1987): 42–43; CSR, Miguel E. Pino, RG94, NA; Pension File, Luz Ortiz [de Pino], RG15, NA.

6. Salazar (*c*1831–*fl*1880) had an extensive career in the territorial legislature including one term as house sergeant, two terms as house clerk, at least four (possibly six) terms as house representative from Rio Arriba County, three terms as council clerk, and two terms as council member from the same county, between 1855 and 1880. He served briefly (October-December 1861) as second lieutenant in the 3rd Rgt., N. Mex. Inf. (mounted). *Off. Army Reg.: Vols.*, 8: 11; Bancroft, *Arizona and New Mexico*, 635–36, 706, 707; CSR, Francisco Salazar, RG94, NA.

From Henry W. Slocum

Confidential—

180 Broadway N.Y.   Dec 8th 1866.

Dear Sir—

If consistent with your views and wishes I hope no appointment of Naval officer at this Port will be made during this present month. You are well aware that in regard to this subject I have not invoked the aid of politicians—have sent no delegations to importune you, and have not even solicited a letter from any person.

My reason for suggesting delay in the selection is that the temper of the Senate may be ascertained before action is taken. I shall soon be able to learn beyond question what my fate would be in the Senate, and to place in your possession more facts bearing on the case. I shall in no event compromise the position I have assumed on political matters, feeling that it would be far better for me to remain a private citizen and earn my living by hard labor than to purchase official position at such a sacrifice. I have *strong reasons* for believing that I can be confirmed if appointed without making any such sacrifice—that my military services and personal relations would secure the result. On this point I can soon give positive proof. In mean time no evil can result from a brief delay in the nom[in]ation. The temper of the Senate will soon become more apparent.

Unless I become perfectly satisfied that I can be confirmed without any sacrifice of principle I shall withdraw my name as a candidate, and cheerfully recommend the appointment of some person who can be confirmed

and who will not become your personal and political enemy in order that
he may effect the result.[1]

                                                              H. W. Slocum

ALS, DLC-JP.
1. Johnson delayed sending Slocum's nomination to the Senate for several months. See
Hugh McCulloch to Johnson, Jan. 12, 1867.

From Edwin M. Stanton

                                         Washington City, Dec. 11: 1866.
Sir,
    In answer to so much of a Resolution of the House of Representatives of
Dec. 6: 1866,[1] hereto annexed, on the subject of *re-appointment by the
President* of persons to office *after rejection by the Senate*, &c, as refers to
this Dept., I have the honor to report—
    1st That no persons after rejection by the Senate, have been re-
appointed by the President.
    2nd That there were no appointments made during the Senates last
session, of persons whose names were intentionally withheld. A few
cases occurred through inadvertence in the Adjt. Genls. Off., but they
were brevet appointments merely. These having expired by constitutional limitation will be nominated at the present session.
    3rd That some 32 persons have been appointed during the recess of
the Senate to fill vacancies made by the ordinary casualties in the Army,
but their names are to be presented to the Senate at the present session.
In this remark are not included Brevet appointments because they are
not supposed to come within the scope of the Resolution, as are not those
appointments made under the provision of the Act of Congress of July
28: 1866[2] to fix the peace establishment. All such appointments, however, are to be submitted to the Senate at this session.
                                    Edwin M. Stanton,   Secy. of War.

LBcopy, DNA-RG107, Lets. Sent, Mil. Bks., Executive, 58-C.
1. See *Congressional Globe*, 39 Cong., 2 Sess., p. 30. The Senate passed a similar resolution on December 12. See Appts. Div., Misc. Lets. Recd., RG48, NA.
2. *U.S. Statutes at Large*, 14: 332–38.

From Timothy O. Howe

                                              Washn.   Dec. 12, 1866.
Mr. President.
    I take the liberty to send you a Newspaper, published in the town
where I live,[1] by one whom you nominated for Assessor of Int. Revenue
for the 5th Dist. of Wis. He was rejected by the Senate.[2]
    During the vacation you appointed him Collector.[3] I ask you to read

his Editorial, on Senotorial Doolittle. The People are informed by your Collector that Senator Doolittle was carried down by *your* short comings.

It is only one of a multitude of Evidences I could furnish you if you wd. hear them—that the patronage you have placed in Senator Doolittles hands is used & has been for nearly one year not to sustain you but to sustain him.

This letter is not confidential. It is written simply to communicate a fact not to obtain any favor or reward.

T. O. Howe

ALS, DLC-JP.

1. No issue of the *Green Bay Gazette* was found with the document. *History of Northern Wisconsin* (Chicago, 1881), 113.

2. George C. Ginty (1840–1890), a newspaper editor and politician who served as major of the 39th Wis. Inf. and colonel of the 47th Wis. Inf., was brevetted a brigadier general of volunteers in September 1865. In March 1866 Ginty and a partner established the *Green Bay Gazette*, a Republican paper, with which Ginty remained connected until May 1868. He was nominated as assessor on May 24, 1866, and rejected on June 30. Ibid.; Hunt and Brown, *Brigadier Generals*; Ser. 6B, Vol. 4: 337, Johnson Papers, LC.

3. Appointed collector on August 23, 1866, during the congressional recess, Ginty was nominated on January 21, 1867, and was once again rejected on February 23, 1867. Ibid., 338; Ser. 6B, Vol. 3: 680, Johnson Papers, LC.

From William H. Ludlow

Oakdale   Sayville, Long Isl.   Dec. 12 1866.

Sir.

If my appointment to the naval office, & the representative strength sustaining it,[1] be regarded by you with favor, I respectfully ask that the wishes & representations of Mr. Thurlow Weed concerning it, be ignored. Since the election, he has avowed his open hostility to my appointment. Previously it was equally strong, but in our State seemingly suppressed. Mr. Dean Richmond informed me, that Mr. Weed gave to him, his pledge of honor at the Saratoga Convention, he would not interfere in this appointment. How far he has redeemed this promise is but known to you, & to the Secretary of the Treasury. I have never been deceived by him, for I never expected his support. Possessing as he does, no political strength, save what he derives from the federal patronage given to him, having no party, and no organization sustaining him, & powerless as he is, either to injure or benefit your cause, my friends, & myself would feel the deepest mortification & regret, if either directly or indirectly, his tactics should be permitted by you, to defeat me. Unless the Senate should take the ground (& they will not), that no friend whatever of yours should be confirmed, I have no doubt that I can pass the ordeal. I am satisfied that Mr. Weed will resort to any course of action & tactics to defeat my appointment, & am equally well satisfied from my thorough knowledge of him, that if I am appointed, he would be the first to claim the merit, & ask the fruits of it. He has no proper cause to complain of it, for he already controls the great bulk of the federal patronage of our State. Pardon the liberty, I take in writing this. I am actuated more by a real regard for your interest, than my own.[2]

Wm. H. Ludlow

ALS, DLC-JP.
1. Backed by a host of strong recommendations, Ludlow had been a candidate for the New York naval officership since early that summer. See John A. Dix to Johnson, June 19, 1866, *Johnson Papers*, 10: 597.
2. Ludlow was not chosen for the post, though he did obtain employment in the New York collector's office. *U.S. Off. Reg.* (1867).

From Lewis D. Campbell

Brasos Santiago, Texas
Thursday, Decr. 13, 1866.

Dear Sir—

I have spent a few days at Brownsville and Metamoras in company with Lieut Gen. Sherman. We had two interviews with Gen. Escobedo on Sunday last.[1] Since then we have been separated from the Susquehanna by a storm which makes it impossible to cross the bar without very great peril. In fact there is no pilot here who will undertake to take us over.

Lieut Gen. Sherman is out fishing and I am housed and suffering from a severe cold.

I have reported officially to the Department of State all my proceedings up to this time, and I desire to say in an unofficial way that the liberals under Juarez in Mexico could make rapid progress if they could but have some of the material of war which is being *thrown away* and *wasted* in the United States. If Congress would pass a joint resolution such as that which is enclosed,[2] speedily, I believe you and Gen. Grant could very soon be instrumental in putting an end to the little that is left of Foreign intervention in Mexico, and to the various petty Combinations that seek to overthrow the legitimate Republic over which Juarez presides.

You may show this hastily written private letter to Mr. Seward if you see fit to do so.

Lewis D. Campbell.

ALS, DLC-JP.
1. Campbell and Sherman reached Brazos Santiago on December 7 and, learning that General Sheridan was in Brownsville, proceeded there on the 8th to speak with him. They crossed over to Matamoras on December 9 to speak with General Escobedo. Campbell to Seward, Dec. 13, 1866, *House Ex. Docs.*, 39 Cong., 2 Sess., No. 76, pp. 579–80 (Ser. 1294).
2. The attached resolution read "That the President be and he is hereby authorized to empower the General of the Armies of the United States to sell such arms clothing and other munitions of war as in the judgment of the General are not now required for the public service, and to receive in payment therefor coin or the bonds of Governments to whom the same may be sold."

From Salmon P. Chase

Home Cor. E. & 6th Street
[Washington]   Decr. 13, [1866][1]

My dear Sir,

A friend, in whom I place every reliance, Mr. Gooch[2] of Massachusetts tells me that there is some talk in Boston of the removal of George Bradburn,[3] a gentleman of about my age, from the position he holds in the Custom House. He is an old personal friend & I know him to be able & honest & am assured he is quite competent to his duties, though afflicted with partial deafness. So I am quite solicitious on his account & will take it as a great kindness if you will endorse on this letter your wish that my wish in his behalf may be gratified & send it to the Secretary or the Collector.[4]

S P Chase

ALS, DNA-RG56, Appts., Customs Service, Subofficer, Boston, George Bradburn.

1. The provenance and date are suggested by both internal and external evidence.

2. Probably Daniel W. Gooch, whom Johnson had removed in August 1866 as naval officer for the district of Boston and Charlestown.

3. Bradburn (1806–1880), a former anti-slavery crusader and member of the Massachusetts legislature (1839–42), was employed at the Boston customhouse from 1861 to at least through 1873. Frances H. Bradburn, *A Memorial of George Bradburn. By His Wife* (Boston, 1883), 1, 4, 25, 234, 237, 246; *U.S. Off. Reg.* (1861–73).

4. A copy of Chase's letter was made and sent to Darius N. Couch, who was then serving as Boston's collector of customs, while the original letter, for some unknown reason, was referred to the secretary of war. A reply from either Couch or Stanton has not been located.

From Lovell H. Rousseau

Washington, D.C.   Dec 14, 1866.

Sir,

I beg leave to call your attention to Colonel W. H. Sidell, 10th U.S. Inf'y, and to ask most respectfully and earnestly that he be promoted by brevet to the rank of Brigadier General. No man of the Army of his rank, rendered more efficient and faithful service during the rebellion than he, and he is entitled to his recognition of his services.

No man has a better personal knowledge of them, Mr President, than yourself, for the scene of much of his labor was in Tennessee, where you was Military Governor.

I happen to know the fact that the line of fortifications, at Nashville, which when built upon, afterward proved so valuable and indispensable, was selected by you and himself he being an educated and professional Engineer. And I know he was with you during all the trying times when Buell and Bragg were up in Kentucky.

Certainly such services should not go unrecognized.[1]

Lovell H Rousseau

ALS, DNA-RG94, ACP Branch, File S-1565-CB-1866, William H. Sidell.
 1. Johnson nominated Sidell for a brevet brigadier generalship on December 24, 1866,
and he was confirmed March 2, 1867, to date March 13, 1865. *Senate Ex. Proceedings*, Vol.
15, pt. 1: 93–94, 328, 337; Hunt and Brown, *Brigadier Generals*.

From Adam Badeau[1]

Executive Mansion   Sunday Decr 15 [1866][2]
7. P.M.

Sir,

 I have the honor to report that the Hon. Secretary of State, after reading the dispatches of General Sherman, which you sent him today by me,
desired me to say to you that he expects information from France by the
next steamer, after the French government shall have received General
Castelnau's[3] report; the Secretary therefore thinks it will be better to
send no word to General Sherman until the information from France
arrives.

 Being quite unwell, I have taken the liberty, after waiting some time, of
leaving my message in writing.

Adam Badeau
Colonel & ADC to the Genl. in Chief

ALS, DLC-JP.
 1. Before the war Badeau (1831–1895), author, soldier, and diplomat, clerked in the
State Department. During the Civil War he served on the staffs of Sherman, Gillmore, and
Grant. Retiring in 1869 as brevet brigadier general, he was appointed by Grant secretary of
the legation at London and in May 1870 consul general. *DAB*.
 2. The year of 1866 is assigned because of internal evidence, particularly the reference
to General Castelnau. He was in Mexico from September 1866 to March 1867. *Diction-
naire de Biographie Française* (Paris, 1954).
 3. Henri-Pierre-Jean-Abdon Castelnau (1814–1890), a professional soldier, served on
the staffs of several generals with several different army units, as well as at times serving as
aide to the minister of war and the emperor Napoleon III. From fall 1866 to spring 1867 he
was envoy of the imperial mission to Mexico to assess the activities of Bazaine and Maximilian and to persuade Maximilian to abdicate if necessary. Castelnau retired from military
life in 1879. Ibid.

From Christopher G. Memminger

Washington   Decr. 15. 1866.

 The Memorial of C. G. Memminger of South Carolina respectfully
sheweth:

 That his application to be admitted to the benefit of the amnesty Proclamation has been on file with the attorney General ever since the formation of the Government in South Carolina in 1865, duly recommended
by Provisional Governor Perry. That since that time your Memorialist
has remained with his family at a residence which he usually occupied in
the summer in Henderson County among the Mountains of North Caro-

lina. Your Memorialist is a Resident of South Carolina, and has for the last twenty years been in the habit of spending four summer months at his summer retreat in North Carolina, and the remainder of the year at his residence in Charleston. His family is large consisting of ten children, and during the late war part of them occupied each of his two houses of residence, and at and before the evacuation of Charleston and for some time after, his house in that City was occupied by his servants and by a tenant placed there during the temporary absence of part of his family. These servants and the tenant were removed by order of the Military after the City was occupied by the forces of the United States, and the House and Lot was taken possession of by the Freedmens Bureau and made use of as an Orphan asylum for Negro children.

Your Memorialist made an application to the Freedmens Bureau setting forth these facts and praying restoration of the property; which has resulted in a recommendation from the head of that Bureau to his asst. Commissioner at Charleston[1] to remove the orphans to some other convenient location, and to admit your memorialist to the possession his house at a reasonable rent to be paid by him.

Your Memorialist has observed in the public newspapers a statement that the President has reached the consideration of cases of the class in which your Memorialist's case is comprehended, two of the members of the Cabinet of the late Confederate Government at the time of its dissolution having been admitted to the benefit of the amnesty.[2] Your Memorialist having resigned his office nearly two years before that dissolution, hopes that his case will be ruled by these precedents and that he will in like manner be admitted to the benefit of the amnesty.[3] But in case any considerations of public policy should render that inexpedient, your Memorialist prays that at least, your Excellency may grant him an order for the unconditional restoration of his home.[4]

C G Memminger.

ALS, DNA-RG94, Amnesty Papers (M1003, Roll 46), S.C., Christopher G. Memminger.
   1. Oliver O. Howard and Robert K. Scott.
   2. George Davis, attorney general, and George A. Trenholm, secretary of the treasury.
   3. Memminger was pardoned December 19, 1866. Amnesty Papers, (M1003, Roll 46), S.C., Christopher G. Memminger, RG94, NA; *Charleston Courier*, Dec. 22, 1866.
   4. Memminger's Charleston home was in the possession of his sons by December 18, 1866. Memminger to W. J. Bennett and W. J. Bennett to Memminger, Dec. 18, 1866, Amnesty Papers (M1003, Roll 46), S.C., Christopher G. Memminger, RG94, NA.

From Rice W. Payne[1]

[December 15, 1866][2]

Sir

The agent of the freedmans Bureau,[3] in this place (Warrenton) is about Collecting all the horses, left with the Citizens, by the army of the

United States, during the War. Upon inquiry by me, under whose order he was acting, replied "Genl Schofield, but that the order *probably* originated with the President."

For that reason I take the liberty of addressing this note to you directly.

Should this order be executed it will, in my opinion, not only defeat public policy—but in very many Cases, the ends of substantial justice also. Your Excellency is doubtless aware of the desolated Condition of the Country, the scarcity of money, and of the utter inability of many of our largest farmers to restock their plantations. With these horses, marked U S, and abandoned as worthless by the UNS army, these farmers have been enabled to cultivate crops, to a sufficient extent to prevent starvation, but deprive them of these horses—where, or how are they to procure others. Enormous Taxation state and Federal has withdrawn from them every dollar that can be spared from the most pressing family necesities, and I can not see how money can be obtained, in a country thus striped to procure a new supply of horses. The fact is, if these horses are reclaimed by the Government many farmers who are now heroicully struggleing against adversity, will be compelled to suspend operations— The products of the country diminished—and our ability to pay taxes greatly curtailed. It is surely against public policy, to produce such results by reclaiming for the government the mere pittance to it, invested in this abandoned stock.

I also respectfully submit: that the Citizens in this part of Virginia, which was in possession and occupancy of the UN States, almost exclusively during the war: have a just claim to the horses left with them by the forces of the UNited States.

It is a fact which investigation will demonstrate, that nine tenths, of the horses left with our people, were worn out in the service of the United States, and exchanged for efficient horses belonging to our citizens. These horses were owned, or purchased by us. We considered them then, as we do now, our property—not just forfeited by the laws of war, but our property still as non Combatants; and so we shall continue to think untill the end of time. We therefore think that the worn out horses left in exchange for our efficient horses are our property, justly and equitably and shall so continue to think untill the government shall think proper to grant us more equitable compensation.

We therefore ask of your Excellency—that the order to deprive us of these horses be recinded.[4]

R W Payne

ALS, DNA-RG92, Claims *re* Services, Horses, and Property.
1. Payne (1818–1884) was a well-to-do lawyer in Fauquier County, Virginia. Nancy C. Baird, *Fauquier County, Virginia, Tombstone Inscriptions* (Delaplane, Va., 1970), 193; 1870 Census, Va., Fauquier, 1st Revenue Dist., Warrenton P.O., 10.
2. The date comes from the docketing.
3. Winfield S. Chase (1835–1910), a watchmaker, was assistant subassistant commis-

sioner for the Freedmen's Bureau in Warrenton, Virginia, from July 1866 to August 1867. During and after the war he served with the 1st N.Y. Vol. Lgt. Arty. and the 18th Rgt., Vet. Res. Corps; he was discharged January 1, 1868. Everly and Pacheli, *Records of Field Officers*, pt. 3: 529; *Off. Army Reg.: Vols.*, 8: 59, 322; Pension File, Georgiana V. Chase, RG15, NA.

    4. Payne's letter was referred to the War Department.

From Louis Schaefer

Canton Ohio   Dcr 15/66.

Dear Sir.

Permit me briefly to present to your consideration the subject of the Collectorship of the 17th District of Ohio. The recent incumbent Hon: L W. Potter[1] died very *suddenly* and *unexpectedly* during the night of the 13th inst. When twice in your city in the latter part of Sept & forepart of October I refrained from enjoying the honor and pleasure of a personal interview, principally for the reason, that I did not desire to add to similar annoyances. As the recent National Union Candidate for Congress of said District I feel a pride to recommend as successor to Hon: L W Potter, General Samuel Beatty[2] a gentleman residing in Stark County in said District, in every respect well worthy and qualified to discharge the duties of said Office. The records of the late War speak of his brave and heroic deeds under Maj: General Thomas on the Cumberland, he was one of the first, and the last in the service, and also served with honor to himself & for the good of our Country in our War with Mexico. The General may be met by slanderers and base caluminators. Their assaults you know how to value and appreciate. The radical element here will recommend and urge the appointment of one Seraphim Meyer[3] a Lawyer of this place, and for a brief space of time Colonel of the 107 Regiment O.V.I. He with the desired approval of his superior Officers resigned and returned home. This same applicant in the only speech he made during our recent Campaign, charged you Sir, with having been a particeps criminis in the assassination of President Lincoln, and made infamous efforts to show circumstances connecting you with that crime.

Another applicant Samuel Lahm[4] of this place will also present his application to your consideration. He is a political huckster, despised by the Republican & repudiated by the Democratic Party, personally, morally and politically a Bankrupt. Those not intimately acquainted with this political Meanderings, may have ignorantly and inocently signed his recommendation. Others may apply for the same position. Stark County, the heaviest Tax-payer & by thousand the greater in Population, the Assessor[5] being located at Steubenville Jefferson County, the other Counties Columbiana & Carrol being the least in point of population and Taxation claims at your hands that consideration which under all the facts and circumstances she believes herself entitled to, & being favored with General Beatty as her Candidate, I hope his competency, his fidelity &

his honesty will be a sufficient passport for him in your estimation, to receive at your hands a favorable consideration, more especially as no one in our District is a more ardent admirer of your Policy than the General. Hoping his application will be crownd with success.[6]

Louis Schaefer

ALS, DNA-RG56, Appts., Internal Revenue Service, Collector, Ohio, 17th Dist., Samuel Beatty.

1. Lyman W. Potter (d. 1866), a New Lisbon, Ohio, lawyer and local judge of common pleas during the late 1850s, had been confirmed as collector the previous June. C. S. Speaker et al., *An Historical Sketch of the Old Village of New Lisbon, Ohio* (New Lisbon, 1903), 111, 113; Ser. 6B, Vol. 4: 256, Johnson Papers, LC.

2. Beatty (1820–1885), a farmer, Mexican War veteran, and former sheriff, rose from captain, 19th Ohio Inf., to brigadier general of volunteers during the Civil War. Warner, *Blue*.

3. Meyer (c1816–fl1890), a native of France who moved to Ohio in the late 1820s, was judge of the court of common pleas during the late 1870s. In 1887 he moved to southern California. Pension File, Seraphim Meyer, RG15, NA; Perrin, *Stark County*, 264.

4. In January, Schaefer again expressed his strong opposition to the appointment of Lahm. See Schaefer to Johnson, Jan. 8, 1867, Appts., Internal Revenue Service, Collector, Ohio, 17th Dist., Samuel Lahm.

5. Anson G. McCook (1835–1917), another member of the "Fighting McCooks" family, had risen to brevet brigadier general of volunteers during the war. Afterward, he was a lawyer, journalist, and Republican congressman (1877–83), moving to New York City in 1873. *BDAC*; Ser. 6B, Vol. 2: 202, Johnson Papers, LC.

6. Both Lahm and Beatty were rejected by the Senate in early 1867. Finally, on March 12, 1867, Kent Jarvis was confirmed as collector of Ohio's Seventeenth District. Ser. 6B, Vol. 4: 258, 259, Johnson Papers, LC.

To Daniel E. Sickles

Washington, D.C., Dec. 15th 1866

It is reported to me that Henry Miller[1] has been tried at Walterborough, S.C. as a Spy and deserter, and sentenced to be hanged on the 4th of January. Have the matter investigated at once and report.[2]

Andrew Johnson.

Tel, DNA-RG107, Tels. Sent, President, Vol. 3 (1865–68).

1. Miller (b. c1842) moved to South Carolina from Ulster County, New York, in 1860. Afterwards, he served in the South Carolina state forces and in the 11th S.C. Inf., CSA, until he deserted in January 1864. In late February 1865 he took the loyalty oath and was employed by the U.S. Army as a guide. After the withdrawal of the U.S. garrison from Walterboro in the summer of 1866, he was arrested and convicted on a charge of highway robbery, stemming from when he accompanied a foraging expedition which took a wagonload of bacon in March 1865. CSR, Henry Miller, RG109, NA; Henry Miller to Daniel E. Sickles, Nov. 25, 1866; Benezet F. Foust to Edward L. Deane, Dec. 17, 1866, Lets. Recd. (Main Ser.), File S-1279-1866 (M619, Roll 517), RG94, NA.

2. A report of Miller's case had already been ordered by Gen. John C. Robinson, commander of the Department of the South during General Sickles's absence, and it was forwarded to the adjutant general's office in Washington, and in turn to Johnson. On December 20, 1866, Governor Orr of South Carolina telegraphed the President that the military investigation was "*ex parte* as the Civil authorities had no notice" and promised to send (and did send) a report of the presiding judge at Miller's trial, noting that he had "respited Miller until March." A copy of the military investigation was ordered by Johnson to be sent to Orr. In January 1867 Orr wrote Johnson that he intended "to commute the sentence of

Miller to imprisonment for a term of years . . . not because his conviction was improper or unjust, but in consequence of the demoralization which pervaded society . . . at the time the offence was committed." John C. Robinson to Johnson, Dec. 16, 1866; James L. Orr to Johnson, Dec. 20, 1866, Johnson Papers, LC; John C. Robinson to Lorenzo Thomas, Dec. 18, 1866; Report of Judge Thomas W. Glover, ca. Dec. 26, 1866; James L. Orr to Johnson, Jan. 6, 1867, Lets. Recd. (Main Ser.), File S-1279-1866 (M619, Roll 517), RG94, NA.

From Jonah D. Hoover[1]

Washington, Decr. 17. 1866

Sir:

I have just received a letter from the Hon: Howell Cobb, of Georgia, in which he requests me to solicit at your hands the favor of an extension of his parole so that he may go where he pleases *in* or *out* of the country. His present parole confines him to Georgia, I believe. His object is to visit the North, and in the settlement of the Estate of Mrs. Cobb's brother,[2] he may wish to go to Havana at an early day.

The like request has been granted in other cases, I believe. Govr. Cobb would regard your prompt compliance as another evidence of your personal regard for him. He would prefer *a pardon*, but if you think it inconsistant with more important considerations, he is willing to sacrifice his personal interests and wishes to the general good.

As the personal friend of Gov. Cobb, I join in this appeal with peculiar pleasure, and shall regard your favorable action as a kindness to myself.

May I request you to leave the necessary paper with Col. Long Col. Rives,[3] or either of your *Aids* so that I can send it this week, if possible.[4]

J. D. Hoover

ALS, DNA-RG94, Amnesty Papers (M1003, Roll 17), Ga., Howell Cobb.
1. Hoover (1821–1870), a merchant and U.S. marshal of the District of Columbia during the 1850s, became the editor of the *Evening Express* a short time before his death. *Evening Star* (Washington), June 6, 1870.
2. Mary Ann Lamar (1818–1889), who married Cobb in the 1830s, and her brother, John Basil Lamar (1812–1862), a congressman in 1843, who administered the numerous properties which their father had left them. John Lamar was a voluntary aide on Gen. Howell Cobb's staff when he was mortally wounded at the battle of Crampton's Gap, Maryland. *NUC Manuscript Collections* (1984), 289; *DAB*; *BDAC*; James C. Bonner, *Milledgeville: Georgia's Antebellum Capital* (Athens, Ga., 1978), 40, 140; *OR*, Ser. 1, Vol. 19, Pt. 1: 871.
3. Andrew K. Long and Wright Rives.
4. Johnson in fact granted an extension of Cobb's parole so that he would be permitted to visit any place in or out of the United States that his business might require. Johnson to [Howell Cobb], Jan. 7, 1866 [1867], Johnson Papers, LC.

From William H. Seward

Department of State
Washington, 17th December 1866.

The Secretary of State, to whom was referred the resolution of the House of Representatives of the sixth instant requesting the President to communicate to that body "at as early a day as possible, 1st the names of all persons reappointed by him after rejection by the Senate, or, the names of others appointed in their stead with a designation of the offices to which they were so appointed, and the dates of their several appointments, and of their nominations to the Senate.

2nd A like list and designation of all persons appointed by him, whose names were with-held from the Senate during its sessions.

3rd A like list and description of all appointments made by him during the recess of the Senate where no vacancy had happened, and if to fill vacancies, then a complete statement of how such vacancies occurred,"[1]— has the honor to state in reply to the 1st interrogatory, that Henry Savage[2] was nominated as Consul to Guatemala, 13th Decr. 1865, and rejected by the Senate 29th May 1866

Edward Uhl[3] of New York was appointed in his stead Novr. 22, 1866, and nominated Decr. 10th 1866

W. W. Holden of North Carolina, nominated as Minister resident at Salvador June 15th 1866 and rejected by the Senate 23d July 1866

A. S. Williams[4] of Michigan, was appointed in his stead, August 16th 1866 and nominated December 10th 1866.

On the subject of the second interrogatory, I have to state that the Department is not aware that any names were withheld from the Senate during its sessions.

In regard to the matter of the third and last interrogatory, I subjoin a list 1st of all appointments made in this Department during the recess of the Senate where no vacancies had occurred.

2nd a list of all appointments made to fill vacancies and showing how said offices became vacant.

I also subjoin a classified list of the whole number of offices under the supervision of this Department, the nominations to which are required by law to be submitted to the Senate.

William H Seward

Copy, DNA-RG59, Reports to President and Congress.
    1. See *Congressional Globe*, 39 Cong., 2 Sess., p. 30; Stanton to Johnson, Dec. 11, 1866.
    2. Not otherwise identified.
    3. Uhl (1843–1906) served as consul to Guatemala until sometime in Grant's administration. Thereafter, he farmed in Ohio and was business manager and later president of the *New York Staats-Zeitung*. *New York Times*, Aug. 2, 1906.
    4. Alpheus S. Williams.

From J. Shearer[1]

Plymouth Wayne Co.   Michigan   December 17, 1866.
Dear Sir

On reading your Statesmanship, patriotic, philanthropic, and able message,[2] it carried me back to the days of our Fathers, and gave me great joy to know that the people had a president of all the united, States, and had done all in his power, to Save their union their peace, and prosperity, *to all*. Every word and line of it is clear, full, just, high, and lofty, and convincing to every rational mind of its truthful goodness and applicability to the uncommon times for which it was written. While reading it, it was impossible to Suppress my feelings of esteem for it, and its author, without Saying God bless Andrew Johnson. May he live long to enjoy the fruits of his auderous labors and see the radical advocates of a *Consolidated Despotism*, laid low in infamy. Sir be of good cheer as you are right, all the childish clamoring of the Radicals, and their press, to the Contrary notwithstanding. During the past history of our common country the people of the North have been clothed from the Cradle to the grave, with the products of the labor of the South, together with untold millions of wealth,—and yet the impious radicals, like the thoughtless Swine pick the acorns not careing from whence they fell. Yet there is one consolation left for conservative men, that when the Radical *Stock* in *trade* which consists of the *negro*, is out of the canvass; which is sure to be in a Short time, down goes their *Shanties*, and they will be numbered with the things that were. Let the constitution, and laws, be the rock of our Safty, and the *Bulwark* of our *liberties*, and we Shall emerge from the ordeal with grateful acknowledgements to the creator of the universe; for his great and bountiful help in times of need.

J Shearer

P.S. My profession is a farmer of the North, but yet I love my brethren of the South, as we are, and Should be all one common family, in Sustaing the general welfare, and good feeling, and let all past difficulties be remembered no more forever. Pardon me for imposing on your time as you have official business enough for your attention. But I thought best to let you know how millions of people think of your Message.

ALS, DLC-JP.
1. Probably either Johnathan Shearer (b. *c*1796) or Joseph Shearer (b. *c*1832), who were both Plymouth, Michigan, farmers and very likely related. 1860 Census, Mich., Wayne, Plymouth, 67.
2. See Message to Congress, Dec. 3, 1866.

From Margaret J. Simmons[1]

Lexington C.H. [S.C.]   Dec 17. 1866

Dear Sir

I hope you will excuse the liberty I take in addressing these few lines to you; but it is in behalf of the colored people of this place. I have been their teacher since Jan 1866 and have just been again appointed by the Episcopal Freedmans Society of New York. We had a hired room till last June when the Gentleman to whom it belonged refused us the use of it any longer.[2] From that time we have had no place. In Sep I hired a small house and have kept in a room under the house. The colored people commenced building a room meaning it for a church and also to keep a school in. Their little means have failed and they are unable to finish it. I have near one hundred scholars all eager to learn but they are very poor. In fact I beleve this to be the poorest District in the state. So I write to see if you will assist them. The smallest Sum will be thankfully received. I am a refugee my native place being Charleston. I have been led to appeal to you seeing your kindness to the colored people of that place.[3] I am unable to do any thing as I have lost all my property and have a Son[4] in tender years to support, I am the Widow of an Episcopal Clergman[5] and also the daughter of one.[6] Please let me hear from you as early as possible. Lexington C H. SoCa.

Mrs J Ward Simmons

ALS, DNA-RG105, Records of the Commr., Lets. Recd. (M752, Roll 42).

1. Mrs. Simmons, the widow of Henry Verdier, married the Reverend Simmons in late 1846. She had at least three children, two of whom died in infancy. Simmons file, Webber Col., ScHi; "The Schrimer Diary," *SCHM*, 69 (1968): 262; Brent H. Holcomb, *Marriage and Death Notices From Columbia, South Carolina, Newspapers 1838–1860* (Columbia, 1988), 74; *Messenger & Register*, 29 (1853): 351.

2. In the late spring of 1866 there was a disturbance at the Simmons school in Lexington. Gov. James L. Orr sought a report from state senator Lemuel Boozer, who investigated the alleged "riot" and afterwards assured the governor that the incident had been a minor disturbance. The events surrounding this incident may have caused Mrs. Simmons to lose the space for her school. For an account of the problems at Lexington regarding the school, see the letters published in the *New York Times*, July 1, 1866.

3. Mrs. Simmons was alluding to Johnson's donation of $1,000 to the Reverend A. Toomer Porter's Theological Institute in Charleston. See A. Toomer Porter to Johnson, July 28, 1866, *Johnson Papers*, 10: 745.

4. Possibly Christopher G. Simmons (b. 1847). Simmons file, Webber Col., ScHi.

5. James Ward Simmons (c1816–1854), who perished in a yellow fever epidemic, had served as deacon at St. Stephen's church in Charleston. After his ordination as priest in 1852, he moved to Spartanburg to become an assistant at the Church of the Advent there. Ibid.; *Charleston Courier*, Oct. 2, 1854; *Messenger & Register*, 25 (1848): 249, 377; 29 (1852): 59, 253.

6. Paul Trapier Gervais (c1785–fl1856), ordained a deacon in 1807 and priest in 1809, later served as rector in St. John's and St. Michael's parishes in Colleton and Charleston districts. 1850 Census, S.C., Charleston, St. Philip and St. Michaels Parishes, 245; Simmons file, Webber Col., ScHi; Charleston directories (1855–56); Frederick Dalcho, *An Historical Account of the Protestant Episcopal Church in South Carolina* (Charleston, 1820), 365.

From Daniel J. Hogan[1]

New York   December 18, 1866

Sir.

I would respectfully call your attention to my application for a commission in the regular army made to the Secretary of War on the 1st of August last.[2]

I forwarded with my application testimonials as to faithful Services &c from Hon. Henry J. Raymond, Major Genl. Weitzel,[3] Brevet Brig Genl

Yeoman[4] and others showing that I had served over two years in the army first as a private in the 5th New Jersey Battery and afterwards a 2d & 1st Lieut. in the 43d U.S. Colored Troops.

I would also call your Excellency's attention to the fact that in view of the fact that some of the new regiments of the regular army to be composed of colored men it is but fair that those officers who were connected with that branch of the Army during the war should receive some, at least, of the appointments in these colored regiments.

The 43d U.S. Cold. Troops, with which I had the honor to serve, was, with a few other colored regiments, connected with *the army of the Potomac* and took an active part in the campaign of Genl. Grant from the crossing of the Rapidan May 5, 1864 to the taking of Richmond April 3, 1865. During that time the regiment participated in fourteen battles comprising the Wilderness, Spotsylvania, Cold Harbor &c &c as the records of the War Department will show. This I believe is as good a record as any colored regiment in the service could show. Much better as far as the amount of fighting is concerned than the great majority of them which were stationed in the South and Southwest.

Yet while the Gazette shows a number of appointments from colored regiments which during the war were stationed at remote points, it does not chronicle a single one, as far as I can ascertain, from those that composed Ferrero's[5] division of the 9th Army Corps *Army of the Potomac* viz: the 19th, 23d, 31st, 29th, 43d &c. A division which in the battle of the mine before Petersburg July 30, 1864 left one half its number killed or wounded before and in the rebel breastworks.[6]

Daniel J. Hogan   late 1st Lieut. 43d U.S.C.T.

No. 224 East 14th Street   New York City

ALS, DNA-RG94, ACP Branch, File H-1463-CB-1866, Daniel J. Hogan.

1. Hogan (1843–1917) worked as a clerk before enlisting in a New Jersey artillery battery in 1863 and later joining the 43rd USCT. After the war Hogan continued clerking in New York City, except for a brief stint in Kansas. CSR, Daniel J. Hogan, RG94, NA; Pension File, Daniel J. Hogan, RG15, NA.

2. Not found, but see Hogan's application for a position in the Freedmen's Bureau. Hogan to Johnson, July 19, 1866, Records of the Commr., Lets. Recd. (M752, Roll 35), RG105, NA.

3. Godfrey Weitzel (1835–1884) graduated from the U.S. Military Academy and served in the army for several years prior to the Civil War, which saw him rise in rank from captain of engineers to major general of volunteers. After the war he returned to the engineering branch of the regular army. Warner, *Blue*.

4. Stephen B. Yeoman (1836–1917), who commanded the 43rd USCT and was brevetted brigadier general in March 1865, worked as a lawyer and mine operator after the war. Hunt and Brown, *Brigadier Generals*.

5. Edward Ferrero (1831–1899), a native of Spain, taught dance at West Point before mustering into the 51st N.Y. Inf. at the start of the war. Promoted to brigadier general in late 1862, his reputation suffered in 1864 after the battle of The Crater, where his lack of leadership contributed to Union defeat. Despite this, he was brevetted major general in December 1864. Following the war he returned to New York and managed a succession of ballrooms. Warner, *Blue*.

6. A regular army commission was not forthcoming for Hogan.

From Lucius B. Marsh[1]

Boston   December 18th. 1866

Dear Sir.

Please read the enclosed correspondence. Adj't. Genl. William Schouler[2] is well known at the War Department, and is a very able and efficient officer, and worthy man. He is removed from office for the simple and *only* reason—he opposed Genl. Butler for "Representative" to Congress, on the ground that he was an *avowed Enemy of the* President.[3] Is not this one of the rare cases, where it would be appropriate and justifiable that the President should give Gen Schouler some good office, *unasked for by him?* He does not know that I have written this letter. He is a very able man and would make a most excellent Assessor or Collector of Internal Revenue, either in our own state or some Southern State. I have known Genl. Schouler for several years, and have had official business with him from the first to the close of the War, and a more faithful and efficient officer we have not in our state.[4]

Lucius B. Marsh—Colonel Late 47th Regt Mass Vols.

ALS, DNA-RG56, Appts., Internal Revenue Service, Assessor, Mass., 6th Dist., Wm. Schouler.

1. Marsh (1818–1901) headed a woolen importing firm in Boston. *NUC*; Boston directories (1867–70).

2. Schouler (1814–1872), a Republican, had a relatively long career in politics and as editor of several newspapers in Massachusetts and Ohio before he was appointed as adjutant general of the former state on the eve of the war. Afterwards he served in the Massachusetts legislature and wrote a two-volume history of the Civil War. The enclosed material consisted of a newspaper clipping, with reprints of several letters, both to and from Schouler, regarding his removal as adjutant general of Massachusetts by Gov. Alexander H. Bullock on December 17, 1866. *DAB*.

3. A few days later Marsh sent the President a reprint of another of Schouler's letters, which boldly defended the Johnson administration and strongly opposed Benjamin Butler's election to Congress. Marsh to Johnson, Dec. 22, 1866, Appts., Internal Revenue Service, Assessor, Mass., 6th Dist., Wm. Shouler, RG56, NA.

4. Marsh's letter was referred to the State Department and then forwarded to Secretary McCulloch. See endorsements attached to the Marsh letter.

From Charles Camper[1]

Washington City.   Dec. 19. 1866.

Sir,

I regret to be obliged, on behalf of myself and other clerks in the employ of the Register of Deeds for the District of Columbia, to make a complaint to your Excellency, and ask you to redress grievances which we suffer as clerks at the hands of the Register, Richard M. Hall. I feel convinced that if your Excellency knew but the half of the injuries we receive and suffer at the hands of the Register, his utter neglect of the duties of the Office, his continued absence during office hours, and the general dissatisfaction of and inconvenience to, the public consequent thereon, you would not hesitate an hour to apply the remedy. But these facts you are not permitted to know and I propose now to inform you.

In the first place we, the clerks, are poor men, dependent on our daily labor for a scanty support, most of us have served our Country in the field, and forced to work for about one half the compensation given in Baltimore and other cities for the same work, and when the work is done, we are paid only when it suits the convenience of Mr. Hall, at such time and in such amounts as pleases him, without regard to the amount due us or to the fact that our families are in need of the money he owes us, and private speculations &c &c.

We learn that the chief arguments made use of by Mr. Hall against his predecessor,[2] to secure his own appointment, was, the clerks were not paid enough for their services, and did not receive their wages when due and that he paid less. It is not because Mr. Hall is not paid; that he does not receive his money in advance &c, he does not pay us. The gross receipts of the office will exceed $9,000 per annum. Clerk hire, blank books, fuel and other office expenses will amount to less than 20 per cent of the receipts. Having a disregard to his official duties, he entrusts the entire business of the office to an offensive and disagreeable man as his chief,[3] while the indexes to the records show an omission, which he neglects to supply.

The law requires him to make proper examination of deeds recorded, which he also totally neglects.

These being facts, which we can abundantly prove if required, we, most respectfully ask your Excellency for some improvement on the present incumbent.[4]

Chas. Camper

ALS, DNA-RG48, Appts. Div., Misc. Lets. Recd.
    1. Camper (fl1886) later served as a clerk in the War Department (1871) and the adjutant general's office (1868, 1872–86). Washington, D.C., directories (1866–86).
    2. Nathaniel C. Towle (1805–1898) was the first recorder of deeds for the District of Columbia (1863–66). A resident of Washington since at least 1838, he was a member of the District bar and served a time as clerk of the Senate. Wilhelmus B. Bryan, A History of the National Capital (2 vols., Norwood, Mass., 1914–16), 2: 521; Job Barnard, "History of the Church of the New Jerusalem in the City of Washington," Records CHS, 24 (1922): 25; Wallace, North American Authors, 462.
    3. Not identified.
    4. In March 1867 a successor to Hall, Edward C. Eddie, was confirmed as recorder of deeds. Bryan, National Capital, 2: 521.

From Hugh McCulloch

December 19th 1866

Sir

I transmit herewith for your approval the nomination of B. P. Carpenter[1] as Assessor of Internal Revenue 12th District of New York in place of James Mackin[2] rejected by the Senate.

Mr Mackin received a temporary appointment vice Carpenter September 24" 66, and was recommended by S. J. Tilden *and* Delegates to the Natl Union Convention Phila. Penna.[3]

The removal of Carpenter was strongly objected to by Thurlow Weed and many others.

Mr Weed now urges his re-appointment and is joined by Hon's H. J Raymond, R. S. Hale,[4] H. H. Van Dyck, H A Smythe, James Kelly, Tho McElrath, Stephen Baker and Hon. J. H Ketchum[5] (member from the District).[6]

H McCulloch   Secretary of the Treasury.

LS, DNA-RG56, Appts., Internal Revenue Service, Assessor, N.Y., 12th Dist., B. P. Carpenter.

1. Benjamin P. Carpenter (1837–1921) had served as assessor of the Twelfth District since 1864, when President Lincoln appointed him. A Republican attorney, judge, and member of the state legislature, Carpenter removed to the Montana Territory in the 1880s, where he served briefly as territorial governor and as member of the Montana constitutional convention. McMullin and Walker, *Territorial Governors*, 217–18; *U.S. Off. Reg.* (1863).

2. After Johnson's recess appointment of Mackin (*c*1822–*fl*1879), a New York assemblyman and onetime state treasurer, the Senate rejected his nomination on December 18. Ser. 6B, Vol. 3: 95; Vol. 4: 51, Johnson Papers, LC; Stephen C. Hutchins, *Civil List and Constitutional History of the Colony and State of New York* (Albany, 1882), 159, 332, 343–45; 1860 Census, N.Y., Dutchess, Fishkill, Matteawan, 292.

3. Henry W. Slocum and John A. Dix also recommended Mackin's appointment, which had been held up by McCulloch on October 1 but ordered "to be perfected" by Johnson five days later. H. W. Slocum to Johnson, Oct. 7, 1866, Appts., Internal Revenue Service, Assessor, N.Y., 12th Dist., James Mackin, RG56, NA.

4. Robert S. Hale (1822–1881) was a New York attorney and judge who served as a Republican in Congress (1866–67, 1873–75). *BDAC*.

5. Stephen Baker (1819–1875) had represented the Twelfth District of New York in Congress as a Republican (1861–63), while John H. Ketchum (1832–1906), a former state legislator and brevet major general during the war, was reelected in November 1866 to his second of a total of seventeen terms as a Republican congressman (1865–73, 1877–93, 1897–1906). Ibid.

6. Carpenter's nomination was sent to the Senate on December 20 and confirmed the following day. Ser. 6B, Vol. 4: 51, Johnson Papers, LC.

From George Jones[1]

City of New York   No. 37. East 27 Street
Decr. 20. 1866

Sir.

By pen and speech I have proved my friendship to you; and my defense of your constitutional deportment as President is proverbial.[2]

The extreme Radicals are circumscribing your legal rights as the Executive; illegally enlarging their own powers by a pseudo Congress; not only to project Impeachment, and suspension from office of the President during trial &c; but, by infamous inuendo, and almost direct accusation, that you had pre-knowledge of the assassination of your predecessor,— the late President of the United States.

Wendell Phillips (see todays N. Y. Herald Decr. 20/66),[3]—writes and

publishes,—in reference to the threatened Impeachment (& Gen'l Butler is pledged to it)—that *You* are "*an Usurper with bloody and unclean
hands*,"—the very words applied by Historians to describe Richard III of
England,—upon ascending his blood-dyed throne, by the assassination
of the rightful occupant & predecessor.

The *New York Times* published as follows,—in the matter of Jefferson
Davis, viz, "*The proclamation of President Johnson,—as a co-assassin of
the late Mr. Lincoln, carries with it a howl and a curse throughout the
world!*"[4]—and that *I* uttered those words!—a Libel, doubly so,—infa-
mously false, and for which malicious Libel, I have sued Henry J. Raymond; and the case will be tried in the Superior Court of the City of New
York in the next month, Jan'y 1867. It stands No. 3053 upon the trial list
of causes Now,—the defense will set up Radical rumors &—therefore,—
I am legally advised, upon my suggestion, to issue a Commission to take
your testimony—of and Concerning the historical event of April 14,
1865,—as to your knowledge of the subject-matter of these infamous &
malicious accusations,—first set afloat by the inuendo letter of Beverly
Tucker.

In the trial of Aaron Burr for treason, he demanded the presence of
President Thomas Jefferson as a Witness. Chief Justice John Marshall
refused the mandate, upon the ground of public inconvenience for the
President to journey from Washington to Richmond,—(a great distance
in those days of travelling); & prolonged absence from the Capital.
But, the Chief Justice Said,—a Commission may issue to take the President's Sworn testimony, and he must obey, as any other Citizen;—yet,—
the President, if he will, can personally visit Richmond, and testify on
oath in open Court. Now—therefore,—upon those legal decisions, I respectfully propound the following questions,—viz 1stly. Will it be your
pleasure to personally attend the said Court in New York City in January
next, to testify on behalf of Plaintiff;—*and forever crush out,—on your
oath,—the Serpent inuendo against You*? for; upon Impeachment, or otherwise, a prisoner cannot testify, or give evidence against the accusation. I
will so arrange as to time, with the Honble. Court,—that your Convenience as to the precise day,—shall be entirely Consulted & arranged.

Your friends here believe, that my suggestion will meet your wisdom
in the premises.

—or 2dly. Will you prefer a Commission to issue by the Court, to take
your deposition upon Interrogatories? If the latter,—then, any suggestive questions on your part,—in addition to those I shall frame,—shall be
inserted in the Commission for examination in chief.

I have thus written to your Excellency as in duty bound,—*before* I
issue,—as is my legal right,—the Commission,—that your pre-decision
in the subject-matter,—shall first be rendered, upon the foregoing propositions as to the manner of taking your evidence.[5]

       George the Count Joannes   (Plaintiff in person)

ALS, DLC-JP.

1. Jones (1810–1879), sometimes called "Count Joannes," was a Welsh-born Shakespearean actor, lecturer, and author, whose eccentric behavior and curious attire won him a great following, though little respect. Irving Browne, "Count Johannes," *The Green Bag*, 8 (1896): 435–39; *New York Tribune Illustrated Supplement*, Jan. 23, 1898.

2. To date, Jones had written several public letters supporting the President and his policies. See, for example, Jones to Johnson, June 26, July 27, Sept. 30, 1865, Johnson Papers, LC.

3. The editorial is entitled "Wendell Phillips on the Impeachment of the President."

4. Here Jones refers to a report which had appeared in the *Times* of June 12, and which he strongly rebutted in his letter to the President later that month. See Jones to Johnson, June 26, 1865, Johnson Papers, LC.

5. Jones sent his letter in care of the President's son, Robert. Not hearing from either Johnson, Jones wrote again in late January 1867, and once more in mid-February, indicating that the trial had been put off until early March. But the case apparently was not called up during the entire year, and the suit is believed to have been discontinued by the defendant. Jones to Robert Johnson, Dec. 20, 1866; Jones to Johnson, Jan. 31, Feb. 19, 1867, ibid.

From Benjamin Rush

11 Upper Seymour Street, Portman Square,
London, 21. Decr. 1866.

Dear Sir,

It was not to be wondered at that your Annual Message[1] should be looked forward to with great eagerness and attract great attention, here, just now.

We got the Telegraphic summary on the day after The Message was delivered. I was in company, on the following day, with three old officers of the British Army, two of them men of rank. Your Message was a natural and prominent topic. Alluding to your firmness in adhering to your convictions on the Reconstruction question, one of the three remarked, in deliberate tones, on the "wonderful determination" it exhibited, "and," he added slowly, "*he'll be very apt to carry his point by it yet*," men in all ages and countries being more or less swayed in their judgments, sooner or later, by the iron firmness of one man in authority, no matter how adverse, at one time, the state of things may have been.

"*Plucky chap*," said another English gentleman to me, who takes great interest in our affairs, and questioned me closely as to the condition of things. I should have been apt to think him not a very civil "chap" by such an allusion to the Chief Magistrate of my Country, and perhaps to have manifested my sense of that feeling, but I knew, from my long residence here formerly, that the term "chap" is often indicative of great friendliness, besides that the whole tenor of his conversation was one of high respect for you, and for our Country, which he longs to visit, and seems to know how to estimate.

"We think a great deal of him in England"; "He's an immense favorite here"; "It doesn't seem right to press so hard upon the South"; "Really a noble character"—these, and similar expressions, uttered in conversation with me, will give you some little idea of the sentiment of the *Clubs* of London. To one of these, "The Travellers," I am in the habit of going a good deal, under an obliging invitation from The Committee, and perhaps there are few better resorts at which, and from which, to catch an occasional glimpse, and reflex, of the educated and enlightened mind and sentiment of England.

But this week the papers have had long articles about you, The Message having been published in London in full on Monday last the 17h inst.

"We are struck anew" said The *Times* "with surprise, *not however wholly unleavened by respect*, at the stubbornness of character which maintains a policy once adopted, although it has since been decisively rejected by those without whose aid it could not possibly be carried into execution."

The *Standard* didn't of course quite like what was said about England, but spoke in a tone of high commendation of your views of Reconstruction, alluding at the same time to the "tremendous responsibility, and fearful difficulty" of your position.

"The future" it continued, "of his country hangs in the balance. If he fails, he gives up eleven States of the Union to a frightful tyranny; to proscription, disfranchisement, the rule of immigrant enemies, malignant renegades and emancipated negroes. If he fails, the hope of true re-union is lost for ever; the South becomes another Mexico in material desolation, another Poland in political misery and disaffection. If he fails, the Radicals triumph, and the government of the Country is handed over to the worst masters it could possibly have."

"The President," it adds, "adheres *firmly* to the advice which he has all along given to the victorious North," and, after recapitulating your views, says, "by the wisdom and justice of this counsel, only men maddened by evil passions and insane fanaticism, can possibly doubt."

It then pays a high tribute to your course during the War, and refers to the fearful perils and sacrifices you encountered and endured on account of your devotion to the Union, and because you were regarded in your own neighborhood, as "*a traitor to the South.*"

It next points out that, after all, under our inevitable arrangement of electoral districts, the large Congressional majority now arrayed against you, is by no means a faithful representation or indication of the actual state of popular feeling, for that in reality, "*of the entire Nation a great majority are on his side*," and that such a "reaction," at no distant day, as would divide and dishearten the majority, and enable The President to resist it, is not improbable."

The article concludes thus:—

"That he is a far better and wiser man than any of his leading adversaries, is certain; that he is honest in his purpose, sound in his views, and well acquainted with the perils that beset him, is almost equally clear;

and not until we can see distinctly that a better mode of attaining his essential object was open to him, shall we be disposed to condemn the resolution with which he has adhered to his original policy."

The article is a very long one, and is characterized by strength and discrimination. It is obviously the production of a thoroughly competent pen, and the subject is handled with as much calmness; as power and truth.

So much for the *Standard*, a paper of immense circulation.

The *Globe*, had a capital article on the same evening.

"The Congress at Washington," it began, is "resolved to undertake the arduous task of treating the Southern States as Russia treats Poland. They are to be deprived of their old rights as Members of The Union; they are to be shorn of power, and deliberately kept in subjection. At present the Southern States have no more voice in the government of The Union, than the Poles have in the Councils of St. Petersburgh. Hence the conflict between Congress and the President.

The Congress—*a sectional one*—elected solely by the North—desires to perpetuate this condition of things; the President is resolved, by all means in his power, to bring it to an end. The policy of the President is the same as that of his predecessor."

After a scathing exposure of the cruel and narrow, "one sided and selfish" policy of the Radicals, the Globe continues:—

"Such at bottom is the policy of Congress. Numerous as is the population whose views it represents, *it is still a sectional policy.* The policy of The President is different. It is not a sectional policy. He is the Chief of the Nation, the Representative of all the States alike. He is the Head of The Union, and as such, he has no interests save those of The Union at large.

He does not say, *this* set of principles is right, and *that* wrong; THAT he says, is for the States themselves to determine. Let *all the Members of The Union meet together on equal terms*, and discuss the questions between them, and let *the vote of the whole*, which exhibits the interests of the majority, decide."

The *Morning Herald* of Tuesday the 18th said:—"The President is alone, with nearly all the world against him. He has a desperate battle to fight, and he is fighting it bravely."

While the article is perhaps a little *sarcastic*, here and there, in reference to what is said in the Message about England, it still pays ill concealed compliments to the Chief Magistrate, whose conciliatory policy it contrasts with the "insolent and cruel dictation" attempted to be practised upon the Southern People, and concludes by the admission that the People of America "in default of him" (The President) "may have a less humane and less enlightened ruler."

The *Pall Mall Gazette* extracted, without comment, your views of Reconstruction.

The *Morning Post* of Wed. the 19h. which I sent you, had one of the best articles which appeared. It spoke of the "singular felicity and conclusiveness of the Message," and dwelled upon the strength of the argument as regards representation and taxation.

Saturday, 22d. Decr.

The *London Review* (Weekly) of to-day, though not inclined to endorse all the Presidents views, admits very frankly that

"the disfranchisement of all prominent Southern whites must just as surely fill the Country with a dangerous agitation. Such a class is not rendered powerless by being disfranchised; its power is only made perilous by being driven into indirect, or concealed channels. It is then hardly to be regretted that the Southern Legislatures have almost unanimously rejected the Constitutional Amendments."

It thus concludes,

"and it will probably be found, as events go on with their infallible logic that no other element of Reconstruction will prove itself so potent, as that which shall secure the free commercial and social mingling of Northern and Southern People."

The *Spectator* has an ill natured article and sides with your opponents, yet is forced notwithstanding, and apparently unconsciously, into the avowal of some truths, as patent, as they are discreditable to the Radicals.

"Again," it says, "the American Liberals have a reason for adopting the extreme course which, *though they will not avow it*, will be exceedingly operative.

They dread, with an unhealthy but natural fear, the return of the Southern Members to the Central Legislature, lest, though victors in the field, they should find themselves overmastered in the forum.

True, the war has placed the North in a position of unquestioned superiority in physical strength. True, the South must come back in greatly diminished numbers and with greatly impaired prestige. Despite all that, a popular assembly, however constituted, *is always much at the mercy of its ablest men*,["] (which it had previously shown was always more or less the case of the Southern representatives) "and in any event," it concludes, "half the energy of the Liberal Party would have to be wasted in incessant watchfulness, lest, in some unlucky moment, the sudden conversion of a few members, say from the South West, should undo the results of the War."

And this is the whole case of the Radicals in a nut shell!

A much esteemed correspondent writes to me from Phila. by the last Steamer as follows:—

"I consider it, (The Message) a very able paper, and one that will do him great credit in years to come." My correspondent is a man of reflection, and was at one time disposed to criticise your course. We have often discussed your policy and views. Hence what he now says may go for all the more.

Though the papers, some or all, from which I have made the above extracts, will doubtless be at your command, it has seemed to me that possibly the extracts might be none the less interesting to you.

Heartily concurring in all that is said in commendation of what I still think your eminently wise and patriotic course, which assuredly the voice of history will endorse, even if the voice of fanaticism and passion should yet be enabled temporarily to overbear and drown, and again thanking you, as one of your constituents in a distant land, for your courageous adherence to your views of duty . . .

Benjamin Rush.

ALS, DLC-JP.
1. See Message to Congress, Dec. 3, 1866.

Interview with Benjamin Eggleston

WASHINGTON, Saturday, Dec. 22, 1866.

The President replied to this[1] that he did not think he had shown a further opposition to the popular verdict than merely to express his opinions to Congress on what he thought would but conduce to the welfare of the country. He thought the Radical Party had made a great mistake in spending so much time as they did last session before announcing upon what terms they would agree to readmit the Southern States, and what great damage to the public welfare had been the result of this delay, and now that Congress had passed the Amendment, and it was about to become part of the Constitution, he could see no guarantee that the Southern States would be admitted, even after the ratification had been fully accomplished.

MR. EGGLESTON replied to this that there was an implied guarantee in the speedy admission of Tennessee after the Legislature had ratified the Amendment, and that he thought the party with which he acted would be nearly a unit on the admission of others of the late rebel States, as soon as they had complied with the conditions exacted from Tennessee.

The President said he hoped this would prove to be true, but he feared there would be strong opposition to such a policy from the extreme Radicals.

MR. EGGLESTON said he felt little doubt on the subject. There might be some opposition from Sumner and Stevens, but it was a good characteristic of Stevens that if he couldn't get what he wanted, he would take the best he could get.

"Yes," said the President, "that's true of Stevens, and I always liked him for it. A practical man, but he seems to me to be working in the wrong direction." The President repeated the hope that the South would be admitted to representation on the adoption of the Amendment. It was useless now, he said, to discuss the propriety or impropriety of the conditions embraced in that measure. It had been agreed upon, and all he could now ask was the guarantee that reconstruction upon that basis should be faithfully kept by the party that had offered it. He expressed regret and surprise that so few members of Congress had called upon him since the opening of the session.

MR. EGGLESTON replied that he did not think members of Congress should carry their antagonism so far as that. He believed in fighting out old political battles before the people, and thought that opposition to the views of the President ought not to deter members from conferring with the Executive or consulting on business matters.

The President concurred in this view exactly. He would like to have men of all political complexions call on him and tell him what they wanted. No harm could possibly come of such an interchange of views, and a great deal of good might come of it, and now that the quarrel had been settled, as most people thought, there was certainly no reason why Senators and Representatives should sedulously so avoid him.

The conversation was concluded by MR. EGGLESTON inquiring what about the Mexican question. The President replied that it didn't look as favorably as he had hoped to have it, but still he thought all would be well.

New York Times, December 26, 1866.
1. Eggleston had asked Johnson whether "it would have been better for him to have surrendered his views and opinions in favor of the popular verdicts in October and November, and not to have pressed his policy in his last message." *New York Times*, Dec. 26, 1866.

From Albert B. Sloanaker

Philadelphia, Decem. 22d 1866

My Dear Sir:

From advices received from Messrs. Cattell, Williams, Yates,[1] and other Senators, I learn that if you withhold my name from the Senate for the present, there is a great probability, if not a certainty of my confirmation, But if I am sent in early a slaughter is inevitable, superinduced by my activity and notoriety in the recent campaign.

In view of our past relations may I not ask for this additional token of your distinguished consideration, if not incompatible with your views of public justice and policy, for I am as ever, willing to make any personal sacrifice that may redound to the credit of yourself or the Administration.

I beg to state here that I unhesitatingly refer you to either the Secretary of the Treasury, or the Commissioner of Internal Revenue,[2] for any endorsement deemed necessary of me as a Public Officer, or as to the general management of this Office in the interest of the Public and the government. Trusting that you may find it in your power to grant this favor, and wishing at the same time in advance to extend to you the compliments of the Season . . . [3]

A B Sloanaker

LS, DNA-RG56, Appts., Internal Revenue Service, Collector, Pa., 1st Dist., A. B. Sloanaker.

1. Alexander G. Cattell, George H. Williams, and Richard Yates. A Republican senator from Oregon (1865–71), Williams (1823–1910) later served as Grant's third attorney general and as mayor of Portland (1902–5). *BDAC*.

2. Edward A. Rollins, whom Sloanaker had written a few days earlier, asking for his help in getting confirmed. Sloanaker to Rollins, Dec. 12, 1866, Johnson Papers, LC.

3. Sloanaker's nomination as collector of the First District of Pennsylvania was, apparently, put off until early February 1867, only to have the Senate reject it that same month. He evidently retained his post, however, through April 1867. *Senate Ex. Proceedings*, Vol. 15, pt. 1: 189, 268; Sloanaker to Johnson, May 18, 1867, Johnson Papers, LC.

From James W. Throckmorton

Austin Texas.
Dated 22d. Recd Dec. 23d 1866

Sir.

A freedman indicted and convicted for an attempt to murder, & escaped.[1] The Bureau Agent Houston[2] resists his arrest by the Sheriff.[3] Is there any redress.[4]

J. W. Throckmorton   Govr.

Tel, DLC-JP.

1. Dick Perkins (c1848–fl1870), freedman, and his former master, Darwin, shot each other, whereupon Perkins was thrown into jail. He escaped five weeks later but then surrendered to the Bureau. While in Bureau custody, Perkins was rearrested and turned over to Darwin. When later asked where and when Perkins had been tried and *convicted*, Throckmorton claimed that his original telegram read: "A freedman, indicted and confined for a deadly assault escaped. The bureau agent at Houston resists his re-arrest by the Sheriff. Is there any redress?" 1870 Census, Tex., Robertson, 1st Prec., Calvert, 53; J. C. De-Gress to Edwin M. Stanton, Dec. 27, 1866, quoted in E. D. Townsend to Throckmorton, Dec. 28, 1866, Tels. Sent, Sec. of War (M473, Roll 91), RG107, NA; J. W. Throckmorton to E. D. Townsend, Jan. 8, 1867, Johnson Papers, LC.

2. Col. Jacob C. DeGress.

3. It is unclear whether DeGress's problems were primarily with law officers in Houston or with officials in Grimes County, where the original assault and imprisonment took place. Richter, *Overreached on All Sides*, 138–39.

4. Although at first Stanton ordered DeGress not to interfere with the civil authorities, when he found out more about the situation, he agreed to transfer the Perkins case to the federal courts under the Civil Rights Act of 1866. DeGress, however, did not trust Throckmorton and therefore helped Perkins "disappear." Bvt. Maj. Gen. Joseph B. Kiddoo, head of the Bureau in Texas, relieved DeGress from his Houston post on December 31, 1866. Edwin M. Stanton to Agent of the Freedmen's Bureau at Houston, Tex., Dec. 24, 1866, Tels. Sent, Sec. of War (M473, Roll 91), RG107, NA; Richter, *Overreached on All Sides*, 139–40. For more of Throckmorton's complaints against the Freedmen's Bureau, see Throckmorton to Johnson, Aug. 20, 1866, and O. M. Roberts and David G. Burnet to Johnson, Dec. 6, 1866.

From Romulus V. Hamilton[1]

Newberry South Carolina   24 December 1866

Sir

I beg leave for reasons which this letter will fully explain to call to your recollection the different interviews with which you were pleased to favor me while you were Governor of Tenesee by my then appellation of R. S. Morrison a federal detective and scout.

The name Morrison was assumed because I was a member of a family devoted to the cause of the rebellion and while serving the Federal cause I was anxious to spare them what they would have considered cause for great mortification.

While acting as scout and detective I was employed by yourself and by Col. Parkhurst[2] Provost General of the Cumberland Department also by Gen. Thomas all of whom were pleased to express the highest satisfaction with my services.

My true name is Romulus V. Hamilton and my address for the present is at Newberry South Carolina where I have been residing since the close of the war.

I have been attending an Academy and School since the close of the war to add to my limited education and from the deliberate and wicked disposition of the people who suspect and perhaps know something of my past life I have been brought under the Suspicion of the Military Authorities upon Charges utterly false that I was concerned in the Murder of a Soldier belonging to Lt. Fout's[3] Command at the jail in Newberry S.C. and also in wounding a Soldier at Cokesberry in Abbeville District S.C.

The Charges are utterly false and but for the determination of the people here who wish to destroy me I could fully vindicate myself. I am fearful to surrender myself because I know my enemies would make those who should be my friends destroy me.

I appeal to you for justice. I ask your interference to rescue me from the net that envelopes me and I do so in memory of the services which I have rendered and for which I am now suffering while represented by my enemies as in opposition to that authority which I have sacrificed so much to sustain. I respectfully ask for a pardon, a general pardon and also to include those specific charges. Were I favored with the permission and had the means to visit Washington I could satisfy your excellency of the entire propriety of your granting my apparently bold request.

Allow me to invite your personal attention to this matter and sincerely hope my prayer may be granted at an early day.[4]

R. V. Hamilton

LS, DNA-RG94, Amnesty Papers (M1003, Roll 45), S.C., Romulus V. Hamilton.
    1. Not further identified. A scout using the name Richard Morrison did make a report to Gen. George H. Thomas's army just prior to the battle of Nashville. Statement of Rich-

ard Morrison, Dec. 13, 1864, Records of Central Office, Correspondence *re* Scouts, Guides, Spies and Detectives, RG110, NA.

2. John G. Parkhurst.

3. William L. Fouts (1840–1920), a farm hand from Morgan County, Ohio, in March 1865 became a first lieutenant in that state's 25th Inf. Rgt. After several postwar moves, he settled in McPherson, Kansas, and worked as a carpenter. 1860 Census, Ohio, Morgan, Bloom Twp., 80; Pension File, Anna E. Fouts, RG15, NA.

4. No pardon of any kind has been located for Hamilton.

From Samuel McKelvy et al.[1]

Pittsburgh Penna.   December 24th 1866

Having learned with regret that George S. Gallupe's appointment as Captain in the Regular Army has been canceled[2] by your order for using violent and disrespectful language towards your administration,

We, the undersigned, who are intimately acquainted and in daily intercourse with Mr. G. certify upon honor that we never have heard or Known Mr. G. to use such language in reference to Your Excellency or Your administration, and Know him to be a good soldier and in every way worthy of the position.[3]

We therefore pray Your Excellency to reconsider your former action and reinstate Mr. Gallupe.[4]

LS, DNA-RG94, ACP Branch, File G-451-CB-1866, G. S. Gallupe.

1. There are seven signatories, including McKelvy, James Lowry, Jr., Robert B. Carnahan, and William G. McCandless, all of whom held political appointments under Johnson.

2. Ending the war as colonel, 5th Pa. Inf., Gallupe (1832–1900), who worked in the oil business before 1861, had held a captain's commission in the 45th U.S. Inf. for several months, until his commission was revoked on November 30, 1866. Heitman, *Register*, 1: 443; *Pittsburgh Post*, Apr. 6, 1900.

3. Not so, according to one Pittsburgh resident who described Gallupe as a "Radical without principle." Sen. Edgar Cowan agreed, adding that Gallupe was both "insolent and abusive." William J. Kountz to Johnson, Dec. 12, 1866, Johnson Papers, LC. Cowan's comments are on the reverse side of Kountz's letter to Johnson.

4. Gallupe also gave his honor as an officer, denying that he had ever spoken disparagingly of the President. Johnson referred the petition to Secretary Stanton, finding that "the explanation is satisfactory." Gallupe was reappointed, this time as captain of the 43rd U.S. Inf., and he continued serving in the army until his retirement in 1878. Ser. 6B, Vol. 2: 113; Gallupe to James K. Moorhead, Dec. 12, 1866, Johnson Papers, LC; Heitman, *Register*, 1: 443.

From Thomas E. Tutt[1]

Washington City D. C   Decr. 24 1866

Sir,

During the pleasant interview had with your Excellency on Saturday, in company with the Honl. John Hogan of Missouri you requested that I present the facts in connection with the Federal appointees of the Territory of Montana.

I most cheerfully comply with the request, and in doing so, I cannot refrain from saying that all the appointees in our young, but rapidly growing Territory, are, I am informed of the Radical school (save the Governor and Secty of the Territory)[2] and nearly all of them, not known to our people, until their advent in their midst with their Commission in their pockets.

Our people are opposed to having foreigners fill these offices, as we think we have an intelligent, brave and loyal people, from whom to make the different appointments; and as our people have been the pioneers of that wild region and have by their intrepid valor and Manhood partially subdued the gold fields of the Territory, and within the three years of its discovery have poured into the lap of the nation not less than Fifty millions of Dollars in gold we feel that we are entitled to some consideration at the hands of the Executive.

I would therefore suggest that as the offices named below are made vacant by resignation, or from other causes, that your Excellency fill the same by appointing the parties named in their regular order.

Chief Justice (now filled by H. L. Hosmer) There is a petition already filed with the Atty General asking that Silas Woodson[3] *of St. Joseph Mo be appointed.*

1st District (now filled by L. E. Munson) I enclose with this a petition from the Bar of Helena and others asking that *Thomas F. Campbell*[4] *be appointed to the position.*

2d District, (now filled by L. P. Willetson) That Lewis McMurtry[5] of the County of Deer Lodge be appointed to fill this position.

Attorney General (now held by E. B. Nealey) That Alexander E. Mayhew[6] now speaker of the Territorial Legislature be appointed to fill *this place.*

U.S. Marshall (now held by Geo. M. Pinney) *That John B. Van Hagin*[7] *be appointed.*

Internal Revenue Collector now filled by N. P. Langford *That Wm. L. Steele*[8] *be appointed to fill the place.*

Assessor of Internal Revenue now filled by T. C. Evarts *That Robert Wiles*[9] be appointed to fill the place.

Postmaster at Helena now held by Jno Potter That John A. Johnson[10] be appointed to fill the place.

Postmaster at Virginia City now held by Jas Gibson That General Andrew Leach[11] be appointed.

All the names I have suggested are good and competent men, and in perfect accord with the administration, and if required, they can send to your Excellency such petitions as will fully endorse them.[12]

Thos. E. Tutt

ALS, DLC-JP.

1. Tutt (1822–1897), a merchant, went to Montana from Missouri in 1864 and served in the abortive constitutional convention of 1866. In 1870 he returned to St. Louis where

he became a bank president. Bancroft, *Washington, Idaho, and Montana*, 650; Hyde and Conrad, *Encyclopedia of St. Louis*, 4: 2319–20.

2. Gov. Green Clay Smith and Secretary Thomas Francis Meagher.

3. Woodson (1819–1896), a lawyer, served in the Kentucky legislature and constitutional convention before moving to St. Joseph, Missouri, in 1854. In addition to several terms as circuit court judge and criminal court judge, Woodson was elected governor of Missouri in 1872 for a single two-year term. *NCAB*, 12: 307.

4. An immigrant from Missouri, Campbell (*fl*1869), a lawyer and probate judge for Lewis and Clark County, eventually became territorial superintendent of public instruction (1867–69). *Historical Sketch and Essay on the Resources of Montana* (Helena, 1868), 140; Bancroft, *Washington, Idaho, and Montana*, 675, 783; *History of Montana*, 669; Members of Helena Bar to Johnson, ca. Oct. 2, 1866, Johnson Papers, LC.

5. Louis McMurtry (*c*1838–*fl*1870), a lawyer, served in the third territorial legislature which convened in November 1866. Bancroft, *Washington, Idaho, and Montana*, 662; 1870 Census, Mont., Deer Lodge, Deer Lodge, 57.

6. Mayhew (*c*1835–*fl*1883), a lawyer born in Pennsylvania, served six terms in the state legislature, four of them as speaker of the house. Bancroft, *Washington, Idaho, and Montana*, 644, 649, 662, 672, 684, 689; Members of Helena Bar to Johnson, ca. Oct. 2, 1866, Johnson Papers, LC; 1880 Census, Mont., Deer Lodge, Deer Lodge, 179.

7. Van Hagen, not further identified, was a member of the third territorial legislature. Bancroft, *Washington, Idaho, and Montana*, 662.

8. New Yorker Nathaniel P. Langford (1832–1911) moved first to Minnesota and later to Montana. In the latter he helped to organize a vigilante group to combat territorial outlaws. Commissioned collector of internal revenue in 1864, Langford was not replaced until 1868 when Johnson twice removed him from office, only to have the Senate reinstate him both times. Johnson then appointed Langford territorial governor, but the Senate refused to confirm the appointment. William L. Steel (*c*1835–*fl*1880), a physician, was a member of the 1866 constitutional convention and by 1870 was serving as sheriff for Lewis and Clark County. Ibid., 650; *DAB*; *History of Montana*, 260; 1870 Census, Mont., Lewis and Clark, Helena, 185; (1880), 293.

9. Truman C. Everts (*c*1826–*fl*1870), a native of Ohio, was commissioned assessor of internal revenue on July 15, 1864, and retained his post until at least mid-summer 1870. Wiles (*c*1821–*fl*1870), an attorney, was residing in Deer Lodge in 1870. *History of Montana*, 260; 1870 Census, Mont., Deer Lodge, Deer Lodge, 59; (1870), Lewis and Clark, Helena, 1st Dist., 172.

10. John Potter (*c*1838–*fl*1885) went to Montana from Minnesota and became the first postmaster at Helena when the post office was established in 1865. He remained in that office until May 6, 1869. He was a U.S. commissioner at Hamilton, Montana, from at least 1877 to at least 1885, as well as a merchant there. Johnston (1825–*fl*1885) practiced law in Iowa and served in that state's senate before moving to Montana in 1862, where he practiced law and served at least three terms as a district attorney. *History of Montana*, 729, 1226; *U.S. Off. Reg.* (1869, 1877–85); *Historical Sketch of Montana*, 154; 1870 Census, Mont., Lewis and Clark, Helena, 187; (1880), Gallatin, Hamilton, 232.

11. James Gibson (*fl*1869) served as postmaster at Virginia City from February 1, 1865, to June 6, 1869, when he was succeeded by former territorial chief justice Hezekiah L. Hosmer. Andrew Leach has not been identified. *U.S. Off. Reg.* (1865–69).

12. None of the officeholders was replaced before the spring of 1867 and in no case did Johnson appoint Tutt's recommendation. Ibid. (1867–69).

From William W. Warren[1]

Brighton   Dec. 24. 1866

Sir;

At the suggestion of leading men in this State, favorable to the administration, and without so much as a request on my own part, I received the appointment of Assessor in this (Mr. Geo. S. Boutwell's) district. I supposed, so far as I gave the subject any attention, that the Senate would act upon the appointment with the others made during the recess; that I should be confirmed or rejected with the rest, and in either case, I should be content with the result.

I am now informed however that special opposition to my confirmation is on foot, at the instance of Mr. Boutwell and in the interest of my predecessor Mr. Esty.[2] It appears that mine is the only office of importance in Mr Boutwell's district where a man upon whom he can count, has been removed to make way for a supporter of the administration; and I infer that this explains the special effort making against me.

The pretended ground of opposition to my confirmation is the allegation that I was only a lukewarm supporter of the war. My opponents have worked in secret, but as I now learn, have procured ex parte affidavits of statements said to have been made by me in public speeches, or in a friend's parlor. Of course I have not been able to ascertain the tenor of these alleged statements, but if they impute to me any sentiments unfriendly to the national cause, they are without foundation in truth. This is susceptible of easy proof, as I occupied a public position in, and was the legal adviser of the town in which I live, during the whole war. An attempt to prevent my reelection to that position, by circulating reports of similar statements to these now charged against me, only succeeded in inducing fifteen voters to vote against me, although the number on the voting list was between six and seven hundred, and parties were about evenly divided. This happened in the spring of 1865. So much feeling was caused by the circulation of the reports then, that I received the largest vote I ever received for the office in question. The truth is that probably not a man in this neighborhood, who is now engaged in furnishing evidence to injure me, did any more (in proportion to his means and ability) for the public cause than I did. At the same time my political opinions have always been opposed to those of the radical leaders in Massachusetts.

I trouble you with this letter, not because I am anxious about the office. I do not *need* it and should not wish to fill it, if I failed to perform a service worth all I may receive for it. But I do not wish by my silence to admit that in my case the administration have appointed a "disloyal man," and on my own account I object to being singled out as a special mark for detraction and misrepresentation.

I have enclosed a copy of the foregoing to the Honorable Secretary of the Treasury for his information, and except to your Excellency & to him I do not feel called upon to make any explanation whatever of my position.[3]

W. W. Warren   Assessor 7th Dist of Mass

ALS, DNA-RG56, Appts., Internal Revenue Service, Assessor, Mass., 7th Dist., W. W. Warren.

1. Warren (1834–1880), a graduate of Harvard University (1856) and an attorney, was

given a recess appointment for the Seventh District assessorship of Massachusetts on September 21, 1866. He later served one term each in the state senate and in Congress as a Democrat (1875–77). *BDAC*; Ser. 6B, Vol. 3: 34, Johnson Papers, LC.

2. Constantine C. Esty (1824–1912) had served as assessor for the Seventh District since the creation of the office in 1862. He, like Warren, was an attorney with postwar experience in the Massachusetts legislature. Esty was also elected to fill an unexpired term in Congress as a Republican (1872–73). *BDAC*.

3. Nominated on December 13, Warren was eventually rejected by the Senate on February 1, 1867. Less than three weeks later, Esty was reappointed by Johnson, and he continued to serve as assessor until 1872. Ser. 6B, Vol. 4: 24, Johnson Papers, LC; *BDAC*.

From Jonathan Worth

Raleigh   December 24th 1866.

Sir:—

In obedience to a resolution of the General Assembly of this State, I have the honor to transmit, herewith an authenticated copy of a Resolution of that body "rejecting the proposed amendment, as the fourteenth article of the Constitution of the United States."

Jonathan Worth   Govr. of N. Carolina.

ALS, DLC-JP.

From Thomas B. Searight[1]

Uniontown Pa.   Dec. 28th 1866

Dear Sir:

Your late annual message, was all that the country could desire. At least it was satisfactory to the real friends of the Union. You have nothing to do but stand firmly in the position you have taken. History will vindicate your course.

I was shown a day or two ago a small copper coin designed to ridicule the firm position taken by Gen. Jackson in opposition to the United States Bank. One side bore the device of a money chest with the inscription "I take the responsibility." The other side had a figure of an Ass, with the inscription—"Roman firmness." Now the man, who was thus attempted to be ridiculed, and brought into public contempt, lives in the hearts of his Countrymen, revered by all.

The Radicals in their mad Scheme of negro suffrage in the District of Columbia, have given you an opportunity to expose them to public condemnation in your veto. I think it will be the turning point of popular reaction against them. Unquestionably an overwhelming majority of the people are opposed to negro suffrage *per se* and independent of all Constitutional objections.[2]

T. B. Searight

ALS, DLC-JP.
  1. Searight (1827–1899) was a prominent Democratic attorney, prothonotary, member of the Pennsylvania legislature, and editor of the *Genius of Liberty*, a Democratic organ. John W. Jordan and James Hadden, eds., *Genealogical and Personal History of Fayette County, Pennsylvania* (3 vols., New York, 1912), 1: 487–88.
  2. See District of Columbia Franchise Law Veto Message, Jan. 5, 1867.

From Jared C. Brown[1]

Port Angeles W. T. [Washington Territory]
Dec 29 *1866*

Respected Sir

Allow me to present to you the name of "Dr. James W. Redfield."[2] He is a Gentleman of Worth, one who would do *honor* to any place that you might appoint him to. He was formily an old acquaintance of yours, in *Tenn*—he was one of the few who took ground for the "*Union*," and, was thrown into prison from which he Escaped and with his wife & two Small Children[3] traveled nearly perishing, to find the "union," lines. At last they made the north after Suffering innumerable hardships foot Sore and weary, ragged and pennyless. There he met the *Hon Victor Smith*,"[4] the former Collector of this Port, who *aided* them to Come to this Territory, and gave him the appointment of Resident Physician at the Marine Hospital where he Continued to remain untill the untimely death of Smith,[5] and the Advent into office of the *Present Collector*,[6] who immediately removed him to give place to others.

Dr. Redfield is one of the ablest and intelligent men on this Coast. He is Strictly Temperate, and attends Strictly to his duties. He has become almost discouraged and disheartened after *braving* all that he has done for the Govt. lossing all and barely Saving his life. And that to be treated as he has been by those who "*Assume power*" *under* the Hypocitical Cry of "*Union.*" Dr. Redfield Came to this place, used a part of his Salery in purchasing a town lot, and improved it. He was Elected School Supervisor and delivered lectures, in behalf of the School used his means as far as he was able to aid in Supporting Schools and the Cause of Christianity. He Delivered the *Address* on the Death of *Lincoln* and I must Say it was one of the best productions I ever listened to. He protraid the Course of the President as well as yours, and than alluded to his own experience in the South, and the Cause of the Refugee, untill not a Single Eye was not wet, with tears. He done all that he could do, and attend to his duty as Physician, in aid of the Election of the "*Union*" *ticket* and with all this he was removed from his possition as Hospital Physician by the Collector of Customs *F. A. Wilson.*

Such has been the treatment "*Union Men*" have receved at the Hands of officials Here.

He having no means, and meeting with Such opposition he managed to Scrape enought together to go to *San Francisco*." And at the present time is Located Somewhere near the Mission with barely Sufficient family practice to Support his family.[7]

You may ask, why will he not push ahead. My reply is that when a man has suffered all Except Death for his Country, and than be [treated?] with a Coldness by the officers of Govt. it Cannot be Expected that he will have any heart to try. A little Encouragement would do much to raise a man up. It is not the worthy Citizen here that get Encouragement, it is those who trim their Sails to Every breeze and, Stoop to Every Act that is vile.

I would most Earnestly urge upon you to take into Consideration, his name and give him the appointment of Some possition Either here or in California. He will do Credit to Any possition that you might give him.

If you would appoint him *Secretary* of this *Territory*, or *Surveyor General* you would be doing an Act of justice to one who is worthy of your kind Consideration.[8]

Jared. C. Brown   Dpt U.S Marshal W T

ALS, NRU-William Henry Seward Col.

1. Brown, apparently from New York but not further identified, seems to have gone to the Washington Territory by way of California. He received his commission as deputy U.S. marshal on August 12, 1863. His letter to Johnson was enclosed in one to Seward. Brown to Seward, Dec. 28, 1866, and Copy of Commission, NRU.

2. Redfield (c1815–fl1867), a native of New York, published books on physiognomy in 1849 and 1852. San Francisco directory (1867–68); S. Austin Allibone, *A Critical Dictionary of English Literature and British and American Authors* (3 vols., Philadelphia, 1874), 2: 1756; 1860 Census, Tenn., Bledsoe, Pikeville P.O., 73.

3. Sarah Redfield (b. c1823) was a native of Vermont. The 1860 census shows a twelve-year-old boy named Edwin, as well as a six-year-old girl and a one-year-old boy whose names are illegible. Ibid.

4. Smith (d. 1865), of Ohio, was an ardent abolitionist and close friend, possibly a cousin, of Salmon P. Chase. He created much turmoil in the territory by moving the customhouse from Port Townsend to Port Angeles. Smith was also a special agent of the Treasury Department. Vincent G. Tegeder, "Lincoln and the Territorial Patronage: The Ascendancy of the Radicals in the West," *MVHR*, 35 (1948–49): 90; Bancroft, *Washington, Idaho, and Montana*, 220–25.

5. Smith and about three hundred other passengers died when the steamer *Brother Jonathan* hit an underwater obstruction and sank off the coast of northern California near Crescent City on July 30, 1865. Ibid., 225; *Oregonian* (Portland), Aug. 2, 3, 1865.

6. Frederick A. Wilson (fl1869), a native of Maine, was appointed collector in May 1863. He served until at least 1869. Wilson appointment, May 11, 1863, Lincoln Papers, LC; *U.S. Off. Reg.* (1865–69).

7. Redfield seems to have left San Francisco permanently in 1867 or 1868. San Francisco directory (1867–68).

8. Redfield was not appointed secretary or surveyor general of the Washington Territory nor does he appear to have received any other post in the territory or California.

From J. Francisco Chaves

House of Representatives, Washington D.C.

Dec. 29th 1866

Your Excellency;

I have the honor to call your attention to the condition of affairs in the Territory of New Mexico, so far as relates to certain Federal official positions. I have heretofore felt impelled to this step, but have been prevented by a sense of delicacy in part, and also because I hoped, that the state of things to be feared, arising from the absence of the Governor, and new Secretary[1] would not become an accomplished fact. My duty to the people of New Mexico, as their Representative in Congress, forbids, that I should longer hesitate to call your attention to their affairs, and ask your intervention in their behalf.

Governor Mitchell was inaugurated in July last, but left the Territory just previous to the assembling of the Legislature, so that officially our people have little Knowledge of him. He has leave of absence granted for six weeks, from the 18th of December inst.[2]

General Este who was appointed Secretary, now over one year since, has never visited the Territory, although he qualified and has given bonds.[3]

The only officer now in the Territory qualified to perform Executive duties is the superseded Secretary,[4] who would be justified, were he to leave the Territory at any time. He is at this time, and has been since Governor Mitchell's departure, performing Executive functions, as Ex-officio Governor and Secretary.

This state of affairs is highly distasteful to the people of New Mexico, as well as injurious to their best interests and their quiet.

The Legislature at its late meeting was for many days, kept in a State bordering upon anarchy, because a large number of the members of the lower House refused to recognize the official character of the Acting Secretary, and Ex-officio Governor; and although that body finally organized, such is the state of dissatisfaction arising out of the absence of the Governor, and the necessity which makes the continuance in performance of executive duties by Secretary Arny necessary, that apprehension exists as to whether any permanent good can be anticipated from the Session of the Legislature, now sitting.

Under this state of affairs, it seems but just, that I respectfully ask and earnestly recommend, that at least the Secretary of the Territory be directed, to proceed to New Mexico, or that a new one be appointed, who will accept the position, and at once undertake the performance of the duties of the office.

In default of General Este's not proceeding directly to the scene of his duties; I would very respectfully recommend the appointment of H. H. Heath,[5] who is a gentleman of undoubted capacity, and sterling integrity, and one to whom from the bright record which he made during the recent Rebellion, in sustaining the glorious cause of the union, no doubt as to his loyalty can for a single moment attach.

In conclusion, I feel justified in stating that his appointment would be entirely satisfactory to a very large majority of my constitutents, and that your Excellency will take these matters into serious consideration.[6]

J. Franco. Chaves   Del. fr. New Mexico

ALS, DNA-RG59, Territorial Papers, N. Mex. (T17, Roll 3).

1. Robert B. Mitchell and George P. Este.

2. When Mitchell received a copy of Chaves's letter two days later, he informed Secretary of State Seward, "I have to say that I did not make a journey of two thousand miles over the plains and at this season of the year for pleasure but as a duty." He came to Washington at the request of the federal territorial officials, the military, and "good citizens" on government business, particularly to protest the prospective removal of federal troops from the Santa Fe and Albuquerque areas and to work out a plan "for the settlement of the vexed Indian question" in the territory. Robert B. Mitchell to W. H. Seward, Dec. 31, 1866, Territorial Papers, N. Mex., (T17, Roll 3), RG59, NA.

3. Este never took his post as secretary. Lawrence R. Murphy, *Frontier Crusader— William F.M. Arny* (Tucson, 1972). For more on the replacement of territorial officers in New Mexico, see New Mexico Citizens to Johnson, Feb. 5, 1866, *Johnson Papers*, 10: 33–35.

4. William F.M. Arny.

5. For more about Herman H. Heath, who was appointed territorial secretary, see Heath to Johnson, Aug. 6, 1866.

6. On the day this letter was written, Johnson endorsed it: "The Special attention of the Secretary State is called to the within statement of facts in regard to affairs in New Mexico."

January 1867

From John H. Young[1]

Washington D.C.   January 1867.

I would most respectfully submit the following protest in regard to my retirement from active service in the Army. The medical commission appointed to examine into my "mental and physical condition," in Mobile Ala. June 1866 was composed of Dr Harvey,[2] *a contract Surgeon, from Canada*, and my most bitter enemy, [(]for what reason I do not know) and Dr Cole[3] asst Surg Vols. I submit that the Board was incompetent, as a commission to make an examination of an officer of the Regular Army, should have been composed of *commissioned* officers of the Regular Army,[4] especially as I was attended from Jany. to August 1866 by a Regular army surgeon.[5] The Report is in itself malicious, in exceeding the bounds given by the order convening the commission. I was not shown that order, and was led to believe by *Dr Cole* that the Report was simply a recommendation for a change of climate. The evidence of asst Surg Phillips U.S.A. who attended me in the Hospital and of Hospital Steward Stevens[6] who saw me daily was not taken, nor any other evidence.[7] The *substance* of the Report is, really, that from the over-use of stimulants I *was insane.* My cessation from, and refusal to continue the use of whiskey, morphine and opium caused temporary delirium.[8] These were prescribed by Dr Harvey himself also by asst Surgeon Phillips at the Hospital and their use continued for nearly a year.[9] Not one word was mentioned of my treatment, but other things uncalled for and about which they knew nothing, were, for instance, the length of time I had not performed duty, the causes and nature of my disease, &c which were misstated.[10] The Report would not have been worthy of notice except for the endorsement of Gen Thomas who recommended that I be sent to the Insane Asylum at Washington and the endorsement of Gen Grant who recommended that I be retired. These recommendations were made on the supposition that the Report was correct. What could Generals Grant & Thomas know of my case, one at Washington, the other at Nashville Tenn. Neither did they know the officers making the Report. My examination before the Retiring Board in Philadelphia was purely a medical one. There really was no examination sufficient to ascertain my "condition physical or mental,"[11] but that report was based on the former one and was unjust to me. Had I been allowed to come North, from Look Out Mountain Tenn, on a short leave of absence, my health would have been restored at once.[12]

My Military History in the letter from the Adjt. Generals' Office to the

President of the Retiring Board is incomplete. I was appointed from civil life, May 14, '61 having previously served in the army.[13] In July I joined my Regt. at Wheeling Va. and was ordered on Recruiting Service to Cleveland, ohio. In August to Bellefontaine Ohio, from there to Columbia Penna., to Newport Barracks Ky, to Cleveland, to New-Port Barracks, then ordered to join my Regt. at Pittsburgh Landing Tenn. Joined May 17, '62, was in all the operations before Corinth, from there marched to Huntsville and Stevenson, also, then to Tulahoma and Manchester Tenn. Was there relieved by the proper Captain of the Corps. In August '62 ordered to proceed to Springfield Ohio and report by letter to the Adjt. General of the Army.[14] At Nashville Tenn the order was countermanded and I was placed on the Staff of General Buell as a Mustering Officer and served in that capacity and as Chief Commissary of Musters on the Staffs of Generals Rosecrans and Thomas until July 1864. I was also on duty at Gen Shermans Hd Qrs Nashville Tenn, on mustering service until Oct 1864. During the month of Sept. '64 I had a sick leave of 30 days, and this is the only leave I ever have had. April '64 I asked Gen Thomas to relieve me, so as to join my Regt. This was not done until July. In Oct I asked to be relieved from Gen Sherman's Hd Qrs to join my Regt. Joined and took command of Regt. in Oct. Remained with Regt. until Aug '65 on Look Out Mountain, and was with the Regt. and in Hospital[15] at Mobile, Ala. until Aug. '66 when I received the order to go before the Retiring Board.

The order retiring me from service conveys a wrong impression. My sickness *was* the result of exposure in the line of duty.[16] On Lookout Mountain in the month of June the water fails, making it necessary heretofore for all the troops to move 3 miles to the Lake and away from the fortifications at an enormous expense to the Government, involving an entire new outfit of Camp and Garrison Equippage. To avoid this with a detail of men I worked daily for 3 months, supplying not only my own but other Regts. It was the exposure during this time that first caused my sickness.

I served as aid to the commanding General at the Battle of Chickamauga[17] had my Horse shot under me received special mention in the Report was at the Battle of Nashville as aid in the Division of General Steedman.

I would respectfully ask that I may be re instated in my former rank and position as I am mentally & physically qualified for service.[18]

John H. Young   Capt 15th Inf. Bvt Maj U.S A

ALS, DNA-RG94, Lets. Recd. (Main Ser.), File Y-3-1867 (M619, Roll 578).

1. Young (c1825–1868), a Mexican War veteran and Painesville, Ohio, merchant, became captain in the 15th Inf. on May 14, 1861, and was brevetted major on September 20, 1863, for gallant and meritorious service at the Battle of Chickamauga. Powell, *Army List*, 694; ACP Branch, File 2225-1884, John H. Young, RG94, NA; 1860 Census, Ohio, Lake, Painesville Village, 427.

2. Canadian John Harvey (*fl*1867) signed on as a contract surgeon in Washington, D.C., in June 1863. From October 1864 to May 1865 he served with the 19th Inf. and from May 1865 to June 1866 with the 15th Inf. He was living in Dahlonega, Georgia, in 1867 and apparently intended to remain in the United States. Harvey Deposition, Mar. 19, 1867, Lets. Recd. (Main Ser.), File Y-3-1867 (M619, Roll 578), RG94, NA.

3. Robert W. Coale (*fl*1867) had served as an acting assistant surgeon for U.S. forces in Tennessee about 1863 and then from January 1865 to June 1866 as an assistant surgeon, U.S. Vols., at the Post Hospital, Mobile, Alabama. Coale Deposition, Mar. 19, 1867, ibid.

4. E. D. Townsend in his rebuttal to Young's letters claimed that "No reply is deemed necessary to the 1st charge as the Officers who composed the Commission were recognized Medical Officers of the Army." Townsend Report, Jan. 21, 1867, ibid.

5. Appointed from New York, Henry J. Phillips (*c*1834–1879), a native of England and former acting assistant surgeon in the Crimea, served as surgeon with the 53rd N.Y. Vols. and then the 102nd N.Y. Vols. early in the war. Although he passed an army medical examination in November 1863, the secretary of war would not commission him until November 1865 after he was naturalized. He was in charge of the Post Hospital at Mobile, Alabama, January-October 1866. He later served as assistant surgeon in Oregon, Alaska, and other posts until retired for disability in 1879. Phillips to Bvt. Maj. Emory, Mar. 16, 1867, ibid.; Powell, *Army List*, 529; H. J. Phillips to Lorenzo Thomas, Dec. 11, 1865; Proceedings of the Army Retiring Board, Apr. 1, 1879; Military History of Henry J. Philips [*sic*], Mar. 22, 1879; Volunteer Organizations in which service was rendered as an officer during the Rebellion, Henry J. Phillips. Oct. 31, 1872; J. W. Barnes to J. M. Schofield, June 11, 1868, all in ACP Branch, File 6126-1872, Henry J. Phillips, RG94, NA.

6. Michael C. Stevens (*fl*1867) had been a hospital steward since October 22, 1862. He went to the Post Hospital at Mobile, Alabama, in late May 1865 and was apparently still working there in March 1867. Stevens Deposition, Mar. 20, 1867, Lets. Recd. (Main Ser.), File Y-3-1867 (M619, Roll 578), RG94, NA.

7. Harvey said that the medical commission personally examined Young, examined two witnesses, whom he identified as himself and Dr. Coale, the other commission member, and then reported on these examinations. Dr. Phillips saw the commission come and go and was certain that they were there for less than a half hour, which he considered an insufficient amount of time. Harvey Deposition, Mar. 19, 1867; Phillips to Emory, Mar. 16, 1867, ibid.

8. Phillips and Stevens admitted that such a reaction was possible but generally attributed Young's difficulties to intemperance and delirium tremens or, as they sometimes called it, *mania a potû*. Harvey, however, flatly stated that ceasing to take the stimulants and opiates he had prescribed did not cause Young to become delirious. Phillips to Emory, Mar. 16, 1867; Stevens Deposition, Mar. 20, 1867; Harvey Deposition, Mar. 19, 1867, ibid.

9. Both doctors agreed that they had prescribed these medications. Records show that the prescriptions could include as much as three bottles of porter, four ounces of whiskey, and various drugs to be taken daily. Phillips to Emory, Mar. 16, 1867; Harvey Deposition, Mar. 19, 1867; J. M. Stephenson Testimony, June 7, 1867, ibid.

10. Harvey and Coale reported that "For the past ten (10) months Captain *John H. Young* 15 U.S. Infantry has done no duty, in consequence of habitual intemperance and mental and physical prostration resulting therefrom; and since Feby. 1866 he has been in Hospital." Report, June 7, 1866, ibid.

11. Young appeared before the retiring board on October 16, 1866. Gen. George G. Meade, president of the board, said that Young was intoxicated at the time. The medical officers on the board found Young suffering from jaundice, which they attributed to "Climatic influences," and concluded that "His physical and mental condition is much impaired, the result of the disease above stated and from habitual excessive intemperance." Records of the retiring board, June 8, 10, 1867, ibid.

12. During the summer of 1865 Young was in charge of a contingent on Lookout Mountain, Tennessee, drilling wells to provide water for the troops. During this time he developed diarrhea, from the exposure, he claimed. In July he went on some business to Chattanooga where he sought out a druggist who gave him a prescription of brandy with some drugs in it. Young was decidedly under the influence by the time he returned to Lookout Mountain. On August 28, 1865, he experienced a similar problem on a return visit to Chattanooga where an army doctor prescribed for him. This time Young was so inebriated

that he had to be carried to the railroad three days later when his command was being transferred to Mobile. As a result he was arrested. After several other drunken indiscretions Young remained under arrest most of the time until he was released from the hospital on August 13, 1866, to appear before the retiring board. Young's summary, June 10, 1867; J. M. Stephenson Testimony, June 7, 1867; Court-martial charges against Young, Dec. 1865; various other documents in ibid.

13. Young was captain and assistant quartermaster in the volunteers during the Mexican War, serving from March 1847 to October 1848. Powell, *Army List*, 694.

14. Lorenzo Thomas.

15. Young was hospitalized January 21, 1866, for delirium tremens. In addition, he was suffering from diarrhea and hemorrhoids. Although Dr. Phillips pronounced Young cured of the alcohol-related condition on March 31, 1866, Gen. Charles R. Woods ordered him kept in the hospital so that he would remain sober in case the authorities wanted to bring him before a court-martial. This had been attempted in December 1865-January 1866, but was aborted at least partly because Young was not sufficiently sober to appear. Various documents in Lets. Recd. (Main Ser.), File Y-3-1867 (M619, Roll 578), RG94, NA.

16. The board had found Young "incapacitated for active service, and that in its judgment, the said incapacity does not result from long and faithful service, from wounds or injury received in the line of duty, from sickness or exposure therein, or from any other incident of service." Board records, June 10, 1867, ibid.

17. William S. Rosecrans.

18. Johnson endorsed this letter calling the "special attention" of the secretary of war "to Capt Youngs case at an early day." Young wrote a second letter to Johnson on January 19 elaborating on some of his points of protest. As a result of the adjutant general's response to these protests, Stanton did not believe that the previous action in Young's case needed to be reversed. However, on January 31, 1867, Johnson directed that the order suspending Young should itself be suspended and Young should appear before the retiring board again. The board, comprised of seven members, three of whom were army surgeons, and headed again by General Meade, convened at Philadelphia in February and again in May. No one but Young could seem to find a connection between his problem and the continued prescription of alcoholic stimulants, opiates, and morphine. Eventually this new board found Young to be incapacitated for duty. Young's original verdict—retired with one year's pay and allowances—was confirmed. Retiring board proceedings, Feb. 6, May 8, June 6–10, 1867; Young to Johnson, Jan. 19, 1867; E. D. Townsend to George G. Meade, Feb. 1, 1867; Phillips to Emory, Mar. 16, 1867; endorsement by E. D. Townsend, July 17, 1867, ibid.; Stanton to Johnson, Lets. Sent, Mil. Bks., Executive, 56-C, RG107, NA; Powell, *Army List*, 694.

From Thomas Cottman

New Orleans   Jany 1st 1866 [1867]

Mr. President

It being New Year and somewhat quiet after the excitement occasioned by the visit of the great men of the nation to our little Provincial Town:[1] I in accord with my promise write simply to keep you au courant with our affairs here. The members of Congress whilst here were the guests of the city & were visited by the citizens generally, without formality or political bias. The visit appeared mutually agreeable and was the occasion of conciliatory demonstration.[2] Govr Wells passed the most of a day with them and there was a pretty free talk generally. The Governor has only prepared the headings for his message and will not make it out for a couple of weeks as yet. I asked him not to do so until I had seen you as I had conversed with leading members of the Legislature and they were in a very different temper from that in which the last Assembly left them.[3] I have not met one who does not regret the appointment of McKee[4] as United States Marshal. Mr Nixon the editor & proprietor of the Crescent who by the way goes to Washington on Sunday next[5] says he is convinced that it was made without all the knowledge of the circumstances being placed before you, of which I think you will be thoroughly convinced of; if the nomination is not placed before the Senate earlier than the 9th of this month. About which time I will do my self the honor to call upon you.[6]

Thos. Cottman

ALS, DLC-JP.
1. A party of sixty to seventy senators, representatives, their wives, other government officials, railroad presidents, and newspaper reporters arrived in New Orleans in the morning of December 28, 1866. They reboarded the train to return to Washington in the evening of December 29. The visit was the brainchild of a group of railroad presidents who financed the excursion. *Picayune* (New Orleans), Dec. 28–30, 1866.
2. Newspaper reports indicated that touchy political questions were scrupulously avoided and that southerners hoped that the congressmen, having experienced southern hospitality and met many notables, would see the South's renewed loyalty and thus not believe every exaggerated report they might hear about southern attitudes and actions. Ibid.
3. Perhaps Cottman is referring to the increased tension between the Democratic legislature and J. Madison Wells, who had become a radical during the summer, which led the new legislature to attempt to oust Wells. Taylor, *La. Reconstructed*, 82.
4. John H. McKee (*fl*1867), a partner in a commission merchant and wholesale grocery firm, was appointed marshal on October 24, 1866, during the congressional recess. William H.C. King, a strong opponent of Cuthbert Bullitt, McKee's predecessor, favored McKee's appointment. New Orleans directory (1866); Ser. 6B, Vol. 3: 386; Vol. 4: 202, Johnson Papers, LC; William H.C. King to Johnson, n.d., Tels. Recd., President, Vol. 5 (1866–67), RG107, NA. See also King to Johnson, Nov. 6, 1866.
5. James O. Nixon was going to Washington to encourage the appointment of Gen. Francis J. Herron as marshal. R. Taylor to Johnson, Jan. 6, 1866[7], Johnson Papers, LC.
6. McKee, who had already been nominated in December 1866, was rejected by the Senate in early March 1867. On April 15 Johnson nominated Herron, who was confirmed and commissioned four days later. Ser. 6B, Vol. 4: 202, 203, Johnson Papers, LC.

From Nathaniel P. Sawyer

Pittsburgh   Jan 3d 1867

My Dear Sir

Enclosed You will find copy of letter written to Fremont in 1864.[1] I have always been his friend. I do not wish to harrass or annoy You. But if You are going to make a change in the War Department and such is the unanimous wish of all Your friends with whom I am brought in contact with, I have no doubt the appointment of Fremont will give general satisfaction to Your friends and prove acceptable to the whole country. Pardon me for intruding on Your time and patience. If I did not like You I would not do it.

N. P. Sawyer

ALS, DLC-JP.
1. In his letter Sawyer predicted "that Lincoln will never fill a second term" and that Johnson would succeed Lincoln as President. Sawyer to John C. Frémont, Sept. 13, 1864, Johnson Papers, LC.

From Edwin M. Stanton

Washington City, January 4 1867.
Mr President:

Pursuant to your request, I have examined and considered the Act, passed at the present session of Congress, entitled an Act to regulate the elective franchise in the District of Columbia, and which Act by its terms extends the elective franchise within said District to every male person (excepting paupers and persons under guardianship) of the age of twenty one years and upwards, who has not been convicted of any infamous crime or offence, (and excepting persons who may have voluntarily given aid and comfort to the rebels in the late rebellion,) and who was born in the United States or naturalized, and who shall have resided in the said District for the period of twelve months next preceeding any election. The effect of this Act is to extend the elective franchise to persons of African descent and to exclude those who have voluntarily given aid and comfort to the rebellion. I am of opinion that in both particulars the law is constitutional; and that Congress has the legislative power to regulate the elective franchise within the District of Columbia, according to its discretion.[1]

Edwin M Stanton   Secretary of War.

LS, DLC-Edwin M. Stanton Papers.
1. See District of Columbia Franchise Law Veto Message, Jan. 5, 1867.

From Joseph W. Allen

Nashville, January 5th 1867.
Dear Sir

I have today valued on you for Sixteen thousand five hundred dollars in favor of W S Huntington Esqr Cashr First National Bank Washington City which I trust you will honor in liquidation of the dft for $20,000:[1] due by you to this bank as M G[2] of Tennessee.

Jos. W Allen   Trustee

ALS, DLC-JP.
1. See Johnson to Burns, Jan. 21, 1867.
2. Military governor.

District of Columbia Franchise Law Veto Message[1]

WASHINGTON, *January 5, 1867.*

To the Senate of the United States:

I have received and considered a bill entitled "An act to regulate the elective franchise in the District of Columbia," passed by the Senate on the 13th of December and by the House of Representatives on the succeeding day. It was presented for my approval on the 26th ultimo—six days after the adjournment of Congress—and is now returned with my objections to the Senate, in which House it originated.

Measures having been introduced at the commencement of the first session of the present Congress for the extension of the elective franchise to persons of color in the District of Columbia, steps were taken by the corporate authorities of Washington and Georgetown to ascertain and make known the opinion of the people of the two cities upon a subject so immediately affecting their welfare as a community. The question was submitted to the people at special elections held in the month of December, 1865, when the qualified voters of Washington and Georgetown, with great unanimity of sentiment, expressed themselves opposed to the contemplated legislation. In Washington, in a vote of 6,556—the largest, with but two exceptions, ever polled in that city—only thirty-five ballots were cast for negro suffrage, while in Georgetown, in an aggregate of 813 votes—a number considerable in excess of the average vote at the four preceding annual elections—but one was given in favor of the proposed extension of the elective franchise. As these elections seem to have been conducted with entire fairness, the result must be accepted as a truthful expression of the opinion of the people of the District upon the question which evoked it. Possessing, as an organized community, the same popular right as the inhabitants of a State or Territory to make known their will upon matters which affect their social and political condition, they could have selected no more appropriate mode of memorializing Congress upon the subject of this bill than through the suffrages of their qualified voters.

Entirely disregarding the wishes of the people of the District of Columbia, Congress has deemed it right and expedient to pass the measure now submitted for my signature. It therefore becomes the duty of the Executive, standing between the legislation of the one and the will of the other, fairly expressed, to determine whether he should approve the bill, and thus aid in placing upon the statute books of the nation a law against which the people to whom it is to apply have solemnly and with such unanimity protested, or whether he should return it with his objections in the hope that upon reconsideration Congress, acting as the representatives of the inhabitants of the seat of Government, will permit them to regulate a purely local question as to them may seem best suited to their interests and condition.

The District of Columbia was ceded to the United States by Maryland and Virginia in order that it might become the permanent seat of Government of the United States. Accepted by Congress, it at once became subject to the "exclusive legislation" for which provision is made in the Federal Constitution. It should be borne in mind, however, that in exercising its functions as the lawmaking power of the District of Columbia the authority of the National Legislature is not without limit, but that Congress is bound to observe the letter and spirit of the Constitution as well in the enactment of local laws for the seat of Government as in legislation common to the entire Union. Were it to be admitted that the right "to exercise exclusive legislation in all cases whatsoever" conferred upon Congress unlimited power within in the District of Columbia, titles of nobility might be granted within its boundaries; laws might be made "respecting an establishment of religion or prohibiting the free exercise thereof, or abridging the freedom of speech or of the press, or the right of the people peaceably to assemble and to petition the Government for a redress of grievances." Despotism would thus reign at the seat of government of a free republic, and as a place of permanent residence it would be avoided by all who prefer the blessings of liberty to the mere emoluments of official position.

It should also be remembered that in legislating for the District of Columbia under the Federal Constitution the relation of Congress to its inhabitants is analogous to that of a legislature to the people of a State under their own local constitution. It does not, therefore, seem to be asking too much that in matters pertaining to the District Congress should have a like respect for the will and interest of its inhabitants as is entertained by a State legislature for the wishes and prosperity of those for whom they legislate. The spirit of our Constitution and the genius of our Government require that in regard to any law which is to affect and have a permanent bearing upon a people their will should exert at least a reasonable influence upon those who are acting in the capacity of their legislators. Would, for instance, the legislature of the State of New York, or of Pennsylvania, or of Indiana, or of any State in the Union, in opposition to the expressed will of a large majority of the people whom they were chosen to represent, arbitrarily force upon them as voters all persons of the African or negro race and make them eligible for office without any other qualification than a certain term of residence within the State? In neither of the States named would the colored population, when acting together, be able to produce any great social or political result. Yet in New York, before he can vote, the man of color must fulfill conditions that are not required of the white citizen; in Pennsylvania the elective franchise is restricted to white freemen, while in Indiana negroes and mulattoes are expressly excluded from the right of suffrage. It hardly seems consistent with the principles of right and justice that representatives of States where suffrage is either denied the colored man or granted to him on qualifications requiring intelligence or property should compel the people of the District of Columbia to try an experiment which their own constituents have thus far shown an unwillingness to test for themselves. Nor does it accord with our republican ideas that the principle of self-government should lose its force when applied to the residents of the District merely because their legislators are not, like those of the States, responsible through the ballot to the people for whom they are the lawmaking power.

The great object of placing the seat of Government under the exclusive legislation of Congress was to secure the entire independence of the General Government from undue State influence and to enable it to discharge without danger of interruption or infringement of its authority the high functions for which it was created by the people. For this important purpose it was ceded to the United States by Maryland and Virginia, and it certainly never could have been contemplated as one of the objects to be attained by placing it under the exclusive jurisdiction of Congress that it would afford to propagandists or political parties a place for an experimental test of their principles and theories. While, indeed, the residents of the seat of Government are not citizens of any State and are not, therefore, allowed a voice in the electoral college or representation in the councils of the nation, they are, nevertheless, American citizens, entitled as such to every guaranty of the Constitution, to every benefit of the laws, and to every right which pertains to citizens of our common country. In all matters, then, affecting their domestic affairs, the spirit of our democratic form of government demands that their wishes should be consulted and respected and they taught to feel that although not permitted practically to participate in national concerns, they are, nevertheless, under a paternal government regardful of their rights, mindful of their wants, and solicitous for their prosperity. It was evidently contemplated that all local questions would be left to their decision, at least to an extent that would not be incompatible with the object for which Congress was granted exclusive legislation over the seat of Government. When the Constitution was yet under consideration, it was assumed by Mr. Madison that its inhabitants would be allowed "a municipal legislature for local purposes, derived from their own suffrages." When for the first time Congress, in the year 1800, assembled at Washington, President Adams, in his speech at its opening, reminded the two Houses that it was for them to consider whether the local powers over the District of Columbia, vested by the Constitution in the Congress of the United States, should be immediately exercised, and he asked them to "consider it as the capital of a great nation, advancing with unexampled rapidity in arts, in commerce, in wealth, and in population, and possessing within itself those resources which, if not thrown away or lamentably misdirected, would secure to it a long course of prosperity and self-government." Three years had not elapsed when Congress was called upon to determine the propriety of retroceding to Maryland and Virginia the jurisdiction of the territory which they had respectively relinquished to the Government of the United States. It was urged on the one hand that exclusive jurisdiction was not necessary or useful to the Government; that it deprived the inhabitants of the District of their political rights; that much of the time of Congress was consumed in legislation pertaining to it; that its government was expensive; that Congress was not competent to legislate for the District, because the members were strangers to its local concerns; and that it was an example of a government without representation—an experiment dangerous to the liberties of the States. On the other hand it was held, among other reasons, and successfully, that the Constitution, the acts of cession of Virginia and Maryland, and the act of Congress accepting the grant all contemplated the exercise of exclusive legislation by Congress, and that its usefulness, if not its necessity, was inferred from the inconvenience which was felt for want of it by the Congress of the Confederation; that the people themselves, who, it was said, had been deprived of their political rights, had not complained and did not desire a retrocession; that the evil might be remedied by giving them a representation in Congress when the District should become sufficiently populous, and in the meantime a local legislature; that if the inhabitants had not political rights they had great political influence; that the trouble and expense of legislating for the District would not be great, but would diminish, and might in a great measure be avoided by a local legislature; and that Congress could not retrocede the inhabitants without their consent. Continuing to live substantially under the laws that existed at the time of the cession, and such changes only having been made as were suggested by themselves, the people of the District have not sought by a local legislature that which has generally been willingly conceded by the Congress of the nation.

As a general rule sound policy requires that the legislature should yield to the wishes of a people, when not inconsistent with the constitution and the laws. The measures suited to one community might not be well adapted to the condition of another; and the persons best qualified to determine such questions are those whose interests are to be directly affected by any proposed law. In Massachusetts, for instance, male persons are allowed to vote without regard to color, provided they possess a certain degree of intelligence. In a population in that State of 1,231,066 there were, by the census of 1860, only 9,602 persons of color, and of the males over 20 years of age there were 339,086 white to 2,602 colored. By the same official enumeration there were in the District of Columbia 60,764 whites to 14,316 persons of the colored race. Since then, however, the population of the District has largely increased, and it is estimated that at the present time there are nearly 100,000 whites to 30,000 negroes. The cause of the augmented numbers of the latter class needs no explanation. Contiguous to Maryland and Virginia, the District during the war became a place of refuge for those who escaped from servitude, and it is yet the abiding place of a considerable proportion of those who sought within its limits a shelter from bondage. Until then held in slavery and denied all opportunities for mental culture, their first knowledge of the Government was acquired when, by conferring upon them freedom, it became the benefactor of their race. The test of their capability for improvement began when the first time the career of free industry and the avenues to intelligence were opened to them. Possessing these advantages but a limited time—the great number perhaps having entered the District of Columbia during the later years of the war, or since its termination—we may well pause to inquire whether, after so brief a probation, they are as a class capable of an intelligent exercise of the right of suffrage and qualified to discharge the duties of official position. The people who are daily witnesses of their mode of living, and who have become familiar with their habits of thought, have expressed the conviction that they are not yet competent to serve as electors, and thus become eligible for office in the local governments under which they live. Clothed with the elective franchise, their numbers, already largely in excess of the demand for labor, would be soon increased by an influx from the adjoining States. Drawn from fields where employment is abundant, they would in vain seek it here, and so add to the embarrassments already experienced from the large class of idle persons congregated in the district. Hardly yet capable of forming correct judgments upon the important questions that often make the issues of a political contest, they could readily be made subservient to the purposes of designing persons. While in Massachusetts, under the census of 1860, the proportion of white to colored males over 20 years of age was 130 to 1, here the black race constitutes nearly one-third of the entire population, whilst the same class surrounds the District on all sides, ready to change their residence at a moment's notice, and with all the facility of a nomadic people, in order to enjoy here, after a short residence, a privilege they find nowhere else. It is within their power in one year to come into the District in such numbers as to have the supreme control of the white race, and to govern them by their own officers and by the exercise of all the municipal authority—among the rest, of the power of taxation over property in which they have no interest. In Massachusetts, where they have enjoyed the benefits of a thorough educational system, a qualification of intelligence is required, while here suffrage is extended to all without discrimination—as well to the most incapable who can prove a residence in the District of one year as to those persons of color who, comparatively few in number, are permanent inhabitants, and, having given evidence of merit and qualification, are recognized as useful and responsible members of the community. Imposed upon an unwilling people placed by the Constitution under the exclusive legislation of Congress, it would be viewed as an arbitrary exercise of power and as an indication by the country of the purpose of Congress to compel the acceptance of negro suffrage by the States. It would engender a feeling of opposition and hatred between the two races, which, becoming deep rooted and ineradicable, would prevent them from living together in a state of mutual friendliness. Carefully avoiding every measure that might tend to produce such a result, and following the clear and well-ascertained popular will, we should assiduously endeavor to promote kindly relations between them, and thus, when that popular will leads the way, prepare for the gradual and harmonious introduction of this new element into the political power of the country.

It can not be urged that the proposed extension of suffrage in the District of Columbia is necessary to enable persons of color to protect either their interests or their rights. They stand here precisely as they stand in Pennsylvania, Ohio, and Indiana. Here as elsewhere, in all that pertains to civil rights, there is nothing to distinguish this class of persons from citizens of the United States, for they possess the "full and equal benefit of all laws and proceedings for the security of person and property as is enjoyed by white citizens," and are made "subject to like punishment, pains, and penalties, and to none other, any law, statute, ordinance, regulation, or custom to the contrary notwithstanding." Nor, as has been assumed, are their suffrages necessary to aid a loyal sentiment here, for local governments already exist of undoubted fealty to the Government, and are sustained by communities which were among the first to testify their devotion to the Union, and which during the struggle furnished their full quotas of men to the military service of the country.

The exercise of the elective franchise is the highest attribute of an American citizen, and when guided by virtue, intelligence, patriotism, and a proper appreciation of our institutions constitutes the true basis of a democratic form of government, in which the sovereign power is lodged in the body of the people. Its influence for good necessarily depends upon the elevated character and patriotism of the elector, for if exercised by persons who do not justly estimate its value and who are indifferent as to its results it will only serve as a means of placing power in the hands of the unprincipled and ambitious, and must eventuate in the complete destruction of that liberty of which it should be the most powerful conservator. Great danger is therefore to be apprehended from an untimely extension of the elective franchise to any new class in our country, especially when the large majority of that class, in wielding the power thus placed in their hands, can not be expected correctly to comprehend the duties and responsibilities which pertain to suffrage. Yesterday, as it were, 4,000,000 persons were held in a condition of slavery that had existed for generations; to-day they are freemen and are assumed by law to be citizens. It can not be presumed, from their previous condition of servitude, that as a class they are as well informed as to the nature of our Government as the intelligent foreigner who makes our land the home of his choice. In the case of the latter neither a residence of five years and the knowledge of our institutions which it gives nor attachment to the principles of the Constitution are the only conditions upon which he can be admitted to citizenship; he must prove in addition a good moral character, and thus give reasonable grounds for the belief that he will be faithful to the obligations which he assumes as a citizen of the Republic. Where a people—the source of all political power—speak by their suffrages through the instrumentality of the ballot box, it must be carefully guarded against the control of those who are corrupt in principle and enemies of free institutions, for it can only become to our political and social system a safe conductor of healthy popular sentiment when kept free from demoralizing influences. Controlled through fraud and usurpation by the designing, anarchy and despotism must inevitably follow. In the hands of the patriotic and worthy our Government will be preserved upon the principles of the Constitution inherited from our fathers. It follows, therefore, that in admitting to the ballot box a new class of voters not qualified for the exercise of the elective franchise we weaken our system of government instead of adding to its strength and durability.

In returning this bill to the Senate I deeply regret that there should be any conflict of opinion between the legislative and executive departments of the Government in regard to measures that vitally affect the prosperity and peace of the country. Sincerely desiring to reconcile the States with one another and the whole people to the Government of the United States, it has been my earnest wish to cooperate with Congress in all measures having for their object a proper and complete adjustment of the questions resulting from our late civil war. Harmony between the coordinate branches of the Government, always necessary for the public welfare, was never more demanded than at the present time, and it will therefore be my constant aim to promote as far as possible concert of action between them. The differences of opinion that have already occurred have rendered me only the more cautious, lest the Executive should encroach upon any of the prerogatives of Congress, or by exceeding in any manner the constitutional limit of his duties destroy the equilibrium which should exist between the several coordinate departments, and which is so essential to the harmonious working of the Government. I know it has been urged that the executive department is more likely to enlarge the sphere of its action than either of the other two branches of the Government, and especially in the exercise of the veto power conferred upon it by the Constitution. It should be remembered, however, that this power is wholly negative and conservative in its character, and was intended to operate as a check upon unconstitutional, hasty, and improvident legislation and as a means of protection against invasions of the just powers of the executive and judicial departments. It is remarked by Chancellor Kent that—

To enact laws is a transcendent power, and if the body that possesses it be a full and equal representation of the people there is danger of its pressing with destructive weight upon all the other parts of the machinery of Government. It has therefore been thought necessary by the most skillful and most experienced artists in the science of civil polity that strong barriers should be erected for the protection and security of the other necessary powers of the Government. Nothing has been deemed more fit and expedient for the purpose than the provision that the head of the executive department should be so constituted as to secure a requisite share of independence and that he should have a negative upon the passing of laws; and that the judiciary power, resting on a still more permanent basis, should have the right of determining upon the validity of laws by the standard of the Constitution.[2]

The necessity of some such check in the hands of the Executive is shown by reference to the most eminent writers upon our system of government, who seem to concur in the opinion that encroachments are most to be apprehended from the department in which all legislative powers are vested by the Constitution. Mr. Madison, in referring to the difficulty of providing some practical security for each against the invasion of the others, remarks that "the legislative department is everywhere extending the sphere of its activity and drawing all power into its impetuous vortex." "The founders of our Republic * * * seem never to have recollected the danger from legislative usurpations, which by assembling all power in the same hands must lead to the same tyranny as is threatened by Executive usurpations." "In a representative republic, where the executive magistracy is carefully limited both in the extent and the duration of its power, and where the legislative power is exercised by an assembly which is inspired, by a supposed influence over the people, with an intrepid confidence in its own strength, which is sufficiently numerous to feel all the passions which actuate a multitude, yet not so numerous as to be incapable of pursuing the objects of its passions by means which reason prescribes, it is against the enterprising ambition of this department that the people ought to indulge all their jealousy and exhaust all their precautions." "The legislative department derives a superiority in our governments from other circumstances. Its constitutional powers being at once more extensive and less susceptible of precise limits, it can with the greater facility mask, under complicated and indirect measures, the encroachments which it makes on the coordinate department." "On the other side, the Executive power being restrained within a narrower compass and being more simple in its nature, and the judiciary being described by landmarks still less uncertain, projects of usurpation by either of these departments would immediately betray and defeat themselves. Nor is this all. As the legislative department alone has access to the pockets of the people and has in some constitutions full discretion and in all a prevailing influence over the pecuniary rewards of those who fill the other departments, a dependence is thus created in the latter which gives still greater facility to encroachments of the former." "We have seen that the tendency of republican governments, is to an aggrandizement of the legislative at the expense of the other departments."[3]

Mr. Jefferson, in referring to the early constitution of Virginia, objected that by its provisions all the powers of government—legislative, executive, and judicial—resulted to the legislative body, holding that "the concentrating these in the same hands is precisely the definition of despotic government. It will be no alleviation that these powers will be exercised by a plurality of hands, and not by a single one. One hundred and seventy-three despots would surely be as oppressive as one." "As little will avail us that they are chosen by ourselves. An elective despotism was not the government we fought for, but one which should not only be founded on free principles, but in which the powers of government should be so divided and balanced among several bodies of magistracy as that no one could transcend their legal limits without being effectually checked and restrained by the others. For this reason that convention which passed the ordinance of government laid its foundation on this basis, that the legislative, executive, and judicial departments should be separate and distinct, so that no person should exercise the powers of more than one of them at the same time. But no barrier was provided between these several powers. The judiciary and executive members were left dependent on the legislative for their subsistence in office, and some of them for their continuance in it. If, therefore, the legislature assumes executive and judiciary powers, no opposition is likely to be made, nor, if made, can be effectual, because in that case they may put their proceedings into the form of an act of assembly, which will render them obligatory on the other branches. They have accordingly in many instances decided rights which should have been left to judiciary controversy; and the direction of the executive, during the whole time of their session, is becoming habitual and familiar."[4]

Mr. Justice Story, in his Commentaries on the Constitution, reviews the same subject, and says:

The truth is that the legislative power is the great and overruling power in every free government. * * * The representatives of the people will watch with jealousy every encroachment of the executive magistrate, for it trenches upon their own authority. But who shall watch the encroachment of these representatives themselves? Will they be as jealous of the exercise of power by themselves as by others? * * *

There are many reasons which may be assigned for the engrossing influence of the legislative department. In the first place, its constitutional powers are more extensive, and less capable of being brought within precise limits than those of either the other departments. The bounds of the executive authority are easily marked out and defined. It reaches few objects, and those are known. It can not transcend them without being brought in contact with the other departments. Laws may check and restrain and bound its exercise. The same remarks apply with still greater force to the judiciary. The jurisdiction is, or may be, bounded to a few objects or persons; or, however general and unlimited, its operations are necessarily confined to the mere administration of private and public justice. It can not punish without law. It can not create controversies to act upon. It can decide only upon rights and cases as they are brought by others before it. It can do nothing for itself. It must do everything for others. It must obey the laws, and if it corruptly administers them it is subjected to the power of impeachment. On the other hand, the legislative power except in the few cases of constitutional prohibition, is unlimited. It is forever varying its means and its ends. It governs the institutions and laws and public policy of the country. It regulates all its vast interests. It disposes of all its property. Look but at the exercise of two or three branches of its ordinary powers. It levies all taxes; it directs and appropriates all supplies; it gives the rules for the descent, distribution, and devises of all property held by individuals; it controls the sources and the resources of wealth; it changes at its will the whole fabric of the laws; it molds at its pleasure almost all the institutions which give strength and comfort and dignity to society.

In the next place, it is the direct visible representative of the will of the people in all the changes of times and circumstances. It has the pride as well as the power of numbers. It is easily moved and steadily moved by the strong impulses of popular feeling and popular odium. It obeys without reluctance the wishes and the will of the majority for the time being. The path to public favor lies open by such obedience, and it finds not only support but impunity in whatever measures the majority advises, even though they transcend the constitutional limits. It has no motive, therefore, to be jealous or scrupulous in its own use of power; and it finds its ambition stimulated and its arm strengthened by the countenance and the courage of numbers. These views are not alone those of men who look with apprehension upon the fate of republics, but they are also freely admitted by some of the strongest advocates for popular rights and the permanency of republican institutions. * * *

  *   *   *   *   *   *   *

* * * Each department should have a will of its own. * * * Each should have its own independence secured beyond the power of being taken away by either or both of the others. But at the same time the relations of each to the other should be so strong that there should be a mutual interest to sustain and protect each other. There should not only be constitutional means, but personal motives to resist encroachments of one or either of the others. Thus ambition would be made to counteract ambition, the desire of power to check power, and the pressure of interest to balance an opposing interest.

  *   *   *   *   *   *   *

* * * The judiciary is naturally and almost necessarily, as has been already said, the weakest department. It can have no means of influence by patronage. Its powers can never be wielded for itself. It has no command over the purse or the sword of the nation. It can neither lay taxes, nor appropriate money, nor command armies, nor appoint to office. It is never brought into contact with the people by constant appeals and solicitations and private intercourse, which belong to all the other departments of Government. It is seen only in controversies or in trials and punishments. Its rigid justice and impartiality give it no claims to favor, however they may to respect. It stands solitary and unsupported, except by that portion of public opinion which is interested only in the strict administration of justice. It can rarely secure the sympathy or zealous support either of the Executive or the Legislature. If they are not, as is not unfrequently the case, jealous of its prerogatives, the constant necessity of scrutinizing the acts of each, upon the application of any private person, and the painful duty of pronouncing judgment that these acts are a departure from the law or Constitution can have no tendency to conciliate kindness or nourish influence. It would seem, therefore, that some additional guards would, under the circumstances, be necessary to protect this department from the absolute dominion of the others. Yet rarely have any such guards been applied, and every attempt to introduce them has been resisted with a pertinacity which demonstrates how slow popular leaders are to introduce

checks upon their own power and how slow the people are to believe that the judiciary is the real bulwark of their liberties. * * *

    *   *   *   *   *   *   *

* * * If any department of the Government has undue influence or absorbing power, it certainly has not been the executive or judiciary.[5]

In addition to what has been said by these distinguished writers, it may also be urged that the dominant party in each House may, by the expulsion of a sufficient number of members or by the exclusion from representation of a requisite number of States, reduce the minority to less than one-third. Congress by these means might be enabled to pass a law, the objections of the President to the contrary notwithstanding, which would render impotent the other two departments of the Government and make inoperative the wholesome and restraining power which it was intended by the framers of the Constitution should be exerted by them. This would be a practical concentration of all power in the Congress of the United States; this, in the language of the author of the Declaration of Independence, would be "precisely the definition of despotic government."

I have preferred to reproduce these teachings of the great statesmen and constitutional lawyers of the early and later days of the Republic rather than to rely simply upon an expression of my own opinions. We can not too often recur to them, especially at a conjuncture like the present. Their application to our actual condition is so apparent that they now come to us a living voice, to be listened to with more attention than at any previous period of our history. We have been and are yet in the midst of popular commotion. The passions aroused by a great civil war are still dominant. It is not a time favorable to that calm and deliberate judgment which is the only safe guide when radical changes in our institutions are to be made. The measure now before me is one of those changes. It initiates an untried experiment for a people who have said, with one voice, that it is not for their good. This alone should make us pause, but it is not all. The experiment has not been tried, or so much as demanded, by the people of the several States for themselves. In but few of the States has such an innovation been allowed as giving the ballot to the colored population without any other qualification than a residence of one year, and in most of them the denial of the ballot to this race is absolute and by fundamental law placed beyond the domain of ordinary legislation. In most of those States the evil of such suffrage would be partial, but, small as it would be, it is guarded by constitutional barriers. Here the innovation assumes formidable proportions, which may easily grow to such an extent as to make the white population a subordinate element in the body politic.

After full deliberation upon this measure, I can not bring myself to approve it, even upon local considerations, nor yet as the beginning of an experiment on a larger scale. I yield to no one in attachment to that rule of general suffrage which distinguishes our policy as a nation. But there is a limit, wisely observed hitherto, which makes the ballot a privilege and a trust, and which requires of some classes a time suitable for probation and preparation. To give it indiscriminately to a new class, wholly unprepared by previous habits and opportunities to perform the trust which it demands, is to degrade it, and finally to destroy its power, for it may be safely assumed that no political truth is better established than that such indiscriminate and all-embracing extension of popular suffrage must end at last in its destruction.

ANDREW JOHNSON.

Richardson, *Messages*, 6: 472–483.
  1. On January 4, Johnson read this veto message to members of his Cabinet who gathered for their regular meeting. All of them, except Stanton, approved the message. See Beale, *Welles Diary*, 3: 3–7.
  2. From James Kent, *Commentaries on American Law*, 8th ed. (4 vols., New York, 1854), 1: 255.
  3. From James Madison, Alexander Hamilton, and John Jay, *The Federalist Papers* (New Rochelle, 1966 [1788]), Nos. 48 and 49, pp. 309–10, 315–16.
  4. From Jefferson's *Notes on the State of Virginia* (1781) as quoted by Madison in Federalist Paper No. 48. Ibid., 310–11.
  5. Taken from Joseph Storey, *Commentaries on the Constitution of the United States* (2 vols., Boston, 1851), 1: 373–75, 378–80.

From Thomas Powell[1]

Cincinnati, Ohio.   January 5, 1867

Sir.

In view of the alarming state of the Union, occasioned by the threatened action of Congress, permit me, as one of your earnest, and most energetic supporters, to offer a few suggestions for your consideration. It has become almost certain now, that the House of Representatives will adopt a resolution preparatory to articles of impeachment of your Excellency: nor will the recklessness of its members pause here. Nullification of the decision of the judiciary, and measures for the final overthrow of the states, will speedily follow.

To warn those members who yet retain a principle of conservatism, and who are not yet irrevocably committed to the measures of the radical leaders—the whole influence of the Secretary of the Treasury ought to be speedily brought to bear on financial circles in New York and New England. I am mistaken, if this course does not bring the powerful influences of those sections to the Capitol to delay, or stop the action about to be taken. If however, such effort prove of no avail, and you should find yourself on the eve before the day of impeachment, there will be only one other course than can be pursued with safety—*Arrest the traitors.* Issue an appeal to the people, and call for half a million of volunteers for the defense of the state. I pledge myself within a few days afterwards to raise a thousand men in my Congressional district—the sixth—and I believe within thirty days fifty thousand men will be under arms in the state of Ohio alone—ready again to do battle for the Union and the Constitution.

In 1797 William Blount[2] a United States Senator from Tennessee, was sequestrated from his office and expelled by the Senate, on *a mere resolution* passed by the House of Representatives, in which it was "Resolved that he be impeached" and at a subsequent session, proceeded to consider the articles of impeachment. If an effort be made in like manner to sequestrate you from your office—nothing but a "Coup d'etat" will save you.

God Almighty grant that you may see the necessity of exerting the nerve which you possess, and at the proper time take such energetic measures, as may prevent the destruction of our government is my earnest and sincere prayer.

Thomas Powell

ALS, DLC-JP.
   1. Powell (*c*1828–*fl*1878) was a Cincinnati lawyer whose actual residence was sometimes listed as Mt. Auburn, Butler County, and Branch Hill, Clermont County, Ohio. 1860 Census, Ohio, Hamilton, Cincinnati, 11th Ward, 273; Cincinnati directories (1859–78).
   2. Blount (1749–1800) had also served as territorial governor and superintendent of Indian affairs. *BDAC.* See also William H. Masterson, *William Blount* (Baton Rouge, 1954).

From Henry Stanbery

Attorney General's Office: January 5' 1867.

Sir:

I have had under consideration the papers referred to me in the matter of the application in behalf of John Twiggs,[1] a minor son of the late General Twiggs,[2] for the restoration of two dwelling houses on Prytanee street,[3] New Orleans, now in possession of the Freedmans Bureau.

This property was seized under a military order of General Butler, in June 1862 as the property of General Twiggs, an officer in the Confederate service.[4]

General Twiggs died in July 1862.[5] After his death proceedings in confiscation were commenced by the District Attorney[6] on the 5th December 1863, against this property under the Act of December 5, 1861. This appears by the letter of Mr. Goodloe,[7] District Attorney to my predecessor,[8] dated March 21, 1866, in which it is stated that General Twiggs died July 15, 1862. The ground laid in the Libel was that this property had been used as the head quarters of General Twiggs whilst in command of the Rebel forces, but the proof was that he only occupied it as his dwelling house.

The District Attorney further stated that he could not make out a case for condemnation and asked authority to dismiss the proceeding. On the

29th March 1866, such authority was given by Mr. Speed, Attorney General, by letter of that date, and at the April Term of the Circuit Court of the United States, for the Eastern District of Louisiana, on motion of the District Attorney, the libel was dismissed and the property was ordered to be restored to the administrator of Twiggs' Estate.

I see no ground upon which the possession of this property can be lawfully retained by the United States. It seems to be conceded in the various reports of military officers found among the papers,[9] and sent here from the War Department that the United States have no title or interest in the property, but an objection is raised against the delivery of the possession to Twiggs' administrator, A. C. Myers,[10] on the ground that he is an unpardoned rebel. It appears that Myers is also Guardian and Curator of the minor John Twiggs.[11]

I think the objection not well taken. The personal disability of the Guardian, if there is such disability, cannot affect his ward, and after the Court has ordered restoration of the property to the Administrator, it is too late to make such an objection.

I am accordingly of opinion that an order should be made that possession of this property be surrendered to the Administrator or his authorized agent.[12]

Henry Stanbery   Attorney General.

LS, DNA-RG94, Lets. Recd. (Main Ser.), File A-11-1867 (M619, Roll 534).

1. John W. Twiggs (c1854–fl1882) was "an infant" at the death of his mother, the second wife of General Twiggs, in March 1855. By 1877 Twiggs was living in San Francisco where he worked as an assayer. Edward Briggs to Johnson, Dec. 1, 1866, Lets. Recd. (Main Ser.), File A-11-1867 (M619, Roll 534), RG94, NA; Northen, *Men in Ga.*, 2: 411; San Francisco directories (1877–81); *U.S. Statutes at Large*, 22: 279.

2. Georgia native David C. Twiggs (1790–1862), a career army man, was dismissed from the service in 1861 for surrendering the Union forces and supplies in Texas to the Confederacy. As the oldest U.S. officer to join the Confederates, Twiggs was too unwell for field command and soon retired. *DAB*; Warner, *Gray*.

3. Actually, Prytania Street. Circuit Court of the U.S., Eastern District of Louisiana, ruling, Apr. 12, 1866, Lets. Recd. (Main Ser.), File A-11-1867 (M619, Roll 534), RG94, NA.

4. Greater detail on the confiscation proceedings can be found in Edward Briggs to Johnson, Dec. 1, 1866, ibid.

5. Twiggs died near Augusta, Georgia. *DAB*; Warner, *Gray*.

6. Rufus Waples (1825–1902) graduated from the University of Louisiana law department in 1852 and practiced in New Orleans. Appointed U.S. district attorney for the eastern district of Louisiana by President Lincoln in 1863, Waples apparently served until mid-1865. He continued to practice law in New Orleans and was involved with the public schools there. In 1878 he moved to Ann Arbor, Michigan. *Who Was Who in America*, 1: 1296; Ser. 6B, Vol. 5, Johnson Papers, LC; Edward Briggs to Johnson, Dec. 1, 1866, Lets. Recd. (Main Ser.), File A-11-1867 (M619, Roll 534), RG94, NA.

7. Kentuckian John K. Goodloe (1823–1892), a lawyer who fought in the Mexican War, served in the Kentucky state house of representatives and senate before being appointed U.S. district attorney for the eastern district of Louisiana in August 1865. He no longer held the post by December 1, 1866. Goodloe returned to Kentucky and practiced corporation law in Louisville for the rest of his life. Ser. 6B, Vol. 5, Johnson Papers, LC; H. Levin, ed., *The Lawyers and Lawmakers of Kentucky* (Chicago, n.d.), 231–36.

8. James Speed.

9. See, for example, Absalom Baird to O. O. Howard, May 30, 1866; Absalom Baird to E. M. Stanton, Aug. 22, 1866; E.R.S. Canby to Stanton, Sept. 3, 1866; J. Holt to Stanton, Dec. 22, 1866, Lets. Recd. (Main Ser.), File A-11-1867 (M619, Roll 534), RG94, NA.

10. Abraham C. Myers (1811–1889), a native of South Carolina, graduated from West Point in 1833 and remained in the army. He served during the Mexican War. As the first quartermaster-general of the Confederacy (1861–63), he grappled with serious supply problems until removed by Jefferson Davis. *DAB*.

11. Myers had applied for pardon on July 24, 1865, from Paris, France. There is no indication that he ever received an individual pardon. Myers was married to Marion Twiggs, John's half-sister. Amnesty Papers (M1003, Roll 46), S.C., A. C. Myers, RG94, NA; *DAB*; Northen, *Men in Ga.*, 2: 411.

12. The matter of the Twiggs property had first been considered by Secretary of War Stanton who referred it to Attorney General Stanbery, resulting in the report printed here. This report was presented to the cabinet on January 8, 1867, and no member objected to a restoration of the property. Johnson endorsed his approval on Stanbery's letter and General Sheridan was directed to restore the Twiggs property to the agent for the estate. Stanton to Johnson, Dec. 31, 1866, Lets. Sent, Mil. Bks., Executive, 58-C, RG107, NA; Randall, *Browning Diary*, 2: 123; E. D. Townsend to P. H. Sheridan, Jan. 9, 1867, Lets. Recd. (Main Ser.), File A-11-1867 (M619, Roll 534), RG94, NA.

To the House of Representatives

WASHINGTON, *January 8, 1867*.

To the House of Representatives:

I transmit the accompanying report from the Attorney-General[1] as a partial reply to the resolution of the House of Representatives of the 10th ultimo, requesting a "list of names of all persons engaged in the late rebellion against the United States Government who have been pardoned by the President from April 15, 1865, to this date; that said list shall also state the rank of each person who has been so pardoned, if he has been engaged in the military service of the so-called Confederate government, and the position if he shall have held any civil office under said so-called Confederate government; and shall also further state whether such person has at any time prior to April 14, 1861, held any office under the United States Government, and, if so, what office, together with the reasons for granting such pardons and also the names of the person or persons at whose solicitation such pardon was granted."

ANDREW JOHNSON.

Richardson, *Messages*, 6: 461.
1. *House Ex. Docs.*, 39 Cong., 2 Sess., No. 31, pp. 2–24 (Ser. 1289).

Remarks at Battle of New Orleans Celebration

[January 8, 1867]

GENTLEMEN: It is not my purpose in rising to make an address on this occasion, and I shall try, at this opportunity at least, if I have not, or cannot, in others, to imitate the example that has been set by the distinguished and illustrious man[1] that has been alluded to here to-night by the chairman of this meeting,[2] to respond to the demonstration you have made this evening by merely proposing a sentiment:

No State of its own will has the right, under the Constitution, to renounce its place in, or to withdraw from, the Union. ⟨Cheers.⟩ Nor has the Congress of the United States, under the Constitution, the power to degrade the people of any State by reducing them to the condition of a mere territorial dependency upon the Federal head. The one is a disruption and dissolution of the Government; the other is consolidation and the exercise of despotic power. The advocates of either are alike the enemies of the Union and of our Federal form of government.

National Intelligencer, January 9, 1867.

1. Andrew Jackson.

2. Francis P. Blair, Sr. The celebration was held under the auspices of the National Democratic Resident Committee. For a complete account, see the *National Intelligencer*, Jan. 9, 1867.

From Henry S. Commager[1]

No 286 "F" Street   Washington D.C.

Jany 9, 1867

I beg leave to respectfully request that the within named William H Huestis Esq.[2] of this District, may be appointed Warden of the Jail. I know him to be a good, capable man, and a sincere friend of the President, & one that is capable of accomplishing very much, in harmonizing the rough political elements, that are now accumulating around the Administration. Here are 17 Radical Senators and one Radical member of the House of Rep. that have endorsed his application. The object in view, in securing the endorsement of these Senators, was to convince the President, that there is not that personal antagonism, existing on the part of opposition Senators, that interested persons who reach the ears of the President, try to induce him to believe there is. It is unnecessary to extend this note. I have only to add, that in my opinion, it could be a wise and judicious step to make this appointment at once.

H. S. Commager   10 Con Dist Ohio.

ALS, DNA-RG48, Appts. Div., Misc. Lets. Recd.

1. Commager (1817–1867) was a prominent lawyer and Democratic politician in Toledo, Ohio. During the war he served with various regiments of the Ohio volunteer infantry and was brevetted brigadier general in February 1865. He was employed by the internal revenue service shortly before his death in Galveston, Texas. Hunt and Brown, *Brigadier Generals*; *Appleton's Cyclopaedia*.

2. Huestis (c1815–1874), a stone contractor and New York native, was appointed warden of the jail by Johnson in July 1867 and served until 1869. 1870 Census, D.C., Washington, 5th Ward, 75; Ser. 6B, Vol. 4: 116, Johnson Papers, LC; Washington, D.C., directories (1866–75); *Evening Star* (Washington), Oct. 26, 1874.

From William T. Sherman

Saint Louis Mo.   Jan 9 1867.

I dislike to approach you in a matter of appointment but I learn that my Brother Charles. T. Sherman is an applicant for the appointment of U.S. Judge of the Northern District of Ohio, now vacant, and believing him highly qualified in every sense I cannot withhold my assistance.

My brother has been a practising Lawyer in Northern Ohio since about 1830, is very well known, and has never taken part in politics that I know of. Regarding the office as one of peculiar honor, I should feel it a compliment to our family to have his claims fairly examined by you. He is now in Washington, but I doubt if he will make much personal exertion in his own interest.[1]

W. T Sherman   Lt Genl.

ALS, DNA-RG60, Appt. Files for Judicial Dists., Ohio, Charles T. Sherman.
1. Sherman received the judgeship on March 2, 1867. Ser. 6B, Vol. 4: 258, Johnson Papers, LC.

From Frank Smith

Private

No 48 Pine Street   New York   Jan 9th 1867

My Dear Sir

Taking it for granted that you would like to hear what effect the proceedings in congress have had in this city I have concluded to write you & also enclose two articles from the "Journal of Commerce["][1] which I think are worthy of perusal. The Journal of Commerce exerts more influence in the commercial community than any paper published here.

Trade is at a stand still and Merchants cannot look for improvement as long as this agitation lasts. The feeling here against congress is rapidly increasing and my conviction is that this impeachment movement has gained you many friends. A great many think that the proceedings will be abandoned while others contend that your enemies will continue to persecute you. I have great faith in the future and feel that you will yet be able to overcome your enemies. If my humble services can be of any use to you at any time I hope you will not fail to call on me. I have some property left and if there should be an emergency in which you might need a *friend* All I have is at your command.[2]

My family are well and wish to be remembered.

Frank Smith

ALS, DLC-JP.
1. Not found.
2. Two weeks later Smith wrote Johnson again, this time relaying the rumor that Rep. James M. Ashley of Ohio had received a bribe to introduce the impeachment resolution in the House. Smith to Johnson, Jan. 23, 1867, Johnson Papers, LC.

From Edwin B. Spinney[1]

Boston   January 9th 1867

Dear Sir.

As an American Citizen humbly do I wish to thank you for the noble and patriotic position you have taken in trying to do all in your power to arrest the fanatical course of the Majority of Congress who are daily subverting the true meaning of the Constitution of our Country and who are fast overturning the very foundation of civil liberty under the pretence of love for the people of color while their true principle in the matter is to sink Country and all for *power* and place, plunder and position. Oh how terrible is the fact that that good old Constitution, that chart by which our Fathers so well clung to that their reverence to that Document, in spite of Geographical bounds and interests made the Union sacred, and led our united Country through so many years of prosperity and peace, how terrible how sad the fact that it is betrayed and trodden under foot by the dominant party who thank God will be in a Minority when the whole Country can speak, as one day they must. So much could I write upon this subject, so full my heart of gratitude to God that you are on the side of the Constitution of our Country, that what little I could *write* at this time would be inadequate to express my thanks to you, for the Manliness and true reasoning Contained in your Veto Message on the Suffrage bill in the District of Columbia, and the position taken by you on all Occasions as chip by chip the enemies of our Republic splinter and destroy the good old constitution of our Country.

My excuse for writing to you is that I feel that you ought to be encouraged by every constitution loving man in the country surrounded as you are by those who are overturning the true principles established by our Fathers in the Constitution as framed by them. May God, in his infinate love keep you and preserve you from harm, and may you live to see our country once more comeing to reason, and all sections, North, South, East & West, liveing under the Constitution of our Fathers as before the Civil War. And to reward you for your noble efforts may you live to see the name of "Andrew Johnson" beloved by his Country men as the Statesman and Patriot who would not allow passion, prejudice, or Sectional Hatred, to despoil his love of country and forget his oath to defend the Constitution.

That time will truly come for the people of the Country are right in heart but are misled by false issues and only want the sober thought in time to become right.

Proceed then in your patriotic duty and your name shall be revered long after your enemies shall be forgotten and an impartial history shall teach future ages to revere the name of him who can be truly called the preserver of the Constitution.

Edwin B. Spinney

ALS, DLC-JP.
  1. Spinney (*fl*1881) was a Boston real estate broker and auctioneer, and later city official. Boston directories (1858–81).

From Paul Williams[1]

Marietta Ga.   Jan 9th 1867

Dear sir
  I set down to drop you a few lines to night. My name is paul Williams. I
am in Marietta Ga.
  My home is in Savannah Ga. I want to Go back thear. I was brote away
from thear in 1863 by my Master. I am ould and 55 years ould & can not
Get money enoft to Go to Savannah.
  Plese Give me stransportion for me & my wife & Child. I Can make
aliveing in savannah. That is my home for 30 years.
  Please Let me now as soon as you get this.[2]

paul. Williams

ALS, DNA-RG105, Chief Quartermaster, Lets. Recd. by Endorsement.
  1. Williams (*c*1811–*fl*1870) was a day laborer. 1870 Census, Ga., Chatham, Savannah, 77.
  2. Williams's application was referred to the War Department and in turn through the
channels of the Freedmen's Bureau to Lt. O. B. Gray, the officer in charge at Marietta. On
February 28, 1867, Gray wrote that he had seen Williams, who was "living on a farm trying
to make a crop" and "he informs me he does not now desire transportation." However,
sometime before 1870 Williams did return to Savannah. Ibid.; Chief Quartermaster, Lets.
Recd. by Endorsement, RG105, NA.

From Alexander Cummings

Denver Col   Jan 10th, 1867

  I am instructed by the House of Representatives of this Territory to
send you the following Resolution passed by that body today. "Whereas it
is announced in the public prints that it is the intention of Congress to
admit Colorado as a State into the Union. Therefore resolved by the
House of Representatives of this Territory that representing as we do the
last & only legal expression of public opinion on this question we earnestly protest against the passage of a law admitting the State without
first having the question submitted to a vote of the people for the reasons
first that we have a right to a voice in the selection of the character of our
Govt. Second that we have not a sufficient population to Support the expense of a State Govt. For these reasons we trust Congress will not force a
Govt on us against our will.["][1]

Alex Cummings   Gov. Colo.

Tel, DLC-JP.
  1. An earlier attempt to admit Colorado had already been vetoed by Johnson. In his
second veto message Johnson quotes this resolution of protest from the Colorado house of

representatives. Colorado Statehood Veto, May 15, 1866, *Johnson Papers*, 10: 506–9; Colorado Statehood Bill Veto Message, Jan. 28, 1867.

Interview with The Times *(London)* Correspondent[1]

WASHINGTON, Thursday, Jan. 10, 1867.

The President said that the light in which he regarded public affairs at the present moment was that a minority in the country was seeking to impose its views upon the majority. That minority knew the scale would be turned against them if the full number of the States were represented in Congress, and hence they were inflexible in their determination to keep them out. If once the people could be brought to understand that the fundamental principles of the Government were at stake, and not mere questions of party supremacy, there would be hope that justice would be done. In the elections last Autumn false issues were dexterously introduced, and upon them the people pronounced a judgment. They were told that if the Southern States were readmitted the national interest would be imperiled, and they did not stop to consider whether this was true or not. They forgot the weakness to which the South had been reduced, and never considered that it would be still unavoidable that it should obey the North, the stronger power—the power with available force at its back.

But, continued the President, it is impossible that the question should rest here. Little by little the Southern States have been brought back into a proper action with the general machinery of Government. The Government and the States had gradually approached each other, law and constituted authority resumed their sway, and everything was completed except the admission of representatives from those States to Congress. But here Congress interposed, and it said, "You are not States at all, and you shall not be represented." From that moment it began to pull to pieces the main fabric of the Government; it began to wipe out the States, from which alone it derived its existence. The States had brought Congress into existence, and now Congress proposed to destroy the States. It proposed to abolish the original and elementary principle of its being. It was as if the creature turned round upon the creator and attempted to destroy him. But suppose these States, with their lawfully-appointed Governors and administrators, refused to obey this summons to depart out of life altogether? Suppose they said, "We are within the scope of the Constitution; we are obeying the laws; the Government recognises us by the infliction of taxes and the appointment of public officers; and no Congress can decree our dissolution!" Could the Government deny or repudiate this argument? If it came before the Courts and they substantiated it, what would remain to Congress but the exercise of force in order to carry out its views? Thus the country would be involved in another revolution;

toward that all the proceedings of Congress in relation to the South were tending. The Executive Government were, at least, endeavoring to fulfill what was the supreme law of the land—the Constitution. There was a time when men considered the Constitution first when they framed laws. Now they occasionally mentioned it in an accidental manner. Some one on looking around discovered the Constitution, with much the same sense of astonishment, apparently, that a man who was watching the stars might experience when he discovered a new planet. But the Constitution was on the side of the Executive; law was on its side, and reason, and justice. The people would eventually perceive that it was interposing to preserve the very basis of this Republican Government, although their attention might be diverted from it now. "There is," added the President, "no answer to this argument—no attempt is made to answer it, except by the use of arbitrary power. You feel sometimes as if you were following up a principle straight to its source, and had got a tight grip upon it; and it is exactly so in this case."

The Constitution, the President further said, had been solemnly received when the people went into the Federation. No section of the people, or their representatives, could ignore or overthrow it, except arbitrarily. By-and-by, when the people heard the crack of the fabric which they had formerly prized so highly, when the sound of the falling timbers reached their ears, and they saw the dust and confusion, they would stop and look up to ascertain who it was that had been doing the work of destruction. That portion of the people which was now unheard would eventually demand by what right a Congress representing a part only of the States had assumed this responsibility. Formerly, when a measure was introduced, the first question asked was, "Is it constitutional?" and the next, "Is it expedient?" Now, Congress only asked, "Is it expedient?" but, in the judgment of the Executive, what was unconstitutional could not be expedient. The Constitution did, indeed, provide for its own enlargement or amendment, and it was competent for the people to change it according to the method prescribed. But now the majority of the people were voiceless on the question: they had no opportunity to make themselves heard. One duty of the Executive was undoubtedly to protect the rights of the minority, and hence Congress was aiming to pull down the Executive, and was even threatening the Supreme Court. It was opposed to the best interests of the people that this attempt should succeed, and the Executive still had confidence that the people would discern that truth for themselves.

The President presently referred to the alleged abuse which had been committed of the appointing power. He said that there was great misconception abroad, as to the good which the Executive might do for itself, or the harm which it might do others, by the bestowal of offices. Suppose, for instance, that there was a post to be given away. There were sure to be twenty applicants for it, and when it was bestowed all that the President had done was to make one lukewarm friend and nineteen enemies. The friend was silenced, for after he received the appointment he had to make favor with the Senate in order to get it confirmed. The man was as likely as not to throw over the President altogether. It was different when the Executive was in harmony with the Senate; then the candidate knew that he could secure a majority of that body, and he could venture to give his adhesion to the President. In point of fact, the Executive had not made more changes than were required by the public service,—not so many as were ordinarily made. There was a great outcry, because the men who were actually in power had filled all the offices with their friends and supporters, and they did not want to see them removed.

With regard to the threatened impeachment, the President said with a smile:

"I had contracted old-world ideas, derived from Magna Charter and so on downward, respecting the right of the accused to be heard and to be fairly tried, but these seem to be going out of date. Now, a committee sitting in secret, and hearing one side only, and that side the enemies of the accused, prejudge his case. It is a consistent part of the general system which we see being pursued."

Frequently during the conversation the President reiterated his belief that the people would eventually begin to look at all the questions now betore them from the Constitutional side. He seemed to be content to be judged by the fidelity and persistence with which he had adhered in his public policy to the Constitution, which his oath obliges him to defend. That oath might as well be rescinded if Congress and the country refused to recognize the Constitution as a law binding upon all alike.

New York Times, February 12, 1867.
    1. Possibly the correspondent was Louis J. Jennings (1836–1893), who was stationed in the United States during the 1865–67 period. *NUC*; *The History of The Times: The Tradition Established 1841–1884* (New York, 1939), 388, 390, 452.

From Wesley Whitaker, Jr.[1]

Office of the "Daily News,"
Goldsboro', Jan. 10, '67.

Sir:

Early in 1865, I sent on, through Provisional Governor, Holden, my application for a pardon, for the offence of acting as Route Agent, under the "Confederate States." I am aware that Gov. H. recommended "a suspension" in my case; but, my name was published among the pardons, through the cols of the "Standard" just before the election at which, Mr. Holden, for the *second time*, was repudiate by the people. I am aware of the recent action of the Radical Congress as regards *pardons*, and I do not now ask you to act in the premises, further than to instruct the Secretary of State, if such a document *has been* made out in my case, to *forward*, &c.[2]

I do not propose to say to you any thing in palliation of my connection with the late rebellion. I served through the war only as *mail agent*; but, the cause of the recommendation of my "suspension" may be inferred, when I tell you, that, knowing W. W. Holden, as I have from boy hood, I have never seen any thing in the man to warrant me in giving him my support and, if *you* have not ascertained this fact, you *will* before the difficulty is finally settled.

I have taken the liberty of sending you an occasional copy of my paper, and from it, you will learn, that I heartily approve your administration— and I can assure you that the oft repeated assertions of the Standard that our people are "traitors still—disloyal," &c, is base fabrication, and *he knows it to be so.*

I trust you will take the trouble to read the "Goldsboro' Daily News," and, if compatible with your wishes and arrangements, will hand it over to the proper Departments to be used as a medium of advertising, when occasion may make it necessary, in the distribution of such patronage.[3]

W. Whitaker, Jr   Ed. Daily News

ALS, DNA-RG94, Amnesty Papers (M1003, Roll 43), N.C., Wesley Whitaker.

1. Whitaker (c1821–fl1874), a Wake County resident, continued in the printing business and was mayor of Raleigh during the 1870s. 1860 Census, N.C., Wake, Raleigh, 77; (1870), 15; Elizabeth R. Murray, *Wake: Capital County of North Carolina* (Raleigh, 1983), Appendix D.

2. Whitaker's pardon was issued May 1, 1867. Amnesty Papers (M1003, Roll 43), N.C., Wesley Whitaker, RG94, NA.

3. The *Goldsboro News* apparently did not receive the patronage of the federal government.

From Robert Berry[1]

Council Chamber   Golden City Colorado Territory
January 11th 1867

Sir

I am instructed by the Council of the Legislative Assembly of the Territory of Colorado (the Secretary of the Territory[2] having refused to do so at the request of the Council) to forward to your Excellency a copy of Resolutions, passed by that body this day, which find enclosed.[3]

R Berry   Secretary of the Council

ALS, DLC-JP.

1. Berry (b. 1830), a native of Ohio, went to Colorado in 1859 where he built a sawmill and then engaged in mining. He held a variety of offices including U.S. marshal, internal revenue collector, member and secretary of the legislative council, county clerk and recorder, and county judge. Bancroft, *Nevada, Colorado, and Wyoming*, 623.

2. Territorial secretary from May 1866 to April 1874, Frank Hall (1836–1917) went to Colorado in 1860 and engaged in mining and newspaper editing. He later wrote a four-

volume history of Colorado. *NUC*; *History of the City of Denver, Arapahoe County, and Colorado* (Chicago, 1880), 455–56; Wallace B. Turner, "Frank Hall: Colorado Journalist, Public Servant, and Historian," *Colorado Magazine*, 53 (1976): 351.

3. The resolutions requested Johnson to remove territorial governor Alexander Cummings and appoint a Colorado resident in his place because "he is Continually in a disgusting and dictatorial manner inter-meddling with the duties of the other Territorial Officers"; and in general was "obnoxious to our people unjust and dishonest in the performance of his official duties." Efforts to remove Cummings had been under way for more than six months. See Frederick J. Stanton to Johnson, June 9, 1866, *Johnson Papers*, 10: 576–77; Allen A. Bradford to Johnson, Feb. 7, 1867, Territorial Papers, Colorado, RG59, NA.

From Hugh McCulloch

Treasury Department.   Jany. 11th. 1867.

Dear Sir:—

I herewith return the letter of Mr. Wm. Montgomery to yourself referred by you to me for report, together with a statement of Mr. Lindsey's case by the Commissioner of Internal Revenue.[1]

When the new law relating to distilled spirits went into operation on the first of September last, I adopted a regulation under which appointments by me of Inspectors in charge of Distilleries were made only upon the joint recommendation of the Assessor and Collector of the District in which service was to be rendered. This was from prudential reasons, as the office of Inspector is one requiring for the protection of the revenue strict integrity and the utmost diligence on the part of its incumbent. When, therefore, Collector Robinson[2] withdrew his recommendation, and represented to me that he lacked confidence in Lindsey, whose appointment was, in some degree, induced through the instance of the distillers whom he was to watch, I did not think it just, nor safe to continue him longer in the Service. The most recent letter received from Mr. Robinson is to the effect that Lindsey should not be reappointed to the charge of the Distillery of Hook & Wise.[3]

H McCulloch   Secretary.

To avoid further trouble in this matter & in order that no injustice should be done to Mr Lindsey, I have appointed him a Clerk in this Department which is satisfactory to him.[4]

H MC

LS, OFH.

1. Montgomery and several other Pennsylvanians had written to the President complaining about the removal of James B. Lindsey (*fl*1867), a distillery inspector, and the appointment of a "bitter enemy" of the Johnson administration in Lindsey's place. The statement from Edward A. Rollins has not been located. Montgomery et al. to Johnson, Dec. 28, 1866, OFH; *U.S. Off. Reg.* (1867).

2. Archibald Robertson.

3. Unidentified.

4. The postscript was written in McCulloch's hand.

From Hugh McCulloch

Treasury Department.   Jany. 12, 1867.

Dear Sir:—

I send you today nominations of General Slocum for Surveyor, and Mr. Franklin[1] for Naval Officer at New York. After giving the subject careful consideration I have come to the conclusion that these nominations are the best that, under the circumstances, can be made.

Mr. Wakeman[2] has held his present office a number of years, and I see no reason why he should continue to hold a position so largely profitable for a longer period. My conviction is very clear that there should be rotation in such offices, and that, without it, the administration will be weakened.

Should you conclude to send General Slocum's name to the Senate for Mr. Wakeman's place, I will thank you to advise me of it a day or two in advance. It is not unlikely, I think, that it can be made acceptable to Messrs. Seward & Weed.

Mr. Franklin has performed for many years the chief duties of the Naval Officer at a compensation which has barely enabled him to support his family with the strictest economy.[3] I think he has fairly earned the promotion, and I doubt not that his nomination would be considered a recognition of valuable service, and be entirely acceptable to the business men of New York. I give you my own views and submit them to your better judgment.[4]

Hugh McCulloch

LS, DLC-JP.
1. Cornell S. Franklin (*fl*1880), a longtime Brooklyn resident, had served as deputy naval officer since the Fillmore administration. *U.S. Off. Reg.* (1851–65); Brooklyn directories (1869–81); E. J. Lowber to McCulloch, Sept. 26, 1866, Appts., Customs Service, Naval Officer, New York, Cornell S. Franklin, RG56, NA.
2. Abram Wakeman, surveyor.
3. Franklin received an annual compensation of $2,000. *U.S. Off. Reg.* (1865).
4. Johnson chose instead to nominate Henry W. Slocum for the naval officership. But after Slocum's nomination was rejected by the Senate in March 1867, Franklin was nominated for the post. Although not confirmed, Franklin apparently continued serving as acting naval officer until the end of Johnson's term. Ser. 6B, Vol. 4: 54–58, Johnson Papers, LC; *U.S. Off. Reg.* (1867).

From David S. Walker

Executive Department   Tallahassee, Florida
January 12th 1867.

Mr. President,

On October 20th 1866 I telegraphed to you the resistance to the civil authority by lawless persons in Fernandina. On 25th Oct. Mr. Stanton desired me to send a detailed statement of the facts. On Nov 5th I complied with Mr. Stanton's request. Since then I have not heard from yourself or Mr. Stanton.

Resistance to civil authority still continues at Fernandina, as you will see by the letter of the Sheriff herewith enclosed mark A.[1] Having no organized and armed militia, with which to assist the Sheriff in the execution of the law, I this day applied to Col. Sprague[2] for the assistance of the U.S. troops under his command, as you will see from copy of my letter to him of this date herewith enclosed, marked B. Col. Sprague, as you will see from his letter to me, dated 14th inst. of which I send you a copy herewith, thinks he cannot give the assistance I ask without orders from the War Department.

I respectfully request that such orders may be issued to him without delay. I am informed that there are not more than a dozen white men in Fernandina who defy the laws, but these induce hundreds of negroes to rebellion against the State authority—and these whites have falsely and fraudulently induced the negroes to believe that they will be sustained by the U.S. troops. If the Officer in Command here[3] were instructed to assist the Sheriff the whole difficulty would be at an end, no further resistance would be made. Those who instigate resistance to the Sheriff are a few persons who purchased lots two or three years ago at the U.S. Tax Commissioners sale. Said sale has been set aside by the U.S. Commissioners, and the lots redeemed by the original owners—the redemption has been ratified by the Secretary of the Treasury of the U.S. and the purchase money refunded to the purchasers, by the United States. This being the case, the Act of Congress expressly requires that the lots be returned to the original owners. But still the purchasers not only refuse to obey this act of Congress, but organize a mob to resist the Sheriff when he attempted to put the owners in possession under the process of the Courts. They thus defy both the laws of the United States and of the State. Referring again to my letter to you of the 5th Novr. and its enclosures I invoke your early action and request that you will inform me thereof.

Gen. Grant on Nov 1st 1866 ordered Gen. Sheridan to instruct Gen Foster in regard to these same writs not to interfere "with the execution of Civil law in Florida," and Concluded by saying "The duty of the Military is to encourage the enforcement of Civil law and order to the fullest extent." Genl. Foster having received this order, obeyed it by ordering the officer to remain strictly neutral, saying to him "In no case will you use the U.S Troops in civil matters except by special orders from these Hd. Qtrs." Believing that the time has now arrived when special orders should be given to assist in the execution of the civil law I respectfully request that it may be done.

I omitted to state that on the day of the last riots alluded to by the Sheriff the insurgents displayed from the building in which they had assembled the National flag, and under it, a pair of hand-cuffs. Why the hand-cuffs were associated with the U.S. flag I do not know, but presume it was done for the purpose of exciting the negroes to greater madness, or to intimate to the Sheriff and his posse that the hand-cuffs would be used on them. Whatever may have been the motive, I trust the Government will punish this insult to its flag.

David S. Walker   Governor of Florida

P.S

January 26th I send by the same mail which takes this, an important communication on the subject of the vacancy in the U.S Dist Court for the northern Dist of Florida. I think those riots have been produced mainly by the absence of a U.S. Dist Judge.

I trust your Excellency will give immediate attention to both these communications and thereby prevent bloodshed & riot for a dreadful conflict grows more and more threatening every day. Dockray, Frasers[4] clerks acts in a most oppressive, tyranical and outrageous manner and appears to be striving to bring about collision.[5]

D. S. Walker

LS, DNA-RG107, Lets. Recd., Executive (M494, Roll 85).

1. The enclosed letter from Sheriff James M. Bennett to Walker was dated January 8, 1867, and reported "a series of lawless and disorderly proceedings" which had recently occurred.

2. John T. Sprague (1810–1878), a career army officer, colonel of the 7th U.S. Inf., and brevet brigadier general, had commanded the District of Florida since December 1866. Hunt and Brown, *Brigadier Generals*; Everly and Pacheli, *Records of Field Officers*, pt. 1: 88.

3. Alonzo A. Cole (c1844–fl1874), captain, 7th U.S. Inf., who was mustered out in 1871 and afterwards moved to Yolo County, California. Walker to Sprague, Jan. 12, 1867, Lets. Recd., Executive (M494, Roll 85), RG107, NA; ACP Branch, File 1415-1874, Alonzo A. Cole, RG94, NA.

4. Either Frederick A. Dockray (b. c1840), a lawyer, or his father, William P. Dockray (b. c1813), and Philip Fraser (c1818–fl1871), all Jacksonville residents. Both Dockrays later were in the local customs office, the senior as inspector, the younger as collector. The younger Dockray was also involved with the *Florida Times* newspaper. Fraser had been U.S. district judge since 1862, and, although he had resided in Florida since before the war, he still maintained a home in Elizabeth, New Jersey, where, because of illness, he spent much of 1866. 1870 Census, Fla., Duval, Jacksonville, 22, 52; Jerrell H. Shofner, *Nor Is It Over Yet: Florida in the Era of Reconstruction, 1863–1877* (Gainesville, 1974), 4, 14, 85, 173, 178, 206; *U.S. Off. Reg.* (1863–71); Lanman, *Biographical Annals*, 155.

5. The postscript was written in Walker's hand.

From Sam Milligan

private

Nashville Tenn.   Jan. 13. 1867

Dear Sir:

I am satisifed from evey indication, the Radicals will nominate Brownlow for Governor at their Convention the 22d prox.[1] Under the franchise law, he will be hard to beat. I have looked the whole State over, and I can think of but one man, who, I think can make a sure thing of it, and that is

General Carter[2]—late Provost Martial General at Knoxville. He is, as to his record, unexceptionable, a Military man of good character & high moral integrity and intelligence. What do you think of it?[3] Where is he? Could he be reached by the Atlantic telegraph?[4] Let me hear from you, if not too much trouble. He could accept, and make the race without being actually present—better if he could be here. *All in confidence.*

Sam Milligan

ALS, DLC-JP.

1. Tennessee Radicals/Republicans did indeed meet in Nashville on February 22 to nominate William G. Brownlow for reelection as governor. Alexander, *Reconstruction*, 141.

2. Samuel P. Carter.

3. The President responded with skepticism, if not outright opposition. See Johnson to Milligan, Jan. 23, 1867.

4. After mustering out of the army, Carter resumed foreign service with the navy, as commander of the steamer *Monocacy* which was part of the Asiatic squadron. *DAB*.

From Calvin A. Anderson[1]

Head Quarters, Post at Grenada
Grenada. Miss.   Jany. 14. 1867

Dr Sir—

It is with feelings of unfeigned pleasure that I seat myself to address you, to return to you my heartfelt and sincere thanks for your kindness and leniency in remitting the sentence in my case and giving me a chance to retrieve the past—and I assure you that I shall ever strive for the future to be worthy of this leniency on your part,—and I trust that the next time my name is brought to your notice it may be in speaking of my efficiency as an Officer and my worth as a Gentleman.

Ten days ago I tendered my Resignation—but, with Your Excellency's permission, I would like to recall it for the present, and re-consider the matter. My reasons for doing it were, I do not like this southern climate, and I was in hopes that I might get an appointment in some Regiment on the frontier, which I know would suit me much better, but on second thought, and owing to a letter I recieved from my Father[2] yesterday, I would like to have the matter dropped for the present, as my Father thinks he can have a transfer effected, which will be better, he thinks, than resigning and trusting to another appointment—or rather, to the chance of getting another appointment. Therefore, I would respectfully ask that Your Excellency let the matter rest for the present, and if my Father succeeds in effecting a transfer I shall only be too happy—for I long to go out on the *plains*, where I spent five of the happiest years of my life.[3]

Calvin A. Anderson   2d Lt. 24th U.S. Infty

ALS, DNA-RG94, ACP Branch, File A-25-CB-1867, Calvin A. Anderson.

1. Anderson (c1834–fl1875), a clerk, had been a private, 7th U.S. Inf. (1857–62), and sergeant, 74th Ind. Inf. (1862–65), before his February 1866 appointment as a lieutenant. CSR, Calvin A. Anderson, RG94, NA; Powell, *Army List*, 161; Fort Wayne directories (1866–75).

2. Calvin Anderson (1803–fl1889) was a Fort Wayne hotel keeper and grocer. *Valley of the Upper Maumee River* (2 vols., Madison, 1889), 2: 47–48.

3. Anderson did not get the transfer and his final resignation date was January 24, 1867. He returned to his Fort Wayne, Indiana, home and clerked in his father's grocery business. Powell, *Army List*, 161; Fort Wayne directories (1866–75).

From William B. Campbell

Washington, D.C. Jany 14th 1867

Sir

I learn that Russell Houston Esqr has resigned the place as Commissioner[1] to settle the claims for the negroes of loyal citizens who were mustered into the United States army, for the state of Tennessee. I therefore recommend William Leillyett Esqr of Nashville Ten, as an active energitic business man—honest & reliable and well qualified to fill said vacancy. I know of no man who would more faithfully discharge the duties, and who is in all respects more worthy & deserving the confidence of the Administration. I beg your particular attention to this case.

W B Campbell

ALS, DNA-RG94, Lets. Recd. (Main Ser.), File W-684-1866 (M619, Roll 528).

1. Actually Houston declined (rather than resigned from) the appointment which had been offered to him in November 1866. On the very day that Campbell penned his letter to the President, the War Department appointed Anthony Keele to replace Houston. The Keele appointment was directed in care of Sen. David T. Patterson; evidently Johnson's son-in-law prevailed over Campbell in this appointment. Edward D. Townsend to O. W. Davis, Jan. 14, 1867; Stanton to Keele, Jan. 14, 1867, Lets. Recd. (Main Ser.), File W-684-1866 (M619, Roll 528), RG94, NA.

From William L. Hodge

Washington   14 Jan 1867

Sir

A short absence from the City has prevented me from sooner thanking you as a resident of the City for your attempt to save us from the degredation of the suffrage bill,[1] which hands us over to a band of ignorant vagabonds runaways & criminals that have congregated here from the surrounding late slave states. Your good intention was frustrated by a fanatical majority but nevertheless your able & conclusive message will be generally read & will make a great impression on the community & produce its good fruit in due time.

The ultra's have taken so much rope that they will undoubtedly hang themselves & those who are disposed either to weep or to rejoice over the dead corpse of radical republicanism will at no very distant period undoubtedly have an opportunity to do so. I certainly shall not be among the *crying* portion of the audience.

Wm. L Hodge

ALS, DLC-JP.
1. See District of Columbia Franchise Law Veto Message, Jan. 5, 1867. The veto was overridden by Congress.

From Fitz John Porter

January 14, 1867, New York, N.Y.; ALS, DLC-JP.
Citing his seventeen years of army service during which he had been "Entrusted at all times with duties of the greatest responsibilities, frequently performed at the peril of life" and "no breath of suspicion had attached itself" to his reputation, Porter asks that the President "appoint a court for the purpose of reconsidering the proceedings" of his trial in January 1863. He cites conditions at that time— "The country was envisioned with perils. Distrust had seized many of the strongest minds. Errors of the greatest magnitude had occured"—as creating "a great and growing sentiment that an example should be had by which faithlessness or incompetency should be promptly dealt with. . . . it was my misfortune to be charged and tried at this most inopportune of periods." Moreover, "Evidence of the most important character to me, at that time totally inaccessible to either the court or myself, is now to be readily obtained" which has persuaded "competent and disinterested persons, including many of those who deemed my trial and condemnation just" that he would now be vindicated.

From Orville H. Browning

Department of the Interior.
Washington D.C.   Jan'y 15", 1867

Sir;

I have the honor, to transmit herewith a copy of a letter received at the Indian Bureau from M. T. Patrick, Indian Agent of the Upper Platt Agency, dated at Fort Laramie, December 26, 1866;[1] also copy of letter this day addressed to me by the Commissioner of Indian Affairs,[2] both relating to the disturbed state of the Indians on our Northwestern frontier, and the threatening attitude now occupied by them.[3]

Unless prompt and efficient measures are taken to pacify and disperse the Indians, war with them will certainly ensue in the spring, and, if hostilities begin, the probability is very strong that the war will be of greater magnitude, more destructive of life and property, and involving a larger expense to the Government than any Indian war we have ever had.

I am anxious, as well on account of our exposed frontier settlements as for the sake of the ignorant and misguided savages, that every possible precaution shall be taken to avert so great a calamity.

I believe that this can be done by prompt, judicious and humane action on our part. But whether it can or not I esteem it a duty to make the effort, and could not but feel that the Government would be justly blameable for the neglect of any means calculated to preserve peaceful relations with the Indians and to escape the many evils of a war.

With this end in view I propose with your sanction, and in co-operation with the Hon. Secretary of War, to send to the hostile bands now reported to be encamped on Tongue River, a Commission composed of four or five prudent and discreet men, selected from gentlemen of Military education and experience, and from civilians acquainted with the habits and character of the Indian tribes, to confer with them, to ascertain their wants; to make to them truthful representations of the power and resources of the government, the absolute impossibility of a successful contest on their part; and the certainty of their extermination should they provoke a war, and also to assure them of the just and humane intentions of the government towards them, and its purpose to deal with them justly, and to provide them reservations for homes, in the event that they disperse their warriors, return to their women and children and remain at peace.

If this be done I believe that war will be prevented, because I believe that if the Indians can be convinced that we mean friendship, justice and fair dealing with them, we will have no further trouble.

I may be mistaken. The effort to pacify them and stifle the War in its incipiency may fail. But even if it does the probabilities of success are such as to justify the effort and leave us without excuse if we neglect to make it. If it succeeds it will save us thousands of lives, millions of money and a vast deal of human suffering. If it fails we will have expended a few thousand dollars in a laudable effort to save our frontier settlements from the horrors of an Indian War, and the Country from the many evils it would bring in its train. We will have done our duty, and the responsibility of the War, if it must come, will not be upon the administration.

I, therefore, most earnestly urge that such a Commission be at once Constituted, and that, in addition to the duties already suggested they be charged with the further duty of making a thorough investigation into the recent massacre at Fort Phil Kearney.[4] This I deem very important. If the Indians are to blame for that atrocity, the leaders who instigated it should be demanded of their tribes and condignly punished. On the other hand if the fault was ours it should be known that proper measures may be taken to prevent a recurrence of similar disasters in the future.[5]

(Signed)   O. H. Browning   Secretary.

Copy, DNA-RG94, Lets. Recd. (Main Ser.), File I-10-1867 (M619, Roll 556).
    1. Pennsylvania native Mathewson T. Patrick (1834–1899) moved to Omaha, Nebraska, in 1856 and dealt in real estate. Lieutenant colonel of the 5th Iowa Cav. during the Civil War, Patrick served in the western theater. He was appointed to the Upper Platte agency on August 3, 1866, and apparently served until 1869, when he became U.S. mar-

shal for the Utah Territory, a post he held until 1873. His letter discussed the large number of warriors camped on the Tongue River in the Dakota Territory. Some Indians who had no wish to participate in a war were reported to be en route to Ft. Laramie. Hill, *Indian Affairs*, 188–89; Arthur C. Wakeley, ed., *Omaha: The Gate City and Douglas County, Nebraska* (2 vols., Chicago, 1917), 2: 328, 331; *OR*, Ser. 1, Vol. 16, Pt. 1: 755–56; Vol. 38, Pt. 2: 904–9; Patrick to H. B. Duncan, Dec. 26, 1866, Lets. Recd. (Main Ser.), File I-10-1867 (M619, Roll 556), RG94, NA.

2. Lewis V. Bogy (1813–1877), a Missouri lawyer, state legislator, and businessman, served a brief (November 1866-March 1867) and controversial term as commissioner of Indian affairs before his appointment was rejected by the Senate. He later became senator from Missouri. His letter to Browning lamented conditions experienced by the Indians and urged an investigative commission which Browning then proposed to the President. Bogy to Browning, Jan. 15, 1865, ibid.; *DAB*; Robert M. Kvasnicka and Herman J. Viola, eds., *The Commissioners of Indian Affairs, 1824–1977* (Lincoln, 1979); Randall, *Browning Diary*, 2: 136.

3. Many of the Indians in the Dakota Territory area were irate because the government had established three forts—Reno, Phil Kearny, and C. F. Smith—during the summer of 1866 to protect the Bozeman Trail. Unfortunately, this trail ran directly through some sacred Indian hunting grounds in the Powder River country. The hostile Sioux, Cheyenne, and Arapaho, determined to prevent white settlement and passage, attacked work parties, supply and emigrant trains, and stock herds whenever possible. Dee Brown, *The Fetterman Massacre* [formerly *Fort Phil Kearny: An American Saga*] (Lincoln, 1971 [1962]), passim.

4. On December 21, 1866, Bvt. Col. William J. Fetterman led a party of troops from Ft. Phil Kearny to rescue the fort's wood procurement train which was under attack. Inexperienced in Indian fighting, he disobeyed explicit orders not to cross Lodge Trail Ridge, thereby leading his troops into an ambush by about 2,000 warriors. The entire contingent of eighty-one died in what is usually known as the Fetterman Massacre. Ibid., chapter 9.

5. The Fetterman Massacre contributed to the continuing rivalry between the peace and negotiation-oriented Bureau of Indian Affairs and the military. Although General Grant disapproved of a commission, Johnson appointed one anyway in early February 1867. While the commission officially determined that fort commander Col. Henry B. Carrington had been undersupplied with men and equipment and was not at fault, this report was buried under adverse and often fictionalized accounts. The commission did hold talks with some of the friendly tribes in the Missouri and Platte river regions, thus preventing General Sherman from sending a punitive military expedition into the area. Ibid., 100, chapters 10 and 11; Utley, *Frontier Regulars*, 114, 118, 120–21, 126; endorsement by Grant, Jan. 21, 1867, Lets. Recd. (Main Ser.), File I-10-1867 (M619, Roll 556), RG94, NA.

From John N. Goodwin

Washington, 15th Jany. 1867.
Sir.

The act which has recently passed Congress, extending the right of suffrage, to all citizens of the United States residing in the Territories, of whatever race or color,[1] confers it upon a large number of Indians in the Territory of Arizona, who have no knowledge of our language, and are ignorant of our customs and laws.

A part of the Territory of Arizona was acquired from Mexico under the treaty of Guadaloupe Hidalgo, dated 2d Feby. 1848, and the remainder under the Gadsden treaty, dated 30th Dec. 1853.

While the whole of the Territory constituted a part of Mexico, a decree was made by that government, giving rights of citizenship to all its Inhabitants, equally, whether *Europeans*, Africans, or Indians. This Decree, which has never been repealed or essentially modified is in the following language.

"Todos los habitantes de la Nueva España, sin distincion alguna, de Europeos, Africanos ni Indios, son ciudadanos de esta monarquia, con opcion, a todo empleo, sigun su merito y virtudes.

Decreto 4. De 5 Octobre, 1821

Pan del Señor Don Augustin de Iturbide 12. Collecion de Ordenos y Decretas Tomo 1, 1821 & 1822.

(Translation—"All the Inhabitants of New Spain, without any distinction, whether Europeans, Africans, or Indians, shall be citizens of this monarchy, with the right to every place—according to their merits and *abilities*.")

I have been informed that under this provision of law, a distinction was made between the Savage and Hostile Indians who roamed through the country, having no settled abode, and the Pueblo Indians, who dwelt in *Villages*, and subsisted by agriculture and the peaceful tools.

If all the rights of citizens were conceded to the Pueblo Indians, by virtue of this decree, it seems very clear, that under the terms of the above named treaties they became citizens of the United States.

The clauses of the treaties bearing upon this point are as follows:

Art. 8. Treaty of Guadaloupe Hidalgo.

"Mexicans now established in Territories previously belonging to Mexico, and which remain for the future within the limits of the United States, as defined by the present treaty, shall be free to continue where they now reside, or to remove at any time to the Mexican republic. Those who shall prefer to remain in the said territories may either retain the title and rights of Mexican citizens or acquire those of citizens of the United States.

But they shall be under the obligation to make their election within one year from the date of the exchange of ratifications of this treaty; and those who shall remain in the said Territories after the expiration of that year without having declared their intention to retain the character of Mexicans, shall be considered to have elected to become citizens of the United States."

Art. 9. "The Mexicans who in the Territories aforesaid shall not preserve the character of citizens of the Mexican Republic conformably with what is stipulated in the preceding article, shall be incorporated into the Union of the United States, and be admitted at the proper time, (to be judged of by the Congress of the United States) to the enjoyment of all the rights of citizens of the United States, according to the provisions of the Constitution."

Art 5. Gadsden Treaty.

"All the provisions of the 8th and 9th Articles of the Treaty of Guadelupe Hidalgo, shall apply to the Territory ceded by the Mexican Republic, in the first article of the present treaty, and to all the rights of persons and property."

If by the term Mexicans, used in the Treaty, is meant citizens of Mexico, and I cannot see how any other meaning can be given it, the Indians remaining in the Territory became citizens of the United States, and are to be admitted at the proper time to be judged of by the Congress of the United States, to all the rights of citizens of the United States.

I submit that the proper time to extend to these people the right of suffrage, will be when they have acquired our language, and with it, some knowledge of our institutions and laws, so that they can exercise the right understandingly.

It is estimated that there are about 40,000 Indians in the Territory of Arizona. The Moquis[2] who are unquestionably Pueblo Indians number according to the estimate of Dr. Ten Broek[3] eight thousand.

The Pinios and Papagoes,[4] who are certainly the most civilized of all the Indian tribes in the Territory, are regarded as Pueblo Indians. They number about twelve thousand.

If this act confers any rights upon Indians, it would certainly make four thousand Indian voters, not one of whom can speak the English language.

The whole vote of the Territory under existing laws will not exceed two thousand.

J. N. Goodwin

LS, DLC-JP.

1. "A bill to regulate the elective franchise of the Territories of the United States," passed by both houses of Congress on January 10, 1867. *Congressional Globe*, 39 Cong., 2 Sess., pp. 381–82, 398–99.

2. Moqui was the name used until the early twentieth century to refer to the group now known as the Hopi. This sedentary tribe lived in northern Arizona villages and, unlike their Navajo neighbors, they were not involved in raiding white settlements. Lamar, *Reader's Encyclopedia*, 511; John C. Connelly, "Hopi Social Organization," in Alfonso Ortiz, ed., *Southwest* (Washington, D.C., 1979), 551–52 [vol. 9 of William C. Sturtevant, ed., *Handbook of North American Indians*].

3. Peter G.S. Ten Broeck (d. 1867) became an assistant army surgeon in 1847, in which capacity he apparently was stationed at Ft. Defiance, near the Pueblo Indian villages, which he visited several times. During the Civil War he served as a surgeon and was brevetted lieutenant colonel in 1865. Frederick J. Dockstader, "Hopi History, 1850–1940," in ibid., 524; Powell, *Army List*, 624.

4. The Piman Indians, including both the Pima and Papago tribes, lived in southern Arizona and northern Sonora, Mexico, and came under United States jurisdiction with the Gadsden Purchase. Residing in relatively stable villages, these Indians never fought against the Americans, but in fact often sided with them to pursue the Apaches. The first Indian reservation in Arizona, the Gila River Indian Reservation, was set aside for the Pima in 1859. Lamar, *Reader's Encyclopedia*, 937–38.

To Lewis E. Parsons

Washington, D.C., January 17 1867

What possible good can be attained by reconsidering the constitutional amendment?[1] I know of none in the present posture of affairs. I do not believe that the people of the whole country will sustain any set of individuals in attempts to change the whole character of our Government, by enabling acts or otherwise. I believe, on the contrary, that they will eventually uphold all who have patriotism and courage to stand by the Constitution, and who place their confidence in the people. There should be no faltering on the part of those who are honest in their determination to sustain the several co-ordinate Departments of the Government, in accordance with its original design.

Andrew Johnson

Tel, DNA-RG107, Tels. Sent, Vol. 3 (1865–68).
1. The Fourteenth Amendment, which had been rejected by the Alabama legislature December 7, 1866. Parsons had indicated in a telegram to Johnson earlier on January 17 that the Alabama legislature was reconsidering its rejection of the Fourteenth Amendment. *Picayune* (New Orleans), Dec. 11, 1866; Parsons to Johnson, Jan. 17, 1867, Johnson Papers, LC.

From Ebenezer W. Peirce[1]

Fall River, Jan 17th 1867.

I beg to assure you that the impeachment movement is decidedly unpopular even here in Radical New England and none speak of it with less favor than leading republicans who begin to feel a strong pressure from the bond holders.

Among your appointments to office in Mass. are three wounded officers and all I think from the Republican party Gen. King, and Col. Stephenson,[2] Assessors, & myself Collector.

If we are rejected by the Senate the fear is that you will then nominate three Democrats and should you do that and either of the Democrats be confirmed our members in congress will have to smart for it. It annoys them when I ask who could blame the President for nominating three denocrats in place of three rejected republicans. When the Senate refuse men who have served in the republican party for many years and served through the war and are disabled by wounds recd. in battle what can the President do to satisfy you but nominate Democrats?[3]

Ebenezer W Peirce   Coll. 1st Dist. Mass.

ALS, DLC-JP.
1. Peirce (1822–1903), a prewar brigadier general of militia, commanded the 29th Mass. Inf. until the fighting before Richmond (1862), where he was wounded and captured, but then escaped. He later served as commandant of the post at Paris, Kentucky, before mustering out of the army in 1864. Given a recess appointment in August 1866 as collector of the First District, Peirce was officially nominated by Johnson for that office on

December 13. *NCAB*, 11: 237; *NUC*; Ser. 6B, Vol. 4: 24, Johnson Papers, LC; Appts. File, Internal Revenue Service, Collector, Mass., 1st Dist., Ebenezer W. Peirce, RG56, NA.

2. William S. King and Luther Stephenson, Jr. Earlier recommended as a candidate for U.S. marshal, King (1818–1882), an attorney and a former commander of a Massachusetts artillery regiment, was given a recess appointment for the Third District assessorship in late September 1866. Stephenson (1830–1921), who was severely wounded at Gettysburg and again at Petersburg, was appointed by Johnson as assessor for the Second District on November 9, 1866. Years later he served as head of the National Home for Disabled Volunteer Soldiers at Togus, Maine (1883–97). Hunt and Brown, *Brigadier Generals*; *NCAB*, 7: 294; Ser. 6B, Vol. 3: 34, Johnson Papers, LC; Appt. Files, Internal Revenue Service, Assessor, Mass., 3rd Dist., William S. King, RG56, NA.

3. King's official nomination was confirmed by the Senate on January 22, 1867, but Stephenson's was rejected. Ser. 6B, Vol. 4: 24, Johnson Papers, LC. For the outcome and aftermath of Peirce's nomination, see his letter to Johnson, Jan. 30, 1867.

From David T. Scott[1]

New Orleans, Jany 17th. 1867.

My Dear Sir

I address you as an old acquaintance who was when you last may recollect me as the Proprietor of the St. Cloud Hotel in Nashville Tennessee.[2] Times, Circumstances and the Casualties of the war has cast my destiny as you perceive in this City to work my way through life and to endeavour to suport and sustain my wife and seven children.[3] In my connexion here in the Cotton & Commission business I have met a great many of my old acquaintances and friends Among the Freedmen who have Served in the Army of the U. States—who have applied to me for aid or information to enable them to adjust their Claims for Bounty &c with the Government. These Claims have pressed so strongly upon me and consumed much of my time without remuneration that I have been advised to apply for a Commission to open an office in this City for the Adjustment of Such Claims. I respectfully ask you therefore to refer my application to the proper Department with instructions to forward me a commission with the requisition forms instructions &c. In the event of the trust being reposed in me I will endeavour faithfully to perform the duties imposed on me to the best of my ability both to the Government as well as the Freedmen. I have never been a politician you know and for my position and deportment during the war I can refer you to no better refference than Genl. Grant who doubtless yet recollects the Circumstances which transpired between us in Memphis Tene. whilst he was in Command there[4] and where I remained with my family during the war. Hoping to hear from you through the proper Channel And Wishing you every Success in all the multiplicity of your Arduous duties . . .[5]

D. T. Scott

ALS, DNA-RG94, USCT Div., Lets. Recd., File P-18-1867.

1. Scott (*c*1806–*fl*1867) was a physician. 1860 Census, Tenn., Davidson, Nashville, 3rd Ward, 85; Nashville directories (1855–61); New Orleans directories (1867–69).

2. Scott was associated with the St. Cloud Hotel during the 1850s and in the early 1860s. Nashville directories (1855–61).

3. Scott and his wife Charity Ann (c1821–fl1869) had three sons and four daughters who, in 1860, ranged in age from two to twenty-two. Sistler, *1850 Tenn. Census*, 6: 29; 1860 Census, Tenn., Davidson, Nashville, 3rd Ward, 85.

4. Grant had his headquarters in Memphis, June 23-July 11, 1862. No evidence of interaction between Grant and Scott has been located.

5. Ten days later C. W. Foster, of the War Department's adjutant general's office, replied to Scott, "I am directed to inform you that such accounts are settled by duly appointed officers of the Government, and as yet there is no necessity, or authority in law, for special appointments of the nature requested by you." Foster to Scott, Jan. 27, 1867, USCT Div., Lets. Recd., File P-18-1867, RG94, NA.

From A. Cameron Hunt

No. 529. H. Street

Washington   Jany 18th 1867

Dear Sir

I desire to call your attention to a fiew facts concering the true condition of things in our Teretory.

1st. The Statements of Mess Evans, Chaffee, Gilpin and Bradford, should be taken with a fair share of allowence, in view of the fact that each of these gentlemen get most lucretive positions under the new State Government—when fuly organized.[1]

2d. The population is fairly stated in the mesage of Governor Cummings, only a little excessive in my judgement,[2] and four years as U.S. Marshal has given me excellent opportunities of knowing pretty correctly.

3d. Out of this population there is not to exceede thre thousand persons who pay taxes at al & near one thousand of this number pay less than five dollars each.

4th If the question was resubmitted to the people the proposition would be voted down by over one thousand majority.

5th. At the election of State officers held in October 1865, there were chosen twenty six members of the House of Representatives and thirteen members of the Senate, (for the new State) al of the lower house were elected for one year and the senior half *ie* six—of the Senate leaving but six members of the two branches, yet in political existance, one member having, decased since.

6th. The proposition for negro suffrage received but a little more than four hundred votes in the entire Teritory, when submitted, with the Constitution.[3]

7th. Every expence incident to the new *State Goverment* will necessarily be double to treble, what it would cost in Iowa or Kansas.

I would gladly have communicated these facts verbaly, but knowing your time must be al absorbed in weightier matters, sought this a (perhaps) less annoying mode.

A. C Hunt   Delegate Elect from Colorado

ALS, DLC-JP.
    1. John Evans and Jerome B. Chaffee, senators-elect, William Gilpin, governor-elect, and Allen A. Bradford, present territorial delegate.
    2. Cummings claimed that a special census, plus informed estimates for non-reported counties, showed a total population of 27,931. Alexander Cummings, Governor's Message, Dec. 13, 1866, Johnson Papers, LC.
    3. Black suffrage received 476 affirmative votes but 4,192 negative votes. Berwanger, *West and Reconstruction*, 144.

From Robert L. Martin[1]

Lenni Mills Delaware Co Penna   Jany 18 1867.

Sir.—

I take the liberty of writing you in relation to the Assessorship of Internal Revenue of this, (the 7 c.) District of Penna. Through your kindness my son Major Archer N Martin[2] was appointed to this office and has discharged the duties thereof since August last. The records of the Dept will shew that he has performed them faithfully, and that in fact, by pursuing frauds and delinquents, he has saved to the Government much more than the emoluments of the office.

But neither this fact, nor his irreproachable integrity nor his three years service in the Army and the honorable and distinguished record he made with Sheridan, will, I apprehend, avail against the Radical rancor against him and myself, for giving you, our earnest and sincere support, and I look therefore for the rejection of his appointment by the Senate.[3] This would be peculiarly hard, as the First Comptroller of the Treasy.,[4] has decided under a law of 1863, that as his appointment *was made to fill a vacancy* that he cannot be paid any thing for his service until his appointment shall be confirmed by the Senate.

Should he be rejected by that body, I beg to ask the favor of you to make no appointment to fill the vacancy, but let the duties of the assessorship (as will the emoluments) devolve on the Depy. Assistant Assessor at West Chester, Captn. J L Englebert,[5] who was appointed by Major Martin, and is a friend and supporter of you and your policy. I apprehend there is no legal or constitutional obligation on you to make such an appointment, where as in this case, the succession in absence of an appointment is provided by law. If the Radicals should practice the injustice of rejecting Major Martin you can foil their malice, by making no appointment and letting the duties and emoluments of the office pertain to Capt Englebert who served gallantly through the War, is a worthy gentleman and a capable and efficient officer of the Department and is politically right.[6]

Robert L Martin

ALS, DNA-RG56, Appts., Internal Revenue Service, Assessor, Pa., 7th Dist., Archer N. Martin.
    1. Martin (c1820–fl1877) was a cotton and woolen manufacturer and a Conservative Republican. 1860 Census, Pa., Delaware, Aston, 162; Henry G. Ashmead, *History of Del-*

aware County, Pennsylvania (Philadelphia, 1884), 297; John M. Broomall to Hugh Mc-Culloch, Aug. 3, 1866; Robert L. Martin to Johnson, Aug. 10, 1867, Appts., Internal Revenue Service, Assessor, Pa., 7th Dist., Archer N. Martin, RG56, NA.

2. Martin (c1844–1894), a brevet major and former aide to General Sheridan who distinguished himself during the war at Fisher's Hill, Virginia, was nominated by Johnson for the Seventh District assessorship on July 18, 1866. Rejected later that month, Martin was given a recess appointment for the same post on August 6. Appt. Files, Internal Revenue Service, Assessor, Pa., 7th Dist., Archer N. Martin, RG56, NA; *Senate Ex. Proceedings*, Vol. 14, pt. 2: 974, 1170; Ser. 6B, Vol. 3: 160, Johnson Papers, LC; Pension File, Archer N. Martin, RG15, NA.

3. Johnson's renomination of Martin as assessor was rejected on February 8, 1867. Ser. 6B, Vol. 4: 84, Johnson Papers, LC.

4. Robert W. Taylor.

5. Jacob Lee Englebert (b. c1840), a Philadelphia clerk, had served in the Army of the Potomac as bugler and captain, 3rd Pa. Cav. CSR, Jacob Lee Englebert, RG94, NA.

6. The President nominated Englebert, who was confirmed by the Senate on March 2, 1867. Ser. 6B, Vol. 4: 86, Johnson Papers, LC. For further developments, see Robert L. Martin to Johnson, Mar. 15, 1867, Appts., Internal Revenue Service, Assessor, 7th Dist., J. Lee Englebert, RG56, NA.

From Edward Stanly[1]

San Francisco   January 18th 1867.

Sir.

Some of your friends, having all confidence in your life-long integrity and well-tried patriotism have united their efforts to form a National Union party.

We have had some correspondence with your friends in Washington City but the distance is so great, that months elapse before we can receive answer to our letters.

We have thought it advisable to request Mr Jesse D. Carr[2] who is about to visit Washington, to call on you, & if you can spare the time, we beg you to learn from him, viva voce, something of the real Condition of affairs in this State: for we know that more satisfactory information can be communicated in half an hour's conversation, than in a multitude of letters.

We recommend Mr Carr as a gentleman of Standing & character, entirely reliable, and an earnest supporter of those measures which distinguish your administration, and we hope will save the country from anarchy.

We beg leave to assure you, that no matter what the headlong spirit of radicalism may attempt, or may do, you will have an earnest sympathy and active support. We only desire the continuance of our friends at Washington, to render our efforts effective, and to know how far we can rely upon the co-operation of the experienced Statesmen enjoying your confidence.

We have requested Mr Carr to confer with Genl. McDougall,[3] before calling on you.

Edw. Stanly Chairman   pro: tem: Nat: Union Com:

ALS, DLC-JP.
1. Appointed by Lincoln military governor of North Carolina in April 1862, Stanly had a largely unsuccessful tenure. After his resignation in early 1863, he resided in California for the rest of his life except for several lengthy trips. Norman D. Brown, *Edward Stanly: Whiggery's Tarheel "Conquerer"* (University, Ala., 1974), 202–4, 249–50, and passim.
2. Carr (c1814–1903) was a "California pioneer, politician, and extensive land owner." *New York Times*, Dec. 12, 1903.
3. California senator James A. McDougall.

From Thomas W. Tipton[1] and John M. Thayer

Washington D C   January 19th 1867

Sir.

In regard to the population of Nebraska, we claim, first that the vote of 9,136 at the October election 1866[2] does not indicate more than 3/4ths of our population! at that time entitled to exercise the right of voting. When the case was tested in several instances by a actual count 1/4th of the voters were absent from the polls. After passing through the Territory last October Gov Saunders[3] Says: "I am well convinced that we have at least 12,000 voters. Several counties in the Territory have almost doubled their population the past season and all who came in after the 9th of April were not voter's at the last election." Two proprietors of Steam Ferry Boats who keep records and are assessed on gross receipts every month reported to the Editor of the Peoples Press at Nebraska City,[4] as follows; "Mr. Beabout[5] Said that for the last four months ending Nov 15th 1866 not less than ten families per day crossed at Nebraska City; and Mr. Morgan[6] of Brownville Said not less than twenty families per day had crossed for Settlement in Nebraska, at that place during the Same time." Hence by these two Ferries not less than 18,450 persons were added to our population in four months, and allowing an equal number crossed at the Steam Ferry Boats at Plattsmouth and Omaha and points above and below, and by all the emigrants roads leading from Kansas during the same time our population could not be less than 96,000; for a vote of 12,000 represents a population of 60,000 itself. After passing 400 miles through the Territory by the Cars and stage and having lectured in the towns and cities of Nebraska during July 1866, Bayard Taylor[7] writes of our populations steady increase, as follows. "It can not be less than 15,000, making the present population of the Territory about 75000" and if we add to this the increase Since the above date it overruns 96,000. While we admit the difficulty of estimating with absolute accuracy Such a Stream of imigration as sets in upon Nebraska we are confident of being near the truth.

T. W. Tipton
John M. Thayer
Senators Elect from Neb.

LS, DLC-JP.
    1. Tipton (1817–1899), a native of Ohio and a lawyer, served in the Ohio state house, in the U.S. Land Office (1849–52), and then became a Methodist minister. About 1859 he moved to Brownsville, Nebraska, where he was a member of the constitutional convention of 1859 and the territorial council. During the war he was chaplain of the 1st Nebr. Vol. Inf. A member of the constitutional convention of 1867, Tipton was one of Nebraska's first two senators, serving 1867 to 1875. *BDAC*.
    2. The October 9 election was for the territorial delegate and congressman. See J. Sterling Morton to Johnson, Oct. 16, 1866.
    3. Alvin Saunders.
    4. Formerly the *Nebraska Press*, established in the spring of 1858, it had a succession of editors. W. H. Miller held the post from some time in 1865 to October 1866. He was succeeded by Col. O. H. Irish, a previous owner, who sold the paper back to Miller and a partner in August 1868. *History of Nebraska*, 1211.
    5. Not identified.
    6. Morgan has not been identified, but Brownsville got a new steam ferry, the *Idona*, in August 1866. Ibid., 1133.
    7. Taylor (1825–1878), of Pennsylvania, was a prolific author of travel accounts and poetry, as well as translator of Goethe's *Faust. DAB*.

From David S. Fraley

                                Batesville Arkansas   Jan 20th/67
Dear Friend
    I have often thought I would write to you. And have as often abandoned the idea as I am aware the ardeous duties you have to Perform leaves you with little leisure for unimportant matters.
    You may remember me as a little N Carolina Tailor that worked for you about 30 years since in Greenville and whose security you went for breaking Old Dicksons[1] oil mill dam on a fishing frolic.
    I came from Greenville to this Place where I married & have now 5 Girls & 1 Boy.[2] At the beginning of this unfortunate war I was worth over fifty thousand dollars[3] and have suffered like Poor Tray for being caught in bad company.
    The Federals took my negroes and me being a Union man the Rebels took the ballance and while they were running you over Tennessee I was acquiring a tolerable Geographical knowlege of this Country in trying to save my neck and did so by going into the Federal lines and went to work for the Goverment until the war closed. At which time I Returned home and found several of my houses torn down & the rest much injured. I am not one of the sort to cry for spilt milk so I went to work and partialy repaired some of them & am renting them out and am able to make buckle & tounge meet by working some at my trade &c as you will see by my [?] and also have a little left to assist my old friends as I have been able to invest Fifty dollars as a help towards starting a Paper here in your interest and for which zeal I had tendered to me the office of Treasurer of a Johnson Club and am discharging the duty faithfully by Paying all that is required out of my own assetts as it would not take two or three National Bank to count the funds on hand contributed. Old Friend I am only sorry

JANUARY 1867

that I can not be of more service to you and the Course you have taken than I am. But who knows but some day, I may be able to assist you more. The cackling of a goose once saved Rome. And as the Fable says a mouse once through grattitude knawed the hunters net from around an entangled Lion. Some day I may be able to both cackle & knaw. As the net seems to be spreading. And in order that you may fully understand the motive that Prompts me to write I will here state that it is pure disinterested friendship for services rendered me in days of yore. I am not in want of an office of any kind unless it would be to further your interest if I could as you are aware many will flatter that thrift may follow others will Damn because the grapes are sour. I am & have been a well wisher to you ever since you befriended me and have been gratified at your steady advancement to high Places and am now as Proud as any man in America that we have a *man* a *Mechanic* and a *North Carolinian* at the helm in these times. I have an unshaken confidence that all will be well yet. You are only an instrument in the hands of Divine Providence to work out his ways and you could not falter or err if you would beleiving that you will tread the Path he has marked for you with no faltering step and that your administration will redound to your good name and that this nation will advance in Prosperity and unity and be to other nations as the Star of Bethlehem to lead them to a Saviour. Hoping God may direct and defend you through all the duties you may have to perform and that you may take the Constitution and the laws of the land in their Purity as your Helmet your Banner & Sheild and defy the host of the Devil arrayed in the livery of the Court of Borraboralagov.[4]

And should I ever get strapped while you are Carrying on I shall certainly kick you for a job. At present I have nothing more to ask only your kind rememberance.

David S. Fraley

ALS, DLC-JP.
1. Probably either William or John Dickson.
2. Isabella E. Fraley (b. *c*1830), David's wife, was a native of Arkansas. By 1860 they had three daughters: Mary A. (b. *c*1853), Martha E. (b. *c*1855), and I. (b. 1859). Mary was apparently the only family member remaining in Arkansas in 1870. 1860 Census, Ark., Independence, Batesville, 8; (1870), Franklin, Lower Twp., 19; Mary Sue Harris and Bobby McLane, *Independence County, Arkansas, Marriage Records, 1826–1877: Books A thru D* (Hot Springs National Park, 1970), 95.
3. The 1860 census showed Fraley with $25,000 of real property and $1,400 of personal property. 1860 Census, Ark., Independence, Batesville, 8.
4. Probably a reference to "Borrioboola Gha," a poem by Orrin Goodrich, first published in 1855.

From Alexander Hawthorn

El Paso Ill, Jany 20 1867

Dear Sir

It may not be out of the way for you to get a line from an old frend.

Well Sir I have been twice down all over the State of Missi and seen for my self the state of things there. The freedmen do not in general work well, the People or Planters are fully disposed to do them full justice so far as I could learn & I was all about among the Planters. I met with a very warm reception as much so as If I had landed in my native land, and it is worse then folly to keep a standing army over the people of the South, and I for one in toto, I disprove the course, the Extreme Radicals, for If your course could have been carried out for the most part, the entire South could have been safly been back into the enjoyment of all their rights and priviledges long ago. I made some short speeches when down among them for which I was called to order for when I came back but I hold the same docterine here and they find that a *Scott* thinks for him self. I pass over the errors of the South and want to do them Justice. The right of voting ought to have been left to the States.

I did think I would have seen you before this but will try and do so in the fall. I would like to fill an office that would pay me. By your appointment the republicans would not dare to defeat me.

Is not the Governorship of Montana now vacant[1]—any such office as that I can fill so far as active determinate business is concerned and can have as good recommendation from the rest as any need for. If you have such an office[2] around about, that wants a man that can put things through remember our youthfull days when first we mett in old Greenville. I want very much to see you. But just go on in your own way and your enemies will have to stand still behold and ponder and parish, in the end. The People of the south will yet come right side up. I told them one and all, just to attend to their planting, and let the Radicals have their way. Just now the state of things was bound to take change. There is some honest men in the north that will yet do them justice.

A. Hawthorn

ALS, NRU-William Henry Seward Col.
  1. Green Clay Smith had been appointed governor of Montana in July 1866 and served until 1869.
  2. No evidence has been uncovered showing Hawthorn receiving any office.

From John W. Smith[1]

Keokuk Iowa   Jan 20th 1867

Dear Sir

Many years have passed since I was intimately acquainted with you in the State of Tennese, was one of your Constituants in the Early history of your public Life. The fortunes of war has changed my condition, having Lost all my substance in the past unholy struggl togeather with two of the Last of my children bereft of Every member of my family, now in the Evening of Life, tottering on the uneven paths, of imbecility & adversity entirely dependant for the sustenance of Life, haveing been appointed by the Masonic bodies as Custodian of the ritual of masonry in the differant grades of the order, by which I am inabled to Support the Corperal frame in the discharge of my duties. I am continually with the public where your administration & your antecedents are the general topics. Now Sir permit me to ask you a plain Question, are you a member of the Masonic fraternity, if so, to what grade of the order have you advanced and where are your memberships.[2] My reason for this inquiry is, I am dayly inquired of by your democratic friends of the mystic tie whether or not you are a Mason. I am satisfied myself, but cannot answer thear Questions from Legal information, a rumer is in Circulation from your political Enemies, that you are an anty mason violenty opposed to the institution which is doing much to your injury. Should your answer be in the affirmative, I will take great pleasure in giving the matter publicity among my democratic friends who are intitled to the information. Let the answer come, over your own Signature, so that the republicans, members of the time honored Society may be convinced of the truth.[3] I shall do Every thing in my power to set the matter right, which will be to your advantage. We know not what may be the state of affairs in our government before the close of your administration. Direct your answer to Keokuk, Iowa to *John W. Smith* in the care of *William Stotts* Esq. P. Box 457.[4]

John W. Smith

ALS, DLC-JP.

1. Not otherwise identified.

2. Johnson joined the Greeneville Lodge No. 3 on May 5, 1851. In late 1866 he became a Thirty-third Degree Mason (the highest). Trefousse, *Johnson*, 80; Harry J. Seymour to Johnson, Oct. 3, 1866, Johnson Papers, LC.

3. There is no evidence that Johnson answered Smith's letter.

4. There were two William Stotts in Keokuk, both natives of Kentucky and probably father and son. The elder (c1800–fl1870), a justice of the peace in 1860, was a retired merchant by 1870. The younger (c1830–fl1870) owned a sawmill. 1860 Census, Iowa, Lee, Keokuk, 3rd Ward, 84; (1870), 5th Ward, 325, 326.

To Michael Burns

Washington, D.C., Jan. 21st 1867

Will Mr. Allen not take twenty (20) State Bonds for the claim.[1] I have the bonds and it would be much easier for me to let them go, than to raise the currency?

If not draw for the $15,000, as stated in my former despatch.[2]

Andrew Johnson—

Tel, DNA-RG107, Tels. Sent, President, Vol. 3 (1865–68).

1. The complicated story of Johnson's indebtedness took additional twists and turns in January. Joseph W. Allen notified the President early in the month that he had sought $16,500 for the First National Bank of Washington to cover the original $20,000 debt. On January 19, Michael Burns informed Johnson that he could arrange with Allen for $15,000 and asked the President what he should do. Johnson immediately telegraphed that Burns should make such an arrangement with Allen. Then on January 21, Burns informed the President that he could not move Allen, meaning perhaps that Burns could not get Allen to agree to accept Johnson's twenty state bonds. Instead, reported Burns, the other deal (evidently the $15,000 agreement) "is the best trade." Allen to Johnson, Jan. 5,

1867; Burns to Johnson, Jan. 19, 21, 1867, Johnson Papers, LC; Johnson to Burns, Jan. 20, 1867, Tels. Sent, President, Vol. 3 (1865–68), RG107, NA.

2. Johnson authorized Burns to draw the $15,000 as payment. Burns immediately did so and notified the President that he had forwarded that amount to the First National Bank of Washington. Johnson to Burns, Jan. 22, 1867, ibid.; Burns to Johnson, Jan. 23, 1867, Johnson Papers, LC.

From Hugh McCulloch

Jany. 21, 1867.
Dear Sir:—
Enclosed I hand you an appointment of Mr. Samuel Milligan to the office of Solicitor of Internal Revenue.[1]

I have not Mr. Milligan's address, and it has occurred to me that it might be agreeable to you to transmit to him the appointment, which you will perceive, is under the control of the Secretary.[2]

H McCulloch

LS, DLC-JP.
1. See McCulloch to Milligan, Jan. 21, 1867, Johnson Papers, LC.
2. Evidently the President did not follow through with the appointment immediately, judging from the lack of future exchange on the matter until July. In that month Johnson offered Milligan either the solicitor's position, which paid $4,000 per annum, or one of two foreign posts, which had somewhat higher salaries. Milligan replied by telegraph at once that he could not accept either one of the State Department jobs; in a letter written the following day he hesitated about the solicitor's post but promised to discuss it with Johnson in Washington. Johnson to Milligan, July 17, 1867, Tels. Sent, President, Vol. 3 (1865–68), RG107, NA; Milligan to Johnson, July 18, 19, 1867, Johnson Papers, LC.

From Henry Stanbery

[Washington, D.C.]   January 21, 1867.
Sir:
I have the honor to acknowledge the receipt of a copy of a Resolution of the Senate of the United States, of January 8th, referred by you to this office, for Report. The Resolution is in these words:

"Resolved; That the President be requested to inform the Senate if any violations of the Act[1] entitled 'An Act to protect all persons in the United States in their civil rights, & furnish the means of their vindication,' have come to his knowledge; and, if so, what steps, if any, have been taken by him to enforce the law, & punish the offenders."[2]

The provisions of the Act which specially refer to the President for Executive action are contained in the 4th, 8th, & 9th sections.

By the first clause of the 4th section, it is provided, "That the District Attorneys, Marshals, & Deputy Marshals, of the United States, the Commissioners appointed by the Circuit and Territorial Courts of the United States, with powers of arresting, imprisoning, or bailing offenders against the laws of the United States, the officers & agents of the

Freedmen's Bureau, & every other officer who may be specially empowered by the President of the United States, shall be, & they are hereby specially authorized & required, at the expense of the United States, to institute proceedings against all & every person who shall violate the provisions of this Act."

The 8th Section provides, "That whenever the President of the United States shall have reason to believe that offences have been or are likely to be committed against the provisions of this Act, within any Judicial District, it shall be lawful for him, in his discretion, to direct the Judge, Marshal, & District Attorney of such District, to attend at such place within the District, & for such time as he may designate, for the purpose of the more speedy arrest & trial of persons charged with a violation of this Act; and it shall be the duty of every Judge, or other officer, when any such requisition shall be received by him to attend at the place, & for the time, therein, designated."

Section 9 provides "that it shall be lawful for the President of the United States, or such person as he may empower for that purpose, to employ such part of the land or naval forces of the United States, or of the militia, as shall be necessary to prevent the violation, & enforce the due execution of this Act."

No report has within my knowledge, been made to you from this office, in relation to any violation of the above-mentioned Act; nor am I advised that any report has been made to this office, of any such violations. A case has been referred to this office by the Secretary of War, which may involve a violation of the provisions of the Act, which forbid a discrimination against people of color, under the penal laws of the States. It is the case of one Wm. Fincher,[3] a person of color in the state of Georgia. The action taken by this office upon this reference appears in the following letter:

Attorney General's Office,
December 11, 1866.

Henry S. Fitch, Esq.
U.S. Attorney, Savannah, Geo.
Sir:

It has been represented to the President that a person has been subjected to, & is now suffering (not as a punishment of crime whereof he has been duly convicted,) a condition of involuntary servitude, within the United States, in contravention of Art. XIII Section 1, of the Constitution of the United States.

If a quesiton so grave, & of such high & prevalent interest, has legitimately arisen, it becomes the duty of the Government, independently of the presumptive indigence of the party, in a case involving vagrancy, to direct the zealous coöperation of the counsel of the United States, with that of the petitioner in the courts of law.

It is alleged that one William Fincher is now performing compulsory labor or service in the chain-gang in Pike County, Georgia, a condition of constraint to which he was forcibly subjected, without having been convicted of, or charged with, any crime, defined as such in the laws of Georgia; that he was indicted as a vagrant & convicted of vagrancy in the county court; that upon a hearing before an appellate court, on certiorari, the prosecution below was sustained, and that the whole proceedings were had upon insufficient evidence of the charge; that the sentence was given with circumstances of severity,—& that the object of the prosecution was to destroy the party's influence & action in the community, as a colored preacher, zealously attached to some society or association which is offensive to public sentiment. Such is the information which has been communicated; but your action in the premises will be grounded exclusively upon the facts as you may discover them upon investigation.

I have to instruct you to inquire into, & immediately report, the substantial circumstances of this case; the law & practice of Georgia, in full, touching the matter, and a full abstract of the record of the prosecution, throughout, stating particulary whether, & if so, when & how, the case has been adjudicated by the highest appellate court of the State, having jurisdiction in the matter.

You will understand, that unless your report shall show that it is entirely impracticable, the object of the President is to have the matter brought forward for adjudication by the Supreme Court of the United States.

I am sir, Very respectfully your obdt servant,

(signed)   Henry Stanbery Attorney General.

It will be observed that this letter purports that the facts of Fincher's case were represented to the President. This expression was according to the usual formula in such cases, but in point of fact, the representation came through the War Department to this office.

From the facts stated, it was supposed, as will be seen by the letter, that they involved a question of the infraction of the late Constitutional Amendment. It may appear when the report of the Dist. Attorney is received, that they involve an infraction of the Civil Rights Bill.

The Dist. Attorney replied to this letter under date of Dec. 15, 1866, acknowledging its receipt, & stating that he would proceed at once to Pike County, & make a rigid investigation of the facts, & report as soon as possible. No report having been received, his attention was again called to the subject, & by a dispatch received from him on the 19th inst. he states that the absence of material witnesses, and the pressure of public business had delayed his report—but says that it will be mailed from Savannah this day.

I am not advised of any other case which requires Executive action under those sections which have been enumerated, or under any other section of the Civil Rights Bill.

Henry Stanbery   Attorney General.

LBcopy, DNA-RG60, Office of Atty. Gen., Lets. Sent, Vol. F (M699, Roll 11).

1. The Civil Rights Bill. For the text, see the *New York Times*, Mar. 16, 1866.

2. *Congressional Globe*, 39 Cong., 2 Sess., p. 326.

3. Fincher (c1822–fl1870), a native of North Carolina, was a minister and married with four children. 1870 Census, Ga., Pike, 167.

From Preston Syll[1]

Columbia, S. Carolina, 21 January, 1867.

May it please Your Excellency,

I humbly presume upon the kindness and generosity of Yr. Excellency's heart, to which none can now be strangers, to address to you the following statement and appeal.

I am by birth a Carolinian—the son of Edward Sill,[2] Esq., M.D., of this town. From the beginning to the end of the late rebellion I was a Unionist—and was forced, in 1862, under pressure of the terrorism then dominant in the South, to escape into the U. States' lines at N. Orleans. Thence I went to the North, seeking employment as journalist—but finding none, left, in despair, for Europe, where I remained till the end of last year, earning a precarious livelihood by tutorial and literary labors— chiefly on the Continent, whither I went to acquire the modern languages and to perfect the education I had already received at some of the best universities in this country. During my absence from Carolina and the course of the war, great changes have found place. At the burning of Columbia, in 1865, my invalid and aged father and my mother and sister[3] were reduced, in the short space of one night, from competency to absolute beggary. They now look to me for maintenance. I cannot, however, aid them here—first, because in the present impoverished condition of things in Carolina, I can earn scarcely my own living, and secondly, because, even were suitable employment to be had here, the bitter prejudice here existing against one who was loyal to the Union would quite mar all my chances of success. In this strait I appeal to Yr. Excellency for some place in Yr. Excellency's gift under Government— preferably *a Consulship or Secretaryship of Legation abroad*—for which I have fitted myself by long and careful study, and which would enable me to educate myself further, and for a still more extended sphere of usefulness to the U. States, and to contribute to the support of those nearest and dearest to me in life. I appeal to Yr. Excellency not on the merits of my loyalty to the Union during the Rebellion—for my loyalty were little worth, did I seek a reward for it—but in behalf of my ruined parents, who, in their declining years and guiltless of participation in the Rebellion, have, as already said, lost their all—and who, permit me to note, are compatriots of Yr. Excellency's—being both N. Carolinians—my father a self-made man, from Wilmington—and who, let me hope, may therefore seem to have some claim on Yr. Excellency's generous heart. By the gift of some office *at home or abroad* to me their son, Yr. Excellency would enable me to provide for them when they most need provision—when old and infirm and penniless.

Proof of my loyalty and attitude during the Rebellion I can furnish from loyalists in the North—from J. R. Gilmore, Esq. (the colleague of Col. Jacques[4] in the Peace Mission to Richmond,)—from Prof. Dr.

Coakley, LL. D., of the University of N. York, and from the Rev. Frederick Sill,[5] Rector of S. Thomas's, N. York, and from many others. I had the honour of meeting the Hon. H. J. Raymond, in N. York, in 1862, and he was, I think, assured of my loyalty. I can further refer to A. G. Mackey, Esq., M.D., Collector of the Port of Charleston, and to the Honble. George Bryan,[6] U.S. Judge, Charleston.

I would most respectfully urge upon Yr. Excellency the pressing nature of the circumstances from which I seek by this appeal to relieve my unfortunate parents—and I trust that Yr. Excellency will freely pardon whatever there be of importunity in my letter, when Yr. Excellency shall have weighed the motives that alone prompt me to address you—filial love and filial duty.

Preston Syll.

ALS, DNA-RG59, Lets. of Appl. and Recomm., 1861–69 (M650, Roll 48), Preston Syll.
    1. Syll (b. c1840) had been a student before the war. 1860 Census, S.C., Richland, Columbia, 116.
    2. Sill (b. c1802) was listed by the census taker as a druggist. Ibid.
    3. Caroline (b. c1810) and Alice Sill (b. c1844). Ibid.
    4. James R. Gilmore and James F. Jaquess.
    5. George W. Coakley (1814–1893) was a mathematics and astronomy teacher in Maryland and New York, who in 1860 published a book about comets. Sill (fl1875) was a Protestant Episcopal minister. John H. Brown, ed., *The Cyclopaedia of American Biographies* (7 vols., Boston, 1897–1903), 2: 82–83; New York City directories (1867–75).
    6. George S. Bryan (1809–1905), a lawyer and one of South Carolina's more prominent unionists, served as U.S. district judge for twenty years (1866–86). Harold Chase et al., comps., *Biographical Dictionary of the Federal Judiciary* (Detroit, 1976), 34.

From John B. Stoll

January 22, 1867, Ligonier, Ind.; ALS, DNA-RG59, Lets. Recd. *re* Publishers of Laws.

Stoll, the editor of the *National Banner*, "the only paper in the state that was started, and has since been maintained, as a purely administration paper," asks that his paper be given the patronage of publishing the laws of the United States, currently enjoyed by the *Howard Tribune* of Kokomo. Stoll has learned that Theophilus Phillips, of the *Tribune*, has sold his paper to S. T. Montgomery, a Radical.

To Sam Milligan

Washington, D.C., Jan. 23d 1867.

Your despatch received.[1] Tennessee delegation meets tonight, and will confer upon the subject matter of your letter of the 13th instant. I doubt the policy of running the candidate referred to in your letter. He has no identity with the people.[2]

You will have the benefit of the consultation here as soon as it is over.

Andrew Johnson

Tel, DNA-RG107, Tels. Sent, President, Vol. 3 (1865–68).
    1. No dispatch from Milligan has been located.
    2. In his letter of January 13, Milligan speculated about the nomination of Brownlow at the Radical convention scheduled for February 22. Milligan promoted the claims of Samuel P. Carter as a possible gubernatorial nominee to rival Brownlow. Yet two days after the Radical conclave, Milligan wrote to Sen. David Patterson about John Caldwell as a possible Conservative nominee and criticized James O. Shackelford's desire to run against Brownlow. Milligan to Johnson, Jan. 13, 1867; Milligan to Patterson, Feb. 24, 1867, Johnson Papers, LC.

From Solomon Cohen

Savannah   24 January 1867

Sir,

As the Representative elect to the Congress of the U.S. from this Congressional district I feel it my duty to call your attention to the conduct of the district attorney.[1] He is attaching the property of our Citizens for confiscation, and from your known liberal and conciliatory course toward the South I feel confident he is acting without your authority.

I would therefore request you to enlighten me on the subject, and if I am right in any conjecture, that you will order the district attorney to suspend his action.

(Signed) Solomon Cohen

Copy, DNA-RG60, Office of Atty. Gen., Lets. Recd., President.
    1. Henry S. Fitch.

From Edwin Croswell[1]

Willard's Hotel   Jan'y 25, 1867.

Dear Sir,

The thought suggested at the interview last evening when we listened with admiration to your impressive conversation,[2]—*that the Minority in Congress should issue an Appeal to the People*,—has occured to my mind with much force since. Something must be done to arouse the People. Apathy and demoralization are subverting the popular mind, and concealing, if not inviting, the approaches of Despotism. The lethargy pervades all classes, and stifles the natural impulses of self preservation,— the natural desire to rescue the country from the grasp of selfish and designing men. Unless this current of evil can be arrested in its course, the constitutional liberties will exist scarcely in name. Whether any thing can be said that will catch and hold the popular attention, is problematical. Certainly not, in any ordinary or hackneyed form. If any thing is done, it must be well done. No one can perform this duty to his country with so much power and significance as yourself. All the great grounds on which the facts and logic of the case rest, are to you "familiar as household words." These presented in your language and with the impress of your feeling, may reach the ear and heart of the People, and move them to action. If not, nothing will—and all the old landmarks, all sacred things, all constitutional guarantees, all hopes of the Republic, are destined to perish.

Allow me therefore to suggest that whenever momentarily released from the pressure of public care, (if you ever enjoy such moments), you note down such thoughts as an effort in this vein and for this majestic purpose shall call out.

Edwin Croswell.

ALS, DLC-JP.
    1. Croswell (1797–1871) was editor of the *Albany Argus*, one of the chief organs of the Democratic party, for thirty years. In 1854 he retired from journalism to pursue other business interests in New York City. *DAB*.
    2. Not found.

From William B. Phillips
Confidential

339 Fourth Avenue,
New York, Jany. 25th, 1867.

Dear Sir,
    From the friendly relations that years ago existed between us and on account of your invariable kind feeling toward me I feel it to be my duty to say a few words to you with regard to the course of the paper with which I am connected. You will give me credit, I hope and beleive, for not favoring such a course. I tried to prevent it, but unavailingly. I consider it not only unjust to you, but revolutionary and dangerous to the country.

    In order to give you an idea of the motives which have led to the articles on impeachment and your administration I will breifly state upon what principle or plan the paper is conducted.

    Mr. Bennett makes everything—yes, the public welfare and everything else—subordinate to what he supposes may promote his interests as proprietor of the paper. It is lamentable to see a great journal so conducted, but it is a fact. Mr. Bennett, however, with all his sagacity, frequently makes mistakes in his calculations of self interest, and I beleive he does so in this instance.

    The question of impeachment is an exciting one, a new and startling sensation, which may occupy the public mind some time and help to give life and circulation to the paper. That is one of the controlling motives of the Herald's course, unworthy as it may be. I must say, however, that Mr. Bennett does not beleive your impeachment or removal would be attended with any serious consequences or any shock to the institutions of the country. He thinks that could be accomplished and pass over like more ordinary events without danger. His mind is so constituted that it is not difficult for him to beleive what suits his purpose. He appears to be firmly persuaded that your impeachment and removal is determined upon by Congress and that the dominant radical party in that body will control its action. He beleives that party will accomplish its object. It is, he says, one of the inevitable phases of the revolution the country is passing through. He, doubtless favors this revolution because he has always been in favor of a strong consolidated government, and thinks this will tend to that end through concentrating its powers in Congress.

Besides, the Herald always endeavors to go with the strongest party or side when its editor discovers which is or is going to be the strongest. Its policy is not to stem the current, but to go with it. As the radical-republican party is so powerful and compact both in Congress and in the State governments it goes along with it even while professing to be independent and to denounce the extremes.

Should the radicals push their measures to an extreme that will create a revulsion in the public mind and a consequent political reaction the Herald will take another tack in accordance with such a change.

Any one with the least reason and sense of justice must be shocked at the wicked and revolutionary programme of the radicals with regard to this impeachment proposition. It is lamentable to think that you, who have labored so honestly and earnestly for the welfare of the whole country, are to be sacrificed on the altar of faction. But these are revolutionary times, and our Jacobins like those of the French are disposed to go any length to carry their objects. If you can not resist the current of radicalism, I would rather see you guide and moderate it for the welfare of the country and to save yourself than to sink under it. Can this be done? I hope you may come through this fiery ordeal triumphantly. I shall lose no opportunity of doing justice to you and your administration whenever I have the power.

W. B. Phillips

ALS, DLC-JP.

From Daniel E. Sickles

Metropolitan [Hotel]   Friday [January 25, 1867][1]

My dear Mr. Johnson,

You have seen, of course, that Stevens abandons his scheme of reconstruction. *Now is your moment—do not lose a day*—it is your opportunity —another may not come. It is in your power to be master of the situation. A Northern man—my old friend Edward Dickerson[2]—assures me that Gov. Walker[3] of Florida whom he knows intimately & has recently left will adopt & can carry out the plan of settlement we have considered together.

D. Sickles

ALS, DLC-JP.

1. The date is based on the Library of Congress's dating and confirmed by accounts in the *National Intelligencer* placing Sickles in Washington during the last half of January and first week of February and reporting Stevens's tabling of his reconstruction bill. Sickles had a personal interview with Johnson on January 24. See the *National Intelligencer*, Jan. 14, 17, Feb. 7, 1867; *Evening Star* (Washington), Jan. 24, 1867.

2. Dickerson (1824–1889), lawyer and mechanical engineer, was the recognized authority on patent law in the U.S by the 1850s. *DAB*.

3. David S. Walker.

From Francis P. Blair, Sr.

Wash   27 Jan '67

My Dear Mr. President

I forgot in my hurry to say that Col Moore,[1] whose claim I urged on you for a majority was twice wounded in battle & suffered for many months. Many of those on the list before you never smelt powder & Meigs[2] will tell you that none excel him in his activity & deligence in his Quarter Master duties.

I am told that Bache[3] at the head of the Coast Survey is at the point of death. I am told that he considered Mr. Patterson[4] his most effecient officer in the conduct of the business of his charge. Patterson was long an active naval officer, before entering on the Survey and it is the general opinion of our navy, as well as that of England, that the Coast Survey shd. be the work of the Navy Dept. & its naval officers. Our Surveys have cost millions more by putting them into the hands of civil Savans instead of our practical & scientific Sailors. I beg you to look into this business as a matter of economy. I have been acquainted with the abuses of this Bureau from the beginning of Pres Jacksons term when old Hasler[5] a german Savan Swallowed the whole concern up in abstractions & by the System of delays introduced made the affair an interminable Job, which has cost millions already and will never end unless it be turned over to the Salaried officers of the navy & made part of their naval duty. I think if Patterson is put at the Head under the Secretary of the Navy, this running sore on the Treasury may be healed & a great Reform introduced.

F P. Blair

ALS, DLC-JP.

1. James M. Moore (1837–1905) of Pennsylvania began his army career by serving in his state volunteers (1861–63) and then in the quartermaster's division of the volunteers and regular army (1863–65). He continued with the Quartermaster Department after war's end, eventually attaining the rank of brigadier general in 1904. *Who Was Who in America*, 1: 860; Powell, *Army List*, 489; Heitman, *Register*, 1: 722.

2. Montgomery C. Meigs.

3. Alexander D. Bache.

4. Carlile P. Patterson (1816–1881) entered the U.S. Navy in 1830 and served in various capacities, including working with the Coast Survey. Having resigned in 1853, he resumed work in 1861 with the Coast Survey and became superintendent in 1874. *NCAB*, 4: 304; Edward W. Callahan, ed., *List of Officers of the Navy of the United States and of the Marine Corps from 1775 to 1900* (New York, 1969 [1901]).

5. Ferdinand R. Hassler (1770–1843), geodesist and mathematician, was a native of Switzerland who eventually emigrated to America in 1805. He was chosen to conduct the coast survey but while witnessing its interminable delays, he held professorships at West Point and at Union College. He traveled to London to purchase the necessary equipment for the coast survey and superintended it from its beginnings in 1816 until his death— except for the fourteen-year period the survey was suspended. *DAB*.

From Jonas H. Ramsey[1]

North Carolina Burke County   Jan the 27th 1867

Dear Sir

I this day do Seat my Self to make nowing how the Rebels ar managing the law. It may be that you now as much a bout the matter as i do but for fear you dont i will write you a letter Stating the facts. Dear Sir i have been indited in Several Cases mearly on Susspison and they will not hardy allow me to prove any thing to the Contrary because i was a union man and would not aide in the Rebelion. They have a Spite at me. They intend to punish me without a Cause. They Can gether up their Rebel Crew and prove any thing they please. The Rebels Can do any thing they please to a union man and not be hurt for it. I will State a Case of that kind. A bout a month after the surrender of all the Rebels troops ther Came a Club of Rebels blacked them Selvs and Came to my house nocked open my dore and Came in to my house and Robed it and Cocked their guns at my breast and Swore they would shoot me if i did not give up my money and abused my famley most Cruel bad and i new them well and my wife[2] new them and Several others that was at my house new them and i indited them and when i went before the Jury and they Said it was no diference they had authority to do Such and Could do So yet if they did so to a union man.

Dear Sir if you do not do Something to Relieve the Sufering union people they will have to leave this Country. After keeping out of the Rebelion and loosing nearly evry thing that i had by the Rebel malitia, I am gitting now So i Can begin to live again and now they intend to take what i have again. I believe if ther is not Somthing Soon don the Rebels will rise and mob the union men. If they would give Justice it would be a good thing to have things that was don in time of the Rebelion tried by law but in as much as they will not give Justice i think to Strike off and let evry thing that was don in war times be killed. Dear Sir president of the U S i do beg of you to aid me and all other union men. If i did not think this was Right my pen would be Silent. All the union people here has ben talking about writing to you a bout this matter but i in my feeble and unegicated Way do write you this letter. A Rebel that did wilful murder in time of the Rebelion ther is nothing don with him at all. They will Call a Cort of three Rebel Squires and Clear him when it Can be proved that he did the Crime. Ther is no law her in faver of the union party.

Dear president for my Sake and for the Sake of my unhelthey famley do parden and forgive me of these Rebels charges. If i was able i would come to you in person with out Stretched arms asking for pardon but i hope you will do Somthing for me and that Shortly. I have always ben in favor of aiding the united States So nothing more only i Remain a friend to you and your Cause.[3]

Jonas. H. Ramsey

Pleas parden and forgive. Direct to Morganton N C.

L, DNA-RG107, Lets. Recd., Executive (M494, Roll 96).

1. Ramsey (c1837–fl1870) was a farm laborer. 1870 Census, N.C., Burke, Upper South Fork Twp., 8.

2. By 1870 Mary A. Ramsey (b. c1845) had four children between ages three and nine. On January 27 she also asked Johnson for a "parden" for her husband and alleged that the "Rebels have bin trying to desstroy the union citisens" of Morganton. Ibid.; Ramsey to Johnson, Jan. 27, 1867, Lets. Recd., Executive (M494, Roll 96), RG107, NA.

3. On February 5, 1867, the Ramsey letters were sent to Governor Worth, who in turn referred them to a two-man Burke County investigating committee. On the 25th of the same month the committee made a lengthy report. Jonas Ramsey had been indicted in the spring and fall terms of 1866 for assault and battery, theft, and forcible trespass. In all the cases, the prosecutors and witnesses, except two, were "union people." The committee noted that during the year after the war when Morganton was garrisoned by U.S. troops Ramsey made no complaint. They believed Union men were "in no danger of being molested, and have nothing to fear, but justice in our courts." They characterized the Ramseys as "ignorant, illiterate and obscure persons neither of whom, from their reputations, are capable of either dictating or writing the letters referred to." B. S. Gaither and T. George Walton to Jonathan Worth, Feb. 25, 1867, ibid.

From David F. Boyd[1]

La. State Seminary & Military Academy,
January 28th, 1867.

Sir:

This Institution is, by the law of the State, a *military* academy. It was organized Jany 1st, 1860, by Lt. Genl. W. T. Sherman U.S.A. During the war its exercises were closed. At the close of the war it was re-organized, but it was *then* thought prudent not resume the military feature. In September last, having learned that the Va. Military Institute, at Lexington, had been fully reinstated in its military rights & privileges by the Government at Washington,[2] I addressed Genl. Sheridan a communication, asking that the same privileges, viz: the use of Drill, musket & uniform, be granted this Institution. Genl. Sheridan referred my communication to the Secretary of War, who *declined* to grant the request.

While this Institution does not *complain* of the action of the honorable Secretary of War in refusing Louisiana what he has granted to Va., yet it begs leave most respectfully to represent to your Excellency the belief that he has acted under some misapprehension as to the danger that would result to the United States from granting the Institution the use of arms &c; and to request you, to whom alone we have been taught to look for even-handed justice, to have the action of the Secretary of War reconsidered, with the hope that the military feature of the school will be speedily restored. But whatever be your decision, it will be most cheerfully abided by.[3]

D. F. Boyd Sup't.

ALS, DNA-RG108, Lets. Recd. *re* Military Discipline.
1. Boyd (1834–1899) had taught school in Louisiana before joining the 19th La. Inf., CSA, in 1861 and serving for the war's duration. Subsequently, he superintended the Louisiana Military Academy (1865–70) and was president and professor of its successor, Louisiana State University (1870–80, 1884–88, 1897–99). Conrad, *La. Biography.*
2. See U. S. Grant to Johnson, Aug. 22, 1866, for the details concerning VMI.
3. When the school reopened in 1865, it retained its military organization and discipline, though without uniforms or arms. Boyd attempted to gain official permission from Sheridan and the secretary of war for uniforms and arms until 1869, at which time he decided on his own to provide cadet uniforms. Walter L. Fleming, *Louisiana State University, 1860–1896* (Baton Rouge, 1936), 130–230 passim.

From Charles Brown[1]

Philada.   Jany. 28th 1867

Dear Sir

Allow an old friend and Colleague to say a few words to you in relation to the appointments to offices in this city, in which he has no other interest or feeling than the success of your administration & the welfare of the country. It is no time now for mere political party or personal consideration. The perils that are impending over our whole constitutional form of government require a higher patriotism. I most sincerely hope that none but men of the most unexceptionable character & qualifications will be appointed by you. These will raise your administration above all impeachments in the eyes of the people—who at last will decide rightly on the acts of their representatives. With these feelings I take the liberty, unsolicited by the parties, to speak to you of some persons I have heard named for some of the principal offices in this city. Wm. Harbeson[2] for *Collector* of the Port. He is the present chief deputy. He entered the custom House some twenty years ago as a clerk in the cashiers department. I found him there in 1853 when collector, & raised him to chief deputy; which office he held under my successor,[3] & also the most part of Mr Lincolns administration. His knowledge, therefore, of the duties of the office cannot be equalled. He has always been a most efficient & popular officer; & of unquestionable integrity. His appointment would give entire satisfaction to all parties, & give high character to your administration. Next comes that of *"Naval Officer."* For this office no man in the state would bring a higher character than the Hon. John K. Findlay.[4] For several years a Judge in our District Court—& a most popular one—he has large acquaintance with mercantile Law; & is also one whose appointment all parties would approve.

Another appointment in the same department is that of *appraiser*, in place of Mr Kilgore.[5] For this office I know no man better qualified, or more likely to meet general approval than George R Berrell,[6] who has also been named for Collector. He was for several years one of the appraisers, while I was collector, & subsequently, & I know him to be an efficient & valuable officer, & well acquainted with the duties he would be required to perform. He is a gentleman of unquestioned integrity.

For Assessor of U S Revenue in place of Mr Thos. Allen[7] decd. Mr. John Cline[8] has been named. Mr Cline was for some years a member of the state Legislature, & U.S. measurer for the Port of Phil. & more recently a candidate for Congress in the 3d district. He is also a Gentlemen of unquestioned integrity, great energy, & well qualified for the place. All the above have been known to me for many years—all are without a stain upon their characters; & their appointment would give *dignity* & character to your administration, & go far to soften or remove a great deal of political party animosity.

A word on general subjects & I am done. I sympathise most sincerely in the troubles & perils that obstruct your patriotic exertions to restore the country to peace & unity. I cannot but believe they will ultimately be crowned with success. In the event, however, of a final attempt of the band of conspirators who now occupy the Halls of Congress to drive you from the executive, the conservative people look to you to allow that issue to be decided no where but by the people themselves. *They* have entrusted to you the power to maintain the constitution & the laws made in *pursuance* thereof against all who attempt to violate or subvert them—no matter how high or how low may be the offenders. To *them*, I think, you may appeal with safety—when the time for that appeal arrives—which seems to be fast approaching.

Chas. Brown

ALS, DNA-RG56, Appts., Customs Service, Subofficer, Philadelphia, Charles Brown.

1. Brown (1797–1883) had an active career in Pennsylvania politics, serving in the state legislature in the 1830s and as a Democrat in Congress during the 1840s, before becoming collector of the port of Philadelphia (1853–57). He also represented Delaware at the National Union Convention in Philadelphia (1866). *BDAC*.

2. Harbeson (c1807–1874) was nominated by Johnson for the collectorship on February 8 in place of William F. Johnston, whose official nomination the Senate rejected on January 22, 1867. Harbeson was likewise rejected, but he later won Senate confirmation in April 1867 as surveyor of the port of Philadelphia. Philadelphia directories (1865–75); *Evening Bulletin* (Philadelphia), Jan. 29, 1874; Ser. 6B, Vol. 4: 84, 90, Johnson Papers, LC.

3. Joseph B. Baker, not further identified.

4. Findlay (1803–1885), a former career army officer and Philadelphia attorney, was not among the ten different nominees Johnson eventually presented to the Senate for confirmation as naval officer. Instead Johnson chose Findlay for the surveyor's position, but he was not confirmed. *Appleton's Cyclopaedia*; Ser. 6B, Vol. 4: 84, 87, 89–90, Johnson Papers, LC.

5. John P. Kilgore (*fl*1868), appointed as appraiser of merchandise for Philadelphia in August 1866, was rejected by the Senate on January 22, 1867. Philadelphia directories (1868–69); Ser. 6B, Vol. 3: 160; Vol. 4: 84, Johnson Papers, LC.

6. Berrell (*fl*1873), a Democrat who worked variously as a clothing merchant and an

auctioneer, was not chosen by Johnson for the appraiser's post in Philadelphia. Philadelphia directories (1867–74); William Bigler to Johnson, Jan. 25, 1867, Appts., Customs Service, Collector, Philadelphia, George R. Berrell, RG56, NA.

7. Allen (c1816–1867) had held a temporary commission for the Third District assessorship since September 1866. *Press* (Philadelphia), Jan. 17, 1867; Ser. 6B, Vol. 3: 161, Johnson Papers, LC.

8. Kline (fl1867), who had earlier run unsuccessfully as a Democrat in the 1860 and 1862 elections, was not appointed by Johnson. *Guide to U.S. Elections*, 608, 611; Frank McCormick to Johnson, Jan. 29, 1867, Appts., Internal Revenue Service, Assessor, Pa., 3rd Dist., John Kline, RG56, NA.

Colorado Statehood Bill Veto Message

WASHINGTON, *January 28, 1867.*

To the Senate of the United States:

I return to the Senate, in which House it originated, a bill entitled "An act to admit the State of Colorado into the Union," to which I can not, consistently with my sense of duty, give my approval. With the exception of an additional section, containing new provisions, it is substantially the same as the bill of a similar title passed by Congress during the last session, submitted to the President for his approval, returned with the objections contained in a message bearing date the 15th of May last,[1] and yet awaiting the reconsideration of the Senate.

A second bill, having in view the same purpose, has now passed both Houses of Congress[2] and been presented for my signature. Having again carefully considered the subject, I have been unable to perceive any reason for changing the opinions which have already been communicated to Congress. I find, on the contrary, that there are many objections to the proposed legislation of which I was not at that time aware, and that while several of those which I then assigned have in the interval gained in strength, yet others have been created by the altered character of the measures now submitted.

The constitution under which the State government is proposed to be formed very properly contains a provision that all laws in force at the time of its adoption and the admission of the State into the Union shall continue as if the constitution had not been adopted. Among those laws is one absolutely prohibiting negroes and mulattoes from voting.[3] At the recent session of the Territorial legislature a bill for the repeal of this law, introduced into the council, was almost unanimously rejected; and at the very time when Congress was engaged in enacting the bill now under consideration the legislature passed an act excluding negroes and mulattoes from the right to sit as jurors. This bill was vetoed by the governor of the Territory, who held that by the laws of the United States negroes and mulattoes are citizens, and subject to the duties, as well as entitled to the rights, of citizenship. The bill, however, was passed, the objections of the governor to the contrary notwithstanding, and is now a law of the Territory. Yet in the bill now before me, by which it is proposed to admit the

Territory as a State, it is provided that "there shall be no denial of the elective franchise or any other rights to any person by reason of race or color, excepting Indians not taxed."

The incongruity thus exhibited between the legislation of Congress and that of the Territory, taken in connection with the protest against the admission of the State hereinafter referred to, would seem clearly to indicate the impolicy and injustice of the proposed enactment.

It might, indeed, be a subject of grave inquiry, and doubtless will result in such inquiry if this bill becomes a law, whether it does not attempt to exercise a power not conferred upon Congress by the Federal Constitution. That instrument simply declares that Congress may admit new States into the Union. It nowhere says that Congress may make new States for the purpose of admitting them into the Union or for any other purpose; and yet this bill is as clear an attempt to make the institutions as any in which the people themselves could engage.

In view of this action of Congress, the house of representatives of the Territory have earnestly protested against being forced into the Union without first having the question submitted to the people. Nothing could be more reasonable than the position which they thus assume; and it certainly can not be the purpose of Congress to force upon a community against their will a government which they do not believe themselves capable of sustaining.

The following is a copy of the protest alluded to as officially transmitted to me:

> Whereas it is announced in the public prints that it is the intention of Congress to admit Colorado as a State into the Union: Therefore,
>
> *Resolved by the house of representatives of the Territory*, That, representing, as we do, the last and only legal expression of public opinion on this question, we earnestly protest against the passage of a law admitting the State without first having the question submitted to a vote of the people, for the reasons, first, that we have a right to a voice in the selection of the character of our government; second, that we have not a sufficient population to support the expenses of a State government. For these reasons we trust that Congress will not force upon us a government against our will.[4]

Upon information which I considered reliable, I assumed in my message of the 15th of May last that the population of Colorado was not more than 30,000, and expressed the opinion that this number was entirely too small either to assume the responsibilities or to enjoy the privileges of a State.

It appears that previous to that time the legislature, with a view to ascertain the exact condition of the Territory, had passed a law authorizing a census of the population to be taken. The law made it the duty of the assessors in the several counties to take the census in connection with the annual assessments, and, in order to secure a correct enumeration of the population, allowed them a liberal compensation for the service by paying them for every name returned, and added to their previous oath of office an oath to perform this duty with fidelity.

From the accompanying official report it appears that returns have been received from fifteen of the eighteen counties into which the State is divided, and that their population amounts in the aggregate to 24,909. The three remaining counties are estimated to contain 3,000, making a total population of 27,909.[5]

This census was taken in the summer season, when it is claimed that the population is much larger than at any other period, as in the autumn miners in large numbers leave their work and return to the East with the results of their summer enterprise.

The population, it will be observed, is but slightly in excess of one-fifth of the number required as the basis of representation for a single Congressional district in any of the States—the number being 127,000.

I am unable to perceive any good reason for such great disparity in the right of representation, giving, as it would, to the people of Colorado not only this vast advantage in the House of Representatives, but an equality in the Senate, where the other States are represented by millions. With perhaps a single exception, no such inequality as this has ever before been attempted.[6] I know that it is claimed that the population of the different States at the time of their admission has varied at different periods, but it has not varied much more than the population of each decade and the corresponding basis of representation for the different periods.

The obvious intent of the Constitution was that no State should be admitted with a less population than the ratio for a Representative at the time of application. The limitation in the second section of the first article of the Constitution, declaring that "each State shall have at least one Representative," was manifestly designed to protect the States which originally composed the Union from being deprived, in the event of a waning population, of a voice in the popular branch of Congress, and was never intended as a warrant to force a new State into the Union with a representative population far below that which might at the time be required of sister members of the Confederacy. This bill, in view of the prohibition of the same section, which declares that "the number of Representatives shall not exceed one for every 30,000," is at least a violation of the spirit if not the letter of the Constitution.

It is respectfully submitted that however Congress, under the pressure of circumstances, may have admitted two or three States with less than a representative population at the time, there has been no instance in which an application for admission has ever been entertained when the population, as officially ascertained, was below 30,000.

Were there any doubt of this being the true construction of the Constitution, it would be dispelled by the early and long-continued practice of the Federal Government. For nearly sixty years after the adoption of the Constitution no State was admitted with a population believed at the time to be less than the current ratio for a Representative, and the first instance in which there appears to have been a departure from the principle was in 1845, in the case of Florida. Obviously the result of sectional strife, we would do well to regard it as a warning of evil rather than as an example for imitation; and I think candid men of all parties will agree that the inspiring cause of the violation of this wholesome principle of restraint is to be found in a vain attempt to balance these antagonisms, which refused to be reconciled except through the bloody arbitrament of arms. The plain facts of our history will attest that the great and leading States admitted since 1845, viz, Iowa, Wisconsin, California, Minnesota, and Kansas, including Texas, which was admitted that year, have all come with an ample population for one Representative, and some of them with nearly or quite enough for two.

To demonstrate the correctness of my views on this question, I subjoin a table containing a list of the States admitted since the adoption of the Federal Constitution, with the date of admission, the ratio of representation, and the representative population when admitted, deduced from the United States census tables, the calculation being made for the period of the decade corresponding with the date of admission.

Colorado, which it is now proposed to admit as a State, contains, as has already been stated, a population less than 28,000, while the present ratio of representation is 127,000.

There can be no reason that I can perceive for the admission of Colorado that would not apply with equal force to nearly every other Territory now organized; and I submit whether, if this bill become a law, it will be possible to resist the logical conclusion that such Territories as Dakota, Montana, and Idaho must be received as States whenever they present themselves, without regard to the number of inhabitants they may respectively contain. Eight or ten new Senators and four or five new members of the House of Representatives would thus be admitted to represent a population scarcely exceeding that which in any other portion of the nation is entitled to but a single member of the House of Representatives, while the average for two Senators in the Union, as now constituted, is at least 1,000,000 people. It would surely be unjust to all other sections of the Union to enter upon a policy with regard to the admission of new States which might result in conferring such a disproportionate share of influence in the National Legislature upon communities which, in pursuance of the wise policy of our fathers, should for some years to come be retained under the fostering care and protection of the National Government. If it is deemed just and expedient now to depart from the settled policy of the nation during all its history, and to admit all the Territories to the rights and privileges of States, irrespective of their population or fitness for such government, it is submitted whether it would not be well to devise such measures as will bring the subject before the country for consideration and decision. This would seem to be eminently wise, because, as has already been stated, if it is right to admit Colorado now there is no reason for the exclusion of the other Territories.

It is no answer to these suggestions that an enabling act was passed authorizing the people of Colorado to take action on this subject. It is well known that that act was passed in consequence of representations that the population reached, according to some statements, as high as 80,000, and to none less than 50,000, and was growing with a rapidity which by the time the admission could be consummated would secure a population of over 100,000. These representations proved to have been wholly fallacious, and in addition the people of the Territory by a deliberate vote decided that they would not assume the responsibilities of a State government. By that decision they utterly exhausted all power that was conferred by the enabling act, and there has been no step taken since in relation to the admission that has had the slightest sanction or warrant of law.

The proceeding upon which the present application is based was in the utter absence of all law in relation to it, and there is no evidence that the votes on the question of the formation of a State government bear any relation whatever to the sentiment of the Territory. The protest of the house of representatives previously quoted is conclusive evidence to the contrary.[7]

But if none of these reasons existed against this proposed enactment, the bill itself, besides being inconsistent in its provisions in conferring power upon a person unknown to the laws and who may never have a legal existence, is so framed as to render its execution almost impossible. It is, indeed, a question whether it is not in itself a nullity. To say the least, it is of exceedingly doubtful propriety to confer the power proposed in this bill upon the "governor elect," for as by its own terms the constitution is not to take effect until after the admission of the State, he in the meantime has no more authority than any other private citizen. But even supposing him to be clothed with sufficient authority to convene the legislature, what constitutes the "State legislature" to which is to be referred the submission of the conditions imposed by Congress? Is it a new body to be elected and convened by proclamation of the "governor elect," or is it that body which met more than a year ago under the provisions of the State constitution? By reference to the second section of the schedule and to the eighteenth section of the fourth article of the State constitution it will be seen that the term of the members of the house of representatives and that of one-half of the members of the senate expired on the first Monday of the present month.[8] It is clear that if there were no intrinsic objections to the bill itself in relation to purposes to be accomplished this objection would be fatal, as it is apparent that the provisions of the third section of the bill to admit Colorado have reference to a period and a state of facts entirely different from the present and affairs as they now exist, and if carried into effect must necessarily lead to confusion.

Even if it were settled that the old and not a new body were to act, it would be found impracticable to execute the law, because a considerable number of the members, as I am informed, have ceased to be residents of the Territory, and in the sixty days within which the legislature is to be convened after the passage of the act there would not be sufficient time to fill the vacancies by new elections, were there any authority under which they could be held.

It may not be improper to add that if these proceedings were all regular and the result to be obtained were desirable, simple justice to the people of the Territory would require a longer period than sixty days within which to obtain action on the conditions proposed by the third section of the bill. There are, as is well known, large portions of the Territory with which there is and can be no general communication, there being several counties which from November to May can only be reached by persons traveling on foot, while with other regions of the Territory, occupied by a large portion of the population, there is very little more freedom of access. Thus, if this bill should become a law, it would be impracticable to obtain any expression of public sentiment in reference to its provisions, with a view to enlighten the legislature, if the old body were called together, and, of course, equally impracticable to procure the election of a new body. This defect might have been remedied by an extension of the time and a submission of the question to the people, with a fair opportunity to enable them to express their sentiments.

The admission of a new State has generally been regarded as an epoch in our history marking the onward progress of the nation; but after the most careful and anxious inquiry on the subject I can not perceive that the proposed proceeding is in conformity with the policy which from the origin of the Government has uniformly prevailed in the admission of new States. I therefore return the bill to the Senate without my signature.

ANDREW JOHNSON.

Richardson, *Messages*, 6: 483–89.

1. See Colorado Statehood Veto, May 15, 1866, *Johnson Papers*, 10: 506–9.
2. The bill passed the House on January 15 and, with the House revisions, the Senate on January 16, 1867. *Congressional Globe*, 39 Cong., 2 Sess., pp. 481, 487.
3. The text of the act can be found in Alexander Cummings, Governor's Message, Dec. 13, 1866, Johnson Papers, LC.
4. Alexander Cummings to Johnson, Jan. 10, 1867.
5. Alexander Cummings to O. H. Browning, Jan. 4, 1867, Johnson Papers, LC. For a contrasting view of territorial statistics and the problems with this census, see Jerome B. Chaffee to Johnson, Dec. 5, 1866.
6. Probably Nevada which, as Johnson indicates in the table at the end of the veto, was admitted in 1864 with a population figure not known.
7. A newspaper report indicated that this "resolution against making Colorado a state was passed in the House in the absence of several who were sick, after having been previously voted down." *Chicago Tribune*, Jan. 16, 1867.
8. See A. Cameron Hunt to Johnson, Jan. 18, 1867.

From Nathaniel Currier[1]

Paris Tenn.   Jany. 28th 1867

Dear Sir

Your Excellency will please allow me to address you a few lines in regard to Mr H. T. Blantons rejection by the Senate as collector for this 7th district of Tenn.[2]

It is well understood here that Mr Bs rejection was brought about by the machinations of a certain clique of extreme radicals, headed by a man who, during the war, was ever active in bringing in medicines and revolvers, and disposing of the same, for gain, to Confederates. Mr Blanton never gave aid to the Enemy—he is Your and the Unions friend[3] and, if his fate is decided, we pray that his enemy (James Worthen)[4] may not find favor in Your sight.

N. Currier

Reference
Hon. I. R. Hawkins M. C
Hon. Em. Etheredge[5]

ALS, DNA-RG56, Appts., Internal Revenue Service, Collector, Tenn., 7th Dist., Horace P. [sic] Blanton.

1. Currier (1807–1877) was a native of Massachusetts who moved to Henry County, Tennessee, in the 1830s. Along with his brother, Currier established a cotton manufacturing business which he continued to operate beyond the Civil War years. Goodspeed's *Carroll, Henry, and Benton*, 899; Charles E. Sanders, comp., *Bible Records of Henry County, Tennessee* (Springville, Tenn., 1988), 19.

2. Horace T. Blanton (b. c1816) was a merchant in Paris, Tennessee, who later, by 1870, became a tax collector, although not a federal collector. The Blanton story in 1866–67 is a bit complicated. Johnson first nominated him as collector of the Seventh District in May 1866 but no action was taken by the Senate. Then in October 1866 the President made a recess appointment of Blanton as collector. Eventually, in January 1867, Johnson nominated Blanton to a permanent position, but the Senate rejected the nomination a week later. 1860 Census, Tenn., Henry, 1st Dist., Paris, 13; (1870), 8; Ser. 6B, Vol. 3: 424; Vol. 4: 227–28, Johnson Papers, LC.

3. In the wake of Blanton's rejection by the Senate, John W. Leftwich, Tennessee congressman, assured the chairman of the Senate finance committee that Blanton "was an original and consistent Union man, thoroughly competent and very poor and needy." Leftwich to William P. Fessenden, Jan. 28, 1867, Appts., Internal Revenue Service, Collector, Tenn., 7th Dist., Horace P. [sic] Blanton.

4. Worthen (b. c1803) was a druggist in Paris who at one time also served briefly as county court clerk for Henry County. 1860 Census, Tenn., Henry, 1st Dist., Paris, 4; Goodspeed's *Carroll, Henry, and Benton*, 821.

5. Isaac R. Hawkins and Emerson Etheridge.

From Henry R. Coggshall[1]

Philadelphia, (Germantown)   Jan. 29 1867

Dear Sir

By reference to the daily papers I perceive that the Guillotine has been applied to me by the U.S. Senate.[2]

You are already aware of my sacrifice of old associates, and of money to an amount far exceeding all the compensation I have received from this office; during the unfortunate campaign of last Autumn.

Allow me to assure you that I still stand with you, firm in the maintenance of those principles for which we are maligned by the radicals on every side; and also to ask as a personal favor that you will *allow no new name* to be sent to the U.S. Senate as a successor in my position until I have an opportunity to see you personally regarding the matter.

Allow me to remind you that I was chairman of the committee who constructed the Phila. "Wigwam" as well as a delegate in that convention, and member of the "*Johnson Union State Central Committee*" and no greater gratification could be given to your political opponents than to see me *summarily slaughtered* and at the same time *apparently deserted by you.*[3]

H. R. Coggshall   Assessor 5th District Penna

LS, DNA-RG56, Appts., Internal Revenue Service, Pa., 5th Dist., Henry R. Coggshall.

1. Coggshall (*fl*1875), also referred to as Harry, was given a temporary commission as assessor of the Fifth District of Pennsylvania in July 1866. Philadelphia directories (1865–76); Joseph R. Flanigen et al. to Johnson, July 4, 1866, Appts., Internal Revenue Service, Assessor, Pa., 5th Dist., Henry R. Coggshall, RG56, NA; Ser. 6B, Vol. 3: 160, Johnson Papers, LC.

2. Johnson's nomination of Coggshall was rejected on January 26. Ibid., Vol. 4: 84.

3. There is no reply by Johnson, who turned to someone else to fill the post.

Nebraska Statehood Bill Veto Message

Washington, *January 29, 1867*.

To the Senate of the United States:

I return for reconsideration a bill entitled "An act for the admission of the State of Nebraska into the Union," which originated in the Senate and has received the assent of both Houses of Congress.[1] A bill having in view the same object was presented for my approval a few hours prior to the adjournment of the last session, but, submitted at a time when there was no opportunity for a proper consideration of the subject, I withheld my signature and the measure failed to become a law.[2]

It appears by the preamble of this bill that the people of Nebraska, availing themselves of the authority conferred upon them by the act passed on the 19th day of April, 1864, "have adopted a constitution which, upon due examination, is found to conform to the provisions and comply with the conditions of said act, and to be republican in its form of government, and that they now ask for admission into the Union." This proposed law would therefore seem to be based upon the declaration contained in the enabling act that upon compliance with its terms the people of Nebraska should be admitted into the Union upon an equal footing with the original States. Reference to the bill, however, shows that while by the first section Congress distinctly accepts, ratifies, and confirms the Constitution and State government which the people of the Territory have formed for themselves, declares Nebraska to be one of the United States of America, and admits her into the Union upon an equal footing with the original States in all respects whatsoever, the third section provides that this measure "shall not take effect except upon the fundamental condition that within the State of Nebraska there shall be no denial of the elective franchise, or of any other right, to any person by reason of race or color, excepting Indians not taxed; and upon the further fundamental condition that the legislature of said State, by a solemn public act, shall declare the assent of said State to the said fundamental condition, and shall transmit to the President of the United States an authentic copy of said act, upon receipt whereof the President, by proclamation, shall forthwith announce the fact, whereupon said fundamental condition shall be held as a part of the organic law of the State; and thereupon, and without any further proceeding on the part of Congress, the admission of said State into the Union shall be considered as complete."³ This condition is not mentioned in the original enabling act; was not contemplated at the time of its passage; was not sought by the people themselves; has not heretofore been applied to the inhabitants of any State asking admission, and is in direct conflict with the constitution adopted by the people and declared in the preamble "to be republican in its form of government," for in that instrument the exercise of the elective franchise and the right to hold office are expressly limited to white citizens of the United States. Congress thus undertakes to authorize and compel the legislature to change a constitution which, it is declared in the preamble, has received the sanction of the people, and which by this bill is "accepted, ratified, and confirmed" by the Congress of the nation.

The first and third sections of the bill exhibit yet further incongruity. By the one Nebraska is "admitted into the Union upon an equal footing with the original States in all respects whatsoever," while by the other Congress demands as a condition precedent to her admission requirements which in our history have never been asked of any people when presenting a constitution and State government for the acceptance of the lawmaking power. It is expressly declared by the third section that the bill "shall not take effect except upon the fundamental condition that within the State of Nebraska there shall be no denial of the elective franchise, or of any other right, to any person by reason of race or color, excepting Indians not taxed." Neither more nor less than the assertion of the right of Congress to regulate the elective franchise of any State hereafter to be admitted, this condition is in clear violation of the Federal Constitution, under the provisions of which, from the very foundation of the Government, each State has been left free to determine for itself the qualifications necessary for the exercise of suffrage within its limits.⁴ Without precedent in our legislation, it is in marked contrast with those limitations which, imposed upon States that from time to time have become members of the Union, had for their object the single purpose of preventing any infringement of the Constitution of the country.

If Congress is satisfied that Nebraska at the present time possesses sufficient population to entitle her to full representation in the councils of the nation, and that her people desire an exchange of a Territorial for a State government, good faith should seem to demand that she should be admitted without further requirements than those expressed in the enabling act, with all of which, it is asserted in the preamble, her inhabitants have complied. Congress may, under the Constitution, admit new States or reject them, but the people of a State can alone make or change their organic law and prescribe the qualifications requisite for electors. Congress, however, in passing the bill in the shape in which it has been submitted for my approval, does not merely reject the application of the people of Nebraska for present admission as a State into the Union, on the ground that the constitution which they have submitted restricts the exercise of the elective franchise to the white population, but imposes conditions which, if accepted by the legislature, may, without the consent of the people, so change the organic law as to make electors of all persons within the State without distinction of race or color. In view of this fact, I suggest for the consideration of Congress whether it would not be just, expedient, and in accordance with the principles of our Government to allow the people, by popular vote or through a convention chosen by themselves for that purpose, to declare whether or not they will accept the terms upon which it is now proposed to admit them into the Union. This course would not occasion much greater delay than that which the bill contemplates when it requires that the legislature shall be convened within thirty days after this measure shall have become a law for the purpose of considering and deciding the conditions which it imposes, and gains additional force when we consider that the proceedings attending the formation of the State constitution were not in conformity with the provisions of the enabling act; that in an aggregate vote of 7,776 the majority in favor of the constitution did not exceed 100; and that it is alleged that, in consequence of frauds, even this result can not be received as a fair expression of the wishes of the people.[5] As upon them must fall the burdens of a State organization, it is but just that they should be permitted to determine for themselves a question which so materially affects their interests. Possessing a soil and a climate admirably adapted to those industrial pursuits which bring prosperity and greatness to a people, with the advantage of a central position on the great highway that will soon connect the Atlantic and Pacific States,[6] Nebraska is rapidly gaining in numbers and wealth, and may within a very brief period claim admission on grounds which will challenge and secure universal assent. She can therefore wisely and patiently afford to wait. Her population is said to be steadily and even rapidly increasing, being now generally conceded as high as 40,000, and estimated by some whose judgment is entitled to respect at a still greater number.[7] At her present rate of growth she will in a very short time have the requisite population for a Representative in Congress, and, what is far more important to her own citizens, will have realized such an advance in material wealth as will enable the expenses of a State government to be borne without oppression to the taxpayer. Of new communities it may be said with special force—and it is true of old ones—that the inducement to emigrants, other things being equal, is in almost the precise ratio of the rate of taxation. The great States of the Northwest owe their marvelous prosperity largely to the fact that they were continued as Territories until they had grown to be wealthy and populous communities.[8]

ANDREW JOHNSON.

Richardson, *Messages*, 6: 489–492.
    1. The bill passed the House on January 15 and, with the House revisions, the Senate on January 16, 1867. *Congressional Globe*, 39 Cong., 2 Sess., pp. 481, 487.
    2. See James M. Woolworth to Johnson, July 30, 1866, *Johnson Papers*, 10: 762–63.
    3. This "fundamental condition" amendment was also known as the "Edmunds Amendment" because it was introduced by Sen. George Edmunds of Vermont. Berwanger, *West and Reconstruction*, 148.
    4. Congress imposed this condition on Colorado at the same time, but Colorado was refused admission for other reasons. *Congressional Globe*, 39 Cong., 2 Sess., pp. 481, 487; Colorado Statehood Bill Veto Message, Jan. 28, 1867.
    5. See James M. Woolworth to Johnson, July 30, 1866, *Johnson Papers*, 10: 762–63.
    6. The transcontinental railroad whose Union Pacific branch ran west through Nebraska from Omaha. James C. Olson, *History of Nebraska* (Lincoln, 1955), 118–19.
    7. See Thomas W. Tipton and John M. Thayer to Johnson, Jan. 19, 1867.
    8. Congress again passed the Nebraska statehood bill, over Johnson's veto, on February 9, 1867. The Nebraska legislature, in special session, approved the "fundamental condition" unanimously on February 21. (If they remained a territory, they would be subject to a new Territorial Suffrage Act which required that blacks be allowed to vote.) Nebraska became the thirty-seventh state on March 1, 1867. Olson, *Nebraska*, 133; Berwanger, *West and Reconstruction*, 148–49.

From James Q. Smith

WASHINGTON, DISTRICT OF COLUMBIA,
January 29, 1867.

RESPECTFUL SIR:

Hearing that an attempt was being made to remove me from the office of district attorney for Alabama, and being unable to ascertain the cause, I repaired immediately to Washington to see you on the subject; but in obtaining an interview for this purpose I have signally failed, after six days' attendance. I would delay longer, but my presence in Alabama is necessary. I would therefore respectfully ask your excellency, as a matter of favor and as a matter of right, to take no action on any representation or charge made against me until I am furnished with a statement of the representation or charge, that I may have an opportunity to refute them, and show to your excellency that it is not the public good my accusers seek, but to gratify a malicious hatred and effect personal interest. No one can know better than your excellency how the position or character of a man can be destroyed, if the *ex parte* statements and representations of enemies or interested persons are received under the cover of "private and confidential" communications, and no opportunity given for explanation. I have good reason to believe, and do believe, this effort to remove me from this office is due entirely to the interested motives of Major General Wager Swayne,[1] Freedmen's Bureau agent at Montgomery, because I would not consent to dismiss cases of confiscation pending in court, and permit him to hold and sell the government property libeled for confiscation, under acts of Congress, by me, and for which I am accountable. He has already sold not less than five hundred thousand dollars' worth of property in Alabama by military orders, under the pretence of aiding the "poor blacks." He is also hostile to me because I won't flood the United States courts in my district with the petty differences of freedmen under the civil rights' bill; and if some selection of his can be obtained as district attorney, then he can use him to his own advantage. I will resign the office before I will consent to be used by a bureau agent as a tool to execute his purposes. The ex-General openly denounces you, and advocates your impeachment as President of the United States, and hopes that a recent order of yours, in reference to the delivering up of C. C. Clay's property,[2] in his possession as bureau agent, will *not* effect this end. I am informed this order has been sent to Congressman Ashley,[3] or some of the committee on impeachment; and if so, you will know where it has come from.

                                                    JAMES Q. SMITH.

P.S.—I had reason to suppose that Governor Parsons was my friend, but I do not now think so, and any interest he takes in my removal may be considered in this light.[4]

                                                              J.Q.S.

House Reports, 40 Cong., 1 Sess., No. 7, p. 551 (Ser. 1314).
    1. Although the validity of Smith's charge against Swayne is unsubstantiated, the general once described the judge as "an ignorant, ferocious scoundrel." John W. DuBose, *Alabama's Tragic Decade: Ten Years of Alabama, 1865–1874* (Birmingham, 1940), 268.
    2. Johnson, on November 25, 1866, had released Clay's property. Clement C. Clay Papers, NcD.
    3. James M. Ashley.
    4. Smith was removed as district attorney of the northern district of Alabama and replaced in early April 1867 by Francis Bugbee. However, sometime thereafter, Smith was appointed to Bugbee's former position as judge of the second judicial district. Ser. 6B, Vol. 4: 180, 181, Johnson Papers, LC; DuBose, *Alabama's Tragic Decade*, 268.

To Edwin M. Stanton

                                    Washington, D.C.   Jany 29 1867.
Dear Sir:
    Will you please furnish me with a copy of the endorsement, and of the telegram upon which it was written, requesting, for publication, copies

of the despatches in reference to the New Orleans riot?[1] Those despatches, you will perhaps remember, were published in the newspapers of this city about the 22d of Decr. last,[2] and I presume that my endorsement upon the telegram to which I refer bore date in that month.

If possible, I should like to have the copies in time for transmission to Congress to day, with the papers upon the subject already furnished by your Department.[3]

Andrew Johnson

LS, DLC-Edwin M. Stanton Papers.
    1. Not found.
    2. No publication of New Orleans riot dispatches has been found in the Washington, D.C., papers about December 22, 1866. The dispatches were, however, published in the *Evening Star* on August 25, 1866.
    3. It is not known if Johnson received these particular items, but he did transmit what papers he had to Congress on January 29. *Congressional Globe*, 39 Cong., 2 Sess., p. 844.

From Edwin M. Stanton

Washington City, Jany. 29 1867.

Sir,

It appears from a report made by Bvt. Maj. Genl. Heinzelman, Comdg. the post of Galveston, to Maj. Genl. Sheridan, and forwarded by the latter to the Adjt. Genl. of the Army,[1] that on the 8 ult. a capias was issued by the Dist. Court of Guadalupe Co. Texas,[2] for the arrest of *General Heinzelman* upon an indictment for taking away papers from the office of the Clerk of the Court,[3] found against him in consequence of certain proceedings under written instructions from his Comdg. Officer requiring him to cause the release of a former Asst. Comr. of the Freedmen's Bu., who was illegally imprisoned for acts done while in the U.S. Service, and in his official capacity, to afford him protection and to cause the cancellation of bonds given by him.[4] Genl. Heintzelman, who states in his report to Genl. Sheridan, that he would not consider his life safe in the hands of the Texas civil authorities, refused to obey the capias. Genl. Grant to whom the papers forwarded by Maj. Genl. Sheridan were referred, reports as follows:—"The course pursued in this matter thus far meets my approval, and I would respectfully request information as to whether Genl. Heintzelman will be sustained by the Govm't."[5]

I submit the case for further instructions as you may deem it proper to give.[6]

Edwin M. Stanton, Secy. of War.

LBcopy, DNA-RG107, Lets. Sent, Mil. Bks., Executive, 58-C.
    1. Samuel P. Heintzelman, Philip H. Sheridan, and Lorenzo Thomas.
    2. John Ireland, judge.
    3. James M. Wilcox.
    4. This relates to the imprisonment of former assistant commissioner of the Freedmen's Bureau Capt. Samuel A. Craig for confiscation and destruction of the papers in the cases

against former Bureau agent William Longworth. See O. M. Roberts and D. G. Burnet to Johnson, Dec. 6, 1866.

    5. Stanton is apparently quoting Grant's January 28, 1867, endorsement on the papers related to the Heintzelman case. Simon, *Grant Papers*, 17: 39.

    6. Johnson ordered Stanton to submit the papers to Attorney General Stanbery. Heintzelman, assisted by David G. Baldwin, federal district attorney for eastern Texas, continued to resist arrest. Stanton to Stanbery, Jan. 30, 1867, Lets. Recd., Executive (M494, Roll 98), RG107, NA; Richter, *Overreached on All Sides*, 135; Richter, *Army in Texas*, 79–80.

From Barnabas Burns[1]

Mansfield O   January 30 1867

Sir

    I See by the procedings of the Senate, that the Nomination and appointment of Capt W. E. Scofield[2] as Assessor for the 8th District of Ohio has been rejected. I am credibly informed that an effort is being, or will be made to procur the appointment of M. W. Worden[3] Esq of this City to the office in room of Capt Scofield. I desire to say, that, Judge Worden is now & always has been a most *bitter & inveterate Radical*, as much so as Thad Stevens himself—his claims will no doubt be pressed on the ground that he was a Soldier & lost a leg at the Surrender of Harpers Ferry in 1862. That is true, but on that Score his claims are not superior to Capt Scofield, except that Capt. S. did not lose a leg, yet he Served *faithfully* from the begining until nearly if not quite the close of the war & made a Splendid record both as a *private* & an officer. I have no interest directly nor indirectly in the matter, but when I see a dignified body, Such as the Senate of the U.S. Should be, refuse to Confirm the appointment of a gallant Soldier to office, on the ground purely because he votes for the men who desire a speedy restoration of the Union, I feel like giving your Excellency Such information as will enable you to act understandingly.[4]

B. Burns

ALS, DNA-RG56, Appts., Internal Revenue Service, Assessor, Ohio, 8th Dist., Wm. E. Schofield.

    1. Burns (1817–*fl*1883), a lawyer and active Democrat, had been a state senator (1847–51) and briefly colonel of the 86th Ohio Inf. *The Biographical Cyclopaedia and Portrait Gallery with an Historical Sketch of the State of Ohio* (6 vols., Cincinnati, 1883–95), 1: 233–34.

    2. William E. Scofield (1834–1883), a Marion County, Ohio, lawyer, had served a three-year enlistment in the 82nd Ohio Inf. J. Wilbur Jacoby, ed., *History of Marion County, Ohio, and Representative Citizens* (Chicago, 1907), 185–86; *Off. Army Reg.: Vols.*, 5: 102.

    3. Milton W. Worden (1839–1869), admitted to the bar just before the war, served in the 32nd Ohio Inf. until 1863, and the next year was elected probate judge of Richland County. A. A. Graham, comp., *History of Richland County, Ohio: Its Past and Present* (Mansfield, Ohio, 1880), 743; *Off. Army Reg.: Vols.*, 5: 102.

    4. Scofield received a recess appointment as assessor August 24, 1866, but he was rejected by the Senate January 26, 1867. Worden served as assessor until his death in January 1869. Ser. 6B, Vol. 3: 495, Johnson Papers, LC; *Mansfield Herald*, Jan. 27, 1869.

From Thomas Miller

Columbus Ohio   January 30th 1867

My Dear Sir

You will I doubt not pardon me for the liberty I now take in thus addressing you at this time. I thought it not amiss to inform you of the Political feeling now existing among our people in Central Ohio. The impeachment question is now I may Say the question of the hour. And in this Connection I am glad to be able to inform Your Excellency; that it meets with little or no favor. Ninety nine out of every hundred of our people of all Political Shades are opposed to and Condem the advocates of it. The Radicals are becoming Very much alarmed lest the finances of the Country may be ruined and Civil War ensue which is enevitable unless Congress refuses to follow the lead of Butler Ashley Stevens & Co.[1] The people are getting thoroughly Sick of them and Should they persist in their evil designs on You for the purpose of unlawfully deposing Your Excellency I am glad to be able to inform You that in less than twenty days this District would furnish twenty Thousand men ready and Willing to fight for your Constitutional rights; their rights and for Constitutional liberty. The action of the Senate in rejecting Your appointees has Completely disgusted the Masses of the people who Seem to think that Congress has fully determined on the total distruction of the whole Country. I am fully of Opinion that from hence forward the power of the Radicals will be departing and every day thank God getting Beautifully less until they sink to rise no more. As for my own case Mr. President I would here state that my appointment and Official actions have given entire Satisfaction to our people save and except Geigher Dewey Baber Hinkle & Co[2] who are all in the employ and keeping of Shellabarger who paid them by having the Senate reject my appointment. This is pay enough for them for all the work they did for Shellabarger during the fall elections. As your appointee Mr President I do not much feel like been deposed by such Wolves in Sheep's clothing. The Assessers Office in a crises like this is of the utmost importance; coming in Connection as it dose; with the masses of our people who are now anxiously looking for correct information Concerning the Radical's proceedings in this and the next Congress. If there is any thing that Your Excellency should think would be proper for me to know I should be quite pleased to hear from you.

Thomas Miller

ALS, DLC-JP.

1. Benjamin F. Butler, James M. Ashley, and Thaddeus Stevens.
2. Joseph H. Geiger, Chauncey Dewey, Richard P.L. Baber, and Saul S. Henkle. Dewey (1796–1880), former law partner of Edwin M. Stanton, was a Cadiz, Ohio, banker, businessman, and active Republican. *Biographical Cyclopaedia of Ohio*, 2: 406–7.

From Ebenezer W. Peirce

Fall River [Mass.], Jan 30th 1867

Mr. President,

I have failed to be confirmed[1] because I would not compromise you. Now one Nathaniel Gilbert[2] is going to ask you to favor him. I can and will if you desire it prove that till within three weeks he has optenly denounced you as ["]a humbug a drunkard & a traitor that ought to be choked with a hemp rope."

If he dont suceed Walter C. Durfee[3] will ask you for my place. He went in hotly against you in the last elections.

If he dont succeed Judge Day[4] who turned against you last fall to get a place will ask for the office.

Now Mr. President having always endeavoured to show my gratitude to you for the office you confered upon me I feel that you will feel bound to take this as an act of intended kindness.

If you do not feel free to reappoint me I will reccomen one of my Deputies, General Timothy Ingraham[5] of New Bedford formerly Provost Marshal Genl. at Washington D.C.[6]

Ebenezer W. Peirce   Collector

ALS, DNA-RG56, Appts., Internal Revenue Service, Collector, Mass., 1st Dist., Timothy Ingraham.

1. Peirce's nomination as collector was rejected by the Senate on January 26, 1867. Ser. 6B, Vol. 4: 24, Johnson Papers, LC.

2. Gilbert (b. c1814), a Republican and former assistant assessor in the First District of Massachusetts, was later recommended for the collectorship by Secretary McCulloch. Appts., Internal Revenue Service, Collector, 1st Dist., Mass., Nathaniel Gilbert, RG56, NA; McCulloch to Johnson, Feb. 4, 1867, ibid., Timothy Ingraham; 1860 Census, Mass., Bristol, 6th Ward, New Bedford, 19.

3. Durfee (c1816–fl1870), who served as collector for the First District from 1862 until Peirce replaced him in August 1866, later worked as an alderman and tax assessor for the city of Fall River. *Our County and Its People: A Descriptive and Biographical Record of Bristol County* (Boston, 1899), 633, 641; Appts., Internal Revenue Service, Collector, 1st Dist., Mass., Walter C. Durfee, RG56, NA; 1860 Census, Mass., Bristol, Fall River, 4th Ward, 265.

4. Joseph M. Day (c1824–fl1892) was a Republican attorney in Barnstable, Massachusetts, who, while on detached duty during the war as a major in the volunteer army, had an interview with Johnson in Nashville. Deyo, *History of Barnstable County*, 104, 211–12; CSR, Joseph M. Day, RG94, NA; Day to Johnson, Mar. 6, 1866, Johnson Papers, LC; Pension File, Joseph M. Day, RG15, NA.

5. Ingraham (1810–1876), who commanded a Massachusetts infantry regiment before becoming provost marshal general for the defenses north of the Potomac, was brevetted a brigadier in October 1865. Hunt and Brown, *Brigadier Generals*; Heitman, *Register*, 563.

6. During the next few days, Peirce continued urging the appointment of Ingraham, whose nomination was finally presented to the Senate in mid-February 1867 but was rejected a few weeks later. Peirce to Johnson, Feb. 8, 1867; Pierce to McCulloch, Feb. 5, 1867, Appts., Internal Revenue Service, Collector, Mass., 1st Dist., Timothy Ingraham, RG56, NA; Ser. 6B, Vol. 4: 24, Johnson Papers, LC.

From Chandler Robbins[1]

Boston, 31st January, 1867.

Dear Sir,

I have requested my valued & intimate friend, Hon. R. C. Winthrop, to convey this note to you—of the contents of which he is ignorant—in order that being of so private a nature it may not fall into other hands than your own, & also that, if you wish, you may ascertain from him who I am & whether I am entirely worthy of your confidence. I beg you to pardon me if I am using undue freedom in what I am about to suggest, & to acquit me of any motive less worthy of your approval than a most sincere & earnest desire to do honor to your official and personal character & to promote the wise and magnanimous policy which I know you have at heart.

Notwithstanding the various malicious charges & insinuations of those, whether in or out of Congress, who are hostile to your administration, there are really only two particulars which unfavorably affect the opinion of your sober-minded fellow citizens—whose judgment is of the most consequence, & determines in the long run the public estimate. Excuse me for saying frankly that these are the unfortunate incident which occured at your inauguration as Vice President, & certain infelicitous words which were drawn from you in your hurried journey to the West, under the pressure of frequent demands for extemperaneous utterance & amidst the excitement of extraordinary provocation. The first is sufficiently explained by the published statement of your predecessor.[2] For the second, candid minds ought to find in the circumstances of the case, if not an adequate excuse, at least a strong palliation.

Now, Dear Sir, I venture to suggest a move in which, consistently with self-respect, you might remove the impression which the incidents alluded to have left upon the minds of many, who otherwise would have been your supporters; & at the same time greatly weaken the power of your enemies; and thus, materialy advance the interests of those patriotic measures with which your name is identified.

Would you not be willing, in the form of a reply to a communication to yourself from some respectable person out of the ranks of the politicians, who should refer, as I have done, to the incidents in question, to say something like this—

The frankness with which you have spoken does not offend me. I have been so inured to abuse from my enemies, that I can more readily bear to be reminded of my faults by a friend. I am glad also to know that there are men like yourself, free from the prejudice of party, who appreciate the trials & perplexities of the President at such a crisis as the present, and whose sense of justice forbids them to give credit to charges of delinquencies & even of crimes, by whomsoever openly made or darkly insinuated, before they have been substantiated. With regard to such accusations I am content to wait & let justice & reason take their own time & course.

Whatever may have been my defects, I am free to confess that the only circumstances which cause me any real uneasiness & regret are precisely those to which you have referred—the unfortunate incident at my inauguration, & the two or three objectionable sentences which were drawn from me in the course of hurried journey to the West, under the pressure of incessant calls for extemporaneous remarks & amidst the excitement of extraordinary provocation. The first is substantially explained by the published statement of my predecessor, which many persons seem to have forgotten. As to the second, I had hoped that men of candid judgment could have found in the circumstances of the case, in connection with my western culture & habits, if not an adequate excuse, at least a strong palliation. But enough of this.

I am not sorry that you have urged upon me the opportunity of saying these few words upon the points to which your letter refers.

Conscious of being governed by no motives aside from the integrity & honor of our common country, I do not fear that, in spite of any infelicitous circumstances & any errors of judgment which may have attended my official career, the main influence of my administration will not be conducive to the national welfare, nor that the ultimate verdict will not be favorable to my intention in respect of patriotism, justice & humanity.

Once more, I beg you to pardon me for presuming to offer these suggestions. Whether they should strike you favorably, or unfavorably, let me assure you that they are made solely with a view to your own honor & the benefit of the policy which I believe to be for the best good of the Nation. Let me also assure you that what I have written is, & shall be, held by me in the strictest & most sacred confidence.

If you should deem it proper to write such a letter as I have sketched, the person to whom it may be addressed might subsequently ask your permission to give it publicity, with a voucher for its genuineness.

Chandler Robbins.

ALS, DLC-JP.

1. Robbins (1810–1882) served as pastor of the Second (Unitarian) Church of Boston for nearly half a century and was actively involved with the Massachusetts Historical Society. *DAB*.

2. In his memoirs published more than two decades later, Secretary McCulloch recalled that Lincoln had told him: "I have known Andy Johnson for many years; he made a bad slip the other day, but you need not be scared; Andy ain't a drunkard." Whether this is the statement to which Robbins refers is not known, however. Hugh McCulloch, *Men and Measures of Half a Century* (New York, 1889), 373.

To the Senate

WASHINGTON, *January 31, 1867.*

To the Senate of the United States:

The accompanying reports from the heads of the several Executive Departments of the Government are submitted in compliance with a resolution of the Senate dated the 12th ultimo,[1] inquiring whether any person appointed to an office required by law to be filled by and with the advice and consent of the Senate, and who was commissioned during the recess of the Senate, previous to the assembling of the present Congress, to fill a vacancy, has been continued in such office and permitted to discharge its functions, either by the granting of a new commission or otherwise, since the end of the session of the Senate on the 28th day of July last, without the submission of the name of such person to the Senate for its confirmation; and particularly whether a surveyor or naval officer of the port of Philadelphia has thus been continued in office without the consent of the Senate, and, if any such officer has performed the duties of that office, whether he has received any salary or compensation therefor.

ANDREW JOHNSON.

Richardson, *Messages*, 6: 465.
1. See Senate Resolution, Dec. 12, 1866, Appts. Div., Misc. Lets. Recd., RG48, NA; Stanton to Johnson, Dec. 11, 1866.

Appendix I

[Adapted from Robert Sobel, ed., *Biographical Directory of the United States Executive Branch, 1774–1971* (Westport, Conn., 1971).]

Office	Name
Secretary of State, 1865–69	William H. Seward
Secretary of the Treasury, 1865–69	Hugh McCulloch
Secretary of War, 1865–68	Edwin M. Stanton
Secretary of War ad interim, 1867–68	Ulysses S. Grant
Secretary of War ad interim, 1868	Lorenzo Thomas
Secretary of War, 1868–69	John M. Schofield
Attorney General, 1865–66	James Speed
Attorney General, 1866–68	Henry Stanbery
Attorney General ad interim, 1868*	Orville H. Browning
Attorney General, 1868–69	William M. Evarts
Postmaster General, 1865–66	William Dennison
Postmaster General, 1866–69	Alexander W. Randall
Secretary of the Navy, 1865–69	Gideon Welles
Secretary of the Interior, 1865	John P. Usher
Secretary of the Interior, 1865–66	James Harlan
Secretary of the interior, 1866–69	Orville H. Browning

*from March 13, 1868, when Stanbery resigned, until July 20, 1868, when Evarts assumed office, Browning discharged the duties of attorney general in addition to his functions as head of the Interior Department.

Appendix II

Veto Messages, Proclamations, and Executive Orders
(August 1866–January 1867)

[Asterisks indicate documents printed in Volume 11; all are printed in James D. Richardson, comp., *A Compilation of the Messages and Papers of the Presidents* (10 vols., Washington, D.C., 1896–99), Volume 6.]

Date	Veto Messages	Richardson, *Messages*
Jan. 5	*District of Columbia Franchise Law Veto Message	472–83
Jan. 28	*Colorado Statehood Bill Veto Message	483–89
Jan. 29	*Nebraska Statehood Bill Veto Message	489–92

	Proclamations	
Aug. 17	*Re Mexican Blockade	433–34
Aug. 20	*Re End of Insurrection	434–38
Oct. 8	Setting day of thanksgiving	438–39

	Executive Orders	
Oct. 26	*Sending Grant with Campbell to Mexico	443
Oct. 30	Replacing Grant with Sherman for Mexican mission	443–44
Nov. 1	Re threat of insurrection in the District of Columbia and Maryland	444
Nov. 2	Re threat of insurrection in Maryland, especially Baltimore	444

Appendix III

Aug. 28	Washington, D.C.; Bladensburg, Md.; Laurel; Annapolis Junction; Baltimore; Havre de Grace; Perryville; Wilmington, Del.; Philadelphia, Pa.
Aug. 29	Philadelphia; Camden, N.J.; Burlington; Bordertown; Trenton; New Brunswick; Newark; Jersey City; New York City
Aug. 30	New York City; West Point, N.Y.; Newburgh; Poughkeepsie; Albany
Aug. 31	Albany, N.Y.; Schenectady; Fonda; Little Falls; Herkimer; Utica; Rome; Syracuse; Auburn
Sept. 1	Auburn, N.Y.; Cuyga; Senaca Falls; Geneva; Clifton Springs; Canandaigua; Rochester; Brockport; Albion; Medina; Lockport; Niagara Falls
Sept. 2	Niagara Falls, N.Y.
Sept. 3	Niagara Falls, N.Y.; Tonawanda; Ft. Porter; Ft. Erie; Buffalo; North Evans; Silver Creek; Dunkirk; Westfield; Erie, Pa.; Girard; Ashtabula, Ohio; Cleveland
Sept. 4	Cleveland; Elyria, Ohio; Oberlin; Norwalk; Clyde; Fremont; Toledo; Monroe, Mich.; Detroit
Sept. 5	Detroit; Ypsilanti, Mich.; Ann Arbor; Jackson; Albion; Marshall; Battle Creek; Galesburg; Kalamazoo; Niles; Michigan City, Ind.; Chicago, Ill.
Sept. 6	Chicago
Sept. 7	Chicago; Lemont, Ill.; Lockport; Joliet; Wilmington; Pontiac; Bloomington; Atlanta; Lincoln; Springfield
Sept. 8	Springfield, Ill.; Carlinville; Alton; St. Louis, Mo.
Sept. 9	St. Louis
Sept. 10	St. Louis; Bunker Hill, Ill.; Mattoon; Charleston; Paris; Terre Haute, Ind.; Greencastle; Indianapolis
Sept. 11	Indianapolis; Franklin, Ind.; Edinburg; Columbus; Seymour; Vienna; Jeffersonville; Louisville, Ky.
Sept. 12	Madison, Ind.; Aurora; North Bend, Ohio; Covington, Ky.; Cincinnati; Morrow, Ohio; Waynesville; Xenia; London; Columbus
Sept. 13	Columbus; Newark, Ohio; Zanesville; New Market; Cadiz Junction; Steubenville; Burgettstown, Pa.; Pittsburgh

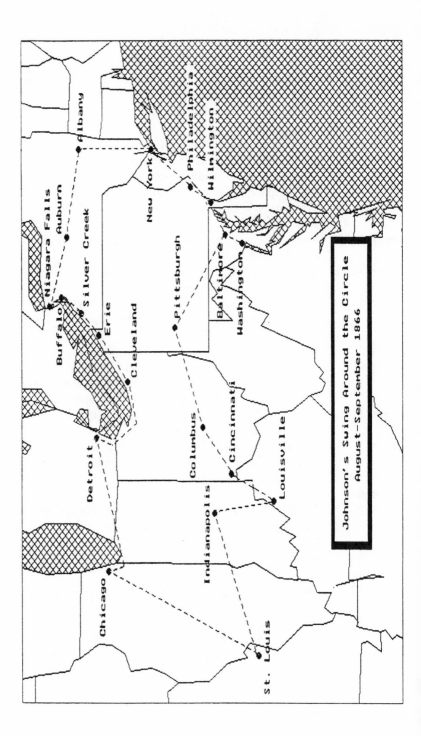

Johnson's Swing Around the Circle
August-September 1866

Sept. 14   Pittsburgh; Irwin, Pa.; Greensburg; Latrobe; Johnstown; Altoona; Huntingdon; Lewistown; Mifflin; Harrisburg

Sept. 15   Harrisburg, Pa.; Baltimore, Md.; Washington, D.C.

Index

Primary identification of a person is indicated by an italic *n* following the page reference. Identifications found in earlier volumes of the *Johnson Papers* are shown by providing volume and page numbers, within parentheses, immediately after the name of the individual. The only footnotes which have been indexed are those that constitute identification notes.